European Yearbook of International
Economic Law

EYIEL Monographs - Studies in European
and International Economic Law

Volume 8

Series Editors
Marc Bungenberg, Saarbrücken, Germany
Christoph Herrmann, Passau, Germany
Markus Krajewski, Erlangen, Germany
Jörg Philipp Terhechte, Lüneburg, Germany
Andreas R. Ziegler, Lausanne, Switzerland

EYIEL Monographs is a subseries of the European Yearbook of International Economic Law (EYIEL). It contains scholarly works in the fields of European and international economic law, in particular WTO law, international investment law, international monetary law, law of regional economic integration, external trade law of the EU and EU internal market law. The series does not include edited volumes. EYIEL Monographs are peer-reviewed by the series editors and external reviewers.

More information about this subseries at http://www.springer.com/series/15744

Sebastián Mantilla Blanco

Full Protection and Security in International Investment Law

 Springer

Sebastián Mantilla Blanco
Bonn, Germany

Inauguraldissertation zur Erlangung des Grades eines Doktors der Rechte durch die Rechts-und Staatswissenschaftliche Fakultät der Rheinischen Friedrich-Wilhelms-Universität Bonn.
Vorgelegt von: Sebastián Mantilla Blanco aus Mainz.
Dekan: Prof. Dr. Jürgen von Hagen.
Erstreferent: Prof. Dr. DDr. h.c. Matthias Herdegen.
Zweitreferent: Prof. Dr. Stefan Talmon LL.M. M.A.
Tag der mündlichen Prüfung: 21. November 2018.

ISSN 2364-8392 ISSN 2364-8406 (electronic)
European Yearbook of International Economic Law
ISSN 2524-6658 ISSN 2524-6666 (electronic)
EYIEL Monographs - Studies in European and International Economic Law
ISBN 978-3-030-24837-6 ISBN 978-3-030-24838-3 (eBook)
https://doi.org/10.1007/978-3-030-24838-3

This Springer imprint is published by the registered company Springer Nature Switzerland AG.
The registered company address is: Gewerbestrasse 11, 6330 Cham, Switzerland

Foreword

The obligation to grant 'full protection and security' is part of the classical repertoire of investment treaties. At the same time, the FPS standard is deeply rooted in the customary law on the status of foreigners. Still, it is only until recently that FPS clauses have emerged from the shadow of related investment principles, such as fair and equitable treatment. The scope of 'full protection and security' up to now remains controversial. The same holds true for the burden which the FPS standard places on the host State, the necessary deployment of the available forces and the degree of diligence which the State owes to the foreign investor.

It is therefore most timely that Dr. Sebastián Mantilla Blanco presents the first comprehensive treatise on 'full protection and security' in international investment law. This book provides a profound analysis of the historical underpinnings of the standard. It provides reliable guidance through the extensive practice of investment arbitration tribunals and the theoretical concepts which underlie treaty interpretation. In the light of often-divergent arbitral practice and scholarly opinions, Sebastián Mantilla's book offers a clear-cut position. His approach is always inspired by a fair balance between the foreign investor's reasonable expectations of effective protection, on the one hand, and the functional capabilities of the host State on the other hand. In this endeavour, Sebastián Mantilla benefits from his familiarity with both the challenges for capital-importing economies, particularly in Latin America, and the perspectives of investors from highly industrialized countries. This double perspective sharpens his sensitivity for the possible contribution of investment protection to the rule of law and good governance, always in context with legitimate political choices.

Sebastián Mantilla's approach also has the merit of linking the standards of investment protection to general rules on State responsibility. This is an important contribution to the coherence of international law against tendencies of fragmentation.

The present study offers most valuable orientation, in principle as well as in detail, to practitioners and academics alike. It has the potential to become the standard treatise on the subject.

University of Bonn   Matthias Herdegen
Bonn, Germany
May 2019

Preface

Almost every investment treaty guarantees covered investments' 'full protection and security' (FPS) within the host state's territory. The binding force of the FPS standard flows not only from international agreements but also from customary law. The obligation to provide security to aliens looks back on a long historical tradition. It has been present in international law and politics since the European Middle Ages and continues to be of the greatest practical importance in the age of bilateral investment treaties and free trade agreements. In the past few decades, the FPS standard took center stage in numerous arbitral proceedings. FPS claims involved a wide array of factual settings, ranging from civil unrest to environmental damages.

Despite its history and relevance for legal practice, the FPS standard continues to be a fundamentally contested concept. The precise contours of the standard in customary law as well as the interpretation of FPS clauses are typical points of contention between the parties in investment arbitrations. Arbitral decisions have followed strikingly divergent approaches with regard to these questions, giving rise to pervasive inconsistencies in the application of the standard. This book provides a comprehensive, deep and systematic analysis of the FPS standard. In so doing, it hopes to contribute to a better understanding and a more consistent application of the oldest and yet least studied international standard of investment protection.

This monograph is the product of more than 3 years of doctoral research at the Institutes of Public Law and International Law of the University of Bonn in Germany. It was awarded the prize of the Konrad Redeker Foundation for outstanding dissertations in public law in 2019.

The book owes much to the many persons and institutions that inspired and supported me throughout this path. I am most grateful to my doctoral supervisor, Professor Matthias Herdegen, for his support and guidance during these years. I also thank my second examiner, Professor Stefan Talmon, for his comments and encouragement for the publication of the dissertation. This project would have never been possible without the generous financial support of the Hanns-Seidel Foundation, which granted me a doctoral scholarship from the funding program of the German Federal Foreign Office.

For the past years, I was fortunate to enjoy the excellent research environment of the University of Bonn, which fostered my intellectual curiosity and provided me with the tools required to complete this project. I am very grateful to my friends and colleagues in Bonn. Thanks to them, this academic endeavour was also an extraordinary personal experience.

I would also like to express my gratitude to the Pontificia Universidad Javeriana and my colleagues and mentors in Bogotá, Colombia, who sparked my interest in the dynamic area of international investment law. Finally, I thank the editors of the *EYIEL Monographs – Studies in European and International Economic Law* for their support to this project.

My parents, Liliana and Ignacio, and my sister, Paula, have provided me strength, confidence and inspiration throughout my life. I dedicate this book to them.

Bonn, Germany   Sebastián Mantilla Blanco
May 2019

Contents

1   Introduction   1

Part I   Formation of the Standard: The Long Path to Customary
         International Law

2   'Full Protection and Security' in Historical Perspective:
    The Challenge of the Sources   17
    2.1   Introductory Remarks   17
    2.2   Obstacles Posed by Historical Sources   21
          2.2.1   Diversity of Intellectual and Political Agendas   21
          2.2.2   The Scope of the Jurisdiction Exercised by Mixed
                  Claims Commissions   24
          2.2.3   Overlapping Causes of Action and All-Encompassing
                  Definitions of Denial of Justice   28
          2.2.4   The Distinction Between Primary and Secondary
                  Rules of International Law. The Limits
                  of a Contemporary Notion   31
    2.3   Overcoming the Obstacles   34

3   The Origins of 'Full Protection and Security'. From Medieval
    Reprisals to the Age of Enlightenment   39
    3.1   Preliminary Issue. Determining the Starting Point   39
    3.2   The Beginnings. The Medieval Practice of Private Reprisals   44
    3.3   The Rationalization of the Protection Obligation. Christian
          von Wolff and the Theory of the Tacit Agreement   49
    3.4   The Reception of Wolff's Theory of the Tacit Agreement
          in the Works of Emer de Vattel   57

3.5   From *Presumed Consent* to *Actual Consent*. The 'Customary'
       Duty upon the Host State to Protect Foreign Citizens   62
       3.5.1   The First Steps. Johann Jakob Moser and the Positive
                Law of Aliens   64
       3.5.2   The Consolidation of the Classical Approach to the
                Law of Aliens. Georg Friedrich von Martens
                and Classic Positivism   67
3.6   The Influence of Eighteenth-Century Legal Scholarship in the
       Subsequent Development of the Law of Aliens. A Dialogue
       Between Theory and Practice   74

4   **A Battle of Gunboats and Books: 'Full Protection and Security'
     and the Minimum Standard of Treatment in Historical
     Perspective**   83
4.1   Preliminary Remarks   83
4.2   Gunboats from the North. The Minimum Standard of
       Treatment, the Gunboat Diplomacy and the Security
       Obligation   85
4.3   Books from the South. The Doctrine of Equality and the
       Security Obligation   96
       4.3.1   The Doctrine of Equality Before Carlos Calvo   97
       4.3.2   The New Guise of an Old Idea: The Calvo Doctrine
                and the Security Obligation   104
       4.3.3   The Long Lasting Debate About the Calvo Doctrine
                and the Extent of the Security Obligation   110

5   **The Calm After the Storm: 'Full Protection and Security' as
     an Element of the Minimum Standard of Treatment**   117
5.1   Preliminary Remarks   117
5.2   The Minimum Standard of Treatment as a Customary Rule
       of Contemporary International Law   119
5.3   The Unsettled Content of the International Minimum Standard
       of Treatment   133
5.4   The Significance of the 'Standard of Civilization' for the
       Determination of the Scope of Application of the Customary
       Security Obligation   140

Part II   Scope of the Customary Standard

6   **Scope of Application of the Customary Standard: Conceptual
     Framework**   145
6.1   Preliminary Remarks   145
6.2   The Notion of Standard and the Formal Structure of 'Full
       Protection and Security'   146
6.3   The Semantics of Security and the Scope of Application
       of 'Full Protection and Security' in Customary International
       Law   154

**7   Subjective Scope of Application of the Customary Standard
of 'Full Protection and Security'**   165
  7.1   Preliminary Remarks   165
  7.2   The Beneficiary of Security. The Foreign National   167
          7.2.1   The Foreignness Requirement   167
          7.2.2   Natural and Juristic Persons   176
  7.3   The Provider of Security. The Host State and the Case of
          Other Internationally Accountable Entities   184

**8   Objective Scope of Application: Protected Interests and Covered
Risks**   197
  8.1   Preliminary Remarks   197
  8.2   First Element. Protected Interests; The Notion of 'Acquired
          Values'   198
  8.3   Second Element. Covered Risks   206
          8.3.1   The Heart of the Standard. Protection Against
                    Private Violence   207
          8.3.2   The Private-Public Divide. Some Grey Areas   224
                    8.3.2.1   Successful Revolutions   225
                    8.3.2.2   Acts of Other States in the Territory
                                of the Host State   233
                    8.3.2.3   Acts of International Organizations   242
                    8.3.2.4   Private Violence Actively Supported
                                by State Agents   245
                    8.3.2.5   Conduct of Soldiers   248
                    8.3.2.6   Risk of Private Violence Materializing
                                in a Public Injury   254
          8.3.3   Beyond the Public-Private Divide   256
                    8.3.3.1   Public Collateral Damages   259
                    8.3.3.2   Natural Disasters and the Risk of Natural
                                Hazards   263

**9   Objective Scope of Application: Irrelevance of the Distinction
Between Physical and Nonphysical Harm**   269
  9.1   Preliminary Remarks   269
  9.2   Physical Security and Nonphysical Security: The Debate
          at a Glance   270
  9.3   The Notion of Legal Security and the Customary Security
          Obligation. Taking Down the House of Cards   279
          9.3.1   The Extensive Understanding of the Security
                    Obligation. The Caveats of Relevant Arbitral
                    Practice   280
          9.3.2   The Extensive Understanding of the Security
                    Obligation. Critique of a Misleading Notion   284
  9.4   The Customary Protection Obligation; Protection Beyond
          Physical Harm   289

**10 The Temporal Scope of Application of the Customary Standard
     of 'Full Protection and Security'** 297
   10.1 Preliminary Remarks 297
   10.2 The Preventive Functional Dimension. The Duty to Prevent
        Injuries to Aliens 303
   10.3 The Repressive Functional Dimension. The Duty to Provide
        Adequate Means for the Redress of Injuries to Aliens 307
   10.4 The Relationship Between the Obligation to Prevent and the
        Obligation of Redress 315

Part III   Content of the Standard

**11 The Characterization of the Obligation to Provide 'Full Protection
     and Security'** 327
   11.1 Preliminary Remarks 327
   11.2 'Full Protection and Security' and the Distinction Between
        Obligations of Conduct and Result 331
        11.2.1 The Concept of Obligations of Conduct and Result:
              From René Demogue to Roberto Ago 332
        11.2.2 'Full Protection and Security': Obligation
              of Conduct or Obligation of Result? A Dichotomy
              That Never Was 335
            11.2.2.1 First Possible Approach: 'Full
                  Protection and Security' as an Obligation
                  of Conduct 336
            11.2.2.2 Second Possible Approach: 'Full
                  Protection and Security' as a Negative
                  Obligation of Result. The ILC and the
                  Notion of 'Obligations of Event' 339
        11.2.3 'Full Protection and Security': Obligation of
              Conduct or Obligation of Result? Intermediate
              Approaches 348
            11.2.3.1 The Application of Different Standards
                  of Liability Depending on the Source
                  of Risk 349
            11.2.3.2 The Distinction Between the *Existence*
                  and the *Use* of the Host State's
                  Municipal Legal, Administrative
                  and Judicial System 353
        11.2.4 The *sui generis* Character of the Standard of
              'Full Protection and Security' 367
   11.3 The Distinction Between Positive and Negative International
        Obligations. 'Full Protection and Security' as a Delict
        of Omission 368

12 Due Diligence in the International Law of Aliens: Conceptual Framework 375
12.1 Preliminary Remarks 375
12.2 Due Diligence: Between Collective Responsibility and Non-responsibility 377
12.3 Due Diligence and the Problem of Fault in the Law of State Responsibility for Injuries to Aliens 383
    12.3.1 Hugo Grotius and the Concept of Fault 386
    12.3.2 Subsequent Theories of Fault 388
        12.3.2.1 Conservative 'Grotian' Approaches 389
        12.3.2.2 Objectivist Approaches 396
    12.3.3 Responsibility Without Fault. The 'Objective Turn' in the International Law of State Responsibility 400
12.4 The Indirect or Direct Character of State Responsibility for Private Injuries to Aliens 405
    12.4.1 The Theories of 'Indirect' Responsibility 406
    12.4.2 The Theories of 'Direct' Responsibility 408
    12.4.3 The 'Separate Delict' Theory 411

13 Due Diligence in the Context of 'Full Protection and Security' Claims 421
13.1 Introductory Remarks 421
13.2 The Distribution of the Burden of Proof 422
13.3 The Subjective or Objective Character of Due Diligence 432
    13.3.1 The 'Subjective' Standard of Due Diligence 433
    13.3.2 The 'Objective' Standard of Due Diligence 436
    13.3.3 The Contemporary Guises of the Objective Standard of Due Diligence 440
        13.3.3.1 Due Diligence as 'Reasonableness' 441
        13.3.3.2 Due Diligence and the Notions of Prudent, Appropriate or Necessary Measures 445
        13.3.3.3 The 'Modified' Objective Standard of Due Diligence 449
13.4 Factual Circumstances Relevant for the Assessment of Diligence 456
    13.4.1 Material Opportunity for Positive Action 457
    13.4.2 Awareness About the Risk 459
    13.4.3 Certainty as to the Legitimacy of the Investor's Rights and Interests 466
    13.4.4 Seriousness of the Situation of Risk 469
    13.4.5 Conduct of the Investor 471
    13.4.6 Differences in the Protection Afforded to Different Groups of Persons 477
    13.4.7 Public Support to Private Wrongdoers 478

13.4.8 Balance Between Private Interests and the Public
Interest 482
13.4.9 Compliance with Relevant Municipal Law 485
13.4.10 Compliance with Other Due Diligence Obligations
Under International Law 487

**Part IV 'Full Protection and Security' Clauses in International
Investment Agreements**

**14 'Protection and Security' Clauses in Investment Treaties:
A Typology** 495
14.1 Preliminary Remarks 495
14.2 References to Customary Law and General International Law
in Protection and Security Clauses 498
14.2.1 Protection and Security Clauses Making Express
Reference to Customary Law or General
International Law 499
14.2.1.1 Treaties Defining the Protection and
Security Obligation by Reference to
Customary Law 499
14.2.1.2 Other References to Customary
International Law 505
14.2.2 Protection and Security Clauses Making No
Express Reference to Customary Law or General
International Law 508
14.3 References to Domestic Law in Protection and Security
Clauses 512
14.4 Qualifying Adjectives in Protection and Security Clauses 516
14.4.1 The Adjective *Full* 516
14.4.1.1 *Full* Security as *Legal* Security 520
14.4.1.2 *Full* Security as *Physical* Security 523
14.4.1.3 *Full* Security as the Object and Purpose
of Other Treaty Provisions 525
14.4.1.4 *Full* Security as a Reference to the
Customary Protection Obligation 526
14.4.2 The Guarantee of *Constant* Protection
and Security 532
14.4.2.1 The Choice Between a Broad
and a Narrow Interpretation of *Constant
Security* Clauses 534
14.4.2.2 *Constant Security* Clauses and
Other Formulations of the Protection
Obligation 540
14.4.3 The Guarantee of *Legal* Protection and Security 542
14.4.4 Protection and Security Clauses Using No Qualifying
Adjectives 549

15 'Full Protection and Security' Clauses and Other Treaty Provisions 553
  15.1 Preliminary Remarks 553
  15.2 'Full Protection and Security' and 'Fair and Equitable Treatment' 554
    15.2.1 The Equating Approach 555
    15.2.2 The General-Particular Approach 563
    15.2.3 'Full Protection and Security' and 'Fair and Equitable Treatment' as Independent Standards 571
  15.3 'Full Protection and Security' and Expropriation 576
    15.3.1 The Substantive Difference Between Protection and Security Clauses and Expropriation Clauses 577
    15.3.2 The Interplay Between Protection and Security Claims and Expropriation Claims in Investment Arbitration 579
  15.4 'Full Protection and Security' and the Prohibition of Discriminatory and Arbitrary Measures 588
  15.5 'Full Protection and Security' and National Treatment 590
  15.6 'Full Protection and Security' and Most-Favored-Nation Treatment 594
  15.7 'Full Protection and Security' and War Clauses 602

16 Conclusion: The Night Watchman State 611

Table of Legal Instruments 615

Table of Cases 631

Table of State Practice 649

Bibliography 659

About the Author

Sebastián Mantilla Blanco was born in 1989 in Mainz, Germany. He holds a law degree (*Abogado*) from the Pontificia Universidad Javeriana (Bogotá, Colombia) and is admitted to practice law in Colombia. After working at the international arbitration team of a law firm in Bogotá, he pursued postgraduate studies at the University of Bonn, obtaining a *Magister Legum* (*LL.M.*) in 2015 and completing his doctoral studies (*Dr. iur.*) in 2018. He currently works as a Research Associate at the Institute of Public Law of the University of Bonn.

Abbreviations

§	Section
AJIL	American Journal of International Law
Am. J. Comp. L.	American Journal of Comparative Law
Am. L. Rev.	American Law Review
Am. U. L. Rev.	American University Law Review
Am. U. Int'l L. Rev.	American University International Law Review
Annals of the Amer. Acad. of Pol. and Soc. Science	Annals of the American Academy of Political and Social Science
Annu. Rep. A.B.A.	Annual Report of the American Bar Association
APPRI	Acuerdo de Promoción y Protección Recíproca de Inversiones
APSR	American Political Science Review
Arb. Int'l.	Arbitration International
ARIA	American Review of International Arbitration
art.	Article
ASIL	American Society of International Law
ASIL Proceedings	Proceedings of the American Society of International Law
AUBLR	American University Business Law Review
AVR	Archiv des Völkerrechts
RBDI	Revue belge de droit international/Belgisch tijdschrift voor internationaal Recht
BGBl.	Bundesgesetzblatt
BIT	Bilateral Investment Treaty
BYIL	British Yearbook of International Law
CA	California
CACM	Central American Common Market
CAFTA-DR	Free Trade Agreement between CACM, the Dominican Republic and the United States of America

Cal. L. Rev.	California Law Review
Chap.	Caput (Chapter)
CETA	Comprehensive Economic and Trade Agreement between Canada and the European Union
Cf./cf.	Confer (compare)
Ch.	Chapter/Chapters
CO	Colorado
CT	Connecticut
Columb. J. Transnat'l L	Columbia Journal of Transnational Law
Colum. L. Rev.	Columbia Law Review
Columb. L. T.	Columbia Law Times
COMESA	Common Market for Eastern and Southern Africa
CPTPP	Comprehensive and Progressive Agreement for Trans-Pacific Partnership
CYIL	Czech Yearbook of Public and Private International Law
Duke L. J.	Duke Law Journal
ECHR	European Convention on Human Rights
ECT	Energy Charter Treaty
ECtHR	European Court of Human Rights
ed/eds	Editor/editors
e.g.	*Exempli gratia*
EHQ	European History Quarterly
et al.	*Et alibi*
etc.	*Et cetera*
et seq	*Et sequens*
EWCA	Court of Appeal Civil Division (England)
FCN Agreement/Treaty	Friendship, Commerce and Navigation Agreement/Treaty
FET	Fair and Equitable Treatment
Fordham Int'l L.J.	Fordham International Law Journal
FPS	Full Protection and Security
FTC	Free Trade Commission (NAFTA)
GG	Grundgesetz (German Fundamental Law)
GoJIL	Goettingen Journal of International Law
GYIL	German Yearbook of International Law
HAHR	The Hispanic American History Review
HILJ	Harvard International Law Journal
Harv. Int'l. L. Club Bull.	Harvard International Law Club Bulletin
Harv. J. L. & Pub. Pol'y	Harvard Journal of Law and Public Policy
Harv. L. Rev.	Harvard Law Review
i.a.	*Inter alia*
ICCPR	International Covenant on Civil and Political Rights

i.e.	*Id est*
ICJ	International Court of Justice
ICJ Rep.	Reports of the International Court of Justice
ICLQ	International and Comparative Law Quarterly
ICSID	International Centre for Settlement of Investment Disputes
ICSID Rev	ICSID Review
IIA	International Investment Agreement
ICtHR	Inter-American Court of Human Rights
IIL	International Investment Law
IL	Illinois
ILA	International Law Association
ILC	International Law Commission
IN	Indiana
infra	Below
Iran–US Cl. Trib. Rep.	Iran–US Claims Tribunal Reports
ISDS	Investor-State Dispute Settlement
Isr. L. Rev.	Israel Law Review
JHIL	Journal of the History of International Law
JILP	New York University Journal of International Law and Politics
J. Int'l Disp. Settlement	Journal of International Dispute Settlement
J. Int'l Econ. L.	Journal of International Economic Law
JPR	Journal of Peace Research
J. World Investment & Trade	Journal of World Investment & Trade
KSzW	Kölner Schrift zum Wirtschaftsrecht
LA	Louisiana
Law Mag. & Rev. Quart. Rev. Juris.	The Law Magazine and Review. A Quarterly Review of Jurisprudence
Lib.	Liber (Book)
LJIL	Leiden Journal of International Law
LNTS	League of Nations Treaty Series
MI	Michigan
MN	Minnesota
MA	Massachusetts
MD	Maryland
Mercosur	Mercado Común del Sur
Mich. J. Int'l L.	Michigan Journal of International Law
Mich. L. Rev.	Michigan Law Review
Moore's Arb.	John Bassett Moore, *History and Digest of the International Arbitrations to Which the United States has been a Party* (Government Printing Office, Washington 1898)
n.	Note(s)/footnote(s)

NAFTA	North American Free Trade Agreement
NC	North Carolina
n.d.	No date
NE	Nebraska
NJ	New Jersey
NILR	Netherlands International Law Review
no.	Number
Nw. J. Int'l L. & Bus	Northwestern Journal of International Law & Business
NY	New York
NYLF	New York Law Forum
OIC	Organisation of the Islamic Conference
OR	Oregon
Or. L. Rev.	Oregon Law Review
p./pp.	Page/pages
P&S	Protection and Security
PCA	Permanent Court of Arbitration
Pol. Sci. Q.	Political Science Quarterly
RCADI	Recueil des Cours de l'Académie de Droit International de La Haye
RDILC	Revue de Droit International et de Législation Comparée
Rev. Int'l St.	Review of International Studies
RGDIP	Revue Générale de Droit International Public
RIAA	Reports on International Arbitral Awards
Sect./Sects.	Section/Sections
Sec. of State	Secretary of State
SIAR	Stockholm International Arbitration Review
sic	*Sic erat scriptum*
Soc. Leg. Stud.	Social & Legal Studies
St. Pap.	British State Papers
Syracuse J. Int'l L. & Com	Syracuse Journal of International Law and Commerce
TN	Tennessee
tr	Translator
TULSA L. Rev.	Tulsa Law Review
Tul. L. Rev.	Tulane Law Review
U. C. Davis J. Int'l L & Pol'y	UC Davis Journal of International Law and Policy
U. Chi. L. Rev.	The University of Chicago Law Review
UCLA L. Rev.	University of California, Los Angeles, Law Review
U. Miami Int'l & Comp. L. Rev.	University of Miami International and Comparative Law Review
UN	United Nations

UNCTAD	United Nations Conference on Trade and Development
UNTS	United Nations Treaty Series
U.K.	United Kingdom
U.S.	United States
USMCA	Agreement between the United States of America, the United Mexican States, and Canada
VA	Virginia
Va. J. Int'l L.	Virginia Journal of International Law
Vand. J. Transnat'l L.	Vanderbilt Journal of Transnational Law
VCLT	Vienna Convention on the Law of Treaties
VT	Vermont
WRV	Weimarer Reichverfassung
ZöR	Zeitschrift für öffentliches Recht
ZöaRV	Zeitschrift für ausländisches öffentliches Recht und Völkerrecht
ZRG	Zeitschrift der Savigny-Stiftung für Rechtsgeschichte

Chapter 1
Introduction

On the daybreak of April 15th, 1856, no inhabitant of Panama City expected to witness a turning point in local history. No one could have predicted that, before midnight, a local peddler and a drunken man would have sparked off a severe diplomatic crisis. That morning, José Manuel Luna had installed his fruit sales stand at an outdoor market nearby a railway station. The day had gone peacefully until an inebriated American citizen, Jake Oliver, took a one *real* (dime) worthy watermelon slice from Luna's stand and did not pay for it. Oliver grabbed his gun and threatened Luna, who then took out a knife. In the hope of preventing a tragic outcome, one of Oliver's companions gave the vendor a dime. As the peddler turned back, a gunshot was fired. The riot had begun. A swiftly growing mob relentlessly attacked U.S. citizens and ransacked their property. Local police intervention proved to be ineffective, if not to say counterproductive. Apparently confused by the events, Governor Francisco de Fábrega authorized Commander Manuel María Garrido to seize the city's railway station, where some Americans had sought refuge. An exchange of gunfire occurred as police officers approached the station. It remains unclear whether it was the police, the locals or the Americans who started the shooting. The fact is that U.S. citizens received injuries from both the local population and Panamanian police forces.[1]

---

[1] For a historical account of the incident see: Mercedes Chen Daley, 'The Watermelon Riot: Cultural Encounters in Panama City, April 15, 1856' (1990) 70(1) HAHR 85, 85-90. For a more detailed account of the facts see: John Bassett Moore, *History and Digest of the International Arbitrations to which the United States has been a Party* (Volume 2: Government Printing Office, Washington 1898) 1362-6. See also: John Bassett Moore, 'The Responsibility of Governments for Mob Violence' (1892) 5 Columb. L. T. 211, 212-3; Michael Donoghue, 'Watermelon Riot, Panama (1856)' in Alan McPherson (ed), *Encyclopedia of U.S. Military Interventions in Latin America* (Volume 1: ABC-Clio, Santa Barbara CA 2013) 688-90; Aimes McGuinness, *Path of Empire. Panama and the California Gold Rush* (Cornell University Press, New York 2008) 1-3, 123 *et seq.*; George Washington Crichfield, *American Supremacy. The Rise and Progress of the Latin American Republics and their Relations to the United States under the Monroe Doctrine* (Volume 2:

© Springer Nature Switzerland AG 2019
S. Mantilla Blanco, *Full Protection and Security in International Investment Law*,
European Yearbook of International Economic Law 8,
https://doi.org/10.1007/978-3-030-24838-3_1

This episode passed to history as the 'watermelon riot'. The United States considered the incident as a violation of the Friendship, Commerce and Navigation Treaty [FCN Treaty] signed with the Republic of New Granada on December 12th, 1846 (so-called 'Mallarino-Bidlack Treaty').[2] The core economic interest underlying the treaty was to ensure the right of way or transit across the Isthmus of Panama to American citizens and their merchandises.[3] The instrument further guaranteed nationals of each contracting party protection within the territory of the other contracting party.[4] These assurances would be at the heart of the forthcoming diplomatic controversy.[5] The United States designated a Special Agent, Mr. Amos Corwine, for the investigation of the facts. In his report of July 18th, 1856, Corwine concluded that 'the Government of New Granada is unable to maintain law and enforce order in this Isthmus, and afford adequate protection to the transit'.[6] The Special Agent went on to recommend taking military action.[7]

Bentano's, New York 1908) 203-9; Óscar Guardiola, *What if Latin America Ruled the World? How the South Will Take the North into the 22nd Century* (Bloomsbury Publishing Plc., London 2010) 223-5. For a description of the facts from the American perspective, see: Amos Corwine, 'The Panama Massacre. Report of the United States Commissioner of July 18, 1856/Evidence Taken at Panama' The New York Times, September 23, 1856.

[2]The Republic of New Granada (*República de la Nueva Granada*) encompassed the present-time national territories of Colombia and Panama. It also included areas that are nowadays part of Ecuador, Nicaragua and Venezuela. The Republic was established in 1832 and was replaced in 1858 by the Granadine Confederation. See generally: David Bushnell, *The Making of Modern Colombia: A Nation in Spite of Itself* (University of California University Press, London 1993) 74-100.

[3]The treaty was explicit in the protection of this core political interest. See: Treaty of Peace, Amity, Navigation, and Commerce between the United States of America and the Republic of New Granada (adopted 12 December 1846, entered into force 18 February 1848) Charles Bevans (ed), *Treaties and Other International Agreements of the United States of America 1776–1949* (Volume 6: U.S. Department of State Publication, Washington 1971) 868, 868 art. 35.

[4]Treaty of Peace, Amity, Navigation, and Commerce between the United States of America and the Republic of New Granada (adopted 12 December 1846, entered into force 18 February 1848) Charles Bevans (ed), *Treaties and Other International Agreements of the United States of America 1776—1949* (Volume 6: U.S. Department of State Publication, Washington 1971) 868, 872 art. 13. The Treaty further guaranteed American citizens 'the most perfect and entire security of conscience without being annoyed, prevented, or disturbed on account of their religious belief' (art. 14).

[5]For a compilation of the most relevant documents of the diplomatic crisis see: Luis Santamaría (ed), *Final Diplomatic Controversy relating to the Occurrences that Took Place at Panama on the 15th of April, 1856* (Mail Office, Liverpool 1857).

[6]Amos Corwine, 'The Panama Massacre. Report of the United States Commissioner of July 18, 1856/Evidence Taken at Panama' The New York Times, September 23, 1856.

[7]Amos Corwine, 'The Panama Massacre. Report of the United States Commissioner of July 18, 1856/Evidence Taken at Panama' The New York Times, September 23, 1856 ("I feel it a duty incumbent on me to recommend the immediate occupancy of the Isthmus, from Ocean to Ocean, by the United States, as the best practicable mode to insure safety and tranquility to the transit; unless New-Granada [. . .] in pursuance of treaty stipulations, can satisfy us as to her ability and inclination to afford the proper protection and make speedy and ample atonement for the wrongs inflicted upon our countrymen by the people and officials of the State of Panama"). See also: 'Note of the Legation of the United States to the Honourables Mssrs. Lino de Pombo and

A few months later, a small contingent of U.S. marines disembarked in Panama and took over effective control of Panama City's railway station.[8] While the intervention did not last long, the 'watermelon riot' would have a long-lasting political impact. It cannot be a mere coincidence for the Colombian statesman José María Torres Caicedo to have written his famous poem *Las dos Américas* (*The Two Americas*), which is often said to have originated the very phrase *Latin America*,[9] precisely in September 1856.[10] The poem fiercely condemned American foreign policy, making express reference to the constant threat of intervention in the isthmus.[11] In an extensive article published a few years later, Torres Caicedo argued that the law of nations does not require states to grant foreigners a higher degree of protection than that enjoyed by nationals, thus formulating, decades before Carlos Calvo (1896), what came to be known as the *Calvo Doctrine*.[12]

At the political and diplomatic level, local authorities continuously insisted on their ability to provide security to foreign nationals and their property in Panama. A

Florentino González, Commissioners on the part of New Granada' (26 February 1857) in Luis Santamaría (ed), *Final Diplomatic Controversy relating to the Occurrences that Took Place at Panama on the 15th of April, 1856* (Mail Office, Liverpool 1857) 37, 39 (underscoring that New Granada seemed to be 'either unable or unwilling to enforce those guarantees, or to give such protection as by the treaty and the charter of the Railroad Company she is pledged to do so').

[8]Robert Harding, *The History of Panama* (Greenwood Press, Westport 2006) 21; Michael Donoghue, 'Watermelon Riot, Panama (1856)' in Alan McPherson (ed), *Encyclopedia of U.S. Military Interventions in Latin America* (Volume 1: ABC-Clio, Santa Barbara CA 2013) 688, 690.

[9]On the influence of the poem see: Aimes McGuinness, *Path of Empire. Panama and the California Gold Rush* (Cornell University Press, New York 2008) 153; João Feres, *La historia del concepto "Latin America" en los Estados Unidos de América* (Universidad de Cantabria, Santander 2008) 60; Walter Mignolo, *The Idea of Latin America* (Blackwell Publishing, Oxford 2005) 79-80. For a critical discussion on the origin of the term 'Latin America' see: Miguel Rojas Mix, *Los cien nombres de América, eso que descubrió Colón* (Universidad de Costa Rica, San José 1997) 343-7.

[10]The poem appeared in a Spanish-language pamphlet titled *El Correo Ultramar* published in Paris on 15th February, 1857. See: Álvaro García San Martín, 'Francisco Bilbao y el proyecto latinoamericano' in Andrés Kozel and Héctor Palma (eds), Heterodoxia y fronteras en América Latina (Teseo, Buenos Aires 2013) 129, 131.

[11]The verses read: "Its large banner needs more stars; its trade requires more regions; but free banners flap in the South. – Let them fall! Says the powerful Union. Central America is being invaded; the Isthmus, constantly threatened; and Walker, the pirate, supported by the North. What a deceitful nation!" Author's translation. The original Spanish text reads: "A su ancho pabellón estrellas faltan, requiere su comercio otras regiones; mas flotan en el Sur libres pendones – Que caigan! dice la potente Unión. La América central es invadida, el Istmo sin cesar amenazado, y Walker, el pirata, es apoyado, por la del Norte pérfida nación!" The full text of the poem was reproduced in a collection of Torres Caicedo's poetic works, published in 1860. See: José María Torres Caicedo, *Religión, patria y amor. Colección de versos escritos* (Th. Ducessoirs, Paris 1860) 448-61.

[12]José María Torres Caicedo, 'Importante cuestión de derecho de gentes. A propósito del conflicto venezolano-hispano en 1860' in José María Torres Caicedo, *Unión Latino-Americana* (Librería de Rosa y Bouret, Paris 1865) 307, 313. On the origins of the Calvo Doctrine see Sect. 4.3.1.

representative example is the Presidential Message to the Congress of New Granada of February 1st, 1857:

> Since the discovery of the gold of California, the Isthmus of Panama has been crossed by an infinitive number of travellers and by immense sums of gold [...] Was there security for the transit at that period? Yes, the most complete [...] There was complete security, there is at present, and there always will be, for passengers and their property without being dependent, in any way, on a numerous armed force [...] In Panama, as well throughout the Republic, all foreigners without distinction have enjoyed, not only the most complete security, but have moreover been the object of the most perfect benevolence. To pretend that any of those who cross over the Isthmus has a right to fire upon the natives, and that these should humbly receive the bow, is the very high of folly and madness [...] The responsibility for the unhappy occurrences of the 15th April, which I sincerely deplore, does not rest upon New Granada, and for the future, I can assure you, nothing is to be feared that can endanger the security of the transit over the Isthmus of Panama.[13]

The 'watermelon riot' eventually resulted in the Herrán-Cass Agreement of September 10th, 1857. Thereby, the Government of New Granada expressly acknowledged its 'privilege and obligation to preserve peace and good order along the transit route'.[14] The first explanatory note to the Agreement made clear that this obligation resulted not only from treaty stipulations, but also from general international law:

> It is understood that the obligation of New Granada to maintain peace and good order on the interoceanic route of the Isthmus of Panama [...] is the same by which all nations are held to preserve peace and order within their territories, in conformity with general principles of the law of nations, and of the public treaties which they may have concluded.[15]

The parties further agreed to constitute a Mixed Claims Commission, which was given jurisdiction to award compensation for damages caused during the riot.[16] The consequences of the occurrences of April 1857 did not however end with this Convention. Historians believe that the 'watermelon riot' was the first in the series

---

[13]'Extract from the Presidential Message to the Congress of New Granada' (1 February 1857) in Luis Santamaría (ed), *Final Diplomatic Controversy relating to the Occurrences that Took Place at Panama on the 15th of April, 1856* (Mail Office, Liverpool 1857) 47, 49-50.

[14]Convention between the United States of America and the Republic of New Granada (adopted 10 September 1857, entered into force 5 November 1860) Charles Bevans (ed), *Treaties and Other International Agreements of the United States of America 1776—1949* (Volume 6: U.S. Department of State Publication, Washington 1971) 888, 889, art. I.

[15]Convention between the United States of America and the Republic of New Granada (adopted 10 September 1857, entered into force 5 November 1860) Charles Bevans (ed), *Treaties and Other International Agreements of the United States of America 1776—1949* (Volume 6: U.S. Department of State Publication, Washington 1971) 888, 891, Explanatory Note No. 1.

[16]Convention between the United States of America and the Republic of New Granada (adopted 10 September 1857, entered into force 5 November 1860) Charles Bevans (ed), *Treaties and Other International Agreements of the United States of America 1776—1949* (Volume 6: U.S. Department of State Publication, Washington 1971) 888, 889-90 art. II. For a detailed account of the Claims Commission's work see: John Bassett Moore, *History and Digest of the International Arbitrations to which the United States has been a Party* (Volume 2: Government Printing Office, Washington 1898) 1361-96.

of incidents and U.S. military interventions that would finally result in the independence of Panama (1903).[17]

From a legal-historical standpoint, there was nothing extraordinary about New Granada's obligation to protect Americans crossing the Isthmus. Since the late eighteenth century, western legal scholars had repeatedly underscored that aliens are entitled to the most constant protection and security within the host state's territory.[18] Treaties, awards and diplomatic correspondence made continuous references to the protection obligation throughout the nineteenth and early twentieth centuries.[19]

From a present-day perspective, the security obligation that came to be known as the standard of 'full protection and security' [FPS] is much more than a somewhat picturesque leftover from the past. The standard made its way into the present through customary international law and, perhaps most importantly, international investment agreements [IIAs].[20] Most bilateral investment treaties [BITs] and investment chapters of free trade agreements [FTAs] accord covered investments 'protection and security'.[21] IIAs have followed this pattern since the very first BIT, which was concluded between Germany and Pakistan in 1959. Article 3(1) of the 1959 treaty provides an indicative example of a modern FPS clause:

> Investments by nationals or companies of either Party shall enjoy security and protection in the territory of the other Party.[22]

Not every treaty uses the same formulation. Diversity signalizes FPS clauses. While some treaties refer to 'protection and security' or 'full protection and security', other instruments ensure covered investments 'the most constant protection and security' or 'legal protection and security.'[23] Needless to say, FPS clauses do not

---

[17]See: Robert Harding, *The History of Panama* (Greenwood Press, Westport 2006) 21-2; Alan McPherson, *Yankee No! Anti Americanism in U.S.–Latin American Relations* (Harvard University Press, Cambridge MA/London 2003), 78-81. Panama declared its independence from Colombia on November 3rd, 1903. The Roosevelt Administration recognized the Republic of Panama on November 6th, 1903. A few days later, the United States and Panama signed the Panama Canal Convention. See: Convention between the United States and the Republic of Panama for the Construction of a Ship Canal to Connect the Waters of the Atlantic and Pacific Oceans (adopted 18 November 1903, entered into force 26 February 1904) *Papers relating to the Foreign Relations of the United States with the Annual Message of the President* (Government Printing Office, Washington 1905) 543-52. For a critical discussion of the recognition of Panama by the United States see: Moorfield Storey, *The Recognition of Panama* (Geo. H. Ellis Co. Printers, Boston 1904).

[18]Chapter 3 presents a survey of early scholarly writings on the subject.

[19]See Chap. 4 *et seq.*

[20]See Chaps. 5, 7, 8 and 14.

[21]For representative examples of international investment treaties containing FPS clauses see: Martin Paparinskis, *Basic Documents on International Investment Protection* (Hart Publishing, Portland OR 2012). See also Chap. 14.

[22]Treaty between the Federal Republic of Germany and Pakistan for the Promotion and Protection of Investments (adopted 25 November 1959, entered into force 28 April 1962) art. 3(1).

[23]Chapter 14 addresses the wording of FPS clauses in detail.

convey a clear meaning from the outset. Taken in isolation, their wording does not reveal much about the FPS standard's precise content and scope of application. In an attempt to reduce the indeterminacy of the FPS standard, numerous treaties have expressly linked the treaty standard to customary international law.[24]

The interpretation of protection and security clauses is not a question of mere academic interest. It is a matter of pivotal practical importance. In fact, FPS is everything but a dormant standard. Since the early 1990s, FPS clauses have been invoked in countless investment arbitration proceedings. To date, at least 90 investment arbitral awards have dealt with the FPS standard. Relevant decisions have been rendered both in arbitral proceedings under the auspices of the International Centre for Settlement of Investment Disputes [ICSID],[25] and in arbitrations outside the

---

[24]Section 14.2 provides representative examples of these treaty clauses.

[25]Adel A Hamadi Al Tamini v Oman, Award, ICSID Case No. ARB/11/33 (3 November 2015) [380, 382 and 448-52]; ADF v United States, Award, ICSID Case No. ARB(AF)/00/1 (9 January 2003) [182-6]; AES Corporation and Tau Power B.V. v Kazakhstan, Award, ICSID Case No. ARB/10/16 (1 November 2013) [337-9]; AES Summit Generation Ltd. and AES-Tisza Erömü Kft. v Hungary, Award, ICSID Case No. ARB/07/22 (23 September 2010) [13.3]; American Manufacturing & Trading Inc. v Zaire, Award, ICSID Case No. ARB 93/1 (21 February 1997) [6.04-6.11]; Ampal-American Israel Corp., Egi-Fund (08-10) Investors LLC, Egi-Series Investments LLC and BSS-EMG Investors LLC v Egypt, Decision on Liability and Heads of Loss, ICSID Case No. ARB/12/11 (21 February 2017) [150, 187, 194-216, 235-47, 271-4, 283-91 and 350(d)]; Anglo American PLC v Venezuela, Award, ICSID Case No. ARB(AF)/14/1 (18 January 2019) [473-85]; Asian Agricultural Products v Sri Lanka, Final Award, ICSID Case No. ARB/87/3 (17 June 1990) [45 et seq.]; Azurix Corp. v Argentina, Award, ICSID Case No. ARB/01/12 (14 July 2006) [406-8]; Bernhard Friedrich Arnd Rüdiger von Pezold et al. v Zimbabwe, Award, ICSID Case No. ARB/10/15 (28 July 2015) [593-9]; Biwater Gauff Ltd. v Tanzania, Award, ICSID Case No. ARB/05/22 (24 July 2008) [724-31]; Československá Obchodní Banka A.S. v Slovakia, Award, ICSID Case No. ARB/97/4 (29 December 2004) [161, 170 and 183]; Compañía de Aguas del Aconquija S.A. and Vivendi Universal S.A. v Argentina, Award, ICSID Case No. ARB/97/3 (20 August 2007) [7.4.13-7.4.17]; Convial Callao S.A. and CCI – Compañía de Concesiones de Infraestructura S.A. v Peru, Laudo Final, ICSID Case No. ARB/10/2 (21 May 2013) [641-62]; Crystallex International Corp. v Venezuela, Award, ICSID Case No. ARB(AF)/11/2 (4 April 2016) [632-5]; Deutsche Bank AG v Sri Lanka, Award, ICSID Case No. ARB/09/02 (31 October 2012) [535-8]; EDF International S.A., Saur International S.A. and Leon Participaciones Argentinas S.A. v Argentina, Award, ICSID Case No. ARB/03/23 (11 June 2012) [403-20 and 1108-12]; Electrabel S.A. v Hungary, Decision on Jurisdiction, Applicable Law and Liability, ICSID Case No. ARB/07/19 (30 November 2012) [7.80 et seq. and 7.145-7]; El Paso Energy International Co. v Argentina, Award, ICSID Case No. ARB/03/15 (31 October 2011) [522-5]; Emilio Agustín Maffezini v Spain, Award, ICSID Case No. ARB/97/7 (13 November 2000) [83]; Enron Corp. and Ponderosa Assets L.P. v Argentina, Award, ICSID Case No. ARB/01/3 (22 May 2007) [284-7]; Gea Group Aktiengesellschaft v Ukraine, Award, ICSID Case No. ARB/08/16 (31 March 2011) [242-67]; Gemplus S.A., SLP S.A. and Gemplus Industrial S.A. de C.V. v Mexico, Award, ICSID Cases No. ARB(AF)/04/3 & ARB(AF)/04/4 (16 June 2010) [9.9-9.14]; Gold Reserve Inc. v Venezuela, Award, ICSID Case No. ARB(AF)/09/1 (22 September 2014) [622-3]; Impregilo S.p.A. v Argentina, Award, ICSID Case No. ARB/07/17 (21 June 2011) [334]; Jan de Nul N.V. and Dredging International N.V. v Egypt, Award, ICSID Case No. ARB/04/13 (6 November 2008) [266-71]; Joseph Charles Lemire v Ukraine, Decision on Jurisdiction and Liability, ICSID Case No. ARB/06/18 (14 January 2010) [246 and 496]; Joseph Houben v Burundi, Sentence, ICSID Case No. ARB/13/7 (12 January 2016) [157-79]; Koch Minerals SÁRL and Koch Nitrogen International

ICSID system.[26] While FPS claims are on the rise, the protection obligation remains

---

SÁRL *v* Venezuela, Award, ICSID Case No. ARB/11/19 (30 October 2017) [8.42-8.46]; LESI S.p.A. and ASTALDI S.p.A. *v* Algeria, Sentence, ICSID Case No. ARB/05/3 (12 November 2008) [152-4]; Liman Caspian Oil BV and NCL Dutch Investment BV *v* Kazakhstan, Award, ICSID Case No. ARB/07/14 (22 June 2010) [289]; Loewen Group Inc. and Raymond L. Loewen *v* United States, Award, ICSID Case No. ARB(AF)/98/3 (26 June 2003) [124 *et seq.*; particularly at 128]; Mamidoil Jetoil Greek Petroleum Products Societe S.A. *v* Albania, Award, ICSID Case No. ARB/11/24 (30 March 2015) [799-829]; Marion Unglaube and Reinhard Unglaube *v* Costa Rica, Award, ICSID Cases No. ARB/01/1 and ARB/09/20 (16 May 2012) [280-8]; M.C.I. Power Group L.C. and New Turbine Inc. *v* Ecuador, Award, ICSID Case No. ARB/03/6 (31 July 2007) [245-6 and 252 *et seq.*]; Mercer International Inc. *v* Canada, Award, ICSID Case No. ARB(AF)/12/ 3 (6 March 2018) [7.80]; Millicom International Operations B.V. and Sentel GMS SA *v* Senegal, Decision on Jurisdiction of the Arbitral Tribunal, ICSID Case No. ARB/08/20 (16 July 2010) [65]; MNSS B.V. and Recupero Credito Acciaio N.V. *v* Montenegro, Award, ICSID Case No. ARB(AF)/ 12/8 (4 May 2016) [348-56]; Mobil Exploration and Development Argentina Inc. Suc. Argentina and Mobil Argentina S.A. *v* Argentina, Decision on Jurisdiction and Liability, ICSID Case No. ARB/04/16 (10 April 2013) [988-1005]; Mondev International *v* United States, Award, ICSID Case No. ARB(AF)/99/2 (11 October 2002) [113-25]; Noble Ventures *v* Romania, Award, ICSID Case No. ARB/01/11 (12 October 2005) [164-7]; OI European Group B.V. *v* Venezuela, Award, ICSID Case No. ARB/11/25 (10 March 2015) [571-81]; Pantechniki S.A. Contractors & Engineers *v* Albania, Award, ICSID Case No. ARB/07/21 (30 July 2009) [71-84]; Parkerings-Compagniet AS *v* Lithuania, Award, ICSID Case No. ARB/05/8 (11 September 2007) [354-61]; Plama Consortium Ltd. *v* Bulgaria, Award, ICSID Case No. ARB/03/24 (27 August 2008) [179-81, 194, 222, 226, 229, 236, 248-55, 259, 270-1, 277-84 and 325]; PSEG Global Inc. and Konya Ilgin Elektrik Üretim ve Ticaret Limited Şirketi *v* Turkey, Award, ICSID Case No. ARB/02/5 (19 January 2007) [257-9]; Rumeli Telekom A.S. and Telsim Mobil Telekomunikasyon Hizmetleri A.S. *v* Kazakhstan, Award, ICSID Case No. ARB/05/16 (29 July 2008) [668-70]; Rusoro Mining Ltd. *v* Venezuela, Award, ICSID Case No. ARB(AF)/12/5 (22 August 2016) [542-54]; Saint-Gobain Performance Plastics Europe *v* Venezuela, Decision on Liability and the Principles of Quantum, ICSID Case No. ARB/12/13 (30 December 2016) [550-65]; SAUR International S.A. *v* Argentina, Décision sur la compétence et sur la responsabilité, ICSID Case No. ARB/04/4 (6 June 2012) [499-501 and 508-11]; Sempra Energy International *v* Argentina, Award, ICSID Case No. ARB/02/16 (28 September 2007) [321-4]; Siemens AG *v* Argentina, Award, ICSID Case No. ARB/02/8 (6 February 2007) [301-9]; Suez Sociedad General de Aguas de Barcelona S.A. and Vivendi Universal S.A. *v* Argentina, Decision on Liability, ICSID Case No. ARB/03/19 (30 July 2010) [158-79]; Spyridon Roussalis *v* Romania, Award, ICSID Case No. ARB/06/1 (7 December 2011) [319-22]; Tecnicas Medioambientales TECMED S.A. *v* Mexico, Award, ICSID Case No. ARB(AF)/00/2 (29 May 2003) [175-81]; Teinver S.A., Transportes de Cercanías S.A. and Autobuses Urbanos del Sur S.A. *v* Argentina, Award, ICSID Case No. ARB/09/1 (21 July 2017) [866-910]; Tenaris S.A. and Talta-Trading E Marketing Sociedade Unipessoal Lda. *v* Venezuela, Award, ICSID Case No. ARB/11/26 (29 January 2016) [438-48]; Tokios Tokelés *v* Ukraine, Award, ICSID Case No. ARB/02/18 (26 July 2007) [85-5 and 123 *et seq.*]; Total S.A. *v* Argentina, Decision on Liability, ICSID Case No. ARB/04/1 (27 December 2010) [343]; Toto Costruzioni Generali S.p.A. *v* Lebanon, Award, ICSID Case No. ARB/07/12 (7 June 2012) [226-30]; Tulip Real Estate Investment and Development Netherlands B.V. *v* Turkey, Award, ICSID Case No. ARB/11/28 (10 March 2014) [419-37]; Vannessa Ventures Ltd. *v* Venezuela, Award, ICSID Case No. ARB(AF)04/6 (16 January 2013) [216-32]; Waguih George Siag and Clorinda Vecchi *v* Egypt, Award, ICSID Case No. ARB/05/15 (1 June 2009) [445-8]; Waste Management *v* Mexico, Award, ICSID Case No. ARB(AF)/00/3 (30 April 2004) [91 and 96]; Wena Hotels Ltd. *v* Egypt, Award, ICSID Case No. ARB/98/4 (8 December 2000) [83-95 and 134].

[26]Achmea B.V. *v* Slovakia (UNCITRAL), Award on Jurisdiction, Arbitrability and Suspension, PCA Case No. 2008-13 (26 October 2010) [259-63 and 284]; Anglia Auto Accessories Ltd. *v* Czech Republic, Final Award, SCC Case No. V 2014/181 (10 March 2017) [190]; BG Group *v* Argentina (UNCITRAL), Final Award (24 December 2007) [323-8]; CC/Devas (Mauritius) Ltd., Devas

one of the least elucidated aspects of international investment law. The increasing number of cases concerning FPS strikingly contrasts with the modest, albeit rapidly growing, attention the standard has received in specialized academic literature.[27]

Employees Mauritius Private Ltd. and Telcom Devas Mauritius Ltd. *v* India (UNCITRAL), Award on Jurisdiction and Merits, PCA Case No. 2013-09 (25 July 2016) [491-500]; CME Czech Republic B.V. *v* Czech Republic (UNCITRAL), Partial Award (13 September 2001) [351-8 and 613]; Eastern Sugar B.V. *v* Czech Republic, Partial Award, SCC Case No. 088/2004 (27 March 2007) [201-7]; Eureko B.V. *v* Poland (*Ad Hoc* Arbitration), Partial Award (19 August 2005) [236-7]; Frontier Petroleum Ltd. *v* Czech Republic (UNCITRAL), Final Award (12 November 2010) [260-73]; Grand River Enterprises Six Nations Ltd. et al. *v* United States of America (UNCITRAL), Award (12 January 2011) [174-6]; Hesham Talaat M. Al-Warraq *v* Indonesia (UNCITRAL), Final Award (15 December 2014) [622-30]; I.P. Busta and J.P. Busta *v* Czech Republic, Final Award, SCC Case No. V 2015/014 (10 March 2017) [165 and 422]; Isolux Netherlands B.V. *v* Spain, Laudo, SCC Case No. V 2013/153 (17 July 2016) [816-9]; Iurii Bogdanov et al. *v* Moldova (SCC), Arbitral Award (22 September 2005) 15; Jan Oostergetel and Theodora Laurentius *v* Slovakia (UNCITRAL), Final Award (23 April 2012) [305-8]; Mohammad Ammar Al-Bahloul *v* Tajikistan, Partial Award on Jurisdiction and Liability, SCC Case No. V 064/2008 (9 September 2009) [243-7]; National Grid P.L.C. *v* Argentina (UNCITRAL), Award (3 November 2008) [187-90]; OAO Tatneft *v* Ukraine (UNCITRAL), Award (29 July 2014) [414-30]; Occidental Exploration and Production Co. *v* Ecuador, Final Award, LCIA Case No. UN 3467 (1 July 2004) [180 and 187]; Oxus Gold *v* Uzbekistan (UNCITRAL), Final Award (17 December 2015) [348 *et seq.* and 829 *et seq.*]; Peter A. Allard *v* Barbados (UNCITRAL), Award (27 June 2016) [239-52]; Ronald Lauder *v* Czech Republic (UNCITRAL), Final Award (3 September 2001) [305-14]; Saluka Investments *v* Czech Republic (UNCITRAL), Partial Award (17 March 2006) [483-96]; Sergei Paushok, CJSC Golden East Co., CJSC Vostoknefte *v* Mongolia (UNCITRAL), Award on Jurisdiction and Liability (28 April 2011) [278-9 and 322-7]; Ulysseas Inc. *v* Ecuador (UNCITRAL), Final Award (12 June 2012) [271-4]; William Ralph Clayton, William Richard Clayton, Douglas Clayton, Daniel Clayton and Bilicon of Delaware Inc. *v* Canada (UNCITRAL), Award on Jurisdiction and Liability, PCA Case No. 2009-05 (17 March 2015) [360, 376, 392-3, 422-3, 427 *et seq.* and 742(a)(ii)]; Windstream Energy LLC *v* Canada (UNCITRAL), Award (27 September 2016) [355-8].

[27]Academic publications about the FPS standard include: Caline Mouawad and Sarah Vasani, 'Energy Disputes in Times of Civil Unrest: Transitional Governments and Foreign Investment Protections' in Arthur Rovine (ed), *Contemporary Issues in International Arbitration and Mediation* (Brill, Leiden/Boston 2015) 234, 242-9; Catharine Titi, 'Full Protection and Security, Arbitrary or Discriminatory Treatment and the Invisible EU Model BIT' (2014) 14 J. World Investment & Trade 534-50; Christoph Schreuer, 'Full Protection and Security' (2010) 1(2) J. Int'l Disp. Settlement 353-69; Eric De Brabandere, 'Fair and Equitable Treatment and (Full) Protection and Security in African Investment Treaties: Between Generality and Contextual Specificity' (2017) Grotius Centre Working Paper 2017/063 1-25; Eric De Brabandere, 'Host States' Due Diligence Obligations in International Investment Law' (2014-5) 42 Syracuse J. Int'l L. & Com. 319-61; Finnur Magnússon, *Full Protection and Security in International Law* (University of Vienna, Vienna 2012); Francisco Endara Flores, 'La protección y seguridad plena de las inversiones. ¿El estándar olvidado de los tratados bilaterales de inversión?' (2009) 2 Revista de Derecho Público 443-60; Geneviève Bastid Burdeau, 'La clause de protection et sécurité pleine et entière' (2015) 119 (1) RGDIP 87-101; George Foster, 'Recovering "Protection and Security": The Treaty Standard's Obscure Origins, Forgotten Meaning, and Key Current Significance' (2012) 45(4) Vand. J. Transnat'l L. 1095-156; Giuditta Cordero Moss, 'Full Protection and Security' in August Reinisch (ed), *Standards of Investment Protection* (Oxford University Press, New York 2008) 131-50; Gleider Hernández, 'The Interaction Between Investment Law and the Law of Armed Conflict in the Interpretation of Full Protection and Security Clauses' in Freya Baetens (ed), *Investment Law within International Law* (Cambridge University Press, Cambridge 2013) 21-50;

Navigating among recent publications one gets the impression that, in the last decades, the standard of 'fair and equitable treatment' [FET] has largely outshined the FPS standard.[28] This academic neglect has not been without practical consequences. In investment arbitral proceedings, the combination of vague treaty language and scarce dogmatic guidance has turned the interpretation of FPS clauses into a true challenge for counsel and arbitrators alike. At least three difficulties have arisen in this regard.

Heather Bray, 'SOI – Save Our Investments! International Investment Law and International Humanitarian Law' (2013) 14 J. World Investment & Trade 578-94; Helge Elisabeth Zeitler, 'Full Protection and Security' in Stephan Schill (ed), *International Investment Law and Comparative Public Law* (Oxford University Press, New York 2010) 183-212; Helge Elisabeth Zeitler, 'The Guarantee of Full Protection and Security in Investment Treaties regarding Harm Caused by Private Parties' (2005) 3 SIAR 1-34; J. Anthony VanDuzer, 'Full Protection and Security' in Thomas Cottier and Krista Nadakavukaren Schefer (eds), *Elgar Encyclopedia of International Economic Law* (Edward Elgar Publishing, Northampton MA 2018) 212-4; John Riggs, 'Investment Protection in Colombia: Can Investors Rely on the Full Protection and Security Clause?' (2014) 7(3) J. World Investment & Trade 264-73; Levon Golendukhin, 'Reference to Intellectual Property Treaty Norms in Full Protection and Security and Fair and Equitable Treatment Claims' in Ian Laird, Borzu Sabahi, Frédéric Sourgens and Todd Weiler (eds), *Investment Treaty Arbitration and International Law* (Juris Net, Huntington NY 2018) 89-110; Lucas Bastin, *State Responsibility for Omissions: Establishing a Breach of the Full Protection and Security Obligation by Omissions* (Oxford University, Oxford 2016) [D.Phil. Thesis]; Lucas Bastin, *Violation of the Full Protection and Security Obligation by Regulatory Omissions* [M.Phil. Thesis] (Oxford University, Oxford 2011); Margarita Sánchez and Robert DeRise, 'The Full Measure of Full Protection and Security' in Ian Laird, Borzu Sabahi, Frédéric Sourgens and Todd Weiler (eds), *Investment Treaty Arbitration and International Law* (Juris Net, Huntington NY 2015) 99-123; Nartnirun Junngam, 'The Full Protection and Security Standard in International Investment Law: What and Who is Investment Fully[?] Protected and Secured From?' (2018) 7(1) AUBLR 1-100; Nicole O'Donnell, 'Reconciling Full Protection and Security Guarantees in Bilateral Investment Treaties with Incidence of Terrorism' (2018) 29(3) ARIA 293-313; Nnaemeka Nwokedi Anozie, *The Full Security and Protection Due Diligence Obligation* (University of Ottawa, Ottawa 2016) [LL.M. Thesis]; Onyema Awa Oyeani, *The Obligation of Host States to Accord the Standard of "Full Protection and Security" to Foreign Investments under International Investment Law* (Brunel University, London 2018) [D. Phil. Thesis]; Petr Stejskal, 'War: Foreign Investments in Danger – Can International Humanitarian Law or Full Protection and Security Always Save It?' (2017) 8 CYIL 529-49; Ralph Alexander Lorz, 'Protection and Security (Including the NAFTA Approach)' in Marc Bungenberg, Jörn Griebel, Stephan Hobe and August Reinisch (eds), *International Investment Law* (Nomos, Baden-Baden 2015) 764-89; Robert Reyes Landicho, 'Enforcing a State's International IP Obligations through Investment Law Standards of Protection – An Ill-Fated Romance' in Ian Laird, Borzu Sabahi, Frédéric Sourgens and Todd Weiler (eds), *Investment Treaty Arbitration and International Law* (Juris Net, Huntington NY 2018) 111-32; Stanimir Alexandrov, 'The Evolution of the Full Protection and Security Standard' in Meg Kinnear, Geraldine Fischer, Jara Mínguez Almeida, Luisa Torres and Mairée Uran Bidegain (eds), *Building International Investment Law. The First 50 Years of ICSID* (Wolters Kluwer/ICSID, Alphen aan den Rijn 2016) 319-29; Todd Weiler, *The Interpretation of International Investment Law: Equality, Discrimination, and Minimum Standards of Treatment in Historical Context* (Brill, Leiden 2013) 59-182. In addition to these academic publications, most textbooks on international investment law include some brief reference to the FPS standard.

[28]Section 15.2 addresses the FET standard and its relationship to the FPS standard.

A first issue pertains to the customary FPS standard. It is a commonplace that FPS is not only a treaty-based obligation, but has, too, a customary character.[29] Nonetheless, the precise scope and content of the customary security obligation remain somewhat uncertain.[30] Arbitral awards too often fail to bolster their assertions about custom with a clear analysis of the relevant sources.[31] A few scholars have made valuable attempts to unveil the meaning of the customary security obligation through systematic and legal-historical analysis.[32] Still, there seems to be more disagreement than agreement on the subject.

A second difficulty refers to the FPS standard's scope of application. The notions of 'physical security' and 'legal security' have largely dominated the assessment of the FPS standard in academic publications and investment arbitral proceedings.[33] Investors often argue that FPS encompasses the notion of *legal security*, which is in turn frequently understood as a guarantee of legal stability. This interpretation typically results in a quandary about the extent of legal stability, possible overlaps with other treaty obligations (particularly the FET standard), and the regard due to the host state's regulatory powers.[34] For its part, the host state usually responds with some appeal to customary law. In this vein, respondent states normally follow one of two lines of argument. A first line of argument consists in defining the scope of FPS by reference to the concept of 'physical' protection, which is said to express the 'traditional' or 'customary' meaning of the standard.[35] A second line of argument draws a line between private and public violence, and suggests that FPS has customarily referred to protection against private injuries.[36]

A third difficulty relates to the applicable standard of liability. With few exceptions, most authorities coincide in stating that the FPS standard does not impose strict liability on the host state.[37] A breach of FPS, it is said, requires a want of diligence on the part of state agents. The linkage between FPS and the notion of due

---

[29]See Chap. 5.

[30]See, for example, the debate on whether FPS encompasses the notion of legal stability (at Sect. 9.3).

[31]Chapter 9 provides some examples of these argumentative deficits. For a detailed analysis of the use of assertion as a means to determine international custom see: Stefan Talmon, 'Determining Customary International Law: The ICJ's Methodology between Induction, Deduction and Assertion' (2015) 26(2) EJIL 417, 434-40 (particularly focusing on ICJ decisions).

[32]For two representative examples see: George Foster, 'Recovering "Protection and Security": The Treaty Standard's Obscure Origins, Forgotten Meaning, and Key Current Significance' (2012) 45 (4) Vand. J. Transnat'l L. 1095, 1095-156; Todd Weiler, *The Interpretation of International Investment Law: Equality, Discrimination, and Minimum Standards of Treatment in Historical Context* (Brill, Leiden 2013) 59-182.

[33]Chapter 9 provides an overview of this particular subject.

[34]Section 9.3 provides a critical analysis of this line of argument.

[35]Sections 9.2 and 9.4 discuss the notions of physical and nonphysical security.

[36]Section 8.3 addresses the sources of risk covered by the customary FPS standard.

[37]It is worth noting that some publicists have suggested that FPS and due diligence are not unavoidably intertwined. According to them, the notion of due diligence is *only* relevant in respect of the *use* of the municipal legal and administrative system in the prevention and punishment of

diligence is perhaps one of the most consistently established premises of contemporary international investment law.[38] At the same time, however, no premise appears to have been more steadily blurred in theory and practice. The obvious question is what due diligence means in this context or, more accurately, the parameters due diligence provides for the assessment of the host state's conduct.[39]

The above list does not intend to be an exhaustive enumeration of all difficulties the FPS standard has posed and continues to pose in practice. Against the backdrop of these ongoing debates, the FPS standard could be taken as a textbook example of the problem of consistency and predictability that has accompanied the development of international investment law throughout the past decades, giving rise to insistent calls for a consistent and predictable application of IIAs.[40] The present monograph represents an effort to analyze the FPS standard in both customary and treaty law, and to scrutinize the wide array of approaches followed by contemporary authorities in dealing with the standard. By so doing, this work hopes to increase certainty in the application of the FPS standard and, at the same time, to foster consciousness about the complexity of its normative structure.

A word of caution should be spoken, however. The FPS standard developed out of sundry and partially inconsistent sources. This work does not pursue the utopian goal of presenting FPS as a legal institution conveying a univocal meaning, entirely free from vagueness and ambiguity. To do so would be to trade off accuracy for consistency.[41] An effort has been made neither to ignore the multitude of doctrinal

---

private injuries to aliens. In all other cases, they argue, a breach of FPS is not dependent on a lack of diligence. Section 11.2.3.2 discusses these views in detail.

[38] See Chap. 11.

[39] See Chaps. 12 and 13.

[40] For an overview of the legitimacy concerns arising out of the inconsistent application of investment protection standards see: Muthucumaraswamy Sornarajah, 'A Coming Crisis: Expansionary Trends in Investment Treaty Arbitration' in Karl Sauvant (ed), *Appeals Mechanism in International Investment Disputes* (Oxford University Press, New York 2008) 39, 41 *et seq.*; Stephan Schill, 'International Investment Law and Comparative Public Law – An Introduction' in Stephan Schill (ed), *International Investment Law and Comparative Public Law* (Oxford University Press, New York 2010) 3, 4-7; Trihn Hai Yen, *The Interpretation of International Investment Treaties* (Brill, Leiden 2014) 9 *et seq.* For some critical remarks about the call for consistency in investment law see: Irene Ten Cate, 'The Costs of Consistency: Precedent in Investment Treaty Arbitration' (2013) 51 Columb. J. Transnat'l L. 418-78; Thomas Schultz, 'Against Consistency in Investment Arbitration' in Zachary Douglas, Joost Pauwelyn and Jorge Viñuales (eds), *The Foundations of International Investment Law. Bringing Theory into Practice* (Oxford University Press, Oxford 2014) 297-316.

[41] The aspiration to accuracy does not only pertain to academic undertakings, but is moreover fundamental to international adjudication. On the role of 'accuracy' in international arbitration see generally: William Park, 'Arbitrators and Accuracy' (2010) 1(1) J. Int'l Disp. Settlement 25-53 (particularly referring to fact-finding but also considering 'the arbitrator's truth-seeking function with respect to legal norms' at pp. 42 *et seq.*). On the trade-off between consistency and accuracy in investment arbitration see: Irene Ten Cate, 'The Costs of Consistency: Precedent in Investment Treaty Arbitration' (2013) 51 Columb. J. Transnat'l L. 418, 457-9 (particularly focusing on consistency as a restraint on the exercise of adjudicatory authority).

projects that have shaped the development of the standard, nor to turn a blind eye to the deep differences of language among FPS clauses, diplomatic correspondence and other relevant sources. Oversimplification is not the answer to such intricacies. The driving forces of international investment law have never been uniformity and doctrinal perfection, but diversity and political compromise. It is not by overlooking discrepancies between sources, but by acknowledging them, that accuracy and certainty in the interpretation of FPS clauses can be achieved.[42]

Simply put, this monograph cannot give a definitive answer to every question about the FPS standard. Some issues must be recognized as unavoidably controversial. In respect of those questions, this work aims at providing a critical account of the state of the art. In this vein, it avoids worshipping some theories as incontestable truths, and disregarding opposite views as false or incorrect. It rather seeks to make a case in favor of those approaches that reduce inconsistencies, find more support from primary sources, or otherwise appear to be more convincing than others. Where none of the existing approaches offers a satisfactory solution, this monograph will take the plunge and propose an alternative.

The argument has been divided in four parts comprising 16 chapters. After this introduction (Chap. 1), Part I (Chaps. 2–5) analyzes the formation of the FPS standard in the international law of aliens. Chapter 2 begins by describing the challenges involved in the selection and assessment of historical sources, and explains this work's methodological response to those obstacles. These preliminary remarks are of a general nature and, hence, relevant for the whole argument.

The historical analysis of the standard properly starts at Chap. 3. The proposition advanced is that the FPS standard roots in the medieval practice of private reprisals, but was first rationalized into a legal obligation in the mid-to-late eighteenth century. These early doctrinal elaborations served the purpose of laying a dogmatic foundation for the sovereign's duty to protect foreigners against private offences. By the end of the century, the standard had been incorporated into the first FCN treaties concluded by the United States, and was thus on the road to its contemporary guise.

Chapter 4 moves on in time and contends that FPS was at the heart of the political struggle for the minimum standard of treatment or civilization, a slippery notion that dominated the legal and political discourse on the law of aliens from the mid-nineteenth century onwards. The minimum standard was resorted to as a means to ensure aliens a 'civilized' treatment by the host state, the measure of which was determined without regard to the treatment enjoyed by the host state's nationals. Chapter 4 contends that the customary status of FPS is not dependent on the recognition of the minimum standard. The debate about the standard of civilization pertained only to the reach of the protection obligation, and not to its existence.

Based on these findings, Chap. 5 explores the normative link between FPS and the minimum standard. The argument is that it was only after World War II, with the advent of IIAs, that the current normative intertwining between both concepts

---

[42]Chapter 2 elaborates further on these ideas.

became apparent. This work argues, however, that this connection is of only limited practical significance for the determination of the FPS standard's scope and content.

Part II then considers the scope of the FPS standard, as delivered by the tradition of the law of aliens. Chapter 6 makes some preliminary remarks about the formal category of 'standard' and the concept of security, which serve as a basis for the subsequent presentation of the customary standard's scope of application.

Chapter 7 begins with the standard's subjective scope of application. It explains the reasons why the customary FPS standard is applicable only in respect of foreign natural and juristic persons, to the exclusion of the host state's own nationals and stateless people. It also considers the close connection between FPS and the principle of territoriality. In this vein, it submits that customary law imposes the protection obligation not only upon states, but also upon other internationally accountable entities exercising territorial control (e.g. *de facto* regimes).

Chapter 8 addresses the FPS standard's objective scope of application. In this connection, it contends that FPS grew out of cases involving mob violence, revolutions and ordinary criminal offences. Accordingly, the quintessence of the standard lies in the prevention and redress of private injuries to aliens. FPS however extends beyond this core and protects foreigners against other risks, the source of which is, as in the case of private violence, *external* to the host state (e.g. acts of other states and natural disasters). The standard also refers to injuries incidentally caused by state action against external threats (public collateral damages).[43]

Chapter 9 then turns into the ongoing debate on the notions of physical security and legal security. In this regard, it suggests that the distinction between physical and nonphysical harm does not belong with the customary standard. Historical evidence is provided that FPS has always protected aliens against nonphysical harm, as long as the injury originates in a source of risk external to the host state (e.g. protection against defamation by private individuals). At the same time, however, Chap. 9 argues that the standard cannot be accurately said to encompass the notion of legal stability. The reason is that the risk of regulatory change is not comparable to the nonphysical risks the FPS standard has traditionally referred to.

Chapter 10 examines the application of the FPS standard *before* and *after* the infliction of an injury. Before the occurrence of an injurious event, the FPS standard consists in a *prevention obligation*. After an injury has been perpetrated, the standard turns into a *redress obligation*. A final section ponders the normative link between both obligations, and evaluates existent doctrinal approaches to this particular issue.

Part III addresses the content of the standard, that is to say, the parameters the FPS standard provides for the assessment of the host state's conduct.[44] Chapter 11 discusses the characterization of FPS under the well-known categories of obligations of conduct and result, on the one hand, and positive and negative obligations on the other. It also refutes novel theories suggesting that the FPS standard could appear

---

[43]Section 8.3.3.1 discusses the notion of 'collateral damages' in detail.

[44]Chapter 6 explains the distinction between the FPS standard's *scope of application* and its *content*.

both as an obligation of conduct (e.g. in respect of private injuries) and as an obligation of result (e.g. in respect of public injuries).

Chapter 12 considers the notion of due diligence in the law of state responsibility for injuries to aliens. The argument is that due diligence appeared in this area of international law as a consequence of the general rule of non-responsibility for acts of individuals, which was first posited by Hugo Grotius in 1625. Grotius made responsibility for private offences dependent on a finding of fault *(culpa)*. The Grotian concept of fault dominated academic debate for centuries. It was only until the late nineteenth century that publicists advancing objective theories of state responsibility found in the notion of due diligence a functional equivalent to the concept of *culpa*. Following Roberto Ago's distinction between primary and secondary norms of international law (in the 1970s) and the ILC's decision to exclude fault as an element of the internationally wrongful act, the element of diligence was formally placed in the realm of the primary norms of international law.

On the basis of these conceptual underpinnings, Chap. 13 goes on to consider the application of the notion of due diligence in the context of FPS claims. In this vein, it begins by addressing the question of the burden of proof of due diligence. Thereafter, it considers whether the notion of due diligence is objective or subjective in character, and addresses the different approaches investment arbitral tribunals have followed in this regard. Chapter 13 argues that there is not, and will never be, a due diligence 'test'. At the same time, however, it identifies multiple criteria which adjudicators should take into consideration when assessing FPS claims (e.g. the host state's awareness about the risk or differences in the protection afforded to different groups of persons).

Part IV discusses the interpretation of FPS treaty clauses. Chapter 14 presents the different formulations used in investment agreements, as well as such wording's interpretation in investment arbitral decisions. The core question addressed throughout the chapter is whether and to which extent those clauses could be said to provide protection *below* or *beyond* the FPS standard's customary core.

Chapter 15 considers the relationship between the FPS standard and other standards of investment protection. In this vein, it specifically analyzes the interplay between the FPS standard and the FET standard, expropriation clauses, the prohibition of discriminatory and arbitrary measures, national treatment, most-favored nation treatment, and war clauses. Finally, Chap. 16 presents an overall summary of the argument.

Part I
Formation of the Standard: The Long Path to Customary International Law

Chapter 2
'Full Protection and Security' in Historical Perspective: The Challenge of the Sources

2.1 Introductory Remarks

Contemporary arbitral awards dealing with the notion of 'full protection and security' normally include some historical remarks about the standard.[1] Historical arguments have moreover taken center stage in recent academic assessments of the subject.[2] This emphasis in history is not accidental. It is true that the first IIAs were concluded at the edge of the 1960s, the first investment treaty arbitrations being decided in the 1990s.[3] Nonetheless, international investment law was not built in a

---

[1]For a representative example see: Suez Sociedad General de Aguas de Barcelona S.A. and Vivendi Universal S.A. *v* Argentina, Decision on Liability, ICSID Case No. ARB/03/19 (30 July 2010) [161-5 and 177].

[2]See, for example: George Foster, 'Recovering "Protection and Security": The Treaty Standard's Obscure Origins, Forgotten Meaning, and Key Current Significance' (2012) 45(4) Vand. J. Transnat'l L. 1095, 1116-20; Todd Weiler, *The Interpretation of International Investment Law: Equality, Discrimination, and Minimum Standards of Treatment in Historical Context* (Brill, Leiden 2013) 59-182.

[3]As noted in the introduction, the first BIT was concluded between Pakistan and Germany in 1959; see: Treaty for the Promotion and Protection of Investments between Pakistan and the Federal Republic of Germany (adopted 25 November 1959, entered into force 28 April 1962). The first ICSID case based on a BIT, which remains one of the leading decisions about the FPS standard, was decided in June 1990. See: Asian Agricultural Products *v* Sri Lanka, Final Award, ICSID Case No ARB/87/3 (27 June 1990).

© Springer Nature Switzerland AG 2019
S. Mantilla Blanco, *Full Protection and Security in International Investment Law*,
European Yearbook of International Economic Law 8,
https://doi.org/10.1007/978-3-030-24838-3_2

vacuum.[4] On the contrary, the system relies on the tradition of the law of state responsibility for injuries to aliens.[5]

The development of the law of aliens bloomed under the shadow of early-modern doctrinal projects during the Age of Enlightenment,[6] reaching its peak in the decades preceding World War II.[7] The years subsequent to 1945 witnessed a striking shift in the international community's focus of attention. Alwyn Freeman, one of the chief publicists in the area both before and after the war, wrote in April 1951:

> Prior to the late war, most of the energies of the international community in the field of individual rights were devoted to the development of the international law respecting the rights of aliens. The five years since the late war afford a striking contrast [...] Probably the atrocities of certain enemy states toward their own subjects on a scale which staggered imagination [...] more than any single factor galvanized the interest of people everywhere into demands that the law of nations provide at least some degree of protection for the individual against his own state.[8]

It is then unsurprising for contemporary international lawyers to take into consideration pre-World War II authorities in their assessment of investment claims. Historical arguments are relevant because the foundations of international investment law lie in a somewhat distant past. This holds especially true for the FPS standard. FPS, as it appears in modern IIAs, resembles formulations that have long

---

[4]For a critical analysis of the relative 'newness' of international investment law see: Todd Weiler, *The Interpretation of International Investment Law: Equality, Discrimination, and Minimum Standards of Treatment in Historical Context* (Brill, Leiden 2013) 3-6.

[5]For a detailed account of the origins of international investment law and its connection to the law of aliens, see: Kate Miles, *The Origins of International Investment Law* (Cambridge University Press, New York 2013) 19-70.

[6]See Sects. 3.3 and 3.4.

[7]For some representative examples of the attention received by the law of aliens in the first decades of the twentieth century see: Alwyn Freeman, *The International Responsibility of States for Denial of Justice* (Klaus Reprint, New York 1970) [first edition: 1938]; Edwin Borchard, *The Diplomatic Protection of Citizens Abroad or the Law of International Claims* (The Banks Law Publishing Co., New York 1916); Frederick Sherwood Dunn, *The Diplomatic Protection of Americans in Mexico* (Klaus Reprint, New York 1971) [first edition: 1933]; Frederick Sherwood Dunn, *The Protection of Nationals. A Study in the Application of International Law* (The Johns Hopkins Press, Baltimore 1932); Hans von Fisch, *Die Staatsrechtliche Stellung der Fremden* (Carl Heymanns Verlag, Berlin 1910).

[8]Alwyn Freeman, 'Human Rights and the Rights of Aliens' (1951) 45 ASIL Proceedings 120, 122-3. It should be noted that the law of aliens continued to be of interest, for example, in connection with the codification of the law of state responsibility. In any case, even in this context, the notion of 'fundamental human rights' would increasingly influence the debate about the substance of the law of aliens. For some representative examples of these intellectual threads see: Francisco García Amador, 'International Responsibility: Report by F. V. García Amador, Special Rapporteur (A/CN.4/96)' (20 January 1956) 2 *Yearbook of the International Law Commission – 1956* 173, 173-221; Francisco García Amador, 'International Responsibility: Second Report by F. V. García Amador, Special Rapporteur (A/CN.4/106)' (15 February 1957) 2 *Yearbook of the International Law Commission – 1957* 104, 112-3; Francisco García Amador, 'State Responsibility. Some New Problems' (1958) 94 RCADI 365, 435-9.

been in use in state practice, arbitral awards and academic publications.[9] A scholar has gone as far as to describe the FPS standard as 'the oldest of the primary obligations in IIL'.[10]

Against this backdrop, a historical assessment of the notion of 'protection and security' serves two purposes. A first goal is to present the development of FPS in international law. This means telling the 'story' of the concept, exploring its roots and discussing its evolution in time. To be sure, a historical account of FPS is not merely ornamental, but fundamental to the legal argument. Borrowing Lassa F. L. Oppenheim's words, 'the exposition of the existing recognized rules of international law is often to a certain extent impossible without a knowledge of the history of the rules concerned'.[11] Oppenheim underscored in this connection the 'historical task' of international law scholarship.[12] Consciousness about this task is spreading fast. Our time is witnessing a 'historiographical turn',[13] that is to say, a 'renaissance' of historical studies about international law.[14] Investment law is not the exception.[15]

The second purpose of the historical survey is to ascertain the scope and content of the customary FPS standard, and to examine to what extent they changed with the passage of time. Historical sources are therefore taken not only as leftovers from the past but, where appropriate, as evidence of long-standing customary norms. The legal argument thus appears enmeshed with the historical argument. There is nothing extraordinary about such interweaving of law and history. As noted by David Kennedy (1999):

> Absent a code or legislature, international lawyers have long read their rules in history, culling famous texts, diplomatic incidents, and judicial pronouncements for insight about what 'the international community', as we would now call it, treated as a binding rule [...] [A]n argument about a rule or principle, or institutional technique in international law is always also an argument about history – that the particular norm proffered has a provenance as law rather than politics, has become general rather than specific, has come through history to stand outside history.[16]

---

[9]See Chaps. 7, 8, 10 and 14.

[10]Todd Weiler, *The Interpretation of International Investment Law: Equality, Discrimination, and Minimum Standards of Treatment in Historical Context* (Brill, Leiden 2013) 59. Section 3.1 discusses Weiler's approach in more detail.

[11]Lassa Francis Laurence Oppenheim, 'The Science of International Law: Its Task and Method' (1908) 2(2) AJIL 313, 315-6.

[12]Lassa Francis Laurence Oppenheim, 'The Science of International Law: Its Task and Method' (1908) 2(2) AJIL 313, 316.

[13]George Rodrigo Bandeira Galindo, 'Martti Koskenniemi and the Historiographical Turn in International Law' (2005) 16(3) EJIL 539, 541. See also: Martti Koskenniemi, 'The Politics of International Law – 20 Years Later' (2009) 20(1) EJIL 7, 17-8.

[14]Emmanuelle Tourme Jouannet and Anne Peters, 'The Journal of the History of International Law: A Forum for New Research' (2014) 16 JHIL 1, 1-4.

[15]See generally: Todd Weiler, *The Interpretation of International Investment Law: Equality, Discrimination, and Minimum Standards of Treatment in Historical Context* (Brill, Leiden 2013) xli-xlv and 1-57.

[16]David Kennedy, 'The Disciplines of International Law and Policy' (1999) 12 LJIL 9, 88.

Inasmuch as historical arguments help elucidate international custom, they also turn relevant for the interpretation and application of 'protection and security' clauses. FPS clauses often contain express references to customary law.[17] Even in the absence of an express reference, investment treaties shall be interpreted in the light of 'relevant rules of international law applicable in the relations between the parties'.[18]

Historical arguments have not been without controversy, though. Publicists have occasionally depicted historical assessments of investment protection standards as a 'conservative force', which could end up 'limiting the interpretation of provisions to a pre-War era'.[19] It is true that customary norms cannot be lightly assumed to convey the same meaning in the present as they did in the past. At the same time, however, taking cognizance of a legal institution's historical underpinnings does not imply turning a blind eye to new developments. Quite the contrary, history allows the identification and critical assessment of waves of change.

It would therefore be naïve to neglect the past and artificially present FPS as the outcome of recent treaty and arbitral practice. Neither can the weight investment arbitral tribunals assign to history be easily ignored. Just to mention a representative example, in *Suez v Argentina* (2010) the arbitrators rejected the interpretation of the FPS standard as a guarantee of legal stability on grounds that tribunals advancing

---

[17]The FTA between Colombia and the United States provides an indicative example of an FPS clause containing a express reference to customary law: "Each Party shall accord to covered investments treatment in accordance with *customary* international law, *including* fair and equitable treatment and *full protection and security*." Emphasis added. Free Trade Agreement between the United States of America and the Republic of Colombia (adopted 22 November 2006, entered into force 15 May 2012) art. 10.5(1). For a detailed analysis of explicit references to customary law in investment treaty practice see: Patrick Dumberry, *The Formation and Identification of Customary International Law in International Investment Law* (Cambridge University Press, Cambridge 2016) 354-64 (making particular reference to FET clauses). Chapter 14 considers the wording of FPS clauses in more detail.

[18]Vienna Convention on the Law of Treaties (adopted 23 May 1969, entered into force 27 January 1980) 1155 UNTS 331 art. 31(3)(c). For a detailed critical analysis of customary international law's relevance for the interpretation and application of treaty-based investment protection standards see: Martins Paparinskis, 'Investment treaty interpretation and customary investment law: Preliminary remarks' in Chester Brown and Kate Miles (eds), *Evolution in Investment Treaty Law and Arbitration* (Cambridge University Press, Cambridge 2011) 65-96. See also: Campbell McLachlan, 'Investment Treaties and General International Law' (April 2008) 57 ICLQ 361, 369-74; Daniel Rosentreter, *Article 31(3)(c) of the Vienna Convention on the Law of Treaties and the Principle of Systemic Integration in International Investment Law and Arbitration* (Nomos, Baden-Baden 2015) 283-462 (particularly at pp. 457-62); Patrick Dumberry, *The Formation and Identification of Customary International Law in International Investment Law* (Cambridge University Press, Cambridge 2016) 367 *et seq.* (particularly at pp. 381-3). Section 14.2.2 elaborates further on this issue.

[19]Campbell McLachlan, 'The Evolution of Treaty Obligations in International Law' in Georg Nolte (ed), *Treaties and Subsequent Practice* (Oxford University Press, Oxford 2013) 69, 80.

such interpretation '[do not] provide a *historical analysis* of the concept of full protection and security'.[20]

This shows that there is some consciousness about the need for a historical assessment of the subject. In spite of this need, anyone seeking to place FPS in historical context will face significant obstacles. While today's notion of 'protection and security' might seem somewhat vague and ambiguous, if not to say obscure, the truth is that the grass was not any greener in the past. A look into primary historical sources reveals deep incongruences, which pose genuine historiographical challenges to the formulation of plausible historical arguments about the FPS standard.[21]

2.2 Obstacles Posed by Historical Sources

Advancing historical arguments about FPS implies dealing with a complex web of slippery and partially inconsistent sources. As a matter of fact, FPS did not originate in a uniform line of cases. Neither can the roots of the standard be placed in a single, clearly distinguishable school of thought. A historical survey of the subject will inescapably face some obstacles, such as: (1) the diversity of intellectual and political projects shaping the formation of the standard; (2) the scope of the jurisdiction exercised by mixed claims commissions, as compared to contemporary investment arbitral tribunals; (3) the existence of overlapping causes of action and the use of all-encompassing definitions of denial of justice; and (4) the limited usefulness of the distinction between primary and secondary rules of international law. The above list does not intend to be exhaustive. On the contrary, it is merely indicative of the difficulties at stake. Needless to say, these challenges do not only affect the analysis of the formation of FPS in the law of aliens (Chaps. 3–5), but also the assessment of the scope and content of the protection obligation (Chaps. 7–13).

2.2.1 Diversity of Intellectual and Political Agendas

Lawyers generally think of international standards of investment protection as positive norms, the source of which is treaty-based, customary, or a combination of both. This approach corresponds to a present-day understanding of international

---

[20]Emphasis added. Suez Sociedad General de Aguas de Barcelona S.A. and Vivendi Universal S.A. *v* Argentina, Decision on Liability, ICSID Case No. ARB/03/19 (30 July 2010) [177]. For a similar appeal see: Todd Weiler, *The Interpretation of International Investment Law: Equality, Discrimination, and Minimum Standards of Treatment in Historical Context* (Brill, Leiden 2013) xli-xlv and 1. Section 9.3.1 provides a more detailed assessment of the *Suez* decision.

[21]These challenges are concerned with how norms of international law are ascertained, established and applied. As such, they may be characterized as 'methodological' challenges. See: Adolf Schüle, 'Methoden der Völkerrechtswissenschaft' (1959/60) 8 AVR 129, 136.

law. Historical sources do not always share this common ground. Let us consider an indicative example. Both Christian von Wolff and Emer de Vattel referred to the notion of protection and security. In this vein, they used a language that bears striking resemblance to contemporary formulations of FPS.[22] However, a closer look reveals that neither of them thought of the protection obligation in the same categories contemporary international lawyers do. They did not derive the duty's binding character from state practice (*usus*) and the sense of a legal obligation (*opinio juris*).[23] Rather, the concept was based on deductive arguments, which appear largely unfamiliar to the modern reader. Their assertions about the security of aliens were enshrined in a different conception of the sources of international law. The security obligation was just a piece of their rationalistic puzzle.[24]

Martti Koskenniemi has suggested that a distinction can be drawn between *theories* and *doctrines* of international law. In Koskenniemi's words:

> It is not obvious where the line between 'theory' and 'doctrine' lies. In general terms, it may be said that where the former asks questions about international law *as a whole* — as a 'system' or an 'instrument' of policy — doctrine deals with particular, substantive aspects of the law, such as, for example, the rules on the use of force [...] the principles of State responsibility, or the role of sanctions in the enforcement of treaties. Nevertheless, if it is usually assumed that doctrine proceeds by interpreting and systematizing the normative materials, how that work is carried out depends on 'theoretical' views about the purpose of interpretation and the types of materials to be included in the system.[25]

Following Koskenniemi's terminology, it could be said that *doctrines* about the law of aliens can only be properly understood in the light of the underlying *theories* of international law. Simply put, the *doctrine* only makes sense within the *theory*. The analysis of historical sources poses a constant, latent risk of placing doctrines from the past into present-day theoretical frameworks. The consequence is that international lawyers could end up twisting doctrines into something they were never meant to be.

---

[22]Christian Freiherr von Wolff, *Ius gentium methodo scientifica perpractatum* (Officina libraria Rengeriana, Magdeburg 1749) 841 *et seq.*; Emer de Vattel, *Le droit des gens ou principes de la loi naturelle appliqués à la conduit et aux affaires des Nations et des Souverains* (1758) (Carnegie Institution, Washington 1916) 329-30. For an English translation see: Christian Wolff, 'Jus gentium methodo scientifica pertractactum' (1749) in James Brown Scott (ed), *Classics of International Law* (Joseph Drake tr, Clarendon Press, Oxford 1934) 536-7 § 1063; Emer de Vattel, *The Law of Nations or Principles of the Law of Nature Applied to the Conduct and Affairs of Nations and Sovereigns* (1758) (G.G. and J. Robinson, London 1797) 173.

[23]For the two constituent elements of custom see: Michael Wood, 'Second Report on Identification of Customary International Law (A/CN.4/672)' (22 May 2014) [http://legal.un.org/ilc/documentation/english/a_cn4_672.pdf] 7-14 [21-31].

[24]Sections 3.3 and 3.4 provide a detailed account of Wolff's and Vattel's views on the subject.

[25]Martti Koskenniemi, 'International Legal Theory and Doctrine' in Rüdiger Wolfrum (ed), *The Max Planck Encyclopedia of Public International Law* (Volume 3: Oxford University Press, New York 2012) 976, 976. See also: Martti Koskenniemi, *From Apology to Utopia. The Structure of International Legal Argument* (Cambridge University Press, New York 2005) 2 *et seq.*

In addition to this diversity of theoretical backbones, historical sources often respond to complex political realities.[26] The reason is that, as noted by Oppenheim, '[the history of dogmatics] is only a branch of the history of Western civilization'.[27] This statement, however Eurocentric, expresses an undeniable feature of international law history. This feature is particularly evident when it comes to the law of aliens. An obvious example is the—nowadays generally abandoned—doctrine of equality, according to which international law does not require host states to give aliens a better treatment than that enjoyed by nationals.[28] The historical record indicates that the development of this doctrine was intrinsically linked to international politics. It was a reaction to the use of force to coerce states into paying compensation for damages suffered by aliens within their territories (so-called 'gunboat diplomacy').[29]

The writings of Hugo Grotius provide an additional, representative example. In his seminal work *De iure belli ac pacis* (1625), Grotius gave full consideration to the Nation's responsibility for the acts of private individuals.[30] In this connection, he delivered a doctrinal edifice which, in some respects, comes close to our modern-day understanding of due diligence.[31] Nonetheless, Grotius' analysis of the subject corresponds to an intellectual project that served a specific practical purpose. It was an attempt to overcome the medieval belief that communities are directly responsible for the acts of their individual members (so-called '*Sippenhaftung*').[32] Consciousness about this practical goal is a fundamental condition for an accurate account of Grotius' opinions and a plausible assessment of their influence.

Resemblances between past and present-day notions must therefore be considered with caution and, perhaps, some restraint. Unreflected uses of historical sources are the breeding ground for unfounded legal-historical narratives, which could end up bolstering misconceptions not only about history, but also about the law. To be sure, doctrinal elaborations are a fundamental shaping factor of legal institutions. But they can only provide a meaningful insight into the development of a legal institution if they are considered in their own theoretical, political and historical contexts.[33]

---

[26]See generally: Martti Koskenniemi, 'The Politics of International Law' (1990) 1 EJIL 4, 31 (suggesting that legal 'conceptual matrices' are always 'arenas of political struggle'). See also: Martti Koskenniemi, 'The Politics of International Law – 20 Years Later' (2009) 20(1) EJIL 7, 14-9 (taking notice of international legal scholarship's growing political awareness).

[27]Lassa Francis Laurence Oppenheim, 'The Science of International Law: Its Task and Method' (1908) 2(2) AJIL 313, 317.

[28]Section 4.3 discusses the doctrine of equality in detail.

[29]See Chap. 4.

[30]Hugonis Groti, *De iure belli ac pacis* (1625) (Leiden, A. W. Sijthoff 1919) 411-29 [Lib. 2 Cap. XXI]. For an English translation see: Hugo Grotius, *The Rights of War and Peace in Three Books* (1625) (The Lawbook Exchange, Clark NJ 2004) 453-73 [Book 2 Chap. XXI].

[31]See Sect. 12.3.1.

[32]See Sect. 12.3.1.

[33]Section 2.3 elaborates further on this issue.

2.2.2 The Scope of the Jurisdiction Exercised by Mixed Claims Commissions

Investment treaty arbitrations primarily refer to specific substantive standards of investment protection (e.g. FPS and FET), which are listed in the applicable IIA.[34] Moreover, ISDS clauses often limit the arbitral tribunal's *ratione materiae* jurisdiction through an express reference to the substantive provisions of the applicable treaty.[35] An often-cited example is the ISDS clause of the ECT, which exclusively covers '[d]isputes between a Contracting Party and an Investor of another Contracting Party relating to an Investment of the latter in the Area of the former, *which concern an alleged breach of an obligation of the former under Part III* [Investment Promotion and Protection]'.[36] Article 8.18(1) of CETA provides an additional, representative example in this regard.[37]

By contrast to modern investment arbitrators, commissioners sitting in mixed claims tribunals did not usually apply any specific, treaty-based substantive protection standards. The scope of the jurisdiction exercised by mixed claims commissions was sometimes narrower, and sometimes broader, than that of present-day investment tribunals. Numerous cases were decided pursuant to special submission

---

[34]For a short overview see: Lucy Reed, Jan Paulsson and Nigel Blackaby, *Guide to ICSID Arbitration* (Kluwer Law International, Alphen aan den Rijn 2011) 59-60 and 74 *et seq.*

[35]See generally: Rudolf Dolzer and Christoph Schreuer, *Principles of International Investment Law* (Oxford University Press, New York 2012) 260-1. The extent of investment tribunals' *ratione materiae* jurisdiction could vary from one treaty to another. Based on an analysis of contemporary IIAs, Zachary Douglas identified four 'prototype provisions'. A first set of treaties grants arbitrators broad jurisdiction, covering 'any' or 'all' investment disputes. The second type refers to investment agreements, investment authorizations and treaty claims. Douglas' third type of clause limits jurisdiction to claims about breaches of the applicable IIA. The fourth type solely covers investment disputes pertaining to 'the quantum payable in the event of a proscribed expropriation'. See: Zachary Douglas, *The International Law of Investment Claims* (Cambridge, Cambridge University Press 2009) 234-5. An ongoing debate concerns the question, whether the first category (which has been sometimes designated 'generic dispute settlement clause') actually extends the tribunal's jurisdiction beyond alleged violations of treaty obligations, thus covering, for example, contractual claims. See: Emmanuel Gaillard, 'Investment Treaty Arbitration and Jurisdiction Over Contract Claims – The SGS Cases Considered' in Todd Weiler (ed), *International Investment Law and Arbitration. Leading Cases from the ICSID, NAFTA, Bilateral Investment Treaties and Customary International Law* (Cameron May, London 2005) 325, 330-6; Eric De Brabandere, *Investment Treaty Arbitration as Public International Law. Procedural Aspects and Implications* (Cambridge University Press, Cambridge 2014) 31-5; James Crawford, 'Treaty and Contract in Investment Arbitration' (2008) 24(3) Arb. Int'l. 351, 361-4; Zachary Douglas, *The International Law of Investment Claims* (Cambridge, Cambridge University Press 2009) 236-40.

[36]Emphasis added. Energy Charter Treaty (adopted 17 December 1994, entered into force 16 April 1998) art. 26(1).

[37]See: Comprehensive Economic and Trade Agreement between Canada and the European Union (signed 30 October 2016, provisionally entered into force 21 September 2017) art. 8.18(1). It should be noted that the dispute settlement provisions of CETA significantly depart from traditional investor-state arbitration. For an overview see: Matthias Herdegen, *Principles of International Economic Law* (Oxford University Press, New York 2016) 477 *et seq.*

agreements concluded between the home and the host state for the purpose of settling one specific dispute.[38] A limited number of covenants referred to 'denial of justice' in the definition of the tribunal's jurisdiction.[39]

Other claims conventions narrowed the commissioners' mandate to claims that would be nowadays decided on the basis of the FPS standard. An example would be the British-Mexican Claims Convention of 1926, which was solely applicable in respect of damages occurred during the Mexican Revolution (1910–1920) and caused, *inter alia*:

> By mutinies or risings or by insurrectionary forces [...] provided that in each case it be established that the competent authorities omitted to take reasonable measures to suppress the insurrections, risings, riots or acts of brigandage in question, or to punish those responsible for the same; or that it be established in like manner that the authorities were blamable in any other way.[40]

In most instances, however, the applicable dispute settlement agreement empowered the commissioners to decide under 'international law, justice and equity' on '*all claims*' of nationals of a contracting party against the other contracting party.[41] This comprehensive wording bears witness to the wide-ranging mandate

---

[38]For example, the Claims Convention concerning the *Venezuela Steam Transportation Company* cases (1892) limited the Commission's mandate to 'the question whether any, and, if any, what indemnity shall be paid by the Government of the United States of Venezuela to the Government of the United States of America for the alleged wrongful seizure, detention and employment in war otherwise of the Steamships *Hero*, *Nutrias* and *San Fernando*, the property of the Venezuela Steam Transportation Company, a corporation existing under the law of the State of New York, and a citizen of the United States, and the imprisonment of its officers, citizens of the United States' (art. I). The Convention did not require the Commission to apply a particular set of substantive protection standards. Rather, adjudicators were directed to decide 'in accordance with justice and equity and the principles of international law' (art. III). Claims Convention concerning the Venezuela Steam Transportation Company (adopted 19 January 1892, entered into force 28 July 1894) Charles Bevans (ed), *Treaties and Other International Agreements of the United States of America 1776–1949* (Volume 12: U.S. Department of State Publication, Washington 1971) 1098, 1098-1100.

[39]That was the case of the agreement providing the basis of jurisdiction for the famous *Fabiani* claim. See: *Antoine Fabiani Case* (31 July 1905) X RIAA 83, 83-139. For a detailed analysis of the *Fabiani* claim see: Floyd Clarke, 'A Permanent Tribunal of International Arbitration: Its Necessity and Value' (1907) 1 AJIL 342, 389-98.

[40]Claims Convention between Great Britain and Mexico (adopted 19 November 1926, entered into force 8 March 1928) V RIAA 7, 8 art. 3. Similar provisions may be found in other conventions signed by Mexico for the compensation of damages inflicted during the Mexican Revolution. See, for example: Special Claims Convention between Mexico and the United States (adopted 10 September 1923, entered into force 19 February 1924) Charles Bevans (ed), *Treaties and Other International Agreements of the United States of America 1776–1949* (Volume 9: U.S. Department of State Publication, Washington 1971) 941, 943 art. III; Claims Convention Between France and the Mexico (adopted 25 September 1924, entered into force 29 December 1924) V RIAA 313, 314 art. 3(5); Claims Convention Between France and Mexico (adopted 2 August 1930, entered into force 6 February 1931) V RIAA 318, 319 art. 3(4).

[41]See, for example: General Claims Convention between the United States of America and the United Mexican States (adopted 8 September 1923, entered into force 1 March 1924) Charles

most commissions enjoyed.[42] But, most importantly, it shows that commissioners did not ordinarily apply a pre-established set of substantive legal provisions.[43] A review of the claims conventions upon which the most influential commissions were established reveals that they usually made no reference to any treaty-based substantive protection standards whatsoever.[44] Some of them referred to 'treaty stipulations' or 'treaty rights' in general, without mentioning a particular agreement.[45] Another

---

Bevans (ed), *Treaties and Other International Agreements of the United States of America 1776–1949* (Volume 9: U.S. Department of State Publication, Washington 1971) 935, 936 art. I. On the interpretation of this provision see: *Illinois Central Railroad Company v Mexico* (31 March 1926) IV RIAA 21[5-6].

[42]In the *Boulton, Bliss & Dallet* case (1904), Commissioner Paúl went on to say: "The amplitude of the phrase "all claims" makes it possible that even the demands which are unforeseen by the law, or which, by the absence of proper agreements, lack juridical foundation entitling them to be examined and confirmed under the proceedings of an ordinary court, must be considered by this tribunal of exceptional jurisdiction, which has to decide them upon their merits and upon a basis of absolute equity." *Boulton, Bliss & Dallett Case* (1904) IX RIAA 136, 137.

[43]For an exhaustive discussion of the scope of jurisdiction (*ratione materiae*) of international mixed claims tribunals, see: Jackson Ralston, *International Arbitral Law and Procedure. Being a Résumé of the Procedure and Practice of International Commissions and Including the Views of Arbitrators upon Questions arising under the Law of Nations* (Ginn & Co., Boston/London 1910) 17-87 and 153-64.

[44]For representative examples of claims conventions entailing no direct reference to treaty stipulations of FCN agreements see: Convention for the Settlement of Claims against Venezuela (adopted 25 April 1866, entered into force 17 April 1867) John Haswell (ed), *Treaties and Conventions Concluded Between the United States of America and Other Powers since July 4, 1776* (U.S. Department of State, Washington 1889) 1140, 1140-3; Convention for the Settlement of Claims between the United States and Peru (adopted 4 December 1868, entered into force 4 June 1869) John Haswell (ed), *Treaties and Conventions Concluded Between the United States of America and Other Powers since July 4, 1776* (U.S. Department of State, Washington 1889) 872, 872-5; Convention Reviving and Modifying the U.S.-Venezuela Convention of April 25, 1866 (adopted 5 December 1885, entered into force 3 June 1889) Charles Bevans (ed), *Treaties and Other International Agreements of the United States of America 1776–1949* (Volume 12: U.S. Department of State Publication, Washington 1971) 1085, 1085-92; Washington Protocol Constituting the French-Venezuelan Claims Commission (adopted 27 February 1903) X RIAA 3, 3-4; Protocol on the Constitution of a Mixed Claims Commission between Venezuela and the German Empire (adopted 13 February 1903) X RIAA 359, 359-60; Protocol on the Constitution of a Mixed Claims Commission between Venezuela and the German Empire (adopted 7 May 1903) X RIAA 361, 361-2; Protocol on the Constitution of a Mixed Claims Commission between Venezuela and the Netherlands (adopted 28 February 1903) X RIAA 709, 709-10; Protocol of an Agreement for Submission to Arbitration of All Unsettled Claims of Spanish Subjects against the Republic of Venezuela (adopted 2 April 1903) X RIAA 737, 737-8; General Claims Convention between the United States of America and the United Mexican States (adopted 8 September 1923, entered into force 1 March 1924) Charles Bevans (ed), *Treaties and Other International Agreements of the United States of America 1776–1949* (Volume 9: U.S. Department of State Publication, Washington 1971) 935, 935-40.

[45]For example, article III of the U.S.-Peru Claims Convention of 1863 provided that disputes were to be decided 'according to the principles of justice and equity, the principles of international law *and treaty stipulations*'. Emphasis added. Convention for the Settlement of Claims between the United States and Peru (adopted 12 January 1863, entered into force 12 April 1863) John Haswell

group of clauses alluded to a specific FCN agreement, but not as a means to limit the commission's material scope of jurisdiction.[46] There were, of course, a few covenants that were specifically concerned with claims arising out of or in connection with a particular FCN agreement.[47] Still, these conventions were more the exception than the rule. It is therefore rather unsurprising that most awards from the 'golden

---

(ed), *Treaties and Conventions Concluded Between the United States of America and Other Powers since July 4, 1776* (U.S. Department of State, Washington 1889) 870, 870-1 art. III. For an additional example see: Special Agreement for the Submission to Arbitration of Pecuniary Claims Outstanding between the United States and Great Britain (adopted 18 August 1910, entered into force 26 April 1912) VI RIAA 9, 10 art. 7.

[46]For instance, article IV of the U.S.-Mexico Claims Convention of 1839 required the commission to decide the claims 'according to the principles of justice, the law of nations *and the stipulations of the treaty of amity and commerce between the United States and Mexico of the 5ᵗʰ of April, 1831*'. Emphasis added. Convention for the Adjustment of Claims of Citizens of the United States against Mexico (adopted 11 April 1839, entered into force 7 April 1840) John Haswell (ed), *Treaties and Conventions Concluded Between the United States of America and Other Powers since July 4, 1776* (U.S. Department of State, Washington 1889) 676, 678 art. IV. References to specific treaties were fairly diverse. For some additional examples see: Protocol establishing a Mixed Claims Commission between Venezuela and Great Britain (adopted 13 February 1903) IX RIAA 351, 352 art. VII ("inasmuch as it may be contended that the establishment of a blockade of Venezuelan ports by the British naval forces has ipso facto created a state of war [...] and that any existing treaty between the two countries has been thereby abrogated, it shall be recorded in an exchange of notes between the undersigned that the Convention between Venezuela and Great Britain of October 29, 1834 [...] shall be deemed to be renewed and confirmed or provisionally renewed and confirmed pending conclusion of a new treaty of Amity and Commerce"); Protocol establishing a Mixed Claims Commission between Venezuela and Italy (adopted 13 February 1903) X RIAA 479, 480 art. VIII (stating that '[t]he Treaty of Amity, Commerce and Navigation between Italy and Venezuela of June 19, 1861, is renewed and confirmed' and including some remarks on the interpretation of the national treatment and MFN clauses of the said FCN agreement; see also art. X). It is worth noting that some treaties made specific reference to a former FCN agreement, but just to determine the *ratione temporis* jurisdiction of the commission. For example, the U.S.-Mexico Claims Convention of 1868 was only applicable to claims arisen after the conclusion of the FCN Agreement signed by the two countries in 1848 (so-called 'Treaty of Guadalupe Hidalgo'). See: Convention for the Settlement of Claims between Mexico and the United States (concluded 4 July 1868, entered into force 1 February 1869) Charles Bevans (ed), *Treaties and Other International Agreements of the United States of America 1776–1949* (Volume 9: U.S. Department of State Publication, Washington 1971) 826, 827-8 arts. I-II. For an additional example see: Convention for the Settlement of Claims between Great Britain and the United States (concluded 8 February 1853, entered into force 26 July 1853) John Haswell (ed), *Treaties and Conventions Concluded Between the United States of America and Other Powers since July 4, 1776* (U.S. Department of State, Washington 1889) 445, 445-6 art. I.

[47]The U.S.-Spain Convention of 1871 provides a good example in this regard. It required the commissioners to decide 'to the best of their judgment and according to public law, and the treaties in force between the two countries, and these present stipulations' (para 2). In addition, the Convention indicated that the Commission could review '[a]djudications of the tribunals in Cuba, concerning citizens of the United States, made in the absence of the parties interested, or in violation of international law, or of the guarantees provided in the treaty of October 27, 1795, between the United States and Spain'. Agreement for Settlement of Certain Claims of Citizens of the United States on Account of Wrongs and Injuries Committed by Authorities of Spain in the Island of Cuba (concluded 11-12 February 1871) John Haswell (ed), *Treaties and Conventions Concluded*

era' of diplomatic protection did not expressly address breaches of the FPS standard, taken as a separate and autonomous international delinquency. The truth is that, in most cases, no distinct FPS clause came into question in the first place.

2.2.3 Overlapping Causes of Action and All-Encompassing Definitions of Denial of Justice

Before the BIT era, cases that contemporary investment tribunals would in all probability decide on the basis of the FPS standard were often presented and adjudicated as denial of justice claims.[48] A prominent example is the *Neer* arbitration, where the United States argued that the Mexican authorities' lack of diligence in investigating the murder of Paul Neer amounted to a failure to do justice.[49] *Neer* was by no means an isolated instance.[50] Only a few prewar decisions drew a fairly clear distinction between 'denial of justice' and other international wrongs, such as 'undue imprisonment'[51] and 'lack of protection'.[52]

This phenomenon is inherently linked to the sound difficulties attached to the notion of 'denial of justice'.[53] The concept was the source of much confusion in the past.[54] Sir Gerald Fitzmaurice observed in 1932 that '[t]o few terms in international

---

Between the United States of America and Other Powers since July 4, 1776 (U.S. Department of State, Washington 1889) 1025, 1025-6.

[48]For a similar observation see: Gordon Christenson, 'Attributing Acts of Omission to the State' (1990) 12 Mich. J. Int'l L. 312, 236; Jan Paulsson, *Denial of Justice in International Law* (Cambridge University Press, New York 2005) 99 and 131 *et seq.*

[49]*LFH Neer and Pauline Neer v Mexico* (15 October 1926) IV RIAA 60 [1]. See also: *Margaret Roper v Mexico* (4 April 1927) IV RIAA 145 [1].

[50]Further examples are provided by many other cases concerning the redress of private injuries to aliens. Chapter 10 assesses the redress obligation in detail.

[51]For an indicative example see the decision of the Italian-Venezuelan Claims Commission in the *Tagliaferro* claim of 1903: *Tagliaferro Case* (1903) X RIAA 592, 593 ("The offences complained of now are double in nature, consisting of unjust imprisonment and denial of justice").

[52]In the *Mallén* case (1927), the United States-Mexico General Claims Commission made an interesting distinction between three causes of actions, including 'lack of protection' and 'denial of justice'. See: *Francisco Mallén v United States* (27 April 1927) IV RIAA 173 [13] ("[T]he United States is liable (a) for illegal acts of the deputy constable Franco on October 12, 1907, (b) for denial of justice on the ground of non-execution of the penalty imposed on November 9, 1907, and (c) for lack of protection").

[53]The author has already addressed the notion of 'denial of justice' elsewhere. See: Sebastián Mantilla Blanco, *Justizielles Unrecht im internationalen Investitionsschutzrecht* (Nomos, Baden-Baden 2016) 51-118. The problems associated to the definition of denial of justice are discussed in greater detail at pp. 51-84 of the said monograph.

[54]Cf. Jan Paulsson, *Denial of Justice in International Law* (Cambridge University Press, New York 2005) 98 (advancing the proposition that the confusion that dominated the literature on 'denial of justice' in the early twentieth century 'was artificial', and further submitting that 'the confusions have dissipated').

law have such a wide variety of meanings or shades of meaning been attributed as to the term denial of justice'.[55] Fitzmaurice's observation was and remains a common place in the literature on the subject.[56]

Doctrinal definitions of 'denial of justice' are not only numerous but also strikingly varied.[57] For present purposes it shall suffice to note that a few (now abandoned) definitions of the term were remarkably broad in scope. In fact, in the early twentieth century 'denial of justice' was frequently understood as a comprehensive notion, which could virtually encompass *any* violation of the law of state responsibility for injuries to aliens. For example, Charles C. Hyde suggested the following definition in 1922:

---

[55] Gerald Fitzmaurice, 'The Meaning of the Term Denial of Justice' (1932) 13 BYIL 93, 93.

[56] For authors making similar statements see: Ali Ehsassi, 'Cain and Abel: Congruence and Conflict in the Application of the Denial of Justice Principle' in Stephan Schill (ed), *International Investment Law and Comparative Public Law* (Oxford University Press, New York 2010) 213, 213; Charles De Visscher, 'La déni de justice en droit international' (1935) 52(2) RCADI 365, 369; Don Wallace, 'Fair and Equitable Treatment and Denial of Justice in *Loewn v. US* and *Chattin v. Mexico*' in Todd Weiler (ed), *International Investment Law and Arbitration. Leading Cases from the ICSID, NAFTA, Bilateral Investment Treaties and Customary International Law* (Cameron May, London 2005) 669, 670; Oliver Lissitzyn, 'The Meaning of the Term Denial of Justice in International Law' (1936) 30(4) AJIL 632, 645-6. For a more detailed discussion of Fitzmaurice's and other authors' concerns regarding the uncertainty of the notion see: Sebastián Mantilla Blanco, *Justizielles Unrecht im internationalen Investitionsschutzrecht* (Nomos, Baden-Baden 2016) 59-60 (citing these and other sources in this connection).

[57] See, for example: Alwyn Freeman, *The International Responsibility of States for Denial of Justice* (Klaus Reprint, New York, 1970) 161 [first edition: 1938] (contending that denial of justice refers to 'all unlawful acts or omissions engaging the State's responsibility in connection with the entire process of administering justice to aliens'); Clyde Eagleton, 'Denial of Justice in International law' (1928) 22 AJIL 538, 558-9 (defining denial of justice as a failure to redress 'an antecedent injury'); Constantin Eustathiades, 'La responsabilité internationale de l'état pour les actes judiciaires et le problème du déni de justice en droit international' (1936) in Constantin Eustathiades, *Études de droit international* 1929-1959 (Volume 1: Editions Klissiounis, Athens 1959) 91-3 (stressing that denial of justice is the violation of the so-called '*obligations générales de protection judiciaire des étrangers*', as opposed to the '*activité juridictionnelle contraire a des obligations internationales spéciales*'); Jan Paulsson, *Denial of Justice in International Law* (Cambridge University Press, New York 2005) 57-99 (explaining denial of justice in terms of 'fundamental procedural fairness', in light of the notion of 'fair trial' in the international law of human rights); League of Nations, 'Questionnaire No. 4/Responsibility of States for Damage done in their Territories to the Person or Property of Foreigners (Doc. Nr. C. 46.M.23.126.V)' in Shabtai Rosenne (ed), *League of Nations Committee of Experts for the Progressive Codification of International Law [1925-1928]* (Volume 2: Oceana Publications, New York 1972) 118, 124-6 (submitting, in line with the *Calvo Doctrine*, that a 'denial of justice' only occurs when foreign citizens are denied *access* to the domestic justice system, provided such denial of access entails discrimination between foreigners and the host state's own citizens). For a critical analysis of each of these approaches see: Sebastián Mantilla Blanco, *Justizielles Unrecht im internationalen Investitionsschutzrecht* (Nomos, Baden-Baden 2016) 59-83.

A denial of justice, in a broad sense, occurs whenever a State, through any department of agency, fails to observe, with respect to an alien, any duty imposed by international law or by treaty with his country.[58]

To be sure, broad definitions of 'denial of justice' were not without practical importance. They turned particularly relevant where the applicable dispute settlement clause limited the adjudicators' jurisdiction to denial of justice claims, the consequence being that the extent of the tribunal's jurisdiction depended on the extent of the concept 'denial of justice'.[59] It must be noted, however, that wide-ranging definitions of the term were usually supplemented by the more-restrictive notion of 'denial of justice in a narrow sense'.[60]

The uncertainty about the meaning of 'denial of justice' turned the concept into an extremely flexible cause of action. A scholar has rightly noted that 'denial of justice' has been traditionally perceived as a 'bewilderingly malleable' legal institution.[61] For that very same reason, it should not come as a surprise that, in cases submitted before international adjudicatory bodies prior to the Second World War, claims pertaining to the protection and security of aliens were often entangled with the slippery notion of 'denial of justice'.

---

[58]Charles Cheney Hyde, *International Law. Chiefly as Interpreted and Applied by the United States* (Volume I: Little Brown & Co., Boston 1922) 491. For some additional examples see: Edwin Borchard, *The Diplomatic Protection of Citizens Abroad or the Law of International Claims* (The Banks Law Publishing Co., New York 1916) 330; *Laura M.B. Janes et al. v Mexico* (16 November 1925) IV RIAA 82 [22]; *LFH Neer and Pauline Neer v Mexico* (15 October 1926) IV RIAA 60, 64 (Separate Opinion of Commissioner Nielsen). For an account and critical discussion of these and further authorities adopting an all-encompassing definition of denial of justice see: Sebastián Mantilla Blanco, *Justizielles Unrecht im internationalen Investitionsschutzrecht* (Nomos, Baden-Baden 2016) 61.

[59]For an indicative example see: *Antoine Fabiani Case* (31 July 1905) X RIAA 83, 83-139 (discussing whether legislative and executive measures adopted by the Venezuelan Government fell within the definition of 'denial of justice', as the term was used in the applicable dispute settlement agreement). On the practical usefulness of the notion of 'denial of justice in a broad sense' see generally: Sebastián Mantilla Blanco, *Justizielles Unrecht im internationalen Investitionsschutzrecht* (Nomos, Baden-Baden 2016) 64-5 (also analyzing the *Fabiani* case in this regard).

[60]See for example: Edwin Borchard, *The Diplomatic Protection of Citizens Abroad or the Law of International Claims* (The Banks Law Publishing Co., New York 1916) 330. For another prominent author distinguishing between broad and narrow understandings of 'denial of justice' see: Hans Kelsen, *Principles of International Law* (The Lawbook Exchange, Clark NJ 2007) 246-7 n. 36 [first edition: 1952]. For an analysis of the dualistic approaches to the concept of denial of justice see: Sebastián Mantilla Blanco, *Justizielles Unrecht im internationalen Investitionsschutzrecht* (Nomos, Baden-Baden 2016) 63-4 (providing a more detailed account of these and further relevant sources).

[61]Ali Ehsassi, 'Cain and Abel: Congruence and Conflict in the Application of the Denial of Justice Principle' in Stephan Schill (ed), *International Investment Law and Comparative Public Law* (Oxford University Press, New York 2010) 213, 213 (referring to the 'bewildering malleability' of the notion).

2.2.4   The Distinction Between Primary and Secondary Rules of International Law. The Limits of a Contemporary Notion

Present-day international lawyers are used to a fairly settled distinction between the *primary rules of international law* establishing the content and extent of an international obligation, on the one hand, and the *secondary rules of international law* governing the consequences of the internationally wrongful act, on the other.[62] One would therefore expect a clear differentiation between a *primary* FPS rule determining the content and scope of the host state's obligation to provide protection and security to aliens, and the general set of *secondary rules* applicable upon a breach of the primary rule. Historical sources on the FPS standard draw no such distinction. This jargon corresponds to a recent—and not entirely undisputed—development, which found particular expression in the *Second Report on State Responsibility* submitted by Roberto Ago to the ILC in 1970.[63] Ago's proposal was successful. The separation of primary and secondary rules would indeed become the 'central organizing device' of the ILC Articles on State Responsibility.[64]

Ago's system implies that the same corpus of (secondary) rules of state responsibility is applicable in respect of any international obligation, regardless of its source, provided the obligation is not subject to a special regime.[65] This premise

---

[62]See generally: Anthony Aust, *Handbook of International Law* (Cambridge University Press, Cambridge 2010) 377.

[63]Ago's influential statement was as follows: "Responsibility differs widely, in its aspects, from the other subjects which the Commission has previously set out to codify. In its previous drafts, the Commission has generally concentrated on defining the rules of international law which, in one sector of inter-state relations or another, impose particular obligations on states, and which may, in a certain sense, be termed "primary", as opposed to the other rules – precisely those covering the field of responsibility – which may be termed "secondary", inasmuch as they are concerned with determining the consequences of failure to fulfill obligations established by the primary rules." Roberto Ago, 'Second Report on State Responsibility – The Origin of International Responsibility (A/CN.4/233)' (10 April 1970) 2 *Yearbook of the International Law Commission – 1970* 177, 179 [11]. During the 415th meeting of the ILC in 1957, Gerald G. Fitzmaurice had already suggested an approach to state responsibility that came close to Ago's 'secondary rules'. See: ILC, 'Summary Records of the 415th Meeting' (12 June 1957) 1 *Yearbook of the International Law Commission – 1957* 162, 163 [13] ("it would be a mistake to try to equate the subject of State responsibility with the whole of international law [. . .] In cases where individuals suffered injury on foreign territory, two questions arose: the first, whether the acts amounted to a breach of international law; and the second whether the circumstances were such that responsibility could be imputed to the State on whose territory the injury was caused. It was [. . .] the second question which was of the real essence of the subject of State responsibility").

[64]James Crawford, 'The ILC's Articles on Responsibility of States for Internationally Wrongful Acts: A Retrospect' (2002) 96(4) AJIL 874, 876. See also: ILC, 'Responsibility of States for Internationally Wrongful Acts. General Commentary' (2001) 2 *Yearbook of the International Law Commission – 2001* 31, 31 [1].

[65]For an overview of the function and practical usefulness of the distinction see generally: James Crawford, *State Responsibility. The General Part* (Cambridge University Press, Cambridge 2013)

was very controversial. For example, Philip Allott observed in 1988 that this approach involves 'generalizing about the effect of unlawful acts without talking too much about any particular unlawful acts'.[66] Allott further disregarded the structure advanced by Ago as the expression of 'a specifically bureaucratic spirit which seeks to get the job done with the minimum of spiritual commitment and the maximum of personal security'.[67] According to him, the whole notion of the 'secondary rules' was a 'dangerous fiction, an unnecessary intrusion into the systematic structure of a legal system'.[68] Other academic studies expressed similar concerns.[69] Confronted with these skeptical views, Special Rapporteur James Crawford acknowledged the limits of Ago's approach:

> [R]ights and duties could be developed by treaty or custom in particular ways for particular states; so, too, might the range of available responses to noncompliance. To this extent, the distinction between primary and secondary obligations was, and is, somewhat relative. A particular rule of conduct might contain its own special rule of attribution or its own rule about remedies. In such a case, there would be little point in arguing about questions of classification. The rule would be applied and it would normally be treated as a *lex specialis*, that is, as excluding the general rule.[70]

While the distinction between 'primary' and 'secondary' rules has proven to be a useful 'organizing device', its accuracy and significance should not be overestimated. This holds particularly true for any study about the FPS standard. An analysis of the evolution of FPS in the law of aliens will necessarily deal with authorities that considered the customary security obligation as an issue that was merely ancillary to more-general questions of state responsibility, such as attribution and fault.[71]

There is nothing extraordinary about this phenomenon. In some measure, the law of aliens was the breeding ground for the modern law of state responsibility.[72] This observation can be easily confirmed by looking into the early codification efforts

---

64-6; Robert Kolb, *The International Law of State Responsibility. An Introduction* (Edward Elgar Publishing, Northampton MA 2017) 6-8.

[66] Philip Allott, 'State Responsibility and the Unmaking of International Law' (1988) 29(1) HILJ 1, 7.

[67] Philip Allott, 'State Responsibility and the Unmaking of International Law' (1988) 29(1) HILJ 1, 10.

[68] Philip Allott, 'State Responsibility and the Unmaking of International Law' (1988) 29(1) HILJ 1, 11.

[69] For an indicative example see: Daniel Bodansky and John R. Crook, 'Symposium: The ILC's State Responsibility Articles. Introduction and Overview' (2002) 96(4) AJIL 773, 779-81. For an skeptical view on the subject see: Rosalyn Higgins, *Problems & Process. International Law and How We Use It* (Clarendon Press, Oxford 1994) 161-5.

[70] James Crawford, 'The ILC's Articles on Responsibility of States for Internationally Wrongful Acts: A Retrospect' (2002) 96(4) AJIL 874, 876-7. See also: James Crawford, *State Responsibility. The General Part* (Cambridge University Press, Cambridge 2013) 64-6.

[71] See Chap. 12.

[72] See generally: Daniel Bodansky and John R. Crook, 'Symposium: The ILC's State Responsibility Articles. Introduction and Overview' (2002) 96(4) AJIL 773, 776-7; Robert Kolb, *The International*

within the League of Nations and the first reports presented by Francisco V. García Amador to the ILC, which focused precisely on state responsibility for injuries to aliens.[73] The notion of the 'secondary rules' has been sometimes described as 'the key that allowed Ago to unlock state responsibility from the box into which García-Amador had placed it through his effort to articulate substantive norms governing the protection of aliens'.[74]

However interesting these debates might be, for present purposes it shall suffice to underscore that historical sources do not deliver the notion of a *primary* FPS obligation, separate from a general corpus of *secondary* rules of state responsibility. A proper understanding of the FPS standard and, particularly, of its link to the due diligence standard of liability, requires some degree of consciousness about the origins and relative character of the *primary rules—secondary rules* divide.[75]

Law of State Responsibility. An Introduction (Edward Elgar Publishing, Northampton MA 2017) 8 *et seq.*

[73]On the codification attempts at the League of Nations see: League of Nations, 'Questionnaire No. 4/Responsibility of States for Damage done in their Territories to the Person or Property of Foreigners (Doc. Nr. C. 46.M.23.126.V)' in Shabtai Rosenne (ed), *League of Nations Committee of Experts for the Progressive Codification of International Law [1925-1928]* (Volume 2, Oceana Publications, New York 1972) 118-31; League of Nations, 'Bases of Discussion drawn up in 1929 by the Preparatory Committee of the Conference for the Codification of International Law (Doc. Nr. C.75.M.69.1929.V)' in Martins Paparinskis, *Basic Documents on International Investment Protection* (Hart Publishing, Portland OR 2012) 20-6; League of Nations, 'Text of Articles Adopted in First Reading by the Third Committee of the Conference for the Codification of International Law (Doc. Nr. C.351(c).M.145(c).929.V)' in Martins Paparinskis, *Basic Documents on International Investment Protection* (Hart Publishing, Portland OR 2012) 26-8. In 1956, Francisco V. García Amador proposed the ILC to adopt a 'gradual approach' to the codification of the law of state responsibility, explaining that '[t]he topic of international responsibility is so broad, and involves such diverse factors, that it is not possible to proceed immediately with the codification of the entire topic. The Commission, as it has done in the case of other topics, should adopt a gradual approach, codifying first that part of the topic which is most ripe for codification and which, at the same time, should receive priority [. . .] The "responsibility of States for damage caused to the person or property of aliens" would appear to fulfil (sic) these two conditions'. Francisco García Amador, 'International Responsibility: Report by F. V. García Amador, Special Rapporteur (A/CN.4/96)' (20 January 1956) 2 *Yearbook of the International Law Commission – 1956* 173, 221. For a brief historical account of these codification projects see: Daniel Bodansky and John R. Crook, 'Symposium: The ILC's State Responsibility Articles. Introduction and Overview' (2002) 96(4) AJIL 773, 776-9.

[74]Daniel Bodansky and John R. Crook, 'Symposium: The ILC's State Responsibility Articles. Introduction and Overview' (2002) 96(4) AJIL 773, 780.

[75]See also Chap. 12.

2.3 Overcoming the Obstacles

Tracing the FPS standard back in the annals of legal history is a demanding undertaking. As shown throughout this chapter, the historical survey must necessarily deal with competing intellectual agendas, complex jurisdictional clauses, the uncertain notion of denial of justice, and general debates about state responsibility. Against this backdrop, it could become a true challenge to distinguish those historical sources that can be genuinely linked to FPS from those that cannot. The underlying reason could be described as a problem of perspective. In his influential work *What is History?* (1961), Edward Carr observed that 'we can view the past, and achieve our understanding of the past, only through the eyes of the present'.[76] According to Carr:

> The historian is of his own age, and is bound by the conditions of human existence. The very words which he uses – words like democracy, empire, war, revolution – have current connotations from which he cannot divorce them.[77]

This holds particularly true for international legal history. Lawyers normally depart from a contemporary notion, and seek to project it into the past. As observed by a legal historian writing on the subject:

> [I]nternational lawyers – whether as scholars searching for rules of customary international law in state practice, or as practitioners fighting their corner in a dispute – will approach historical material with a view to garner from it some insight or rule of contemporaneous relevance.[78]

As a corollary, historical narratives about the law are at permanent risk of becoming 'skewed from the outset'.[79] The risk is particularly high when it comes to customary law. Arguments about customary law are, in the final analysis, 'argument[s] about history'.[80] Nonetheless, their ultimate purpose is not historical, but normative: they resort to history as a *means* to understand a contemporary legal institution and could hence be depicted as 'unabashedly instrumental'.[81]

This instrumental use of history is not wrong for and by itself. As observed by Randall Lesaffer, 'there is nothing wrong with the desire to learn something useful

---

[76]Edward Hallett Carr, *What is History?* (Penguin Books, New York 1987) 24 [first edition: 1961].

[77]Edward Hallett Carr, *What is History?* (Penguin Books, New York 1987) 24-5 [first edition: 1961].

[78]Matt Craven, 'International Law and its Histories' in Matt Craven, Malgosia Fitzmaurice and Maria Vogiatzi (eds), *Time, History and International Law* (Martinus Nijhoff, Leiden/Boston 2011) 1, 16.

[79]Matt Craven, 'International Law and its Histories' in Matt Craven, Malgosia Fitzmaurice and Maria Vogiatzi (eds), *Time, History and International Law* (Martinus Nijhoff, Leiden/Boston 2011) 1, 16.

[80]David Kennedy, 'The Disciplines of International Law and Policy' (1999) 12 LJIL 9, 88.

[81]Matt Craven, 'International Law and its Histories' in Matt Craven, Malgosia Fitzmaurice and Maria Vogiatzi (eds), *Time, History and International Law* (Martinus Nijhoff, Leiden/Boston 2011) 1, 7. See also pp. 15-23.

for the present from the past'.[82] The clue is to approach the past with some restraint. When examining historical material, international lawyers must be mindful not only of their own normative goals, but also of their 'historical task'.[83] They should avoid falling into an exercise of 'foreign office international legal history' in which historical material is 'distorted or perverted, in order to make some point that has no basis in fact or reality'.[84] In practice, this implies acknowledging historical sources as they are, that is to say, as 'remnants from the past'.[85] Normative arguments—e.g. statements about customary law—should be built on the historical rationale of the sources, and not the other way around; as noted by Lesaffer, 'before one can learn something from the past other than what one knows from the present, one first has to let the past be the past – at least as far as this is humanly possible'.[86]

Professional historians could possibly link this call with the 'Rankean' classical historiographical ideal of presenting the past 'as it actually was', as a sort of incontestable fact or truth.[87] For the sake of clarity, this monograph does not pursue

---

[82]Randall Lesaffer, 'International Law and its History: The Story of an Unrequired Love' in Matt Craven, Malgosia Fitzmaurice and Maria Vogiatzi (eds), *Time, History and International Law* (Martinus Nijhoff, Leiden/Boston 2011) 27, 37.

[83]On the 'historical task' of international law scholarship see generally: Lassa Francis Laurence Oppenheim, 'The Science of International Law: Its Task and Method' (1908) 2(2) AJIL 313, 315 *et seq.*

[84]David Bederman, 'Foreign Office International Legal History' in Matt Craven, Malgosia Fitzmaurice and Maria Vogiatzi (eds), *Time, History and International Law* (Martinus Nijhoff, Leiden/Boston 2011) 43, 46. Bederman proposes the label 'foreign office legal history' as the equivalent in international law to the phenomenon American constitutional historians describe as 'law office history'. According to Bederman, this phenomenon has the following features: "(1) a lack of analytical rigour in historical investigations; (2) selective use of historical materials; (3) sloppy or strategic methodologies in the review of historical sources; (4) overt or implicit instrumentalism in the selection of historic data and/or the conclusions drawn from such material; and (5) an unwillingness or inability to reconcile conflicting sources, or an inability to accept ambiguity or incompleteness in the historic record" (at p. 46). See also: Matt Craven, 'International Law and its Histories' in Matt Craven, Malgosia Fitzmaurice and Maria Vogiatzi (eds), *Time, History and International Law* (Martinus Nijhoff, Leiden/Boston 2011) 1, 15 *et seq.*

[85]See generally: Mark Gilderhus, *History and Historians. A Historiographical Introduction* (Prentice Hall, Upper Saddle River NJ 2007) 86-7.

[86]Randall Lesaffer, 'International Law and its History: The Story of an Unrequired Love' in Matt Craven, Malgosia Fitzmaurice and Maria Vogiatzi (eds), *Time, History and International Law* (Martinus Nijhoff, Leiden/Boston 2011) 27, 37.

[87]In the preface to the 1824 edition of his *Geschichten der romanischen und germanischen Völker*, Leopold von Ranke (1795-1886) described the role of the historian as presenting the past 'as it actually was' ('wie es eigentlich gewesen [ist]'). See: Leopold von Ranke, *Geschichten der romanischen und germanischen Völker von 1494 bis 1514* (Leipzig, Ducker & Humblot 1885) vii [first edition: 1824]. The 'Rankean ideal' has been the subject of intense controversy. For example, in his assessment of nineteenth century historiography, Walter Benjamin observed that '[t]he history that showed things "as they really were" was the strongest narcotic of the century'. Walter Benjamin, *The Arcades Project* (Howard Eiland and Kevin McLaughlin tr, Harvard University Press, Cambridge MA 1999) 463. For a discussion of the 'Rankean ideal' in connection with international law history see: Matt Craven, 'International Law and its Histories' in Matt Craven, Malgosia Fitzmaurice and Maria Vogiatzi (eds), *Time, History and International Law* (Martinus

such an idealistic goal. Following the thread of other works in legal history, it does not claim to provide an entirely 'neutral' or 'correct' description of the past.[88] The historical survey intends to deliver a merely *plausible* narrative, which should lead the way to a reasonable normative argument.[89]

The fact that the narrative is merely *plausible* should not diminish its value or practical significance. On the contrary, *plausible* historical arguments are likely to foster objectivity in the application of investment protection standards. Borrowing Todd Weiler's words, history helps investment lawyers avoid 'embarking upon a rudderless excursion in subjective analysis'.[90] Plausible accounts of the past have the effect of placing a burden upon those sailing against the wind of history or, more accurately, a version of history. Those rejecting the argument shall either refute it, which implies suggesting an alternative historical narrative, or provide evidence that the legal institution at stake changed or evolved with the passage of time.

In any case, the plausibility of a historical argument depends on both the adequate selection of relevant historical materials, and a conscious effort to interpret them in their own temporal context.[91] In its endeavor to fulfill these criteria, the historical survey could seem close to historiographical contextualism, in the sense that it attempts to 'reconstruct' contexts and 'interpret' written sources on that basis.[92]

Nijhoff, Leiden/Boston 2011) 1, 16. For a critical assessment of classic historicism see: Edward Hallett Carr, *What is History?* (Penguin Books, New York 1987) 8 *et seq.* [first edition: 1961].

[88] In the field of international legal history, influential scholars have also opted to renounce to the Rankean ideal. For instance, in *The Gentle Civilizer of Nations*, Martti Koskenniemi presented his work as 'a kind of experimentation in the writing about the disciplinary past in which the constrains of any rigorous "method" have been set aside in an effort to create intuitively plausible and politically engaged narratives [...] The essays do not seek a neutral description of the past "as it actually was" – that sort of knowledge is not open to us'. Martti Koskenniemi, *The Gentle Civilizer of Nations. The Rise and Fall of International Law 1870-1960* (Cambridge University Press, New York 2008) 9-10.

[89] For an overview of the use of 'historical narratives' in modern historiography see: Lawrence Stone, 'The Revival of Narrative: Reflections on a New Old History' (1979) 85 Past & Present 3, 3-24.

[90] Todd Weiler, *The Interpretation of International Investment Law: Equality, Discrimination, and Minimum Standards of Treatment in Historical Context* (Brill, Leiden 2013) 1. See also Charles Brower's Foreword to Weiler's book (at p. xxxv).

[91] These two points are intrinsically related to basic historiographical concerns. On the use and implications of historiographical methodology for international legal history see: Randall Lesaffer, 'International Law and its History: The Story of an Unrequired Love' in Matt Craven, Malgosia Fitzmaurice and Maria Vogiatzi (eds), *Time, History and International Law* (Martinus Nijhoff, Leiden/Boston 2011) 27, 37 *et seq.* See also: David Bederman, 'Foreign Office International Legal History' in Matt Craven, Malgosia Fitzmaurice and Maria Vogiatzi (eds), *Time, History and International Law* (Martinus Nijhoff, Leiden/Boston 2011) 43, 62-3; Matt Craven, 'International Law and its Histories' in Matt Craven, Malgosia Fitzmaurice and Maria Vogiatzi (eds), *Time, History and International Law* (Martinus Nijhoff, Leiden/Boston 2011) 1, 15-23.

[92] For a presentation of contextualism in legal historiography see: William Fisher, 'Texts and Contexts: The Application to American Legal History of the Methodologies of Intellectual History' (1997) 49 Stan. L. Rev. 1065, 1068-9 and 1076-9. Fischer also discusses the use of contextualism by American constitutional originalists (at pp. 1103-8). See also: David Rabban, 'The

For the avoidance of doubt, the present monograph does not intend to follow a strictly contextualist line of argument. The argument could be best portrayed as a halfway between a moderate contextualism and what some legal historians would describe as a 'playful' history, that is to say, a narrative which hopes to remain 'sensitive to the subtle interaction of arguments' and 'prone to punning and unexpected juxtapositions'.[93] This approach crystalizes in two features of the survey.

First. The historical argument departs from a *label* rather than from a previously determined *meaning*. It primarily relies on authorities using the expressions 'protection' and 'security', or a similar wording, when referring to the duties of the host state toward foreigners and their home states. Sources have been selected regardless of whether these terms appear in the context of denial of justice claims, or in connection with other causes of action. In the interpretation of primary historical sources, attention is drawn to the theoretical and factual background of each particular source. In this vein, for example, the analysis of early modern doctrinal approaches to the protection of aliens (e.g. in the works of Christian von Wolff or Emer de Vattel) is preceded by a brief presentation of their understanding of the sources of international law. Additional historical material has been included whenever relevant for a contextual understanding of the subject.

Second. The structure of the argument aims at avoiding, as far as possible, *a priori* assumptions about the origins and meaning of the FPS standard. For that very same reason, the historical survey begins by justifying its own starting point and considering possible alternative approaches. Most importantly, the development of the FPS standard is not presented as a history of continuities. A conscious effort has been made not to hide historical sources' disparities, contradictions and conflicting political backgrounds. On the contrary, such struggles constitute a fundamental ingredient of the narrative. This will be particularly evident in the analysis of state practice and scholarly writings from the nineteenth and early twentieth centuries.[94]

The resulting legal-historical background shall serve as a basis for identifying those features of the standard which, borrowing David Kennedy's words, 'have come through history to stand outside history'.[95] In order to make the leap from historical arguments into normative statements about customary law, this

---

Historiography of Late Nineteenth-Century American Legal History' (2003) 4(2) Theoretical Inquiries in Law 541, 547 *et seq.* (referring to the particular case of American legal historiography).

[93]William Fisher, 'Texts and Contexts: The Application to American Legal History of the Methodologies of Intellectual History' (1997) 49 Stan. L. Rev. 1065, 1108-9. It should be noted that Fischer's idea of a 'playful history' does *not* represent a separate historiographical approach. Rather, it is a *feature* of historical narratives, which usually results from 'textualist' (the text transcends the context) and 'new historicist' (enhanced interest in written sources' influence on historical realities) historiographical approaches (at pp. 1108-9). See also pp. 1069-70 (on textualism) and pp. 1070-2 (on new historicism).

[94]See Chap. 4.

[95]David Kennedy, 'The Disciplines of International Law and Policy' (1999) 12 LJIL 9, 88.

monograph primarily relies on inductive reasoning.[96] Induction reveals the common threads between past and present-day sources. An inductive approach does not however imply renouncing to every form of deduction; it simply sets an accent.[97]

[96]For the primacy of inductive reasoning for the determination of customary international law, see: *Delimitation of the Maritime Boundary in the Gulf of Maine Area (Canada v United States of America)* [1984] ICJ Rep 246, 299 [111]. See also: Adolf Schüle, 'Methoden der Völkerrechtswissenschaft' (1959/60) 8 AVR 129, 148 (underscoring the necessity for inductive reasoning); Stefan Talmon, 'Determining Customary International Law: The ICJ's Methodology between Induction, Deduction and Assertion' (2015) 26(2) EJIL 417, 421 (analyzing the role of induction and also considering the *Gulf Maine* decision at pp. 423 and 430).

[97]For a similar remark on inductive arguments in international law see: Georg Schwarzenberger, *The Inductive Approach to International Law* (Stevens & Sons, London 1965) 37-8. For the use of deductive arguments for ascertaining international customary rules see: Stefan Talmon, 'Determining Customary International Law: The ICJ's Methodology between Induction, Deduction and Assertion' (2015) 26(2) EJIL 417, 423-34.

Chapter 3
The Origins of 'Full Protection and Security'. From Medieval Reprisals to the Age of Enlightenment

3.1 Preliminary Issue. Determining the Starting Point

Foreignness is as old a concept as statehood itself. National identities are inclusive of the natives and exclusive of those not belonging to the national community, who are accordingly designated as *hostis*, strangers, foreigners, or aliens.[1] The interest of home states in ensuring their citizens' protection abroad has been traditionally attached to broader debates on the legal status of aliens.[2] An unavoidable difficulty for tracing back the roots of FPS in history is hence to determine the starting point. One could indeed go back to antiquity,[3] or even to the geneses of mankind. For instance, Todd Weiler places the origins of FPS in the Bronze Age:

> The roots of the P&S standard lay in over two millennia of promises of examples and protection and security [...] The concept of hospitality, which encompasses the practice of according protection and security to aliens, appears to have been a recurring theme from the start of human civilisation. While shared understandings of concepts such as: sovereignty, territory, property rights, economy and States may have all evolved over the millennia and between cultures, the concept of hospitality itself has remained largely immutable.[4]

---

[1]For a philosophical analysis of the notion of 'foreignness' and its relationship to the idea of 'otherness' see: Jacques Derrida, *Of Hospitality* (Rachel Bowlby tr, Stanford University Press, Stanford CA 2000) 21-2, 43 *et seq* and 71-2.

[2]For a general analysis of the historical development of the legal status of aliens see: Borchard, *The Diplomatic Protection of Citizens Abroad or the Law of International Claims* (The Banks Law Publishing Co., New York 1916) 33-6.

[3]Cf. Nartnirun Junngam, 'The Full Protection and Security Standard in International Investment Law: What and Who is Investment Fully[?] Protected and Secured From?' (2018) 7(1) AUBLR 1, 8 *et seq.*, 85-6, 90, 94 and 99 (arguing that the origins of the FPS standard can be placed in the antiquity, particularly in Greece and Rome).

[4]Todd Weiler, *The Interpretation of International Investment Law: Equality, Discrimination, and Minimum Standards of Treatment in Historical Context* (Brill, Leiden 2013) 61. See also: Nicole O'Donnell, 'Reconciling Full Protection and Security Guarantees in Bilateral Investment Treaties

© Springer Nature Switzerland AG 2019
S. Mantilla Blanco, *Full Protection and Security in International Investment Law*,
European Yearbook of International Economic Law 8,
https://doi.org/10.1007/978-3-030-24838-3_3

The 'hospitality approach' is not entirely convincing. This view poses at least four concerns. The first concern refers to the contention that hospitality has been a consistent and 'largely immutable' notion in utterly different historical and geographical contexts, as suggested by Weiler.[5] The concept of hospitality is anything but straightforward. There is no universal, univocal notion of hospitality (*hospitalité/ Hospitalität/Wirthbarkeit*). Numerous theories have been advanced in this regard. The participants in the conceptual debate include Immanuel Kant, Emmanuel Levinas, Jacques Derrida and Pierre Klossowski, just to mention some prominent examples.[6] Moreover, studies from other disciplines suggest that people's understanding of hospitality could considerably vary from one culture or religion to another.[7]

A second concern arises from the assumption that the FPS standard is embedded within the notion of hospitality, so that FPS can be properly styled as a 'hospitality obligation'.[8] The link between the two notions is unsure. For instance, it is a common ground that, as a minimum, FPS assures foreigners physical protection against private wrongs.[9] The host state is thus pledged to protect aliens from its own citizens.[10] Whether *hospitality* truly implies that guests shall be protected against members of the 'host family' or the 'host community' is dubious, if to say the least.

with Incidence of Terrorism' (2018) 29(3) ARIA 293, 297-8 (following Weiler's views); Timothy Foden, 'Back to Bricks and Mortar: The case of a "Traditional" Definition of Investment that Never Was' in Ian Laird, Borzu Sabahi, Frédéric Sourgens and Todd Weiler (eds), *Investment Treaty Arbitration and International Law* (Juris Net, Huntington NY 2015) 145-8 (relying on Weiler's approach).

[5]Todd Weiler, *The Interpretation of International Investment Law: Equality, Discrimination, and Minimum Standards of Treatment in Historical Context* (Brill, Leiden 2013) 61.

[6]See: Immanuel Kant, *Zum ewigen Frieden. Ein philosophischer Entwurf* (Frankfurt/Leipzig, 1796) 36-7; Emmanuel Levinas, *Totalité et infini. Essai sur l'extériorité* (Brodard at Taupin, Paris 1990) 12, 166-7, 187-8, 224 284, 332-4 and 341; Jacques Derrida, *Of Hospitality* (Rachel Bowlby tr, Stanford University Press, Stanford CA 2000); Jacques Derrida, *Adieu to Emmanuel Levinas* (Pascale-Anne Brault/Michael Naas tr, Stanford University Press, Stanford CA 1999) 15 *et seq*; Pierre Klossowski, *Les lois de l'hospitalité* (Gallimard, Paris 1970).

[7]Cf. Julian Pitt-Rivers, 'The Law of Hospitality' (2012) 2(1) HAU Journal of Ethnographic Theory 501, 501-17. For other authors addressing the concept see: Amy G. Oden (ed), *And You Welcomed Me. A Sourcebook on Hospitality in Early Christianity* (Abingdon Press, Nashville TN 2001); Hanns Boersma, *Violence, Hospitality, and the Cross: Reappropriating the Atonement Tradition* (Baker Publishing, Grand Rapids MI 2004); James A. Heffernan, *Hospitality and Treachery in Western Literature* (Yale University Press, New Haven CT 2014); Jessica Wrobleski, *The Limits of Hospitality* (Liturgical Press, Collegeville MN 2012); Judith Still, *Derrida and Hospitality. Theory and Practice* (Edinburgh University Press, Edinburgh 2013); Réal Robert Fillion, *Multicultural Dynamics and the Ends of History. Exploring Kant, Hegel, and Marx* (University of Ottawa Press, Ottawa 2008) 61-8.

[8]Todd Weiler, *The Interpretation of International Investment Law: Equality, Discrimination, and Minimum Standards of Treatment in Historical Context* (Brill, Leiden 2013) 61-2.

[9]Chapters 8 and 9 discuss this aspect of the FPS standard in greater detail.

[10]See Sect. 8.3.1.

The third concern is that *hospitality* could be too broad a notion. The whole question of foreignness has been occasionally assessed as a question of hospitality.[11] Without entering into the philosophical debate, one observes that, under some understandings of the term, hospitality could actually embody the whole substance of the law of aliens.[12] From this standpoint, FPS would be a *particular content* within the broader notion of hospitality (as a *general content*). This relationship is implicit in Weiler's use of the term, as he states that 'the concept of hospitality [...] encompasses the practice of according protection and security to aliens'.[13] This is not without consequences. Not every reference to the *general* (hospitality) concerns the *particular* (FPS). It is therefore little surprising that some of the earliest authorities quoted by Weiler, while arguably referring to hospitality, do not *expressly* refer to 'protection' or 'security'.[14]

Lastly, a fourth concern pertains to the very idea of an international 'hospitality *obligation*'.[15] In his celebrated essay *Zum ewigen Frieden* (1795), Immanuel Kant conceived the idea of 'universal hospitality' as a condition for peace.[16] Hospitality, said Kant, 'signifies solely the right every stranger has of not being treated as an enemy in the country in which he arrives'.[17] Kant believed, however, that hospitality

---

[11]See, for example: Jacques Derrida, *Of Hospitality* (Rachel Bowlby tr, Stanford University Press, Stanford CA 2000) 3-73.

[12]For example, Jacques Derrida draws a careful distinction between the (absolute) 'law of hospitality' and the '*laws* of hospitality'. The said 'laws' include the whole body of rights and duties, which hosts and guests owe to each other. If a similar terminology were to be used in the context of international law, these 'laws' would embody all rules and principles of the law of aliens. See: Jacques Derrida, *Of Hospitality* (Rachel Bowlby tr, Stanford University Press, Stanford CA 2000) 75-6. For an additional example see: Julius Goebel, 'The International Responsibility of States for Injuries Sustained by Aliens on Account of Mob Violence, Insurrections and Civil Wars' (1914) 8 AJIL 802, 803 (suggesting that the law of aliens arose out of the primitive notion of a *Gastrecht* among Germanic peoples).

[13]Todd Weiler, *The Interpretation of International Investment Law: Equality, Discrimination, and Minimum Standards of Treatment in Historical Context* (Brill, Leiden 2013) 61.

[14]See, for example: Todd Weiler, *The Interpretation of International Investment Law: Equality, Discrimination, and Minimum Standards of Treatment in Historical Context* (Brill, Leiden 2013) 68-79 (quoting, among others, the Buddhacarita of Aśvaghosa, the Mencious Text, the Torah, the Tanakh, the New Testament and the Qur'an).

[15]Todd Weiler, *The Interpretation of International Investment Law: Equality, Discrimination, and Minimum Standards of Treatment in Historical Context* (Brill, Leiden 2013) 61-2.

[16]Immanuel Kant, *Project for a Perpetual Peace: A Philosophical Essay* (Vernor & Hood, London 1796) 28-31; Immanuel Kant, *Zum ewigen Frieden. Ein philosophisher Entwurf* (Frankfurt/Leipzig 1796) 36-42.

[17]Immanuel Kant, *Project for a Perpetual Peace: A Philosophical Essay* (Vernor & Hood, London 1796) 28. The original German text reads as follows: "da bedeutet Hospitalität (Wirthbarkeit) das Recht eines Fremdlings, seines Ankunft auf dem Boden eines andern wegen, von diesem nicht feindselig behandelt zu werden". See: Immanuel Kant, *Zum ewigen Frieden. Ein philosophisher Entwurf* (Frankfurt/Leipzig 1796) 36 [first edition: 1795].

could be conditional and granted on a merely temporary basis.[18] Jacques Derrida famously criticized Kant's definition of hospitality and decried it as a blatant contradiction.[19] According to Derrida, hospitality can only be pure if it is unconditional, for conditions are inhospitable gestures, that is to say, acts of inhospitality.[20] But this kind of hospitality, which Derrida calls *'the law of hospitality'*, constitutes an outright impossible demand.[21] It indeed implies opening the door to 'the absolute, unknown, anonymous, other'.[22] Consequently, in the real world, absolute hospitality is unavoidably and necessarily impossible.[23]

Following Derrida, hospitality has therefore always been restricted through the *'laws of hospitality'*, namely, 'the norms, the rights and the duties that are imposed on host and hostesses, on the men or women who give a welcome as well as the men or women who receive it'.[24] These conditions 'transgress' and 'challenge' *'the law of absolute, unconditional, hyperbolical hospitality'*.[25] As a result, '[t]he antinomy of hospitality irreconcilably opposes *The* law, in its universal singularity, to a plurality that is not only a dispersal (laws in the plural), but a structured multiplicity, determined by a process of division and differentiation'.[26] The *law* and the *laws*, as understood by Derrida, 'both imply and exclude each other, simultaneously'.[27] The antinomy is tragic:

> The tragedy, for it is a tragedy of destiny, is that the two antagonistic terms of this antinomy are not symmetrical. *The* law is above the laws [. . .] But even while keeping itself above the

---

[18]Immanuel Kant, *Project for a Perpetual Peace: A Philosophical Essay* (Vernor & Hood, London 1796) 28-31; Immanuel Kant, *Zum ewigen Frieden. Ein philosophisher Entwurf* (Frankfurt/Leipzig 1796) 36-42. For the interpretation of the Kantian concept of hospitality see: Jacques Derrida, *Adieu to Emmanuel Levinas* (Pascale-Anne Brault/Michael Naas tr, Stanford University Press, Stanford CA 1999) 87 *et seq.*

[19]Jacques Derrida, *Adieu to Emmanuel Levinas* (Pascale-Anne Brault/Michael Naas tr, Stanford University Press, Stanford CA 1999) 87 *et seq*; Jacques Derrida, *Of Hospitality* (Rachel Bowlby tr, Stanford University Press, Stanford CA 2000) 43 *et seq.*

[20]Jacques Derrida, *Of Hospitality* (Rachel Bowlby tr, Stanford University Press, Stanford CA 2000) 25-7.

[21]Jacques Derrida, *Of Hospitality* (Rachel Bowlby tr, Stanford University Press, Stanford CA 2000) 25-7 and 71-81.

[22]Jacques Derrida, *Of Hospitality* (Rachel Bowlby tr, Stanford University Press, Stanford CA 2000) 25-6.

[23]Jacques Derrida, *Of Hospitality* (Rachel Bowlby tr, Stanford University Press, Stanford CA 2000) 25-7, 71-81, 75 *et seq.*

[24]Jacques Derrida, *Of Hospitality* (Rachel Bowlby tr, Stanford University Press, Stanford CA 2000) 77.

[25]Jacques Derrida, *Of Hospitality* (Rachel Bowlby tr, Stanford University Press, Stanford CA 2000) 75-7.

[26]Jacques Derrida, *Of Hospitality* (Rachel Bowlby tr, Stanford University Press, Stanford CA 2000) 79.

[27]Jacques Derrida, *Of Hospitality* (Rachel Bowlby tr, Stanford University Press, Stanford CA 2000) 81.

laws of hospitality, *the* unconditional law of hospitality needs the laws, it *requires* them. This demand is constitutive.[28]

What Weiler understands under 'hospitality obligation' is not entirely clear.[29] But this terminology could entail a paradox. Following Derrida, if hospitality is pure, it cannot be conditional; but unconditional hospitality implies an unbearable burden.[30] And then the question turns into whether an impossible demand can or should constitute a binding international obligation. Against this setting it seems that clarity is better served if one avoids linking FPS to the disputed notion of hospitality. Such linkage is further unnecessary. FPS has a meaning of its own.

This chapter traces the geneses of FPS back not to the Bronze Age, but to the Western-European Middle Ages. The starting point has been determined on the basis of a factual observation. Present-day investment protection standards were inspired by prewar treaty practice and academic publications.[31] In the nineteenth and early twentieth centuries, it was not unusual for foreign offices and international law scholars to seek inspiration from eighteenth century treatises, such as Emer de Vattel's celebrated *Le droit des gens*.[32] A look into the works of Vattel and other authors of the time reveals that the principles on the treatment of aliens were consistently linked to the notion of private reprisals, a medieval institution that had already drawn the attention of some of the 'fathers' of international law, including Hugo Grotius (1583–1645).[33]

This chapter submits that the medieval practice of reprisals was 'rationalized' in the mid-to-late eighteenth century through the *theory of the tacit agreement*. Aliens were thereby understood to 'tacitly' adhere to the social contract by the act of entering into a foreign sovereign's realms. The host sovereign was in turn presumed to agree to extend his protection to them, in return for obedience. Upon certain conditions, the breach of such protection obligation entitled the foreigner's home state to undertake or authorize reprisals. This approach was not free from controversy at the time. German classic positivists sought to establish the principles of the law of aliens, not on the basis of legal fictions, but through an *inductive* analysis of European state practice. Not surprisingly, their treatises were the first to characterize the protection obligation as a *customary* duty. In spite of their methodological disparities, both approaches set out a doctrinal, rational, basis for the emerging

---

[28] Jacques Derrida, *Of Hospitality* (Rachel Bowlby tr, Stanford University Press, Stanford CA 2000) 79.

[29] Todd Weiler, *The Interpretation of International Investment Law: Equality, Discrimination, and Minimum Standards of Treatment in Historical Context* (Brill, Leiden 2013) 61-2.

[30] Jacques Derrida, *Of Hospitality* (Rachel Bowlby tr, Stanford University Press, Stanford CA 2000) 75-81.

[31] See Sect. 2.1.

[32] See Sect. 3.6 (addressing the influence of Vattel and other eighteenth century international law scholars).

[33] See Sect. 3.2.

FPS standard. This chapter shows that these doctrinal foundations had a recognizable influence on the first generation of FCN agreements.

3.2 The Beginnings. The Medieval Practice of Private Reprisals

The roots of the sovereign's duty to protect aliens can be placed in the medieval practice of private reprisals (*repreaesaliae* or *pignerationes*).[34] In their most rudimentary origins, reprisals were a form of 'self-redress', which allowed the victim of an unjustified injury to directly seize the wrongdoer's property.[35] Reprisals could be employed not only against the initial wrongdoer, but also against the person and belongings of any member of the wrongdoer's family, clan or national community.[36] Reprisals are therefore believed to originate from the combination of an instinctive sense of 'self-help' and a primitive notion of collective responsibility.[37]

---

[34]The English term 'reprisals' seems to have appeared at some point during the thirteenth century. However, Medieval Latin texts usually used the expression *repraesaliae* or *repressaliae*. In an attempt to establish a link between the concept and earlier roman institutions, some sources chose the word *pignerationes*. See: Geoffrey Butler and Simon Maccoby, *The Development of International Law* (Longmans, Green & Co., New York 1928) 173. This chapter uses these expressions interchangeably.

[35]For an overview of the rudimentary origins of private reprisals see: Geoffrey Butler and Simon Maccoby, *The Development of International Law* (Longmans, Green & Co., New York 1928) 173-5.

[36]A representative example may be found in the authorization for reprisals granted by King Edward I of England, to Bernard Dongresilli (1295). The letter was first issued by John, 'lieutenant of the King' in Gascony, and later confirmed by the King. Dongresilli had sought 'shelter from bad weather' in a Portuguese port. According to the document, 'some sons of perdition' ransacked his vessel, taking with them the merchant's valuable possessions. The King of Portugal had allegedly received himself a part of the spoils. The letter of reprisals read as follows: "Yielding to the prayer of the said merchant, [we] have given and granted, and now give and grant to him, Bernard, his heirs, successors, and posterity, liberty to make reprisals upon the people of the realm of Portugal, and particularly upon those of the city of Lisbon aforesaid, and upon their goods, wheresoever he may find them, whether within the dominion of our lord, the King and Duke, or without, [and] to retain and keep them for himself, until he and his heirs or successors or posterity, shall be fully satisfied for [the loss of] his goods so spoiled as aforesaid, or their value as declared above, together with the expenses reasonably incurred by him in that behalf." For a detailed account of the incident and the original historical sources see: Grover Clark, 'The English Practice with Regard to Reprisals by Private Persons' (1933) 27(4) AJIL 694, 696 (citing the original documents in length). See also: Hans Planitz, 'Studien zur Geschichte des deutschen Arrestprozesses. Der Fremdenarrest' (1919) 40 Zeitschrift der Savigny Stiftung für Rechtsgeschichte 87, 168 and 178 *et seq.*

[37]See: Antônio Augusto Cançado Trindade, 'Origin and Historical Development of the Rule of Exhaustion of Local Remedies in International Law' (1976) 12 RBDI 499, 501; Friedrich Rudolf Hohl, *Bartolus a Saxoferrato: Seine Bedeutung für die Entwicklungsgeschichte des Repressaliensrechts* [unpublished doctoral dissertation] (Volume 1: Universität Bonn, Bonn 1954) 33-7; Geoffrey Butler and Simon Maccoby, *The Development of International Law*

Medieval *repreaesaliae* were not a static institution. Quite the contrary, they were dynamic and in constant evolution. With the passage of time, sovereigns progressively limited the use of reprisals through a public-law mechanism, which could be accurately characterized as an embryonic form of diplomatic intervention: *letters of marque,* also known as *letters or reprisals* or *letters de requête.*[38] A *letter of marque* embodied a formal authorization for reprisals, which could be obtained from the monarch only, and constituted a mandatory requirement for self-redress.[39] Letters of reprisals were hence an instrument to ensure that the sovereign maintained, at least in some measure, control over his subjects' use of reprisals.[40] In this vein, international law historians have observed that '[p]rinces would see that reprisals undertaken privately by the subjects of one of them against the subjects of another would be likely to lead from outrage to outrage to a state of war'.[41]

The regulation of letters of marque through internal ordinances became increasingly abstract, general and complex throughout the years.[42] In addition, there was a dense network of treaties addressing the practice of reprisals.[43] Treaties typically circumscribed the right declare or authorize *repreaesaliae* to cases entailing a *denial of justice* (*déni de justice* or *denegata justitia*), attributable to the host sovereign, and further conditioned the issuance of *letters de requête* upon the prior exhaustion of

---

(Longmans, Green & Co., New York 1928) 173-5; Guha Roy, 'Is the Law of Responsibility of States for Injuries to Aliens a Part of Universal International Law?' (1963) 55(4) AJIL 863, 864; Hans Spiegel, 'Origin and Development of Denial of Justice' (1938) 32(1) AJIL 63, 64.

[38] Antônio Augusto Cançado Trindade, 'Origin and Historical Development of the Rule of Exhaustion of Local Remedies in International Law' (1976) 12 RBDI 499, 501-2; Geoffrey Butler and Simon Maccoby, *The Development of International Law* (Longmans, Green & Co., New York 1928) 174-5; Peter Haggermacher, 'L'ancêtre de la protection diplomatique: les représailles de l'ancien droit' (2010) 143 Relations Internationales 7, 7-12. Some scholars have observed that the expression 'letter of marque' conveys the meaning of an authorization to undertake reprisals abroad, that is to say, outside the home state's territory. For this terminological precision see: Ernest Nys, *Le droit de la guerre et les précurseurs de Grotius* (C. Muquardt, Brussels 1882) 48; Stephen Neff, *Justice Among Nations. A History of International Law* (Harvard University Press, Cambridge MA 2014) 89. This work uses the terms 'letter of reprisals', 'letter of marque' and 'letter de requête' indistinctly.

[39] Antônio Augusto Cançado Trindade, 'Origin and Historical Development of the Rule of Exhaustion of Local Remedies in International Law' (1976) 12 RBDI 499, 501 *et seq.*; Geoffrey Butler and Simon Maccoby, *The Development of International Law* (Longmans, Green & Co., New York 1928) 175-6.

[40] Geoffrey Butler and Simon Maccoby, *The Development of International Law* (Longmans, Green & Co., New York 1928) 175-6.

[41] Geoffrey Butler and Simon Maccoby, *The Development of International Law* (Longmans, Green & Co., New York 1928) 174-5. For a similar approach to the rationale of letters of reprisals see: Arthur Nussbaum, *Geschichte des Völkerrechts in gedrängter Darstellung* (C.H. Beck, München/ Berlin 1960) 28-9.

[42] See generally: Geoffrey Butler and Simon Maccoby, *The Development of International Law* (Longmans, Green & Co., New York 1928) 173 *et seq.*

[43] See generally: Hans Spiegel, 'Origin and Development of Denial of Justice' (1938) 32(1) AJIL 63, 64 *et seq.*

local remedies by the offended party.[44] The aforesaid restraints have been tracked back to a handful of covenants concluded between Italian free states from the mid-ninth century onwards.[45] The notion of denial of justice (as a requirement for reprisals) attracted the attention of the most prominent legal scholars of that time, including Bartolus de Sassoferrato,[46] Giovanni Legnano,[47] Alberico Gentili,[48] and Hugo Grotius.[49] Nowadays, the proposition that the medieval practice of reprisals

---

[44]Friedrich Rudolf Hohl, *Bartolus a Saxoferrato: Seine Bedeutung für die Entwicklungsgeschichte des Repressaliensrechts* [unpublished doctoral dissertation] (Volume 1: Universität Bonn, Bonn 1954) 37. On the relation between reprisals and the law of denial of justice see: Hans Spiegel, 'Origin and Development of Denial of Justice' (1938) 32(1) AJIL 63, 63-79; Peter Haggermacher, 'L'ancêtre de la protection diplomatique: les représailles de l'ancien droit' (2010) 143 Relations Internationales 7, 9-10. On the origins of the modern local remedies rule in the law of reprisals see: Antônio Augusto Cançado Trindade, 'Origin and Historical Development of the Rule of Exhaustion of Local Remedies in International Law' (1976) 12 RBDI 499, 501-14. For an exhaustive survey of early English legal authorities providing evidence of the close historical relationship between the institution of reprisals, the exhaustion of local remedies and the concept of denial of justice see: Arnold Duncan McNair (First Baron McNair), *International Law Opinions* (Volume 2: Cambridge University Press, Cambridge 1956) 297-304. For an analysis of the link between reprisals and denial of justice in medieval Germany see: Hans Planitz, 'Studien zur Geschichte des deutschen Arrestprozesses. Der Fremdenarrest' (1919) 40 Zeitschrift der Savigny Stiftung für Rechtsgeschichte 87, 178-83 and 189-90.

[45]For detailed examples of this treaty practice see: Hans Spiegel, 'Origin and Development of Denial of Justice' (1938) 32(1) AJIL 63, 64-5. See also: Antônio Augusto Cançado Trindade, 'Origin and Historical Development of the Rule of Exhaustion of Local Remedies in International Law' (1976) 12 RBDI 499, 502 *et seq.*; Stephen Neff, *Justice Among Nations. A History of International Law* (Harvard University Press, Cambridge MA 2014) 90.

[46]Bartolus Sassoferratus prepared an influential *Tractatus Represaliarum* in 1354. For an overview on Sassoferrato's theory of reprisals see: Cecil Sidney Woolf, *Bartolus of Sassoferrato. His position in the History of Medieval Political Thought* (Cambridge University Press, Cambridge 1913) 203-7. For a deeper analysis of his *Tractatus Represaliarum* see: Friedrich Rudolf Hohl, *Bartolus a Saxoferrato: Seine Bedeutung für die Entwicklungsgeschichte des Repressaliensrechts* [unpublished doctoral dissertation] (Volume 1: Universität Bonn, Bonn 1954). Hohl discusses Sassoferrato's theory of denial of justice at pp. 88-100.

[47]For an English translation of the treatise see: Giovanni da Legnano, 'Tractatus De Bello, De Represaliis et De Duello' (1393) in James Brown Scott (ed), *Classics of International Law* (James Leslie Brierly tr, Carnegie Institution, Washington 1917) 209, 307-30.

[48]Gentili addressed the issue in *De iure belli libri tres* (Book I, § XXI), which was devoted to offences committed by private individuals. See: Alberico Gentili, 'De iure belli libri tres' (1598) in James Brown Scott (ed), *Classics of International Law* (John C. Rolfe tr, Carnegie Institution, Washington 1917) 99-104.

[49]Grotius discussed the medieval law of reprisals in *De iure belli ac pacis* (Book 3, Chap. II). For the original text see: Hugonis Groti, *De iure belli ac pacis* (1625) (Leiden, A. W. Sijthoff 1919) 495-500. For an English translation see: Hugo Grotius, *The Rights of War and Peace in Three Books* (1625) (The Lawbook Exchange, Clark NJ 2004) 538-49.

prepared the ground for the modern law of denial of justice seems to enjoy general acceptance.[50]

Reprisals have much to do with the protection of foreign citizens and, thus, with the FPS standard.[51] The reasons are three. *First*, reprisals were a means of redress for injuries suffered by private citizens as a result of acts of violence attributable to foreign subjects.[52] While the distinction between the *private* and *public* spheres was somewhat obscure during the Middle Ages, one could say in a modern jargon that the essence of reprisals referred more to harm done to private individuals than to harm done to the state or prince.[53] As a matter of fact, when the monarch was the victim of the original wrong, the injurious act had much more severe consequences and could even be considered as a cause for war.[54]

Second, the liability of the national community for its individual members, triggered by a failure to do justice by the prince, could be seen as an emergent form of state responsibility for injuries to aliens.[55] Some authors have suggested that private reprisals are the origin of the whole international law of state responsibility.[56]

---

[50]See, for example: Ali Ehsassi, 'Cain and Abel: Congruence and Conflict in the Application of the Denial of Justice Principle' in Stephan Schill (ed), *International Investment Law and Comparative Public Law* (Oxford University Press, New York 2010) 213, 217; Alwyn Freeman, *The International Responsibility of States for Denial of Justice* (Klaus Reprint, New York, 1970) 53-67 [first edition: 1938]; Borzu Sabahdi, *Compensation and Restitution in Investor-State Arbitration* (Oxford University Press, New York 2011) 35-6; Charles De Visscher, 'Le déni de justice en droit international' (1935) 52(2) RCADI 369, 370-4; Don Wallace, 'Fair and Equitable Treatment and Denial of Justice in *Loewn v. US* and *Chattin v. Mexico*' in Todd Weiler, *International Investment Law and Arbitration. Leading Cases from the ICSID, NAFTA, Bilateral Investment Treaties and Customary International Law* (Cameron May, London 2005) 669, 672-4; Eduardo Jiménez de Aréchega, 'International responsibility' in Max Sørensen (ed), *Manual of Public International Law* (St. Martin's Press, New York 1968) 531, 553; Friedrich August von der Heydte, *Die Geburtsstunde des souveränen Staates. Ein Beitrag zur Geschichte des Völkerrechts, der allgemeinen Staatslehre und des politischen Denkens* (Druck und Verlag Josef Habbel, Regensburg 1952) 291-3; Jan Paulsson, *Denial of Justice in International Law* (Cambridge University Press, New York 2005) 13-4. See also: Sebastián Mantilla Blanco, *Justizielles Unrecht im internationalen Investitionsschutzrecht* (Nomos, Baden-Baden 2016) 56-7 (quoting these and other sources in particular reference to the origins of the concept of 'denial of justice').

[51]Cf. also Nartnirun Junngam, 'The Full Protection and Security Standard in International Investment Law: What and Who is Investment Fully[?] Protected and Secured From?' (2018) 7 (1) AUBLR 1, 14-5.

[52]Wilhelm Grewe, *The Epochs of International Law* (Walter de Gruyter, Berlin 2000) 202-3; Grover Clark, 'The English Practice with Regard to Reprisals by Private Persons' (1933) 27 (4) AJIL 694, 722-3.

[53]For a similar observation see: Stephen Neff, *Justice Among Nations. A History of International Law* (Harvard University Press, Cambridge MA 2014) 88.

[54]Wilhelm Grewe, *The Epochs of International Law* (Walter de Gruyter, Berlin 2000) 202.

[55]See generally: Antônio Augusto Cançado Trindade, 'Origin and Historical Development of the Rule of Exhaustion of Local Remedies in International Law' (1976) 12 RBDI 499, 501 *et seq.*

[56]Albert Geuffre de Lapradelle and Nicolas Politis, *Recueil des arbitrages internationaux* (A. Pedone, Paris 1904) 213; Charles De Visscher, 'Le déni de justice en droit international' (1935) 52(2) RCADI. 369, 370.

An important difference cannot go unnoticed, however. In the present day, international responsibility for the acts of non-state actors is not based on a personal bond between the sovereign and the individual wrongdoer.[57] Rather, it rests upon the control exercised by the state over the territory where the wrongful act occurred.[58] The late medieval period witnessed a gradual move from the early medieval prevalence of personal loyalties to territoriality as the defining feature of both sovereign power and state responsibility.[59] This work will elaborate later on the legal implications this fundamental change holds for the customary notion of 'protection and security'.[60]

Third, European sovereigns increasingly conditioned the granting of *letters of marque* to a previous, fruitless, attempt to obtain justice from the wrongdoer's sovereign.[61] This condition entails a subtle implication, namely, that sovereigns were expected to offer aliens adequate means of redress.[62] The resemblance of this obligation to the present-day FPS standard is striking. FPS is generally considered to encompass an obligation of redress or, more precisely, an obligation to offer a fair opportunity of redress.[63]

---

[57] On the abandonment of the 'personal bond' as the basis for state responsibility see: Heinrich Triepel, *Völkerrecht und Landesrecht* (Verlag von C. L. Hirschfeld, Leipzig 1899) 325. Chapter 12 discusses this issue in more detail, in particular connection with the notion of 'due diligence'.

[58] See: Heinrich Triepel, *Völkerrecht und Landesrecht* (Verlag von C. L. Hirschfeld, Leipzig 1899) 325.

[59] See: Adolf Jess, *Politische Handlungen Privater gegen das Ausland und das Völkerrecht* (Verlag von M. & H. Marcus, Breslau 1923) 8 *et seq.*; Jan Arno Hessbruegge, 'The Historical Development of the Doctrines of Attribution and Due Diligence in International Law' (2003/4) 36(4) JILP 265, 280-1. For a historical analysis of the foundations of sovereign power in the Middle Ages see: Heinrich Mitteis, *Der Staat des hohen Mittelalters. Grundlinien einer vergleichenden Verfassungsgeschichte des Lehnszeitalters* (Hermann Böhlaus, Weimar 1953) 3 *et seq.*; Theodor Mayer, 'Die Ausbildung der Grundlagen des modernen deutschen Staates im hohen Mittelalter' (1939) 159(3) Historische Zeitschrift 457, 462 *et seq.*; Theodor Mayer, 'Die Entstehung des "modernen" Staates im Mittelalter und die freien Bauern' (1937) 57(1) ZRG 210, 211-4. Some legal historians have consistently placed the origin of the 'modern state' in the late medieval period, particularly between the 13th and 14th centuries. See, for example: Friedrich August von der Heydte, *Die Geburtsstunde des souveränen Staates. Ein Beitrag zur Geschichte des Völkerrechts, der allgemeinen Staatslehre und des politischen Denkens* (Druck und Verlag Josef Habbel, Regensburg 1952) 41 *et seq.*

[60] See Sect. 7.3. Cf. also Sect. 12.2.

[61] See generally: Antônio Augusto Cançado Trindade, 'Origin and Historical Development of the Rule of Exhaustion of Local Remedies in International Law' (1976) 12 RBDI 499, 501 *et seq.*

[62] See generally: Antônio Augusto Cançado Trindade, 'Origin and Historical Development of the Rule of Exhaustion of Local Remedies in International Law' (1976) 12 RBDI 499, 501 (referring to the historical roots of the idea that foreigners have 'a right to be accorded justice').

[63] Section 10.3 addresses the redress obligation in detail.

3.3   The Rationalization of the Protection Obligation. Christian von Wolff and the Theory of the Tacit Agreement

The late-seventeenth and eighteenth centuries were a groundbreaking period for political and legal thinking in general, and for the development of modern theories about international law in particular.[64] This period witnessed what Otto von Gierke (1871) believed to be the fatal consequence of cultural development: *abstraction*.[65] In Gierke's words: '[a]bstract, yes, abstract, often up to the edge of death, will become law and language, belief and morals, the state itself'.[66] Among the many jurists contributing to the gradual abstraction of international law during those years there was however one, a real master of abstraction, whose vast intellectual contributions would earn him the reputation of being 'a monarch in the realm of thought'[67] or, in more delightful words, 'the very prince of pedants'.[68] His name was Christian von Wolff.[69]

In *Jus gentium method scientifica pertractactum* (1749), Wolff took up the challenge of developing a scientific presentation of the law of nations.[70] And he successfully did so. His work continues to be acclaimed and praised as a legal masterpiece; some international law historians go as far as to say that '[n]ever had

---

[64]See generally: Alexander Orakhelashvili, 'The Origins of Consensual Positivism – Pufendorf, Wolff and Vattel' in Alexander Orakhelashvili (ed), *Research Handbook on the Theory and History of International Law* (Edward Elgar Publishing, Northampton MA 2011) 93, 93-110; Stephen Neff, *Justice Among Nations. A History of International Law* (Harvard University Press, Cambridge MA 2014) 179-213.

[65]Otto von Gierke, *Der Humor im Deutschen Recht* (Weidmannsche Buchhandlung, Berlin 1871) 4.

[66]Author's translation. The original German text reads: "Abstrakt, ja abstrakt oft bis an die Grenze des Todten, werden Recht und Sprache, Glaube und Sitte, wird selbst der Staat". Otto von Gierke, *Der Humor im Deutschen Recht* (Weidmannsche Buchhandlung, Berlin 1871) 4.

[67]Otfried Nippold used this expression in his introductory note to a reprint of Wolff's *Jus gentium method scientifica pertractactum*. See: Christian Wolff, 'Jus gentium methodo scientifica pertractactum' (1749) in James Brown Scott (ed), *Classics of International Law* (Joseph Drake tr, Clarendon Press, Oxford 1934) lii. For the original Latin text of the treatise, see: Christian Freiherr von Wolff, *Ius gentium methodo scientifica perpractatum* (Officina libraria Rengeriana, Magdeburg 1749). This work primarily relies on the English translation prepared by Joseph Drake in 1934. The English version has however been verified, where relevant, against the original Latin text.

[68]Stephen Neff, *Justice Among Nations. A History of International Law* (Harvard University Press, Cambridge MA 2014) 183.

[69]For a brief overview of Wolff's contribution to international law see: Thomas Kleinlein, 'Christian Wolff. System as an Episode?' in Stefan Kadelbach, Thomas Kleinlein and David Roth-Isigkeit (eds), *System, Order and International Law. The Early History of International Legal Thought from Machiavelli to Hegel* (Oxford University Press, Oxford 2017) 216, 216 *et seq.*

[70]See generally: Thomas Kleinlein, 'Christian Wolff. System as an Episode?' in Stefan Kadelbach, Thomas Kleinlein and David Roth-Isigkeit (eds), *System, Order and International Law. The Early History of International Legal Thought from Machiavelli to Hegel* (Oxford University Press, Oxford 2017) 216, 221-5.

an academic spider woven so marvelous a conceptual web'.[71] Most importantly, at least for present purposes, Wolff delivered a sophisticated theory on the status of foreign citizens and a dogmatic foundation for the duty placed upon host states to provide security to aliens. Wolff's theory can yet only be properly understood against the background of his general approach to the sources of international law. This section therefore begins by briefly summarizing Wolff's system of international law. It then examines his views on the status of aliens.

Wolff departed from the premise that nature established a society of mankind, which did not disappear with the emergence of nations, but rather endured in the form of a society of nations.[72] He accordingly described nations as 'individual free persons living in a state of nature'.[73] Wolff considered that nations are primarily bound by natural law, but not in the same manner as individuals, for nations do not share a 'human nature'.[74] The members of this society of nations are driven by the ultimate goal of 'promoting the common good by their combined powers'.[75] Defining the state as 'a society of men united for the purpose of promoting the common good by their combined powers', Wolff concluded that '[a]ll nations are understood to have come together into a state, whose separate members are separate nations, or individual states'.[76] He named this supreme state *'civitas maxima'*.[77]

In Wolff's system, nations are therefore subject to two different legal orders. *First*, 'the law of nature applied to nations', which embodies the law necessary for the existence of the *civitas maxima* itself (*ius gentium necessarium*).[78] *Second*, the law emanating from the 'will of nations' or 'positive law of nations' (*ius gentium*

---

[71] Stephen Neff, *Justice Among Nations. A History of International Law* (Harvard University Press, Cambridge MA 2014) 184.

[72] Christian Wolff, 'Jus gentium methodo scientifica pertractactum' (1749) in James Brown Scott (ed), *Classics of International Law* (Joseph Drake tr, Clarendon Press, Oxford 1934) 11 § 7.

[73] Christian Wolff, 'Jus gentium methodo scientifica pertractactum' (1749) in James Brown Scott (ed), *Classics of International Law* (Joseph Drake tr, Clarendon Press, Oxford 1934) 9 § 2.

[74] Christian Wolff, 'Jus gentium methodo scientifica pertractactum' (1749) in James Brown Scott (ed), *Classics of International Law* (Joseph Drake tr, Clarendon Press, Oxford 1934) 9 §§ 2 and 3.

[75] Christian Wolff, 'Jus gentium methodo scientifica pertractactum' (1749) in James Brown Scott (ed), *Classics of International Law* (Joseph Drake tr, Clarendon Press, Oxford 1934) 12 § 9.

[76] Christian Wolff, 'Jus gentium methodo scientifica pertractactum' (1749) in James Brown Scott (ed), *Classics of International Law* (Joseph Drake tr, Clarendon Press, Oxford 1934) 12 § 9.

[77] Christian Wolff, 'Jus gentium methodo scientifica pertractactum' (1749) in James Brown Scott (ed), *Classics of International Law* (Joseph Drake tr, Clarendon Press, Oxford 1934) 12 § 9. For an overview of the concept of the *civitas maxima* in the international law theory of Christian Wolff see: Anne Kühler, 'Societas Humana bei Christian Wolff' in Tilmann Altwicker, Francis Cheneval and Oliver Diggelmann (eds), *Völkerrechtsphilosophie der Frühaufklärung* (Mohr Siebeck, Tübingen 2015) 119-24; Thomas Kleinlein, 'Christian Wolff. System as an Episode?' in Stefan Kadelbach, Thomas Kleinlein and David Roth-Isigkeit (eds), *System, Order and International Law. The Early History of International Legal Thought from Machiavelli to Hegel* (Oxford University Press, Oxford 2017) 216, 225-8.

[78] Christian Wolff, 'Jus gentium methodo scientifica pertractactum' (1749) in James Brown Scott (ed), *Classics of International Law* (Joseph Drake tr, Clarendon Press, Oxford 1934) 10 § 4.

positivum).[79] Wolff's positive law is based on three forms of consent: *presumed*, *express* and *tacit*. Presumed consent (*consensus praesumtus*) is the source of Wolff's 'voluntary law of nations' (*ius voluntarium*), which flows from the *civitas maxima* and 'is considered to have been laid down by its fictitious ruler and so to have proceeded from the will of nations'.[80] Express consent (*consensus expressus*) provides the basis for the 'stipulative law of nations' or law of treaties (*ius gentium pactitium).*[81] Finally, tacit consent (*consensus tacitus*) is the backbone of customary international law (*ius gentium consuetudinarium*), i.e., that which 'is so called, because it has been brought in by long usage and observed as law'.[82] It is in the context of this very abstract system that Wolff assessed the status of aliens.[83]

Wolff believed that individuals are born as natives of the country where their parents are domiciled, and remain citizens of that nation notwithstanding whether they subsequently establish their domicile abroad.[84] Naturalization, albeit legitimate, is a legal fiction.[85] Individuals may decide to leave their own country or be compelled to do so.[86] Exile may hence be voluntary or involuntary.[87] Voluntary exile may occur against the will of the sovereign (e.g. in the case of those evading punishment for a crime), or in the exercise of the so-called 'right to emigrate', that is, when the prince authorizes a subject to leave his realms (e.g. in the case of those who follow a religion which the monarch 'does not wish to tolerate').[88] The aforesaid 'right to emigrate' arises either from the sovereign's own discretion or from a treaty

---

[79]Christian Wolff, 'Jus gentium methodo scientifica pertractactum' (1749) in James Brown Scott (ed), *Classics of International Law* (Joseph Drake tr, Clarendon Press, Oxford 1934) 19 § 25.

[80]Christian Wolff, 'Jus gentium methodo scientifica pertractactum' (1749) in James Brown Scott (ed), *Classics of International Law* (Joseph Drake tr, Clarendon Press, Oxford 1934) 17-8 § 22. This notion is consistent with Wolff's characterization of the supreme state as a democratic one, in which the nations as a whole hold some sovereignty over each individual nation (at pp. 15-7 §§ 15-20, and particularly at p. 16 §19).

[81]Christian Wolff, 'Jus gentium methodo scientifica pertractactum' (1749) in James Brown Scott (ed), *Classics of International Law* (Joseph Drake tr, Clarendon Press, Oxford 1934) 18 § 23.

[82]Christian Wolff, 'Jus gentium methodo scientifica pertractactum' (1749) in James Brown Scott (ed), *Classics of International Law* (Joseph Drake tr, Clarendon Press, Oxford 1934) 18-9 § 24.

[83]For a more detailed account of Wolff's approach to the sources of the law of nations see: Thomas Kleinlein, 'Christian Wolff. System as an Episode?' in Stefan Kadelbach, Thomas Kleinlein and David Roth-Isigkeit (eds), *System, Order and International Law. The Early History of International Legal Thought from Machiavelli to Hegel* (Oxford University Press, Oxford 2017) 216, 228-31.

[84]Christian Wolff, 'Jus gentium methodo scientifica pertractactum' (1749) in James Brown Scott (ed), *Classics of International Law* (Joseph Drake tr, Clarendon Press, Oxford 1934) 77 § 140 and 78 § 144.

[85]Christian Wolff, 'Jus gentium methodo scientifica pertractactum' (1749) in James Brown Scott (ed), *Classics of International Law* (Joseph Drake tr, Clarendon Press, Oxford 1934) 74-5 § 134.

[86]Christian Wolff, 'Jus gentium methodo scientifica pertractactum' (1749) in James Brown Scott (ed), *Classics of International Law* (Joseph Drake tr, Clarendon Press, Oxford 1934) 79 § 145.

[87]Christian Wolff, 'Jus gentium methodo scientifica pertractactum' (1749) in James Brown Scott (ed), *Classics of International Law* (Joseph Drake tr, Clarendon Press, Oxford 1934) 79 § 145.

[88]Christian Wolff, 'Jus gentium methodo scientifica pertractactum' (1749) in James Brown Scott (ed), *Classics of International Law* (Joseph Drake tr, Clarendon Press, Oxford 1934) 83 § 153.

with another sovereign; but it is not based on the law of nature, 'for this [right] assumes that there are established states'.[89] The individual leaving his country has the natural right, triggered by the act of abandoning his nation's territory, 'to dwell anywhere in the world'.[90] He may thus submit a request for 'admittance' to other sovereigns.[91] But princes can under no circumstances be compelled to welcome foreigners into their realms.[92]

Individuals admitted into a foreign territory automatically acquire the status of *'temporary citizens'*.[93] This status is based on a complex fiction: by the very act of entering into a foreign monarch's dominions, aliens *'tacitly* bind themselves that they wish to subject their acts to the laws of the place, and the laws have the same force over them as over citizens'.[94] From the standpoint of the foreign national, the tacit agreement may therefore be best described as an adherence to the social contract. On his part, the host state enters into the tacit agreement by virtue of *presumed consent.*[95] Indeed, according to Wolff, '[t]he ruler of the territory is not *presumed* to desire that the actions of foreigners should be exempt from the law'.[96]

In spite of being domiciled abroad, individuals continue to be citizens of their home state.[97] Along these lines, Wolff advances the proposition that not only the host state, but also the home state, shall be *presumed* to have consented to the

---

[89]Christian Wolff, 'Jus gentium methodo scientifica pertractactum' (1749) in James Brown Scott (ed), *Classics of International Law* (Joseph Drake tr, Clarendon Press, Oxford 1934) 83 § 154.

[90]Christian Wolff, 'Jus gentium methodo scientifica pertractactum' (1749) in James Brown Scott (ed), *Classics of International Law* (Joseph Drake tr, Clarendon Press, Oxford 1934) 80 § 147.

[91]Christian Wolff, 'Jus gentium methodo scientifica pertractactum' (1749) in James Brown Scott (ed), *Classics of International Law* (Joseph Drake tr, Clarendon Press, Oxford 1934) 80-1 § 148.

[92]Christian Wolff, 'Jus gentium methodo scientifica pertractactum' (1749) in James Brown Scott (ed), *Classics of International Law* (Joseph Drake tr, Clarendon Press, Oxford 1934) 80-1 § 148. Nonetheless, Wolff clarified that the refusal to admit a foreigner must be justified by 'special reasons' (at p. 81 § 149).

[93]Christian Wolff, 'Jus gentium methodo scientifica pertractactum' (1749) in James Brown Scott (ed), *Classics of International Law* (Joseph Drake tr, Clarendon Press, Oxford 1934) 152-3 § 303.

[94]Emphasis added. Christian Wolff, 'Jus gentium methodo scientifica pertractactum' (1749) in James Brown Scott (ed), *Classics of International Law* (Joseph Drake tr, Clarendon Press, Oxford 1934) 152-3 § 303. A similar statement appears at pp. 151-2 § 300. In Wolff's theory, aliens are accordingly bound only 'to do and not to do the things which must be done or not done by citizens at the time under same circumstances, except in so far as particular laws introduce something else concerning foreigners' (at p. 153 § 304). Those particular laws are regarded as additional conditions incorporated to the tacit agreement (at pp. 153-4 § 304).

[95]Christian Wolff, 'Jus gentium methodo scientifica pertractactum' (1749) in James Brown Scott (ed), *Classics of International Law* (Joseph Drake tr, Clarendon Press, Oxford 1934) 151 § 299.

[96]Emphasis added. Christian Wolff, 'Jus gentium methodo scientifica pertractactum' (1749) in James Brown Scott (ed), *Classics of International Law* (Joseph Drake tr, Clarendon Press, Oxford 1934) 151 § 299.

[97]Christian Wolff, 'Jus gentium methodo scientifica pertractactum' (1749) in James Brown Scott (ed), *Classics of International Law* (Joseph Drake tr, Clarendon Press, Oxford 1934) 536-7 § 1063.

subjection of its subjects to the 'laws of the place'.[98] The tacit agreement might hence be regarded, at least to some extent, as a tripartite agreement between the individual, the home state and the host state.

Like the social contract, the tacit agreement is by no means a one-way street. The foreign sovereign also assumes a fundamental obligation towards aliens and their home state: to protect them.[99] In Wolff's system, 'the right of security belongs to every man by nature'.[100] When an individual establishes his domicile abroad, the host state assumes his protection, so that 'between the ruler of the territory and the foreigner living in it there exists a tacit agreement, by which the latter promises temporary obedience, the former protection'.[101] The notion of protection encompasses the duty to prevent harm, on the one hand, and the duty to offer adequate means of redress if harm is inflicted, on the other:

> Foreigners, as long as they live in alien territory, ought to be safe from every injury, and the ruler of the state is bound to defend them against it, that is, security is to be assured to foreigners living in alien territory [...] The ruler of a state ought not to allow any one of his subjects to cause a loss or do a wrong to the citizen of another nation, and if this has been done, he ought to compel him to repair the loss caused and to punish him; unless he does this, since he tacitly approves the act, the nation itself must be assumed to have done the wrong or inflicted the injury.[102]

Scholars have suggested that '[b]y using terms such as "injury", "loss" and "wrong", Wolff made clear that the duty required protection against *non*physical as well physical harms'.[103] Based on such observation, they rely on Wolff to advance the proposition that FPS, as delivered by the tradition of the law of aliens, 'obliges the host state to have a system capable of protecting and securing the investment (both legally and physically)'.[104] This line of argument is misleading. It turns a blind eye to the fact that, according to Wolff, protection is granted in

---

[98]Christian Wolff, 'Jus gentium methodo scientifica pertractactum' (1749) in James Brown Scott (ed), *Classics of International Law* (Joseph Drake tr, Clarendon Press, Oxford 1934) 151-2 §§ 299-300.

[99]Christian Wolff, 'Jus gentium methodo scientifica pertractactum' (1749) in James Brown Scott (ed), *Classics of International Law* (Joseph Drake tr, Clarendon Press, Oxford 1934) 537 § 1063.

[100]Christian Wolff, 'Jus gentium methodo scientifica pertractactum' (1749) in James Brown Scott (ed), *Classics of International Law* (Joseph Drake tr, Clarendon Press, Oxford 1934) 537 § 1063.

[101]Christian Wolff, 'Jus gentium methodo scientifica pertractactum' (1749) in James Brown Scott (ed), *Classics of International Law* (Joseph Drake tr, Clarendon Press, Oxford 1934) 537 § 1063.

[102]Christian Wolff, 'Jus gentium methodo scientifica pertractactum' (1749) in James Brown Scott (ed), *Classics of International Law* (Joseph Drake tr, Clarendon Press, Oxford 1934) 536-7 § 1063.

[103]George Foster, 'Recovering "Protection and Security": The Treaty Standard's Obscure Origins, Forgotten Meaning, and Key Current Significance' (2012) 45(4) Vand. J. Transnat'l L. 1095, 1117. For a similar observation cf. Nartnirun Junngam, 'The Full Protection and Security Standard in International Investment Law: What and Who is Investment Fully[?] Protected and Secured From?' (2018) 7(1) AUBLR 1, 31.

[104]George Foster, 'Recovering "Protection and Security": The Treaty Standard's Obscure Origins, Forgotten Meaning, and Key Current Significance' (2012) 45(4) Vand. J. Transnat'l L. 1095, 1156.

exchange for *obedience*.[105] Wolff did not envisage a right to an enhanced stability of the national legal system. The duty was conceived in terms of protection *through* the state against *private* violence, not against local law. Wolff himself began his presentation of the protection obligation by indicating that '[the prince] ought not to allow *any one of his subjects* to cause a loss or do a wrong to the citizen of another nation'.[106] He was thus essentially referring to private wrongs, and not to the public act of amending local legislation.

It should further be noted that the agreement is *tacit*, but only from the perspective of the foreign national. The attainment of the status of 'temporary citizen', which implies subjection to municipal law, is based on the foreigner's own will.[107] This consent is normally not expressed in words, but through the *act* of crossing a border and setting foot on foreign soil.[108] The home state and the host state also give their consent to the foreigner's subjection to the laws of the place; still, Wolff did not characterize their consent as *tacit* but as *presumed*.[109] This terminology is not merely ornamental. Rather, it indicates that the protection obligation is neither treaty-based nor customary, but properly belongs to Wolff's *ius voluntarium*.[110]

Contemporary writers have acknowledged that the notion of the 'voluntary law' could be confusing to the modern eye.[111] In fact, the notion cannot be properly understood if *presumed consent* is expected to be a form of *real consent*.[112] Wolff's voluntary law flows from a natural law-influenced 'objectivized' will of the states, and not from their 'actual' will.[113] Plainly stated, the voluntary law does not refer to rules and principles states have *truly* consented to; rather, it embodies the rules and

---

[105]Christian Wolff, 'Jus gentium methodo scientifica pertractactum' (1749) in James Brown Scott (ed), *Classics of International Law* (Joseph Drake tr, Clarendon Press, Oxford 1934) 537 § 1063.

[106]Christian Wolff, 'Jus gentium methodo scientifica pertractactum' (1749) in James Brown Scott (ed), *Classics of International Law* (Joseph Drake tr, Clarendon Press, Oxford 1934) 536 § 1063.

[107]Christian Wolff, 'Jus gentium methodo scientifica pertractactum' (1749) in James Brown Scott (ed), *Classics of International Law* (Joseph Drake tr, Clarendon Press, Oxford 1934) 151-2 § 300.

[108]Christian Wolff, 'Jus gentium methodo scientifica pertractactum' (1749) in James Brown Scott (ed), *Classics of International Law* (Joseph Drake tr, Clarendon Press, Oxford 1934) 151-2 § 300.

[109]Christian Wolff, 'Jus gentium methodo scientifica pertractactum' (1749) in James Brown Scott (ed), *Classics of International Law* (Joseph Drake tr, Clarendon Press, Oxford 1934) 151 § 299.

[110]This interpretation of Wolff's work is based on the language of §§ 299-300, where reference is made to the 'presumed consent' of the home and host states. The wording of the English translation prepared by Joseph Drake is consistent with the original Latin text, which uses the verb *praesumere*. See: Christian Freiherr von Wolff, *Ius gentium methodo scientifica perpractatum* (Officina libraria Rengeriana, Magdeburg 1749) 231-3 § 299-300.

[111]On the difficulties attached to the proper understanding of Wolff's system of international law from a modern perspective, see: Martti Koskenniemi, *From Apology to Utopia. The Structure of International Legal Argument* (Cambridge University Press, New York 2005) 110-2.

[112]Cf. Martti Koskenniemi, *From Apology to Utopia. The Structure of International Legal Argument* (Cambridge University Press, New York 2005) 110.

[113]On this understanding of Wolff's voluntary law, see: Martti Koskenniemi, *From Apology to Utopia. The Structure of International Legal Argument* (Cambridge University Press, New York 2005) 110.

principles sovereigns *would* agree upon *if* they could reach a rational and complete understanding of the national interests they represent.[114]

Wolff believed that the breach of the rights and duties derived from the tacit agreement could entitle a nation to resort to reprisals.[115] He however rejected the early medieval idea of an individual right to reprisals and was explicit in stating that 'the right of reprisal belongs only to nations and to their rulers'.[116] In Wolff's system, an authorization for reprisals can be granted where 'a nation refuses to do justice to another nation or to its citizens'.[117] Therefore, a failure to grant adequate protection can only justify reprisals where, as a result of the host state's failure to do justice, an injury remains without redress.[118]

The rationale of reprisals rests on the idea of collective responsibility: with respect of foreign nations, Wolff said, all members of a nation shall be considered as a single person, so that 'their property also taken as a whole cannot be regarded otherwise than as the property of this person, that is, of the nation'.[119] This principle derives from the cornerstone of the *civitas maxima*: in respect of each other, nations may be seen as free 'individual persons', so that each nation embodies the sum of its individual citizens.[120] The practical implication is that the rights of one nation towards another can be enforced on the property of its (private) citizens.[121] Wolff went as far as to recognize the institute of the 'adrolepsy or viricaption', whereby foreign nationals may eventually be taken 'by way of pledge' too.[122]

---

[114]For this interpretation of Wolff see: Martti Koskenniemi, *From Apology to Utopia. The Structure of International Legal Argument* (Cambridge University Press, New York 2005) 110.

[115]Christian Wolff, 'Jus gentium methodo scientifica pertractatum' (1749) in James Brown Scott (ed), *Classics of International Law* (Joseph Drake tr, Clarendon Press, Oxford 1934) 302 *et seq.* §§ 589 *et seq.*

[116]Christian Wolff, 'Jus gentium methodo scientifica pertractatum' (1749) in James Brown Scott (ed), *Classics of International Law* (Joseph Drake tr, Clarendon Press, Oxford 1934) 302-3 § 590.

[117]Christian Wolff, 'Jus gentium methodo scientifica pertractatum' (1749) in James Brown Scott (ed), *Classics of International Law* (Joseph Drake tr, Clarendon Press, Oxford 1934) 300-1 § 586 and 302 § 589. Delay in rendering judgment and cases of manifest injustice are embedded within Wolff's notion of refusals to do justice (at pp. 301-2 §§ 587-8).

[118]Christian Wolff, 'Jus gentium methodo scientifica pertractatum' (1749) in James Brown Scott (ed), *Classics of International Law* (Joseph Drake tr, Clarendon Press, Oxford 1934) 302 § 589.

[119]Christian Wolff, 'Jus gentium methodo scientifica pertractatum' (1749) in James Brown Scott (ed), *Classics of International Law* (Joseph Drake tr, Clarendon Press, Oxford 1934) 146-7 § 289.

[120]Christian Wolff, 'Jus gentium methodo scientifica pertractatum' (1749) in James Brown Scott (ed), *Classics of International Law* (Joseph Drake tr, Clarendon Press, Oxford 1934) 146-7 § 289.

[121]Christian Wolff, 'Jus gentium methodo scientifica pertractatum' (1749) in James Brown Scott (ed), *Classics of International Law* (Joseph Drake tr, Clarendon Press, Oxford 1934) 147 § 290 and 256 § 495. Wolff clearly supports his principle on the law of nature; according to him, 'the property of citizens is bound by nature for the debts of the state, and also the private property itself of the ruler of the state' (at p. 300 § 586).

[122]Christian Wolff, 'Jus gentium methodo scientifica pertractatum' (1749) in James Brown Scott (ed), *Classics of International Law* (Joseph Drake tr, Clarendon Press, Oxford 1934) 303 § 592.

In sum, Christian von Wolff delivered a unique, systematic theory of the law of aliens. Observing the medieval practice of reprisals and based on a complex—but fully rational—approach to the sources of international law, he established a logical nexus between reprisals and a corpus of substantive guarantees for foreign citizens. The whole system was based on the idea that, in virtue of a tacit agreement, foreigners are at the same time subject to the laws of the host state and entitled to protection and security against private wrongs.

It should be noted, however, that the 'tacit agreement' was not a completely novel idea in Wolff's days. Samuel Pufendorf had already proposed a similar construct in 1672, without much elaboration, as an example of how natural freedom could be restricted as a result of 'tacit consent'.[123] Pufendorf's argument was however inserted into a different understanding of the law of nations.[124] Pufendorf's short remarks could have inspired Wolff. But the extraordinary theoretical backbone behind the fiction is certainly Wolff's own accomplishment.

---

[123]See: Samuel Pufendorf, 'Of the Law of Nature and of Nations in Eight Books' (1672) in Craig Carr (ed) *The Political Writings of Samuel Pufendorf* (Michael Seidler tr, Oxford University Press, New York 1994) 171. In his *De jure naturae et gentium libri octo*, Pufendorf addressed the issue of consent as the normative basis for promises and pacts, which 'as a rule restrict our freedom and impose on us a burden of necessarily doing something we were formerly free to do or not to do' (at p. 171). In this connection, he explained that consent might be *express* or *tacit*; for Pufendorf, a tacit pact 'occurs when consent is expressed not by such signs as are regularly accepted in human transactions, but when it is clearly inferred from the nature of the affair and other circumstances' (at p. 171). Aiming to provide an example of what would be a 'tacit pact', Pufendorf stated: "Suppose a foreigner comes as a friend to some state that commonly treats outsiders in a friendly manner. He is thought to have promised tacitly, and by his very act of coming, to conform himself to that state's laws as they pertain to his status as soon as he has come to know that such laws apply generally to all who desire to go about in that state's territory, even though he has never given a express promise to that effect. And for this reason he is in turn tacitly promised by the state that it will temporarily defend him and administer justice on his behalf." (at p. 171).

[124]In his *Elementorum jurisprudentiae universalis libri duo* (1660), Pufendorf famously equalized the law of nations to natural law. See: Samuel Pufendorf, 'Elementorum Jurisprudentiae Universalis Libri Duo' in James Brown Scott (ed), *Classics of International Law* (William Abbott tr, Clarendon Press, Oxford 1931) 165 ("Something must be added now also on the subject of the Law of Nations, which, in the eyes of some men, is nothing other than the law of nature, in so far as different nations, not united with another by a supreme command, observe it, who must render one another the same duties in their fashion, as are prescribed for individuals by the law of nature. On this point there is no reason for our conducting any special discussion here, since what we recount on the subject of the law of nature and of the duties of individuals, can be readily applied to whole states and nations which have also coalesced into one moral person. Aside from this law, we are of the opinion that there is no law of nations").

3.4   The Reception of Wolff's Theory of the Tacit Agreement in the Works of Emer de Vattel

The system of international law developed by Christian von Wolff was certainly not without controversy. Nonetheless, criticism was mainly concerned with his well-known fiction of a *'civitas maxima'*.[125] In contrast, and partly thanks to the works of Emmer de Vattel (1714-1767), Wolff's theory of the tacit agreement had an impressive reception in western international law scholarship. It is by no means a secret that Wolff had a significant influence on his Swiss colleague. Vattel's celebrated *Le droit des gens* (1758) bears witness to this uncontestable truth.[126] In the Preamble, Vattel himself stated:

> Those who have read Monsieur Wolf's treatises on the law of nature and the law of nations, will see what advantage I have made of them. Had I everywhere pointed out what I have borrowed, my pages would be crowded with quotations equally useless and disagreeable to the reader.[127]

In spite of their striking resemblance, the two theories were not identical. Vattel was skeptical about the fiction of the *civitas maxima*.[128] He believed that the application of natural law to nations could be better explained through the idea of the 'natural liberty of nations', without recourse to Wolff's fictional 'republic of nations'.[129]

Still, Vattel's understanding of the sources of international law was clearly inspired by Wolff's work. Vattel adopted the fundamental distinction between a natural law-based 'necessary law of nations' (*droit des gens naturel ou nécessaire*) and a consensual 'positive law of nations' (*droit des gens positif*),[130] further recognizing Wolff's three forms of consent: express (*consentement exprès/droit conventionnel*), tacit (*consentement tacite/droit coutumier*) and presumed (*consentement présumé/droit volontaire*).[131] For Vattel, conventional law and customary law were part of the 'special law of nations' (*droit particulier*), which was founded on the agreement of a limited number of particular states.[132] Vattel ascribed a universal character (*droit universel*) only to his *necessary law of nations* (a form of

---

[125]Otfried Nippold's introductory note to Wolff's *Jus gentium* provides a detailed account of the debate: Christian Wolff, 'Jus gentium methodo scientifica pertractactum' (1749) in James Brown Scott (ed), *Classics of International Law* (Joseph Drake tr, Clarendon Press, Oxford 1934) xli-xlv.

[126]This section uses an English translation of the original French treatise, which was published in London in 1797. Emer de Vattel, *The Law of Nations* (1758) (G.G. and J. Robinson, London 1797). References to the original French text will be included where necessary.

[127]Emer de Vattel, *The Law of Nations* (1758) (G.G. and J. Robinson, London 1797) xii.

[128]Emer de Vattel, *The Law of Nations* (1758) (G.G. and J. Robinson, London 1797) xiii-xiv.

[129]Emer de Vattel, *The Law of Nations* (1758) (G.G. and J. Robinson, London 1797) xv.

[130]Emer de Vattel, *The Law of Nations* (1758) (G.G. and J. Robinson, London 1797) lxvi.

[131]Emer de Vattel, *The Law of Nations* (1758) (G.G. and J. Robinson, London 1797) xvii-xviii and lxv-lxvi.

[132]Emer de Vattel, *The Law of Nations* (1758) (G.G. and J. Robinson, London 1797) lxv.

natural law), and to the *voluntary law of nations*, which had the complex character of being simultaneously *positive* and *natural law-based*.[133] His work focused on the *droit universel* and accordingly followed a deductive method.[134]

Just as Wolff, Vattel devoted much of his work to citizenship and to the law of aliens. In this vein, he departed from the fundamental natural law-based premise that children acquire the legal status of their parents.[135] Vattel further followed Wolff in recognizing a 'right to emigrate'.[136] Still, he did not give this right an absolute character.[137] It was only in a few cases, mostly concerned with serious breaches of the social contract on the part of the sovereign, that Vattel characterized emigration as an absolute right.[138] Like Wolff, Vattel linked emigration to the concept of exile,

---

[133]Emer de Vattel, *The Law of Nations* (1758) (G.G. and J. Robinson, London 1797) lxv. Vattel admits Wolff's complex distinction between the *necessary* and the *voluntary* law of nations (at pp. xvi and lxix). Nonetheless, his understanding of these concepts subtly differs from Wolff. Avoiding recourse to the notion of the *civitas maxima* and its fictional legislator, Vattel explains that both 'are established *by nature*' (at p. xvi). The *necessary law* could be depicted as the 'immutable' conscience of a nation: it is a 'sacred', 'absolute' and 'internal' law, which 'contains the precepts prescribed by the law of nature to states' (at pp. xvi and lviii). By contrast, the *voluntary law* is not an '*internal law*', but an '*external law*': it is not the conscience of the individual nation, but a set of rational rules governing the relationships between states (at p. lxvi). According to Vattel, it applies 'as a rule which the general welfare and safety *oblige them to admit* in their transactions to each other' (at p. xvi). Vattel's *voluntary law* is thus based on *consent*, and consistently belongs to the broader category of the '*positive law of nations*' (at p. lxvi). Still, the consent upon which it is founded is neither *actually* nor *freely* given; it is always *presumed* (at p. lxvi). For a critical account of Vattel's theory of the sources of international law see: Charles Fenwick, 'The Authority of Vattel' (1913) 7(3) APSR 395, 400-5.

[134]Cf. Emer de Vattel, *The Law of Nations* (1758) (G.G. and J. Robinson, London 1797) xvi-xvii.

[135]Citizenship is thus primarily transmitted by blood (*ius sanguinis*) (at pp. 101-2). This premise has far-reaching consequences for the status of aliens who have obtained the right of permanent residence (at p. 102). The children of such aliens, Vattel says, 'follow the condition of their fathers' and do not acquire citizenship by birth, but just 'the right of perpetual residence' (at p. 102). It should be noted that Vattel slightly departs from Wolff's views on citizenship. While Wolff believed that children were citizens of the country in which their parents had their (permanent) domicile, Vattel develops an autonomous notion of citizenship, which is entirely detached from the concept of domicile. Cf. Christian Wolff, 'Jus gentium methodo scientifica pertractatum' (1749) in James Brown Scott (ed), *Classics of International Law* (Joseph Drake tr, Clarendon Press, Oxford 1934) 77 § 140; Emer de Vattel, *The Law of Nations* (1758) (G.G. and J. Robinson, London 1797) 102-3.

[136]Emer de Vattel, *The Law of Nations* (1758) (G.G. and J. Robinson, London 1797) 106. By contrast to Wolff, however, Vattel held that the right to emigrate originates in each person's natural freedom (at pp. 103-4). Vattel also recognized that emigration could be founded on domestic law, the prince's graciousness and international agreements (at p. 106).

[137]Emer de Vattel, *The Law of Nations* (1758) (G.G. and J. Robinson, London 1797) 104.

[138]For Vattel, a citizen has an absolute right to definitively abandon his country in three cases: (i) if he lacks the means to earn his own subsistence; (ii) when the state 'absolutely fails' in its duties towards a citizen; and (iii) if domestic law places inacceptable burdens upon a citizen (e.g. prohibiting his religion). See: Emer de Vattel, *The Law of Nations* (1758) (G.G. and J. Robinson, London 1797) 105-6.

which could also be either *voluntary* or *involuntary*.[139] Vattel made however clear that exiled men do under no circumstances lose their natural human condition.[140]

According to Vattel, foreigners are always entitled to the protection of the host state.[141] The basis for the host state's protection obligation was strikingly similar to Wolff's theory of the tacit agreement:

> The sovereign ought not to grant an entrance into his state for the purpose of drawing foreigners into a snare; as soon as he admits them, *he engages to protect them as his own subjects, and to afford them perfect security* [*entière sûreté*], *as far as depends on him.*[142]

Protection by the host state has its counterpart in the foreigner's submission to the domestic legal order. In Vattel's view, the act of entering into the territory of another nation involves a 'tacit submission' to municipal law.[143] From this perspective, the admission of foreigners is always conditional:

> [T]he sovereign *is supposed* to allow him access only upon this tacit condition, that he be subject to the laws [. . .] which have no relation to the title of citizen.[144]

Even though the language used by Vattel is less explicit than that chosen Wolff, it is clear that the consent of the host state is *presumed*: the sovereign *is supposed* (*est supposé*) to have consented to the tacit agreement[145] The obligation to protect would hence belong to the positive *voluntary law of nations*. This conclusion is consistent with the fact that Vattel's work focuses on the *universal* law of nations, which he considered to be 'susceptible of demonstration'.[146] It is also worth noting that Vattel explicitly stated that the host state is bound to ensure the security of aliens 'as far as it depends on him'.[147] The implication is that the protection obligation does *not* have an absolute character.

---

[139]Emer de Vattel, *The Law of Nations* (1758) (G.G. and J. Robinson, London 1797) 108.

[140]Emer de Vattel, *The Law of Nations* (1758) (G.G. and J. Robinson, London 1797) 108.

[141]Emer de Vattel, *The Law of Nations* (1758) (G.G. and J. Robinson, London 1797) 102 (particularly referring to inhabitants) and 173-4 (particularly referring to travellers). For the classification of foreigners in these two categories see pp. 102 and 171.

[142]Emphasis added. Emer de Vattel, *The Law of Nations* (1758) (G.G. and J. Robinson, London 1797) 173. On his part, the foreigner shall, 'from a sense of gratitude for the protection granted to him' contribute to the protection of the nation, 'as far as [this] is consistent with his duty as citizen of another state' (at p. 173). For the original French text see: Emer de Vattel, *Le droit des gens* (1758) (Volume 1: Carnegie Institution, Washington 1916) 331.

[143]Emer de Vattel, *The Law of Nations* (1758) (G.G. and J. Robinson, London 1797) 172.

[144]Emphasis added. Emer de Vattel, *The Law of Nations* (1758) (G.G. and J. Robinson, London 1797) 172. This wording is consistent with the French original text, where Vattel states: 'le Souverain *est supposé* ne lui donner accès que sous cette condition tacite, qu'il sera soumis aux Loix'. Emphasis added. Emer de Vattel, *Le droit des gens* (1758) (Volume 1: Carnegie Institution, Washington 1916) 329.

[145]Emer de Vattel, *The Law of Nations* (1758) (G.G. and J. Robinson, London 1797) 172. For the original French text see: Emer de Vattel, *Le droit des gens* (1758) (Volume 1: Carnegie Institution, Washington 1916) 329.

[146]Emer de Vattel, *The Law of Nations* (1758) (G.G. and J. Robinson, London 1797) xvi-xvii.

[147]Emer de Vattel, *The Law of Nations* (1758) (G.G. and J. Robinson, London 1797) 173.

At his point one may speculate whether Vattel referred to physical security only, or whether his concept of security comprised some measure of protection against nonphysical harm too, as some scholars have suggested.[148] The most accurate answer would be that Vattel did not consider this particular issue at all. But he did certainly not envisage a right to an enhanced stability of the legal system. Just as Wolff, Vattel believed the tacit agreement to be reciprocal: the sovereign assures aliens security in exchange for an unconditioned submission to domestic law.[149] Moreover, Vattel's main concern seemed to be private violence and the possible attribution of private citizens' conduct to the host state:

> [A]s it is impossible for the best regulated state, or for the most vigilant and absolute sovereign, to model at his pleasure all the actions of his subjects, and to confine them on every occasion to the most exact obedience, it would be unjust to impute to the nation or the sovereign every fault committed by the citizens. We ought not to say in general, that we have received an injury from a nation, because we have received it from one of its subjects. But if a nation or its chief approves and ratifies the act of the individual, it then becomes a public concern; and the injured party is to consider the nation as the real author of the injury of which the citizen was perhaps only the instrument.[150]

Vattel submitted that, wherever a private wrong has been done to a foreign citizen, the home state can still demand justice from the host state.[151] And in this case it is a failure to do justice what could trigger international responsibility.[152] Hence, the host nation bears a duty to do its best efforts to *prevent* and *redress* private injures to aliens.[153] These duties are owed not only to the person of the foreign national, but also to his home state: '[w]hoever uses a citizen ill, indirectly offends the state, who is bound to protect this citizen'.[154] Accordingly:

> If a sovereign, who might keep his subjects within the rules of justice and peace, suffers them to injure a foreign nation either in its body or its members, he does no less injury to that nation, than if he injured it himself.[155]

Thus, the breach of the tacit agreement by the host state entails an international delinquency. It is at this point that Vattel analyzes the practice of reprisals. According to Vattel, '[r]eprisals are used between nation and nation, to do themselves justice when they cannot otherwise obtain it'.[156] This right is, of course,

---

[148]For this interpretation of Vattel see: George Foster, 'Recovering "Protection and Security": The Treaty Standard's Obscure Origins, Forgotten Meaning, and Key Current Significance' (2012) 45 (4) Vand. J. Transnat'l L. 1095, 1117-8.

[149]Emer de Vattel, *The Law of Nations* (1758) (G.G. and J. Robinson, London 1797) 172.

[150]Emer de Vattel, *The Law of Nations* (1758) (G.G. and J. Robinson, London 1797) 162.

[151]Emer de Vattel, *The Law of Nations* (1758) (G.G. and J. Robinson, London 1797) 162-3.

[152]Emer de Vattel, *The Law of Nations* (1758) (G.G. and J. Robinson, London 1797) 287.

[153]Cf. Emer de Vattel, *The Law of Nations* (1758) (G.G. and J. Robinson, London 1797) 162.

[154]Emer de Vattel, *The Law of Nations* (1758) (G.G. and J. Robinson, London 1797) 162. This statement is also known as the 'Vattelian fiction' in the law of diplomatic protection.

[155]Emer de Vattel, *The Law of Nations* (1758) (G.G. and J. Robinson, London 1797) 162.

[156]Emer de Vattel, *The Law of Nations* (1758) (G.G. and J. Robinson, London 1797) 283.

extraordinary: *réprésailles* are only admissible in the case of 'a well-ascertained and undeniable debt'.[157] They also require the exhaustion of local remedies, so that the one resorting to reprisals must show 'that he has ineffectually demanded justice, or at least that he has every reason to think it would be in vain for him to demand it'.[158] In this connection, Vattel submitted that reprisals are only admissible where the sovereign has incurred in a 'denial of justice'.[159]

Vattel considered that it was for the sovereign, and not for private citizens, to determine whether reprisals are justified.[160] Vattel observed that this was the rationale behind letters of reprisals.[161] Reprisals may be enforced on the property of the offender and on the property of his co-nationals.[162] The reason is that, following Vattel, 'the property of the individuals is, in the aggregate, to be considered as the property of the nation, with respect to other states'.[163] Accordingly, 'if one nation has a right to any part of the property of another, she has an indiscriminate right to the property of the citizens of the latter nation, until the debt be discharged'.[164] Reprisals could also involve the detention of another nation's citizens 'in order to compel her to do justice'.[165]

The views of Vattel are strikingly similar to those expressed by Wolff. Still, at least in the area of state responsibility for injuries to aliens, one could say that, while Wolff has the greater intellectual merit, Vattel enjoyed an undoubtedly wider exposure.[166] Wolff's work was only available in Latin.[167] For his part, Vattel did

---

[157]Emer de Vattel, *The Law of Nations* (1758) (G.G. and J. Robinson, London 1797) 283-4.

[158]Emer de Vattel, *The Law of Nations* (1758) (G.G. and J. Robinson, London 1797) 284.

[159]Emer de Vattel, *The Law of Nations* (1758) (G.G. and J. Robinson, London 1797) 285-7 (at p. 287, Vattel explains: "we ought not to make reprisals, except when we are unable to obtain justice. Now justice is refuted in several ways: – First, by denial of justice, properly so called, or by a refusal to hear our complaints or those of your subjects, or to admit them to establish their right before the ordinary tribunals. Secondly, by studied delays, for which no good reasons can be given, – delays equivalent to refusal, or still more ruinous. Thirdly, by an evidently unjust and partial decision.").

[160]Emer de Vattel, *The Law of Nations* (1758) (G.G. and J. Robinson, London 1797) 285.

[161]Emer de Vattel, *The Law of Nations* (1758) (G.G. and J. Robinson, London 1797) 285.

[162]Emer de Vattel, *The Law of Nations* (1758) (G.G. and J. Robinson, London 1797) 284.

[163]Emer de Vattel, *The Law of Nations* (1758) (G.G. and J. Robinson, London 1797) 165. This results from the fact that 'nations act and treat together as bodies, in their quality of political societies, and are considered as so moral persons' (at p. 165).

[164]Emer de Vattel, *The Law of Nations* (1758) (G.G. and J. Robinson, London 1797) 165.

[165]Emer de Vattel, *The Law of Nations* (1758) (G.G. and J. Robinson, London 1797) 287. Vattel however insisted that the prisoner's lives shall be respected (at p. 287).

[166]Charles Fenwick, 'The Authority of Vattel' (1913) 7(3) APSR 395, 395 *et seq*. On the influence of Vattel in other regions of the world see: Stephen Neff, *Justice Among Nations. A History of International Law* (Harvard University Press, Cambridge MA 2014) 312.

[167]For Wolff's original text see: Christian Freiherr von Wolff, *Ius gentium methodo scientifica perpractatum* (Officina libraria Rengeriana, Magdeburg 1749).

not write in Latin, but in French.[168] In addition, just a few years after the first edition of his treatise, a handful of English translations were already circulating both in Europe and in America. Vattel was hence much more accessible than Wolff.[169] Writing in 1913, Charles Fenwick observed:

> Vattel's treatise on the law of nations was quoted by judicial tribunals, in speeches before legislative assemblies, and in the decrees and correspondence of executive officials. It was the manual of the student, the reference work of the statesman, and the text from which the political philosopher drew inspiration.[170]

Vattel's opinions increasingly lost their almost mystical authority as a reflection of *actual* international law.[171] His treatise would often receive the honorable discharge of being labeled as a 'classic' and placed on the shelf of legal history.[172] His influence in the shaping of the institutions of the law of aliens and, particularly, of the FPS standard, is however undeniable.

3.5   From *Presumed Consent* to *Actual Consent*. The 'Customary' Duty upon the Host State to Protect Foreign Citizens

Based on the theory of the tacit agreement, Wolff and Vattel envisaged an embryonic *positive* FPS standard founded on the *presumed* consent of states, and indirectly based on natural law.[173] The security obligation was consistently linked to the uniquely complex *mélange* of natural and positive law represented in the idea of the *voluntary law of nations*.[174] The theory of the tacit agreement was not

---

[168]For a reprint of the original French text see: Emer de Vattel, *Le droit des gens* (1758) (Volume 1: Carnegie Institution, Washington 1916).

[169]For a similar observation see: Charles Fenwick, 'The Authority of Vattel' (1913) 7(3) APSR 395, 396-7.

[170]Charles Fenwick, 'The Authority of Vattel' (1913) 7(3) APSR 395, 395.

[171]Charles Fenwick, 'The Authority of Vattel' (1913) 7(3) APSR 395, 395.

[172]Charles Fenwick, 'The Authority of Vattel' (1913) 7(3) APSR 395, 395.

[173]See Sects. 3.3 and 3.4. For a discussion of the influence of Wolff and Vattel in the development of the FPS standard cf. also George Foster, 'Recovering "Protection and Security": The Treaty Standard's Obscure Origins, Forgotten Meaning, and Key Current Significance' (2012) 45(4) Vand. J. Transnat'l L. 1095, 1117-8; Nartnirun Junngam, 'The Full Protection and Security Standard in International Investment Law: What and Who is Investment Fully[?] Protected and Secured From?' (2018) 7(1) AUBLR 1, 31; Onyema Awa Oyeani, *The Obligation of Host States to Accord the Standard of "Full Protection and Security" to Foreign Investments under International Investment Law* (Brunel University, London 2018) [D.Phil. Thesis] 33-6, 58 and 318.

[174]See Sects. 3.3 and 3.4.

naturalistic, at least in the pure sense of the term: Wolff and Vattel were themselves 'forerunners' of the concept of a 'positive law of nations'.[175] Wolff rejected Samuel Pufendorf's strict naturalism,[176] which reduced the whole substance of the law of nations to natural law.[177] Vattel followed Wolff's line of argument, but was more concerned about the practical aspects of international law than about the theoretical backbone of the system.[178] Notwithstanding their criticism to Pufendorf, neither Wolff nor Vattel could entirely abandon naturalism; in the end, by the time they were writing, natural law was still widely regarded as the keystone of the law.[179]

In the decades that followed the publication of Wolff's and Vattel's treatises, there was a radical change in the mainstream of international law scholarship.[180] As noted by Leo Gross (1969):

---

[175]Cf. Stephen Neff, *Justice Among Nations. A History of International Law* (Harvard University Press, Cambridge MA 2014) 227 (explaining that 'pragmatist' scholars from the eighteenth century were certainly not 'true positivists', but could still be considered as 'forerunners of positivism'). It must be observed, however, that Neff only classifies Vattel as a 'pragmatist' (at p. 196). By contrast, he describes Wolff as a 'rationalist' (at pp. 183 *et seq.*). On the relationship of Wolff and Vattel to positivism see: Alexander Orakhelashvili, 'The Origins of Consensual Positivism – Pufendorf, Wolff and Vattel' in Alexander Orakhelashvili (ed), *Research Handbook on the Theory and History of International Law* (Edward Elgar Publishing, Northampton MA 2011) 93, 93-110 (providing a detailed, general analysis of their influence). See also: Leo Gross, 'The Peace of Westphalia 1648-1948' in ASIL, *International Law in the Twentieth Century* (Meredith Corp., New York 1969) 25, 41-3 (particularly referring to Vattel).

[176]Otfried Nippold summarized Wolff's contributions in this regard in an introductory note to a reprint of *Jus gentium method scientifica pertractactum*. See: Christian Wolff, 'Jus gentium methodo scientifica pertractactum' (1749) in James Brown Scott (ed), *Classics of International Law* (Joseph Drake tr, Clarendon Press, Oxford 1934) xxxvii.

[177]Samuel Pufendorf, 'Of the Law of Nature and of Nations in Eight Books' (1672) in Craig Carr (ed) *The Political Writings of Samuel Pufendorf* (Michael Seidler tr, Oxford University Press, New York 1994) 95-268. For an early criticism to naturalism see: Samuel Rachel, 'De Jure Naturae et Gentium Dissertationes' (1676) in James Brown Scott (ed), *Classics of International Law* (John Pawley Bate tr, Carnegie Institution, Washington 1916) 209 § XCIV. On the so-called 'early positivists' see: Arthur Nussbaum, *Geschichte des Völkerrechts in gedrängter Darstellung* (C.H. Beck, München/Berlin 1960) 182-93.

[178]This circumstance may be evidenced in some parts of Vattel's Preface. See: Emer de Vattel, *The Law of Nations* (1758) (G.G. and J. Robinson, London 1797) xi-xii and xviii-xix. Charles Fenwick would describe Vattel's work as an attempt to 'popularize the larger and less accessible work of Wolff'. Charles Fenwick, 'The Authority of Vattel' (1913) 7(3) APSR 395, 396-7. Fenwick does however acknowledge that Vattel 'did not borrow blindly' (at p. 397).

[179]For authors making similar observations see: Alexander Orakhelashvili, 'The Origins of Consensual Positivism – Pufendorf, Wolff and Vattel' in Alexander Orakhelashvili (ed), *Research Handbook on the Theory and History of International Law* (Edward Elgar Publishing, Northampton MA 2011) 93, 93-110; Stephen Neff, *Justice Among Nations. A History of International Law* (Harvard University Press, Cambridge MA 2014) 179 *et seq.*; Martti Koskenniemi, 'Into Positivism: Georg Friedrich von Martens (1756-1821) and modern international law' (2008) 15 *Constellations* 189, 189-93.

[180]Martti Koskenniemi, 'Into Positivism: Georg Friedrich von Martens (1756-1821) and modern international law' (2008) 15 *Constellations* 189, 189 *et seq.*

From the 18th century and, particularly, from Vattel onward, however, there can be no doubt as to the trend of the development. It was predominantly positivist and consensual.[181]

This approach would have its peak at the edge of the nineteenth century when, as explained by Martti Koskenniemi, Europe would witness 'the conceptualisation of the international world in terms of the formal relationships between European sovereigns'.[182] In this context, the law of nations 'would now be needed less to explain the legitimacy of the system than to law out how those relationships ought to be conducted for the benefit of all'.[183]

This modest intellectual revolution had direct consequences for the development of the FPS standard. It is precisely in the last decades of the eighteenth century that international law scholars would begin to conceive the duty to give foreigners some measure of protection as a *customary duty*. The security obligation would hence no longer be based on *presumed* consent, but on *actual* consent. Moreover, as opposed to Wolff and Vattel, positivists would follow a primarily *inductive* method for the identification of the institutions of the law of aliens.

3.5.1 The First Steps. Johann Jakob Moser and the Positive Law of Aliens

Just a few years before the publication of Vattel's renowned treatise, Johann Jakob Moser published one of the first classic positivist treatises on international law: *Grundsätze des jetzt üblichen Europäischen Völkerrechts in Friedenszeiten* (1750).[184] While not denying the existence or authority of natural law,[185] Moser warned his readers that he did not pursue the goal of presenting a 'rationalized international law' (*raisonniertes Völkerrecht*).[186] He believed that, in most cases,

---

[181]Leo Gross, 'The Peace of Westphalia 1648-1948' in ASIL, *International Law in the Twentieth Century* (Meredith Corp., New York 1969) 25, 37. Leo Gross rightfully observed that the basis of the binding character of international law would be placed on the will of each individual state, so that '[t]he concept of the family of nations recedes in the background' (at p. 37). See also: Stephen Neff, *Justice Among Nations. A History of International Law* (Harvard University Press, Cambridge MA 2014) 217-9.

[182]Martti Koskenniemi, 'Into Positivism: Georg Friedrich von Martens (1756-1821) and modern international law' (2008) 15 *Constellations* 189, 190.

[183]Martti Koskenniemi, 'Into Positivism: Georg Friedrich von Martens (1756-1821) and modern international law' (2008) 15 *Constellations* 189, 190.

[184]Johann Jakob Moser, *Grundsätze des jetzt üblichen Europäischen Völkerrechts in Friedenszeiten* (Hanau 1750). On Moser's importance for classic positivism see: Martti Koskenniemi, 'Into Positivism: Georg Friedrich von Martens (1756-1821) and modern international law' (2008) 15 *Constellations* 189, 194 *et seq.*

[185]Johann Jakob Moser, *Grundsätze des jetzt üblichen Europäischen Völkerrechts in Friedenszeiten* (Hanau 1750) 9.

[186]Johann Jakob Moser, *Grundsätze des jetzt üblichen Europäischen Völkerrechts in Friedenszeiten* (Hanau 1750) iv.

rationalist approaches to the law of nations reflected no more than each scholar's very own thoughts and passions.[187] His project was to lay down the rules of international law on the basis of the *actual* practice of European states:

> My international law is only and solely based on what has actually and usually occurred in practice, no matter whether it might be just or unjust under the laws written by god, as well as under natural and human laws.[188]

Moser devoted only a few sections of his treatise to the law of aliens.[189] His method was clearly inductive, as shown by the constant references made to the actual practice of European states, and the acknowledgement of certain areas in which the lack of sufficient evidence made it impossible to identify a clear rule.[190] In spite of this noteworthy methodological difference, Moser's conclusions were thorough similar to those reached by Wolff and Vattel.

According to Moser, sovereigns have the right to freely decide on the admission of foreign subjects.[191] Upon their admission, aliens become subject to the laws in force in the host territory.[192] Moser acknowledged certain limits to the sovereign's authority over foreign citizens,[193] but made clear that a nation bears no obligation to place foreigners in a footing of equality with her own citizens.[194] When an alien is admitted into a country, Moser argued, the host sovereign always assumes certain duties *vis-à-vis* the alien's home state.[195] The assurance of some degree of protection and security to foreign subjects is at the heart of these obligations:

---

[187] Johann Jakob Moser, *Grundsätze des jetzt üblichen Europäischen Völkerrechts in Friedenszeiten* (Hanau 1750) iv.

[188] Author's translation. The original German text reads: "[Es ist also dies mein Völkerrecht] lediglich und ganz allein auf das gegründet, was wirklich geschehen ist und zu geschehen pfleget, es mag nun nach denen Göttlichen geschriebenen und natürlichen auch menschliche Rechten recht oder unrecht seyn". Johann Jakob Moser, *Grundsätze des jetzt üblichen Europäischen Völkerrechts in Friedenszeiten* (Hanau 1750) iv; see also p. 6.

[189] Johann Jakob Moser, *Grundsätze des jetzt üblichen Europäischen Völkerrechts in Friedenszeiten* (Hanau 1750) 393 *et seq.* and 469 *et seq.*

[190] Johann Jakob Moser, *Grundsätze des jetzt üblichen Europäischen Völkerrechts in Friedenszeiten* (Hanau 1750) 393 *et seq.*

[191] Johann Jakob Moser, *Grundsätze des jetzt üblichen Europäischen Völkerrechts in Friedenszeiten* (Hanau 1750) 393-5. Moser went as far as to assert that a sovereign may even require – as a condition for admission – foreign subjects to renounce to their former sovereign and promise him obedience (at p. 393).

[192] Johann Jakob Moser, *Grundsätze des jetzt üblichen Europäischen Völkerrechts in Friedenszeiten* (Hanau 1750) 393-5.

[193] For example, Moser expressed the view that foreigners cannot be compelled to enroll in the host state's military. See: Johann Jakob Moser, *Grundsätze des jetzt üblichen Europäischen Völkerrechts in Friedenszeiten* (Hanau 1750) 396.

[194] Johann Jakob Moser, *Grundsätze des jetzt üblichen Europäischen Völkerrechts in Friedenszeiten* (Hanau 1750) 396.

[195] Johann Jakob Moser, *Grundsätze des jetzt üblichen Europäischen Völkerrechts in Friedenszeiten* (Hanau 1750) 398.

Princes are responsible for the protection of servants and subjects of other sovereigns against any form of violence or slander, [as long as they] lawfully dwell within their states.[196]

This passage is remarkable because it indicates that Moser's protection obligation did not refer to physical injuries to aliens only, but also to nonphysical private offences, such as defamation or slander (*Beleidigungen*).[197] Moser additionally observed that, whenever a foreigner receives an injury, it was not unusual for the aggrieved party's sovereign to take the matter into his own hands.[198] On his part, the sovereign whose subject caused the injury normally granted satisfaction, either willingly or in response to a complaint.[199]

Interestingly, Moser made some specific remarks about the exercise of police authority in respect of aliens.[200] In the absence of a specific treaty-based obligation, sovereigns are not *required* to take into consideration the concerns of other nations when adopting police measures, though it could be sometimes *advisable* to do so.[201] As a corollary, even if their own subjects are affected by police measures undertaken by another sovereign, princes ought not to raise complaints about such measures.[202] Moser did not however conceive this rule in absolute terms and held it to be inapplicable in cases involving breaches of international treaties, failures to do justice and the placing of inequitably heavy burdens on foreign citizens.[203] Moser additionally addressed the practice of reprisals, linking the right to pursue reprisals to the notion of denial of justice.[204] He further submitted that reprisals could be practiced not only on the property of the sovereign who denies justice, but also on the person and properties of his subjects.[205]

---

[196]Author's translation. The original German text reads as follows: "Landesherrn seynd schuldig, anderer Souvereinen Bediente und Unterthanen, so sich aus rechtsmäßigen Ursachen in ihren Staaten aufhalten, gegen allen Gewalt, oder andere Beleidigungen, zu schützen". Johann Jakob Moser, *Grundsätze des jetzt üblichen Europäischen Völkerrechts in Friedenszeiten* (Hanau 1750) 398.

[197]Johann Jakob Moser, *Grundsätze des jetzt üblichen Europäischen Völkerrechts in Friedenszeiten* (Hanau 1750) 398.

[198]Johann Jakob Moser, *Grundsätze des jetzt üblichen Europäischen Völkerrechts in Friedenszeiten* (Hanau 1750) 398.

[199]Johann Jakob Moser, *Grundsätze des jetzt üblichen Europäischen Völkerrechts in Friedenszeiten* (Hanau 1750) 398.

[200]Johann Jakob Moser, *Grundsätze des jetzt üblichen Europäischen Völkerrechts in Friedenszeiten* (Hanau 1750) 469-70.

[201]Johann Jakob Moser, *Grundsätze des jetzt üblichen Europäischen Völkerrechts in Friedenszeiten* (Hanau 1750) 469.

[202]Johann Jakob Moser, *Grundsätze des jetzt üblichen Europäischen Völkerrechts in Friedenszeiten* (Hanau 1750) 469-70.

[203]Johann Jakob Moser, *Grundsätze des jetzt üblichen Europäischen Völkerrechts in Friedenszeiten* (Hanau 1750) 470.

[204]Johann Jakob Moser, *Grundsätze des jetzt üblichen Europäischen Völkerrechts in Friedenszeiten* (Hanau 1750) 597.

[205]Johann Jakob Moser, *Grundsätze des jetzt üblichen Europäischen Völkerrechts in Friedenszeiten* (Hanau 1750) 598.

To anyone acquainted with the treatises of Wolff and Vattel, it is conspicuous that Moser's views on the treatment of foreigners were by no means revolutionary. Moser's contribution lies more in his method than in his particular conclusions about the law of aliens. By relying on actual state practice, he placed the host state's obligation to protect foreign citizens, as well as the notions of collective responsibility and denial of justice, in an inductively ascertained corpus of *customary* international law.

3.5.2 The Consolidation of the Classical Approach to the Law of Aliens. Georg Friedrich von Martens and Classic Positivism

More than three decades after the first edition of Moser's treatise, another German public law scholar would follow his steps, bringing the positivist approach to the law of nations to one of its most sophisticated expressions.[206] His name remains firmly etched in the intellectual history of international law: Georg Friedrich von Martens.[207] In spite of being an active politician and diplomat, Martens had a very prolific academic activity.[208] His *Primae lineae iuris gentium europearum* (1785),[209] were followed by his legendary *Précis du droit des gens moderne de l'Europe* (1789),[210] of which he would prepare a revised edition in German language a few years later (1796).[211]

---

[206]See generally: Martti Koskenniemi, 'Into Positivism: Georg Friedrich von Martens (1756-1821) and modern international law' (2008) 15 *Constellations* 189, 193 *et seq.*

[207]On Marten's importance for the development of international law see: Stephen Neff, *Justice Among Nations. A History of International Law* (Harvard University Press, Cambridge MA 2014) 198-201.

[208]See: Martti Koskenniemi, 'Into Positivism: Georg Friedrich von Martens (1756-1821) and modern international law' (2008) 15 *Constellations* 189, 194; Stephen Neff, *Justice Among Nations. A History of International Law* (Harvard University Press, Cambridge MA 2014) 198-9.

[209]The *Primae lineae iuris gentium europearum* were not only used in academic debate, but also as teaching material for Martens' lectures at the University of Göttingen. For a brief presentation of Martens' teaching activity and an enlightening summary of his approach to the law of nations see: Georg Friedrich von Martens, *Versuch über die Existenz eines positiven Europäischen Völkerrechts und den Nutzen dieser Wissenschaft* (Johann Christian Dieterich, Göttingen 1787). The *Vesuch* was used as an introduction to the international law course Martens held at Göttingen in the fall semester of 1787. The *Vesuch* already contains many of the defining features of Martens' positive law of nations (at pp. 6-12).

[210]Georg Friedrich von Martens, *Précis du droit moderne de l'Europe* (Guillaumin et cir. Libraires, Paris 1858) [first edition: 1789].

[211]Georg Friedrich von Martens, *Einleitung in das positive Europäische Völkerrecht auf Verträge und Herkommen gegründet* (Johann Christian Dieterich, Göttingen 1796). Martens explained the differences between his French first edition and the revisited German second edition in the Preamble

In his commentary to the *Déclaration du droit des gens*, unsuccessfully submitted by Henri Grégoire (better known as Abbé Grégoire) to the French National Assembly in 1795, Martens delivered a very representative synthesis of his own views on the law of nations.[212] He sharply criticized Grégoire's ambitious endeavor to set down a list of (idealistic) principles of the law of nations, pointing out the perils, uncertainties and ineffectiveness attached to the essentially naturalistic assertions made in the Abbot's Declaration.[213] Beyond his critical remarks on Grégoire's choice of language, Martens made clear that he was pleading for realism.[214] He believed the *Déclaration* to be at best a 'delightful dream' (*lieblicher Traum*), suitable for pleasing conversations.[215]

In spite of his positivist spirit, Martens did not deny the *existence* of a natural law of nations.[216] On the contrary, he drew a careful distinction between natural international law (*natürliches Völkerrecht*) and positive international law (*positives Völkerrecht*).[217] Nations are moral persons in a natural state (*Naturstand*).[218] The natural law of nations is therefore the law of nature, as may be suitable for the relations among peoples (*Völker*).[219] This law is *general* and *necessary* because it is binding upon all peoples regardless of their actual will.[220] But Martens did not believe this natural law to actually provide a corpus of rules capable of governing the relations of nations to each other:

> [F]rom the very moment in which two peoples enter into relations with each other, natural international law is no longer sufficient to determine their rights.[221]

(*Vorbericht*) to the German book (at iii-xvi). This chapter primarily relies on the 1796 German edition.

[212]For a similar observation see: Martti Koskenniemi, 'Into Positivism: Georg Friedrich von Martens (1756-1821) and modern international law' (2008) 15 *Constellations* 189, 199 (observing that Martens' commentaries were considered 'as a kind of methodological and political *credo* of its author').

[213]Georg Friedrich von Martens, *Einleitung in das positive Europäische Völkerrecht auf Verträge und Herkommen gegründet* (Johann Christian Dieterich, Göttingen 1796) v-xiv.

[214]Cf. Georg Friedrich von Martens, *Einleitung in das positive Europäische Völkerrecht auf Verträge und Herkommen gegründet* (Johann Christian Dieterich, Göttingen 1796) v *et seq.*

[215]Georg Friedrich von Martens, *Einleitung in das positive Europäische Völkerrecht auf Verträge und Herkommen gegründet* (Johann Christian Dieterich, Göttingen 1796) vii.

[216]Georg Friedrich von Martens, *Einleitung in das positive Europäische Völkerrecht auf Verträge und Herkommen gegründet* (Johann Christian Dieterich, Göttingen 1796) 2.

[217]Georg Friedrich von Martens, *Einleitung in das positive Europäische Völkerrecht auf Verträge und Herkommen gegründet* (Johann Christian Dieterich, Göttingen 1796) 2.

[218]Georg Friedrich von Martens, *Einleitung in das positive Europäische Völkerrecht auf Verträge und Herkommen gegründet* (Johann Christian Dieterich, Göttingen 1796) 2.

[219]Georg Friedrich von Martens, *Einleitung in das positive Europäische Völkerrecht auf Verträge und Herkommen gegründet* (Johann Christian Dieterich, Göttingen 1796) 2.

[220]Georg Friedrich von Martens, *Einleitung in das positive Europäische Völkerrecht auf Verträge und Herkommen gegründet* (Johann Christian Dieterich, Göttingen 1796) 2.

[221]The original German text reads: "Sobald zwey Völker mit einander in Verkehr treten, so reicht das natürliche Völkerrecht allein nicht mehr hin, um ihre Rechte zu bestimmen." Georg Friedrich

From the rights and obligations of a state towards another state, said Martens, 'there appears – in opposition to the natural, general and necessary international law – a positive, particular and arbitrary international law for these two peoples'.[222] Martens' understanding of the positive law of nations excluded Wolff's notion of a (positive) *voluntary law*, based on a presumed consent of states and ultimately derived from the idea of a *civitas maxima*.[223] According to Martens, most of the general rules advanced by Wolff would more properly belong to the natural law of nations (*natürliches Völkerrecht*) or to the public morals of the peoples (*Völkermoral*).[224]

The sources of Martens' positive international law are thus treaty law (*Vertragsrecht*) and customary law (*Gewohnheitsvölkerrecht*).[225] The treaty and customary rules applicable to each particular state constitute the said state's external public law (*auswärtiges Staatsrecht*).[226] Martens further provided a detailed assessment of the notion of customary international law, explaining that international custom is not based on the silent consent of states (*stillschweigende Einwilligung*), but on the will each state has tacitly expressed through its own actions.[227] The actions of the state may indeed create an expectation on other states that the same course of action will be followed in the future.[228] The normative force of custom (*Herkommen*) is however incomplete (*unvolkommene Verbindlichkeit*), and its content could therefore change in time; but the state still has the duty towards its fellow states to observe it and to provide a clear indication of its intention to adopt a different pattern of conduct.[229] Martens' sources of international law are not

---

von Martens, *Einleitung in das positive Europäische Völkerrecht auf Verträge und Herkommen gegründet* (Johann Christian Dieterich, Göttingen 1796) 3.

[222]The original German text reads: "[Aus dem Inbegriff dieser Bestimmungen] entsteht im Gegensatz des natürlichen, allgemeinen und nothwendigen Völkerrechts, ein positives, besonderes, willkürliches Völkerrecht dieser beyden Völker." Georg Friedrich von Martens, *Einleitung in das positive Europäische Völkerrecht auf Verträge und Herkommen gegründet* (Johann Christian Dieterich, Göttingen 1796) 3.

[223]Georg Friedrich von Martens, *Einleitung in das positive Europäische Völkerrecht auf Verträge und Herkommen gegründet* (Johann Christian Dieterich, Göttingen 1796) 6-7.

[224]Georg Friedrich von Martens, *Einleitung in das positive Europäische Völkerrecht auf Verträge und Herkommen gegründet* (Johann Christian Dieterich, Göttingen 1796) 7.

[225]Georg Friedrich von Martens, *Einleitung in das positive Europäische Völkerrecht auf Verträge und Herkommen gegründet* (Johann Christian Dieterich, Göttingen 1796) 3.

[226]Georg Friedrich von Martens, *Einleitung in das positive Europäische Völkerrecht auf Verträge und Herkommen gegründet* (Johann Christian Dieterich, Göttingen 1796) 3.

[227]Georg Friedrich von Martens, *Einleitung in das positive Europäische Völkerrecht auf Verträge und Herkommen gegründet* (Johann Christian Dieterich, Göttingen 1796) 72.

[228]Georg Friedrich von Martens, *Einleitung in das positive Europäische Völkerrecht auf Verträge und Herkommen gegründet* (Johann Christian Dieterich, Göttingen 1796) 72.

[229]Georg Friedrich von Martens, *Einleitung in das positive Europäische Völkerrecht auf Verträge und Herkommen gegründet* (Johann Christian Dieterich, Göttingen 1796) 72-3.

completely separate compartments.[230] Customary rules may reflect natural law, in which case they should suffer no changes with the passage of time.[231] Treaties may reproduce customary rules.[232] And customary law may, too, reproduce or change rules that were originally treaty-based.[233]

It is against this theoretical background that Martens' approach to the law of aliens can be properly assessed. As a corollary of its exclusive property right over its own territory, every state has the right of admission of foreign citizens.[234] In contrast, states cannot prevent aliens from abandoning their territory, as far as they have not committed crimes, assumed debts or become the object of reprisals.[235] A foreigner may also lose his right to leave the country by the act of naturalization.[236]

Martens drew particular attention to the treatment of aliens who have been admitted into the host state's territory.[237] He believed that the core function of the state is to provide some measure of security to the members of the national community.[238] For the achievement of this goal, every state is entitled to exercise its sovereign powers within its borders, in respect of natives and aliens alike.[239] Local law is thus fully applicable to foreign citizens.[240] Martens emphasized that the host state must be able to assure the maintenance of internal security, peace and order; foreigners should hence refrain from undertaking any actions against this

---

[230]Cf. Georg Friedrich von Martens, *Einleitung in das positive Europäische Völkerrecht auf Verträge und Herkommen gegründet* (Johann Christian Dieterich, Göttingen 1796) 74.

[231]Georg Friedrich von Martens, *Einleitung in das positive Europäische Völkerrecht auf Verträge und Herkommen gegründet* (Johann Christian Dieterich, Göttingen 1796) 74.

[232]Georg Friedrich von Martens, *Einleitung in das positive Europäische Völkerrecht auf Verträge und Herkommen gegründet* (Johann Christian Dieterich, Göttingen 1796) 74.

[233]Georg Friedrich von Martens, *Einleitung in das positive Europäische Völkerrecht auf Verträge und Herkommen gegründet* (Johann Christian Dieterich, Göttingen 1796) 74.

[234]Georg Friedrich von Martens, *Einleitung in das positive Europäische Völkerrecht auf Verträge und Herkommen gegründet* (Johann Christian Dieterich, Göttingen 1796) 94-5. Martens observed, however, that European sovereigns had usually granted some freedom of entry and establishment to each other's subjects (at pp. 94-5).

[235]Georg Friedrich von Martens, *Einleitung in das positive Europäische Völkerrecht auf Verträge und Herkommen gegründet* (Johann Christian Dieterich, Göttingen 1796) 100.

[236]Georg Friedrich von Martens, *Einleitung in das positive Europäische Völkerrecht auf Verträge und Herkommen gegründet* (Johann Christian Dieterich, Göttingen 1796) 100.

[237]Georg Friedrich von Martens, *Einleitung in das positive Europäische Völkerrecht auf Verträge und Herkommen gegründet* (Johann Christian Dieterich, Göttingen 1796) 94 *et seq.*

[238]Georg Friedrich von Martens, *Einleitung in das positive Europäische Völkerrecht auf Verträge und Herkommen gegründet* (Johann Christian Dieterich, Göttingen 1796) 92.

[239]Georg Friedrich von Martens, *Einleitung in das positive Europäische Völkerrecht auf Verträge und Herkommen gegründet* (Johann Christian Dieterich, Göttingen 1796) 92-3.

[240]Georg Friedrich von Martens, *Einleitung in das positive Europäische Völkerrecht auf Verträge und Herkommen gegründet* (Johann Christian Dieterich, Göttingen 1796) 97 and 101. Martens excluded from this rule diplomatic envoys (*Gesandte*) and reigning princes (*regierende Prinzen*) (at p. 97).

superior purpose.[241] If they do so, the state may exercise its criminal prosecution powers (*Criminal-Gewalt*) against them.[242] Nonetheless, Martens acknowledged that foreigners could be entitled to a special treatment under treaty and customary law:

> [F]oreign powers [usually] have the right to request – on behalf of their own subjects entering into a foreign territory, establishing their residence therein or conducting businesses with the subjects of that state – [measures] which [the host] state would not be bound to tolerate, refrain from applying or undertake under the strict principles of the said state's natural law.[243]

In this connection, Martens compared the reciprocal rights of states concerning each other's subjects to a sort of public law easement (*Staatsdienstbarkeit*), which is partly based on custom (*servitutes iuris publici generales*) and partly based on international treaties (*servitutes iuris publici particulares*).[244] Like Moser, Martens considered that aliens are particularly entitled to the host state's protection.[245] This entitlement provides, in turn, the basis for more specific customary obligations:

> [A]s a result of the protection it owes to the person and property of foreign residents, the state shall investigate and prosecute crimes committed within its territory against [such foreign residents] with the same diligence and strength as if [the crimes] had been committed against its own, native subjects.[246]

---

[241] Georg Friedrich von Martens, *Einleitung in das positive Europäische Völkerrecht auf Verträge und Herkommen gegründet* (Johann Christian Dieterich, Göttingen 1796) 98.

[242] Georg Friedrich von Martens, *Einleitung in das positive Europäische Völkerrecht auf Verträge und Herkommen gegründet* (Johann Christian Dieterich, Göttingen 1796) 122.

[243] Author's translation. The original German text reads: "[Sieht man hingegen auf die, theils auf Herkommen, theils auf Verträge gegründete Praxis der Europäischen Völker, so zeigt sich sehr häufig, daß] fremde Mächte für ihre Unterthanen welche in ein fremdes Gebiet eintreten, oder sich dort niederlassen, oder von Haus aus mit den Unterthanen dieses Staates in Verkehr sind, manches zu fordern berechtigt sind, was nach den strengen Grundsätzen des natürlichen Rechts dieser Staat zu ihrem Vortheil zu leiden, zu unterlassen oder zu unternehmen nicht verbunden wäre." Georg Friedrich von Martens, *Einleitung in das positive Europäische Völkerrecht auf Verträge und Herkommen gegründet* (Johann Christian Dieterich, Göttingen 1796) 93.

[244] Georg Friedrich von Martens, *Einleitung in das positive Europäische Völkerrecht auf Verträge und Herkommen gegründet* (Johann Christian Dieterich, Göttingen 1796) 93. Martens elaborated further on the concept of the 'international law easements' (*Völkerrechts-Dienstbarkeiten*) in a later section of his treatise (at pp. 135-6). These concepts continued to be used in German-speaking countries for centuries. For an indicative example see: Eduard Otto von Waldkirch, *Das Völkerrecht in seinen Grundzügen dargestellt* (Verlag von Helbing & Lichtenhahn, Basel 1926) 201.

[245] Georg Friedrich von Martens, *Einleitung in das positive Europäische Völkerrecht auf Verträge und Herkommen gegründet* (Johann Christian Dieterich, Göttingen 1796) 124.

[246] Author's translation. The original German text reads: "Kraft des Schutzes welchen der Staat den fremden Einwohnern für Ihre Person und Güter zu leisten schuldig ist, muß er die in seinem Gebiet wider selbige begangenen Verbrechen mit eben der Sorgfalt und Strenge untersuchen und bestrafen, als wenn sie gegen seine Eingebohrne Unterthanen begangen worden wären." Georg Friedrich von Martens, *Einleitung in das positive Europäische Völkerrecht auf Verträge und Herkommen gegründet* (Johann Christian Dieterich, Göttingen 1796) 124.

Martens additionally considered that foreigners have a right to be protected against specific nonphysical offences, such as defamation.[247] This shows that, in the same manner as Moser, Martens extended the protection obligation beyond physical security. Still, in his assessment of the security of aliens, Martens was essentially referring to private wrongs. His examples leave the impression that Martens thought of the protection of aliens as protection *through* and not *against* the host state.

As regards to the redress of injuries to aliens, Martens departed from the fundamental premise that aliens are subject to the jurisdiction of local courts.[248] In this connection, he devoted several sections of his treatise to the status and rights of foreigners in the context of local court proceedings, developing his own doctrine of denial of justice.[249] According to Martens, foreign citizens have the duty to resort to local justice administration, avoiding any recourse to private violence.[250] But this duty has its counterpart in the host state's obligation to do justice:

> [E]ach state is entirely liable to foreigners, as well as to its own citizens, to grant them access to the courts and to provide them with prompt and impartial justice.[251]

States are however not required, unless otherwise agreed in a particular treaty, to create special jurisdictions for foreigners or to give priority to cases involving aliens.[252] If these obligations are met, both the foreign citizen and his home state have no cause of complaint against the host state; furthermore, neither of them may question the local court's decision on the merits.[253] The home state may only intervene where justice has been delayed or denied.[254]

---

[247]Georg Friedrich von Martens, *Einleitung in das positive Europäische Völkerrecht auf Verträge und Herkommen gegründet* (Johann Christian Dieterich, Göttingen 1796) 98-9.

[248]Georg Friedrich von Martens, *Einleitung in das positive Europäische Völkerrecht auf Verträge und Herkommen gegründet* (Johann Christian Dieterich, Göttingen 1796) 115.

[249]Georg Friedrich von Martens, *Einleitung in das positive Europäische Völkerrecht auf Verträge und Herkommen gegründet* (Johann Christian Dieterich, Göttingen 1796) 115-22.

[250]Georg Friedrich von Martens, *Einleitung in das positive Europäische Völkerrecht auf Verträge und Herkommen gegründet* (Johann Christian Dieterich, Göttingen 1796) 116.

[251]Author's translation. The original German text reads: "[Dagegen ist aber] jeder Staat vollkommen schuldig den Fremden, so wie seinen eigenen Unterthanen, die Wege des Rechtens zu eröffnen, und ihnen eine schleunige und unpartheiyliche Justitz angedenken zu lassen." Georg Friedrich von Martens, *Einleitung in das positive Europäische Völkerrecht auf Verträge und Herkommen gegründet* (Johann Christian Dieterich, Göttingen 1796) 116.

[252]Georg Friedrich von Martens, *Einleitung in das positive Europäische Völkerrecht auf Verträge und Herkommen gegründet* (Johann Christian Dieterich, Göttingen 1796) 116.

[253]Georg Friedrich von Martens, *Einleitung in das positive Europäische Völkerrecht auf Verträge und Herkommen gegründet* (Johann Christian Dieterich, Göttingen 1796) 116-7. Martens clarified that his conclusion was inapplicable to cases where local courts have decided on the basis of international law: no state can impose on other states its own understanding of the law of nations (at p. 117).

[254]Georg Friedrich von Martens, *Einleitung in das positive Europäische Völkerrecht auf Verträge und Herkommen gegründet* (Johann Christian Dieterich, Göttingen 1796) 118 (in general) and 293 (in particular reference to reprisals).

In such instances, the home state has the right to retaliation, reprisals or even to declare war.[255] Upon a denial of justice, reprisals can be exercised against the person or property not only of those who caused the original injury and their home state, but also against any subject of that state.[256] However, Martens observed, in the practice of European states from the fourteenth century onwards, private reprisals required a *letter de marque* (*Markbrief*).[257] Martens further noted that letters of marque had become rather uncommon with the passage of time: sovereigns often preferred not to leave reprisals in the hands of private citizens, and consistently opted to take reprisals into their own hands.[258]

Martens' rules were throughout similar to those laid down by Wolff and Vattel. His method was nonetheless different. There was no recourse to the fiction of a tacit agreement or to the presumed consent of states. In order to identify the rules of the law of aliens and determine their binding force, Martens considered whether and to which extent Western European nations had actually come to accept those rules as legally binding.[259] At some instances, he took note of changes in the practice of states, and gave weight to those changes in the assessment of the customary character of specific legal institutions.[260] Against this backdrop, it is safe to say that, with Moser, Martens was one of the first scholars to place on the host state a *customary* obligation to protect foreign subjects within its territory.

---

[255]Georg Friedrich von Martens, *Einleitung in das positive Europäische Völkerrecht auf Verträge und Herkommen gegründet* (Johann Christian Dieterich, Göttingen 1796) 118.

[256]Georg Friedrich von Martens, *Einleitung in das positive Europäische Völkerrecht auf Verträge und Herkommen gegründet* (Johann Christian Dieterich, Göttingen 1796) 293-4.

[257]Georg Friedrich von Martens, *Einleitung in das positive Europäische Völkerrecht auf Verträge und Herkommen gegründet* (Johann Christian Dieterich, Göttingen 1796) 294-5.

[258]Georg Friedrich von Martens, *Einleitung in das positive Europäische Völkerrecht auf Verträge und Herkommen gegründet* (Johann Christian Dieterich, Göttingen 1796) 294-5.

[259]This is evident in the language used in the assessment of the rules applicable to the treatment of aliens. Cf. Georg Friedrich von Martens, *Einleitung in das positive Europäische Völkerrecht auf Verträge und Herkommen gegründet* (Johann Christian Dieterich, Göttingen 1796) 94 *et seq.*

[260]A clear example is Martens' presentation of the *ius albinagii* or *droit d'aubaine* (i.e. the institution allowing the host state, upon the death of a foreign citizen, to requisition or inherit the foreigner's properties), which, Martens observed, was already in disuse in most European states and did hence no longer belong to customary international law. Georg Friedrich von Martens, *Einleitung in das positive Europäische Völkerrecht auf Verträge und Herkommen gegründet* (Johann Christian Dieterich, Göttingen 1796) 112-4.

3.6   The Influence of Eighteenth-Century Legal Scholarship in the Subsequent Development of the Law of Aliens. A Dialogue Between Theory and Practice

Eighteenth century international law scholars made a great contribution to the development of the law of aliens.[261] Their works rendered a great service not only to legal science, but also to the foreign offices of countless states.[262] This section shows that these academic treatises and, particularly, Vattel's *Le droit des gens*, were actively used in the negotiation of the first generation of American FCN agreements, the 'forerunners' of today's IIAs.[263] FCN agreements were one of the most significant concerns of American foreign policy in the immediate aftermath of the Declaration of Independence.[264] As plausibly suggested by some scholars:

---

[261] See Sects. 3.3, 3.4 and 3.5.

[262] Cf. Charles Fenwick, 'The Authority of Vattel' (1913) 7(3) APSR 395, 395 (particularly referring to Vattel); Stephen Neff, *Justice Among Nations. A History of International Law* (Harvard University Press, Cambridge MA 2014) 200 (referring to Martens' reputation in academic circles).

[263] On the historical connection between FCN treaties and BITs see: Kate Miles, *The Origins of International Investment Law* (Cambridge University Press, New York 2013) 24-5 (characterizing FCN treaty practice 'as a forerunner of modern investment treaties'). See also: Jeswald Salacuse, *The Law of Investment Treaties* (Oxford University Press, Oxford 2015) 92-4; John Coyle, 'The Treaty of Friendship, Commerce and Navigation in the Modern Era' (2013) 51 Columb. J. Transnat'l L. 302, 327-30; Kenneth Vandevelde, 'A Brief History of International Investment Agreements' (2005) 12 U. C. Davis J. Int'l L. & Pol'y 157, 157-61; O. Thomas Johnson and Jonathan Gimblett, 'From Gunboats to BITs: The Evolution of Modern International Investment Law' in Karl Sauvant (ed), *Yearbook on International Law & Policy* 649, 676-9; Rumana Islam, *The Fair and Equitable Treatment Standard (FET) in International Investment Arbitration* (Springer, Singapore 2018) 32; Stephan Schill, *The Multilaterization of International Investment Law* (Cambridge University Press, Cambridge 2009) 29-30; Wolfgang Alschner, 'Americanization of the BIT Universe: The Influence of Friendship, Commerce and Navigation (FCN) Treaties on Modern Investment Treaty Law' (2013) 5(2) GoJIL 455, 468-8. For a different view on the influence of FCN agreements on contemporary IIAs see: Muthucumaraswamy Sornarajah, *The International Law on Foreign Investment* (Cambridge University Press, New York 2010) 180 ("The FCN treaty contained almost a charter of the rights that the alien was to enjoy in the host state [. . .] to the extent that the early FCN treaty was not specific to investment, the FCN treaty may not be the precursor of the modern bilateral investment treaty, but its investment provisions contain many features which are now found in a more refined way in bilateral investment treaties"). On early FCN treaty practice as a shaping factor of the FPS standard cf. George Foster, 'Recovering "Protection and Security": The Treaty Standard's Obscure Origins, Forgotten Meaning, and Key Current Significance' (2012) 45(4) Vand. J. Transnat'l L. 1095, 1118-20 (particularly focusing on the correspondence of Alexander Hamilton and briefly noting the possible influence of European scholars); Onyema Awa Oyeani, *The Obligation of Host States to Accord the Standard of "Full Protection and Security" to Foreign Investments under International Investment Law* (Brunel University, London 2018) [D.Phil. Thesis] 36-9 (providing an overview and citing the papers of Alexander Hamilton at p. 38).

[264] Cf. Alfred Eckes Jr., *Opening America's Market. U.S. Foreign Trade Policy Since 1776* (The University of North Carolina Press, Chapel Hill NC 1995) 4 *et seq.*

Eager to obtain foreign diplomatic recognition and break the British stranglehold on Atlantic commerce, the Americans prepared to offer the only meaningful lure available: access to U.S. market.[265]

A look into the signatures at the bottom of eighteenth century U.S. FCN treaties suffices to confirm the importance these agreements had for the new republic. The names include some of America's founding fathers, including John Adams, Benjamin Franklin, Alexander Hamilton, John Jay and Thomas Jefferson.[266] It is no secret that Franklin was in charge of the negotiations of the Treaty of Amity and Commerce concluded in 1778 between the United States and the Government of Louis XVI of France.[267] The treaty was moreover drafted on the basis of the so-called 'Model Treaty' of 1776, an astonishingly modern trade policy document authored by John Adams.[268] The security of aliens was a recurrent issue in the 1778 treaty. The clearest example appears in article 6:

> The Most Christian King [of France] shall endeavor by all the means in his power to *protect and defend* all vessels and the effects belonging to the subjects, people or inhabitants of the said United States, or any of them, being in his ports, havens or roads, or on the seas near to his countries, islands or towns.[269]

Article 7 imposed a similar obligation upon the United States.[270] Other provisions of the agreement contained further references to the protection of aliens, thus reinforcing the treaty-based security obligation.[271] This type of clauses was not

---

[265] Alfred Eckes Jr., *Opening America's Market. U.S. Foreign Trade Policy Since 1776* (The University of North Carolina Press, Chapel Hill NC 1995) 4-5.

[266] Specific examples are provided later in this section.

[267] For a historical account of Franklin's role in the negotiation of the treaty see: Jonathan Dull, *Franklin the Diplomat: the French Mission* (The American Philosophical Society, Philadelphia 1982) 19-32. For a detailed analysis of American foreign policy during the period at issue see: Willem Theo Oosterveld, *The Law of Nations in Early American Foreign Policy. Theory and Practice from the Revolution to the Monroe Doctrine* (Brill, Leiden 2015) 97-116 (particularly considering the French Alliance in historical context).

[268] On the 'Model Treaty' or 'Plan of Treaties' of 1776 see: Gregg Lint, 'John Adams on the Drafting of the Treaty Plan of 1776' 2(4) Diplomatic History (1978) 313, 313-20.

[269] Emphasis added. Treaty of Amity and Commerce between the United States of America and the Kingdom of France (adopted 6 February 1778, entered into force 17 July 1778) Hunter Miller (ed), *Treaties and Other International Acts of the United States of America* (Volume 2: Government Printing Office, Washington 1931) 3, 7 art. 6.

[270] Treaty of Amity and Commerce between the United States of America and the Kingdom of France (adopted 6 February 1778, entered into force 17 July 1778) Hunter Miller (ed), *Treaties and Other International Acts of the United States of America* (Volume 2: Government Printing Office, Washington 1931) 3, 8 art. 8.

[271] Treaty of Amity and Commerce between the United States of America and the Kingdom of France (adopted 6 February 1778, entered into force 17 July 1778) Hunter Miller (ed), *Treaties and Other International Acts of the United States of America* (Volume 2: Government Printing Office, Washington 1931) 3, 9-21 art. 8 (creating an obligation upon the French monarch to 'employ his good offices and interposition' with African sovereigns 'in order to provide as full and efficaciously as possible for the Benefit, Convenience and Safety of the said United States and each of them, their Subjects, People and Inhabitants, and their Vessels and Effects, against all Violence, Insult, Attacks,

particular to the 1778 treaty. Similar provisions appear, for example, in the FCN agreements concluded with the Netherlands in 1782 (signed by Adams)[272] and Prussia in 1785 (signed by Adams, Franklin and Jefferson).[273] Another example would be the Treaty of Amity, Commerce and Navigation between the United States and Great Britain of 1794, which has been described as the 'most crucial' and 'most bitterly debated' international agreement in U.S. history.[274]

The historical record indicates that Chief Justice John Jay led the negotiations.[275] Nonetheless, other prominent American politicians, including Alexander Hamilton, played a material role in the process too.[276] Despite the fact that the protection of aliens was not the main political concern of the negotiators, they managed to incorporate an embryonic FPS clause into the Jay Treaty:

> Article 14. [. . .] The people and Inhabitants of the Two Countries respectively, shall have liberty, *freely and securely, and without hindrance and molestation,* to come with their Ships and Cargoes to the Lands, Countries, Cities, Ports Places and Rivers within the Dominions and Territories, to enter into the same, and to remain and reside there [. . .] and generally the Merchants and Traders on each side, shall enjoy the *most complete protection and Security*

---

or Depredations on the Part of the said Princes and States of Barbary, or their Subjects'), art. 17 (providing that 'the more effectual Care may be taken for the Security of the Subjects and Inhabitants of both Parties, that they suffer no injury by the men of War or Privateers of the other Party, all the Commanders of the Ships of his most Christian Majesty & the said United States and all their Subjects and Inhabitants shall be forbid doing any Injury or Damage to the other Side; and if they act to the contrary, they shall be punished and shall moreover be bound to make Satisfaction for all the Matter of Damage, and the Interest thereof, by reparation, under the Pain and obligation of their Person and Goods') and art. 25 (concerning the right to sail and trade with 'Liberty and Security').

[272]Treaty of Amity and Commerce between the United States of America and the Netherlands (adopted 8 October 1782, entered into force 23 June 1783) Hunter Miller (ed), *Treaties and Other International Acts of the United States of America* (Volume 2: Government Printing Office, Washington 1931) 59, 64-5 art. 5.

[273]Treaty of Amity and Commerce between the United States of America and the Kingdom of Prussia (adopted 10 September 1785, entered into force 17 May 1786) Hunter Miller (ed), *Treaties and Other International Acts of the United States of America* (Volume 2: Government Printing Office, Washington 1931) 162, 167 art. 7.

[274]Jerald Combs, *The Jay Treaty: Political Battleground of the Founding Fathers* (University of California Press, Berkeley 1970) ix. Among others, Thomas Jefferson and James Madison actively opposed the treaty, which they considered to be nothing more than technical 'surrender' to Britain (at ix).

[275]For a detailed account on the negotiation of the Jay Treaty see: Jerald Combs, *The Jay Treaty: Political Battleground of the Founding Fathers* (University of California Press, Berkeley 1970) 137-58.

[276]On the role of Alexander Hamilton in the history of the Anglo-American relations see: Jerald Combs, *The Jay Treaty: Political Battleground of the Founding Fathers* (University of California Press, Berkeley 1970) 31-64. The participation of Hamilton in the shaping of the Jay Treaty is also a well-documented historical fact (at pp. 137-58).

for their Commerce; but subject always, as to what respects this article, to the Laws and Statutes of the Two Countries respectively.[277]

Article 19 of the Treaty also enshrined an FPS obligation, whereby 'more abundant Care may be taken for the security of the respective Subjects and Citizens of the Contracting Parties'.[278] These clauses resemble, at least to some extent, the views of Emmer de Vattel. In fact, the treaty envisaged the security obligation as a best efforts obligation. In addition, it directly linked the duty to the subjection of foreign citizens to local law. In 1758, Vattel had already advanced the proposition that the sovereign assures security to aliens only 'as far as it depends on him'.[279] Vattel also followed Wolff in conceiving the protection granted to aliens as a right that was yielded in exchange for obedience.[280]

In his *Remarks on the Treaty of Commerce and Navigation Lately Made Between the United States and Great Britain* of July 1795, Alexander Hamilton explained the content of the Jay Treaty, heavily relying on Vattel's treatise.[281] Hamilton's comments on article 14 are however somewhat disappointing. He merely observed that '[t]his article is a general formula without any special or remarkable feature.'[282] A similar comment was made with regard to article 19.[283] While these observations do not tell much about the rationale of the protection obligation, Hamilton was certainly aware of the theory of the tacit agreement. In his *Report on a Plan for the Further Support of Public Credit*, submitted to Congress just 2 months after the conclusion of the Jay Treaty and before the exchange of ratification instruments, Hamilton cited Vattel and made express reference to the tacit agreement:

[T]he right to property always implies the right to be protected & secured in the enjoyment of that property. And a nation by the very act of permitting the Citizen of a foreign country to

---

[277]Emphasis added. Treaty of Amity, Commerce, and Navigation between the United States and Great Britain (adopted 19 November 1794, entered into force 28 October 1795) Hunter Miller (ed), *Treaties and Other International Acts of the United States of America* (Volume 2: Government Printing Office, Washington 1931) 245, 257 art. 14.

[278]Treaty of Amity, Commerce, and Navigation between the United States and Great Britain (adopted 19 November 1794, entered into force 28 October 1795) Hunter Miller (ed), *Treaties and Other International Acts of the United States of America* (Volume 2: Government Printing Office, Washington 1931) 245, 259 art. 19.

[279]Emer de Vattel, *The Law of Nations* (1758) (G.G. and J. Robinson, London 1797) 172.

[280]Emer de Vattel, *The Law of Nations* (1758) (G.G. and J. Robinson, London 1797) 172.

[281]'Remarks on the Treaty of Amity Commerce and Navigation Lately Made between the United States and Great Britain' (9 11 July 1795) *United States National Archives: Founders Online Project* [http://founders.archives.gov/documents/Hamilton/01-18-02-0281].

[282]'Remarks on the Treaty of Amity Commerce and Navigation Lately Made between the United States and Great Britain' (9-11 July 1795) *United States National Archives: Founders Online Project* [http://founders.archives.gov/documents/Hamilton/01-18-02-0281].

[283]In relation to articles 19 and 20, Hamilton stated: "These articles require no comment. They are usual and every way unexceptionable." 'Remarks on the Treaty of Amity Commerce and Navigation Lately Made between the United States and Great Britain' (9-11 July 1795) *United States National Archives: Founders Online Project* [http://founders.archives.gov/documents/Hamilton/01-18-02-0281].

acquire property within its territory, whether to Lands, funds or to any other thing, *tacitly engages to give protection and security to that property and to allow him as full enjoyment of it as any other proprietor*; an engagement which no state of things between the two nations can justly or reasonably affect.[284]

The link between early FCN treaties and Vattel goes far beyond Hamilton. At the time when the first FCN agreements were being negotiated, the views of Vattel enjoyed widespread acceptance in the highest circles of the American society.[285] John Adams, Benjamin Franklin, Thomas Jefferson and John Jay had full access to his treatise.

Adams had learned international law from the books of Vattel, whom he once called 'one of my preceptors'.[286] In 1811 he would himself recall his youth years in Boston, remembering Richard Gridley's 'comprehensive' study plan.[287] Gridley's reading list on the 'law of nature and nations' included, he said, Vattel's treatise.[288] He had furthermore quoted Vattel in two speeches held in 1773.[289] It is also a documented fact that Franklin brought him a new edition of *Le droit des gens* in 1776.[290] Adams had a sincere admiration for Vattel. In 1790 he would give William Cranch 'some hints' on the study of law, recommending—among others—*Le droit*

---

[284]Emphasis added. 'Report for a Plan for the Further Support of Public Debt' (16 January 1795) *United States National Archives: Founders Online Project* [http://founders.archives.gov/documents/Hamilton/01-18-02-0052-0002].

[285]For a detail presentation of Vattel's influence on the American founding fathers see: Vincent Chetail, 'Vattel and the American Dream: An Inquiry into the Reception of the *Law of Nations* in the United States' in Vincent Chetail and Pierre Marie Dupuy (eds), *The Roots of International Law. Liber Amicorum Peter Haggenmacher* (Martinus Nijhoff Publishers, Leiden 2013) 251, 253-62.

[286]'John Adams to Benjamin Rush' (24 July 1789) *United States National Archives: Founders Online Project* [http://founders.archives.gov/documents/Adams/99-02-02-0700]. For a further example of Adams' admiration for Vattel see: 'John Adams to Richard Cranch Norton' (20 March 1812) *United States National Archives: Founders Online Project* [http://founders.archives.gov/documents/Adams/99-03-02-2127].

[287]'John Adams to Richard Rush' (14 April 1811) *United States National Archives: Founders Online Project* [http://founders.archives.gov/documents/Adams/99-02-02-5631].

[288]'John Adams to Richard Rush' (14 April 1811) *United States National Archives: Founders Online Project* [http://founders.archives.gov/documents/Adams/99-02-02-5631].

[289]'Reply of the House to Hutchinson's First Message' (26 January 1773) in Robert Taylor, *The Adams Papers. Papers of John Adams* (Volume 1: Harvard University Press, Cambridge MA 1977) 315, 320 and 330-1. See also: 'Reply of the House to Hutchinson's Second Message' (2 March 1773) in Robert Taylor, *The Adams Papers. Papers of John Adams* (Volume 1: Harvard University Press, Cambridge MA 1977) 344 and 346.

[290]Franklin referred to this event in a letter addressed to his friend, James Bowdoin. See: 'Benjamin Franklin to James Bowdoin' (24 March 1776) *United States National Archives: Founders Online Project* [http://founders.archives.gov/documents/Franklin/01-22-02-0231].

des gens as one of the books 'most in use' in the field.[291] In his older years, he would give a similar advice to his own grandson, George Washington Adams.[292]

Benjamin Franklin also belonged to the circle of Vattel's American readers. Just a year before assuming the office of American Commissioner to France, where he famously negotiated the first FCN agreement in U.S. history, Franklin received from Charles Dumas three copies of the last (French) edition of Vattel's treatise.[293] On December 9th, 1775, Franklin wrote to Dumas:

> I am much obliged by the kind present you have made us of your edition of Vattel. It came to us in good season, when the circumstances of a rising state make it necessary frequently to consult the law of nations.[294]

In subsequent correspondence, Frankin would sometimes refer to Vattel's 'excellent Treatise entitled *Le Droit des Gens*'.[295] For his part, Thomas Jefferson frequently quoted the works of Vattel in his personal correspondence.[296] In a letter to

---

[291] 'John Adams to William Cranch' (30 December 1790) *United States National Archives: Founders Online Project* [http://founders.archives.gov/documents/Adams/99-02-02-1118].

[292] 'John Adams to George Washington Adams' (9 December 1821) *United States National Archives: Founders Online Project* [http://founders.archives.gov/documents/Adams/99-03-02-3989]; 'John Adams to George Washington Adams' (13 January 1822) *United States National Archives: Founders Online Project* [http://founders.archives.gov/documents/Adams/99-03-02-3995]. John Adams also seems to have transmitted some of his high esteem for the Swiss scholar to his son, the later President John Quincy Adams. The diary of President John Quincy Adams suggests that he read the entire treatise in 1787 (at the young age of 21 years). On September 15th, 1787, Adams wrote: '[Vattel's] sentiments and principles appear to be dictated by good sense and real virtue. They appear all to derive from that law of nature, which every person of common sense and common honesty must wish to prevail'. 'September 15th' in Robert Taylor & Marc Fredlaender, *The Adams Papers. Diary of John Quincy Adams* (Volume 2: Harvard University Press, Cambridge MA 1981) 289. For a further example of Adams' admiration for Vattel see his note of September 22nd, 1787 (at pp. 292-3).

[293] 'Original Letter from Dr. Franklin to Monsieur Dumas' (9 December 1775) 45 *The European Magazine and London Review* (1804) 347, 347.

[294] 'Original Letter from Dr. Franklin to Monsieur Dumas' (9 December 1775) 45 *The European Magazine and London Review* (1804) 347, 347. In the same letter, Franklin briefly referred to the reception of Vattel's work. In this connection, he wrote: "[A] copy, which I kept, (after depositing one in our own public library here, and sending the other to the College of Massachusetts Bay, as you directed), has been continually in the hands of the members of our Congress, now sitting, who are much pleased with your notes and preface, and have entertained a high and just esteem for their author" (at pp. 347-8).

[295] See, for example: 'Benjamin Franklin to Andreas Peter Graf von Bernstorff' (22 December 1779) *United States National Archives: Founders Online Project* [http://founders.archives.gov/documents/Franklin/01-31-02-0175].

[296] For instance, in a letter to John Garland Jefferson, Thomas Jefferson proposed him a reading list, recommending the study of Vattel's treatise. See: 'Thomas Jefferson to John Garland Jefferson' (11 June 1790) *United States National Archives: Founders Online Project* [http://founders.archives.gov/documents/Jefferson/01-16-02-0278]. See also: 'Report on the Negotiations with Spain' (18 March 1792) *United States National Archives: Founders Online Project* [http://founders.archives.gov/documents/Jefferson/01-23-02-0259]; 'Thomas Jefferson to George Hammond' (20 May 1792) [http://founders.archives.gov/documents/Jefferson/01-23-02-0506].

James Madison dated August 3rd, 1793, he would state that '[in order to obtain] lights from the law of nations on the construction of treaties [...] Vattel has been most generally the guide'.[297] In the same letter, he made a short reference to Wolff.[298] In another letter Jefferson had referred to Vattel as the most 'enlightened and distinguished judge' in international affairs.[299] Allusions to Vattel may also be found in the archives of John Jay.[300]

It should be noted that the role of Vattel was not just that of another book of reference. *Le droit des gens* had a prominent position in U.S. early treaty and diplomatic practice, being at the heart of delicate political debates, such as the one concerning the validity of the 1778 Treaty signed with King Louis XVI in the aftermath of the French Revolution.[301]

The historical record does not provide as much evidence of Martens' influence on the negotiators of the first FCN agreements. It is clear that he could not have provided any guidance for the 1778 treaty because his *Primae lineae iuris gentium europearum* were first published in 1785, the French edition appearing in 1789.[302] However, leading American statesmen consulted his work at the time when the debate on the negotiation and ratification of the Jay Treaty was taking place. Hamilton quoted Martens' *Law of Nations* (an English translation of the *Précis*) in

---

[297]'Thomas Jefferson to James Madison' (3 August 1793) *United States National Archives: Founders Online Project* [http://founders.archives.gov/documents/Madison/01-15-02-0044].

[298]'Thomas Jefferson to James Madison' (3 August 1793) *United States National Archives: Founders Online Project* [http://founders.archives.gov/documents/Madison/01-15-02-0044].

[299]'Thomas Jefferson to Edmond Charles Genet' (17 June 1793) *United States National Archives: Founders Online Project* [http://founders.archives.gov/documents/Jefferson/01-26-02-0276].

[300]See, for example: 'John Jay to George Washington' (28 August 1790) *United States National Archives: Founders Online Project* [http://founders.archives.gov/documents/Washington/05-06-02-0170].

[301]Hamilton contended that the 1778 treaty could be declared void after the French Revolution and supported his argument on a passage of Vattel. Others were skeptical. Jefferson would write to John Madison: "Would you suppose it possible that it should have been seriously proposed to declare our treaties with France void on the authority of an ill-understood scrap in Vattel 2.§.197. ('toutefois si ce changement &c—gouvernement') and that it should be necessary to discuss it?" See: 'Thomas Jefferson to James Madison' (28 April 1793) *United States National Archives: Founders Online Project* [http://founders.archives.gov/documents/Madison/01-15-02-0013]. For a record of the discussions about Hamilton's proposal see: 'Cabinet Meeting. Opinion on a Proclamation of Neutrality and on Receiving the French Minister' (19 April 1793) *United States National Archives: Founders Online Project* [http://founders.archives.gov/documents/Hamilton/01-14-02-0226].

[302]Georg Friedrich von Martens, *Précis du droit moderne de l'Europe* (Guillaumin et cir. Libraires, Paris 1858) [first edition: 1789].

his comments to the Jay Treaty (in 1795), as well as in other documents from the same decade.[303] Jefferson also had early access to the *Précis*.[304] He would once refer to Martens as 'the latest and most respected writer' on the law of nations.[305] The correspondence of John Adams indicates that he received a copy of the book in 1794.[306]

These examples reveal some connection between the drafters of early FCN treaties and the theories developed by European legal scholars in the Age of Enlightenment. There was a constant dialogue between theory and practice. This was particularly relevant for the FPS standard. As it has been shown throughout this section, eighteenth century FCN treaties contain some of the earliest examples of modern FPS clauses.[307] The importance of FCN treaties for the law of aliens cannot be underestimated.[308] As noted by Stephen C. Neff (2014):

> There is no better illustration of the process by which international law is built from the bottom up, by conscious state practice, than the network of treaties of amity and commerce that began to be a common feature of the European landscape in about the middle of the seventeenth century.[309]

---

[303]See: 'Remarks on the Treaty of Amity Commerce and Navigation Lately Made between the United States and Great Britain' (9-11 July 1795) *United States National Archives: Founders Online Project* [http://founders.archives.gov/documents/Hamilton/01-18-02-0281]. For a further example see: 'No Jacobin No. II' (5 August 1793) *United States National Archives: Founders Online Project* [http://founders.archives.gov/documents/Hamilton/01-15-02-0145].

[304]William Short sent Jefferson a copy of the *Recueil des Traités* in 1792, referring to Martens as 'the same author on the *Droit des gens moderne de l'Europe*'. This suggests that Jefferson had access to the *Précis* before 1792. See: 'William Short to Thomas Jefferson' (31 August 1792) *United States National Archives: Founders Online Project* [http://founders.archives.gov/documents/Jefferson/01-24-02-0313].

[305]'Thomas Jefferson to Edmund Pendleton' (14 February 1799) *United States National Archives: Founders Online Project* [http://founders.archives.gov/documents/Jefferson/01-31-02-0024]. In 1800, Jefferson would include Martens' manual in a reading list suggested for Joseph Cabell. See: 'A Course of Reading for Joseph C. Cabell' (September 1800) *United States National Archives: Founders Online Project* [http://founders.archives.gov/documents/Jefferson/01-32-02-0110].

[306]'John Quincy Adams to John Adams' (9 November 1794) *United States National Archives: Founders Online Project* [http://founders.archives.gov/documents/Adams/99-02-02-1580]; 'John Quincy Adams to John Adams' (3 December 1794) *United States National Archives: Founders Online Project* [http://founders.archives.gov/documents/Adams/99-02-02-1610]. The latter communication suggests that Adams received the *Précis* after the conclusion of the Jay Treaty but at the time when the debate on its ratification was taking place.

[307]For an arbitral tribunal expressly recognizing the influence of FCN treaty practice on contemporary FPS clauses see: Suez Sociedad General de Aguas de Barcelona S.A. and Vivendi Universal S.A. *v* Argentina, Decision on Liability, ICSID Case No. ARB/03/19 (30 July 2010) [161-3].

[308]See generally: Kenneth Vandevelde, 'A Brief History of International Investment Agreements' 12 U. C. Davis J. Int'l L. & Pol'y 157, 158-61.

[309]Stephen Neff, *Justice Among Nations. A History of International Law* (Harvard University Press, Cambridge MA 2014) 201.

FCN treaties would take center stage in numerous diplomatic incidents during the nineteenth and early twentieth centuries, and would be a fairly important ingredient in the well-known debate about the notion of an international minimum standard of treatment. Chapter 4 explores the historical background of this debate and its role in the evolution of the FPS standard.

Chapter 4
A Battle of Gunboats and Books: 'Full Protection and Security' and the Minimum Standard of Treatment in Historical Perspective

4.1 Preliminary Remarks

The evolution of the FPS standard after the Age of Enlightenment was tied to the most significant and fiercely debated problem in the history of the law of aliens: the question, whether international law recognizes an objective minimum standard for the treatment of foreign citizens, or whether aliens are under no circumstances entitled to a better treatment than the local population (doctrine of equality).[1] The debate would have a long-lasting impact on the FPS standard. Present-day IIAs often envisage the FPS standard as an element of a more-general 'international minimum standard of treatment'.[2] A representative example would be article 9.6 of the Trans-Pacific Partnership Agreement [TPP] of 2016, which is an integral part of the Comprehensive and Progressive Agreement for Trans-Pacific Partnership [CPTPP] of 2018[3]:

Minimum Standard of Treatment.

1. Each Party shall accord to covered investments treatment in accordance with applicable customary international law principles, *including* fair and equitable treatment and *full protection and security.*

2. For greater certainty, paragraph 1 prescribes the *customary international law minimum standard of treatment of aliens* as the standard of treatment to be afforded to covered investments. The concepts of "fair and equitable treatment" and *"full protection and*

---

[1]For an excellent overview of the overall debate see: Martins Paparinskis, *The International Minimum Standard and Fair and Equitable Treatment* (Oxford University Press, Oxford 2013) 20-63.

[2]Chapter 14 addresses the language of FPS clauses in greater detail.

[3]Article 1 of the CPTPP incorporates into the treaty framework most articles of the TPP. Cf. Comprehensive and Progressive Agreement for Trans-Pacific Partnership (adopted 8 March 2018, partially entered into force 30 December 2018) art. 1(1).

© Springer Nature Switzerland AG 2019

S. Mantilla Blanco, *Full Protection and Security in International Investment Law,*
European Yearbook of International Economic Law 8,
https://doi.org/10.1007/978-3-030-24838-3_4

security" do not require treatment in addition to or beyond that which is required by that standard, and do not create additional substantive rights.[4]

This chapter explores the relationship between the FPS standard and the minimum standard of treatment from a historical perspective. The proposition advanced is that the security of aliens was at the heart of the debate about the minimum standard. Western powers resorted to the notion of a 'minimum standard of civilization' to justify military interventions in fragile states, which were too-often unwilling to compensate aliens for losses sustained as a result of revolutions, civil disorders or widespread criminality.[5] Semi-peripheral states could not match the military power of their counterparts.[6] But they could challenge the legal basis of the interventions. The doctrine of equality was hence advanced as a means to oppose the 'gunboat diplomacy'[7] and to avoid responsibility for mob injuries, revolutionary damages and their like.[8] To be sure, neither party in this battle of gunboats and books disputed the *existence* of a customary obligation to provide protection and security to

---

[4]Emphasis added. Trans-Pacific Partnership Agreement (adopted 4 February 2016) art. 9.6(1) and (2).

[5]Section 4.2 elaborates further on this idea.

[6]On the term 'semi-periphery' see: Arnulf Becker Lorca, *Mestizo International Law. A Global Intellectual History 1842-1933* (Cambridge University Press, New York 2014) 18. Becker Lorca explains that the 'semi-periphery' refers to the idea of a 'world system', in which 'the organization of the international world depends on the establishment of a global division of labor' (at p. 18). From this standpoint, some states belong to the 'core' or the 'centre' and are accordingly capable of setting the conditions applicable to 'global production and exchange' (at p. 18). The 'periphery' finds pre-established conditions and ends up satisfying the necessities of the 'core states' (at p. 18). I this vein, Becker Lorca states: "[t]he relationship between centre and periphery is not fixed, but historically fluid. The semi-periphery specifically describes those states that have acquired some margin of autonomy to insert themselves strategically in the global economy and that aspire to move upwards, but that because of geopolitical or economic reasons still do not amass enough power to become part of the world's core." Arnulf Becker Lorca, *Mestizo International Law. A Global Intellectual History 1842-1933* (Cambridge University Press, New York 2014) 18. For a description of 'semi peripheral states' in the nineteenth and early twentieth centuries see: Arnulf Becker Lorca, 'Universal International Law: Nineteenth-Century Histories of Imposition and Appropriation' (2010) 51(2) HILJ 475, 482-4 (arguing that, in those years, the world's 'semi periphery' would include the Latin American republics, the Ottoman Empire and Japan).

[7]'Gunboat diplomacy' might be defined as 'the treat or use of naval force to secure diplomatic concessions'. See: David Nicholson, 'Gunboat Diplomacy' in James Bradford (ed) *International Encyclopedia of Military History* (Routledge, New York 2006) 574, 574. A more detailed definition would be 'the use or threat of limited naval force, otherwise than as an act of war, in order to secure advantage or to avert loss, either in the furtherance of an international dispute or else against foreign nationals within the territory or the jurisdiction of their own state'. See: James Cable, *Gunboat diplomacy 1919-1979. Political Applications of Limited Naval Force* (McMillan, London 1994) 14. See also: Christer Jönsson, 'Gunboat Diplomacy' in Keith Dowding (ed), *Encyclopedia of Power* (SAGE Publications, Los Angeles CA 2011) 300. Interventions for the protection of aliens abroad could also include the landing of small contingents in foreign territory. See: Milton Offutt, *The Protection of Citizens Abroad by the Armed Forces of the United States* (Klaus Reprint, New York 1972) 1 [first edition: 1928]. This chapter uses the term 'gunboat diplomacy' in a broad sense, encompassing all of the abovementioned forms of intervention.

[8]Section 4.3 explores the historical context of the doctrine of equality.

aliens. The bone of contention was whether the security enjoyed by the host state's citizens was the ultimate measure of the security owed to aliens.

4.2 Gunboats from the North. The Minimum Standard of Treatment, the Gunboat Diplomacy and the Security Obligation

Contemporary international law assumes the existence of a general, universal and objective 'international minimum standard of treatment'.[9] Every state must ensure that aliens enjoy that 'minimum treatment', irrespective of the treatment given to the host state's own citizens.[10] The minimum standard has a puzzling effect.[11] As expressed by Sir Hersch Lauterpacht (1945):

> The result, which is somewhat paradoxical, is that the individual in his capacity as an alien enjoys a larger measure of protection by international law than in his character as a citizen of his own State.[12]

This principle is neither self-evident, nor has always enjoyed general acceptance. The minimum standard seems to be of Victorian origin.[13] However, its proclamation as a well-established customary norm does not reach back beyond the first decades of the twentieth century.[14] The perhaps earliest account of the 'minimum standard', properly so-called, was a speech delivered by the American Nobel Prize laureate Elihu Root in 1910:

---

[9]See: Georg Schwarzenberger, *Foreign Investments and International Law* (Stevens & Sons, London 1969) 21-6.

[10]Hersch Lauterpacht, *An International Bill of the Rights of Man* (Columbia University Press, New York 1945) 48.

[11]Hersch Lauterpacht, *An International Bill of the Rights of Man* (Columbia University Press, New York 1945) 48. See also: ILC, 'Summary Records of the 370th Meeting' (19 June 1956) 1 *Yearbook of the International Law Commission – 1956* 226, 229-30 [28-9] (statement of Francisco García Amador).

[12]Hersch Lauterpacht, *An International Bill of the Rights of Man* (Columbia University Press, New York 1945) 48.

[13]See generally: Georg Schwarzenberger, *Foreign Investments and International Law* (Stevens & Sons, London 1969) 22-3 (particularly referring to the growing network of FCN agreements); Georg Schwarzenberger, *The Inductive Approach to International Law* (Stevens & Sons, London 1965) 34 n. 81 (placing the origins of the minimum standard in the '*pax Britannica*' preceding World War I and further discussing the issue at pp. 55 and 78).

[14]In the nineteenth century, international law scholarship did not usually refer to a 'minimum standard of treatment' in the assessment of the law of aliens and the 'gunboat diplomacy'. For a representative example see: Robert Phillimore, *Commentaries upon International Law* (Volume 2: Butterworths, London 1871) 3-19 (referring to '[the] right of protecting citizens in foreign countries').

> There is a standard of justice, very simple, very fundamental, and of such general acceptance by all civilized countries as to from part of the international law of the world. The condition upon which any country is entitled to measure the justice due from it to an alien by the justice it accords to its own citizens is that its system of law and administration shall conform to this general standard. If any country's system of law and administration does not conform to that standard, although the people of the country may be compelled to live under it, no other country can be compelled to accept it as furnishing a satisfactory measure of treatment to its citizens.[15]

As observed by Martins Paparinskis, these words would have 'almost a mystical effect' in international law scholarship.[16] Root seems indeed to be the first influential authority to ever use the phrase 'minimum standard' and expressly proclaim the customary character of the principle.[17] The speech is not far from the modern idea of a 'minimum standard' as 'an absolute bottom below which conduct is not accepted by the international community'.[18] Read in context, however, it is striking that Root's main concern in 1910 was the security aliens abroad and the justification of the use of force as a means to enforce the host state's protection obligation.[19] Just before announcing the 'minimum standard', Root stated:

> [A]rmed forces have often been landed from men-of-war for the protection of the life and property of their national citizens during revolutionary disturbances [. . .] [Such a course] can be justified only by unquestionable facts which leave no practical doubt of the incapacity of the government of the country to perform its international duty of protection [. . .] As between countries which maintain effective government for the maintenance of order within their territories, the protection of one country for its nationals in foreign territory can be exercised only by calling upon the government of the other country for the performance of its international duty, and the measure of one country's international obligation is the measure of the other country's right. The rule of obligation is perfectly distinct and settled. Each country is bound to give to the nationals of another country in its territory the benefit of the same laws, the same administration, the same protection, and the same redress for injury which it gives to its own citizens, an neither more nor less: provided the protection which the country gives to its own citizens conforms to the established standard of civilization.[20]

In advancing this principle, Root heavily relied on a famous speech held in 1850 by the British Foreign Secretary, Viscount Palmerston, at the House of Commons[21]:

---

[15]Elihu Root, 'The Basis of Protection of Citizens Residing Abroad' (1910) 4(3) AJIL 517, 521-22.

[16]On the influence of Roots's address of 1910 see: Martins Paparinskis, *The International Minimum Standard and Fair and Equitable Treatment* (Oxford University Press, Oxford 2013) 39.

[17]Martins Paparinskis, *The International Minimum Standard and Fair and Equitable Treatment* (Oxford University Press, Oxford 2013) 39 *et seq.*; William Slomanson, *Fundamental Perspectives on International Law* (Wadsworth, Boston 2010) 227 (observing that Root's words constitute 'the most definitive' definition of the standard).

[18]For this definition of the 'minimum standard' see: *Glamis Gold v United States*. See: Glamis Gold *v* United States of America (UNCITRAL), Award (8 June 2009) [615].

[19]Elihu Root, 'The Basis of Protection of Citizens Residing Abroad' (1910) 4(3) AJIL 517, 521-22. See also the examples provided at pp. 523 *et seq.* (particularly referring to mob injuries).

[20]Elihu Root, 'The Basis of Protection of Citizens Residing Abroad' (1910) 4(3) AJIL 517, 521.

[21]Elihu Root, 'The Basis of Protection of Citizens Residing Abroad' (1910) 4(3) AJIL 517, 522 (quoting Palmerston in length).

We shall be told, perhaps, as we have already been told, that if the people of the country are liable to have heavy stones placed upon their breasts, and police officers to dance upon them; if they are liable to have their heads tied to their knees, and to be left for hours in that state; or to be swung like a pendulum, and to be bastinadoed as they swing, foreigners have no right to be better treated than the natives, and have no business to complain if the same things are practiced upon them. We may be told this, but that is not my opinion, nor do I believe it is the opinion of any reasonable man. [...] I therefore fearlessly challenge the verdict which this House [...] is to give on the question now brought before it; whether the principles on which the foreign policy of Her Majesty's Government has been conducted, and the sense of duty which has led us to think ourselves bound to afford protection to our fellow subjects abroad, are proper and fitting guides for those who are charged with the Government of England; and whether, as the Roman, in days of old, held himself free from indignity, when he could say *Civis Romanus sum*; so also a British subject, in whatever land he may be, shall feel confident that the watchful eye and the strong arm of England, will protect him against injustice and wrong.[22]

Viscount Palmerston's statement would be pass to history as the *Civis Romanus sum* ('I am a citizen of Rome') speech.[23] The background of the speech was the Don Pacifico affair, one of the sharpest diplomatic disputes between Britain and Greece in the nineteenth century.[24] In 1847, private citizens caused severe damages to the property of David Pacifico, a Gibraltar-born British national, under the passive eyes of Greek authorities.[25] The case of Mr. Pacifico was one of several incidents involving grievances to British subjects on Greek soil.[26] The official position of Greece was that Mr. Pacifico could only seek diplomatic intervention by the British

---

[22]Henry John Temple (Third Viscount Palmerston), 'Speech on the *Don Pacifico* affair' (28 June 1850) Hansard's Parliamentary Debates CXII (Commons), Third Series 380, 387 and 444.

[23]Horst Dippel, 'A Nineteenth-Century Truman Doctrine *avant la lettre*? Constitutional Liberty Abroad and the Parliamentary Debate about British Foreign Policy from Castlereagh to Palmerston' in Kelly Grotke and Markus Prutsch (eds), *Constitutionalism, Legitimacy, and Power. Nineteenth-Century Experiences* (Oxford University Press, Oxford 2014) 23, 44. For a more detailed account of the debate and the reception of Palmerston's speech in the House of Commons see: Anthony Tollope, *Lord Palmerston* (Wm. Isbister Ltd., London 1882) 122-7.

[24]For a historical account of the *Don Pacifico* affair, see: Anthony Tollope, *Lord Palmerston* (Wm. Isbister Ltd., London 1882) 112-28; David Brown, *Palmerston and the Politics of Foreign Policy 1846-55* (Manchester University Press, New York 2002) 101-34; David Hannell, 'Lord Palmerston and the 'Don Pacifico Affair' of 1850. The Ionian Connection' (1989) 19 EHQ 495, 497 *et seq.*; James Brown Scott, *Cases on International Law* (West Publishing Co., St. Paul MN 1922) 510-3.

[25]David Hannell, 'Lord Palmerston and the 'Don Pacifico Affair' of 1850. The Ionian Connection' (1989) 19 EHQ 495, 497 (shortly summarizing the facts of the case); James Brown Scott, *Cases on International Law* (West Publishing Co., St. Paul MN 1922) 510-3 (providing a more detailed presentation of the incident).

[26]See generally: David Hannell, 'Lord Palmerston and the 'Don Pacifico Affair' of 1850. The Ionian Connection' (1989) 19 EHQ 495, 497.

Government upon a failed attempt to obtain justice from domestic courts.[27] Foreign Secretary Palmerston sought to force Greece to afford compensation and, to the surprise of the international community, ordered the naval blockade of the harbor of Pireaus.[28] Numerous states opposed Palmerston's 'gunboat diplomacy'.[29] As noted by a historian writing on the incident:

> Practically the whole of Europe was outraged with the measures pursued by Palmerston; both France and Russia sent strong protests to London.[30]

The naval blockade would have the most severe political consequences in Britain: Lord Stanley (Conservative Party) successfully brought a motion of censure against the administration of Prime Minister John Russel.[31] An opposite motion of confidence was however masterly submitted at the lower house,[32] opening the door to a vigorous discussion, which historians have depicted as 'the most splendid debate which ever occurred in the English House of Commons'.[33] A tight majority approved the motion.[34] Observers have stressed that '[t]here is no doubt that Palmerston's career and reputation were saved by the Commons' vote'.[35] It was precisely during this parliamentary debate at the House of Commons, which represented one of the most serious challenges he would face in his entire political career, that Viscount Palmerston held the *Civis Romanus sum* speech.[36]

Root's reliance on Palmerston's speech indicates that, in the prewar era, the minimum standard and the gunboat diplomacy were two sides of the same coin. Most importantly, the facts that motivated the blockade of Pireaus confirm that there was a close linkage between the emerging idea of a minimum standard of treatment and western powers' concern for the security of their citizens abroad.

---

[27]James Brown Scott, *Cases on International Law* (West Publishing Co., St. Paul MN 1922) 510.

[28]David Hannell, 'Lord Palmerston and the 'Don Pacifico Affair' of 1850. The Ionian Connection' (1989) 19 EHQ 495, 498.

[29]David Hannell, 'Lord Palmerston and the 'Don Pacifico Affair' of 1850. The Ionian Connection' (1989) 19 EHQ 495, 498.

[30]David Hannell, 'Lord Palmerston and the 'Don Pacifico Affair' of 1850. The Ionian Connection' (1989) 19 EHQ 495, 498.

[31]David Brown, *Palmerston and the Politics of Foreign Policy 1846-55* (Manchester University Press, New York 2002) 102; David Hannell, 'Lord Palmerston and the 'Don Pacifico Affair' of 1850. The Ionian Connection' (1989) 19 EHQ 495, 498.

[32]David Hannell, 'Lord Palmerston and the 'Don Pacifico Affair' of 1850. The Ionian Connection' (1989) 19 EHQ 495, 498.

[33]John McGilchrist, *Lord Palmerston. A Biography* (George Routledge & Sons, London 1865) 196.

[34]David Brown, *Palmerston and the Politics of Foreign Policy 1846-55* (Manchester University Press, New York 2002) 103; David Hannell, 'Lord Palmerston and the 'Don Pacifico Affair' of 1850. The Ionian Connection' (1989) 19 EHQ 495, 498.

[35]David Hannell, 'Lord Palmerston and the 'Don Pacifico Affair' of 1850. The Ionian Connection' (1989) 19 EHQ 495, 498.

[36]Henry John Temple (Third Viscount Palmerston), 'Speech on the *Don Pacifico* affair' (28 June 1850) Hansard's Parliamentary Debates CXII (Commons), Third Series 380, 380-444.

The gunboat diplomacy was not exclusively British. The German Empire also pursued a *Kanonenbootpolitik* for the advancement of Prussian economic interests overseas.[37] The peak of the gunboat diplomacy was precisely the Venezuelan blockade of 1902, a joint naval operation of Germany, Italy and Great Britain.[38] The operation sought to force the Government of Cipriano Castro to award adequate compensation to German, Italian and British subjects for injuries and losses sustained in the context of civil unrest.[39] The *Kanonenbootpolitik* was not without controversy in Berlin. Even before the blockade, prominent German politicians looked at other powers' interventions against weaker states with a critical eye.[40]

---

[37]For an analysis of the German *Kanonenbootpolitik* in Latin America see: Gerhard Wiechmann, 'Die Königlich Preußische Marine in Lateinamerika 1851 bis 1867. Ein Versuch deutscher Kanonenbootpolitik in Übersee' in Sandra Carreras and Günter Maihold (eds), *Preußen und Lateinamerika. Im Spannungsfeld von Kommerz, Macht und Kultur* (LIT Verlag, Münster 2004) 105-44. For a survey of Prussian interventions other regions of the world see: Cord Eberspächer, *Die deutsche Yangste-Patrouille. Deutsche Kanonenpolitik im Zeitalter des Imperialismus 1900-1914* (Winkler, Bochum 2004) 17-318 (particularly referring to interventions in China).

[38]See generally: Nancy Mitchell, *The Danger of Dreams. German and American Imperialism in Latin America* (The University of North Carolina Press, Chapel Hill NC 1999) 64-103.

[39]For detailed account of the events that motivated the blockade see: 'Grossbritanien – Denkschrift über die Beschwerde gegen Venezuela' in Gustav Roloff (ed), *Das Staatsarchiv. Sammlung der offiziellen Aktenstücke zur Geschichte der Gegenwart* (Volume 68: Duncker & Humblot, Berlin 1904) 121-5. See also: 'Der Reichskanzler Graf von Bülow an Kaiser Wilhelm' (1 September 1902) in Johanes Lepsius, Albrecht Mendelssohn and Friedrich Thimme (eds), *Die Große Politik der Europäischen Kabinette 1871-1914. Sammlung der Diplomatischen Akten des Auswärtigen Amtes* (Volume 17: Deutsche Verlagsgesellschaft für Politik und Geschichte, Berlin 1924) 244-5. For a historical analysis of the Venezuelan blockade see: Nancy Mitchell, *The Danger of Dreams. German and American Imperialism in Latin America* (The University of North Carolina Press, Chapel Hill NC 1999) 64-103.

[40]An interesting example appears in the records of the parliamentary debates regarding the FCN Agreement between the German Empire and the Republic of Colombia. Ludwig von Bar, who was simultaneously Member of the *Reichstag* and of the *Institut de Droit International*, questioned the effectiveness of the American interventions in South America. Von Bar considered that such measures usually caused the nationals of the intervening states to be treated with suspicion and distrust in the aftermath of the intervention. See: Reichstag, 'Protokoll – 68. Sitzung' (16 March 1893) *Stenographische Berichte über die Verhandlungen des Reichtags, VIII. Legislaturperiode, II. Session 1892/3* (Volume 3: Verlag der Norddeutschen Buchdruckerei, Berlin 1893) 1671, 1673.

The effectiveness and costs of the naval intervention were at the heart of intense debates at the *Reichstag*, particularly in January[41] and March[42] 1903. The joint action against Venezuela was intrinsically entangled with the emerging idea of an international minimum standard. In a communication addressed to German Emperor Wilhelm II, Chancellor Bernhard Graf von Bülow stated:

> The Venezuelan Government has repeatedly rejected our diplomatic intervention, invoking its own municipal legal provisions; we have pointed out that, under such principles, the national legislature would be able to exclude every form of diplomatic intervention [...] The actions of the Venezuelan Government shall be seen as a frivolous attempt to detach itself from its legal obligations [...] in the current civil wars significant German interests have been affected [...] *The Venezuelan rulers have apparently taken the view that German subjects living in their territories are unprotected, abandoned to their arbitrariness.* A severe action against Venezuela is urgently desirable, taking into consideration our image in Central and South America, as well as the substantial German interests to be protected there.[43]

---

[41] See: Reichstag, 'Protokoll – 241. Sitzung' (19 January 1903) *Stenographische Berichte über die Verhandlungen des Reichtags, X. Legislaturperiode, II. Session 1900/3* (Volume 8: Verlag der Norddeutschen Buchdruckerei, Berlin 1903) 7393, 7396-7 (intervention by Freiherr v. Thielman pertaining to the costs of the blockade); Reichstag, 'Protokoll – 242. Sitzung' (20 January 1903) *Stenographische Berichte über die Verhandlungen des Reichtags, X. Legislaturperiode, II. Session 1900/3* (Volume 8: Verlag der Norddeutschen Buchdruckerei, Berlin 1903) 7413, 7414 (intervention by v. Vollmar criticizing the use of force against Venezuela) and 7431-2 (response by Chancellor v. Büllow); Reichstag, 'Protokoll – 243. Sitzung' (21 January 1903) *Stenographische Berichte über die Verhandlungen des Reichtags, X. Legislaturperiode, II. Session 1900/3* (Volume 8: Verlag der Norddeutschen Buchdruckerei, Berlin 1903) 7437, 7451 (intervention by Mr. Schrader, making particular emphasis on the costs of the blockade and the role played by the Roosevelt administration); Reichstag, 'Protokoll – 244. Sitzung' (22 January 1903) *Stenographische Berichte über die Verhandlungen des Reichtags, X. Legislaturperiode, II. Session 1900/3* (Volume 8: Verlag der Norddeutschen Buchdruckerei, Berlin 1903) 7467, 7473 (intervention of Mr. Bebel, underscoring that those who made business in South America were well aware of the political risks attached to their ventures).

[42] Reichstag, 'Protokoll – 287. Sitzung' (19 March 1903) *Stenographische Berichte über die Verhandlungen des Reichtags, X. Legislaturperiode, II. Session 1900/3* (Volume 10: Verlag der Norddeutschen Buchdruckerei, Berlin 1903) 8717, 8718 (intervention by Freiherr v. Hertling, in defense of the German intervention), 8722-4 (intervention by Mr. Hasse, concluding Germany could have obtained a better result, and also discussing the role of the United States in the crisis), 8727-8 (intervention by Mr. Oertel, stating that Germany obtained the best result it could have possibly obtained out of the blockade) and 8734-5 (intervention by Mr. Gradnauer, criticizing the Government's actions). See also Chancellor v. Bülow's statements at pp. 8719-20 and 8729.

[43] Emphasis added. Author's translation. The original German text reads as follows: "Die venezolanische Regierung hat wiederholt unter Berufung auf ihre landesrechtlichen Vorschriften unsere diplomatische Einmischung abgelehnt, obwohl sie darauf hingewiesen wurde, daß bei solchen Grundsätzen jede diplomatische Vertretung durch die Landesgesetzgebung ausgeschlossen werden könnte [...] Das ganze Verhalten der venezolanischen Regierung muß als ein frivoler Versuch, sich ihren rechtlichen Verpflichtungen zu entziehen, bezeichnet werden [...] In dem gegenwärtigen Bürgerkriege sind von neuem erhebliche deutsche Interessen geschädigt worden [...] *Die Venezolanische Machthaber scheinen der Ansicht zu sein, daß die in ihrem Lande lebenden Deutschen ihrer Willkür schutzlos preisgegeben sind.* Ein scharfes Vorgehen gegen Venezuela dürfte daher schon im Hinblick auf unser Ansehen in Zentral- und Südamerika und

The Venezuelan blockade and, more generally, the use of the gunboat diplomacy in the American continent, cannot be properly understood without considering an additional political ingredient: the *Monroe Doctrine*. In 1823, President James Monroe announced that the United States would see the colonization by European powers of Latin American states as a threat to its own national security interests.[44] The reaction of Washington was the perhaps most significant concern of European powers considering military action as a means to enforce their citizens' claims against Latin American states. For example, the German Ambassador in London, Count Wolff-Metternich, described the concerns of the German Empire with regard to the Venezuelan Blockade in the following terms:

> I am well aware of the fact that the Imperial Government desires to diligently avoid any [action] which could understandably excite susceptibilities in the United States. I do not believe to be wrong in assuming that the British Government also has this very same wish. Good relations with the United States are for England as much useful and valuable as for us. On the other hand, if the one or the other American disapproves our plan against Venezuela based on an untenable interpretation of the Monroe doctrine, we should neither let him influence us, nor take [such statements] too seriously. The U.S. Government is conscious of the fact that we do not desire to establish ourselves in Venezuela, and it could have given us free hand to proceed against recalcitrant debtors.[45]

---

die dort zu schützenden großen deutschen Interessen dringend erwünscht sein." Emphasis added. 'Der Reichskanzler Graf von Bülow an Kaiser Wilhelm' (1 September 1902) in Johanes Lepsius, Albrecht Mendelssohn and Friedrich Thimme (eds), *Die Große Politik der Europäischen Kabinette 1871-1914. Sammlung der Diplomatischen Akten des Auswärtigen Amtes* (Volume 17: Deutsche Verlagsgesellschaft für Politik und Geschichte, Berlin 1924) 244-5. For a similar statement see: 'Der Reichskanzler Graf von Bülow an Kaiser Wilhelm' (3 November 1902) in Johanes Lepsius, Albrecht Mendelssohn and Friedrich Thimme (eds), *Die Große Politik der Europäischen Kabinette 1871-1914. Sammlung der Diplomatischen Akten des Auswärtigen Amtes* (Volume 17: Deutsche Verlagsgesellschaft für Politik und Geschichte, Berlin 1924) 248.

[44] The original formulation of the Monroe Doctrine appears in President James Monroe's message to the U.S. Congress of December 2nd, 1823: 'Message of the President of the United States, at the Commencement of the First Session of the Eighteenth Congress' 5 American State Papers: Foreign Relations (1858) 245, 246 and 250 ("the occasion has been judged proper for asserting as a principle in which the rights and interests of the United States are involved, that the American continents, by the free an independent condition which they have assumed and maintain, are henceforth not to be considered as subjects for future colonization by any European powers [. . .] We owe it, therefore, to candor, and to the amicable relations existing between the United States and those powers, to declare that we should consider any attempt on their part to extend their system, to any portion of this hemisphere as dangerous to our peace and safety"). For an analysis of the origin and historical context of the Monroe Doctrine see: Alejandro Álvarez, *The Monroe Doctrine. Its Importance in the International Life of the States of the New World* (Oxford University Press, New York 1924) 3-31.

[45] Author's translation. The original German text reads: "Ich wisse, daß die Kaiserliche Regierung den Wunsch hege, alles sorgfältig zu vermeiden, was in den Vereinigten Staaten berechtigte Empfindlichkeiten erregen könnte, und ich glaubte in der Annahme nicht fehl zu gehen, wenn ich auch bei der englischen Regierung diesen Wunsch voraussetze, da gute Beziehungen zu den Vereinigten Staaten für England ebenso nützlich und wertvoll seien wie für uns. Auf der anderen Seite dürften wir es aber nicht zu ernst nehmen und uns nicht davon beeinflussen lassen, wenn der eine oder der andere Amerikaner, auf einer unhaltbaren Auslegung der Monroedoktrin fußend, unser Vorgehen gegen Venezuela mißbillige. Die amerikanische Regierung wisse sehr wohl, daß

Wolff-Metternich might have underestimated the importance of the Monroe Doctrine in America. In the aftermath of the naval operation in Venezuela, the Roosevelt administration would reinterpret the Monroe Doctrine and claim a monopoly on military interventions in Latin America.[46] This policy crystallized in the so-called *Roosevelt Corollary*.[47] The new policy was announced in the President's annual message to Congress of December 6th, 1904:

> All that this country desires is to see the neighboring countries stable, orderly, and prosperous. Any country whose people conduct themselves well can count upon our hearty friendship. *If a nation shows that it knows how to act with reasonable efficiency and decency in social and political matters, if it keeps order and pays its obligations*, it need fear no interference from the United States. Chronic wrongdoing, *or an impotence which results in a general loosening of the ties of civilized society may in America*, as elsewhere, ultimately require intervention by some civilized nation, and in the Western Hemisphere the adherence of the United States to the Monroe Doctrine may force the United States, however reluctantly, in flagrant cases of such wrongdoing or impotence, to the exercise of an *international police power* [. . .] Our interests and those of our southern neighbors are in reality identical. They have great natural riches, and if within their borders the reign of law and justice obtains, prosperity is sure to come to them. While they thus obey the primary laws of civilized society they may rest assured that they will be treated by us in a spirit of cordial and helpful sympathy. We would interfere with them only in the last resort, and then only *if it came evident that their inability or unwillingness to do justice at home* and abroad had

---

wir uns nicht in Venezuela festzusetzen wünschten, und wir hätten von Ihr freie Hand erhalten, gegen den widerspenstigen Schuldner vorzugehen". 'Der Botschafter in London Graf von Metternich an das Auswärtige Amt' (15 December 1902) in Johanes Lepsius, Albrecht Mendelssohn and Friedrich Thimme (eds), *Die Große Politik der Europäischen Kabinette 1871-1914. Sammlung der Diplomatischen Akten des Auswärtigen Amtes* (Volume 17: Deutsche Verlagsgesellschaft für Politik und Geschichte, Berlin 1924) 262, 262-3. The note was addressed to the German Foreign Office and described Count Wolff-Metternich's own statements in a private meeting with the British Secretary of Foreign Affairs, Lord Lansdowne. For some additional examples see: 'Der Geschäftsträger in Washington Graf von Quadt an das Auswärtige Amt' (23 November 1902) in Johanes Lepsius, Albrecht Mendelssohn and Friedrich Thimme (eds), *Die Große Politik der Europäischen Kabinette 1871-1914. Sammlung der Diplomatischen Akten des Auswärtigen Amtes* (Volume 17: Deutsche Verlagsgesellschaft für Politik und Geschichte, Berlin 1924) 256, 256; 'Der Reichskanzler Graf von Bülow an Kaiser Wilhelm' (12 December 1902) in Johanes Lepsius, Albrecht Mendelssohn and Friedrich Thimme (eds), *Die Große Politik der Europäischen Kabinette 1871-1914. Sammlung der Diplomatischen Akten des Auswärtigen Amtes* (Volume 17: Deutsche Verlagsgesellschaft für Politik und Geschichte, Berlin 1924) 258, 258-9; 'Der Staatssekretär des Auswärtigen Amtes Freiherr von Richthofen an den Botschafter in London Grafen von Metternich' (14 December 1902) in Johanes Lepsius, Albrecht Mendelssohn and Friedrich Thimme (eds), *Die Große Politik der Europäischen Kabinette 1871-1914. Sammlung der Diplomatischen Akten des Auswärtigen Amtes* (Volume 17: Deutsche Verlagsgesellschaft für Politik und Geschichte, Berlin 1924) 260, 260-1.

[46]'Message of the President of the United States to the Senate and House of Representatives' (6 December 1904) *Papers relating to the Foreign Relations of the United States with the Annual Message of the President* (Government Printing Office, Washington 1905) ix, xli-xlii.

[47]On the political motivation of the 'Roosevelt Corollary' see: John Matthews, 'Roosevelt's Latin-American Policy' (1935) 29 Am. Pol. Sci. Rev. 805, 806-8. See also: Russell Crandall, *Gunboat Democracy. U.S. Interventions in the Dominican Republic, Grenada, and Panama* (Rowman & Littlefield, Lanham MD 2006) 11-16.

violated the rights of the United States *or had invited foreign aggression to the detriment of the entire body of American nations.*[48]

The reference to an 'impotence which results in a general loosening of the ties of civilized society', as opposed to a 'chronic wrongdoing', indicates that Roosevelt's policy was not only directed against states which actively commit international wrongs, but also against those states which are incapable of ensuring some measure of order and security within their borders.[49] President Theodore Roosevelt's own autobiography bears witness to this rationale:

> There are [. . .] weak nations so utterly incompetent either to protect the rights of foreigners against their own citizens, or to protect their own citizens against foreigners, that it becomes a matter of sheer duty for some outside power to interfere in connection with them.[50]

In those cases, Roosevelt seems to have applied what he believed to be 'the only safe rule' in U.S. foreign policy, namely, 'to promise little, and faithfully to keep every promise; to speak softly and carry a big stick'.[51] American military interventions were not an unusual phenomenon, neither before nor after Roosevelt's presidency. In many cases, the Department of the Navy merely sent warships to the shores of other states and threatened local authorities with the use of force.[52] In other cases, U.S. marines conducted operations on the ground.[53] This policy would be abandoned during the Hoover administration, and would come to a definitive end with the

---

[48]Emphasis added. 'Message of the President of the United States to the Senate and House of Representatives' (6 December 1904) *Papers relating to the Foreign Relations of the United States with the Annual Message of the President* (Government Printing Office, Washington 1905) ix, xli-xlii. President Roosevelt further stated that '[t]he strong arm of the Government in respect for its just rights in international matters is the Navy of the United States [. . .] There is no more patriotic duty before us as a people than to keep the Navy adequate to the needs of this country's position' (at p. xliii).

[49]'Message of the President of the United States to the Senate and House of Representatives' (6 December 1904) *Papers relating to the Foreign Relations of the United States with the Annual Message of the President* (Government Printing Office, Washington 1905) ix, xli-xlii.

[50]Theodore Roosevelt, *Theodore Roosevelt. An Autobiography* (The Macmillan Company, New York 1913) 576.

[51]Theodore Roosevelt, *Theodore Roosevelt. An Autobiography* (The Macmillan Company, New York 1913) 580. See also: 'Message of the President of the United States to the Senate and House of Representatives' (6 December 1904) *Papers relating to the Foreign Relations of the United States with the Annual Message of the President* (Government Printing Office, Washington 1905) ix, xxxix ("It is not merely unwise, it is contemptible, for a nation, as for an individual, to use high-sounding language to proclaim its purposes, or to take positions which are ridiculous if unsupported by potential force, and then to refuse to provide this force. If there is no intention of providing and of keeping the force necessary to back up a strong attitude, then it is far better not to assume such an attitude").

[52]See, for example: Martin Manning, 'Gunboat Diplomacy' in Alan McPherson (ed), *Encyclopedia of U.S. Military Interventions in Latin America* (ABC-Clio, Santa Barbara CA 2013) 261, 261-3.

[53]Milton Offutt, *The Protection of Citizens Abroad by the Armed Forces of the United States* (Klaus Reprint, New York 1972) 1 [first edition: 1928].

'good-neighbor policy' introduced by Secretary of State Cordell Hull and President Franklin D. Roosevelt in the 1930s.[54]

This bellicose policy of intervention was mostly applied in cases concerning the protection and security of U.S. citizens and their property in instable countries, which were the scenario of an unending cycle of insurrections, civil wars, revolutions and counterrevolutions.[55] The U.S. Navy Regulations of 1909 provide clear indication of the kind of cases in which the United States would pursue its 'gunboat diplomacy':

> The use of force against a foreign and friendly state, or against anyone within the territories thereof, is illegal. The right of self-preservation, however, is a right which belongs to states as well as to individuals, and in the case of states it includes the protection of the State, its honor, and its possessions, *and the lives and property of its citizens against arbitrary violence, actual or impending, whereby the State or its citizens may suffer irreparable injury* [. . .] In no case shall force be exercised in time of peace otherwise than as an application of the right of self-preservation as above defined. It must be used only as a last resort.[56]

The *Regulations* further included specific rules for the use of force, providing further evidence of the close connection between America's gunboat diplomacy and the host state's obligation to provide protection and security to aliens:

> Whenever in the application of the above-mentioned principles, it shall become necessary to land an armed force in foreign territory on occasions of political disturbance *where the local*

---

[54]On this policy change see generally: Alexander DeConde, *Herbert Hoover's Latin American Policy* (Stanford University Press, Stanford CA 1951) 13-89; Eric Paul Roorda, 'Good Neighbor Policy' in Alan McPherson (ed), *Encyclopedia of U.S. Military Interventions in Latin America* (ABC-Clio, Santa Barbara CA 2013) 235-9.

[55]See generally: Edwin Borchard, *The Diplomatic Protection of Citizens Abroad or the Law of International Claims* (The Banks Law Publishing Co., New York 1916) 448-50 (stating at p. 448 that 'the army or the navy have been frequently used for the protection of citizens or their property in foreign countries in cases of emergency where the local government has failed, through inability or unwillingness, to afford adequate protection to the persons or property of the foreigners in question' and elaborating further at pp. 448-53); Milton Offutt, *The Protection of Citizens Abroad by the Armed Forces of the United States* (Klaus Reprint, New York 1972) 1-2 [first edition: 1928] ("[Military interventions constitute a legitimate exercise of] the right of a state to protect by force its citizens living in a foreign country when sudden disturbances in the foreign state threaten the safety of their lives and property, and when the government under whose jurisdiction they reside has shown itself unwilling or unable to afford them reasonable protection"); Frederick Sherwood Dunn, *The Diplomatic Protection of Americans in Mexico* (Klaus Reprint, New York 1971) 1-2 [first edition: 1933] (explaining that the causes of diplomatic interposition in favor of American citizens in Mexico were mostly related to Mexico's 'long periods of political disorder, revolutions, inefficiency and corruption in governmental agencies, and constant financial difficulties, all of which made it extremely difficult, if not impossible, to provide the degree of security for life and property normally found in civilized states'; see also pp. 152-65). See also: Martin Manning, 'Gunboat Diplomacy' in Alan McPherson (ed), *Encyclopedia of U.S. Military Interventions in Latin America* (ABC-Clio, Santa Barbara CA 2013) 261-3; Arnulf Becker Lorca, *Mestizo International Law. A Global Intellectual History 1842-1933* (Cambridge University Press, New York 2013) 145-58.

[56]Emphasis added. *Regulations for the Government of the Navy of the United States* (Government Printing Office, Washington 1909) 86-7 § 342.

authorities are unable to give adequate protection to life and property, the assent of such authorities, or of some of them, shall be first obtained, *if it can be done without prejudice to the interests involved.*[57]

By contrast to the cases described in the *Regulations*, the United States maintained a policy of non-intervention in respect of other types of claims, including contract claims.[58] For a long time, prominent American international law scholars consistently considered that a breach of contract did not provide a suitable basis for diplomatic protection,[59] except for claims based on instruments of public debt.[60]

The examples discussed throughout this section reveal a close historical and political connection between the gunboat diplomacy, the emerging notion of a minimum standard of treatment, and the idea of an obligation upon the host state to ensure the protection and security of aliens within its territory. This political and historical context is also the reason why the protection obligation would also take center stage in Latin America's response to the interventions: the Calvo Doctrine.

---

[57]Emphasis added. *Regulations for the Government of the Navy of the United States* (Government Printing Office, Washington 1909) 87 § 343.

[58]United States Department of State, *Personal Instructions to the Diplomatic Agents of the United States* (Government Printing Office, Washington 1885) 28 § 134 ("[t]he interposition of diplomatic representatives is often asked by their countrymen to aid in the collection of claims against the government which they are accredited. If the claim is founded in contract, they must not interfere without specific instructions to do so. If it is founded in tort, they will, as a general rule, in like manner, seek previous instructions before interfering, unless the person of the claimant be assailed or there be pressing necessity for action in his behalf before they can communicate with the Department of State; in which event they will communicate in full the reasons for their actions"). This principle was reiterated in subsequent versions of the *Personal Instructions*. On the interpretation of this instruction, in its version of 1906, see: Edwin Borchard, *The Diplomatic Protection of Citizens Abroad or the Law of International Claims* (The Banks Law Publishing Co., New York 1916) 656-8. On practice of the U.S. Department of State as regards to contract claims see generally: Philip Jessup, 'Responsibility of States for Injuries to Individuals' (1946) 46 Colum. L. Rev. 903, 916; Philip Jessup, *A Modern Law of Nations* (The Macmillan Company, New York 1949) 109; Robert Jennings, 'State Contracts in International Law' (1961) 37 BYIL 156, 158-9. For the British approach to the exercise of diplomatic protection in connection with contract claims see: Richard Lillich, *International Claims: Postwar British Practice* (Syracuse University Press, New York 1967) 76.

[59]See, for example: Edwin Borchard, *The Diplomatic Protection of Citizens Abroad or the Law of International Claims* (The Banks Law Publishing Co., New York 1916) 282-3; Charles Cheney Hyde, *International Law. Chiefly as Interpreted and Applied by the United States* (Volume I: Little Brown & Co., Boston 1922) 375.

[60]Edwin Borchard, *The Diplomatic Protection of Citizens Abroad or the Law of International Claims* (The Banks Law Publishing Co., New York 1916) 282; Robert Jennings, 'State Contracts in International Law' (1961) 37 BYIL 156, 159.

4.3   Books from the South. The Doctrine of Equality and the Security Obligation

The gunboat diplomacy and the minimum standard were never without controversy. They were actively opposed in the south of the American continent. The Latin American republics could certainly not counter the naval and military power of Great Britain, the German Empire or the United States. So they resorted to the most effective means at their disposal: their intellectual elite. It has been observed that the members of this elite 'were as prolific as they were strategic'.[61] They not only managed to present their arguments within the existing canons of international law, but also to disseminate their ideas in Paris, London and other major centers of intellectual exchange.[62]

International law scholars from the semi-periphery would fiercely defend the interests of their home states, shaking the legal basis of both the Palmerston formula and the minimum standard.[63] In this regard, Latin American jurists resorted to a principle that already had some tradition in international law: the doctrine of equality. The argument of equality was simple: no state has an obligation to give foreigners a better treatment than the one afforded to its own nationals.[64] As a corollary, they argued, international responsibility can never attach where nationals and aliens are placed in the same conditions.[65] In the mid-nineteenth century the doctrine of equality would be increasingly associated to the name of a Uruguay-born Argentinean diplomat: Carlos Calvo.[66]

This section explores the relationship between the argument of equality and the customary security obligation. In this vein, it begins by analyzing the origins of the argument of equality before the publication of Calvo's treatise (1868) and providing evidence of its close connection with the problem of state responsibility for acts of individuals (e.g. mob violence). Thereafter, it considers the context and structure of Calvo's argument, making particular emphasis on his understanding of the security obligation. Finally, it presents a brief overview of the subsequent debate on Calvo's ideas before World War II.

---

[61] Arnulf Becker Lorca, *Mestizo International Law. A Global Intellectual History 1842-1933* (Cambridge University Press, New York 2014) 50.

[62] See generally: Arnulf Becker Lorca, *Mestizo International Law. A Global Intellectual History 1842-1933* (Cambridge University Press, New York 2014) 49-50.

[63] On the partial victories of Latin American international law scholars see, particularly, Sect. 4.3.3.

[64] Section 4.3.2 elaborates further on the content of the doctrine of equality.

[65] See Sects. 4.3.1 and 4.3.2.

[66] For a short presentation of the Calvo Doctrine see: Patrick Julliard, 'Calvo Doctrine/Calvo Clause' in Rüdiger Wolfrum (ed), *The Max Planck Encyclopedia of Public International Law* (Volume 1: Oxford University Press, New York 2012) 1086, 1086-7.

4.3.1   The Doctrine of Equality Before Carlos Calvo

As stated beforehand, Latin American jurists pleading against the minimum standard posited that states fully discharge their obligations in respect of foreign citizens by giving them the same treatment as to their own nationals.[67] To be sure, the doctrine of equality never entailed a rejection of the host state's obligation to give protection and security to aliens. Evidence of the notion of FPS can be found in the sometimes called 'prehistory of international law', long before the idea of an objective minimum standard of treatment appeared in the international arena.[68] For that very same reason, it was possible for scholars and diplomats to simultaneously oppose the 'minimum standard' and recognize the existence of the customary security obligation.

Moreover, in the first decades of the nineteenth century it was not unusual to define the obligation to grant protection and security to aliens in terms of national treatment.[69] A noteworthy example is the FCN Treaty concluded between Chile and the United States on May 16th, 1832.[70] While establishing that aliens shall enjoy 'special protection', the treaty defined the content of the obligation by reference to the doctrine of equality.[71] The Chilean Congress moreover conditioned ratification upon approval of an Explanatory Convention limiting the scope of the judicial

---

[67]Martins Paparinskis, *The International Minimum Standard and Fair and Equitable Treatment* (Oxford University Press, Oxford 2013) 24 (particularly referring to Carlos Calvo).

[68]For the historical origins of the FPS standard see Chap. 3. For the notion of a 'prehistory of international law' see: Martti Koskenniemi, 'International Law and *raison d'état*: Rethinking the Prehistory of International Law' in Benedict Kingsbury and Benjamin Straumann (eds), *The Roman Foundations of the Law of Nations. Alberico Gentili and the Justice of Empire* (Oxford University Press, New York 2010) 297, 297-99 (arguing that the actual origins of modern international law lie, not in the Western-European sixteenth century, but in the late 1860s; according Koskenniemi earlier theories and developments are better characterized 'as a 'prehistory of international law') See also: Martti Koskenniemi, *The Gentle Civilizer of Nations. The Rise and Fall of International Law 1870-1960* (Cambridge University Press, New York 2008) 3-4.

[69]See: Frank Griffith Dawson, 'The Influence of Andrés Bello on Latin-American Perceptions on Non-Intervention and State Responsibility' (1986) 57 BYIL 253, 289-92 (providing numerous examples of this treaty practice, including the Chile-US treaty of 1832).

[70]Treaty of Peace, Amity, Navigation, and Commerce between the United States of America and the Republic of Chile (adopted 16 May 1832, entered into force 29 April 1834) Hunter Miller (ed), *Treaties and Other International Acts of the United States of America* (Volume 3: Government Printing Office, Washington 1971) 671, 671-95.

[71]Treaty of Peace, Amity, Navigation, and Commerce between the United States of America and the Republic of Chile (adopted 16 May 1832, entered into force 29 April 1834) Hunter Miller (ed), *Treaties and Other International Acts of the United States of America* (Volume 3: Government Printing Office, Washington 1971) 671, 677-8 art. 10 ("Both the contracting parties promise and engage formally to give their *special protection* to the persons and property of the citizens of each other, of all occupations, who may be in the territories subject to the jurisdiction of the one or the other, transient or dwelling therein, leaving open and free to them the tribunals of justice *on the same terms which are usual and customary with the natives or citizens of the country in which they may be"* – emphasis added).

protection owed to American citizens to the 'most perfect equality' with Chilean citizens,[72] a condition that would be finally accepted by the United States.[73] These provisions represented a small victory of Chilean foreign policy. Chile took international affairs seriously. The Government entrusted the negotiations to the Venezuelan jurist Andrés Bello, one of the forerunners of international law scholarship in Latin America.[74] Acting on behalf of Chile, Bello signed both the FCN treaty and the Explanatory Convention.[75] To-date, many specialists believe that Bello was the true father of the 'Calvo Doctrine'.[76] The Chile-US treaty of 1832 seems thus premonitory of the Latin American appeal to the doctrine of equality, which would be at the heart of numerous diplomatic controversies during the subsequent decades,[77] and is still present in the municipal legal systems of some South American states.[78]

---

[72]See: 'Mr. Hamm, *Chargé d'Affaires*, to Mr. Livingston, Sec. of State' (5 October 1832) Hunter Miller (ed), *Treaties and Other International Acts of the United States of America* (Volume 3: Government Printing Office, Washington 1971) 704.

[73]Additional and Explanatory Convention to the Treaty of Peace, Amity, Commerce and Navigation concluded in the City of Santiago on the 16th Day of May of 1832 between the United States of America and the Republic of Chile (adopted 1 September 1833, entered into force 29 April 1834) Hunter Miller (ed), *Treaties and Other International Acts of the United States of America* (Volume 3: Government Printing Office, Washington 1971) 695, 697-8 art. 2 ("[I]t is mutually understood, that the Republic of Chile is only bound by the aforesaid stipulation to maintain the most perfect equality in this respect between American and Chilean citizens, the former to enjoy all the rights and benefits of the present or future provisions which the laws grant to the latter in their judicial tribunals, but not special favors of privileges"). For the diplomatic note containing the instructions of U.S. Secretary of State Edward Livingston on the Chilean proposal see: 'Instructions from Secretary of State Livingston on the Additional and Explanatory Convention to the Treaty of Peace, Amity, Commerce and Navigation between the United States of America and the Republic of Chile' (19 April 1833) in Hunter Miller (ed), *Treaties and Other International Acts of the United States of America* (Volume 3: Government Printing Office, Washington 1971) 704.

[74]On Bello's role in the negotiations see: Frank Griffith Dawson, 'The Influence of Andrés Bello on Latin-American Perceptions on Non-Intervention and State Responsibility' (1986) 57 BYIL 253, 260.

[75]Treaty of Peace, Amity, Navigation, and Commerce between the United States of America and the Republic of Chile (adopted 16 May 1832, entered into force 29 April 1834) Hunter Miller (ed), *Treaties and Other International Acts of the United States of America* (Volume 3: Government Printing Office, Washington 1971) 671, 695; Additional and Explanatory Convention to the Treaty of Peace, Amity, Commerce and Navigation concluded in the City of Santiago on the 16th Day of May of 1832 between the United States of America and the Republic of Chile (adopted 1 September 1833, entered into force 29 April 1834) Hunter Miller (ed), *Treaties and Other International Acts of the United States of America* (Volume 3: Government Printing Office, Washington 1971) 695, 699.

[76]For some representative examples see: Edwin Borchard, 'The "Minimum Standard" of the Treatment of Aliens' (1940) 38(4) Mich. L. Rev. 445, 450; Frank Griffith Dawson, 'The Influence of Andrés Bello on Latin-American Perceptions on Non-Intervention and State Responsibility' (1986) 57 BYIL 253, 285-303 and 311-15; Santiago Montt, *State Liability in Investment Treaty Arbitration* (Hart Publishing, Oxford 2009) 41-4.

[77]Examples are provided later in this section.

[78]An indicative example of a modern appeal to the doctrine may be found in article 320(II) of the Bolivian Constitution, whereby: "[e]very foreign investment shall be subject to the jurisdiction, the laws and the authorities of Bolivia, and no one shall be entitled to invoke exceptions or to resort to

The doctrine of equality was not a Latin American invention, though. Its origins could be traced as far back as to the works of prominent representatives of Spanish Scholasticism.[79] Most importantly, the argument of equality had also been advanced by some capital-exporting states in the mid-nineteenth century.[80] In times of the gunboat diplomacy the United States itself had occasionally pursued this line of argument.[81] The perhaps clearest examples of this position appear in the correspondence of Secretary of State Daniel Webster during the Fillmore administration.[82] In a communication to the President pertaining to the *Trasher* incident (1851), Webster stated:

> No man can carry the aegis of his national American liberty into a foreign country, and expect to hold it up for his exemption from the dominion and authority of the laws and the

---

diplomatic claims to obtain a more favorable treatment." Author's translation. The original Spanish text reads: "Toda inversión extranjera estará sometida a la jurisdicción, a las leyes y a las autoridades bolivianos; y nadie podrá invocar situación de excepción, ni apelar a reclamaciones diplomáticas para obtener un tratamiento más favorable." Constitución del Estado Plurinacional de Bolivia (adopted 7 February 2009) [https://www.oas.org/dil/esp/Constitucion_Bolivia.pdf] art. 320(I).

[79]For a representative example see: Francisco de Vitoria, 'De Indis et de Iure Belli Reflectiones' (1532) in James Brown Scott (ed), *Classics of International Law* (John Pawley Bate tr, Carnegie Institution, Washington 1917) 154 ("[I]f there be any persons who wish to acquire a domicile in some State of the Indians [...] *they enjoy the privileges of citizens just as others do, provided that they also submit to the burdens to which others submit*" – emphasis added). On the doctrine of equality in the theories of Vitoria see: Anthony Anghie, 'Francisco de Vitoria and the Colonial Origins of International Law' (1996) 5 Soc. Leg. Stud. 321, 325-7; Orestes Araújo, *Las doctrinas internacionalistas de Fray Francisco de Vitoria* (Universidad de Montevideo, Montevideo 1948); Muthucumaraswamy Sornarajah, *The International Law on Foreign Investment* (Cambridge University Press, New York 2010) 19. See also: Sebastián Mantilla Blanco, *Justizielles Unrecht im internationalen Investitionsschutzrecht* (Nomos, Baden-Baden 2016) 53 n. 120 (quoting these and other sources in this regard).

[80]An indicative example appears in a note sent by Prince Felix zu Schwarzenberg to the Austrian Embassy in London on April 14th, 1850. On that occasion, the Prince instructed his Ambassador to present a strong protest against the actions undertaken by Lord Palmerston for the protection of British subjects affected by the Italian civil disturbances of 1849. In this connection, Schwarzenberg claimed that foreigners are not entitled to a greater protection from the host state than that enjoyed by the natives. See: 'Note du Cabinet de Vienne' (14 April 1850) in Carlos Calvo, 'De la non-responsabilité des états a raison des pertes et dommages éprouvés par des étrangers en temps de troubles intérieurs ou de guerres civiles' (1869) 1 Revue de droit international et de législation comparée 417, 419 ("quelque disposées que pussent être les nations civilisées d'Europe à étendre les limites du droit de protection, jamais cependant elles ne la seraient au point d'accorder aux étrangers des privilèges que les lois territoriales ne garantissent pas aux nationaux").

[81]See: J. Patrick Kelly, 'Customary International Law in Historical Context: The Exercise of Power Without General Acceptance' in Brian Lepard (ed), Reexamining Customary International Law (Cambridge University Press, Cambridge 2017) 47, 70; Martins Paparinskis, *The International Minimum Standard and Fair and Equitable Treatment* (Oxford University Press, Oxford 2013) 28; Sebastián Mantilla Blanco, *Justizielles Unrecht im internationalen Investitionsschutzrecht* (Nomos, Baden-Baden 2016) 54.

[82]Cf. Charles Fenwick, *International Law* (The Century Co., New York 1924) 392-3 (particularly mentioning the New Orleans riots of 1851, discussed later in this section).

sovereign power of that country, unless he be authorized to do so by virtue of treaty stipulations.[83]

In the same document, Webster explained:

[Public law] does in no case impart to foreigners residing in any country privileges which are denied to its own citizens or subjects, except, perhaps, that of leaving the country.[84]

These statements were consistent with Webster's response to claims filed by foreign governments against the United States.[85] In 1851, for example, private individuals had damaged the property of Spanish nationals in Louisiana, apparently enraged by the prosecution of a group of American outlaws in Cuba.[86] The crowd further destroyed the Spanish Consulate in New Orleans, forcing the Consul to leave the city for security reasons.[87] The Government of Queen Isabella II of Spain raised a claim for compensation before the State Department.[88] While the administration of President Millard Fillmore admitted responsibility on account of the damages inflicted to the Consul, the U.S. Government denied any liability for the losses sustained by private Spanish subjects.[89] In this regard, Secretary Webster explained:

[Spanish subjects] are entitled to such protection as is afforded to our own citizens. While, therefore, the losses of individuals, private Spanish subjects, are greatly to be regretted, yet it is understood that many American citizens suffered equal loses from the same cause. And these private individuals, subjects of Her Catholic Majesty, coming voluntary to reside in the United States, have certainly no cause of complaint, if they are protected by the same law and by the same administration of law, as native born citizens of this country.[90]

---

[83]'Mr. Webster to the President of the United States' (23 December 1851) *The Works of Daniel Webster* (Volume 6: Charles C. Little and James Brown, Boston 1851) 521, 528. The *Trasher* incident concerned the case of Mr. John Trasher, an American citizen resident in Cuba, who had been convicted for treason against the Spanish Crown, and sentenced to prison and forced labor in Spain (at p. 522).

[84]'Mr. Webster to the President of the United States' (23 December 1851) *The Works of Daniel Webster* (Volume 6: Charles C. Little and James Brown, Boston 1851) 521, 528.

[85]See: John Bassett Moore, *A Digest of International Law* (Volume 6: Government Printing Office, Washington 1906) 811-5 (referring to the New Orleans riots of 1851).

[86]For a short account of the facts see: Francis Mitchell, 'International Liability for Mob Injuries' (1900) 34 Am. L. Rev. 709, 714-5.

[87]Francis Mitchell, 'International Liability for Mob Injuries' (1900) 34 Am. L. Rev. 709, 714; Henry St. George Tucker, *Limitations on the Treaty Making Power under the Constitution of the United States* (Little, Brown, and Co., Boston 1915) 240.

[88]Henry St. George Tucker, *Limitations on the Treaty Making Power under the Constitution of the United States* (Little, Brown, and Co., Boston 1915) 240.

[89]For the full text of the diplomatic note see: 'Mr. Webster to Mr. Calderón' (13 November 1851) in Henry St. George Tucker, *Limitations on the Treaty Making Power under the Constitution of the United States* (Little, Brown, and Co., Boston 1915) 242-4. For a more detailed account of the diplomatic incident see: Francis Mitchell, 'International Liability for Mob Injuries' (1900) 34 Am. L. Rev. 709, 714-5.

[90]'Mr. Webster to Mr. Calderón' (13 November 1851) in Henry St. George Tucker, *Limitations on the Treaty Making Power under the Constitution of the United States* (Little, Brown, and Co., Boston 1915) 242, 243.

In the following decades, there was no clarity within the State Department as to whether Webster's note of 1851 represented the settled diplomatic doctrine of the U.S. Government. In 1875, in the context of a diplomatic incident involving private injuries to American citizens in Brazil, Secretary Hamilton Fish would take distance from Webster's approach by stating that '[Webster's views] might have been different, especially if the sufferers should have been without remedy through the courts'.[91] Nonetheless, in 1881 and 1882, the State Department would rely once again on the doctrine of equality in its response to a Chinese diplomatic complaint pertaining to injuries inflicted to Chinese residents by a xenophobic mob in the State of Colorado.[92] A few years later, in 1887, Secretary of State Frelinghuysen quoted Webster's note of 1851 and stressed:

> This principle is therefore to be regarded as adjudicated and established by the highest international and domestic authority in accordance with the enunciation above given.[93]

In many other cases, the U.S. Government agreed to compensate the victims of violent crowds, but carefully clarified that such payments entailed no recognition of international responsibility.[94] The varying and somewhat erratic diplomatic practice of the State Department in this regard turned the doctrine of equality into a valuable

---

[91]'Note of Mr. Fish, Sec. of State, to Mr. Partidge' (27 February 1875) in Francis Wharton (ed), *A Digest of the International Law of the United States. Documents issued by Presidents and Secretaries of State* (Volume 2: Government Printing Office, Washington 1887) 602, 602.

[92]See: 'Mr. Blaine to Chen Lan Pin' (25 March 1881) *Papers relating to the Foreign Relations of the United States with the Annual Message of the President* (Government Printing Office, Washington 1882) 335, 336 (observing that the US-China FCN agreement of 1858 did not grant Chinese nationals protection beyond national treatment and explaining that '[t]he subjects of China, in respect of their rights and security of person and property, are placed under the protection of the laws of the United States in manner and measure equal to that extended to native citizens of this country'); 'Mr. Evarts to Chen Lan Pin' (30 December 1880) *Papers relating to the Foreign Relations of the United States with the Annual Message of the President* (Government Printing Office, Washington 1882) 319, 319 ("[i]t affords me pleasure to assure you that no only in Denver, but in every other part of the United States, the protection of this Government will always be, as it always has been, freely and fully given to the natives of China resident in the country, in the same manner and to the same extent as it is afforded to our own citizens"). On the Denver riot see also: John Bassett Moore, *A Digest of International Law* (Volumes 1-6: Government Printing Office, Washington 1906) 820 *et seq.* For an additional example of this diplomatic practice see: John Bassett Moore, *A Digest of International Law* (Volume 4: Government Printing Office, Washington 1906) 2 (at § 534). For a discussion of these and other incidents see: Francis Mitchell, 'International Liability for Mob Injuries' (1900) 34 Am. L. Rev. 709, 716 *et seq.*; Charles Fenwick, *International Law* (The Century Co., New York 1924) 392-3.

[93]'Note of Mr. Frelinghuysen, Sec. of State, to Mr. Morgan' (15 November 1883) in Francis Wharton (ed), *A Digest of the International Law of the United States. Documents issued by Presidents and Secretaries of State* (Volume 2: Government Printing Office, Washington 1887) 679, 687.

[94]For a critical analysis of nineteenth-century American state practice in this area, see: Francis Mitchell, 'International Liability for Mob Injuries' (1900) 34 Am. L. Rev. 709, 714-21; Charles Cheney Hyde, *International Law. Chiefly as Interpreted and Applied by the United States* (Volume I: Little Brown & Co., Boston 1922) 516-22; Charles Fenwick, *International Law* (The Century Co., New York 1924) 392-3.

tool for Latin American diplomats dealing with the threat of the gunboat diplomacy. The Chilean Ministry of Foreign Affairs, for example, masterly quoted Secretary Webster's note of 1851 in its response to claims for compensation formulated by the United States in 1852.[95]

The Chilean diplomatic correspondence from those years provides some of the earliest examples of the use of the argument of equality in Latin America. The argument was normally advanced in cases concerning mob injuries to European nationals and U.S. citizens.[96] There are good reasons to believe that the man behind the argument was precisely the Venezuelan jurist Andrés Bello, who was by then employed as a Chief Legal Officer at the Ministry of Foreign Affairs.[97] The first example would be a communication from Foreign Minister Antonio Varas to the American *chargé d'affaires* in Santiago de Chile, dated December 20th, 1852:

> The duty upon the state to protect the person and property of the foreign national is discharged in the most favorable and generous manner when he [the foreigner] is treated in the same way as the native; no nation can be demanded to establish a privilege in respect of them [...] With regard to the liability arising from acts of the subjects of a state, the rule is that the state only assumes responsibility when those acts are executed under its shelter, [i.e.] when it authorizes them through its own sovereignty or by according the perpetrators protection. In the present case, the acts were directed against the authority of the state itself; they echoed a rebellion that the Government would readily repress, and which it has [now] repelled with determination by all available means. Such calamities, which all countries have faced at some point [in history], are among the many events that cause harm both to the natives and to aliens dwelling in the country.[98]

---

[95] 'Antonio Varas al señor Peyton, Enviado Extraordinario y Ministro Plenipotenciario de los Estados Unidos de América' (20 December 1852) in Rafael Caldera (ed), *Obras completas de Andrés Bello/Derecho internacional IV. Documentos de la Cancillería Chilena* (Volume XIII: Fundación La Casa de Bello, Caracas 1981) 481, 482-3. For another example see: 'Antonio Varas al señor Cazotte, Encargado de Negocios de la República Francesa' (29 December 1852) in Rafael Caldera (ed), *Obras completas de Andrés Bello/Derecho internacional IV. Documentos de la Cancillería Chilena* (Volume XIII: Fundación La Casa de Bello, Caracas 1981) 490, 498-9.

[96] For some examples see: Rafael Caldera (ed), *Obras completas de Andrés Bello/Derecho internacional IV. Documentos de la Cancillería Chilena* (Volume XIII: Fundación La Casa de Bello, Caracas 1981) 481 *et seq.* (discussed later in this section).

[97] Frank Griffith Dawson, 'The Influence of Andrés Bello on Latin-American Perceptions on Non-Intervention and State Responsibility' (1986) 57 BYIL 253, 260.

[98] Author's translation. The original Spanish text reads: "El deber de protección del Estado respecto a la persona y propiedad del extranjero, se cumple del modo más favorable y generoso cuando se trata de la misma manera que al nacional, sin que de país alguno pueda exigirse que establezca respecto de ellos preferencia [...] En materia de responsabilidad por actos de súbditos de un Estado, la regla es que el Estado sólo asume responsabilidad cuando bajo su amparo se ejecutan estos actos, cuando los autoriza con su soberanía o protección dispensada a los autores. En el presente caso los actos han sido dirigidos contra la autoridad misma del Estado, han sido un eco de la sublevación que el Gobierno combaría en ese momento y que ha combatido con todo empeño, empleando todos los elementos que estaban en su mano. Esa calamidad a que todos los países se han visto sujetos, entra en la línea de otros mil acontecimientos que perjudican a los naturales y extranjeros que habitan el país." 'Antonio Varas al señor Peyton, Enviado Extraordinario y Ministro Plenipotenciario de los Estados Unidos de América' (20 December 1852) in Rafael Caldera (ed), *Obras completas de*

A few days later, a similar note was sent to the French Minister. The second diplomatic note also referred to the duty to provide security for foreign citizens, and went on to characterize national treatment as the greatest liberality a host state can offer as regards to the treatment of aliens.[99] This note was much more detailed than the one addressed to the American Government and may, without hesitation, be regarded as a true legal masterpiece. The Chilean Minister based his argument on principles of natural justice, heavily relying on prominent European scholars, such as Vattel.[100] The note further explained the inconvenience of recognizing a special right to compensation in favor of foreign nationals.[101] Such privilege could awake resentment against aliens and would also place an unbearable burden upon states.[102] In this vein, the Chilean Government observed:

> [I]nternal disorders, riots and civil revolutions have been extremely recurrent, and almost no country from those who call themselves "civilized" has remained free from such scourges.[103]

The letter additionally quoted a handful of cases where western powers actually relied on the doctrine of equality, amusingly qualifying those states as '[the] nations which in the general community conform the aristocracy, i.e., those transforming their own principles into rules'.[104] In response to the French Government's appeal to reciprocity, the Chilean Note included a deep analysis of French municipal

---

Andrés Bello/Derecho internacional IV. Documentos de la Cancillería Chilena (Vol. XIII: Fundación La Casa de Bello, Caracas 1981) 481, 488.

[99] For the full text of the note see: 'Antonio Varas al señor Cazotte, Encargado de Negocios de la República Francesa' (29 December 1852) in Rafael Caldera (ed), *Obras completas de Andrés Bello/ Derecho internacional IV. Documentos de la Cancillería Chilena* (Vol. XIII: Fundación La Casa de Bello, Caracas 1981) 490, 490-505.

[100] See: 'Antonio Varas al señor Cazotte, Encargado de Negocios de la República Francesa' (29 December 1852) in Rafael Caldera (ed), *Obras completas de Andrés Bello/Derecho internacional IV. Documentos de la Cancillería Chilena* (Vol. XIII: Fundación La Casa de Bello, Caracas 1981) 490, 492-3.

[101] 'Antonio Varas al señor Cazotte, Encargado de Negocios de la República Francesa' (29 December 1852) in Rafael Caldera (ed), *Obras completas de Andrés Bello/Derecho internacional IV. Documentos de la Cancillería Chilena* (Vol. XIII: Fundación La Casa de Bello, Caracas 1981) 490, 496.

[102] 'Antonio Varas al señor Cazotte, Encargado de Negocios de la República Francesa' (29 December 1852) in Rafael Caldera (ed), *Obras completas de Andrés Bello/Derecho internacional IV. Documentos de la Cancillería Chilena* (Vol. XIII: Fundación La Casa de Bello, Caracas 1981) 490, 496.

[103] Author's translation. The original Spanish text reads: "las revueltas intestinas, los motines y revoluciones civiles han sido en extremo frecuentes, y raro país, de los que se llaman civilizados, se han visto libres de este azote". 'Antonio Varas al señor Cazotte, Encargado de Negocios de la República Francesa' (29 December 1852) in Rafael Caldera (ed), *Obras completas de Andrés Bello/ Derecho internacional IV. Documentos de la Cancillería Chilena* (Vol. XIII: Fundación La Casa de Bello, Caracas 1981) 490, 496.

[104] Author's translation. The original Spanish text reads: "las naciones que en la comunidad general forman la aristocracia, las que hacen pasar a regla los principios que adoptan." 'Antonio Varas al señor Cazotte, Encargado de Negocios de la República Francesa' (29 December 1852) in Rafael

legislation and convincingly explained that a reasonable French court applying local law would reject the arguments of the French *chargé d'affaires*.[105]

The argument of equality would soon make its way from diplomatic correspondence and international treaties to scholarly writings. In the 1860s, the Colombian statesman José María Torres Caicedo published one of the most detailed defenses of the doctrine of equality of the nineteenth century.[106] The core of Torres' argument was that 'neither positive nor customary international law grant to foreigners greater rights than [those enjoyed by] nationals'.[107] It must be noted, however, that Torres Caicedo postulated the equality argument in particular connection with the question of state responsibility for revolutions and civil disorders.[108] This is hardly surprising. This was precisely what the political dispute had always been about.

4.3.2   The New Guise of an Old Idea: The Calvo Doctrine and the Security Obligation

By the end of the 1860s, the argument of equality would find its most famous and influential expression in Carlos Calvo's *Derecho internacional teórico y práctico de Europa y América* (1868):

> One of the most important international law issues that have been discussed in recent times concerns the liability of governments for the losses and damages caused by factions to foreigners. This matter has such a paramount importance that it could not only affect the international rights of states but even their own legislation, which is exclusive and particular to each people [. . .] But the implications [of such liability] would go far beyond that. It

---

Caldera (ed), *Obras completas de Andrés Bello/Derecho internacional IV. Documentos de la Cancillería Chilena* (Vol. XIII: Fundación La Casa de Bello, Caracas 1981) 490, 497-8.

[105]See: 'Antonio Varas al señor Cazotte, Encargado de Negocios de la República Francesa' (29 December 1852) in Rafael Caldera (ed), *Obras completas de Andrés Bello/Derecho internacional IV. Documentos de la Cancillería Chilena* (Vol. XIII: Fundación La Casa de Bello, Caracas 1981) 490, 500-4.

[106]José María Torres Caicedo, 'Importante cuestión de derecho de gentes. A propósito del conflicto venezolano-hispano en 1860' in José María Torres Caicedo, *Unión Latino-Americana* (Librería de Rosa y Bouret, Paris 1865) 307, 307-81. A first edition of Torres Caicedo's work had appeared some years before, in the *Correo de Ultramar*. For an author attributing the Calvo Doctrine to Torres Caicedo see: Luis A. Podestá Costa, 'La responsabilidad del Estado por daños irrogados a la persona o a los bienes de extranjeros en luchas civiles' (1938) 67/8 Revista de Derecho Internacional 5, 7-8 (and n. 5-6).

[107]Author's translation. The original Spanish text reads: "[e]l derecho de gentes positivo y el consuetudinario no acuerdan á los extranjeros mas derechos que á los nacionales." José María Torres Caicedo, 'Importante cuestión de derecho de gentes. A propósito del conflicto venezolano-hispano en 1860' in José María Torres Caicedo, *Unión Latino-Americana* (Librería de Rosa y Bouret, Paris 1865) 307, 313.

[108]See: José María Torres Caicedo, 'Importante cuestión de derecho de gentes. A propósito del conflicto venezolano-hispano en 1860' in José María Torres Caicedo, *Unión Latino-Americana* (Librería de Rosa y Bouret, Paris 1865) 307, 307-81.

would imply granting an unjustifiable privilege to the benefit of foreigners and to the detriment of nationals. If these [nationals] do not have any right to request compensation for losses and damages, how could others earn such a right? The immediate, and indeed unavoidable, implication of recognizing that principle would be to accept two great inequalities and two enormous privileges: an internal [inequality], as a privilege for foreign nationals, and an external [inequality], as a [privilege] for the strongest State.[109]

Calvo elaborated further on this argument in a second (revisited and extended) edition of the treatise, which was written in French and was therefore much more accessible for the Western-European audience.[110] Contemporary authors have argued that the exclusion or restraint of international responsibility for private violence was the political core of the Calvo Doctrine.[111] This might be true. As it had been the case of other champions of the doctrine of equality, such as José M. Torres Caicedo,[112] Calvo's views on the law of aliens were closely and essentially linked to his rejection of the Palmerston formula and the recurrent use of the gunboat diplomacy in the Western Hemisphere.[113]

In his Spanish treatise (1868), Calvo quoted Vattel's exposition of the obligation to provide security to aliens, emphasizing its non-absolute character.[114] The works for Vattel were useful for advancing Latin American political interests. To begin with, the views of Vattel were generally accepted as an authoritative exposition of

---

[109]Author's translation. The original Spanish text reads as follows: "Una de las cuestiones más importantes de derecho internacional discutida en los tiempos modernos, es la referente á la responsabilidad que incumbe a los gobiernos por los daños y perjuicios que causen las facciones á los extranjeros. Es tal la importancia de este asunto, que su desenlace puede afectar no sólo á los derechos internacionales de los Estados, sino también á la legislación propia, exclusiva, particular de cada pueblo [...] Mas no supondría solamente lo que acabamos de decir, sino que equivaldría á conceder un privilegio injustificable á favor de los extranjeros y contrario á los naturales. Si estos no tienen derecho alguno á exigir que se les resarza de los daños y perjuicios que hayan sufrido ¿cómo han de tenerle los demás? La consecuencia inmediata, ineludible, de reconocer semejante principio sería el sostenimiento de dos grandes desigualdades y de dos enormes privilegios: una interior, privilegio de los extranjeros, y otra exterior, que lo sería del Estado mas fuerte." Carlos Calvo, *Derecho internacional teórico y práctico de Europa y América* (Volume 1: D'Amyot Librairie Diplomatique & Durand et Pedone, Paris 1868) 387-8 § 291.

[110]Carlos Calvo, *Le droit international théorique et pratique précédé d'un exposé historique des progrès de la science du droit des gens* (Volume 3: Rousseau, Paris 1896) 142 § 1280.

[111]See, for example: Martins Paparinskis, *The International Minimum Standard and Fair and Equitable Treatment* (Oxford University Press, Oxford 2013) 23 n. 72 and 26.

[112]See Sect. 4.3.1.

[113]See: Carlos Calvo, *Derecho internacional teórico y práctico de Europa y América* (Volume 1: D'Amyot Librairie Diplomatique & Durand et Pedone, Paris 1868) 136-96 at § 76-94; Carlos Calvo, *Le droit international théorique et pratique précédé d'un exposé historique des progrès de la science du droit des gens* (Volume 1: Rousseau, Paris 1896) 266-355 §§ 110-209; Carlos Calvo, *Le droit international théorique et pratique précédé d'un exposé historique des progrès de la science du droit des gens* (Volume 3: Rousseau, Paris 1896) 142-3 § 1281.

[114]Carlos Calvo, *Derecho internacional teórico y práctico de Europa y América* (Volume 1: D'Amyot Librairie Diplomatique & Durand et Pedone, Paris 1868) 392 at § 293. See also: Carlos Calvo, *Le droit international théorique et pratique précédé d'un exposé historique des progrès de la science du droit des gens* (Volume 2: Rousseau, Paris 1896) 348 § 865.

the Law of Nations, both in Europe and in the United States.[115] Moreover, the theory of the tacit agreement provided a convincing dogmatic foundation for the subjection of foreigners to domestic legislation.[116] Perhaps most importantly, Vattel had admitted that 'it is impossible for the best regulated state, or for the most vigilant and absolute sovereign, to model at his pleasure all the actions of his subjects'.[117] For that very same reason, Vattel said, '[w]e ought not to say in general, that we have received an injury from a nation, because we have received it from one of its subjects'.[118] Calvo welcomed Vattel's approach, observing that 'at present, almost all publicists approve the substance of this doctrine'.[119] In this vein, Calvo explained:

> This question is related to the very serious issue of the constant claims of the great European powers against American states. They have all been based on *personal offences*, sometimes real, sometimes inflated by their agents, and always portrayed with the most vivid colors. The rule which in more than one case the [European powers] have tried to impose on the [American republics] is that foreigners deserve a higher consideration, and more respect and privileges, than the very natives of the country where they live. This principle, which application is notoriously unjust and contrary to the rule of equality of states, and which consequences are essentially disturbing, is not applicable in the relations of European peoples to each other. In all cases where the rule has been advanced by any state, the answer of the other has been negative. And so it must be. Otherwise, relatively weak states would be at the mercy of powerful states. And the citizens of one state would [moreover] have less rights and guarantees than resident aliens.[120]

---

[115]See generally: Charles Fenwick, 'The Authority of Vattel' (1913) 7(3) APSR 395, 395 *et seq.*

[116]For a detailed account of the theory of the tacit agreement see Sects. 3.3 and 3.4. For a representative example of the reception of Vattel's theory of the tacit agreement in Latin America see: Andrés Bello, Principios de derecho de jentes (Valentín Espinal, Caracas 1837) 54-5 [first edition: 1832].

[117]Emer de Vattel, *The Law of Nations or Principles of the Law of Nature Applied to the Conduct and Affairs of Nations and Sovereigns* (1758) (G.G. and J. Robinson, London 1797) 284.

[118]Emer de Vattel, *The Law of Nations or Principles of the Law of Nature Applied to the Conduct and Affairs of Nations and Sovereigns* (1758) (G.G. and J. Robinson, London 1797) 284. See also Sect. 3.4.

[119]Author's translation. The original Spanish text reads: "[c]on el fondo de esta doctrina se hallan hoy conformes casi todos los publicistas." Carlos Calvo, *Derecho internacional teórico y práctico de Europa y América* (Volume 1: D'Amyot Librairie Diplomatique & Durand et Pedone, Paris 1868) 392 at § 293. See also: Carlos Calvo, *Le droit international théorique et pratique précédé d'un exposé historique des progrès de la science du droit des gens* (Volume 2: Rousseau, Paris 1896) 348 § 865.

[120]Emphasis added. Author's translation. The original Spanish text reads: "[c]on esta cuestion (sic), se relaciona el gravísimo asunto de las constantes reclamaciones de las grandes potencias europeas cerca (sic) de los gobiernos de los Estados americanos. Todas se han fundado en ofensas personales, reales unas veces, otras abultadas por sus agentes, pintadas siempre con vivos colores. Y la regla que en mas de un caso han tratado de imponer las primeras á los segundos, es, que los extranjeros merecen mas consideración y mayores respetos y privilegios que los mismos naturales del país en que residen. Este principio, cuya aplicación es notoriamente injusta y atentatoria á la ley de la igualdad de los Estados, y cuyas consecuencias son esencialmente perturbadoras, no constituye regla de derecho aplicable en las relaciones internacionales de los de Europa, porque de lo contrario los pueblos relativamente débiles estarian (sic) á merced de los poderosos, y los ciudadanos de un

Similar formulations of the argument appear, in like contexts, at may other instances of the treatise.[121] The expression 'personal offences' (*ofensas personales*) already suggests that Calvo's argument of equality primarily referred to injuries originating in the conduct of private citizens.[122] Nonetheless, as shown by Calvo's reliance on Vattel, Calvo's doctrine of equality was never an argument against the *existence* of a customary security obligation.[123] The French edition of the treatise suggests that Calvo's point was that, in cases involving private injuries to aliens, international responsibility could only be established upon a failure by local authorities to properly redress the original injury:

> The state does not only have the right, but also the duty, to protect and defend its nationals abroad by all means allowed by the law of nations, whenever they are subject to arbitrary proceedings or wrongs committed against them. *[Protection is] due even if the abuse or damage does not directly result from the act of the foreign state, in case it [the host state] has done nothing to counteract it.* In such cases, the home state of the injured [alien] has the right to seek redress of the injustice, compensation of damages, and guarantees of non-repetition, as the case may be. *When private persons (robbers, thieves, etc.) have caused the damage, the state in whose territory the grievance has been committed bears the obligation to prosecute the wrongdoers. The victim, even if she were to possess another nationality, shall first resort to the authorities of the host state. But if it [the host state] refuses to do justice, [the injured person] may request protection from her home country,* which is then entitled to exercise diplomatic intervention. This intervention is only justified in cases where a violation of international law has occurred and the foreign person has been injured, or when learned attorneys from her own country believe a judgment passed against her to be unfair.[124]

---

país tendrian (sic) menos derechos y garantías que los residentes extranjeros". Carlos Calvo, *Derecho internacional teórico y práctico de Europa y América* (Volume 1: D'Amyot Librairie Diplomatique & Durand et Pedone, Paris 1868) 392-3 at § 293.

[121] See, for example: Carlos Calvo, *Derecho internacional teórico y práctico de Europa y América* (Volume 1: D'Amyot Librairie Diplomatique & Durand et Pedone, Paris 1868) 387-88 § 291.

[122] Cf. Carlos Calvo, *Derecho internacional teórico y práctico de Europa y América* (Volume 1: D'Amyot Librairie Diplomatique & Durand et Pedone, Paris 1868) 392-3 at § 293.

[123] Cf. Carlos Calvo, *Derecho internacional teórico y práctico de Europa y América* (Volume 1: D'Amyot Librairie Diplomatique & Durand et Pedone, Paris 1868) 392 at § 293.

[124] Emphasis added. Author's translation. The original French text reads: "L'État a non seulement le droit, mais encore le devoir de protéger et de défendre, par tous les moyens qu'autorise le droit des gens, ses nationaux à l'étranger, lorsqu'ils sont l'objet de poursuites arbitraires ou de lésions commises à leur préjudice, quand même les mauvais *traitements ou les dommages éprouvés par eux ne sont pas directement le fait de l'État étranger, mais quand celui-ci n'a rien fait pour s'y opposer.* En pareils cas, l'État auquel appartient la personne lésée a le droit de demander la réparation de l'injustice, une indemnité pour le dommage causé et, selon les circonstances, des garanties contre le renouvellement d'actes semblables. *Quand le dommage provient de personnes ayant un caractère privé (brigands, voleurs, etc.), c'est à l'État sur le territoire duquel le délit a été commis qu'incombe l'obligation de punir les coupables ; la personne lésée, même si elle appartient à une autre nationalité, doit donc s'adresser d'abord aux autorités de l'État où elle habite; mais si l'on refuse de lui rendre justice, alors elle pourra réclamer la protection de son pays d'origine,* qui pourra intervenir diplomatiquement en sa faveur. Cette intervention n'est justifiée que dans le cas où le droit international a été enfreint et la personne de l'étranger lésée, ou lorsque le jugement que le condamne est déclaré inique par les jurisconsultes de son pays." Emphasis added. Carlos Calvo, *Le*

Generally speaking, Calvo's views were not much revolutionary.[125] At his time it was often argued that international responsibility for injuries to aliens can only arise from a failure to do justice: if a private wrong has occurred, the state is liable to redress it; and it is then the failure to redress such a primary wrong what originates international responsibility.[126]

This premise holds true for *most* cases involving private injuries to aliens. In the specific area of revolutionary damages and civil unrest, Calvo's position was slightly different. In an article published in 1869, he argued that damages suffered by aliens in the context of severe civil disturbances do not normally entail international responsibility.[127] The argument was partly based on Calvo's distinctive equality rationale:

> [Such responsibility would imply creating an] exorbitant and devious privilege, essentially favorable to powerful states and detrimental to the most fragile nations [and], in the end, *establishing an unjustifiable inequality between natives and foreigners.*[128]

Calvo further submitted that the principle of territorial jurisdiction implies that the decision on claims arising from such events should remain the 'exclusive domain' of

---

droit international théorique et pratique précédé d'un exposé historique des progrès de la science du droit des gens (Volume 2: Rousseau, Paris 1896) 347-8 § 863.

[125]For a similar observation see: Martins Paparinskis, *The International Minimum Standard and Fair and Equitable Treatment* (Oxford University Press, Oxford 2013) 24 (noting that, in the final analysis, Calvo's arguments were 'quite unremarkable'). Paparinskis also provides a detailed analysis of the Calvo Doctrine at pp. 23 *et seq.*

[126]There was some debate as to the point in time in which a 'denial of justice' takes place. Charles C. Hyde argued that a want of protection could in itself entail a failure to do justice. Charles Cheney Hyde, *International Law. Chiefly as Interpreted and Applied by the United States* (Volume I: Little Brown & Co., Boston 1922) 522. Hyde's renowned student, Clyde Eagleton, would however observe that, while responsibility could arise before a failure to redress has occurred, '[i]t is ordinarily true that the responsibility of the state appears as the result of a failure in duties in redress, rather than in duties of restraint'. Clyde Eagleton, *The Responsibility of States in International Law* (Klaus Reprint, New York 1970) 93 [first edition: 1928]. See also Sects. 2.2.3 and 10.4.

[127]Carlos Calvo, 'De la non-responsabilité des états a raison des pertes et dommages éprouvés par des étrangers en temps de troubles intérieurs ou de guerres civiles' (1869) 1 Revue de droit international et de législation comparée 417, 417 ("[l]es gouvernements sont-ils ou non responsables des pertes et préjudices éprouvés par des étrangers en temps de troubles intérieurs ou de guerres civiles? Cette question a été longuement discutée et finalement résolue par la négative").

[128]Emphasis added. Author's translation. The original French text reads as follows: "[Admettre, dans l'espèce, la responsabilité des Gouvernements, c'est-à-dire le principe d'une indemnité], ce serait créer un privilège exorbitant et funeste, essentiellement favorable aux États puissants, et nuisible aux nations plus faibles, enfin établir une inégalité injustifiable entre les nationaux et les étrangers'. Carlos Calvo, 'De la non-responsabilité des états a raison des pertes et dommages éprouvés par des étrangers en temps de troubles intérieurs ou de guerres civiles' (1869) 1 Revue de droit international et de législation comparée 417, 417.

ordinary courts.[129] As a corollary, those injuries provide no immediate cause for diplomatic intervention.[130] The aforesaid statements resemble the formulation of the doctrine of equality Calvo used at several instances, both in his Spanish treatise of 1868 and in the French edition of 1896.[131]

While equality certainly played a role in this regard, the doctrine of equality was only an element of Calvo's argument against state responsibility for revolutionary damages. Calvo referred in this connection to a speech held at the British Parliament by Lord Stanley, one of Vicount Palmerston's political adversaries in the times of the *Don Pacifico* affair.[132] Based on that speech, he suggested that civil disorders could constitute an event of *force majeure* excluding international responsibility.[133] In Latin America, the *force majeure* argument was not exclusively Calvo's; it was part of the usual repertoire of semi-peripheral lawyers opposing the gunboat diplomacy.[134]

---

[129]Carlos Calvo, 'De la non-responsabilité des états a raison des pertes et dommages éprouvés par des étrangers en temps de troubles intérieurs ou de guerres civiles' (1869) 1 Revue de droit international et de législation comparée 417, 417.

[130]Carlos Calvo, 'De la non-responsabilité des états a raison des pertes et dommages éprouvés par des étrangers en temps de troubles intérieurs ou de guerres civiles' (1869) 1 Revue de droit international et de législation comparée 417, 427.

[131]See: Carlos Calvo, *Derecho internacional teórico y práctico de Europa y América* (Volume 1: D'Amyot Librairie Diplomatique & Durand et Pedone, Paris 1868) 387-88 § 291; Carlos Calvo, *Le droit international théorique et pratique précédé d'un exposé historique des progrès de la science du droit des gens* (Volume 3: Rousseau, Paris 1896) 142 § 1280.

[132]Carlos Calvo, 'De la non-responsabilité des états a raison des pertes et dommages éprouvés par des étrangers en temps de troubles intérieurs ou de guerres civiles' (1869) 1 Revue de droit international et de législation comparée 417, 418. On the *Don Pacifico* affair see Sect. 4.2.

[133]See: Carlos Calvo, 'De la non-responsabilité des états a raison des pertes et dommages éprouvés par des étrangers en temps de troubles intérieurs ou de guerres civiles' (1869) 1 Revue de droit international et de législation comparée 417, 418. See also: Carlos Calvo, *Derecho internacional teórico y práctico de Europa y América* (Volume 1: D'Amyot Librairie Diplomatique & Durand et Pedone, Paris 1868) 388 § 291; Carlos Calvo, *Le droit international théorique et pratique précédé d'un exposé historique des progrès de la science du droit des gens* (Volume 3: Rousseau, Paris 1896) 143 § 1280.

[134]For a representative example see: Harmodio Arias, 'The Non-Liability of States for Damages Suffered by Foreigners in the Course of a Riot, an Insurrection, or a Civil War' (1913) 7(4) AJIL 724, 764; Simón Planas Suárez, *Los extranjeros en Venezuela. Su condición ante el derecho público y privado de la república* (Centro Tipográfico Colonial, Lisboa 1917) 179-85. For an opposite view on the point of *force majeure* see: Emilio Brusa, 'Responsabilité des États à raison des dommages soufferts par des étrangers en cas d'émeute ou de guerre civile' (1898) 17 Annuaire de l'Institut de Droit International 96, 97 *et seq.*

4.3.3   The Long Lasting Debate About the Calvo Doctrine and the Extent of the Security Obligation

Calvo's work was as controversial as it was influential. For a long time, his treatises were frequently quoted in diplomatic correspondence, both in Latin America and in other regions of the world.[135] The question of state responsibility for acts of individuals remained at the heart of the debate. There were times in which the doctrine of equality seemed to enjoy more acceptance than the minimum standard.

In Latin America, the dominance of the Calvo Doctrine in the first years of the twentieth century crystalized in the *Convention on the Rights of Aliens*.[136] The Convention was enthusiastically adopted by *most* states of the American continent (with the particular exception of Haiti and the United States) at the Second Pan-American Conference, hosted by Mexico in 1902.[137] The treaty had a clear political motivation. The year of its adoption coincides with the Venezuelan blockade.[138] Article 2 of the Convention was unmistakably clear as to the extent of the rights of aliens, and made particular reference to the contentious and intricate issue of revolutionary damages:

> The States do not owe to, nor recognize in, favor of foreigners, any obligations or responsibilities other than those established by their Constitutions and laws in favor of their citizens. Therefore, the States are not responsible for damages sustained by aliens through acts of rebels or individuals, and in general, for damages originating from fortuitous causes of any kind, considering as such the acts of war whether civil or national; except in the case of failure on the part of the constituted authorities to comply with their duties.[139]

The principle laid down in the Convention would also find support in arbitral decisions. A good example is the *Rosa Gelbtrunk* case (1902), where Arbitrator Henry Strong expressly held that foreign citizens are not entitled to a higher degree

---

[135]Examples of Calvo's early reception appear in the correspondence of the Mexican Government regarding damages inflicted during the unsuccessful revolution leaded by General Porfirio Díaz in 1871. See: Frederick Sherwood Dunn, *The Diplomatic Protection of Americans in Mexico* (Klaus Reprint, New York 1971) 152-61 (particularly at p. 155) [first edition: 1933]. For further examples see: Martins Paparinskis, *The International Minimum Standard and Fair and Equitable Treatment* (Oxford University Press, Oxford 2013) 27 *et seq.*

[136]Convention Relative to the Rights of Aliens (adopted 1902) *Report of the Delegates of the United States to the Second International Conference of American States, Held at the City of Mexico from October 22, 1901, to January 22, 1902* (Government Printing Office, Washington 1902) 226-30 (Appendix GG).

[137]Convention Relative to the Rights of Aliens (adopted 1902) *Report of the Delegates of the United States to the Second International Conference of American States, Held at the City of Mexico from October 22, 1901, to January 22, 1902* (Government Printing Office, Washington 1902) 226-30 (Appendix GG).

[138]On the Venezuelan blockade see Sect. 4.2.

[139]Convention Relative to the Rights of Aliens (adopted 1902) *Report of the Delegates of the United States to the Second International Conference of American States, Held at the City of Mexico from October 22, 1901, to January 22, 1902* (Government Printing Office, Washington 1902) 226, 228.

of protection than that which the host state provides for its own nationals, and cannot legitimately expect to be exempt from the 'political vicissitudes' of the country.[140] Strong's statement was however weakened by a later observation, which called into question the applicability of the rule in cases involving mob injuries that could have been avoided through the proper exercise of 'due diligence'.[141] A clearer example would be Commissioner Zuloaga's Supplementary Opinion in the *Sambiaggio* case (1903).[142] On that occasion, Zuloaga stated:

> Setting aside all discussion as to principles of international law [...] I would ask, Is it equitable that foreigners domiciled in Venezuela should expect to escape the political condition of the country, and obtain, as an advantage over the natives, not only payment for damages inflicted on them by the Government, but also for those caused by the rebels the Government was combatting, and against whom it was expending all its energies, blood, and treasure? Is it equitable that, as between a Venezuelan and a foreigner, the former should say, "My home is in mourning for cherished members of my family who have perished in defense of the state; I myself am ruined from the enforced neglect of my business: I have been the victim of the enemy," while the foreigner may say, "I have lost nothing by the war, I am as safe as in times of peace; not only does the government (which I do not defend) pay me for the losses which it has inflicted on me but for those occasioned by its enemies as well.[143]

Many versions of Calvo's theories circulated around the globe for decades. Some were quite extreme. For instance, in a report submitted to the League of Nations in 1926, José Gustavo Guerrero and Wang-Chung Hui would go as far as to suggest that private violence belongs to the realm of municipal law, thus having a 'slight

---

[140]For the opinion of Arbitrator Strong see: *Rosa Gelbtrunk v El Salvador* (26 April 1902) *Papers relating to the Foreign Relations of the United States with the Annual Message of the President* (Government Printing Office, Washington 1902) 876, 877-8 ("The principle which I hold to be applicable to the present case may thus be stated: A citizen or subject of one nation who, in the pursuit of commercial enterprise, carries trade within the territory and under the protection of the sovereignty of a nation other than its own is to be considered as having cast in his lot with the subjects or citizens of the State in which he resides and carries business. Whilst on the one hand he enjoys the protection of that State, so far as the police regulations and other advantages are concerned, on the other hand he becomes liable to the political vicissitudes of the country in which he thus has a commercial domicile in the same manner as the subjects or citizens of that State are liable to the same. The State to which he owes national allegiance has no right to claim for him as against the nation in which he is resident any other or different treatment in case of loss by war – either foreign or civil – revolution, insurrection, or other internal disturbance caused by organized military force or soldiers, than that which the later country metes out to its own subjects or citizens. This I conceive to be now a well-established doctrine of international law"). The remaining two arbitrators issued no dissenting or separate opinion in this case.

[141]*Rosa Gelbtrunk v El Salvador* (26 April 1902) *Papers relating to the Foreign Relations of the United States with the Annual Message of the President* (Government Printing Office, Washington 1902) 876, 879 ("It is, however, not to be assumed that this rule would apply in a case of mob violence which might, if due diligence had been used, have been prevented by civil authorities alone or by such authorities aided by an available military force").

[142]*Sambiaggio Case* (1903) X RIAA 499, 511-2.

[143]*Sambiaggio Case* (1903) X RIAA 499, 511-2.

relevance' in international law.[144] It is also worth noting that Calvo enjoyed some acceptance outside the semi-periphery. In Germany, Emanuel von Ullman would echo the argument of equality in 1908, albeit only in connection with revolutionary damages.[145] In 1924, the renowned American scholar Charles Fenwick recognized Calvo's importance and positive reception in specialized legal literature:

> Leaving out of account the possibility that the government may have failed to use promptly the means at its disposal to maintain its constitutional authority, it would appear that the Calvo Doctrine is a correct statement of the law, in so at least as concerns the practice of the larger states among themselves.[146]

Support for the Calvo Doctrine was never unanimous, however. Even in Latin America there were strong voices advocating for a minimum standard.[147] The choice between the doctrine of equality and the minimum standard was one of the most divisive questions of international law during the prewar years. The working papers of The Hague Codification Conference of 1930 provide unequivocal evidence of the deep disagreements of the international community in this regard. The Chinese delegate, C. C. Wu, expressed the view that an alien setting foot in foreign territory 'must be prepared for all the local conditions, political and physical, as he is prepared for the weather'.[148] Wu further argued that '[the foreigner] must take what he finds and cannot complain of a defective or corrupt administration anymore than nationals

---

[144]See: League of Nations, 'Questionnaire No. 4/Responsibility of States for Damage done in their Territories to the Person or Property of Foreigners (Doc. Nr. C. 46.M.23.126. V)' in Shabtai Rosenne (ed), *League of Nations Committee of Experts for the Progressive Codification of International Law [1925-1928]* (Volume 2: Oceana Publications, New York 1972) 118, 124.

[145]Emanuel von Ullmann, *Völkerrecht* (J. C. B. Mohr, Tübingen 1908) 153.

[146]Charles Fenwick, *International Law* (The Century Co., New York 1924) 394. Cf. also Amos Hershey, *The Essentials of International Public Law and Organization* (The Macmillan Co., New York 1927) 162-3 and n. 6.

[147]An example may be found in the *Déclaration des grandes principes du droit international moderne* of April 12th, 1938, authored by Alejandro Álvarez. Article 25 of the Declaration read as follows: "Les Etats doivent: b) Maintenir une organisation politique et juridique qui permette à toutes les personnes résidant sur leur territoire d'exercer les droits et de jouir des avantages que le sentiment de la justice internationale impose aujourd'hui à tout peuple civilisé." Alejandro Álvarez, *Exposé de motifs et déclaration des grands principes du droit international moderne* (Editions Internationales, Paris 1938) 54-5. For an additional example see: Isidoro Ruiz Moreno, *Manual de derecho internacional público* (Editorial Juan Castagnola, Buenos Aires 1943) 152. For a critical discussion of this position see: Edwin Borchard, 'The "Minimum Standard" of the Treatment of Aliens' (1940) 38(4) Mich. L. Rev. 445, 457 (providing an English translation of the proposal of Álvarez, and discussing the views of Ruiz and other Latin American scholars).

[148]Edwin Borchard, 'The "Minimum Standard" of the Treatment of Aliens' (1940) 38(4) Mich. L. Rev. 445, 450-1 (describing the declarations of Mr. Wu). Interestingly, Ludwig von Bar had made a similar remark in a speech held at the *Reichstag* in 1893. See: Reichstag, 'Protokoll – 68. Sitzung' (16 March 1893) *Stenographische Berichte über die Verhandlungen des Reichtags, VIII. Legislaturperiode, II. Session 1892/3* (Volume 3: Verlag der Norddeutschen Buchdruckerei, Berlin 1893) 1671, 1672 (referring only to the risk of civil unrest, and making some important caveats at p. 1673).

can'.[149] In this connection, China submitted a draft article, which was fully in line with Calvo's views:

> A State is only responsible for damage caused by private persons to the person or property of foreigners if it has manifestly failed to take such preventive or punitive measures as in the circumstances might reasonably be expected of *if had the persons injured been its own nationals*.[150]

The vote on the draft article was tight: a slim majority dismissed the Chinese proposal at the Conference's Third Committee, with a difference of only six votes.[151] Not only Latin American states were against the minimum standard.[152] Support for the doctrine of equality came from all over the world; even Portugal was on Calvo's side.[153] As observed by Oliver Lissitzyn (1965):

> Had all the Latin American states and the Soviet Union participated in the vote, there probably would have been a majority against the international standard.[154]

After Conference, the doctrine of equality continued to be a leading principle in the southern part of the American continent.[155] In 1933, the widespread support the

---

[149]Edwin Borchard, 'The "Minimum Standard" of the Treatment of Aliens' (1940) 38(4) Mich. L. Rev. 445, 450-1 (describing the declarations of Mr. Wu).

[150]Emphasis added. Green Hackworth, 'Responsibility of States for Damages Caused in their Territory to the Person or Property of Foreigners. The Hague Conference for the Codification of International Law' (1930) 24(3) AJIL 500, 513.

[151]Green Hackworth, 'Responsibility of States for Damages Caused in their Territory to the Person or Property of Foreigners. The Hague Conference for the Codification of International Law' (1930) 24(3) AJIL 500, 514; Oliver Lissitzyn, *International Law Today and Tomorrow* (Oceana Publications, New York 1965) 78.

[152]Oliver Lissitzyn, *International Law Today and Tomorrow* (Oceana Publications, New York 1965) 78.

[153]Oliver Lissitzyn, *International Law Today and Tomorrow* (Oceana Publications, New York 1965) 78.

[154]Oliver Lissitzyn, *International Law Today and Tomorrow* (Oceana Publications, New York 1965) 78. For a description of the political interests represented at the Conference see: Frederick Sherwood Dunn, *The Protection of Nationals. A Study in the Application of International Law* (The Johns Hopkins Press, Baltimore 1932) 64-6.

[155]A resolution that embodied both the Calvo Doctrine and the Drago Doctrine was approved at the Fifth Plenary Session of the Seventh Inter-American Conference, which took place in 1933. U.S. Secretary of State Cordell Hull was present at the Session, but raised no objection against the draft resolution. See: 'Actas de la Quinta Sesión Plenaria' (24 December 1933) in *Actas y antecedentes de las sesiones plenarias de la Séptima Conferencia Internacional Americana* (Montevideo 1933) 107, 119-20. Interestingly, a few days before, at the Fifth Session of the Second Committee (held on December 11th, 1933), Hull had voted in favor of the provision in question, without making any reservation or clarification as regards to the doctrine of equality. See: 'Acta de la Quinta Sesión' in *Actas y antecedentes de la primera, segunda y octava comisiones de la Séptima Conferencia Internacional Americana* (Montevideo 1933) 111, 131 and 137. It is worth noting, however, that Hull would take a stance against Latin America's understanding of the doctrine of equality years later. In 1938 he stated with some irony that, under this misleading and 'wholly inapplicable' equality principle, 'it is wholly justifiable to deprive an individual of his rights if all other persons are equally deprived, and if no victim is allowed to escape'. 'Communication of the

doctrine enjoyed in the region found clear expression in article 9 of the *Montevideo Convention on Rights and Duties of States*, which expressly established that 'foreigners may not claim rights other or more extensive than those of the nationals'.[156]

Besides the doctrine of equality, there was another front in the Latin American resistance against the gunboat diplomacy: the legitimacy of the use of force as such. In this regard, the position of the Latin American republics crystalized in the *Drago Doctrine* (1902), which spurned the use of military force for the collection of public debt.[157] The father of the doctrine, Luis M. Drago, was well aware of the *Don Pacifico* incident and would expressly criticize Palmerston's intervention in Greece in an article published in 1907.[158] The Drago Doctrine was also linked to the idea that the gunboat diplomacy was inconsistent with the role of the United States as the guarantor of the freedom and independence of all Latin American republics, a then not uncommon interpretation of the Monroe Doctrine.[159] Leading Latin American

---

U.S. Secretary of State to the Mexican Ambassador at Washington' (22 August 1938) 32(4) AJIL 191, 198. For a short overview of the longstanding debate about the interpretation of article 9 of the Convention see: Edwin Borchard, 'The "Minimum Standard" of the Treatment of Aliens' (1940) 38 (4) Mich. L. Rev. 445-7 and 460-1.

[156]Convention on the Rights and Duties of States (adopted 26 December 1933, entered into force 26 December 1934) 165 LNTS 19, 27 art. 9. See also the reservation made by the U.S. Government in this regard: 'Reservation of the United States of America to the Convention on the Rights and Duties of States' (26 December 1933) 165 LNTS 28, 29 ("the United States Government in all of its international associations and relationships and conduct will follow scrupulously the doctrines and policies which it has pursued since March 4th which are embodied in the different addresses of President Roosevelt since that time and in the recent peace address of myself [Hull] on the 15th day of December before this Conference and in the law of nations as generally recognized and accepted").

[157]For the original formulation of the Drago Doctrine see: 'Letter of Mr. Drago, Minister of Foreign Relations of the Argentine Republic, to Mr. Mérou, Argentine Minister to the United States' (29 December 1902) in Alejandro Álvarez, *The Monroe Doctrine. Its Importance in the International Life of the States of the New World* (Oxford University Press, New York 1924) 187, 191 (Annex XXIX) ("In a word, the principle which she [the Argentine Republic] would like to see recognized is: that the public debt can not (sic) occasion armed intervention or even the actual occupation of the territory of American nations by an European power").

[158]Luis María Drago, 'State Loans in Their Relation to International Policy' (1907) 1(3) AJIL 692, 710-11 ("[f]inancial interventions are to-day and have always been a political weapon in the hands of governments. They have all proceeded in accordance with the formula of Lord Palmerston. The right to interfere for the collection of debts is declared indisputable [. . .] These interventions are always directed against nations that are weak or without allies and in consequence unable to resist them"). See also Drago's discussion of Palmerston's views at pp. 697-8.

[159]See, for example: Alejandro Álvarez, *The Monroe Doctrine. Its Importance in the International Life of the States of the New World* (Oxford University Press, New York 1924) 3-31 (arguing at p. 20 that the United States had invoked the original Monroe Doctrine to pursue an unacceptable 'policy of hegemony' and pleading at p. 21 for the proclamation of a new 'Pan-American doctrine', which renounces to every form of imperialism). See also: Alejandro Álvarez, *Le droit international américain* (A. Pedone, Paris 1910) 125-84 (providing a critical analysis of U.S. foreign policy in Latin America during the nineteenth and early twentieth centuries). For a discussion of these views from an American perspective, see: Elihu Root, 'The Real Monroe Doctrine' (1914) 8 ASIL Proceedings 6, 15-6 and 21-2 (arguing at pp. 15-6 that '[i]f the Monroe Doctrine had never been

international lawyers enthusiastically acclaimed the Drago Doctrine; 3 years before his death, Carlos Calvo himself would express his deep sympathy and sincere support for the doctrine.[160] The campaign for the Drago Doctrine yielded positive results. Article 1 of the Drago-Porter Convention of 1907 elevated the Drago Doctrine into a binding rule of international law.[161]

The intense battle of gunboats and books described in this chapter did hence not have an entirely clear outcome. While the gunboat diplomacy would be defeated by semi-peripheral states advancing the Drago Doctrine, the substantive debate about the choice between the notion of a 'minimum standard of treatment' and the doctrine of equality would remain far from settled.

---

declared or thought of [. . .] [t]he United States would have had the right to demand from every other American state observance of treaty obligations and of the rules of international law. *It would have had the right to insist upon due protection for the lives and property of its citizens within the territory of every other American states, and upon the treatment of its citizens in that territory according to the rules of international law* [. . .] All these rights which the United States would have had as against other American states it has now. They are not in the slightest degree affected by the Monroe Doctrine' – emphasis added). Root had a privileged access to the debate. In his capacity as Secretary of State, he had himself travelled to Latin America to participate in the Third Panamerican Conference, which took place in Rio de Janeiro on July 31st, 1906. For a short account of this event see: 'Mr. Root's South American Trip' (1907) 1(1) AJIL 143, 143-4.

[160]Carlos Calvo, 'Lettre-Circulaire à quelques-uns de ses collègues de l'Institut de France et de l'Institut de Droit International' (17 April 1903) in *La Doctrine de Monroe* (A. Eyméoud, Paris 1903) 14-5.

[161]See: Convention on the Limitation of Employment of Force for Recovery of Contract Debts (adopted 18 October 1907, entered into force 26 January 1910) in Charles Bevans (ed), *Treaties and Other International Agreements of the United States of America 1776-1949* (Volume 1: Government Printing Office, Washington 1968) 607, 614. See also: Wolfgang Benedek, 'Drago-Porter Convention' in Rüdiger Wolfrum (ed), *The Max Planck Encyclopedia of Public International Law* (Volume 3: Oxford University Press, New York 2012) 234-6.

Chapter 5
The Calm After the Storm: 'Full Protection and Security' as an Element of the Minimum Standard of Treatment

5.1 Preliminary Remarks

The notion of an international minimum standard of treatment was one of the most contentious questions of international law before World War II.[1] Notwithstanding the deep inconsistencies and lively discussions that signalized the development of the standard in the prewar era, contemporary authors generally recognize the existence of a minimum standard.[2] Moreover, it is a common place that the customary obligation to provide protection and security to aliens is an element of the minimum standard.[3]

---

[1] See Chap. 4.

[2] For some indicative examples, see: Alfred Verdross and Bruno Simma, *Universelles Völkerrecht* (Duncker & Humblot, Berlin 1984) 801-5; Andreas Lowenfeld, *International Economic Law* (Oxford University Press, New York 2008) 468-70 and 557-8; Fausto de Quadros, *A proteção da propriedade privada pelo direito internacional público* (Livraria Almedina, Coimbra 1998) 133-48; Hans Roth, *The Minimum Standard of International Law Applied to Aliens* (IMP F.A.A. Sijhoff, The Hague 1949) 178-85; Ioana Tudor, *The Fair and Equitable Treatment in the International Law of Foreign Investment* (Oxford University Press, New York 2008) 60-5; James Crawford, *Brownlie's Principles of Public International Law* (Oxford University Press, Oxford 2012) 613-4; John Humphrey, 'The International Law of Human Rights in the Middle Twentieth Century' in Maarten Bos (ed), *The Present State of International Law. International Law Association 1873-1973* (Springer Science/Business Media, New York 1973) 75-6; Malcolm Shaw, *International Law* (Cambridge University Press, New York 2003) 733-7; Martins Paparinskis, *The International Minimum Standard and Fair and Equitable Treatment* (Oxford University Press, Oxford 2013) 13-63; Matthias Herdegen, *Völkerrecht* (C.H. Beck, Munich 2017) 215-6; Rudolf Dolzer and Christoph Schreuer, *Principles of International Investment Law* (Oxford University Press, New York 2012) 3 *et seq.*

[3] For a decision implying this link between the international minimum standard and the customary duty to provide protection and security to aliens see: *Case Concerning Elettronica Sicula S.p.A. (ELSI) (United States of America v Italy)* [1989] ICJ Rep 15, 66 [111]. On the relationship between the FPS standard and the minimum standard see: Andrew Newcombe and Lluís Paradell,

© Springer Nature Switzerland AG 2019
S. Mantilla Blanco, *Full Protection and Security in International Investment Law*,
European Yearbook of International Economic Law 8,
https://doi.org/10.1007/978-3-030-24838-3_5

This chapter explores this conspicuous change in the perception of the minimum standard and its relationship to the customary security obligation. The argument has been divided in three parts. A first section considers the legal basis for the present-day recognition of the minimum standard as an institution of customary international law, which embodies, among many other elements, the FPS standard. A second section discusses the content of the minimum standard and shows that, while the minimum standard enjoys broad acceptance, its substance remains largely contentious.[4] Finally, the third section submits that, as a consequence of its own vagueness, the minimum standard does not provide a suitable basis for the determination of the FPS standard's scope of application. Therefore, a top-bottom approach, which seeks establish the meaning of FPS based on the more-general notion of a minimum standard, will in all likelihood lead to inaccurate or inconclusive results.

Law and Practice of Investment Treaties. Standards of Treatment (Kluwer Law International, Alphen aan den Rijn 2009) 235, 246 and 307-14; Rudolf Dolzer and Christoph Schreuer, *Principles of International Investment Law* (Oxford University Press, New York 2012) 166; Francisco Endara Flores, 'La protección y seguridad plena de las inversiones. ¿El estándar olvidado de los tratados bilaterales de inversión?' (2009) 2 Revista de Derecho Público 443, 447-8; George Foster, 'Recovering "Protection and Security": The Treaty Standard's Obscure Origins, Forgotten Meaning, and Key Current Significance' (2012) 45(4) Vand. J. Transnat'l L. 1095, 1121-2; Gus Van Harten, *Investment Arbitration and Public Law* (Oxford University Press, Oxford 2008) 87; Helge Elisabeth Zeitler, 'Full Protection and Security' in Stephan Schill (ed), *International Investment Law and Comparative Public Law* (Oxford University Press, New York 2010) 183, 184-90; Martins Paparinskis, *The International Minimum Standard and Fair and Equitable Treatment* (Oxford University Press, Oxford 2013) 8; Patrick Dumberry, *The Formation and Identification of Customary International Law in International Investment Law* (Cambridge University Press, Cambridge 2016) 107 and 109; Ralph Alexander Lorz, 'Protection and Security (Including the NAFTA Approach)' in Marc Bungenberg, Jörn Griebel, Stephan Hobe and August Reinisch (eds), *International Investment Law. A Handbook* (Nomos, Baden-Baden 2015) 764, 766. Some authors have gone as far as to present the notion of a 'minimum standard of full protection and security' (as opposed to the 'minimum standard of fair and equitable treatment'). For an author using this terminology see: José Antonio Rivas, 'Colombia' in Chester Brown (ed), *Commentaries on Selected Model Investment Treaties* (Oxford University Press, Oxford 2013) 183, 213-7. Cf. also: Christoph Schreuer, 'Full Protection and Security' (2010) 1(2) J. Int'l Disp. Settlement 353, 364 (suggesting that, while the *treaty-based* FPS standard is autonomous from the 'minimum standard', 'the international minimum standard does contain certain duties to protect foreign investors against adverse action').

[4]For a similar observation see: Patrick Dumberry, *The Formation and Identification of Customary International Law in International Investment Law* (Cambridge University Press, Cambridge 2016) 97-110 (arguing that the minimum standard is a 'firmly established rule [...] with an undefined content').

5.2   The Minimum Standard of Treatment as a Customary Rule of Contemporary International Law

One of the most intricate problems in the international law of aliens is the question, how the standard of civilization, which was the perhaps most contentious legal principle of the prewar era, gained a customary character.[5] The question is intrinsically linked to the broader debate on the formation, ascertainment and definition of international custom.[6] The establishment of customary international law has been the subject of infinite scholarly studies and has consistently given rise to a large and varied array of theoretical approaches.[7] As expressed by Stefan Talmon:

> There are probably few topics in international law that are more over-theorized than the creation and determination of custom. Indeed, at times one might get the impression that the topic has been theorized to death.[8]

Notwithstanding the foregoing, there is some agreement on a basic premise: a rule can only be characterized as customary if it embodies a general practice (objective element), which is accepted as law (subjective element).[9] These two elements are easily stated but not so easily proven.[10] As put forward by Judge Philip Jessup:

> No survey of State practice can, strictly speaking, be comprehensive and the practice of a single State may vary from time to time – perhaps depending on whether it is in the position of plaintiff or defendant.[11]

---

[5]For an excellent account of the evolution of the minimum standard of treatment after World War II see: Martins Paparinskis, *The International Minimum Standard and Fair and Equitable Treatment* (Oxford University Press, Oxford 2013) 65-103.

[6]On the identification and determination of customary norms of international law see generally: Michael Wood, 'Second Report on Identification of Customary International Law (A/CN.4/672)' (22 May 2014) [http://legal.un.org/ilc/documentation/english/a_cn4_672.pdf].

[7]Stefan Talmon, 'Determining Customary International Law: The ICJ's Methodology between Induction, Deduction and Assertion' (2015) 26(2) EJIL 417, 429.

[8]Stefan Talmon, 'Determining Customary International Law: The ICJ's Methodology between Induction, Deduction and Assertion' (2015) 26(2) EJIL 417, 429.

[9]This standard formulation of the elements of international custom derives from the language used in article 38(1)(b) of the ICJ Statute. See: Statute of the International Court of Justice (adopted 26 June 1945, entered into force 24 October 1945) art. 38(1)(b) (referring to 'international custom, as evidence of a general practice accepted as law'). For a detailed account of the 'two-elements approach' see: Michael Wood, 'Second Report on Identification of Customary International Law (A/CN.4/672)' (22 May 2014) [http://legal.un.org/ilc/documentation/english/a_cn4_672.pdf] 7-15 [21-31].

[10]For an overview of the difficulties and differences of opinion arising out of the two elements in theory and practice see: Matthias Herdegen, *Völkerrecht* (C.H. Beck, Munich 2017) 147-56.

[11]*Barcelona Traction Light and Power Company Ltd. (Belgium v Spain)* [1970] ICJ Rep 3, Separate Opinion of Judge Jessup 161, 197 [60]. See also: Albert Bleckmann, *Grundprobleme und Methoden des Völkerrechts* (Karl Alber, München/Frankfurt 1982) 112 (from a general perspective); Stefan Talmon, 'Determining Customary International Law: The ICJ's Methodology between Induction, Deduction and Assertion' (2015) 26(2) EJIL 417, 427 (making reference to Jessup's opinion in this regard).

The general rule is that customary norms are to be determined from the bottom to the top, by inductive reasoning, albeit some forms of deduction have also been common in practice.[12] Prior to the BIT era, inductive arguments did not provide solid justification for the characterization of the international minimum standard as a customary rule of international law: there was no consistent state practice in this regard, not even in the United States.[13] The proclamation of the minimum standard as a customary rule was always based on a selective use of legal sources favoring the standard of civilization, and a conscious disregard of sources favoring the doctrine of equality.[14] Taking Elihu Root's speech of 1910 as an example, one gets the impression that he was merely *asserting* the minimum standard, hiding the weakness of his argument behind a strikingly pompous rhetoric.[15]

In the mid-twentieth century efforts were made to justify the international minimum standard through deductive reasoning. For example, in 1940, Edwin Borchard resorted to normative deduction (i.e. the inference of a customary rule from customary norms enjoying general acceptance)[16] for rejecting and refuting the doctrine of equality.[17] In this regard, Borchard argued that '[i]f it is true that the doctrine of equality is the final test of international responsibility, then the source of international responsibility lies in municipal law'.[18] In other words, following this view, the minimum standard can be deduced from the very 'supremacy of international law'.[19]

---

[12]Adolf Schüle, 'Methoden der Völkerrechtswissenschaft' (1959/60) 8 AöR 129, 148; Stefan Talmon, 'Determining Customary International Law: The ICJ's Methodology between Induction, Deduction and Assertion' (2015) 26(2) EJIL 417, 421 *et seq.*

[13]See Sect. 4.3.1.

[14]For a detailed analysis of these inconsistencies see Sects. 4.2 and 4.3.

[15]On Elihu Root's 1910 speech see Sect. 4.2. For a detailed analysis of the argumentative weakness of Root's speech, see: Martins Paparinskis, *The International Minimum Standard and Fair and Equitable Treatment* (Oxford University Press, Oxford 2013) 39-46. On the determination of customary international law by means of assertion see: Stefan Talmon, 'Determining Customary International Law: The ICJ's Methodology between Induction, Deduction and Assertion' (2015) 26 (2) EJIL 417, 434 *et seq.* (particularly addressing ICJ adjudicatory practice). For an example of an arbitral tribunal assuming (or asserting) the international minimum standard see: *Harry Roberts v Mexico* (2 November 1926) IV RIAA 77, 80.

[16]For this definition of 'normative deduction' see: Stefan Talmon, 'Determining Customary International Law: The ICJ's Methodology between Induction, Deduction and Assertion' (2015) 26(2) EJIL 417, 423.

[17]Edwin Borchard, 'The "Minimum Standard" of the Treatment of Aliens' (1940) 38(4) Mich. L. Rev. 445, 447.

[18]Edwin Borchard, 'The "Minimum Standard" of the Treatment of Aliens' (1940) 38(4) Mich. L. Rev. 445, 447. This argument has not been unusual in international legal scholarly writings. For some additional examples see: Alfred Verdross, 'Les règles internationales concernant le traitement des étrangers' (1931) 37(3) RCADI 322, 350; Samy Friedman, *Expropriation in International Law* (Steven & Sons, London 1953) 130-1. On the different methods of deduction used by international adjudicatory bodies see: Stefan Talmon, 'Determining Customary International Law: The ICJ's Methodology between Induction, Deduction and Assertion' (2015) 26(2) EJIL 417, 423 *et seq.*

[19]Edwin Borchard, 'The "Minimum Standard" of the Treatment of Aliens' (1940) 38(4) Mich. L. Rev. 445, 452.

Borchard further considered that the doctrine of equality was inconsistent with the maxim that privileges and rights under international law are correlative to international obligations:

> Sovereignty is more emotionally invoked by the less mature than by older states. These weaker countries often disregard the rule, axiomatic in fact, that a state claiming the privileges of international law must comply with its duties.[20]

Borchard's argument, however appealing, did not provide a conclusive or convincing justification for the minimum standard. A first objection would be that, in the absence of a settled standard, the treatment of aliens could have been regarded as an area that was not yet (or not fully) regulated by international law.[21] From this standpoint, there would be no conflict between international and municipal law at all, but just a gap.[22] This observation is consistent with Sir Hersch Lauterpacht's contention in 1933 that the treatment of foreign citizens could serve as an example of a lacuna in international law caused by 'revealed discrepancies in the practice of states'.[23] In continental Europe, some authors had already stressed in the 1920s that the law of aliens was a subject of municipal rather than international law.[24] For

---

[20]Edwin Borchard, 'The "Minimum Standard" of the Treatment of Aliens' (1940) 38(4) Mich. L. Rev. 445, 451. Nonetheless, when arguing why the measure of protection required by international law is not limited to the guarantees of municipal law, Borchard resorted, too, to inductive reasoning. See: Edwin Borchard, 'The "Minimum Standard" of the Treatment of Aliens' (1940) 38 (4) Mich. L. Rev. 445, 447-60.

[21]See: Hersch Lauterpacht, *The Function of Law in the International Community* (Clarendon Press, Oxford 1933) 76-8.

[22]Cf. Hersch Lauterpacht, *The Function of Law in the International Community* (Clarendon Press, Oxford 1933) 76-8.

[23]Hersch Lauterpacht, *The Function of Law in the International Community* (Clarendon Press, Oxford 1933) 76. The acknowledgement of this kind of gaps was not inconsistent with Lauterpacht's well-known advocacy for the 'completeness' of international law; Lauterpacht summarized his own views on the subject as follows: "[i]f consent is the essential condition for the existence of a rule of international law, then a revealed and deliberate absence of agreement should clearly point to the existence of a gap on the subject [...] It is submitted that this view can be adopted only subject to the qualification that the gap is virtually filled when the States recognize the authority of obligatory judicial settlement [...] in the absence of an agreed rule, the judge would have to reject the demand of the plaintiff State on the ground that no evidence of a rule of international law limiting the freedom of action of the defendant State has been produced. The fundamental principle of the formal completeness of the international legal system cannot be affected by the mere fact of a number of States disagreeing on a particular subject" (at p. 77). For a historical analysis of Lauterpacht's approach see: Martti Koskenniemi, *The Gentle Civilizer of Nations. The Rise and Fall of International Law 1870-1960* (Cambridge University Press, New York 2008) 361-9.

[24]See, for example: Ernst Isay, *Das deutsche Fremdenrecht. Ausländer und Polizei* (Verlag von Georg Stilke, Berlin 1923) 21.

instance, the German public law scholar Ernst Isay claimed in 1923 that 'the legal status of foreigners in a state cannot be governed [by a law] different to the law of that state'.[25] Isay explained:

> Even if general guidelines could be obtained from international law in this connection, international law fails as soon as it comes to the assessment of the specifics.[26]

Isay further noted that, in any case, specific international commitments regarding the protection of aliens would not be applied in practice as rules of international law, but as rules of German domestic law, since they would be incorporated into the local legal order under article 4 of the Weimar Constitution (1919).[27] In 1965, Karl Doehring would sharply criticize Isay's approach, considering it inadequate for the assessment of the status of aliens and inconsistent with the German Constitution of 1949.[28]

---

[25] Author's translation. The original German text reads: "Allein die Rechtslage der Ausländer in einem bestimmten Staat kann gar nicht anders behandelt werden, als nach dem Recht eben dieses Staates." Ernst Isay, *Das deutsche Fremdenrecht. Ausländer und Polizei* (Verlag von Georg Stilke, Berlin 1923) 21.

[26] Author's translation. The original German text reads: "Sollten selbst aus dem Völkerrecht in dieser Beziehung gewisse allgemeine Richtlinien zu gewinnen sein, so versagt doch das Völkerrecht, sobald es sich um die Beurteilung der Einzelheiten handelt." Ernst Isay, *Das deutsche Fremdenrecht. Ausländer und Polizei* (Verlag von Georg Stilke, Berlin 1923) 22.

[27] Article 4 of the Weimar Constitution provided: "Generally recognized rules of international law shall be applicable as binding elements of the law of the German Empire." Author's translation. The original German text reads: "Die allgemein anerkannten Regeln des Völkerrechts gelten als bindende Bestandteile des deutschen Reichsrechts." Verfassung des deutschen Reiches (11 August 1929) (Reichszentrale für Heimatdienst, Berlin 1929) art. 4. For Isay's interpretation of this provision see: Ernst Isay, *Das deutsche Fremdenrecht. Ausländer und Polizei* (Verlag von Georg Stilke, Berlin 1923) 21-3.

[28] Karl Doehring, *Die allgemeinen Regeln des völkerrechtlichen Fremdenrechts und das deutsche Verfassungsrecht* (Carl Heymanns Verlag, Köln/Berlin 1963) 1-8. Doehring partially based his argument on Article 25 of the German Constitution of 1949, according to which '[t]he general rules of international law form part of German federal law. They take precedence over the laws and directly give rise to rights and obligations for the inhabitants of the [German] territory'. Author's translation. The original German text reads: "Die allgemeinen Regeln des Völkerrechtes sind Bestandteil des Bundesrechtes. Sie gehen den Gesetzen vor und erzeugen Rechte und Pflichten unmittelbar für die Bewohner des Bundesgebietes." Grundgesetz für die Bundesrepublik Deutschland (23 May 1949) BGBl. 1 art. 25. According to Doehring: "Article 25 GG does not only declare, as did Article 4 WRV, international law as domestic law, but it further gives [international law] precedence over [municipal] law. [The norm moreover] allows deriving from [international law] rights and obligations not only for the state, but also for individuals. No national legal directive concerning the law of aliens shall collide with the international law of aliens. International law is not only a means of interpretation of the municipal law of aliens, or an instruction by the international community that the state shall adopt the correspondent regulations, but a direct source of substantive law. Whoever looks into the German law of aliens shall, *unu actu*, deal with international law." Author's translation. The original German text reads: "Art. 25 GG erklärt nicht nur, wie Art. 4 WRV, das Völkerrecht zu nationalem Recht, sondern ordnet es den Gesetzen vor und läßt aus ihm neben Rechten und Pflichten der Staatsgewalt auch solche der Individuen entstehen. Kein nationaler Rechtssatz, der sich auf das Fremdenrecht bezieht, darf mit den Normen des völkerrechtlichen Fremdenrechts kollidieren. Das Völkerrecht ist nicht mehr nur Auslegungsmittel des nationalen

A second objection to Borchard's argument is that the doctrine of equality does not necessarily imply turning around the hierarchy between municipal law and international law. At least in theory, the treatment owed to foreigners could be defined in terms of non-discrimination.[29] Such approach would not shatter any fundamental principles of international law: it would merely require some resort to local law, in order to establish a *tertium comparationis* and verify whether unjustified discrimination has actually taken place.[30]

This shows that, even well into the twentieth century, the minimum standard could not be convincingly established as a customary rule, neither through induction nor through deduction.[31]

Most importantly, the academic debate on the minimum standard was far from over: the minimum standard would face yet another challenge in the 1960s. In 1961, Guha Roy advocated for a 'modernization' of the law in line with the doctrine of equality.[32] His argument was much more radical than that pursued decades before by Carlos Calvo and other Latin American jurists.[33] Roy called into question the binding character of the law of aliens in respect of the third world.[34] In this vein, he submitted that this was a dogmatically weak area of law, which had developed in pursuit of imperialistic policies in the interest of the handful of Western states that conformed the international community before World War II.[35] Roy noted that

---

Fremdenrechts oder ein Auftrag der Völkergemeinschaft an den Staat, entsprechende Regelungen zu treffen, sondern unmittelbare Rechtsquelle des materiellen Rechts. Wer sich mit dem nationalen Fremdenrecht befaßt, muß *unu actu* das Völkerrecht behandeln" (at p. 1).

[29] Section 4.3.1 provides examples of treaties and other sources following this approach. Cf. also Sect. 14.3.

[30] For a similar argument see: Karl Doehring, *Die allgemeinen Regeln des völkerrechtlichen Fremdenrechts und das deutsche Verfassungsrecht* (Carl Heymanns Verlag, Köln/Berlin 1963) 92-3. It is not uncommon for norms of international law to entail some *renvoi* to municipal legal systems. For a detailed analysis of the issue of *renvoi* in international law and, particularly, in international investment law, see: Monique Sasson, *Substantive Law in Investment Treaty Arbitration* (Kluwer Law International, Alphen aan den Rijn 2010) xi-xxxii and 195-208; Nils Börnsen, *Nationales Recht in Investitionsschiedsverfahren* (Mohr Siebeck, Tübingen 2016) 82 *et seq.*

[31] See also Sects. 2.3 and 4.3.3.

[32] Guha Roy, 'Is the Law of Responsibility of States for Injuries to Aliens a Part of Universal International Law?' (1963) 55(4) AJIL 863, 884-5. Following Roy, upon admitting an alien into its territory '[the host state] does not in any way guarantee his life and property beyond the point to which its laws may guarantee them to its own nationals' (at p. 884). In the end, Roy observed, '[a]n alien entering foreign territory of his own free will does so entirely at his own risk and with the full knowledge of the conditions there' (at p. 884). In addition, '[t]he most effective form of security for a foreigner lies in the confidence he can create around him in the state where he lives or owns property and also in the laws of that state' (at p. 885).

[33] Section 4.3.2 discusses the Calvo Doctrine in detail.

[34] Guha Roy, 'Is the Law of Responsibility of States for Injuries to Aliens a Part of Universal International Law?' (1963) 55(4) AJIL 863, 867-8 and 881 *et seq.*

[35] Roy's argument focused on the 'Vattelian fiction' and other traditional premises of the law of diplomatic protection. See: Guha Roy, 'Is the Law of Responsibility of States for Injuries to Aliens a Part of Universal International Law?' (1963) 55(4) AJIL 863, 863-80 (particularly at pp. 865 and

'[b]eyond the frontiers of this community there was a vaster world'.[36] According to him, the idea that the present-day international community is a mere 'expanded version of the old' implies 'an analogy between this community and a club' which, 'like most analogies, seems superficial and misleading'.[37] Based on these observations, Roy concluded:

> The new born world community must have a new set of laws to govern the interrelations of its members as well as other matters. This new set of laws may, of course, be built round a nucleus of as much of the old law as may be found to be conducive to the larger interests, not only of some members of this new community, but of all.[38]

For what reason does then a state owe foreign nationals a treatment consistent with a 'minimum standard' or, using a nineteenth century terminology, a 'standard of civilization'? From a contemporary perspective, it is the increasing number of IIAs containing references to the customary standard what most clearly confirms the existence, that is to say, the present-day existence, of the minimum standard.[39] A survey of post-Second World War treaty practice indeed suggests that states have mostly given up their insistence on the doctrine of equality,[40] embracing both the

---

888). For an overview of the more-general historical debate about the binding character of international law in respect of developing countries see: Anna Krueger, *Die Bindung der Dritten Welt an das postkoloniale Völkerrecht* (Springer, Heidelberg 2017) 41 *et seq.* and 359-62.

[36]Guha Roy, 'Is the Law of Responsibility of States for Injuries to Aliens a Part of Universal International Law?' (1963) 55(4) AJIL 863, 881.

[37]Guha Roy, 'Is the Law of Responsibility of States for Injuries to Aliens a Part of Universal International Law?' (1963) 55(4) AJIL 863, 881.

[38]Guha Roy, 'Is the Law of Responsibility of States for Injuries to Aliens a Part of Universal International Law?' (1963) 55(4) AJIL 863, 882. For a discussion of Roy's views and the enduring debate on the subject cf. Rumana Islam, *The Fair and Equitable Treatment Standard (FET) in International Investment Arbitration* (Springer, Singapore 2018) 57.

[39]Resorting to BITs as a means to establish the existence and scope of customary international law is by no means a novel approach. For an author relying on investment agreements to prove the existence of the minimum standard see: Karl Doehring, 'Gewohnheitsrecht aus Verträgen' (1976) 36 ZaöRV 77, 90-1. For a more recent example see: Patrick Dumberry, *The Formation and Identification of Customary International Law in International Investment Law* (Cambridge University Press, Cambridge 2016) 98-9 (additionally referring to arguments advanced by respondent states in investment arbitral proceedings). However, Dumberry is critical of scholars considering that IIAs entail an expression of a new corpus of customary law (at pp. 160-205 and 415-7). See also: Francis A. Mann, 'British Treaties for the Promotion and Protection of Investments' (1981) 52 BYIL 241, 249-50; Stephen Schwebel, 'Investor-State Disputes and the Development of International Law. The Influence of Bilateral Investment Treaties on Customary International Law' (2004) 98 ASIL Proceedings 27, 27-30. This line of argument has always been somewhat controversial. For skeptical views see: Andrew Guzmán, 'Why LDCs Sign Treaties That Hurt Them: Explaining the Popularity of Bilateral Investment Treaties' (1997) 38 Va. J. Int'l L. 639, 686; Bernard Kishoiyian, 'The Utility of Bilateral Investment Treaties in the Formulation of Customary International Law' (1993-4) 14 Nw. J. Int'l L. & Bus. 327, 327-75.

[40]See generally: Patrick Dumberry, *The Formation and Identification of Customary International Law in International Investment Law* (Cambridge University Press, Cambridge 2016) 98-9.

ideas and the terminology Elihu Root advocated for in 1910.[41] Not only treaties
between traditional capital-exporting economies evidence this trend, but also IIAs
between capital-exporting and capital-importing states.[42] Clauses acknowledging
the customary 'minimum standard of treatment' may be found even in investment
agreements concluded by developing or newly industrialized states among themselves (so-called 'south-south agreements').[43]

---

[41]On the relevance of Root's speech for the subsequent development of the law of aliens see
generally: Martins Paparinskis, *The International Minimum Standard and Fair and Equitable
Treatment* (Oxford University Press, Oxford 2013) 39 *et seq.* (also providing a critical assessment
of Root's argument). It must be noted, however, that Paparinskis considers that the postwar period
was signalized by a 'shift of the paradigm the standard was meant to regulate' (at p. 64). The new
'paradigm' relates to 'business interests of corporate investors' (at p. 64).

[42]See, for example: Agreement between Canada and Mali for the Promotion and Protection of
Investments (adopted 28 November 2014) art. 6(1) and (2); Agreement between Japan and the
Oriental Republic of Uruguay for the Liberalization, Promotion and Protection of Investment
(adopted 26 January 2015) art. 5; Agreement between Japan and the Republic of Colombia for
the Liberalization, Promotion and Protection of Investment (adopted 12 September 2011) art. 4
(1) and (2); Agreement between Japan and the Republic of Peru for the Promotion, Protection and
Liberalization of Investment (adopted 22 November 2008, entered into force 10 December 2009)
art. 5(1) and (2); Agreement between the Belgium-Luxembourg Economic Union and the Republic
of Colombia on the Reciprocal Promotion and Protection of Investments (adopted 4 February 2009)
art. III(4); Agreement between the Government of the United Kingdom and the Government of the
United Mexican States for the Promotion and Reciprocal Protection of Investments (adopted
12 May 2006, entered into force 25 July 2007) art. 3; Bilateral Investment Treaty between the
Government of Canada and the Republic of Côte d'Ivoire (adopted 30 November 2014) art. 6
(1) and (2); Free Trade Agreement between Australia and the Republic of Korea (adopted 8 April
2014) art. 11(5); Free Trade Agreement between CACM, the Dominican Republic and the United
States of America (adopted 5 August 2004, entered into force 1 January 2009) art. 10(5)(1) and (2);
Free Trade Agreement between the Government of the United States of America and the Government of Chile (adopted 6 June 2003, entered into force 1 January 2004) art. 10(4)(1) and (2); Free
Trade Agreement between the Kingdom of Morocco and the United States of America (adopted
15 June 2004, entered into force 1 January 2006) art. 10(5)(1) and (2); Free Trade Agreement
between the United States of America and the Republic of Colombia (adopted 22 November 2006,
entered into force 15 May 2012) art. 10(5)(1) and (2); Free Trade Agreement between the United
States of America and the Sultanate of Oman (adopted 19 January 2006, entered into force
1 January 2009) art. 10(5)(1) and (2); Free Trade Agreement between the United States of America
and the Republic of Peru (adopted 12 April 2006, entered into force 1 February 2009) art. 10(5)
(1) and (2); North American Free Trade Agreement (adopted 17 December 1992, entered into force
1 January 1994) art. 1105; Protocol to the Agreement between the Government of Australia and the
Government of the United Mexican States on the Promotion and Reciprocal Protection of Investments (adopted 23 August 2005, entered into force 21 July 2007) art. 4(1) and (2); Treaty between
Australia and Japan for an Economic Partnership (adopted 8 July 2014), art. 14(5).

[43]For some representative examples see: Agreement between the Government of the Republic of
Azerbaijan and the Government of the Syrian Arab Republic on the Promotion and Reciprocal
Protection of Investments (adopted 8 July 2009, entered into force 4 January 2010) art. 2(2);
Agreement between the Government of the Republic of Croatia and the Government of the
Republic of Azerbaijan on the Promotion and Reciprocal Protection of Investments (adopted
2 November 2007, entered into force 30 May 2008) art. 2(2); Agreement between the Government
of the Republic of Mauritius and the Government of the Arab Republic of Egypt in the Reciprocal
Promotion and Protection of Investments (adopted 25 June 2014) art. 4(2); Agreement between the

The FPS standard is nowadays widely regarded as an element of the customary minimum standard of treatment.[44] In the NAFTA context, the NAFTA Free Trade Commission [FTC] has made clear that it is the contracting states' understanding that the FPS clause of NAFTA constitutes a codification of a particular element of the minimum standard.[45] In this vein, in *Mondev v United States* (2002), the arbitrators observed:

> [T]he phrase "Minimum standard of treatment" has historically been understood as a reference to a minimum standard under customary international law, whatever controversies there may have been over the content of that standard [...] The FTC interpretation makes it clear that in Article 1105(1) *the terms "fair and equitable treatment" and "full protection and security" are, in the view of the NAFTA Parties, references to existing elements of the*

Government of the Republic of Turkey and the Government of the Islamic Republic of Pakistan concerning the Reciprocal Promotion and Protection of Investments (adopted 22 May 2012) art. 3 (2); Agreement between the Government of the United Mexican States and the Government of the Republic of Belarus on the Promotion and Reciprocal Protection of Investments (adopted 4 September 2008, entered into force 27 August 2009) art. 5; Agreement between the Government of the United Mexican States and the Government of the Republic of India on the Promotion and Protection of Investments (adopted 21 May 2007, entered into force 23 February 2008) art. 5(3)(a); Agreement between the Republic of Guatemala and the Republic of Trinidad and Tobago on the Reciprocal Promotion and Protection of Investments (adopted 13 August 2013) art. 4; Agreement between the Republic of Turkey and the Government of the Gabonese Republic concerning the Reciprocal Promotion and Protection of Investments (adopted 18 July 2012) art. 3(2); Agreement between the United Mexican States and the Slovak Republic on the Promotion and Reciprocal Protection of Investments (adopted 26 October 2007, entered into force 8 April 2009) art. 5(2)(a); Agreement for the Promotion and Protection of Investments between the Republic of Colombia and the Republic of India (adopted 10 November 2009, entered into force 3 July 2013) art. 3(4)(c); Comprehensive Economic Cooperation Agreement between the Government of Malaysia and the Government of the Republic of India (adopted 18 February 2011, entered into force 1 July 2011) art. 10(5)(2); Free Trade Agreement between the Government of the People's Republic of China and the Government of the Republic of Peru (adopted 28 April 2009, entered into force 1 March 2010) art. 132(2)(a); Free Trade Agreement between the Republic of China (Taiwan) and the Republic of Nicaragua (adopted 23 June 2006, entered into force 1 January 2008) art. 10(5); Investment Agreement for the COMESA Common Investment Area (adopted 23 May 2007) art. 14(2). On south-south IIAs see generally: UNCTAD, *South-South Cooperation in International Investment Arrangements* (United Nations, New York/Geneva 2005). For an analysis of south-south IIAs from a political perspective see: Lauge Skovgaard Poulsen, 'The Politics of South-South Bilateral Investment Treaties' in Tomer Broude, Marc Busch and Amelia Porges (eds), *The Politics of International Economic Law* (Cambridge University Press, New York 2011) 186, 186-211. For an analysis of FPS clauses in African treaties, including those containing references to the minimum standard, see: Eric De Brabandere, 'Fair and Equitable Treatment and (Full) Protection and Security in African Investment Treaties: Between Generality and Contextual Specificity' (2017) Grotius Centre Working Paper Series 1, 9 *et seq.* (arguing that, generally speaking, there is no difference in substance between African IIAs and IIAs from other regions; Brabandere analyzes intra-African treaties at pp. 12 *et seq.*).

[44]This statement is a common place in specialized literature about the FPS standard. See n. 3 above.

[45]NAFTA Free Trade Commission, *Notes of Interpretation of Certain Chapter 11 Provisions* (31 July 2001) [http://www.sice.oas.org/tpd/nafta/Commission/CH11understanding_e.asp] § B (1) and (2).

customary international law standard and are not intended to add novel elements to that standard.[46]

Beyond the particular context of NAFTA, numerous BITs and FTAs style FPS as an element of the 'minimum standard'.[47] This phenomenon is rather unusual in

---

[46]Emphasis added. Mondev International *v* United States, Award, ICSID Case No. ARB(AF)/99/2 (11 October 2002) [121-2]. See also para 124. The tribunal additionally expressed support for 'a reasonable evolutionary interpretation' of the customary standard (at paras 123 and 125). For an author commenting on the statement quoted in the principal text see: Martins Paparinskis, *The International Minimum Standard and Fair and Equitable Treatment* (Oxford University Press, Oxford 2013) 18 (also mentioning the problem of the influence of IIAs on international custom).

[47]For a representative example see: Free Trade Agreement between CACM, the Dominican Republic and the United States of America (adopted 5 August 2004, entered into force 1 January 2009) art. 10(5)(1) and (2) ("1. Each Party shall accord to covered investments treatment in accordance with customary international law, including fair and equitable treatment and full protection and security. 2. For greater certainty, paragraph 1 prescribes the customary international law minimum standard of treatment of aliens as the minimum standard of treatment to be afforded to covered investments. The concepts of "fair and equitable treatment" and "full protection and security" do not require treatment in addition to or beyond that which is required by that standard, and do not create additional substantive rights"). For some additional examples see: Agreement between Canada and Mali for the Promotion and Protection of Investments (adopted 28 November 2014) art. 6; Agreement between Japan and the Oriental Republic of Uruguay for the Liberalization, Promotion and Protection of Investment (adopted 26 January 2015) art. 5; Agreement between Japan and the Republic of Colombia for the Liberalization, Promotion and Protection of Investment (adopted 12 September 2011) art. 4(1) and (2); Agreement between Japan and the Republic of Peru for the Promotion, Protection and Liberalization of Investment (adopted 22 November 2008, entered into force 10 December 2009) art. 5(1) and (2); Agreement between the Government of the Republic of Azerbaijan and the Government of the Syrian Arab Republic on the Promotion and Reciprocal Protection of Investments (adopted 8 July 2009, entered into force 4 January 2010) art. 2 (2); Agreement between the Government of the Republic of Croatia and the Government of the Republic of Azerbaijan on the Promotion and Reciprocal Protection of Investments (adopted 2 November 2007, entered into force 30 May 2008) 2(2); Agreement between the Government of the Republic of Turkey and the Government of the Islamic Republic of Pakistan concerning the Reciprocal Promotion and Protection of Investments (adopted 22 May 2012) art. 3(2); Agreement between the Government of the United Kingdom and the Government of the United Mexican States for the Promotion and Reciprocal Protection of Investments (adopted 12 May 2006, entered into force 25 July 2007) art. 3(1); Agreement between the Government of the United Mexican States and the Government of the Republic of Belarus on the Promotion and Reciprocal Protection of Investments (adopted 4 September 2008, entered into force 27 August 2009) art. 5(1); Agreement between the Republic of Turkey and the Government of the Gabonese Republic concerning the Reciprocal Promotion and Protection of Investments (adopted 18 July 2012) art. 3(2); Agreement between the United Mexican States and the Slovak Republic on the Promotion and Reciprocal Protection of Investments (adopted 26 October 2007, entered into force 8 April 2009) art. 5(1); Bilateral Investment Treaty between the Government of Canada and the Republic of Côte d'Ivoire (adopted 30 November 2014) art. 6(1); Comprehensive Economic Cooperation Agreement between the Government of Malaysia and the Government of the Republic of India (adopted 18 February 2011, entered into force 1 July 2011); Free Trade Agreement between Australia and the Republic of Korea (adopted 8 April 2014) 11(5)(1); Free Trade Agreement between the Government of the United States of America and the Government of Chile (adopted 6 June 2003, entered into force 1 January 2004) 10(4)(1); Free Trade Agreement between the Kingdom of Morocco and the United States of America (adopted 15 June 2004, entered into force 1 January 2006) art. 10(5)(1); Free

international law.[48] Judge Richard Reeve Baxter observed in 1970 that 'treaties that assert on their face that they incorporate customary international law are rare'.[49] Considering the particular case of explicit 'declaratory statements' in multilateral treaties, Baxter noted that '[j]uridically, they would count for no more and no less than proof of the State practice of each of the States parties, taken in their totality'.[50] Hence, these treaties primarily *facilitate* proof of the [customary] law'.[51] Baxter also underscored that such statements entail an astonishingly clear expression of the subjective element of international custom (*opinio juris*):

> [A] sense of a legal obligation [. . .] is unambiguously present in a treaty, to which States become parties with full realization that they thereby assume legal obligations and may claim legal rights.[52]

Trade Agreement between the Republic of China (Taiwan) and the Republic of Nicaragua (adopted 23 June 2006, entered into force 1 January 2008) art. 10(5)(1); Free Trade Agreement between the United States of America and the Republic of Colombia (adopted 22 November 2006, entered into force 15 May 2012) art. 10(5)(1); Free Trade Agreement between the United States of America and the Sultanate of Oman (adopted 19 January 2006, entered into force 1 January 2009) art. 10(5)(1); Free Trade Agreement between the United States of America and the Republic of Peru (adopted 12 April 2006, entered into force 1 February 2009) art. 10(5)(1); North American Free Trade Agreement (adopted 17 December 1992, entered into force 1 January 1994) 1105(1); Reciprocal Investment Promotion and Protection Agreement between the Government of the Kingdom of Morocco and the Government of the Federal Republic of Nigeria (adopted 3 December 2016) art. 7; Treaty between Australia and Japan for an Economic Partnership (adopted 8 July 2014) art. 14(5). Some agreements use a different wording, by acknowledging FPS as a customary rule without *expressly* labeling it *as an element* of the international minimum standard. However, these treaties typically clarify that FPS imposes no obligation beyond the 'minimum standard'. For an indicative example see: Agreement between the Belgium-Luxembourg Economic Union and the Republic of Colombia on the Reciprocal Promotion and Protection of Investments (adopted 4 February 2009) art. 3(2) and (4)(a). See also the interpretation of article V of the US-Italy FCN Agreement of 1948 in the *ELSI case* of 1989: *Case Concerning Elettronica Sicula S.p.A. (ELSI) (United States of America v Italy)* [1989] ICJ Rep 15, 66 [111] (stating that '[t]he primary standard laid down by Article V is "the full protection and security required by international law", in short the "protection and security" must conform to the international minimum standard').

[48]Richard Reeve Baxter, 'Treaties and Custom' (1970) 129 RCADI 25, 38.

[49]Richard Reeve Baxter, 'Treaties and Custom' (1970) 129 RCADI 25, 38.

[50]Richard Reeve Baxter, 'Treaties and Custom' (1970) 129 RCADI 25, 43. It should be noted that Baxter was considering at this point the hypothesis of a fictional multilateral treaty, ratified by all but one state in the world, having the specific aim of declaring customary law and using the 'clearest possible language' for this purpose (at p. 36).

[51]Richard Reeve Baxter, 'Treaties and Custom' (1970) 129 RCADI 25, 43. Treaties cannot only provide proof of customary law, but can also influence the formation of customary norms. See: *North Sea Continental Shelf (Germany v Denmark/Germany v Netherlands)* [1969] ICJ Rep. 3, 41 [71]. Judge Baxter analyzed this decision in detail (at pp. 43 and 45 *et eq.*). See also: Brian Lepard, *Customary International Law. A New Theory with Practical Applications* (Cambridge University Press, New York 2011) 31.

[52]Richard Reeve Baxter, 'Treaties and Custom' (1970) 129 RCADI 25, 37-8. For a critical assessment of Baxter's approach to the *opinio juris* element see: Karl Doehring, 'Gewohnheitsrecht aus Verträgen' (1976) 36 ZaöRV 77, 93 (arguing that the sense of a legal obligation cannot be deduced from the mere fact that state practice crystalized in international treaties; it is required that

The use of treaties as evidence of international custom has long been debated in academic circles, and continues to be controversial.[53] However, there seems to be some agreement that, where a treaty *expressly* declares that one of its provisions codifies a customary norm, such treaty clause provides genuine evidence of the 'sense of a legal obligation'.[54]

This effect can be derived not only from multilateral treaties, but also from bilateral treaties.[55] Judge Baxter suggested that the repeated use of the same wording in bilateral treaties could originate a 'form contract', which, like a multilateral agreement, could also be considered as an expression of international custom.[56] More explicitly, Karl Doehring observed in 1963:

---

states perceive the obligation as binding beyond the legal relationship between the parties to the treaty).

[53] A clear example would be the debate between Anthony D'Amato and Arthur M. Weisburd regarding D'Amato's contention that 'generalizable provisions in bilateral and multilateral treaties generate customary rules of law binding upon all states'. See: Anthony D'Amato, *The Concept of Custom in International Law* (Cornell University Press, Ithaca/London 1971) 104 (and pp. 103-66). See also: Anthony D'Amato, *Treaties as a Source of General International Law* (1961-2) 3 (2) Harv. Int'l. L. Club Bull. 1, 1-43 (first version of D'Amato's argument, which was based on a student paper written under supervision of Judge Baxter). For the D'Amato-Weisburd debate see: Arthur Weisburd, 'Customary International Law: The Problem of Treaties' (1988) 21 Vand. J. Transnat'l L. 1, 10-46; Anthony D'Amato, 'Custom and Treaty: A Response to Professor Weisburd' (1988) 21 Vand. J. Transnat'l L. 459, 459-72; Arthur Weisburd, 'A Reply to Professor D'Amato' (1988) 21 Vand. J. Transnat'l L. 473, 473-88; Anthony D'Amato, 'A Brief Rejoinder' (1988) 21 Vand. J. Transnat'l L. 489, 489-90.

[54] Even the most skeptical authors agreed on this point. For a representative example see: Arthur Weisburd, 'Customary International Law: The Problem of Treaties' (1988) 21 Vand. J. Transnat'l L. 1, 23 ("[the *opinio juris* requirement] means that a state acknowledges the right of states to whom it owes a putative duty to inquire about possible breaches of the duty and also acknowledges its obligation to make reparation for any breaches of the duty. *With respect to many treaties, this determination can lead to the conclusion that the treaty is not merely an example of practice, but in addition, an example of practice believed to be legally binding. This is most obviously true of treaties that state explicitly that they are declarative of custom. Even when this type of statement is an inaccurate description of the state of law as of the date of the treaty's conclusion, it amounts to an explicit acknowledgement by the parties to the treaties that they would be legally bound to the treaty's rules even if the treaty did not exist. This acknowledgement makes it easy to include those parties in the tally of states that not only follow a given practice but do so in the belief that the practice is law.*" – emphasis added).

[55] Karl Doehring, 'Gewohnheitsrecht aus Verträgen' (1976) 36 ZaöRV 77, 85 *et seq.*

[56] Richard Reeve Baxter, 'Treaties and Custom' (1970) 129 RCADI 25, 77. Baxter did not address the international minimum standard as such. He did however consider some issues related to the law of aliens, such as the so-called 'lump-sum agreements' on nationalized foreign property (at pp. 87-8). On the use of bilateral treaties as evidence of international custom see also: Richard Reeve Baxter, 'Multilateral Treaties as Evidence of Customary International Law' (1965-6) 41 BYIL 275, 276-7; Brian Lepard, *Customary International Law. A New Theory with Practical Applications* (Cambridge University Press, New York 2011) 30-2.

[Q]uantity may become quality when a series of new treaties stipulates the same rights and obligations, which were not originally conceived as self-evident.[57]

In a later article (1976), Doehrig elaborated further on this idea:

Neither the quantity of the treaties, nor the number or quality of the parties can for themselves create such effect [i.e. giving a rule a binding character in respect of third states]. It is always additionally required that the treaty practice in question confirms an unavoidable, intense and vital interest of the community of states, or an interest that entails no severe contradiction with the maintenance of state sovereignty.[58]

Doehring believed that postwar FCN treaty practice fulfilled these requirements and, hence, provided evidence of the customary character of the minimum standard.[59] This view is not far from contemporary literature on investment law.[60] A similar line of argument has been followed in arbitral decisions.[61] The award

---

[57] Author's translation. The original German text reads: "[Der Einfluß des Vertragsrechts auf das Gewohnheitsrecht ist nicht geringer.] Die Quantität kann zur Qualität werden, wenn eine Reihe neuerer Verträge gleiche, zunächst nicht als selbstverständlich empfundene Rechte und Pflichten stipuliert." Karl Doehring, *Die allgemeinen Regeln des völkerrechtlichen Fremdenrechts und das deutsche Verfassungsrecht* (Carl Heymanns Verlag, Köln/Berlin 1963) 15.

[58] Author's translation. The original German text reads: "Weder die Zahl der Verträge, noch ihre Teilnehmerzahl oder Teilnehmerqualität allein können diesen Effekt herbeiführen. Immer müßte hinzukommen, daß festgestellt werden kann, die angeführte Vertragspraxis bestätige ein unabwendbares, intensives und als lebensnotwendig empfundenes Interesse der Staatengemeinschaft oder auch ein solches Interesse, dem dasjenige an der Aufrechterhaltung der staatlichen Souveränität nicht in besonderem Maße entgegengesetzt werden kann." Karl Doehring, 'Gewohnheitsrecht aus Verträgen' (1976) 36 ZaöRV 77, 92-3 (also analyzing at pp. 84-6 the requirement that the treaty-based rule be capable of generalization, and discussing at pp. 90 *et seq.* the particular case of the minimum standard).

[59] Karl Doehring, 'Gewohnheitsrecht aus Verträgen' (1976) 36 ZaöRV 77, 90-1 (particularly focusing on the obligation to provide judicial protection to aliens and the notion of denial of justice). For a detailed analysis of the role of investment treaties in the formation of customary law see: Patrick Dumberry, *The Formation and Identification of Customary International Law in International Investment Law* (Cambridge University Press, Cambridge 2016) 160-205 and 415-7. For an overview see: Matthias Herdegen, *Völkerrecht* (C.H. Beck, Munich 2017) 156-8.

[60] See, for example: Patrick Dumberry, *The Formation and Identification of Customary International Law in International Investment Law* (Cambridge University Press, Cambridge 2016) 98-9 (referring to the minimum standard) and 354 *et seq.* (referring to FET treaty provisions).

[61] Pope & Talbot Inc. *v* Canada (UNCITRAL), Award in respect of Damages (31 May 2002) [62] (concluding that investment treaties constitute state practice for the purposes of establishing customary international law); Loewen Group Inc. and Raymond L. Loewen *v* United States, Award, ICSID Case No. ARB(AF)/98/3 (26 June 2003) [131] (noting that BITs express 'the content of custom in international law' and quoting *Pope & Talbot v Canada* in this connection); Murphy Exploration & Production Co. *v* Ecuador (UNCITRAL), Partial Final Award (6 May 2016) [207-8] (taking cognizance of the approach followed in other cases and noting at para 208 that '[t]he international minimum standard and the treaty standard continue to influence each other and, in the view of the Tribunal, these standards are increasingly aligned'). For the opposite view see the claimant's argument in *ADF v USA* (2003): ADF *v* United States, Award, ICSID Case No. ARB (AF)/00/1 (9 January 2003) [70] (arguing that, if there was a customary FPS standard, 'there would have been no need for the multitude of bilateral investment treaties [. . .] which are now in force').

rendered in *Mondev v United States* (2002) provides a clear example of this approach:

> [T]he vast number of bilateral and regional investment treaties (more than 2000) almost uniformly provide for fair and equitable treatment of foreign investments, and largely provide for full protection and security of investments. Investment treaties between North and South, and East and West, and between States in these spheres *inter se*. On a remarkably widespread basis, States have repeatedly obliged themselves to accord foreign investment such treatment. In the Tribunal's view, such a body of concordant practice will necessarily have influenced the content of rules governing the treatment of foreign investment in current international law.[62]

The constant references to a customary minimum standard made in contemporary IIAs, as well as the frequent declaration of FPS as a constituent element of such general standard, may thus be taken as evidence of both state practice and the sense of a legal obligation.[63]

A possible objection to this analysis should not remain unattended: Andrew Guzmán suggested in 1998 that BITs could not be regarded as evidence of customary international law because there was a lack of *opinio juris* on the part of least developed countries ["LDCs"].[64] While Guzmán primarily referred to protection against expropriation, his views could be also relevant for the assessment of other standards:

> LDCs face a prisoner's dilemma in which it is optimal for them, as a group, to reject the Hull Rule [i.e. no expropriation without prompt, adequate and effective compensation], but in which each individual LDC is better off "defecting" from the group by signing a BIT that gives it the advantage over other LDCs in the competition to attract foreign investors.[65]

Guzmán summarized his own argument in the following terms:

> If BITs are signed out of a sense of obligation or to clarify a legal obligation, they must be considered evidence of customary international law. On the other hand, if BITs are signed for reasons unrelated, or even contrary, to a country's sense of obligation, BITs are not evidence of customary international law [. . .] That BITs have been signed in large numbers merely demonstrates the magnitude of the perceived benefits associated with the ability to avoid the dynamic inconsistency problem. Thus, if countries have signed BITs out of

---

[62]Mondev International *v* United States, Award, ICSID Case No. ARB(AF)/99/2 (11 October 2002) [117] (also applying this reasoning to the FPS standard at para 125). The *Mondev* award has influenced subsequent arbitral decisions. For a representative example see: Murphy Exploration & Production Co. *v* Ecuador (UNCITRAL), Partial Final Award (6 May 2016) [207-8]. See also n. 42, 43 and 47 above.

[63]See generally: Patrick Dumberry, *The Formation and Identification of Customary International Law in International Investment Law* (Cambridge University Press, Cambridge 2016) 98-9.

[64]Andrew Guzmán, 'Why LDCs Sign Treaties That Hurt Them: Explaining the Popularity of Bilateral Investment Treaties' (1997) 38 Va. J. Int'l L. 639, 685 *et seq.*

[65]Andrew Guzmán, 'Why LDCs Sign Treaties That Hurt Them: Explaining the Popularity of Bilateral Investment Treaties' (1997) 38 Va. J. Int'l L. 639, 666-7.

economic motives, the treaties should not be interpreted as evidence of customary international law.[66]

This argument has met with sharp criticism.[67] José E. Álvarez has observed that the vast majority of customary rules came into existence as a result of 'economic' or 'political' interests of states.[68] According to Álvarez, '[t]hese rationales do not undercut the existence of *opinio juris*'.[69] Thus, while the 'economic concerns' of developing states could be what motivates some of them to enter into IIAs, 'this economic rationale for concluding a BIT does not necessarily undercut the potential for BITs to affirm or otherwise affect customary international law'.[70]

The Guzmán-Álvarez debate should not affect the conclusion that IIAs provide irrefutable evidence of the present-day acceptance of the minimum standard, and of FPS as one of its constituting elements. The reason is that, in contemporary IIAs, this recognition is normally unequivocal and express.[71] Guzmán himself stressed that '[c]learly, the BIT's effect on international law would be simplified if these treaties included an *explicit acknowledgement* that the treaty merely codified rules of customary law'.[72]

---

[66]Andrew Guzmán, 'Why LDCs Sign Treaties That Hurt Them: Explaining the Popularity of Bilateral Investment Treaties' (1997) 38 Va. J. Int'l L. 639, 686. See also: Bernard Kishoiyian, 'The Utility of Bilateral Investment Treaties in the Formulation of Customary International Law' (1993-4) 14 Nw. J. Int'l L. & Bus. 327, 327-75.

[67]See: José Álvarez, *The Public International Law Regime Governing International Investment* (Hague Academy of International Law, The Hague 2011) 143.

[68]José Álvarez, *The Public International Law Regime Governing International Investment* (Hague Academy of International Law, The Hague 2011) 143.

[69]José Álvarez, *The Public International Law Regime Governing International Investment* (Hague Academy of International Law, The Hague 2011) 143.

[70]José Álvarez, *The Public International Law Regime Governing International Investment* (Hague Academy of International Law, The Hague 2011) 143.

[71]n. 42, 43 and 47 above provide representative examples of this recognition.

[72]Emphasis added Andrew Guzmán, 'Why LDCs Sign Treaties That Hurt Them: Explaining the Popularity of Bilateral Investment Treaties' (1997) 38 Va. J. Int'l L. 639, 686. For an author discussing the views of Álvarez and Guzmán in connection with the 'Hull formula' see: Patrick Dumberry, *The Formation and Identification of Customary International Law in International Investment Law* (Cambridge University Press, Cambridge 2016) 86-7.

5.3   The Unsettled Content of the International Minimum Standard of Treatment

The characterization of the minimum standard of treatment as a customary norm of international law leaves the question open as to the meaning of the standard.[73] The minimum standard is intrinsically vague, faltering and ambiguous.[74] Using a more optimistic formulation, Edwin Borchard once characterized the standard of civilization as 'mild, flexible and variable'.[75] At the 372nd meeting of the ILC (June 21st, 1956), Sir Gerald Fizmaurice noted that '[t]he standard had never been satisfactorily defined'.[76] During the decades preceding the Second World War, he observed, international adjudicators usually 'refrained from specifying what the standard was'.[77]

At least two approaches have been suggested for the definition of the minimum standard: the human rights approach and the *Neer* approach.[78] The first approach consists in the definition of the minimum standard by recourse to international human rights law.[79] The use of human rights to fill the open-textured international

---

[73]On the indeterminacy of the minimum standard see generally: Patrick Dumberry, *The Formation and Identification of Customary International Law in International Investment Law* (Cambridge University Press, Cambridge 2016) 97-110. See also: ILC, 'Summary Records of the 372nd Meeting' (21 June 1956) 1 *Yearbook of the International Law Commission – 1956* 239, 243 [40].

[74]Cf. Edwin Borchard, 'The "Minimum Standard" of the Treatment of Aliens' (1940) 38(4) Mich. L. Rev. 445, 458. On the indeterminate character of the minimum standard cf. also El Paso Energy International Co. *v* Argentina, Award, ICSID Case No. ARB/03/15 (31 October 2011) [335]; CC/Devas (Mauritius) Ltd., Devas Employees Mauritius Private Ltd. and Telcom Devas Mauritius Ltd. *v* India (UNCITRAL), Award on Jurisdiction and Merits, PCA Case No. 2013-09 (25 July 2016) [456].

[75]Edwin Borchard, 'The "Minimum Standard" of the Treatment of Aliens' (1940) 38(4) Mich. L. Rev. 445, 458.

[76]See: ILC, 'Summary Records of the 372nd Meeting' (21 June 1956) 1 *Yearbook of the International Law Commission – 1956* 239, 243 [40].

[77]See: ILC, 'Summary Records of the 372nd Meeting' (21 June 1956) 1 *Yearbook of the International Law Commission – 1956* 239, 243 [40].

[78]These approaches have been critically discussed in international investment law literature. For a representative example see: Martins Paparinskis, *The International Minimum Standard and Fair and Equitable Treatment* (Oxford University Press, Oxford 2013) 48 *et seq.* (critically discussing the *Neer* decision) and 74 *et seq.* and 171 *et seq.* (analyzing the relationship between the minimum standard, international investment law and human rights, and expressing some support for certain human rights analogies).

[79]For some representative examples see: Alwyn Freeman, 'Human Rights and the Rights of Aliens' (1951) 45 ASIL Proceedings 120, 120-30; Charles Fenwick, 'The Progress of International Law During the Past Forty Years' (1951) 79 RCADI 1, 44; Francisco García Amador, 'International Responsibility: Second Report by F. V. García Amador, Special Rapporteur (A/CN.4/106)' (15 February 1957) 2 *Yearbook of the International Law Commission – 1957* 104, 112-3; Francisco García Amador, 'State Responsibility. Some New Problems' (1958) 94 RCADI 365, 435-9; Karl Doehring, *Die allgemeinen Regeln des völkerrechtlichen Fremdenrechts und das deutsche Verfassungsrecht* (Carl Heymanns Verlag, Köln/Berlin 1963) 68-85; Richard Lillich, *The Human*

minimum standard is a creative but at the same time questionable line of argument.[80] The reasons are many.[81]

To begin with, human rights have developed on the basis of concrete—and mostly regional—treaties.[82] Some human rights may arguably have already gained a customary character, but it is unclear which specific guarantees may be accurately styled as customary.[83] Moreover, as opposed to the minimum standard, human rights are not just a minimum: they provide a degree of protection that could well go

---

Rights of Aliens in Contemporary International Law (Manchester University Press, Manchester 1984) 1-4 and 121-4. For a detailed analysis of the human rights approach see: Martins Paparinskis, *The International Minimum Standard and Fair and Equitable Treatment* (Oxford University Press, Oxford 2013) 74 *et seq.* See also: Sebastián Mantilla Blanco, *Justizielles Unrecht im internationalen Investitionsschutzrecht* (Nomos, Baden-Baden 2016) 77 *et seq.* While the human rights approach, properly so-called, arose in the aftermath of World War II, prewar authorities had already discussed similar ideas. For a representative example see: Edwin Borchard, 'Basic Elements of Diplomatic Protection of Citizens Abroad' (1913) 7(3) AJIL 497, 506-9. For nineteenth century authorities arguing that individuals could be entitled to fundamental guarantees under international law irrespective of their nationality see: Pasquale Fiore, *Il Diritto Internazionale Codificato e la Sua Sanzione Giuridica* (Unione Tipografico-Editrice, Turin 1890) 164 § 367 ("Devono essere riguardati come diritti dell'uomo di fronte al Diritto internazionale quelli, che ad esso spettano come persona in confronto di tutti gli Stati, di tutti gli altri uomini, e di tutte le altre persone che coesistono nella *Magna civitas*"); Paul Heilborn, *Das System des Völkerrechts entwickelt aus den völkerrechtlichen Begriffen* (Verlag von Julius Springer, Berlin 1896) 64-84 (considering the possible recognition of individuals as subjects of rights and duties under the law of aliens and addressing the notion of 'general human rights' [*allgemeine Menschenrechte*]).

[80]This approach has always been somewhat controversial. For a recent discussion of the subject see: Anthea Roberts, 'Clash of Paradigms: Actors and Analogies Shaping the Investment Treaty System' (2013) 107 AJIL 45, 69-74; Dominik Kneer, *Investitionsschutz und Menschenrechte. Eine Untersuchung zum Einfluss menschenrechtlicher Standards auf die Investitionssicherung* (Nomos, Baden-Baden 2012) 27-46; Gus Van Harten, *Investment Arbitration and Public Law* (Oxford University Press, Oxford 2008) 136-4; Pierre Marie Dupuy and Jorge E. Viñuales, 'Human Rights and Investment Disciplines: Integration in Progress' in Marc Bungenberg, Jörn Griebel, Stephan Hobe and August Reinisch (eds), *International Investment Law* (Nomos, Baden-Baden 2015) 1739, 1739-67. For a defense of a (careful) reliance on human rights in the interpretation of international investment protection standards see: Martins Paparinskis, *The International Minimum Standard and Fair and Equitable Treatment* (Oxford University Press, Oxford 2013) 171-80. For an analysis of the role human rights obligations have played in the adjudicatory practice of investment tribunals see: Eric De Brabandere, *Investment Treaty Arbitration as Public International Law. Procedural Aspects and Implications* (Cambridge University Press, Cambridge 2014) 129 *et seq.*

[81]The author has already advanced this argument elsewhere, providing additional references to the ongoing academic debate on the human rights approach: Sebastián Mantilla Blanco, *Justizielles Unrecht im internationalen Investitionsschutzrecht* (Nomos, Baden-Baden 2016) 77-83 (addressing the minimum standard, but particularly focusing on the definition of denial of justice through analogies to the notion of a fair trial).

[82]See: Walter Kälin and Jörg Künzli, *The Law of International Human Rights Protection* (Oxford University Press, New York 2010) 37-66.

[83]Walter Kälin and Jörg Künzli, *The Law of International Human Rights Protection* (Oxford University Press, New York 2010) 67-74.

beyond the minimum standard.[84] Finally, while individuals are at the very heart of universal and regional human rights systems, the law of aliens protects them only in their character as foreign nationals and gives more weight to the interests of their home states.[85] From a historical perspective, the substantive guarantees enjoyed by foreign citizens were believed to be 'not so much rights of the alien *per se*, as they are rights of the state of which the alien is a subject'.[86] The reason is that the law of aliens evolved hand-in-hand with the practice of diplomatic protection, which has traditionally departed from the Vattelian idea that the infliction of an injury to a foreigner entails an 'indirect injury' against his or her home state.[87] The law of state

---

[84] Sir Gerald Fitzmaurice advanced a similar argument in 1956; see: ILC, 'Summary Records of the 372nd Meeting' (21 June 1956) 1 *Yearbook of the International Law Commission – 1956* 239, 243 [40] ("[T]he two concepts of "international standard of justice" and "observance of fundamental human rights" might be found not completely to coincide. The international standard having been set hitherto at a rather low level, cases might arise where fundamental human rights had been denied, and yet it would be difficult to claim that the international standard of justice had not been achieved. On the other hand, cases might arise where no denial of human rights was involved, but where there had nevertheless been a departure from the international standard of justice"). The author has already discussed this statement elsewhere: Sebastián Mantilla Blanco, *Justizielles Unrecht im internationalen Investitionsschutzrecht* (Nomos, Baden-Baden 2016) 80-1.

[85] Cf. Chittharanjan Felix Amerasinghe, *Diplomatic Protection* (Oxford University Press, New York 2008) 344 (warning against 'the temptation to over-emphasize the interests of the individual and to ignore those of the respondent state', in particular reference to the law of diplomatic protection). For a similar view see: Annemarieke Vermeer-Künzli, 'As If: The Legal Fiction in Diplomatic Protection' (2007) 18(1) EJIL 37, 65-8. For some critical approaches see: Richard Lillich, *The Human Rights of Aliens in Contemporary International Law* (Manchester University Press, Manchester 1984) 1-3 (describing the traditional basis of the law of aliens from a critical perspective); *Ahmadou Sadio Diallo (Guinea v Congo)* [2010] ICJ Rep 639, Separate Opinion of Judge Cançado Trindade 729, 798-9 [205-6] (criticizing the traditional focus on the state rather than the individual in the law of diplomatic protection). See also: Sebastián Mantilla Blanco, *Justizielles Unrecht im internationalen Investitionsschutzrecht* (Nomos, Baden-Baden 2016) 79-80.

[86] Julius Goebel, 'The International Responsibility of States for Injuries Sustained by Aliens on Account of Mob Violence, Insurrections and Civil Wars' (1914) 8 AJIL 802, 811. For a similar approach see: Felix Stoerk, 'Staatsunterthanen und Fremde' in Franz von Holtzendorff (ed), *Handbuch des Völkerrechts auf Grundlage europäischer Staatspraxis* (Volume 2: Verlag von F. F. Richter, Hamburg 1887) 582, 585-96. Prewar international law normally regarded individuals to be not 'subjects', but 'objects of the Law of Nations': Lassa Francis Laurence Oppenheim, *International Law. A Treatise* (Volume 1: Longmans, Green & Co., London 1905) 344-7 [290-2].

[87] Emer de Vattel, *The Law of Nations* (1758) (G.G. and J. Robinson, London 1797) 162 ('[w]hoever uses a citizen ill, indirectly offends the state, who is bound to protect this citizen'). See also: *Mavrommatis Palestine Concessions (Greece v UK)* (Jurisdiction) [1924] PCIJ Rep Series A No 2, 12; *Barcelona Traction Light and Power Company Ltd. (Belgium v Spain)* [1970] ICJ Rep 3, 33 [36]. For a critique of the 'Vattelian fiction' see: *Ahmadou Sadio Diallo (Guinea v Congo)* [2010] ICJ Rep 639, Separate Opinion of Judge Cançado Trindade 729, 798-9 [205-6] (stressing at para 205 that 'it is about time for this Court to overcome the *acrobaties intellectuelles* ensuing from an undue reliance on the old Vattelian fiction, revived by the PCIJ in the *Mavrommatis* fiction' and further contending that this idea '[is] not a principle, [but] simply a largely surpassed fiction'). See also Trindade's remarks at para 221 (pp. 804-5). For other critical views see: Guha Roy, 'Is the Law of Responsibility of States for Injuries to Aliens a Part of Universal International Law?' (1963)

responsibility for injuries to aliens was therefore described as the result of an overlap between the *personal jurisdiction* of the home state and the *territorial jurisdiction* of the host state.[88] The bond between the individual and his or her home state continues to be an essential ingredient of the minimum standard.[89] Analogies to human rights might of course be permissible at some particular instances.[90] As a general approach, however, the human rights argument is not entirely accurate.[91]

More conservative arbitral decisions and scholarly studies have occasionally defined the minimum standard by reference to the decision rendered by the United States – Mexico General Claims Commission in the legendary *Neer* case (1926).[92]

55(4) AJIL 863, 863-80; Richard Lillich, *The Human Rights of Aliens in Contemporary International Law* (Manchester University Press, Manchester 1984) 1-3. For an excellent overview of the debate on the 'Vattelian fiction' see: Annemarieke Vernmeer-Künzli, 'As If: The Legal Fiction in Diplomatic Protection' (2007) 18(1) EJIL 37, 68 (concluding that 'abandoning the legal fiction now would be premature'). See also: ILC, 'Report of the International Law Commission on the Work of its Fifty-Eighth Session – Diplomatic Protection' (2006) 2(2) *Yearbook of the International Law Commission – 2006* 23, 27 art. 1 (Commentary) [3-5] (leaving the question open). The author has already addressed the debate on the 'Vattelian fiction' in a previous publication: Sebastián Mantilla Blanco, *Justizielles Unrecht im internationalen Investitionsschutzrecht* (Nomos, Baden-Baden 2016) 79.

[88]For some representative examples see: Emanuel von Ullmann, *Völkerrecht* (J. C. B. Mohr, Tübingen 1908) 360. For a similar observation see: Paul Heilborn, *Das System des Völkerrechts entwickelt aus den völkerrechtlichen Begriffen* (Verlag von Julius Springer, Berlin 1896) 77 and 81. See also Sect. 7.3.

[89]For a contemporary analysis of the traditional notion of the 'bond of nationality' see: Annemarieke Vermeer-Künzli, 'Nationality and Diplomatic Protection. A reappraisal' in Alessandra Annoni and Serena Forlati (eds), *The Changing Role of Nationality in International Law* (Routledge, New York 2013) 76, 77-8 (focusing on the law of diplomatic protection). For an argument against the classic approach see: Karl Doehring, *Die allgemeinen Regeln des völkerrechtlichen Fremdenrechts und das deutsche Verfassungsrecht* (Carl Heymanns Verlag, Köln/Berlin 1963) 68-85. Section 7.2.1. addresses the implications of this premise for the scope of application of the customary FPS standard.

[90]Efforts have been made to build a reliable theoretical framework for such analogies: Martins Paparinskis, *The International Minimum Standard and Fair and Equitable Treatment* (Oxford University Press, Oxford 2013) 74-83 and 171-80. Paparinskis concludes that, even though analogies from human rights law are *prima facie* permissible, this 'does not mean that the approaches followed by the ECtHR are applicable *verbatim* or even *mutatis mutandis* within investment protection law' (at p. 179). See also: Martins Paparinskis, 'Analogies and Other Regimes of International Law' in Zachary Douglas, Joost Pauwelyn and Jorge Viñuales (eds), *The Foundations of International Investment Law. Bringing Theory into Practice* (Oxford University Press, Oxford 2014) 73, 79-81.

[91]The author has already made this point elsewhere: Sebastián Mantilla Blanco, *Justizielles Unrecht im internationalen Investitionsschutzrecht* (Nomos, Baden-Baden 2016) 82 (also discussing Paparinskis' approach and the permissibility of human rights analogies, but particularly focusing in the relationship of denial of justice to the notion of fair trial).

[92]*LFH Neer and Pauline Neer v Mexico* (15 October 1926) IV RIAA 60-6. The author has already discussed some aspects of the *Neer* case and its use in investment arbitral decisions in a previous publication: Sebastián Mantilla Blanco, *Justizielles Unrecht im internationalen Investitionsschutzrecht* (Nomos, Baden-Baden 2016) 55-6 and 58-9 (in particular connection with the notion of denial of justice).

The United States submitted the claim on behalf of the widow and the daughter of Paul Neer, an American citizen resident in Mexico.[93] Mr. Neer had been murdered in the presence of his wife in the evening of November 16th, 1924.[94] The State Department contended that 'Mexican authorities showed an unwarrantable lack of intelligent investigation in prosecuting the culprits'.[95] In its assessment of Mexico's international responsibility, the US-Mexico General Claims Commission held:

[T]he treatment of an alien, in order to constitute an international delinquency, should amount to an outrage, to bad faith, to willful neglect of duty, or to an insufficiency of governmental action so far short of international standards that every reasonable and impartial man would readily recognize its insufficiency.[96]

This statement has been of paramount influence in contemporary international investment law, being relied upon by respondent states, scholars and adjudicating bodies alike.[97] As rightly noted by Jan Paulsson and Georgios Petrochilos:

[There is] a hasty assumption, namely that the minimum standard of treatment looks to a single, generally applicable standard of review with respect to all types of state conduct, and that the test was set forth in the 1926 Neer decision.[98]

---

[93]LFH Neer and Pauline Neer v Mexico (15 October 1926) IV RIAA 60 [1].

[94]LFH Neer and Pauline Neer v Mexico (15 October 1926) IV RIAA 60 [1].

[95]LFH Neer and Pauline Neer v Mexico (15 October 1926) IV RIAA 60 [1].

[96]LFH Neer and Pauline Neer v Mexico (15 October 1926) IV RIAA 60 [4].

[97]For a detailed survey on the influence of the Neer decision arbitral practice and academic publications see: Martins Paparinskis, The International Minimum Standard and Fair and Equitable Treatment (Oxford University Press, Oxford 2013) 48-54 (making a similar observation at p. 48). On the relevance of the Neer standard in contemporary investment law cf. also: Martins Paparinskis, 'Fair and Equitable Treatment' in Thomas Cottier and Krista Nadakavukaren Schefer (eds), Elgar Encyclopedia of International Economic Law (Edward Elgar Publishing, Northampton MA 2018) 208, 210. J. Paulsson and G. Petrochilos have argued that the Neer decision would not gain particular importance until the 2000s. See: Jan Paulsson and Georgios Petrochilos, 'Neer-ly Misled?' (2007) 22(2) ICSID Rev 242, 247 ('[a]fter languishing three-quarters of century in relative obscurity, Neer was, it seems, resuscitated in Canada's pleadings in the SD Myers and Poper & Talbot cases').

[98]Jan Paulsson and Georgios Petrochilos, 'Neer-ly Misled?' (2007) 22(2) ICSID Rev 242, 242. Paulsson and Petrochilos have suggested that, instead of Neer, it would be preferable to rely on the General Claims Commission's Roberts award of 1926 (at p. 257). For the full text of the Roberts award see: Harry Roberts v Mexico (2 November 1926) IV RIAA 77-81. For a critical assessment of Paulsson's and Petrochilos' argument see: Martins Paparinskis, The International Minimum Standard and Fair and Equitable Treatment (Oxford University Press, Oxford 2013) 51-4. For some examples of investment arbitral decisions defining the minimum standard based on the Roberts award see: Flughafen Zürich A.G. and Gestión de Ingeniería IDC S.A. v Venezuela, Laudo, ICSID Case No. ARB/10/19 (18 November 2014) [562-4]; Joseph Charles Lemire v Ukraine, Decision on Jurisdiction and Liability, ICSID Case No. ARB/06/18 (14 January 2010) [248-9]; SAUR International S.A. v Argentina, Décision sur la compétence et sur la responsabilité, ICSID Case No. ARB/04/4 (6 June 2012) [493]; OI European Group B.V. v Venezuela, Award, ICSID Case No. ARB/11/25 (10 March 2015) [486-8]; Rusoro Mining Ltd. v Venezuela, Award, ICSID Case No. ARB(AF)/12/5 (22 August 2016) [518].

Many arguments have been advanced against the use of the *Neer* standard as a definition of the minimum standard.[99] The main objections are four. First, in the *Neer* decision, the General Claims Commission particularly referred to the concept of denial of justice and expressly warned that it did not intend to 'announce a precise formula'.[100] In other denial of justice claims, and particularly in cases related to failures to investigate crimes against aliens, the Commission would consistently use a terminology bearing striking resemblance to the *Neer* standard without presenting it as a general standard.[101]

A second argument is that the General Claims Commission merely asserted the *Neer* test, without submitting actual evidence that the *Neer* standard enjoyed acceptance within the international community.[102] The Commission quoted several authorities in the very same paragraph containing its much-celebrated formulation.[103] Nonetheless, its sources were mostly academic, and pertained only to the customary notion of 'denial of justice'.[104] These deficiencies have led some

---

[99]For a detailed presentation of the objections against the *Neer* standard see: Jan Paulsson and Georgios Petrochilos, '*Neer*-ly Misled?' (2007) 22(2) ICSID Rev 242, 242-57; Martins Paparinskis, *The International Minimum Standard and Fair and Equitable Treatment* (Oxford University Press, Oxford 2013) 48-54.

[100]*LFH Neer and Pauline Neer v Mexico* (15 October 1926) IV RIAA 60 [4]. See also: Martins Paparinskis, *The International Minimum Standard and Fair and Equitable Treatment* (Oxford University Press, Oxford 2013) 49 *et seq.* (particularly discussing the relationship between the *Neer* formula and the concept of 'denial of justice'); Railroad Development Corp. *v* Guatemala, Award, ICSID Case No. ARB/07/23 (29 June 2012) [216] (emphasizing the careful words chosen by the General Claims Commission).

[101]For a clear statement of the actual (or actually intended) scope of the '*Neer* formula' see: *Gertrude Parker Massey v Mexico* (15-16 April 1927) IV RIAA 155, 162-3 (opinion of Commissioner Fernández stating that '[i]n the *Neer* case [...] the Commission, [was] expressing its idea of denial of justice'). See also: *B. E. Chattin v Mexico* (23 July 1927) IV RIAA 282 [10] (indicating that the *Neer* formula was only applicable to: (i) acts of the judiciary; and (ii) 'indirect' state responsibility for acts of individuals, such as failures to prevent private injuries to aliens; see also paras 11 and 29 and the dissent of Commissioner Fernández at p. 308); *H. G. Venable v Mexico* (8 July 1927) IV RIAA 219 [14] (particularly referring to deficiencies in the administration of justice); *Louis B. Gordon v. Mexico* (8 October 1930) IV RIAA 586, 590 (applying the *Neer* standard in respect of acts of the judicial branch of public power); *Teodoro García and M. A. Garza v United States of America* (3 December 1926) IV RIAA 119 [8] (using the *Neer* formula in specific connection with the notion of denial of justice; cf. also Nielsen's dissent at p. 127). For a critical assessment of the General Claims Commission's application of the *Neer* formula in subsequent cases see: Jan Paulsson and Georgios Petrochilos, '*Neer*-ly Misled?' (2007) 22(2) ICSID Rev 242, 253-7 (making particular emphasis on the *B. E. Chattin* case); Martins Paparinskis, *The International Minimum Standard and Fair and Equitable Treatment* (Oxford University Press, Oxford 2013) 48-52 (additionally addressing Paulsson's and Petrochilos' arguments).

[102]Railroad Development Corp. *v* Guatemala, Award, ICSID Case No. ARB/07/23 (29 June 2012) [216-7] (noting at para 216 that the *Neer* award 'did not formulate the minimum standard after an analysis of State practice' and further observing at para 217 that the *Neer* decision, as such, cannot be said to constitute state practice).

[103]*LFH Neer and Pauline Neer v Mexico* (15 October 1926) IV RIAA 60 [4].

[104]*LFH Neer and Pauline Neer v Mexico* (15 October 1926) IV RIAA 60 [4]. For an analysis of this aspect of the award see: Martins Paparinskis, *The International Minimum Standard and Fair and*

contemporary investment tribunals to reject the *Neer* standard as an authoritative statement of the law.[105] For instance, in *Rail Road Development v Guatemala* (2012), the arbitrators stated:

> It is ironic that the decision considered reflecting the expression of the minimum standard of treatment in customary international law is based on the opinions of commentators and, on its own admission, went further than their views without an analysis of State practice followed because of a sense of obligation.[106]

Third, in any case, the *Neer* decision did not elaborate much on the precise content of the minimum standard.[107] Its emphasis on a 'willful neglect of duty' could be arguably read as referring to the FPS standard, the implication being that— following *Neer*—FPS constitutes a due diligence obligation.[108]

Finally, a fourth objection is that, even if one were to accept that *Neer* reflected the stand of customary law at the time the decision was rendered,[109] it is hard to believe that the minimum standard has remained untouched and unchanged since the second decade of the twentieth century.[110]

Equitable Treatment (Oxford University Press, Oxford 2013) 49 *et seq*. For this criticism see: Railroad Development Corp. *v* Guatemala, Award, ICSID Case No. ARB/07/23 (29 June 2012) [216] (noting that the *Neer* award was mostly based on scholarly opinions).

[105]For a representative example see: Railroad Development Corp. *v* Guatemala, Award, ICSID Case No. ARB/07/23 (29 June 2012) [216-8].

[106]Railroad Development Corp. *v* Guatemala, Award, ICSID Case No. ARB/07/23 (29 June 2012) [216].

[107]For this objection see: Martins Paparinskis, *The International Minimum Standard and Fair and Equitable Treatment* (Oxford University Press, Oxford 2013) 50.

[108]For this line of argument see: Mondev International *v* United States, Award, ICSID Case No. ARB(AF)/99/2 (11 October 2002) [115] (holding that *Neer* 'concerned not the treatment of foreign investment as such but the physical security of the alien'). See also: ADF *v* United States, Award, ICSID Case No. ARB(AF)/00/1 (9 January 2003) [180-1] (quoting the *Mondev* tribunal in this regard). For a detailed analysis of this understanding of the *Neer* case see: Jan Paulsson and Georgios Petrochilos, '*Neer*-ly Misled?' (2007) 22(2) ICSID Rev 242, 250 *et seq*. (particularly analyzing the *Mondev* and *ADF* decisions); Martins Paparinskis, *The International Minimum Standard and Fair and Equitable Treatment* (Oxford University Press, Oxford 2013) 50-4 (particularly at 50-1, making emphasis on the obligation to investigate and punish criminal offences against foreign citizens).

[109]For an arbitral decision accepting *Neer* as a presentation of the law as it stood in the 1920s see: Glamis Gold *v* United States (UNCITRAL), Award (8 November 2009) [21-2, 600 *et seq*. and 612-6] (observing at para 21 that 'the parties in this case and other two NAFTA State Parties agree that the customary international law standard is at least that set forth in the 1926 *Neer* arbitration' and concluding at para 616 that '[t]he fundamentals of *Neer* still apply today').

[110]ADF *v* United States, Award, ICSID Case No. ARB(AF)/00/1 (9 January 2003) [121, 125, 179-86]; CC/Devas (Mauritius) Ltd., Devas Employees Mauritius Private Ltd. and Telcom Devas Mauritius Ltd. *v* India (UNCITRAL), Award on Jurisdiction and Merits, PCA Case No. 2013-09 (25 July 2016) [457]; Crystallex International Corp. *v* Venezuela, Award, ICSID Case No. ARB(AF)/11/2 (4 April 2016) [534-6]; Gami Investments *v* Mexico (UNCITRAL), Final Award (15 November 2004) 144 [95]; Mondev International *v* United States, Award, ICSID Case No. ARB(AF)/99/2 (11 October 2002) [114-7]; Gold Reserve Inc. *v* Venezuela, Award, ICSID Case No. ARB(AF)/09/1 (22 September 2014) [567]; Railroad Development Corp. *v* Guatemala,

5.4   The Significance of the 'Standard of Civilization' for the Determination of the Scope of Application of the Customary Security Obligation

Investment treaty practice indicates that, nowadays, states generally accept the existence of the customary minimum standard of treatment.[111] Moreover, present-day IIAs indicate that numerous states consider that the FPS standard is a constituent element of the more-general minimum standard.[112] In spite of its widespread acceptance, the exact meaning and precise content of the minimum standard continue to be unclear.[113] The question therefore arises as to whether the vague concept of a minimum standard actually provides a suitable basis for the determination of the content and scope of the FPS standard.

This question could be given an intuitive, and perhaps even self-evident, answer. There is but one feature of the minimum standard that is neither contentious, nor disputable: the minimum standard has always served the purpose of laying down a bottom line, which is established under international law and is therefore autonomous from the host state's municipal legal order.[114] The rationale of the minimum standard results, in fact, from long decades of sharp political and academic controversy concerning the choice between the 'standard of civilization' and the 'doctrine of equality'.[115] For this reason, the acknowledgement of FPS as an element of the minimum standard implies that the security obligation is *not necessarily* satisfied when the host state affords foreigners and nationals the same protection.[116] Factual scenarios could arise in which the FPS standard requires a state to provide aliens a greater degree of security than that which it provides for its own citizens.[117] As explained by U.S. Secretary of State Hamilton Fish (1873):

> It may, in general, be true that when foreigners take up their abode in a country, they must expect to share the fortune of the other inhabitants and cannot expect a preference over them. While, however, a government may construe according to its pleasure its obligation to protect its own citizens from injury, foreign governments have a right and it is their duty to

---

Award, ICSID Case No. ARB/07/23 (29 June 2012) [218]; Waste Management *v* Mexico, Award, ICSID Case No. ARB(AF)/00/3 (30 April 2004) [93]. See also: OI European Group B.V. *v* Venezuela, Award, ICSID Case No. ARB/11/25 (10 March 2015) [489] (using the same 'evolutionary' argument in respect of the *Roberts* decision); Rusoro Mining Ltd. *v* Venezuela, Award, ICSID Case No. ARB(AF)/12/5 (22 August 2016) [519] (referring to the *Roberts* award and quoting *OI European* in this connection).

[111]See Sect. 5.2.

[112]See Sect. 5.2.

[113]See Sect. 5.3.

[114]See Sect. 4.2.

[115]See Sects. 4.2 and 4.3.

[116]Cf. Chap. 4.

[117]This is, precisely, the most controversial effect of the minimum standard. For a detailed analysis of this particular question in historical perspective see Chap. 4.

judge whether their citizens have received the protection due to them pursuant to public law and treaties.[118]

The FPS standard should not, however, place an unreasonably heavy burden on the host state. The classification of FPS under the umbrella concept of the minimum standard implies that FPS is, too, a *bottom line* or *minimum*.[119] The logical consequence is that the threshold for a breach of FPS is always high: in order to constitute an international delinquency, a want of protection must fall beyond the absolute minimum that every state can expect from any other state.[120]

Beyond these effects, however fundamental, the minimum standard is of limited significance for the determination of the FPS standard. This holds particularly true for the ascertainment of the scope of the security obligation.[121] The answer to the most fundamental questions about the reach of FPS (e.g. whether FPS refers to physical security only or also covers the notion of legal stability) cannot be derived from the notion of the customary minimum standard.[122] The reason is that, if one accepts that the FPS standard is only an *element* of the minimum standard, it follows that its scope of application is *narrower* than that of the minimum standard. Thus, even if one were to conclude that risks such as the instability of the domestic legal order are covered by the general minimum standard, this mere fact does not imply that they also fall within the scope of the more-specific FPS standard.

---

[118]'Mr. Fish, Sec. of State, to Mr. Foster' (16 December 1873) in Francis Wharton (ed), *A Digest of the International Law of the United States. Documents issued by Presidents and Secretaries of State* (Volume 2: Government Printing Office, Washington 1887) 617-8.

[119]On the notion of the minimum standard as a 'bottom line' see Sect. 4.2.

[120]This might be relevant, for example, for the definition of the degree of diligence required under the FPS standard. On this particular issue see Sects. 13.3.2 and 13.4.10.

[121]For the scope of the customary security obligation see Chaps. 6–10.

[122]Cf. Chap. 6 *et seq.*

Part II
Scope of the Customary Standard

Chapter 6
Scope of Application of the Customary Standard: Conceptual Framework

6.1 Preliminary Remarks

The foregoing sections presented the origins of the customary standard of 'full protection and security' in the international law of aliens. The eighteenth century witnessed an academic debate on the source of the sovereign's duty to protect foreign citizens, which was signalized by the dogmatic struggle between naturalist and classic positivist approaches to the law of nations.[1] In the nineteenth and early twentieth centuries, the sharp political dispute about the so-called 'standard of civilization' took center stage in international politics.[2] The bone of contention was whether national treatment could or should be regarded as the 'ceiling' of the host state's obligation to protect aliens and their property.[3]

At present, most of these controversies are fairly settled. Contemporary state practice indicates that the FPS standard has acquired a customary character.[4] Moreover, FPS is generally considered as an element of the international minimum standard of treatment.[5] The present-day international consensus is that the host state does not necessarily satisfy its obligation to provide security to aliens by ensuring that they enjoy the same conditions as its own citizens.[6]

The question remains open, however, as to the actual extent of the customary security obligation. This chapter seeks to provide a conceptual roadmap for the assessment of state and arbitral practice regarding the reach of the obligation. In this vein, it draws a distinction between the FPS standard's *scope of application* and its

---

[1] See Chap. 3.
[2] See Chap. 4.
[3] See Chap. 4.
[4] See Sect. 5.2.
[5] See Sect. 5.2.
[6] Cf. Chap. 5.

© Springer Nature Switzerland AG 2019   145
S. Mantilla Blanco, *Full Protection and Security in International Investment Law*,
European Yearbook of International Economic Law 8,
https://doi.org/10.1007/978-3-030-24838-3_6

content. These categories are used as an organizing device, which should allow the identification and presentation of the standard's substance. The argument has been divided in two parts.

A first section explores the notion of 'standard' as a formal category, underscoring its value as an explanatory tool of the FPS standard's formal structure. The second section analyzes the concept of 'security' as the key notion FPS refers to. As will be shown below, a semantic scrutiny of the term indicates that *security* always describes a *relationship* between an identifiable set of elements: securing agent, secured agent, secured values, and secured risks.[7] Thus, while the meaning of FPS cannot be derived from the concept of security as such, the recognition of security as a 'relational notion' facilitates the determination of the defining elements of FPS as an international obligation.

6.2   The Notion of Standard and the Formal Structure of 'Full Protection and Security'

International investment law generally designates substantive guarantees for the protection of foreign investments as 'standards'.[8] This label contrasts with the terminology used in other areas of law, where reference is usually made to rights, rules or principles, but not so often to standards.[9] The concept of standard is relevant for the assessment of FPS.[10] The obvious question is: are we looking for a general principle, for a rule, or for something different? The answer is not straightforward. The notion of standard, however widespread, conveys no univocal meaning in legal

---

[7]For this understanding of the notion of security see: Rhonda Powell, 'The Concept of Security' (2012) 1 Oxford Socio-Legal Review 1, 5-6. Section 6.3 discusses Powell's and other authors' views in greater detail.

[8]For a short account of the rules-standards divide in international investment law see: Gebhard Bücheler, *Proportionality in Investor-State Arbitration* (Oxford University Press, Oxford 2015) 40.

[9]It must be however noted that, in international law, the notion of standard has not been peculiar to the law of investment protection. For some examples from other areas of international law see: Amicahi Cohen, 'Rules and Standards in the Application of International Humanitarian Law' (2008) 41 Isr. L. Rev. 1, 2 *et seq.*; Daniel Bodansky, *Rules and Standards in International Law* (New York University, New York 2003) [Preliminary Draft]; Daniel Bodansky, 'Rules vs. Standards in International Environmental Law' (2004) 98 ASIL Proceedings 275, 276.

[10]For an author considering the notion of 'standard' in connection with FPS see: Finnur Magnússon, *Full Protection and Security in International Law* (University of Vienna, Vienna 2012) 141 *et seq.* For another scholar underscoring the standard-like structure of FPS see: Geneviève Bastid Burdeau, 'La clause de protection et sécurité pleine et entière' (2015) 119 (1) RGDIP 87, 88.

science.[11] To mention just a few representative examples, Ronald Dworkin used the term as a genre embodying rules and principles.[12] Other scholars have made fascinating attempts to distinguish standards from other types of norms, thus avoiding their use as an all-encompassing umbrella concept.[13] For instance, Roscoe Pound (1919) considered standards as a separate category, which he believed to be characteristic of developed legal systems.[14] In this connection, Pound observed:

> In framing standards the law seeks neither to generalize by eliminating the circumstances nor to particularize by including them; instead, the law seeks to formulate the general expectation of society as to how individuals will act in the course of their undertakings, and thus to guide the common sense or expert intuition of jury or commission when called on to judge a particular conduct under particular circumstances [...] Standards are devised for special situations in which we are compelled to take special circumstances into account; for classes of cases in which each is necessarily unique. For such cases we must rely on the common sense of the common man as to common things. And this common sense cannot be put in the form of a syllogism.[15]

Pound carefully distinguished standards from rules, principles and conceptions.[16] According to him, rules 'prescribe a fixed and definite result for a fixed and definite situation of fact'.[17] Principles 'are general premises for judicial and juristic reasoning, to which we turn to apply new rules, to interpret old rules, to meet new situations, to measure the scope and application of rules and standards and to

---

[11]For an analysis of the many possible uses of the term see: Alexandra Diehl, *The Core Standard of International Investment Protection: Fair and Equitable Treatment* (Kluwer Law International, Alpen aan den Rijn 2012) 23 *et seq.*

[12]Ronald Dworkin, *Taking Rights Seriously* (Bloomsbury Academic, New York 1977) 38 *et seq.* and 93 *et seq.* Dworkin's terminology has already drawn the attention of international investment law scholars. For a representative example see: Alexandra Diehl, *The Core Standard of International Investment Protection: Fair and Equitable Treatment* (Kluwer Law International, Alpen aan den Rijn 2012) 26.

[13]See, for example: Roscoe Pound, 'The Administrative Application of Legal Standards' (1919) 42 Annu. Rep. A.B.A. 445, 445 *et seq.* Pound's views have already been considered in academic publications in the area of international investment law. For some examples see: Alexandra Diehl, *The Core Standard of International Investment Protection: Fair and Equitable Treatment* (Kluwer Law International, Alpen aan den Rijn 2012) 24 *et seq.*; Finnur Magnússon, *Full Protection and Security in International Law* (University of Vienna, Vienna 2012) 141 *et seq.*; Ioana Tudor, *The Fair and Equitable Standard in the International Law of Foreign Investment* (Oxford University Press, New York 2008) 119.

[14]Roscoe Pound, 'The Administrative Application of Legal Standards' (1919) 42 Annu. Rep. A.B.A. 445, 456.

[15]Roscoe Pound, 'The Administrative Application of Legal Standards' (1919) 42 Annu. Rep. A.B.A. 445, 456-7 and 463.

[16]Roscoe Pound, 'The Administrative Application of Legal Standards' (1919) 42 Annu. Rep. A.B.A. 445, 454-6.

[17]Roscoe Pound, 'The Administrative Application of Legal Standards' (1919) 42 Annu. Rep. A.B.A. 445, 455.

reconcile them when they conflict'.[18] Legal conceptions 'are more or less well-defined types to which we refer or by which we classify cases, so that when a particular case is so classified we may attribute to it the legal consequences attached to the type' (e.g. 'contract').[19] Finally, 'legal standards' are 'legally defined measures of conduct, to be applied by or under the discretion of the tribunal'.[20] In later publications, Pound would describe standards as 'general limits of permissible conduct to be applied according to the circumstances of each case'.[21]

The concept of 'standard' is not a merely descriptive device: scholars have argued that decisionmakers (legislative bodies, ordinary tribunals, constitutional courts, etc.) may choose to formulate a legal directive as a rule or as a standard.[22] In American legal thinking, resort to the rules-standards divide has been made to describe the difference between 'categorization' and 'balancing' in the Supreme Court's jurisprudence.[23] The classical examples would be the Court's decisions in *Baltimore & Ohio RR Co v Goodman* (1927) and *Pokora v Wabash Rail Co* (1934).[24] Both cases referred to accidents involving a crash between a car and a train.[25] In *Goodman*, Justice Oliver W. Holmes devised a rule: if a train is coming, the driver must 'stop and get out of his vehicle, although obviously he will not often be required to do more than stop and look'.[26] In *Pokora*, Justice Benjamin Cardozo formulated a standard requiring the driver to exercise 'reasonable' care.[27] Cardozo further criticized Holmes' approach, underlining 'the need for caution in framing standards of behavior that amount to rules of law'.[28]

---

[18]Roscoe Pound, 'The Administrative Application of Legal Standards' (1919) 42 Annu. Rep. A.B.A. 445, 455.

[19]Roscoe Pound, 'The Administrative Application of Legal Standards' (1919) 42 Annu. Rep. A.B.A. 445, 455.

[20]Roscoe Pound, 'The Administrative Application of Legal Standards' (1919) 42 Annu. Rep. A.B.A. 445, 456.

[21]Roscoe Pound, 'Hierarchy of Sources and Forms in Different Systems of Law' (1933) 7(4) Tul. L. Rev. 475, 485.

[22]See: Kathleen Sullivan, 'Foreword: The Justices of Rules and Standards' (1992) 106 Harv. L. Rev. 22, 57 *et seq.* See also pp. 26-7 and 122-3.

[23]See: Kathleen Sullivan, 'Foreword: The Justices of Rules and Standards' (1992) 106 Harv. L. Rev. 22, 59.

[24]See: *Baltimore & Ohio RR Co v Goodman* (1927) 275 US 66, 69-70; *Pokora v Wabash Rail Co* (1934) 292 US 98, 104-6. For an account of the approaches followed in these two cases and the contrast between them see: Antonin Scalia, 'The Rule of Law as a Law of Rules' 55(4) U. Chi. L. Rev. 1175, 1187-8; Pierre Schlag, 'Rules and Standards' (1985-6) 33 UCLA L. Rev. 379, 379-80 and 403.

[25]See: *Baltimore & Ohio RR Co v Goodman* (1927) 275 US 66, 69-70; *Pokora v Wabash Rail Co* (1934) 292 US 98, 104-6.

[26]*Baltimore & Ohio RR Co v Goodman* (1927) 275 US 66, 69-70. On the significance of the *Goodman* case see: G. Edward White, *Justice Oliver Wendell Holmes. Law and the Inner Self* (Oxford University Press, New York 1993) 384-6.

[27]*Pokora v Wabash Rail Co* (1934) 292 US 98, 104-6.

[28]*Pokora v Wabash Rail Co* (1934) 292 US 98, 104-6.

In her foreword to the *Harvard Law Review* of 1992, Kathleen Sullivan made a meticulous comparison between the rationales of rules and standards.[29] According to her, '[a] legal directive is "rule"-like when it binds a decisionmaker to respond in a determinate way to the presence of delimited triggering facts'.[30] Hence, '[r]ules aim to confine the decisionmaker to facts, leaving irreducibly arbitrary and subjective value choices to be worked out elsewhere'.[31] For its part, a standard 'tends to collapse decisionmaking back into the direct application of the background principle or policy to a fact situation'.[32] For that reason, '[s]tandards allow for the decrease of errors of under- and over-inclusiveness by giving the decisionmaker more discretion than do rules'.[33] Notwithstanding the foregoing, when repeatedly applied in the same manner, standards may end up acquiring the normative structure of a rule.[34] It has been therefore suggested that 'a rule is a standard that has reached epistemological maturity'.[35] Other scholars have argued that the core difference between rules and standards is 'whether the law is given content *ex ante* or *ex post*'[36] or, in plain

---

[29]Kathleen Sullivan, 'Foreword: The Justices of Rules and Standards' (1992) 106 Harv. L. Rev. 22, 22-123. Sullivan notes that, while some Supreme Court justices are more prone to rules ('justices of rules'), some tend to formulate standards ('justices of standards') (particularly at 122-3).

[30]Kathleen Sullivan, 'Foreword: The Justices of Rules and Standards' (1992) 106 Harv. L. Rev. 22, 58.

[31]Kathleen Sullivan, 'Foreword: The Justices of Rules and Standards' (1992) 106 Harv. L. Rev. 22, 58.

[32]Kathleen Sullivan, 'Foreword: The Justices of Rules and Standards' (1992) 106 Harv. L. Rev. 22, 58.

[33]Kathleen Sullivan, 'Foreword: The Justices of Rules and Standards' (1992) 106 Harv. L. Rev. 22, 58-9. See also Sullivan's remarks at p. 61. For another author addressing this particular issue see: Frederick Schauer, 'Rules and the Rule of Law' (1991) 14 Harv. J. L. & Pub. Pol'y 645, 653. For a different perspective see: Joseph Blocher, 'Roberts' Rules: The Assertiveness of Rules-Based Jurisprudence' (2011) 46 TULSA Law Review 431, 437 and 439 (arguing that 'rules are means of allocating decisionmaking authority, not destroying it [. . .] it is too simple to say that rules limit judicial power. Within the judiciary, they do no more than transfer power from one court to another. And even when one considers the power of the judiciary as against the political branches, rules are not necessarily power-denying. The real issue is who has the power to set the rules and how they go about doing so').

[34]Pierre Schlag, 'Rules and Standards' (1985-6) 33 UCLA L. Rev. 379, 428-9; Kathleen Sullivan, 'Foreword: The Justices of Rules and Standards' (1992) 106 Harv. L. Rev. 22, 62 (citing Schlag at n. 254). Cf. also: Rusell Korobkin, 'Behavioral Analysis and Legal Form: Rules vs. Standards Revisited' (2000) 79 Or. L. Rev. 23, 29.

[35]Kathleen Sullivan, 'Foreword: The Justices of Rules and Standards' (1992) 106 Harv. L. Rev. 22, 62.

[36]Louis Kaplow, 'Rules versus Standards: An Economic Analysis' (1992) 42 Duke L. J. 557, 559. For a similar view see: Friedrich Rosenfeld, 'The Trend from Standards to Rules in International Investment Law and its Impact upon the Interpretative Power of Arbitral Tribunals' (2014) 108 ASIL Proceedings 191, 191.

words, 'the extent to which efforts to give content to the law are undertaken before or after individuals act'.[37]

This work does not aim to enter into a legal-philosophical quest for a precise definition of 'standard'. For present purposes it suffices to note that the term 'standard' is normally used to describe an open-textured and flexible normative structure, which has the practical effect of enhancing adjudicatory discretion.[38] In this vein, Charles de Visscher explained in his Hague Lecture of 1954:

> Le terme standard implique qu'il s'agit moins ici d'une règle ferme aux contours nettement définis que d'un principe ou, mieux encore, d'une directive dont l'application peut dépendre d'éléments variables, particuliers à chaque espèce.[39]

The threshold issue for the present survey is whether and how the notion of 'standard', taken as a *formal* category,[40] might be useful or relevant for the assessment of the FPS standard.[41] A similar question has been posed in respect of the 'fair and equitable treatment' standard.[42] In one of the first comprehensive studies on the subject, Ioana Tudor attempted to explain the standard of 'fair and equitable treatment' based on the distinction between rules and standards.[43] Her conclusion was that, 'given the flexibility of the notion and the ways in which it is adapted and applied to a case, the FET has no stable or fixed content'.[44] This statement has met with sharp criticism.[45] Stephan Schill has suggested that Tudor's conclusion is inconsistent with the FET standard's customary character:

---

[37]Louis Kaplow, 'Rules versus Standards: An Economic Analysis' (1992) 42 Duke L. J. 557, 560.

[38]For a similar understanding of the term see: Charles De Visscher, 'Cours général de principes de droit international public' (1954) 86 RCADI 445, 508. See also: Duncan Kennedy, 'Form and Substance in Private Law Adjudication' (1976) 89 Harv. L. Rev. 1685, 1688; Ioana Tudor, *The Fair and Equitable Treatment Standard in the International Law of Foreign Investment* (Oxford University Press, New York 2008) 115.

[39]Charles De Visscher, 'Cours général de principes de droit international public' (1954) 86 RCADI 445, 508 (making specific reference to the customary minimum standard of treatment).

[40]Pierre Schlag has explained that the concept of 'standard' refers to the *'formal* dimensions' of 'legal directives' (e.g. whether norms are general/specific, narrow/broad, etc.): Pierre Schlag, 'Rules and Standards' (1985-6) 33 UCLA L. Rev. 379, 381-2.

[41]This is not the first academic study considering the formal category of standard in connection with FPS. See: Finnur Magnússon, *Full Protection and Security in International Law* (University of Vienna, Vienna 2012) 141 *et seq.*

[42]Alexandra Diehl, *The Core Standard of International Investment Protection: Fair and Equitable Treatment* (Kluwer Law International, Alpen aan den Rijn 2012) 17 *et seq.*; Ioana Tudor, *The Fair and Equitable Treatment Standard in the International Law of Foreign Investment* (Oxford University Press, New York 2008) 109 *et seq.*

[43]Ioana Tudor, *The Fair and Equitable Treatment Standard in the International Law of Foreign Investment* (Oxford University Press, New York 2008) 109-33.

[44]Ioana Tudor, *The Fair and Equitable Treatment Standard in the International Law of Foreign Investment* (Oxford University Press, New York 2008) 133.

[45]Ronald Kläger, *'Fair and Equitable Treatment' in International Investment Law* (Cambridge University Press, New York 2011) 124; Stephan Schill, 'Ioana Tudor. The Fair and Equitable Treatment Standard in the International Law of Foreign Investment' (2009) 20 EJIL 229, 237.

Tudor is right in stressing the central role of arbitrators in bringing FET to life. Yet, her conclusion on the lack of a fixed content reinforces the contradiction addressed earlier, namely how a norm without a fixed content can become a norm of customary international law.[46]

Similarly, Ronald Kläger considered Tudor's analysis 'unsatisfactory',[47] noting that 'Tudor's category of a standard and her reference to an average social conduct are relatively indeterminate concepts themselves'.[48]

This controversy should not lead to a definitive rejection of the standard as an explanatory tool in this area of international law.[49] A standard, however flexible, is not a blank space: a flexibly formulated content (such as 'reasonable care') is still a defined content.[50] Moreover, there is no reason why a customary norm of international law cannot have a standard-like normative structure.[51] For instance, it is a commonplace in legal literature that 'undue delays' in the administration of justice constitute a denial of justice, and thus entail a breach of the customary law of

---

[46]Stephan Schill, 'Ioana Tudor. The Fair and Equitable Treatment Standard in the International Law of Foreign Investment' (2009) 20 EJIL 229, 237. On the debate between Tudor and Schill see also: Patrick Dumberry, *The Formation and Identification of Customary International Law in International Investment Law* (Cambridge University Press, Cambridge 2016) 184.

[47]Ronald Kläger, *'Fair and Equitable Treatment' in International Investment Law* (Cambridge University Press, New York 2011) 125.

[48]Ronald Kläger, *'Fair and Equitable Treatment' in International Investment Law* (Cambridge University Press, New York 2011) 124.

[49]Cf. Finnur Magnússon, *Full Protection and Security in International Law* (University of Vienna, Vienna 2012) 145 (recognizing – without particular reference to Tudor's approach – that 'the standard, as a concept, still enjoys an important role in international law', but making some important caveats at pp. 146 *et seq.*).

[50]Roscoe Pound, 'The Administrative Application of Legal Standards' (1919) 42 Annu. Rep. A.B.A. 445, 456 (providing at p. 456 a definition of 'standard' as a 'legally defined' parameter for the assessment of conduct, and noting at p. 458 that standards have 'limits', which are 'fixed by deduction or interpretation or the appropriate means of finding the law').

[51]Cf. Alexandra Diehl, *The Core Standard of International Investment Protection: Fair and Equitable Treatment* (Kluwer Law International, Alpen aan den Rijn 2012) 135 (making particular reference to the FET standard); Karl Doehring, *Die allgemeinen Regeln des völkerrechtlichen Fremdenrechts und das deutsche Verfassungsrecht* (Carl Heymanns Verlag, Köln/Berlin 1963) 83-4 (stating that indeterminacy should not affect a norm's customary status). There has been, however, some debate as to whether vagueness could actually impair a legal directive from being acknowledged as a customary norm. For the debate see: Jean D'Aspremont, 'International Customary Investment Law: Story of a Paradox' in Tarcisio Gazzini and Eric De Brabandere (eds), *International Investment Law: The Sources of Rights and Obligations* (Martinus Nijhoff, Leiden 2012) 1, 34 (arguing that 'many candidates for customary status in investment law [. . .] fail to meet the minimum threshold in terms of normative content that is necessary for such norms possibly to constitute [. . .] a customary rule'); Patrick Dumberry, *The Formation and Identification of Customary International Law in International Investment Law* (Cambridge University Press, Cambridge 2016) 105, 181 and 185 (discussing the views of D'Aspremont both in general and in particular connection with the minimum standard, and also addressing Diehl's arguments at p. 185).

aliens.[52] In such scenario, the applicable customary norm clearly has a 'standard-like' structure.[53] But it is still customary.[54] Many international legal directives have a changing and more or less flexible content.[55] In 1963, Karl Doehring observed:

> [I]f the indeterminacy of an alleged international legal directive were a sufficient reason for denying its existence, there would be little left for positive international law, properly so-called.[56]

In the final analysis, the absence of a 'fixed content' should not impair a norm's existence or binding character.[57] Most importantly, standards do not exist in a factual vacuum: just as rules, they refer to more or less specific factual settings and, consequently, have a more-or-less delimited *scope of application*.[58] As explained by Pierre Schlag:

---

[52]For two representative examples see: *El Oro Mining and Railway Co. v Mexico* (18 June 1931) V RIAA 191 [9]; *The Interoceanic Railway of Mexico Ltd. et al. v Mexico* (18 June 1931) V RIAA 178 [7-11]. It should be noted that in *El Oro Mining*, the British-Mexican Commission formulated a standard-like directive requiring consideration of the circumstances of each particular case (at para 9). Nonetheless, it also formulated a rule-like directive indicating that, under any circumstances, a nine-year delay can hardly be considered reasonable (at para 9). For a detailed analysis of the maxim 'justice delayed is justice denied' see: Alwyn Freeman, *The International Responsibility of States for Denial of Justice* (Klaus Reprint, New York 1970) 242-63 [first edition: 1938]. The author has already discussed the issue of denial of justice resulting from delays elsewhere: Sebastián Mantilla Blanco, *Justizielles Unrecht im internationalen Investitionsschutzrecht* (Nomos, Baden-Baden 2016) 95-9.

[53]Other authors have mentioned 'due process' as a textbook example of a standard. See: Roscoe Pound, 'The Administrative Application of Legal Standards' (1919) 42 Annu. Rep. A.B.A. 445, 456.

[54]See generally: Alwyn Freeman, *The International Responsibility of States for Denial of Justice* (Klaus Reprint, New York 1970) 242-63 [first edition: 1938].

[55]This feature of customary norms gave rise to intense discussions in the past. For an example see the Isay-Doehring debate on the relevance of international law for the regulation of the status and treatment of aliens: Ernst Isay, *Das deutsche Fremdenrecht. Ausländer und Polizei* (Verlag von Georg Stilke, Berlin 1923) 22 (noting the changing character of customary norms and arguing that international law does not provide a clear regulatory framework for the status of aliens); Karl Doehring, *Die allgemeinen Regeln des völkerrechtlichen Fremdenrechts und das deutsche Verfassungsrecht* (Carl Heymanns Verlag, Köln/Berlin 1963) 3 (observing that, while customary norms are constantly changing and too-often have a disputed content, they are still applicable under art. 25 of the German Fundamental Law). See also Doehring's remarks at p. 9 (mentioning the law of aliens as one of the areas of international law where these features are most clearly recognizable).

[56]Author's translation. The original German text reads: "Wäre die Unbestimmtheit eines angeblichen Rechtsatzes im Völkerrecht ein genügender Grund, seinen Bestand zu leugnen, bliebe nur wenig übrig, was als positives Recht bezeichnet werden könnte." Karl Doehring, *Die allgemeinen Regeln des völkerrechtlichen Fremdenrechts und das deutsche Verfassungsrecht* (Carl Heymanns Verlag, Köln/Berlin 1963) 83-4.

[57]See: Karl Doehring, *Die allgemeinen Regeln des völkerrechtlichen Fremdenrechts und das deutsche Verfassungsrecht* (Carl Heymanns Verlag, Köln/Berlin 1963) 83-4.

[58]Cf. Pierre Schlag, 'Rules and Standards' (1985-6) 33 UCLA L. Rev. 379, 381-3 (describing the features of '[legal] directives' in general).

The formula of a legal directive [rule or standard] is "if this, then that." A directive thus has two parts: a "trigger" that identifies some phenomenon and a "response" that requires or authorizes a legal consequence when that phenomenon is present.[59]

The difference between rules and standards lies in the fact that, while a rule has a 'hard empirical trigger and a hard determinate response',[60] standards have 'a soft evaluative trigger and a soft modulated response'.[61] Following Schlag, an example of a rule would be: 'sounds above 70 decibels shall be punished by a ten dollar fine'.[62] In contrast, a standard would say: 'excessive loudness shall be enjoinable upon a showing of irreparable harm'.[63] Other scholars have suggested that, in the end, there are neither 'pure rules' nor 'pure standards': legal directives are always placed somewhere between the two poles.[64] Another line of argument submits that the application of standards involves an interplay between the standard and a rule (properly so-called).[65] For example, Roscoe Pound observed in 1933 that, when standard is applied, 'there is a rule (in the narrower sense) prescribing adherence to the standard and imposing consequences if the standard is not lived up to'.[66]

The application of a standard to a particular situation of fact presupposes that the case falls within the scope of the standard or, using Pound's explanatory model, within the scope of the 'rule (in the narrower sense) prescribing adherence to the standard'.[67] The broadness or specificity of the trigger does not in itself impair a legal directive's standard-like structure.[68] As explained by Duncan Kennedy (1976):

A rule setting the age of legal majority at 21 is more general than a rule setting the age of capacity to contract at 21. A standard of reasonable care in the use of firearms is more particular than a standard of reasonable care in the use of "any dangerous instrumentality".

---

[59]Pierre Schlag, 'Rules and Standards' (1985-6) 33 UCLA L. Rev. 379, 381.

[60]Pierre Schlag, 'Rules and Standards' (1985-6) 33 UCLA L. Rev. 379, 382.

[61]Pierre Schlag, 'Rules and Standards' (1985-6) 33 UCLA L. Rev. 379, 383.

[62]Pierre Schlag, 'Rules and Standards' (1985-6) 33 UCLA L. Rev. 379, 383.

[63]Pierre Schlag, 'Rules and Standards' (1985-6) 33 UCLA L. Rev. 379, 383.

[64]Rusell Korobkin, 'Behavioral Analysis and Legal Form: Rules vs. Standards Revisited' (2000) 79 Or. L. Rev. 23, 25-30.

[65]See: Roscoe Pound, 'Hierarchy of Sources and Forms in Different Systems of Law' (1933) 7 (4) Tul. L. Rev. 475, 485.

[66]Roscoe Pound, 'Hierarchy of Sources and Forms in Different Systems of Law' (1933) 7(4) Tul. L. Rev. 475, 485. Pound however emphasized that standards are more flexible than rules; in this vein, he explained that 'the significant thing is the standard, to be applied, not absolutely as in case of a rule, but in view of the facts of each case' (at p. 485).

[67]Roscoe Pound, 'Hierarchy of Sources and Forms in Different Systems of Law' (1933) 7(4) Tul. L. Rev. 475, 485. Cf. also Pierre Schlag, 'Rules and Standards' (1985-6) 33 UCLA L. Rev. 379, 381-3.

[68]Duncan Kennedy, 'Form and Substance in Private Law Adjudication' (1976) 89 Harv. L. Rev. 1685, 1689. The expression 'standard-like' is not Kennedy's. Other authors have used the terms 'rule-like' and 'standard-like' to refer to the different approaches that could be followed for the formulation of a 'legal directive'. For some indicative examples see: Kathleen Sullivan, 'Foreword: The Justices of Rules and Standards' (1992) 106 Harv. L. Rev. 22, 60-1 and 70; Pierre Schlag, 'Rules and Standards' (1985-6) 33 UCLA L. Rev. 379, 428-9.

Generality means that the framer of the legal directive is attempting to kill many birds with one stone. The wide scope of the rule or standard is an attempt to deal with as many as possible of the different imaginable fact situations in which a substantive issue may arise [. . .] we can have general or particular standards, and general or particular rules.[69]

Against this backdrop, the notion of standard could help distinguish two separate questions. The first question refers to the *scope of application* or factual trigger of the FPS standard.[70] Using the terminology chosen by some scholars, this would be the 'rule in a narrower sense' determining the cases in which adjudicators are called upon to apply the FPS standard.[71] The second question concerns the FPS standard's *actual content*, i.e., the parameters it provides for the evaluation of conduct.[72] If a distinction were to be drawn between the *standard* and the *rule* requiring its application in a specific case, this would be the question about the standard as such.[73] In respect of FPS, the said parameters for the evaluation of conduct are embodied in the open-textured 'due diligence' standard of liability.[74]

6.3   The Semantics of Security and the Scope of Application of 'Full Protection and Security' in Customary International Law

At the outset, the standard of 'full protection and security' poses a semantic question. Do 'protection' and 'security' convey different meanings? What does the adjective 'full' reveal about the standard? The expression 'full protection and security' is a term of art designating a customary standard of the law of aliens.[75] While the adjective 'full' could have some significance for the interpretation of FPS *treaty clauses*, its use in connection with the customary standard is not intended to add any substantive meaning to the term.[76] To avoid confusion, some scholars prefer to use

---

[69]Duncan Kennedy, 'Form and Substance in Private Law Adjudication' (1976) 89 Harv. L. Rev. 1685, 1689.

[70]See Chaps. 7–10.

[71]Cf. Roscoe Pound, 'Hierarchy of Sources and Forms in Different Systems of Law' (1933) 7 (4) Tul. L. Rev. 475, 485.

[72]See Chaps. 11–13.

[73]Cf. Roscoe Pound, 'Hierarchy of Sources and Forms in Different Systems of Law' (1933) 7 (4) Tul. L. Rev. 475, 485.

[74]See Chaps. 11–13. The term 'standard' should facilitate the presentation of the FPS standard and not turn into a terminological straitjacket. Therefore, unless otherwise stated, the use of the terms 'rule', 'principle' or 'standard' in other sections does not intend to ascribe to the norm in question a 'standard-like' or a 'rule-like' structure.

[75]On the customary character of FPS see Sect. 5.2.

[76]Section 14.4.1 discusses the significance of the adjective *full* in the interpretation of FPS treaty clauses.

the label 'P&S'.[77] Still, 'FPS' continues to be the most common designation of the standard.[78]

The *Oxford English Dictionary* indicates that both *protection* and *security* refer to the 'condition of being protected' and convey the idea of 'freedom' or 'preservation' from injury or threat.[79] The phrase 'protection and security' could therefore seem somewhat redundant. And it is. Sometimes more words are used than needed to describe or designate a concept or idea, thus forming a pleonasm.[80] This phenomenon is fairly common in investment law; a well-known example is 'fair and equitable treatment'.[81]

Against this background, the FPS standard could be accurately described as a guarantee of *security*. Looking for a definition of security is by no means an easy task, and could readily turn into a truly frustrating undertaking.[82] Lucia Zedner has described the notion as 'promiscuous',[83] observing that 'security is a slippery and contested term that conveys many meanings and has many referent objects, ranging from the individual to the state to the biosphere'.[84] Other scholars have depicted

---

[77]See, for example: Todd Weiler, *The Interpretation of International Investment Law: Equality, Discrimination, and Minimum Standards of Treatment in Historical Context* (Brill, Leiden 2013) xxxvii *et seq.*

[78]See, for example: David Collins, 'Applying the Full Protection and Security Standard of Protection to Digital Investments' (2011) 12(2) J. World Investment & Trade 225, 225; Eric De Brabandere, 'Host States' Due Diligence Obligations in International Investment Law' (2014-5) 42 Syracuse J. Int'l L. & Com. 319, 332; Eric De Brabandere, *Investment Treaty Arbitration as Public International Law. Procedural Aspects and Implications* (Cambridge University Press, Cambridge 2014) 25; Helge Elisabeth Zeitler, 'Full Protection and Security' in Stephan Schill (ed), *International Investment Law and Comparative Public Law* (Oxford University Press, New York 2010) 183, 183.

[79]'protection, n' (June 2015) *Oxford English Dictionary Online* [http://www.oed.com/view/Entry/153134?redirectedFrom=protection]; 'security, n' (June 2015) *Oxford English Dictionary Online* [http://www.oed.com/view/Entry/174661?redirectedFrom=security&]. For an author relying on the Oxford English Dictionary for the assessment of the FPS standard see: Finnur Magnússon, *Full Protection and Security in International Law* (University of Vienna, Vienna 2012) 107-12.

[80]On the notion of pleonasm in linguistics see: Francesco Gardani, 'Affix Pleonasm' in Peter Müller, Ingeborg Ohnheiser, Susan Olsen and Franz Rainer (eds), *Word Formation. An International Handbook of the Languages of Europe* (Volume 1: Walter de Gruyter, Berlin/Boston 2015) 537, 537-50 (particularly at pp. 538-9).

[81]See: Ronald Kläger, *'Fair and Equitable Treatment' in International Investment Law* (Cambridge University Press, New York 2011) 41-2. In 1969, Georg Schwarzenberger had already suggested that the expression 'fair and equitable' 'appears to suffer from a proclivity to redundancy'. Georg Schwarzenberger, *Foreign Investments and International Law* (Stevens & Sons, London 1969) 116.

[82]Cf. Lucia Zedner, *Security* (Routledge, New York 2009) 9.

[83]Lucia Zedner, *Security* (Routledge, New York 2009) 9.

[84]Lucia Zedner, *Security* (Routledge, New York 2009) 10.

security as an 'essentially contested concept'.[85] The underlying problem is that security cannot be defined in precise terms: any abstract, general definition of security will be incapable of delivering a both accurate and meaningful idea of the concept.[86]

Let us consider a traditional definition as an example. In his analysis of the Latin term *securitas*, John T. Hamilton explains that the word has the following components: 'the prefix *sē-* (apart, aside, away from); the noun *cura* (care, concern, attention, worry); and the suffix-*tas* (denoting a condition of state of being)'.[87] Thus, *securitas* 'denotes a condition of being separated from care, a state wherein worries have been put off to the side'.[88] In this line of thought, security could be understood as *freedom from fear*.[89] If taken as a general definition, however, the notion of 'freedom from fear' might prove both insufficient and inaccurate.

This understanding of *securitas* links security to a subjective state of mind or, in other words, the idea of 'tranquility of mind'.[90] This effect is not accidental. This was precisely the meaning intended by some influential Roman sources.[91] For instance, Cicero resorted to the noun *securitas* to describe stoic psychological tranquility.[92] In contrast, he used the term *salus* to denote corporal safety, safety

---

[85]Barry Buzan, 'Peace, Power, and Security: Contending Concepts in the Study of International Relations' (1984) 21(2) JPR 109, 125 n. 1. Buzan uses the notion of 'essentially contested concept' based on the influential work of the Scottish philosopher Walter Bryce Gallie (at p. 125 n. 1). See: Walter Bryce Gallie, 'Essentially Contested Concepts' (1956) 56 Proceedings of the Aristotelian Society 167, 171-80. This characterization of the concept of security has not been without criticism. For a critical view see: David Baldwin, 'The Concept of Security' (1997) 23 Rev. Int'l St. 5, 10-2.

[86]Barry Buzan, 'Peace, Power, and Security: Contending Concepts in the Study of International Relations' (1984) 21(2) JPR 109, 118 (arguing that notions such as security 'cannot be, or have not yet been, reduced to standard formulas'); Rhonda Powell, 'The Concept of Security' (2012) 1 Oxford Socio-Legal Review 1, 9 (pointing out that 'substantive definitions of security' are always inaccurate).

[87]John Hamilton, *Security: Politics, Humanity, and the Philology of Care* (Princeton University Press, Princeton NJ 2013) 5.

[88]John Hamilton, *Security: Politics, Humanity, and the Philology of Care* (Princeton University Press, Princeton NJ 2013) 5.

[89]Hamilton also elaborates further on the notion of 'freedom from fear' in another chapter of his book. See: John Hamilton, *Security: Politics, Humanity, and the Philology of Care* (Princeton University Press, Princeton NJ 2013) 296.

[90]John Hamilton, *Security: Politics, Humanity, and the Philology of Care* (Princeton University Press, Princeton NJ 2013) 51 *et seq.* (addressing the notion of security as 'tranquility of mind' in Roman sources).

[91]John Hamilton, *Security: Politics, Humanity, and the Philology of Care* (Princeton University Press, Princeton NJ 2013) 51 *et seq.* (particularly referring to Cicero's *De Officiis*).

[92]For this interpretation see: John Hamilton, *Security: Politics, Humanity, and the Philology of Care* (Princeton University Press, Princeton NJ 2013) 51 *et seq.* (particularly at p. 53). This interpretation refers to a famous passage of *De Officiis* (at Book 1 para 69), where Cicero stated: "[a]gain, we must keep ourselves free from every disturbing emotion, not only from desire and fear, but also from excessive pain and pleasure, and from anger, so that we may enjoy the calm of soul and freedom from care [*securitas*] which brings both moral stability and dignity of character." Marcus Tullius Cicero, *De Officiis* (Walter Miller tr, Macmillan Co., New York 1921) 71 [bilingual edition]. The original Latin text reads: "[v]acandum autem omni est animi perturbatione, cum

from more objectively determined threats or, most importantly, public safety.[93] Roman sources would soon give up this distinction between *securitas* and *salus*.[94] Hamilton has observed that the differentiation would progressively disappear or, at least, 'become less rigorous' with the passage of time.[95] *Security* would gradually be untied from the individual's private sphere and extend beyond its original subjective essence.[96] For instance, later Roman sources often qualified the term with adjectives pointing to the *security of the state*.[97] Some examples would be '*securitas augusta*', '*securitas publica*', '*securitas orbi*' and '*securitas rei publica*'.[98] At many instances, *securitas* would become the Latin equivalent of *asphaleia* in Epicurean philosophy, thus conveying the meaning of 'protection from others'.[99] In this vein, Hamilton explains that '*asphaleia* guarantees that institutions will not crumble'.[100]

Modern theories of security usually draw a distinction between *subjective security* (i.e. a psychological state or feeling of peace and tranquility) and *objective*

---

cupiditate et metu, tum etiam aegritudine et voluptate nimia et iracundia, ut tranquilitas animi et securitas adsit, quae affert cum constantiam, tum etiam dignitatem." (at p. 70). For an analysis of the Latin term *securitas* see also: Emma Rothschild, 'What is Security?' (1995) 124(3) Daedalus 53, 61-2.

[93]In *De Legibus*, Cicero uses the word *salus* to denote the 'safety of the people', by stating: "[t]here shall be two magistrates with royal powers. Since they lead, judge, and confer, from these functions they shall be called praetors, judges and consuls. In the field they shall hold the supreme military power; they shall be subject to no one; *the safety [salus] of the people shall be their highest law.*" Emphasis added. Marcus Tullius Cicero, *On the Republic. On the Laws* (Clinton Keyes tr, Harvard University Press, Cambridge MA 1928) 465 and 467 [bilingual edition]. The original Latin text reads: "Regio imperio duo sunto, iique praeeundo, iudicando, consulendo praetores, iudices, consules appellamino; militiae summum ius habento, nemini parento; *ollis salus populi suprema lex esto*." (at pp. 464 and 466). For a detailed study of the use of the terms *securitas* and *salus* in Cicero's works and other Roman sources see: John Hamilton, *Security: Politics, Humanity, and the Philology of Care* (Princeton University Press, Princeton NJ 2013) 51-67 (referring to Cicero's *De Legibus* at p. 59).

[94]John Hamilton, *Security: Politics, Humanity, and the Philology of Care* (Princeton University Press, Princeton NJ 2013) 59.

[95]John Hamilton, *Security: Politics, Humanity, and the Philology of Care* (Princeton University Press, Princeton NJ 2013) 59.

[96]John Hamilton, *Security: Politics, Humanity, and the Philology of Care* (Princeton University Press, Princeton NJ 2013) 59.

[97]John Hamilton, *Security: Politics, Humanity, and the Philology of Care* (Princeton University Press, Princeton NJ 2013) 58-9.

[98]John Hamilton, *Security: Politics, Humanity, and the Philology of Care* (Princeton University Press, Princeton NJ 2013) 58-9 (referring to coin inscriptions using these and similar expressions). See also Hamilton's examples at p. 58 n. 13.

[99]John Hamilton, *Security: Politics, Humanity, and the Philology of Care* (Princeton University Press, Princeton NJ 2013) 60.

[100]John Hamilton, *Security: Politics, Humanity, and the Philology of Care* (Princeton University Press, Princeton NJ 2013) 60.

security (i.e. a use of the term that makes specific reference to an objectively identified threat).[101] The two notions are not completely separate compartments.[102] For some scholars, 'it can be argued that in fact, objective and subjective security are symbiotic and synchronised'.[103]

To be clear, there is nothing wrong about the use of the term 'security' to describe individual tranquility or peace of mind.[104] This could well be one of the concept's numerous dimensions or shades of meaning.[105] But a merely individualist, psychological notion of security can still not be taken as a general definition: it would indeed leave aside many widespread usages of the term.[106] What is more, it is nowadays contested whether security must be necessarily linked or reduced to the subjective notion of *fear*.[107] For instance, in its assessment of 'human security', the United Nations has long considered that the concept comprises, among others, 'freedom from fear' and 'freedom from want'.[108]

---

[101]On the distinction between objective and subjective security see: Alexandra Walker, 'Conscious and Unconscious Security Responses' in Hitoshi Nasu and Kim Rubenstein, *Legal Perspectives on Security Institutions* (Cambridge University Press, Cambridge 2015) 27, 29-31; Arnold Wolfers, 'National Security as an Ambiguous Symbol' (1952) 67(4) Pol. Sci. Q. 481, 485; Lucia Zedner, *Security* (Routledge, New York 2009) 13-9; Rhonda Powell, 'The Concept of Security' (2012) 1 Oxford Socio-Legal Review 1, 16-20.

[102]Alexandra Walker, 'Conscious and Unconscious Security Responses' in Hitoshi Nasu and Kim Rubenstein, *Legal Perspectives on Security Institutions* (Cambridge University Press, Cambridge 2015) 30.

[103]Alexandra Walker, 'Conscious and Unconscious Security Responses' in Hitoshi Nasu and Kim Rubenstein, *Legal Perspectives on Security Institutions* (Cambridge University Press, Cambridge 2015) 30.

[104]On the notion of 'subjective security' see generally: Alexandra Walker, 'Conscious and Unconscious Security Responses' in Hitoshi Nasu and Kim Rubenstein, *Legal Perspectives on Security Institutions* (Cambridge University Press, Cambridge 2015) 29.

[105]Cf. Rhonda Powell, 'The Concept of Security' (2012) 1 Oxford Socio-Legal Review 1, 18-20 (summarizing the discussion on subjective and objective security).

[106]For a general discussion of possible difficulties arising from the subjective notion of security see: Lucia Zedner, *Security* (Routledge, New York 2009) 16-9 (particularly at p. 19). See also: Rhonda Powell, 'The Concept of Security' (2012) 1 Oxford Socio-Legal Review 1, 18-20.

[107]Cf. Ashok Swain, *Understanding Security Challenges. Threats and Opportunities* (Routledge, New York 2013) 132 *et seq.* (particularly referring to the evolution of the notion of 'human security').

[108]United Nations Development Programme, *Human Development Report 1994* (Oxford University Press, New York 1994) 23-33 (particularly at 23). For an overview of the evolution of the notion of human security see: Caroline Thomas, 'Globalization and Human Security' in Anthony McGrew and Nana K. Poku, *Globalization, Development and Human Security* (Polity Press, Cambridge 2007) 107, 108-16; Ronald Behringer, *The Human Security Agenda. How Middle Power Leadership Defied US Hegemony* (Continuum International Publishing Group, New York 2012) 13-6; Shahrbanou Tadjbakhsh, 'In Defense of the Broad View of Human Security' in Mary Martin and Taylor Owen (eds), *Routledge Handbook of Human Security* (Routledge, New York 2014) 43, 50-4.

On the other hand, the notion of 'absence of fear' or 'freedom from fear' seems too vague as a basis for a meaningful definition of security.[109] Security could indeed easily become a highly abstract, unachievable ideal.[110] Hamilton suggests that this problem is immanent to the etymology of the Latin word *securitas* itself.[111] In one of his *fabulae*, Gauis Julius Hyginus portrayed a divine figure called Cura (literally meaning 'care' or 'concern') forming the first human being out of clay (*humus*).[112] In Roman times the deity was believed to possess men during their entire mortal existence: only death could bring human soul to Janus and the body to Tellus (Earth), finally freeing men from Cura, their maker.[113] As a corollary, a perfect *securitas* (literally meaning 'freedom from cura/concern') is never possible in a mortal life.[114] This Roman legend may be taken as a warning: women and men will never be entirely free from fear, anxiety and worries.[115] For present purposes, this somewhat picturesque story indicates that, if security is defined as freedom from any possible fear, a legal obligation to ensure security could entail an impossible commitment.[116]

---

[109] See: Rhonda Powell, 'The Concept of Security' (2012) 1 Oxford Socio-Legal Review 1, 18-20.

[110] John Hamilton, *Security: Politics, Humanity, and the Philology of Care* (Princeton University Press, Princeton NJ 2013) 5-6 (referring to the origins of the term *securitas* and suggesting at p. 6 that security could be 'the history of an ambition to evade time and its contingencies').

[111] John Hamilton, *Security: Politics, Humanity, and the Philology of Care* (Princeton University Press, Princeton NJ 2013) 3-6.

[112] R. Scott Smith and Stephen Trzaskoma, *Apollodorus' Library and Hyginus' Fabulae* (Hackett Publishing, Indianapolis IN 2007) 166-7. Discussed at: John Hamilton, *Security: Politics, Humanity, and the Philology of Care* (Princeton University Press, Princeton NJ 2013) 3-6.

[113] The story presents the Roman deity Cura using clay *(humus)* to form a man. At Cura's request, Jove accepted to give the figure true life, but then claimed that the figure should not be named after Cura, but after himself. The goddess of the Earth (*Tellus*) became aware of the figure's existence and claimed that, since she had provided the clay, the new being should carry her name. Saturn, the god of time, was called upon to settle the dispute. The god chose to call the figure *homo*, noting that it was made out of *humus*. Saturn sought to do justice to the three deities by giving the figure's soul to Jove and the body to Tellus. Jove and Tellus would obtain their parts after the figure's death. Finally, the divine arbiter granted Cura the right to possess and control the figure during its entire life. For an English translation of Hyginus' text see: R. Scott Smith and Stephen Trzaskoma, *Apollodorus' Library and Hyginus' Fabulae* (Hackett Publishing, Indianapolis IN 2007) 166-7. It should be noted that this myth has already been the subject of philosophical reflection. For an outstanding example see: Martin Heidegger, *Sein und Zeit* (Max Niemeyer Verlag, Tübingen 1967) 196-200. For a detailed discussion of the story and its significance for the concept of security see: John Hamilton, *Security: Politics, Humanity, and the Philology of Care* (Princeton University Press, Princeton NJ 2013) 3-6.

[114] John Hamilton, *Security: Politics, Humanity, and the Philology of Care* (Princeton University Press, Princeton NJ 2013) 3-6.

[115] See: John Hamilton, *Security: Politics, Humanity, and the Philology of Care* (Princeton University Press, Princeton NJ 2013) 6.

[116] Cf. Lucia Zedner, *Security* (Routledge, New York 2009) 18-9 (noting the difficulties attached to unqualified, expansive notions of subjective security, but without making particular reference to security obligations).

Such impossibility would ultimately result from the broadness of the definition itself.[117] In the end, the term *security* would remain somewhat meaningless unless the subject and object of fear are somehow delimited.[118] This phenomenon is evident in most uses of the term.[119] For instance, in his *Theory of Moral Sentiments*, Adam Smith stated:

> [Security] is the first and the principal object of prudence. It is adverse to expose our health, our fortune, our rank, or reputation, to any sort of hazard.[120]

In this passage, security conveys the meaning of freedom from fear *of* any hazard *to* certain values.[121] It is thus striking that security is circumscribed by a number of external elements: a subject (implicit), specific values (health, fortune, rank, reputation) and a threat (any sort of hazard).[122] A similar analysis could be made in respect of any practical use of the concept.[123] This circumstance may be taken as an indication that security is, in the end, a blank space.[124]

Social scientists have observed that '[s]ecurity has no inherent meaning outside its relations with other concepts, there is no one 'security' but multiple securities'.[125] In a similar line of thought, political science studies have concluded that, in order to be meaningful, the concept of security always requires some sort of 'specification' or 'contextual information'.[126] Barry Buzan notes that any discussion on the subject presupposes an external 'referent object'.[127] David Baldwin considers that security involves a problem of 'specification', observing that there are many means—i.e.,

---

[117]On the need for 'meaningful' discussions of the security concept see: Rhonda Powell, 'The Concept of Security' (2012) 1 Oxford Socio-Legal Review 1, 6 *et seq.*

[118]For a similar observation see: Rhonda Powell, 'The Concept of Security' (2012) 1 Oxford Socio-Legal Review 1, 6 *et seq.* Cf. also: David Balwin, 'The Concept of Security' (1997) 23 Rev. Int'l St. 5, 13.

[119]See: Rhonda Powell, 'The Concept of Security' (2012) 1 Oxford Socio-Legal Review 1, 6 *et seq.*

[120]Adam Smith, *The Theory of Moral Sentiments* (1759) (Cambridge University Press, Cambridge 2002) 249. For a discussion of Smith's notion of security see: Emma Rothschild, 'What is Security?' (1995) 124(3) Daedalus 53, 61-2.

[121]Cf. Adam Smith, *The Theory of Moral Sentiments* (1759) (Cambridge University Press, Cambridge 2002) 249.

[122]Cf. Adam Smith, *The Theory of Moral Sentiments* (1759) (Cambridge University Press, Cambridge 2002) 249. For an analysis of these elements as components of the notion of security see: Rhonda Powell, 'The Concept of Security' (2012) 1 Oxford Socio-Legal Review 1, 5 (from a general perspective).

[123]See: Rhonda Powell, 'The Concept of Security' (2012) 1 Oxford Socio-Legal Review 1, 5.

[124]Cf. Rhonda Powell, 'The Concept of Security' (2012) 1 Oxford Socio-Legal Review 1, 5 (arguing that security, as a concept, 'is not substantive').

[125]Mike Bourne, *Understanding Security* (MacMillan, New York 2014) 2.

[126]David Balwin, 'The Concept of Security' (1997) 23 Rev. Int'l St. 5, 6 and 12 *et seq.* (referring to 'specification'); Rhonda Powell, 'The Concept of Security' (2012) 1 Oxford Socio-Legal Review 1, 6 (referring to 'contextual information').

[127]Barry Buzan, Ole Waever and Jaap de Wilde, *Security. A New Framework for Analysis* (Lynne Rienner Publishers, Boulder CO 1998) 21-3 and 36.

external factors—through which such 'specification' can be achieved.[128] According to him, 'one could specify security with respect to the actor whose values are to be secured, the values concerned, the degree of security, the kinds of threats, the means for coping with such threats, the costs of doing so, and the relevant period of time'.[129] Baldwin is nonetheless cautious in explaining that '[n]ot all of the dimensions need to [be] specified all the time'.[130] Quite the contrary:

> The question remains, however: 'How much specification is enough? Must all of these dimensions be specified in detail every time one uses the concept of security? Obviously not. Both the number of dimensions in need of specifications and the degree of specificity required will vary with the research task at hand.[131]

Arbitral tribunals interpreting FPS treaty clauses or applying the customary FPS standard are necessarily faced with and challenged by these complexities.[132] In *Suez v Argentina*, the arbitrators expressly acknowledged the problem in the following terms:

> This Tribunal is confronted initially with two basic questions: Protection from whom? Protection against what? In other words, from whom is a Contracting Party to protect an investor and against what specific actions by such person is a Contracting Party to secure protection?[133]

Bearing the foregoing in mind, the concept of security has been characterized as 'formal' or 'relational'.[134] As noted by Rhonda Powell (2012):

> Meaningful discussions of security rely upon appropriate contextual information about whose security is in question, which value or interest is to be secured, which risk or threat is posed and who is best placed to protect and provide. The concept of security does not contain this information. Security is a relational concept because it describes the relation between these four factors [i.e., agent, provider of security, secured values and risks] and derives its meaning, in any particular context, from them.[135]

The notion of security, taken as a 'relational concept', is a powerful tool for explaining the diversity of meanings and shades of meaning that have been ascribed to a term which, as some scholars observe, 'is vertiginously ubiquitous, serving a vast array of discourses for practically every area of human society'.[136]

---

[128]David Balwin, 'The Concept of Security' (1997) 23 Rev. Int'l St. 5, 12 *et seq.*

[129]David Balwin, 'The Concept of Security' (1997) 23 Rev. Int'l St. 5, 17.

[130]David Balwin, 'The Concept of Security' (1997) 23 Rev. Int'l St. 5, 17.

[131]David Balwin, 'The Concept of Security' (1997) 23 Rev. Int'l St. 5, 17.

[132]Cf. Suez Sociedad General de Aguas de Barcelona S.A. and Vivendi Universal S.A. *v* Argentina, Decision on Liability, ICSID Case No. ARB/03/19 (30 July 2010) [160].

[133]Suez Sociedad General de Aguas de Barcelona S.A. and Vivendi Universal S.A. *v* Argentina, Decision on Liability, ICSID Case No. ARB/03/19 (30 July 2010) [160].

[134]Rhonda Powell, 'The Concept of Security' (2012) 1 Oxford Socio-Legal Review 1, 6. For a similar terminology, see: Mike Bourne, *Understanding Security* (MacMillan, New York 2014) 2.

[135]Rhonda Powell, 'The Concept of Security' (2012) 1 Oxford Socio-Legal Review 1, 6.

[136]John Hamilton, *Security: Politics, Humanity, and the Philology of Care* (Princeton University Press, Princeton NJ 2013) 7.

Most importantly, such characterization could help identify the defining elements of the FPS standard's scope of application. In fact, if FPS is understood as a guarantee of security, following Powell, at least four questions must be answered for the standard to be meaningful: '(a) security for whom (an agent); (b) security of what (a value or interest); (c) security against what (a threat or risk), and (d) security by whom (a provider of protection)'.[137] Following David Baldwin's theories, each element does not need to be specified in the same degree at the same time.[138] For instance, a broad definition of the secured values does not necessarily undermine the determinacy of the concept, provided other elements of the security relation (e.g. the threats or risks) are specified to a reasonable degree.[139]

These questions may be easily translated into a terminology much more familiar to international lawyers. It could be said that the FPS standard has both a *subjective* scope of application (protected persons and protecting agents) and an *objective* scope of application (protected values or interests, and threats or risks against which security is afforded).[140]

As will be shown below, no element has greater significance for the definition of FPS than the threats or risks to which the standard refers.[141] In this respect, the FPS standard poses three fundamental questions. First, the source or origin of risk (i.e. the entity or phenomenon that produces the threat), the threshold issue being whether and to which extent the FPS standard relates to both public and non-public hazards.[142] The second question concerns the material—i.e., physical or nonphysical—nature of the threat, another usual controversy in the debate about the scope of the FPS standard.[143] Thirdly, the question arises as to whether the FPS standard is only relevant *before* the materialization of the risk or threat, or whether it also encompasses obligations that are applicable *after* an injury has been inflicted. This question therefore refers to the FPS standard's *temporal* scope of application.[144]

These elements—determining the subjective, objective and temporal scope of application of the standard—are *external* to the notion of security and can only be

---

[137]Rhonda Powell, 'The Concept of Security' (2012) 1 Oxford Socio-Legal Review 1, 5.

[138]David Balwin, 'The Concept of Security' (1997) 23 Rev. Int'l St. 5, 17.

[139]Section 8.3 argues that, while the values secured by the customary FPS standard are a broad category, FPS refers to very specific risks.

[140]See Chaps. 7 and 8. A scholar has used a similar terminology in connection with the FPS standard, but has ascribed a different meaning to the terms '*ratione materiae*' (which he uses to refer to the 'physical' or 'legal' character of harm) and '*ratione personae*' (which he uses to refer to the distinction between harm originating in the acts of private parties and harm originating in the acts of state agents). Cf. Nartnirun Junngam, 'The Full Protection and Security Standard in International Investment Law: What and Who is Investment Fully[?] Protected and Secured From?' (2018) 7 (1) AUBLR 1, 60-74. All these aspects are considered here under the standard's objective scope of application and, particularly, under the notion of covered risks.

[141]See Sect. 8.3. Cf. also Chap. 9.

[142]See Sect. 8.3.

[143]See Chap. 9.

[144]See Chap. 10.

established on the basis of contextual evidence.[145] In the case of the customary FPS standard, this contextual evidence is provided, among others, by diplomatic correspondence, official statements, negotiating instruments, and arbitral decisions.

---

[145]Cf. Rhonda Powell, 'The Concept of Security' (2012) 1 Oxford Socio-Legal Review 1, 6.

Chapter 7
Subjective Scope of Application of the Customary Standard of 'Full Protection and Security'

7.1 Preliminary Remarks

The personal or subjective scope of application of the customary FPS standard is intrinsically and unavoidably linked to the definition of the law of aliens itself. The key to the definition of this area of international law is, in turn, the concept of nationality.[1] Felix Stoerk explained in 1887, at a time when individuals were not yet generally regarded as subjects of rights and duties under international law, that 'nationality is the point of passage an individual needs to reach to come into the light of international law'.[2] More specifically, Edwin Borchard observed in 1913:

---

[1]The concept of nationality requires a short clarification. There has been some controversy as to whether nationality is a *legal relationship* between a state and an individual (*Rechtsverhältnis*), or whether it is a *status* implicating certain rights and obligations (*rechtliche Eigenschaft*). The latter theory is based on the observation that the bond of nationality, if taken as a state-individual legal relationship, always presupposes that the individual fulfills the conditions for acquiring nationality. In other words, he or she must have the *legal condition* or *status* of a national. The implication is subtle: nationality is *not* a legal relationship with the home state. Such relationship would be, at best, an *implication* of nationality. In this line of thought, nationality could be described as a *legal status* (*Zustand*). Some authors (e.g. Alexander Makarov) preferred to take the best of both worlds, considering nationality to be *at the same time* a legal relationship and a legal status (so-called *vermittlende Theorie*). For a detailed, critical presentation of these theories: Alexander Makarov, *Allgemeine Lehren des Staatsangehörigkeitsrechts* (W. Kohlhammer Verlag, Heidelberg 1962) 19-29; Bernhard Dubois, *Die Frage der völkerrechtlichen Schranken landesrechtlicher Regelung der Staatsangehörigkeit* (Verlag Stämpfli & Cie., Bern 1955) 1-4; Eduard Goldstein, *Die Staatsangehörigkeit der juristischen Person* (Junge & Sohn, Erlangen 1912) 13.

[2]Author's translation. The original German text reads: "die Staatsangehörigkeit bildet den Durchgangspunkt, den das Individuum erreicht haben muß, um in das Licht völkerrechtlicher Betrachtung zu gelangen." Felix Stoerk, 'Staatsunterthanen und Fremde' in Franz von Holtzendorff (ed), *Handbuch des Völkerrechts auf Grundlage europäischer Staatspraxis* (Volume 2: Verlag von F. F. Richter, Hamburg 1887) 582, 589.

© Springer Nature Switzerland AG 2019
S. Mantilla Blanco, *Full Protection and Security in International Investment Law*,
European Yearbook of International Economic Law 8,
https://doi.org/10.1007/978-3-030-24838-3_7

A discussion of the subject [i.e. the protection of citizens abroad] [. . .] involves a preliminary study of three distinct legal relations, first, between the state and its own citizen; secondly, between the state and aliens resident within it; and, lastly, the relations of states among themselves with respect to their rights over and their international responsibility for delinquencies toward aliens.[3]

From this standpoint, the subjective scope of application of the FPS standard can be best portrayed as a triangular relationship between the home state, the host state and the foreigner.[4] The home state plays a role in the analysis of reciprocity, the rules applicable to nationality and the exercise of diplomatic protection.[5] From a substantive perspective, however, the alien's home state generally remains in the backstage: protection is granted *by the host state* (the provider of security) to the *foreign national* (the subject whose interests or values are being secured).[6] This relationship is, plainly stated, the heart of the FPS standard.

Bearing the foregoing in mind, this section begins by addressing the *beneficiary* of the security obligation. In this connection, it submits two basic propositions. First, only a foreign *national* and not every *alien* is entitled to protection under the customary FPS standard. A bond with a state *different* from the host state (i.e. the home state) has always been—and continues to be—a *conditio sine qua non* for the standard to be applicable. As a corollary, the customary FPS standard is *not* applicable in respect of the host state's own nationals and stateless people. Second, the customary FPS standard does not only refer to *foreign natural persons*; it is a commonplace that it also protects *foreign juristic persons*.

The second part of the argument refers to the *provider* of security. The rationale of the FPS standard, it is argued, is to provide security for persons subject to foreign *territorial jurisdiction*. For that very same reason, as a rule, the customary security obligation refers to the *territorial state*. Nonetheless, statehood, as such, is not a necessary condition of the application of the standard. FPS is also applicable in respect of internationally accountable non-state entities exercising actual territorial control (e.g. *de facto* regimes).

---

[3]Edwin Borchard, 'Basic Elements of Diplomatic Protection of Citizens Abroad' (1913) 7(3) AJIL 497, 497. For a similar remark see: Eduard Otto von Waldkirch, *Das Völkerrecht in seinen Grundzügen dargestellt* (Verlag von Helbing & Lichtenhahn, Basel 1926) 247.

[4]See generally: Edwin Borchard, 'Basic Elements of Diplomatic Protection of Citizens Abroad' (1913) 7(3) AJIL 497, 497.

[5]Some of these issues will be considered in Sect. 7.2.1, in particular connection with the protection of stateless people.

[6]Section 6.3 provides an overview of the subjective elements of the security relationship, from a general theoretical perspective (i.e. 'secured agent' and 'provider of security'). For a similar observation regarding the role of the home state see: Emanuel von Ullmann, *Völkerrecht* (J. C. B. Mohr, Tübingen 1908) 360 (referring to the law of aliens in general).

7.2   The Beneficiary of Security. The Foreign National

7.2.1   *The Foreignness Requirement*

At the outset, the proposition that foreignness is a defining element of the law of aliens seems to be self-explanatory. In the final analysis, this is the idea underlying the traditional understanding of the law of aliens as the law governing a triangular relationship between a home state, a host state, and a foreign national.[7] This view, however prevalent, has not been without controversy. The German public law scholar Karl Doehring contested some of these classical premises in 1963.[8] Doehring's arguments can be summarized in two main objections. In the first place, Doehring pointed out that the fact that individuals are nowadays generally recognized as subjects of rights and obligations under international law, along with the swift development of human rights law, could have major consequences for law of state responsibility for injuries to aliens.[9] In this connection, he explained:

> In international treaty law it is clearly no longer uncommon for a state to assume the obligation – before another state, a group of states, or the community of states – to recognize certain rights not only to aliens, but also to its own nationals. In such cases, if a state violates rights established under international law in respect of its own citizens, it would be, at the same time, in breach of a rule of the law of aliens (in the broadest sense). In this scenario a foreign state could assert the rights of a non-national. Hence, a violation of the law of aliens would arise despite the wrongful act having no relation whatsoever to any territory different to that of the affected individual's [home state]. The legal relationship under the law of aliens appears here between an individual and a foreign state on the sole ground that the latter state is the holder of a right established under international law to the benefit of such individual.[10]

---

[7]Cf. Edwin Borchard, 'Basic Elements of Diplomatic Protection of Citizens Abroad' (1913) 7 (3) AJIL 497, 497.

[8]See: Karl Doehring, *Die allgemeinen Regeln des völkerrechtlichen Fremdenrechts und das deutsche Verfassungsrecht* (Carl Heymanns Verlag, Köln/Berlin 1963) 19-29.

[9]Karl Doehring, *Die allgemeinen Regeln des völkerrechtlichen Fremdenrechts und das deutsche Verfassungsrecht* (Carl Heymanns Verlag, Köln/Berlin 1963) 9-11 and 38 *et seq.*

[10]Author's translation. The original German text reads: "Schon im völkerrechtlichen Vertragsrecht ist es durchaus nicht mehr ungewöhnlich, daß ein Staat sich gegenüber einem anderen Staat, einer Staatengruppe oder der Staatengemeinschaft verpflichtet, nicht nur fremden, sondern auch eigenen Staatsangehörigen bestimmte Rechte einzuräumen; verletzt der Staat in diesem Falle völkerrechtlich garantierte Rechte durch Verhalten gegenüber eigenen Staatsangehörigen, so ist damit gleichzeitig eine Regel des Fremdenrechts im weitesten Sinne mißachtet; denn der fremde Staat kann in diesem Falle die Rechte eines für ihn fremden Staatsangehörigen geltend machen. Es wäre also das Fremdenrecht verletzt, obwohl der verletzende Akt selbst in keiner Beziehung zu einem für das betroffene Individuum fremden Territorium steht. Die Fremdenrechtsbeziehung besteht hier zwischen einem Individuum und einem fremden Staat nur deswegen, weil dieser Staat Inhaber eines zu Gunsten des Individuums eingeräumten völkerrechtlichen Anspruchs ist." Karl Doehring, *Die allgemeinen Regeln des völkerrechtlichen Fremdenrechts und das deutsche Verfassungsrecht* (Carl Heymanns Verlag, Köln/Berlin 1963) 23-4.

Doehring's first objection is not entirely convincing. As a preliminary matter, it must be observed that his argument was based on a definition advanced by Ernst Isay in 1923, according to which:

> [T]he law of aliens is the sum of the legal directives which take a person's foreign or national condition as an element of [the legal directive's] factual trigger.[11]

Making specific reference to international obligations states assume *before other states* but *in respect of their own nationals* (particularly in the ECHR and in treaties concerning minority rights), Doehring confidently stated that such treaty-based rules could be accurately placed within the broad scope of the law of aliens, as conceived by Isay.[12] The reason was that, in respect of the states before which such treaty obligations had been assumed (e.g. the parties to multilateral human rights conventions), the protected individual would be an alien.[13]

At this point, Doehring seems to have partially misunderstood Isay's definition.[14] Isay never contended that any legal relation involving an individual and a foreign state falls within the scope of the law of aliens.[15] He merely observed that the norms of the law of aliens are signalized by the fact that *foreignness* is an element of the legal directive's factual trigger.[16] Isay further clarified that such norms must draw a *legally significant* distinction between nationals and non-nationals.[17] As an example of a norm *not* belonging to the law of aliens Isay mentioned article 3 of the Prussian Passport Act of 1867, whereby 'federal [German] nationals and foreigners have the duty to sufficiently identify themselves upon request of the competent authority'.[18]

---

[11] Author's translation. The original German text reads: "Fremdenrecht ist die Gesamtheit der Sätze, welche die Aus- oder Inländereigenschaft einer Person als Tatbestandsmerkmal verwenden." Ernst Isay, *Das deutsche Fremdenrecht. Ausländer und Polizei* (Verlag von Georg Stilke, Berlin 1923) 4. In support of his definition, Isay also provided a detailed analysis of the term *Fremdenrecht* ('law of aliens') (at pp. 1-24).

[12] Karl Doehring, *Die allgemeinen Regeln des völkerrechtlichen Fremdenrechts und das deutsche Verfassungsrecht* (Carl Heymanns Verlag, Köln/Berlin 1963) 25. In this connection, attention should be drawn to the fact that, while Doehring was referring exclusively to the *international* law of aliens, Isay referred to the law of aliens in general (including *domestic* rules pertaining to the treatment of foreigners). Cf. Ernst Isay, *Das deutsche Fremdenrecht. Ausländer und Polizei* (Verlag von Georg Stilke, Berlin 1923) 1-24.

[13] Karl Doehring, *Die allgemeinen Regeln des völkerrechtlichen Fremdenrechts und das deutsche Verfassungsrecht* (Carl Heymanns Verlag, Köln/Berlin 1963) 25.

[14] Doehring discussed some of Isay's remarks on this particular subject at other instances of his treatise. See: Karl Doehring, *Die allgemeinen Regeln des völkerrechtlichen Fremdenrechts und das deutsche Verfassungsrecht* (Carl Heymanns Verlag, Köln/Berlin 1963) 32 *et seq.*

[15] Cf. Ernst Isay, *Das deutsche Fremdenrecht. Ausländer und Polizei* (Verlag von Georg Stilke, Berlin 1923) 1-4.

[16] Ernst Isay, *Das deutsche Fremdenrecht. Ausländer und Polizei* (Verlag von Georg Stilke, Berlin 1923) 1-4.

[17] Ernst Isay, *Das deutsche Fremdenrecht. Ausländer und Polizei* (Verlag von Georg Stilke, Berlin 1923) 1-3.

[18] Ernst Isay, *Das deutsche Fremdenrecht. Ausländer und Polizei* (Verlag von Georg Stilke, Berlin 1923) 1.

According to Isay, provisions of this kind, albeit referring to foreigners, should not be classified under the (domestic) law of aliens.[19] In fact, 'they only state that a specific feature (i.e. a person's foreignness) shall have no legal consequences at all'.[20] Much the same could be said about Doehring's examples. Human rights generally draw no distinction by reason of nationality.[21] In turn, minority rights are granted to members of a minority group; whether they are foreigners or nationals in respect of any specific state is an ancillary and rather inconsequential issue.[22] Simply put, foreignness is not the defining element of the factual trigger.

Furthermore, at least from a present-day perspective, Doehring's own understanding of the law of aliens seems excessively broad. Doehring believed that, in international law, the scope of the law of aliens (*Fremdenrecht*) could be defined in the following terms:

> [A]ny legal relation between a state and individuals who are not in possession of [that state's] nationality, *as well as any legal relation between states concerning the rights or legally protected interests of individuals.*[23]

The implication of Doehring's definition was that the law of aliens could protect individuals against their own home states, for example, in cases where the home state has entered into an obligation towards third states to protect and respect such individuals' rights (e.g. in human rights treaties).[24] In those scenarios, third states have a right to demand from the home state compliance with the obligation, even if the beneficiary is, in respect of them, an alien.[25] Doehring himself recognized, however, that relations of this nature were unknown to classical international law.[26]

---

[19]See: Ernst Isay, *Das deutsche Fremdenrecht. Ausländer und Polizei* (Verlag von Georg Stilke, Berlin 1923) 2.

[20]Author's translation. The original German text reads: "sie besagen nur, daß eine bestimmte Tatsache (nämlich die Ausländereigenschaft einer Person) keine Rechtswirkung habe." Ernst Isay, *Das deutsche Fremdenrecht. Ausländer und Polizei* (Verlag von Georg Stilke, Berlin 1923) 2.

[21]See also the discussion of the 'human rights approach' to the minimum standard of treatment in Sect. 5.3.

[22]For a detailed analysis of the protection of minorities in international law see: Sarah Pritchard, *Der völkerrechtliche Minderheitenschutz. Historische und neuere Entwicklungen* (Duncker & Humblot, Berlin 2001). See particularly pp. 49-50 (providing some general remarks about the purpose of the protection of minority groups in international law).

[23]Emphasis added. Author's translation. The original German text reads: "[Für die Belange der hier vorgenommenen Untersuchung soll die Definition des völkerrechtlichen Fremdenrechts lauten:] Jede Rechtsbeziehung, in welcher ein Staat zu Individuen steht, die nicht seine Staatsangehörigen sind *und jede Rechtsbeziehung zwischen Staaten, die Rechte oder rechtlich geschützte Interessen von Individuen zum Gegenstand haben.*" Karl Doehring, *Die allgemeinen Regeln des völkerrechtlichen Fremdenrechts und das deutsche Verfassungsrecht* (Carl Heymanns Verlag, Köln/Berlin 1963) 29.

[24]Karl Doehring, *Die allgemeinen Regeln des völkerrechtlichen Fremdenrechts und das deutsche Verfassungsrecht* (Carl Heymanns Verlag, Köln/Berlin 1963) 23 *et seq.*

[25]Karl Doehring, *Die allgemeinen Regeln des völkerrechtlichen Fremdenrechts und das deutsche Verfassungsrecht* (Carl Heymanns Verlag, Köln/Berlin 1963) 23 *et seq.*

[26]Karl Doehring, *Die allgemeinen Regeln des völkerrechtlichen Fremdenrechts und das deutsche Verfassungsrecht* (Carl Heymanns Verlag, Köln/Berlin 1963) 24.

Doehring was hence advancing a novel definition, which was ultimately contrary to the traditional, if not to say customary, understanding of the law of aliens.[27] His conclusion was of the greatest significance. If successful, his thesis could have ended up definitively blurring any distinction between human rights and the minimum standard.[28] Not surprisingly, Doehring was also one of the most passionate advocates of the human rights approach to the minimum standard of treatment.[29] Still, to stand against the pre-World War II consensus was an act of intellectual bravery, and brave acts usually leave their champions alone. Doehring's extensive definition of the law of aliens would never find sufficient acceptance within the international community.

Forty years later, in the second edition of his treatise on international law (2004), Doehring would himself acknowledge that 'the distinction of the rules of the law of aliens from those of general international human rights law always poses difficulties'.[30] This statement has a subtle implication, namely, that there is a difference and that a line must be accordingly drawn between these two areas of international law.

---

[27] For an example of this 'traditional' conception of the law of aliens see: Edwin Borchard, 'Basic Elements of Diplomatic Protection of Citizens Abroad' (1913) 7(3) AJIL 497, 497.

[28] Cf. Karl Doehring, *Die allgemeinen Regeln des völkerrechtlichen Fremdenrechts und das deutsche Verfassungsrecht* (Carl Heymanns Verlag, Köln/Berlin 1963) 23-9 and 68-121.

[29] Karl Doehring, *Die allgemeinen Regeln des völkerrechtlichen Fremdenrechts und das deutsche Verfassungsrecht* (Carl Heymanns Verlag, Köln/Berlin 1963) 68-121. This point requires some elaboration. Doehring advanced the proposition that the material content of the law of aliens is twofold (so-called '*Zweiteilung des Fremdenrechts*') (at pp. 108 and 110). On the one hand, there are certain institutions of the law of aliens which primarily concern the home state's own rights (e.g. non-discrimination, expulsion and extradition) (at pp. 56-68; see also pp. 119-20). On the other hand, the law of aliens additionally provides a set of individual rights (*Individualrechte*), which Doehring identified with the notion of the minimum standard of treatment (at pp. 68-118; see also pp. 119-20). From a substantive standpoint, it is the minimum standard and not the whole of the law of aliens what Doehring linked to the notion of human rights (at pp. 70-6). This approach leads to a distinction between three possible factual settings, which Doehring described in the following terms: "In respect of the responsibility of the state under the law of aliens a distinction shall be drawn between the following cases: 1. [State] conduct towards an alien [that] violates the rights of his or her home state only; 2. [State] conduct [that] violates the foreigner's individual rights (minimum standard) and *unu actu* the rights of the home state; 3. [State] conduct [that] solely violates the individual rights of an alien (minimum standard), e.g. where the home state has consented [to such conduct] or in the case of stateless people." Author's translation. The original German text reads: "Bei der Verantwortlichkeit der Staaten im Fremdenrecht sind also folgende Fälle zu unterscheiden: 1. Das Verhalten gegenüber einem Fremden verletzt nur die Rechte seines Heimatstaates; 2. Das Verhalten verletzt subjektive Rechte des Fremden (Mindeststandard) und *unu actu* Rechte seines Heimatstaates; 3. Das Verhalten verletzt nur subjektive Rechte des Fremden (Mindeststandard), z.B. bei Einwilligung des Heimatstaates oder bei Staatenlosen." (at p. 113).

[30] Author's translation. The original German text reads: "Schwierigkeiten bereitet immer wieder die Abgrenzung von Regeln des Fremdenrechts zu solchen der allgemeinen völkerrechtlichen Menschenrechte." Karl Doehring, *Völkerrecht. Ein Lehrbuch* (C. F. Müller Verlag, Heidelberg 2004) 374.

In that very same chapter, Doehring moreover limited the scope of the law of aliens to 'any legal relation established between a state and natural or legal persons not possessing that state's nationality'.[31] To the careful listener, Doehring was renouncing here to the second part of his 1963 definition and, consequently, to the extension of the law of aliens beyond its traditional scope of application.[32]

Doehring's second objection to the classical understanding of the law of aliens referred to the protection of stateless people.[33] In this regard, Doehring's observations shed substantial doubts as to whether the institutions of the law of aliens necessarily involve a triangular relation involving two states (i.e. the home and the host state), and a foreign natural or juristic person.[34] In his terminological assessment of the terms 'foreigner' (*Ausländer*) and 'alien' (*Fremde*), Doehring noted that, while every foreigner is an alien, not every alien is a foreigner.[35] Foreigners are nationals of other states; aliens are plainly non-nationals.[36] As a result, he said, the term 'alien' encompasses both stateless persons and individuals whose nationality is unclear (e.g. dual nationals).[37] Doehring further explained that the law of aliens does not serve the sole purpose of protecting the interests of states: if individuals can be subjects of rights under international law, the guarantees of the law of aliens could arguably encompass individual rights too.[38] From this standpoint, there would be no reason to exclude stateless people from the law of aliens' scope of application.[39]

---

[31] Author's translation. The original German text reads: "[Das völkerrechtliche Fremdenrecht betrifft] alle Rechtsbeziehungen, die zwischen einem Staat und natürlichen oder juristischen Personen bestehen, die nicht die Staatsangehörigkeit dieses Staates innehaben." Karl Doehring, *Völkerrecht. Ein Lehrbuch* (C. F. Müller Verlag, Heidelberg 2004) 374.

[32] Cf. Karl Doehring, *Die allgemeinen Regeln des völkerrechtlichen Fremdenrechts und das deutsche Verfassungsrecht* (Carl Heymanns Verlag, Köln/Berlin 1963) 29.

[33] Karl Doehring, *Die allgemeinen Regeln des völkerrechtlichen Fremdenrechts und das deutsche Verfassungsrecht* (Carl Heymanns Verlag, Köln/Berlin 1963) 19-20 and 26-9.

[34] On this triangular relationship see: Edwin Borchard, 'Basic Elements of Diplomatic Protection of Citizens Abroad' (1913) 7(3) AJIL 497, 497 (discussed in Sect. 7.1).

[35] Karl Doehring, *Die allgemeinen Regeln des völkerrechtlichen Fremdenrechts und das deutsche Verfassungsrecht* (Carl Heymanns Verlag, Köln/Berlin 1963) 19-20.

[36] Karl Doehring, *Die allgemeinen Regeln des völkerrechtlichen Fremdenrechts und das deutsche Verfassungsrecht* (Carl Heymanns Verlag, Köln/Berlin 1963) 19-20.

[37] Karl Doehring, *Die allgemeinen Regeln des völkerrechtlichen Fremdenrechts und das deutsche Verfassungsrecht* (Carl Heymanns Verlag, Köln/Berlin 1963) 19-20 and 26-9.

[38] Karl Doehring, *Die allgemeinen Regeln des völkerrechtlichen Fremdenrechts und das deutsche Verfassungsrecht* (Carl Heymanns Verlag, Köln/Berlin 1963) 9-12 and 28.

[39] Karl Doehring, *Die allgemeinen Regeln des völkerrechtlichen Fremdenrechts und das deutsche Verfassungsrecht* (Carl Heymanns Verlag, Köln/Berlin 1963) 28. For another author advocating for the extension of the law of aliens to stateless people see: Hans Roth, *The Minimum Standard of International Law Applied to Aliens* (IMP F.A.A. Sijhoff, The Hague 1949) 35 (arguing, on the one hand, that the law of aliens concerns 'general international law' rather than reciprocal obligations between particular states and, on the other hand, that stateless people 'would be absolutely at the mercy of their State of residence, if international law did not intervene in their favour').

Doehring's arguments are persuasive. Still, when it comes to statelessness, state practice did not (and does not yet) fully support his conclusion. The FPS standard and other substantive guarantees of the law of aliens developed hand-in-hand with the exercise of diplomatic protection, which, at least from a historical perspective, referred only to *nationals of other states.*[40] It remains in fact somewhat unclear to which extent states actually conceived principles like the minimum standard of treatment as applicable with regard to stateless persons.[41] Historical sources suggest that, for a long time, they did not.[42] Taking the writings of Edwin Borchard as an example, it seems that the traditional conception of the law of aliens was based on the following, fundamental assumption:

> The migration of the citizen of one state to another and his residence in the latter brings about in constitutional theory a double citizenship, of primary and organic nature with respect of his home state and of a temporary and qualified nature with respect of the state of residence. It subjects the individual for different purposes and in different degrees to the sovereignty of two states.[43]

While terminology varies from one author to another, the underlying idea is usually the same.[44] The consequence is that, for many years, the law of aliens was generally believed to be inapplicable in respect of stateless people.[45] The *Dickson Car Wheel Company Case* (1931) provides a clear statement of the crude practical effect of this majority view.[46] In that case, Commissioner Fernández MacGregor stated:

---

[40]At this point, Doehring observed that the exercise of diplomatic protection in cases involving individual rights (as opposed to rights of the home state, properly so-called) could be characterized as a 'representative action' (*Prozeßstandschaft*), i.e. an action in which the plaintiff advances another person's right but still acts in his or her own name. See: Karl Doehring, *Die allgemeinen Regeln des völkerrechtlichen Fremdenrechts und das deutsche Verfassungsrecht* (Carl Heymanns Verlag, Köln/Berlin 1963) 112-3.

[41]For a historical account of the minimum standard of treatment see Chap. 4.

[42]Cf. Lassa Francis Laurence Oppenheim, *International Law. A Treatise* (Volume 1: Longmans, Green & Co., London 1905) 366 [312].

[43]Edwin Borchard, 'Basic Elements of Diplomatic Protection of Citizens Abroad' (1913) 7(3) AJIL 497, 505.

[44]For some indicative examples see: Emanuel von Ullmann, *Völkerrecht* (J. C. B. Mohr, Tübingen 1908) 360; Paul Heilborn, *Das System des Völkerrechts entwickelt aus den völkerrechtlichen Begriffen* (Verlag von Julius Springer, Berlin 1896) 77 and 81.

[45]Cf. Lassa Francis Laurence Oppenheim, *International Law. A Treatise* (Volume 1: Longmans, Green & Co., London 1905) 366 [312]; *Dickson Car Wheel Co. v Mexico* (July 1931) IV RIAA 669, 678. Cf. also: ILC, 'Report of the International Law Commission on the Work of its Fifty-Eighth Session – Diplomatic Protection' (2006) 2(2) *Yearbook of the International Law Commission – 2006* 23, 35-6 [1] (also citing the *Dickson Car Wheel Co.* case in this connection).

[46]*Dickson Car Wheel Co. v Mexico* (July 1931) IV RIAA 669.

[A] State [. . .] does not commit an international delinquency in inflicting an injury upon an individual lacking nationality, and consequently, no State is empowered to intervene or complain on his behalf either before or after the injury.[47]

In support of this conclusion Fernández MacGregor invoked, among others, the authority of L. F. L. Oppenheim, who stressed in 1905:

[S]tateless individuals are in most States treated more or less as though they were subjects of foreign States, but as a point of international legality there is no restriction whatever upon a State's maltreating them to any extent.[48]

The protection of stateless people under customary law would continue to pose major difficulties in the years that followed World War II.[49] Even Richard B. Lillich, one of the best-known advocates for the modernization of the law of aliens on the basis of postwar human rights developments, acknowledged that stateless persons could not be easily assimilated to nationals of other states:

A stateless person differs from an 'ordinary' alien in that he is an alien everywhere and a national nowhere, whereas ordinary aliens are typically nationals of one State and aliens anywhere else. This apparently minor distinction should not lull one into thinking that the problems of stateless persons differ only in minor ways from the problems of other aliens. One important difference is that stateless persons are unable to benefit from the law of diplomatic protection of nationals abroad, since the right of protection, with certain minor exceptions, is available only when the link of nationality is present.[50]

Lillich therefore expressed the view that 'the traditional doctrine of diplomatic protection [. . .] leaves a stateless person entirely unprotected as far as the pursuit of a claim is concerned'.[51] He further mentioned other differences between stateless persons and foreigners, noting that '[s]till more serious is the fact that a stateless person may find himself effectively unable to travel internationally, since he usually lacks a passport'.[52] A passport, he explained, is not just a means of 'identification' but additionally embodies 'a guarantee on the part of the issuing State to other States that it will accept the passport holder back into its territory in the event of the holder

---

[47]*Dickson Car Wheel Co. v Mexico* (July 1931) IV RIAA 669, 678. For a critical assessment of this statement see: ILC, 'Report of the International Law Commission on the Work of its Fifty-Eighth Session – Diplomatic Protection' (2006) 2(2) *Yearbook of the International Law Commission – 2006* 23, 35-6 [1] (commenting on the *Dickson Car Wheel Co.* case).

[48]Lassa Francis Laurence Oppenheim, *International Law. A Treatise* (Volume 1: Longmans, Green & Co., London 1905) 366 [312]. For the use of Oppenheim's opinion in the *Dickson Car Wheel Co.* case see: *Dickson Car Wheel Co. v Mexico* (July 1931) IV RIAA 669, 678.

[49]Cf. Richard Lillich, *The Human Rights of Aliens in Contemporary International Law* (Manchester University Press, Manchester 1984) 64-5.

[50]Richard Lillich, *The Human Rights of Aliens in Contemporary International Law* (Manchester University Press, Manchester 1984) 64.

[51]Richard Lillich, *The Human Rights of Aliens in Contemporary International Law* (Manchester University Press, Manchester 1984) 12.

[52]Richard Lillich, *The Human Rights of Aliens in Contemporary International Law* (Manchester University Press, Manchester 1984) 64.

being expelled or deported'.[53] Lillich observed that '[i]n the absence of such a guarantee, countries are very reluctant to accept an alien into their territory'.[54]

From a substantive standpoint, doubts arise from the fact that considerations of reciprocity, which have always been present in the law of aliens, presuppose the existence of a state other than the host state, from which reciprocity can be expected.[55] In addition, it cannot be easily ignored that some institutions of the law of aliens are *per definitionem* dependent on the link or bond of nationality between the foreigner and the home state.[56] An example would be the prohibition upon the host state to coerce foreigners into disloyalty toward their home states (e.g. compelling foreign citizens to serve in the military against their country of origin).[57]

The ILC, taking cognizance of the traditional 'general rule' excluding the diplomatic protection of stateless people, introduced in article 8 of its *Draft Articles on Diplomatic Protection* (2006) an exception allowing interposition by the state in whose territory such persons 'lawfully and habitually' reside.[58] This provision could be the first step towards a new approach to the question of statelessness; still, the ILC has recognized and several states have emphasized that Draft Article 8 is *not* a codification of present-day customary international law.[59] In *Al Rawi et al. v Foreign*

---

[53]Richard Lillich, *The Human Rights of Aliens in Contemporary International Law* (Manchester University Press, Manchester 1984) 64.

[54]Richard Lillich, *The Human Rights of Aliens in Contemporary International Law* (Manchester University Press, Manchester 1984) 64.

[55]Interestingly, in a study on the status of foreigners in Germany published in 1974, Karl Doehring emphasized the role of reciprocity as a shaping factor of international obligations concerning the treatment of aliens. See: Karl Doehring, 'Der Status des Fremden im Verfassungsrecht der Bundesrepublik Deutschland unter Gesichtspunkt der normativen Verschränkung von Völkerrecht und Verfassungsrecht' in Karl Doehring and Josef Isensee (eds), *Die staatsrechtliche Stellung der Ausländer in der Bundesrepublik Deutschland. Vertrauensschutz im Verwaltungsrecht* (De Gruyter, Berlin 1974) 7, 17-8. Doehring also discussed reciprocity at some instances of his 1963 treatise. See: Karl Doehring, *Die allgemeinen Regeln des völkerrechtlichen Fremdenrechts und das deutsche Verfassungsrecht* (Carl Heymanns Verlag, Köln/Berlin 1963) 32 and 64-8.

[56]Doehring analyzed some of these features of the law of aliens in his 1963 monograph. Cf. Karl Doehring, *Die allgemeinen Regeln des völkerrechtlichen Fremdenrechts und das deutsche Verfassungsrecht* (Carl Heymanns Verlag, Köln/Berlin 1963) 31-2.

[57]Doehring acknowledged that this prohibition is a well-established principle of the law of aliens. See: Karl Doehring, *Die allgemeinen Regeln des völkerrechtlichen Fremdenrechts und das deutsche Verfassungsrecht* (Carl Heymanns Verlag, Köln/Berlin 1963) 31.

[58]ILC, 'Report of the International Law Commission on the Work of its Fifty-Eighth Session – Diplomatic Protection' (2006) 2(2) *Yearbook of the International Law Commission – 2006* 23, 35 art. 8.

[59]ILC, 'Report of the International Law Commission on the Work of its Fifty-Eighth Session – Diplomatic Protection' (2006) 2(2) *Yearbook of the International Law Commission – 2006* 23, 36 [2-4]. In its commentaries, the ILC itself emphasized the *lege ferenda* character of the provision in question (at p. 36 paras 2 and 4, and n. 88). In this vein, the Commission described article 8 as 'an exercise in progressive development of the law', which 'departs from traditional rule that only nationals may benefit from the exercise of diplomatic protection' and constitutes 'an exceptional measure introduced *de lege ferenda*' (at p. 36 paras 2 and 4). Several governments made similar

Secretary (2006), the English Court of Appeal expressed the view that 'Article 8 is, in the argot of international lawyers, *lex ferenda*, that is, proposed law, as opposed to *lex lata* (existing law, law already laid down)'.[60]

In sum, the *customary* FPS standard cannot yet be said to protect stateless persons. State practice on the FPS standard mostly concerns the exercise of diplomatic protection and has therefore traditionally referred to nationals of other states.[61] This does not however mean that international law has turned a blind eye to the possible mistreatment and abuse of stateless people.[62] The ILC has noted that the extreme view expressed in the *Dickson Car Wheel Co.* case, definitively excluding any international protection for stateless people, 'no longer reflects' those persons' status under international law.[63] In this vein, the ILC underscored that there are multilateral treaties specifically addressing the issue, such as the 1954 *Convention on the Status of Stateless Persons* and the 1961 *Convention on the Reduction of Statelessness*.[64] In addition, it has been plausibly contended that host states might

---

remarks in their comments to the ILC Draft. See: ILC, 'Documents of the Fifty-Eighth Session – Comments and Observations received from Governments on Diplomatic Protection' (2006) 2 (1) *Yearbook of the International Law Commission – 2006* 34, 46 (statement of Morocco, noting that '[d]raft article 8 is not part of customary international law or codified international law, but rather represents progressive development of the law') and 47 (statement of the United Kingdom expressing the following view: "[i]n relation to article 8, the protection of stateless persons and refugees is not a matter which the United Kingdom regards as falling within the scope of the concept of diplomatic protection as that is understood in current international law. The United Kingdom considers that the provisions of draft article 8 are *lex ferenda*. Whether the United Kingdom would exceptionally, for example on humanitarian grounds, be prepared to make representations or take other action on behalf of stateless persons or refugees would depend on the circumstances of the case and would be in its own discretion, but it would not *strictu sensu* be an exercise of diplomatic protection").

[60] *Al Rawi et al. v Foreign Secretary* [2006] EWCA Civ 1219, 1265 [118]. See also: ILC, 'Report of the International Law Commission on the Work of its Fifty-Eighth Session – Diplomatic Protection' (2006) 2(2) *Yearbook of the International Law Commission – 2006* 23, 36 [2] n. 88 (quoting the *Al Rawi* decision).

[61] For a classical example of the exercise of diplomatic protection in connection with FPS claims see: *Case Concerning Elettronica Sicula S.p.A. (ELSI) (United States of America v Italy)* [1989] ICJ Rep 15, 66-7 [111].

[62] Cf. ILC, 'Report of the International Law Commission on the Work of its Fifty-Eighth Session – Diplomatic Protection' (2006) 2(2) *Yearbook of the International Law Commission – 2006* 23, 35-6 [1] (recognizing that '[c]ontemporary international law reflects a concern for the status of [stateless people]').

[63] ILC, 'Report of the International Law Commission on the Work of its Fifty-Eighth Session – Diplomatic Protection' (2006) 2(2) *Yearbook of the International Law Commission – 2006* 23, 35-6 [1].

[64] Convention relating to the Status of Stateless Persons (adopted 28 September 1954, entered into force 6 June 1960) 360 UNTS 117; Convention on the Reduction of Statelessness (adopted 30 August 1961, entered into force 13 December 1975) 989 UNTS 175. See also: ILC, 'Report of the International Law Commission on the Work of its Fifty-Eighth Session – Diplomatic Protection' (2006) 2(2) *Yearbook of the International Law Commission – 2006* 23, 36 [1].

bear an obligation towards 'the international community as a whole' to give some degree of protection to stateless people.[65]

This chapter neither intends to disregard these new developments, nor to take a stance in the underlying debates. The proposition advanced is far more modest. While it is true that stateless people nowadays enjoy some protection under international law, protection obligations in respect of stateless people are different from, and should not be confused with, the FPS standard. The FPS standard is one of the oldest institutions of the law of aliens and, as such, has customarily referred to nationals of other states.[66] There is no indication that customary law has evolved in such way as to extend to stateless people the specific, substantive guarantee embodied in the FPS standard. Even if one were to accept that each state has an obligation to the whole international community to protect stateless people,[67] such obligation would have a different rationale and scope than the FPS standard.[68]

7.2.2   Natural and Juristic Persons

Nationality is the legal institution which defines, *par excellence*, the personal scope of application of the law of aliens, in general, and of the customary security obligation in particular.[69] As explained above, foreign nationality is a *conditio*

---

[65]See: William Conklin, *Statelessness. The Enigma of an International Community* (Hart Publishing, Oxford 2014) 58-63 and 235-301. The issue of statelessness has also been discussed in the context of international human rights law; for a detailed survey of the human rights dimension of statelessness see: Manuela Sissy Kraus, *Menschenrechtliche Aspekte der Staatenlosigkeit* (Berliner Wissenschaftsverlag, Berlin 2013) 174-262.

[66]Chapter 3 provides a general account of the historical origins of the FPS standard.

[67]Cf. William Conklin, *Statelessness. The Enigma of an International Community* (Hart Publishing, Oxford 2014) 58-63 and 235-301 (analyzing the rationale of international obligations in respect of stateless people in general). Conklin discussed at several instances the notion of 'obligations *erga omnes*' suggested by the ICJ in *Barcelona Traction* (see particularly Conklin's comments at pp. 38, 53-5 and 274-5).

[68]Cf. *Barcelona Traction Light and Power Company Ltd. (Belgium v Spain)* [1970] ICJ Rep 3, 32 [33] and [35] ("an essential distinction should be drawn between the obligations of a State towards the international community as a whole, and those arising vis-à-vis another State in the field of diplomatic protection. By their very nature the former are the concern of all States. In view of the importance of the rights involved, all States can be held to have a legal interest in their protection; they are obligations *erga omnes* [...] Obligations the performance of which is the subject of diplomatic protection *are not of the same category. It cannot be held, when one such obligation in particular is in question, in a specific case, that all States have a legal interest in its observance.* In order to bring a claim in respect of such an obligation, a State must first establish its right to do so." – emphasis added). Cf. also: William Conklin, *Statelessness. The Enigma of an International Community* (Hart Publishing, Oxford 2014) 273-4 (discussing this particular passage of the *Barcelona Traction* decision).

[69]See Sect. 7.2.1.

sine qua non for the enjoyment of protection under the customary FPS standard.[70] This requirement might give the impression that the customary standard primarily refers to the protection of *natural* rather than *juristic* persons. While the present-day state of international law is that juristic persons enjoy protection under the customary FPS standard,[71] for a long time it was not entirely clear whether *foreign companies* were entitled to the same protection as *foreign nationals*.[72]

The extension of the notion of *nationality* to juristic persons was the source of sharp academic controversy up to the first decades of the twentieth century.[73] Paul Ruegger stated in 1918 that 'the public law relationship between a person and a state, which constitutes nationality, is conceptually different when it comes to a physical or to a juristic person'.[74] Baron Edward Hilton Young noted in 1908 that the term *nationality* 'introduces some danger of confusion'.[75] According to him, '[i]n its ordinary meaning its content is not purely juridical; it is partly political also'.[76] Young believed that the question, whether a juristic person may possess the political quality embodied in the idea of nationality, should be left to political science.[77] He therefore excluded the 'political part' of the term from legal analysis, in order to 'imply only [a] purely legal consequence, – that to the juristic person in question the rules of law of a certain state must be applied as its personal law'.[78] These debates

---

[70]See Sect. 7.2.1.

[71]For a statement of the current state of the law see: *Barcelona Traction Light and Power Company Ltd. (Belgium v Spain)* [1970] ICJ Rep 3, 32 [33] (discussed later in this section).

[72]This section presents the historical debate in detail, particularly focusing on postwar FCN treaty practice.

[73]For a defense of the extension of the concept of nationality to juristic persons see: Ernst Isay, *Die Staatsangehörigkeit der juristischen Personen* (Mohr, Tübingen 1907) 64 *et seq.*; Paul Ruegger, *Die Staatsangehörigkeit der juristischen Personen. Die völkerrechtlichen Grundlagen* (Schweizerische Vereinigung für Internationales Recht, Zürich 1918) 15. For a rejection of the extension of the concept of nationality to corporate entities see: Eduard Goldstein, *Die Staatsangehörigkeit der juristischen Person* (Junge & Sohn, Erlangen 1912) 14 *et seq.* and 58. See also: Max Seydel, *Commentar zur Verfassungs-Urkunde für das Deutsche Reich* (A. Stuber's Buchhandlung, Würzburg 1873) 52-3. For an overview of the debate see: Eduard Otto von Waldkirch, *Das Völkerrecht in seinen Grundzügen dargestellt* (Verlag von Helbing & Lichtenhahn, Basel 1926) 247-8.

[74]Author's translation. The original German text reads: "Das öffentlich-rechtliche Verhältnis zwischen Person und Staat, welches die Staatsangehörigkeit ausmacht, ist daher begrifflich ein anderes, wenn es sich um physische und wenn es sich um juristische Personen handelt." Paul Ruegger, *Die Staatsangehörigkeit der juristischen Personen. Die völkerrechtlichen Grundlagen* (Schweizerische Vereinigung für Internationales Recht, Zürich 1918) 15. It should however be noted that Ruegger believed that the term *Nationalität* could also be employed in relation to corporate entities (at p. 15).

[75]Edward Hilton Young, 'The Nationality of a Juristic Person' (1908) 22(1) Harv. L. Rev. 1, 2.

[76]Edward Hilton Young, 'The Nationality of a Juristic Person' (1908) 22(1) Harv. L. Rev. 1, 2.

[77]Edward Hilton Young, 'The Nationality of a Juristic Person' (1908) 22(1) Harv. L. Rev. 1, 2.

[78]Edward Hilton Young, 'The Nationality of a Juristic Person' (1908) 22(1) Harv. L. Rev. 1, 2. For a similar, though not identical, approach see: Hans Kelsen, *General Theory of Law and State* (Anders Wedberg tr., Lawbook Exchange, Clark NJ 2009) 240.

might have influenced present-day terminology. German-speaking public law scholarship usually draws a terminological distinction between *Staatsangehörigkeit* (which refers to natural persons) and *Staatszugehörigkeit* (which refers to juristic persons).[79] Still, the noun *Nationalität* is used in respect of both natural and legal persons.[80]

In the particular context of the law of aliens, the protection of juristic persons appears to be a fairly recent concern. Eighteenth century theories about the security of aliens had a humanistic and naturalistic tint.[81] Moreover, most relevant diplomatic incidents and cases filed with Mixed Claims Commissions concerned the protection of individuals.[82] While a few nineteenth century claims conventions allowed the submission of claims on behalf of corporations, the protection of juristic persons was not a major issue in international treaty making until the early twentieth century.[83] In the United States, the first FCN agreement containing express provisions on the rights of juristic persons was concluded in 1911.[84] A clear policy favoring the extension of equal rights to natural and juristic persons was only set decades later, in the early aftermath of World War II.[85] In an often-quoted statement delivered before a Subcommittee of the U.S. Senate on May 9th, 1952, Deputy Assistant Secretary of State for Economic Affairs Harold Linder explained:

> Perhaps the most striking advance of the postwar treaties over earlier treaties is the cognizance taken of the widespread use of the corporate form of business organization in present-day economic affairs. In the treaties antedating World War II American corporations were specifically assured only small protection against possible discriminatory treatment in foreign countries. In the postwar treaties, however, corporations are accorded essentially the same treaty rights as individuals.[86]

---

[79]For some indicative examples see: Jost Delbrück and Rüdiger Wolfrum, *Völkerrecht. Begründet von Georg Dahm* (Volume 1: De Gruyter, Berlin 2002) 100-3; Florian Becker, 'Gebiets- und Personalhoheit des Staates' in Josef Isensee and Paul Kirchhof (eds), *Handbuch des Staatsrechts* (Volume 9: C. F. Müller 2013) 193, 234-5.

[80]For an indicative example see: Paul Ruegger, *Die Staatsangehörigkeit der juristischen Personen. Die völkerrechtlichen Grundlagen* (Schweizerische Vereinigung für Internationales Recht, Zürich 1918) 15 *et seq.*

[81]See Sects. 3.3 and 3.4.

[82]Examples are provided, particularly, in Sect. 8.3.1.

[83]Herman Walker, 'Provisions on Companies in United States Commercial Treaties' (1956) 50 (2) AJIL 373, 373-80.

[84]Herman Walker, 'Provisions on Companies in United States Commercial Treaties' (1956) 50 (2) AJIL 373, 373 and 378 (referring in this connection to article VII of the US-Japan FCN Agreement of 1911).

[85]Herman Walker, 'Provisions on Companies in United States Commercial Treaties' (1956) 50 (2) AJIL 373, 380 (stating that this policy was 'inaugurated with the China treaty of 1946'). Cf. also: Lucas Bastin, *State Responsibility for Omissions: Establishing a Breach of the Full Protection and Security Obligation by Omissions* (Oxford University, Oxford 2016) [D.Phil. Thesis] 94-6.

[86]'Statement of Harold F. Linder, Deputy Assistant Secretary of State for Economic Affairs, Department of State' (9 May 1952) *Hearing before a Subcommittee of the Committee on Foreign Relations, United States Senate, Eighty-Second Congress, 2nd Session on Treaties of Friendship, Commerce, and Navigation between the United States and Colombia, Israel, Ethiopia, Italy,*

This change was not a merely formal or terminological update: in the 1950s there was a widespread perception that the treaty language of previous FCN agreements, which normally referred to 'citizens' or 'nationals', did not provide an adequate framework for the protection of corporate entities.[87] In an academic article published in 1956, Herman Walker, an Advisor on Commercial Treaties at the U.S. State Department, explained:

> An artificial person cannot in fact enjoy a number of rights commonly granted to "nationals" or the like, in commercial treaties (e.g., liberty of conscience, exception from compulsory military service). Strictly speaking, indeed, it cannot be a "national" or "citizen," since these terms imply relations of personal allegiance to a sovereign state which only natural persons can have. At no time have corporations been subsumed under the expression "nationals," or the like, in the formal structure of United States commercial treaties [...] The now established official view, accordingly, is that in general corporations are not deemed to be within the purview of a commercial treaty *except there may be express provision to that effect*.[88]

Against this backdrop, the question arises as to whether the *customary* law of aliens and, particularly, the customary FPS standard, do actually protect juristic persons. Writing in 1949, J. M. Jones noted that shareholder claims had only taken center stage in the international arena after the Mexican Revolution and socialist revolutions in the European continent.[89] In Jones' view, this circumstance explained the paucity of sources addressing the customary status of corporations and their shareholders:

> [A]ll this intense economic development and profound social change has happened in the short space of less than half a century. Customary international law does not generally develop so quickly; it is hardly surprising, therefore, that a student of international law, looking for rules on the subject, has to search hard, and, when the search is ended, may be unable to say that the law is settled in all respects.[90]

Denmark, and Greece (Government Printing Office, Washington 1952) 2, 4. On this aspect of the postwar U.S. FCN program see: Herman Walker, 'Provisions on Companies in United States Commercial Treaties' (1956) 50(2) AJIL 373, 373-93 (also quoting Lindman at p. 373); Kenneth Vandevelde, *The First Bilateral Investment Treaties: U.S. Postwar Friendship, Commerce and Navigation Treaties* (Oxford University Press, New York 2017) 389-90 (quoting Lindman at p. 389). See also: Herman Walker, 'Treaties for the Encouragement and Protection of Foreign Investment: Present United States Practice' (1956) Am. J. Comp. L. 229, 232 *et seq.*

[87] Cf. Kenneth Vandevelde, *The First Bilateral Investment Treaties: U.S. Postwar Friendship, Commerce and Navigation Treaties* (Oxford University Press, New York 2017) 389-90.

[88] Emphasis added. Herman Walker, 'Provisions on Companies in United States Commercial Treaties' (1956) 50(2) AJIL 373, 377-8.

[89] John Mervyn Jones, 'Claims on Behalf of Nationals Who are Shareholders in Foreign Companies' (1949) 26 BYIL 225, 225.

[90] John Mervyn Jones, 'Claims on Behalf of Nationals Who are Shareholders in Foreign Companies' (1949) 26 BYIL 225, 225-6.

This issue played a fairly important role in the drafting of 'protection and security' clauses in the decade of 1950.[91] For example, the treaties concluded by the United States with Israel (1951), Denmark (1951), Japan (1953), Korea (1956), and Pakistan (1959) contained two separate FPS clauses; the first clause provided:

> *Nationals* of either Party within the territories of the other Party shall be free from [unlawful] molestations of every kind, and *shall receive the most constant protection and security, in no case less than that required by international law*.[92]

For its part, the second clause read as follows:

> Property of *nationals and companies* of either Party shall receive the most constant protection and security within the territories of the other Party.[93]

It is conspicuous that these treaties made express reference to the 'protection and security [...] required by international law' only in connection with the protection of *nationals*, as opposed to the protection of *companies*. The same pattern appears in

---

[91]Kenneth Vandevelde, *The First Bilateral Investment Treaties: U.S. Postwar Friendship, Commerce and Navigation Treaties* (Oxford University Press, New York 2017) 413-4 (analyzing the changes in the formulation of the 'most constant protection and security' standard in U.S. treaties after World War II, and providing multiple examples of American treaty practice in this specific area). See also: Robert Renbert Wilson, *United States Commercial Treaties and International Law* (The Houser Press, New Orleans LA 1960) 119-21 (also providing examples and detailed analysis of U.S. treaty practice, particularly at pp. 119 *et seq.*).

[92]Emphasis added. Treaty of Friendship, Commerce and Navigation between the United States of America and Israel (adopted 23 August 1951, entered into force 3 April 1954) 219 UNTS 237, art. III(1); Treaty of Friendship, Commerce and Navigation between the United States of America and the Kingdom of Denmark (adopted 1 October 1951, entered into force 30 July 1961) 421 UNTS 105, art. III(1); Treaty of Friendship, Commerce and Navigation between the United States of America and Japan (adopted 2 April 1953, entered into force 30 October 1953) 206 UNTS 191, art. II(1); Treaty of Friendship, Commerce and Navigation between the United States of America and the Republic of Korea (adopted 28 November 1956, entered into force 7 November 1957) 302 UNTS 281, art. III(1); Treaty of Friendship and Commerce between the United States of America and Pakistan (adopted 12 November 1959, entered into force 12 February 1961) 404 UNTS 259, art. III(1). It should be noted that the adjective 'unlawful' only appears in the treaties concluded with Israel, Denmark and Japan.

[93]Emphasis added. Treaty of Friendship, Commerce and Navigation between the United States of America and Israel (adopted 23 August 1951, entered into force 3 April 1954) 219 UNTS 237, art. VI(1); Treaty of Friendship, Commerce and Navigation between the United States of America and the Kingdom of Denmark (adopted 1 October 1951, entered into force 30 July 1961) 421 UNTS 105, art. VI(1); Treaty of Friendship, Commerce and Navigation between the United States of America and Japan (adopted 2 April 1953, entered into force 30 October 1953) 206 UNTS 191, art. VI(1); Treaty of Friendship, Commerce and Navigation between the United States of America and the Republic of Korea (adopted 28 November 1956, entered into force 7 November 1957) 302 UNTS 281, art. VI(1); Treaty of Friendship and Commerce between the United States of America and Pakistan (adopted 12 November 1959, entered into force 12 February 1961) 404 UNTS 259, art. VI(1).

the FCN agreements concluded with Germany (1954) and The Netherlands (1956), which used a slightly different language.[94]

This treaty language poses the question, whether it was the United States' understanding that customary law protected natural persons only, so that an autonomous treaty-based standard was needed in order to ensure the security of American companies abroad.[95] Internal documents suggest that there was widespread concern within the State Department about the effect that express references to customary law could have on the interpretation of FCN agreements, taking into account the uncertainties of customary law in this area.[96]

While particular doubts could have arisen as to the protection of juristic persons under the customary law of aliens, the fact is that U.S. treaty practice was not entirely consistent in this regard. Other postwar FCN agreements included an express reference to international law not only in respect of *nationals*, but also of *companies*; a representative example would be the U.S.-Ireland FCN Agreement of 1950:

> Property of nationals *and companies* of either Party shall receive the most constant protection and security within the territories of the other Party, *in no case less than that required by international law.*[97]

Article V of the FCN agreement between Italy and the United States (1948) followed a similar approach:

> 1. The nationals of each High Contracting Party shall receive, within the territories of the other High Contracting Party, *the most constant protection and security* for their persons and property, *and shall enjoy in this respect the full protection and security required by international law* [...] *In so far as the term "nationals" where used in this paragraph is*

---

[94]Treaty of Friendship, Commerce and Navigation between the United States of America and the Federal Republic of Germany (adopted 29 October 1954, entered into force 14 July 1956) 273 UNTS 3, arts. III(1) and V(1); Treaty of Friendship, Commerce and Navigation between the Kingdom of the Netherlands and the United States of America (adopted 27 March 1956, entered into force 5 December 1957) 285 UNTS 231, arts. III(1) and VI(1).

[95]Cf. Kenneth Vandevelde, *The First Bilateral Investment Treaties: U.S. Postwar Friendship, Commerce and Navigation Treaties* (Oxford University Press, New York 2017) 414-5.

[96]On this concern see: Kenneth Vandevelde, *The First Bilateral Investment Treaties: U.S. Postwar Friendship, Commerce and Navigation Treaties* (Oxford University Press, New York 2017) 414-5 (providing references to multiple internal State Department documents from that period).

[97]Emphasis added. Treaty of Friendship, Commerce and Navigation between the United States of America and Ireland (adopted 21 January 1950, entered into force 14 September 1950) 206 UNTS 269, art. VIII(2). For a short discussion of this wording see: Kenneth Vandevelde, *The First Bilateral Investment Treaties: U.S. Postwar Friendship, Commerce and Navigation Treaties* (Oxford University Press, New York 2017) 413-5 (specifically referring to the US-Ireland FCN Agreement).

applicable in relation to property it shall be construed to include corporations and associations [. . .]

3. The nationals, *corporations and associations* of either High Contracting Party shall within the territories of the other High Contracting Party receive *protection and security* with respect to the matters enumerated in paragraphs 1 and 2 of this Article.[98]

This clause was the basis of the ICJ's decision on the *ELSI* case (1989), where the FPS standard was invoked and applied in connection with corporate entities.[99]

Beyond this specific treaty context, present-day international law leaves no doubt as to the protection of juristic persons under the customary law of aliens. For the purposes of diplomatic protection it is out of question that, just like natural persons, juristic persons have a *state of nationality*: the ILC's *Draft Articles on Diplomatic Protection* devote a whole chapter to legal persons, using the term 'state of nationality' to denote a legal entity's home state.[100] To the same effect, in the *Ahmadou Sadio Diallo* case (2007), the ICJ observed:

Conferring independent corporate personality on a company implies granting it rights over its own property, rights which it alone is capable of protecting. As a result, only the State of nationality may exercise diplomatic protection on behalf of the company when its rights are injured by a wrongful act of another State.[101]

In practice, recent debate has referred more to the determination of the nationality of corporations than to the possibility of exercising diplomatic protection on their

---

[98]Emphasis added. Treaty of Friendship, Commerce and Navigation between the United States of America and the Italian Republic (adopted 2 February 1948, entered into force 26 July 1949) Charles Bevans (ed), *Treaties and Other International Agreements of the United States of America 1776—1949* (Volume 9: U.S. Department of State Publication, Washington 1971) 261, 264-5 arts. V(1) and (3).

[99]In the *ELSI* case, the Government of the United States alleged that Italy had violated its obligations under the 1948 FCN Agreement 'by reason of its acts and omissions in relation to, and its treatment of, *two United States corporations*, the Raytheon Company ("Raytheon") and the Machlett Laboratories Incorporated ("Machlett"), in relation to the Italian corporation Raytheon-Elsi S.p.A.'. Emphasis added. *Case Concerning Elettronica Sicula S.p.A. (ELSI) (United States of America v Italy)* [1989] ICJ Rep 15, 12 [12]. The Court's analysis of the FPS standard appears at 63-5 [102-8].

[100]In fact, article 9 of the Articles on Diplomatic Protection (2006) reads as follows: "For the purposes of the diplomatic protection of a corporation, the State of nationality means the State under whose law the corporation was incorporated. However, when the corporation is controlled by nationals of another State or States and has no substantial business activities in the State of incorporation, and the seat of management and the financial control of the corporation are both located in another State, that State shall be regarded as the State of nationality." ILC, 'Report of the International Law Commission on the Work of its Fifty-Eighth Session – Diplomatic Protection' (2006) 2(2) *Yearbook of the International Law Commission – 2006* 23, 37 art. 9. In its official commentary to this provision, the ILC noted that '[d]raft article 9 recognizes that diplomatic protection may be extended to corporations' (at p. 37 para 1). The ILC defined corporations as 'profit-making enterprises with limited liability whose capital is generally represented by shares' (at p. 37 para 2). Article 13 of the Draft Articles deals with the protection of legal persons other than corporations (at pp. 43-4).

[101]*Ahmadou Sadio Diallo (Guinea v Congo)*, Preliminary Objections, Judgment, [2007] ICJ Rep 582, 605 [61].

behalf.[102] Being diplomatic protection the breeding ground of the customary FPS standard, the standard may without hesitation be said to protect the interests of foreign juristic persons. As stated by the ICJ in the *Barcelona Traction* case (1970):

> When a State admits into its territory foreign investments or foreign nationals, *whether natural or juristic persons, it is bound to extend to them the protection of the law* and assumes obligations concerning the treatment to be afforded to them.[103]

Investment treaties reflect this premise. Many IIAs combine a definition of 'investor' which encompasses juristic persons, on the one hand, and a formulation of the FPS standard which entails a express reference to 'international law' or 'customary international law' on the other.[104] These treaty provisions may be taken as a direct statement of the contracting parties' understanding of the current state of customary law.[105] As such, they evidence the existence of broad consensus among the international community as regards to the protection of juristic persons under the customary FPS standard. Interestingly, legal advisors of the U.S. Department of State had anticipated this development as early as in the

---

[102]The general rule in this regard continues to be the one drawn by the ICJ in the *Barcelona Traction* case. On that occasion, the Court held: "In allocating corporate entities to States for purposes of diplomatic protection, international law is based, but only to a limited extent, on an analogy with the rules governing the nationality of individuals. The traditional rule attributes the right of diplomatic protection of a corporate entity to the State under the laws of which it is incorporated and in whose territory it has its registered office. These two criteria have been confirmed by long practice and by numerous international instruments. This notwithstanding, further or different links are at times said to be required in order that a right of diplomatic protection should exist. Indeed, it has been the practice of some States to give a company incorporated under their law diplomatic protection solely when it has its seat (*siège social*) or management or centre of control in their territory, or when a majority or a substantial proportion of the shares has been owned by nationals of the State concerned. Only then, it has been held, does there exist between the corporation and the State in question a genuine connection of the kind familiar from other branches of international law. However, in the practical field of the diplomatic protection of corporate entities, no absolute text of the 'genuine connection' had found general acceptance. Such tests as have been applied are of a relative nature, and sometimes links with one state had to be weighted against those with another." *Barcelona Traction Light and Power Company Ltd. (Belgium v Spain)* [1970] ICJ Rep 3, 42 [70]. For an overview of the diplomatic protection of juristic persons see: Markus Krajewski, *Wirtschaftsvölkerrecht* (C. H. Müller, Heidelberg 2009) 29-30.

[103]Emphasis added. *Barcelona Traction Light and Power Company Ltd. (Belgium v Spain)* [1970] ICJ Rep 3, 32 [33].

[104]For a representative example see: Free Trade Agreement between the United States of America and the Republic of Colombia (adopted 22 November 2006, entered into force 15 May 2012) art. 10.5(1) (FPS clause including a express reference to 'treatment in accordance with customary international law') and art. 10.28 (broad definition of 'investor of a Party'). See also Sect. 14.2.1. For a detailed presentation of the protection of juristic persons under contemporary IIAs as well as of the notion of corporate nationality see: Markus Burgstaller, 'Nationality of Corporate Investors and International Claims against the Investor's Own State' (2006) 7 J. World Investment & Trade 857, 860-3; Markus Perkams, 'Protection of Legal Persons' in Marc Bungenberg, Jörn Griebel, Stephan Hobe and August Reinisch (eds), *International Investment Law* (Nomos, Baden-Baden 2015) 638, 638-52.

[105]Section 5.2 discusses the use of investment treaties as evidence of customary international law.

1950s. Making reference to the U.S. State Department's decision to expressly include corporations as beneficiaries of FCN agreements, Herman Walker observed in 1956:

> The growth of this pattern, if and as it occurs with the accretion in time of additional examples, should be conducive to the development of international standards of practice, not to say to the crystallization of principles international law, with respect to the treatment of companies. This consummation would seem especially appropriate in an age when international trade and business are so predominantly conducted through the corporate medium.[106]

In addition to investment treaties, arbitral decisions confirm that corporate entities currently enjoy protection under the customary FPS standard. Most contemporary investment claims concerning the interpretation or application of the FPS standard involve a corporate investor.[107] The application of the standard to juristic persons has not been an issue in any of these cases, including those in which the arbitrators defined the FPS standard by reference to customary law.[108]

7.3   The Provider of Security. The Host State and the Case of Other Internationally Accountable Entities

This chapter has already considered the protected agent or beneficiary of the customary security obligation.[109] The present section therefore focuses on the provider of security, which corresponds to the internationally accountable entity holding territorial jurisdiction over a foreign citizen.[110] Territoriality is deeply rooted in the FPS standard's origins in international law. Christian von Wolff and Emmer de Vattel argued that the act of entering into a *foreign territory* triggered both the foreigner's submission to the laws of the country and the host state's corresponding

---

[106]Herman Walker, 'Provisions on Companies in United States Commercial Treaties' (1956) 50 (2) AJIL 373, 393.

[107]For a list of investment arbitration cases involving FPS claims see Chap. 1. In most of the cases, the claimant was a juristic person.

[108]Some of these cases are discussed in Sect. 14.2.

[109]See Sect. 7.2.

[110]This section uses the expression 'internationally accountable entity' to refer to any body that is subject of rights and duties under international law, regardless of whether it is a *state*, properly so-called; using a Kelsenian terminology, the entities in question would be all those falling within the 'personal sphere of validity of international law'. See: Hans Kelsen, *Principles of International Law* (The Lawbook Exchange, Clark NJ 2007) 96-190 (particularly at pp. 96-100 and 158 *et seq.*) [first edition: 1952].

protection obligation.[111] The ICJ followed a similar line of argument centuries later in the *Barcelona Traction* case.[112]

Classic positivist scholars recognized, too, the importance of the territorial principle in this regard. Georg Friedrich von Martens placed the origin of the security obligation in the act of admitting a foreign citizen into the host country; the right of admission, in turn, was founded in the state's exclusive property right (*ausschließliches Eigenthumsrecht*) over the territory.[113] Consequently, the provider of security coincided with the entity exercising *territorial* jurisdiction over a foreign national.[114] To the same effect, in 1845, Karl Theodor Pütter defined the law of aliens as follows:

> [T]he European law of aliens is the general Christian law of nations applicable to the rights, legal transactions and legal relations of the subjects of one state in the *territory of another [state].*[115]

In 1908, Emanuel von Ullmann plausibly suggested that, in the essence, the law of aliens refers to a situation where the personal jurisdiction of a state overlaps with the territorial jurisdiction of another state:

> [When an alien enters into a foreign territory] a concurrence appears between the sovereign authority of the home and foreign states, with the legal bond to the home state (i.e. nationality) maintaining decisive importance at the backstage. The factual subjection [of the individual] to the territorial sovereignty of the host state, however, limits and adjusts the home state's personal sovereignty. A parallel effectiveness of both concurring [sovereign] powers is impracticable.[116]

---

[111]See Sects. 3.3 and 3.4.

[112]*Barcelona Traction Light and Power Company Ltd. (Belgium v Spain)* [1970] ICJ Rep 3, 32 [33] (placing the origin of the protection obligation in the act of *admitting* foreigners or their investments).

[113]Georg Friedrich von Martens, *Einleitung in das positive Europäische Völkerrecht auf Verträge und Herkommen gegründet* (Johann Christian Dieterich, Göttingen 1796) 94-5. Martens observed that, in spite of having the right of admission, European sovereigns had usually granted some freedom of entry and establishment to each other's subjects (at pp. 94-5). For a detailed presentation of Martens' views see Sect. 3.5.2.

[114]See Sect. 3.5.2.

[115]Emphasis added. Author's translation. The original German text reads: "Das europäische Fremdenrecht ist das allgemeine christliche Völkerrechtsgesetz für die Rechte, Rechtsgeschäfte und –verhältnisse der Unterthanen des einen Staates im Gebiete des andern." Karl Theodor Pütter, *Das praktische europäische Fremdenrecht* (J. C. Hinrichs'schen Buchhandlung, Leipzig 1845) 11.

[116]Author's translation. The original German text reads: "[Im ganzen] ergibt sich eine Konkurrenz der heimatlichen und der fremden Staatsgewalt, wobei zwar die rechtliche Verbindung mit dem Heimatstaat (die Staatsangehörigkeit) in der letzten Reihe entscheidende Bedeutung behält, die faktische Subjektion unter die Territorialhoheit des Aufenthaltsstaats aber doch die Wirksamkeit der Personalhoheit des Heimatstaats einschränkt und modifiziert, also eine parallele Wirksamkeit der beiden konkurrierenden Gewalten nicht durchführbar ist." Emanuel von Ullmann, *Völkerrecht* (J. C. B. Mohr, Tübingen 1908) 360. For a similar observation see: Paul Heilborn, *Das System des Völkerrechts entwickelt aus den völkerrechtlichen Begriffen* (Verlag von Julius Springer, Berlin 1896) 77 and 81. For an analysis of the historical origins and significance of the interplay between

Following a similar line of thought, Edwin Borchard observed in 1913 that '[t]he principles of territorial jurisdiction and personal sovereignty are mutually corrective forces'.[117] In this vein, Borchard argued that submission to the authority of the territorial state is complemented by the idea that the foreigner 'still owes allegiance to his own state'.[118] In this interplay between territorial and personal jurisdiction, the security obligation is placed always on the territorial state, which is better positioned to protect the foreigner against physical violence and other possible grievances.[119] As noted by William E. Hall (1890):

> The exclusive force possessed by the will of an independent community *within the territory* occupied by it is necessarily attended with corresponding responsibility. A state must not only itself obey the law, *but it must take reasonable care that illegal acts are not done within its dominions* [. . .] Hence it becomes necessary to provide by municipal law, to a reasonable extent, against the commission by private persons of acts which are injurious to the rights of other states.[120]

Based on Hall's argument, Clyde Eagleton would state in 1928:

> The responsibility of the state for the acts of individuals is therefore based upon the *territorial control* which it enjoys, and which enables it, and it alone, to restrain and punish individuals, whether nationals or not, within its limits.[121]

This rationale and the underlying principles hold only true under the assumption that the host state exercises actual *territorial control*; the partial, gradual or complete loss of effective control poses a complex and challenging situation, which could raise serious doubts as to the applicability of the security obligation.[122]

---

the principles of territoriality and personal jurisdiction see: Cedric Ryngaert, *Jurisdiction in International Law* (Oxford University Press, Oxford 2015) 50-77.

[117]Edwin Borchard, 'Basic Elements of Diplomatic Protection of Citizens Abroad' (1913) 7 (3) AJIL 497, 515.

[118]Edwin Borchard, 'Basic Elements of Diplomatic Protection of Citizens Abroad' (1913) 7 (3) AJIL 497, 518. For similar statements see: Clyde Eagleton, *The Responsibility of States in International Law* (Klaus Reprint, New York 1970) 78 [first edition: 1928]; Hans Roth, *The Minimum Standard of International Law Applied to Aliens* (IMP F.A.A. Sijhoff, The Hague 1949) 34.

[119]Cf. Clyde Eagleton, *The Responsibility of States in International Law* (Klaus Reprint, New York 1970) 78 [first edition: 1928] (particularly referring to state responsibility for private violence).

[120]Emphasis added. William Edward Hall, *A Treatise on International Law* (Clarendon Press, Oxford 1890) 56.

[121]Emphasis added. Clyde Eagleton, *The Responsibility of States in International Law* (Klaus Reprint, New York 1970) 78 [first edition: 1928] (also quoting Hall in support of the argument).

[122]The *George H. Bowley* award provides a clear example in this regard. In that case, private individuals had stolen American property in the vicinity of San Juan del Sur shortly before Costa Rican troops assumed control over the area. In his decision on the case, Umpire Bertinatti stated: "The troops of Costa Rica had that day arrived before the town, but occupied it only the next morning [. . .] As a matter of course, the police of a town belongs to the local authorities, and they alone are responsible for neglect in that duty. *A military occupant may claim to exercise the police, but no responsibility can be conceived to fall upon him before he makes such a claims and enters upon such duty.* General Cañas, who commanded the Costaricans, immediately upon entering in

Generally speaking, two factual scenarios can be distinguished in this regard. In the first scenario, no distinct internationally accountable entity assumes control over the troubled area. In such case, while the state continues to be the passive subject of the customary security obligation, responsibility for losses suffered within the disputed area is unlikely to attach: failures to prevent or redress injuries to aliens could be justified under the *force majeure* exception or another circumstance precluding wrongfulness.[123] Even if these exceptions are considered to be

that town gave orders to punish the authors of that crime and protect the person and property of citizens of the United States. It was all that could be reasonably expected of him." Emphasis added. *George H. Bowley & Co. v Costa Rica* (21 December 1862) 3 Moore's Arb. 3032-3.

[123]The ILC has indicated that '[m]aterial impossibility of performance giving rise to *force majeure* may be due to a natural or physical event [. . .] or to human intervention (e.g. loss of control over a portion of the State's territory as a result of an insurrection or devastation of an area by military operations carried out by a third state), or some combination of the two'. ILC, 'Responsibility of States for Internationally Wrongful Acts. General Commentary' (2001) 2 *Yearbook of the International Law Commission – 2001* 31, 76 art. 23 (Commentary) [3]. For some indicative examples of the use of the force majeure exception in connection with omissions in the protection of foreigners see: *Frederick Wipperman v United States of Venezuela* (10 July 1890) *United States and Venezuelan Claims Commission. Opinions Delivered by the Commissioners in the Principal Cases* (Gibson Bros., Washington 1890) 132, 136-7 (non-responsibility for the depredation of a vessel by 'savage tribes' in Venezuela; the decision was largely based on implicit considerations of *force majeure*); *Naomi Russell v Mexico* (24 April 1931) IV RIAA 805, 855-6 (murder of an American citizen by Mexican rebels; the Commissioners recognized *force majeure* as a possible circumstance precluding a finding of responsibility); *James Crossman v Venezuela* (1903) IX RIAA 356, 356 and 360 [interlocutory opinion by Umpire Plumley] (failure to prevent the theft of valuable objects in a city under rebel control; the respondent government alleged *force majeure*); *Charles de Lemos and Guillermina Dalton de Lemos v Venezuela* (1903) IX RIAA 360, 364 (damage to the property of British subjects and consular agents during the Bombardment of Ciudad Bolívar, Venezuela, which had been taken over by insurgents; Commissioner Grisanti qualified the event as a case of *force majeure*); *Sambiaggio Case* (1903) X RIAA 499, 513 and 516 (case concerning revolutionary damages; Umpire Ralston noted that 'the very existence of a flagrant revolution presupposes that a certain set of men have gone temporarily or permanently beyond the power of the authorities', later quoting a handful of authorities on the *force majeure* exception and further characterizing some forms of civil strife as 'a fortuitous case for which no responsibility exists'). More recent examples can be found in several decisions of the Iran-US Claims Tribunal. See: Gould Marketing Inc. *v* Ministry of National Defense, Award, Case No. 49 (17 July 1983) 3 Iran – US Cl. Trib. Rep. 147, 153 ("By December 1978, strikes, riots and other civil strife in the course of the Islamic Revolution had created classic *force majeure* conditions at least in Iran's major cities. By *force majeure* we mean social and economic forces beyond the power of the state to control through the exercise of *due diligence*. Injuries caused by the operation at such forces are therefore not attributable to the state for purposes of its responding for damages"). Cf. also: International Technical Products Corp. *v* Iran, Award, Case No. 302 (19 August 1985) 9 Iran – US Cl. Trib. Rep. 10, 23-5; Sylvania Technical Systems Inc. *v* Iran, Award, Case No. 64 (28 June 1985) 8 Iran – US Cl. Trib. Rep. 298, 308-10. For an overview of the Iran-US Claims Tribunal's case law in this area see: Anaconda Iran Inc. *v* Iran, Award, Case No. 167 (10 December 1986) 13 Iran – US Cl. Trib. Rep. 199, 212-3 [47-8] (quoting these and other relevant decisions). For investment cases involving some allegation of *force majeure* in connection with civil disorders, terrorism and their like see: Ampal-American Israel Corp., Egi-Fund (08-10) Investors LLC, Egi-Series Investments LLC and BSS-EMG Investors LLC *v* Egypt, Decision on Liability and Heads of Loss, ICSID Case No. ARB/12/11 (21 February 2017) [237 *et seq.*, 255, 271 *et seq.* and 330] (allegation of *force*

inapplicable,[124] lack of territorial control could indicate that there was no want of diligence on the part of the host state because local authorities had no reasonable opportunity to take positive action.[125]

Notwithstanding the foregoing, the inability to control a given territory does not *in itself* relieve the host state from its duties under the customary FPS standard. This premise can be exemplified through article 9 of the *ILC Articles on State Responsibility*.[126] The rule provides for the attribution of an action or omission to the state, where the following conditions are met:

> A person or group of persons is in fact exercising elements of the governmental authority *in the absence or default of the official authorities and in circumstances such as to call for the exercise of those elements of authority.*[127]

---

majeure in relation to a contractual claim regarding the operation of a pipeline, which had been the target of several terrorist attacks; the ICSID award referred in this vein to the findings of a previous ICC tribunal); Autopista Concesionada de Venezuela C.A. *v* Venezuela, Award, ICSID Case No. ARB/00/5 (23 September 2003) [107-29] (allegation that civil disorders constituted a *force majeure* event which, according to the respondent state, justified the decision not to grant a toll increase under a concession agreement); Toto Costruzioni Generali S.p.A. *v* Lebanon, Decision on Jurisdiction, ICSID Case No. ARB/07/12 (11 September 2009) [165-8] (acknowledging civil unrest as a possible justification for delays in local court proceedings, but not expressly referring to the *force majeure* exception); RSM Production Corp. *v* Central African Republic, Décision sur la compétence et la responsabilité, ICSID Case No. ARB/07/2 (7 December 2010) [143-213] (holding that a civil unrest leading to a *coup d'état* was a *force majeure* event; the case referred to a contract claim and involved a contractual definition of *force majeure*). It should also be noted that *force majeure* is not a one-way street. In some cases foreign investors have successfully invoked *force majeure* as a means to avoid responsibility for contractual breaches. For an indicative example see: Gujarat State Petroleum Corp. Ltd., Alkor Petroo Ltd. and Western Drilling Contractors Private Ltd. *v* Republic of Yemen and The Yemen Ministry of Oil and Minerals, ICC Case No. 19299/MCP, Final Award (10 July 2015) [211-24] (concerning the applicability of a contractual *force majeure* clause in the context of the Yemeni revolution of 2011; see particularly paras 202 and 212-3).

[124]Resort to the *force majeure* exception in the context of civil unrest has not been without controversy. In a report presented to the *Institut de Droit International* in 1898, Emilio Brusa famously argued that the foreigner suffering a revolutionary damage sacrifices his individual interest for the benefit of a foreign national community (so-called 'theory of expropriation'). Consequently, Brusa said, the foreigner shall be indemnified irrespective of whether the host state's actions or omissions appear to be justified on grounds of *force majeure* or otherwise. See: Emilio Brusa, 'Responsabilité des États à raison des dommages soufferts par des étrangers en cas d'émeute ou de guerre civile' (1898) 17 Annuaire de l'Institut de Droit International 96, 97 *et seq.*, 106-9 and 134-7. Brusa's theories were the subject of sharp criticism. For a critical assessment of the subject see: Carl Ludwig von Bar, 'A raison des dommages soufferts par des étrangers en cas de troubles, d'émeute ou de guerre civile' (1899) 31 (1) RDILC 464, 466-70; Luis A. Podestá Costa, 'La responsabilidad del Estado por daños irrogados a la persona o a los bienes de extranjeros en luchas civiles' (1938) 67/8 Revista de Derecho Internacional 5, 49-52.

[125]Section 13.4.1 addresses this aspect of the notion of due diligence in detail.

[126]Cf. ILC, 'Responsibility of States for Internationally Wrongful Acts. General Commentary' (2001) 2 *Yearbook of the International Law Commission – 2001* 31, 49 art. 9.

[127]Emphasis added. ILC, 'Responsibility of States for Internationally Wrongful Acts. General Commentary' (2001) 2 *Yearbook of the International Law Commission – 2001* 31, 49 art. 9.

The ILC has noted that this situation is extremely unusual in practice:

The exceptional nature of the circumstances envisaged by the article is indicated by the phrase "in circumstances such as to call for". Such cases occur only rarely, such as during revolution, armed conflict or foreign occupation, where the regular authorities dissolve, are disintegrating, have been suppressed or are for the time being inoperative. They may also cover cases where lawful authority is being gradually restored, e.g., after foreign occupation. The principle underlying article 9 owes something to the old idea of the *levée en masse*, the self-defense of the citizenry in the absence of regular forces: in effect it is a form of agency of necessity.[128]

James Crawford has observed that the rule normally applies in cases where 'the state apparatus has suffered total or partial collapse, for example in cases where it has lost control of the territory concerned'.[129] This special rule could thus turn particularly relevant where the host state is unable to effectively control a given area, and no other internationally accountable authority is in a position to take its place.[130] For instance, in the years that followed the Islamic Revolution, Iran witnessed a proliferation of armed 'revolutionary committees' ('*Komitehs*'), which had no formal place in the structure of the Iranian state.[131] In *Yeager v Iran*, the Iran-US Claims Tribunal assessed the attribution of acts committed by such *Komitehs* in the light of this exceptional rule of attribution.[132]

In factual scenarios of this kind, omissions in the protection of aliens, which are imputable to private individuals exercising elements of governmental authority, could be arguably measured against the FPS standard.[133] In virtue of the

---

[128]ILC, 'Responsibility of States for Internationally Wrongful Acts. General Commentary' (2001) 2 *Yearbook of the International Law Commission – 2001* 31, 49 art. 9 (Commentary) [1-2].

[129]James Crawford, *State Responsibility. The General Part* (Cambridge University Press, Cambridge 2013) 169 (also citing the case *Yeager v Iran*).

[130]Cf. James Crawford, *State Responsibility. The General Part* (Cambridge University Press, Cambridge 2013) 169.

[131]Cf. Kenneth P. Yeager *v* Iran, Award, Case No. 10199 (2 November 1987) 17 Iran – US Cl. Trib. Rep. 92, 97 [23] and 102 *et seq.* [39 *et seq.*]

[132]See: Kenneth P. Yeager *v* Iran, Award, Case No. 10199 (2 November 1987) 17 Iran – US Cl. Trib. Rep. 92, 103 [42] (quoting articles 8(a) and (b) of the then-available version of the ILC Draft Articles, which envisaged a rule similar to present-day article 9). See also: ILC, 'Responsibility of States for Internationally Wrongful Acts. General Commentary' (2001) 2 *Yearbook of the International Law Commission – 2001* 31, 49 art. 9 (Commentary) [2] (quoting the *Yeager* case as an example).

[133]It must be noted, however, that the *Yeager* case was not specifically concerned with a want of diligence in the protection of foreign citizens; the case referred to the expulsion of a foreign citizen from Iranian territory. See: Kenneth P. Yeager *v* Iran, Award, Case No. 10199 (2 November 1987) 17 Iran – US Cl. Trib. Rep. 92, 94-6 [12-6]. Nonetheless, the Iran-US Claims Tribunal acknowledged that the *Komitehs* played a major role in different areas, including 'the maintenance of public security' (at p. 105 para 45). See also the Tribunal's remarks at pp. 97 para 23 and pp. 102 *et seq.* paras 39 *et seq.* For another decision addressing state responsibility in cases where neither the titular government nor an insurgent movement exercises effective territorial control see: Alfred L. Short *v* Iran, Award, Case No. 11135 (14 July 1987) 16 Iran – US Cl. Trib. Rep. 76, 84-5 [33-4] (concerning the attribution of acts committed by private supporters of the Islamic revolution).

abovementioned rule, those omissions could be attributed to the host state.[134] As a corollary, under these exceptional circumstances, the host state could incur in a breach of the customary security obligation despite absence of territorial control.

More fraught is the second scenario, which refers to cases where another internationally accountable entity fills the space left by a weak state, and exercises control over a part of the host territory. For instance, a foreign power could assume direct control over some territorial unit, thus becoming responsible for the security of aliens in the area.[135] A similar situation could arise in respect of international organizations. In this vein, in its *Report on Due Diligence* of 2016, the International Law Association [ILA] explained:

> [A] potential source [of obligations upon international organizations] is due diligence obligations accompanying obligations sourced in general customary international law [...] In the context of territorial administration where an international organisation is directly engaged in the governance of territory, there is a strong argument to be made that it should consider itself bound more extensively by customary international law obligations compared with its more routine activities.[136]

Another example would be a *de facto* government.[137] When an insurrectionary group succeeds in gaining *de facto* control over a portion of the host state's

---

Cf. also: Alfred L. Short *v* Iran, Dissenting Opinion of Justice Brower, Case No. 11135 (14 July 1987) 16 Iran – US Cl. Trib. Rep. 86, 84-5 [33-4] and 93-5 [13-6].

[134]It is worth underscoring that the rule of attribution set forth in article 9 of the ILC Articles is applicable in respect of both actions and omissions. Cf. ILC, 'Responsibility of States for Internationally Wrongful Acts. General Commentary' (2001) 2 *Yearbook of the International Law Commission – 2001* 31, 34 art. 2 and 49 art. 9.

[135]An indicative example may be found in a diplomatic note sent by the Japanese Minister of Foreign Affairs to the American Ambassador in Tokyo in 1911, in the early aftermath of the annexation of the Korean peninsula to the Japanese Empire. On that occasion, the Japanese Minister promised that 'it will be the constant and sincere aim of the Imperial Government to afford to all legitimate interests, foreign as well as national, in all parts of the Empire, full protection and security'. 'The [Japanese] Minister of Foreign Affairs to the American Ambassador' (6 October 1911) *Papers relating to the Foreign Relations of the United States with the Annual Message of the President* (Government Printing Office, Washington 1911) 323, 324. For the related discussion of the applicability of FPS *treaty clauses* in cases of foreign occupation cf. Petr Stejskal, 'War: Foreign Investments in Danger – Can International Humanitarian Law or Full Protection and Security Always Save It?' (2017) 8 CYIL 529, 537 *et seq.* (also referring the possible use of the *force majeure* defense at p. 538).

[136]ILA Study Group on Due Diligence in International Law, 'Second Report by Mr. Tim Stephens (Rapporteur) and Mr. Duncan French (Chair)' (20 July 2016) 42 (without specific reference to the FPS standard).

[137]The use of the expression *'de facto* government' has been somewhat inconsistent in legal literature and state practice; the term could therefore convey different meanings. See generally: Stefan Talmon, *Recognition of Governments in International Law. With Particular Reference to Governments in Exile* (Clarendon Press, Oxford 1998) 60. For another author analyzing the meaning of the term see: Antoine Rougier, *Les guerres civiles et le droit des gens* (Larose & Forcel, Paris 1903) 483-8.

territory,[138] it is that group, and not the titular Government, the one accountable for the protection of aliens.[139] In the *Salvador Prats* affair, a case concerning areas subject to confederate control in the course of the American Civil War, Commissioner Wadsworth stated:

> [The Government of the United States] was under no obligation, by treaty or the law of nations, to protect the property of aliens situate (sic) inside the enemy country against the enemy. The international duty of the United States or its engagements by treaty to extend protection to aliens, transient or dwelling, in its territories, ceased inside the territory held by the insurgents from the time such territory was withdrawn by war from the control of that government, and until her authority and jurisdiction were again established over it.[140]

The *Institut de Droit International* recognized in 1900 the possibility of directing requests for compensation to revolutionary movements, provided they (and not the legitimate government) exercise authority over a foreign national.[141] Diplomatic

---

[138]Insurgent or revolutionary movements that have gained control over a given area and recognition as a 'belligerent power' have been traditionally considered as subjects of international law, being sometimes characterized as 'statelike communities'. See: Hans Kelsen, *Principles of International Law* (The Lawbook Exchange, Clark NJ 2007) 161 [first edition: 1952]. Cf. also: Roberto Ago, 'Fourth Report on State Responsibility – The Internationally Wrongful Act of the State, Source of International Responsibility (Continued)' (A/CN.4/264)' (20 June 1972 and 9 April 1973) 2 *Yearbook of the International Law Commission – 1972* 71, 129-30 ("the [insurrectional] movement is essentially a "provisional" subject of international law. The duration of its existence coincides with the duration of its fight against the pre-existing State or its Government"); Malcolm Shaw, *International Law* (Cambridge University Press, New York 2003) 219-20 (classifying these groups as a 'special case' of international legal subjectivity). On the protection of investments in territories under insurgent control cf. also Petr Stejskal, 'War: Foreign Investments in Danger – Can International Humanitarian Law or Full Protection and Security Always Save It?' (2017) 8 CYIL 529, 542-3 and 547 (arguing that FPS imposes no obligations on insurgents as such, but focusing on the application of FPS *treaty* clauses rather than the *customary* FPS standard).

[139]Specifically on the international responsibility of *de facto* regimes under the customary law of aliens see: Daoud L. Khairallah, *Insurrection under International Law with Emphasis on the Rights and Duties of Insurgents* (Lebanese University, Beirut 1973) 270-1 ("Notwithstanding the restrictions which may be imposed as a consequence of the exceptional circumstances generated by civil strife, both the lawful government and the insurgents have an interest in respecting the aliens' rights and in guaranteeing their safety. The lawful government is under a legal obligation to protect the rights of aliens in the fighting against insurgents and in all other situations. *The insurgents, however, come under the same responsibility, as soon as they establish an effective de facto authority over part of the state territory and they claim representing the state*" – emphasis added). See also: Jochen Abr. Frowein, *Das de facto-Regime im Völkerrecht. Eine Untersuchung zur Rechtsstellung nichtanerkannter Staaten und ähnlicher Gebilde* (Carl Heymanns Verlag, Köln/Berlin 1968) 86-93 (particularly at 89-90); Ulrich Erdmann, *Nichtanerkannte Staaten und Regierungen* (Institut für Völkerrecht der Universität Göttingen, Göttingen 1966) 29-38.

[140]*Salvador Prats v United States* (undated) 3 Moore's Arb. 2886, 2890.

[141]Institut de Droit International, 'Règlement sur la responsabilité des États à raison des dommages soufferts par les étrangers en cas d'émeute, d'insurrection ou de guerre civile' (1900) 18(I) Annuaire de l'Institut de Droit International 254, 254-5 art. 2 ("Tant que ce dernier [le gouvernement insurrectionnel] est considéré par le gouvernement de la personne soi-disant lésée comme Puissance belligérante, les demandes ne pourront être adressées [. . .] qu'au gouvernement insurrectionnel et non au gouvernement légitime").

practice corroborates this premise. In the context of the American civil war, Earl Russel summarized the position of the British Government as regards the security of aliens within territories under control of the Confederate States in the following terms:

> Her Majesty's Government hold it to be an undoubted principle of international law that when the persons or the property of the subjects or citizens of a state are injured by a *de facto* government, the state so aggrieved has a right to claim from the *de facto* government redress and reparation; and also that in cases of apprehended losses or injury to their subjects states may lawfully enter into communication with *de facto* governments to provide for the temporary security of the persons and property of their subjects.[142]

Another relevant example would be the Greytown incident of 1854.[143] On that occasion, U.S. Secretary of State William L. Marcy held the people of the vicinity of San Juan del Norte, who had proclaimed their independence from Nicaragua and adopted 'Greytown' as the official designation of their new territorial and political unit, to be responsible for the security of aliens within the territory under their control.[144] Specifically, Mr. Marcy emphasized that foreigners had placed their personal integrity and properties in the hands of the community of Greytown, and that 'by receiving them within its jurisdiction it [the community] assumed the *obligation of protecting them*'.[145] For that very same reason, the U.S. Government considered that the people of Greytown were accountable under international law for any 'want of that protection' affecting the interests of foreign nationals.[146]

An additional example may be found in the instructions sent by Secretary of State John Milton Hay to the American legation in La Paz (Bolivia) in March 1899, when

---

[142]'Earl Russel to Mr. Adams' (26 November 1861) in John Bassett Moore, *A Digest of International Law* (Volume 1: Government Printing Office, Washington 1906) 209.

[143]For a description of the facts see: John Bassett Moore, *A Digest of International Law* (Volume 7: Government Printing Office, Washington 1906) 346-54. The Greytown incident will also be discussed in Sect. 8.3.2.2.

[144]'Mr. Marcy, Sec. of State, to Count Sartiges, French min.' (26 February 1857) in John Bassett Moore, *A Digest of International Law* (Volume 6: Government Printing Office, Washington 1906) 927, 928.

[145]Emphasis added. 'Mr. Marcy, Sec. of State, to Count Sartiges, French min.' (26 February 1857) in John Bassett Moore, *A Digest of International Law* (Volume 6: Government Printing Office, Washington 1906) 927, 928.

[146]'Mr. Marcy, Sec. of State, to Count Sartiges, French min.' (26 February 1857) in John Bassett Moore, *A Digest of International Law* (Volume 6: Government Printing Office, Washington 1906) 927, 928. For the purposes of state responsibility, Greytown could be characterized as a *de facto* government not recognized by the United States; on the status of Greytown under international law see: Jochen Abr. Frowein, *Das de facto-Regime im Völkerrecht. Eine Untersuchung zur Rechtsstellung nichtanerkannter Staaten und ähnlicher Gebilde* (Carl Heymanns Verlag, Köln/Berlin 1968) 73.

a revolutionary government was established in the city.[147] On that occasion, Secretary Hay stated:

> You will understand that you can have no diplomatic relations with the insurgents implying their recognition by the United States as the legitimate Government of Bolivia, *but that, short of such recognition, you are entitled to deal with them as the responsible parties in local possession,* to the extent of demanding for yourself, *and for all Americans within reach of insurgent authority within the territory controlled by them, fullest protection for life and property.* If the situation at La Paz becomes unendurable or more perilous, you should collect all Americans within reach and quit the city, taking them with you, demanding adequate escort to the nearest place of safety.[148]

In 1911, Secretary of State Philander Knox referred to the 'usual practice' of the State Department of holding *de facto* authorities responsible for the security of American citizens within territories under their control.[149] This practice did not change much with the passage of time. For instance, in 1964 an insurgent group took control of the Congolese city of Stanleyville (nowadays Kisangani) and threatened to execute the American missionary Paul Carlston.[150] U.S. Secretary of State Dean Rusk encouraged both the titular government and the Organization of African Unity 'to take rapid and effective action to protect the lives of innocent civilians'.[151] This request was not however meant to relieve the insurgents from their own responsibility:

---

[147]'Mr. Hay to Mr. Bridgman' (14 March 1899) *Papers relating to the Foreign Relations of the United States with the Annual Message of the President* (Government Printing Office, Washington 1899) 105, 105.

[148]Emphasis added. 'Mr. Hay to Mr. Bridgman' (14 March 1899) *Papers relating to the Foreign Relations of the United States with the Annual Message of the President* (Government Printing Office, Washington 1899) 105, 105.

[149]'The Secretary of State to the American Minister' (20 January 1911) *Papers relating to the Foreign Relations of the United States with the Annual Message of the President* (Government Printing Office, Washington 1911) 649, 649 ("On October 11, 1909, Gen. Juan J. Estrada, governor of one of the eastern Provinces of Nicaragua [. . .] issued a manifesto reciting the evils of the Zelaya administration, proclaimed himself the provision president of the Republic, and solicited the recognition of the United States. The Department, *following its usual practice in such cases,* made no response to his request, but shortly thereafter notified the leaders of the revolution, as it did the representative of Zelaya, *that the Government of the United States would hold strictly accountable for the protection of American life and property the factions de facto control in control of the eastern and western portions, respectively, of the Republic of Nicaragua*" – emphasis added).

[150]See: 'Message from Secretary of State Rusk to Chairman of the Ad Hoc Commission of the Congo Prime Minister Jomo Kenyatta' (16 November 1964) Jules Davids (ed), *Documents on American Foreign Relations – 1964* (Harper & Row Publishers, New York 1965) 345, 345.

[151]'Message from Secretary of State Rusk to Chairman of the Ad Hoc Commission of the Congo Prime Minister Jomo Kenyatta' (16 November 1964) Jules Davids (ed), *Documents on American Foreign Relations – 1964* (Harper & Row Publishers, New York 1965) 345, 346.

My Government holds the rebel leaders directly responsible for the safety of Dr. Carlston and all other American citizens in areas under rebel control.[152]

These examples suggest that the security obligation is placed on the state formally holding sovereignty over the host territory *only as long as* no other internationally answerable entity assumes territorial control over the relevant area. This principle could pose significant difficulties in practice. The reason lies in the fact that, as rightly observed by some scholars, 'territorial control is a question of degree'.[153] The question therefore arises as to the point in time when a state can be said to have lost control over a portion of its territory or, put differently, how much control is it required for another entity (e.g. a revolutionary group) to become responsible for the security of foreigners. In the particular case of insurrectionary movements, the

---

[152]'Message from Secretary of State Rusk to Chairman of the Ad Hoc Commission of the Congo Prime Minister Jomo Kenyatta' (16 November 1964) Jules Davids (ed), *Documents on American Foreign Relations – 1964* (Harper & Row Publishers, New York 1965) 345, 346.

[153]Nina Caspersen, 'Making Peace with De Facto States' in Martin Riegl and Bohumil Doboš (eds), *Unrecognized States and Secession in the 21st Century* (Springer, Cham 2017) 13.

traditional criterion has been the recognition of belligerency.[154] In 1928, Clyde Eagleton summarized the mainstream view on the subject in the following terms:

> If belligerent status is accorded to the rebels, it may be taken as an admission of inability to control them; and, consequently, as a warning of non-liability for their actions. Such admission may be made by the parent state itself, in which case notice is served upon all other nations; or recognition of belligerency may be granted by other states, thereby incapacitating themselves from the later presentation of claims for damages done to their citizens through insurgent action.[155]

This opinion was shared by some of the most prominent scholars in the area,[156] and has also been adopted in diplomatic correspondence.[157] This view found notable

---

[154]See generally: Clyde Eagleton, *The Responsibility of States in International Law* (Klaus Reprint, New York 1970) 147 [first edition: 1928].

[155]Clyde Eagleton, *The Responsibility of States in International Law* (Klaus Reprint, New York 1970) 147 [first edition: 1928].

[156]See, for example: Alf Ross, *A Textbook of International Law. General Part* (Longmans, Green and Co., London 1947) 166; Antoine Pillet, *Les lois actuelles de la guerre* (Rousseau, Paris 1901) 29; Arnold Duncan McNair (First Baron McNair), *International Law Opinions* (Volume 2: Cambridge University Press, Cambridge 1956) 245; Edwin Borchard, *The Diplomatic Protection of Citizens Abroad or the Law of International Claims* (The Banks Law Publishing Co., New York 1916) 235; Edwin Borchard, 'The Law of Responsibility of States for Damage Done in Their Territory to the Person or Property of Foreigners. Comments to the Draft Convention' (April 1929) 23 AJIL 140, 195 art. 13; Hans Kelsen, *Principles of International Law* (The Lawbook Exchange, Clark NJ 2007) 291-2 [first edition: 1952]; Ian Brownlie, *System of the Law of Nations. State Responsibility* (Clarendon Press, Oxford 1983) 177. Even some of the most consistent advocates for a far-reaching responsibility of the host state for the acts of rebels and insurrects, such as Carlos Wiesse and Emilio Brusa, recognized this principle. Wiesse, while submitting that states are generally responsible for injuries received by aliens within their territories, believed the rule not to be applicable in respect of portions of the territory where social order has not yet been established; in later publications, Wiesse went on to concede that recognition of an insurrectionary movement as a belligerent power relieves the host state from responsibility for damages occurred within areas subject to rebel control. See: Carlos Wiesse, *Le droit international apliqué aux guerres civiles* (B. Benda Libraire-Éditeur, Lausanne 1898) 44-5; Carlos Wiesse, *Reglas de derecho internacional aplicables á las guerras civiles* (Imp. Torres Aguirre, Lima 1905) 82-3. For his part, Brusa expressed in 1898 the view that the host state is generally responsible for revolutionary damages to aliens. However, in a subsequent document presented to the *Institut de Droit International* in 1900, he acknowledged that, whenever a belligerent power has gained control over a portion of the host state's territory, it had been the practice of some states to direct their claims to the insurrectionary government and not to the titular government. See: Emilio Brusa, 'Responsabilité des États à raison des dommages soufferts par des étrangers en cas d'émeute ou de guerre civile' (1898) 17 Annuaire de l'Institut de Droit International 96, 97 *et seq.*, 106-9 and 134-7; Emilio Brusa, 'Responsabilité des États à raison des dommages soufferts par des étrangers en cas d'émeute ou de guerre civile. Nouvelles thèses présentées par MM. Brusa, rapporteur, et L. de Bar' (1900) 18 Annuaire de l'Institut de Droit International 47, 47-8.

[157]For a clear example of state practice in support of the principle see: 'Mr. Seward, Sec. of State, to Mr. Dayton, min. to France' (12 January 1864) in John Bassett Moore, *A Digest of International Law* (Volume 6: Government Printing Office, Washington 1906) 957 ("France, by recognizing the insurgents as belligerents, may be expected to have accepted all the responsibility of that measure, and to be content to regard her subjects domiciled in belligerent territory as identified with belligerent themselves").

support in the Neuchâtel (1900)[158] and Lausanne (1927)[159] Sessions of the *Institut de Droit International*. It must be observed, however, that the recognition of belligerency by a given state has a merely *evidentiary value* and does not, for and by itself, change anything in the *substance* of the security relationship.[160]

The underlying reason can be best explained through a hypothetical example. Let us assume that a xenophobic mob attacks foreigners and ransacks their property in a city, which is under effective control of an insurrectionary group. Rebel troops witness the attacks, but choose not to take any action against the rioters. The titular government has not yet recognized the rebels as a belligerent group, and only a few states have given the insurrects belligerent status. In such scenario, it seems utterly artificial to say that the revolutionaries are responsible for the security of those individuals whose home states have issued a recognition of belligerency, and that the titular government remains responsible for the protection of citizens of other states.

Responsibility does not switch from the titular government to the rebels as a consequence of the recognition of belligerency as such, but as a corollary of the change in the entity holding actual territorial control. The act of according belligerent status entails a formal recognition by the issuing state of such change in control. As such, it prevents the issuing state from successfully pursuing claims against the titular government for injuries inflicted upon its citizens within belligerent territory.[161]

---

[158]Institut de Droit International, 'Règlement sur la responsabilité des États à raison des dommages soufferts par les étrangers en cas d'émeute, d'insurrection ou de guerre civile' (1900) 18(I) Annuaire de l'Institut de Droit International 254, 254-5 art. 2 ("Cependant, certaines demandes d'indemnité peuvent être écartées, quand elles se rapportent à des faits qui se sont produits après que le gouvernement de l'Etat auquel appartient la personne lésée a reconnu le gouvernement insurrectionnel comme Puissance belligérante, et quand la personne lésée a continué de garder son domicile ou son habitation sur le territoire du gouvernement insurrectionnel").

[159]Institut de Droit International, 'Résolutions votées par l'Institut au cours de sa XXXI Vᵉ Session – Responsabilité internationale des États à raison des dommages causés sur leur territoire à la personne ou aux biens des étrangers (XIIIᵉ Commission)' (1927) 33(II) Annuaire de l'Institut de Droit International 330, 332 art. 7 ("La responsabilité de l'Etat en raison d'actes commis par des insurgés, cesse lorsqu'il a reconnu ces derniers comme partie belligérante, et, en tous cas, à l'égard des Etats qui les ont reconnus comme tels"). See also: Leo Strisower, 'Responsabilité internationale des États à raison des dommages causés sur leur territoire à la personne ou aux biens des étrangers' (1927) 33(I) Annuaire de l'Institut de Droit International 455, 484.

[160]On the legal effects of recognition see generally: Malcolm Shaw, *International Law* (Cambridge University Press, New York 2003) 393 *et seq.* (noting at p. 393 that recognition 'is a legal acknowledgement of a factual state of affairs'). On belligerency see also pp. 1040 *et seq.*

[161]Cf. n. 155, 156 and 157 above.

Chapter 8
Objective Scope of Application: Protected Interests and Covered Risks

8.1 Preliminary Remarks

Two elements determine the objective scope of application of application of the FPS standard. The first element corresponds to the legal interests or values protected under the standard; the second concerns the risks against which security is provided.[1] This chapter explores these two elements of the security obligation. In this vein, it submits that the object of protection is broad in scope, and cannot be limited to a pre-established catalogue of individual rights. Taking inspiration from political science theories about the concept of security, it could be said that, in customary law, the FPS standard protects the 'acquired values' of foreign citizens (as a general category).[2] These 'values' are not only those which foreigners acquire *through* the state (e.g. property over specific assets), but also those which liberal legal theorists would characterize as 'natural' or 'inherent' values (e.g. life and bodily integrity).[3]

This chapter identifies the risks covered by the FPS standard on the basis of their *source*, that is to say, the *public* or *non-public* origin of the threat. In this connection, it argues that the essence of the FPS standard refers to the host state's reaction against *non-public* threats, i.e. risks that do not originate in the host state's conduct.[4] This

---

[1]See generally Chap. 6.

[2]Cf. Arnold Wolfers, 'National Security as an Ambiguous Symbol' (1952) 67(4) Pol. Sci. Q. 481, 484-5; David Baldwin, 'The Concept of Security' (1997) 23 Rev. Int'l St. 5, 13. Section 8.2 elaborates further on this terminology.

[3]See Sect. 8.2.

[4]For some examples of arbitral decisions formulating the FPS standard in terms of the host state's 'reaction' or 'response' against a threat see: Ampal-American Israel Corp., Egi-Fund (08-10) Investors LLC, Egi-Series Investments LLC and BSS-EMG Investors LLC v Egypt, Decision on Liability and Heads of Loss, ICSID Case No. ARB/12/11 (21 February 2017) [245-6, 254 and 288] (particularly referring to the alleged failure by the host state to protect a pipeline from armed attacks); Bernhard Friedrich Arnd Rüdiger von Pezold et al. v Zimbabwe, Award, ICSID Case

© Springer Nature Switzerland AG 2019
S. Mantilla Blanco, *Full Protection and Security in International Investment Law*,
European Yearbook of International Economic Law 8,
https://doi.org/10.1007/978-3-030-24838-3_8

implies that the standard is applicable in respect of failures to prevent or redress injuries occasioned by private actors or natural phenomena.[5] In addition, the FPS standard covers public injuries incidentally caused by state action against such external threats (e.g. collateral damages inflicted in the course of counterinsurgency operations).[6]

8.2   First Element. Protected Interests; The Notion of 'Acquired Values'

In order to be meaningful, a security obligation must refer to some value or object of protection.[7] The customary FPS standard could be therefore reasonably expected to point to a well-defined set of rights, such as life, liberty and property. The host state would be accordingly pledged to protect foreign nationals *in the exercise of those rights* within its territory. Such an approach poses the obvious difficulty of formulating a catalogue of rights as a 'referent object' for the security obligation.[8] This problem is not particular to the FPS standard; it also affects the assessment of the more-general minimum standard. Despite many attempts to establish the content of

---

No. ARB/10/15 (28 July 2015) [596] (stating that 'the Respondent breached this [FPS] standard in relation to the non-responsiveness of the police to various violent incidents'); Convial Callao S.A. and CCI – Compañía de Concesiones de Infraestructura S.A. *v* Peru, Laudo Final, ICSID Case No. ARB/10/2 (21 May 2013) [651-2] (requiring that the state 'reacts in a reasonable manner to the circumstances that could affect the investment' ['*reaccione de manera razonable ante las circunstancias que pudieran afecta la inversión*'], and underscoring that the basis for responsibility is the state's passive response to such circumstances); Tecnicas Medioambientales TECMED S.A. *v* Mexico, Award, ICSID Case No. ARB(AF)/00/2 (29 May 2003) [177] (considering whether the authorities of the Mexican vicinity of Hermosillo 'reacted reasonably' toward local demonstrations against an industrial waste landfill).

[5]See particularly Sects. 8.3.1 (private violence) and 8.3.3.2 (natural phenomena).

[6]See particularly Sect. 8.3.3.1.

[7]See generally: Barry Buzan, Ole Waever and Jaap de Wilde, *Security. A New Framework for Analysis* (Lynne Rienner Publishers, Boulder CO 1998) 21-3 and 36 (also discussed in Sect. 6.3).

[8]For a discussion of the notion of 'referent object' as an element of the concept of security see: Barry Buzan, Ole Waever and Jaap de Wilde, *Security. A New Framework for Analysis* (Lynne Rienner Publishers, Boulder CO 1998) 21-3 and 36. See also Sect. 6.3.

the minimum standard of treatment through an inventory of specific individual rights,[9] no 'bill of rights' seems to provide a suitable definition of the standard.[10] Enumerations of the rights of aliens, however appealing, are always either too broad or too narrow in scope; they are therefore unlikely to be correct, precise and exhaustive at the same time.[11]

Let us consider an indicative example. An inventory of the individual rights comprised by the minimum standard could be limited to the liberal *trias* of life, liberty and property.[12] If this approach were to be followed, the elements of the list would be precise and correct; they would in fact correspond to specific rights, which can be reasonably placed within the general corpus of the law of aliens.[13] But the list would not be comprehensive enough. There seems indeed to be no reason to exclude, for example, personal integrity, the recognition of legal personality, and due process.[14] One could go even further. Numerous FCN agreements assured aliens

---

[9]For some representative examples see: Alfred Verdross and Bruno Simma, *Universelles Völkerrecht* (Ducker & Humblot, Berlin 1984) 802-3 (particularly at p. 802, no. 6); Carmen Tiburcio, *The Human Rights of Aliens under International and Comparative Law* (Martinus Nijhoff Publishers, The Hague 2001) xiii-xxiv and 75 *et seq.*; Erich Kaufmann, 'Règles générales du droit de la paix' (1935) 54(4) RCADI 309, 427-33; Fausto de Quadros, *A proteção da propriedade privada pelo direito internacional público* (Livraria Almedina, Coimbra 1998) 133-44; Georg Dahm, *Völkerrecht* (Volume 1: W. Kohlhammer Verlag, Stuttgart 1958) 506-11; Hans Roth, *The Minimum Standard of International Law Applied to Aliens* (IMP F.A.A. Sijhoff, The Hague 1949) 134-85; Isidoro Ruiz Moreno, *Manual de derecho internacional público* (Editorial Juan Castagnola, Buenos Aires 1943) 152-4; Knut Ipsen, *Völkerrecht* (C.H. Beck, Munich 2014) 856-7.

[10]For an author discussing the attempts to enumerate the rights encompassed by the minimum standard see: Karl Doehring, *Die allgemeinen Regeln des völkerrechtlichen Fremdenrechts und das deutsche Verfassungsrecht* (Carl Heymanns Verlag, Köln/Berlin 1963) 80-3.

[11]For the debate on the content of the minimum standard see Sect. 5.3.

[12]For instance, the Brazilian diplomat and international law scholar Hildebrando Accioly defined the scope of the customary protection obligation by recourse to the *trias* of life (*direito à vida*), liberty (*direito à liberdade individual*) and property (*direito de propriedade*); nonetheless, Accioly considered the list to be non-exhaustive. See: Hildebrando Accioly, *Manual de Direito Internacional Publico* (São Paulo, Edição Saraiva 1958) 90. For another example see: Han Tao Wu, *Responsibility of States for Injuries Sustained by Aliens on Account of Acts of Insurgents* (University of Illinois, Urbana IL 1930) 4 (referring to the foreigner's rights to 'life, liberty, and property, and access to the competent courts for the sake of securing his protection').

[13]Cases concerning the life and property of aliens are uncountable. For some indicative examples see: *Elvira Almaguer v Mexico* (13 May 1929) IV RIAA 523, 523-9 (life); *Laura M.B. Janes et al. v Mexico* (16 November 1925) IV RIAA 82, 82-98 (life); *LFH Neer and Pauline Neer v Mexico* (15 October 1926) IV RIAA 60, 60-6 (life); *French Company of Venezuelan Railroads Case* (31 July 1905) X RIAA 285, 285-355 (property); *Puerto Cabello and Valencia Railway Company Case* (1903) IX RIAA 510, 510-33 (property). For an example of a case involving the liberty of a foreign national see: 'Turkey. Abduction by Brigands, Ransom, and Release of Miss Ellen M. Stone, An American Missionary' (5 September 1901 – 8 May 1902) *Papers relating to the Foreign Relations of the United States with the Annual Message of the President* (Government Printing Office, Washington 1902) 997, 997-1023.

[14]For an exhaustive survey of cases concerning the right of aliens to the recognition of their legal personality before judicial bodies see: Alwyn Freeman, *The International Responsibility of States for Denial of Justice* (Klaus Reprint, New York 1970) 215 *et seq.* [first edition: 1938] (in particular

freedom of conscience and religion; some treaties went as far as to provide for 'the most perfect and entire security of conscience'.[15] One could hence be tempted to include freedom of religion on the list of rights comprised by the minimum standard in general, and the FPS standard in particular. However, the enumeration would then soon become a venture beyond the safe waters of existing customary law (*lex lata*), and could easily turn into an argument of proposed law (*lege ferenda*).

Taking cognizance of this difficulty, this study follows a different approach. The proposition advanced is that, in order to properly establish the scope of the FPS standard in customary law, there is no need for a catalogue of specifically defined individual rights. Rather, the FPS standard could be said to protect a broad, but still clearly delimited, category of interests: the '*acquired values*' of foreign citizens. This approach is not entirely novel. Political science studies on the concept of security have used the notion of 'acquired values' for decades; in his influential article *National Security as an Ambiguous Symbol* (1952), Arnold Wolfers explained:

> Security points to some protection of values previously acquired [...] security, in an objective sense, measures the absence of threats to acquired values, in a subjective sense, the absence of fear that such values will be attacked.[16]

---

connection with the right of access to local courts). For some indicative examples of cases involving the bodily integrity of foreign citizens see: *George Adams Kennedy v Mexico* (6 May 1927) IV RIAA 194, 194-203; *Bond Coleman v Mexico* (3 October 1928) IV RIAA 364, 364-8. For a representative example of a claim concerning due process see: *Cotesworth & Powell Case* (August 1875) 4 Moore's Arb. 2050, 2052-85.

[15]For a clear example see: Treaty of Peace, Amity, Navigation, and Commerce between the United States of America and the Republic of New Granada (adopted 12 December 1846, entered into force 18 February 1848) Charles Bevans (ed), *Treaties and Other International Agreements of the United States of America 1776–1949* (Volume 6: U.S. Department of State Publication, Washington 1971) 868, 872 art. 14 ("The citizens of the United States residing in the territories of the Republic of New Granada, *shall enjoy the most perfect and entire security of conscience without being annoyed, prevented, or disturbed on account of their religious beliefs*. Neither shall they be annoyed, molested or disturbed in the proper exercise of their religion in private houses or in the Chapels or places of worship appointed for that purpose, provided that in so doing they observe the decorum of divine worship, and the respect due to the laws, usages and customs of the country [...] In like manner the citizens of New Granada shall enjoy, within the Government and territories of the United States, *a perfect and unrestrained liberty of conscience and of exercising their religion, publicly or privately, within their own dwelling houses, or in the chapels and places of worship appointed for that purpose, agreeably to the laws, usages & customs of the United States*" – emphasis added). German FCN agreements also guaranteed freedom of conscience and religion but did not use the expression 'security of conscience'. For some indicative examples see: Freundschafts-, Handels- und Schifffahrtsvertrag zwischen dem Deutschen Reich und dem Freistaat Columbien (adopted 23 July 1892, entered into force 12 April 1894) Felik Stoerk (ed), *Martens Nouveau Recueil Général des Traités, 2me Série* (Volume 19: Librairie Dietrich, Göttingen 1895) 831, 835-6 art. 8; Freundschafts-, Handels- und Schifffahrtsvertrag zwischen dem Deutschen Reich und Samoa (adopted 24 January 1879) Friedrich Heinrich Geffcken (ed) *Martens Recueil Manuel et Pratique de Traités et Conventions, 2me Série* (Volume 3: F. A. Brockhaus, Leipzig 1888) 1, 1 art. 3.

[16]Arnold Wolfers, 'National Security as an Ambiguous Symbol' (1952) 67(4) Pol. Sci. Q. 481, 484-5.

Following Walter Lippman's contention that national security refers to the 'core values' of a nation,[17] Wolfers stated:

> Security, like other aims, may be an intermediate rather than an ultimate goal, in which case it can be judged as a means to these more ultimate ends.[18]

Decades later, David Baldwin noted that Wolfer's characterization 'seems to capture the basic intuitive notion underlying most uses of the term security'.[19] This observation is correct. Generally speaking, the values the notion of security refers to are *preexistent* to the security relationship; security is generally provided for what subjects already have, not for what they expect to obtain in the future.[20]

The notion of *'acquired values'* could appear to be too broad a notion. The broadness of the concept might give the impression that it is incapable of actually *delimiting* the customary FPS standard. A closer look however reveals that, if the notion is considered in conjunction with other criteria defining the security obligation's scope of application, broadness ceases to be a problem. Not every element of a security relationship must be specified in the same degree.[21] In the particular case of the FPS standard, it is the *risk* or *threat* what narrows the scope of the customary protection obligation to a greater extent.[22] This chapter submits that the host state is pledged to exercise due diligence in the protection of the 'acquired values' of foreign citizens against *non-public risks*.[23] Thus, the broad notion of 'acquired values', when read in context, appears as a sufficiently determinate notion. Several factors define the values protected by the FPS standard in customary law. To begin with, they are vulnerable to a specific category of risks.[24] In addition, they are held by a specific group of persons, namely, foreign natural and juristic persons.[25] Finally, they are *acquired values* rather than mere expectations.[26]

While an exhaustive list of the rights protected under the customary FPS standard might be desirable, a choice must be made between an enumeration of specific rights, which will be necessarily incomplete or inaccurate, and a broadly defined criterion. In a quandary about these alternatives, accuracy should be preferred over a higher degree of determinacy.

---

[17]Walter Lippman, *U.S. Foreign Policy: Shield of the Republic* (Little & Brown, Boston 1943) 51. See also: Arnold Wolfers, 'National Security as an Ambiguous Symbol' (1952) 67(4) Pol. Sci. Q. 481, 484.

[18]Arnold Wolfers, 'National Security as an Ambiguous Symbol' (1952) 67(4) Pol. Sci. Q. 481, 492.

[19]David Baldwin, 'The Concept of Security' (1997) 23 Rev. Int'l St. 5, 13.

[20]Cf. David Baldwin, 'The Concept of Security' (1997) 23 Rev. Int'l St. 5, 13. Section 6.3 addresses Baldwin's and other authors' views on the concept of security.

[21]David Balwin, 'The Concept of Security' (1997) 23 Rev. Int'l St. 5, 17. See also Sect. 6.3.

[22]Section 8.3 addresses the risks covered by the FPS standard in detail.

[23]See Sect. 8.3.

[24]Cf. Sect. 8.3.

[25]Cf. Chap. 7.

[26]Section 9.3.2 analyzes the applicability of the FPS standard to the protection of 'legitimate expectations' in detail.

The broadness of the notion of 'acquired values' is consistent with the diversity of interests FPS claims could refer to. Some cases concern the protection of the life, property or personal integrity of a foreign citizen threatened, for example, by mobs or insurgents.[27] In such factual settings, the host state will be required to take preventive measures of protection, as well as to provide adequate means of redress for injuries resulting from these forms of violence.[28] At other instances, the values at stake could coincide, for example, with a foreign citizen's rights under a private contract or with rights recognized by a civil court judgment. A foreign creditor holding a proper payment order or writ of execution must be provided with proper means to enforce his or her title against the debtor (e.g. seizure of assets by competent authorities); the absence of such means could involve a breach of the protection obligation.[29]

As the foregoing examples already suggest, acquired values may coincide with rights created by domestic law, that is to say, rights obtained from the host state (e.g. property rights over specific assets).[30] The notion is, however, not necessarily limited to this kind of rights. Under the theory of the tacit agreement, for example, the security obligation was envisaged as encompassing a duty to protect natural rights.[31] The specific rights conveyed by the notion of 'natural rights' in liberal legal thought may vary from one theory to another. John Locke would say that there are

---

[27]Mob violence and similar forms of private violence will be discussed in detail in Sect. 8.3.1.

[28]See Chap. 10.

[29]An unjustified failure or refusal to enforce a civil court judgment could indeed entail a violation of the customary law of aliens. See generally: Alwyn Freeman, *The International Responsibility of States for Denial of Justice* (Klaus Reprint, New York 1970) 392-7 [first edition: 1938]. For a classical example see: *Montano v United States of America* (2 November 1863) 2 Moore's Arb. 1630, 1630-8. In the *Montano* case, a U.S. court had rendered civil judgment in favor of E. G. Montano, a national of Peru, in a claim raised against an American private organization (at pp. 1630-1). The local court ordered the District Marshal to execute the decision against the respondent's property (at pp. 1631 and 1634-5). As the marshal sought to enforce the decision, however, an individual alleged to be the true owner of the asset on which execution was pursued (at p. 1635). The marshal then (unlawfully) required Mr. Montano to provide a 'bond of indemnity' (at p. 1635). Upon Montano's failure to do so, the Marshal returned the court's original writ of execution with the annotation '*nulla bona*' (at p. 1635). In his opinion on the case, Umpire Pedro Alcántara Herrán stated: "The marshal is under obligations to employ all necessary efforts to execute the writs placed in his hands by the court upon which he depends, and nothing is more important than the execution of a judgment [. . .] The sentence of the court was not made effective through the fault of the public officer who was under obligation to execute it. And in this case the denial of justice is the more palpable [. . .] because it is not now a subject for examination and decision whether this claim be just, but that a writ decreed in the sovereign name of the country be executed by which is recognized and defined the rights of the aggrieved party who sought reparation" (at pp. 1635-6).

[30]Alfred Verdross, 'Les règles internationales concernant le traitement des étrangers' (1931) 37 (3) RCADI 322, 357-8 (deriving the duty to respect and protect 'legally acquired rights' from the theory of the tacit agreement).

[31]On the theory of the tacit agreement see Sects. 3.3 and 3.4.

three natural rights—i.e., life, liberty and estate, which are covered under the far-reaching Lockean concept of property.[32] Other thinkers, such as Thomas Hobbes and Jean-Jacques Rousseau, dismissed the characterization of property (or 'estate' in Locke's terminology) as a natural right.[33]

For present purposes, it suffices to emphasize that, conceptually, a right or value does not require express recognition from the host state in order to fall within the scope of the host state's protection obligation. Christian von Wolff observed in 1749 that 'exiles do not cease to be men'.[34] Similarly, Emmer de Vattel noted in 1758 that '[a] man, by being exiled or banished, does not forfeit the human character'.[35] These statements show that, in the tradition of the law of aliens, foreigners entering into a new country are nothing like a passenger without baggage: they come into the host territory as holders of a preexistent set of rights or values, which the sovereign, upon their admission, is obliged to protect.[36]

Two final remarks should be made with regard to the notion of 'acquired values'. First, this study has resorted to this broad concept in connection with the *customary protection obligation*. In investment treaty arbitration, however, the applicable

---

[32]See: John Locke, *Two Treatises of Government* (A. Millar et al., London 1764) 269 Book I § 87 [first edition: 1689] ("Man being born, as has been proved, with a title to perfect freedom and an uncontrolled enjoyment of all the rights and privileges of the law of Nature, equally with any other man, or number of men in the world, hath by nature a power not only to preserve his *property— that is, his life, liberty, and estate*, against the injuries and attempts of other men, but to judge of and punish the breaches of that law in others, as he is persuaded the offence deserves, even with death itself, in crimes where the heinousness of the fact, in his opinion, requires it" – emphasis added).

[33]In particular reference of the state of nature, Hobbes stated that '[w]here there is no common Power, there is no Law: where no Law, no Injustice. Force, and Fraud, are in warre, the two Cardinall vertues. Justice, and Injustice are none of the Faculties neither of the Body, nor Mind [...] They are Qualities, that Relate to men in Society, not in Solitude. *It is consequent also to the same condition, that there be no Propriety, no Dominion, no Mine and Thine distinct; but onely that to every mans, that he can get; and for so long, as he can keep it'*. Emphasis added. Thomas Hobbes, *Leviathan* (Cambridge University Press, Cambridge 1904) 85 [first edition: 1651]. Rousseau believed that, through the social contract, every individual waives his or her natural liberty ('*liberté naturelle*'), and obtains in return both civil liberty (*liberté civile*) and property over his or her possessions ('*propriété de tout ce qu'il possede*'). Rousseau considered that every person has a natural right to the goods necessary to satisfy her fundamental needs, and acknowledged that persons living in a state of nature could actually possess goods. Nonetheless, he was emphatic in stating that property, as a 'true right' ('*vrai droit*'), could not precede the formation of the state. See: Jean-Jacques Rousseau, *Du contract social ou principes du droit politique* (M.M. Rey, Amsterdam 1763) 23-6 [first edition: 1762]. For an overview of the status of property in early modern liberal theories of law see: Christian Hillgruber, 'Ist privates Eigentum ein Menschenrecht? Philosophische und verfassungshistorische Überlegungen' in Anton Rauscher (ed), *Das Eigentum als eine Bedingung der Freiheit* (Dunckler & Humblot, Berlin 2013) 111, 112-22 (discussing the views of Hobbes, Rousseau and Locke).

[34]Christian Wolff, 'Jus gentium methodo scientifica pertractatum' (1749) in James Brown Scott (ed), *Classics of International Law* (Joseph Drake tr, Clarendon Press, Oxford 1934) 80 § 147.

[35]Emer de Vattel, *The Law of Nations or Principles of the Law of Nature Applied to the Conduct and Affairs of Nations and Sovereigns* (1758) (G.G. and J. Robinson, London 1797) 108.

[36]See generally Sects. 3.3 and 3.4.

instrument will define the *object of protection* in more or less precise terms. The *treaty-based* protection obligation will normally refer only to *investments*, as defined by the applicable IIA.[37] Thus, the object of protection of FPS clauses is typically narrower in scope than that provided for the standard under general customary international law.[38] Resort to the notion of 'acquired values' could, however, be still useful for the assessment of FPS treaty claims in some cases. For instance, some treaties grant protection under the FPS standard not only to *investments*, but also to *investors*, so that 'acquired values' of investors not properly constituting 'investments' (e.g. life, personal integrity, etc.) could be arguably protected under the relevant clause.[39] The notion of 'acquired values' could also be relevant for cases where the investor seeks protection of mere expectations: investors can indeed be required to show that they have actually acquired the rights in respect of which they invoke the FPS standard.[40]

Second, the expression 'acquired values' is not to be confused with the *doctrine of acquired rights*, which has been at the heart of sharp academic controversy in the context of postcolonial nationalization disputes.[41] The doctrine of acquired rights

---

[37] For an indicative example see: U.S. Model BIT (2012) art. 5(1).

[38] For an analysis of FPS treaty clauses see Chap. 14.

[39] For example, the BIT between Argentina and Mexico grants 'full legal protection to [admitted] investors *and* their investments'. Emphasis added. Author's translation. The original Spanish text reads 'plena protección legal a tales inversores [admitidos] y a sus inversiones'. Acuerdo entre el Gobierno de los Estados Unidos Mexicanos y el Gobierno de la República Argentina para la promoción y protección recíproca de las inversiones (adopted 13 November 1996, entered into force 22 June 1996) art. 3(2). For an arbitral tribunal considering this treaty clause and taking note of the fact that other treaties refer only to 'investments' see: Gemplus S.A., SLP S.A. and Gemplus Industrial S.A. de C.V. *v* Mexico, Award, ICSID Cases No. ARB(AF)/04/3 & ARB(AF)/04/4 (16 June 2010) [9.9]. In *Hesham Talaat M. Al-Warraq v Indonesia*, the tribunal gave some weight to the fact that the applicable treaty referred to the protection of 'investments' rather than to the protection of 'investors'. Cf. Hesham Talaat M. Al-Warraq *v* Indonesia (UNCITRAL), Final Award (15 December 2014) [627 and 629]. See also the arguments of the parties at paras 427 *et seq*. For an author discussing the difference between protection of 'investors' and 'investments' cf. Nartnirun Junngam, 'The Full Protection and Security Standard in International Investment Law: What and Who is Investment Fully[?] Protected and Secured From?' (2018) 7(1) AUBLR 1, 59 and 88 (also commenting on relevant investment cases).

[40] Marion Unglaube and Reinhard Unglaube *v* Costa Rica, Award, ICSID Cases No. ARB/01/1 and ARB/09/20 (16 May 2012) [287] ("If Claimants had succeeded in establishing by appropriate evidence that they possessed certain specific development rights [. . .] and that, as a result, the Respondent had assumed corresponding legal obligations, then failure of Respondent to accord protection to those rights might have constituted a valid claim based on failure to provide full protection and security."). Section 9.3.2 elaborates further on the issue of legitimate expectations.

[41] For authors expressing reluctance towards the 'doctrine of acquired rights' see: Muthucumaraswamy Sornarajah, *The International Law on Foreign Investment* (Cambridge University Press, New York 2010) 419-20; Muthucumaraswamy Sornarajah, *The Pursuit of National-ized Property* (Martinus Nijhoff Publishers, Dordrecht 1986) 112-3 and 212-3; Yilma Makonnen, 'State Succession in Africa: Selected Problems' (1986) 200(5) RCADI 93, 194-204. See also: Kate Miles, *The Origins of International Investment Law* (Cambridge University Press, New York 2013) 81-2.

can be summarized in the idea that, once alien has 'acquired' a right, there is an obligation to respect it, even if there is, for example, a change in government.[42] The notion of 'acquired right' that underlies this doctrine does not necessarily overlap with the concept of 'acquired values' as a defining element of the security obligation.

The doctrine of acquired rights usually refers to *private rights* and, particularly, *private pecuniary rights*.[43] Its application in respect of values that do not perfectly fit within these categories, such as rights derived from concession agreements (sometimes characterized as 'mixed rights') or administrative contracts, has been the subject of some controversy in the past.[44] Another contentious area would be, for example, 'good will and clientele'.[45]

---

[42]For a general presentation of the 'doctrine of acquired rights' see: Pierre Lalive, 'The Doctrine of Acquired Rights' in International and Comparative Law Center, *Rights and Duties of Private Investors Abroad* (Matthew Bender & Co., New York 1965) 145, 145 *et seq*.

[43]See, for example: Daniel Patrick O'Connell, *The Law of State Succession* (Cambridge University Press, Cambridge 2015) 81 [first edition: 1956] (defining acquired rights as 'any things, corporeal or incorporeal, properly vested in a natural or juristic person, and of an assessable monetary value' and further linking the term to the German notion of '*Vermögensrechte*'); Paul Guggenheim, *Lehrbuch des Völkerrechts* (Volume 1: Verlag für Recht und Gesellschaft, Basel 1948) 301-2 (referring solely to 'acquired property rights' or '*wohlerworbene Vermögensrechte*'); Pierre Lalive, 'The Doctrine of Acquired Rights' in International and Comparative Law Center, *Rights and Duties of Private Investors Abroad* (Matthew Bender & Co., New York 1965) 145, 183-9 and 200 (linking the doctrine of acquired rights to 'pecuniary rights' and providing a review of the literature on the subject). For a broader understanding of the notion of 'acquired rights' see: Georges Kaeckenbeeck, 'La protection internationale des droits acquis' (1937) 59(1) RCADI 317, 324-38.

[44]For authors considering that the 'doctrine of acquired rights' is applicable in respect of rights derived from concession agreements see: Daniel Patrick O'Connell, *The Law of State Succession* (Cambridge University Press, Cambridge 2015) 106 *et seq*. (particularly at p. 129) [first edition: 1956]; Pierre Lalive, 'The Doctrine of Acquired Rights' in International and Comparative Law Center, *Rights and Duties of Private Investors Abroad* (Matthew Bender & Co., New York 1965) 145, 185; Robert Jennings, 'State Contracts in International Law' (1961) 37 BYIL 156, 173-5. For authors expressing skepticism towards this use of the doctrine see: James Crawford, *Brownlie's Principles of Public International Law* (Oxford University Press, Oxford 2012) 628-9; Kate Miles, *The Origins of International Investment Law* (Cambridge University Press, New York 2013) 81-2; Muthucumaraswamy Sornarajah, *The Pursuit of Nationalized Property* (Martinus Nijhoff Publishers, Dordrecht 1986) 112-3; Yilma Makonnen, 'State Succession in Africa: Selected Problems' (1986) 200(5) RCADI 93, 200-4. On the question of concessions see also: Isi Foighel, *Nationalization. A Study in the Protection of Alien Property in International Law* (Stevens & Sons, London 1957) 73-4; Mohammed Bedjaoui, 'Sixth Report on Succession of States in respect of Matters other than Treaties (A/CN.4/267)' (20 May 1973) 2 *Yearbook of the International Law Commission – 1973* 3, 27 [15-17]. For an overview of the debate and, particularly, the discussions at the ILC, see: Anna Krueger, *Die Bindung der Dritten Welt an das postkoloniale Völkerrecht* (Springer, Heidelberg 2017) 335 *et seq*. As regards to administrative contracts, Daniel P. O'Connell famously argued that '[c]ontracts of this kind differ from concessionary contracts in lacking any interest in realty' (at p. 137). Following O'Connell, 'administrative contracts' typically concern 'ordinary governmental routine' (e.g. supply of goods) (at p. 137). O'Connell therefore believed that, in these cases, 'the contractual relationship expires with the change of sovereignty' (at p. 137).

[45]In respect of 'good will and clientele' see: Pierre Lalive, 'The Doctrine of Acquired Rights' in International and Comparative Law Center, *Rights and Duties of Private Investors Abroad* (Matthew Bender & Co., New York 1965) 145, 187-91.

Furthermore, academic debate on the doctrine of acquired rights has chiefly focused on whether new states and governments are bound to recognize property rights that have been previously acquired by alien nationals, particularly in the aftermath of a 'transfer of sovereignty'.[46] This debate, however interesting, is immaterial for the notion of 'acquired values' as an element of the customary FPS standard, and does not affect the normative structure of the security obligation.

8.3   Second Element. Covered Risks

The notion of security necessarily refers to a threat or risk.[47] Risks are definable by numerous criteria. For example, the risk of a house or building being entirely consumed by an intentional fire could be described, among others, by its origin (e.g. 'human' as opposed to 'natural' risks), by the threatened object (e.g. risks affecting immovable goods), or by its effects (e.g. risk of total/partial destruction of property). Therefore, the elucidation of the threats the FPS standard is directed against implies establishing, as a preliminary matter, some identification criterion. This chapter submits that the risks FPS refers to are identifiable by their *source* or *origin*. In this vein, a first section presents protection against private violence as the heart of the customary FPS standard.[48] A second section analyzes instances where the line between private and public conduct might not be entirely clear.[49] Finally, the last section considers the application of the FPS standard beyond the specific area of private and third party violence.[50]

The core of the argument is that the rationale of the FPS standard consists in the protection of foreign nationals against risks that do not originate in the host state's own acts. As will be shown throughout this chapter, while the most usual example of this type of risks is private violence, the same rationale is applicable in respect of other sources of risk (e.g. natural disasters, acts of other states, etc.).

---

[46]See: Pierre Lalive, 'The Doctrine of Acquired Rights' in International and Comparative Law Center, *Rights and Duties of Private Investors Abroad* (Matthew Bender & Co., New York 1965) 145, 162 *et seq.* See also Lalive's remarks on cases not involving a 'transfer of sovereignty' at pp. 172 *et seq.* For other authors addressing the issue see: Daniel Patrick O'Connell, *The Law of State Succession* (Cambridge University Press, Cambridge 2015) 81 *et seq.* [first edition: 1956]; Francisco García Amador, 'International Responsibility: Fourth Report by F. V. García Amador, Special Rapporteur (A/CN.4/119)' (26 February 1959) 2 *Yearbook of the International Law Commission – 1959* 1, 4 [9]; Georges Kaeckenbeeck, 'La protection internationale des droits acquis' (1937) 59(1) RCADI 317, 339-68; Mohammed Bedjaoui, 'Sixth Report on Succession of States in respect of Matters other than Treaties (A/CN.4/267)' (20 May 1973) 2 *Yearbook of the International Law Commission – 1973* 3, 27 [15-17].

[47]See Sect. 6.3.

[48]See Sect. 8.3.1.

[49]See Sect. 8.3.2.

[50]See Sect. 8.3.3.

8.3.1 The Heart of the Standard. Protection Against Private Violence

The most usual area of application of the FPS standard in the customary law of aliens is the prevention and redress of *private injuries* to the 'acquired values' of foreign citizens.[51] A growing number of investment arbitral decisions have held that protection against private actors or, more generally, third parties, represents and exhausts the substance of the FPS standard.[52]

A representative example would be the award rendered in *El Paso v Argentina* (2011).[53] In that case, an American energy company claimed that governmental measures adopted in response to the economic depression faced by Argentina in 2001 had severely affected its investments.[54] Among others, the investor invoked the FPS standard.[55] In this connection, it claimed that the FPS clause enshrined in the US-Argentinian BIT granted covered investors a greater degree of protection than the customary FPS standard.[56] According to the claimant, this treaty-based standard encompassed a guarantee of legal security in terms of predictable 'legal and regulatory frameworks'.[57] For its part, the Argentinian Government contended that the treaty did not provide for protection beyond the customary security obligation, and went on to advance the following argument:

> [T]he protection and security standard is no more than the traditional obligation to protect aliens under international customary law. It is a residual obligation provided for the cases in

---

[51]For the sake of clarity, this work characterizes an *injury* as private, natural or public, depending on the origin of the respective *threat* or *risk*. The notion of 'acquired values' has been discussed in detail in Sect. 8.2.

[52]The author has considered some of these decisions elsewhere. See: Sebastián Mantilla Blanco, *Justizielles Unrecht im internationalen Investitionsschutzrecht* (Nomos, Baden-Baden 2016) 130-1 (particularly at n. 401) (discussing the relationship between FPS and denial of justice, and briefly mentioning this and other arbitral approaches to the interpretation of the FPS standard); Max Baumgart and Sebastián Mantilla Blanco, 'Electrabel v. Ungarn: Aktuelle Entwicklungen beim Schutz von Auslandsinvestitionen nach dem Vertrag über die Energiecharta' (2016) 7(3) KSzW 179, 183 (specifically discussing the *Electrabel v Hungary* case and the interpretation of the ECT).

[53]El Paso Energy International Co. *v* Argentina, Award, ICSID Case No. ARB/03/15 (31 October 2011).

[54]For a detailed account of the facts see: El Paso Energy International Co. *v* Argentina, Award, ICSID Case No. ARB/03/15 (31 October 2011) [48 *et seq.*].

[55]El Paso Energy International Co. *v* Argentina, Award, ICSID Case No. ARB/03/15 (31 October 2011) [520].

[56]El Paso Energy International Co. *v* Argentina, Award, ICSID Case No. ARB/03/15 (31 October 2011) [520]. The FPS clause used the following language: "Investment shall at all times be accorded fair and equitable treatment, shall enjoy full protection and security and shall in no case be accorded treatment less than that required by international law." Treaty between the United States of America and the Argentine Republic concerning the Reciprocal Encouragement and Protection of Investment (adopted 14 November 1991, entered into force 20 October 1994) art. 2(a).

[57]El Paso Energy International Co. *v* Argentina, Award, ICSID Case No. ARB/03/15 (31 October 2011) [520].

which the challenged acts may not be in themselves attributed to the Government, but to a third party. In these assumptions, the Government must act diligently to prevent and penalize illegitimate acts by third parties damaging aliens.[58]

The state further alleged that, since the claim only referred to measures which originated in governmental conduct, Argentina could not have possibly breached its obligations under the FPS standard.[59] The tribunal agreed with the respondent's interpretation of the BIT:

> The BIT requires that Argentina provide "full protection and security" to El Paso's investment. The Tribunal considers that the full protection and security standard is no more than the traditional obligation to protect aliens under international customary law and that it is a residual obligation provided for those cases in which the acts challenged may not in themselves be attributed to the Government, but to a third party [. . .] El Paso does not complain about a violation by Argentina of an obligation of prevention or repression [. . .] all the impugned acts that allegedly violate the FPS standard are directly attributable to the GOA [Government of Argentina] and not to any third party. In the present case, none of the measures challenged by El Paso were taken by a third party; they all emanated from the State itself. Consequently, these measures should only be assessed in the light of the other BIT standards and cannot be examined from the angle of full protection and security. The conclusion is that there is no trace of a violation of the full protection and security standard by any of the GOA's measures impugned by the Claimant.[60]

This holding bears resemblance to the Partial Award issued some years earlier by a SCC tribunal in *Eastern Sugar v Czech Republic* (2007).[61] The dispute arose out of several measures aimed at the gradual adaptation of the Czech sugar industry to the European Union's relevant regulatory standards.[62] The investor, a Dutch company, alleged that the measures in question were inconsistent with the FPS clause of the Netherlands-Czech and Slovak Federal Republic BIT of 1991.[63] When considering the FPS standard, as embodied in Article 3(2) of the BIT, the arbitrators stated:

> As the tribunal understands it, the criterion in Art. 3(2) of the BIT concerns the obligation of the host state to protect the investor from *third* parties, in the cases cited by the Parties, mobs,

---

[58]El Paso Energy International Co. *v* Argentina, Award, ICSID Case No. ARB/03/15 (31 October 2011) [521].

[59]El Paso Energy International Co. *v* Argentina, Award, ICSID Case No. ARB/03/15 (31 October 2011) [521].

[60]El Paso Energy International Co. *v* Argentina, Award, ICSID Case No. ARB/03/15 (31 October 2011) [522 and 524-5].

[61]Eastern Sugar B.V. *v* Czech Republic, Partial Award, SCC Case No. 088/2004 (27 March 2007).

[62]Eastern Sugar B.V. *v* Czech Republic, Partial Award, SCC Case No. 088/2004 (27 March 2007) [222 *et seq.*].

[63]Eastern Sugar B.V. *v* Czech Republic, Partial Award, SCC Case No. 088/2004 (27 March 2007) [202]. Article 3(2) of the BIT read as follows: "More particularly, each Contracting Party shall accord to such investments full security and protection which in any case shall not be less than that accorded either to investments of its own investors or to investments of investors of any third State, whichever is more favorable to the investor concerned." Agreement between the Kingdom of the Netherlands and the Czech and Slovak Federal Republic on the Encouragement and Reciprocal Protection of Investments (adopted 24 April 1991, entered into force 1 October 1992) art. 3(2) (also quoted at para 201 of the Partial Award).

insurgents, rented thugs and others engaged in physical violence against the investor in violation of the state monopoly of physical force. Thus, where a host state fails to grant full protection and security, it fails to *prevent* actions by third parties that it is required to prevent [. . .] In the present case, for the most part, Eastern Sugar complains about acts committed by the Czech Republic itself, not acts of third parties. Eastern Sugar does not claim that disgruntled sugar beet growers were dumping sugar beet on the entrance stairs of Eastern Sugar, and policemen were looking with a grin on their face. Sugar beet was dumped on the stairs of the Ministry of Agriculture, and the Ministry of Agriculture then allegedly reacted with the Third Sugar Decree, targeting Eastern Sugar.[64]

Despite the fact that the *Eastern Sugar* tribunal did not elaborate on whether Article 3(3) of the BIT actually incorporated the *customary* FPS standard into the applicable IIA, the rationale of the *Eastern Sugar* award is strikingly similar to the findings in *El Paso v Argentina*.[65] The latter award would in turn influence the interpretation of the FPS standard advanced in *Electrabel v Hungary* (2012), an ECT case.[66] The *Electrabel* tribunal summarized its understanding of FPS in the following terms:

The Tribunal considers that, by promising full protection and security, Hungary assumed an obligation actively to create and maintain measures that promote security. *The necessary measures must be capable of protecting the covered investment against action by private persons.*[67]

In *Mobil v Argentina* (2013) the arbitrators agreed with the third party approach, as developed in *El Paso*.[68] In this vein, they held that FPS embodies the customary protection obligation of the law of aliens.[69] Accordingly, the tribunal stated that FPS has a 'residual' character and is applicable where 'the acts challenged cannot be

---

[64]Eastern Sugar B.V. *v* Czech Republic, Partial Award, SCC Case No. 088/2004 (27 March 2007) [203-4]. Similarly, in *Saluka v Czech Republic*, another tribunal linked the standard to 'civil strife and physical violence', but avoided limiting its scope to private violence. See: Saluka Investments *v* Czech Republic (UNCITRAL), Partial Award (17 March 2006) [483].

[65]Cf. Eastern Sugar B.V. *v* Czech Republic, Partial Award, SCC Case No. 088/2004 (27 March 2007) [203-4]; El Paso Energy International Co. *v* Argentina, Award, ICSID Case No. ARB/03/15 (31 October 2011) [522 and 524-5].

[66]On that occasion, after quoting in length the award rendered in *El Paso v Argentina*, the arbitrators stated: "The Tribunal generally concurs with the description given by the *El Paso* award on the scope of the FPS standard." Electrabel S.A. *v* Hungary, Decision on Jurisdiction, Applicable Law and Liability, ICSID Case No. ARB/07/19 (30 November 2012) [7.83].

[67]Emphasis added. Electrabel S.A. *v* Hungary, Decision on Jurisdiction, Applicable Law and Liability, ICSID Case No. ARB/07/19 (30 November 2012) [7.145]. For a discussion of the *Electrabel* decision see: Max Baumgart and Sebastián Mantilla Blanco, 'Electrabel v. Ungarn: Aktuelle Entwicklungen beim Schutz von Auslandsinvestitionen nach dem Vertrag über die Energiecharta' (2016) 7(3) KSzW 179, 183.

[68]Mobil Exploration and Development Argentina Inc. Suc. Argentina and Mobil Argentina S.A. *v* Argentina, Decision on Jurisdiction and Liability, ICSID Case No. ARB/04/16 (10 April 2013) [999].

[69]Mobil Exploration and Development Argentina Inc. Suc. Argentina and Mobil Argentina S.A. *v* Argentina, Decision on Jurisdiction and Liability, ICSID Case No. ARB/04/16 (10 April 2013) [999].

attributed to the Government, but to a third party'.[70] The arbitrators noted that the claims of the investors referred to acts of the state.[71] They therefore concluded that 'the measures should only be assessed in the light of other BIT standards and cannot be examined from the angle of full protection and security'.[72]

The decision rendered in *El Paso* also influenced the assessment of the FPS standard in *Oxus Gold v Uzbekistan* (2015).[73] In that case, the arbitrators relied on *El Paso* to hold that FPS refers to protection from acts of non-state actors.[74] In the tribunal's view, in cases involving conduct which is directly attributable to state agents, other standards of investment protection, such as FET, come into play.[75] The arbitrators recognized, however, that specific treaty clauses could deviate from the general standard's scope of application.[76] Similarly, in *CC/Devas v India* (2016), the tribunal held that '[t]he nature of that provision [FPS] has been aptly described in the *El Paso* award'.[77] The arbitrators consistently found that FPS only provides protection against acts of third parties, as opposed to acts that are directly attributable to the host state.[78]

In *Ulysseas v Ecuador* (2012), the tribunal limited the scope of application of the FPS standard to the prevention and redress of 'wrongful injuries inflicted by *third parties* to persons or property of aliens in its [the host state's] territory'.[79] In *Vannessa Holdings v Venezuela* (2013), the investor claimed that Venezuela breached the FPS standard on account of the Ministry of Energy and Mines' '[failure] to exercise its obligations of supervision and control',[80] as well as the absence of a proper investigation of claimant's complaints about an alleged

---

[70]Mobil Exploration and Development Argentina Inc. Suc. Argentina and Mobil Argentina S.A. *v* Argentina, Decision on Jurisdiction and Liability, ICSID Case No. ARB/04/16 (10 April 2013) [999].

[71]Mobil Exploration and Development Argentina Inc. Suc. Argentina and Mobil Argentina S.A. *v* Argentina, Decision on Jurisdiction and Liability, ICSID Case No. ARB/04/16 (10 April 2013) [1004].

[72]Mobil Exploration and Development Argentina Inc. Suc. Argentina and Mobil Argentina S.A. *v* Argentina, Decision on Jurisdiction and Liability, ICSID Case No. ARB/04/16 (10 April 2013) [1004].

[73]Oxus Gold *v* Uzbekistan (UNCITRAL), Final Award (17 December 2015) [353].

[74]Oxus Gold *v* Uzbekistan (UNCITRAL), Final Award (17 December 2015) [353 and 834-6].

[75]Oxus Gold *v* Uzbekistan (UNCITRAL), Final Award (17 December 2015) [353]. Cf. also Sect. 15.2.3.

[76]Oxus Gold *v* Uzbekistan (UNCITRAL), Final Award (17 December 2015) [353].

[77]CC/Devas (Mauritius) Ltd., Devas Employees Mauritius Private Ltd. and Telcom Devas Mauritius Ltd. *v* India (UNCITRAL), Award on Jurisdiction and Merits, PCA Case No. 2013-09 (25 July 2016) [499].

[78]CC/Devas (Mauritius) Ltd., Devas Employees Mauritius Private Ltd. and Telcom Devas Mauritius Ltd. *v* India (UNCITRAL), Award on Jurisdiction and Merits, PCA Case No. 2013-09 (25 July 2016) [499].

[79]Emphasis added. Ulysseas Inc. *v* Ecuador (UNCITRAL), Final Award (12 June 2012) [272].

[80]Vannessa Ventures Ltd. *v* Venezuela, Award, ICSID Case No. ARB(AF)04/6 (16 January 2013) [218].

expropriation.[81] In this vein, the investor explained that 'FPS applies to the protection by the State of foreign investments from actions of the State's officials and agencies'.[82] For its part, the respondent argued that FPS primarily refers to physical violence, and cannot be said to cover the kind of risks referred to by the investor.[83] The arbitrators dismissed the claim.[84] As regards to the interpretation of the FPS standard, they explained:

> [A]s far as the content of the FPS standard is concerned, the Tribunal is broadly in agreement that it applies at least in situations *where actions of third parties involving either physical violence or the disregard of legal rights occur* [. . .] While members of the Tribunal do not consider that there is a more precise formulation of the content of the standard that is universally accepted, they are in agreement that even the most demanding formulation of the FPS standard for which Claimant contended was not violated in the present case.[85]

A similar approach was followed a few years later in *Joseph Houben v Burundi* (2016), where the arbitrators reached the following conclusion:

> Il est généralement admis que le standard de sécurité et protection constantes, sans autre qualification, s'applique principalement pour protéger l'intégrité physique des investisseurs et de leurs investissements lorsqu'ils sont menacés *par l'action de tiers*, comme cela a été rappelé dans un certain nombre d'affaires CIRDI.[86]

In *Mercer v Canada* (2018), the arbitral tribunal held that the FPS clause in NAFTA 'addresses a third person causing harm to the Claimant, other than the Respondent (or persons whose acts are attributable to the Respondent under international law)'.[87] The arbitrators observed that an FPS claim would be unsuccessful since '[t]here is no malign third person in this case'.[88] In *Koch v Venezuela* (2017), the arbitral tribunal stated:

---

[81]Vannessa Ventures Ltd. *v* Venezuela, Award, ICSID Case No. ARB(AF)04/6 (16 January 2013) [218].

[82]Vannessa Ventures Ltd. *v* Venezuela, Award, ICSID Case No. ARB(AF)04/6 (16 January 2013) [218].

[83]Vannessa Ventures Ltd. *v* Venezuela, Award, ICSID Case No. ARB(AF)04/6 (16 January 2013) [220].

[84]Vannessa Ventures Ltd. *v* Venezuela, Award, ICSID Case No. ARB(AF)04/6 (16 January 2013) [237].

[85]Emphasis added. Vannessa Ventures Ltd. *v* Venezuela, Award, ICSID Case No. ARB(AF)04/6 (16 January 2013) [223].

[86]Emphasis added. Joseph Houben *v* Burundi, Sentence, ICSID Case No. ARB/13/7 (12 January 2016) [157] (also quoting *El Paso v Argentina* at para 159). The arbitrators however observed that the FPS clause of the Belgium-Burundi BIT could, at least in theory, reach beyond the FPS standard's traditional core (at para 160). In any case, the tribunal did not consider the latter question to be relevant for the resolution of the dispute (at para 160). It is worth noting that the limitation of the FPS standard to injuries caused by third parties has become an increasingly usual line of argument, which is typically pursued by respondent states in investment arbitrations. For a recent example see: Eurogas Inc. and Belmont Resources Inc. *v* Slovakia, Award, ICSID Case No. ARB/14/14 (18 August 2017) [365].

[87]Mercer International Inc. *v* Canada, Award, ICSID Case No. ARB(AF)/12/3 (6 March 2018) [7.80].

[88]Mercer International Inc. *v* Canada, Award, ICSID Case No. ARB(AF)/12/3 (6 March 2018) [7.80].

Under its meaning well-settled in customary international law, the FPS standard is confined to physical protection of aliens against acts of third persons not attributable to the host State. As such, it can give rise to a limited form of liability where the host State has failed to exercise reasonable diligence to prevent such acts.[89]

Other tribunals, albeit not *expressly* restricting the scope of the FPS standard to private violence, have drawn special attention to the public or private origin of the wrongdoings at stake.[90] An early UNCTAD report on investment treaties (1998) recognized that what is special about the FPS standard is that it requires action against private threats; nonetheless, the report also stated that this somewhat peculiar aspect of the standard does not exhaust its content:

> [T]he term "full protection and security" connotes the assurance of full protection and security for foreign investors as contemplated or required by customary international law. At the same time, the clause on *full protection and security is unusual in that it contemplates protecting investment against private as well as public action*, that is, the clause requires that the host country should exercise reasonable care to protect the investment against injury by private parties.[91]

---

[89]Koch Minerals SÁRL and Koch Nitrogen International SÁRL *v* Venezuela, Award, ICSID Case No. ARB/11/19 (30 October 2017) [8.46].

[90]Gemplus S.A., SLP S.A. and Gemplus Industrial S.A. de C.V. *v* Mexico, Award, ICSID Cases No. ARB(AF)/04/3 & ARB(AF)/04/4 (16 June 2010) [9.11-9.12] (basing the distinction between FPS and other treaty-based standards on the fact that FPS clauses '*also* involve the host state protecting the investment from a third party' and observing that 'the harm alleged by the Claimants is attributed to the Respondent itself and not to any third party' – emphasis added); OI European Group B.V. *v* Venezuela, Award, ICSID Case No. ARB/11/25 (10 March 2015) [580] (stating that 'The FPP guarantee entails an obligation by the State to deploy its police force or take other coercive measures to prevent *others* from disrupting the peaceful possession and enjoyment of the investment' – emphasis added); SAUR International S.A. *v* Argentina, Décision sur la compétence et sur la responsabilité, ICSID Case No. ARB/04/4 (6 June 2012) [500] (referring to the notions of 'violence physique' and 'troubles civils'); Sergei Paushok et al. *v* Mongolia (UNCITRAL), Award on Jurisdiction and Liability (28 April 2011) [327] (observing that 'in the present instance there is no claim of a negative action taken by *third parties* that the State is accused of not having prevented' – emphasis added); Suez Sociedad General de Aguas de Barcelona S.A. and Vivendi Universal S.A. *v* Argentina, Decision on Liability, ICSID Case No. ARB/03/19 (30 July 2010) [165] ("*Traditionally*, the cases applying full protection and security have dealt with injuries to physical assets of investors committed by *third parties* where host governments have failed to exercise due diligence in preventing the damage or punishing the perpetrators. In the present case, the Claimants are attempting to apply the protection and security clause to a different type of situation. They do not complain that *third parties* have injured their physical assets or persons, *as in the traditional protection and security case*" – emphasis added). The private or public origin of the original injury has also been considered in cases pertaining to alleged failures to provide adequate means of redress. For some representative examples see: Frontier Petroleum Ltd. *v* Czech Republic (UNCITRAL), Final Award (12 November 2010) [263 and 296]; Jan Oostergetel and Theodora Laurentius *v* Slovakia (UNCITRAL), Final Award (23 April 2012) [226]. Section 10.3 provides a detailed analysis of the application of the FPS standard to failures of redress.

[91]Emphasis added. UNCTAD, *Bilateral Investment Treaties in the Mid-1990s* (United Nations, New York/Geneva 1998) 55. See also the investor's argument in *Rumeli Telekom v Kazakhstan*: Rumeli Telekom A.S. and Telsim Mobil Telekomunikasyon Hizmetleri A.S. *v* Kazakhstan, Award, ICSID Case No. ARB/05/16 (29 July 2008) [660] (relying on UNCTAD's report and arguing that the private or public origin of an injury is 'inconsequential' for the application of the FPS standard; the tribunal did not address this particular argument in detail).

Arbitral tribunals have sometimes expressed doubts as to the accuracy of the definition of FPS as protection against private or third-party conduct.[92] Academic opinions are also divided in this regard. On the one side of the spectrum, a few studies have expressed some support or, at least, sympathy, for this theory.[93] On the other side of the spectrum, some scholars have characterized this understanding of

---

[92]AES Summit Generation Ltd. and AES-Tisza Erömü Kft. *v* Hungary, Award, ICSID Case No. ARB/07/22 (23 September 2010) [13.3.2] ("In the Tribunal's view, the duty to provide most constant protection and security to investments is a state's obligation to take reasonable steps to protect its investors – or to enable its investors to protect themselves – against harassment *by third parties and/or state actors*" – emphasis added); Biwater Gauff Ltd. *v* Tanzania, Award, ICSID Case No. ARB/05/22 (24 July 2008) [730] ("[t]he Arbitral Tribunal also does not consider that the "full security" standard is limited to a State's failure to prevent actions by third parties, *but also extends to actions by organs and representatives of the State itself*. That is also implied by the term "full," as well as the purposes of the BIT and the Wena and AMT awards" – emphasis added); Emilio Agustín Maffezini *v* Spain, Award, ICSID Case No. ARB/97/7 (13 November 2000) [83] (stating that 'lack of transparency' in a loan operation, which was held to be attributable to the host state, contravened Spain's protection obligation under the applicable BIT; the tribunal did not however make any reference whatsoever to the *customary* security obligation); Frontier Petroleum Ltd. *v* Czech Republic (UNCITRAL), Final Award (12 November 2010) [261] ("the host state is under an obligation to take active measures to protect the investment from adverse effects that stem *from private parties or from the host state and its organs*" – emphasis added); Isolux Netherlands B.V. *v* Spain, Laudo, SCC Case No. V 2013/153 (17 July 2016) [817] (stating that FPS protects investors against both 'state agents' ['*agentes del Estado*'] and 'third parties' ['*terceros*']); Parkerings-Compagniet AS *v* Lithuania, Award, ICSID Case No. ARB/05/8 (11 September 2007) [355] ("The injury could be committed *either by the host State*, or by its agencies *or by an individual*" – emphasis added); Tenaris S.A. and Talta-Trading E Marketing Sociedade Unipessoal Lda. *v* Venezuela, Award, ICSID Case No. ARB/11/26 (29 January 2016) [439] ("The Tribunal accepts Claimants' submission that the obligation is *not exclusively* limited to physical protection from third parties" – emphasis added).

[93]See, for example: August Reinisch, 'Internationales Investitionsschutzrecht' in Christian Tietje (ed), *Internationales Wirtschaftsrecht* (De Gruyter, Berlin 2015) 398, 417; Jörn Griebel, *Internationales Investitionsrecht* (C.H. Beck, Munich 2008) 74-5; Stephan Hobe, *Einführung in das Völkerrecht* (A. Francke Verlag, Tübingen 2014) 389. Cf. also Robert Reyes Landicho, 'Enforcing a State's International IP Obligations through Investment Law Standards of Protection – An Ill-Fated Romance' in Ian Laird, Borzu Sabahi, Frédéric Sourgens and Todd Weiler (eds), *Investment Treaty Arbitration and International Law* (Juris Net, Huntington NY 2018) 111, 126-7. Other authors express some sympathy for this approach, but do not exclude the applicability of FPS in respect of public violence. For an indicative example see: Matthias Herdegen, *Principles of International Economic Law* (Oxford University Press, New York 2016) 466 (noting at p. 466 that '[a]s a rule, full protection and security refers to protection by the host State's authorities against physical violence and other threats, particularly from non-State actors', and also referring to public violence at p. 468); Stephan Schill, *The Multilateralization of International Investment Law* (Cambridge University Press, Cambridge 2009) 80-1 (addressing the issue in specific connection with the distinction between the FPS standard and the FET standard). For a much more cautious view cf. Nartnirun Junngam, 'The Full Protection and Security Standard in International Investment Law: What and Who is Investment Fully[?] Protected and Secured From?' (2018) 7(1) AUBLR 1, 93-4 (stating that 'it might be advisable to limit an application of the FPS standard only to harms perpetrated by third parties' in order to prevent inconsistencies, but arguing that the third-party approach does not correspond with the historical origins and current scope of the standard, which covers both private and public harm).

the FPS standard as 'a stray position'.[94] In this vein, it has been further observed that 'this approach of limiting the full protection and security standard to third parties alone is remarkable, as it does not have foundation in the writings of scholars of international law'.[95] In his analysis of the FPS standard, Kenneth J. Vandevelde advanced a teleological argument against this approach:

> This reading [...] clearly is too narrow [...] *The purpose of this standard is to protect the investment, not to protect the host state's monopoly on the use of force.* Indeed, for purposes of investment protection, the situation where the state itself attacks the investment may be more worrisome than where the attacks come from private third parties, precisely because the state does have a monopoly on the use of force. Private parties are in some measure deterred from physical assaults on foreign investment by the knowledge that they would be acting outside the law. If the state itself undertakes to destroy the physical security of an investment, no countervailing force exists to deter it. *Investment security is not promoted by a rule that simply reserves to the state the power to undermine the security of foreign investment.*[96]

Vandevelde's critique is at first sight appealing. On a closer look, however, it becomes apparent that the argument is based on two false assumptions. First, it is not true that the restriction of FPS to private violence has the effect of turning the standard into a tool for the protection of 'the host state's monopoly on the use of force'.[97] The interpretation advanced in *El Paso* and similar awards simply limits the risks covered by the standard on account of their source.[98] Nothing more. Neither is the host state turned into the beneficiary of protection, nor does its 'monopoly of force' become the object of protection. The host state remains the *provider* of security, and the investor the *beneficiary* of security. It could even be said that the ultimate effect of this approach is quite the opposite of that envisaged by Vandevelde: the interpretation adopted in *El Paso* puts the host state's 'monopoly of force' at the service of foreign investors.

Second, Vandevelde seems to assume that limiting FPS to private violence leaves investments unprotected from public violence.[99] To say that some conduct falls outside the scope of a specific international obligation, however, is not to say that

---

[94]Ralph Alexander Lorz, 'Protection and Security (Including the NAFTA Approach)' in Marc Bungenberg, Jörn Griebel, Stephan Hobe and August Reinisch (eds), International Investment Law (Nomos, Baden-Baden 2015) 764, 776.

[95]Finnur Magnússon, Full Protection and Security in International Law (University of Vienna, Vienna 2012) 154.

[96]Emphasis added. Kenneth Vandevelde, *Bilateral Investment Treaties: History, Policy, and Interpretation* (Oxford University Press, New York 2010) 252.

[97]Kenneth Vandevelde, *Bilateral Investment Treaties: History, Policy, and Interpretation* (Oxford University Press, New York 2010) 252.

[98]Cf. El Paso Energy International Co. *v* Argentina, Award, ICSID Case No. ARB/03/15 (31 October 2011) [522 and 524-5].

[99]Cf. Kenneth Vandevelde, *Bilateral Investment Treaties: History, Policy, and Interpretation* (Oxford University Press, New York 2010) 252. For a similar view see: Elisabeth Zeitler, 'Full Protection and Security' in Stephan Schill (ed), *International Investment Law and Comparative Public Law* (Oxford University Press, New York 2010) 183, 192.

such conduct is not internationally wrongful; public violence could fit into *other* standards of investment protection.[100] It is therefore simply not true that this interpretation 'reserves to the state the power to undermine the security of foreign investment', as Vandevelde suggests.[101]

Notwithstanding this widespread skepticism, and however 'remarkable',[102] 'stray'[103] or 'narrow'[104] the restriction of FPS to private or third party violence might appear to be, this view truly captures the quintessence of the customary standard.

Many contemporary instances of application of the FPS standard have referred to injurious actions committed by private parties.[105] Furthermore, it is precisely in

---

[100]See also: Sebastián Mantilla Blanco, *Justizielles Unrecht im internationalen Investitionsschutzrecht* (Nomos, Baden-Baden 2016) 130 n. 401 (briefly addressing the issue).

[101]Kenneth Vandevelde, *Bilateral Investment Treaties: History, Policy, and Interpretation* (Oxford University Press, New York 2010) 252.

[102]Finnur Magnússon, Full Protection and Security in International Law (University of Vienna, Vienna 2012) 154.

[103]Ralph Alexander Lorz, 'Protection and Security (Including the NAFTA Approach)' in Marc Bungenberg, Jörn Griebel, Stephan Hobe and August Reinisch (eds), International Investment Law (Nomos, Baden-Baden 2015) 764, 776.

[104]Kenneth Vandevelde, *Bilateral Investment Treaties: History, Policy, and Interpretation* (Oxford University Press, New York 2010) 252.

[105]Adel A Hamadi Al Tamini v Oman, Award, ICSID Case No. ARB/11/33 (3 November 2015) [448-52] (alleged failure to prevent the theft of equipment and other property); Bernhard Friedrich Arnd Rüdiger von Pezold et al. v Zimbabwe, Award, ICSID Case No. ARB/10/15 (28 July 2015) [3, 110-5 and 582 et seq.] (alleged want of diligence in the removal of illegal settlers from private property); Frontier Petroleum Ltd. v Czech Republic (UNCITRAL), Final Award (12 November 2010) [26-31, 260-73, 296, 417, 431-8, 452, 464-8] (failure to enforce a commercial arbitral award against locally incorporated private companies, to prosecute a private individual, and to grant the investor protection against private debtors); Gea Group Aktiengesellschaft v Ukraine, Award, ICSID Case No. ARB/08/16 (31 March 2011) [211-2, 239-67] (failure to investigate a series of criminal offences; it should be however noted that, in this case, the private or public nature of some of the original injuries was contentious); Jan Oostergetel and Theodora Laurentius v Slovakia (UNCITRAL), Final Award (23 April 2012) [94-5, 226, 305-8 and 341] (alleged denial of justice in bankruptcy proceedings involving private creditors); Joseph Houben v Burundi, Sentence, ICSID Case No. ARB/13/7 (12 January 2016) [157-79] (alleged failure to protect the investor's property against illegal settlers); LESI S.p.A. and ASTALDI S.p.A. v Algeria, Sentence, ICSID Case No. ARB/05/3 (12 November 2008) [11 et seq. and 152-4] (private threats to the investment's physical security which were attributable to Islamic extremist groups); Mamidoil Jetoil Greek Petroleum Products Societe S.A. v Albania, Award, ICSID Case No. ARB/11/24 (30 March 2015) [819-29] (case concerning 'smuggling, fuel adulteration and tax evasion'); MNSS B.V. and Recupero Credito Acciaio N.V. v Montenegro, Award, ICSID Case No. ARB(AF)/12/8 (4 May 2016) [348-56] (physical occupation of premises by members of a labor union); Noble Ventures v Romania, Award, ICSID Case No. ARB/01/11 (12 October 2005) [160-7] (protests, intimidations and theft of property by private individuals); Pantechniki S.A. Contractors & Engineers v Albania, Award, ICSID Case No. ARB/07/21 (30 July 2009) [1-2, 71-84] (plundering of an investor's road work site by private looters in the context of civil disturbances); Parkerings-Compagniet AS v Lithuania, Award, ICSID Case No. ARB/05/8 (11 September 2007) [354-61] (private acts of vandalism; however, in this case the Claimant also invoked the FPS standard in

cases concerning private violence that the standard of 'protection and security' has taken the center stage in investment arbitration proceedings.[106] In cases involving damages inflicted by state organs, tribunals tend to focus on other standards of investment protection, such as fair and equitable treatment or protection against expropriation.[107]

---

respect of certain public acts); Plama Consortium Ltd. *v* Bulgaria, Award, ICSID Case No. ARB/03/24 (27 August 2008) [229, 236, 248-55 and 325] (actions of the syndics appointed in bankruptcy proceedings, and riot violence allegedly incited by one of them; while the syndics were held not to be organs of the state, it should be noted that the FPS standard was also invoked in respect of public conduct); Tecnicas Medioambientales TECMED S.A. *v* Mexico, Award, ICSID Case No. ARB (AF)/00/2 (29 May 2003) [175-82] (alleged support, promotion and encouragement of social movements against the operation of the investor's landfill of industrial waste, and alleged failure by Mexican competent judicial and police authorities to take action against protestors); Tenaris S.A. and Talta-Trading E Marketing Sociedade Unipessoal Lda. *v* Venezuela, Award, ICSID Case No. ARB/11/26 (29 January 2016) [447] (alleged collusion between public authorities and a labor union, which, according to the Claimant, had 'spearheaded a radical and violent movement' against the investor); Toto Costruzioni Generali S.p.A. *v* Lebanon, Award, ICSID Case No. ARB/07/12 (7 June 2012) [171, 195-206 and 226-30] (failure to remove a group of protesters, whose properties had been expropriated by the host state, who blocked access to the investor's construction site; the case also was also concerned with the presence of foreign troops allegedly preventing the investor from initiating a construction project); Wena Hotels Ltd. *v* Egypt, Award, ICSID Case No. ARB/98/4 (8 December 2000) [17, 80-95] (illegal seizure of hotel facilities by officers of the Egyptian Hotel Company, a state-owned company with an independent legal personality and essentially commercial functions; the acts of the said entity were held not to be directly attributable to the state). On the question of attribution in the *Wena v Egypt* case see: Wena Hotels Ltd. *v* Egypt, Decision on Annulment, ICSID Case No. ARB/98/4 (5 February 2002) [30-5]. It should be noted that, albeit most of these claims were ultimately unsuccessful, in none of them did the arbitrators deny the applicability of the FPS standard to cases involving private violence.

[106]For an indicative example see: William Ralph Clayton, William Richard Clayton, Douglas Clayton, Daniel Clayton and Bilicon of Delaware Inc. *v* Canada (UNCITRAL), Award on Jurisdiction and Liability, PCA Case No. 2009-05 (17 March 2015) [360, 376, 392-3, 422-3, 427 *et seq.* and 742(a)(ii)] (while the tribunal declared a breach of NAFTA Article 1105, including FET and FPS, its legal analysis largely focused on the FET standard and the protection of legitimate expectations; the parties had submitted separate arguments about the FPS standard).

[107]Section 15.2 discusses the relationship between the FPS standard and the FET standard in detail. Section 15.3 considers the relationship between FPS and expropriation.

Claims invoking the FPS standard in respect of actions that were directly attributable to state organs have been usually unsuccessful, though in most of the cases the origin of the injury was not the reason (or main reason) for the dismissal of the FPS claim.[108] The linkage of the customary security obligation to the

---

[108] ADF v United States, Award, ICSID Case No. ARB(AF)/00/1 (9 January 2003) [182-6 and 199] (regulatory and administrative restrictions to the use of imported steel in highway projects funded by the U.S. Federal Government); AES Summit Generation Ltd. and AES-Tisza Erömü Kft. v Hungary, Award, ICSID Case No. ARB/07/22 (23 September 2010) [13.3 and 16.1] (reintroduction of regulated pricing in the energy sector); Alex Genin, Eastern Credit Ltd. and A.S. Baltoil v Estonia, Award, ICSID Case No. ARB/99/2 (25 June 2001) [66-71, 336-47 and 385] (complicity of the Bank of Estonia in a series of misrepresentations in the balance sheet of a local financial institution; while the claim was presented as a violation to the obligation to provide protection *and* fair and equitable treatment, the tribunal largely focused on the FET standard. The case also involved a harassment claim [at paras 95-7 and 374-5] and an alleged failure to provide means of asserting rights [at paras 92-4], which were, however, not presented in terms of failures to provide protection); BG Group v Argentina (UNCITRAL), Final Award (24 December 2007) [323-8] (concerning measures adopted by Argentina in the aftermath of the 2001 financial crisis); CC/Devas (Mauritius) Ltd., Devas Employees Mauritius Private Ltd. and Telcom Devas Mauritius Ltd. v India (UNCITRAL), Award on Jurisdiction and Merits, PCA Case No. 2013-09 (25 July 2016) [491 and 500] (acts of the Cabinet of India and other governmental actions, which allegedly affected and devaluated the investment); Deutsche Bank AG v Sri Lanka, Award, ICSID Case No. ARB/09/02 (31 October 2012) [526-38] (alleged 'coordinated efforts' of the Sri Lankan Central Bank and the local Supreme Court for preventing a state-owned company from making payments due under a Hedging Agreement); Enron Corp. and Ponderosa Assets L.P. v Argentina, Award, ICSID Case No. ARB/01/3 (22 May 2007) [284-7] (measures adopted by Argentina in the aftermath of the 2001 financial crisis); Eureko B.V. v Poland (*Ad Hoc* Arbitration), Partial Award (19 August 2005) [236-7] (harassment by local authorities of the investor's representatives); Gemplus S.A., SLP S.A. and Gemplus Industrial S.A. de C.V. v Mexico, Award, ICSID Cases No. ARB(AF)/04/3 & ARB(AF)/04/4 (16 June 2010) [9.11-9.13] (administrative measures concerning a concession contract); Gold Reserve Inc. v Venezuela, Award, ICSID Case No. ARB (AF)/09/1 (22 September 2014) [622-3] (termination of a concession agreement and seizure of the investor's assets); Isolux Netherlands B.V. v Spain, Laudo, SCC Case No. V 2013/153 (17 July 2016) [816-9] (modification of the legislative framework applicable to the Spanish solar energy sector); Iurii Bogdanov et al. v Moldova (SCC), Arbitral Award (22 September 2005) [1.2.3 and 4.2.3] (regulatory and administrative measures restricting the state-owned shares eligible for being assigned as 'compensation shares' for the value of the assets transferred by private investors under a privatization contract); Jan de Nul N.V. and Dredging International N.V. v Egypt, Award, ICSID Case No. ARB/04/13 (6 November 2008) [266-70] (measures attributable to the Suez Canal Authority, a Egyptian state entity, and possible omissions of the Prime Minister in respect of the acts of the said Authority); M.C.I. Power Group L.C. and New Turbine Inc. v Ecuador, Award, ICSID Case No. ARB/03/6 (31 July 2007) [245-6 and 373] (bad faith in the liquidation of a state contract, cancellation of an operating permit, and alleged harassment of the investor by state agents); Mobil Exploration and Development Argentina Inc. Suc. Argentina and Mobil Argentina S.A. v Argentina, Decision on Jurisdiction and Liability, ICSID Case No. ARB/04/16 (10 April 2013) [60 et seq. and 988-1005] (regulatory measures and alleged acts of harassment and coercion affecting a concession in the natural gas sector); Mondev International v United States, Award, ICSID Case No. ARB(AF)/99/2 (11 October 2002) [140, 144, 147, 150-7] (statutory immunity of the Boston Redevelopment Authority as a bar to the right of access to the local justice system); OI European Group B.V. v Venezuela, Award, ICSID Case No. ARB/11/25 (10 March 2015) [571-81] (expropriation of two major glass production plants in Venezuela); Oxus Gold v Uzbekistan (UNCITRAL), Final Award (17 December 2015) [348 *et seq.* and 834 *et seq.*] (FPS claims involving the revocation of concession rights for the development of a mine, criminal enquiries

and modification of tax rules); Parkerings-Compagniet AS *v* Lithuania, Award, ICSID Case No. ARB/05/8 (11 September 2007) [358-9] (alleged omissions of the Prime Minister in respect of acts attributable to municipal authorities); Plama Consortium Ltd. *v* Bulgaria, Award, ICSID Case No. ARB/03/24 (27 August 2008) [194, 271, 277, 325] (alleged breaches of a privatization agreement and local environmental regulations, amendment of local environmental regulations, measures concerning taxation on paper profits, privatization of a state company allegedly leading the investor to incur significant losses, and measures affecting the relationship between the investor and a state-owned commercial bank that was subsequently privatized); PSEG Global Inc. and Konya Ilgin Elektrik Üretim ve Ticaret Limited Şirketi *v* Turkey, Award, ICSID Case No. ARB/02/5 (19 January 2007) [257-9] (adverse effects of certain legal amendments and administrative actions); Ronald Lauder *v* Czech Republic (UNCITRAL), Final Award (3 September 2001) [305-14] (reform of the Czech domestic media law, initiation of administrative procedures against a joint company with participation of the foreign investor, and alleged failure to intervene in a dispute between the investor and a private television broadcasting company); Rumeli Telekom A.S. and Telsim Mobil Telekomunikasyon Hizmetleri A.S. *v* Kazakhstan, Award, ICSID Case No. ARB/05/16 (29 July 2008) [662, 669-70] (alleged collusion between a private individual and state organs against the investor; official security agents were said to have obstructed the investor's access to a locally-incorporated company's physical premises and information); Rusoro Mining Ltd. *v* Venezuela, Award, ICSID Case No. ARB(AF)/12/5 (22 August 2016) [542-54] (regulatory measures concerning the Venezuelan gold industry and the local currency market); Saluka Investments *v* Czech Republic (UNCITRAL), Partial Award (17 March 2006) [485-96 and 505] (invasive inspection of the investor's offices and freezing of the foreign investor's shareholding in a privatized financial institution); SAUR International S.A. *v* Argentina, Décision sur la compétence et sur la responsabilité, ICSID Case No. ARB/04/4 (6 June 2012) [499-500 and 508-11] (enforcement of an administrative intervention ['*intervention administrative*'] order by Argentinean police officers); Sempra Energy International *v* Argentina, Award, ICSID Case No. ARB/02/16 (28 September 2007) [321-4] (measures adopted in the aftermath of the 2001 Argentinian financial crisis; it should however be noted that the *Sempra* award was annulled in 2010 for reasons related to the state of necessity exception); Sergei Paushok et al. *v* Mongolia (UNCITRAL), Award on Jurisdiction and Liability (28 April 2011) [322-8] (enactment and enforcement of a law imposing windfall taxes on certain commodities); Suez Sociedad General de Aguas de Barcelona S.A. and Vivendi Universal S.A. *v* Argentina, Decision on Liability, ICSID Case No. ARB/03/19 (30 July 2010) [158-79] (measures adopted in the aftermath of the 2001 Argentinian financial crisis affecting a waste water treatment concession); Spyridon Roussalis *v* Romania, Award, ICSID Case No. ARB/06/1 (7 December 2011) [147-57, 259-89, 319-22, 358-9, 362 and 609] (intervention of the General Prosecutor before the local Supreme Court in support of a request filed by a government agency to vacate a lower court decision favorable to the investor, and alleged lack of impartiality in municipal court proceedings, among other measures); Tokios Tokelés *v* Ukraine, Award, ICSID Case No. ARB/02/18 (26 July 2007) [4, 12-4, 31 *et seq.*, 85-6, 113-6, 123 *et seq.* and 147] (the case, as described at para 4 of the award, concerned '[an alleged] long-running campaign of oppression by State agencies, instigated for political reasons by a person or persons in high authority, and taking the shape of numerous episodes of unjustified interference [...] under the guise of investigations into breaches of Ukrainian economic laws'). In some cases, the arbitral tribunal acknowledged the existence of a possible issue of attribution, but left the question open and dismissed the FPS claim on other grounds. For an indicative example see: Mohammad Ammar Al-Bahloul *v* Tajikistan, Partial Award on Jurisdiction and Liability, SCC Case No. V 064/2008 (9 September 2009) [173 and 245] (considering that, regardless of the issue of attribution, the claim would fail for lack of evidence). For an example of a successful FPS claim regarding public action see: CME Czech Republic B.V. *v* Czech Republic (UNCITRAL), Partial Award (13 September 2001) [613] (regulatory and administrative measures having an indirect effect over a private contractual relationship). Cf. also Sect. 9.3.1.

notion of private violence implies building a bridge between the contemporary FPS standard and a rich array of state and arbitral practice from the late nineteenth century onwards. Cases concerning private injuries to aliens have indeed been at the core of international disputes for centuries. Claims have referred to ordinary criminal offences,[109] acts of brigandage and banditry,[110] damages occurred in the course of inmate disturbances,[111] mob violence,[112] acts of rebels or

---

[109]See, for example: *Elvira Almaguer v Mexico* (13 May 1929) IV RIAA 523, 523-9 (particularly at p. 525); *George Adams Kennedy v Mexico* (6 May 1927) IV RIAA 194, 194-203 (particularly at p. 199 para 8); *Irma Eitelman Miller et al. v Mexico* (26 September 1928) IV RIAA 336, 336-7 [1-5]; *J. J. Boyd v Mexico* (12 October 1928) IV RIAA 380, 380-1 (particularly at p. 381); *John Chase v Mexico* (26 September 1928) IV RIAA 337, 337-9; *Laura M.B. Janes et al. v Mexico* (16 November 1925) IV RIAA 82, 82-98 (particularly at pp. 86-7 paras 19-20); *LFH Neer and Pauline Neer v Mexico* (15 October 1926) IV RIAA 60, 60-6 (particularly at p. 60 para 3); *Louise O. Canahl v Mexico* (15 October 1928) IV RIAA 389, 389-91; *Sarah Ann Gorham v Mexico* (24 October 1930) IV RIAA 639, 639-45 (particularly at p. 645); *Sophie B. Sturtevant v Mexico* (5 November 1930) IV RIAA 665-9 (particularly at p. 667); *Vernon Monroe Greenlaw v Mexico* (24 October 1930) IV RIAA 626, 626-32 (particularly at p. 632).

[110]A historically significant example would be the case of the kidnapping of Ellen Stone, a U.S. national, in the Ottoman Empire. For the diplomatic correspondence on the case see: 'Turkey. Abduction by Brigands, Ransom, and Release of Miss Ellen M. Stone, An American Missionary' (5 September 1901 – 8 May 1902) *Papers relating to the Foreign Relations of the United States with the Annual Message of the President* (Government Printing Office, Washington 1902) 997, 997-1023. See also: Teresa Carpenter, *The Miss Stone Affair. America's First Modern Hostage Crisis* (Simon & Schuster, New York 2003). For a legal analysis of the case in light of the customary law of aliens see: George Phillimore, 'Current Notes on International Law' (1902) 27 Law Mag. & Rev. Quart. Rev. Juris. 330, 337-8. For an additional example see: 'Correspondence between Great Britain, Italy, Turkey and Greece, respecting the Capture and Murder by Brigands of the Secretaries of the British and Italian Legations at Athens (Mr. Herbert and Count de Boyl) and of other British Subjects' (1870-1871) 65 St. Pap. 667, 667-723. For a representative example of arbitral practice in this area see: *Frederick Wipperman v United States of Venezuela* (10 July 1890) *United States and Venezuelan Claims Commission. Opinions Delivered by the Commissioners in the Principal Cases* (Gibson Bros., Washington 1890) 132. See also: *Christina Patton v Mexico* (8 July 1931) V RIAA 224, 224-9; *J. J. Boyd v Mexico* (12 October 1928) IV RIAA 380, 380-1 (particularly at p. 380); *William E. Bowerman and Messrs. Burberry's Ltd. v Mexico* (15 February 1930) V RIAA 104, 104-8 (particularly at p. 106 para 7).

[111]*Frederick H. Lovett et al. v. Chile* (10 April 1894) XXIX RIAA 319, 319-21.

[112]For academic writings specifically dealing with international responsibility for mob injuries and providing an account of the case law on the subject see: Ernest Wilson Huffcut, 'International Liability for Mob Injuries' (1891) 2 Annals of the Amer. Acad. of Pol. and Soc. Science 69, 69-84; Francis Mitchell, 'International Liability for Mob Injuries' (1900) 34 Am. L. Rev. 709, 709-21; John Bassett Moore, 'The Responsibility of Governments for Mob Violence' (1892) 5 Columb. L. T. 211, 211-5; Julius Goebel, 'The International Responsibility of States for Injuries Sustained by Aliens on Account of Mob Violence, Insurrections and Civil Wars' (1914) 8 AJIL 802, 812-52. For some indicative examples of adjudicatory practice in this area see: *Cecelia Dexter Baldwin et al. v Panama* (26 June 1933) VI RIAA 328, 328-33; *Charlie R. Richeson et al. v Panama* (26 June 1933) VI RIAA 325, 325-8; *Hampden Osborne Banks et al. v Panama* (29 June 1933) VI RIAA 349-52; *Home Frontier and Foreign Missionary Society of the United Brethren in Christ v Great Britain* (18 December 1929) VI RIAA 42, 42-4; *Jennie L. Underhill Case* (1903-5) IX RIAA 158, 159-60; *Thomas H. Youmans v Mexico* (23 November 1926) IV RIAA 110, 110-7 (particularly at pp. 114-5 paras 11-2); *Walter A. Noyes v Panama* VI RIAA 308, 309-11.

revolutionists,[113] and even hooligan attacks.[114] Despite of such diversity of factual settings, these cases share an important common thread. From a legal standpoint, they all involve a problem of attribution, posing the question of whether and on which account the host state may be held accountable for injuries committed by non-state actors.[115] This is also the reason why international responsibility in this area has been consistently said to arise out of a failure to exercise due diligence in the protection of foreign citizens.[116]

The host state, albeit not an 'insurer' against all possible wrongs taking place within its borders,[117] is considered accountable for its own failure to provide foreign

---

[113]For some indicative examples see: *Amelia de Brissot et al. v. United States of Venezuela* (26 August 1890) *United States and Venezuelan Claims Commission. Opinions Delivered by the Commissioners in the Principal Cases* (Gibson Bros., Washington 1890) 457-89; *Aroa Mines Ltd. v Venezuela* (1903) IX RIAA 402, 402-45 (particularly at p. 445); *Bolívar Railway Company Case* (1903) IX RIAA 445, 451-3; *Bond Coleman v Mexico* (3 October 1928) IV RIAA 364, 364-8; *Dix Case* (1903-5) IX RIAA 119, 119-20; *French Company of Venezuelan Railroads Case* (31 July 1905) X RIAA 285, 285-355; *Georges Pinson v Mexico* (19 October 1928) V RIAA 327, 422-33 [50-6]; *G. L. Solis v Mexico* (3 October 1928) IV RIAA 358, 361-2; *Guastini Case* (1903) X RIAA 561, 561-82; *Guerrieri Case* (1903) X RIAA 583; *Heny Case* (1903-5) IX RIAA 125, 128; *Naomi Russell v Mexico* (24 April 1931) IV RIAA 805, 832-3, 855-6, 858-76 and 889-91 (including the discussion of the subject in the commissioners' separate and dissenting opinions); *Puerto Cabello and Valencia Railway Company Case* (1903) IX RIAA 510, 513; *Salas Case* (1903) X RIAA (1903) 720, 720-1; *Sambiaggio Case* (1903) X RIAA 499-535 (particularly at pp. 515 and 529); *Salvador Prats v United States* (undated) 3 Moore's Arb. 2886, 2886-900; *Santa Gertrudis Jute Mill Co. Ltd. v Mexico* (15 February 1930) V RIAA 108-15 (particularly at pp. 110-3); *The Home Insurance Company v Mexico* (31 March 1926) IV RIAA 48, 48-53 (particularly at p. 52). See also: Frederick Sherwood Dunn, *The Diplomatic Protection of Americans in Mexico* (Klaus Reprint, New York 1971) 152-65 [first edition: 1933].

[114]See: 'Note from the Soviet Foreign Ministry to the Turkish Embassy in Moscow' (30 August 1964) in Ian Brownlie, *System of the Law of Nations. State Responsibility* (Clarendon Press, Oxford 1983) 118 (diplomatic claim concerning a hooligan attack on Soviet citizens at an international fair in Izimir on August 29th, 1963; Soviet authorities underscored that '[t]he life of Soviet citizens – the personnel of the [Soviet] pavilion – was in danger, and considerable damage was done to Soviet property' and noted that '[t]he hooligans shouted abusive words addressed to the Soviet Union').

[115]For an indicative example see: Gordon Christenson, 'Attributing Acts of Omission to the State' (1990) 12 Mich. J. Int'l L. 312, 326-7. Some scholars have argued that a line should be drawn between 'responsibility by attribution' and 'responsibility due to failure to exercise due diligence'. See: Jan Arno Hessbruegge, 'The Historical Development of the Doctrines of Attribution and Due Diligence in International Law' (2003/4) 36(4) JILP 265, 268. The problem with Hessbruegge's terminology is that, in order to trigger international responsibility, a failure to exercise due diligence must, too, be attributable to the state. Chapter 12 discusses the concept of due diligence and its relation to the problem of attribution in more detail.

[116]Chapter 12 provides a detailed account of the historical and conceptual relationship between the due diligence standard of liability and state responsibility for acts of individuals.

[117]For the rejection of the depiction of the host state as an 'insurer' see: Mr. Bayard, Sec. of State, to Mr. Stuphen' (6 January 1888) in John Bassett Moore, *A Digest of International Law* (Volume 6: Government Printing Office, Washington 1906) 961, 962 (expressly stating that host governments are not required to act as 'an insurer' in their response to civil disorders).

citizens protection and security against third party violence (so-called 'separate delict theory').[118] Omissions in the form of wants of diligence in the prevention and redress of private injuries to aliens thus constitute *public acts* of the state, which, just as actions, can be internationally wrongful and consistently entail international responsibility.[119] Not surprisingly, most theories of due diligence in international law were developed in the particular context of state responsibility for acts of individuals.[120] There is hence a close link between private wrongs, due diligence, and the duty to provide security to aliens.[121]

At some instances, this conceptual linkage found direct expression in treaty stipulations. A good illustration may be found in the FCN agreement concluded between Colombia and the German Empire in 1899, which expressly excluded liability for acts of revolutionaries in the absence of a 'want of diligence' in the protection of German citizens in Colombia.[122] A similar approach was followed in articles 10–12 of the *Harvard Draft Convention on the Responsibility of States for Damage Done in their Territory to the Person or Property of Foreigners* (1929), a document that has been described as a 'high-water mark' of the modern law of aliens.[123] Article 11 of the *Harvard Draft* provided:

> Article 11. A state is responsible if an injury to an alien results from an act of an individual or from mob violence, if the state has failed to exercise due diligence to prevent such injury and if local remedies have been exhausted without adequate redress for such failure, or if there has been denial of justice.[124]

---

[118]Section 12.4.3 addresses the 'separate delict theory' in detail.

[119]Section 11.3 explains the characterization of FPS as a 'delict of omission'.

[120]Cf. also Chap. 12.

[121]Cf. also Chap. 12.

[122]For the English text of the clause see: Jackson Ralston, *Venezuelan Arbitrations of 1903* (Government Printing Office, Washington 1904) 384 ("the German Government will not attempt to hold the Colombian Government responsible, *unless there be due want of diligence on the part of the Colombian authorities or their agents*, for the injuries, oppressions, or extortions occasioned in time of insurrection or civil war to German subjects in the territory of Colombia, through rebels, or caused by salvage tribes beyond the control of the Government" – emphasis added). For the original German text see: Freundschafts-, Handels- und Schifffahrtsvertrag zwischen dem Deutschen Reich und dem Freistaat Columbien (adopted 23 July 1892, entered into force 12 April 1894) Felik Stoerk (ed), *Martens Nouveau Recueil Général des Traités, 2me Série* (Volume 19: Librairie Dietrich, Göttingen 1895) 831, 842-3 art. 20.

[123]Campbell McLachlan, 'Investment Treaties and General International Law' (April 2008) 57 ICLQ 361, 366. For the text of the draft articles see: 'Responsibility of States for Damage done in their Territory to the Person and Property of Foreigners' (1929) 23 AJIL 131, 134 arts. 10-2.

[124]'Responsibility of States for Damage done in their Territory to the Person and Property of Foreigners' (1929) 23 AJIL 131, 134 art. 11.

In his commentary to this provision, Edwin Borchard observed that '[w]here an alien suffers injury inflicted by an individual or a group of individuals, the situation is to be distinguished from that where injury results from an act of the state'.[125] The reason is simple. Following Borchard:

> No state can be held to guarantee that aliens entering its territory will suffer no injury whatsoever; but a state has a duty to prevent injuries to aliens where this is possible by the exercise of due diligence.[126]

For that very same reason, Borchard explained, '[only] if there has been a failure to exercise due diligence the state is responsible, provided local remedies have been exhausted without adequate redress for its failure'.[127] Finally, Borchard noted that 'a long line of cases has established responsibility where injury results from the wrongful act of private individuals *under these special conditions*'.[128]

The ILC considered, too, the question of state responsibility for acts of individuals. Chapter III of Francisco García Amador's Revised Draft on State Responsibility (1961) was particularly concerned with cases involving 'negligence and other acts and omissions in connection with the protection of aliens'.[129] Article 7 established the rules applicable to acts of individuals under the suggestive title '*Negligence in the performance of the duty of protection*'.[130] In his *Fourth Report on*

---

[125]Edwin Borchard, 'The Law of Responsibility of States for Damage Done in Their Territory to the Person or Property of Foreigners. Comments to the Draft Convention' (April 1929) 23 AJIL 140, 189 art. 10.

[126]Edwin Borchard, 'The Law of Responsibility of States for Damage Done in Their Territory to the Person or Property of Foreigners. Comments to the Draft Convention' (April 1929) 23 AJIL 140, 189 art. 10.

[127]Edwin Borchard, 'The Law of Responsibility of States for Damage Done in Their Territory to the Person or Property of Foreigners. Comments to the Draft Convention' (April 1929) 23 AJIL 140, 189 art. 10.

[128]Emphasis added. Edwin Borchard, 'The Law of Responsibility of States for Damage Done in Their Territory to the Person or Property of Foreigners. Comments to the Draft Convention' (April 1929) 23 AJIL 140, 189 art. 10.

[129]Francisco García Amador, 'International Responsibility: Sixth Report by F. V. García Amador, Special Rapporteur (A/CN.4/134 and Add. 1)' (26 January 1961) 2 *Yearbook of the International Law Commission – 1961* 1, 47.

[130]Francisco García Amador, 'International Responsibility: Sixth Report by F. V. García Amador, Special Rapporteur (A/CN.4/134 and Add. 1)' (26 January 1961) 2 *Yearbook of the International Law Commission – 1961* 1, 47 art. 7. Similar principles appear in a previous version of the Draft, which was submitted to the ILC in 1957. See: Francisco García Amador, 'International Responsibility: Second Report by F. V. García Amador, Special Rapporteur (A/CN.4/106)' (15 February 1957) 2 *Yearbook of the International Law Commission – 1957* 104, 130 arts. 10 and 11.

State Responsibility (1972), Roberto Ago also made a valuable attempt to codify the rules governing the responsibility of states for wrongs committed by private individuals, using a language that was strikingly reminiscent of the *Harvard Draft*.[131] The ILC would finally remove these provisions for reasons unrelated to their substance and customary status in international law.[132]

Against this background, the reasoning followed in *El Paso v Argentina* and other cases can hardly be said to be counterintuitive or remarkable. The approach of these investment tribunals simply recognizes the pattern of many instances of application of the notion of 'protection and security' in the customary law of aliens, and interprets the contemporary FPS standard accordingly.

---

[131] See: Roberto Ago, 'Fourth Report on State Responsibility – The Internationally Wrongful Act of the State, Source of International Responsibility (Continued) (A/CN.4/264)' (20 June 1972 and 9 April 1973) 2 *Yearbook of the International Law Commission – 1972* 71, 126 art. 11 ("Article 11. Conduct of private individuals. 1. The conduct of a private individual or group of individuals, acting in that capacity, is not considered to be an act of the State in international law. 2. However, the rule enunciated in the preceding paragraph is without prejudice to the attribution to the State of any omission on the part of its organs, where the latter ought to have acted to prevent or punish the conduct of the individual or group of individuals and failed to do so"). Ago's lengthy comments on this provision provide clear evidence of the strong link between state responsibility for acts of individuals and the customary security obligation: "[w]ithout undertaking to provide precise details on the matter which are not necessary here, we may take it to be generally acknowledged that every State must, under international law, ensure that foreign States, their appointed representatives and, to a lesser degree, their individual nationals, *are effectively protected against attacks by individuals*" – emphasis added (at p. 98 para 67). Interestingly, at the 1309th Meeting of the ILC, Milan Šahović emphasized that the cases mentioned by Ago were mostly concerned with 'the status of aliens' and went on to state that 'it would be desirable to consider, in the commentary to article 11, whether that provision could really be applied to all possible cases'. ILC, 'Summary Records of the 1309th Meeting' (14 May 1975) 1 *Yearbook of the International Law Commission – 1975* 28, 31-2 [38]. In addition, Šahović suggested that the provision should be titled 'Conduct of organs acting by omission' (at p. 32 para 42).

[132] At the 1309th meeting of the ILC, Paul Reuter questioned the inclusion of the provision in the Draft Articles, famously characterizing it as 'essentially self-evident'. See: ILC, 'Summary Records of the 1309th Meeting' (14 May 1975) 1 *Yearbook of the International Law Commission – 1975* 28, 31 [30]. See also: ILC, 'Summary Records of the 1345th Meeting' (7 July 1975) 1 *Yearbook of the International Law Commission – 1975* 213, 214-5 [10-7]. Similarly, Special Rapporteur James Crawford recommended in 1998 the elimination of the provision in question, which he believed to be 'circular and potentially misleading' because the '[t]he issue in such cases is not whether the acts of private individuals as such are attributable to the state (they are not), but rather, what is the extent of the obligation of the state to prevent or respond to those acts'. James Crawford, 'First Report on State Responsibility (A/CN.4/490 and Add. 1-7)' (April-August 1998) 2(1) *Yearbook of the International Law Commission – 1998* 1, 48 [244]. The discussion at the ILC was therefore particularly related to the characterization of the Draft Article as a rule of attribution (rather than as a primary rule), and its apparent redundancy; the substance of the rule was, however, never put into question. For a detailed account of the drafting history of this provision at the ILC and the final decision to delete it see: Olivier de Frouville, 'Attribution of Conduct to the State: Private Individuals' in James Crawford, Alain Pellet and Simon Olleson (eds), *The Law of International Responsibility* (Oxford University Press, New York 2010) 257, 262-3.

8.3.2 The Private-Public Divide. Some Grey Areas

The preceding section has provided evidence of the close connection between state responsibility for acts of private individuals, on the one hand, and the customary FPS standard on the other. FPS does not however refer only to cases involving injuries that are clearly and unquestionably 'private' (e.g. acts of outlaws and ordinary criminal offences). To begin with, in numerous cases the characterization of conduct as 'public' or 'private' could sow significant confusion.[133] As explained by Gordon Christenson (1983):

> Nothing is better established in theory or more blurred in practice than the distinction between acts done in a purely private capacity, such as mob violence or common murders, and those done in a public capacity, such as failure to provide protection that meets the international standard, failure of the judicial system, failure to apprehend or punish, or State complicity in or tacit approval of private acts.[134]

To be sure, difficulties are not limited to the problem of attribution.[135] In many cases, while there is no doubt that the original injury was *not* attributable to the host state, its classification as a 'private' wrong seems inadequate from the outset. That is the case, for example, of acts of other states in the host state's territory. This section submits that wrongs of this kind, albeit not private, can still be assessed under the FPS standard. Even though these cases certainly have a special character, in these scenarios the customary security obligation is applicable under the same rationale as in the case of private injuries. In the end, harm originates in the conduct of an entity *different* from the host state.

A detailed analysis of every possible factual scenario in which the line between private and public acts might be obscure would exceed the scope of the present study. This section therefore focuses on factual settings which, from a legal-historical perspective, are particularly relevant for the customary FPS standard, namely: (1) successful revolutions; (2) acts of other states in the territory of the host state; (3) acts of international organizations; (4) private violence actively supported by officers of the host state; (5) conduct of soldiers; and (6) risk of private violence materializing in a public injury.

---

[133]Cf. Gordon Christenson, 'The Doctrine of Attribution in State Responsibility' in Richard Lillich (ed), *International Law of State Responsibility for Injuries to Aliens* (University Press of Virginia, Charlottesville VA 1983) 321, 335.

[134]Gordon Christenson, 'The Doctrine of Attribution in State Responsibility' in Richard Lillich (ed), *International Law of State Responsibility for Injuries to Aliens* (University Press of Virginia, Charlottesville VA 1983) 321, 335.

[135]Section 8.3.1 addresses the problem of attribution posed by cases of state responsibility for acts of individuals. Chapter 12 below considers the issue from the standpoint of due diligence.

8.3.2.1 Successful Revolutions

Acts of revolutionaries are not substantially different from acts of regular private individuals.[136] For the purposes of the law of state responsibility for injuries to aliens, an uprising against the host state's government, however severe, can hardly be distinguished from an ordinary case of mob violence, widespread banditry or other civil disturbances.[137] Terms such as 'mob', 'rebellion', 'insurrection' or 'revolution' do not have fixed meanings in international law.[138] Scholars and adjudicators have sometimes described the difference as one of degree.[139] In the 1970s, Roberto Ago argued that the differentiation is not just 'quantitative' in nature, but has, too, a qualitative character:

> What, in fact, characterizes the situation created by the emergence of an insurrectional movement as defined in international law is the very existence, parallel with the State and in a portion of the territory under its sovereignty of a *separate subject of international law*.[140]

---

[136]See generally: Edwin Borchard, 'The Law of Responsibility of States for Damage Done in Their Territory to the Person or Property of Foreigners. Comments to the Draft Convention' (April 1929) 23 AJIL 140, 193 art. 12.

[137]For a similar observation see: Edwin Borchard, 'The Law of Responsibility of States for Damage Done in Their Territory to the Person or Property of Foreigners. Comments to the Draft Convention' (April 1929) 23 AJIL 140, 193 art. 12 ("In principle, there is no difference between this case [act of insurgents] and that of mob violence, with respect to responsibility"). The ILC has expressed a similar view; see: ILC, 'Responsibility of States for Internationally Wrongful Acts. General Commentary' (2001) 2 *Yearbook of the International Law Commission – 2001* 31, 50 art. 10 (Commentary) [2] ("At the outset, the conduct of the members of the movement presents itself purely as the conduct of private individuals. It can be placed on the same footing as that of persons or groups who participate in a riot or mass demonstration and is likewise not attributable to the State. Once an organized movement comes into existence as a matter of fact, it will be even less possible to attribute conduct to the State, which will not be in a position to exert effective control over its activities").

[138]Cf. *Georges Pinson v Mexico* (19 October 1928) V RIAA 327, 424 [51.4] and 426 [53].

[139]For an indicative example see: *Georges Pinson v Mexico* (19 October 1928) V RIAA 327, 424 [51.4] and 426 [53] ("Le terme "révolution" n'a pas de contenu précis en droit international [...] Ainsi que je l'ai fait observer ci-dessus (§ 51) la doctrine et la pratique du droit international n'attachent point au mot "révolution" un ses bien déterminé. Si les auteurs et les tribunaux internationaux tâchent de classer un peu les différents mouvements qui peuvent mettre en péril l'ordre public dans un Etat, tels que: émeutes, troubles, désordres, soulèvements, séditions, insurrections, révoltes, rébellions, révolutions, guerres civiles, guerres intestines, etc., et leurs équivalents également nombreux en d'autres langues, ou bien ils ne font pas de distinction nette entre celles-ci et les autres troubles, ni entre ces derniers entre eux, pour se borner à la remarque générale que tous ces mouvements forment, pour ainsi dire, une échelle de désordres, ascendante selon leur caractère plus ou moins grave pour l'ordre public"). For a similar observation see: Karl Strupp, *Handbuch des Völkerrechts. Das völkerrechtliche Delikt* (Volume 3: Verlag von W. Kohlhammer 1920) 97 n. 1; Daniel Patrick O'Connell, *International Law* (Volume 2: Stevens & Sons, London 1970) 967 *et seq.*; Edwin Borchard, *The Diplomatic Protection of Citizens Abroad or the Law of International Claims* (The Banks Law Publishing Co., New York 1916) 228.

[140]Emphasis added. Roberto Ago, 'Fourth Report on State Responsibility – The Internationally Wrongful Act of the State, Source of International Responsibility (Continued) (A/CN.4/264)' (20 June 1972 and 9 April 1973) 2 *Yearbook of the International Law Commission – 1972* 71, 129 [153].

Other authors suggested that, in the final analysis, a revolution can only be said to be such when it succeeds,[141] a view that was much criticized in the past.[142] Besides this somewhat inconsistent terminology, a basic proposition has long enjoyed general acceptance within the international community.[143] As stated by U.S. Secretary of State William Seward (1868):

> It is a well-established principle of international law [. . .] that no government can be held responsible for the act of rebellious bodies of men, committed in violation of its authority, where it is itself guilty of no breach of good faith or of no negligence in suppressing insurrection.[144]

This statement may be fairly said to reflect the opinions expressed in countless academic publications and arbitral decisions, though the justification of the rule could significantly vary from one source to another.[145] These principles, which fully

---

[141]Commissioner González Roa advanced this position in the *Naomi Russel* arbitration. See: *Naomi Russell v Mexico* (24 April 1931) IV RIAA 805, 870-1.

[142]For a detailed discussion of the subject see: *Georges Pinson v Mexico* (19 October 1928) V RIAA 327, 427-9 [54].

[143]On the terminological debate see generally: *Georges Pinson v Mexico* (19 October 1928) V RIAA 327, 424 [51.4] and 426 [53].

[144]'Mr. Seward, Sec. of State, to Mr. Smith' (9 July 1868) in John Bassett Moore, *A Digest of International Law* (Volume 6: Government Printing Office, Washington 1906) 956. The US-Mexico General Claims Commission relied on this statement in the *Solis* claim of 1928. See: *G. L. Solis v Mexico* (3 October 1928) IV RIAA 358, 361.

[145]*Aroa Mines Ltd. v Venezuela* (1903) IX RIAA 402, 439-40; *De Caro Case* (1903) X RIAA 635, 635 and 642; *Guastini Case* (1903) X RIAA 561, 561 and 577-8; *Guerrieri Case* (1903) X RIAA 583; *G. L. Solis v Mexico* (3 October 1928) IV RIAA 358, 361-2; *Home Frontier and Foreign Missionary Society of the United Brethren in Christ v Great Britain* (18 December 1929) VI RIAA 42, 44; *Naomi Russell v Mexico* (24 April 1931) IV RIAA 805, 831 *et seq.* and 858-63; *N. H. Henriquez Case* (1903) X RIAA 713, 716; *Salas Case* (1903) X RIAA (1903) 720, 720-1; *Salvador Prats v United States* (undated) 3 Moore's Arb. 2886, 2890; *Sambiaggio Case* (1903) X RIAA 499, 499 and 512-3 (but note the opinion of Mr. Ruffillo Agnoli, the Italian Commissioner, at pp. 504-5; the case was decided by Umpire Ralston). For scholarly writings confirming the rule (and providing further references to state and arbitral practice) see: Antoine Rougier, *Les guerres civiles et le droit des gens* (Larose & Forcel, Paris 1903) 473-4; Charles de Visscher, *Théories et réalités en droit international public* (A. Pedone, Paris 1960) 352; Charles Fenwick, *International Law* (The Century Co., New York 1924) 394; Clyde Eagleton, *The Responsibility of States in International Law* (Klaus Reprint, New York 1970) 140-7 [first edition: 1928]; Edwin Borchard, *The Diplomatic Protection of Citizens Abroad or the Law of International Claims* (The Banks Law Publishing Co., New York 1916) 229; Edwin Borchard, 'The Law of Responsibility of States for Damage Done in Their Territory to the Person or Property of Foreigners. Comments to the Draft Convention' (April 1929) 23 AJIL 140, 195-6 art. 13; Georg Muszack, *Ueber die Haftung einer Regierung für Schäden, welche Ausländer gelegentlich innerer Unruhen in ihren Landen erlitten haben* (Heiz u. Mündel, Strasbourg 1905) 13-4; Gordon Christenson, 'Attributing Acts of Omission to the State' (1990) 12 Mich. J. Int'l L. 312, 322-3; Haig Silvanie, *Responsibility of States for the Acts of Unsuccessful Insurgent Governments* (AMS Press, New York 1968) 135 *et seq.* [first edition: 1939]; Hans Kelsen, *Principles of International Law* (The Lawbook Exchange, Clark NJ 2007) 292 [first edition: 1952]; James Crawford, *State Responsibility. The General Part* (Cambridge University Press, Cambridge 2013) 170; Pascuale Fiore, *Nouveau droit international public suivant les besoins de la civilisation moderne* (Volume 1: Charles Antoine tr, A. Durand et Pedone-Lauriel

resemble the rationale of the rules applicable in respect of private injuries to aliens, hold true, however, only as far as the insurgents are *unsuccessful*.[146] Whenever a revolution succeeds, either by establishing a new state or a new government, an entirely different legal situation arises.[147] The applicable customary rule crystalized in articles 10(1) and 10(2) of the *ILC Articles on State Responsibility* (2001), which read as follows:

Article 10. Conduct of an insurrectional or other movement.

1. The conduct of an insurrectional movement which becomes the new Government of a State shall be considered as an act of that State under international law.

2. The conduct of a movement, insurrectional or other, which succeeds in establishing a new state in part of the territory of a pre-existing State or in a territory under its administration shall be considered as an act of the new State under international law.[148]

In cases where a new state emerges, the assessment of the security obligation should pose no difficulties.[149] In application of the rule codified in article 10(2) of the ILC Articles, the new state will be considered accountable for any failure *by the rebels* to prevent or redress injuries to aliens in the territorial areas under their control, provided the insurrectionary movement could be reasonably regarded as the passive subject of the customary security obligation at the time of the injury.[150]

Éditeurs 1885) 583-4. For a particularly detailed analysis of state responsibility for acts of insurgents see: Roberto Ago, 'Fourth Report on State Responsibility – The Internationally Wrongful Act of the State, Source of International Responsibility (Continued) (A/CN.4/264)' (20 June 1972 and 9 April 1973) 2 *Yearbook of the International Law Commission – 1972* 71, 128-52 [151-214]. A few authors, however, virtually denied any form of state responsibility for conduct of insurgents, even in cases where most authors would consider the host state accountable for a want of due diligence. For a representative example see: Harmodio Arias, 'The Non-Liability of States for Damages Suffered by Foreigners in the Course of a Riot, an Insurrection, or a Civil War' (1913) 7 (4) AJIL 724, 724-66 (particularly at 736 and 764-5). Arias' views are discussed in greater detail in Sect. 12.2, in connection with the concept of due diligence.

[146]For a similar remark see: Roberto Ago, 'Fourth Report on State Responsibility – The Internationally Wrongful Act of the State, Source of International Responsibility (Continued) (A/CN.4/264)' (20 June 1972 and 9 April 1973) 2 *Yearbook of the International Law Commission – 1972* 71, 131 [157].

[147]See: Roberto Ago, 'Fourth Report on State Responsibility – The Internationally Wrongful Act of the State, Source of International Responsibility (Continued) (A/CN.4/264)' (20 June 1972 and 9 April 1973) 2 *Yearbook of the International Law Commission – 1972* 71, 131-2 [157 and 159].

[148]ILC, 'Responsibility of States for Internationally Wrongful Acts. General Commentary' (2001) 2 *Yearbook of the International Law Commission – 2001* 31, 50 art. 10.

[149]For a detailed, critical analysis of article 10(2) of the *ILC Articles on State Responsibility* see: Patrick Dumberry, 'New State Responsibility for Internationally Wrongful Acts by an Insurrectional Movement' (2006) 17(3) EJIL 605, 605-21 (concluding at p. 620 that the rule in question 'has long been considered as a well-established principle of international law' but also taking note of the fact that state practice is 'limited' in this area; Dumberry's article also provides an account of different dogmatic approaches regarding the justification of the rule).

[150]Cf. ILC, 'Responsibility of States for Internationally Wrongful Acts. General Commentary' (2001) 2 *Yearbook of the International Law Commission – 2001* 31, 50 art. 10(2). For the

In turn, as explained by James Crawford, 'any acts undertaken by the predecessor state in attempting to suppress the insurgency will *not* be attributed to the new state'.[151]

More fraught is the event in which the revolutionaries manage to establish a new government rather than a new state, in which case conduct of said victorious insurgents is imputable or, using Ago's words, 'retroactively' attributable to the host state.[152] The rule envisaged by the ILC for this situation (quoted above) has a long tradition in international law.[153] A similar provision appeared in article 13(b) of the *Harvard Draft* of 1929:

> [T]he state whose government is established thereby is responsible under article 7 [responsibility for acts of authorities of the state], if an injury to an alien has resulted from an *act or omission of the revolutionists* committed *at any time after the inception of the revolution*.[154]

This principle has additionally enjoyed broad and consistent support in international case law and international law scholarship.[155] The rule seems, furthermore,

---

characterization of a revolutionary movement and other non-state actors as passive subjects of the customary security obligation see Sect. 7.3.

[151]Emphasis added. James Crawford, *State Responsibility. The General Part* (Cambridge University Press, Cambridge 2013) 176. Roberto Ago, while acknowledging this general rule, also observed that 'one might consider the possible succession of the new State to certain *ex delicto* obligations of the pre-existing State, but it is evident that the new State then assumes such obligations as a matter of State succession, not of international responsibility for its own acts'. Roberto Ago, 'Fourth Report on State Responsibility – The Internationally Wrongful Act of the State, Source of International Responsibility (Continued) (A/CN.4/264)' (20 June 1972 and 9 April 1973) 2 *Yearbook of the International Law Commission – 1972* 71, 144 [195].

[152]Roberto Ago, 'Fourth Report on State Responsibility – The Internationally Wrongful Act of the State, Source of International Responsibility (Continued) (A/CN.4/264)' (20 June 1972 and 9 April 1973) 2 *Yearbook of the International Law Commission – 1972* 71, 149-1 [210-1]. See also the authorities quoted by Ago at p. 150 n. 489. On this question cf. also Petr Stejskal, 'War: Foreign Investments in Danger – Can International Humanitarian Law or Full Protection and Security Always Save It?' (2017) 8 CYIL 529, 544.

[153]Cf. ILC, 'Responsibility of States for Internationally Wrongful Acts. General Commentary' (2001) 2 *Yearbook of the International Law Commission – 2001* 31, 50 art. 10(1); Roberto Ago, 'Fourth Report on State Responsibility – The Internationally Wrongful Act of the State, Source of International Responsibility (Continued) (A/CN.4/264)' (20 June 1972 and 9 April 1973) 2 *Yearbook of the International Law Commission – 1972* 71, 140 *et seq.* [182 *et seq.*].

[154]Emphasis added. 'Responsibility of States for Damage done in their Territory to the Person and Property of Foreigners' (1929) 23 AJIL 131, 134-5 art. 13.

[155]Alfred L. Short *v* Iran, Award, Case No. 11135 (14 July 1987) 16 Iran – US Cl. Trib. Rep. 76, 84-5 [33]; *Bolívar Railway Company Case* (1903) IX RIAA 445, 452-3; *Georges Pinson v Mexico* (19 October 1928) V RIAA 327, 429-31 [55] (particularly at p. 431); *Dix Case* (1903-5) IX RIAA 119, 119-20; *French Company of Venezuelan Railroads Case* (31 July 1905) X RIAA 285, 354; *Heny Case* (1903-5) IX RIAA 125, 128; *Naomi Russell v Mexico* (24 April 1931) IV RIAA 805, 858-66 (particularly at pp. 863 and 866); *Puerto Cabello and Valencia Railway Company Case* (1903) X RIAA 510, 513. See also: Clyde Eagleton, *The Responsibility of States in International Law* (Klaus Reprint, New York 1970) 147-8 [first edition: 1928]. A similar principle was acknowledged by the U.S. Supreme Court in *Williams v Bruffy*. See: *Williams v Bruffy* (1 October 1877) 96 U.S. 176. This decision was quoted both in the *Bolívar Railway*

not to have changed much with the passage of time.[156] There has been, however, some debate as to the moment from which the 'retroactive' international responsibility of the state attaches.[157] While some scholars submit that this form of 'retroactive' attribution presupposes that the insurgent group exercised a minimum measure of territorial control, other authors contend—in line with the *Harvard Draft*—that the state is responsible for all acts committed by the rebels from the very beginning of the revolutionary war.[158]

The effect of this rule of attribution is, in any case, utterly complex. As a general proposition, the rule makes the host state responsible for the actions and omissions of *both* the rebels *and* former governmental authorities.[159] This effect is not self-

---

Company Case (at p. 453) and in the *Heny Case* (at p. 128). For an account of the customary rules governing responsibility for conduct of successful revolutionaries see: Alfred Verdross and Bruno Simma, *Universelles Völkerrecht* (Duncker & Humblot, Berlin 1984) 862; Charles de Visscher, *Théories et réalités en droit international public* (A. Pedone, Paris 1960) 352; Clyde Eagleton, *The Responsibility of States in International Law* (Klaus Reprint, New York 1970) 147-8 [first edition: 1928]; Edwin Borchard, *The Diplomatic Protection of Citizens Abroad or the Law of International Claims* (The Banks Law Publishing Co., New York 1916) 241-2; Edwin Borchard, 'The Law of Responsibility of States for Damage Done in Their Territory to the Person or Property of Foreigners. Comments to the Draft Convention' (April 1929) 23 AJIL 140, 195-6 art. 13; Frank Schorkopf, *Staatsrecht der internationalen Beziehungen* (C.H. Beck, Munich 2017) 426; Karl Strupp, *Handbuch des Völkerrechts. Das völkerrechtliche Delikt* (Volume 3: Verlag von W. Kohlhammer 1920) 92; Ian Brownlie, *System of the Law of Nations. State Responsibility* (Clarendon Press, Oxford 1983) 177-8; Jochen Abr. Frowein, *Das de facto-Regime im Völkerrecht. Eine Untersuchung zur Rechtsstellung nichtanerkannter Staaten und ähnlicher Gebilde* (Carl Heymanns Verlag, Köln/Berlin 1968) 85-6 and 200-2. For a critical analysis of article 10 of the *ILC Articles on State Responsibility* see: Jean D'Aspremont, 'Rebellion and State Responsibility: Wrongdoing by Democratically Elected Insurgents' (2009) 58 ICLQ 427, 427-42 (particularly focusing on the scenarios of 'national reconciliation' as well as 'power sharing-agreements').

[156]Cf. 'Responsibility of States for Damage done in their Territory to the Person and Property of Foreigners' (1929) 23 AJIL 131, 134-5 art. 13; ILC, 'Responsibility of States for Internationally Wrongful Acts. General Commentary' (2001) 2 *Yearbook of the International Law Commission – 2001* 31, 50 art. 10(2).

[157]See generally: James Crawford, *State Responsibility. The General Part* (Cambridge University Press, Cambridge 2013) 173-4.

[158]For the first position see: James Crawford, *State Responsibility. The General Part* (Cambridge University Press, Cambridge 2013) 173-4 (observing that the ILC avoided taking a stance on this particular issue, but citing sources suggesting that some measure of territorial control could be required for the application of the rule); Roberto Ago, 'Fourth Report on State Responsibility – The Internationally Wrongful Act of the State, Source of International Responsibility (Continued) (A/CN.4/264)' (20 June 1972 and 9 April 1973) 2 *Yearbook of the International Law Commission – 1972* 71, 129 [153] *et seq.* (emphasizing the importance of the moment in which an insurgent organization obtains autonomous international legal personality). For representative examples of authorities claiming that responsibility should be assumed for any acts committed from the start of the revolutionary war see: Alfred L. Short v Iran, Dissenting Opinion of Justice Brower, Case No. 11135 (14 July 1987) 16 Iran – US Cl. Trib. Rep. 86, 99-100 [28-9]; Daniel Patrick O'Connell, *International Law* (Volume 2: Stevens & Sons, London 1970) 968.

[159]For this effect see: Clyde Eagleton, *The Responsibility of States in International Law* (Klaus Reprint, New York 1970) 147-8 [first edition: 1928]; James Crawford, *State Responsibility. The General Part* (Cambridge University Press, Cambridge 2013) 173-4.

evident and could even appear to be counterintuitive.[160] Edwin Borchard justified the rule by resort to the somewhat questionable fiction that 'the revolution represented *ab initio* a changing national will, crystallizing in the final successful result'.[161] The same rationale underlies the *Bolívar Railway Co.* award of 1903, where Umpire Plumley stated:

> Responsibility [for the acts of successful revolutionists] comes because it is the same nation. Nations do not die when there is a change of their rules or in their forms of government. These are but expressions of a change of national will. "The king is dead; long live the king!" has typified this thought for ages. The nation is responsible for the debts contracted by its titular government, and that responsibility continues through all changing forms of government until the obligation is discharged. The nation is responsible for the obligations of a successful revolution from its beginning, because, in theory, it represented *ab initio a* changing national will, crystalizing in the finally successful result.[162]

This reasoning has not been without controversy. Roberto Ago would note in 1972 that 'the very concept of "national will" is to be treated with caution'.[163] In his usual vigorous style, he observed:

> [I]t is difficult to maintain that the outcome of the fighting in a civil war should, like a judgment of God, establish retrospectively that those who triumphed were, from the outset of the civil war, more representative of the national will than those who lost.[164]

Following Ago, the rationalization of the rule advanced in the *Bolívar Railway Co.* award is additionally contrary to the enduring responsibility of the state for the acts of the deposed government, which, under this rationale, would not represent the 'true national will' (as a result of its defeat).[165] As an alternative, Ago pointed out that 'what is important is to determine whether that attribution is or not made in the real world of international relations'.[166] Ago's refreshing call was not entirely new. Almost 50 years earlier, the German public law scholar Karl Strupp had similarly

---

[160]For a short presentation of different attempts to justify the rule see: James Crawford, *State Responsibility. The General Part* (Cambridge University Press, Cambridge 2013) 173 *et seq.* (referring, among others, to the *Bolívar Railway Co. Case* of 1903 at n. 53, and discussing the views of Roberto Ago).

[161]Edwin Borchard, *The Diplomatic Protection of Citizens Abroad or the Law of International Claims* (The Banks Law Publishing Co., New York 1916) 241 (citing the *Bolívar Railway Co.* case and other examples at n. 3).

[162]*Bolívar Railway Company Case* (1903) IX RIAA 445, 452-3.

[163]Roberto Ago, 'Fourth Report on State Responsibility – The Internationally Wrongful Act of the State, Source of International Responsibility (Continued) (A/CN.4/264)' (20 June 1972 and 9 April 1973) 2 *Yearbook of the International Law Commission – 1972* 71, 145 [198].

[164]Roberto Ago, 'Fourth Report on State Responsibility – The Internationally Wrongful Act of the State, Source of International Responsibility (Continued) (A/CN.4/264)' (20 June 1972 and 9 April 1973) 2 *Yearbook of the International Law Commission – 1972* 71, 145 [198].

[165]Roberto Ago, 'Fourth Report on State Responsibility – The Internationally Wrongful Act of the State, Source of International Responsibility (Continued) (A/CN.4/264)' (20 June 1972 and 9 April 1973) 2 *Yearbook of the International Law Commission – 1972* 71, 145 [198].

[166]Roberto Ago, 'Fourth Report on State Responsibility – The Internationally Wrongful Act of the State, Source of International Responsibility (Continued) (A/CN.4/264)' (20 June 1972 and 9 April 1973) 2 *Yearbook of the International Law Commission – 1972* 71, 145 [199].

noted that this exceptional rule of attribution could only be legally justified if accepted as a 'special liability' founded on international custom.[167]

In one or the other way, the acts of the rebels are directly imputable to the state.[168] In spite of the change in power, there is 'continuity' in the state as a single moral person.[169] It has been suggested that the actions and omissions of insurgents could be understood as acts of a state *'in statu nascendi'*.[170] Those acts therefore involve the immediate and direct responsibility of the state whose government has changed.[171] James Crawford has characterized this rule as 'a *negative attribution clause* to which is attached a curious form of secondary, contingent responsibility based on the successful outcome of the insurgency'.[172]

To be sure, the change in power does not relieve the state from responsibility for international wrongs imputable to agents of the deposed government; *forma regiminis mutate, non mutatur civitas ipsa*.[173] As put forward by Roberto Ago:

> The State does not cease to exist and its organization persists, even if it undergoes some alterations, with the result that, after the success of the insurrectional movement, the previous acts or omissions of members of that organization will continue to be attributed to the State.[174]

According to Ago, as a result of these principles, '[t]he possibility then arises for the State's being called upon to answer *at the same time* for acts emanating from two different organizations'.[175] These rules, when applied in cases involving the customary FPS standard, lead to two possible factual scenarios.

---

[167]Karl Strupp, *Handbuch des Völkerrechts. Das völkerrechtliche Delikt* (Volume 3: Verlag von W. Kohlhammer 1920) 92.

[168]ILC, 'Responsibility of States for Internationally Wrongful Acts. General Commentary' (2001) 2 *Yearbook of the International Law Commission – 2001* 31, 50 art. 10(1).

[169]For this idea of 'continuity' see: ILC, 'Responsibility of States for Internationally Wrongful Acts. General Commentary' (2001) 2 *Yearbook of the International Law Commission – 2001* 31, 50-1 [4-7].

[170]Jochen Abr. Frowein, *Das de facto-Regime im Völkerrecht. Eine Untersuchung zur Rechtsstellung nichtanerkannter Staaten und ähnlicher Gebilde* (Carl Heymanns Verlag, Köln/ Berlin 1968) 209.

[171]See generally: Clyde Eagleton, *The Responsibility of States in International Law* (Klaus Reprint, New York 1970) 147 [first edition: 1928] (noting that, in these cases, 'the acts of the insurgents now become the acts of the government, for which it must accept responsibility').

[172]Emphasis added. James Crawford, *State Responsibility. The General Part* (Cambridge University Press, Cambridge 2013) 171.

[173]For an author using this Latin maxim see: Clyde Eagleton, *The Responsibility of States in International Law* (Klaus Reprint, New York 1970) 148 [first edition: 1928].

[174]Roberto Ago, 'Fourth Report on State Responsibility – The Internationally Wrongful Act of the State, Source of International Responsibility (Continued) (A/CN.4/264)' (20 June 1972 and 9 April 1973) 2 *Yearbook of the International Law Commission – 1972* 71, 145 [197].

[175]Emphasis added. Roberto Ago, 'Fourth Report on State Responsibility – The Internationally Wrongful Act of the State, Source of International Responsibility (Continued) (A/CN.4/264)' (20 June 1972 and 9 April 1973) 2 *Yearbook of the International Law Commission – 1972* 71, 145 [197].

In a first scenario, the host state could be considered responsible for the injurious *actions* of the rebels and, in addition, for wants of diligence (i.e. *omissions*) by the defeated government in the prevention and redress of revolutionary damages. In these cases, as a rule, the FPS standard will be relevant with regard to *omissions* of the former government only. While the *actions* of the rebels could certainly be internationally wrongful, they are more properly measured against *other* primary rules (e.g. protection against expropriation).[176]

This situation can be best visualized through an example. In the Peruvian revolutionary conflict of 1884–1885 (also known as Cáceres-Iglesias civil war), troops of the rebel General Andrés Avelino Cáceres confiscated a certain amount of guano, which was the property of a U.S. company, in the vicinity of Mollendo.[177] The constitutional government of Peru was said to be incapable of adopting any effective measures to secure or recover American property in the area.[178] Andrés Avelino Cáceres would eventually succeed in his quest for power, being officially proclaimed President of Peru in 1886.[179] The State Department decided to seek compensation from the new government.[180] In his instructions to the U.S. diplomatic representative in Peru, Secretary of State Thomas Bayard stated:

> The guano which was seized was appropriated to sustain a cause which has become national by the voluntary action of the people of Peru, its chief representative being at the present time the duly elected and installed constitutional executive of the Republic.[181]

In this case, two different potential legal issues were at stake. First, a confiscation of property committed by the rebel army, which, upon the triumph of the insurrection, was imputable to the host state.[182] This internationally wrongful *action* would be best assessed as an expropriation, and not as a failure to provide protection and security.[183] Second, the (former) titular government of Peru could have incurred in a want of due diligence in the prevention of the taking or, more generally, in the protection of foreign property. Such omissions, if any, would continue to be attributable to the host state because the victory of Cáceres did neither affect the legal personality of Peru nor its identity as a subject of international law.[184] In the specific

---

[176]For the characterization of FPS as a 'delict of omission' see Sect. 11.3.

[177]John Bassett Moore, *A Digest of International Law* (Volume 6: Government Printing Office, Washington 1906) 992.

[178]John Bassett Moore, *A Digest of International Law* (Volume 6: Government Printing Office, Washington 1906) 992.

[179]John Bassett Moore, *A Digest of International Law* (Volume 6: Government Printing Office, Washington 1906) 992.

[180]John Bassett Moore, *A Digest of International Law* (Volume 6: Government Printing Office, Washington 1906) 992.

[181]'Mr. Bayard, Sec. of State, to Mr. Buck, min. to Peru' (13 August 1886) in John Bassett Moore, *A Digest of International Law* (Volume 6: Government Printing Office, Washington 1906) 992.

[182]Cf. ILC, 'Responsibility of States for Internationally Wrongful Acts. General Commentary' (2001) 2 *Yearbook of the International Law Commission – 2001* 31, 50 art. 10(1).

[183]For a detailed analysis of the relationship between FPS and expropriation see Sect. 15.3.

[184]Cf. Roberto Ago, 'Fourth Report on State Responsibility – The Internationally Wrongful Act of the State, Source of International Responsibility (Continued) (A/CN.4/264)' (20 June 1972 and 9 April 1973) 2 *Yearbook of the International Law Commission – 1972* 71, 145 [197].

case of the confiscation of guano in Mollendo, the State Department's complaint referred only to the first issue (i.e. the question of expropriation).[185] The reason might have been that a want of diligence was hard to establish because, at the time of the taking, the official troops had apparently lost control of the town.[186]

In a second scenario, the acts of the *rebels* could be arguably measured against the customary FPS standard. This situation is likely to occur where the rebels have gained control over a portion of the host territory.[187] As far as they are in control, the revolutionaries can indeed be expected to assume responsibility for the security of foreigners in the area; this duty does not only require them to provide protection against ordinary private individuals, but also against other insurgent movements as well as regular or counterrevolutionary forces.[188] A failure by the rebels to provide such protection is, upon their seizure of power, an omission attributable to the host state.[189]

Interestingly, this hypothesis could give rise to scenarios where the host state is considered responsible for a failure *by the insurgents* to protect aliens *from the titular government*. Let us consider a hypothetical example. A is an alien resident in a territory controlled by revolutionary forces, which exercise *de facto* authority in the area. The rebels have knowledge that the titular government is planning a minor military operation, in the course of which damages could be done to the person and property of A. The damages are entirely avoidable by minimal precautionary measures. The revolutionaries fail to take any measures to protect A, in spite of having all means to do so. The governmental forces eventually destroy the property of A, and cause her severe corporal injuries. If the insurgents are victorious and establish a new government, their want of protection will be attributable to the host state under article 10(1) of the *ILC Articles on State Responsibility*.[190]

8.3.2.2 Acts of Other States in the Territory of the Host State

Injuries to aliens may directly result from the actions of a state other than the territorial state. This hypothesis poses the question, whether the host state could incur in a breach the FPS standard by failing to prevent *other states* from injuring

---

[185]Cf. 'Mr. Bayard, Sec. of State, to Mr. Buck, min. to Peru' (13 August 1886) in John Bassett Moore, *A Digest of International Law* (Volume 6: Government Printing Office, Washington 1906) 992.

[186]Cf. John Bassett Moore, *A Digest of International Law* (Volume 6: Government Printing Office, Washington 1906) 992.

[187]On the relevance of territorial control for the application of the FPS standard see Sect. 7.3.

[188]On the violation of the FPS standard by *de facto* governments and other non-state actors see Sect. 7.3.

[189]Cf. ILC, 'Responsibility of States for Internationally Wrongful Acts. General Commentary' (2001) 2 *Yearbook of the International Law Commission – 2001* 31, 50 art. 10(1).

[190]Cf. ILC, 'Responsibility of States for Internationally Wrongful Acts. General Commentary' (2001) 2 *Yearbook of the International Law Commission – 2001* 31, 50 art. 10(1).

foreign citizens within its territory. Investment arbitral tribunals have already been confronted with this factual scenario. A noteworthy example is *Toto Construzioni v Lebanon* (2012).[191] In that case, a foreign corporate investor claimed that troops of the Syrian Army had obstructed a major construction project in Lebanese territory.[192] In the claimant's view, the passivity of the host government in respect of Syrian military units amounted to a breach of its international obligation to ensure the security of Italian investments in areas subject to its territorial jurisdiction.[193] The arbitrators unanimously dismissed the claim.[194] Notwithstanding this finding, the *Toto Construzioni* tribunal did not question the applicability of the FPS standard to this situation of fact:

> The Tribunal finds that Toto was – or should have been – aware that the Syrian troops occupied areas along the alignment. Taking into account the circumstances, the Tribunal is satisfied that Lebanon did whatever was within its power to obtain the Syrian troop's departure. *Lebanon did not neglect its obligation under Article 2 of the Treaty to protect Toto's investment*: the measures it undertook to obtain the evacuation of the Syrian troops were not unreasonable or discriminatory, and they proved to be adequate [. . .] the Tribunal's view is that Toto did not establish that Lebanon behaved negligently or capriciously, or that it acted discriminatorily or violated the international minimum standard by not obtaining immediately the departure of foreign troops. *If in fact it had been established that the presence of Syrian troops for a limited period on part of the site materially prejudiced Toto's operations, Toto would have had a good claim, because, as between Lebanon and*

---

[191]Toto Construzioni Generali S.p.A. *v* Lebanon, Award, ICSID Case No. ARB/07/12 (7 June 2012). On the application of the FPS standard with regard to acts of third states in the host state's territory cf. also Petr Stejskal, 'War: Foreign Investments in Danger – Can International Humanitarian Law or Full Protection and Security Always Save It?' (2017) 8 CYIL 529, 535 *et seq*.

[192]Toto Construzioni Generali S.p.A. *v* Lebanon, Award, ICSID Case No. ARB/07/12 (7 June 2012) [99]. It is worth noting that the Syrian units concentrated in a small area (at para 100). Nothing suggests that Syria actually displaced Lebanon as the state exercising actual territorial control and, as such, as the passive subject of the security obligation. On the 'passive subject' of the security obligation and the relevance of territorial control see Sect. 7.3.

[193]Toto Construzioni Generali S.p.A. *v* Lebanon, Award, ICSID Case No. ARB/07/12 (7 June 2012) [171 and 195-206]. The Italy-Lebanon BIT contains two separate FPS provisions, namely, article 2(3) and article 4(1). See: Agreement between the Italian Republic and the Lebanese Republic on the Promotion and Reciprocal Protection of Investments (adopted 7 November 1997, entered into force 9 February 2000) art. 2(3) ("Each Contracting Party shall *protect* within its territory investments made in accordance with its laws and regulations by investors of the other Contracting Party" – emphasis added) and art. 4(1) ("Investments by investors of either Contracting Party *shall enjoy full protection and security* in the territory of the other contracting party" – emphasis added). In *Toto Construzioni*, the claimant based its argument about the non-removal of Syrian military units on article 2(3) of the BIT (at para 171). In this regard, the tribunal observed: "Toto [. . .] did not elaborate on the possibility that the failure to remove the Syrian troops from the site could be a breach of Article 4.1 as well. This being as it is, the Tribunal sees a strong overlap between protection and security under Article 4.1. of the Treaty, and protection of the investment under Article 2.3 of the Treaty. Consequently, the finding that a claim is not covered by Article 2.3 will also entail that it is not covered by Article 4.1" (at para 171).

[194]Toto Construzioni Generali S.p.A. *v* Lebanon, Award, ICSID Case No. ARB/07/12 (7 June 2012) [261].

Toto, the burden of the presence of Syrian troops on the Lebanese territory would have to be borne by Lebanon. In the view of the Tribunal, Toto has not so established.[195]

In this type of cases, a distinction must always be drawn between the responsibility the state whose actions caused the injury, on the one hand, and the responsibility of the territorial state on the other.[196] The FPS standard is applicable in respect of the *territorial state*.[197] It requires the host state to exercise due diligence in the prevention of harmful acts of other states in areas subject to its territorial jurisdiction.[198] A clear statement of the rule appeared in the *Harvard Draft* of 1929:

> A state is responsible if an injury to an alien results from an act, committed within its territory, which is attributable to another state, only if it has failed to use due diligence to prevent such injury.[199]

This rule has long been present in the diplomatic practice of western states.[200] During the golden years of U.S. gunboat diplomacy, it was most consistently invoked in incidents involving naval bombardments in Central and South

---

[195]Emphasis added. Toto Construzioni Generali S.p.A. *v* Lebanon, Award, ICSID Case No. ARB/07/12 (7 June 2012) [200 and 205]. It must be noted that the *Toto Construzioni* tribunal's remarks on the customary minimum standard were made in specific connection with article 3(1) of the Italy-Lebanon BIT (i.e. fair and equitable treatment).

[196]Cf. 'Stanbery, At. Gen., in response to a request of Mr. Seward, Sec. of State, for an opinion on the claims of Wheelwright & Co. and Loring & Co. for loses of merchandises in the conflagration caused by the bombardment of Valparaiso by the Spanish fleet' (1866) in John Bassett Moore, *A Digest of International Law* (Volume 6: Government Printing Office, Washington 1906) 941, 941-2 (discussed later in this section).

[197]See Sect. 7.3 (also addressing the application of the FPS standard in respect of other entities exercising territorial control).

[198]Cf. Toto Construzioni Generali S.p.A. *v* Lebanon, Award, ICSID Case No. ARB/07/12 (7 June 2012) [205]. See also: Toto Costruzioni Generali S.p.A. *v* Lebanon, Decision on Jurisdiction, ICSID Case No. ARB/07/12 (11 September 2009) [118].

[199]'Responsibility of States for Damage done in their Territory to the Person and Property of Foreigners' (1929) 23 AJIL 131, 138 art. 14. See also: ILC, 'Report of the International Law Commission on the Work of its Twenty-Seventh Session – State Responsibility' (1975) 2 *Yearbook of the International Law Commission – 1975* 51, 84 ("the actions of foreign organs in the territory of a State, while not attributable to that State, may in certain cases afford material opportunity for the territorial State to engage in conduct which might entail international responsibility. For example, the organs of the territorial State might be guilty, in connection with the actions of a foreign State in the national territory, of failing to discharge an international obligation towards a third State to protect that State, its representatives *or its nationals*" – emphasis added). For an additional example see: ILC, 'Revised Draft on the Responsibility of States for Injuries Caused in its Territory to the Person or Property of Aliens' (1961) 2 *Yearbook of the International Law Commission – 1961* 46, 48 art. 15.

[200]'Responsibility of States for Damage done in their Territory to the Person and Property of Foreigners' (1929) 23 AJIL 131, 196-8 (commentary on Draft Article 14, also providing examples of state and arbitral practice in this area).

America.[201] One of the most flamboyant examples was the Greytown incident of 1852–1854.[202]

On May 1st, 1852, the people of San Juan del Norte declared their independence from Nicaragua and adopted the name of 'Greytown'.[203] Shortly thereafter, the City Council ordered the Accessory Transit Co. (USA) to demolish its facilities and leave the town.[204] The new authorities sent armed men to enforce the Council's resolution.[205] A few days later, the *U.S.S. Cyanne*, an American warship, approached Greytown.[206] The Secretary of the Navy authorized the deployment of American troops to counter the measures adopted by Greytown's *de facto* authorities.[207] U.S. citizens and their properties were formally placed under the protection of the Navy.[208] In spite of the Navy's display of strength, the situation did not improve. There were several incidents with the local population, including a crowd attack on the U.S. representative in the area, Solon Bordland.[209]

The United States demanded from the people of Greytown proper compensation for all damages caused to both the Accessory Transit Co. and to Mr. Borland.[210] Navy Captain Hollins, who was in command of the *U.S.S. Cyanne*, further threatened with a naval bombardment of the city in case of refusal.[211] Hollins' threat was not a bluff. The bombardment actually took place on the morning of July 13th,

---

[201]For an overview of this type of cases see: John Bassett Moore, *A Digest of International Law* (Volume 6: Government Printing Office, Washington 1906) 926-48 (particularly referring to the Greytown and Valparaíso bombardments, which are discussed in greater detail later in this section).

[202]This example has been often cited in the past. It was referred to, for example, in Edwin Borchard's commentary to article 14 of the *Harvard Draft* of 1929. See: 'Responsibility of States for Damage done in their Territory to the Person and Property of Foreigners' (1929) 23 AJIL 131, 197-8. Cf. also: Roberto Ago, 'Fourth Report on State Responsibility – The Internationally Wrongful Act of the State, Source of International Responsibility (Continued) (A/CN.4/264)' (20 June 1972 and 9 April 1973) 2 *Yearbook of the International Law Commission – 1972* 71, 127 [149] n. 322.

[203]John Bassett Moore, *A Digest of International Law* (Volume 7: Government Printing Office, Washington 1906) 346.

[204]John Bassett Moore, *A Digest of International Law* (Volume 7: Government Printing Office, Washington 1906) 346.

[205]John Bassett Moore, *A Digest of International Law* (Volume 7: Government Printing Office, Washington 1906) 346.

[206]John Bassett Moore, *A Digest of International Law* (Volume 7: Government Printing Office, Washington 1906) 347.

[207]John Bassett Moore, *A Digest of International Law* (Volume 7: Government Printing Office, Washington 1906) 347.

[208]John Bassett Moore, *A Digest of International Law* (Volume 7: Government Printing Office, Washington 1906) 347.

[209]John Bassett Moore, *A Digest of International Law* (Volume 7: Government Printing Office, Washington 1906) 348-9.

[210]John Bassett Moore, *A Digest of International Law* (Volume 7: Government Printing Office, Washington 1906) 350-1.

[211]John Bassett Moore, *A Digest of International Law* (Volume 7: Government Printing Office, Washington 1906) 351.

1854.[212] The military action undertaken by the U.S. Navy caused severe damages not only to the local population, but also to French, German and British citizens resident in the city.[213]

Count Eugène de Sartiges, the French Ambassador to the United States, demanded compensation for the injuries sustained by French nationals at Greytown.[214] U.S. Secretary of State William Marcy informed the French Minister that 'the President has not been able to find any grounds of right, or even equity, upon which such reclamation can be sustained'.[215] The American argument was that 'there would be no difficulty in justifying the bombardment on well-settled principles of international law'.[216] Most importantly, at least for present purposes, the State Department contended that French citizens whose property had been damaged were under protection of the people and authorities of Greytown, and not of the United States:

> If there were persons in Greytown when it was bombarded who did not belong to the political organization there established, and who suffered in consequence of that bombardment, they can only resort for indemnity, if entitled to it, to that community. *It was to that community they committed their persons and property, and by receiving them within its jurisdiction it assumed the obligation of protecting them. Nothing can be more clearly established than the principle that a foreigner domiciled in a country can only look to that country for the protection he is entitled to receive while within its territory, and that if he sustains injury for the want of that protection, the country of his domicil* (sic) *must indemnify him.*[217]

Marcy supported his position with a comprehensive account of the diplomatic practice of European states.[218] Years later, the U.S. Government would give a similar response to a request presented by Prussia pertaining to the wrongs done to

---

[212]John Bassett Moore, *A Digest of International Law* (Volume 7: Government Printing Office, Washington 1906) 352.

[213]For the diplomatic correspondence on the Greytown incident see: John Bassett Moore, *A Digest of International Law* (Volume 6: Government Printing Office, Washington 1906) 926-40. See also: John Bassett Moore, *A Digest of International Law* (Volume 7: Government Printing Office, Washington 1906) 353-4.

[214]'Count Sartriges, French min., to Mr. Marcy, Sec. of State' (13 January 1857) in John Bassett Moore, *A Digest of International Law* (Volume 6: Government Printing Office, Washington 1906) 926, 926-8.

[215]'Mr. Marcy, Sec. of State, to Count Sartiges, French min.' (26 February 1857) in John Bassett Moore, *A Digest of International Law* (Volume 6: Government Printing Office, Washington 1906) 927, 927.

[216]'Mr. Marcy, Sec. of State, to Count Sartiges, French min.' (26 February 1857) in John Bassett Moore, *A Digest of International Law* (Volume 6: Government Printing Office, Washington 1906) 927, 928.

[217]Emphasis added. 'Mr. Marcy, Sec. of State, to Count Sartiges, French min.' (26 February 1857) in John Bassett Moore, *A Digest of International Law* (Volume 6: Government Printing Office, Washington 1906) 927, 928.

[218]'Mr. Marcy, Sec. of State, to Count Sartiges, French min.' (26 February 1857) in John Bassett Moore, *A Digest of International Law* (Volume 6: Government Printing Office, Washington 1906) 927, 929-34.

German subjects during the Greytown bombardment.[219] In contrast to the German and French foreign offices, the British Government abstained from exercising diplomatic protection.[220] In a speech delivered in the House of Commons, Lord Palmerston expressed support for the position of President Pierce's administration, and declared before the House that any claim against the U.S. Government for damages to the persons or property of British subjects at Greytown would be baseless.[221]

American foreign policy followed the same line in subsequent incidents.[222] A clear example is the Spanish bombardment of the Chilean port of Valparaíso in 1866.[223] On that occasion, Secretary of State William Seward requested Attorney General Henry Stanbery a legal opinion about the possible exercise of diplomatic protection in support of American companies, which had sustained material losses as a corollary of the Spanish naval assault.[224] Stanbery considered that there was no basis for a diplomatic claim.[225] Most importantly, he made clear that the actions of Spain and the possible omissions of Chile were two different legal issues:

> The question presented for my opinion is, Whether a case is made for the intervention of the United States on behalf of these citizens for indemnity against Spain or Chile? I do not see any ground upon which such intervention is allowable in respect of either of those Governments. The [Spanish] bombardment [. . .] can not be said to have been contrary to the laws of war [. . .] as to the Chilean authorities, it does not appear that they did or omitted any act for which our citizens there domiciled have a right to complain, or that the measure of protection

---

[219] 'Mr. Fish, Sec. of State, to Baron Gerolt, Prussian min.' (15 April 1870) in John Bassett Moore, *A Digest of International Law* (Volume 6: Government Printing Office, Washington 1906) 937, 937-8.

[220] For the British position see: Henry John Temple (Third Viscount Palmerston), 'Intervention before the House of Commons on the Greytown Bombardment' (19 June 1857) Hansard's Parliamentary Debates CXLVI (Commons), Third Series 40, 40-3.

[221] See: Henry John Temple (Third Viscount Palmerston), 'Intervention before the House of Commons on the Greytown Bombardment' (19 June 1857) Hansard's Parliamentary Debates CXLVI (Commons), Third Series 40, 40-3.

[222] See generally: John Bassett Moore, *A Digest of International Law* (Volume 6: Government Printing Office, Washington 1906) 940 *et seq.*

[223] For a detailed account of the Valparaíso incident see: John Bassett Moore, *A Digest of International Law* (Volume 6: Government Printing Office, Washington 1906) 940 *et seq.*; John Bassett Moore, *A Digest of International Law* (Volume 7: Government Printing Office, Washington 1906) 354-60. This example has been often used in academic literature, along with the Greytown incident. Cf. Roberto Ago, 'Fourth Report on State Responsibility – The Internationally Wrongful Act of the State, Source of International Responsibility (Continued) (A/CN.4/264)' (20 June 1972 and 9 April 1973) 2 *Yearbook of the International Law Commission – 1972* 71, 127 [149] n. 322.

[224] John Bassett Moore, *A Digest of International Law* (Volume 6: Government Printing Office, Washington 1906) 940-1; John Bassett Moore, *A Digest of International Law* (Volume 7: Government Printing Office, Washington 1906) 358.

[225] 'Stanbery, At. Gen., in response to a request of Mr. Seward, Sec. of State, for an opinion on the claims of Wheelwright & Co. and Loring & Co. for loses of merchandises in the conflagration caused by the bombardment of Valparaiso by the Spanish fleet' (1866) in John Bassett Moore, *A Digest of International Law* (Volume 6: Government Printing Office, Washington 1906) 941, 941-2.

they were bound by public law to extend to those citizens and their property was withheld.[226]

This kind of cases has long drawn the attention of international law scholars. The issue was at the heart of a thrilling academic debate between Friedrich Klein and Alfred Verdross in the 1940s.[227] Klein (1941) considered that these cases involved the *indirect responsibility* ('*mittelbare Haftung*') of a state for the acts of another state.[228] For his part, Verdross (1948) submitted that in such events there was no 'indirect responsibility' whatsoever:

> [A]s a general rule, the territorial state is only liable for the damages caused by other states to aliens in its territory, if it has breached its international obligation to provide protection. In such a case, the territorial state is not indirectly liable, but directly responsible.[229]

Verdross' views enjoyed widespread acceptance in academic circles. A prominent example would be Roberto Ago, who contended in 1972 that the argument of 'indirect responsibility' was largely based on a misguided understanding of relevant state practice:

> [W]hat is alleged in such cases to be a source of responsibility of the "territorial" State is certainly not the act committed by foreign organs but the passive or negligent attitude considered to have been adopted by the organs of that State towards the acts committed.[230]

Verdross' and Ago's views are correct. The responsibilities of the territorial state and of the state whose agents directly caused the injury must be assessed in a separate manner.[231] The fact alone that the conduct of a state different from the

---

[226]'Stanbery, At. Gen., in response to a request of Mr. Seward, Sec. of State, for an opinion on the claims of Wheelwright & Co. and Loring & Co. for loses of merchandises in the conflagration caused by the bombardment of Valparaiso by the Spanish fleet' (1866) in John Bassett Moore, *A Digest of International Law* (Volume 6: Government Printing Office, Washington 1906) 941, 941-2.

[227]Cf. Friedrich Klein, *Die mittelbare Haftung im Völkerrecht* (Vittorio Klostermann, Frankfurt am Main 1941) 265-8; Alfred Verdross, 'Theorie der mittelbaren Staatenhaftung' (1948) 1 ÖZÖR 388, 421-2.

[228]Friedrich Klein, *Die mittelbare Haftung im Völkerrecht* (Vittorio Klostermann, Frankfurt am Main 1941) 265-8. For a concise presentation of the concept of indirect responsibility see: Dionisio Anzilotti, *Lehrbuch des Völkerrechts* (Volume 1: Walter de Gruyter, Berlin/Leipzig 1929) 417. See also Sect. 12.4.1.

[229]Author's translation. The original German text reads: "Grundsätzlich ist also der Territorialstaat für die von anderen Staaten auf seinem Gebiete verursachten, von Ausländern erlittenen Schäden nur dann verantwortlich, wenn er seine völkerrechtliche Schutzpflicht verletzt hat. Ist das aber der Fall, dann ist der Territorialstaat nicht mittelbar haftbar, sondern unmittelbar verantwortlich." Alfred Verdross, 'Theorie der mittelbaren Staatenhaftung' (1948) 1 ÖZÖR 388, 421-2 (see also pp. 405-8).

[230]Roberto Ago, 'Fourth Report on State Responsibility – The Internationally Wrongful Act of the State, Source of International Responsibility (Continued) (A/CN.4/264)' (20 June 1972 and 9 April 1973) 2 *Yearbook of the International Law Commission – 1972* 71, 128 [150] (also addressing the debate between Verdross and Klein at p. 127 para 148).

[231]Cf. Roberto Ago, 'Fourth Report on State Responsibility – The Internationally Wrongful Act of the State, Source of International Responsibility (Continued) (A/CN.4/264)' (20 June 1972 and 9 April 1973) 2 *Yearbook of the International Law Commission – 1972* 71, 128-9 [151].

host state provided the occasion for a want of protection does not imply that international responsibility can or should be collectively attributed to both states.[232] Neither does the responsibility of the territorial (host) state depend on the wrongfulness of the original harmful act: even if an injury results from a *lawful* action by a third state (e.g. self-defense), the host state could still be responsible for its own lack of due diligence in the prevention of harm.[233]

Hence, in the classical examples discussed in this section, two potential responsibilities were at stake: (1) the responsibility of the state conducting the bombardment, which depended on the wrongfulness of said military action; and (2) the responsibility of the territorial state for its lack of diligence in the adoption of adequate measures of protection.[234] There could be, thus, an *internationally wrongful* omission in the protection of aliens from injuries produced by the *internationally permissible* conduct of another state.[235]

Difficulties may however arise in the unlikely event that a claim relates to acts committed by agents of the *home state* in the host territory. The customary security obligation cannot be properly said to cover risks originating in conduct imputable to the foreigner's home state.[236] There seems to be no place for an analogy to the rules applicable in respect of injuries inflicted by third states; the position of the home state is, in fact, hardly comparable to that of another state, which is a true outsider to the legal relationship governed by the law of aliens.[237]

Moreover, if the injury originated in the home state's wrongful conduct, a diplomatic claim by said state is likely to fail under considerations of good faith. International law prevents states from obtaining benefits out of their own misdemeanors; *nullus commodum capere potest de injuria sua propia*.[238] This well-

---

[232]Cf. Roberto Ago, 'Fourth Report on State Responsibility – The Internationally Wrongful Act of the State, Source of International Responsibility (Continued) (A/CN.4/264)' (20 June 1972 and 9 April 1973) 2 *Yearbook of the International Law Commission – 1972* 71, 127-9 [148-51].

[233]Cf. Roberto Ago, 'Fourth Report on State Responsibility – The Internationally Wrongful Act of the State, Source of International Responsibility (Continued) (A/CN.4/264)' (20 June 1972 and 9 April 1973) 2 *Yearbook of the International Law Commission – 1972* 71, 127 [148] (referring to the hypothesis of the original harmful conduct constituting 'legitimate acts of war').

[234]This principle is implicit in Mr. Marcy's note on the Greytown incident. Cf. 'Mr. Marcy, Sec. of State, to Count Sartiges, French min.' (26 February 1857) in John Bassett Moore, *A Digest of International Law* (Volume 6: Government Printing Office, Washington 1906) 927, 927-8.

[235]Cf. Roberto Ago, 'Fourth Report on State Responsibility – The Internationally Wrongful Act of the State, Source of International Responsibility (Continued) (A/CN.4/264)' (20 June 1972 and 9 April 1973) 2 *Yearbook of the International Law Commission – 1972* 71, 127 [148] (also referring to the Greytown and Valparaíso incidents at n. 322).

[236]The author is not aware of any finding of liability against a host state on account of an alleged want of due diligence in the protection of foreign nationals from agents of their own home states.

[237]The role of the home state in this area has been discussed in detail in Sects. 7.1 and 7.2.

[238]For the relationship between the Latin maxim '*nullus commodum capere potest de injuria sua propia*' and the good faith principle see: Bin Cheng, *General Principles of Law as Applied by International Courts and Tribunals* (Cambridge University Press, New York 2006) 149-55 [first edition: 1953] (also providing an account of the maxim's status in international law). These cases could also involve the principle according to which the foundation of a legal action cannot lie in a breach of the law: '*ex delicto non oritur actio*' (discussed by Cheng at pp. 155-8).

known maxim could also be invoked by the respondent state in investment arbitration proceedings, if the investor's direct action against the host state is considered as a 'substitute' for diplomatic protection.[239] In the later scenario, the argument's success will however depend on whether applicable substantive standards are considered as 'direct' individual rights vested upon the foreign investor, or are regarded as rights of the investor's home state.[240]

The situation described above should not be confused with cases where a threat originates in the territory of the *home state*, but is *not attributable* to it. In such events, the customary security obligation is fully applicable. The case *William W. Mills v Mexico* provides a good example of this scenario.[241] The case referred to the American Civil War.[242] William Mills, an American citizen and a loyal supporter of the U.S. Government, was forced to flee from his hometown in (Confederate) Texas, eventually finding refuge in El Paso del Norte (Mexico).[243] Confederate troops arrested Mills in Mexico and took him back to Texas, where he was brutally mistreated.[244] The Claims Commission considered the possible responsibility of Mexico for a want of diligence in the protection of Mills, while the latter was under Mexican territorial jurisdiction.[245] The Commissioners took notice of the peculiarities of the facts of the case, and observed:

> The violence which injured him [Mills] came from the territory and jurisdiction of his own country and, accomplishing its circuit, returned to the place from whence it came.[246]

---

[239]For instance, the investor's decision to submit an investment dispute to arbitration under the Washington Convention of 1965 excludes the exercise of diplomatic protection by the respective home state. See: Convention on the Settlement of Investment Disputes between States and Nationals of Other States (submitted 18 March 1965, entered into force 14 October 1966) 575 UNTS 159 art. 27. For an author characterizing arbitration under the ICSID Convention as 'a substitute for the traditional system of diplomatic protection' see: Eric De Brabandere, *Investment Treaty Arbitration as Public International Law. Procedural Aspects and Implications* (Cambridge University Press, Cambridge 2014) 67.

[240]For an analysis of possible theoretical approaches to the classification of substantive standards of investment protection as rights of the foreign investor or, in the alternative, as rights of the home state see: Tilmann Rudolf Braun, 'Globalization-Driven Innovation: The Investor as a Partial Subject in Public International Law – An Inquiry into the Nature and Limits of Investor Rights' (2013) 04/13 JMWP 1, 1-63 (also considering the possibility that investors are said to have mere procedural rights, so that substantive standards would be more properly understood as rights of their respective home states; at pp. 35-8 Braun expresses support for the 'direct rights approach' and the recognition of investors as 'partial subjects'). For a more detailed presentation of the argument see: Tilmann Rudolf Braun, *Ausprägungen der Globalisierung: Der Investor als Partielles Subjekt im Internationalen Investitionsrecht* (Nomos, Baden-Baden 2012) 72-161. Cf. also: Eric De Brabandere, *Investment Treaty Arbitration as Public International Law. Procedural Aspects and Implications* (Cambridge University Press, Cambridge 2014) 55-73 (heavily relying on the classification of rights as 'substantive' or 'procedural', particularly at pp. 55-6).

[241]*William W. Mills v Mexico* (6 July 1870) 3 Moore's Arb. 3033, 3033-5.

[242]*William W. Mills v Mexico* (6 July 1870) 3 Moore's Arb. 3033, 3033.

[243]*William W. Mills v Mexico* (6 July 1870) 3 Moore's Arb. 3033, 3033.

[244]*William W. Mills v Mexico* (6 July 1870) 3 Moore's Arb. 3033, 3033.

[245]*William W. Mills v Mexico* (6 July 1870) 3 Moore's Arb. 3033, 3033-5.

[246]*William W. Mills v Mexico* (6 July 1870) 3 Moore's Arb. 3033, 3033-5.

Notwithstanding this circumstance, the Commissioners emphasized that, upon crossing the Mexican border, an American national 'is entitled to protection to his person and property from the authorities of Mexico'.[247] They however concluded that, in the specific case of Mr. Mills, there had been no internationally wrongful omission on the part of competent Mexican authorities.[248]

In sum, the customary protection obligation is applicable with regard to acts of third states in the host territory. Leaving injuries caused by the home state aside, the rationale of these cases is generally the same as in cases pertaining to private violence. The reason is that the immediate cause of the injury is, too, *external to the host state*.[249] It must be acknowledged, however, that the *application* of the FPS standard cannot ignore the peculiarities of these factual settings: while the structure of the security obligation is certainly the same, it is also true that privileges, immunities, among others, could have a decisive impact on the assessment of the host state's conduct.[250] For instance, a failure by the host state to provide adequate redress to a foreign citizen could appear as justified where the perpetrator enjoys immunity under international law.[251]

8.3.2.3   Acts of International Organizations

Third states are not the only internationally accountable entities, different from the host state, whose conduct has the potential of causing harm to foreign nationals in the host territory. Other entities are likely to generate similar risks. In this regard,

---

[247] *William W. Mills v Mexico* (6 July 1870) 3 Moore's Arb. 3033, 3033.

[248] *William W. Mills v Mexico* (6 July 1870) 3 Moore's Arb. 3033, 3034.

[249] Cf. Sect. 8.3.1.

[250] The ILC considered some of these issues in its Report to the UN General Assembly of 1975. See: ILC, 'Report of the International Law Commission on the Work of its Twenty-Seventh Session – State Responsibility' (1975) 2 *Yearbook of the International Law Commission – 1975* 51, 84-6. The ILC observed that 'in the case of ordinary private individuals it is natural to postulate the existence of a set of obligations incumbent on the State with regard to the prevention and punishment of acts committed by such persons to the prejudice of foreign states or their nationals' (at p. 84). However, according to the ILC, where the injury is inflicted by agents of another state, 'it is less natural to imagine that the State could fail in an international obligation of that kind' (at p. 84). The reason is that 'the organs of a foreign state are not subject in foreign territory to the same authority as private individuals' (at p. 84). In this hypothesis, the ILC explained, 'it will be necessary to take into account the incidence of the privileges and immunities enjoyed by the organs of the foreign state, any special status which they may possess, the possibility that the foreign state concerned has reserved for itself the exclusive performance of certain supervisory or punitive functions, etc.' (at p. 86).

[251] For a similar observation see: ILC, 'Report of the International Law Commission on the Work of its Twenty-Seventh Session – State Responsibility' (1975) 2 *Yearbook of the International Law Commission – 1975* 51, 84. The ILC also acknowledged that, in spite of these singularities, the duty of redress is also applicable in these complex factual settings (at p. 86).

particular attention should be drawn to the acts of international organizations.[252] In the last few decades the world has witnessed an unprecedented proliferation of international organizations, which are nowadays active in nearly every state around the globe.[253] Their activities are therefore an increasingly important source of risk not only for the local population, but also for foreign nationals.[254] As in the case of harm caused by private individuals and foreign states, the host state cannot be deemed to be *directly* responsible for injuries to aliens that originate in acts of international organizations.[255] The 1975 version of the ILC *Articles on State Responsibility* codified the rule applicable in this scenario as follows (Draft Article 13):

> The conduct of an organ of an international organization acting in that capacity shall *not* be considered as an act of a State under international law by reason only of the fact that such conduct has taken place in the territory of that State or in any other territory under its jurisdiction.[256]

This rule should not exclude the possible responsibility of the territorial state for wants of diligence in the protection of citizens of other states.[257] Draft Article 15 of the ILC's *Revised Draft on the Responsibility of States for Injuries Caused in its Territory to the Person or Property of Aliens* of 1961 formulated this principle in the following terms:

> Acts and omissions of a third State or of an *international organization shall be imputable to the State in whose territory they were committed* only if the latter could have avoided the injurious act and did not exercise such *diligence* as was possible in the circumstances.[258]

---

[252]The *ILC Draft Articles on the Responsibility of International Organizations* (2011), define 'international organization' as 'an organization established by a treaty or other instrument governed by international law and possessing its own international legal personality. International organizations may include as members, in addition to States, other entities'. ILC, 'Responsibility of International Organizations, with Commentaries (A/66/10)' (2011) [http://legal.un.org/ilc/texts/instruments/english/commentaries/9_11_2011.pdf] art. 2(a).

[253]See generally: Mosche Hirch, *The Responsibility of International Organizations toward Third Parties* (Martinus Nijhoff Publishers, Dordrecht 1995) 1-5.

[254]For a similar observation see: Mosche Hirch, *The Responsibility of International Organizations toward Third Parties* (Martinus Nijhoff Publishers, Dordrecht 1995) 5 (without particular reference to foreign nationals).

[255]See generally: Mosche Hirch, *The Responsibility of International Organizations toward Third Parties* (Martinus Nijhoff Publishers, Dordrecht 1995) 77-82 (providing an overview of the work of the ILC and academic publications addressing the issue).

[256]Emphasis added. ILC, 'Report of the International Law Commission on the Work of its Twenty-Seventh Session – State Responsibility' (1975) 2 *Yearbook of the International Law Commission – 1975* 51, 87.

[257]See generally: Mosche Hirch, *The Responsibility of International Organizations toward Third Parties* (Martinus Nijhoff Publishers, Dordrecht 1995) 78-82 (particularly at pp. 80-1).

[258]Emphasis added. ILC, 'Revised Draft on the Responsibility of States for Injuries Caused in its Territory to the Person or Property of Aliens' (1961) 2 *Yearbook of the International Law Commission – 1961* 46, 48 art. 15. The final version of the *ILC Articles* does not address this particular issue. See: ILC, 'Responsibility of States for Internationally Wrongful Acts. General Commentary' (2001) 2 *Yearbook of the International Law Commission – 2001* 31, 141-2 art. 57.

The wording of Draft Article 15 was not entirely fortunate. Failure to provide protection against harmful acts of an international organization should not lead to the *imputation* (i.e. *attribution*) of such organization's conduct to the territorial (host) state.[259] The host state's omission, if internationally wrongful, is more properly styled and assessed as a separate and autonomous international delinquency.[260] Notwithstanding its imprecise language, the 1961 Draft evidences that the source of responsibility in these factual settings is an *omission* in the protection of aliens, which takes the form of a *want of diligence*.[261] From this standpoint, these events are analogous to private violence and can be accordingly considered through the prism of the customary FPS standard.[262]

Particular difficulties could however arise in cases where either the host state or the home state is a member of the organization whose agents inflicted the injury. The threshold issue at any such instances is the responsibility of states for the harmful conduct of international organizations they are members of.[263] In his presentation of the *ILC Articles on the Responsibility of International Organizations* (2011), ICJ Judge Giorgio Gaja explained that 'given the separate legal personality of the organization, responsibility does not as a rule fall on its members'.[264] The ILC Articles of 2011 set forth several exceptions to this general principle (e.g. cases where the state 'has accepted responsibility for that act' or 'has led the injured party to rely on its responsibility').[265] These exceptions, however important, do not impair the validity of the general rule described by Judge Gaja.[266] In the words of the ILC:

---

[259]The question of indirect responsibility has already been discussed in connection with acts of third states, in Sect. 8.3.2.2. The issue will also be considered in the assessment of the concept of due diligence, in Sect. 12.4.1.

[260]For a similar observation see: Mosche Hirch, *The Responsibility of International Organizations toward Third Parties* (Martinus Nijhoff Publishers, Dordrecht 1995) 81-2 (arguing at p. 81 that in these cases the host state breaches 'an obligation of control').

[261]Cf. also Mosche Hirch, *The Responsibility of International Organizations toward Third Parties* (Martinus Nijhoff Publishers, Dordrecht 1995) 81-2 (without particular reference to the 1961 Draft).

[262]Cf. Ignaz Seidl-Hohenveldern, *Collected Essays on International Investments and on International Organizations* (Kluwer Law International, The Hague 1998) 63-4 ("Such responsibility would thus be parallel to that incurred by a State in situations where that State failed to prevent or punish the conduct of a person or group of persons not acting on behalf of that State causing damage to foreign interests, which the State was under a duty to protect, in virtue of international law"). For a similar observation see: Roberto Ago, 'Fourth Report on State Responsibility – The Internationally Wrongful Act of the State, Source of International Responsibility (Continued) (A/CN.4/264)' (20 June 1972 and 9 April 1973) 2 *Yearbook of the International Law Commission – 1972* 71, 128-9.

[263]On this question see generally: Cedric Ryngaert and Holly Buchanan, 'Member State Responsibility for the Acts of International Organizations' (2011) 7(1) Utrecht Law Review 131, 131-46.

[264]Giorgio Gaja, *Articles on the Responsibility of International Organizations* (United Nations Audiovisual Library, 2014) [Written version: http://legal.un.org/avl/ha/ario/ario.html] 7.

[265]ILC, 'Responsibility of International Organizations, with Commentaries (A/66/10)' (2011) [http://legal.un.org/ilc/texts/instruments/english/commentaries/9_11_2011.pdf] 96 art. 62.

[266]Giorgio Gaja, *Articles on the Responsibility of International Organizations* (United Nations Audiovisual Library, 2014) [Written version: http://legal.un.org/avl/ha/ario/ario.html] 7 (discussing

While it would be [. . .] inappropriate to include in the draft a provision stating a residual, and negative, rule for those cases in which responsibility is not considered to arise for a State in connection with the act of an international organization, *such a rule is clearly implied.* Therefore, *membership does not as such entail for member States international responsibility when the organization commits an internationally wrongful act.*[267]

This normative framework has significant implications for the FPS standard. As a corollary of an international organization's 'separate legal personality', its conduct cannot be automatically characterized as conduct of its individual member states.[268] *As far as this principle holds*, acts and omissions of said organization are, for all practical purposes, *external* to the host state.[269] For that very same reason, a want of diligence in the prevention or redress of the harmful act could, in principle, be assessed under the FPS standard.[270] By contrast, whenever the acts of an international organization have been found to be attributable to the host state (e.g. agents of the host state coerced the organization into the internationally wrongful conduct), the case would fall outside the scope of the FPS standard.[271] Neither should the FPS standard be applied where a foreigner's *home state* was behind the harmful conduct of an international organization: FPS does not and should not serve the purpose of ensuring the security of aliens against risks originating in the acts of their own home states.[272]

8.3.2.4 Private Violence Actively Supported by State Agents

The distinction between private and public injuries could seem somewhat obscure where private violence against foreign nationals has enjoyed active support from state agents.[273] These intricate factual settings can be best portrayed through the example of the *Youmans* case, a most puzzling dispute decided by the United States-Mexico General Claims Commission in 1926.[274]

---

the specific exceptions set forth by the *Draft Articles* and expressly stating that 'these exceptions do not contradict the principle').

[267]Emphasis added. ILC, 'Responsibility of International Organizations, with Commentaries (A/66/10)' (2011) [http://legal.un.org/ilc/texts/instruments/english/commentaries/9_11_2011.pdf] 96 art. 62 (Commentary) [2].

[268]Giorgio Gaja, *Articles on the Responsibility of International Organizations* (United Nations Audiovisual Library, 2014) [Written version: http://legal.un.org/avl/ha/ario/ario.html] 7.

[269]Cf. Giorgio Gaja, *Articles on the Responsibility of International Organizations* (United Nations Audiovisual Library, 2014) [Written version: http://legal.un.org/avl/ha/ario/ario.html] 7.

[270]Cf. Sect. 8.3.1.

[271]For the hypothesis of coercion see: ILC, 'Responsibility of International Organizations, with Commentaries (A/66/10)' (2011) [http://legal.un.org/ilc/texts/instruments/english/commentaries/9_11_2011.pdf] 92, art. 60(a).

[272]For this argument see Sect. 8.3.2.2. See also Chap. 7 above.

[273]See also Sect. 13.4.7 (addressing the relevance of public authorities' support for the assessment of due diligence).

[274]*Thomas Youmans v Mexico* (23 November 1926) IV RIAA 110, 110-7.

The case concerned the murder of Thomas H. Youmans, John A. Connelly, and George Arnold by a violent crowd in Mexican territory.[275] The three men were contractors of a British firm.[276] Their tragedy originated in an argument between John Connelly and Cayetano Medina, a Mexican worker.[277] Medina demanded payment of a negligible sum as part of his salary, and Connelly refused.[278] As animosity escalated, other workers took sides with Medina and threatened the Americans with physical violence.[279] In a blundering attempt to protect his own life, Connelly ended up wounding Medina with a gunshot.[280] The three Americans sought refuge in Connelly's private house, which would soon be surrounded by an immense crowd of infuriated Mexican workers.[281] The British firm turned to the Mayor for protection.[282] The Mayor made a swift attempt to soothe the violent crowd, without success.[283] Fearing for the lives of the Americans, he sent a small contingent of the State of Michoacán's army to protect the three men.[284] This well-intentioned measure led to an outcome no one could have anticipated.[285] The U.S. Consul General described the subsequent events as follows:

> It is believed by those who seem well acquainted with all the circumstances that the appearance of the troops on the ground in behalf of public order, would of itself alone have been sufficient to have quelled the riot and put an end to all further turbulent and unlawful proceedings, but to the astonishment of all, they at one took position and opened fire on the Americans in the house. This act encouraged the mob to reopen their attack with redoubled fury. The soldiers continued their fire until they had expended their ammunition.[286]

A regiment from the Federal Government took over control of the place within a day.[287] The President of the United Mexican States required the State of Michoacán to investigate the case and to bring the culprits to justice.[288] Still, while available evidence suggested that roughly a thousand people had taken part in the riot, no more

---

[275] *Thomas Youmans v Mexico* (23 November 1926) IV RIAA 110, 111 [1-2]. The General Claims Commission issued separate decision on the murder of John Connelly, which was largely based on the findings of the *Youmans* award. See: *Agnes Connelly et al. v Mexico* (23 November 1926) IV RIAA 117, 117-8.

[276] *Thomas Youmans v Mexico* (23 November 1926) IV RIAA 110, 111 [2].

[277] *Thomas Youmans v Mexico* (23 November 1926) IV RIAA 110, 111 [2].

[278] *Thomas Youmans v Mexico* (23 November 1926) IV RIAA 110, 111 [2].

[279] *Thomas Youmans v Mexico* (23 November 1926) IV RIAA 110, 111 [2].

[280] *Thomas Youmans v Mexico* (23 November 1926) IV RIAA 110, 111 [2].

[281] *Thomas Youmans v Mexico* (23 November 1926) IV RIAA 110, 111 [2].

[282] *Thomas Youmans v Mexico* (23 November 1926) IV RIAA 110, 111 [2].

[283] *Thomas Youmans v Mexico* (23 November 1926) IV RIAA 110, 111 [2].

[284] *Thomas Youmans v Mexico* (23 November 1926) IV RIAA 110, 111 [2].

[285] *Thomas Youmans v Mexico* (23 November 1926) IV RIAA 110, 111 [2] and 113 [6-7].

[286] *Thomas Youmans v Mexico* (23 November 1926) IV RIAA 110, 113 [6].

[287] *Thomas Youmans v Mexico* (23 November 1926) IV RIAA 110, 112 [3].

[288] *Thomas Youmans v Mexico* (23 November 1926) IV RIAA 110, 112 [3].

than twenty-nine persons were indicted.[289] Only five suspects were actually tried and sentenced to death, but their death penalties would be eventually commuted.[290]

In the *Youmans* case, the parties and the commissioners made constant references to the host state's obligation to provide security to aliens. The claim submitted by the State Department pertained to both an alleged want of due diligence in the protection of Mr. Youmans from the crowd, and to Mexico's failure to properly punish the offenders.[291] As to the redress obligation, the commissioners had no difficulty in making a finding of responsibility against Mexico.[292]

By contrast, the assessment of the prevention obligation was fraught with considerable difficulty.[293] The Mexican Government disputed the facts and argued that the acts of the soldiers were not attributable to Mexico.[294] The Commission acknowledged that available evidence did not reveal whether it had been the soldiers or the rioters who immediately caused Youmans' death.[295] As to the military operation, it held that the soldiers had acted as agents of the state, since 'at the time of the commission of these acts the men were on duty under the immediate supervision and in the presence of a commanding officer'.[296] In this connection, the commissioners observed:

> It can not be properly said that adequate protection is afforded to foreigners in a case in which the proper agencies of the law to afford protection participate in the murder.[297]

This statement gives the preliminary impression that the General Claims Commission characterized an *action*, which it had found to be *directly attributable* to Mexico (namely, the shooting by the soldiers), as a *failure to provide protection*. This approach seems somewhat counterintuitive: If A willingly causes harm to B, it is artificial to say that A 'failed to give protection' to B.

In the analysis of these situations of fact, the point of departure must be the distinction between the *acts of state agents*, on the one hand, and the *acts of private individuals* on the other.[298] Taking the *Youmans* case as an example, a clear line must be drawn between the conduct of the State of Michoacán's soldiers and the conduct of the workers in revolt.[299] Nothing indicates that the acts of the latter

---

[289]*Thomas Youmans v Mexico* (23 November 1926) IV RIAA 110, 112 [3].

[290]*Thomas Youmans v Mexico* (23 November 1926) IV RIAA 110, 112 [3].

[291]*Thomas Youmans v Mexico* (23 November 1926) IV RIAA 110, 114-5 [11].

[292]*Thomas Youmans v Mexico* (23 November 1926) IV RIAA 110, 115 [12].

[293]*Thomas Youmans v Mexico* (23 November 1926) IV RIAA 110, 115-6 [13-4].

[294]*Thomas Youmans v Mexico* (23 November 1926) IV RIAA 110, 115-6 [13-4].

[295]*Thomas Youmans v Mexico* (23 November 1926) IV RIAA 110, 115 [12].

[296]*Thomas Youmans v Mexico* (23 November 1926) IV RIAA 110, 116 [14]. Section 8.3.2.5 discusses the question of state responsibility for acts of soldiers in detail.

[297]*Thomas Youmans v Mexico* (23 November 1926) IV RIAA 110, 115 [12].

[298]See also the discussion of the 'separate delict theory' in Sect. 12.4.3.

[299]Cf. *Thomas Youmans v Mexico* (23 November 1926) IV RIAA 110, 111 [2].

were attributable to the state (as it would have been the case, for example, if the workers had acted under 'control', 'instructions' or 'direction' of Mexico).[300]

Bearing in mind the differentiation between these two groups of persons (i.e. workers and soldiers), it becomes clear that, in reality, two *different* acts of the state were at stake: (1) the *action* of shooting at the Americans; and (2) the *failure* to prevent the laborers from attacking U.S. citizens.[301] Only the second act, that is, the act of *omission*, can be properly styled as a *failure* to provide protection.[302]

To say that the action and the omission are conceptually distinct is not, however, the same as saying that they are immaterial to each other. As explained by Clyde Eagleton in 1928, the action of state agents could still be relevant as *evidence* of the host state's want of diligence.[303] Contemporary investment arbitral decisions seem to coincide with Eagleton's approach. Several investment tribunals have indeed given weight to local authorities' active support to a private wrongdoer in their assessment of the host state's diligence.[304]

8.3.2.5 Conduct of Soldiers

During the nineteenth and early twentieth centuries, the territorial state's obligation to provide protection and security to aliens was frequently invoked in connection with conduct of soldiers.[305] The acts in question were not always accessory to mobs, riots or other classical examples of private wrongdoing.[306] There were many instances where acts of members of the host state's military were the direct and only source of the injury.[307] These decisions might raise doubts as to whether the customary FPS standard can be truly limited to risks that do not originate in the host state's own conduct.[308] This section submits that awards issued by mixed claims

---

[300]Cf. ILC, 'Responsibility of States for Internationally Wrongful Acts. General Commentary' (2001) 2 *Yearbook of the International Law Commission – 2001* 31, 47-9 art. 8.

[301]Cf. also the discussion of the 'separate delict theory' in Sect. 12.4.3.

[302]For the characterization of FPS as a 'delict of omission' see Sect. 11.3.

[303]Clyde Eagleton, *The Responsibility of States in International Law* (Klaus Reprint, New York 1970) 92 [first edition: 1928].

[304]Section 13.4.7 discusses these arbitral decisions in detail, in particular connection with the concept of 'due diligence'.

[305]For an overview see: John Bassett Moore, *A Digest of International Law* (Volume 6: Government Printing Office, Washington 1906) 758-65 (providing numerous examples of state practice in this area).

[306]Section 8.3.2.4 discussed the particular hypothesis of active support by state agents to private wrongdoers. On this scenario see also Sect. 13.4.7.

[307]For a representative example see: John Bassett Moore, *A Digest of International Law* (Volume 6: Government Printing Office, Washington 1906) 762-5 (referring to the *Pears* case, discussed later in this section).

[308]Cf. Sect. 8.3.1.

commissions in these cases are generally consistent with the definition of the customary FPS standard as protection against non-public risks.

In the contemporary law of state responsibility, attribution does not depend on the 'higher' or 'lower' hierarchy of an organ within a state's internal structure.[309] The threshold issue is whether state officials are acting in an 'official capacity' or in a merely 'private capacity'.[310] These present-day principles did not always enjoy general acceptance. For instance, U.S. Secretary of State Thomas Bayard stressed in 1885 that the United States 'is not responsible for collateral misconduct of individual soldiers dictated by private malice'.[311] This statement conveys a Grotian idea. In *De Iure Belli ac Pacis* (1625), Hugo Grotius famously argued that 'Kings [are not] bound to make Reparation, if their Soldiers, either by Sea or Land, shall do their Allies any Damage, contrary to their Command.'[312]

Mixed claims commissions often followed this Grotian line of argument. While upholding the host state's responsibility for injuries inflicted by soldiers under command and control of officers, they regularly assessed acts performed by soldiers in the absence of a commanding officer, or in violation of an officer's orders, as private conduct.[313] In the *Solis* claim of 1928, Commissioner Fred K. Nielsen observed:

[309]ILC, 'Responsibility of States for Internationally Wrongful Acts. General Commentary' (2001) 2 *Yearbook of the International Law Commission – 2001* 31, 40 art. 4(1) ("The conduct of any State organ shall be considered an act of that State under international law [. . .] *whatever position it holds in the organization of the State*" – emphasis added). See also the ILC's commentary to this provision.

[310]See: ILC, 'Responsibility of States for Internationally Wrongful Acts. General Commentary' (2001) 2 *Yearbook of the International Law Commission – 2001* 31, 41 [7] ("Nor is any distinction made at the level of principle between the acts of "superior" and "subordinate" officials, provided they are acting in their official capacity. This is expressed in the phrase "whatever position it holds in the organization of the State" in article 4. No doubt lower-level officials may have a more restricted scope of activity and they may not be able to make final decisions. But conduct carried out by them in their official capacity is nonetheless attributable to the State for the purposes of article 4").

[311]'Mr. Bayard, Sec. of State, to Mr. Buck, min. to Peru' (28 October 1885) in John Bassett Moore, *A Digest of International Law* (Volume 6: Government Printing Office, Washington 1906) 758, 758.

[312]For the English translation quoted in the main text see: Hugo Grotius, *The Rights of War and Peace in Three Books* (1625) (The Lawbook Exchange, Clark NJ 2004) 374 [Book 2 Chap. XVII, § XX(2)]. For the original Latin text see: Hugonis Groti, *De iure belli ac pacis* (1625) (Leiden, A. W. Sijthoff 1919) 332 [Lib. 2 Cap. XVII § XX(2)].

[313]Cf. *Case of the "Topas"* (undated) 3 Moore's Arb. 2992, 2992-3; *Case of Thomas K. Foster* (9 May 1874) 3 Moore's Arb. 2999, 2999; *D. Earnshaw et al. v United States of America* (30 November 1925) VI RIAA 160, 163-5; *Dunbar & Belknap v Mexico* (17 April 1875) 3 Moore's Arb. 2998, 2998; *G. L. Solis v Mexico* (3 October 1928) IV RIAA 358, 362-3; *Jean Jeannaud v United States of America* (undated) 3 Moore's Arb. 3000, 3001; *Louis Castelain and Marie Castelain v United States of America* (undated) 3 Moore's Arb. 2999, 3000; *Mildred Standish v Mexico* (12 March 1875) 3 Moore's Arb. 3004, 3005; *Theodore Webster v Mexico* (undated) 3 Moore's Arb. 3004; *Vidal v United States of America* (undated) 3 Moore's Arb. 2999, 2999. See generally: John Bassett Moore, *History and Digest of the International Arbitrations to Which the United States has been a Party* (Volume 3: Government Printing Office, Washington 1898) 2996-7 (providing a compilation and presentation of numerous decisions on the subject, including

[C]ertain cases coming before international tribunals may have revealed some uncertainty whether acts of soldiers should properly be regarded as private acts for which there is no liability on the state, or acts for which the state should be held responsible. In the absence of definite information concerning the precise situation of the troops, the Commission must consider whether it is warranted in assuming that the soldiers encamped on the claimant's ranch were a band of stragglers for whom there was no responsibility, or that they must have been under the direct command of some officer, or that responsibility for their location and activities rested with some officer, in the seemingly strange event that no responsible officer was in immediate command. I am of the opinion that it cannot be reasonably assumed that the soldiers were stragglers for whom there is no responsibility. I think it must be taken for granted that some officer was charged with responsibility for their station and acts.[314]

It was precisely in cases where no officer was in control that the host state's responsibility for soldiers' conduct was predicated on an *omission* in the protection of foreign nationals and their property.[315] This rationale applied not only to the prevention of harm as such, but also to the *redress* this kind of injuries.[316]

The *Pears* case (1899–1900) provides a representative example of this hypothesis.[317] Private Cruz Rosales, a recruit in the Honduran military, fired a gunshot against a U.S. citizen, causing his death.[318] Rosales was arrested and expelled from the armed forces, but was released shortly thereafter.[319] Criminal investigations against Rosales continued for a long time.[320] The U.S. State Department filed a

---

most of the cases mentioned above). See also: Frederick Sherwood Dunn, *The Diplomatic Protection of Americans in Mexico* (Klaus Reprint, New York 1971) 279 and 283-4 [first edition: 1933] (providing some additional examples from cases decided by the US-Mexico Claims Commission of 1868); John Bassett Moore, *A Digest of International Law* (Volume 6: Government Printing Office, Washington 1906) 758 *et seq.* (providing examples of diplomatic practice in this area).

[314] *G. L. Solis v Mexico* (3 October 1928) IV RIAA 358, 362-3.

[315] For this hypothesis see generally: John Bassett Moore, *A Digest of International Law* (Volume 6: Government Printing Office, Washington 1906) 758 *et seq.*

[316] For the obligation to punish 'subordinate officers' responsible for a wrongful act see: Francis Mitchell, 'International Liability for Mob Injuries' (1900) 34 Am. L. Rev. 709, 712.

[317] For a short description of the case see: John Bassett Moore, *A Digest of International Law* (Volume 6: Government Printing Office, Washington 1906) 762-5. For a detailed account of the facts see: 'Mr. Hay, Sec. of State, to Mr. Hunter' (16 March 1899) *Papers relating to the Foreign Relations of the United States with the Annual Message of the President* (Government Printing Office, Washington 1900) 674, 674-6.

[318] 'Mr. Hay, Sec. of State, to Mr. Hunter' (16 March 1899) *Papers relating to the Foreign Relations of the United States with the Annual Message of the President* (Government Printing Office, Washington 1900) 674, 674-5; John Bassett Moore, *A Digest of International Law* (Volume 6: Government Printing Office, Washington 1906) 762.

[319] 'Mr. Hay, Sec. of State, to Mr. Hunter' (16 March 1899) *Papers relating to the Foreign Relations of the United States with the Annual Message of the President* (Government Printing Office, Washington 1900) 674, 674-5; John Bassett Moore, *A Digest of International Law* (Volume 6: Government Printing Office, Washington 1906) 762.

[320] 'Mr. Hay, Sec. of State, to Mr. Hunter' (16 March 1899) *Papers relating to the Foreign Relations of the United States with the Annual Message of the President* (Government Printing Office, Washington 1900) 674, 675.

claim for compensation with the Honduran Office of Foreign Relations.[321] In its response, Honduras argued that the American claim was baseless:

> [T]he Government of Honduras, owing to the knowledge which it has of the facts verified, believes that responsibility cannot be deduced against the State, inasmuch as they were not done by its order nor received its approval.[322]

Secretary of State John Hay acknowledged that 'Rosales [...] was a raw recruit, ignorant and illiterate'.[323] Hay however underscored 'the sentinel's gross ignorance of his duty' as well as 'the gross ignorance or negligence of the officers of the guard and of the post in failing to properly instruct him'.[324]

Notwithstanding these remarks, the true bone of contention was the redress obligation. Honduras had initially submitted that 'the deed cannot justify a diplomatic claim, because the investigation is being carried out in accordance with prescribed laws'.[325] This explanation fell short as a Honduran criminal court declared that the death of the American had been accidental, and found Rosales innocent on all counts.[326] Secretary Hay expressed that 'there has appeared no serious purpose on the part of the Honduran Government to punish either the sentinel or his superiors'.[327] Honduran Secretary of Foreign Relations César Bonilla, albeit

---

[321] 'Mr. Hay, Sec. of State, to Mr. Hunter' (16 March 1899) *Papers relating to the Foreign Relations of the United States with the Annual Message of the President* (Government Printing Office, Washington 1900) 674, 676; John Bassett Moore, *A Digest of International Law* (Volume 6: Government Printing Office, Washington 1906) 762.

[322] 'Mr. Bonilla to Mr. Hunter' (25 April 1899) *Papers relating to the Foreign Relations of the United States with the Annual Message of the President* (Government Printing Office, Washington 1900) 679, 680.

[323] 'Mr. Hay, Sec. of State, to Mr. Hunter' (20 March 1900) *Papers relating to the Foreign Relations of the United States with the Annual Message of the President* (Government Printing Office, Washington 1900) 685, 689.

[324] 'Mr. Hay, Sec. of State, to Mr. Hunter' (20 March 1900) *Papers relating to the Foreign Relations of the United States with the Annual Message of the President* (Government Printing Office, Washington 1900) 685, 689.

[325] 'Mr. Bonilla to Mr. Hunter' (25 April 1899) *Papers relating to the Foreign Relations of the United States with the Annual Message of the President* (Government Printing Office, Washington 1900) 679, 680. The Honduran Minister of Justice made a similar statement in a separate document, which was attached to the diplomatic note: 'Mr. Fiallos, Honduran minister of justice, to the minister of Honduras' (4 March 1899) *Papers relating to the Foreign Relations of the United States with the Annual Message of the President* (Government Printing Office, Washington 1900) 681, 684.

[326] See: 'Mr. Hay, Sec. of State, to Mr. Hunter' (20 March 1900) *Papers relating to the Foreign Relations of the United States with the Annual Message of the President* (Government Printing Office, Washington 1900) 685, 688. See also: 'Mr. Bonilla to Mr. Hunter' (30 June 1899) *Papers relating to the Foreign Relations of the United States with the Annual Message of the President* (Government Printing Office, Washington 1900) 684, 684-5.

[327] 'Mr. Hay, Sec. of State, to Mr. Hunter' (20 March 1900) *Papers relating to the Foreign Relations of the United States with the Annual Message of the President* (Government Printing Office, Washington 1900) 685, 689.

insisting on Honduras' non-responsibility for these tragic events, eventually authorized payment of monetary damages.[328]

In sum, as far as an act committed by members of the military is considered as *not* attributable to the host state, there is nothing extraordinary about the application of the customary FPS standard. The original injury is, in the final analysis, *non-public* (i.e. *external* to the state).[329]

Closer to our times, the ICSID award rendered in *AMT v Zaire* (1997) provides an excellent example of this rationale.[330] The case concerned the investments of an American corporation, *American Manufacturing & Trading Inc.* [AMT], in Zairian territory (nowadays Democratic Republic of Congo).[331] AMT held a shareholding of over 90% in *Société Industrielle Zaïrois SPRL* [SINZA], a locally incorporated company.[332] In the period between 1991 and 1993, members of the local military plundered and severely damaged SINZA's industrial premises on multiple occasions.[333] AMT therefore filed a request for ICSID arbitration, invoking the United States-Zaire BIT of 1984.[334] In its arbitration claim, AMT specifically alleged that Zaire had breached its obligations under the BIT's FPS clause.[335] The US-Zaire BIT defined the extent of the security obligation by reference to customary law:

> [The] protection and security of investments [...] may not be less than that recognized by international law.[336]

The arbitrators thus held that the FPS standard, as envisaged by the BIT, was 'an objective obligation which must not be inferior to the minimum standard of vigilance

---

[328]The Honduran Secretary of Foreign Relations used a careful language, making the following suggestion to the Minister of the United States: "as this Government earnestly desires the maintenance of the harmony happily existing between the two countries, it is ready to take part in a friendly settlement, which would remove the difficulty, and that through whatever means which might impair neither the honor nor the dignity of the State, and which could not establish any precedent in cases that may unfortunately occur in the future." 'Mr. Bonilla to Mr. Hunter' (2 July 1900) *Papers relating to the Foreign Relations of the United States with the Annual Message of the President* (Government Printing Office, Washington 1900) 692, 693.

[329]See also the presentation of the 'core' of the FPS standard in Sect. 8.3.1.

[330]American Manufacturing & Trading Inc. *v* Zaire, Award, ICSID Case No. ARB 93/1 (21 February 1997).

[331]American Manufacturing & Trading Inc. *v* Zaire, Award, ICSID Case No. ARB 93/1 (21 February 1997) [1.01 and 1.05].

[332]American Manufacturing & Trading Inc. *v* Zaire, Award, ICSID Case No. ARB 93/1 (21 February 1997) [1.05].

[333]American Manufacturing & Trading Inc. *v* Zaire, Award, ICSID Case No. ARB 93/1 (21 February 1997) [3.04].

[334]American Manufacturing & Trading Inc. *v* Zaire, Award, ICSID Case No. ARB 93/1 (21 February 1997) [1.03].

[335]American Manufacturing & Trading Inc. *v* Zaire, Award, ICSID Case No. ARB 93/1 (21 February 1997) [6.04].

[336]Treaty between the United States of America and the Republic of Zaire concerning the Reciprocal Encouragement and Protection of Investment (adopted 3 August 1984, entered into force 28 July 1989) art. II.

and care required by international law'.[337] They consequently defined FPS as an 'obligation of vigilance', which requires the state to 'take all measures necessary to ensure the full enjoyment of protection and security of its [the investor's] investment'.[338] Consistent with this characterization of the standard, the arbitrators concluded:

> Zaire has breached its obligation by taking no measure whatever that would serve to ensure the protection and security of the investment in question [...] Zaire is responsible for its inability to prevent the disastrous consequences of these events adversely affecting the investments of AMT which Zaire had the obligation to protect [...] Zaire has manifestly failed to respect the minimum standard required of it by international law [...] The responsibility of the State of Zaire is incontestably engaged by the very fact of an omission by Zaire to take every measure necessary to protect and ensure the security of the investment made by AMT in its territory.[339]

The arbitral tribunal then assessed the war clause of the US-Zaire BIT, which specifically regulates compensation for 'riots' or other 'acts of violence'.[340] In this regard, the tribunal held that said clause 'more specifically reinforced' the treaty's FPS provision.[341] As to AMT's claims, the arbitrators stated:

> [I]t suffices to confirm once more the engagement of the responsibility of the State of Zaire [...] Such is the case without the Tribunal enquiring as to the identity of the author of the acts of violence committed on the Zairian territory. It is of little or no consequence whether it be a member of the Zairian armed forces or any burglar whatsoever [...] the Republic of Zaire is inevitably responsible for the losses and damages resulting from the events [...] without having to determine by whom these losses were caused.[342]

The later statement gives the impression that the ICSID tribunal considered that the FPS standard was equally applicable to state agents, such as members of the Zairian military, and private individuals. It is therefore little surprising for some authors to cite the *AMT* case as an example of the application of FPS in cases involving public violence.[343] A closer look reveals, however, that this understanding

---

[337]American Manufacturing & Trading Inc. *v* Zaire, Award, ICSID Case No. ARB 93/1 (21 February 1997) [6.06].

[338]American Manufacturing & Trading Inc. *v* Zaire, Award, ICSID Case No. ARB 93/1 (21 February 1997) [6.05].

[339]American Manufacturing & Trading Inc. *v* Zaire, Award, ICSID Case No. ARB 93/1 (21 February 1997) [6.08 and 6.10-6.11].

[340]Treaty between the United States of America and the Republic of Zaire concerning the Reciprocal Encouragement and Protection of Investment (adopted 3 August 1984, entered into force 28 July 1989) art. IV(2).

[341]American Manufacturing & Trading Inc. *v* Zaire, Award, ICSID Case No. ARB 93/1 (21 February 1997) [6.12 *et seq.*] (particularly at para 6.14). Section 15.7 discusses this aspect of the AMT case in greater detail.

[342]American Manufacturing & Trading Inc. *v* Zaire, Award, ICSID Case No. ARB 93/1 (21 February 1997) [6.13-6.14].

[343]For this understanding of the case see: Christoph Schreuer, 'Full Protection and Security' (2010) 1(2) J. Int'l Disp. Settlement 353, 357-8. See also: Christoph Schreuer, 'The Protection of Investments in Armed Conflicts' in Freya Baetens (ed), *Investment Law within International Law* (Cambridge University Press, Cambridge 2013) 3, 7-8.

of the AMT award is incorrect. The reason is that the AMT tribunal held that the plundering of SINZA's premises, despite resulting from actions of military men, had been committed in a merely private capacity:

> AMT maintains that the destructions [...] were committed by the Zairian armed forces from Camp Kokolo. It is true that they appeared to be (in whole or in part – in this regard, the Tribunal is not certain) soldiers with weapons of the army, including grenades and automatic weapons belonging to the armed forces [...] In the present case, it is true from the information received that there were the military, at least persons in military attire who manifestly acted individually without any one being able to show either that they were organized or that they were under order nor indeed that they were concerted. *The nature of the looting and the destruction of property which were (sic) looted show clearly that it was not "the army" or "the armed forces" that acted as such in the circumstance [...] they were separate individuals and not the forces that performed the action.*[344]

Against this background, it can be safely said that the *AMT v Zaire* case actually fits into the pattern of private violence cases.[345] This is also the reason why Zaire was held responsible, not for the *actions* of the soldiers who plundered SINZA's premises, but for an *omission* in the protection of foreign property.[346]

8.3.2.6 Risk of Private Violence Materializing in a Public Injury

In some rare occasions, a risk of private violence calling upon the host state to take preventive measures of protection does not materialize in a private injury, but in an injury that, as such, is directly imputable to the state. The United States – Mexico General Claims Commission was confronted with this intricate scenario in the *Francisco Mallén* incident of 1927.[347]

---

[344]Emphasis added. American Manufacturing & Trading Inc. *v* Zaire, Award, ICSID Case No. ARB 93/1 (21 February 1997) [7.06 and 7-08-7.10].

[345]Following a similar line of argument, some scholars have also classified AMT as a case pertaining to private violence. See for example: Elisabeth Zeitler, 'Full Protection and Security' in Stephan Schill (ed), *International Investment Law and Comparative Public Law* (Oxford University Press, New York 2010) 183, 192-3; Eric De Brabandere, 'Host States' Due Diligence Obligations in International Investment Law' (2014-5) 42 Syracuse J. Int'l L. & Com. 319, 335-6; Finnur Magnússon, *Full Protection and Security in International Law* (University of Vienna, Vienna 2012) 241-2.

[346]American Manufacturing & Trading Inc. *v* Zaire, Award, ICSID Case No. ARB 93/1 (21 February 1997) [6.10-6.11].

[347]The *Mallén* claim pertained to the security of a consular officer and not of an ordinary foreign national; nonetheless, the General Claims Commission considered that the difference between the protections owed to these two groups of persons was one of degree. See: *Francisco Mallén v United States* (27 April 1927) IV RIAA 173, 175 [6] ("The question has been raised whether consuls are entitled to a "special protection" for their persons. *If they should indicate that, apart from prerogatives extended to consuls either by treaty or by unwritten law, the Government of their temporary residence is bound to grant them other prerogatives not enjoyed by common citizens (be it citizens or aliens), the answer is in the negative.* But if "special protection" means that in executing the laws of the country, especially those concerning police and penal law, the

The case concerned two assaults against Mr. Francisco Mallén, the Mexican Consul in El Paso, Texas.[348] In the first attack, Juan Franco, a local police officer with a personal hatred towards Consul Mallén, used the shelter of the night to perpetrate the crime.[349] The prompt intervention of an eyewitness, whose possible affiliation to the local police remained unclear, saved Consul Mallén from dying at Deputy Franco's hands.[350] Both the United States and Mexico agreed that the U.S. Government was not directly responsible for Franco's initial physical assault.[351] In its decision of April 27th, 1927, the General Claims Commission qualified the action as 'the malevolent and unlawful act of a private individual who happened to be an official, not the act of an official'.[352] The Commission further held that '[l]ack of protection *during* this occurrence cannot be maintained; the second policemen, or the private citizen, did all what was necessary, and the incident was closed'.[353]

Local courts characterized the assault as a mere 'disturbance of the peace'.[354] For this reason, they merely imposed Franco a trifling fine.[355] While Franco was discharged from the police, he would eventually be allowed to assume the office of Deputy Sheriff.[356] The decision to reappoint Franco would be at the heart of the Mexican Government's subsequent diplomatic claim. A few months after the first incident, Consul Mallén was on his way from Ciudad Juárez (Mexico) to the United States.[357] Deputy Sheriff Franco followed the Consul from the Mexican side of the border.[358] Once the vehicle had arrived to the United States, Franco brutally assaulted Mallén and took him to jail.[359] The Commission did not spare words of censure against these actions:

> It is essential to state that the whole act was of a most savage, brutal and humiliating character. It is also essential to note that both Governments consider Franco's acts as the acts

---

Government should *realize* that foreign Governments are sensitive regarding the treatment accorded [to] their representatives, and that therefore the consul's residence *should exercise greater vigilance in respect to their security and safety,* the answer as evidently shall be in the affirmative" – emphasis added).

[348] *Francisco Mallén v United States* (27 April 1927) IV RIAA 173, 173-4 [1].

[349] *Francisco Mallén v United States* (27 April 1927) IV RIAA 173, 173-5 [1 and 4].

[350] *Francisco Mallén v United States* (27 April 1927) IV RIAA 173, 174-5 [4].

[351] *Francisco Mallén v United States* (27 April 1927) IV RIAA 173, 175 [5].

[352] *Francisco Mallén v United States* (27 April 1927) IV RIAA 173, 174 [4].

[353] *Francisco Mallén v United States* (27 April 1927) IV RIAA 173, 175 [5] (emphasis in the original).

[354] *Francisco Mallén v United States* (27 April 1927) IV RIAA 173, 175 [5].

[355] On the court proceedings see: *Francisco Mallén v United States* (27 April 1927) IV RIAA 173, 174-5 [4-5].

[356] *Francisco Mallén v United States* (27 April 1927) IV RIAA 173, 178 [12]. See also Commissioner Nielsen's remarks at p. 181.

[357] *Francisco Mallén v United States* (27 April 1927) IV RIAA 173, 176 [7].

[358] *Francisco Mallén v United States* (27 April 1927) IV RIAA 173, 176 [7].

[359] *Francisco Mallén v United States* (27 April 1927) IV RIAA 173, 176-7 [7].

of an official on duty (though he came from the Mexican side), and that the evidence establishes his showing his badge to assert his official capacity. Franco could not have taken Mallén to jail if he had not been acting as a police officer. *Though his act would seem to have been a private act of revenge which was disguised, once the first thirst of revenge had been satisfied, as an official act of arrest, the act as a whole can only be considered as the act of an official.*[360]

In the *Mallén* case, the initial physical attack indicated that a new attempt against Consul Mallén's life could occur at any time. This risk was of a *private* nature; it originated in the personal relationship between Mallén and Franco, who had been discharged from duty.[361] The United States, however, allowed Mallén to return to the police.[362] By so doing, U.S. authorities boosted existing risks to Mallen's life and personal integrity.[363] It is therefore little surprising that the General Claims Commission declared that the United States was not only responsible for the second attack, which was attributable to the state, but also for an internationally wrongful *omission* in the protection of Mr. Mallén:

> Lack of protection on the part of the Texas authorities lies in the fact that so dangerous an official as Franco, after having had his appointment as deputy contestable cancelled on October 14, 1907, was reappointed shortly afterwards [...] this time as deputy sheriff. This reappointment means lack of protection in so serious a form that it amounts to a challenge; it is exactly the reverse from that protection to all peaceful residents, whether aliens or nationals [...] the United States is liable: (a) for illegal acts of the deputy constable Franco on October 13, 1907; (b) for denial of justice on the ground of nonexecution of the penalty imposed on November 9, 1907, and (c) for lack of protection.[364]

In these scenarios, the host state could hence be responsible for at least two delinquencies: (1) the internationally wrongful action that has directly caused the injury; and (2) a lack of protection, which is to be established in terms of due diligence and properly falls within the scope of the customary FPS standard.[365]

8.3.3 Beyond the Public-Private Divide

This chapter has shown that the heart of the customary FPS standard lies in the protection of foreigners against the risk of private violence.[366] While the line between private and public wrongs could be somewhat obscure or blurred in specific factual scenarios, the application of the security obligation in such contexts follows the same rationale as in ordinary cases of private violence. In the end, the *source of*

---

[360]Emphasis added. *Francisco Mallén v United States* (27 April 1927) IV RIAA 173, 177 [7].

[361]On the personal relationship between the two men see: *Francisco Mallén v United States* (27 April 1927) IV RIAA 173, 175 [5].

[362]Cf. *Francisco Mallén v United States* (27 April 1927) IV RIAA 173, 178 [12].

[363]Cf. *Francisco Mallén v United States* (27 April 1927) IV RIAA 173, 177 [7].

[364]*Francisco Mallén v United States* (27 April 1927) IV RIAA 173, 178 [12].

[365]Cf. *Francisco Mallén v United States* (27 April 1927) IV RIAA 173, 178 [12].

[366]Cf. Sect. 8.3.1.

risk is always the conduct of a *third party* and, as such, is *external* to the host state.[367] Following a similar line of argument, German scholars have attempted to explain the normative structure of protection obligations (*Schutzpflichten*) in international law based on well-known categories of domestic public law:

> Rights to protection can only exist in the absence of an overreach by the state ('*Eingriff*'). In the case of an overreach, the breach of duty concerns a conventional right protecting individuals against public authorities ('*Abwehrecht*'), which is directly affected by state organs/the state. A right to protection presupposes a non-public infringement ('*Übergriff*'), that is to say, an impairment originating in a cause different from the mere exercise of sovereign authority.[368]

If one were to use the terminology proposed by Georg Jellinek in his celebrated *System der subjektiven öffentlichen Rechte* (1882), the duty to respect would correspond to the individual's freedom *from* the state ('*status libertatis*' or '*negativer Status*'), and the duty to protect would coincide with freedom *through* positive action by the state ('*status civitatis*' or '*positiver Status*').[369]

The FPS standard imposes a duty to protect individual rights from *external* threats and, from this perspective, would most perfectly coincide with Jellinek's *status civitatis*.[370] The underlying notion of security is well-known in legal science. Constitutional law scholars have submitted that the protection dimensions

---

[367]Cf. Sect. 8.3.2.

[368]Author's translation. The original German text reads: "Schutzrechte können nur dann entstehen, wenn kein staatlicher Eingriff vorliegt. Im Fall eines Eingriffs nämlich handelt es sich um eine Verletzung einer aus konventionellen staatsgerichteten Rechten (insbesondere Abwehrrechten) folgenden Pflicht *unmittelbar durch Staatliche Organe/den Staat* [...] [e]in Schutzrecht [setzt] aber einen sogenannten *Übergriff* voraus, d.h. die Beeinträchtigung, die durch eine nichthoheitliche Ursache hervorgerufen wurde." Sandra Stahl, *Schutzpflichten im Völkerrecht. Ansatz einer Dogmatik* (Springer, Heidelberg 2012) 122.

[369]Georg Jellinek, *System der subjektiven öffentlichen Rechte* (Akademische Verlagsbuchhandlung von J.C.B. Mohr 1892) 81-2. Jellinek believed that, in his relation to the state, the individual appears under a multitude of *statuses*, namely: (i) a passive status ('*passiver Status*' or '*status subjectionis*'), understood as a condition of subjugation towards the state; (ii) a negative status ('*negativer Status*' or '*status libertatis*'), which can be best portrayed as freedom *from* the (otherwise almighty) state; (iii) a positive status ('*positiver Status*' or '*status civitatis*'), which consists in freedom *through* the state or, put differently, a right to positive action by state organs for the security and protection of individual interests; and (iv) an active status ('*activer Status*' or '*Status activer Cività*'), which corresponds to the exercise of political rights (at pp. 81-2). According to Jellinek, the recognition of individual personality ('*individuelle Persönlichkeit*') should gradually reduce the scope of the passive status, and hence decrease the power of the state; the sovereign will thus cease to rule over slaves and can be consequently expected to treat his subjects as free men (at pp. 81-2). For an author using some of Jellinek's categories in connection with the FPS standard see: Helge Elisabeth Zeitler, 'Full Protection and Security' in Stephan Schill (ed), *International Investment Law and Comparative Public Law* (Oxford University Press, New York 2010) 183, 183 and n. 3 (Zeitler's views are discussed later in this section).

[370]Cf. Georg Jellinek, *System der subjektiven öffentlichen Rechte* (Akademische Verlagsbuchhandlung von J.C.B. Mohr 1892) 81-2. For these constitutional law distinctions see also: Josef Isensee, 'Abwehrecht und Schutzpflicht' in Josef Isensee and Paul Kirchhof (eds), *Handbuch des Staatsrechts* (Volume 9: C. F. Müller 2013) 413, 414-6.

(*Schutzaspekte*) of fundamental rights, taken as a whole, could be regarded as elements of a general 'fundamental right to security' (*Grundrecht auf Sicherheit*).[371] This constitutional approach might well describe the 'core' of the FPS standard. Nonetheless, in the law of aliens, the customary security obligation also covers risks that do not perfectly fit into these categories. For example, in cases involving public collateral damages caused *by state action* against external threats (e.g. destruction of private property in the course of counterinsurgency operations), it is doubtful whether the international delinquency can be accurately classified under Jellinek's *status civitatis*.[372]

Taking into consideration these circumstances, scholars have occasionally gone as far as to ascribe to the FPS standard a primarily negative function (in terms of freedom from the state).[373] They have consistently presented the positive aspect of FPS as an *additional*, if not to say *accessory*, function of the standard.[374] In this regard, Helgue Elizabeth Zeitler advances the following argument:

> The principle of 'full protection and security' requires, *as a minimum, the abstention of the host state from interference with the rights of the investor*, in particular violations of his or her property. But for all awards that have addressed the principle, one common observation may be made: the required standard *goes further* and is known from other areas of law, such as human rights and fundamental freedoms in national constitutional law. *It requires positive action by the host state to protect foreign investment through preventive and repressive action, and also against harm caused by private actors.* What is often described as the *status positivus* of fundamental rights has been translated in different ways into the investment law jurisprudence.[375]

Zeitler is right in observing that, while FPS certainly entails an obligation to take action as required under the *status civitatis*, this aspect does not exhaust the standard.[376] She goes, however, too far in placing a duty of abstention (or duty to respect) at the core of the FPS standard, implicitly leaving the positive aspect (*status civitatis*) in the backstage.[377] This section submits that cases where the customary

---

[371]See: Josef Isensee, *Das Grundrecht auf Sicherheit. Zu den Schutzpflichten des freiheitlichen Verfassungsstaates* (Walter de Gruyter, Berlin 1983) 33-4.

[372]For the concept of 'collateral damage' see Sect. 8.3.3.1.

[373]Cf. Helge Elisabeth Zeitler, 'Full Protection and Security' in Stephan Schill (ed), *International Investment Law and Comparative Public Law* (Oxford University Press, New York 2010) 183, 183.

[374]Cf. Helge Elisabeth Zeitler, 'Full Protection and Security' in Stephan Schill (ed), *International Investment Law and Comparative Public Law* (Oxford University Press, New York 2010) 183, 183.

[375]Emphasis added. Helge Elisabeth Zeitler, 'Full Protection and Security' in Stephan Schill (ed), *International Investment Law and Comparative Public Law* (Oxford University Press, New York 2010) 183, 183.

[376]Cf. Helge Elisabeth Zeitler, 'Full Protection and Security' in Stephan Schill (ed), *International Investment Law and Comparative Public Law* (Oxford University Press, New York 2010) 183, 183.

[377]Cf. Helge Elisabeth Zeitler, 'Full Protection and Security' in Stephan Schill (ed), *International Investment Law and Comparative Public Law* (Oxford University Press, New York 2010) 183, 183. In a previous article, Zeitler had focused on the application of the FPS standard in the specific context of private violence. See: Helge Elisabeth Zeitler, 'The Guarantee of Full Protection and Security in Investment Treaties Regarding Harm Caused by Private Actors' (2005) 3 SIAR 1, 2 *et seq.* (also drawing a distinction between duties of abstention and positive obligations at pp. 10 and 24).

FPS standard might actually be detached from the notion of third party conduct can be reduced to no more than two hypotheses: (1) the risk of public collateral damages; and (2) the risk of natural disasters.

8.3.3.1 Public Collateral Damages

Some of the best-known instances of application of the FPS standard have been concerned with injuries *incidentally* caused by the host state to a foreign citizen, especially in the course of operations aimed at the prevention or repression of private violence (e.g. military action against insurgents).[378] The present chapter designates such injuries as 'public collateral damages'.

The concept of 'collateral damages' has particularly developed in the area of international humanitarian law, in specific connection with the interpretation of articles 51(5)(b) ('protection of the civilian population') and 57 ('precautions in attack') of the *First Additional Protocol* to the Geneva Conventions.[379] The term roots, however, in a 'military jargon' describing injuries inflicted to the civilian population in the course of security maneuvers.[380] As used by contemporary sources, the notion is potentially broad in scope.[381] In international humanitarian law debate has chiefly focused on the issue of compensation for 'collateral damages' resulting from legitimate military operations.[382] The present chapter does not intend to use the phrase 'collateral damage' in this technical sense. Its choice of language merely seeks to underscore the *incidental* character of the injuries at stake.

---

[378]Cf. Asian Agricultural Products *v* Sri Lanka, Final Award, ICSID Case No ARB/87/3 (27 June 1990) (discussed later in this section).

[379]See: Protocol Additional to the Geneva Conventions of 12 August 1949, and relating to the Protection of Victims of International Armed Conflicts (adopted 8 June 1977, entered into force 7 December 1978) XVI ILM 1391, 1413 art. 51(5)(b) and 1415-6 art. 57.

[380]See: Giovanni Carlo Bruno, 'Collateral Damages of Military Operations: Is Implementation of International Humanitarian Law Possible Using International Human Rights Law Tools?' in Roberta Arnold and Noëlle Quénivet (eds), *International Humanitarian Law and Human Rights Law* (Brill, Leiden 2008) 295, 295.

[381]On the concept of 'collateral damage' in international humanitarian law see: Christine Byron, 'Collateral Damage' in Vincent Parrillo (ed), *Encyclopedia of Social Problems* (SAGE Publications, Thousand Oaks CA 2008) 140, 140-2; Giovanni Carlo Bruno, 'Collateral Damages of Military Operations: Is Implementation of International Humanitarian Law Possible Using International Human Rights Law Tools?' in Roberta Arnold and Noëlle Quénivet (eds), *International Humanitarian Law and Human Rights Law* (Brill, Leiden 2008) 295, 295-6; Hans-Peter Gasser and Knut Dörmann, 'Protection of the Civilian Population' in Dieter Fleck (ed), *The Handbook of International Humanitarian Law* (Oxford University Press, Oxford 2013) 231, 243-7; Louise Doswald-Beck et al., *San Remo Manual on International Law Applicable to Armed Conflicts at Sea* (Cambridge University Press, Cambridge 1995) 87; Neta Crawford, *Accountability for Killing: Moral Responsibility for Collateral Damage in America's Post-9/11* (Oxford University Press, New York 2013) 7-9.

[382]For the ongoing debate on compensation for 'collateral damages' see: Michael Reisman, 'Compensating Collateral Damage in Elective International Conflict' (2013) 8 Intercultural Hum. Rts. L. Rev. 1, 1-18.

This section submits that the customary FPS standard covers the risk of collateral damage to the 'acquired values' of foreign nationals.[383] International adjudicators have already been confronted with these factual scenarios. An interesting historical example would be the award rendered in *Luzon Sugar Refining Co. Ltd. v United States of America* (1925).[384] The case pertained to the damages suffered by a British company during an American counterinsurgency operation in the Philippines, which by then was under U.S. rule.[385] In that case, the commissioners could not reach a finding of responsibility:

> This is a claim for injury to the plant of the claimant during the Philippine insurrection. It appears that the insurgents entrenched about fifty yards on each side of the pumping station of the claimant and that during the operation of driving them out the plant was damaged by shells. It is clear from the report of General Otis that the damage was an incident of the military operations whereby the insurgents were driven from their capital. The foreign residents, whose property unhappily chanced to stand in the field of those operations, have no ground of complaint against the United States *which had no choice but to conduct them where the enemy was to be found. No complaint is made that the troops were out of hand or did anything beyond what the operations necessarily involved.*[386]

Contemporary investment tribunals have also addressed the issue of public collateral damages. A representative example would be the *AAPL v Sri Lanka* case of 1990.[387] The claimant was Asian Agricultural Products Ltd. [AAPL], a company incorporated under the laws of Hong Kong.[388] AAPL had made a substantial investment in *Serebid Seafoods Ltd.*, a public company registered in Sri Lanka, which conducted shrimp culture projects across the country.[389] The investor claimed that the local company's main production facilities had suffered severe damages in the course of a counterinsurgency operation undertaken by the host state's armed forces.[390] AAPL therefore submitted a request for ICSID arbitration under the Sri Lanka – United Kingdom BIT of 1980 (which covered Hong Kong investments).[391] The FPS standard was at the heart of the decision. In spite of the case being

---

[383]On the notion of 'acquired value' see Sect. 8.2.

[384]*Luzon Sugar Refining Co. Ltd. v United States of America* (30 November 1925) VI RIAA 165.

[385]*Luzon Sugar Refining Co. Ltd. v United States of America* (30 November 1925) VI RIAA 165.

[386]Emphasis added. *Luzon Sugar Refining Co. Ltd. v United States of America* (30 November 1925) VI RIAA 165. Roberto Ago cited this case in 1939 as an example of the role of fault (*culpa*) in the international law of state responsibility: Roberto Ago, *La colpa nell'illecito internazionale* (CEDAM – Casa Editrice Dott. A. Milani, Pavia 1939) 29.

[387]Asian Agricultural Products v Sri Lanka, Final Award, ICSID Case No ARB/87/3 (27 June 1990).

[388]Asian Agricultural Products v Sri Lanka, Final Award, ICSID Case No ARB/87/3 (27 June 1990) [1].

[389]Asian Agricultural Products v Sri Lanka, Final Award, ICSID Case No ARB/87/3 (27 June 1990) [3].

[390]Asian Agricultural Products v Sri Lanka, Final Award, ICSID Case No ARB/87/3 (27 June 1990) [3].

[391]Asian Agricultural Products v Sri Lanka, Final Award, ICSID Case No ARB/87/3 (27 June 1990) [1].

concerned with a specific FPS clause, the arbitrators also took into consideration customary international law.[392] In this connection, they held:

> It is a *generally accepted rule of International Law*, clearly stated in international arbitral awards and in the writings of the doctrinal authorities, that: (i) A State on whose territory an insurrection occurs is not responsible for the loss of damage sustained by foreign investors *unless it can be shown that the Government of that state failed to provide the standard of protection required, either by treaty, or under general customary law, as the case may be*; and (ii) Failure to provide the standard of protection required entails that state's international responsibility for losses suffered, *regardless of whether the damages occurred during an insurgents' offensive act or resulting from governmental counter-insurgency activities.*[393]

At first sight, this statement seems to be entirely straightforward. A closer look however reveals a possible inconsistency. In the case of a counterinsurgency operation, injuries to aliens result from a *state action*. If—following the argument of the *AAPL* tribunal—liability is established here for a *want of due diligence* in the protection of foreigners, a possible self-reference problem becomes apparent. FPS would require the state to exercise *due diligence* in respect of *its own conduct*, as opposed to some *external* phenomenon. It seems however artificial to say that the state whose *actions* immediately caused the harmful outcome is responsible for an *omission* in the protection of aliens.[394]

It has been argued that the *AAPL v Sri Lanka* award does not actually refer to public violence.[395] In this vein, a scholar has claimed that the *AAPL* tribunal never measured the acts of Sri Lanka, as such, against a due diligence standard of liability.[396] Rather, he says, the arbitrators' analysis of diligence pertained solely and only to omissions in the adoption of precautionary measures *prior* to the counterinsurgency operation.[397] He thus draws the following conclusion:

> In *AAPL v Sri Lanka*, the Tribunal indeed did not apply the due diligence standard to the acts of State organs which had caused harm [. . .] [T]he Tribunal considered that Sri Lanka, by failing to take precautionary measures to remove suspected staff members from the farm through peaceful means *before launching the attack*, violated its due diligence obligation [. . .] This finding was not applied to the acts of the State organ which had caused the killings

---

[392]See: Asian Agricultural Products *v* Sri Lanka, Final Award, ICSID Case No ARB/87/3 (27 June 1990) [22-3 and 40(D)].

[393]Emphasis added. Asian Agricultural Products *v* Sri Lanka, Final Award, ICSID Case No ARB/87/3 (27 June 1990) [72].

[394]Cf. also Lucas Bastin, *State Responsibility for Omissions: Establishing a Breach of the Full Protection and Security Obligation by Omissions* (Oxford University, Oxford 2016) [D.Phil. Thesis] 204 (observing that '[i]t is intuitively odd to speak of a State's failure to exercise due diligence to forestall damage which is the result of the State's own actions'). Bastin reaches, however, a different conclusion as to the scope of the FPS standard, and was not referring at this point to the hypothesis of collateral damages.

[395]Cf. Eric De Brabandere, 'Host States' Due Diligence Obligations in International Investment Law' (2014-5) 42 Syracuse J. Int'l L. & Com. 319, 335.

[396]Eric De Brabandere, 'Host States' Due Diligence Obligations in International Investment Law' (2014-5) 42 Syracuse J. Int'l L. & Com. 319, 335.

[397]Eric De Brabandere, 'Host States' Due Diligence Obligations in International Investment Law' (2014-5) 42 Syracuse J. Int'l L. & Com. 319, 335.

and destruction of property, since the Tribunal had found that there was no conclusive evidence that the Sri Lankan security forces had in fact killed the staff members and destroyed the farm, nor that the acts had been caused by the rebels [...] *This assessment thus was alien to the application of the due diligence standard to the acts of the destruction of the property itself by the Government forces.*[398]

This understanding of the case is not entirely consistent with the actual wording of the award. It is true that the arbitrators distinguished between state conduct before and after the military operation, but the *AAPL* tribunal was explicit and insistent in stating that: (1) the FPS standard is applicable in respect of *both* injuries caused by the insurgents and injuries inflicted by the armed forces[399]; and (2) FPS entails an obligation of vigilance and does under no circumstance impose 'strict liability' on the host state.[400] While it is true that the *AAPL* tribunal could not establish the effective cause of the injuries, the arbitrators drew no distinction whatsoever between the prevention of private harm, on the one hand, and the prevention of public damages on the other.[401] The rationale behind the arbitral tribunal's line of argument becomes clear in the following statement:

> The Tribunal is of the opinion that reasonably the Government should have at least tried to use such peaceful available high level channel of communication in order to get any suspect elements excluded from the farm's staff. This would have been essential to *minimize the risks* of the killings and destruction when planning to undertake a vast military counterinsurgency operation in that area for regaining lost control [...] the Tribunal considers that the *Respondent through said inaction and omission violated its due diligence obligation* which requires undertaking all possible measures that could be reasonably expected to prevent the *eventual occurrence* of killings and property destructions.[402]

This holding provides a clear indication that responsibility was established for an *omission* in the exercise of *due diligence* in the *mitigation* of damages, including public damages, that could *eventually* occur in connection with the military maneuver planned by the Sri Lankan army. It could hence be said that the state was held liable not only for failing to prevent injuries by the rebels but, most importantly, at least for present purposes, for *failing to mitigate collateral damages* associated to its *own actions.*

The *risk of collateral damages* is always incidental to an original, external, threat.[403] In counterinsurgency operations and similar sets of facts, the harmful

---

[398]Emphasis added. Eric De Brabandere, 'Host States' Due Diligence Obligations in International Investment Law' (2014-5) 42 Syracuse J. Int'l L. & Com. 319, 335.

[399]Asian Agricultural Products *v* Sri Lanka, Final Award, ICSID Case No ARB/87/3 (27 June 1990) [72].

[400]Asian Agricultural Products *v* Sri Lanka, Final Award, ICSID Case No ARB/87/3 (27 June 1990) [53 and 72]. For a detailed analysis of this aspect of the award see: Stephen Vasciannie, 'Bilateral Investment Treaties and Civil Strife: The AAPL/Sri Lanka Arbitration' (1992) 39(3) NILR 332, 344-6 and 353.

[401]Cf. Asian Agricultural Products *v* Sri Lanka, Final Award, ICSID Case No ARB/87/3 (27 June 1990) [72].

[402]Emphasis added. Asian Agricultural Products *v* Sri Lanka, Final Award, ICSID Case No ARB/87/3 (27 June 1990) [85(b)].

[403]For authors addressing the notion of 'collateral damages' see n. 381 above.

actions of the state are not *directed* against foreign citizens. State organs *react* against some *outside* phenomenon and aliens get injured in the process. The initial, original, threat is always external to the state; the risk of damage through the state is merely incidental. The original threat is, moreover, too, a potential threat against the values that become incidentally affected by state action. For instance, property damaged in the course of counterinsurgency operations is as much threatened by insurgent action (original threat) as by state action (incidental/collateral threat). For that very same reason, the direct source of the injury (state action) is, perhaps paradoxically, at the same time a means to prevent the materialization of a pre-existent, original, risk.

This paradox has an important corollary: the *values* impaired by collateral damages are necessarily *capable* of being affected by the original threat, which in turn corresponds to some outside phenomenon (usually private violence). The latter feature marks a fundamental difference in respect of cases pertaining, for example, to legal stability. Legitimate expectations concerning the stability of the investment's legal environment can only be frustrated by state action itself (e.g. through administrative or regulatory measures); private acts cannot by themselves produce a direct change in the host state's regulatory framework.[404]

Attention should also be drawn to the fact that, in cases concerning collateral damages, the breach of the FPS standard never refers to the *action* of the state as such, but to an *omission* by the state (i.e. the *failure* to exercise *due diligence* in the *mitigation* of collateral damages). This omission is autonomous and conceptually different from the action constituting the immediate cause of the injury. Even if the positive act (e.g. the counterinsurgency operation) is adjusted to international law, the failure to prevent or mitigate collateral damages could still be internationally wrongful.[405]

8.3.3.2 Natural Disasters and the Risk of Natural Hazards

Natural disasters are not an obvious concern of international investment law. Against the backdrop of massive losses of life, irreparable environmental damages and widespread misery, the protection of foreign nationals and their property cannot be more than an ancillary issue. States facing such extreme situations cannot be expected to give priority to foreign interests.[406] Not surprisingly, studies assessing the relationship between foreign investment and natural catastrophes have chiefly focused on circumstances precluding wrongfulness, such as the necessity defense and *force majeure*.[407]

---

[404]For the notion of 'legal stability' see Sect. 9.3.

[405]Section 8.3.2.2 advances a similar argument in respect of acts of third states in the host territory.

[406]Cf. also Sect. 13.4.8.

[407]For an indicative example, see: Ibironke Odumosu-Ayanu, 'International Investment Law and Disasters: Necessity, Peoples and the Burden of Economic Emergencies' in David Caron, Michael Kelly and Anastasia Telesetsky (eds), *The International Law of Disaster Relief* (Cambridge

Much less attention has been given to treaty clauses that expressly envisage these extraordinary situations. Such provisions are fairly common in investment treaties. A representative example would be article 8.11 of the *Comprehensive Economic and Trade Agreement* between the European Union and Canada [CETA]:

> Each Party shall accord to investors of the other Party, whose covered investments suffer losses owing to armed conflict, civil strife, a state of emergency or *natural disaster* in its territory, treatment no less favourable than that it accords to its own investors or to the investors of a third country, whichever is more favourable to the investor concerned, as regards to restitution, indemnification, compensation or other settlement.[408]

Similar clauses can be found in numerous IIAs.[409] A subsequent section assesses these provisions and their interplay with the treaty-based FPS standard in detail.[410] Two observations shall suffice for the purposes of this chapter. First, international law often assimilates natural disasters to events such as 'armed conflict' or 'civil strife', which are produced by human conduct.[411] Second, natural disasters are not

---

University Press, New York 2014) 314-37. See also: William Burke-White and Andreas von Staden, 'Investment Protection in Extraordinary Times: The Interpretation and Application of Non-Precluded Measures Provisions in Bilateral Investment Treaties' (2007-8) 48 Va. J. Int'l L. 307, 358 and 407. In this connection, the ILC has observed that '[m]aterial impossibility of performance giving rise to *force majeure* may be due to a natural or physical event [. . .] or to human intervention (e.g. loss of control over a portion of the State's territory as a result of an insurrection or devastation of an area by military operations carried out by a third state), or some combination of the two'. ILC, 'Responsibility of States for Internationally Wrongful Acts. General Commentary' (2001) 2 *Yearbook of the International Law Commission – 2001* 31, 76 art. 23 (Commentary) [3]. On natural disasters as an event of *force majeure* see also: ILC, 'Force Majeure and Fortuitous Event as Circumstances Precluding Wrongfulness: Survey of State Practice, International Judicial Decisions and Doctrine' (27 June 1977) 2(1) *Yearbook of the International Law Commission – 1978* 61, 72. For a similar statement in the field of international investment law see: José Álvarez, *Expert Opinion in Sempra Energy International v Argentina (ICSID Case No. ARB/02/16 and ARB/03/02)* (12 August 2005) [57].

[408]Emphasis added. Comprehensive Economic and Trade Agreement between Canada and the European Union (signed 30 October 2016, provisionally entered into force 21 September 2017) art. 8.11.

[409]This clause has been particularly usual in Canadian treaty practice. For some indicative examples see: Agreement between Canada and the Federal Republic of Senegal for the Promotion and Protection of Investments (adopted 27 November 2014) art. 7; Agreement between Canada and the Republic of Costa Rica for the Promotion and Protection of Investments (adopted 18 March 1998, entered into force 29 September 1999) art. 7; Agreement between Canada and the Republic of Croatia for the Promotion and Protection of Investments (adopted 3 February 1997, entered into force 30 January 2001) art. 7; Agreement between Canada and the Republic of Venezuela for the Promotion and Protection of Investments (adopted 1 July 1996, entered into force 28 January 1998) art. 6. See also: Canadian Model BIT (2004) art. 12(1).

[410]Cf. Sect. 15.7.

[411]Cf. Eduardo Valencia-Ospina, 'Preliminary Report on the Protection of Persons in the Event of Disasters (A/CN.4/598)' (5 May 2008) 2(1) *Yearbook of the International Law Commission – 2008* 143, 152 [48] (relying on a broad understanding of 'disaster', which would encompass both 'natural' calamities and 'man-made' calamities). The distinction between 'natural' and 'man-made' disasters was discussed during the sixtieth session of the ILC. See: ILC, 'Report of the International Law Commission on the Work of its Sixtieth Session – Protection of Persons in the Event of Disasters' (2008) 2(2) *Yearbook of the International Law Commission – 2008* 129, 132 [233-7].

only relevant in view of possible circumstances precluding wrongfulness, but could also trigger specific obligations of the host state.[412]

In a detailed survey on the subject (2007), the ILC observed that, as a consequence of its 'territorial sovereignty', every state 'has the primary responsibility for the protection of persons on its territory or subject to its jurisdiction or control during a disaster'.[413] This fundamental premise found clear expression in the *Draft Articles on the Protection of Persons in the Event of Disasters* (2016):

> The affected State has the duty to ensure the protection of persons and provision of disaster relief assistance in its territory, or in territory under its jurisdiction or control.[414]

The 2016 Draft further provides:

> Each State shall reduce the risk of disasters by taking appropriate measures, including through legislation and regulations, to prevent, mitigate and prepare for disasters.[415]

The ILC Draft shows that failures to prevent or mitigate the hazardous effects of a natural disaster could constitute violations of protection obligations under international law.[416] While these obligations certainly resemble the customary security obligation, they do not entirely coincide with the FPS standard. To begin with, they are applicable to the benefit of citizens and aliens alike.[417] Moreover, some of the territorial state's obligations in this area have been characterized in the past as 'obligations of result'.[418]

---

[412]Cf. Comprehensive Economic and Trade Agreement between Canada and the European Union (signed 30 October 2016, provisionally entered into force 21 September 2017) art. 8.11.

[413]ILC, 'Protection of Persons in the Event of Disasters: Memorandum by the Secretariat (A/CN.4/590)' (11 December 2007) [http://legal.un.org/docs/?symbol=A/CN.4/590] 23 [23].

[414]ILC, 'Draft Articles on the Protection of Persons in the Event of Disasters (A/71/10)' (2016) [http://legal.un.org/ilc/texts/instruments/english/commentaries/6_3_2016.pdf] 28 art. 10(1).

[415]ILC, 'Draft Articles on the Protection of Persons in the Event of Disasters (A/71/10)' (2016) [http://legal.un.org/ilc/texts/instruments/english/commentaries/6_3_2016.pdf] 22 art. 9(1).

[416]Please note that protection obligations are usually aimed at the *prevention* of harm. They are consequently triggered by the *risk* of a disaster, rather than by the *occurrence* of a disaster. In his *Preliminary Report on the Protection of Persons in the Event of Disasters*, Eduardo Valencia-Ospina suggested the distinction of at least three 'successive phases' in this regard: (i) pre-disaster stage; (ii) disaster response; and (iii) post-disaster stage. Eduardo Valencia-Ospina, 'Preliminary Report on the Protection of Persons in the Event of Disasters (A/CN.4/598)' (5 May 2008) 2(1) *Yearbook of the International Law Commission – 2008* 143, 154 [57-8].

[417]Cf. ILC, 'Draft Articles on the Protection of Persons in the Event of Disasters (A/71/10)' (2016) [http://legal.un.org/ilc/texts/instruments/english/commentaries/6_3_2016.pdf] 16 [7].

[418]In 2013, the Chairman of the Drafting Committee characterized the obligation to 'reduce the risk of disasters' as an obligation of result; see: ILC, 'Protection of Persons in the Event of Disasters: Statement of the Chairman of the Drafting Committee' (26 July 2013) [http://legal.un.org/docs/?path=./ilc/sessions/65/pdfs/protection_of_persons_dc_statement_2013.pdf&lang=E] 3-4. However, the ILC's commentary to Draft Article 9(1) suggests that said duty constitutes an obligation of conduct; see: ILC, 'Draft Articles on the Protection of Persons in the Event of Disasters (A/71/10)' (2016) [http://legal.un.org/ilc/texts/instruments/english/commentaries/6_3_2016.pdf] 26 [10].

The threshold issue is whether the customary FPS obligation (i.e. a specific international protection obligation) may be said to comprise the risk of *natural disasters* or, broadly speaking, the risk of *natural hazards*. Before going any further, attention should be drawn to the fact that not every *natural hazard* can be properly characterized as a *natural disaster*. The expression *natural disaster* (particular category), as used by the ILC, conveys the meaning of a *natural hazard* (general category) that is signalized by its exceptionally acute or severe effects.[419]

In its *First Report* of 2014, the *ILA Study Group on Due Diligence in International Law* included protection against natural hazards within the scope of the FPS standard.[420] However, the report did not elaborate much on this idea. Neither does investment adjudicatory practice yet provide clear guidance in this regard. To date, the perhaps most relevant investment case about protection against environmental risks is *Peter Allard v Barbados* (2016).[421] In that case, the investor argued 'that damage to private property caused by pollution is an actionable injury under customary international law'.[422] Particularly, he claimed that 'physical interference with property through the unlawful trespass of pollutants' constituted a violation of the FPS standard.[423] Barbados questioned these premises.[424] The tribunal did not deem it necessary to take a stance in the debate and dismissed the FPS claim:

> Even accepting the Claimant's articulation of the FPS standard as including an obligation of the host State to protect foreign investments against environmental damage, and assuming (*quod non*) that environmental damage was proven in the present case, the Tribunal finds that no violation of the FPS standard arising under Article II(2)(b) of the [Canada-Barbados] BIT is established.[425]

These sources convey some skepticism as to whether the FPS standard covers the risk of environmental damage. Even from a more general perspective, attempts to codify rules of international law addressing natural hazards are often perceived as suggestions *de lege ferenda*, which lack a genuine *lex lata* character.[426] The reason

---

[419]ILC, 'Protection of Persons in the Event of Disasters' (2006) 2(2) *Yearbook of the International Law Commission – 2006* 206, 206 [3-4] (qualifying 'natural disasters' as 'natural hazards' and further noting that '[t]he fact that such events become "disasters" speaks more of the susceptibility of human beings to the adverse effects of natural hazards').

[420]ILA Study Group on Due Diligence in International Law, 'First Report by Mr. Tim Stephens (Rapporteur) and Mr. Duncan French (Chair)' (7 March 2014) 9 (making express reference to 'natural disasters').

[421]Peter A. Allard v Barbados (UNCITRAL), Award (27 June 2016).

[422]Peter A. Allard v Barbados (UNCITRAL), Award (27 June 2016) [231].

[423]Peter A. Allard v Barbados (UNCITRAL), Award (27 June 2016) [231].

[424]Peter A. Allard v Barbados (UNCITRAL), Award (27 June 2016) [236].

[425]Peter A. Allard v Barbados (UNCITRAL), Award (27 June 2016) [252].

[426]Cf. ILC, 'Protection of Persons in the Event of Disasters' (2006) 2(2) *Yearbook of the International Law Commission – 2006* 206 [1] (stating that '[t]he topic "Protection of persons in the event of disasters" would fall within the category of "new developments in international law and pressing concerns of the international community as a whole" as contemplated by the Commission, at its forty-ninth session, upon establishing guidelines for the inclusion of topics in the long-term programme of work').

is, perhaps, that state practice in this specific area is rather scant. As a corollary, an inductive analysis about the protection of foreigners against natural hazards would pose insurmountable difficulties. Arguments placing the risk of natural hazards within the customary protection obligation thus require resort to deductive reasoning and, particularly, to 'analogical deduction'.[427] As observed by Hersch Lauterpacht in 1933:

> It happens frequently that when an international tribunal is confronted with a seemingly novel situation, although there is no rule of international law directly applicable to case before the Court, international law regulates expressly some similar situation. It is to these rules that the Tribunal has recourse in dealing with a case *prima impressionis*.[428]

The question would hence be whether and to which extent the risk of natural hazards is *analogous* to risks that can be safely said to fall within the scope of the customary security obligation (e.g. private violence). Natural hazards are similar to third party conduct in that they are *external* to the host state. It is precisely this *external character* what ultimately defines the objective scope of application of the FPS standard in the customary law of aliens.[429] This quality explains why the standard may be said to comprise, beyond the risk of private violence properly so-called, the risk of injuries caused by foreign states and international organizations.[430] Following this line of argument, there seems to be no reason for the exclusion natural hazards.

Let us consider a hypothetical example. A is a foreign national whose property is at risk of being flooded. Public authorities have been timely alerted of the situation and are in a position to actually prevent or diminish the hazardous consequences of the imminent flood. Nonetheless, the host state fails to undertake any step in that direction. The risk subsequently materializes, causing a total loss of property. Consider now the case of B, a foreign national facing the imminent risk of his property being damaged by a mob. Assume that, except for the source of the risk, the situation of B is identical to that of A. In the situation portrayed above, it makes little sense to hold the FPS obligation applicable in the case of B, but not in the case of A. In respect of the host state, the situation of A is *analogous* to that of B. Both A and B are facing threats that do *not* originate in positive conduct by the host state, and which call for positive action by local authorities.

---

[427]For the concept of 'analogical deduction' and its use in the identification of customary rules of international law see: Stefan Talmon, 'Determining Customary International Law: The ICJ's Methodology between Induction, Deduction and Assertion' (2015) 26(2) EJIL 417, 426-7 (particularly addressing the practice of the ICJ).

[428]Hersch Lauterpacht, *The Function of International Law in the International Community* (Clarendon Press, Oxford 1933) 111.

[429]Cf. Sects. 8.3.1 and 8.3.2.

[430]See Sects. 8.3.2.2 and 8.3.2.3.

Chapter 9
Objective Scope of Application: Irrelevance of the Distinction Between Physical and Nonphysical Harm

9.1 Preliminary Remarks

Chapter 8 has shown that the risks covered by the customary FPS standard are identifiable by their source.[1] As a rule, the standard refers to risks that do *not* originate in the host state's conduct, such as private violence and natural phenomena. A look into academic publications and arbitral awards reveals, however, that another criterion has been *en vogue* for decades: the material nature of the threat. The bone of contention has been whether the FPS standard refers only to the *physical security* of investments or encompasses, too, the notion *nonphysical* security. Specifically, the question has been raised as to whether FPS guarantees investors *legal security*, a particular form of nonphysical protection, in the sense of a stable and secure legal framework for the investment.[2]

The adjective 'physical' has remained largely undefined in both arbitral decisions and academic publications. In spite of relevant sources providing no elaboration on the term, nothing suggests that *physical* has ever conveyed a notion other than its ordinary meaning. For present purposes, a dictionary definition of *physical* may be resorted to as a guideline for ascertaining the word's meaning in common linguistic usage. The Webster English Dictionary defines *physical* as something 'having material existence: perceptible through the senses and subject to the laws of nature'.[3] Similarly, the Oxford English Dictionary describes the term as follows:

---

[1] See particularly Sect. 8.3.

[2] See Sect. 9.3.

[3] 'physical' in *Merriam Webster Collegiate Dictionary* (Merriam-Webster, Springfield MA 2004) 935. To this effect, the Dictionary's definition relies on Thomas De Quincey's *The Caesars*, where De Quincey observed that 'everything physical is measurable by weight, motion, and resistance'. Thomas De Quincey, *The Caesars* (Ticknor & Fields, Boston 1860) 21 (De Quincey was however referring only to *physical power*).

© Springer Nature Switzerland AG 2019
S. Mantilla Blanco, *Full Protection and Security in International Investment Law*,
European Yearbook of International Economic Law 8,
https://doi.org/10.1007/978-3-030-24838-3_9

Of or relating to natural phenomena perceived through the senses (as opposed to the mind); of or relating to matter or the material world; natural; tangible, concrete [. . .] Involving or inclined towards bodily contact or activity; tactile; strenuous, vigorous. Also: bodily aggressive or violent.[4]

Departing from these definitions, this chapter examines the ongoing discussion about the notions of *physical* and *nonphysical* security. In this vein, it submits that these categories are irrelevant for the determination of the customary standard's scope of application. The argument begins with a presentation of pertinent arbitral decisions and academic publications. Based on this overview of the debate, a second section considers the specific question of whether the *customary* FPS standard encompasses a guarantee of legal security. The proposition advanced is that *legal risks* have never belonged with the customary security obligation. Attempts to introduce this type of risks into the standard are ill founded and unsound.

Finally, a third section seeks to determine whether there are forms of nonphysical violence that could actually fall within the scope of the FPS standard. On the basis of some indicative examples of state practice, it contends that the standard is applicable in respect of both physical and nonphysical risks, provided the *source of risk* is *external* to the host state. Plainly stated: it is not the material nature of the risk, but only its *source*, what is relevant for the definition of the obligation's scope of application. The conclusion is that the physical-nonphysical divide, which has for a long time dominated academic debate on the subject, is largely misleading.

9.2 Physical Security and Nonphysical Security: The Debate at a Glance

Many, if not to say most, instances of application of the FPS standard have been some way or other concerned with physical violence. In an effort to overcome the uncertainties attached to the meaning and scope of the FPS standard, arbitral tribunals have frequently held that the protection obligation refers to *physical security* only. Adjudicators often go on to characterize this approach as the 'traditional' or 'more commonly accepted' understanding of the standard. An example may be found in *Gold Reserve v Venezuela* (2014), where the arbitrators stated:

The Tribunal finds that Claimant's claim under Article II(2) of the BIT, to the extent that it provides for the duty to accord full protection and security to Claimant's investments, is to be dismissed. While some investment treaty tribunals have extended the concept of full protection and security to an obligation to provide regulatory and legal protections, *the more traditional, and commonly accepted view, as confirmed in the numerous cases cited by Respondent is that this standard of treatment refers to protection against physical harm to persons and property. Accordingly, the Tribunal finds that the obligation to accord full protection and security under the BIT refers to the protection from physical harm.* There has

---

[4]'physical, adj.' (May 2016) *Oxford English Dictionary Online* [http://www.oed.com/view/Entry/143120?rskey=KMtVVv&result=2&isAdvanced=false#eid].

been no suggestion in the present case that Respondent failed to protect Claimant's investment from physical harm, and therefore no breach of the full protection and security standard occurred.[5]

To the same effect, in *BG Group Plc. v Argentina* the tribunal noted that 'notions of protection and security or full protection and security in international law have *traditionally* been associated with situations where the *physical security* of the investor or its investment is compromised' and considered 'inappropriate' to extend the standard beyond this core.[6] Similar statements have been recurrent in investment arbitral awards.[7] Perhaps inspired by these developments, recent treaty practice, too,

---

[5]Emphasis added. Gold Reserve Inc. *v* Venezuela, Award, ICSID Case No. ARB(AF)/09/1 (22 September 2014) [622-3].

[6]BG Group *v* Argentina (UNCITRAL), Final Award (24 December 2007) [324] (heavily relying on *AAPL v Sri Lanka* and *AMT v Zaire* and dismissing the claimant's argument that the standard encompasses the notion of 'legal security').

[7]For some representative examples see: Bernhard Friedrich Arnd Rüdiger von Pezold et al. *v* Zimbabwe, Award, ICSID Case No. ARB/10/15 (28 July 2015) [596] (stating that FPS 'relates to physical security and threats of violence'); Crystallex International Corp. *v* Venezuela, Award, ICSID Case No. ARB(AF)/11/2 (4 April 2016) [632-5] (relying on the 'ordinary meaning' of the words 'protection' and 'security', as well as on the need of avoiding an overlap with the FET standard; in addition, the tribunal observed at n. 862 that its conclusion would have been the same had the treaty used the formula 'in accordance with principles of international law'); Deutsche Bank AG *v* Sri Lanka, Award, ICSID Case No. ARB/09/02 (31 October 2012) [535 and 538] (indicating that the 'prevailing interpretation of the clause' is that FPS protects the 'physical integrity of the investment', but making no finding on the alleged breach of the standard); Marion Unglaube and Reinhard Unglaube *v* Costa Rica, Award, ICSID Cases No. ARB/01/1 and ARB/09/20 (16 May 2012) [280 *et seq.*] (observing at para 280 that 'full protection and security has traditionally been interpreted as referring to government protection of the physical facilities and personnel related to an investment', but adopting a broader interpretation of the treaty clause at stake at paras 281 *et seq.*); Mohammad Ammar Al-Bahloul *v* Tajikistan, Partial Award on Jurisdiction and Liability, SCC Case No. V 064/2008 (9 September 2009) [246] (stating that FPS has 'principally developed in the context of physical security', but supporting a broader interpretation of the 'most constant protection and security' clause of the ECT); OI European Group B.V. *v* Venezuela, Award, ICSID Case No. ARB/11/25 (10 March 2015) [571-6] (referring to a treaty clause using the phrase 'full *physical* security and protection' – emphasis added); PSEG Global Inc. and Konya Ilgin Elektrik Üretim ve Ticaret Limited Şirketi *v* Turkey, Award, ICSID Case No. ARB/02/5 (19 January 2007) [258-9] (also acknowledging that the standard has been extended beyond physical security in 'exceptional situations'); Rumeli Telekom A.S. and Telsim Mobil Telekomunikasyon Hizmetleri A.S. *v* Kazakhstan, Award, ICSID Case No. ARB/05/16 (29 July 2008) [668] (specifically making reference to the notion of 'physical damage'); SAUR International S.A. *v* Argentina, Décision sur la compétence et sur la responsabilité, ICSID Case No. ARB/04/4 (6 June 2012) [499-501] (however noting that that the distinction between physical and nonphysical protection was immaterial for the resolution of the dispute); Tenaris S.A. and Talta-Trading E Marketing Sociedade Unipessoal Lda. *v* Venezuela, Award, ICSID Case No. ARB/11/26 (29 January 2016) [438] (stating that 'the standard of constant protection refers principally to the physical protection of the investor and its assets'); Toto Construzioni Generali S.p.A. *v* Lebanon, Award, ICSID Case No. ARB/07/12 (7 June 2012) [228-9] (making reference to the 'physical integrity' of the investment). Some tribunals have delimited the scope of application of the FPS standard through both the notion of *private violence* and the concept of *physical violence*. If this approach were to be followed, FPS would refer only to acts of *physical* violence committed by *third* parties. For some representative examples see: Eastern

has resorted to the concept of *physical violence* as a means to delimit the scope of FPS clauses. These novel provisions can be classified in two groups. A first group of clauses defines the scope of FPS without making any reference whatsoever to customary law.[8] Those provisions pose a question of interpretation, the threshold

---

Sugar B.V. *v* Czech Republic, Partial Award, SCC Case No. 088/2004 (27 March 2007) [203] (referring to acts committed by '*third parties* [. . .] engaged in *physical violence* against the investor in violation of the state monopoly of *physical force*'); Saluka Investments *v* Czech Republic (UNCITRAL), Partial Award (17 March 2006) [483-4] (describing the scope of application of FPS as referred to 'civil strife and physical violence', but qualifying this statement with the phrase 'essentially', thus potentially opening the door for extensive interpretations of the standard); Suez Sociedad General de Aguas de Barcelona S.A. and Vivendi Universal S.A. *v* Argentina, Decision on Liability, ICSID Case No. ARB/03/19 (30 July 2010) [164-7, 173-5, 179] (particularly at paras 165 and 174-5) (heavily relying on the wording of a specific FPS provision). Cf. also: Mobil Exploration and Development Argentina Inc. Suc. Argentina and Mobil Argentina S.A. *v* Argentina, Decision on Jurisdiction and Liability, ICSID Case No. ARB/04/16 (10 April 2013) [999-1005] (following the third party approach throughout the analysis of the FPS claims, but using the phrase 'physical protection' in connection with the prevention obligation, at para 1002).

[8] An example would be article 3(1) of the Netherlands – Dominican Republic BIT, whereby '[e]ach Contracting Party shall accord to such investments *full physical security and protection*'. Emphasis added. Agreement on Encouragement and Reciprocal Protection of Investments between the Kingdom of the Netherlands and the Dominican Republic (adopted 3 March 2006, entered into force 1 October 2007) art. 3(1). This wording has not been uncommon in Dutch treaty practice. For some additional examples see: Agreement between the Kingdom of the Netherlands and the Macao Special Administrative Region of the People's Republic of China on Encouragement and Reciprocal Protection of Investments (adopted 22 May 2008, entered into force 1 May 2009) art. 3(1); Agreement on Encouragement and Reciprocal Protection of Investments between the Government of the Republic of Tajikistan and the Government of the Kingdom of the Netherlands (adopted 24 July 2002, entered into force 1 April 2004) art. 3(1); Agreement on Encouragement and Reciprocal Protection of Investments between the Republic of Armenia and the Kingdom of the Netherlands (adopted 10 June 2005, entered into force 1 August 2006) art. 3(1); Agreement on Encouragement and Reciprocal Protection of Investments between the Kingdom of the Netherlands and the Republic of Suriname (adopted 31 March 2005, entered into force 1 September 2006) art. 3 (1); Agreement on Encouragement and Reciprocal Protection of Investments between the Kingdom of the Netherlands and the Republic of Venezuela (adopted 22 October 1991, entered into force 1 November 1993, terminated 1 November 2008) art. 3(2) (see also ad article 3 in the Protocol to the BIT, referring to the minimum standard *only* in connection with the FET standard, and not in respect of FPS); Agreement on Encouragement and Reciprocal Protection of Investments between the Lao People's Democratic Republic and the Kingdom of the Netherlands (adopted 16 May 2003, entered into force 1 May 2005) art. 3(1). Other treaties use the phrase 'adequate physical protection and security'. For some indicative examples see: Agreement between the Government of the Kingdom of Cambodia and the Government of the Republic of Cuba concerning the Promotion and Protection of Investments (adopted 26 September 2001) art. 3(1); Agreement between the Government of the Kingdom of Cambodia and the Government of the Socialist Republic of Vietnam concerning the Promotion and Protection of Investments (adopted 1 September 2001) art. 3(1); Agreement between the Government of the Kingdom of Cambodia and the Government of the Republic of the Philippines concerning the Promotion and Protection of Investments (adopted 16 August 2000) art. 3(1); Agreement between the Government of the Republic of Singapore and the Government of the Republic of Indonesia on the Promotion and Protection of Investments (adopted 16 February 2005, entered into force 21 June 2006) art. 2(2). Cf. also: Indian Model BIT (2015) art. 3.2 (expressly clarifying that FPS 'only refers to a Party's obligations relating to physical security').

issue being whether and to which extent the treaty-based protection obligation overlaps with the customary security obligation.[9] In other clauses, the contracting parties clearly incorporate the *customary* FPS standard into the treaty, and define such customary standard in terms of *physical security*. An indicative example would be article 10 of the New Zealand-Taiwan Economic Cooperation Agreement:

> Minimum Standard of Treatment. 1. Each Party shall accord to covered investments treatment in accordance with the customary international law minimum standard of treatment, including fair and equitable treatment and full protection and security. 2. The obligation in paragraph 1 to provide: [. . .] (b) "full protection and security" requires each party to take such measures as may be reasonably necessary to ensure the *physical protection and security* of covered investments. 3. The concepts of "fair and equitable treatment" and "full protection and security" do not require treatment in addition to or beyond that which is required by the customary international law minimum standard of treatment, and do not create additional substantive rights.[10]

The qualification of the customary standard with the adjective *physical* has found support in some academic publications.[11] Still, many authors remain skeptical. The debate is generally presented as a dichotomy between the restriction of the standard to *physical security* and its extension to *legal security* (understood as *legal*

The Indian Model BIT does not refer to customary law with regard to the FPS standard, but art. 3.1 refers to other customary rules (e.g. denial of justice). On the FPS clause of the Indian Model BIT cf. Prabhash Ranjan, 'Investment Protection and Host State's Right to Regulate in the Indian Model Bilateral Investment Treaty: Lessons for Asian Countries' in Julien Chaisse, Tomoko Ishikawa and Sufian Jusoh (eds), *Asia's Changing International Investment Regime: Sustainability, Regionalization, and Arbitration* (Springer, Singapore 2017) 47, 58-9.

[9]Chapter 14 addresses the relationship between the customary standard and the interpretation of FPS treaty clauses in detail.

[10]Emphasis added. Agreement between New Zealand and the Separate Customs Territory of Taiwan, Penghu, Kinmen, and Matsu on Economic Cooperation (adopted 10 July 2013) art. 10. For some additional examples of treaties using a similar wording see: Free Trade Agreement between Malaysia and Australia (adopted 22 May 2012, entered into force 1 January 2013) art. 12.7; Protocol on Investment to the New Zealand-Australia Closer Economic Relations Trade Agreement (adopted 16 February 2011, entered into force 1 March 2013) art. 12.

[11]For examples of academic publications expressing support for the 'physical security' criterion see: Burkhard Schöbener, Jochen Herbst and Markus Perkams, *Internationales Wirtschaftsrecht* (C.F. Müller, Heidelberg 2010) 278; Carsten Kern, *Schiedsgericht und Generalklausel: Zur Konkretisierung des Gebots des fair and equitable treatment in der internationalen Schiedsgerichtsbarkeit* (Mohr Siebeck, Tübingen 2017) 158-62; Giuditta Cordero Moss, 'Full Protection and Security' in August Reinisch (ed), *Standards of Investment Protection* (Oxford University Press, New York 2008) 131, 131-2; Zachary Douglas, 'Property, Investment, and the Scope of Investment Protection Obligations' in Zachary Douglas, Joost Pauwelyn and Jorge Viñuales (eds), *The Foundations of International Investment Law. Bringing Theory into Practice* (Oxford University Press, Oxford 2014) 363, 379; Vasyl Chornyi, Marianna Nerushay and Jo-Ann Crawford, *A Survey of Investment Provisions in Regional Trade Agreements*, WTO Working Paper ERSD-2016-07 (World Trade Organization/Economic Research and Statistics Division, Geneva 2016) 27.

stability).[12] Scholars disregarding the restrictive, physical approach have usually resorted to historical arguments about customary law.

With a particular focus on U.S. treaty practice, George Foster (2012) argues that limiting the scope of the standard to physical protection is 'untenable'.[13] He further criticizes recent U.S. treaties, which limit the FPS standard to *police protection*, a notion that Foster considers to be closely connected with the concept of *physical security*.[14] According to Foster, the State Department is 'perpetuating the misunderstanding that the customary norm of protection and security is somehow limited to police protection, which is not and never has been'.[15] Todd Weiler (2013) also advocates for a broad understanding of the standard:

> The heretical version of the P&S standard, too commonly espoused today, is that it requires the host State to take reasonable steps, as are within its means, to police its territory so as to prevent the alien's tangible, physical investments from coming to harm (such as being vandalised, looted and/or gutted during a period of unrest). The history of the P&S standard does not support such a narrow construction any more than does the unadorned text of most IIL treaties. The P&S standard applies to more than just 'bricks and mortar' investments and it requires more of a host state than just maintaining a police force so as to provide non-discriminatory protection and security to foreigners during a riot.[16]

Building up on Weiler's work, Timothy Foden (2015) observes that limiting the FPS standard to protection against 'physical' threats implies, too, that the standard will only be applicable in respect of physical—that is to say, tangible—property.[17] Foden underscores that this result is inconsistent with the fact that the concepts of 'investment' and 'property' usually encompass both tangible and intangible assets.[18]

---

[12]The notion of 'legal security' as 'legal stability' will be addressed in detail in Sect. 9.3.

[13]George Foster, 'Recovering "Protection and Security": The Treaty Standard's Obscure Origins, Forgotten Meaning, and Key Current Significance' (2012) 45(4) Vand. J. Transnat'l L. 1095, 1149.

[14]George Foster, 'Recovering "Protection and Security": The Treaty Standard's Obscure Origins, Forgotten Meaning, and Key Current Significance' (2012) 45(4) Vand. J. Transnat'l L. 1095, 1155-6. The wording Foster criticizes has crystalized in the latest versions of the U.S. Model BIT (2004/2012), which include a clause whereby 'full protection and security requires each Party to provide the level of *police protection* required under customary international law'. Emphasis added. U.S. Model BIT (2004) art. 5(2)(b); U.S. Model BIT (2012) art. 5(2)(b). The same wording appears in the USMCA of 2018: Agreement between the United States of America, the United Mexican States, and Canada (adopted 30 November 2018) art. 14.6(2)(b).

[15]George Foster, 'Recovering "Protection and Security": The Treaty Standard's Obscure Origins, Forgotten Meaning, and Key Current Significance' (2012) 45(4) Vand. J. Transnat'l L. 1095, 1155.

[16]Todd Weiler, *The Interpretation of International Investment Law: Equality, Discrimination, and Minimum Standards of Treatment in Historical Context* (Brill, Leiden 2013) 59-61.

[17]Timothy Foden, 'Back to Bricks and Mortar: The case of a "Traditional" Definition of Investment that Never Was' in Ian Laird, Borzu Sabahi, Frédéric Sourgens and Todd Weiler (eds), *Investment Treaty Arbitration and International Law* (Juris Net, Huntington NY 2015) 139-66.

[18]Timothy Foden, 'Back to Bricks and Mortar: The case of a "Traditional" Definition of Investment that Never Was' in Ian Laird, Borzu Sabahi, Frédéric Sourgens and Todd Weiler (eds), *Investment Treaty Arbitration and International Law* (Juris Net, Huntington NY 2015) 139-66. For a similar argument see: John Riggs, 'Investment Protection in Colombia: Can Investors Rely on the Full Protection and Security Clause?' (2014) 7(3) J. World Investment & Trade 264, 271; Nartnirun

Foden's argument has some tradition in international investment law. UNCTAD advanced a thorough similar proposition in a study published in 2004.[19] The argument reappeared years later in the claimants' submissions in *National Grid v Argentina* (2008), *OI European Group B.V. v Venezuela* (2015) and *Teinver v Argentina* (2017).[20] It has also played a fairly important role in arbitral decisions. For example, the *National Grid* tribunal agreed with the investor's argument, and held:

> Given that these terms ['protection and constant security' in article 2(2) of the Argentina-UK BIT] are closely associated with fair and equitable treatment, which is not limited to such physical situations, *and in the context of the protection of investments broadly defined to include intangible assets*, the Tribunal finds no rationale for limiting the application of a substantive protection of the treaty to a category of assets – physical assets – when it was not restricted in that fashion by the Contracting Parties.[21]

The argument also served as a basis for the extensive interpretation of the FPS standard adopted by the tribunal in *Siemens v Argentina* (2007):

> As a general matter and based on the definition of investment, which includes tangible and intangible assets, the Tribunal considers that the obligation to provide full protection and security is wider than "physical" protection and security. It is difficult to understand how the physical security of an intangible asset would be achieved.[22]

Junngam, 'The Full Protection and Security Standard in International Investment Law: What and Who is Investment Fully[?] Protected and Secured From?' (2018) 7(1) AUBLR 1, 89-90. Cf. also Junngam's view on the scope of the standard at p. 93.

[19]In its survey, UNCTAD concludes: "As the term "investment" has expanded to include a broader variety of intangible forms of property, the range of protection that an investor may argue is required by the obligation of full protection and security has potentially expanded. For example, where "investment" includes intellectual property, an investor may contend that the obligation to exercise reasonable care to protect intellectual property against private infringement may provide some form of remedy against those who infringe copyrights or patents." UNCTAD, *International Investment Agreements: Key issues* (Volume 1: United Nations, New York/Geneva 2004) 136. For a similar view see: Caline Mouawad and Sarah Vasani, 'Energy Disputes in Times of Civil Unrest: Transitional Governments and Foreign Investment Protections' in Arthur Rovine (ed), *Contemporary Issues in International Arbitration and Mediation* (Brill, Leiden/Boston 2015) 234, 247-8; Joshua Robins, 'The Emergence of Positive Obligations in Bilateral Investment Treaties' (2005-6) U. Miami Int'l & Comp. L. Rev. 403, 430. A similar argument has been advanced in connection with the standard of 'most constant protection and security' under ECT article 10(1). See: Thomas Roe and Matthew Happold, *Settlement of Investment Disputes under the Energy Charter Treaty* (Cambridge University Press, Cambridge 2011) 116.

[20]National Grid P.L.C. *v* Argentina (UNCITRAL), Award (3 November 2008) [182] (quoting UNCTAD's survey in this connection); OI European Group B.V. *v* Venezuela, Award, ICSID Case No. ARB/11/25 (10 March 2015) [562 and 572]; Teinver S.A., Transportes de Cercanías S.A. and Autobuses Urbanos del Sur S.A. *v* Argentina, Award, ICSID Case No. ARB/09/1 (21 July 2017) [900].

[21]Emphasis added. National Grid P.L.C. *v* Argentina (UNCITRAL), Award (3 November 2008) [187].

[22]Siemens AG *v* Argentina, Award, ICSID Case No. ARB/02/8 (6 February 2007) [303].

A decade later, in *Teinver v Argentina* (2017), another ICSID arbitral tribunal reached a similar conclusion:

> [T]he Tribunal is of the view [that] while the traditional notion of full protection and security addresses the protection of property from physical threats and injury, it can, in appropriate circumstances, include the protection of intangible assets which fall within the scope of the definition of an investment in the relevant treaty.[23]

There have also been serious efforts to overcome the contradiction between the definition of FPS in terms of *physical protection* and the fact that IIAs actually protect *nonphysical* assets. Finnur Magnússon has suggested that, in the case of intangible assets, 'the protection owed to the investor cannot be physical in the literal sense'.[24] Rather, he says, the host state has to provide 'structures of protection' (e.g. ensure the availability of the legal system, grant 'police protection' to the owner of the intangible asset, etc.).[25] This approach, while interesting, does not actually reconcile the understanding of FPS as *physical security* with the broad definitions of *investment* enshrined in most IIAs. The reason is that Magnússon's examples do not actually pertain to the assurance of *physical* protection for *intangible* assets. In some cases, it is doubtful whether the form of protection he refers to can be understood as physical security (e.g. his example of the 'availability of the legal system'). In other cases, it seems that physical security is being granted not to an *intangible* asset as such, but to some *tangible* object or *physical* person having some relation to the intangible asset (e.g. police protection for the owner of intangible property).

In sum, the *Siemens* tribunal was right in noting that it is not possible to give physical protection to an intangible asset. The fact that most IIAs protect intangible property raises genuine doubts about the definition of FPS in terms of *physical security*. The shortcomings of the notions of 'physical security' and 'physical protection' are of great practical relevance. As a matter of fact, these widespread criteria pose serious difficulties with regard to digital assets and cybersecurity.[26] The

---

[23]Teinver S.A., Transportes de Cercanías S.A. and Autobuses Urbanos del Sur S.A. *v* Argentina, Award, ICSID Case No. ARB/09/1 (21 July 2017) [905].

[24]Finnur Magnússon, *Full Protection and Security in International Law* (University of Vienna, Vienna 2012) 187.

[25]Finnur Magnússon, *Full Protection and Security in International Law* (University of Vienna, Vienna 2012) 187-8.

[26]The application of the FPS standard to digital assets and intellectual property has gained considerable attention in specialized legal literature. Cf. David Collins, 'Applying the Full Protection and Security Standard of Protection to Digital Investments' (2011) 12(2) J. World Investment & Trade 225, 225-43; Levon Golendukhin, 'Reference to Intellectual Property Treaty Norms in Full Protection and Security and Fair and Equitable Treatment Claims' in Ian Laird, Borzu Sabahi, Frédéric Sourgens and Todd Weiler (eds), *Investment Treaty Arbitration and International Law* (Juris Net, Huntington NY 2018) 89, 89-110; Nicole O'Donnell, 'Reconciling Full Protection and Security Guarantees in Bilateral Investment Treaties with Incidence of Terrorism' (2018) 29 (3) ARIA 293, 302; Onyema Awa Oyeani, *The Obligation of Host States to Accord the Standard of "Full Protection and Security" to Foreign Investments under International Investment Law* (Brunel University, London 2018) [D.Phil. Thesis] 232 *et seq.*; Robert Reyes Landicho, 'Enforcing a State's International IP Obligations through Investment Law Standards of Protection – An

physical security approach would imply, for example, that failures in the exercise of due diligence against cyberattacks and cyberterrorism would not fall under the scope of the FPS standard unless some form of 'physical' property (e.g. a hard drive or server) is affected.[27]

Most importantly, the *physical security* approach does not always provide a clear parameter for the delimitation of the FPS standard's scope of application. Recent cases have shown the shortcomings of this criterion. In *Peter Allard v Barbados* (2016), a Canadian investor alleged that the respondent state had breached the FPS clause of the Canada-Barbados BIT by failing to prevent environmental damage to a natural sanctuary in the west coast of Barbados, which the investor had acquired for the purpose of developing an ecotourism project.[28] The respondent argued that the applicable FPS clause 'merely reflects customary international law'[29] and 'is limited to protection against *direct physical harm* to an investor or its property by a State, its agents or as the result of the State's gross negligence in protecting the investment against *physical harm*'.[30] Barbados further contended that FPS could not be said to 'impose liability on the host state for alleged violations by third parties of domestic environmental legislation'.[31] For his part, the claimant alleged that FPS was not limited to 'physical interference with property' or 'physical violence'.[32] As an alternative argument, the investor submitted that his claim could be considered as 'one of physical interference with property *through the unlawful trespass of pollutants*'.[33]

The *Peter Allard* case poses an interesting question. Despite there was no *physical attack* whatsoever on the investor or his property, the claimant rightly

---

Ill-Fated Romance' in Ian Laird, Borzu Sabahi, Frédéric Sourgens and Todd Weiler (eds), *Investment Treaty Arbitration and International Law* (Juris Net, Huntington NY 2018) 111, 111-32; Simon Klopschinski, *Der Schutz geistigen Eigentums durch völkerrechtliche Investitionsverträge* (Carl Heymanns Verlag, Cologne 2011) 190-1, 217, 341, 344-5 and 351-4; Timothy Nelson et al., 'Full Protection and "Cyber" Security?' in Ian Laird, Borzu Sabahi, Frédéric Sourgens and Todd Weiler (eds), *Investment Treaty Arbitration and International Law* (Juris Net, Huntington NY 2018) 133, 133-57 (panel discussion on the subject, moderated by T. Nelson).

[27]For a detailed analysis of this possible implication of the criterion of 'physical security' cf. Robert Reyes Landicho, 'Enforcing a State's International IP Obligations through Investment Law Standards of Protection – An Ill-Fated Romance' in Ian Laird, Borzu Sabahi, Frédéric Sourgens and Todd Weiler (eds), *Investment Treaty Arbitration and International Law* (Juris Net, Huntington NY 2018) 111, 127-31 (mentioning the example of cyberattacks which affect physical servers).

[28]For the facts of the case see: Peter A. Allard *v* Barbados (UNCITRAL), Award (27 June 2016) [33-46]. It should be noted that the respondent considered that the relevant treaty clause 'merely reflects customary international law' (at para 236).

[29]Peter A. Allard *v* Barbados (UNCITRAL), Award (27 June 2016) [236].

[30]Emphasis added. Peter A. Allard *v* Barbados (UNCITRAL), Award (27 June 2016) [235].

[31]Peter A. Allard *v* Barbados (UNCITRAL), Award (27 June 2016) [235].

[32]Peter A. Allard *v* Barbados (UNCITRAL), Award (27 June 2016) [239-52]. It should be additionally noted that, in this case, the investor was unable to prove any damage attributable to the host state's acts or omissions (see para 167).

[33]Emphasis added. Peter A. Allard *v* Barbados (UNCITRAL), Award (27 June 2016) [231].

noted that the trespass of pollutants into the environmental sanctuary could be reasonably said to produce a *physical impact* on the investment.[34] This shows that *physical harm* does not always result from a *physical harmful act*. Thus, the question turns into what *physical protection* actually means: Is it the act directly originating the injury what has to be physical? Does physical security mean that the measures of protection omitted by the state must be of a physical nature? Does it suffice that some physical event appears somewhere in the chain of causation? Or is it the injury itself what needs to have a physical character?

In the *Peter Allard* case, the issue did not have much significance for the resolution of the dispute. The arbitrators avoided entering into a debate about the FPS standard's scope or the physical or nonphysical nature of the interferences at stake.[35] They analyzed the measures undertaken by Barbados for the protection of the natural environment in the area and concluded that, regardless of these questions, no breach of the FPS standard had been proven.[36]

Scholars and arbitral tribunals have sometimes avoided taking a stance in the ongoing debate on the *physical security* approach. For example, Ralph Alexander Lorz characterizes 'protection against physical harm' as the 'uncontested core' of the FPS standard, further observing that 'at least those types of assets which can be physically protected are supposed to enjoy this protection under the standard'.[37] In *Enron v Argentina* (2008) the arbitrators were similarly cautious in this regard. In view of the inconsistencies signalizing relevant sources, the tribunal stated:

> There is no doubt that historically this particular standard has been developed in the context of physical protection and security of the company's officials, employees or facilities. The Tribunal cannot exclude as a matter of principle that there might be cases where a broader interpretation could be justified, but then it becomes difficult to distinguish such situation from one resulting in the breach of fair and equitable treatment, and even from some form of expropriation.[38]

---

[34]Section 8.3.3.2 argues that natural phenomena could actually trigger the protection obligation. The issue is however contentious. In the *Peter Allard* case, the tribunal avoided taking a stance on this particular issue. See: Peter A. Allard *v* Barbados (UNCITRAL), Award (27 June 2016) [252].

[35]Peter A. Allard *v* Barbados (UNCITRAL), Award (27 June 2016) [231].

[36]Peter A. Allard *v* Barbados (UNCITRAL), Award (27 June 2016) [252].

[37]Ralph Alexander Lorz, 'Protection and Security (Including the NAFTA Approach)' in Marc Bungenberg, Jörn Griebel, Stephan Hobe and August Reinisch (eds), *International Investment Law* (Nomos, Baden-Baden 2015) 764, 775-6. For an additional example of a scholarly writing describing the debate without taking a stance on the particular issue of the physical/nonphysical divide see: Stanimir Alexandrov, 'The Evolution of the Full Protection and Security Standard' in Meg Kinnear, Geraldine Fischer, Jara Mínguez Almeida, Luisa Torres and Mairée Uran Bidegain (eds), *Building International Investment Law. The First 50 Years of ICSID* (Wolters Kluwer/ICSID, Alphen aan den Rijn 2016) 319, 324-9 (particularly at p. 329).

[38]Enron Corp. and Ponderosa Assets L.P. *v* Argentina, Award, ICSID Case No. ARB/01/3 (22 May 2007) [286].

Other arbitral tribunals have expressed similar views.[39] These eclectic opinions seek to find a way through the many different and inconsistent approaches to the scope of FPS. But, in the end, they also depart from the assumption that the customary or traditional standard actually refers to physical security.

This assumption is questionable. This section has shown that many authorities are still skeptical about the *physical security* approach. The notion of *physical security* needlessly introduces an inconsistency into investment treaties providing broad definitions of 'investment'. Moreover, as shown by the parties' arguments in the *Peter Allard* case, it does not provide absolute certainty as to the scope of the standard.

9.3   The Notion of Legal Security and the Customary Security Obligation. Taking Down the House of Cards

As an alternative to the *physical security* approach, arbitral tribunals and scholars have advanced a broad understanding of FPS, according to which the standard encompasses the concept of legal security and, particularly, the protection of the investor's legitimate expectations related to the stability of the investment's legal and regulatory framework.

This section contends that the customary protection obligation has never referred to the stability of the investment's legal environment. The argument has been divided in two parts. Section 9.3.1 examines the arbitral decisions usually cited in support of the interpretation of FPS as a guarantee of legal stability. In this vein, it argues that these decisions have important caveats and argumentative deficiencies, which are often overlooked by those advancing the broad interpretation of FPS. It is therefore submitted that the 'extensive approach' is a textbook example of what Anthea Roberts (2010) has cleverly described as the 'house of cards' of investment arbitration:

> [Investment arbitral practice] frequently resembles a house of cards built largely by reference to other tribunal awards and academic opinions, with little consideration of the views and practices of states in general or the treaty parties in particular.[40]

---

[39]For an identical observation see: Sempra Energy International *v* Argentina, Award, ICSID Case No. ARB/02/16 (28 September 2007) [323]. For other tribunals taking cognizance of the different approaches as to the meaning of the standard, but avoiding to take a stance on the matter, see: Gemplus S.A., SLP S.A. and Gemplus Industrial S.A. de C.V. *v* Mexico, Award, ICSID Cases No. ARB(AF)/04/3 & ARB(AF)/04/4 (16 June 2010) [9.12-9.13]; Spyridon Roussalis *v* Romania, Award, ICSID Case No. ARB/06/1 (7 December 2011) [320-1].

[40]Anthea Roberts, 'Power and Persuasion in Investment Treaty Arbitration: The Dual Role of States' (2010) 104 AJIL 179, 179.

Section 9.3.2 then explains the reasons why this understanding of FPS is not only methodologically unfounded, but moreover contravenes the very essence of the FPS standard.

9.3.1 The Extensive Understanding of the Security Obligation. The Caveats of Relevant Arbitral Practice

The development of the FPS standard has been signalized by a remarkable array of divergent approaches as to the scope of the protection obligation. One of the most significant debates pertains to the question, whether FPS entails a guarantee of legal security. Investors often rely on broad interpretations of the security obligation, arguing that FPS ensures a *secure* legal environment.[41] The notion of legal security

---

[41]For some examples of such a broad interpretation of the FPS standard being advanced by the claimant in investment arbitral proceedings see: Achmea B.V. *v* Slovakia (UNCITRAL), Award on Jurisdiction, Arbitrability and Suspension, PCA Case No. 2008-13 (26 October 2010) [260-1]; ADF *v* United States, Award, ICSID Case No. ARB(AF)/00/1 (9 January 2003) [72]; AES Corporation and Tau Power B.V. *v* Kazakhstan, Award, ICSID Case No. ARB/10/16 (1 November 2013) [337]; AES Summit Generation Ltd. and AES-Tisza Erömü Kft. *v* Hungary, Award, ICSID Case No. ARB/07/22 (23 September 2010) [13.1.1-13.1.5]; Alasdair Ross Anderson et al. *v* Costa Rica, Award, ICSID Case No. ARB(AF)/07/3 (19 May 2010) [16]; Ampal-American Israel Corp., Egi-Fund (08-10) Investors LLC, Egi-Series Investments LLC and BSS-EMG Investors LLC *v* Egypt, Decision on Liability and Heads of Loss, ICSID Case No. ARB/12/11 (21 February 2017) [150]; Anglo American PLC *v* Venezuela, Award, ICSID Case No. ARB(AF)/14/1 (18 January 2019) [475-6]; Azurix Corp. *v* Argentina, Award, ICSID Case No. ARB/01/12 (14 July 2006) [395-6]; Bear Creek Mining Corp. *v* Peru, Award, ICSID Case No. ARB/14/21 (30 November 2017) [536-8]; BG Group *v* Argentina (UNCITRAL), Final Award (24 December 2007) [317-8]; Biwater Gauff Ltd. *v* Tanzania, Award, ICSID Case No. ARB/05/22 (24 July 2008) [715]; Burlington Resources Inc. *v* Ecuador, Decision on Jurisdiction, ICSID Case No. ARB/08/5 (2 June 2010) [212-5]; CC/Devas (Mauritius) Ltd., Devas Employees Mauritius Private Ltd. and Telcom Devas Mauritius Ltd. *v* India (UNCITRAL), Award on Jurisdiction and Merits, PCA Case No. 2013-09 (25 July 2016) [491]; Compañía de Aguas del Aconquija S.A. and Vivendi Universal S.A. *v* Argentina, Award, ICSID Case No. ARB/97/3 (20 August 2007) [7.4.13]; Crystallex International Corp. *v* Venezuela, Award, ICSID Case No. ARB(AF)/11/2 (4 April 2016) [625]; Deutsche Bank AG *v* Sri Lanka, Award, ICSID Case No. ARB/09/02 (31 October 2012) [527-8]; Deutsche Telekom AG *v* India (UNCITRAL), Interim Award, PCA Case No. 2014-10 (13 December 2017) [417]; EDF International S.A., Saur International S.A. and Leon Participaciones Argentinas S.A. *v* Argentina, Award, ICSID Case No. ARB/03/23 (11 June 2012) [403-6]; Enron Corp. and Ponderosa Assets L.P. *v* Argentina, Award, ICSID Case No. ARB/01/3 (22 May 2007) [284]; Fraport AG Frankfurt Airport Services Worldwide *v* Philippines, Award, ICSID Case No. ARB/11/12 (10 December 2014) [285]; Garanti Koza LLP *v* Turkmenistan, Award, ICSID Case No. ARB/11/20 (19 December 2016) [277]; Gemplus S.A., SLP S.A. and Gemplus Industrial S.A. de C.V. *v* Mexico, Award, ICSID Cases No. ARB(AF)/04/3 & ARB(AF)/04/4 (19 June 2010) [2.30-2.31]; Hesham Talaat M. Al-Warraq *v* Indonesia (UNCITRAL), Final Award (15 December 2014) [425-6 and 627]; Isolux Netherlands B.V. *v* Spain, Laudo, SCC Case No. V 2013/153 (17 July 2016) [428, 816]; Merril & Ring Forestry L.P. *v* Canada (UNCITRAL/ICSID Administered Case), Award (31 March 2010) [154] (see also Canada's counterargument at

underlying this line of argument comes close to the idea of legal stability. This all-encompassing understanding of the FPS standard found expression in an Opinion delivered by the Advocate General of the European Court of Justice on September 19th, 2017.[42] Notwithstanding the fact that the Advocate General's argument was particularly concerned with the possible inconsistency of intra-EU BITs with the law of the European Union,[43] his statement can be cited as a clear example of the extensive interpretation of FPS:

[Full protection and security] places the State under a positive obligation to take measures to protect the investment, which includes the physical protection of the investor and his investment against violent acts on the part of individuals or bodies of the State *and the legal protection of the investor and his investment. There is no directly equivalent rule in EU law.* Admittedly, the fundamental freedoms may be applicable in the same factual contexts as the guarantee of full protection and security, since they have direct vertical and horizontal effect. However, the contents are different, whether in relation to the physical protection of the investor or the *legal protection which includes the State's obligation to ensure that the level of protection and security of investments agreed with foreign investors will not be*

---

para 172); Mobil Exploration and Development Argentina Inc. Suc. Argentina and Mobil Argentina S.A. *v* Argentina, Decision on Jurisdiction and Liability, ICSID Case No. ARB/04/16 (10 April 2013) [989-93]; OAO Tatneft *v* Ukraine (UNCITRAL), Award (29 July 2014) [415]; OI European Group B.V. *v* Venezuela, Award, ICSID Case No. ARB/11/25 (10 March 2015) [562-3, 565-6]; Oxus Gold *v* Uzbekistan (UNCITRAL), Final Award (17 December 2015) [348 and 829]; Peter A. Allard *v* Barbados (UNCITRAL), Award (27 June 2016) [231]; PSEG Global Inc. and Konya Ilgin Elektrik Üretim ve Ticaret Limited Şirketi *v* Turkey, Award, ICSID Case No. ARB/02/5 (19 January 2007) [257]; Ronald Lauder *v* Czech Republic (UNCITRAL), Final Award (3 September 2001) [305-6]; Rusoro Mining Ltd. *v* Venezuela, Award, ICSID Case No. ARB (AF)/12/5 (22 August 2016) [450 and 543]; Saint-Gobain Performance Plastics Europe *v* Venezuela, Decision on Liability and the Principles of Quantum, ICSID Case No. ARB/12/13 (30 December 2016) [544-6]; SAUR International S.A. *v* Argentina, Décision sur la compétence et sur la responsabilité, ICSID Case No. ARB/04/4 (6 June 2012) [471 and 499]; Sempra Energy International *v* Argentina, Award, ICSID Case No. ARB/02/16 (28 September 2007) [321]; Sergei Paushok et al. *v* Mongolia (UNCITRAL), Award on Jurisdiction and Liability (28 April 2011) [258 (1), 279 and 322]; Siemens AG *v* Argentina, Award, ICSID Case No. ARB/02/8 (6 February 2007) [274, 286 and 301]; Suez Sociedad General de Aguas de Barcelona S.A. and Vivendi Universal S.A. *v* Argentina, Decision on Liability, ICSID Case No. ARB/03/19 (30 July 2010) [160 and 165]; Supervisión y Control S.A. *v* Costa Rica, Award, ICSID Case No. ARB/12/4 (18 January 2017) [233-4]; Teinver S.A., Transportes de Cercanías S.A. and Autobuses Urbanos del Sur S.A. *v* Argentina, Award, ICSID Case No. ARB/09/1 (21 July 2017) [898-900]; Ulysseas Inc. *v* Ecuador (UNCITRAL), Final Award (12 June 2012) [260 and 271]; Vincent J. Ryan, Schooner Capital LLC and Atlantic Investment Partners LLC *v* Poland, Award, ICSID Case No. ARB(AF)/ 11/3 (24 November 2015) [275(iv)]; William Ralph Clayton, William Richard Clayton, Douglas Clayton, Daniel Clayton and Bilicon of Delaware Inc. *v* Canada (UNCITRAL), Award on Jurisdiction and Liability, PCA Case No. 2009-05 (17 March 2015) [360 and 392-3].

[42]Slovak Republic *v* Achmea B.V., Case C-284/16, Opinion of Advocate General Wathelet (19 September 2017) [211-2].

[43]Slovak Republic *v* Achmea B.V., Case C-284/16, Opinion of Advocate General Wathelet (19 September 2017) [180 and 210-2].

abolished or reduced in any way whatsoever by a change in its laws or by acts of its administration.[44]

Following a similar line of argument, some tribunals have adopted broad interpretations of FPS.[45] A few scholars have welcomed this approach and characterized it as the 'predominant trend in investment treaty jurisprudence'.[46] This remark goes too far. It turns a blind eye to the fact that restrictive interpretations of the FPS standard have been much more common in practice.[47]

Most importantly, supporters of the expansive interpretation of the FPS standard often disregard the caveats of relevant arbitral decisions. In investment arbitral practice, far-reaching interpretations of the FPS standard are normally based on the assumption that the applicable FPS *treaty clause* uses a particularly broad language or otherwise extends beyond the *customary* FPS obligation.[48] In some cases, the arbitrators held that the applicable treaty-based standard comprised a guarantee of legal stability but, having already declared a breach of FET, abstained

---

[44]Emphasis added. Slovak Republic *v* Achmea B.V., Case C-284/16, Opinion of Advocate General Wathelet (19 September 2017) [180 and 210-2].

[45]For a recent example cf. Anglo American PLC *v* Venezuela, Award, ICSID Case No. ARB(AF)/14/1 (18 January 2019) [482].

[46]Timothy Foden, 'Back to Bricks and Mortar: The case of a "Traditional" Definition of Investment that Never Was' in Ian Laird, Borzu Sabahi, Frédéric Sourgens and Todd Weiler (eds), *Investment Treaty Arbitration and International Law* (Juris Net, Huntington NY 2015) 139, 148 (particularly commenting on the approach followed in *Siemens v Argentina*).

[47]See Sect. 9.2.

[48]Azurix Corp. *v* Argentina, Award, ICSID Case No. ARB/01/12 (14 July 2006) [408 and 442 No. 3] (further linking the FPS standard to the FET standard); Biwater Gauff Ltd. *v* Tanzania, Award, ICSID Case No. ARB/05/22 (24 July 2008) [730] (heavily underscoring the adjective 'full' used in the relevant FPS clause); Frontier Petroleum Ltd. *v* Czech Republic (UNCITRAL), Final Award (12 November 2010) [263-4 and 268] (extending the FPS standard to 'legal protection' at para 263, but observing at para 268 that the applicable FPS clause is not 'equivalent to customary international law'. It should be noted that the *Frontier* tribunal primarily used the expression 'legal protection' in connection with the duty of redress and went on to state at para 264 that 'protection and security is not restricted to physical protection but extends to legal protection *through domestic courts*' – emphasis added); National Grid P.L.C. *v* Argentina (UNCITRAL), Award (3 November 2008) [187-90] (further linking the FPS standard to the FET standard); Sergei Paushok et al. *v* Mongolia (UNCITRAL), Award on Jurisdiction and Liability (28 April 2011) [326] (stating that, in the presence of an FPS clause using the adjective 'legal', there is 'no reason to limit the protection guaranteed to mere physical protection'); Siemens AG *v* Argentina, Award, ICSID Case No. ARB/02/8 (6 February 2007) [301-9 and 403] (underscoring the use of the adjective 'legal' in the respective FPS clause); Spyridon Roussalis *v* Romania, Award, ICSID Case No. ARB/06/1 (7 December 2011) [321] (recalling the significance of the adjective 'full' for the interpretation of FPS treaty clauses, but without endorsing the extensive interpretation of the standard); Total S.A. *v* Argentina, Decision on Liability, ICSID Case No. ARB/04/1 (27 December 2010) [343] (basing its approach on the 'plain reading' of the applicable treaty clause, which guaranteed FPS 'in accordance with the principle of fair and equitable treatment'). Chapter 14 addresses the interpretation of specific formulations of the FPS standard.

from making any explicit finding on FPS.[49] In another group of cases, tribunals equalized the FET and the FPS standards, finding that a violation of the latter 'automatically' entails a breach of the former.[50] Finally, in many cases adjudicators merely *asserted* that the FPS standard generally includes an obligation to ensure the stability of the investment's legal environment, without elaborating much on the argument. For instance, the tribunal in *Anglo American PLC v Venezuela* (2019) held that, unless otherwise established by the applicable treaty in express terms, the FPS standard entails a guarantee of 'legal security'.[51] The arbitrators did not provide any reasons beyond an argument of authority in support of their statement.[52] Similarly, in its Partial Award in the case *CME v Czech Republic* (2001), an UNCITRAL arbitral tribunal held:

> The Media Council's actions in 1996 and its actions and inactions in 1999 were targeted to remove the security and legal protection of the Claimant's investment in the Czech Republic. The Media Council's (possible) motivation to regain control of the operation of the broadcasting after the Media Law had been amended as of January 1, 1996 is irrelevant. *The host State is obligated to ensure that neither by amendment of its laws nor by actions of its administrative bodies is the agreed and approved security and protection of the foreign investor's investment withdrawn or devalued. This is not the case. The Respondent therefore is in breach of this obligation.*[53]

The sureness and conviction flowing from this passage strikingly contrasts with the frailty of the underlying argument. Besides a summary of the parties' claims, the *CME* tribunal failed to provide any evidence underpinning its extensive understanding of the FPS standard. Subsequent tribunals have recognized this deficit. In *Suez v Argentina*, the arbitrators strongly criticized the *CME* Partial Award and other arbitral decisions following a similar line of argument:

---

[49]Total S.A. *v* Argentina, Decision on Liability, ICSID Case No. ARB/04/1 (27 December 2010) [343] (see also para 116 n. 113). Cf. also Anglo American PLC *v* Venezuela, Award, ICSID Case No. ARB(AF)/14/1 (18 January 2019) [482-5].

[50]See, for example: Azurix Corp. *v* Argentina, Award, ICSID Case No. ARB/01/12 (14 July 2006) [406-8]; Occidental Exploration and Production Co. *v* Ecuador, Final Award, LCIA Case No. UN 3467 (1 July 2004) [187]. Section 15.2 provides a more detailed analysis of the relationship between the FET standard and the FPS standard. The so-called 'equating approach' is discussed in Sect. 15.2.1.

[51]Anglo American PLC *v* Venezuela, Award, ICSID Case No. ARB(AF)/14/1 (18 January 2019) [482].

[52]Anglo American PLC *v* Venezuela, Award, ICSID Case No. ARB(AF)/14/1 (18 January 2019) [482].

[53]Emphasis added. CME Czech Republic B.V. *v* Czech Republic (UNCITRAL), Partial Award (13 September 2001) [613]. It must be noted that the *CME* tribunal was divided on this claim. See: CME Czech Republic B.V. *v* Czech Republic (UNCITRAL), Dissenting Opinion of Arbitrator Jaroslav Hándl against the Partial Award (11 September 2001) 16. In *Suez v Argentina* the tribunal took into account this dissent and observed that 'the precedential effect of the *CME* case might be reduced by the fact that it was not a unanimous decision'. Suez Sociedad General de Aguas de Barcelona S.A. and Vivendi Universal S.A. *v* Argentina, Decision on Liability, ICSID Case No. ARB/03/19 (30 July 2010) [167].

> While strict textual interpretation of the treaty language would lead this Tribunal to conclude that the applicable BITs in the present cases do not have the expansive scope on which the Claimants are basing their claim, there is another reason for the Tribunal not to follow the interpretation made in, *inter alia*, *CME* and *Azurix*. Neither the *CME* nor *Azurix* awards provide a historical analysis of the concept of full protection and security or give any clear reason as to why it was departing from the historical interpretation traditionally employed by courts and tribunals and expanding that concept to cover non-physical actions and injuries.[54]

Decisions extending FPS to legal security in unqualified terms are typically based on *a priori* assumptions. Particularly, they assume that a standard of 'protection and security' must necessarily cover the notion of security in general. The problem is, precisely, that *security* is a 'relational concept': if the term is considered in isolation, it is nothing more than an empty glass.[55] Moreover, the fact that the law of aliens and most investment treaties establish an obligation to provide *security* does not mean that the standard must cover *every thinkable form of security*.

The debate on the subject bears some resemblance with a problem Jan Paulsson ingeniously addressed in his famous conference *International Arbitration Is Not Arbitration* (2008). On that occasion, Paulsson appealingly introduced the topic with the following words:

> What are you to make of the title of this lecture? [...] You don't think that international arbitration is arbitration because it has 'arbitration' in its name, do you? Do you think a sea elephant is an elephant? International arbitration is no more a "type" of arbitration than a sea elephant is a type of elephant. True, one reminds us of the other. Yet the essential difference of their nature is so great that their similarities are largely illusory.[56]

Borrowing Paulsson's clever comparison, one could say that, in the absence of sufficient evidence pointing to another direction, 'legal security' is no more a 'type' of security under 'full protection and security' than a 'sea elephant is a type of elephant'. The stability of the legal environment might be desirable, at least from the perspective of foreign investors. But, as will be shown in the following pages, the risk of subsequent changes in the law does not properly belong to the customary notion of FPS.

9.3.2   The Extensive Understanding of the Security Obligation. Critique of a Misleading Notion

All-encompassing definitions of the customary protection obligation should be considered with caution. In their quest to achieve the greatest possible degree of

---

[54]Suez Sociedad General de Aguas de Barcelona S.A. and Vivendi Universal S.A. *v* Argentina, Decision on Liability, ICSID Case No. ARB/03/19 (30 July 2010) [177].

[55]Section 6.3 discusses the 'relational' concept of security in detail.

[56]Jan Paulsson, 'International Arbitration Is Not Arbitration' (2008) 2 Stockholm International Arbitration Review 1, 1. The paper is based on a conference delivered by Paulsson at McGill University in May 2008.

protection for investors, interpreters too-often take the FPS standard out of its historical context and disregard its customary meaning. This section argues that the *customary* FPS standard cannot be properly said to ensure the stability of the investment's legal framework. The reasons are three.

The first reason concerns the historical origins of the standard. As shown in Chap. 3, eighteenth century scholars explained the foundations of the security obligation with the fiction of a 'tacit agreement' between the host sovereign and the foreigner entering into his dominions. The fiction was based on the idea that security was granted *in exchange for* obedience: by coming into the host territory, aliens tacitly submit to the laws of the place and, *in return*, the sovereign extends his protection to them.[57] Recognizing a guarantee of enhanced legal stability to the benefit of foreigners would imply acknowledging a *conditional submission* to local law, which would in turn contravene the very rationale of the theory.[58] Neither do early positivist justifications of the protection obligation provide any indication that the concept of security was meant to encompass legal stability.[59]

A second reason against this understanding of the FPS standard lies in the fact that *changes* in the legal system are events which, in most cases, originate entirely in the active exercise of public authority.[60] The harmful outcome flowing from regulatory changes always results from a state *action*; by contrast, the customary FPS standard refers to the host state's *omissions*.[61] While the FPS standard could certainly apply, in some exceptional circumstances, to cases where injuries are *materially caused* by an *action* attributable to the state (e.g. in the event of a counterinsurgency operation), in those events responsibility results from an *omission* in the mitigation of the injurious consequences of state action against some *external risk*.[62] Such public damages are merely *collateral*—that is to say, *incidental*—to state action, and are closely related to a non-public (i.e. private or natural) source of risk.[63]

---

[57] See Sects. 3.3 and 3.4. See also: Emilio Brusa, 'Responsabilité des États à raison des dommages soufferts par des étrangers en cas d'émeute ou de guerre civile' (1898) 17 Annuaire de l'Institut de Droit International 96, 101-2 (advancing the proposition that any right to compensation for revolutionary damages is conditional upon compliance with applicable rules of public order).

[58] Cf. Sects. 3.3 and 3.4.

[59] Cf. Sect. 3.5.

[60] A *change* or *modification* of existing regulations always occurs through an *action* by the host state. The scenario referred to at this point is in this sense different to regulatory or administrative omissions, which will be discussed in Sect. 9.4. For an excellent study on the notion of 'regulatory omissions' see: Lucas Bastin, *Violation of the Full Protection and Security Obligation by Regulatory Omissions* [M.Phil. Thesis] (Oxford University, Oxford 2011) 59-89. Cf. also: Lucas Bastin, *State Responsibility for Omissions: Establishing a Breach of the Full Protection and Security Obligation by Omissions* (Oxford University, Oxford 2016) [D.Phil. Thesis] 162 *et seq.* Cf. also pp. 208 *et seq.*

[61] This feature will be analyzed in detail in Sect. 11.3.

[62] See Sect. 8.3.3.1.

[63] See Sect. 8.3.3.1.

These conditions will hardly be met in cases concerning changes in an investment's regulatory framework. In such instances, there is usually nothing but a *state action*, which is generally not specifically directed against any private or otherwise external source of risk. In cases about *legal security* it is therefore artificial to say that responsibility arises out of a failure to exercise 'due diligence' in the protection of foreigners. In the end, the host state would be required to exercise diligence in respect of *itself*. That is why some scholars have suggested that, in this kind of cases, the FPS standard entails a strict liability.[64] This view, however interesting, ends up disregarding the most outstanding element of FPS, which is due diligence.[65]

A third reason for excluding legal security from the scope of application of the customary security obligation concerns the object of protection. Legal stability is usually attached to the notion of *legitimate expectations*. In contrast, the security obligation refers to values that are not merely *expected*, but have already been *acquired*.[66] *Legitimate expectations* do not fit into the notion of *acquired values*.[67] An *expectation* implies looking into the *future*. In *Parkerings v Lithuania*, for example, the tribunal described expectations as a particular form of 'hope'.[68] Moreover, even if one were to accept that expectations are 'acquired values', the interests protected under the FPS standard are always susceptible of being affected or impaired by third party conduct or natural phenomena.[69] This is not the case of expectations concerning the stability of the legal environment, which can only be frustrated by the host state's regulatory actions.[70]

---

[64]Some scholars have indeed advanced the proposition that the FPS standard may be generally said to cover 'damages by state organs', in which case a strict liability standard applies. See: Ralph Alexander Lorz, 'Protection and Security (Including the NAFTA Approach)' in Marc Bungenberg, Jörn Griebel, Stephan Hobe and August Reinisch (eds), *International Investment Law* (Nomos, Baden-Baden 2015) 764, 776-7. Section 11.2.3.1 provides a critical assessment of this theory.

[65]See Chap. 11. For an author rejecting the application of a strict liability standard in these cases see: Gleider Hernández, 'The Interaction Between Investment Law and the Law of Armed Conflict in the Interpretation of Full Protection and Security Clauses' in Freya Baetens (ed), *Investment Law within International Law* (Cambridge University Press, Cambridge 2013) 21, 39.

[66]See Sect. 8.2. See also Sect. 6.3.

[67]On the notion of 'acquired values' see Sect. 8.2.

[68]Parkerings-Compagniet AS *v* Lithuania, Award, ICSID Case No. ARB/05/8 (11 September 2007) [344] (stating that 'not every hope amounts to an expectation under international law', and thus implying that expectations are some form of 'hope'). The question may however arise as to whether an *expectation* could, for itself, be a *value* susceptible of being *acquired*. If this view were to be followed, the *acquired value* would not be *what is being expected*, but *the expectation itself*. This approach should be avoided. Elevating the notion of 'acquired values' to such an excessively abstract level could end up depriving the concept of any meaningful content.

[69]See Sect. 8.3.3.1.

[70]Zachary Douglas has suggested that private actions could also have adverse effects on the investment's legal environment; he considers, however, that the FPS standard is inapplicable in respect of such risks. See: Zachary Douglas, 'Property, Investment, and the Scope of Investment Protection Obligations' in Zachary Douglas, Joost Pauwelyn and Jorge Viñuales (eds), *The Foundations of International Investment Law. Bringing Theory into Practice* (Oxford University Press, Oxford 2014) 363, 379-80 (advocating for the restriction of the FPS standard to 'physical

The protection of legitimate expectations through the customary security obligation poses an additional problem: the actual status of legitimate expectations in international law remains largely unclear. The ICJ has held that general international law imposes no obligation to protect legitimate expectations.[71] Arbitral decisions do not provide a solid foundation for a general doctrine of legitimate expectations in international investment law. As observed by a scholar writing on the subject:

> [T]hrough a mechanical and not thoroughly thought-through reference to previous awards, tribunals evade their duty to explain the roots, the exact contours and possible limits of the issue of protection of the investor's legitimate expectations under the applicable investment treaty.[72]

The protection of investors' expectations has been a controversial subject in academic writings and investment arbitral practice.[73] In the particular context of the FPS standard, some arbitral tribunals have noted that placing the notion of 'legal

---

violence'). The present section is only concerned with expectations pertaining to the *stability* of the legal system; the notion of the 'legal or commercial environment', as used by Douglas, is therefore broader in scope.

[71]Cf. *Obligation to Negotiate Access to the Pacific Ocean (Bolivia v Chile)* [2018] ICJ General List No. 153 [162] ("The Court notes that references to legitimate expectations may be found in arbitral awards concerning disputes between a foreign investor and the host State that apply *treaty clauses* providing for fair and equitable treatment. It does not follow from such references that there exists in general international law a principle that would give rise to an obligation on the basis of what could be considered a legitimate expectation. Bolivia's argument based on legitimate expectations thus cannot be sustained" – emphasis added).

[72]Michele Potestà, 'Legitimate Expectations in Investment Treaty Law: Understanding the Roots and Limits of a Controversial Concept' (2013) 28(1) ICSID Review 88, 91. In this connection, Potestà suggests that the 'duty to protect legitimate expectations' originates in municipal administrative law principles and could be characterized as a 'general principle of law' under article 38(1) (c) of the Statute of the ICJ (at pp. 92-8). For a critical analysis of this approach cf. Fulvio Maria Palombino, *Fair and Equitable Treatment and the Fabric of General Principles* (Springer, Berlin 2018) 87 *et seq.*

[73]Controversy has arisen even in connection with the FET standard, which has been more or less consistently said to protect the investor's legitimate expectations. A flawless example of the uncertainties still surrounding the concept may be found in Pedro Nikken's Separate Opinion in *Suez v Argentina*, where he stated that '[t]he assertion that fair and equitable treatment includes an obligation to satisfy or not to frustrate the legitimate expectations of the investor at the time of his/her investment does not correspond, in any language, to the ordinary meaning to be given to the terms 'fair and equitable' [. . .] the interpretation that tends to give the standard of fair and equitable treatment the effect of a legal stability provision has no basis in the BITs or in the customary rules applicable to the interpretation of treaties'. Suez Sociedad General de Aguas de Barcelona S.A. and Vivendi Universal S.A. *v* Argentina, Separate Opinion of Arbitrator Pedro Nikken, ICSID Case No. ARB/03/19 (30 July 2010) [3]. For another example of an arbitrator taking a cautious stance with regard to the protection of legitimate expectations cf. Greentech Energy Systems A/S, NovEnergia II Energy & Environment (SCA) SICAR and NovEnergia II Italian Portfolio SA *v* Italy, Dissenting Opinion of Arbitrator Giorgio Sacerdoti, SCC Case No. V 2015/095 (5 December 2018) [5-6]. It should be noted, however, that the most common view is the one extending the FET standard to the protection of legitimate expectations. For a detailed analysis of the protection of legitimate expectations under the FET standard see: Ronald Kläger, *'Fair and Equitable Treatment' in International Investment Law* (Cambridge University Press, New York 2011) 164-87. See also:

security' within the protection obligation has the ultimate effect of introducing a questionable 'stability agreement' into the standard. In *AES v Hungary*, for example, the arbitrators explained:

> To conclude that the right to constant protection and security implies that no change in the law that affects the investor's rights could take place, would be practically the same as to recognizing the existence of a non-existent stability agreement as a consequence of the full protection and security standard. The Tribunal finds that there can have been no breach of the obligation to provide constant protection and security as a result of Hungary's reintroduction of regulated pricing in 2006-2007, such reintroduction being based on rational public policy grounds.[74]

Following a similar line of argument, in *CME v Czech Republic* the respondent observed that '[t]here can be no legitimate expectation that provisions and laws become frozen the minute they touch the interests of a foreign investor'.[75]

It is most doubtful whether the *customary* minimum standard, in general, or the *customary* FPS standard, in particular, protect legitimate expectations.[76] In several written statements concerning the interpretation of NAFTA and CAFTA-DR, the U.S. Government has made a compelling argument against the idea that the customary law of aliens protects such expectations:

> An investor may develop its own expectations about the legal regime governing its investment, but those expectations impose no obligations on the State under the minimum standard of treatment. The United States is aware of no general and consistent State practice and *opinio juris* establishing an obligation under the minimum standard of treatment not to frustrate the investors' expectations; instead, something more is required than the mere interference with those expectations.[77]

These views influenced the USMCA of 2018, the trade agreement negotiated by the Trump Administration with Mexico and Canada to replace NAFTA. Article 14.6 (4) of the USMCA Agreement provides:

Michele Potestà, 'Legitimate Expectations in Investment Treaty Law: Understanding the Roots and Limits of a Controversial Concept' (2013) 28(1) ICSID Review 88, 90-2 and 98-121.

[74] AES Summit Generation Ltd. and AES-Tisza Erömü Kft. *v* Hungary, Award, ICSID Case No. ARB/07/22 (23 September 2010) [13.3.5-6].

[75] CME Czech Republic B.V. *v* Czech Republic (UNCITRAL), Partial Award (13 September 2001) [356]. Cf. also the respondent's argument in *CC/Devas v India*: CC/Devas (Mauritius) Ltd., Devas Employees Mauritius Private Ltd. and Telcom Devas Mauritius Ltd. *v* India (UNCITRAL), Award on Jurisdiction and Merits, PCA Case No. 2013-09 (25 July 2016) [494-5].

[76] On the characterization of the FPS standard as an element of the minimum standard of treatment see Sect. 5.2.

[77] Eli Lilly and Co. *v* Canada (UNCITRAL), NAFTA Article 1128 Submission of the United States of America, Case No. UNCT/14/2 (18 March 2016) [13]; Windstream Energy LLC *v* Canada (UNCITRAL), NAFTA Article 1128 Submission of the United States of America (12 January 2016) [16]; Spence International Investments LLC., Berkowitz et al. *v* Costa Rica (UNCITRAL), CAFTA-DR Article 10.20.2 Submission of the United States of America, Case No. UNCT/13/2 (17 April 2015) [18].

> For greater certainty, the mere fact that a Party takes or fails to take an action that may be inconsistent with an investor's expectations does not constitute a breach of this Article [Minimum Standard of Treatment], even if there is loss or damage to the covered investment as a result.[78]

An entirely different question, which will be assessed at a later stage, is whether specific FPS *treaty* clauses could be said to deviate from customary law, and protect legitimate expectations.[79] In any case, the *customary* FPS standard cannot be extended this far.

9.4 The Customary Protection Obligation; Protection Beyond Physical Harm

This chapter has shown that neither the definition of FPS in terms of 'physical security' nor the extension of the standard to 'legal security' provide a suitable basis for the definition of the standard's scope of application. The dichotomy between physical and legal security is, moreover, utterly artificial. To say that the FPS standard does not include a guarantee of legal stability does not necessarily imply limiting the scope of the customary protection obligation to physical security. *Legal* is not the opposite of *physical*. Not every form of *nonphysical* security is concerned with *legal stability*.

A few arbitral decisions have sought to overcome these problems by focusing only on whether the injury was produced by third parties, regardless of whether it was physical or not.[80] These decisions provide an appealing alternative to the (false) dichotomy between 'physical' and 'legal' security, which has dominated academic debate for decades.[81] The implication is that the FPS standard covers not only

---

[78]Agreement between the United States of America, the United Mexican States, and Canada (adopted 30 November 2018) art. 14.6(4).

[79]See Chap. 14.

[80]For some indicative examples see: Electrabel S.A. *v* Hungary, Decision on Jurisdiction, Applicable Law and Liability, ICSID Case No. ARB/07/19 (30 November 2012) [7.145]; El Paso Energy International Co. *v* Argentina, Award, ICSID Case No. ARB/03/15 (31 October 2011) [522 and 524]; Ulysseas Inc. *v* Ecuador (UNCITRAL), Final Award (12 June 2012) [272]; Vannessa Ventures Ltd. *v* Venezuela, Award, ICSID Case No. ARB(AF)04/6 (16 January 2013) [223]. Section 8.3.1 presents these and other cases following similar approaches (e.g. the qualification of the injury by *both* the origin of the threat and its physical character).

[81]The approach followed by a specific arbitral tribunal will depend on the wording of the applicable FPS clause. Chapter 14 provides an overview of the alternative approaches to the interpretation of the main types of FPS clauses. Cf. also: Max Baumgart and Sebastián Mantilla Blanco, 'Electrabel v. Ungarn: Aktuelle Entwicklungen beim Schutz von Auslandsinvestitionen nach dem Vertrag über die Energiecharta' (2016) 7(3) KSzW 179, 183 (particularly focusing on the interpretation of the ECT in *Electrabel v Hungary*); Sebastián Mantilla Blanco, *Justizielles Unrecht im internationalen Investitionsschutzrecht* (Nomos, Baden-Baden 2016) 130-1 n. 401 (providing a brief description of the main alternatives).

physical but also *nonphysical* threats, *provided* the source of risk is external to the host state. Refuting the 'physical security' approach requires showing that the customary protection obligation, as delivered by the tradition of the law of aliens, also refers to some forms of *nonphysical* harm.

The historical record suggests that the customary notion of FPS has traditionally encompassed the notion of *nonphysical* private acts of hostility against foreigners. The works of Georg Friedrich von Martens provide a classical example in this regard. As early as 1796, Martens advanced the proposition that insulting or otherwise injurious acts which tarnish the honor of a foreign subject call for positive protective action by the host sovereign:

> [T]he police shall be watchful that not only aliens dwelling in the territory, who anyway enjoy the protection of the state, but also foreign Regents and their subjects, are not offended in their honor through slanderous rumors, pamphlets, etc.[82]

These words were not unqualified. Following a surprisingly modern line of argument, Martens underscored the need for a balance between the protection of aliens and other values, such as the freedom of the press.[83] Later scholarly studies also considered the question of state responsibility for the acts of the press, unmistakably addressing cases of reputational damage by private press agencies as breaches of the customary protection obligation.[84] Beyond Martens' textbook example, historical illustrations of nonphysical violence actually falling within the scope of the FPS standard may be found in some pieces of diplomatic correspondence from the last decades of the nineteenth century and the first decades of the twentieth century.

A first example refers to an unfortunate series of nonphysical acts of hostility against Chinese and Japanese citizens occurred in the city of Butte, Silverbow County (Montana), from 1896 to 1898. The episode would be the subject of both local court proceedings and a diplomatic claim filed with the State Department by the Chinese Legation in Washington. The local court decision on the case, issued in 1900, contains a detailed account of the facts.[85] A number of labor unions of the city

---

[82]Author's translation. The original German text reads: "[Auch dahin hat unter unzähligen anderen Puncten] die Policey zu wachen, daß nicht durch beleidigende Gerüchte, Druckschriften u.s.f. die Ehre, nicht nur der im Lande befindlichen Fremden, welche ohnehin des Schutzes des Staates genießen, sondern auch auswärtiger Regenten und ihrer Unterthanen ungestraft angetastet werde." Georg Friedrich von Martens, *Einleitung in das positive Europäische Völkerrecht auf Verträge und Herkommen gegründet* (Johann Christian Dieterich, Göttingen 1796) 98-9 (also discussed in Sect. 3.5.2). For another prominent scholar placing the protection of reputation ('*Ehre*') within the customary security obligation see: Hans Kelsen, 'Unrecht und Unrechtsfolge im Völkerrecht' (1932) 12 ZöR 481, 531.

[83]See: Georg Friedrich von Martens, Einleitung in das positive Europäische Völkerrecht auf Verträge und Herkommen gegründet (Johann Christian Dieterich, Göttingen 1796) 99.

[84]See: Edward Zellweger, *Die völkerrechtliche Verantwortlichkeit des Staates für die Presse unter besonderer Berücksichtigung der schweizerischen Praxis* (Polygraphischer Verlag, Zurich 1949) 7-39.

[85]For the full text of the decision, see: Hum Fay et al. *v* Frank Balwin et al. (1900) *Papers relating to the Foreign Relations of the United States with the Annual Message of the President* (Government Printing Office, Washington 1901) 117-24.

had declared a boycott against Chinese and Japanese residents, which the court qualified as a 'willful and malicious conspiracy' against Asian immigrants.[86] The conspirators had not acted in the shadows. Quite the contrary, the boycott had been openly announced in a local newspaper, in the following terms:

> A general boycott has been declared upon all Chinese and Japanese restaurants, tailor shops, and washhouses by the Silver Bow Trades and Labor Assembly. All the friends and sympathizers of organized labor will assist us in this fight against the lowering Asiatic standards of living and morals. America v. Asia, progress v. retrogression are the considerations now involved. American manhood and American womanhood must be protected from competition [...] and further reduction of the wages of native labor by the employment of these people must be strenuously resisted.[87]

The unions went even further. A man had been employed to drive through the city with insulting cartoons, which, in words of the Court, 'were designed to, and would, excite in the spectators feelings of prejudice and hostility against the Chinese'.[88] Members of the labor associations disturbed the customers of the Chinese and compelled them to leave the stores.[89] Some plotters additionally threatened American employers of Asian immigrants, aggressively requesting them to discharge their foreign workers; the boycott was extended to those refusing.[90]

The U.S. Court acknowledged that the complainants were 'entitled to the protection which is accorded in the United States to subjects of the Empire of Chins'.[91] In the court's view, the Government had failed in its duty to provide such protection:

> [T]he public authorities and officers of said city of Butte and said county of Silver Bow and said State of Montana did not protect any of said complainants [...] [and] never caused any of said defendants to be arrested or punished in any manner for the commission of any of said acts.[92]

---

[86]Hum Fay et al. v Frank Balwin et al. (1900) *Papers relating to the Foreign Relations of the United States with the Annual Message of the President* (Government Printing Office, Washington 1901) 117, 119 [6].

[87]Hum Fay et al. v Frank Balwin et al. (1900) *Papers relating to the Foreign Relations of the United States with the Annual Message of the President* (Government Printing Office, Washington 1901) 117, 120 [8].

[88]Hum Fay et al. v Frank Balwin et al. (1900) *Papers relating to the Foreign Relations of the United States with the Annual Message of the President* (Government Printing Office, Washington 1901) 117, 120 [9].

[89]Hum Fay et al. v Frank Balwin et al. (1900) *Papers relating to the Foreign Relations of the United States with the Annual Message of the President* (Government Printing Office, Washington 1901) 117, 120-1 [10-1].

[90]Hum Fay et al. v Frank Balwin et al. (1900) *Papers relating to the Foreign Relations of the United States with the Annual Message of the President* (Government Printing Office, Washington 1901) 117, 120-4 [12-26].

[91]Hum Fay et al. v Frank Balwin et al. (1900) *Papers relating to the Foreign Relations of the United States with the Annual Message of the President* (Government Printing Office, Washington 1901) 117, 119 [2].

[92]Hum Fay et al. v Frank Balwin et al. (1900) *Papers relating to the Foreign Relations of the United States with the Annual Message of the President* (Government Printing Office, Washington 1901) 117, 124 [27].

The Court further concluded that the effect of the Unions' acts 'was to deprive said Chinese residents of said city of Butte of work and the means of earning a livelihood, and compelled them to go to other places'.[93] The Court issued a restraining order.[94] Some sources indicate that the boycott nonetheless continued, albeit clandestinely.[95]

For that reason, the Chinese Minister to the United States, Wu Tingfang, presented a formal claim before the State Department. The Ambassador did not spare adjectives in describing the situation of his countrymen, noting that 'false and slanderous stories' were used to 'inflame the public mind against the Chinese subjects'.[96] He also outlined the 'spirit of lawlessness and hatred created by this conspiracy'.[97] Ambassador Tingfang noted that 'the police did not and would not protect or endeavor to protect them'.[98] The Governor of Montana had also failed to 'interpose his higher authority and influence to secure them the protection which had been guaranteed to them by treaty and by public law'.[99] Only the courts had undertaken some effort to protect the Chinese. However, due to the fact that the boycott had continued in a 'clandestine' manner, China requested compensation from the U.S. Federal Government.[100]

In his response to the Chinese legation, Secretary of State John Hay noted that the U.S. court system had provided and continued to provide Chinese residents with sufficient means of redress, as shown by the fact that a local court had ruled in their favor; under such circumstances, he saw no reason justifying diplomatic

---

[93]Hum Fay et al. *v* Frank Balwin et al. (1900) *Papers relating to the Foreign Relations of the United States with the Annual Message of the President* (Government Printing Office, Washington 1901) 117, 124 [29].

[94]Hum Fay et al. *v* Frank Balwin et al. (1900) *Papers relating to the Foreign Relations of the United States with the Annual Message of the President* (Government Printing Office, Washington 1901) 117, 124 [29].

[95]'Mr. Wu to Mr. Hill' (6 July 1901) *Papers relating to the Foreign Relations of the United States with the Annual Message of the President* (Government Printing Office, Washington 1901) 100, 102 (noting that 'the conspirators, while ceasing from open acts of violence, are still seeking to execute their conspiracy by clandestine means').

[96]'Mr. Wu to Mr. Hill' (6 July 1901) *Papers relating to the Foreign Relations of the United States with the Annual Message of the President* (Government Printing Office, Washington 1901) 100, 100.

[97]'Mr. Wu to Mr. Hill' (6 July 1901) *Papers relating to the Foreign Relations of the United States with the Annual Message of the President* (Government Printing Office, Washington 1901) 100, 100.

[98]'Mr. Wu to Mr. Hill' (6 July 1901) *Papers relating to the Foreign Relations of the United States with the Annual Message of the President* (Government Printing Office, Washington 1901) 100, 100.

[99]'Mr. Wu to Mr. Hill' (6 July 1901) *Papers relating to the Foreign Relations of the United States with the Annual Message of the President* (Government Printing Office, Washington 1901) 100, 100.

[100]'Mr. Wu to Mr. Hill' (6 July 1901) *Papers relating to the Foreign Relations of the United States with the Annual Message of the President* (Government Printing Office, Washington 1901) 100, 102-3.

interposition.[101] Secretary Hay did not deny, however, that Asian residents were entitled to protection by U.S. authorities. Quite the contrary, he stated:

> The Department is glad to be able to assure you that while the action of the Federal court is sufficient proof that the rights of the subjects of the Empire of China domiciled in the city of Butte will be protected and enforced by the judiciary, *it may yet add that the Executive will not fail, should the case arise justifying its interposition, to use all its power to secure to them all the rights, privileges, immunities and exemptions* guaranteed by the United States Constitution and by treaty between the Governments of the United States and China.[102]

This diplomatic note clearly recognizes the obligation placed upon the host state, in this case the United States, to extend its protection to foreign citizens threatened by private hate and violence. Furthermore, by acknowledging that the state shall 'use all its power to secure' certain values, Secretary Hay ultimately described the underlying duty as a non-absolute obligation.[103] More importantly, at least for present purposes, Secretary Hay's words are clearly related to the risk of *nonphysical* harm. That was, in the end, what the diplomatic incident was all about.

An additional historical example of events of nonphysical violence falling within the scope of the FPS standard appears in the British diplomatic correspondence pertaining to the rights of British subjects in Canton (1849).[104] In a communication sent to the Chinese Imperial Commissioner, Seu Kwang Tsin, Sir Samuel George Bonham, then British Governor of Hong Kong, stated:

> I have recently received from the Consul at Canton copies of certain resolutions drawn up and promulgated by the woolen drapers, cotton and cotton-yarn merchants of Canton, expressing the determination of these traders to suspend, for the present, all transactions with British merchants [...] In the resolutions of the guilds, moreover, not only are indecorous epithets applied to my countrymen, but their language throughout is in a strain calculated to engender and preserve ill-feeling between our respective nations by misleading the well-thinking and quietly disposed. Their whole proceeding has, in short, a strong tendency to instigate the mob, at the present crisis, to acts of hostility. I have, heretofore, refrained from taking any provisional steps towards the security of British subjects residing at Canton from the violence of the people, relying, as I still do, upon the disposition of your Government, and, in particular, of your Excellency, to afford them the protection to which they are entitled; and until I am informed that it is out of your power to ensure the security of their persons and property, I shall remain quietly where I am [...] I think, therefore, that these combinations on the part of the Chinese guilds, as being hostile in their tendency, should be immediately taken notice of, and the anonymous writers and propagators of the

---

[101]'Mr. Hay to Mr. Wu' (4 December 1901) *Papers relating to the Foreign Relations of the United States with the Annual Message of the President* (Government Printing Office, Washington 1901) 127, 127-8.

[102]Emphasis added. 'Mr. Hay to Mr. Wu' (4 December 1901) *Papers relating to the Foreign Relations of the United States with the Annual Message of the President* (Government Printing Office, Washington 1901) 127, 127-8.

[103]Cf. 'Mr. Hay to Mr. Wu' (4 December 1901) *Papers relating to the Foreign Relations of the United States with the Annual Message of the President* (Government Printing Office, Washington 1901) 127, 127-8.

[104]For a short historical account of the crisis see: George Beer Endacott, *A Biographical Sketch-Book of Early Hong Kong* (Hong Kong University Press, Hong Kong 2005) 34 *et seq.*

inflammatory and insulting placards, to the existence of which your attention has been of late frequently directed, should be, as your laws require, severely punished.[105]

This note shows that the security obligation refers to *nonphysical* harm originating from private parties. In fact, Governor Bonham was seeking the protection of nonphysical values (the reputation and honor of British subjects), from nonphysical actions.

These nowadays somewhat forgotten diplomatic incidents provide uniquely clear examples of nonphysical violence originating in the acts of private parties. Risks of this kind are not as unusual or exotic as it might appear at first sight. Local merchants and businessmen are often hostile towards foreign competitors entering into the local market. When resentment escalates and turns into a boycott or a similar event, the FPS standard requires the host state to intervene. Local authorities cannot become passive witnesses of nonphysical outrages against foreign citizens.

Beyond these cases, there is a wide array of injuries that could genuinely fall within the scope of the customary protection obligation, and yet cannot be accurately described as 'physical'. Further examples would be cases involving forced loans imposed by revolutionists, or extortion by non-state agents.[106] In such cases, while physical violence could have been used to coerce the victim, neither the actions of the direct wrongdoers nor the injuries inflicted upon the foreign national are necessarily 'physical' in nature.[107]

Contemporary examples might be less obvious or extreme than those described above. For instance, a failure by municipal antitrust authorities to take any steps to prevent or sanction collusion among local competitors against a foreign investor could constitute an internationally wrongful omission contrary to the customary FPS standard. In such case, no actual risk of physical harm is at stake. Still, the relevant threat clearly originates in the actions of private individuals, namely, the investor's market competitors. This circumstance explains the applicability of the FPS standard and the due diligence standard of liability. Cases involving omissions in the enforcement of laws protecting intellectual property against piracy or hacking follow the same logic.[108]

---

[105]'Mr. Bonham to Commissioner Seu' (13 March 1849) 38 (1) St. Pap. 856, 856-7.

[106]See, for example: *De Caro Case* (1903) X RIAA 635, 638 (forced loans imposed by Paolo Guzmán, a General of the so-called 'libertadora revolution'); *George Creswell Delamain v Mexico* (10 July 1931) V RIAA 229, 231 (extortion by a 'bandit leader' and payment of a ransom; it should be noted that the case involved the kidnapping of a foreign national); *Naomi Russell v Mexico* (24 April 1931) IV RIAA 805, 837 and 839 (case involving extortion by revolutionists to a foreign citizen, who was subsequently murdered by the outlaws).

[107]Cf. n. 106 above.

[108]For an analysis of these scenarios cf. Robert Reyes Landicho, 'Enforcing a State's International IP Obligations through Investment Law Standards of Protection – An Ill-Fated Romance' in Ian Laird, Borzu Sabahi, Frédéric Sourgens and Todd Weiler (eds), *Investment Treaty Arbitration and International Law* (Juris Net, Huntington NY 2018) 111, 118 and 126 *et seq*. Cf. also David Collins, 'Applying the Full Protection and Security Standard of Protection to Digital Investments' (2011) 12 (2) J. World Investment & Trade 225, 234 *et seq*. (drawing a parallel between cyberattacks and 'civil disturbances').

The importance of these areas of application of the FPS standard cannot be underestimated. In his comment on the guarantee of 'most constant protection and security' under article 10(1) of the ECT, Thomas Wälde (2004) suggested that this treaty clause should '[be linked] to the economic police in the traditional sense'.[109] In this connection, he explained:

> Where many of the former Communist States' previously State-operated activities now rest in delegated or private hands, but there is often a dominant economic power in implicit collusion with the political and administrative forces, the standard could therefore rather be read to stand for an obligation of the State to use its "police" and economic regulatory powers in a wider sense to ensure that the foreign investor can operate its business in a context not only free from direct physical harassment but also free from harassment by administrative powers and abusively used dominant economic powers derived from control over natural monopolies, essential facilities and other sources of dominant economic power.[110]

For the sake of accuracy, Wälde generally supported a broad interpretation of the ECT rather than a limitation of the security obligation to protection against physical and nonphysical harm *by third parties*.[111] Wälde's view on the standard was that, despite guaranteeing security against omissions by local authorities, article 10(1) of the ECT was *primarily* aimed at giving protection against '[the] *active* and abusive exercise of State powers'.[112] While one may disagree on this extensive reading of the ECT,[113] this does not diminish the enlightening potential of Wälde's idea that the standard could encompass omissions in the exercise of economic police functions in respect of private parties.

Investment arbitral tribunals have already been confronted with cases involving nonphysical harm caused by third parties. In *Eastern Sugar v Czech Republic* (2007) the question arose as to whether the Czech Republic could be held responsible for failing to prevent the investor's 'newcomer competitors' from selling beyond a previously-established quota on sugar.[114] Regrettably, the *Eastern Sugar* tribunal's position as to the applicability of the FPS standard in respect of this claim remained somewhat unclear. While the arbitral tribunal considered that the FPS standard primarily refers to protection against acts of third parties, it also observed that the

---

[109]Thomas Wälde, 'Energy Charter Treaty-based Investment Arbitration. Controversial Issues' (2004) 5 J. World Investment & Trade 373, 391.

[110]Thomas Wälde, 'Energy Charter Treaty-based Investment Arbitration. Controversial Issues' (2004) 5 J. World Investment & Trade 373, 391.

[111]Thomas Wälde, 'Energy Charter Treaty-based Investment Arbitration. Controversial Issues' (2004) 5 J. World Investment & Trade 373, 390-1.

[112]Thomas Wälde, 'Energy Charter Treaty-based Investment Arbitration. Controversial Issues' (2004) 5 J. World Investment & Trade 373, 391.

[113]Section 14.4.2 addresses the interpretation of the ECT in more detail.

[114]Eastern Sugar B.V. *v* Czech Republic, Partial Award, SCC Case No. 088/2004 (27 March 2007) [205].

protection obligation usually concerns 'the state monopoly of physical force'.[115] The arbitrators did not elaborate further on the 'physical' criterion. The 'newcomer competitors' issue was not one of the investor's principal claims and the tribunal decided to focus on the claims pertaining to the acts of Czech authorities, under the FET standard.[116]

In *Hesham Talaat M. Al-Warraq v Indonesia* (2014) one of the claims referred to the alleged breach of the guarantee of 'adequate protection and security' in article 2 of the OIC Agreement on account of alleged negligence of governmental authorities in the supervision of a bank.[117] The claim was however dismissed for insufficient evidence.[118] Another example would be *Mamidoil v Albania* (2015). In that case, an ICSID tribunal considered an FPS claim concerning the host state's alleged failure to take action against 'smuggling, fuel adulteration and tax evasion'.[119] While the arbitral tribunal did not reach a finding of liability, it had no difficulty in assessing the facts under the FPS standard.[120]

---

[115]Eastern Sugar B.V. *v* Czech Republic, Partial Award, SCC Case No. 088/2004 (27 March 2007) [203].

[116]Eastern Sugar B.V. *v* Czech Republic, Partial Award, SCC Case No. 088/2004 (27 March 2007) [207 and 333-47].

[117]Hesham Talaat M. Al-Warraq *v* Indonesia (UNCITRAL), Final Award (15 December 2014) [627].

[118]Hesham Talaat M. Al-Warraq *v* Indonesia (UNCITRAL), Final Award (15 December 2014) [627].

[119]Mamidoil Jetoil Greek Petroleum Products Societe S.A. *v* Albania, Award, ICSID Case No. ARB/11/24 (30 March 2015) [824].

[120]In the *Mamidoil* case, the investor was unable to prove the impact of such activities on its investment; for the rejection of the claim see: Mamidoil Jetoil Greek Petroleum Products Societe S.A. *v* Albania, Award, ICSID Case No. ARB/11/24 (30 March 2015) [825-6 and 829].

Chapter 10
The Temporal Scope of Application of the Customary Standard of 'Full Protection and Security'

10.1 Preliminary Remarks

The temporal scope of application of FPS refers to the *moment in time* or, more precisely, *moments in time*, in which the host state is pledged to take positive steps for the protection of aliens. The said moments may be most accurately defined by reference to the *harmful event*, i.e. the point in time in which the injury consummates. *Before* damage is inflicted, the FPS standard imposes an obligation to *prevent* harm. This obligation includes a duty *prevent additional harm* (i.e. a duty to *mitigate* damages) whenever the harmful event cannot be entirely avoided. In turn, *after* an injury has been inflicted upon a foreign citizen, the host state is required to provide *means of redress* in respect of it. From a historical perspective, the latter obligation chiefly developed in connection with the punishment of crimes against foreigners.[1] It

---

[1]For a similar remark see: Suez Sociedad General de Aguas de Barcelona S.A. and Vivendi Universal S.A. *v* Argentina, Decision on Liability, ICSID Case No. ARB/03/19 (30 July 2010) [165]. For some historical examples see: *Amelia de Brissot et al. v. United States of Venezuela* (26 August 1890) *United States and Venezuelan Claims Commission. Opinions Delivered by the Commissioners in the Principal Cases* (Gibson Bros., Washington 1890) 457, 484-9 (opinions of Commissioners Little and Findlay); Hum Fay et al. *v* Frank Balwin et al. (1900) *Papers relating to the Foreign Relations of the United States with the Annual Message of the President* (Government Printing Office, Washington 1901) 117, 124 [27]; *Lina Balderas de Díaz v United States of America* (16 November 1926) IV RIAA 106, 107-8 [3-6]; 'Murder of Charles W. Renton– Diplomatic Correspondence' (1895) *Papers relating to the Foreign Relations of the United States with the Annual Message of the President* (Government Printing Office, Washington 1895) 882, 882-935; 'Settlement of the Claims of Mrs. Charles W. Renton, of Ella Miller Renton, and of the Estate of Jacob Baiz' (1904) *Papers relating to the Foreign Relations of the United States with the Annual Message of the President* (Government Printing Office, Washington 1904) 352, 352-69 (particularly at 357-9); *Sarah Bryant, Countess D'Etchegoyen v. Mexico* (6 August 1932) V RIAA 305, 306 [5]; *Thomas Youmans v Mexico* (23 November 1926) IV RIAA 110, 114-5 [11]; *William E. Bowerman and Messrs. Burberry's Ltd. v Mexico* (15 February 1930) V RIAA 104, 106 [7]. On the *Renton* case see also: John Bassett Moore, *A Digest of International Law* (Volume 6:

© Springer Nature Switzerland AG 2019
S. Mantilla Blanco, *Full Protection and Security in International Investment Law*,
European Yearbook of International Economic Law 8,
https://doi.org/10.1007/978-3-030-24838-3_10

is therefore often referred to as an *obligation of repression*.[2] In *El Paso v Argentina* (2011) the arbitral tribunal described these two aspects of the standard in the following terms:

> The minimum standard of vigilance and care set by international law comprises a duty of prevention and a duty of repression. A well-established aspect of the international standard of treatment is that States must use "due diligence" to prevent wrongful injuries to the person or property of aliens caused by third parties within their territory, and, if they did not succeed, exercise at least "due diligence" to punish such injuries.[3]

The FPS standard may hence be said to perform two different functions in two different moments, namely, a *preventive* function and a *repressive/redress* function. The standard's *temporal dimensions* are therefore, too, *functional dimensions*. These two functional dimensions root in more general distinctions, which have been traditionally drawn in the context of state responsibility for acts of private parties. Back in the seventeenth century, Hugo Grotius advanced the fundamental proposition that the host state can only be held responsible for injuries to aliens caused by acts of individuals in two exceptional scenarios. First, if the sovereign is aware of the imminence of harm and fails to prevent, that is to say, tolerates, the harmful conduct (*patientia*); second, if the state receives and gives refuge to the offender, by neither punishing him nor accepting to extradite him (*receptus*).[4]

The differentiation between preventive and repressive action, albeit probably originating in—and being without doubt essential to—the Grotian doctrine of

---

Government Printing Office, Washington 1906) 794-9. For an arbitral decision recognizing the preventive and repressive dimension of the protection obligation without making particular reference to criminal offences see: *H. G. Venable v Mexico* (8 July 1927) IV RIAA 219, 257 [17].

[2]For some recent examples of this terminology being used in connection with the FPS standard see: Electrabel S.A. *v* Hungary, Decision on Jurisdiction, Applicable Law and Liability, ICSID Case No. ARB/07/19 (30 November 2012) [7.146] (referring to an 'obligation of repression'); El Paso Energy International Co. *v* Argentina, Award, ICSID Case No. ARB/03/15 (31 October 2011) [523] (using the expression 'duty of repression'); Sergei Paushok, CJSC Golden East Co., CJSC Vostoknefte *v* Mongolia (UNCITRAL), Award on Jurisdiction and Liability (28 April 2011) [324] (using the phrase 'duty of repression'); Ulysseas Inc. *v* Ecuador (UNCITRAL), Final Award (12 June 2012) [272] (making reference to 'repression and punishment'); Helge Elisabeth Zeitler, 'Full Protection and Security' in Stephan Schill (ed), *International Investment Law and Comparative Public Law* (Oxford University Press, New York 2010) 183, 183 (observing that the FPS standard requires 'repressive action'). For the sake of precision, however, the more-general expression 'obligation of redress' seems preferable.

[3]El Paso Energy International Co. *v* Argentina, Award, ICSID Case No. ARB/03/15 (31 October 2011) [523].

[4]Hugonis Groti, *De iure belli ac pacis* (1625) (Leiden, A. W. Sijthoff 1919) 411-29 [Lib. 2 Cap. XXI]; Hugo Grotius, *The Rights of War and Peace in Three Books* (1625) (The Lawbook Exchange, Clark NJ 2004) 453-73 [Book 2 Chap. XXI]. On the Grotian theory of fault see Sect. 12.3.1. See also: Riccardo Pisillo Mazzeschi, *"Due diligence" e responsabilità internazionale degli stati* (Giuffrè Editore, Milan 1989) 28-30.

fault, cannot be said to be particular to it; quite the contrary, the distinction is also at the heart of most modern theories of state responsibility for acts of individuals.[5] Academic studies generally recognize the host state's prevention and repression obligations under customary international law.[6] In the specific field of international

---

[5] Cf. Chap. 12. Some drafts for the codification of the law of state responsibility also considered the distinction between the prevention obligation and the obligation of redress. For a representative example see: Roberto Ago, 'Fourth Report on State Responsibility – The Internationally Wrongful Act of the State, Source of International Responsibility (Continued) (A/CN.4/264)' (20 June 1972 and 9 April 1973) 2 *Yearbook of the International Law Commission – 1972* 71, 126 art. 11 (drawing the distinction in connection with state responsibility for acts of individuals).

[6] See, for example: Alfred Verdross and Bruno Simma, *Universelles Völkerrecht* (Duncker & Humblot, Berlin 1984) 863-5 (analyzing the host state's responsibility for lacks of diligence in the prevention or repression of private wrongs to foreign citizens); Alf Ross, *A Textbook of International Law. General Part* (Longmans, Green and Co., London 1947) 165 ("[t]he state is bound to provide reasonable police measures for the protection of threatened aliens and for the effective prosecution and punishment of the criminals, should crime occur in spite of all. The state is responsible if it does not show due diligence and care in any of these respects"); Andrés Bello, *Principios de derecho de jentes* (Valentín Espinal, Caracas 1837) 54-5 (considering the issue in particular connection with the sovereign's duties towards nationals and foreigners); Clyde Eagleton, The Responsibility *of States in International Law* (Klaus Reprint, New York 1970) 87 ("The state has two duties: a duty of prevention, and a duty of redress. It may incur responsibility for insufficient effort to prevent an injury as well as for failure in its subsequent duty of providing redress") and 93 (concluding that '[the state is] not responsible for acts of individuals, except when it has failed in its duties of prevention and punishment, of restraint and redress') [first edition: 1928]; Emanuel von Ullmann, *Völkerrecht* (J. C. B. Mohr, Tübingen 1908) 152-3 (analyzing the protection obligation in its preventive and repressive dimensions, and expressing some restrictive views on responsibility for revolutionary damages); Franz von Liszt, *Das Völkerrecht systematisch dargestellt* (Verlag von O. Häring, Berlin 1906) 192 (advancing the proposition that, in those cases, the state appears as an 'indirect subject of the international delict' – *mittelbares Deliktsubjekt*); Gaetano Morelli, *Nozioni di diritto internazionale* (CEDAM – Casa Editrice Dott. A. Milani, Padua 1958) 341 (referring to preventive and repressive measures of protection in connection with the concept of fault in international law); Hans-Jürgen Schlochauer, 'Die Entwicklung des völkerrechtlichen Deliktsrechts' (1975) 16 AVR 239, 254 *et seq.* (with particular reference to the Grotian notions of *patientia* and *receptus*); Hans Kelsen, 'Collective and Individual Responsibility in International Law with Particular Regard to the Punishment of War Crimes' (1943) 31 Cal. L. Rev. 531, 536 (observing that, in the case of acts of individuals, 'the State, in whose territory the acts have been committed, is responsible in so far as the State is obliged to prevent these acts, and, if prevention is not possible, to punish the delinquents and compel them to pay damages'); Hans Kelsen, 'Unrecht und Unrechtsfolge im Völkerrecht' (1932) 12 ZöR 481, 513-4 and 532-3 (considering the duties of prevention and repression in specific connection with state responsibility for acts of private individuals); John Thomas Abdy (ed), *Kent's Commentary on International Law* (Steven & Sons, London 1878) 113 (stating that '[w]hen foreigners are admitted into a state upon free and liberal terms, the public faith becomes pledged for their protection. The courts of justice ought to be freely open to them to resort to for the redress of their grievances'); Karl Strupp, *Grundzüge des positiven Völkerrechts* (Ludwig Röhrscheid, Bonn 1922) 132 (recognizing both obligations in particular connection with acts of private individuals); Marcel Sirbert, *Traité de droit international public* (Volume 1: Librairie Dalloz, Paris 1951) 317 (making particular emphasis on the concept of '*diligence nécessaire*'); Pavlos Alextrandou Zannas, *La responsabilité internationale des Etats pour les actes de négligence* (Ganguin & Laubscher, Geneva 1952) 57-63 (distinguishing between the 'fonction préventive' and the 'fonction

investment law, scholars tend to acknowledge the two functional dimensions of the FPS standard without digging much deeper into the question.[7]

The dual purpose of FPS enjoys broad recognition in contemporary investment arbitration practice too. A clear example may be found in the award issued in *Parkerings v Lithuania* (2007). In that case, the arbitral tribunal observed that '[a] violation of the standard of *full protection and security* could arise in case of failure of the State to prevent the damage, to restore the previous situation or to

---

répressive'); Richard Lillich and John Paxman, 'State Responsibility for Injuries to Aliens Occasioned by Terrorist Activities' (1977) 26(2) Am. U. L. Rev. 217, 221 (recognizing both the 'duty of a state to prevent the commission of acts injurious to foreign states, including acts injurious to their nationals as well' and the 'duty to take reasonable steps to apprehend and punish [the offender]'); Richard Lillich, *The Human Rights of Aliens in Contemporary International Law* (Manchester University Press, Manchester 1984) 13 ("the original injury is sometimes inflicted by a private party independent from the host government, or by an official of the host government acting outside the scope of his authority. In these latter types of cases, the responsibility of the host State may arise from the State's failure to prevent or redress the substantive injury"); Robert Jennings and Arthur Watts (eds), *Oppenheim's International Law* (Volume 1: Longman Group, Essex 1993) 549 (noting, in reference to state responsibility for acts of individuals, that '[the state's] duty is to exercise due diligence to prevent internationally injurious acts on the part of private persons, and, in case such acts have nevertheless been committed, to punishing the offenders and compelling them to pay damages where required'; see also p. 551).

[7]For scholarly writings recognizing these two functional dimensions see, for example: David Collins, 'Applying the Full Protection and Security Standard of Protection to Digital Investments' (2011) 12(2) J. World Investment & Trade 225, 225 and 236-41 (with particular reference to the protection of digital assets); Geneviève Bastid Burdeau, 'La clause de protection et sécurité pleine et entière' (2015) 119(1) RGDIP 87, 99 (discussing the *El Paso* award in this connection); Giuditta Cordero Moss, 'Full Protection and Security' in August Reinisch (ed), *Standards of Investment Protection* (Oxford University Press, New York 2008) 131, 131 (referring to '[t]he protection that the legal system affords in order to prevent or prosecute actions that threaten or impair the physical safety of the investment'); Helge Elisabeth Zeitler, 'Full Protection and Security' in Stephan Schill (ed), *International Investment Law and Comparative Public Law* (Oxford University Press, New York 2010) 183, 183 (noting that the standard 'requires positive action by the host state to protect foreign investment through preventive and repressive action'); Helge Elisabeth Zeitler, 'The Guarantee of Full Protection and Security in Investment Treaties regarding Harm Caused by Private Parties' (2005) 3 SIAR 1, 9 (stating that '[b]ased on the same principle of protection, obligations exist both on the level of protection and of repression'); Finnur Magnússon, *Full Protection and Security in International Law* (University of Vienna, Vienna 2012) 183-7 (providing an overview of arbitral practice indicating that FPS guarantees the availability of the local legal system); Lucas Bastin, *State Responsibility for Omissions: Establishing a Breach of the Full Protection and Security Obligation by Omissions* (Oxford University, Oxford 2016) [D.Phil. Thesis] 88 and 151 *et seq.* (also analyzing cases concerning the redress obligation at pp. 151 *et seq.*); Ralph Alexander Lorz, 'Protection and Security (Including the NAFTA Approach)' in Marc Bungenberg, Jörn Griebel, Stephan Hobe and August Reinisch (eds), *International Investment Law* (Nomos, Baden-Baden 2015) 764, 782 ('the host State does not only owe the prevention of physical impairment of the investment, but also the availability of remedies if such attacks occur'; see also p. 767); Todd Weiler, *The Interpretation of International Investment Law: Equality, Discrimination, and Minimum Standards of Treatment in Historical Context* (Brill, Leiden 2013) 166 (linking the FPS standard to the customary minimum legal standard of treatment of aliens and expressing that '[t]he CLIMSTA was a manifestation of the P&S standard which, of logical necessity, included prohibitions against both administrative and judicial denials of justice').

punish the author of the injury'.[8] A similar approach was followed in *Sergei Paushok v Mongolia* (2011). In their award on jurisdiction and liability, the arbitrators expressly recognized the two functional dimensions of the FPS standard:

> The minimum standard of vigilance and care set by international law comprises a duty of prevention and a duty of repression. A well-established aspect of the international standard of treatment is that States must exercise "due diligence" to prevent wrongful injuries to the person or property of aliens within their territory and, if they did not succeed, to exercise at least "due diligence" to punish such injuries.[9]

To the same effect, in *Ulysseas v Ecuador* (2012) the arbitrators summarized the two aspects of the protection obligation in the following terms:

> Full protection and security [...] imposes [the host state] an obligation of vigilance under international law comprising a duty of due diligence for the prevention of wrongful injuries inflicted by third parties to persons or property of aliens in its territory or, if not successful, the repression and punishment of such injuries.[10]

In *Electrabel v Hungary* (2012), an ECT arbitral tribunal noted that FPS imposes upon the host state an obligation to undertake measures to 'protect the covered investment against adverse action by private parties' and to provide 'tools for obtaining redress', and went on to characterize the latter element as an 'obligation of repression'.[11] The tribunal in *Mobil v Argentina* (2013) adopted a similar interpretation of the FPS standard, observing that '[FPS] must be understood as the obligation of the host State to act with due diligence providing investors' physical protection and, if it comes to that, facilitate investor's access to justice'.[12] As they dismissed the FPS claim, the arbitrators underscored that none of the investors' claims referred to such obligations.[13]

In *Oxus Gold v Uzbekistan* (2015), the arbitral tribunal considered that the FPS standard goes beyond the duty to prevent wrongs by third parties, and further requires the state to 'punish' the offenders.[14] In *Joseph Houben v Burundi* (2016), too, the arbitrators unambiguously acknowledged the dual function of the FPS standard:

---

[8]Parkerings-Compagniet AS *v* Lithuania, Award, ICSID Case No. ARB/05/8 (11 September 2007) [355].

[9]Sergei Paushok, CJSC Golden East Co., CJSC Vostoknefte *v* Mongolia (UNCITRAL), Award on Jurisdiction and Liability (28 April 2011) [324].

[10]Ulysseas Inc. *v* Ecuador (UNCITRAL), Final Award (12 June 2012) [272].

[11]Electrabel S.A. *v* Hungary, Decision on Jurisdiction, Applicable Law and Liability, ICSID Case No. ARB/07/19 (30 November 2012) [7.145-6].

[12]Mobil Exploration and Development Argentina Inc. Suc. Argentina and Mobil Argentina S.A. *v* Argentina, Decision on Jurisdiction and Liability, ICSID Case No. ARB/04/16 (10 April 2013) [1002].

[13]Mobil Exploration and Development Argentina Inc. Suc. Argentina and Mobil Argentina S.A. *v* Argentina, Decision on Jurisdiction and Liability, ICSID Case No. ARB/04/16 (10 April 2013) [1003].

[14]Cf. Oxus Gold *v* Uzbekistan (UNCITRAL), Final Award (17 December 2015) [353, 355 and 834].

[U]n aspect bien établi de la norme est que les États doivent utiliser une «diligence raisonnable» pour prévenir les dommages injustifiés à la personne ou aux biens des étrangers sur leur territoire et, s'ils n'y ont pas réussi, exercer au moins une «diligence raisonnable» pour punir les auteurs de tels dommages.[15]

In other arbitral decisions, despite the tribunal making no explicit recognition of the obligation of redress, the repressive function seems to be at least implicit in the arbitrators' line of argument.[16] Taking into consideration this line of cases, investors have sometimes invoked the FPS standard in connection with the 'inactivity' of the host state's judiciary.[17]

---

[15]Joseph Houben v Burundi, Sentence, ICSID Case No. ARB/13/7 (12 January 2016) [161].

[16]Frontier Petroleum Ltd. v Czech Republic (UNCITRAL), Final Award (12 November 2010) [273] (observing that FPS encompasses 'an obligation to make a functioning system of courts and legal remedies available to the investor'); Gemplus S.A., SLP S.A. and Gemplus Industrial S.A. de C.V. v Mexico, Award, ICSID Cases No. ARB(AF)/04/3 & ARB(AF)/04/4 (16 June 2010) [9.12] (stating that 'the existence of many legal proceedings involving the Concession and the Concessionaire [...] demonstrate that it was never a case about a failure by the Respondent to afford, indirectly, legal protection to the Claimants or their investments under Mexican law within the Mexican legal system [...] the Concessionaire was itself entitled to resort and did resort to domestic legal remedies in the Respondent's state courts'); Mohammad Ammar Al-Bahloul v Tajikistan, Partial Award on Jurisdiction and Liability, SCC Case No. V 064/2008 (9 September 2009) [246] (holding that 'miscarriage of justice' could constitute a breach of the FPS standard); Ronald Lauder v Czech Republic (UNCITRAL), Final Award (3 September 2001) [314] (making reference to the availability of the local judicial system); Suez Sociedad General de Aguas de Barcelona S.A. and Vivendi Universal S.A. v Argentina, Decision on Liability, ICSID Case No. ARB/03/19 (30 July 2010) [165] (the tribunal considered the historical evolution of FPS, and noted that most instances of application of the standard have been related to '[failures] to exercise due diligence in preventing the damage or punishing the perpetrators'); Wena Hotels Ltd. v Egypt, Award, ICSID Case No. ARB/98/4 (8 December 2000) [84] (the case was related to the wrongful seizure of the investor's hotels in Egypt; in relation to FPS, the arbitrators noted that competent authorities 'took no immediate action to restore the hotels promptly to Wena's control' and further observed that 'Egypt never imposed substantial sanctions on EHC or its senior officials, suggesting Egypt's approval of EHC's actions').

[17]For some examples see: Anglia Auto Accessories Ltd. v Czech Republic, Final Award, SCC Case No. V 2014/181 (10 March 2017) [130] (the tribunal did not consider this allegation in detail; the arbitrators found that the FPS claim fell outside the tribunal's material scope of jurisdiction at para 190); Vannessa Ventures Ltd. v Venezuela, Award, ICSID Case No. ARB(AF)04/6 (16 January 2013) [226-7] (stating that, while there were delays in the assessment of the investor's claims, Venezuela's conduct had not reached the 'high threshold' for a treaty breach; see also the analysis of other allegations related to the redress obligation at paras 228 et seq.).

10.2 The Preventive Functional Dimension. The Duty to Prevent Injuries to Aliens

Most contemporary instances of application of the FPS standard have been concerned with the *prevention* of injuries to foreign investors and their property.[18] It is the *preventive* function, rather than the *repressive* function, that has taken center stage in contemporary arbitral practice. The underlying reason might be that, while claims pertaining to failures of redress are often presented under a wide variety of headings (e.g. denial of justice, fair and equitable treatment or effective means clauses), FPS often appears to be the only standard against which omissions in the prevention of harm can be properly assessed.[19]

It is therefore little surprising for some authors to consider the FPS standard only in its preventive dimension, without turning much attention to the obligation of redress. Just to mention a prominent example, Kenneth J. Vandelvelde describes the scope of the customary standard in the following terms:

> The requirement of full protection and security is an established standard of customary international law that requires the host state to exercise due diligence or reasonable care *to prevent injury to the property (and persons) of foreign nationals.*[20]

The preventive functional dimension of the customary FPS standard enjoys a long tradition in international law. It found expression in most of the 'classic'

---

[18]For some representative examples see: Adel A Hamadi Al Tamini *v* Oman, Award, ICSID Case No. ARB/11/33 (3 November 2015) [448-52] (alleged failure to prevent acts of vandalism); American Manufacturing & Trading Inc. *v* Zaire, Award, ICSID Case No. ARB 93/1 (21 February 1997) [6.08] (failure to prevent physical damage to a protected investment); LESI S.p.A. and ASTALDI S.p.A. *v* Algeria, Sentence, ICSID Case No. ARB/05/3 (12 November 2008) [11 *et seq.* and 152-4] (alleged insufficiency of state action against Islamic extremist groups); Noble Ventures *v* Romania, Award, ICSID Case No. ARB/01/11 (12 October 2005) [160-7] (preventive action against occupations, intimidations and thefts); Pantechniki S.A. Contractors & Engineers *v* Albania, Award, ICSID Case No. ARB/07/21 (30 July 2009) [1-2, 71-84] (failure to prevent the plundering of an investor's road work site); Parkerings-Compagniet AS *v* Lithuania, Award, ICSID Case No. ARB/05/8 (11 September 2007) [354-61] (prevention of certain private acts of vandalism); Plama Consortium Ltd. *v* Bulgaria, Award, ICSID Case No. ARB/03/24 (27 August 2008) [236, 248-55 and 325] (prevention of riot violence); Tecnicas Medioambientales TECMED S.A. *v* Mexico, Award, ICSID Case No. ARB(AF)/00/2 (29 May 2003) [175] (alleged failure to 'prevent or put an end to the adverse social demonstrations expressed through disturbances in the operation [of the investment]'); Toto Costruzioni Generali S.p.A. *v* Lebanon, Award, ICSID Case No. ARB/07/12 (7 June 2012) [171, 195-206 and 226-30] (preventive measures of protection against owners of expropriated parcels and foreign troops); Wena Hotels Ltd. *v* Egypt, Award, ICSID Case No. ARB/98/4 (8 December 2000) [80-95] (failure to prevent the illegal seizure of the investor's property).

[19]Chapter 15 provides a detailed analysis of the relationship between FPS and other standards of investment protection, including the FET standard.

[20]Emphasis added. Kenneth Vandelvelde, *Bilateral Investment Treaties: History, Policy, and Interpretation* (Oxford University Press, New York 2010) 243. For an arbitral decision emphasizing the preventive dimension of the FPS standard cf. Koch Minerals SÁRL and Koch Nitrogen International SÁRL *v* Venezuela, Award, ICSID Case No. ARB/11/19 (30 October 2017) [8.46].

treatises on the law of nations, including the works of Hugo Grotius, Christian von Wolff and Emer de Vattel.[21] Edwin Borchard summarized in 1916 the core of the obligation with the following words:

> The failure of a government to use due diligence to prevent a private injury is a well-recognized ground of state responsibility. The state is thus responsible for every injury which by the exercise of reasonable care it could have averted.[22]

This statement resembles the formulation used by Francis Wharton in a legal opinion prepared for the U.S. Department of State in 1885. The report referred to the seizure of some ships of the United Magdalena Steam Navigation Co. by armed rebels in Colombia. In his analysis of the case, Wharton drew the following conclusion:

> The Government of the United States of Colombia is liable not only for any injury done by it or with its permission to citizens of the United States or their property, *but for any such injury which by the exercise of reasonable care it could have averted, and it is also liable for damages done to such vessels when by reasonable care it could have averted such damage.*[23]

For the purposes of this section, it suffices to emphasize that the duty to prevent injuries to aliens is *triggered* by the *risk* of an injury. It is the external *threat* to the acquired values of a foreign citizen what calls upon the adoption of preventive measures by local authorities. To be clear, this does not imply that the *actual occurrence* of a harmful event is immaterial for a finding of responsibility. For instance, the ILC concluded in 1997 that a *breach* of the customary obligation to prevent injuries to aliens requires both a failure to exercise due diligence *and* the *occurrence* of the injurious event, i.e. the actual infliction of an injury.[24] In the

---

[21]Hugonis Groti, *De iure belli ac pacis* (1625) (Leiden, A. W. Sijthoff 1919) 411-29 [Lib. 2 Cap. XXI]; Hugo Grotius, *The Rights of War and Peace in Three Books* (1625) (The Lawbook Exchange, Clark NJ 2004) 453-73 [Book 2 Chap. XXI]; Christian Wolff, 'Jus gentium methodo scientifica pertractactatum' (1749) in James Brown Scott (ed), *Classics of International Law* (Joseph Drake tr, Clarendon Press, Oxford 1934) 536-7 § 1063; Emer de Vattel, *The Law of Nations or Principles of the Law of Nature Applied to the Conduct and Affairs of Nations and Sovereigns* (1758) (G.G. and J. Robinson, London 1797) 173. Cf. Chap. 3. See also Chap. 12.

[22]Edwin Borchard, *The Diplomatic Protection of Citizens Abroad or the Law of International Claims* (The Banks Law Publishing Co., New York 1916) 217.

[23]Emphasis added. 'Report of Mr. Wharton to the Department of State' (18 May 1885) *Papers relating to the Foreign Relations of the United States with the Annual Message of the President* (Government Printing Office, Washington 1885) 212, 212. Wharton had already used this formulation in a previous communication on the same matter. See: 'Mr. Wharton to the Department of State' (21 April 1885) *Papers relating to the Foreign Relations of the United States with the Annual Message of the President* (Government Printing Office, Washington 1885) 212, 212. Wharton's report was also quoted in academic writings as an expression of the customary protection obligation. See, for example: Clyde Eagleton, *The Responsibility of States in International Law* (Klaus Reprint, New York 1970) 87 n. 33 [first edition: 1928].

[24]ILC, 'Draft Articles on State Responsibility with Commentaries thereto adopted by the International Law Commission on First Reading (Doc. No. 97-02583)' (January 1997) [http://legal.un.org/ilc/texts/instruments/english/commentaries/9_6_1996.pdf] 174-7 [7-16].

Commission's opinion, these two conditions are both cumulative and necessary for a declaration of liability under this heading.[25]

A fundamental distinction must be therefore drawn between the point in time in which the prevention obligation requires positive action by the state, and the moment in which insufficiency of preventive measures can be properly qualified as an international wrong. These two moments never coincide. As a matter of sheer logic, preventive action must necessarily take place *prior to* the infliction of harm. In turn, if the view of the ILC is followed, a *breach* of the prevention obligation can only be established upon the occurrence of the injurious event.

This section is concerned only with the temporal scope of application of FPS. It therefore focuses on the point in time in which the prevention obligation is *triggered*. Chapter 11 addresses the conditions upon which a breach of FPS can be established and the role that the actual injury plays in that context.

As stated beforehand, the very notion of a prevention obligation implies that state action is required *before* the injury consummates. State practice specifically referring to threats that have not yet materialized in an injury is, however, rather scarce. Diplomatic correspondence is usually directed at the assertion of some claim for compensation and, for that very same reason, normally refers to injuries that have already been inflicted. Still, Governments have sometimes made specific requests for protection *before* the occurrence of the harmful event.

A historical example may be found in an exchange of diplomatic notes between the Mexican Minister of Foreign Affairs and the U.S. Ambassador to Mexico in 1911. In a first note, the American Ambassador stated:

> Representations have been made to me today by a large delegation of American merchants and business men residing in the City of Mexico, relative to the inadequate protection which, in case of danger being threatened to life and property by the disorderly elements of society, the Government of your excellency could afford [. . .] the military and police forces [. . .] are not sufficient to come with any formidable attack which might be made [. . .] I am obliged to say to you that in case of American lives or property being injured as a result of turbulent disturbances my Government will be obliged to assume, prima facie, that insufficient protection has been afforded.[26]

In his response to the American Embassy, the Mexican Foreign Minister did not contest the duty placed upon local authorities to prevent these imminent injuries to U.S. citizens. Quite the contrary, he readily expressed his Government's commitment to comply with such international obligation:

> I can assure your excellency that the interests and persons of American citizens and members of other foreign countries in the City of Mexico are not in any way in danger of suffering any

---

[25]ILC, 'Draft Articles on State Responsibility with Commentaries thereto adopted by the International Law Commission on First Reading (Doc. No. 97-02583)' (January 1997) [http://legal.un.org/ilc/texts/instruments/english/commentaries/9_6_1996.pdf] 174-7 [7-16]. Section 11.2.2.2 provides a detailed analysis of the ILC's position in this regard.

[26]'The American Ambassador to the Mexican Minister of Foreign Affairs' (13 May 1911) *Papers relating to the Foreign Relations of the United States with the Annual Message of the President* (Government Printing Office, Washington 1911) 492, 492.

injury at all, *as the necessary precautions have been taken to prevent not only the perpe-tration of attacks, but also the slightest disturbances.* Therefore your excellency may appease the minds of the merchants and businessmen who called at the embassy and inform them that *the Government will endeavor by all means to avoid any danger for them; but in the remote case that an incident of that class should happen, your excellency may be sure that the Government will at the same time prevent the injury and try the case in accordance with the provisions of international law.*[27]

These communications have the particular feature that, at the time they were dispatched, no injuries had yet been inflicted. It becomes thus conspicuous that the United States was demanding fulfillment of an international obligation, which it considered to be triggered by the *risk* of an injurious event. Mexico did not challenge, but rather confirmed, this fundamental proposition.

Investment arbitral decisions also confirm that the prevention obligation is trig-gered by the *risk* of an injury, which in turn implies drawing a fundamental conceptual distinction between the host state's conduct *before* and *after* the infliction of harm. A good example appears in *Joseph Houben v Burundi* (2016). In that case, illegal settlers had invaded the property of Mr. Joseph Houben, a Belgian national, in Bujumbura.[28] Despite Houben repeatedly requesting police intervention, local authorities did not take sufficient steps to protect his property.[29]

In the arbitral proceedings, Burundi argued that local law provided for the protection of the actual holders of the land and, moreover, that their expulsion could be inconsistent with Article 17 of the ICCPR (protection of 'privacy, family, home and correspondence').[30] The Tribunal observed that, for the purposes of the FPS claim, the threshold issue was not whether Burundi could or should have expelled the invaders.[31] The FPS standard required the host state to take reasonable measures to prevent them from illegally invading Mr. Houben's property in the first place.[32] This is but another way of saying that the prevention obligation concerns the host state's conduct *before* risk materializes in an injury; the duty to take action is triggered by the *risk* of harm and not by the *occurrence* of harm:

> [L]a question n'est pas de savoir si le Burundi était tenu d'expulser les usurpateurs après que ces derniers furent entrés en possession du terrain, ni si leur expulsion, une fois les habitations construites, aurait été contraire au droit international des droits de l'homme, mais si le Burundi a pris les mesures nécessaires pour empêcher, *a priori*, que ces usurpateurs ne prennent possession du terrain. Les circonstances de faits décrites ci-dessus démontrent que tel n'est pas le cas.[33]

---

[27]Emphasis added. 'The [Mexican] Minister of Foreign Affairs to the American Ambassador' (16 May 1911) *Papers relating to the Foreign Relations of the United States with the Annual Message of the President* (Government Printing Office, Washington 1911) 493, 493.

[28]For a detailed account of the facts of the case see: Joseph Houben v Burundi, Sentence, ICSID Case No. ARB/13/7 (12 January 2016) [86-102].

[29]Joseph Houben v Burundi, Sentence, ICSID Case No. ARB/13/7 (12 January 2016) [165-9].

[30]Joseph Houben v Burundi, Sentence, ICSID Case No. ARB/13/7 (12 January 2016) [177].

[31]Joseph Houben v Burundi, Sentence, ICSID Case No. ARB/13/7 (12 January 2016) [177].

[32]Joseph Houben v Burundi, Sentence, ICSID Case No. ARB/13/7 (12 January 2016) [177].

[33]Joseph Houben v Burundi, Sentence, ICSID Case No. ARB/13/7 (12 January 2016) [177].

10.3   The Repressive Functional Dimension. The Duty to Provide Adequate Means for the Redress of Injuries to Aliens

State and arbitral practice leave no doubt that the customary FPS standard encompasses not only a duty to take positive action to prevent an impending injury, but also an obligation of redress. As a general rule, the individual affected by an act of violence that is not attributable to state action shall seek redress before local authorities; in such scenario, the host state is pledged to provide adequate means of redress against the offender. In *Amelia de Brisot et al. v Venezuela*, the United States—Venezuela Claims Commission (established under the bilateral convention of December 5th, 1885) considered this element of the customary protection obligation in detail. The case concerned the rebel assault of the steamer *Apure*, property of *The Orinoco Steam Navigation Co.* (USA), in the Venezuelan port of Apurito. In his opinion on the case, Commissioner Findlay stated:

> The attack was in the nature of an ambuscade and complete surprise. It would be wholly unwarranted, therefore, to hold Venezuela responsible for not anticipating and preventing an outbreak, of which the persons more interested in knowing and the very actors on the spot, had no knowledge. *A state, however, is liable for wrongs inflicted upon the citizens of another state in any case where the offender is permitted to go at large without being called to account or punished for his offence, or some honest endeavor made for his arrest and punishment.*[34]

As it may be deduced from Commissioner Findlay's words, the obligation of redress—just as the prevention obligation—is not of an absolute nature. In other words, the host state's customary duty does not reach as far as to impose an obligation to ensure that reparation is actually effected. On the contrary, the state will have discharged its duties under the customary FPS standard if it has exercised diligence in providing proper means of redress. As expressed by U.S. Attorney General Levi Lincoln in 1802:

> By the law of nations, if the citizens of one state do an injury to the citizens of another, the government of the offending subject ought to take every reasonable measure to cause reparation be made by the offended (sic). But if the offender is subject to the ordinary

---

[34]Emphasis added. *Amelia de Brissot et al. v. United States of Venezuela* (26 August 1890) *United States and Venezuelan Claims Commission. Opinions Delivered by the Commissioners in the Principal Cases* (Gibson Bros., Washington 1890) 457, 486. For his part, Commissioner Little noted that 'Venezuela's responsibility and liability in the matter are to be determined and measured by her conduct in ascertaining and bringing to justice the guilty parties. If she did all that could reasonably be required in that behalf, she is to be held blameless; otherwise not. Without entering upon a discussion of the investigation instituted and conducted by her, it seems that there was fault in not causing the leaders, at least, of this lawless band to be arrested. It was notorious who they were. It does not seem that any attempt was made before any local authority to bring them or any of the band to justice' (at pp. 482-3). These opinions had some influence on other arbitral decisions. See, for example: *Poggioli Case* (1903) X RIAA 669-92 (quoting both Commissioner Findlay and Commissioner Little).

processes of law, it is believed this principle does not generally extend to oblige the government to make satisfaction in case of the inability of the offender.[35]

In more recent years, in *Frontier Petroleum v Czech Republic* (2010), an UNCITRAL arbitral tribunal made clear that the host state's redress obligation under the FPS standard is not an absolute guarantee.[36] The tribunal confined protection under the standard to the issuance of a 'reasonably tenable' decision on any particular dispute.[37] Most importantly, it acknowledged that states enjoy a broad margin of discretion in the design of local redress mechanisms.[38]

To be sure, the redress obligation is not necessarily satisfied by rendering a decision which formally puts an end to an ongoing dispute or clarifies the investor's legal position. The FPS standard further requires such decision to be actually enforced. The award rendered in *Siag v Egypt* (2009) provides a clear example of this aspect of the standard. In that case, municipal courts had issued several judgments declaring that the taking of the investors' property had been illegal.[39] Notwithstanding the foregoing, property was never returned to the foreign investors.[40] The arbitrators characterized this situation as 'the most egregious element in the whole affair' and went on to declare that Egypt had breached the applicable FPS clause.[41]

Proper redress does not always consist in providing access to the local judiciary. The obligation of redress could require police protection or immediate administrative action. An indicative example appears in *Wena Hotels v Egypt* (2000). The case concerned the illegal seizure of the investor's property by the Egyptian Hotel Company [EHC].[42] In their assessment of the FPS claims, the arbitrators considered that Egypt had breached its protection obligation not only by failing to prevent the seizure of the investor's properties but also by failing to restore the illegally-seized properties:

> Even if the Tribunal were to accept this explanation for Egypt's failure to act *before* the seizures, it does not justify the fact that neither the police nor the Ministry of Tourism took

---

[35]Emphasis added. 'Lincoln, At. Gen.' (1802) in John Bassett Moore, *A Digest of International Law* (Volume 6: Government Printing Office, Washington 1906) 787, 787.

[36]Frontier Petroleum Ltd. *v* Czech Republic (UNCITRAL), Final Award (12 November 2010) [269 and 273].

[37]Frontier Petroleum Ltd. *v* Czech Republic (UNCITRAL), Final Award (12 November 2010) [273].

[38]Frontier Petroleum Ltd. *v* Czech Republic (UNCITRAL), Final Award (12 November 2010) [273].

[39]Waguih George Siag and Clorinda Vecchi *v* Egypt, Award, ICSID Case No. ARB/05/15 (1 June 2009) [43-64, 67-75, 81-2 and 85-7].

[40]Waguih George Siag and Clorinda Vecchi *v* Egypt, Award, ICSID Case No. ARB/05/15 (1 June 2009) [448].

[41]Waguih George Siag and Clorinda Vecchi *v* Egypt, Award, ICSID Case No. ARB/05/15 (1 June 2009) [448].

[42]Wena Hotels Ltd. *v* Egypt, Award, ICSID Case No. ARB/98/4 (8 December 2000) [17 *et seq*].

any immediate action to protect Wena's investments *after* EHC had illegally seized the hotels.[43]

In sum, it may be safely stated that the customary protection obligation encompasses an obligation of redress. Further, it is undisputed that said 'repression' obligation is an obligation of *diligence*. The question arises, however, as to the actual scope of the redress obligation. Unless FPS is elevated to the category of an all-encompassing obligation and thus deprived from any meaningful content, not every failure to redress an injury done to a foreign national can be measured against the FPS standard. The duty of redress cannot be held to encompass every imaginable grievance sustained by an alien while in the host state's territory.

This section advances one simple, fundamental proposition: the distinction between the FPS standard's preventive and repressive functional dimensions refers only to the standard's *temporal* scope of application. All other elements of the security relationship (secured/securing subjects, secured values and, most importantly, covered risks) remain the same regardless of whether the standard is being applied in connection with the prevention of an impending injury or the redress of an inflicted injury.

The definition of the repressive obligation's scope of application has been signalized by generalizations and imprecise formulas. Vagueness has opened the door to significant practical difficulties. If the repressive functional dimension is given too broad a scope, the FPS standard may end up significantly overlapping with other international obligations, particularly with those related to the redress of wrongful injuries and the exercise of judicial authority. An extensive approach could thus end up blurring any meaningful distinction between FPS and other standards of investment protection, such as the FET standard.[44]

A brief look into some instances of application of the redress obligation provides evidence of the aforesaid difficulties. Thus, for example, in *Ronald Lauder v Czech Republic* the arbitrators noted that, under the FPS standard, the host state is required to 'keep its judicial system available for the Claimant and any entities he controls to bring their claims, and for such claims to be properly examined and decided in accordance with domestic and international law'.[45] This formulation gives the

---

[43]Wena Hotels Ltd. *v* Egypt, Award, ICSID Case No. ARB/98/4 (8 December 2000) [88].

[44]Section 15.2 provides a detailed assessment of the relationship between the FPS standard and the FET standard.

[45]Ronald Lauder *v* Czech Republic (UNCITRAL), Final Award (3 September 2001) [314]. This issue was discussed in detail in the parties' submissions in *EDF v Argentina*. See: EDF International S.A., Saur International S.A. and Leon Participaciones Argentinas S.A. *v* Argentina, Award, ICSID Case No. ARB/03/23 (11 June 2012) [409-10 and 419-20]. The tribunal took cognizance of the arguments, but abstained from digging deeper into the question (at paras 1108-12). For a claim based on a broad understanding of the redress obligation cf. Hesham Talaat M. Al-Warraq *v* Indonesia (UNCITRAL), Final Award (15 December 2014) [622] (investor's argument concerning an alleged breach of the guarantee of 'adequate protection and security' of the OIC Agreement 'by the conduct of the prosecutorial authorities and of the courts of law who applied the criminal legislation in an arbitrary and discriminatory manner').

impression that the FPS standard encompasses the whole protection of aliens through the local judiciary.

To be clear, placing the availability of the municipal judicial system or some procedural guarantees within the FPS standard is by no means unsound. The issue is rather that an *unqualified* application of the FPS standard to the administration of justice is inaccurate and might lead to unintended results. Measuring *every* act of the local judiciary against the FPS standard could give rise to at least two logical inconsistencies.

In the first place, the repression obligation would cease to be an obligation of redress. Not every international delict committed in connection with the administration of justice can be accurately characterized as a failure to redress a previous injury. For instance, if a lawsuit is brought against a foreign investor and competent domestic courts arbitrarily favor a local claimant, thus failing to provide the respondent due process in law, the foreign respondent would be the victim of an internationally wrongful act of the judiciary. Such act, however, does not constitute a failure to redress a *previous* injury to the respondent; rather, it would be the first injury inflicted on such foreign citizen.[46]

Second, adopting the broad definition of the repressive functional dimension advanced in *Ronald Lauder v Czech Republic* would imply ascribing a much wider scope of application to the obligation of redress than to the prevention obligation. Not every 'failure of redress' refers to injuries originating in a source of risk *external* to the host state. For example, arbitrariness or gross procedural unfairness in court proceedings instituted against a public entity could constitute a failure to comply with such a broadly defined obligation of redress, in spite of having no particular connection with an external source of damage.[47]

Most of these inconsistencies can be avoided by accepting the proposition announced in the introduction to this section, namely, that the FPS standard's repressive functional dimension refers only to the standard's *temporal* scope of application. As a corollary, the subjects, object and risks conforming the protection obligation remain the same both *before* and *after* the consummation of an injury. The FPS standard hence requires the host state to provide means of redress for injuries done to the acquired values of foreign citizens, provided such injuries are the result of events (risks/threats) external to the state, or constitute collateral damages occasioned by state action against an external source of danger. Arbitral decisions provide some authority in support of this conclusion. For instance, in *Frontier Petroleum v Czech Republic* (2010), the arbitrators stated:

---

[46]In 1932, Gerald G. Fitzmaurice used this example as an argument against the definition of 'denial of justice' as a failure to redress a previous injury. See: Gerald Fitzmaurice, 'The Meaning of the Term Denial of Justice' (1932) 13 BYIL 93, 108.

[47]In *Mondev v United States*, the arbitral tribunal envisaged this effect, but did not go deeper into the issue. Mondev International *v* United States, Award, ICSID Case No. ARB(AF)/99/2 (11 October 2002) [152].

This Tribunal notes that nearly all of the decisions dealing with procedural propriety and due process in the context of fair and equitable treatment have concerned proceedings involving disputes with the host state or with state entities. *This may suggest that complaints about lack of due process in disputes with private parties are better dealt with in the context of the full protection and security standard.*[48]

In *El Paso v Argentina* (2011), an ICSID arbitral tribunal rejected the investor's claims under the FPS standard on the following grounds:

El Paso does not complain about a violation by Argentina of *an obligation of prevention or repression* [. . .] In the present case, *none of the measures challenged by El Paso were taken by a third party; they all emanated from the State itself.* Consequently, these measures should only be assessed in the light of the other BIT standards and cannot be examined from the angle of full protection and security.[49]

In *Jan Oostergetel v Slovakia* (2012), an UNCITRAL arbitral tribunal quoted the *Frontier Petroleum* award and was explicit in stating that '[c]oncerning the possible link between due process and procedural property and the standard of full protection and security, the Tribunal agrees, in principle, with the opinion of the *Frontier* tribunal'.[50] In *Electrabel v Hungary* (2012), another arbitral tribunal, after considering whether the acts of *Magyar Villamos Müvek Zrt* (a state owned electricity company) could be attributed to the host state, made the following observation:

[Under the FPS standard] necessary measures must be capable of protecting the investment against adverse action by third parties. *If MVM were considered as such private person, Hungary provided Electrabel the means for obtaining redress (obligation of repression).*[51]

Similarly, in *Ulysseas v Ecuador* (2012), the arbitrators underscored that the FPS standard refers to the prevention and repression of 'wrongful injuries inflicted by third parties to persons or property of aliens'.[52] In *Oxus Gold v Uzbekistan* (2015), the tribunal restricted the scope of both the duty of prevention and the duty of redress to protection from wrongful conduct by third parties.[53] In *Joseph Houben v Burundi*

---

[48]Emphasis added. Frontier Petroleum Ltd. *v* Czech Republic (UNCITRAL), Final Award (12 November 2010) [296]. Attention should be drawn to the very cautious words chosen by the tribunal in this connection (e.g. the expression 'this might suggest'). The arbitrators moreover went on to state that 'full protection and security obliges the host state to provide a legal framework that grants security and protects the investment against adverse action by private persons as well as state organs, whereas fair and equitable treatment consists mainly of an obligation on the host state's part to desist from behavior that is unfair and inequitable' (at para 296).

[49]Emphasis added. El Paso Energy International Co. *v* Argentina, Award, ICSID Case No. ARB/03/15 (31 October 2011) [523].

[50]Jan Oostergetel and Theodora Laurentius *v* Slovakia (UNCITRAL), Final Award (23 April 2012) [226]. It should however be noted that this holding had little significance for the decision on the dispute. Indeed, the arbitrators stated: "In the present case, however, given that the BIT introduces full protection and security as a specific application of FET, the distinction between the two types of complaints seems to lack relevance." (at para 226).

[51]Emphasis added. Electrabel S.A. *v* Hungary, Decision on Jurisdiction, Applicable Law and Liability, ICSID Case No. ARB/07/19 (30 November 2012) [7.146].

[52]Ulysseas Inc. *v* Ecuador (UNCITRAL), Final Award (12 June 2012) [272].

[53]Oxus Gold *v* Uzbekistan (UNCITRAL), Final Award (17 December 2015) [353, 355 and 834].

(2016) the arbitrators limited the scope of application of the FPS standard to protection against acts of third parties (*action de tiers*) without making an exception for the redress obligation, which existence and binding character was explicitly recognized in the award.[54] A similar approach was implicit in *Gemplus v Mexico* (2010).[55] In other cases, while the repressive functional dimension was not expressly restricted to private injuries, the issue of judicial protection was considered against the backdrop of a dispute between non-state parties.[56]

Adjudicatory practice is, however, not entirely straightforward. Some tribunals have expressed the view that the FPS standard encompasses an obligation of redress for injuries resulting from state action. These decisions should be read with caution. To begin with, these assertions have not carried much weight in the resolution of the underlying disputes. Furthermore, they are typically based on the assumption that the FPS standard encompasses a protection obligation with regard to physical harm caused by state entities, and that the obligation of redress necessarily refers to the same kind of injuries as such broadly-defined prevention obligation. An example would be the award rendered in *Siag v Egypt* (2009), where the arbitrators considered that the non-enforcement of judicial decisions declaring an expropriation as illegal constituted a breach of the FPS standard.[57] Another example appears in *Suez v Argentina* (2010). In that case, the arbitral tribunal stated:

> [T]his Tribunal is of the view that the stability of the business environment and legal security are more characteristic of the standard of fair and equitable treatment, while the full protection and security standard primarily seeks to protect investment from physical harm.

---

[54]Joseph Houben *v* Burundi, Sentence, ICSID Case No. ARB/13/7 (12 January 2016) [157 and 161].

[55]Gemplus S.A., SLP S.A. and Gemplus Industrial S.A. de C.V. *v* Mexico, Award, ICSID Cases No. ARB(AF)/04/3 & ARB(AF)/04/4 (16 June 2010) [9.11-9.12].

[56]A prominent example would be the arbitral award rendered in the case *Ronald Lauder v Czech Republic*. Despite the arbitrators advancing a broad definition of the redress obligation, the underlying case concerned a judicial dispute between private parties. See: Ronald Lauder *v* Czech Republic (UNCITRAL), Final Award (3 September 2001) [314] (referring to the duty to keep the local judiciary available for the resolution of a private contractual dispute). For some additional examples see: Parkerings-Compagniet AS *v* Lithuania, Award, ICSID Case No. ARB/05/8 (11 September 2007) [355-61] (alleged violations of the FPS standard, which were partly related to state actions, and partly referred to private acts of vandalism; see particularly para 356); Tecnicas Medioambientales TECMED S.A. *v* Mexico, Award, ICSID Case No. ARB(AF)/00/2 (29 May 2003) [177] (recognizing that Mexican judicial authorities had acted reasonably 'in relation to the efforts made to take action against the community's opposing demonstrations'; it should be however noted that, in this very same connection, the tribunal also considered judicial actions pertaining to municipal administrative measures); Wena Hotels Ltd. *v* Egypt, Award, ICSID Case No. ARB/98/4 (8 December 2000) [84] (seizure of hotel facilities by a state-owned company whose acts were held not to be directly attributable to the Egypt).

[57]Waguih George Siag and Clorinda Vecchi *v* Egypt, Award, ICSID Case No. ARB/05/15 (1 June 2009) [448]. While the *Siag* award was right in noting that the FPS standard requires the actual enforcement of local court decisions granting redress to a foreign investor (see discussion above), it seems that the case involved a source of risk which was entirely public and, thus, did not entirely fit into the FPS standard's scope of application.

This said, this latter standard may also include an obligation to provide adequate mechanisms and legal remedies for prosecuting the *State organs or private parties* responsible for the injury caused to the investor.[58]

The *Suez* tribunal was advancing two different propositions. In the first place, the arbitrators indicated that FPS 'primarily' refers to private and public *physical* harm. This proposition is unsound. As explained in Chap. 9, the physical/nonphysical divide is largely misleading and does not provide a suitable basis for delimiting the FPS standard's scope of application.[59] A second proposition, which is—at least implicitly—present in the *Suez* award, is that the obligation of redress refers to the same risks as the prevention obligation. In other words, the host state shall exercise due diligence in the avoidance of *certain* (impending) injuries and, if *such* injuries come to materialize, it is then pledged to provide means of redress in respect of those very *same* (now inflicted) injuries. This view is correct. If the argument advanced throughout this survey were to be followed, however, the injuries in question would not be those having a physical nature, as the *Suez* tribunal suggested, but those originating in a source other than state action.

There are a few cases in which adjudicating bodies seem to have actually considered the FPS standard in respect of harm directly and exclusively arising out of public actions. A prominent—and often quoted—example is the ICJ judgment in *Elettronica Sicula*.[60] In that case, the Major of Palermo requisitioned the property of an American-owned company.[61] The company filed an administrative appeal with the competent City Prefect.[62] In its diplomatic protection claim, the U.S. Government alleged that the Prefect's delays in ruling on the appeal amounted to a 'procedural denial of justice' and, thus, were in breach of Article V of the FCN treaty between Italy and the United States.[63]

The ICJ recognized that '[t]he primary standard laid down by Article V is the full protection and security required by international law',[64] further noting that 'the

---

[58]Emphasis added. Suez Sociedad General de Aguas de Barcelona S.A. and Vivendi Universal S.A. *v* Argentina, Decision on Liability, ICSID Case No. ARB/03/19 (30 July 2010) [173]. It should be additionally noted that the *Suez* tribunal heavily focused on the wording of a specific treaty clause (see, for example, para 175).

[59]On the physical-nonphysical divide see particularly Sect. 9.2.

[60]For academic studies quoting the *Elettronica Sicula* decision in this connection see: Finnur Magnússon, *Full Protection and Security in International Law* (University of Vienna, Vienna 2012) 183-4; Christoph Schreuer, 'Full Protection and Security' (2010) 1(2) J. Int'l Disp. Settlement 353, 359.

[61]*Case Concerning Elettronica Sicula S.p.A. (ELSI) (United States of America v Italy)* [1989] ICJ Rep 15, 32-3 [30].

[62]*Case Concerning Elettronica Sicula S.p.A. (ELSI) (United States of America v Italy)* [1989] ICJ Rep 15, 33 [32].

[63]For the United States' argument about the delay see: *Case Concerning Elettronica Sicula S.p.A. (ELSI) (United States of America v Italy)* [1989] ICJ Rep 15, 66 [110].

[64]*Case Concerning Elettronica Sicula S.p.A. (ELSI) (United States of America v Italy)* [1989] ICJ Rep 15, 66 [111].

"protection and security" must conform to the minimum international standard'.[65] It additionally observed that, in the specific treaty under consideration, FPS and the minimum standard are 'supplemented by the criteria of national treatment and most-favoured-nation treatment'.[66] The Court did not however consider the Prefect's delays to constitute a breach of the FPS standard:

> The Chamber is here called upon to apply the provisions of a treaty which sets *standards* – in addition to the reference to general international law – *which may go further in protecting nationals of the High Contracting Parties than general international law requires*; but the United States has not – save in one respect – suggested that these requirements do in this respect set *higher standards than the international standard*. It must be doubted whether in all the circumstances, the delay in the Prefect's ruling in this case can be regarded as falling below *that standard*. Certainly, the Applicant's use of so serious a charge as to call it a "denial of procedural justice" might be thought exaggerated.[67]

The *ELSI* case should not be taken as evidence of an all-encompassing obligation of redress being embedded within the FPS standard. The ICJ did not intend to extend FPS to any administrative or judicial proceeding concerning every imaginable kind of injury. It is true that the Court expressly mentioned FPS in this particular connection.[68] Nonetheless, the ICJ did not actually *apply* the FPS standard in respect of the administrative delays; there was no finding of liability under this heading. Moreover, the Court was considering a specific treaty clause which, despite being 'primarily' concerned with the FPS standard, also encompassed other standards, such as national treatment, most favored nation treatment, protection against expropriation and, most importantly, a detailed list of procedural guarantees.[69] The ICJ further recognized that such treaty-based *standards* (in plural) did not necessarily correspond to the customary minimum standard of treatment. Noting that the United States had not submitted evidence of any such clauses establishing standards 'higher' than those provided by customary law, it measured the delays against the

---

[65]*Case Concerning Elettronica Sicula S.p.A. (ELSI) (United States of America v Italy)* [1989] ICJ Rep 15, 66 [111].

[66]*Case Concerning Elettronica Sicula S.p.A. (ELSI) (United States of America v Italy)* [1989] ICJ Rep 15, 66 [111].

[67]Emphasis added. *Case Concerning Elettronica Sicula S.p.A. (ELSI) (United States of America v Italy)* [1989] ICJ Rep 15, 66-7 [111].

[68]*Case Concerning Elettronica Sicula S.p.A. (ELSI) (United States of America v Italy)* [1989] ICJ Rep 15, 66 [111].

[69]See: Treaty of Friendship, Commerce and Navigation between the United States of America and the Italian Republic (adopted 2 February 1948, entered into force 26 July 1949) Charles Bevans (ed), *Treaties and Other International Agreements of the United States of America 1776–1949* (Volume 9: U.S. Department of State Publication, Washington 1971) 261, 264-5 arts. V(2) (expropriation), V(3) (national treatment and most-favored nation treatment) and V(4) (access to municipal courts and procedural guarantees). Nonetheless, it should be noted that the United States did not base its argument on the procedural guarantees set forth in the treaty. See: *Case Concerning Elettronica Sicula S.p.A. (ELSI) (United States of America v Italy)* [1989] ICJ Rep 15, 66 [110].

(general) customary minimum standard, but seemingly not against the more-specific FPS standard.[70]

10.4   The Relationship Between the Obligation to Prevent and the Obligation of Redress

As explained throughout this chapter, the FPS standard encompasses both a prevention obligation and a redress obligation. This circumstance poses the question as to the relationship between both elements and, particularly, as to whether they may be considered as autonomous obligations providing different bases for international responsibility. A first possible approach would be to limit responsibility to cases where local authorities fail to redress an injury. From this perspective, the prevention and repression obligations would not be separate, independent compartments. Rather, a breach of the prevention obligation would trigger the obligation of redress. In turn, a subsequent failure to give redress would constitute a condition necessary for a finding of international responsibility.

In this line of argument, the 1977 Annual Report of the ILC described the customary protection obligation as an 'obligation of result' signalized by the possibility of the host state discharging its duties by producing an 'alternative result instead of that originally required'.[71] The ILC noted that such 'alternative result' is 'different from that aimed at by the obligation, but in a way equivalent to it'.[72] In this connection, the Commission explained:

> [A] State cannot be charged with a final breach of the obligation to exercise vigilance to prevent unlawful attacks against the person and property of foreigners, or of the obligation to protect every person against arbitrary arrest or detention, merely because it has not been able to prevent the commission of such misdeeds. If the State is to be found guilty of such a breach, it must have failed to achieve not only the priority result but also the alternative result: that is to say, it must have failed to ensure that the victims of these misdeeds receive

---

[70]Chapter 5 considers the relationship between FPS and the more-general international minimum standard. For other interpretations of the ELSI case see: Frontier Petroleum Ltd. *v* Czech Republic (UNCITRAL), Final Award (12 November 2010) [264] (stating that, following the *ELSI* case, '[FPS] is not restricted to physical protection but extends to legal protection through domestic courts'); Christoph Schreuer, 'Full Protection and Security' (2010) 1(2) J. Int'l Disp. Settlement 353, 359 (observing that '*ELSI* may be quoted in support of the argument that the protection and security standard is not restricted to physical protection but extends to legal protection by domestic courts'); Finnur Magnússon, *Full Protection and Security in International Law* (University of Vienna, Vienna 2012) 184 (suggesting that the ICJ was considering a possible violation of the 'international minimum standard of full protection and security').

[71]ILC, 'Report of the International Law Commission on the Work of its Twenty-Ninth Session – State Responsibility' (1977) 2(2) *Yearbook of the International Law Commission – 1977* 5, 29 [33].

[72]ILC, 'Report of the International Law Commission on the Work of its Twenty-Ninth Session – State Responsibility' (1977) 2(2) *Yearbook of the International Law Commission – 1977* 5, 29 [33].

full and complete compensation for the injury sustained. It is this second failure which, added to the first, transforms it into a complete and final breach.[73]

These views are hardly compatible with the contemporary understanding of the FPS standard. For instance, the ILC Report ignores the well-established 'due diligence' component of the security obligation. The debate on the characterization of the security obligation as an obligation of result or conduct will be addressed in Chap. 11. For the purposes of this section, the threshold issue is whether, as the 1977 Report suggests, a failure of redress is a condition necessary for establishing responsibility under this heading. Some historical sources seem to indicate, at least implicitly, that it is. An example appears in the *Harvard Draft* of 1929, which, making particular reference to events of mob violence, set forth the following rule:

> Article 11. A state is responsible if an injury to an alien results from an act of an individual or from mob violence, *if the state has failed to exercise due diligence to prevent such injury and if local remedies have been exhausted without adequate redress for such failure, or if there has been denial of justice.*[74]

The *Harvard Draft* included a similar provision for the case of injuries caused by insurgents.[75] This approach has the advantage of establishing a clear link between the two functional dimensions of the FPS standard. However, a closer look reveals that it is ultimately defective and unsound. Three arguments speak against this view.

First, sources indicating that a breach of the customary protection obligation requires a failure to provide local means of redress should be taken with caution.[76] These statements are usually related to the debate on the substantive or procedural

---

[73]ILC, 'Report of the International Law Commission on the Work of its Twenty-Ninth Session – State Responsibility' (1977) 2(2) *Yearbook of the International Law Commission – 1977* 5, 29 [33]. An almost identical statement appears in Roberto Ago's Sixth Report on State Responsibility. See: Roberto Ago, 'Sixth Report on State Responsibility – The Internationally Wrongful Act of the State, Source of International Responsibility (A/CN.4/302 and Add.1-3)' (1977) 2(1) *Yearbook of the International Law Commission – 1977* 3, 20 [45].

[74]Emphasis added. 'Responsibility of States for Damage done in their Territory to the Person and Property of Foreigners' (1929) 23 AJIL 131, 134 art. 11. This work has already considered this provision in Sect. 8.3.1. In his comments on article 11, Edwin Borchard underscored the distinction between private and public injuries and observed that the abovementioned conditions for the establishment of responsibility may be viewed as 'certain manifestations of the actual or implied complicity of the government in the act, before of after it, either by directly ratifying or approving it, or by an implied, tacit or constructive approval in the negligent failure to prevent the injury, or to investigate the case, or to punish the guilty individual, or to enable the victim to pursue his civil remedies against the offender'. Edwin Borchard, 'The Law of Responsibility of States for Damage Done in Their Territory to the Person or Property of Foreigners. Comments to the Draft Convention' (April 1929) 23 AJIL 140, 189 art. 11.

[75]'Responsibility of States for Damage done in their Territory to the Person and Property of Foreigners' (1929) 23 AJIL 131, 134 art. 12.

[76]In a previous publication, the author has analyzed the relationship between the local remedies rule and the notion of denial of justice. See: Sebastián Mantilla Blanco, *Justizielles Unrecht im internationalen Investitionsschutzrecht* (Nomos, Baden-Baden 2016) 28-45 and 110-7.

nature of the local remedies rule,[77] and the understanding of denial of justice as an all-encompassing notion, which would cover the whole substance of the law of aliens and constitute the general ground of diplomatic intervention.[78] For example, the ILC's Annual Report of 1977 was largely based on Roberto Ago's Sixth Report on State Responsibility.[79] For his part, Ago was one of the most prominent champions of the characterization of the local remedies rule as a substantive condition for the establishment of international responsibility, a position that found specific expression in the abovementioned Sixth Report.[80] Much the same can be said in respect of the *Harvard Draft*. The *Draft* included a substantive requirement of exhaustion of local remedies not only with regard to private injuries, but in respect of public injuries too.[81] Furthermore, in his comment to article 6 (local remedies rule), Edwin Borchard unmistakably characterized the nature of the rule as substantive:

> The resort to local remedies [. . .] is a necessary condition, both of the duty to respond internationally (international responsibility) and of the correlative right of the "injured state" to demand reparation on behalf of its national [. . .] local remedies must be exhausted, even when officials of the state have committed the injury.[82]

Second, the redress obligation is not triggered by the *breach of the prevention obligation*, but by the *occurrence of a harmful event*. This idea has appeared in different guises throughout the years. Just to mention a prominent example, Heinrich Triepel distinguished in 1899 between two possible forms of state responsibility for acts of individuals.[83] The first form is the duty to make reparation (*Pflicht zur Reparation*) and is contingent upon a prior finding of *fault* (*Schuld*) on the part of

---

[77] For a detailed recent survey on the legal nature of the local remedies rule see: Michael Gindler, *Die local remedies rule im Investitionsschutzrecht* (Nomos, Baden-Baden 2013) 74-102.

[78] On the definition of denial of justice and its relevance for the assessment of historical sources pertaining to the FPS standard see Sect. 2.2.3.

[79] See: Roberto Ago, 'Sixth Report on State Responsibility – The Internationally Wrongful Act of the State, Source of International Responsibility (A/CN.4/302 and Add.1-3)' (1977) 2(1) *Yearbook of the International Law Commission – 1977* 3, 20 [45].

[80] See: Roberto Ago, 'Sixth Report on State Responsibility – The Internationally Wrongful Act of the State, Source of International Responsibility (A/CN.4/302 and Add.1-3)' (1977) 2(1) *Yearbook of the International Law Commission – 1977* 3, 20-43 [47-113], particularly at 22 [52] ("It is our contention that the principle of the exhaustion of local remedies applies necessarily, and primarily, to the determination of the existence of an internationally wrongful act arising through the breach of an international obligation, and thus to the genesis of international responsibility").

[81] 'Responsibility of States for Damage done in their Territory to the Person and Property of Foreigners' (1929) 23 AJIL 131, 133-4 arts. 6-8.

[82] Edwin Borchard, 'The Law of Responsibility of States for Damage Done in Their Territory to the Person or Property of Foreigners. Comments to the Draft Convention' (April 1929) 23 AJIL 140, 151-2 art. 6.

[83] Heinrich Triepel, *Völkerrecht und Landesrecht* (Verlag von C. L. Hirschfeld, Leipzig 1899) 334-5.

state agents (e.g. lack of diligence in the prevention of an injury).[84] The second form corresponds to the duty to grant satisfaction (*Genugthuung*).[85] As understood by Triepel, satisfaction usually consists in adequately punishing the offenders.[86] This obligation applies irrespective of any prior faulty conduct by the state; thus, the state must punish the wrongdoers, even if it bears no fault in failing to prevent the injury.[87] Private wrongs can therefore give rise to *both* reparation *and* satisfaction (if the state is at fault), or *only* to satisfaction (if no prior faulty conduct is attributable to state organs).[88] This is but another way of saying that the 'punishment obligation' arises out of the very *occurrence* of the private wrong, regardless of whether there has been a prior lack of diligence on the part of competent authorities.[89] Simply put, an antecedent international wrong is not a necessary condition for the activation of the duty of redress.

Let us consider an indicative example. In principle, the breach of a contract between private parties is not attributable to the state and, consequently, cannot be properly styled as an international delinquency. Neither can an impending breach of contract be considered as a situation of risk calling for active preventive intervention by public authorities: before a competent organ has established the existence and extent of a breach, the legitimacy of the investor's interests will be largely uncertain.[90]

In spite of the absence of an international wrong, a breach of contract causing damages to a foreign national does actually trigger the international obligation of redress. In those cases, the threshold issue is not whether the acts of a contracting party are, *as such*, attributable to the host state, as some arbitral decisions

---

[84]Heinrich Triepel, *Völkerrecht und Landesrecht* (Verlag von C. L. Hirschfeld, Leipzig 1899) 334-5.

[85]Heinrich Triepel, *Völkerrecht und Landesrecht* (Verlag von C. L. Hirschfeld, Leipzig 1899) 335.

[86]Heinrich Triepel, *Völkerrecht und Landesrecht* (Verlag von C. L. Hirschfeld, Leipzig 1899) 334 n. 1, 335 and 337.

[87]Heinrich Triepel, *Völkerrecht und Landesrecht* (Verlag von C. L. Hirschfeld, Leipzig 1899) 335-6.

[88]Heinrich Triepel, *Völkerrecht und Landesrecht* (Verlag von C. L. Hirschfeld, Leipzig 1899) 335. For a critical analysis of Triepel's approach to this particular subject see: Dionisio Anzilotti, *Teoria generale della responsabilità dello stato nel diritto internazionale* (F. Lumachi Libraio-Editore, Florence 1902) 173-4 (particularly at n. 1); Dionisio Anzilotti, *Lehrbuch des Völkerrechts* (Volume 1: Walter de Gruyter, Berlin/Leipzig 1929) 380-1.

[89]Chapter 12 explores the relationship between the concepts of 'fault' and 'due diligence', as used in international legal thinking.

[90]This holds true even where a state-owned company was a party to the contract. For a representative example see: Saint-Gobain Performance Plastics Europe *v* Venezuela, Decision on Liability and the Principles of Quantum, ICSID Case No. ARB/12/13 (30 December 2016) [559-60] (referring to a contract between a foreign investor and a state-owned company; the tribunal clarified at para 536 that it would make no decision as to the attribution of the company's acts to Venezuela). Section 13.4.3 analyzes this aspect of the case in greater detail.

misleadingly suggest.[91] Regardless of this often-intricate question of attribution, the host state is pledged to provide means of asserting contractual rights before domestic authorities. A failure to do so could be characterized as an omission, attributable to the host state, which entails a violation of FPS.[92] Arbitral tribunals have recognized that a breach of contract, albeit not internationally wrongful, activates the host state's duty of redress under the FPS standard.[93] This shows that redress is required whenever an *injury* has been *inflicted*. The existence of a *prior* international wrong, committed in connection with that injury, is immaterial for the activation of the redress obligation.

Third, this approach drastically reduces the significance of the prevention obligation. If this view were to be followed, a failure to exercise due diligence in the prevention of an injury would never constitute an international wrong in itself. Neither would diligence in the prevention of harm have a clear impact on the assessment responsibility. Liability would solely arise from a breach of the redress obligation; a separate breach of the prevention obligation would be impossible. In consequence, the host state's preventive actions would only be relevant if they achieve the result of actually avoiding the injurious event, thus eliminating the material opportunity for a failure of redress. In all other cases, the diligence exercised by state agencies before the occurrence of the injury would be irrelevant in the eyes of international law.

Some authorities sought to overcome this effect by stating that compliance with the prevention obligation 'excuses' a breach of the obligation of redress. For instance, in a communication sent to Charles F. Adams (then U.S. Minister to the United Kingdom), U.S. Secretary of State William Seward stated:

> It seems to the President an incontestable principle, that whatever injury is committed by the subjects of Great Britain upon citizens of the United States, either within the British dominions or upon the high seas, in expeditions thus proceeding from British ports and posts, ought to be redressed by her Majesty's government, *unless they shall be excused from*

---

[91]In *Gea Group Aktiengesellschaft v Ukraine*, the investor submitted an FPS claim related to the alleged failure to punish an individual who was responsible for a misrepresentation in a repayment agreement. The tribunal dismissed the claim on the ground that such misrepresentation was not attributable to Ukraine. This approach is unpersuasive. The legal issue in this case was the alleged *omission* to take action against a private individual, and not the attribution of that individual's conduct to the host state. See: Gea Group Aktiengesellschaft *v* Ukraine, Award, ICSID Case No. ARB/08/16 (31 March 2011) [256-66].

[92]On the example of a failure to redress a private breach of contract as an situation giving rise to international responsibility see: Chittharanjan Felix Amerasinghe, *Local Remedies in International Law* (Cambridge University Press, Cambridge 2004) 100.

[93]For some representative examples see: Ronald Lauder *v* Czech Republic (UNCITRAL), Final Award (3 September 2001) [314] (making reference to the duty of redress in the case of a private breach of contract); Parkerings-Compagniet AS *v* Lithuania, Award, ICSID Case No. ARB/05/8 (11 September 2007) [360] (referring to a contract concluded with the City of Vilius, a public entity). Section 13.4.3 elaborates further on the issue of contractual rights.

liability upon the ground that the government had made all reasonable efforts to prevent the injury from being inflicted.[94]

Diplomatic and arbitral practice do not support this approach.[95] Moreover, reasonable efforts to prevent harm do not (and should not) exclude responsibility for denial of access to justice, unreasonable delays or arbitrariness in local instances of redress. Secretary Seward's statement is therefore unsound. There is no reason why due diligence in the prevention of an injury should exclude responsibility for subsequent acts of competent agencies of redress.

There are good reasons for considering that the duties of prevention and redress constitute two distinct, separate legal bases for international responsibility. It must be acknowledged that the occurrence of an injury creates the *material opportunity* for a breach of the duty of redress, which in turn implies that harm could not—or was otherwise not—prevented. This does not however mean that a *breach* of the preventive obligation is a condition precedent for a violation of the *redress obligation*. Two scenarios should be distinguished in this regard.

On the one hand, the injurious event might have occurred in spite of diligent preventive efforts by local authorities. In such case, the host state will have fulfilled its prevention obligation. But it is still required to exercise diligence in the redress of the injury, and may be held accountable for a failure to do so. In this scenario, a failure of redress would be the first and only act engaging the host state's international responsibility. On the other hand, if the host state's omissions in the prevention of the injury are internationally wrongful, its responsibility is immediately engaged. A subsequent failure of redress would constitute an *additional* international wrong.

There is nothing extraordinary or novel about this conclusion. Writing before the BIT-era, in a time in which international claims were generally raised through diplomatic interposition and treaty-based exceptions to the local remedies rule

---

[94]Emphasis added. 'Mr. Seward to Mr. Adams' (8 December 1862) *Papers relating to the Foreign Relations of the United States with the Annual Message of the President* (Government Printing Office, Washington 1863) 16, 17. Secretary Seward's note should however be taken with caution. In spite of the explicit reference to the security of American citizens 'within the British dominions', the case was not particularly related to the security of aliens in British territory. Rather, it referred to failures by local authorities to prevent the use of British ports for outfitting private ships, which were later engaged in the plundering of American vessels in the high seas. For a detailed description of the factual background of the incident and the basis of the American claims see: 'Mr. Adams to Earl Russell' (20 November 1862) *Papers relating to the Foreign Relations of the United States with the Annual Message of the President* (Government Printing Office, Washington 1863) 7, 7-9.

[95]For an indicative example see: 'The [Mexican] Minister of Foreign Affairs to the American Ambassador' (16 May 1911) *Papers relating to the Foreign Relations of the United States with the Annual Message of the President* (Government Printing Office, Washington 1911) 493, 493 (noting that in the 'remote event' that, in spite of the efforts of Mexican authorities, an injury occurs, the Mexican Government would 'try the case').

were virtually unknown,[96] Clyde Eagleton (1928) observed that local redress fulfills two different functions:

> Some difficulty arises from the double function served by local remedies. They may be regarded, on the one hand, as a means of repairing a breach of international law for which responsibility is already existent; and, on the other hand, as a duty whose improper execution will itself responsibility upon the state [. . .] if the alien has received an injury which is not in itself internationally illegal, his failure to secure proper redress from the state may, at this point, for the first time, engage the responsibility of the state. Whether the state has an anterior responsibility or not, it must usually be permitted to use its own agencies of redress where it has provided them; and the failure of these agencies may either create an original responsibility where none has existed hitherto, or serve to carry the case on to diplomatic procedure if responsibility was already engaged.[97]

As stated beforehand, where the state has committed an internationally wrongful omission in the prevention of an injury, it may already be held accountable for such conduct. In consequence, a subsequent failure to redress the inflicted damages will only play secondary role. As expressed by Eagleton:

> The state has [. . .] the duty of using due diligence for the prevention of injury to an alien, a duty entirely different from that of redress. Where a lack of diligence is established, it may not be necessary to resort to local remedies, and consequently no denial of justice would appear; but the state might nevertheless be responsible. The failure of the United States, for instance, to give proper protection in mob cases should not be regarded as a denial of justice, but as another violation of international law. It may subsequently become responsible, if its courts fail to give redress, on another count: that of denial of justice in the courts.[98]

---

[96]For a long time, exceptions to the local remedies requirement were rather rare in practice. Still, during the early and mid-twentieth century some arbitral tribunals actually came to the conclusion that the parties to the applicable arbitration agreement had the intention of excluding the application of the rule. For some indicative examples see: Edwin Borchard, 'The Law of Responsibility of States for Damage Done in Their Territory to the Person or Property of Foreigners. Comments to the Draft Convention' (April 1929) 23 AJIL 140, 154 art. 6. In the BIT-era, exceptions to the rule have ceased to be uncommon. The most prominent example would be article 26 of the ICSID Convention. See: Convention on the Settlement of Investment Disputes between States and Nationals of Other States (submitted 18 March 1965, entered into force 14 October 1966) 575 UNTS 159, art. 26 ("Consent of the parties to arbitration under this Convention shall, unless otherwise stated, be deemed consent to such arbitration to the exclusion of any other remedy. A Contracting State may require the exhaustion of local administrative or judicial remedies as a condition of its consent to arbitration under this Convention").

[97]Clyde Eagleton, *The Responsibility of States in International Law* (Klaus Reprint, New York 1970) 98-9 [first edition: 1928].

[98]Clyde Eagleton, *The Responsibility of States in International Law* (Klaus Reprint, New York 1970) 113 [first edition: 1928]. For the sake of accuracy, it should be observed that Eagleton defined the term 'denial of justice' as a failure to redress an 'antecedent injury'; for that reason, in Eagleton's theory of state responsibility, local redress and denial of justice are 'interlocking and inseparable' (at p. 113). See also: Clyde Eagleton, 'Denial of Justice in International law' (1928) 22 AJIL 538, 538-59 (particularly at 542). Eagleton's definition of denial of justice was the subject of much debate in the past. Leading international scholars rejected the notion, considering that it fell too short, at least as a general formulation of the notion. See, for example: Alwyn Freeman, *The International Responsibility of States for Denial of Justice* (Klaus Reprint, New York 1970) 151-60 [first edition: 1938]; Gerald Fitzmaurice, 'The Meaning of the Term Denial of Justice' (1932)

The repressive functional dimension therefore gains particular importance in cases where the failure to prevent an injury is not *in itself* internationally wrongful. It is precisely in these cases that responsibility emanates originally, firstly and most genuinely, from a breach of the redress obligation. This will generally be the case where the injury originates in acts of individuals, that is, the customary core of the FPS standard. In fact, those acts are *per definitionem* not attributable to the host state. In addition, omissions in the *prevention* of private injuries are internationally wrongful only under exceptional circumstances. In most such cases, the material opportunity for an international wrong will first appear in the context of local redress, or will arise out of the very absence of municipal means of redress (e.g. in the case of an amnesty).[99] This factual circumstance does not however affect the fundamental argument advanced throughout this section: a failure to exercise due diligence in the prevention of an injury may be in itself internationally wrongful and constitute an autonomous source of international responsibility. In words of Eagleton:

> The state, it may be said in summary, is [...] not responsible for acts of individuals, except when it has failed in its duties of prevention and punishment, of restraint and redress. While, *as a matter of statistical calculation*, the responsibility of the state usually appears after its local machinery of redress has failed to give satisfaction, it can not be admitted that the state is, in principle, never liable before that point. It is conceivable that its liability may have existed from the moment the alien was injured.[100]

The proposition that the prevention and redress obligations are autonomous from each other entails an important implication: compliance with the redress obligation does not excuse a breach of the prevention obligation. As a matter of principle, if the breach of the prevention obligation is established, subsequent redress does not eliminate the wrongful character of such omission under international law. As stated in *Mondev v United States*:

> An investor whose local staff had been assaulted by the police while at work could well claim that its investment was not accorded "treatment in accordance with international law, including... full protection and security" if the government were immune from suit for the assaults. *In such a case, the availability of an action in tort against individual (possibly*

---

13 BYIL 93, 106-8; Jan Paulsson, *Denial of Justice in International Law* (Cambridge University Press, New York 2005) 57-8; Oliver Lissitzyn, 'The Meaning of the Term Denial of Justice in International Law' (1936) 30(4) AJIL 632, 638-9. Cf. also Sect. 2.2.3.

[99] On the example of an amnesty preventing aliens from obtaining local redress for revolutionary damages see: Francisco García Amador, 'International Responsibility: Sixth Report by F. V. García Amador, Special Rapporteur (A/CN.4/134 and Add. 1)' (26 January 1961) 2 *Yearbook of the International Law Commission – 1961* 1, 47 art. 7(3); Jacques Dumas, 'La responsabilité des États a raison des crimes et délits commis sur leur territoire au préjudice d'Étrangers' (1931) 36 RCADI 183, 258.

[100] Emphasis added. Clyde Eagleton, *The Responsibility of States in International Law* (Klaus Reprint, New York 1970) 93 [first edition: 1928]. See also: Oliver Lissitzyn, 'The Meaning of the Term Denial of Justice in International Law' (1936) 30(4) AJIL 632, 638 (particularly referring to diplomatic practice using the term 'denial of justice' 'as a synonym for failure or absence of local remedies').

unidentifiable) officers might not be a sufficient basis to avoid the situation being characterised as a breach of Article 1105(1).[101]

Notwithstanding the foregoing, the fact that the state has provided local redress *could* imply that the alien has obtained *reparation* for the injury. *Reparation* is conceptually different from *redress*. The obligation to make full reparation (by restitution, compensation or satisfaction) is a *consequence* of the internationally wrongful act. It is distinguishable from the obligation of redress, which refers to the provision—under municipal law—of adequate means of obtaining remedies for an injury done to an alien, and does not presuppose an international illegality.

If the state has committed an internationally wrongful omission by failing to adopt adequate measures to prevent an injury, it has a duty to make reparation. As far as local courts diligently redress the injury and grant the alien adequate compensation, the host state will not only have fulfilled its obligation of redress, but also the reparation obligation originating in the breach of the prevention obligation. In this kind of cases, even if the host state is liable under international law for breach of the prevention obligation, an international claim for compensation will most likely be unsuccessful; local agencies of redress will have discharged the obligation to make full reparation for the internationally wrongful act.

Thus, for example, in *Saluka v Czech Republic* (2006), the investor alleged that a series of police searches affected the enjoyment of its privacy and property rights, and constituted a violation of the FPS standard.[102] The arbitral tribunal did neither declare a breach of the prevention obligation nor elaborate on the applicability of the standard to this factual setting.[103] It simply observed that, irrespective of the existence of a breach, local courts had already issued a decision in favor of the investor.[104] For that reason, the arbitrators said, 'the Claimant can no longer be aggrieved'.[105] The FPS claim was consistently dismissed.[106]

These observations are in line with the approach followed in *Pantechniki v Albania*. In that case, the investor alleged that Albania's failure to take active measures of protection against a looting amounted to a breach of the FPS standard.[107] In addition, the Claimant contended that the host state's failure to compensate the damages caused by the looting constituted an additional violation of the FPS

---

[101]Emphasis added. Mondev International *v* United States, Award, ICSID Case No. ARB(AF)/99/2 (11 October 2002) [152]. However, this observation was not material for the resolution of the dispute, as it becomes clear at [153].

[102]Saluka Investments *v* Czech Republic (UNCITRAL), Partial Award (17 March 2006) [494].

[103]Saluka Investments *v* Czech Republic (UNCITRAL), Partial Award (17 March 2006) [494-6].

[104]Saluka Investments *v* Czech Republic (UNCITRAL), Partial Award (17 March 2006) [495].

[105]Saluka Investments *v* Czech Republic (UNCITRAL), Partial Award (17 March 2006) [496].

[106]Saluka Investments *v* Czech Republic (UNCITRAL), Partial Award (17 March 2006) [496 and 505].

[107]Pantechniki S.A. Contractors & Engineers *v* Albania, Award, ICSID Case No. ARB/07/21 (30 July 2009) [73].

standard.[108] Acting as Sole Arbitrator, Jan Paulsson underscored the distinction between a breach of the FPS standard and a failure to make reparation:

> The Claimant also curiously seeks to establish a violation of the duty to provide full protection and security by reason of Albania's failure to give compensation for the events of March 1997. This argument is put in a number of ways. *They all founder for the same simple reason: they confuse breach and the failure to provide remedy.* The latter is not a breach in the absence of predicate acts or omissions. *If those predicates are extant the breach is consummated without any need to refer to a failure of compensation.* The Claimant has not shown that Albania failed to comply with its duty to extend full protection and security in the circumstances that gave rise to this case.[109]

In sum, if the host state has failed to exercise due diligence in the prevention of harm in a case calling for the application of the customary FPS standard, responsibility is immediately established as a result of such internationally wrongful omission; an additional failure to provide means of redress is not a condition for a finding of liability.

---

[108]Pantechniki S.A. Contractors & Engineers *v* Albania, Award, ICSID Case No. ARB/07/21 (30 July 2009) [84].

[109]Emphasis added. Pantechniki S.A. Contractors & Engineers *v* Albania, Award, ICSID Case No. ARB/07/21 (30 July 2009) [84].

Part III
Content of the Standard

Chapter 11
The Characterization of the Obligation to Provide 'Full Protection and Security'

11.1 Preliminary Remarks

The foregoing chapters have focused on the subjective, objective and temporal scope of application of the customary FPS standard. The question was left open as to the parameters the standard provides for the assessment of the host state's conduct. In other words, this work has not yet considered the 'actual content' of FPS or, using the terminology coined by some scholars, the 'standard as such'.[1] For all practical purposes, the content of FPS refers to the conditions required for establishing a breach of the standard. These conditions have been and continue to be contentious in international legal literature.

The debate has appeared in different guises in the past. The issue is sometimes presented in connection with the question whether FPS always imposes a duty of due diligence, or whether it could also entail strict liability under some specific circumstances. Scholars have also studied the conditions for a breach as a problem pertaining to the classification of the protection obligation under more general categories. In this vein, they have drawn particular attention to the notions of *obligations of conduct* and *obligations of result*, as well as to the conceptual distinction between *positive* and *negative* obligations (i.e. duties of action and duties of abstention).

Investment arbitral decisions generally coincide in placing within the security obligation a positive duty to exercise due diligence in the protection of aliens, and

---

[1]Section 6.2 assesses the concept of 'standard' as a legal category and explains the terminology used in the main text.

© Springer Nature Switzerland AG 2019

S. Mantilla Blanco, *Full Protection and Security in International Investment Law*,
European Yearbook of International Economic Law 8,
https://doi.org/10.1007/978-3-030-24838-3_11

sometimes go on to expressly characterize the obligation as one of means or vigilance.[2] Some tribunals have chosen a negative formulation to this effect, stating

---

[2]For some examples of awards making express reference to the notion of 'due diligence' in connection with the FPS standard see: Ampal-American Israel Corp., Egi-Fund (08-10) Investors LLC, Egi-Series Investments LLC and BSS-EMG Investors LLC v Egypt, Decision on Liability and Heads of Loss, ICSID Case No. ARB/12/11 (21 February 2017) [241] (noting that 'the State is obliged to exert due diligence in order to protect a claimant's investment'); Asian Agricultural Products v Sri Lanka, Final Award, ICSID Case No. ARB/87/3 (17 June 1990) [53] (linking the FPS standard to the notion of due diligence); Bernhard Friedrich Arnd Rüdiger von Pezold et al. v Zimbabwe, Award, ICSID Case No. ARB/10/15 (28 July 2015) [596] (agreeing with the parties' statement that FPS is a standard of 'due diligence'); Biwater Gauff Ltd. v Tanzania, Award, ICSID Case No. ARB/05/22 (24 July 2008) [725] (stating that 'in international law, the duty of protection implies a duty of due diligence'); CC/Devas (Mauritius) Ltd., Devas Employees Mauritius Private Ltd. and Telcom Devas Mauritius Ltd. v India (UNCITRAL), Award on Jurisdiction and Merits, PCA Case No. 2013-09 (25 July 2016) [498] (describing FPS 'as an obligation of vigilance and due diligence'); Convial Callao S.A. and CCI – Compañía de Concesiones de Infraestructura S.A. v Peru, Laudo Final, ICSID Case No. ARB/10/2 (21 May 2013) [643] (describing FPS as a diligence obligation and underscoring the non-absolute character or the standard); Deutsche Bank AG v Sri Lanka, Award, ICSID Case No. ARB/09/02 (31 October 2012) [537] (indicating that 'the full protection and security standard only involves a best efforts obligation, a duty of due diligence'); Electrabel S.A. v Hungary, Decision on Jurisdiction, Applicable Law and Liability, ICSID Case No. ARB/07/19 (30 November 2012) [7.83] (quoting arbitral decisions which define the content of FPS in terms of due diligence); El Paso Energy International Co. v Argentina, Award, ICSID Case No. ARB/03/15 (31 October 2011) [522] (noting that '[t]he case law and commentators generally agree that this standard imposes an obligation of vigilance and due diligence upon the government' and further elaborating on the notion of 'due diligence' at para 523); Frontier Petroleum Ltd. v Czech Republic (UNCITRAL), Final Award (12 November 2010) [270] (concluding that 'the standard is one of due diligence'); Jan de Nul N.V. and Dredging International N.V. v Egypt, Award, ICSID Case No. ARB/04/13 (6 November 2008) [269] (expressing that 'this concept [FPS] refers to the exercise of due diligence by the State'); Joseph Charles Lemire v Ukraine, Decision on Jurisdiction and Liability, ICSID Case No. ARB/06/18 (14 January 2010) [496] (stressing that '[n]ot every lack of diligence by a supervisory authority opens the door to a claim under the BIT'); Joseph Houben v Burundi, Sentence, ICSID Case No. ARB/13/7 (12 January 2016) [161] (explicitly defining the content of FPS in terms of 'diligence raisonnable'); Koch Minerals SÁRL and Koch Nitrogen International SÁRL v Venezuela, Award, ICSID Case No. ARB/11/19 (30 October 2017) [8.46] (linking FPS to the notion of 'reasonable diligence'); LESI S.p.A. and ASTALDI S.p.A. v Algeria, Sentence, ICSID Case No. ARB/05/3 (12 November 2008) [153] (characterizing the obligation as an 'obligation de moyens'); Mamidoil Jetoil Greek Petroleum Products Societe S.A. v Albania, Award, ICSID Case No. ARB/11/24 (30 March 2015) [821] (taking cognizance of the widespread consensus that FPS 'obliges States to use due diligence to prevent harassment and injuries to investors'); MNSS B.V. and Recupero Credito Acciaio N.V. v Montenegro, Award, ICSID Case No. ARB(AF)/12/8 (4 May 2016) [351] (stating that FPS entails 'an obligation of vigilance and due diligence'); Mobil Exploration and Development Argentina Inc. Suc. Argentina and Mobil Argentina S.A. v Argentina, Decision on Jurisdiction and Liability, ICSID Case No. ARB/04/16 (10 April 2013) [999] (stating that 'this standard imposes an obligation of vigilance and due diligence upon the government'); Noble Ventures v Romania, Award, ICSID Case No. ARB/01/11 (12 October 2005) [164] (holding that '[FPS] is not a strict standard, but one requiring due diligence to be exercised by the State'); Oxus Gold v Uzbekistan (UNCITRAL), Final Award (17 December 2015) [353 and 834] (stating that FPS comprises 'an obligation of vigilance and due diligence'); Pantechniki S.A. Contractors & Engineers v Albania, Award, ICSID Case No. ARB/07/21 (30 July 2009) [76-81] (providing a detailed analysis of the

that FPS does *not* impose strict liability upon the host state.[3] No other feature of the

meaning of due diligence in the context of FPS); Plama Consortium Ltd. *v* Bulgaria, Award, ICSID Case No. ARB/03/24 (27 August 2008) [222] (rejecting the FPS claims on the ground that the Claimant could not identify – nor the arbitrators establish – a 'lack of due diligence' attributable to the Respondent); Ronald Lauder *v* Czech Republic (UNCITRAL), Final Award (3 September 2001) [308] (concluding that the applicable FPS clause 'obliges the Parties to exercise such due diligence in the protection of foreign investment as reasonable under the circumstances'); Rumeli Telekom A.S. and Telsim Mobil Telekomunikasyon Hizmetleri A.S. *v* Kazakhstan, Award, ICSID Case No. ARB/05/16 (29 July 2008) [668] (relying on arbitral decisions which indicate that 'in international law, the full protection and security obligation is one of due diligence and no more'); Saint-Gobain Performance Plastics Europe *v* Venezuela, Decision on Liability and the Principles of Quantum, ICSID Case No. ARB/12/13 (30 December 2016) [553] (acknowledging that 'there is common ground between the Parties that Article 3(2) of the Treaty [FPS] imposes a duty of due diligence on Respondent'); Sergei Paushok et al. *v* Mongolia (UNCITRAL), Award on Jurisdiction and Liability (28 April 2011) [323-5] (noting that '[t]he case law and commentators generally agree that this standard imposes an obligation of vigilance and due diligence upon the government' and further holding the due diligence standard applicable in respect of both the prevention obligation and the duty of redress); Suez Sociedad General de Aguas de Barcelona S.A. and Vivendi Universal S.A. *v* Argentina, Decision on Liability, ICSID Case No. ARB/03/19 (30 July 2010) [162] (explaining that '[t]raditionally, courts and tribunals have interpreted the content of this standard of treatment as imposing a positive obligation upon the host state to exercise due diligence to protect the investor and his property', see also paras 164 and 179); Spyridon Roussalis *v* Romania, Award, ICSID Case No. ARB/06/1 (7 December 2011) [322] (quoting arbitral decisions to the effect that 'the full protection and security obligation is one of due diligence and no more'); Toto Construzioni Generali S.p.A. *v* Lebanon, Award, ICSID Case No. ARB/07/12 (7 June 2012) [227] (noting that 'the obligation of full protection and security is not a strict liability standard, but requires due diligence'); Ulysseas Inc. *v* Ecuador (UNCITRAL), Final Award (12 June 2012) [272] (holding that the FPS standard 'imposes an obligation of vigilance and care' and comprises 'a duty of due diligence'); Waguih George Siag and Clorinda Vecchi *v* Egypt, Award, ICSID Case No. ARB/05/15 (1 June 2009) [447] (noting that the FPS standard 'is not absolute' and that 'a host state must exercise due diligence in preventing harm to an investment').

[3] AES Summit Generation Ltd. and AES-Tisza Erömü Kft. *v* Hungary, Award, ICSID Case No. ARB/07/22 (23 September 2010) [13.3.2.]; Ampal-American Israel Corp., Egi-Fund (08-10) Investors LLC, Egi-Series Investments LLC and BSS-EMG Investors LLC *v* Egypt, Decision on Liability and Heads of Loss, ICSID Case No. ARB/12/11 (21 February 2017) [241 and 243-4]; Asian Agricultural Products *v* Sri Lanka, Final Award, ICSID Case No. ARB/87/3 (17 June 1990) [48 and 53]; Bernhard Friedrich Arnd Rüdiger von Pezold et al. *v* Zimbabwe, Award, ICSID Case No. ARB/10/15 (28 July 2015) [596]; Frontier Petroleum Ltd. *v* Czech Republic (UNCITRAL), Final Award (12 November 2010) [269-70]; Gemplus S.A., SLP S.A. and Gemplus Industrial S.A. de C.V. *v* Mexico, Award, ICSID Cases No. ARB(AF)/04/3 & ARB(AF)/04/4 (16 June 2010) [9.10]; LESI S.p.A. and ASTALDI S.p.A. *v* Algeria, Sentence, ICSID Case No. ARB/05/3 (12 November 2008) [153]; Mamidoil Jetoil Greek Petroleum Products Societe S.A. *v* Albania, Award, ICSID Case No. ARB/11/24 (30 March 2015) [821]; MNSS B.V. and Recupero Credito Acciaio N.V. *v* Montenegro, Award, ICSID Case No. ARB(AF)/12/8 (4 May 2016) [351]; Mohammad Ammar Al-Bahloul *v* Tajikistan, Partial Award on Jurisdiction and Liability, SCC Case No. V 064/2008 (9 September 2009) [246]; Noble Ventures *v* Romania, Award, ICSID Case No. ARB/01/11 (12 October 2005) [164]; Parkerings-Compagniet AS *v* Lithuania, Award, ICSID Case No. ARB/05/8 (11 September 2007) [357]; Plama Consortium Ltd. *v* Bulgaria, Award, ICSID Case No. ARB/03/24 (27 August 2008) [181]; Ronald Lauder *v* Czech Republic (UNCITRAL), Final Award (3 September 2001) [308]; Saluka Investments *v* Czech Republic (UNCITRAL), Partial Award (17 March 2006) [484]; Suez Sociedad General de Aguas de Barcelona S.A. and

standard seems to be more clearly and consistently established in practice. In the *ELSI* case, the ICJ observed that '[t]he reference in Article V [of the US-Italy FCN Agreement] to the provision of "constant protection and security" cannot be construed as the giving of a warranty that property shall never in any circumstances be occupied or disturbed'.[4] The Court was certainly referring to a specific treaty clause. Still, investment tribunals have often relied on this passage in their assessment of FPS claims.[5]

The issue is nonetheless not as straightforward as it might seem at first sight. As will be shown throughout this chapter, new approaches tend to restrict the due diligence standard of liability to some specific areas of application of FPS. According to these novel theories, there are factual scenarios in which a failure to exercise diligence is not required for international responsibility to arise under this heading.[6]

The present survey, after careful consideration of these views, advances three fundamental propositions. First, a breach of the FPS standard can only be declared where the host state has failed to exercise *diligence* in the protection of foreign citizens' acquired values. Plainly stated, the host state will never be in violation of the standard if it has made a diligent effort to prevent the injury or to redress it, as the case may be. Second, the FPS standard is, at the same time, by no means a 'pure' obligation of diligence. A failure to exercise due diligence is a *necessary* but not *sufficient* condition for a violation of the standard. An *additional* requirement must be met. The breach is contingent upon the occurrence of the *injurious event*, i.e. the actual infliction of harm or damage. Third, as a corollary of the 'diligence' element, the protection obligation can be accurately characterized as a *positive obligation*.

Vivendi Universal S.A. *v* Argentina, Decision on Liability, ICSID Case No. ARB/03/19 (30 July 2010) [164]; Spyridon Roussalis *v* Romania, Award, ICSID Case No. ARB/06/1 (7 December 2011) [322]; Tecnicas Medioambientales TECMED S.A. *v* Mexico, Award, ICSID Case No. ARB (AF)/00/2 (29 May 2003) [177]; Toto Construzioni Generali S.p.A. *v* Lebanon, Award, ICSID Case No. ARB/07/12 (7 June 2012) [227]; Tulip Real Estate Investment and Development Netherlands B.V. *v* Turkey, Award, ICSID Case No. ARB/11/28 (10 March 2014) [430]; Wena Hotels Ltd. *v* Egypt, Award, ICSID Case No. ARB/98/4 (8 December 2000) [84].

[4]*Case Concerning Elettronica Sicula S.p.A. (ELSI) (United States of America v Italy)* [1989] ICJ Rep 15, 65 [108].

[5]See for example: Ampal-American Israel Corp., Egi-Fund (08-10) Investors LLC, Egi-Series Investments LLC and BSS-EMG Investors LLC *v* Egypt, Decision on Liability and Heads of Loss, ICSID Case No. ARB/12/11 (21 February 2017) [242]; Suez Sociedad General de Aguas de Barcelona S.A. and Vivendi Universal S.A. *v* Argentina, Decision on Liability, ICSID Case No. ARB/03/19 (30 July 2010) [162]; Toto Construzioni Generali S.p.A. *v* Lebanon, Award, ICSID Case No. ARB/07/12 (7 June 2012) [228]. Cf. also: Convial Callao S.A. and CCI – Compañía de Concesiones de Infraestructura S.A. *v* Peru, Laudo Final, ICSID Case No. ARB/10/2 (21 May 2013) [643] (using a similar formulation and citing the Parties' memorials) and [646] (making an indirect reference to the *ELSI* case); SAUR International S.A. *v* Argentina, Décision sur la compétence et sur la responsabilité, ICSID Case No. ARB/04/4 (6 June 2012) [483] (using a similar language without quoting the *ELSI* decision).

[6]See Sect. 11.2.3.

FPS requires the host state to undertake *positive acts*. Consequently, a breach of FPS always takes the form of an *omission*.

11.2 'Full Protection and Security' and the Distinction Between Obligations of Conduct and Result

In considering the characterization of the obligation to provide 'full protection and security' under more general categories of international law, the present section pays particular attention to the distinction between *obligations of conduct* (or *obligations of means*) and *obligations of result*. The reason is that academic works on the subject have often drawn a link between these dogmatic categories, on the one side, and the notion of due diligence on the other.[7] Thus, at least from the outset, the concepts appear to be unavoidably interlocked.

This being said, the use of the expressions 'obligation of conduct' and 'obligation of result' has not been entirely consistent in international legal literature. This section therefore begins by considering the origins and dogmatic implications of the classification of international obligations under these two general categories. On the basis

---

[7]For some indicative examples see: Eric De Brabandere, 'Host States' Due Diligence Obligations in International Investment Law' (2014-5) 42 Syracuse J. Int'l L. & Com. 319, 323-4; Finnur Magnússon, *Full Protection and Security in International Law* (University of Vienna, Vienna 2012) 171-4; Giuditta Cordero Moss, 'Full Protection and Security' in August Reinisch (ed), *Standards of Investment Protection* (Oxford University Press, New York 2008) 131, 139; Joanna Kulesza, *Due Diligence in International Law* (Brill, Leiden 2016) 135 et seq.; Jörn Griebel, *Internationales Investitionsrecht* (C.H. Beck, Munich 2008) 75; Levon Golendukhin, 'Reference to Intellectual Property Treaty Norms in Full Protection and Security and Fair and Equitable Treatment Claims' in Ian Laird, Borzu Sabahi, Frédéric Sourgens and Todd Weiler (eds), *Investment Treaty Arbitration and International Law* (Juris Net, Huntington NY 2018) 89, 95-6; Lucas Bastin, *Violation of the Full Protection and Security Obligation by Regulatory Omissions* [M.Phil. Thesis] (Oxford University, Oxford 2011) 68; Maria Fanou and Vassilis Tzevelekos, 'The Shared Territory of the ECHR and International Investment Law' in Yannick Radi (ed), *Research Handbook on Human Rights and Investment* (Edward Elgar Publishers, Northampton MA 2018) 93, 126; Riccardo Pisillo-Mazzeschi, 'The Due Diligence Rule and the Nature of the International Responsibility of States' in René Provost (ed), *State Responsibility in International Law* (Ashgate Publishing Co., Burlington VT 2002) 97, 135-7; Timo Koivurova, 'Due Diligence' in Rüdiger Wolfrum (ed), *The Max Planck Encyclopedia of Public International Law* (Volume 3: Oxford University Press, New York 2012) 236, 236. See also: ILA Study Group on Due Diligence in International Law, 'Second Report by Mr. Tim Stephens (Rapporteur) and Mr. Duncan French (Chair)' (20 July 2016) 1-2, 7, 19-20 and 22-3. Some arbitral awards also provide evidence of the linkage between the notion of due diligence, and the concepts of obligations of conduct/result. For a representative example see: LESI S.p.A. and ASTALDI S.p.A. *v* Algeria, Sentence, ICSID Case No. ARB/05/3 (12 November 2008) [153]. International adjudicatory bodies have made similar statements in respect of other areas of international law: *Responsibilities and Obligations of States Sponsoring Persons and Entities with Respect to Activities in the Area (Advisory Opinion)* [2011] 50 ILM 458 [111]; *Case Concerning Pulp Mills on the River Uruguay (Argentina v Uruguay)* [2010] ICJ Rep 14, 77 [187] and 83 [204].

of these remarks, it then discusses this conceptual divide's significance for the assessment of the FPS standard.

11.2.1 The Concept of Obligations of Conduct and Result: From René Demogue to Roberto Ago

The classification of civil obligations as obligations of conduct and result roots in the continental legal tradition and was brought into international law by Roberto Ago in the 1970s.[8] In French private law, the distinction dates back to the writings of René Demogue. In his *Traité des obligations en général* (1925), Demogue introduced it as an analytical tool for determining the place of negligence in the law of obligations.[9]

Demogue's idea was simple. If a specific obligation is interpreted as requiring the debtor to achieve some result, non-performance is established when such result has not been accomplished (*obligation de résultat*); in order to escape liability, the debtor thus needs to prove *cas fortuit* or *force majeure*.[10] In contrast, whenever an obligation imposes a mere *duty to endeavor* the attainment of some result (*obligation de moyens*), liability is dependent upon verified fault or negligence on the part of the debtor.[11] For that very same reason, a successful allegation of non-performance becomes particularly burdensome in respect of this kind of obligations.[12]

Special Rapporteur Ago's use of these categories in the Draft Articles of State Responsibility significantly diverged from the meaning they ordinarily convey in

---

[8]See: Roberto Ago, 'Sixth Report on State Responsibility – The Internationally Wrongful Act of the State, Source of International Responsibility (A/CN.4/302 and Add.1-3)' (1977) 2(1) *Yearbook of the International Law Commission – 1977* 4-43 [1-113]. On the civil law origin of the distinction and its use in international law see: ILC, 'Report of the International Law Commission on the Work of its Fifty-First Session – State Responsibility' (1999) 2(2) *Yearbook of the International Law Commission – 1999* 48, 57 [132-3]; James Crawford, 'Second Report on State Responsibility (A/CN.4/490 and Add. 1-7)' (1999) 2(1) *Yearbook of the International Law Commission – 1999* 3, 21 [57]; James Crawford, *State Responsibility. The General Part* (Cambridge University Press, Cambridge 2013) 221; Pierre Marie Dupuy, 'Reviewing the Difficulties of Codification: On Ago's Classification of Obligations of Means and Obligations of Result in Relation to State Responsibility' (1999) 10(2) EJIL 371, 374-8. See also: Finnur Magnússon, *Full Protection and Security in International Law* (University of Vienna, Vienna 2012) 171-2 (considering the issue in particular connection with the FPS standard).

[9]René Demogue, *Traité des obligations en général* (Volume 5: Rousseau: Paris 1925) 538 *et seq.* For an overview of the distinction's current use in French private law see: Simon Whittaker, 'The Law of Obligations' in John Bell, Sophie Boyron and Simon Whittaker (eds), *Principles of French Law* (Oxford University Press, New York 2008) 294, 342-3. See also: James Gordley and Arthur von Mehren, *An Introduction to the Comparative Study of Private Law* (Cambridge University Press, Cambridge 2006) 499-500.

[10]René Demogue, *Traité des obligations en général* (Volume 5: Rousseau: Paris 1925) 538-9.

[11]René Demogue, *Traité des obligations en général* (Volume 5: Rousseau: Paris 1925) 538-9.

[12]On the burden of proof see generally: René Demogue, *Traité des obligations en général* (Volume 5: Rousseau: Paris 1925) 538-9.

continental legal systems.[13] Ago defined obligations of conduct as those prescribing a 'specific course of conduct'.[14] These obligations are therefore signalized by their high degree of determinacy and create a particularly rigid yardstick for the assessment of conduct.[15] In turn, Ago's obligations of result require the state to achieve some particular outcome, usually *by the means of its own choice*.[16] One of the most important defining features of this second kind of obligations is the 'special character of the conditions for their breach' which, in the particular case of obligations referring to the protection of aliens, include the exhaustion of local remedies by the affected individual.[17] The underlying idea is that the host state may satisfy its duties by achieving the result originally envisaged in the primary norm (*main result*) or, in the alternative, by making reparation (*alternative result*).[18]

In the late 1990s, scholars and states questioned the relevance and accuracy of Ago's categories and, particularly, his departure from 'classic' civil law concepts.[19] James Crawford would go as far as to make the following statement:

---

[13]The distinction was envisaged in Articles 20, 21 and 22 of the Draft Articles. See: ILC, 'Report of the International Law Commission on the Work of its Twenty-Ninth Session – State Responsibility' (1977) 2(2) *Yearbook of the International Law Commission – 1977* 5, 11 arts. 20-2. On the inconsistency between Ago's use of the distinction and its original civil law meaning see: Pierre Marie Dupuy, 'Reviewing the Difficulties of Codification: On Ago's Classification of Obligations of Means and Obligations of Result in Relation to State Responsibility' (1999) 10(2) EJIL 371, 374-8.

[14]Roberto Ago, 'Sixth Report on State Responsibility – The Internationally Wrongful Act of the State, Source of International Responsibility (A/CN.4/302 and Add.1-3)' (1977) 2(1) *Yearbook of the International Law Commission – 1977* 3, 5 [4].

[15]Roberto Ago, 'Sixth Report on State Responsibility – The Internationally Wrongful Act of the State, Source of International Responsibility (A/CN.4/302 and Add.1-3)' (1977) 2(1) *Yearbook of the International Law Commission – 1977* 3, 4-8 [4-13].

[16]Roberto Ago, 'Sixth Report on State Responsibility – The Internationally Wrongful Act of the State, Source of International Responsibility (A/CN.4/302 and Add.1-3)' (1977) 2(1) *Yearbook of the International Law Commission – 1977* 3, 4 [3-4] and 20-1 [47-8].

[17]Roberto Ago, 'Sixth Report on State Responsibility – The Internationally Wrongful Act of the State, Source of International Responsibility (A/CN.4/302 and Add.1-3)' (1977) 2(1) *Yearbook of the International Law Commission – 1977* 3, 12 [23] and 21 [49].

[18]Roberto Ago, 'Sixth Report on State Responsibility – The Internationally Wrongful Act of the State, Source of International Responsibility (A/CN.4/302 and Add.1-3)' (1977) 2(1) *Yearbook of the International Law Commission – 1977* 3, 12 [23] and 21 [49]. For a critical perspective on Ago's understanding of obligations of conduct and result see: Pierre Marie Dupuy, 'Reviewing the Difficulties of Codification: On Ago's Classification of Obligations of Means and Obligations of Result in Relation to State Responsibility' (1999) 10(2) EJIL 371, 376. For an overview of the link between this classification of international obligations and the local remedies rule see: Alfred Verdross and Bruno Simma, *Universelles Völkerrecht* (Duncker & Humblot, Berlin 1984) 884-5.

[19]ILC, 'Report of the International Law Commission on the Work of its Fifty-First Session – State Responsibility' (1999) 2(2) *Yearbook of the International Law Commission – 1999* 48, 57 [132-3] and 68 [180]. See also: Pierre Marie Dupuy, 'Reviewing the Difficulties of Codification: On Ago's Classification of Obligations of Means and Obligations of Result in Relation to State Responsibility' (1999) 10(2) EJIL 371, 374-8 (with further references to state practice and scholarly writings); James Crawford, 'Second Report on State Responsibility (A/CN.4/490 and Add. 1-7)' (1999)

It is not unusual for domestic analogies to be modified in the course of transplantation to international law. Indeed, it is unusual for them not to be. But I know no other example where the effect of a national law analogy has been reversed in the course of transplantation. In French law, obligations of result are stricter than obligations of conduct. According to Ago, obligations of result were less strict because the state had a discretion as to the means which it did not have with obligations of conduct.[20]

Efforts have been made to return to the original private law meaning of the terms. For example, Riccardo Pisillo-Mazzeschi bases his analysis of the concept of due diligence in international law on the civil law distinction between obligations of conduct and result, making the following remark:

> The distinction we suggest [...] comes close, in its principle elements, to the one between obligations of diligent conduct and obligations of result which has progressively developed in the domestic civil law of various States. In substance, on the basis of the distinction, we have an obligation of result when the contract or the law requires a certain conduct in itself, regardless of its outcome. For the obligation of result, non-fulfillment arises from the absence of the promised result, while for the obligation of conduct, non-fulfillment results from the fact that the debtor did not use the diligence required by the circumstances. In summary, the obligation of result is an obligation to *succeed* while the obligation of diligent conduct is an obligation to *make every effort*.[21]

While this chapter resorts at many particular instances to this civil law-based taxonomy, it also considers Roberto Ago's work on the subject in detail, making the pertinent terminological clarifications. Notwithstanding the foregoing, this survey does not seek to catalogue FPS under one of these dogmatic categories. Rather, it uses the distinction as a means to better illustrate the content of and dogmatic debates on the FPS standard or, borrowing Ian Brownlie's words, 'as a useful tool of analysis, that is, as a servant and not a master'.[22] In so doing, it also takes cognizance of the fact that international obligations do not always perfectly fit into these categories.[23] It furthermore acknowledges that, as accurately noted by James

---

2(1) *Yearbook of the International Law Commission – 1999* 3, 21 [56] (summarizing Governments' comments on the distinction). For an overview see: James Crawford, 'Revisiting the Draft Articles on State Responsibility' (1999) 10(2) EJIL 435, 441-2.

[20]James Crawford, 'Revisiting the Draft Articles on State Responsibility' (1999) 10(2) EJIL 435, 441. See also: James Crawford, 'Second Report on State Responsibility (A/CN.4/490 and Add. 1-7)' (1999) 2(1) *Yearbook of the International Law Commission – 1999* 3, 21-2 [58].

[21]Riccardo Pisillo-Mazzeschi, 'The Due Diligence Rule and the Nature of the International Responsibility of States' in René Provost (ed), *State Responsibility in International Law* (Ashgate Publishing Co., Burlington VT 2002) 97, 135-6. For another example see: ILA Study Group on Due Diligence in International Law, 'Second Report by Mr. Tim Stephens (Rapporteur) and Mr. Duncan French (Chair)' (20 July 2016) 22.

[22]It should be however noted that, in this particular instance, Brownlie was referring to the notions of 'obligations of conduct' and 'obligations of result', as used in the ILC Annual Report of 1977 (which was un turn largely based on Ago's work). See: Ian Brownlie, *System of the Law of Nations. State Responsibility* (Clarendon Press, Oxford 1983) 241.

[23]See, generally: James Crawford, *State Responsibility. The General Part* (Cambridge University Press, Cambridge 2013) 223-4. See also: Göran Lysén, *State Responsibility and International Liability of States for Lawful Acts* (Iustus Förlag, Uppsala 1997) 62. Some scholars have sought

Crawford, '[t]axonomy may assist in, but is no substitute for, the interpretation and application of primary rules'.[24]

Hence, for present purposes, the threshold issue is whether a specific international legal directive, namely the FPS standard, requires the state to achieve a particular result (e.g. the non-occurrence of the injury, in the case of the prevention obligation), or whether the host state is simply pledged to adopt some course of conduct (i.e. diligence aimed at the prevention and redress of certain injuries). This question is the subject of the following subsections.

11.2.2 'Full Protection and Security': Obligation of Conduct or Obligation of Result? A Dichotomy That Never Was

At first sight, the qualification of the security obligation as an obligation of means or result could appear to be a dogmatic debate of little practical interest. This might hold true in cases where a foreseeable injury has been inflicted on an alien and the host state has taken no action whatsoever to prevent it, despite having a reasonable opportunity to do so. In such scenarios, the breach of the FPS standard is apparent, regardless of whether the prevention obligation is said to be one of means or one of result: neither was the injury avoided (result), nor did the state act with diligence. This was the case in *AMT v Zaire*, where the arbitrators upheld a FPS claim on the following grounds:

> It would not appear useful for the Tribunal to enter into the debate whether in the case on hand Zaire is bound by an obligation of result or simply an obligation of conduct. The Tribunal deems it sufficient to ascertain, as it has done, that Zaire has breached its obligation by taking no measure whatever that would serve to ensure the protection and security of the investment in question. The Tribunal finds that Zaire has breached the obligation it has contracted by signing the above-cited provisions of the BIT in the face of events from which the ensuing disastrous consequences have been sufficiently described in the documents filed with the Tribunal. Zaire is responsible for its inability to prevent the disastrous consequences

---

to further develop this widespread classification of international obligations and, underscoring its insufficiency, have proposed some additional categories. See: Rüdiger Wolfrum, 'Obligations of Result Versus Obligations of Conduct: Some Thoughts About the Implementation of International Obligations' in Mahnoush Arsanjani, Jacob Katz Cogan, Robert Sloane and Siegfried Wiessner (eds), *Looking into the Future. Essays on International Law in Honor of W. Michael Reisman* (Martinus Nijhoff, Leiden/Boston 2011) 363, 369-83 (these additional categories include 'goal-oriented obligations', 'international obligations addressing natural or juridical persons' and 'obligations of conduct as well as of result'). For an additional example see: Georg Dahm, Jost Delbrück and Rüdiger Wolfrum, *Völkerrecht* (Volume 3: De Gruyter, Berlin 2002) 876.

[24]James Crawford, *State Responsibility. The General Part* (Cambridge University Press, Cambridge 2013) 223. See also: James Crawford, 'Second Report on State Responsibility (A/CN.4/490 and Add. 1-7)' (1999) 2(1) *Yearbook of the International Law Commission – 1999* 3, 24 [68]. For a similar remark in specific connection with the FPS standard see: Giuditta Cordero Moss, 'Full Protection and Security' in August Reinisch (ed), *Standards of Investment Protection* (Oxford University Press, New York 2008) 131, 139.

of these events adversely affecting the investments of AMT which Zaire had the obligation to protect.[25]

In other cases, however, the use of the distinction could have significant implications. In the first place, if FPS were considered to entail an obligation of means (in the civil law sense of the term), the party asserting the breach would need to provide evidence of a lack of diligence on the part of the host state. In contrast, if FPS is characterized as an obligation of result, the claimant could successfully invoke responsibility by simply proving that the result envisaged by the standard was not achieved.[26]

A second possible effect of the classification of FPS under these general categories pertains to the determination of the *tempus commissi delicti*, i.e. the moment in which a breach of the standard—and, particularly, the prevention obligation—consummates.[27] In fact, if FPS were classified as a 'pure' obligation of means, the breach would *not* be contingent upon the actual infliction of harm. Responsibility would be consistently engaged from the very moment in which the state fails to adopt preventive measures of protection in the face of some specific threat or risk, regardless of the outcome.[28]

11.2.2.1   First Possible Approach: 'Full Protection and Security' as an Obligation of Conduct

As stated in the introduction to this chapter, one of the most salient features of the FPS standard is the duty to exercise 'due diligence' in the protection of aliens. This element of FPS has been recognized since the very first award ever issued in investment treaty arbitration, in the case *AAPL v Sri Lanka*, back in 1990. In that case, the tribunal observed that the investor's claims departed from the idea that the applicable FPS clause 'created a strict liability which renders the Sri Lankan Government liable for any destruction of the investment even if caused by persons whose acts are not attributable to the Government and under circumstances beyond the State's control'.[29] The tribunal unmistakably rejected the Claimant's understanding of the security obligation:

---

[25] American Manufacturing & Trading Inc. *v* Zaire, Award, ICSID Case No. ARB 93/1 (21 February 1997) [6-08] (failure to prevent physical damage to a protected investment) [6.08].

[26] This first effect is a direct consequence of the civil law understanding of 'obligations of conduct' and 'obligations of result'. See Sect. 11.2.1.

[27] On this effect see: ILC, 'Summary Records of the 1478th Meeting' (12 May 1978) 1 *Yearbook of the International Law Commission – 1978* 13, 14 [5] (statement by Willem Riphagen). On the practical relevance of the *tempus commissi delicti* see: Göran Lysén, *State Responsibility and International Liability of States for Lawful Acts* (Iustus Förlag, Uppsala 1997) 71 *et seq*.

[28] See Sect. 11.2.2.1.

[29] Asian Agricultural Products *v* Sri Lanka, Final Award, ICSID Case No. ARB/87/3 (17 June 1990) [45].

The arbitral Tribunal is not aware of any case in which the obligation assumed by the host State to provide the nationals of the other Contracting State with full protection and security was construed as absolute obligation which guarantees that no damages will be suffered, in the sense that any violation thereof creates automatically a "strict liability" on behalf of the host State [. . .] the Tribunal declares unfounded the Claimant's main plea aiming to consider the Government of Sri Lanka assuming strict liability under Article 2(2) of the Bilateral Investment Treaty, without any need to prove that the damages suffered were attributable to the State or its agents, and to establish the State's responsibility for not acting with due diligence.[30]

Just as investment arbitral awards,[31] scholarly writings, too, have generally acknowledged that FPS requires diligent conduct on the part of the host state.[32]

---

[30] Asian Agricultural Products v Sri Lanka, Final Award, ICSID Case No. ARB/87/3 (17 June 1990) [48 and 53].

[31] Additional examples of awards recognizing the due diligence element are provided in Sect. 11.1.

[32] For some representative examples see: August Reinisch, 'Internationales Investitionsschutzrecht' in Christian Tietje (ed), *Internationales Wirtschaftsrecht* (De Gruyter, Berlin 2015) 398, 417-8; Burkhard Schöbener, Jochen Herbst and Markus Perkams, *Internationales Wirtschaftsrecht* (C.F. Müller, Heidelberg 2010) 278; Christoph Schreuer, 'Full Protection and Security' (2010) 1 (2) J. Int'l Disp. Settlement 353, 366-8; George Foster, 'Recovering "Protection and Security": The Treaty Standard's Obscure Origins, Forgotten Meaning, and Key Current Significance' (2012) 45 (4) Vand. J. Transnat'l L. 1095, 1103-4; Giuditta Cordero Moss, 'Full Protection and Security' in August Reinisch (ed), *Standards of Investment Protection* (Oxford University Press, New York 2008) 131, 139-40; Gleider Hernández, 'The Interaction Between Investment Law and the Law of Armed Conflict in the Interpretation of Full Protection and Security Clauses' in Freya Baetens (ed), *Investment Law within International Law* (Cambridge University Press, Cambridge 2013) 21, 39; Heather Bray, 'SOI – Save Our Investments! International Investment Law and International Humanitarian Law' (2013) 14 J. World Investment & Trade 578, 583 and 590 *et seq.*; Joshua Robins, 'The Emergence of Positive Obligations in Bilateral Investment Treaties' (2005-6) U. Miami Int'l & Comp. L. Rev. 403, 427; Kenneth Vandevelde, *Bilateral Investment Treaties: History, Policy, and Interpretation* (Oxford University Press, New York 2010) 243-4; Krista Nadakavukaren Schefer, *International Investment Law. Text, Cases and Materials* (Edward Elgar Publishing, Northampton MA 2013) 321; Lucas Bastin, *State Responsibility for Omissions: Establishing a Breach of the Full Protection and Security Obligation by Omissions* (Oxford University, Oxford 2016) [D.Phil. Thesis] 50 *et seq.*; Lucas Bastin, *Violation of the Full Protection and Security Obligation by Regulatory Omissions* [M.Phil. Thesis] (Oxford University, Oxford 2011) 65, 68, 76-81; Nartnirun Junngam, 'The Full Protection and Security Standard in International Investment Law: What and Who is Investment Fully[?] Protected and Secured From?' (2018) 7(1) AUBLR 1, 94-6; Maria Fanou and Vassilis Tzevelekos, 'The Shared Territory of the ECHR and International Investment Law' in Yannick Radi (ed), *Research Handbook on Human Rights and Investment* (Edward Elgar Publishers, Northampton MA 2018) 93, 126; Michael Gindler, *Die local remedies rule im Investitionsschutzrecht* (Nomos, Baden-Baden 2013) 120; Nnaemeka Nwokedi Anozie, *The Full Security and Protection Due Diligence Obligation* (University of Ottawa, Ottawa 2016) [LL.M. Thesis] 6 and 23 *et seq.*; Petr Stejskal, 'War: Foreign Investments in Danger – Can International Humanitarian Law or Full Protection and Security Always Save It?' (2017) 8 CYIL 529, 532, 535 and 548; Robert Reyes Landicho, 'Enforcing a State's International IP Obligations through Investment Law Standards of Protection – An Ill-Fated Romance' in Ian Laird, Borzu Sabahi, Frédéric Sourgens and Todd Weiler (eds), *Investment Treaty Arbitration and International Law* (Juris Net, Huntington NY 2018) 111, 126; Rudolf Dolzer and Margrete Stevens, *Bilateral Investment Treaties* (Martinus Nijhoff, The Hague 1995) 61; Rudolf Dolzer and Christoph Schreuer, *Principles of International Investment Law* (Oxford University Press, New York 2012)

Notwithstanding the foregoing, little has been said as to whether it is truly possible to characterize FPS as a 'pure' obligation of means or conduct, in the traditional sense of the terms. Some tribunals seem to assume that it is. For instance, in *LESI & ASTALDI v Algeria*, the arbitrators stated:

> L'obligation de sécurité est une obligation de moyens et non pas une obligation de résultat garantissant à l'investisseur que jamais rien n'arriverait à son investissement [...] L'obligation de sécurité implique dès lors que l'Etat d'accueil fasse tout ce qui est dans son pouvoir pour éviter qu'un dommage ne soit infligé aux investissements.[33]

This view has important practical consequences. In fact, if this categorization is correct, the breach of the FPS standard would not depend, in any way, on the *result* of the host state's conduct. It would be contingent on its diligence, and nothing more. A failure to exercise diligence would hence not only be a *necessary condition*, but also a *sufficient condition* for a breach of the FPS standard. As a corollary, the existence of an injury would be immaterial to the question of responsibility.[34] Thus, if in the face of an imminent peril the host state has left the integrity of an investment to fate and destiny, the mere circumstance that no injury was finally inflicted would not imply that authorities have discharged their protection obligation under

---

161; Stanimir Alexandrov, 'The Evolution of the Full Protection and Security Standard' in Meg Kinnear, Geraldine Fischer, Jara Mínguez Almeida, Luisa Torres and Mairée Uran Bidegain (eds), *Building International Investment Law. The First 50 Years of ICSID* (Wolters Kluwer/ICSID, Alphen aan den Rijn 2016) 319, 320 and 322-3; Todd Weiler, *The Interpretation of International Investment Law: Equality, Discrimination, and Minimum Standards of Treatment in Historical Context* (Brill, Leiden 2013) 61; Valériane König, *Präzedenzwirkung internationaler Schiedssprüche. Domatisch-empirische Analysen zur Handels- und Investitionsschiedsgerichtsbarkeit* (De Gruyter, Berlin 2013) 235 *et seq.*; Zachary Douglas, 'Property, Investment, and the Scope of Investment Protection Obligations' in Zachary Douglas, Joost Pauwelyn and Jorge Viñuales (eds), *The Foundations of International Investment Law. Bringing Theory into Practice* (Oxford University Press, Oxford 2014) 363, 379.

[33]LESI S.p.A. and ASTALDI S.p.A. *v* Algeria, Sentence, ICSID Case No. ARB/05/3 (12 November 2008) [153].

[34]Cf. Lucas Bastin, *Violation of the Full Protection and Security Obligation by Regulatory Omissions* [M.Phil. Thesis] (Oxford University, Oxford 2011) 68 ("As the course of jurisprudence considering the full protection and security obligation has now resolved, *it is an obligation of means, not of ends*. A state can therefore take action in an effort to secure protection and security for the foreign investment, but if that action is not sufficient to satisfy the due diligence standard, the State will nevertheless have breached its obligation and international responsibility will attach. Conversely, if a State does act to secure protection and security for the investment, and that action is deemed by the arbiter of fact sufficient to satisfy the due diligence standard, then, *irrespective of any material or moral harm suffered by the claimant*, the State will have fulfilled its obligation and cannot be held internationally responsible" – emphasis added). In later works, Bastin, while classifying FPS as a 'non-absolute positive obligation', has suggested that damage could actually be required. See: Lucas Bastin, *State Responsibility for Omissions: Establishing a Breach of the Full Protection and Security Obligation by Omissions* (Oxford University, Oxford 2016) [D.Phil. Thesis] 50-1 and 74-5 (characterizing FPS as an obligation under this category at pp. 50-1, and stating at p. 75 that '[w]hile not all omissions that cause damage are wrongful, all omissions that are wrongful must have caused some variety of damage'). Cf. also Bastin's analysis of the concept of damage at pp. 37-9.

customary international law.[35] Their omissions could still amount to an international wrong, and their responsibility be genuinely compromised.[36]

It is out of question that due diligence is an element of the FPS standard. Nonetheless, there are good reasons for rejecting the classification of FPS as a pure obligation of means. As will be shown below, a lack of diligence, despite being a fundamental requirement for a violation of FPS, is not the only condition that must be satisfied in order to establish a breach of the standard.[37]

11.2.2.2   Second Possible Approach: 'Full Protection and Security' as a Negative Obligation of Result. The ILC and the Notion of 'Obligations of Event'

During the drafting process of the ILC Articles on State Responsibility, distinguished international law scholars presented the customary obligation to provide protection and security to aliens as an example of an obligation of result. In this regard, they particularly referred to the prevention obligation, the 'result' envisaged by the obligation being the non-occurrence of a harmful event. The core of the debate took place at the 30th Session of the ILC (1978), in connection with Draft Article 23. Through this provision, Special Rapporteur Roberto Ago sought to introduce the special category of 'obligations of event' or 'obligations of prevention' into the international law of state responsibility. Ago's initial draft read as follows:

> There is no breach by a State of an international obligation requiring it to prevent a given event unless, following a lack of prevention on the part of the State, the event in question occurs.[38]

In his Second,[39] Third,[40] Sixth[41] and Seventh[42] Reports on State Responsibility (1970–1978), Ago resorted to the customary protection obligation as an example of

---

[35]Cf. n. 34 above.

[36]Cf. n. 34 above.

[37]See Sect. 11.2.2.2.

[38]Roberto Ago, 'Seventh Report on State Responsibility – The Internationally Wrongful Act of the State, Source of International Responsibility (A/CN.4/307 and Add.1 and 2)' (1978) 2(1) *Yearbook of the International Law Commission – 1978* 31, 37.

[39]Roberto Ago, 'Second Report on State Responsibility – The Origin of International Responsibility (A/CN.4/233)' (10 April 1970) 2 *Yearbook of the International Law Commission – 1970* 177, 194 [51-2].

[40]Roberto Ago, 'Third Report on State Responsibility – The Origin of International Responsibility (A/CN.4/246 and Add. 1-3)' (1971) 2(1) *Yearbook of the International Law Commission – 1971* 199, 222 [71].

[41]See: Roberto Ago, 'Sixth Report on State Responsibility – The Internationally Wrongful Act of the State, Source of International Responsibility (A/CN.4/302 and Add.1-3)' (1977) 2(1) *Yearbook of the International Law Commission – 1977* 3, 20 [45]. See also: ILC, 'Report of the International Law Commission on the Work of its Twenty-Ninth Session – State Responsibility' (1977) 2 (2) *Yearbook of the International Law Commission – 1977* 5, 29 [33].

[42]Roberto Ago, 'Seventh Report on State Responsibility – The Internationally Wrongful Act of the State, Source of International Responsibility (A/CN.4/307 and Add.1 and 2)' (1978) 2(1) *Yearbook of the International Law Commission – 1978* 31, 32 [2], 33-4 [5, 7-9, 11] and 36 [16].

an obligation falling into this formal category, making specific reference to the host state's duty to protect aliens from mobs and other forms of private violence. In his Seventh Report, he went on to observe that scholars usually considered the prevention of private injuries—including those inflicted on aliens—to be the 'typical example' of an 'international obligation requiring preventive action on the part of the State'.[43]

At the 30th Session of the ILC, several members expressed some concern as to the relationship between obligations of conduct and result, on the one hand, and the type of obligations addressed by Draft Article 23, on the other. Ago agreed to clarify this point by introducing into Draft Article 23 a clear reference to the general classification criteria.[44] The provision's redrafted version was as follows:

> When the result required of a State by an international obligation is the prevention, by means of its own choice, of the occurrence of a given event, there is a breach of that obligation only if, by the conduct adopted, the State does not achieve that result.[45]

The ILC adopted this version of Draft Article 23 in 1978 (in first reading),[46] but decided to delete it decades later, considering that these dogmatic intricacies refer more to the content of primary rules of international law than to the secondary rules governing state responsibility.[47] This decision does not however diminish the significance of the ILC's work on the subject, particularly when it comes to the assessment of the customary norm which the Special Rapporteur regarded to be the 'typical example' of this kind of obligations.[48]

In its comments to the 1997 version of the Draft, the ILC characterized the obligations in question as 'obligations of event'.[49] The Commission defined event

---

[43]Roberto Ago, 'Seventh Report on State Responsibility – The Internationally Wrongful Act of the State, Source of International Responsibility (A/CN.4/307 and Add.1 and 2)' (1978) 2(1) *Yearbook of the International Law Commission – 1978* 31, 36 [16].

[44]ILC, 'Summary Records of the 1477th Meeting' (11 May 1978) 1 *Yearbook of the International Law Commission – 1978* 9, 11 [11] (statement of Roberto Ago).

[45]A Drafting Committee chaired by Stephen Schwebel prepared this version of Draft Article 23; the text was submitted and discussed at the 1513th meeting of the ILC. See: ILC, 'Summary Records of the 1513th Meeting' (6 July 1978) 1 *Yearbook of the International Law Commission – 1978* 206, 206 [1].

[46]ILC, 'Summary Records of the 1513th Meeting' (6 July 1978) 1 *Yearbook of the International Law Commission – 1978* 206, 208 [18].

[47]See: James Crawford, 'Second Report on State Responsibility (A/CN.4/490 and Add. 1-7)' (1999) 2(1) *Yearbook of the International Law Commission – 1999* 3, 28-9 [89-90]; ILC, 'Report of the International Law Commission on the Work of its Fifty-First Session – State Responsibility' (1999) 2(2) *Yearbook of the International Law Commission – 1999* 48, 58 [142] and 62 [181].

[48]Roberto Ago, 'Seventh Report on State Responsibility – The Internationally Wrongful Act of the State, Source of International Responsibility (A/CN.4/307 and Add.1 and 2)' (1978) 2(1) *Yearbook of the International Law Commission – 1978* 31, 36 [16].

[49]ILC, 'Draft Articles on State Responsibility with Commentaries thereto adopted by the International Law Commission on First Reading (Doc. No. 97-02583)' (January 1997) [http://legal.un.org/ilc/texts/instruments/english/commentaries/9_6_1996.pdf] 176 [13].

as 'an act of man or nature *which, as such, involves no action by the State*'.[50]
Attention should be drawn to the fact that, as Special Rapporteur Ago explained in
1978, the concept of 'event' was considered to be conceptually distinct from the
notions of 'injury' or 'damage'.[51] For example, in diplomatic law, the obligation
upon receiving states to prevent intrusions in an embassy's premises refers to the
event of the intrusion and, consequently, could be breached regardless of whether the
intruder actually causes damages.[52]

This dogmatic distinction is, however, usually immaterial for the customary duty
to prevent injuries to aliens. If the event the obligation refers to is the *infliction* of
harm or damage, it follows that the very *occurrence of the event* implies the *existence
of damage*. The only exception would be that of injuries which do not consum-
mate—or, at least, not in full extent—simultaneously with the injurious event
(e.g. mob violence against a foreigner who survives the harmful event, but dies
some days later).

For all practical purposes, classifying this particular obligation as an 'obligation
of event' implies turning the existence of an injury into a prerequisite for successfully invoking responsibility.[53] There is nothing extraordinary about this effect.
Despite it being common ground that an internationally wrongful act does not
necessarily presuppose the occurrence of an injury, it is also generally accepted
that damage may be an element of specific *primary norms* of international law.[54] As

---

[50]ILC, 'Draft Articles on State Responsibility with Commentaries thereto adopted by the International Law Commission on First Reading (Doc. No. 97-02583)' (January 1997) [http://legal.un.org/
ilc/texts/instruments/english/commentaries/9_6_1996.pdf] 173 [4].

[51]See: ILC, 'Summary Records of the 1477th Meeting' (11 May 1978) 1 *Yearbook of the
International Law Commission – 1978* 9, 10 [6].

[52]Paul Reuter brought a similar example into the debate on Draft Article 23, noting that in such
cases responsibility could arise even in the absence of damage. Ago responded by drawing the
distinction between 'event' and 'damage'. See: ILC, 'Summary Records of the 1476th Meeting'
(10 May 1978) 1 *Yearbook of the International Law Commission – 1978* 4, 7 [21-2] (Reuter's
remarks); ILC, 'Summary Records of the 1477th Meeting' (11 May 1978) 1 *Yearbook of the
International Law Commission – 1978* 9, 10 [6] (Ago's response). See also: ILC, 'Draft Articles on
State Responsibility with Commentaries thereto adopted by the International Law Commission on
First Reading (Doc. No. 97-02583)' (January 1997) [http://legal.un.org/ilc/texts/instruments/
english/commentaries/9_6_1996.pdf] 173 [5].

[53]Cf. Robert Kolb, *The International Law of State Responsibility. An Introduction* (Edward Elgar
Publishing, Northampton MA 2017) 39-40 (referring to the notions of 'due diligence' and 'obligations of prevention'). For the sake of accuracy, it should be noted that some members of the ILC
expressed doubts as to this principle. For a prominent example see: ILC, 'Summary Records of the
1476th Meeting' (10 May 1978) 1 *Yearbook of the International Law Commission – 1978* 4, 7
[21-3] (intervention of Paul Reuter suggesting that 'when the risk could be precisely defined in
advance, the State ought to take preventive measures in proportion to it' and further stressing that
'any default on that obligation would of itself constitute a breach').

[54]This section does not intend to draw a dogmatic distinction between 'injury' and 'damage'. It
should however be noted that terminology is not entirely uniform in legal literature, with some
authorities ascribing each term a different meaning. For an overview of the terminological debate
see: James Crawford, *State Responsibility. The General Part* (Cambridge University Press, Cambridge 2013) 54-5.

accurately noted by James Crawford, 'particular rules of international law may require actual damage to have been caused before any issue of responsibility is raised'.[55]

Much more interesting is the fact that the ILC considered obligations of event to be a subtype of the more general category of obligations of result.[56] In his Second Report on State Responsibility, Special Rapporteur James Crawford provides some insight into the underlying reason:

> It is tempting to analyse obligations of prevention as "negative" obligations of result. For such obligations, the result in question is not the occurrence of something but its non-occurrence.[57]

The notion of 'negative obligations of result' must be taken with caution.[58] If the phrase 'obligation of result' were to convey its traditional civil law meaning, classifying the customary protection obligation under this heading would imply imposing an excessively heavy burden on the host state. The state would in fact be pledged to *achieve a result*, such result seemingly being that, while in the host territory, aliens remain free from harm arising from some specific risks.

This was not the sense intended by the ILC.[59] At the Commission's 1477th Meeting, Roberto Ago explained that Draft Article 23 was not aimed at turning obligations of prevention into 'absolute' obligations. The record of the meeting is unmistakably clear in this fundamental respect:

> Mr. AGO (Special Rapporteur), in response to the questions which article 23 had given rise, said first that the international obligations referred to in that article were not normally absolute obligations, and that the rule was by no means aimed at transforming them into absolute obligations, as some members of the Commission feared. If they were absolute obligations, they would require that the State prevent the occurrence of a given event in any

---

[55]James Crawford, *State Responsibility. The General Part* (Cambridge University Press, Cambridge 2013) 59. See also: James Crawford, 'Revisiting the Draft Articles on State Responsibility' (1999) 10(2) EJIL 435, 438.

[56]For an overview of the Commission's approach see: ILC, 'Summary Records of the 1513th Meeting' (6 July 1978) 1 *Yearbook of the International Law Commission – 1978* 206, 208 [4] (statement of Stephen Schwebel).

[57]James Crawford, 'Second Report on State Responsibility (A/CN.4/490 and Add. 1-7)' (1999) 2(1) *Yearbook of the International Law Commission – 1999 3*, 28 [85]. See also: James Crawford, *State Responsibility. The General Part* (Cambridge University Press, Cambridge 2013) 228.

[58]At the ILC, the classification of these obligations as obligations of result was somewhat controversial. The question was raised as to whether 'obligations of event' could be said to actually constitute a third, additional category of international obligations. See, for example: ILC, 'Summary Records of the 1476th Meeting' (10 May 1978) 1 *Yearbook of the International Law Commission – 1978 4*, 7 [25] (intervention of Nikolai Ushakov).

[59]For an overview of the debates on Draft Article 23 in particular connection with the notion of fault see: Karl Zemanek, 'Schuld- und Erfolgshaftung im Entwurf der Völkerrechtskommission über Staatenverantwortlichkeit. Zugleich Bemerkungen zum Prozess der Kodifikation im Rahmen der Vereinten Nationen' in Emanuel Diez, Jean Monnier, Jörg Müller, Heinrich Reimann and Luzius Wildhaber (eds), *Festschrift für Rudolf Bindschedler zum 65. Geburtstag am 8. Juli 1980* (Verlag Stämpfli & cie., Bern 1980) 315, 322-31.

case whatsoever; consequently, the mere occurrence of the event would constitute a breach of the obligation. However, *under this proposed article 23, there was a breach of the obligation to prevent an event only if the event occurred following a lack of prevention on the part of the State. Accordingly, two conditions had to be fulfilled: the event to be prevented must have occurred and it must have been made possible by lack of vigilance on the Part of the State.* Therefore the case in which the event occurred despite the State's having taken all the adequate preventive measures had to be excluded.[60]

Thus, if the customary obligation to prevent injuries to aliens were said to belong with Ago's category of 'obligations of event', a finding of liability under this heading would depend on *both* the infliction of harm and a lack of due diligence attributable to the host state. As noted in the ILC's Commentary to Draft Article 23, '[when consenting to an obligation of event] States are not underwriting some kind of insurance to cover contracting States against the occurrence, whatever the conditions, of events of the kind contemplated'.[61]

There would be, therefore, no departure from the well-established principle that the FPS standard is intrinsically linked to the notion of due diligence. Ago's opening statement at the 1476th Meeting of the ILC provides a summary of his views on the subject. The record states:

> For a breach of an obligation of that type to occur, the event that should have been prevented must have taken place as a result of the State's negligence [. . .] Thus, two conditions must be fulfilled in order that there should be a breach of an obligation: first, the event to be prevented must have occurred, and secondly, it must have occurred owing to the State's failure to prevent it. Neither of those conditions alone sufficed to prove the existence of a breach; in other words, it was not enough that there should have been a negligence on the part of the State, or that the event had occurred: both conditions must be fulfilled.[62]

From a strictly formal perspective, the obligations in question are neither obligations of conduct nor obligations of result, in the civil law sense of the terms. As put forward by James Crawford:

> [O]bligations of prevention are not warranties or guarantees that an event will not occur; rather, they are inherently obligations to take all reasonable or necessary measures to ensure that the event does not occur. Although it has been said that an obligation of prevention is essentially regarded as a duty of due diligence, when it comes to assessing the breach, *obligations of prevention may be distinguished from obligations of due diligence in the*

---

[60]Emphasis added. ILC, 'Summary Records of the 1477th Meeting' (11 May 1978) 1 *Yearbook of the International Law Commission – 1978* 9, 9-10 [4]. See also: ILC, 'Summary Records of the 1513th Meeting' (6 July 1978) 1 *Yearbook of the International Law Commission – 1978* 206, 207-8 [3-4] (statement of Stephen Schwebel). For an overview see: Alfred Verdross and Bruno Simma, *Universelles Völkerrecht* (Duncker & Humblot, Berlin 1984) 852-3.

[61]ILC, 'Draft Articles on State Responsibility with Commentaries thereto adopted by the International Law Commission on First Reading (Doc. No. 97-02583)' (January 1997) [http://legal.un.org/ilc/texts/instruments/english/commentaries/9_6_1996.pdf] 173 [6].

[62]ILC, 'Summary Records of the 1476th Meeting' (10 May 1978) 1 *Yearbook of the International Law Commission – 1978* 4, 5 [9]. See also: ILC, 'Draft Articles on State Responsibility with Commentaries thereto adopted by the International Law Commission on First Reading (Doc. No. 97-02583)' (January 1997) [http://legal.un.org/ilc/texts/instruments/english/commentaries/9_6_1996.pdf] 173-4 [6-8].

ordinary sense. A true obligation of prevention is not breached unless the apprehended event occurs, whereas an obligation of due diligence would be breached by a failure to exercise due diligence, even if the apprehended result did not (or not yet) occur. Thus obligations of due diligence are relative, not absolute.[63]

For present purposes, the threshold issue is whether the customary protection obligation actually meets the features described above. To be sure, it is generally accepted that a breach of the FPS standard requires some 'negligence' or 'lack of diligence' on the part of the host state.[64] For that very same reason, the aforementioned dogmatic and terminological intricacies may be reduced to one fundamental question: Is the occurrence of the injurious event (i.e. the infliction of an injury) a *conditio sine qua non* for establishing a breach of the customary protection obligation?

There are good reasons to say that it is. The issue was raised on several occasions both at international conferences and in scholarly works. Relevant sources were chiefly concerned with state responsibility for acts of individuals.[65] For instance, in the context of the Hague Codification Conference of 1930, the Austrian Government stated:

> It is obvious that mere failure to exercise due diligence in protecting the person of foreigners does not in itself involve the responsibility of the State: such responsibility would arise only if a foreigner suffered injury through an act of a private person.[66]

The Hague Conference's working documents did not escape Ago's attention. After careful consideration of those examples of state practice, as well as of early arbitral decisions addressing subject, Ago reached the following conclusion:

> [I]t seems beyond doubt that the view generally shared by all the governments represented is that a State could not be held responsible for the breach of the obligation to prevent an event such as an injurious act by a private person affecting a foreigner, so long as that event had not occurred [. . .] a State has never asserted that such a breach has been perpetrated on the sole ground of negligence or failure to prevent a purely hypothetical event which did not actually occur.[67]

---

[63]Emphasis added. James Crawford, *State Responsibility. The General Part* (Cambridge University Press, Cambridge 2013) 227. A prominent example would be the obligation to prevent genocide. After a careful analysis of the ICJ's decision in the *Bosnian Genocide* case, Crawford notes that '[t]he obligation to prevent genocide requires both a failure to take steps *and* the occurrence of genocide before responsibility is triggered' (at p. 232).

[64]Section 11.2.3 provides a critical analysis of novel theories considering that the FPS standard imposes strict liability in some factual scenarios.

[65]For an early example see: Adolf Jess, *Politische Handlungen Privater gegen das Ausland und das Völkerrecht* (Verlag von M. & H. Marcus, Breslau 1923) 140. Further examples will be provided below.

[66]Quoted in: Roberto Ago, 'Seventh Report on State Responsibility – The Internationally Wrongful Act of the State, Source of International Responsibility (A/CN.4/307 and Add.1 and 2)' (1978) 2 (1) *Yearbook of the International Law Commission – 1978* 31, 34 [8] (also providing other examples of relevant state practice).

[67]Roberto Ago, 'Seventh Report on State Responsibility – The Internationally Wrongful Act of the State, Source of International Responsibility (A/CN.4/307 and Add.1 and 2)' (1978) 2(1) *Yearbook of the International Law Commission – 1978* 31, 34 [9-10].

This opinion found broad support within the ILC. At the Commission's 1478th Meeting, Willem Riphagen went as far as to say that Draft Article 23 was 'tautological'.[68] Similarly, Stephen Schwebel considered it to be a 'truism' that '[there is] no breach by a State of an international obligation requiring it to prevent a given event unless that event occurred'.[69] For his part, Sir Francis Vallat appealingly noted that a 'theoretically established failure of prevention' does not suffice for a violation of this kind of obligations to be declared.[70] The breach, Vallat said, is contingent upon 'a failure of prevention made concrete by the actual occurrence of an event'.[71] Despite these declarations did not specifically refer to the customary obligation to grant protection and security to aliens, there was no single statement questioning Ago's resort to this example.

There is no reason to depart from Ago's conclusion. It may be however added that, in some cases, states have requested protection for their nationals *before* the occurrence of any injury whatsoever.[72] These pieces of diplomatic correspondence should not be taken as an indication that responsibility is not necessarily dependent on the actual infliction of harm. As expressed by Schwebel when addressing the issue, states may 'make representations, raise questions, express anxieties and even protest at the possibility of occurrences without alleging actual violations of international law'.[73]

In *Burlington Resources Inc. v Ecuador* (2010), the investor alleged that local authorities had failed provide it 'full protection and security' against intense indigenous opposition to its operations in Ecuador.[74] The applicable dispute settlement clause allowed the submission of a request for arbitration only after 6 months 'from the data (sic) on which the dispute arose'.[75] In the arbitral proceedings, the parties

---

[68]See: ILC, 'Summary Records of the 1478th Meeting' (12 May 1978) 1 *Yearbook of the International Law Commission – 1978* 13, 14 [5] (statement by Willem Riphagen). See also p. 17 [25] (statement of Robert Q. Quentin-Baxter) and p. 18 [24] (response of Roberto Ago).

[69]ILC, 'Summary Records of the 1478th Meeting' (12 May 1978) 1 *Yearbook of the International Law Commission – 1978* 13, 16 [17].

[70]ILC, 'Summary Records of the 1478th Meeting' (12 May 1978) 1 *Yearbook of the International Law Commission – 1978* 13, 15 [11].

[71]ILC, 'Summary Records of the 1478th Meeting' (12 May 1978) 1 *Yearbook of the International Law Commission – 1978* 13, 15 [11].

[72]For some indicative examples see: 'The American Ambassador to the Mexican Minister of Foreign Affairs' (13 May 1911) *Papers relating to the Foreign Relations of the United States with the Annual Message of the President* (Government Printing Office, Washington 1911) 492, 492; 'The [Mexican] Minister of Foreign Affairs to the American Ambassador' (16 May 1911) *Papers relating to the Foreign Relations of the United States with the Annual Message of the President* (Government Printing Office, Washington 1911) 493, 493. Section 10.2 discusses this exchange of diplomatic notes.

[73]ILC, 'Summary Records of the 1478th Meeting' (12 May 1978) 1 *Yearbook of the International Law Commission – 1978* 13, 16 [19].

[74]Burlington Resources Inc. v Ecuador, Decision on Jurisdiction, ICSID Case No. ARB/08/5 (2 June 2010) [216, 250 *et seq.*].

[75]Treaty between the United States of America and the Republic of Ecuador concerning the Encouragement and Reciprocal Protection of Investment (adopted 17 August 1993, entered into force 11 May 1997) art. 6(3)(a).

disagreed as to whether the investor's 'requests for assistance' indicated the existence of '[a] dispute sufficiently expressed in legal terms' for the purposes of the waiting period.[76] In this connection, the tribunal held:

> [T]his request for assistance does not express disagreement with the manner in which the Respondent has fulfilled its obligation to provide protection and security [...] In and for itself, a request for assistance does not express disagreement on the parties' rights and obligations [...] unless the surrounding context suggests otherwise, i.e. that the party whose assistance is requested has thus far failed to abide by its duty to assist.[77]

This statement, despite referring to a particular procedural question, substantially coincides with Schwebel's observation. The mere existence of communications requesting prompt state action against some risk does not necessarily imply that a breach of FPS has already taken place. Generally speaking, the moment in which state action is required is different from the moment in which a violation of the protection obligation can be properly established.

Bearing the foregoing in mind, it could be said that the customary prevention obligation is *triggered* by the risk of an injury but, following the opinion of the ILC, the *actual infliction of damage* is necessary for considering the state's omissions 'as constituting a completed breach of an international obligation, and hence as being a source of international responsibility'.[78] This idea has found expression in multiple investment arbitral awards. A representative example appears in *Noble Ventures v Romania* (2005). In that case, the arbitrators dismissed an FPS claim, among others, on the ground that 'it has not been established that non-compliance with the [protection] obligation prejudiced the Claimant, to a material degree'.[79] In *Ronald Lauder v Czech Republic* (2001), the arbitrators gave weight to the fact that the acts which the investor considered to be contrary to the FPS standard had not 'caused a direct or indirect damage to Mr. Lauder's investment'.[80] To the same effect, in

---

[76]Burlington Resources Inc. *v* Ecuador, Decision on Jurisdiction, ICSID Case No. ARB/08/5 (2 June 2010) [250 *et seq.*] (particularly at para 316).

[77]Burlington Resources Inc. *v* Ecuador, Decision on Jurisdiction, ICSID Case No. ARB/08/5 (2 June 2010) [298] (further declaring at para 317 that the FPS claim was inadmissible and upholding Ecuador's jurisdictional objection pertaining to this claim at para 318).

[78]ILC, 'Report of the International Law Commission on the Work of its Twenty-Seventh Session – State Responsibility' (1975) 2 *Yearbook of the International Law Commission – 1975* 51, 72 [8] n. 100. This statement is quoted in length in Ago's Seventh Report. See: Roberto Ago, 'Seventh Report on State Responsibility – The Internationally Wrongful Act of the State, Source of International Responsibility (A/CN.4/307 and Add.1 and 2)' (1978) 2(1) *Yearbook of the International Law Commission – 1978* 31, 33 [5].

[79]Noble Ventures *v* Romania, Award, ICSID Case No. ARB/01/11 (12 October 2005) [166].

[80]Ronald Lauder *v* Czech Republic (UNCITRAL), Final Award (3 September 2001) [313].

Ampal et al. v Egypt (2017) the arbitrators emphasized that the standard of due diligence 'must be assessed according to the particular circumstances *in which the damage occurs*'.[81] A few scholars have also recognized this requirement.[82] In some cases, respondent states have requested dismissal of FPS claims on the ground that no damage was inflicted.[83]

This analysis has focused on the preventive functional dimension of the FPS standard. The redress obligation should pose no difficulties. As shown throughout this section, beyond all terminological and dogmatic technicalities, the threshold issue at this stage is whether the occurrence of an *injury* is a condition necessary for successfully invoking responsibility under the FPS standard. The redress obligation does certainly not fit into the formal category of 'obligation of event'. Nonetheless, as in the case of the prevention obligation, a breach of the redress obligation presupposes both the occurrence of an injurious event and a lack of diligence on the part of the host state.

The infliction of harm is the event that ultimately triggers the obligation of redress.[84] It is indeed self-evident that, in the absence of an injurious event, there will be no injury to redress in the first place. As to the due diligence element, it must be conceded that arbitral decisions usually refer to the due diligence standard of liability only in relation to the preventive functional dimension of the FPS standard. Nonetheless, some tribunals have expressly defined the obligation of redress in terms of due diligence too. A clear example may be found in the award rendered in *El Paso v Argentina* (2011):

> A well-established aspect of the international standard of treatment is that States must use "due diligence" to prevent wrongful injuries to the person or property of aliens caused by third parties within their territory, *and, if they did not succeed, exercise at least "due diligence" to punish such injuries. If a State fails to exercise due diligence to prevent or punish such injuries, it is responsible for this omission and is liable for the ensuing damage*.[85]

---

[81]Emphasis added. Ampal-American Israel Corp., Egi-Fund (08-10) Investors LLC, Egi-Series Investments LLC and BSS-EMG Investors LLC *v* Egypt, Decision on Liability and Heads of Loss, ICSID Case No. ARB/12/11 (21 February 2017) [241].

[82]See, for example: Helge Elisabeth Zeitler, 'The Guarantee of Full Protection and Security in Investment Treaties regarding Harm Caused by Private Parties' (2005) 3 SIAR 1, 8 (observing that '[n]on-action may only give rise to state responsibility if private persons cause a certain damage' and mentioning Draft Article 23 in this connection).

[83]For an example cf. Karkey Karadeniz Elektrik Uretim A.S. *v* Pakistan, Award, ICSID Case No. ARB/13/1 (22 August 2017) [407].

[84]See Sect. 10.3.

[85]Emphasis added. El Paso Energy International Co. *v* Argentina, Award, ICSID Case No. ARB/03/15 (31 October 2011) [523]. For similar statements cf. Joseph Houben *v* Burundi, Sentence, ICSID Case No. ARB/13/7 (12 January 2016) [161]; Oxus Gold *v* Uzbekistan (UNCITRAL), Final Award (17 December 2015) [355]; Sergei Paushok, CJSC Golden East Co., CJSC Vostoknefte *v* Mongolia (UNCITRAL), Award on Jurisdiction and Liability (28 April 2011) [324-5]. Section 11.2.3 discusses some dissident views on this particular issue.

In sum, it may be agreed that a breach of the FPS standard presupposes both the infliction of an injury and a lack of diligence on the part of the host state. Even if the host state has failed to exercise due diligence in the face of a clear threat towards an alien, the state will not have breached its prevention obligation unless harm was actually inflicted. At the same time, the mere fact that a foreigner has sustained an injury, and that municipal authorities have not provided adequate means of redress, does not suffice for successfully invoking international responsibility. In addition to the injury, the host state must have failed to exercise the diligence required by the circumstances of the case. As a corollary, it could be said that the FPS standard cannot be accurately characterized under the traditional categories of 'obligation of conduct' and 'obligation of result'. The standard belongs somewhere in between.

11.2.3 *'Full Protection and Security': Obligation of Conduct or Obligation of Result? Intermediate Approaches*

Recent scholarly writings and a few arbitral decisions suggest that FPS does not impose a sole, univocal standard of liability. Rather, it is argued that the standard may entail strict liability in some cases, and due diligence liability in other cases. A textbook example would be the award rendered in *National Grid v Argentina* (2008). In that case, the arbitrators adopted a broad interpretation of the applicable FPS clause and concluded that some changes in the regulatory framework relevant for the investment were 'contrary to the protection and constant security which the Respondent agreed to provide investments under the Treaty'.[86] Interestingly, the tribunal took cognizance of previous arbitral decisions (quoted by Argentina), which referred to physical injuries caused by private parties and defined FPS in terms of due diligence.[87] In this connection, the arbitrators stated:

> [The decisions] adduced by the Respondent do not deal with the question before this Tribunal. They all deal with questions of disturbances, rebellion, physical threats, destruction of company assets, but none considered whether the scope of the protection and constant security obligation embraced non-physical situations. In the cases of *AAPL* and *AMT* the issue was whether the obligation was of an absolute character or simply an obligation of due diligence of the State to protect aliens under customary international law, a matter different from the issue in the instant case.[88]

The notion of due diligence did not play any role in the *National Grid* tribunal's analysis of Argentina's responsibility.[89] It is thus apparent that the arbitrators considered 'due diligence' to be inapplicable to FPS claims concerning (positive)

---

[86]National Grid P.L.C. *v* Argentina (UNCITRAL), Award (3 November 2008) [189].

[87]National Grid P.L.C. *v* Argentina (UNCITRAL), Award (3 November 2008) [188].

[88]National Grid P.L.C. *v* Argentina (UNCITRAL), Award (3 November 2008) [188].

[89]National Grid P.L.C. *v* Argentina (UNCITRAL), Award (3 November 2008) [187-90].

regulatory measures.[90] Regrettably, the arbitrators did not elaborate much on this idea.

Scholarly works are more clear in this regard. Extant 'eclectic' academic approaches to the applicable standard of liability may be classified in two groups. A first trend consists in drawing a line between different sources of risk. In this line of argument, the host state would be strictly liable for harmful actions attributable to its agents. The due diligence standard of liability would hence be applicable only in respect of harm caused by third parties.[91]

A second trend considers that the FPS standard requires the host state both to ensure the *existence* of an adequate administrative and judicial system, and to properly *use* that system for the purpose of protecting aliens. As regards to the *existence* of some degree of institutional organization, the state's liability is strict. For the adequate *use* of the system, in turn, the host state's conduct is measured against a standard of due diligence.[92]

This section argues that these dogmatic approaches are unsound. They transform FPS into a complex and increasingly abstract conceptual web embedding a wide array of international obligations, which, on a closer look, do not properly belong with the customary notion of FPS. They furthermore turn a blind eye on consistent arbitral and state practice indicating that FPS and due diligence are two sides of the same coin.

11.2.3.1 The Application of Different Standards of Liability Depending on the Source of Risk

One of the most controversial issues surrounding the determination of the FPS standard's scope of application is the question whether, beyond the risk of private violence, the standard provides protection against public injuries too.[93] Among those accepting that FPS is generally applicable in respect of injuries which directly result from the actions of state agents, it seems to be common ground that, as expressed by Helge Elisabeth Zeitler, 'the standard of obligation owed differs depending on whether it is state actors who are causing harm (the state owes abstention) or private actors (the state owes due diligence to prevent and to investigate in case damage occurred)'.[94]

---

[90]For the sake of accuracy, the tribunal heavily relied on the wording of the applicable FPS clause, which was considered to be autonomous from the customary protection obligation. See: National Grid P.L.C. *v* Argentina (UNCITRAL), Award (3 November 2008) [187-9].

[91]See Sect. 11.2.3.1.

[92]See Sect. 11.2.3.2.

[93]Section 8.3 provides a detailed assessment of this issue.

[94]Helge Elisabeth Zeitler, 'Full Protection and Security' in Stephan Schill (ed), *International Investment Law and Comparative Public Law* (Oxford University Press, New York 2010) 183, 191.

Some authors have dug deeper into the private-public divide and, based on a careful analysis of relevant rules of state responsibility, advanced the proposition that the notion of due diligence is applicable only in cases involving some form of private violence.[95] In respect of public injuries, they say, the FPS standard imposes strict liability. In this line of argument, Eric De Brabandere explains:

> [T]he State's duty to abstain from infringing the *physical* protection and security of aliens, which applies to all State organs and entities the acts of which are attributable to the State, is not tested by reference to the due diligence standard [...] In this case, contrary to the responsibility of States for acts of third parties other than State organs, the wrongful act is *the act that has caused harm*. In case of acts of third parties other than State organs, the internationally wrongful act is the *failure to prevent* the occurrence of the act or the failure to apprehend or punish those responsible for the act, assessed through the due diligence standard. This explains why due diligence is of no relevance in the first case, but is in the latter.[96]

Similarly, Ralf Alexander Lorz suggests that '[under the FPS standard] [t]he level of protection to be expected from the host State may vary, which in turn influences the type of liability incurred by the State'.[97] In this connection, he identifies two possible scenarios. A first scenario refers to cases where harm originates in the actions of state organs:

> With regard to those actions, the host State simply owes abstention from behavior harmful to the investor. The standard of liability that applies in case of a violation is not exactly clear. Considering the comprehensive responsibility standard laid down in Art 4 of the ILC Draft Articles on State Responsibility, though, much speaks in favour of imposing strict liability on the host State for the conduct of its organs.[98]

The second scenario pertains to damages originating in the conduct of private actors, in which case liability is established in terms of due diligence. In Lorz's words:

> [A] host State cannot be held strictly liable for any damage to investments on its territory [...] Strict liability is therefore out of the question with regard to damages caused by private parties. Whereas [...] other standards mainly prohibit certain behaviour by the host State and its organs that would damage the investment, the pivotal thrust of protection and security goes beyond that: it imposes on the host State not only a duty to refrain from certain actions, but an obligation to take active measures for the protection of the investment, namely, to

---

[95]See: Eric De Brabandere, 'Host States' Due Diligence Obligations in International Investment Law' (2014-5) 42 Syracuse J. Int'l L. & Com. 319, 334-5; Ralph Alexander Lorz, 'Protection and Security (Including the NAFTA Approach)' in Marc Bungenberg, Jörn Griebel, Stephan Hobe and August Reinisch (eds), *International Investment Law* (Nomos, Baden-Baden 2015) 764, 776-7.

[96]Eric De Brabandere, 'Host States' Due Diligence Obligations in International Investment Law' (2014-5) 42 Syracuse J. Int'l L. & Com. 319, 333-4.

[97]Ralph Alexander Lorz, 'Protection and Security (Including the NAFTA Approach)' in Marc Bungenberg, Jörn Griebel, Stephan Hobe and August Reinisch (eds), *International Investment Law* (Nomos, Baden-Baden 2015) 764, 776.

[98]Ralph Alexander Lorz, 'Protection and Security (Including the NAFTA Approach)' in Marc Bungenberg, Jörn Griebel, Stephan Hobe and August Reinisch (eds), *International Investment Law* (Nomos, Baden-Baden 2015) 764, 777.

prevent private actors from harming it. This means that a different standard of liability is needed. Tribunals and authors alike usually call this standard due diligence.[99]

These arguments are based on a dubious premise. They in fact assume that FPS is generally applicable in respect of public violence. This study does not share this view. On the contrary, as explained in Chap. 8, it argues that the customary protection obligation refers only to the host state's reaction towards threats originating in an *external* source of risk. When advancing their arguments on the scope of FPS, De Brabandere and Lorz were well aware of arbitral practice restricting the scope of application of the FPS standard to private violence. They however disregarded those tribunals' understanding of the standard without elaborating much on the underlying rationale. Lorz described it as 'a stray position'.[100] For his part, De Brabandere invoked the authority of other tribunals pointing at the opposite direction:

> It is interesting to note in this respect that certain tribunals, such as the Tribunal in *El Paso*, have implied that in case of acts of the State or State organs, the FPS standard does not apply, being limited to acts of third parties only. Other tribunals have however, correctly, posited that the FPS standard applies to both State and third party acts.[101]

De Brabandere's argument of authority is inconclusive. Arbitral practice is inconsistent. For that very same reason, restricting the scope of application of FPS to 'private violence' or other specific risks necessarily implies rejecting authorities adopting more extensive approaches. And so, too, extending the standard to public violence necessarily implies dismissing more restrictive interpretations of FPS. In the end, one will always find authorities on both sides of the spectrum.

The solution proposed by De Brabandere and Lorz is moreover unsound. If the host state is said to assume strict liability in respect of public injuries, and due diligence responsibility for private injuries, it seems artificial to qualify these obligations as elements of a single standard. The risks they refer to are different, and so are the parameters they provide for the assessment of conduct. Simply put, their theory presents an FPS standard which is much like Dr. Jekyll and Mr. Hyde,[102] swinging between strict liability and due diligence liability depending on the circumstances of the case. To be sure, it may be agreed that *due diligence* is not applicable in respect of public injuries (except, perhaps, failures to mitigate collateral damages caused in the course of state action against external threats).[103] But this

---

[99]Ralph Alexander Lorz, 'Protection and Security (Including the NAFTA Approach)' in Marc Bungenberg, Jörn Griebel, Stephan Hobe and August Reinisch (eds), *International Investment Law* (Nomos, Baden-Baden 2015) 764, 778.

[100]Ralph Alexander Lorz, 'Protection and Security (Including the NAFTA Approach)' in Marc Bungenberg, Jörn Griebel, Stephan Hobe and August Reinisch (eds), International Investment Law (Nomos, Baden-Baden 2015) 764, 776.

[101]Eric De Brabandere, 'Host States' Due Diligence Obligations in International Investment Law' (2014-5) 42 Syracuse J. Int'l L. & Com. 319, 334.

[102]Robert Louis Stevenson, *The Strange Case of Dr. Jekyll and Mr. Hyde* (Longmans, Green and Co., London 1901) [first edition: 1886].

[103]On the issue of collateral damages see Sect. 8.3.3.1.

circumstance should not be taken as evidence of the 'duality' of the FPS standard. Rather, it seems to be an indication of the inapplicability of FPS in most cases involving harmful actions which are attributable to the state.

De Brabandere and Lorz make a valuable effort to reconcile arbitral decisions extending the FPS standard to public injuries with authorities describing the standard in terms of due diligence. Their views, however, bring more uncertainty than certainty to the interpretation and application of FPS. As a matter of fact, no arbitral decision has ever expressly held FPS to impose strict liability on the host state.

Quite the contrary, if there is any point of agreement in current arbitral practice, it is that FPS is *not* attached to a standard of strict liability. Explicit statements to this effect appeared already in some of the first investment arbitral awards addressing the FPS standard, such as *AAPL v Sri Lanka* (1990) and *Wena v Egypt* (2000).[104] Later on, in *Ronald Lauder v Czech Republic* (2001), the arbitrators noted that strict liability would require 'a specific provision in the Treaty'.[105] In *Tecmed v Mexico* (2003), the arbitrators stated:

> The Arbitral Tribunal agrees with the Respondent, and with the case law quoted by it, that the guarantee of full protection and security is not absolute and does not impose strict liability upon the State that grants it.[106]

In *Noble Ventures v Romania* (2005), the tribunal explained that FPS 'is not a strict standard'.[107] Similar statements appear in *Saluka v Czech Republic* (2006), *Parkerings v Lithuania* (2007) and *LESI & ASTALDI v Algeria* (2008).[108] In *Suez v Argentina* (2010), the arbitrators underscored that 'the full protection and security standard implies only an obligation of due diligence, as opposed to strict liability'.[109] In *AES v Hungary* (2010), the tribunal noted that 'the [FPS] standard is certainly not one of strict liability'.[110] A similar conclusion was reached in *Frontier Petroleum v Czech Republic* (2010).[111] In *Spyridon Roussalis v Romania* (2011), the arbitral tribunal observed that 'it is generally accepted that the obligation to provide

---

[104]Asian Agricultural Products *v* Sri Lanka, Final Award, ICSID Case No. ARB/87/3 (17 June 1990) [48 and 53]; Wena Hotels Ltd. *v* Egypt, Award, ICSID Case No. ARB/98/4 (8 December 2000) [84].

[105]Ronald Lauder *v* Czech Republic (UNCITRAL), Final Award (3 September 2001) [308].

[106]Tecnicas Medioambientales TECMED S.A. *v* Mexico, Award, ICSID Case No. ARB(AF)/00/2 (29 May 2003) [177].

[107]Noble Ventures v Romania, Award, ICSID Case No. ARB/01/11 (12 October 2005) [164].

[108]Saluka Investments *v* Czech Republic (UNCITRAL), Partial Award (17 March 2006) [484]; Parkerings-Compagniet AS *v* Lithuania, Award, ICSID Case No. ARB/05/8 (11 September 2007) [357]; LESI S.p.A. and ASTALDI S.p.A. *v* Algeria, Sentence, ICSID Case No. ARB/05/3 (12 November 2008) [153].

[109]Suez Sociedad General de Aguas de Barcelona S.A. and Vivendi Universal S.A. *v* Argentina, Decision on Liability, ICSID Case No. ARB/03/19 (30 July 2010) [164].

[110]AES Summit Generation Ltd. and AES-Tisza Erömü Kft. *v* Hungary, Award, ICSID Case No. ARB/07/22 (23 September 2010) [13.3.2].

[111]Frontier Petroleum Ltd. *v* Czech Republic (UNCITRAL), Final Award (12 November 2010) [269-70].

protection and security does not create absolute liability'.[112] To the same effect, in *Toto Costruzioni v Lebanon* (2012), the arbitrators held that 'the obligation of full protection and security is not a strict liability standard'.[113]

In sum, investment arbitral decisions coincide in rejecting the definition of FPS in terms of strict liability. At the same time, however, De Brabandere and Lorz are right in pointing out that the due diligence standard of liability is generally unsuitable for the assessment of public injuries. In the face of a state action targeting foreign nationals, it seems artificial to measure state conduct against the yardstick of due diligence. These circumstances may therefore best be taken as an indication that FPS is not applicable in respect of injuries which are unrelated to a source of risk that is *external* to the host state. They hence confirm the proposition advanced in Chap. 8 above. For the avoidance of doubt, this conclusion does not have the effect of allowing host states to avoid accountability for their own actions. Public injuries can be measured against *other* standards of investment protection, which, in turn, could certainly impose strict liability.

11.2.3.2 The Distinction Between the *Existence* and the *Use* of the Host State's Municipal Legal, Administrative and Judicial System

Recent academic works about the FPS standard have pointed out that the standard encompasses different obligations, which generally correspond to its preventive and repressive functional dimensions, albeit scholars have also introduced some additional categories.[114] A few authors have gone a step further, and have suggested that each of these obligations entails both a duty to *possess* local mechanisms of prevention and redress, and a duty to *use* those mechanisms for the purpose of protecting foreign nationals. Each duty, they say, is subject to a different standard of liability. For the sake of accuracy, it must be noted that these theories have been developed in particular connection with private injuries to aliens, though their followers generally consider the FPS standard to be applicable in respect of public injuries too.

The argument seems to be inspired by historical sources indicating that the host state bears a duty to maintain some 'adequate governmental organization' within its territory. For instance, Ricardo Pisillo-Mazzeschi refers to the obligation 'of *possessing*, on a permanent basis, a legal and administrative apparatus normally able to guarantee respect for the international norm on prevention'.[115] Pisillo-

---

[112]Spyridon Roussalis *v* Romania, Award, ICSID Case No. ARB/06/1 (7 December 2011) [322].

[113]Toto Construzioni Generali S.p.A. *v* Lebanon, Award, ICSID Case No. ARB/07/12 (7 June 2012) [227].

[114]Chapter 10 discusses the FPS standard's functional dimensions in detail.

[115]Riccardo Pisillo-Mazzeschi, 'The Due Diligence Rule and the Nature of the International Responsibility of States' in René Provost (ed), *State Responsibility in International Law* (Ashgate Publishing Co., Burlington VT 2002) 97, 114. See also p. 116.

Mazzeschi considers this obligation to be distinguishable from 'that of *using* such apparatus with the diligence that circumstances require'.[116] According to him, only the latter obligation may be accurately defined in terms of due diligence; in contrast, 'the duty of the State to *possess* a minimum legal and administrative apparatus is not in any way conditioned by the due diligence rule'.[117] Pisillo-Mazzeschi takes the same approach in respect of the *redress* obligation.[118]

In particular connection with the FPS standard, Eric De Brabandere does not only distinguish between the standard of liability applicable to state organs and acts of individuals.[119] Building on Pisillo-Mazzeschi's argument, De Brabandere submits that the duty to protect aliens from private violence comprises three different obligations, which cannot always be properly defined in terms of due diligence:

> The duty to protect the security of aliens and their property from acts of third parties in their territory has been accepted since long in international law. This obligation can be decomposed into three subcomponents: 1) the obligation of States to prevent acts of individuals that may harm the security of aliens and their property, by making use of their administrative and judicial apparatus to that effect; 2) the obligation of States to apprehend and bring to justice those responsible for injuries caused to aliens by making use of their administrative and judicial apparatus to that effect, and 3) the obligation of States to possess and make available to aliens a judicial and administrative system capable of preventing acts, and of punishing and apprehending those responsible for the acts.[120]

De Brabandere argues that the third of these obligations is not an obligation of diligence, thus implicating that responsibility is established irrespective of whether there was negligent or diligent conduct on the part of the host state:

> This distinction between these three obligations is important, since practice shows that the third obligation – States' obligation *to possess and make available a judicial and administrative system* – is tested not by reference to the due diligence standard, while States' other obligations have been assessed by reference to the due diligence standard.[121]

---

[116]Riccardo Pisillo-Mazzeschi, 'The Due Diligence Rule and the Nature of the International Responsibility of States' in René Provost (ed), *State Responsibility in International Law* (Ashgate Publishing Co., Burlington VT 2002) 97, 114. See also p. 116.

[117]Riccardo Pisillo-Mazzeschi, 'The Due Diligence Rule and the Nature of the International Responsibility of States' in René Provost (ed), *State Responsibility in International Law* (Ashgate Publishing Co., Burlington VT 2002) 97, 115.

[118]Riccardo Pisillo-Mazzeschi, 'The Due Diligence Rule and the Nature of the International Responsibility of States' in René Provost (ed), *State Responsibility in International Law* (Ashgate Publishing Co., Burlington VT 2002) 97, 116-8. For a more detailed presentation of the argument see: Riccardo Pisillo Mazzeschi, *"Due diligence" e responsabilità internazionale degli stati* (Giuffrè Editore, Milan 1989) 231-5. Cf. also: Helge Elisabeth Zeitler, 'The Guarantee of Full Protection and Security in Investment Treaties Regarding Harm Caused by Private Actors' (2005) 3 SIAR 1, 12 (quoting Pisillo-Mazzeschi in this connection).

[119]On De Brabandere's distinction between public and private injuries see Sect. 11.2.3.1.

[120]Eric De Brabandere, 'Host States' Due Diligence Obligations in International Investment Law' (2014-5) 42 Syracuse J. Int'l L. & Com. 319, 324-5.

[121]Eric De Brabandere, 'Host States' Due Diligence Obligations in International Investment Law' (2014-5) 42 Syracuse J. Int'l L. & Com. 319, 325. See also pp. 341-5.

In the same line of argument, Finnur Magnússon contends that FPS requires the host state 'to establish and maintain a structure, e.g. a police force, judiciary, penal system, etc.'.[122] According to him, this element of the standard 'entails an *obligation of result* due to the fact that the structure has to be in place'.[123] Magnússon further explains that '[a]nother part of the obligation is to use the structure to fulfill the obligation owed to the investor'.[124] This second duty, he says, 'entails an *obligation of conduct*, namely the state has to use its best efforts to prevent, apprehend and punish the parties who intend to inflict or have inflicted damage to the investment'.[125]

In plain terms, these authors consider that host states are strictly liable for the *existence* and *availability* of administrative and judicial mechanisms capable of preventing and redressing injuries to aliens. The *use* of those mechanisms, in turn, is said to constitute a conceptually distinct obligation, which measures state conduct against the yardstick of *due diligence*. The present section analyzes this argument in respect of both the prevention and the redress of private injuries to aliens. In this connection, it submits that these dogmatic utterances are unfounded and unsound. The notions of FPS and due diligence cannot be detached from each other. The FPS standard does not impose, under any circumstance, a strict liability on the host state.

The Prevention of Private Injuries to Aliens

Let us examine first the prevention of harm. Following the views of De Brabandere and Pisillo-Mazzeschi, states are pledged under customary international law to provide a system *capable* of averting private injuries to aliens; moreover, both authors seem to consider states to be strictly liable for the absence of such system.[126] These views find virtually no support in contemporary arbitral practice. De Brabandere recognizes that this obligation, as such, 'has not been addressed by investment tribunals'.[127] Historical sources do not support the theory either. Authors

---

[122]Finnur Magnússon, *Full Protection and Security in International Law* (University of Vienna, Vienna 2012) 174.

[123]Finnur Magnússon, *Full Protection and Security in International Law* (University of Vienna, Vienna 2012) 174.

[124]Finnur Magnússon, *Full Protection and Security in International Law* (University of Vienna, Vienna 2012) 174.

[125]Finnur Magnússon, *Full Protection and Security in International Law* (University of Vienna, Vienna 2012) 174.

[126]Eric De Brabandere, 'Host States' Due Diligence Obligations in International Investment Law' (2014-5) 42 Syracuse J. Int'l L. & Com. 319, 324-5 and 360; Riccardo Pisillo Mazzeschi, *"Due diligence" e responsabilità internazionale degli stati* (Giuffrè Editore, Milan 1989) 231-5; Riccardo Pisillo-Mazzeschi, 'The Due Diligence Rule and the Nature of the International Responsibility of States' in René Provost (ed), *State Responsibility in International Law* (Ashgate Publishing Co., Burlington VT 2002) 97, 114-6.

[127]Eric De Brabandere, 'Host States' Due Diligence Obligations in International Investment Law' (2014-5) 42 Syracuse J. Int'l L. & Com. 319, 342.

following this approach usually invoke the authority of early-twentieth century arbitral commissions, as well as Article 4 of the *Harvard Draft* of 1929.[128] Draft Article 4 read as follows:

> A state has a duty to maintain a governmental organization adequate, under normal conditions, for the performance of its obligations under international law and treaties. In the event of emergencies temporarily disarranging its governmental organization, a state has a duty to use the means at its disposal for the performance of these obligations.[129]

In his comments to this provision, Edwin Borchard explained that '[Draft Article 4] is a statement of the general duty of every state to maintain a minimum amount of governmental organization'.[130] He further underscored the link between this general directive and the customary protection obligation, noting that '[t]he performance of this primary duty is of importance to other states because of the increased likelihood of injury they may sustain as a consequence of injuries to their nationals'.[131] At first sight, Borchard hence appears to be in line with De Brabandere and Pisillo-Mazzeschi. From the outset, he even seems to share the view that this duty is not an obligation of diligence:

> The term "means at its disposal" is employed because it is desired to emphasize the instrumentalities of government that may be available for use. The term is thus different from the term "due diligence" used in Article 10 [prevention of injuries to aliens], which has reference to the efficiency and diligence with which the instrumentalities of government are employed.[132]

These statements should be considered with caution. While it is undeniable that the *Harvard Draft* recognized a duty to establish some degree of governmental organization, it did not—at least expressly—held the state to be strictly liable for the existence of such organization. The qualification of the duty with phrases such as 'normal conditions' and the explicit reference to events of emergency confirm this observation. Moreover, the distinction between 'due diligence' and 'means at its disposal' in Borchard's commentary, rather than creating a strict liability, had the ultimate effect of lowering the standard applicable in case of emergency. Borchard was simply emphasizing that, in such scenarios, the state is not required to anything more than using the (limited) means *available* to it. In other words, in the context of

---

[128]See, for example: Riccardo Pisillo Mazzeschi, *"Due diligence" e responsabilità internazionale degli stati* (Giuffrè Editore, Milan 1989) 231-4 (quoting the *Harvard Draft* at p. 234).

[129]'Responsibility of States for Damage done in their Territory to the Person and Property of Foreigners' (1929) 23 AJIL 131, 133 art. 4.

[130]Edwin Borchard, 'The Law of Responsibility of States for Damage Done in Their Territory to the Person or Property of Foreigners. Comments to the Draft Convention' (April 1929) 23 AJIL 140, 146 art. 4.

[131]Edwin Borchard, 'The Law of Responsibility of States for Damage Done in Their Territory to the Person or Property of Foreigners. Comments to the Draft Convention' (April 1929) 23 AJIL 140, 146 art. 4.

[132]Edwin Borchard, 'The Law of Responsibility of States for Damage Done in Their Territory to the Person or Property of Foreigners. Comments to the Draft Convention' (April 1929) 23 AJIL 140, 146 art. 4.

an emergency, the host state's diligence is determined in view of the means it *actually* disposes of, and not of the means a state *should*—ideally or hypothetically—have at its disposal.

A review of the sources quoted in Borchard's commentary suggests that Draft Article 4 was intended to prevent states from alleging the inadequacy of their own governmental organization, their own municipal law or their own wrongs as a means to avoid responsibility. Borchard himself noted that '[t]he failure to perform the duty, under normal conditions, may make impossible for a state to avoid responsibility in certain cases where responsibility otherwise would not have existed'.[133] It is therefore little surprising that some of the sources quoted in this connection have been invoked, too, in support of maxims such as *nullus commodum capere de sua injuria propria*, i.e. '[n]o one should be allowed to reap advantages from his own wrong'.[134]

This understanding of the *Harvard Draft* and other relevant sources is by no means a novelty in international legal literature. Back in 1977, in his study on the concept of due diligence in international law, Pierre Marie Dupuy advanced the proposition that an obligation of due diligence has two constitutive elements. The first element is the existence of an 'internationally indispensable municipal legal order' (*droit interne internationalement indispensable*) and the corresponding 'minimal administrative apparatus' (*appareil administrative minimum*) necessary for executing international obligations.[135] According to Dupuy, this first element has the practical implication that states cannot rely on their own domestic law and governmental organization to escape responsibility.[136] At the same time, he argued that 'from a material standpoint' there is a duty to create such a system, and quoted Article 4 of the *Harvard Draft* in support of his opinion.[137] Dupuy's second element, in turn, pertains to the actual implementation of the system and the use of an

---

[133]Edwin Borchard, 'The Law of Responsibility of States for Damage Done in Their Territory to the Person or Property of Foreigners. Comments to the Draft Convention' (April 1929) 23 AJIL 140, 146 art. 4.

[134]Bin Cheng, *General Principles of Law as Applied by International Courts and Tribunals* (Cambridge University Press, New York 2006) 150 [first edition: 1953]. Cheng quotes in this connection the *Montijo* case (at p. 149), which is also referenced in Borchard's commentary to Draft Article 4. See: Edwin Borchard, 'The Law of Responsibility of States for Damage Done in Their Territory to the Person or Property of Foreigners. Comments to the Draft Convention' (April 1929) 23 AJIL 140, 146-7 art. 4. Pisillo Mazzeschi also relies on this case. See: Riccardo Pisillo Mazzeschi, *"Due diligence" e responsabilità internazionale degli stati* (Giuffrè Editore, Milan 1989) 232. Section 13.3.3.3 discusses the *Montijo* award in detail.

[135]Pierre Marie Dupuy, 'La diligence due dans le droit international et la responsabilité' in OECD, *Aspects juridiques de la pollution transfrontière* (OECD, Paris 1977) 396, 400-1.

[136]Pierre Marie Dupuy, 'La diligence due dans le droit international et la responsabilité' in OECD, *Aspects juridiques de la pollution transfrontière* (OECD, Paris 1977) 396, 401.

[137]Pierre Marie Dupuy, 'La diligence due dans le droit international et la responsabilité' in OECD, *Aspects juridiques de la pollution transfrontière* (OECD, Paris 1977) 396, 401 ("D'un point de vue matériel, il est obligé de se doter d'un appareil administratif minimum, nécessaire à l'exécution de ses obligations").

appropriate degree of diligence, adjusted to the circumstances of each particular case.[138] Dupuy held both elements to be part of a single whole.[139]

Most of Dupuy's observations are correct. Still, his choice of words when addressing the first element (and, particularly, the idea of a 'material' duty or obligation to create a legal and administrative system) is somewhat misleading. Dupuy relied in this connection on the works of Heinrich Triepel (1899). A look into Triepel's argument confirms that the first of Dupy's 'elements' should not be considered as an international obligation of its own. Following Triepel, the fulfillment of international obligations usually requires the existence of some municipal legal provisions or administrative structures without which states will be unable to comply with their international commitments. But such domestic norms and structures are not themselves the *object* of an international obligation. In this vein, Triepel introduced the notion of 'internationally indispensable [municipal] law' (*international unentbehrliches Recht*):

> The character of the internationally indispensable [municipal] law may be perhaps portrayed through an [example] I take from transactions among private individuals. Someone who assumes a contractual obligation to deliver some goods that he does not yet possess is not "obliged" to acquire them. He [surely] needs to do so, if he has the intention to fulfill his obligation. But this obligation consists in something different, namely, in the delivery of the goods as such. No court in the world would accept a claim requesting that the debtor be sentenced to acquire the goods. The situation is similar in respect of the state in a given case. International law does not oblige [the state], for example, to enact legislation allowing it – in order to safeguard its neutrality – to prevent warships from being equipped in or departing from its harbours. If [the state] has failed to comply with its prevention obligation, it cannot invoke before [foreign powers] the shortcomings of necessary legislation. For, if there is any uncontested principle of international law, it is that no state can refuse compliance with or excuse the breach of its international obligations on the [sole] ground that the acts necessary to this effect are not permitted by its [own] legislation.[140]

---

[138]Pierre Marie Dupuy, 'La diligence due dans le droit international et la responsabilité' in OECD, *Aspects juridiques de la pollution transfrontière* (OECD, Paris 1977) 396, 402.

[139]Pierre Marie Dupuy, 'La diligence due dans le droit international et la responsabilité' in OECD, *Aspects juridiques de la pollution transfrontière* (OECD, Paris 1977) 396, 401-2.

[140]Author's translation. The original German text reads: "Der Charakter des international unentbehrlichen Rechts wird vielleicht durch ein Bild ins Klare gestellt, das ich dem Rechtsverkehre der Privaten entnehme. Wer in einem Vertrage die Lieferung von Waaren übernimmt, der ist, wenn er diese nicht besitz, nicht etwa "verpflichtet", sie anzuschaffen. Es ist genöthigt, das zu thun, wenn er seine Pflicht erfüllen will; aber diese Pflicht besteht in etwas anderem, nämlich in der Uebergabe der Waaren selbst. Kein Gericht der Welt würde einem Klageantrage entsprechen, der den Lieferungspflichtigen zur Anschaffung verurtheilt wissen wollte; dieser kann sich nur nicht zur Vertheidigung gegen die Leistungsanklage darauf berufen, dass er die Waare nicht besitze. Ahnlich verhält es sich im angenommenen Falle mit dem Staate. Er wird durch das Völkerrecht nicht verpflichtet, etwa Polizeigesetze zu erlassen, die es ihm zur Wahrung seiner Neutralität ermöglichen, Ausrüstung und Abfahrt von Kreuzern in seinen Häfen zu hindern; hat er aber einmal dieser seiner Pflicht zur Verhinderung nicht genügt, so kann er dem Auslande gegenüber nicht den Einwand erheben, es gebreche ihm an dem dazu erforderlichen Landesgesetze. Denn – wenn es einen unbestrittenen Satz des internationalen Rechtes giebt, so ist der, dass kein Staat die Erfüllung völkerrechtlicher Pflichten deshalb verweigern oder die Nichterfüllung damit entschuldigen könne, dass ihm seine Gesetzgebung die Vornahme der erforderlichen Akte nicht erlaube." Heinrich Triepel, *Völkerrecht und Landesrecht* (Verlag von C. L. Hirschfeld, Leipzig 1899) 302-3.

Triepel quoted at this point Sir James F. Stephen's comments on the *Alabama* claims. Stephen, a well-known English criminal lawyer, was particularly referring to the British Foreign Enlistment Act, which the U.S. Government decried as incapable of preventing British harbors from being used to support the Confederate Army. In his analysis of the case, Stephen stated:

> As for the Foreign Enlistment Act, it was obvious enough that it had nothing to do with the question between the two nations. The American complaint was equally well or ill founded whether the Foreign Enlistment Act did or did not enable the government to prevent British harbours from being turned into naval stations for the Confederates. If it did, their complaint was that it was not used. If it did not, their complaint was that it was ineffectual. If your fire burns my house it matters little whether you have a bad fire-engine, or having a good one neglect to use it. My complaint is that your fire burns my house. The efficiency of your fire engine is a matter not for me but for you.[141]

International law does not usually require states to enact specific pieces of legislation. Express obligations to do so are extremely rare in practice, and cannot be easily derived from broad legal directives, such as the FPS standard. In an article published in 1906, Dionisio Anzilotti presented the underlying principle in clear and compelling terms:

> Les plus souvent [. . .] le droit international n'impose pas à l'État les règles de droit interne qu'il doit ou ne doit pas avoir; le droit international se borne à déterminer la conduite que l'État doit tenir en telles ou telles circonstances, en lui laissant toute liberté de se donner les lois qu'il juge propres à assurer cette conduite. Dans ces cas, la loi, en soi, est *indifférente* au point de vue de droit international: elle ne saurait donc en constituer une violation, bien qu'elle puisse déterminer une activité de l'État contraire au droit international. *Le fait illicite n'est pas la loi mais l'action qui dérivera de la loi*; seule, cette action pourra engager la responsabilité internationale de l'État.[142]

The existence of some domestic legal, administrative and judicial system is necessary for the state to be in a position to exercise diligence in the protection of aliens.[143] But, as such, it is not the object of the security obligation, and the host state is certainly not strictly liable for its absence. It is therefore understandable that, while some historical sources use a positive language indicating that states have a 'duty' to ensure the existence of some governmental organization, none of them expressly recognizes a separate obligation which imposes a strict liability on the host state.[144]

---

[141] James Fitzjames Stephen, *A History of the Criminal Law of England* (Volume 3: Macmillan & Co., London 1883) 261. Also discussed in: Heinrich Triepel, *Völkerrecht und Landesrecht* (Verlag von C. L. Hirschfeld, Leipzig 1899) 304.

[142] Emphasis in the original. Dionisio Anzilotti, 'La responsabilité internationale des états a raison des dommages soufferts par des étrangers' (1906) 13 RGDIP 285, 294.

[143] For a similar view see: Alf Ross, *A Textbook of International Law. General Part* (Longmans, Green and Co., London 1947) 265 (specifically referring to the need for 'penal rules' allowing the prevention and prosecution of criminal offences against foreigners, and qualifying their existence as a 'requisite' or 'requirement').

[144] Consider, for example, the cases referred to by Pisillo Mazzeschi in this connection. See: Riccardo Pisillo Mazzeschi, *"Due diligence" e responsabilità internazionale degli stati* (Giuffrè Editore, Milan 1989) 231-4.

To be sure, the host state cannot justify a failure to grant protection and security on its own failure to create a proper administrative and judicial system. The reason, however, is not the existence of a separate obligation to create such system, but the well-known principle that no state can avail itself of its own domestic law as a means to escape international responsibility.[145] Investment arbitral tribunals have underscored that '[under the FPS standard, the host state] shall take all measures necessary to ensure the full enjoyment of protection and security of its investment *and should not be permitted to invoke its own legislation to detract from any such obligation*'.[146]

The dogmatic distinction between the *existence* of some governmental organization and its *setting in motion* could moreover become moot in practice. If governmental organization does not exist at all (i.e. if it is absolutely absent in the whole of the host state's territory), the question arises as to whether the criteria of statehood set forth in the Montevideo Convention of 1933 are fulfilled in the first place.[147] In the more likely case that governmental organization *exists*, but is not present in some areas of the state's territory for reasons *not attributable* to the host state (e.g. civil war or natural catastrophes causing a partial loss of territorial control), the state could, in all probability, successfully invoke some circumstance precluding the wrongfulness of its failure to protect (e.g. force majeure).

Finally, if governmental organization exists but is utterly defective as a result of circumstances which are attributable to or controllable by the host state (e.g. applicable municipal legislation), the shortcomings of governmental organization may be taken as an indication of a want of diligence in the prevention of injuries to aliens. Such absence of diligence, however, cannot be assessed in the abstract. Rather, it must be considered in view of a specific risk materializing in a particular injury. This is consistent with the idea that a breach of the prevention obligation is contingent upon the occurrence of the harmful event.[148]

There is an additional reason for rejecting this intermediate approach. If the theory were to have any practical consequence, states could be considered

---

[145]For a similar argument see: Paul Schoen, *Die völkerrechtliche Haftung der Staaten aus unerlaubten Handlungen* (J. U. Kern's Verlag, Breslau 1917) 60 (observing that the state cannot invoke its own municipal law to justify an omission in the protection of aliens).

[146]Emphasis added. American Manufacturing & Trading Inc. *v* Zaire, Award, ICSID Case No. ARB 93/1 (21 February 1997) [6.05]. Other arbitral decisions have quoted this passage in their assessment of FPS claims: Wena Hotels Ltd. *v* Egypt, Award, ICSID Case No. ARB/98/4 (8 December 2000) [84] (quoting *AMT v Zaire*); Saluka Investments *v* Czech Republic (UNCITRAL), Partial Award (17 March 2006) [484] (making reference to both *AMT v Zaire* and *Wena v Egypt*).

[147]Convention on the Rights and Duties of States (adopted 26 December 1933, entered into force 26 December 1934) 165 LNTS 19, 25 art. 1 ("The State as a person of international law should possess the following qualifications: (a) a permanent population; (b) a defined territory; (c) government; and (d) capacity to enter into relations with other states"). On the notion of 'government', as used in the Montevideo Convention, see generally: Malcolm Shaw, *International Law* (Cambridge University Press, New York 2003) 180-1.

[148]See Sect. 11.2.2.2.

internationally responsible for their defective governmental organization, irrespective of the actual occurrence of an injurious event or any specific want of diligence. In practice, enforcing this 'duty' would imply scrutinizing the manner how each state is organized. Such scrutiny would entail an intense interference in the host state's sovereignty. Even if the level of governmental organization required by international law is said to be a minimum, such 'minimum' will be hard to determine *before* the system's defects have materialized in some form of harm. Adjudicators would therefore end up deciding whether a state is 'duly' organized in the abstract. This effect risks at opening the door to significant incongruences with existent international law. As stated by the ICJ in its Advisory Opinion on the *Western Sahara* (1975), '[n]o rule of international law, in the view of the Court, requires the structure of a State to follow any particular pattern, as is evident from the diversity of the forms of State found in the world today'.[149]

Recent arbitral practice has underscored that, in the application of investment protection standards, some deference should be given to the sovereign public policy choices made by the host state in the pursuit of the general interest; some arbitral tribunals have gone as far as to recognize that states enjoy a broad 'margin of appreciation' in some sensitive areas.[150]

The spirit of these developments would be seriously compromised if investment protection standards were interpreted as to allow the scrutiny of the most elementary sovereign choices, such as those pertaining to the state's governmental organization, in the abstract. Only when an injury has occurred may the defective organization of the state be considered as one of many elements relevant for determining whether authorities were negligent in the prevention of harm, thus engaging the host state's responsibility under the FPS standard.

There is, in sum, no compelling reason for conceptually dividing the prevention obligation into two separate duties subject to different standards of liability and, by so doing, departing from a consistent line of cases indicating that the FPS standard does not create a strict liability. This theory does not only misconstrue relevant historical sources. It further has the effect of undermining state sovereignty to a degree which, in all probability, no state could reasonably foresee when agreeing to extend its protection to foreign citizens within its territory.

---

[149]*Western Sahara (Advisory Opinion)* [1975] ICJ Rep 12, 43-4 [94]. For a similar argument (in specific connection with the notion of due diligence in international law) see: Pavlos Alextrandou Zannas, *La responsabilité internationale des Etats pour les actes de négligence* (Ganguin & Laubscher, Geneva 1952) 84-5.

[150]For a express recognition of the host state's 'margin of appreciation' see: Philip Morris Brands Sàrl, Philip Morris Products S.A. and Abal Hermanos S.A. *v* Uruguay, Award, ICSID Case No. ARB/10/7 (8 July 2016) [399] (in particular connection with the FET standard). See also: AES Summit Generation Ltd. and AES-Tisza Erömü Kft. *v* Hungary, Award, ICSID Case No. ARB/07/22 (23 September 2010) [13.3.2] (recognizing the host state's margin of discretion in the context of an FPS claim pertaining to legal security).

The Redress of Private Injuries to Aliens

As De Brabandere rightly points out, some investment tribunals have considered that the FPS standard encompasses a duty to make the municipal judicial system available to foreign investors.[151] This element, he says, 'does not entail any due diligence obligation'.[152] De Brabandere further emphasizes that 'the due diligence standard here is inapplicable'.[153] Other authors have also underscored the idea that the existence and availability of the domestic judicial system constitutes a separate obligation, which they characterize as 'objective in nature' and, thus, as an 'obligation of result'.[154] In support of this argument, De Brabandere quotes the decisions issued in *Frontier Petroleum v Czech Republic, Parkerings v Lithuania, Ronald Lauder v Czech Republic* and *Saluka Investments v Czech Republic*.[155]

These awards, however, do not fully support his views. As a matter of fact, nothing in these decisions indicates that the availability of local redress mechanisms constitutes an autonomous obligation, separate and distinguishable from the diligence with which those mechanisms operate. Moreover, the tribunals in question did not explicitly measure the host state's conduct against a standard of strict liability or otherwise different from due diligence. Quite the contrary, most of them were explicit in rejecting such approach. Let us consider first the award issued in *Frontier Petroleum v Czech Republic* (2010), in which De Brabandere most heavily relies. The *Frontier* tribunal stated:

> In this Tribunal's view, where the acts of the host state's judiciary are at stake, 'full protection and security means that the state is under an obligation to make a functioning system of courts and legal remedies available to the investor.[156]

It is accurate to say that the arbitrators recognized an obligation to make the judicial system available to foreign investors. Nonetheless, they did not—neither

---

[151]Eric De Brabandere, 'Host States' Due Diligence Obligations in International Investment Law' (2014-5) 42 Syracuse J. Int'l L. & Com. 319, 341 *et seq.*

[152]Eric De Brabandere, 'Host States' Due Diligence Obligations in International Investment Law' (2014-5) 42 Syracuse J. Int'l L. & Com. 319, 342.

[153]Eric De Brabandere, 'Host States' Due Diligence Obligations in International Investment Law' (2014-5) 42 Syracuse J. Int'l L. & Com. 319, 342.

[154]Finnur Magnússon, *Full Protection and Security in International Law* (University of Vienna, Vienna 2012) 174. See also: Riccardo Pisillo Mazzeschi, *"Due diligence" e responsabilità internazionale degli stati* (Giuffrè Editore, Milan 1989) 239; Riccardo Pisillo-Mazzeschi, 'The Due Diligence Rule and the Nature of the International Responsibility of States' in René Provost (ed), *State Responsibility in International Law* (Ashgate Publishing Co., Burlington VT 2002) 97, 116-7.

[155]Eric De Brabandere, 'Host States' Due Diligence Obligations in International Investment Law' (2014-5) 42 Syracuse J. Int'l L. & Com. 319, 341-5.

[156]Frontier Petroleum Ltd. *v* Czech Republic (UNCITRAL), Final Award (12 November 2010) [273]. De Brabandere heavily relies on this decision in support of his argument that, under the FPS standard, the state is strictly liable for granting foreign investors access to domestic courts. See: Eric De Brabandere, 'Host States' Due Diligence Obligations in International Investment Law' (2014-5) 42 Syracuse J. Int'l L. & Com. 319, 342 and 344.

expressly nor impliedly—endorsed the classification of this element of the security obligation as an obligation of result or as a strict liability. Quite the opposite, the tribunal made the following general remark about the FPS standard:

> There is broad agreement that the obligation to provide protection and security does not create an obligation of result or absolute liability [...] Rather, as noted by Claimant, the standard is one of due diligence.[157]

This observation was unqualified. The arbitrators made no exception for any particular element of the FPS standard. Hence, the *Frontier* award does not actually support the view that FPS entails an 'obligation of result' regarding the availability of local redress mechanisms.[158]

Moving on to the second case, in *Parkerings v Lithuania* the arbitrators noted that, in virtue of the FPS standard, the host state shall 'keep its judicial system available' to foreign investors and ensure that claims are 'properly examined in accordance with domestic and international law by an impartial and fair court'.[159] This statement must be read in context. In the *Parkerings* case, the investor alleged that the 'passivity' of the respondent state in respect of a breach of contract committed by the City of Vilnius amounted to a violation of the FPS clause set forth in the Norway-Lithuania BIT.[160]

The tribunal began by clarifying that 'the investment Treaty created no duty of due diligence on the part of the Respondent to intervene in the dispute between the Claimant and the City of Vilnius over the nature of their legal relationships'.[161] This remark does not call into question the qualification of FPS as a duty of due diligence. It simply indicates that FPS does not go as far as to require the host state to take sides with a foreign investor by actively intervening in a contractual dispute. The arbitrators additionally noted that Lithuania had fulfilled its duties under the applicable FPS clause by providing an opportunity of redress through the local judiciary, and properly examining those claims:

> The Claimant had the opportunity to raise the violation of the Agreement and to ask for reparation before the Lithuanian Courts. The Claimant failed to show that it was prevented to do so. As a result, the Arbitral Tribunal considers that the Respondent did not violate its obligation of full protection and security.[162]

---

[157]Frontier Petroleum Ltd. *v* Czech Republic (UNCITRAL), Final Award (12 November 2010) [269-70].

[158]Section 13.3.3.3 considers the application of the standard of due diligence in the *Frontier* award in more detail.

[159]Parkerings-Compagniet AS *v* Lithuania, Award, ICSID Case No. ARB/05/8 (11 September 2007) [360].

[160]Parkerings-Compagniet AS *v* Lithuania, Award, ICSID Case No. ARB/05/8 (11 September 2007) [359].

[161]Parkerings-Compagniet AS *v* Lithuania, Award, ICSID Case No. ARB/05/8 (11 September 2007) [359].

[162]Parkerings-Compagniet AS *v* Lithuania, Award, ICSID Case No. ARB/05/8 (11 September 2007) [361].

In any case, the issue was considered briefly since, in the arbitral tribunal's view, there was 'no evidence – not even an allegation – that the Respondent violated this obligation'.[163] One may speculate whether, had Lithuania failed to provide access to justice, the *Parkerings* tribunal would have held the respondent state strictly liable for the unredressed injury. The fact is, however, that the arbitrators did not reach such conclusion. What is more, in their analysis of another FPS claim, the arbitrators quoted *Tecmed v Mexico* to the effect that the FPS standard is neither 'absolute' nor imposes 'strict liability' on the host state.[164] The tribunal recognized no exception to this principle.

Similarly, in *Ronald Lauder v Czech Republic* the tribunal concluded that the FPS standard imposes upon the host state an obligation 'to keep its judicial available' to foreign investors.[165] It further emphasized that FPS does not establish 'a duty of due diligence on the Part of the Czech Republic to intervene [in a private dispute]'.[166] Rather, the arbitrators said, the state discharges its protection obligation by providing a justice system capable of giving proper consideration to the claims.[167] The *Ronald Lauder* tribunal did not consider responsibility for the availability of means of redress to be absolute. The award was clear as to the applicable standard of liability:

> The Arbitral Tribunal is of the opinion that the Treaty obliges the Parties to exercise such due diligence in the protection of foreign investment as reasonable under the circumstances. However, the Treaty does not oblige the Parties to protect foreign investment against any possible loss of value caused by persons whose acts could not be attributed to the State. Such protection would indeed amount to strict liability, which can not be imposed to a State absent any specific provision in the Treaty.[168]

Finally, in *Saluka Investments v Czech Republic*, police authorities had frozen the investor's shares in IPB, a Czech bank.[169] The Supreme Public Prosecutor's Office upheld the freezing orders.[170] The investor alleged that these measures constituted a breach of the FPS clause set forth in the Czech Republic-Netherlands BIT.[171] The

---

[163]Parkerings-Compagniet AS *v* Lithuania, Award, ICSID Case No. ARB/05/8 (11 September 2007) [360].

[164]Parkerings-Compagniet AS *v* Lithuania, Award, ICSID Case No. ARB/05/8 (11 September 2007) [357]. This statement appears in the very same page where the tribunal referred to the availability of the local judicial system (p. 76). See also: Tecnicas Medioambientales TECMED S.A. *v* Mexico, Award, ICSID Case No. ARB(AF)/00/2 (29 May 2003) [177].

[165]Ronald Lauder *v* Czech Republic (UNCITRAL), Final Award (3 September 2001) [314].

[166]Ronald Lauder *v* Czech Republic (UNCITRAL), Final Award (3 September 2001) [314].

[167]Ronald Lauder *v* Czech Republic (UNCITRAL), Final Award (3 September 2001) [314]. The formulation of these duties in the *Ronald Lauder* award is almost identical to the wording used years later by the *Parkerings* tribunal.

[168]Ronald Lauder *v* Czech Republic (UNCITRAL), Final Award (3 September 2001) [308].

[169]Saluka Investments *v* Czech Republic (UNCITRAL), Partial Award (17 March 2006) [491].

[170]It should be noted that Saluka had a partial success before the Supreme Public Prosecutor's Office. Still, the Office upheld the freezing of the investor's shares in IPB. Saluka then filed an action with the Constitutional Court. See: Saluka Investments *v* Czech Republic (UNCITRAL), Partial Award (17 March 2006) [492].

[171]Saluka Investments *v* Czech Republic (UNCITRAL), Partial Award (17 March 2006) [485 and 491-3].

Claimant further considered that the decision upholding the freezing orders amounted to a procedural denial of justice.[172] These allegations were unsuccessful. The arbitrators made no statement to the effect that FPS establishes a separate obligation to make a system of justice available to foreign investors. They further avoided taking a stance as to the applicability of the FPS standard to this factual scenario:

> Even assuming that the freezing of the IPB shares held by Saluka may be State conduct within the scope of the "full security and protection" clause, the Tribunal, *without deciding that question*, fails to see a procedural denial of justice that would violate the Czech Republic's Treaty obligations. The absence of further appeals against decisions of the last instance for appeals is not *per se* a denial of justice [. . .] Nothing therefore emerges from the facts before the Tribunal that would amount to a manifest lack of due process leading to a breach of international justice and to a failure of the Czech Republic to provide "full protection and security" to Saluka's investment.[173]

It should be additionally noted that, before considering this specific FPS claim, the *Saluka* tribunal made some general remarks on the meaning of FPS in international investment law,[174] and was explicit in stating that '[t]he standard does not imply strict liability of the host State'.[175] The *Saluka* tribunal neither qualified this observation, nor mentioned any exception concerning specific elements of the standard.

In sum, these awards do not support the argument that the FPS standard encompasses an independent duty to make the local judicial system available to foreign investors. Much less do they support the definition of such obligation in terms other than due diligence. None of them contains an express statement to this effect, and they all seem rather to reject the possibility of measuring state conduct against a standard of strict liability.

The distinction between the *existence* and the *setting in motion* of local redress mechanisms as separate elements of FPS additionally poses major practical difficulties. This theory opens the door to significant overlaps between FPS, the traditional notion of denial of justice and other standards of investment protection, such as the FET standard. Authors following these views are well aware of this effect. Thus, De Brabandere observes that the obligation to grant access to justice 'has been considered more broadly to form part of the IMS or the FET standard, especially when seen in relation to the obligations relating to due process and the prohibition of denial of justice'.[176]

It must be conceded that there might be cases in which the host state's conduct could simultaneously constitute a denial of justice, a breach of the FET standard and

---

[172]Saluka Investments *v* Czech Republic (UNCITRAL), Partial Award (17 March 2006) [492].

[173]Emphasis added. Saluka Investments *v* Czech Republic (UNCITRAL), Partial Award (17 March 2006) [493].

[174]Saluka Investments *v* Czech Republic (UNCITRAL), Partial Award (17 March 2006) [483-4].

[175]Saluka Investments *v* Czech Republic (UNCITRAL), Partial Award (17 March 2006) [484].

[176]Eric De Brabandere, 'Host States' Due Diligence Obligations in International Investment Law' (2014-5) 42 Syracuse J. Int'l L. & Com. 319, 342.

a violation of FPS. The conditions for a finding of liability, however, deeply vary from one obligation to another. A breach of FPS never results from the mere absence of adequate local redress mechanisms, but from the host state's lack of diligence in providing a reasonable opportunity of redress. To be certain, the absence or unavailability of agencies of local redress *could* indicate that the host state has not displayed the diligence required under the redress obligation. In the likely case that an unreasonable restriction of access constitutes a violation of another international obligation (e.g. a denial of justice), it seems clear that such international wrong cannot exclude or excuse a breach of FPS; *nullus commodum capere de sua injuria propria*.[177] Even in the absence of an additional international delinquency, the state should not be allowed to justify its want of diligence and escape responsibility by merely invoking its own municipal legislation or the defects of its own governmental organization.[178]

In any case, a breach of FPS must be established on a separate, autonomous basis. The redress obligation embedded within the FPS standard consists in making a diligent effort to grant aliens an opportunity of redress. As noted by Arbitrator Max Huber in the *Case of British Property in Spanish Morocco* (1925):

> La responsabilité de l'État peut être engage [. . .] non seulement par un manqué de vigilance dans la prévention des actes dommageables, *mais aussi par un manque de diligence dans la poursuite pénale des fauteurs, ainsi que dans l'application des sanctions civiles voulues.*[179]

The redress obligation is, just like the prevention obligation, an obligation of diligence. The FPS standard does not entail a separate, absolute guarantee of access to the local judiciary. This conclusion has important practical implications. Some of the most usual areas of application of the FPS standard are situations in which the state apparatus faces some external threat, or local authorities lack absolute control over a given area. Thus, for example, the state cannot be held strictly liable for not possessing an 'adequate' judicial and administrative system in areas ravaged by or recovering from civil disorders or natural catastrophes. Even if such conditions do not amount to a circumstance excluding the wrongfulness of the host state's omissions (e.g. force majeure), in the analysis of an FPS claim, the evaluation of the diligence displayed by the host state must give due consideration to such an extraordinary situation. As stated by Sole Arbitrator Jan Paulsson in *Pantechniki v Albania*:

> There is an important distinction between the two [denial of justice and FPS] in terms of the *consciousness* of state behavior in each case. A legal system and the dispositions it generates are the products of deliberate choices and conduct developed or neglected over long periods. The minimum requirement is not high in light of the great value placed on the rule of law. There is a warrant for its consistent application. *A failure of protection and security is to the*

---

[177]Bin Cheng, *General Principles of Law as Applied by International Courts and Tribunals* (Cambridge University Press, New York 2006) 150 [first edition: 1953].

[178]See the section "The Prevention of Private Injuries to Aliens".

[179]Emphasis added. *Affaire des biens britanniques au Maroc espagnol* (1 May 1925) II RIAA 615, 645.

contrary likely to arise in an unpredictable instance of civil disorder which could have been readily controlled by a powerful state but which overwhelms the limited capacities of one which is poor and fragile. There is no issue of incentives or disincentives with regard to unforeseen breakdowns of public order; it seems difficult to maintain that a government incurs in international responsibility for failure to plan for unprecedent trouble of unprecedent magnitude in unprecedent places. The case for an element of proportionality in applying the international standard is stronger than with respect to claims of denial of justice.[180]

A denial or restriction of access to justice may thus be measured against a stricter standard in the context of a denial of justice or FET claim than in connection with an FPS claim. The reason is that the availability of local redress mechanisms is not a separate obligation under the FPS standard. As stated beforehand, the nonexistence of proper agencies of redress might indicate a want of diligence on the part of the host state, but does not constitute a breach of the FPS standard for and by itself. Cases in which the absence of adequate means of redress could be considered as entailing a breach of FPS may hence be explained without shattering the standard's dogmatic structure. There is no need to disavow the more or less consistent arbitral practice indicating that FPS does not impose strict liability. There is no compelling reason to say that, by promising 'protection and security', the host state offers an absolute guarantee of access to its own agencies of redress. The redress obligation, as an element of the FPS standard, is an obligation of diligence, nothing more.

11.2.4 The sui generis *Character of the Standard of 'Full Protection and Security'*

The foregoing analysis indicates that the customary protection obligation can neither be qualified as a 'pure' obligation of conduct nor as an obligation of result. Rather, the standard is of a *sui generis* nature. A breach of FPS requires *both* a lack of diligence on the part of the host state and the actual occurrence of an injury. The exercise of diligence is usually the threshold issue for a finding of liability under the standard, albeit the occurrence of an injury might be relevant for determining the *tempus commissi delicti* (i.e. the moment in which the breach has occurred). Novel theories dividing the FPS standard in separate obligations and attaching them to different standards of liability are unsound. They are usually based on an inaccurate interpretation of historical sources, and do not provide a reasonable solution to any real problem concerning the interpretation or application of the FPS standard.

As shown in the previous sections, the applicable standard of liability does not vary depending on the (public or private/natural) source of the risks at stake, as some authors suggest. The question in these cases does not actually pertain to the content

---

[180]Emphasis added. Pantechniki S.A. Contractors & Engineers *v* Albania, Award, ICSID Case No. ARB/07/21 (30 July 2009) [77].

of the security obligation, but to the applicability of the FPS standard. Cases involving purely public injuries fall outside the standard's scope of application.

Furthermore, the existence or availability of municipal agencies of prevention and redress does not constitute a separate, absolute obligation under the FPS standard. A breach of the security obligation is always contingent upon a failure to exercise due diligence in the protection of aliens. There is no doubt that a legal and administrative system must be in place for the host state to be in a position to exercise diligence, and that a want of diligence cannot be justified on the mere failure to create such system. But these premises neither affect the content of the security obligation, nor imply that the host state assumed strict liability for the existence of the system. The FPS standard is therefore better understood as a *sui generis* obligation, in the terms described above.

11.3 The Distinction Between Positive and Negative International Obligations. 'Full Protection and Security' as a Delict of Omission

International obligations may either require the adoption of some course of conduct or proscribe some course of conduct. Depending on their content, they may consistently be described as *positive obligations* (i.e. obligations 'to do') or *negative obligations* (i.e. obligations 'not to do').[181] The foregoing sections have shown that the notions of FPS and due diligence are unavoidably conjoined.[182] The FPS standard demands *diligent action* on the part of the host state.[183] This premise admits no exception, neither in view of particular elements of the standard,[184] nor in respect of any particular source of risk.[185]

If this proposition is true, it can be safely said that FPS belongs to the first category.[186] The link between due diligence and the notion of positive international

---

[181]See generally: Roberto Ago, 'Le délit international' (1939) 68 RCADI 415, 500-6; James Crawford, *State Responsibility. The General Part* (Cambridge University Press, Cambridge 2013) 219.

[182]See Sects. 11.1 and 11.2.

[183]See Sects. 11.1 and 11.2.

[184]See Sect. 11.2.3.2.

[185]See Sect. 11.2.3.1.

[186]For a explicit characterization of the FPS standard as a positive obligation see: Joshua Robins, 'The Emergence of Positive Obligations in Bilateral Investment Treaties' (2005-6) U. Miami Int'l & Comp. L. Rev. 403, 426-31; Lucas Bastin, *State Responsibility for Omissions: Establishing a Breach of the Full Protection and Security Obligation by Omissions* (Oxford University, Oxford 2016) [D.Phil. Thesis] 50 *et seq.*; Lucas Bastin, *Violation of the Full Protection and Security Obligation by Regulatory Omissions* [M.Phil. Thesis] (Oxford University, Oxford 2011) 67.

obligations is beyond doubt.[187] An obligation requiring the exercise of diligence is *per definitionem* an obligation to *take action*, to *do something*. Not surprisingly, some scholars have classified obligations of diligence as a subtype of positive obligations.[188] Against this background, it appears that a breach of the FPS standard always takes the form of an *omission*, i.e. a *failure to do* something.[189] This premise, albeit correct, is not without controversy. At least two objections could be raised in this regard.

In the first place, the question may arise as to whether it is actually accurate to define FPS as a delict of omission. In most cases state agents do not remain entirely inactive in the face of some external peril or actual impairment to the security of foreign nationals. Public authorities normally adopt some positive measures of protection. A breach of the FPS standard can certainly be established whenever the measures adopted prove to be inadequate or insufficient. The result is that a breach of FPS may occur in the presence of *positive* state conduct.

This issue is not particular to the FPS standard. Another example is the obligation to prevent genocide. In its decision on the *Bosnian Genocide Case*, the ICJ drew a distinction between the violation of the obligation to prevent genocide, on the one hand, and complicity in the commission of genocide on the other. The Court concluded that 'while complicity results from commission, violation of the obligation to prevent results from omission'.[190] This statement has been the subject of

---

[187]See generally: Joanna Kulesza, Due Diligence in International Law (Brill, Leiden 2016) 265. See also: Maja Janmyr, *Protecting Civilians in Refugee Camps. Unable and Unwilling States, UNCHR and International Responsibility* (Martinus Nijhoff, Leiden 2013) 179; Vladyslav Lanovoy, Complicity and its Limits in the Law of International Responsibility (Hart Publishing, Portland OR 2016) 216.

[188]For an indicative example see: Lucas Bastin, *State Responsibility for Omissions: Establishing a Breach of the Full Protection and Security Obligation by Omissions* (Oxford University, Oxford 2016) [D.Phil. Thesis] 50 *et seq.*; Lucas Bastin, *Violation of the Full Protection and Security Obligation by Regulatory Omissions* [M.Phil. Thesis] (Oxford University, Oxford 2011) 22-33.

[189]For an arbitral tribunal expressly linking the FPS standard to the notion of internationally wrongful omissions see: Sergei Paushok, CJSC Golden East Co., CJSC Vostoknefte *v* Mongolia (UNCITRAL), Award on Jurisdiction and Liability (28 April 2011) [325] (observing that '[i]f a State fails to use due diligence to prevent or punish such injuries [covered by the FPS standard], it is responsible *for this omission*' – emphasis added). Cf. also Oxus Gold *v* Uzbekistan (UNCITRAL), Final Award (17 December 2015) [355]. On the connection of the customary protection obligation and the concept of 'delicts of omission' see: Hans Kelsen, 'Unrecht und Unrechtsfolge im Völkerrecht' (1932) 12 ZöR 481, 515. For a detailed analysis of the conceptual link between the notions of due diligence and internationally wrongful omissions see: Karl Zemanek, 'Schuld- und Erfolgshaftung im Entwurf der Völkerrechtskommission über Staatenverantwortlichkeit. Zugleich Bemerkungen zum Prozess der Kodifikation im Rahmen der Vereinten Nationen' in Emanuel Diez, Jean Monnier, Jörg Müller, Heinrich Reimann and Luzius Wildhaber (eds), *Festschrift für Rudolf Bindschedler zum 65. Geburtstag am 8. Juli 1980* (Verlag Stämpfli & cie., Bern 1980) 315, 322-3.

[190]*Case Concerning the Application of the Convention on the Prevention and Punishment of the Crime of Genocide (Bosnia and Herzegovina v Serbia and Montenegro)* [2007] ICJ Rep 43, 223 [432]. For a similar approach to the distinction between complicity and negligence see: Richard Lillich and John Paxman, 'State Responsibility for Injuries to Aliens Occasioned by Terrorist Activities' (1977) 26(2) Am. U. L. Rev. 217, 236.

intense academic debate.[191] Among others, James Crawford has expressed doubts as to the Court's resort to the distinction between actions and omissions.[192] As a matter of fact, he notes, a state could have adopted positive measures for the prevention of genocide and, at the same time, be in breach of its prevention obligation.[193] In such cases, Crawford says, the breach arises out of 'the commission of *positive* acts'.[194] Taking cognizance of these situations, some scholars have coined the expression 'omission by action'.[195]

These dogmatic utterances must be considered with caution. In ordinary language, an action consists in *doing* something.[196] Actions involve movement, that is to say, a change or alteration in the state of things.[197] In contrast, an omission conveys the idea of inaction or abstention. Some dictionaries define the term as '[t]he non-performance or neglect of an action'.[198] It seems therefore counterintuitive to say that an internationally wrongful omission was committed through positive acts. The underlying problem is, however, more apparent than real.

In his 1939 Hague lectures, Roberto Ago gave detailed consideration to these conceptual and terminological intricacies. Ago submitted that the distinction between *délits d'action* and *délits d'omission* is not *material* but *legal* in nature.[199] Plainly stated, the difference is not that an action implies 'movement' (*mouvement*) and an omission consists in 'inaction' or 'stasis' (*stase*).[200] Rather, the difference lies in the applicable legal duty.[201] A delict of action is the breach of a legal obligation *not to perform* a certain action.[202] In contrast, a delict of omission is the breach of a

---

[191]For a detailed analysis on the subject see: Helmut Philip Aust, *Complicity and the Law of State Responsibility* (Cambridge University Press, New York 2011) 225 *et seq.* (advancing the argument that, contrary to the ICJ's view, there could also be cases of 'complicity through omission'). For a similar remark see: Vladyslav Lanovoy, *Complicity and its Limits in the Law of International Responsibility* (Hart Publishing, Portland OR 2016) 96 and 284. This section does not address the issue of complicity in detail. Section 12.4.3 makes some remarks on notion of complicity by omission, and the – sometimes seemingly blurred – line between complicity and due diligence.

[192]James Crawford, *State Responsibility. The General Part* (Cambridge University Press, Cambridge 2013) 218-9.

[193]James Crawford, *State Responsibility. The General Part* (Cambridge University Press, Cambridge 2013) 218-9.

[194]Emphasis added. James Crawford, *State Responsibility. The General Part* (Cambridge University Press, Cambridge 2013) 219. See also Sect. 12.4.3.

[195]Franck Latty, 'Actions and Omissions' in James Crawford, Alain Pellet and Simon Olleson (eds), *The Law of International Responsibility* (Oxford University Press, New York 2010) 355, 361.

[196]'action, n' (October 2016) *Oxford English Dictionary Online* [http://www.oed.com/view/Entry/1938?rskey=k9Re6P&result=1&isAdvanced=false#eid].

[197]'action' in *Merriam Webster Collegiate Dictionary* (Merriam-Webster, Springfield MA 2004) 12.

[198]'omission, n' (October 2016) *Oxford English Dictionary Online* [http://www.oed.com/view/Entry/131211?redirectedFrom=omission#eid].

[199]Roberto Ago, 'Le délit international' (1939) 68 RCADI 415, 501.

[200]Roberto Ago, 'Le délit international' (1939) 68 RCADI 415, 501.

[201]Roberto Ago, 'Le délit international' (1939) 68 RCADI 415, 501.

[202]Roberto Ago, 'Le délit international' (1939) 68 RCADI 415, 501.

legal obligation *to perform* a certain action.[203] In the latter case, a *positive obligation* is what ultimately allows identifying the action which the state was *required to* perform and, hence, what it *failed to* perform: A legally relevant omission can only be recognized in the light of a legal duty.[204]

Crawford is right in noting that a breach of an obligation 'to do' may arise *even* in cases where the state has adopted some positive conduct. At the same time, however, it is not entirely accurate to say that obligations 'to do' may be breached *through* or *by* positive conduct, as Crawford and other contemporary legal scholars suggest.[205] Following Ago, the content of the primary obligation is what determines the positive or negative character of conduct capable of constituting a breach.[206] In the example referred to by Crawford (i.e. insufficient measures to prevent genocide), the obligation requires *positive* preventive measures. Responsibility is consistently established not for what the state *did*, but for what it *failed to do*.

Much the same can be said in respect of the adoption of clearly inadequate measures for the protection of aliens against, for example, mob violence.[207] In such an event, the possible breach of the protection obligation arises from the *failure to adopt adequate measures* (i.e. an *omission*), and not from the *actions* undertaken by the host state. These situations, therefore, cannot be properly styled as omissions *through* or *by* action. A more accurate designation would be 'omissions *in spite* of an action'.

The concurrence of actions and omission in cases involving FPS claims has not escaped the attention of investment arbitral tribunals. The award rendered in *Ampal et al. v Egypt* (2017) provides a clear example. In that case, the arbitrators considered an FPS claim pertaining to an alleged failure to prevent terrorist attacks to an oil pipeline during the Egyptian Arab spring.[208] In this vein, they stated:

> The duty imposed by the international standard is one that rests upon the State. However, since it concerns an obligation of diligence, the Tribunal is of the view that the operation of the standard does not depend upon whether the acts that give rise to the damage to the Claimant's investment are committed by agents of State (which are thus directly attributable to the State) or by third parties. *Rather the focus is on the acts or omissions of the State in*

---

[203]Roberto Ago, 'Le délit international' (1939) 68 RCADI 415, 501.

[204]Roberto Ago, 'Le délit international' (1939) 68 RCADI 415, 500-6.

[205]James Crawford, *State Responsibility. The General Part* (Cambridge University Press, Cambridge 2013) 219; Franck Latty, 'Actions and Omissions' in James Crawford, Alain Pellet and Simon Olleson (eds), *The Law of International Responsibility* (Oxford University Press, New York 2010) 355, 361.

[206]Roberto Ago, 'Le délit international' (1939) 68 RCADI 415, 500-6.

[207]It should be noted that, in his analysis of the subject, Roberto Ago gave express consideration to the example of mob injuries to aliens. See: Roberto Ago, 'Le délit international' (1939) 68 RCADI 415, 503.

[208]Ampal-American Israel Corp., Egi-Fund (08-10) Investors LLC, Egi-Series Investments LLC and BSS-EMG Investors LLC *v* Egypt, Decision on Liability and Heads of Loss, ICSID Case No. ARB/12/11 (21 February 2017) [235-8 and 275-7] (including extensive quotations from an ICC Award referring to the same facts in connection with a contractual claim; para 277 contains a detailed description of the attacks).

addressing the unrest that gives rise to the damage [...] *the Tribunal will now review the acts and omissions of the Respondent in reaction to the attacks on the pipeline.*[209]

Thus, the arbitrators recognized that the FPS standard entails an obligation of diligence and refers to the *reaction* of state against external threats (e.g. civil unrest, terrorist attacks).[210] They further noted that the analysis of an FPS claim often implies dealing with both actions and omissions of the host state.[211] Regrettably, the *Ampal* tribunal missed the opportunity to make clear that, even in the presence of state actions (e.g. existent, albeit utterly inadequate, positive measures of protection), a breach of FPS is established on account of a *failure* to exercise diligence, that is to say, an *omission*.

These terminological and conceptual remarks do not however remove all possible objections to the characterization of FPS as a delict of omission. The terminology used by some states and arbitral tribunals is likely to sow confusion in this regard. For instance, the arbitrators in *Sergei Paushok v Mongolia* (2011) considered that the FPS standard could be breached where there was 'negative action taken by third parties that the State is accused of not having prevented',[212] as well as 'through actions of the State or its agents'.[213] In *CME v Czech Republic* (2001), the respondent argued that the investor had to show that the breach of the standard 'is the result of the *actions* of the Czech Republic'.[214] The Czech Republic did not elaborate further on this idea and went on to describe the FPS standard as 'an obligation of *due diligence relating to the activities of the state*'.[215]

Similarly, in *Eureko v Poland* (2005), the arbitrators refrained from declaring that certain 'acts of harassment' constituted a breach of the FPS standard because 'there is no clear evidence before the Tribunal that the RoP [Republic of Poland] was the *author or instigator* of the *actions* in question'.[216] It then stated, without more elaboration, that 'if such actions were to be repeated and sustained, it may be that

---

[209]Emphasis added. Ampal-American Israel Corp., Egi-Fund (08-10) Investors LLC, Egi-Series Investments LLC and BSS-EMG Investors LLC *v* Egypt, Decision on Liability and Heads of Loss, ICSID Case No. ARB/12/11 (21 February 2017) [245-6].

[210]Ampal-American Israel Corp., Egi-Fund (08-10) Investors LLC, Egi-Series Investments LLC and BSS-EMG Investors LLC *v* Egypt, Decision on Liability and Heads of Loss, ICSID Case No. ARB/12/11 (21 February 2017) [245-6].

[211]Ampal-American Israel Corp., Egi-Fund (08-10) Investors LLC, Egi-Series Investments LLC and BSS-EMG Investors LLC *v* Egypt, Decision on Liability and Heads of Loss, ICSID Case No. ARB/12/11 (21 February 2017) [245-6].

[212]Sergei Paushok, CJSC Golden East Co., CJSC Vostoknefte *v* Mongolia (UNCITRAL), Award on Jurisdiction and Liability (28 April 2011) [327].

[213]Sergei Paushok, CJSC Golden East Co., CJSC Vostoknefte *v* Mongolia (UNCITRAL), Award on Jurisdiction and Liability (28 April 2011) [327].

[214]CME Czech Republic B.V. *v* Czech Republic (UNCITRAL), Partial Award (13 September 2001) [352].

[215]Emphasis added. CME Czech Republic B.V. *v* Czech Republic (UNCITRAL), Partial Award (13 September 2001) [354].

[216]Eureko B.V. *v* Poland (*Ad Hoc* Arbitration), Partial Award (19 August 2005) [237].

the responsibility of the Government of Poland would be incurred by a failure to prevent them'.[217] These statements give the impression that, for the *Eureko* tribunal, a breach of the FPS standard usually takes the form of an *action*. By contrast, the 'failure to prevent' appears to have a rather exceptional character.

Most academic studies of the FPS standard avoid expressly classifying the standard as a positive obligation. While scholars generally recognize that FPS could require positive conduct in some specific factual settings, they usually ascribe, too, negative obligations to the standard. This approach typically departs from the assumption that FPS is applicable in respect of public acts of violence.[218] It is, in fact, in relation to *those* (public) acts that the security obligation is often described as a *duty of abstention*.[219]

Chapter 8 refutes this widespread view. The proposition advanced throughout this monograph is that the FPS standard grants protection against risks *external* to the host state. Thus, as a rule, the standard is *not* applicable to acts of public violence, which should accordingly be considered in the light of other standards of investment protection.[220]

The only exception would be the case of collateral injuries occasioned in the course state action against some external threat.[221] In such events, actions of state agents are the material, immediate cause of the injury. Nonetheless, the breach of FPS is not established on account of those *actions*; FPS requires authorities to *exercise diligence* to reduce the risk of *collateral injuries* to aliens.[222] The obligation is, hence, an obligation *to do*. Recalling once again Ago's 1939 lecture, it is the content of the primary duty what allows the identification of the conduct capable of constituting a breach.[223] Being the duty at stake a *positive* obligation, the breach takes the form of an *omission* in the mitigation of damages. It could therefore be said

---

[217]Eureko B.V. *v* Poland (*Ad Hoc* Arbitration), Partial Award (19 August 2005) [237].

[218]See, for example, Sect. 11.2.3. Cf. also Sect. 8.3.3.

[219]See, for example: Eric De Brabandere, 'Host States' Due Diligence Obligations in International Investment Law' (2014-5) 42 Syracuse J. Int'l L. & Com. 319, 324 and 333-7 (referring to the host state's 'duty to abstain'); Finnur Magnússon, *Full Protection and Security in International Law* (University of Vienna, Vienna 2012) 162 (concluding that '[a] state can violate its obligation towards the investor by a breach of a duty to abstain'); Helge Elisabeth Zeitler, 'Full Protection and Security' in Stephan Schill (ed), *International Investment Law and Comparative Public Law* (Oxford University Press, New York 2010) 183, 191 (explaining that, in respect of harm caused by state agents, 'the state owes abstention'); Ralph Alexander Lorz, 'Protection and Security (Including the NAFTA Approach)' in Marc Bungenberg, Jörn Griebel, Stephan Hobe and August Reinisch (eds), *International Investment Law* (Nomos, Baden-Baden 2015) 764, 777 (noting that, in respect of damages caused by state organs, 'the host State simply owes abstention from behavior harmful to the investor').

[220]See Sect. 8.3.

[221]See Sect. 8.3.3.1.

[222]See Sect. 8.3.3.1.

[223]Roberto Ago, 'Le délit international' (1939) 68 RCADI 415, 500-6.

that the *action* (e.g. a counterinsurgency operation) creates the *material opportunity* for the *omission* (i.e. the *failure to mitigate* collateral damages).[224] Thus, in spite of being correlated, the action and the omission remain conceptually and, most importantly, legally distinct.[225]

These remarks shall suffice to reaffirm that the FPS standard is, without exception, *positive* in character. In consequence, a breach of the standard always appears in the form of an *omission*. As accurately observed by the arbitrators in *El Paso v Argentina*, FPS protects investors against injuries 'caused by third parties' and, thus, '[i]f a State fails to exercise due diligence to prevent or punish such injuries, it is responsible for *this omission*'.[226]

---

[224]Cf. Sect. 8.3.3.1. From a more general perspective, some authors have observed that it is not uncommon for state actions to originate the factual situation in the context of which a wrongful omission takes place. See: Lucas Bastin, *Violation of the Full Protection and Security Obligation by Regulatory Omissions* [M.Phil. Thesis] (Oxford University, Oxford 2011) 37-8.

[225]Cf. also Sect. 12.4.3.

[226]Emphasis added. El Paso Energy International Co. *v* Argentina, Award, ICSID Case No. ARB/03/15 (31 October 2011) [523]. Cf. also Oxus Gold *v* Uzbekistan (UNCITRAL), Final Award (17 December 2015) [355].

Chapter 12
Due Diligence in the International Law of Aliens: Conceptual Framework

12.1 Preliminary Remarks

Due diligence is a ubiquitous concept in contemporary international law. The notion has in fact permeated the most diverse areas of the international legal order, from human rights to international environmental law. Its widespread use has not escaped the attention of scholars and international institutions. Academic publications seeking to provide detailed accounts of the dogmatic grounding and practical uses of due diligence are on the rise.[1] Moreover, the *International Law Association* [ILA] constituted a Study Group with the mandate of considering 'the extent to which there is a commonality of understanding between the distinctive areas in which the notion of due diligence is applied'.[2] The Group presented its First Report in 2014,[3] and concluded its activities with a Second Report in 2016.[4]

---

[1]See, for example: Eric De Brabandere, 'Host States' Due Diligence Obligations in International Investment Law' (2014-5) 42 Syracuse J. Int'l L. & Com. 319-61; Jan Arno Hessbruegge, 'The Historical Development of the Doctrines of Attribution and Due Diligence in International Law' (2003/4) 36(4) JILP 265-306; Joanna Kulesza, *Due Diligence in International Law* (Brill, Leiden 2016); Riccardo Pisillo Mazzeschi, *"Due diligence" e responsabilità internazionale degli stati* (Giuffrè Editore, Milan 1989); Riccardo Pisillo-Mazzeschi, 'The Due Diligence Rule and the Nature of the International Responsibility of States' in René Provost (ed), *State Responsibility in International Law* (Ashgate Publishing Co., Burlington VT 2002) 97-139; Robert Barnidge, 'The Due Diligence Principle under International Law' (2006) Int'l Comm. L. Rev. 81-121; Timo Koivurova, 'Due Diligence' in Rüdiger Wolfrum (ed), *The Max Planck Encyclopedia of Public International Law* (Volume 3: Oxford University Press, New York 2012) 236-46.

[2]ILA, 'Mandate of the Study Group on Due Diligence in International Law' (n.d.) 1.

[3]ILA Study Group on Due Diligence in International Law, 'First Report by Mr. Tim Stephens (Rapporteur) and Mr. Duncan French (Chair)' (7 March 2014).

[4]ILA Study Group on Due Diligence in International Law, 'Second Report by Mr. Tim Stephens (Rapporteur) and Mr. Duncan French (Chair)' (20 July 2016).

© Springer Nature Switzerland AG 2019

S. Mantilla Blanco, *Full Protection and Security in International Investment Law*, European Yearbook of International Economic Law 8, https://doi.org/10.1007/978-3-030-24838-3_12

Extant works on the subject reveal that due diligence, albeit ever-present, is still a concept signalized by complexity and some degree of uncertainty. The ILA made a remarkable effort to bring about the notion by ascertaining its 'normative core' and 'the factors that might influence the variability in its operation'.[5] However, the meaning of 'due diligence' remains somewhat unsure. For instance, the ILA Study Group recognized that 'due diligence is not one, but many standards of conduct'.[6] It further stated that the notion is 'an expansive, sectorally-specific yet overreaching concept'.[7] To the same effect, scholars have described due diligence as a thoroughly 'ambiguous' term, which 'has become a short hand reference to a set of criteria for assessing the level of care given by state authorities in a particular case'.[8] In its *Seabed Advisory Opinion*, the International Tribunal for the Law of the Sea depicted due diligence as a 'variable concept' and went on to observe that '[t]he content of due diligence obligations may not easily be described in precise terms'.[9]

The present chapter does not intend to find a definitive solution to the manifold intricacies surrounding the concept. Neither does it intend to generally address the multifarious expressions of due diligence in international law. Rather, it considers the notion in the specific context of the law of aliens. Its main purpose is to identify and analyze the dogmatic struggles that shaped the present-day concept of due diligence. By so doing, it hopes to foster consciousness about the foundations of the notion and, at the same time, to facilitate the assessment of diligence in practice. With these goals in mind, this chapter advances three main propositions.

First. From a legal-historical perspective, the concept of due diligence is a halfway between the pre-modern idea that the nation is responsible for the acts of its individual members (collective responsibility) and doctrines acknowledging no international responsibility whatsoever for private injuries to aliens. Thus, due diligence appeared in the law of aliens as a means to justify state responsibility for private violence against foreign nationals without falling back into collective responsibility. For that very same reason, theories of due diligence always place the basis of state responsibility on territorial control, and not on the personal bond of nationality.

Second. The phrase 'due diligence' is nothing but the new guise of the longstanding debate on the concept of fault (*culpa*) in international law. A look into academic publications on the subject reveals that, ever since the late-nineteenth century 'objective turn' in the law of state responsibility, due diligence has been used

---

[5]ILA Study Group on Due Diligence in International Law, 'Second Report by Mr. Tim Stephens (Rapporteur) and Mr. Duncan French (Chair)' (20 July 2016) 47.

[6]ILA Study Group on Due Diligence in International Law, 'Second Report by Mr. Tim Stephens (Rapporteur) and Mr. Duncan French (Chair)' (20 July 2016) 47.

[7]ILA Study Group on Due Diligence in International Law, 'Second Report by Mr. Tim Stephens (Rapporteur) and Mr. Duncan French (Chair)' (20 July 2016) 47.

[8]Joanna Kulesza, *Due Diligence in International Law* (Brill, Leiden 2016) 1.

[9]*Responsibilities and Obligations of States Sponsoring Persons and Entities with Respect to Activities in the Area (Advisory Opinion)* [2011] 50 ILM 458 [117].

as a 'functional equivalent'[10] to the notion of fault.[11] As a corollary, the label 'due diligence' is the tip of an iceberg of theoretical and dogmatic struggles, which have attracted the attention of nearly every school of thought in the law of aliens.

Third. The contemporary notion of due diligence relies on the idea that the state is not *indirectly responsible* for the acts of individuals (theories of indirect responsibility), but *directly responsible* for its own conduct in connection with those acts (separate delict theory). This feature is the result of an early twentieth century academic debate, which became one of the most important shaping factors of the concept of due diligence.

12.2   Due Diligence: Between Collective Responsibility and Non-responsibility

The definition of the customary protection obligation in terms of due diligence may be best described as a halfway between two opposite approaches to state responsibility for acts of individuals. On the one side of the spectrum there was the theory of collective responsibility.[12] This theory considered that the national community, as a whole, was directly responsible for the acts of its individual members.[13] The aforesaid premise served as a basis for the widespread practice of private reprisals throughout the European Middle Ages.[14]

The placement of a collective personal bond as the cornerstone of responsibility was a natural corollary of the medieval understanding of authority. The influential Austrian historian Theodor Mayer explained in 1939 that, in their early medieval origins, European states were much more personal organizations (*Personenverbandstaaten*) than institutionalized territorial states (*institutionelle*

---

[10]This monograph resorts to the term 'functional equivalent' to express the idea that different schools of thought may come to similar, 'equivalent solutions' to the same conceptual problems. The notion of the 'functional equivalent' is a key analytical tool in the social sciences. Its development owes much to Niklas Luhmann's systems theory and, particularly, to his idea of 'functionally equivalent solutions' (*funktional äquivalente Problemlösungen*). See: Niklas Luhmann, *Soziale Systeme. Grundriß einer allgemeinen Theorie* (Suhrkamp Verlag, Frankfurt 1984) 33.

[11]On the linkage of the concepts of due diligence and fault see particularly Sect. 12.3.

[12]Section 3.2 discusses this theory in more detail, in connection with the Medieval practice of private reprisals.

[13]See generally: Adolf Jess, *Politische Handlungen Privater gegen das Ausland und das Völkerrecht* (Verlag von M. & H. Marcus, Breslau 1923) 8-14. See also: Jan Arno Hessbruegge, 'The Historical Development of the Doctrines of Attribution and Due Diligence in International Law' (2003/4) 36(4) JILP 265, 279-81. On the notion of collective responsibility in the context of the medieval law of reprisals see Sect. 3.2.

[14]See Sect. 12.2.

Flächenstaaten).[15] The foundation of political power did thus not lie in territorial control, but in vassalage and personal loyalties.[16] Some scholars have therefore plausibly characterized this incipient idea of international responsibility as a form of 'tribal responsibility' (*Sippenhaftung*).[17] In this system of collective responsibility, the attribution of acts of individuals to the sovereign was not an issue. Neither did liability for acts of individuals arise from a want of diligence. Quite the opposite, if one were to use a contemporary terminology, responsibility was strict and direct.[18]

During the late medieval period, the western world witnessed a gradual turn from the medieval prevalence of *personality* to a primacy of *territoriality* as the chief defining element of sovereignty.[19] The growing role of territoriality as the most significant feature of sovereign power prepared the ground for the recognition of the state as a legal entity that is both separate and autonomous from the sum of its members (i.e. the individual members of the national community).[20]

The emergence of the modern territorial state had a pivotal importance for the law of state responsibility for private injuries to aliens. Acts of individuals became at this point acts of *others*. The seed of this abstraction was already present in Hugo Grotius' rejection of collective responsibility.[21] Nineteenth century German positivist scholars would refine this conceptual edifice through an analogy to the private law notion of the *corporation*: the state, as a moral person, is necessarily different from

---

[15]Heinrich Mitteis, *Der Staat des hohen Mittelalters. Grundlinien einer vergleichenden Verfassungsgeschichte des Lehnszeitalters* (Hermann Böhlaus, Weimar 1953) 3-5; Theodor Mayer, 'Die Ausbildung der Grundlagen des modernen deutschen Staates im hohen Mittelalter' (1939) 159(3) Historische Zeitschrift 457, 462 *et seq.*; Theodor Mayer, 'Die Entstehung des "modernen" Staates im Mittelalter und die freien Bauern' (1937) 57(1) ZRG 210, 211-4.

[16]The present-day notion of (territorial) sovereignty has therefore been plausibly labeled as a post-medieval concept. See: Robert Jackson, *Sovereignty. Evolution of an idea* (Polity Press, Malden MA 2007) Ch. 1.

[17]See: Adolf Jess, *Politische Handlungen Privater gegen das Ausland und das Völkerrecht* (Verlag von M. & H. Marcus, Breslau 1923) 8. See also: Dionisio Anzilotti, *Lehrbuch des Völkerrechts* (Volume 1: Walter de Gruyter, Berlin/Leipzig 1929) 376-7.

[18]For a similar observation see: Hans Kelsen, *Principles of International Law* (The Lawbook Exchange, Clark NJ 2007) 12 [first edition: 1952] (noting that 'collective responsibility is, by its very nature, absolute responsibility' and explaining that 'in the case of collective responsibility a sanction is directed against individuals who have not committed the delict').

[19]For a detailed legal historical study on the subject see: Simeon Guterman, 'The First Age of European Law: The Origin and Character of the Conflict of Laws in the Early Middle Ages' (1961) 7(2) NYLF 131, 133 et seq. See also: Theodor Mayer, 'Die Ausbildung der Grundlagen des modernen deutschen Staates im hohen Mittelalter' (1939) 159(3) Historische Zeitschrift 457, 462 et seq. (focusing on the German medieval ages).

[20]On the connection between the rise of the modern Western state and the proliferation of legal theories on state responsibility for acts of individuals, which directly or indirectly addressed the underlying question of attribution see: Jan Arno Hessbruegge, 'The Historical Development of the Doctrines of Attribution and Due Diligence in International Law' (2003/4) 36(4) JILP 265, 281 *et seq.*

[21]See Sect. 12.3.1.

both its individual subjects (*Unterthanen*) and the people (*Volk*).[22] Adolf Lasson's conception of the state provides a clear example of this line of thought:

> [T]he state is not the people, and the will of the people is not the will of the state; this follows from the concept of the corporation.[23]

The legal consequence of this premise is striking. If the actions of individual citizens are not considered as acts of the state, the principle logically turns from the (medieval) general rule *responsibility* to a (modern) general rule of *non-responsibility* for private wrongs.[24]

In the late nineteenth and early twentieth centuries, a few Latin American scholars would turn the aforesaid principle of non-responsibility into a rule conveying a virtually absolute character. An article published in the seventh volume of the *American Journal of International Law* (1913) delivers the perhaps most clear, if not to say extreme, expression of this approach.[25] The author was Harmodio Arias Madrid, a young Panamanian lawyer who would later serve two terms as President of Panama, first in an interim capacity (in 1931), and then as Constitutional President (from 1932 to 1936).[26]

In his seminal article, Arias construed the duty to provide protection and security to aliens in conspicuously narrow terms.[27] His argument was particularly concerned with some of the customary standard's most traditional areas of application, such as revolutions, civil wars and other severe civil disorders.[28] In those cases, he explained, the host state faces a threat to its most essential interests, including its very own existence.[29] Arias considered that such factual settings usually pose a case

---

[22]For a representative example see: Adolf Lasson, *Princip und Zukunft des Völkerrechts* (Verlag von Wilhelm Hertz, Berlin 1871) 122-40.

[23]Author's translation. The original German text reads: "[Vor allem ist es wichtig festzustellen, dass] der Staat nicht das Volk und der Volkswille nicht der Staatswille ist. Das folgt aus dem Begriffe der Corporation." Adolf Lasson, *Princip und Zukunft des Völkerrechts* (Verlag von Wilhelm Hertz, Berlin 1871) 136.

[24]Cf. Sect. 12.3.1.

[25]Harmodio Arias, 'The Non-Liability of States for Damages Suffered by Foreigners in the Course of a Riot, an Insurrection, or a Civil War' (1913) 7(4) AJIL 724, 724-66.

[26]See: Thomas M. Leonard, *Historical Dictionary of Panama* (Rowman & Littlefield, Lanham MD 2015) 36.

[27]Harmodio Arias, 'The Non-Liability of States for Damages Suffered by Foreigners in the Course of a Riot, an Insurrection, or a Civil War' (1913) 7(4) AJIL 724, 732 *et seq.*

[28]Harmodio Arias, 'The Non-Liability of States for Damages Suffered by Foreigners in the Course of a Riot, an Insurrection, or a Civil War' (1913) 7(4) AJIL 724, 732 *et seq.*

[29]Harmodio Arias, 'The Non-Liability of States for Damages Suffered by Foreigners in the Course of a Riot, an Insurrection, or a Civil War' (1913) 7(4) AJIL 724, 732 *et seq.*

of 'intrinsic impossibility', which excludes responsibility,[30] and invoked 'the well known maxim *nemo tenetur ad impossibile*' in this connection.[31]

Arias additionally argued that, if state conduct is measured against a standard of negligence, the result will most likely be a finding of non-responsibility.[32] The reasons are twofold. First, civil disorders usually constitute 'contingencies [. . .] which the most prudent legislator cannot foresee, or the most powerful and well constituted government prevent'.[33] Second, in any such scenarios, the assessment of diligence normally faces insurmountable evidentiary difficulties and could moreover open the door to logical contradiction.[34] As a matter of fact, the state cannot be seriously assumed to have acted recklessly in respect of affairs which pertain not only to the wellbeing of aliens, but also to the state's very own fundamental interests:

> [G]ranting the existence of the above set of circumstances, it would not be possible to allow the supposition to be entertained that damages have resulted owing to carelessness. For how can a state be thought to be negligent as to a matter that vitally affects its existence? Moreover – and this will apply to cases in which the existence of the constituted authorities is not so deeply involved in the prevention of the injurious acts, and damages accrue to foreigners either on account of measures taken by the state in the recovery of its authority, or through acts done by the rebels – it will not be possible, owing to the complicated nature of the case, to obtain proof of the carelessness of the government.[35]

Besides generally rejecting responsibility in the aforesaid factual settings, Arias presented the duty to protect as a self-judging obligation.[36] Any dispute concerning the protection of aliens in such scenarios would hence belong in the realm of national law.[37] According to Arias, no one can scrutinize the host state's sovereign choices in this regard:

---

[30]Harmodio Arias, 'The Non-Liability of States for Damages Suffered by Foreigners in the Course of a Riot, an Insurrection, or a Civil War' (1913) 7(4) AJIL 724, 735.

[31]Harmodio Arias, 'The Non-Liability of States for Damages Suffered by Foreigners in the Course of a Riot, an Insurrection, or a Civil War' (1913) 7(4) AJIL 724, 736.

[32]Cf. Harmodio Arias, 'The Non-Liability of States for Damages Suffered by Foreigners in the Course of a Riot, an Insurrection, or a Civil War' (1913) 7(4) AJIL 724, 735-6.

[33]Harmodio Arias, 'The Non-Liability of States for Damages Suffered by Foreigners in the Course of a Riot, an Insurrection, or a Civil War' (1913) 7(4) AJIL 724, 735.

[34]Cf. Harmodio Arias, 'The Non-Liability of States for Damages Suffered by Foreigners in the Course of a Riot, an Insurrection, or a Civil War' (1913) 7(4) AJIL 724, 736.

[35]Harmodio Arias, 'The Non-Liability of States for Damages Suffered by Foreigners in the Course of a Riot, an Insurrection, or a Civil War' (1913) 7(4) AJIL 724, 736.

[36]Cf. Harmodio Arias, 'The Non-Liability of States for Damages Suffered by Foreigners in the Course of a Riot, an Insurrection, or a Civil War' (1913) 7(4) AJIL 724, 736. On the concept of *self-judging* obligations see: Martti Koskenniemi, *The Gentle Civilizer of Nations. The Rise and Fall of International Law 1870-1960* (Cambridge University Press, New York 2008) 358 (linking the concept to Hersch Lauterpacht's theories of international law). For Lauterpacht's analysis of the subject see: Hersch Lauterpacht, *The Function of International Law in the International Community* (Clarendon Press, Oxford 1933) 165-8.

[37]Cf. Harmodio Arias, 'The Non-Liability of States for Damages Suffered by Foreigners in the Course of a Riot, an Insurrection, or a Civil War' (1913) 7(4) AJIL 724, 735-6 (particularly arguing at p. 735 that the right to compensation depends on domestic law).

> The most honest and obliging state will not always be willing to grant individuals or foreign nations the right to inquire into its acts to ascertain when some of its officials have been negligent in the performance of their duties. Public policy naturally prevents such a course. The state is the sole judge of its internal acts. International law cannot demand of a state to permit an investigation of this nature.[38]

This line of argument thus excludes international responsibility for injuries inflicted in the context of civil wars, revolutions and their like.[39] Arias believed that foreign citizens affected by such events are not entitled to an '*indemnity*'; a reparation claim, he said, is dependent on, and entirely subject to, municipal law.[40] To be sure, he acknowledged that host states could decide to grant the victims some compensation; and yet, in the eyes of international law, such payment would constitute a generous act of giving, a payment *ex gratia*, and nothing more.[41] This view on compensation was consistent with some claims conventions, which, despite subjecting revolutionary claims to arbitral determination, used a language that was carefully designed to avoid the recognition of a legal obligation to compensate.[42]

Arias' view was an extreme version of semi-peripheral theories on the subject. Latin American international law scholars were reluctant to accept responsibility for acts of private individuals and, particularly, for acts of revolutionaries, in the terms advanced by their American and European peers.[43] In contrast to Arias, however, they usually did not contest that states are liable for their own negligence in the protection of aliens; their argument was rather that international law does not require protection beyond the security enjoyed by the host state's citizens.[44] A prominent representative of this approach was Carlos Calvo.[45]

To be fair, theories of non-responsibility did not usually exclude *every* form of state responsibility for acts of individuals. The argument was normally concerned with the prevention obligation, rather than with the obligation of redress. Arias, for

---

[38]Harmodio Arias, 'The Non-Liability of States for Damages Suffered by Foreigners in the Course of a Riot, an Insurrection, or a Civil War' (1913) 7(4) AJIL 724, 736.

[39]Cf. Harmodio Arias, 'The Non-Liability of States for Damages Suffered by Foreigners in the Course of a Riot, an Insurrection, or a Civil War' (1913) 7(4) AJIL 724, 732 *et seq.*

[40]Harmodio Arias, 'The Non-Liability of States for Damages Suffered by Foreigners in the Course of a Riot, an Insurrection, or a Civil War' (1913) 7(4) AJIL 724, 735.

[41]Harmodio Arias, 'The Non-Liability of States for Damages Suffered by Foreigners in the Course of a Riot, an Insurrection, or a Civil War' (1913) 7(4) AJIL 724, 735.

[42]For a representative example see: Claims Convention between Great Britain and Mexico (adopted 5 December 1930, entered into force 9 March 1931) V RIAA 10, 11 art. 2.

[43]Cf. Sect. 4.3.

[44]Cf. Sect. 4.3.

[45]See, particularly: Carlos Calvo, 'De la non-responsabilité des états a raison des pertes et dommages éprouvés par des étrangers en temps de troubles intérieurs ou de guerres civiles' (1869) 1 Revue de droit international et de législation comparée 417, 417-27. Arias also resorted to the doctrine of equality, as an additional argument in support of his views. See: Harmodio Arias, 'The Non-Liability of States for Damages Suffered by Foreigners in the Course of a Riot, an Insurrection, or a Civil War' (1913) 7(4) AJIL 724, 736. Section 4.3.2 discusses the Calvo doctrine in more detail.

example, assumed that a failure to redress an injury could, under extraordinary circumstances, indicate that the state had become 'a moral accomplice to the original offence'.[46]

Most academic approaches to state responsibility for acts of individuals may be placed somewhere between the theory of collective responsibility and the theory of non-responsibility.[47] Extant theories usually share two common threads. In the first place, most of them recognize that, *as a general rule*, states are *not* responsible for injuries caused by private individuals.[48] As expressed by Heinrich Triepel in his celebrated treatise *Völkerrecht und Landesrecht* (1899):

> It is sure that, at present, the responsibility of the state for acts of individuals is not based on the affiliation of the individual to the national community. The early-medieval idea of a liability of the community for the acts of its members is alien to modern international law.[49]

Second, publicists generally recognize that cases involving private injuries to aliens *could* seriously compromise the host state's international responsibility. They diverge, however, as to the conditions upon which liability is established. Dogmatic approaches range from the roman law-inspired Grotian theory of fault (*culpa*) to complex theories of risk insurance. These theories are the subject of the following sections.

---

[46]Harmodio Arias, 'The Non-Liability of States for Damages Suffered by Foreigners in the Course of a Riot, an Insurrection, or a Civil War' (1913) 7(4) AJIL 724, 735. As will be shown in Sect. 12.4.1, this use of the concept of complicity enjoyed some support in distinguished academic circles both in Europe and in the United States.

[47]Cf. Sect. 12.2.

[48]For a representative example of an author questioning such a general rule see: Franz von Liszt, *Das Völkerrecht systematisch dargestellt* (Verlag von O. Häring, Berlin 1906) 192 (discussed in detail in Sect. 12.4.1).

[49]Author's translation. The original German text reads: "Nun ist zunächst sicher, dass die Haftung des Staats für Handlungen Einzelner ihren Grund heutigen Tages nicht findet in der Zugehörigkeit des Thäters zum Staatenverbande. Der frühmittelalterliche Gedanke einer Haftung der Gemeinschaft für ihre Glieder ist dem modernen Völkerrecht fremd." Heinrich Triepel, *Völkerrecht und Landesrecht* (Verlag von C. L. Hirschfeld, Leipzig 1899) 325. For a similar observation see: Clyde Eagleton, *The Responsibility of States in International Law* (Klaus Reprint, New York 1970) 76-80 [first edition: 1928]; Dionisio Anzilotti, *Lehrbuch des Völkerrechts* (Volume 1: Walter de Gruyter, Berlin/Leipzig 1929) 376-7; Georg Muszack, *Ueber die Haftung einer Regierung für Schäden, welche Ausländer gelegentlich innerer Unruhen in ihren Landen erlitten haben* (Heiz u. Mündel, Strasbourg 1905) 37.

12.3 Due Diligence and the Problem of Fault in the Law of State Responsibility for Injuries to Aliens

The notion of 'due diligence' did not originate in international law. As will be shown throughout this section, the concept came into the law of nations behind the cloak of a Roman law analogy, and under the designation of *culpa* (fault).[50] These Roman law underpinnings already suggest a strong interweaving between *fault* and *due diligence*. As noted by William L. Burdick:

> Culpa and diligentia are [. . .] inseparably associated, since culpa is the lack of due diligence, and the degree of diligentia or care required in any given case regulates inversely the degree of culpa or negligence that will subject one to liability in case of loss.[51]

This connection has not escaped the attention of international law scholars. Hersch Lauterpacht observed in 1927 that 'care and due care are conceptions indissolubly connected with the idea of fault'.[52] To the same effect, Francisco García Amador noted in 1957 that 'the rule of due diligence is the expression *par excellence* of the so-called theory of fault (*culpa*)'.[53] Others have considered due diligence to be the ultimate test for establishing fault.[54] Jost Delbrück and Rüdiger Wolfrum expressed the view that, perhaps as a result of the uncertainty that still surrounds the concept of fault in international law, scholars and states often prefer resorting to the concept of due diligence as an element of the international obligation.[55] Similarly, in his Dissenting Opinion in *AAPL v Sri Lanka*, Arbitrator Samuel K.B. Asante equalized the concepts of 'due diligence' and 'culpable conduct'.[56] Some authors have considered the difference to be merely terminological in character. For instance, Alf Ross stated in 1947 that 'the typical estimate of culpability [is] expressed in ordinary linguistic usage by such terms as "neglect", "due diligence" and the like'.[57]

---

[50]See Sect. 12.3.1.

[51]William Livesey Burdick, *The Principles of Roman Law and Their Relation to Modern Law* (Lawbook Exchange, Clark NJ 2004) 415. See also: Paul Jörs and Wolfgang Kunkel, *Römisches Privat Recht* (Springer, Berlin 1949) 179. For a more detailed study on the subject see: Johann Christian Hasse, *Die Culpa des Römischen Rechts. Eine Civilistische Abhandlung* (Akademische Buchhandlung, Kiel 1815) 199 *et seq.*

[52]Hersch Lauterpacht, *Private Law Sources and Analogies of International Law (With Special Reference to International Arbitration)* (Longmans, Green and Co. Ltd., London 1927) 139.

[53]Francisco García Amador, 'International Responsibility: Second Report by F. V. García Amador, Special Rapporteur (A/CN.4/106)' (15 February 1957) 2 Yearbook of the International Law Commission – 1957 104, 122 [7].

[54]Antoine Favre, 'Fault as an Element of the Illicit Act' (1963-4) 52 Geo. L. J. 555, 558.

[55]Jost Delbrück and Rüdiger Wolfrum, Völkerrecht. Begründet von Georg Dahm (Volume 3: De Gruyter, Berlin 2002) 948.

[56]Asian Agricultural Products v Sri Lanka, Dissenting Opinion of Samuel K.B. Asante, ICSID Case No. ARB/87/3 (27 June 1990), 6(2) ICSID Review 574, 581.

[57]Alf Ross, *A Textbook of International Law. General Part* (Longmans, Green and Co., London 1947) 256.

Be as it may be, for a long time, questions which present-day international lawyers would in all probability address in terms of 'primary due diligence obligations' were considered as questions of fault.[58] This was particularly the case of state responsibility for private injuries to aliens. Nearly every scholar addressing the question of fault in international law referred to the example of private offences against foreign citizens.[59] Contemporary scholars have designated these traditional approaches to due diligence as 'subjective theories', in opposition to those theories which seek to 'objectivize' the assessment of diligence.[60]

The well-informed reader might feel tempted to reject subjective theories from the outset. Private law analogies, albeit widespread, have never been free from controversy in international law.[61] Moreover, international lawyers often perceive fault as a notion which confusing effects largely overshadow its advantages and enlightening potential. The concept has always been contentious, if not to say convoluted. A young Roberto Ago observed in 1939:

> [T]he problem of fault, among the topics of international responsibility, is generally considered as one of the most fascinating and complex [subjects] of the entire general theory of international law.[62]

The ILC's decision not to include fault as an element of the internationally wrongful act boosted skepticism towards subjective approaches to due diligence.[63] These initial concerns can be addressed shortly.

---

[58] See Sects. 12.3.1 and 12.3.2. Some of these issues have been introduced in Sect. 2.2.4, in connection with the present-day distinction between primary and secondary norms of international law.

[59] For a similar observation see: Roberto Ago, *La colpa nell'illecito internazionale* (CEDAM – Casa Editrice Dott. A. Milani, Pavia 1939) 27 (however providing examples of other possible uses of the notion of fault in international law at pp. 27 *et seq.*, and claiming that 'fault *lato sensu* constitutes a necessary subjective condition for the attribution of an internationally wrongful act' ['la colpa *lato sensu* costituisce una condizione soggettiva indispensabile per l'imputazione di un fatto illecito internazionale'] at p. 32). Cf. also Robert Kolb, *The International Law of State Responsibility. An Introduction* (Edward Elgar Publishing, Northampton MA 2017) 22-3.

[60] On this classification of theories of due diligence, and for a detailed analysis of the subjective character of the underlying notion of fault, see: Riccardo Pisillo Mazzeschi, *"Due diligence" e responsabilità internazionale degli stati* (Giuffrè Editore, Milan 1989) 26 (also discussing the Grotian theory of fault at 28-9). See also: Roberto Ago, *La colpa nell'illecito internazionale* (CEDAM – Casa Editrice Dott. A. Milani, Pavia 1939) 3 *et seq.*

[61] Hersch Lauterpacht, *Private Law Sources and Analogies of International Law (With Special Reference to International Arbitration)* (Longmans, Green and Co. Ltd., London 1927) 50-1 (with particular reference to the positivist doctrine of international law). For some critical comments on the use of analogies in international law see: Heinrich Triepel, *Völkerrecht und Landesrecht* (Verlag von C. L. Hirschfeld, Leipzig 1899) 213-25.

[62] Author's translation. The original Italian text reads: "Il problema della colpa, in tema di responsabilità internazionale, è generalmente noto come uno dei più interessanti e dei più complessi di tutta la teoria generale del diritto internazionale." Roberto Ago, *La colpa nell'illecito internazionale* (CEDAM – Casa Editrice Dott. A. Milani, Pavia 1939) 3.

[63] ILC, 'Responsibility of States for Internationally Wrongful Acts. General Commentary' (2001) 2 *Yearbook of the International Law Commission – 2001* 31, 34 art. 2 (Commentary) [3]. Cf. also

First, it may be conceded that analogies sometimes lead to inaccurate statements about the law.[64] But it would go too far to consider them to be generally inadmissible. Analogy has always accompanied the formation of rules and principles of international law.[65] Distinguished publicists have gone as far as to characterize it as a 'vehicle of progress'.[66] Subjective theories of due diligence should hence not be disregarded on the sole ground that they rely on analogies. The threshold issue is rather whether the specific analogy they propose is substantiated, adequate and useful.

Second, while fault does not appear in the ILC's definition of the internationally wrongful act, the notion still has manifold manifestations in international law. In 1999, Andrea Gattini recalled a former member of the ILC explaining the place of fault in the ILC's Draft Articles of State Responsibility with the following words:

> It is like when you enter a room, and you can tell that somebody has just smoked a cigarette. You can't see the smoker, but you know he's there.[67]

The linkage between due diligence and fault seems to subsist in international lawyers' subconscious, and often resurfaces in their assessment of questions of diligence. For instance, the ILA Study Group on Due Diligence in International Law stated in its *Second Report* (2016) that '[a]t its heart, due diligence is concerned with supplying a standard of care against which fault can be assessed'.[68] Bearing the foregoing in mind, it seems appropriate to properly consider the notion of fault, and to analyze its influence in present-day approaches to due diligence.

Göran Lysén's discussion of the question of fault and its relationship to the notion of due diligence: Göran Lysén, *State Responsibility and International Liability of States for Lawful Acts* (Iustus Förlag, Uppsala 1997) 90-6 (specifically addressing the ILC's approach at p. 94). See also Sect. 12.4.3. below.

[64]Hersch Lauterpacht, *Private Law Sources and Analogies of International Law (With Special Reference to International Arbitration)* (Longmans, Green and Co. Ltd., London 1927) 84-7.

[65]Hersch Lauterpacht, *Private Law Sources and Analogies of International Law (With Special Reference to International Arbitration)* (Longmans, Green and Co. Ltd., London 1927) 43-87.

[66]Hersch Lauterpacht, *Private Law Sources and Analogies of International Law (With Special Reference to International Arbitration)* (Longmans, Green and Co. Ltd., London 1927) 84.

[67]Andrea Gattini, 'Smoking/No Smoking: Some Remarks on the Current Place of Fault in the ILC Draft Articles on State Responsibility' (1999) 10(2) EJIL 397, 397. For an appraisal of the ILC's approach to the question of fault cf. Oliver Diggelmann, 'Fault in the Law of State Responsibility – Pragmatism *ad infinitum?*' (2006) 49 GYIL 293, 293 *et seq.*

[68]ILA Study Group on Due Diligence in International Law, 'Second Report by Mr. Tim Stephens (Rapporteur) and Mr. Duncan French (Chair)' (20 July 2016) 2. For an scholar recognizing the connection between the contemporary notion of 'due diligence' and the concept of 'fault' see: Sandra Stahl, *Schutzpflichten im Völkerrecht. Ansatz einer Dogmatik* (Springer, Heidelberg 2012) 190. Cf. also Nnaemeka Nwokedi Anozie, *The Full Security and Protection Due Diligence Obligation* (University of Ottawa, Ottawa 2016) [LL.M. Thesis] 41 *et seq.* (addressing the use of domestic law analogies) and 47 *et seq.* (assessing the due diligence obligation in the context of FPS by recourse to the common law notion of negligence).

12.3.1 Hugo Grotius and the Concept of Fault

The advent of fault into international law was the product of a legal transplant.[69] The transplant crystalized in Hugo Grotius' acclaimed treatise *De iure belli ac pacis* (1625).[70] In the essence, the Grotian theory of fault consisted in an analogy to private law.[71] Invoking the authority of classic Roman sources, Grotius observed:

> [N]either is a Father responsible for his Children's Crimes, not a Master for his Servants, nor any other Superior for the Faults of those under his Care; if there be nothing criminal in his Conduct, with respect of the Faults of those, over whom he has Authority.[72]

Taking cognizance of these principles, Grotius assimilated the position of the state in respect of private individuals to that of a 'Father' or 'Master' in respect of his children or servants:

> No civil Society, or other public Body, is accountable for the Faults of its particular Members, unless it has concurred with them, or has been negligent in attending to its Charge.[73]

---

[69]The term 'legal transplant' originated in Alan Watson's theory of comparative law, and designates the borrowing of legal institutions from one legal system to another. See: Alan Watson, *Legal Transplants: An Approach to Comparative Law* (University of Georgia Press, Athens GA 1993) 21-30 (particularly at 22) [first edition: 1974].

[70]For the original Latin text of the treatise, see: Hugonis Groti, *De iure belli ac pacis* (1625) (Leiden, A. W. Sijthoff 1919) 411-29 [Lib. 2 Cap. XXI]. This section primarily relies on the English translation printed for W. Inns and R. Manby (London) in 1738. The text quoted corresponds to a reprint of the original 1738 translation, published in 2004: Hugo Grotius, *The Rights of War and Peace in Three Books* (1625) (The Lawbook Exchange, Clark NJ 2004) 453-73 [Book 2 Chap. XXI]. At each particular instance, the English version has been verified against the original Latin text. For a more general outlook on Grotius' theory of fault see: Andrea Gattini, *Zufall und force majeure im System der Staatenverantwortlichkeit anhand der ILC-Kodifikationsarbeit* (Duncker & Humblot, Berlin 1989) 18-9 (presenting a short summary of the Grotian theory of fault); Hersch Lauterpacht, *Private Law Sources and Analogies of International Law (With Special Reference to International Arbitration)* (Longmans, Green and Co. Ltd., London 1927) 135-7 (providing a detailed analysis of Grotius' analogy to Roman private law); Riccardo Pisillo Mazzeschi, *"Due diligence" e responsabilità internazionale degli stati* (Giuffrè Editore, Milan 1989) 28-30 (particularly focusing on the emerging concept of the due diligence standard of liability); Renaud Gagné, *Ancestral Fault in Ancient Greece* (Cambridge University Press, Cambridge 2013) 97-111 (particularly at 101; Gagné provides a detailed analysis of Grotius' use of classical sources); Roberto Ago, *La colpa nell'illecito internazionale* (CEDAM – Casa Editrice Dott. A. Milani, Pavia 1939) 3-4 (providing an overview of the Grotian approach to the question of fault). For an author expressing doubts as to whether the notion of fault can be traced back to Grotius see: Margarete Kuhn, *Verschuldens- oder Verursachungshaftung der Staaten im allgemeinen Völkerrecht* (Imprimerie Photo-Landa, Frankfurt 1961) 75-6.

[71]For a detailed assessment of the private law origins of the Grotian theory of fault see: Hersch Lauterpacht, *Private Law Sources and Analogies of International Law (With Special Reference to International Arbitration)* (Longmans, Green and Co. Ltd., London 1927) 135-7.

[72]Hugo Grotius, *The Rights of War and Peace in Three Books* (1625) (The Lawbook Exchange, Clark NJ 2004) 454 [Book 2 Chap. XXI, § II(1)].

[73]Hugo Grotius, *The Rights of War and Peace in Three Books* (1625) (The Lawbook Exchange, Clark NJ 2004) 454 [Book 2 Chap. XXI, § II(1)].

Having thus established the foundation for his argument, Grotius went on to note that there are two situations in which public bodies must assume responsibility for the acts of private parties, namely, toleration (*patientia*) and refuge (*receptus*).[74]

The concept of *patientia* was based on the idea that 'a Man who is privy to a Fault and does not hinder it, when in a Capacity and under an Obligation of so doing, may properly be said to be the author of it'.[75] In the Grotian system, responsibility on this account is contingent upon the host state being *aware* of the threat and having the *means to avoid* the infliction of harm.[76] The threshold for *receptus* was not any lower. In Grotius' words:

> [S]ince for one State to admit within its Territories another foreign Power upon the Score of exacting Punishment is never practiced, nor indeed convenient, it seems reasonable, that that State where the convicted Offender lives or has taken Shelter, should, upon Application being made to it, either punish the demanded Person according to his Demerits, or else deliver him up to be treated at the Discretion of the injured Party.[77]

The requirement of an 'Application' entails a subtle implication, namely, that the state cannot be held responsible on this account unless it acquired *actual knowledge* of both the occurrence of the offence and the offender's presence in its territory. In addition, the affected party bears the burden of seeking redress. The Grotian theory of fault was a groundbreaking development in the law of nations. Its main contributions to the subsequent evolution of the international law of state responsibility were twofold.

First. Grotius' theory presupposes that the state is distinct and separate from its individual subjects.[78] This might seem obvious to the modern eye. Against the backdrop of the then widespread practice of private reprisals, however, the issue appears much less straightforward. To the careful listener, Grotius was defeating by one stroke the very foundations of collective responsibility.[79] The theory further

---

[74] Hugo Grotius, *The Rights of War and Peace in Three Books* (1625) (The Lawbook Exchange, Clark NJ 2004) 454 [Book 2 Chap. XXI, § II(2)]. The English edition used throughout this work translates *receptus* as *protection*. This translation is not only inaccurate, but could also be somewhat misleading. In his student edition of *De iure belli ac pacis*, Stephen Neff translates *receptus* as *refuge*. At this point, this section makes use of Neff's translation. See: Hugo Grotius, *On the Law of War and Peace* (Stephen Neff tr, Cambridge University Press, Cambridge 2012) 292. For the original Latin text see: Hugonis Groti, *De iure belli ac pacis* (1625) (Leiden, A. W. Sijthoff 1919) 412 [Lib. 2 Cap. XXI § II(2)].

[75] Hugo Grotius, *The Rights of War and Peace in Three Books* (1625) (The Lawbook Exchange, Clark NJ 2004) 454 [Book 2 Chap. XXI, § II(2)].

[76] Hugo Grotius, *The Rights of War and Peace in Three Books* (1625) (The Lawbook Exchange, Clark NJ 2004) 455 [Book 2 Chap. XXI, § II(4)].

[77] Hugo Grotius, *The Rights of War and Peace in Three Books* (1625) (The Lawbook Exchange, Clark NJ 2004) 457 [Book 2 Chap. XXI, § IV(1)].

[78] Cf. also Sect. 12.3.2.1.

[79] For a more detailed analysis of the legal-historical context of the Grotian theory of fault see: Hersch Lauterpacht, *Private Law Sources and Analogies of International Law (With Special Reference to International Arbitration)* (Longmans, Green and Co. Ltd., London 1927) 136 (underscoring that, by objecting the Medieval notion of collective responsibility, Grotius

broke with the medieval emphasis on personal bonds and individual allegiances as the keystone of political power, and gave clear preeminence to the territorial principle.[80] This contribution is confirmed by the fact that Grotius justified the notion of *receptus* by the need of avoiding foreign intrusions in the host state's territory.[81]

Second. For present purposes, the perhaps most important corollary of the Grotian theory of fault is that the state is *not responsible* for private harm *as a general rule*. Acts and omissions committed by private individuals cannot be directly attributed to their home state. The concepts of *patientia* and *receptus* could be consistently characterized as regimes of *exception*. This powerful idea was of the greatest influence for the evolution of the law of aliens. Scholars writing on the law of nations echoed Grotius' general non-responsibility rule for centuries.[82]

12.3.2   Subsequent Theories of Fault

Alan Watson observed in 1974 that '[a] successful legal transplant – like that of a human organ – will grow in its new body, and become part of that body just as the rule or institution would have continue to develop in its parent system'.[83] It should therefore not come as a surprise that, in spite of its private law origins, the concept of fault acquired a more or less autonomous identity as an institution of the law of nations. An important caveat must be kept in mind, though. The reception of *culpa* in international law can barely be described as a story of evolution, development or continuity. Quite the contrary, the notion was the source of constant struggle. The debate on the subject did not only involve opposing views as to the suitability of the concept for the law of state responsibility. Even among those acknowledging the element of fault, there were deep disagreements as to the definition and practical implications of the notion.

---

rendered a 'great historical service'). For a similar observation see: Francisco García Amador, 'International Responsibility: Fifth Report by F. V. García Amador, Special Rapporteur (A/CN.4/125)' (9 February 1960) 2 *Yearbook of the International Law Commission – 1960* 41, 60-1 [80].

[80]Section 12.2 considers the contrast between modern territorial states and medieval forms of political power in more detail.

[81]Hugo Grotius, *The Rights of War and Peace in Three Books* (1625) (The Lawbook Exchange, Clark NJ 2004) 457 [Book 2 Chap. XXI, § IV(1)].

[82]See generally: Dionisio Anzilotti, *Lehrbuch des Völkerrechts* (Volume 1: Walter de Gruyter, Berlin/Leipzig 1929) 375-8 (underscoring the importance of Grotius' theory for the law of state responsibility); Riccardo Pisillo Mazzeschi, *"Due diligence" e responsabilità internazionale degli stati* (Giuffrè Editore, Milan 1989) 29 (providing additional references on the early reception of the Grotian theory of fault).

[83]Watson, *Legal Transplants: An Approach to Comparative Law* (University of Georgia Press, Athens GA 1993) 27 [first edition: 1974].

This section does not pursue the goal of delivering an exhaustive presentation of the theories of fault in international law. It will merely identify two different doctrinal leanings in the reception of the Grotian analogy. A first tendency could be described as 'Grotian' or 'conservative' in the sense that it preserved the essence of the Grotian theory of fault. These approaches reflect the fundamental idea that fault cannot be presumed, thus maintaining Grotius' general non-responsibility rule. They furthermore conceived fault as a human quality, thus keeping unspoiled the spirit of the Grotian Roman law analogy.

The second group of theories corresponds to those which, while formally preserving the element of *culpa*, attempted to 'objectivize' the assessment of conduct. They introduced fundamental modifications to the original Grotian model and, by so doing, ended up transforming the theory of fault into something new. Some authors went a step further and, without renouncing to the concept of fault, explicitly broke with the Grotian tradition. Taking into consideration their resemblance of purpose, these theories can be characterized as *objectivist approaches*.[84]

12.3.2.1   Conservative 'Grotian' Approaches

The private law-inspired Grotian notion of fault could be depicted as subjective, that is to say, psychological in character. Grotius conceived *culpa* as an inherently human feature.[85] This has significant implications for international law. Abstract entities— including the state—are incapable of incurring in *culpa* for and by themselves. Grotius did not elaborate much on this particular issue. By leaving this fundamental question unsettled, Grotius challenged the ability and imagination of legal scholars and sowed the seed of uncountable dogmatic elaborations.

Contemporary authors have sought to explain this gap by suggesting that the Grotian theory of fault did not actually refer to the responsibility of the state as a moral entity, but to the responsibility of the *physical person* of the sovereign.[86] This

---

[84]The phrase 'objectivist approach', as used in this section, should not be confused with the 'objective approaches' or 'objective theories' of state responsibility, which will be introduced in Sect. 12.3.3.

[85]For the characterization of the Grotian theory of fault as an expression of a psychological conception of fault see: Riccardo Pisillo-Mazzeschi, 'The Due Diligence Rule and the Nature of the International Responsibility of States' in René Provost (ed), *State Responsibility in International Law* (Ashgate Publishing Co., Burlington VT 2002) 97, 99. This section, while conceding that Grotius conceived fault as a psychological quality, does not share some aspects of Pisillo-Mazzeschi's interpretation of *De iure belli ac pacis*.

[86]For some indicative examples see: Andrea Gattini, *Zufall und force majeure im System der Staatenverantwortlichkeit anhand der ILC-Kodifikationsarbeit* (Duncker & Humblot, Berlin 1989) (arguing that Grotius focused on the responsibility of the sovereign or, more precisely, '*reges*' and '*magistratus*'); Antoine Favre, 'Fault as an Element of the Illicit Act' (1963-4) 52 Geo. L. J. 555, 555 (noting that, after the original formulation of the theory, 'the Person-State' replaced the king as the subject of state responsibility); Jan Arno Hessbruegge, 'The Historical Development of the Doctrines of Attribution and Due Diligence in International Law' (2003/4) 36(4) JILP

interpretation is inaccurate. Grotius' choice of words indicates that he was not referring to the prince, but to the nation: *state agents (rectores)* are the ones who engage in culpable conduct,[87] but such conduct gives rise to the responsibility of the *national community (communitas)*.[88] Grotius did hence not confuse the person of the monarch with the body of the nation, but rather *imputed* the (faulty) conduct of the agent to the body of the nation. Grotius surely did not think of the world as a world of autocrats. His own country was by then a republic.[89] What is more, the republican form of government had already attracted Grotius' attention in his younger years.[90] Leading international scholars seem to share this understanding of *De iure belli ac pacis*. A prominent example would be Hersch Lauterpacht, who wrote in 1927:

> It is not possible to expatiate here the merits of the doctrine introduced by him [Grotius], but it may be stated with confidence that it became a part not only of the science of international law but also of the practice of governments. *It is believed that it corresponds with the*

265, 283 (noting that '[f]or Grotius, responsibility in international law meant responsibility of the sovereign as a natural person' and further arguing that 'the doctrine of attribution was unknown to him') and 296 (emphasizing that 'Grotius viewed responsibility as the responsibility among kings'); Margarete Kuhn, *Verschuldens- oder Verursachungshaftung der Staaten im allgemeinen Völkerrecht* (Imprimiere Photo-Landa, Frankfurt 1961) 77 (arguing that Grotius limited responsibility to acts of the sovereign, because 'only he [the sovereign] is identical to the state'); Riccardo Pisillo Mazzeschi, *"Due diligence" e responsabilità internazionale degli stati* (Giuffrè Editore, Milan 1989) 30 (equalizing the Grotian notion of state with the person of the sovereign).

[87] Hugonis Groti, *De iure belli ac pacis* (1625) (Leiden, A. W. Sijthoff 1919) 412 [Lib. 2 Cap. XXI § II(2)]. The Latin term '*rectores*' has been used in diverse contexts and could convey different meanings. In medieval and late-medieval Latin, '*Rector*' can designate the 'territorial prince', but also a wide array of higher state officials. The use of the plural form in Grotius' work suggests that he was not necessarily referring to the person of the sovereign, but simply to a state agent. See: '*Rector*' in *Glossarium Mediae et Infimae Latinitatis* (Volume 7: Niort, L. Favre 1886) 61; '*Rector*' in *Mediae Latinitatis Lexicon Minus – Medieval Latin Dictionary* (Volume 2: Brill, Leiden 2002) 1164-5.

[88] Hugonis Groti, *De iure belli ac pacis* (1625) (Leiden, A. W. Sijthoff 1919) 412 [Lib. 2 Cap. XXI § II(1)]. Grotius resorted in this connection to the expression '*communitas ut alia ita et civiles*'. The term '*communitas*' was often used to designate the sum of a city or village's population. See: 'communitas' in *Glossarium Mediae et Infimae Latinitatis* (Volume 2: Niort, L. Favre 1886) 459. In other glossaries, the term is defined more generally as a body of people. See: 'communitas' in *Mediae Latinitatis Lexicon Minus – Medieval Latin Dictionary* (Volume 1: Brill, Leiden 2002) 1027. The Oxford English Dictionary traces the origins of the English word 'community' back to Latin and Anglo-Norman sources. A 'now rare' use of the term was, according to the Dictionary, '[a] commonwealth, a nation or state'. See: 'community, n' (January 2017) *Oxford English Dictionary Online* [http://www.oed.com/view/Entry/37337?redirectedFrom=community#eid] (quoting Latin, French and English sources from the fourteenth century onwards).

[89] For an excellent study of Grotius' complex relationship with the Dutch Republic see: Henk Nellen, *Hugo Grotius: A Lifelong Struggle for Peace in Church and State, 1583-1645* (J.C. Grayson tr., Brill, Leiden 2015) 71-462.

[90] Grotius is generally regarded as the author of a short work titled *De republica enmendada*, albeit there is still some controversy about its authorship. The book criticized the organization of the Dutch republic and advocated for aristocracy. See generally: Henk Nellen, *Hugo Grotius: A Lifelong Struggle for Peace in Church and State, 1583-1645* (J.C. Grayson tr., Brill, Leiden 2015) 71-3.

conception of States as moral entities accountable for their acts and omissions in proportion to the mens rea of their agents, the real addressees of international duties – a conception which must form the foundation of any legal theory of responsibility.[91]

Lauterpacht's interpretation of Grotius is not only accurate, but additionally provides an excellent example of the so-called 'subjective' or 'psychological' theories of fault in international law.[92] To be sure, this was a widespread view in the twentieth century. Those who favored the use of fault in the law of state responsibility mostly linked the concept to a subjective, individual quality. In spite of this common ground, the role of fault was the subject of intense academic debate. Theories of fault oscillated between those reducing *culpa* to its traditional 'Grotian' core and those abstracting fault into a general principle of state responsibility.

The perhaps most clear illustration of the 'restrictive' side of the spectrum appears in the works of Paul Schoen. In a monograph published in 1917, Schoen observed that 'any will and conduct of the state is in the final analysis only will and conduct of human beings, namely, of the individuals who have been appointed as state agents'.[93] In this vein, he considered that it is beyond doubt that the concept of fault applies in connection with state responsibility for failures to prevent and repress private injuries to aliens.[94] Along these lines, Schoen made a strong defense of the Grotian analogy.[95] His conclusion was that it is only in this specific context that international law calls upon the application of the principle of fault.[96] In the last

---

[91]Emphasis added. Hersch Lauterpacht, *Private Law Sources and Analogies of International Law (With Special Reference to International Arbitration)* (Longmans, Green and Co. Ltd., London 1927) 137.

[92]On the theories of psychological fault see generally: Riccardo Pisillo Mazzeschi, "Due diligence" e responsabilità internazionale degli stati (Giuffrè Editore, Milan 1989) 61-9 (particularly focusing on the writings of Roberto Ago, but also providing some notes on Morelli and mentioning other relevant authors, such as Dahm and Ross). For an English summary of the argument see: Riccardo Pisillo-Mazzeschi, 'The Due Diligence Rule and the Nature of the International Responsibility of States' in René Provost (ed), *State Responsibility in International Law* (Ashgate Publishing Co., Burlington VT 2002) 97, 99-101. For an overview of the theories of fault in the international law of aliens see: Francisco García Amador, 'International Responsibility: Fifth Report by F. V. García Amador, Special Rapporteur (A/CN.4/125)' (9 February 1960) 2 *Yearbook of the International Law Commission – 1960* 41, 60-3 [79-87] (including references to the most significant dogmatic approaches to the subject).

[93]Author's translation. The original German text reads: "[A]lles staatliche Wollen und Handeln [ist] doch nur Wollen und Handeln von Menschen, nämlich der zu staatlichen Organträgern bestellten Individuen." Paul Schoen, *Die völkerrechtliche Haftung der Staaten aus unerlaubten Handlungen* (J. U. Kern's Verlag, Breslau 1917) 51.

[94]Paul Schoen, *Die völkerrechtliche Haftung der Staaten aus unerlaubten Handlungen* (J. U. Kern's Verlag, Breslau 1917) 51.

[95]Paul Schoen, *Die völkerrechtliche Haftung der Staaten aus unerlaubten Handlungen* (J. U. Kern's Verlag, Breslau 1917) 58 *et seq*. Schoen expressly mentions the Grotian origins of the concept of fault at 50.

[96]Paul Schoen, *Die völkerrechtliche Haftung der Staaten aus unerlaubten Handlungen* (J. U. Kern's Verlag, Breslau 1917) 62. For a critical analysis of Schoen's views see: Adolf Jess, *Politische Handlungen Privater gegen das Ausland und das Völkerrecht* (Verlag von M. &

decades of the twentieth century, some publicists shared the fundamental proposition that fault, though not a general condition for responsibility, could constitute a requirement for specific violations of international law, such as the customary obligation to protect foreign citizens.[97] Thus, Ingo von Münch argued in 1963 that, as a rule, fault is a requirement of state responsibility in cases involving acts of individuals.[98]

Other authors proposed a solution which, despite bearing a striking resemblance to Schoen's approach,[99] resorted to much more abstract conceptual devices. An often-cited example is a monograph published by Karl Strupp in 1922. Strupp argued that, while a state's responsibility for its organs' actions (*Handlungen*) is based on a standard of strict liability (*Erfolgshaftung*), the wrongfulness of an omission (*Unterlassungshandlungen*) is always determined on the basis of the principle of fault (*Verschuldensprinzip*).[100] He thus extended the role of fault beyond its original core but, at the same time, sought to maintain its essence through the concept of *delicts of omission*.[101] Prominent German-speaking scholars shared this opinion in the first decades of the twentieth century.[102] Moreover, a few

---

H. Marcus, Breslau 1923) 122-8. See also: Margarete Kuhn, *Verschuldens- oder Verursachungshaftung der Staaten im allgemeinen Völkerrecht* (Imprimiere Photo-Landa, Frankfurt 1961) 90-3 (particularly focusing on the differences and similarities between the views of Schoen and Dionisio Anzilotti's approach to state responsibility for acts of individuals).

[97]For a representative example see: Benedetto Conforti, 'Cours general de droit international public' (1988) 212 RCADI 9, 175-6 (also establishing a link between the notions of *faute* and *diligence nécessaire dans la protection*); Hans-Jürgen Schlochauer, 'Die Entwicklung des völkerrechtlichen Deliktsrechts' (1975) 16 AVR 239, 262 (further characterizing the faulty lack of protection as a 'secondary state conduct').

[98]Ingo von Münch, *Das völkerrechtliche Delikt in der modernen Entwicklung der Völkerrechtsgemeinschaft* (P. Keppler Verlag, Frankfurt 1963) 169. Cf. also n. 97 above.

[99]The similarity between Schoen and Strupp has not remained unnoticed. See, for example: Adolf Jess, *Politische Handlungen Privater gegen das Ausland und das Völkerrecht* (Verlag von M. & H. Marcus, Breslau 1923) 128; Francisco García Amador, 'International Responsibility: Fifth Report by F. V. García Amador, Special Rapporteur (A/CN.4/125)' (9 February 1960) 2 *Yearbook of the International Law Commission – 1960* 41, 61-2 [84].

[100]Karl Strupp, *Grundzüge des positiven Völkerrechts* (Ludwig Röhrscheid, Bonn 1922) 129-30.

[101]Cf. Karl Strupp, *Grundzüge des positiven Völkerrechts* (Ludwig Röhrscheid, Bonn 1922) 129-30. For an analysis of Strupp's views in context see: Pavlos Alextrandou Zannas, *La responsabilité internationale des Etats pour les actes de négligence* (Ganguin & Laubscher, Geneva 1952) 35-6.

[102]For an indicative example see: Eduard Otto von Waldkirch, *Das Völkerrecht in seinen Grundzügen dargestellt* (Verlag von Helbing & Lichtenhahn, Basel 1926) 230-1.

contemporary authors have followed Strupp's views.[103] Nonetheless, at least at present, this view has met with more criticism than praise.[104]

Most supporters of the concept of fault went a step beyond Strupp and elevated *culpa* to a general principle of state responsibility. This entailed liberating fault from its original, 'Grotian' scope of application. At the same time, however, there was still something inherently Grotian in the underlying understanding of fault as a human or psychological quality. For example, Georg Dahm advocated in 1961 for the recognition of fault (*Schuld*) as a necessary condition for state responsibility, further distinguishing between intent (*Vorsatz*) and negligence (*Fahrlässigkeit*).[105] In this

---

[103]For a representative example see: Karl Zemanek, 'Schuld- und Erfolgshaftung im Entwurf der Völkerrechtskommission über Staatenverantwortlichkeit. Zugleich Bemerkungen zum Prozess der Kodifikation im Rahmen der Vereinten Nationen' in Emanuel Diez, Jean Monnier, Jörg Müller, Heinrich Reimann and Luzius Wildhaber (eds), *Festschrift für Rudolf Bindschedler zum 65. Geburtstag am 8. Juli 1980* (Verlag Stämpfli & cie., Bern 1980) 315, 322-3. But cf. also: Karl Zemanek, Gerhard Hafner and Stephan Wittich, 'Die völkerrechtliche Verantwortlichkeit und die Sanktionen des Völkerrechts' in Hanspeter Neuhold, Waldemar Hummer and Christoph Schreuer (eds), *Österreichisches Handbuch des Völkerrechts* (Volume 1: Manz, Vienna 2004) 505, 510 (adopting a more cautious terminology on this particular subject). Alfred Verdross and Bruno Simma have also expressed some sympathy for Strupp's distinction. Their choice of words is however very careful in this regard. They rely on the distinction between actions and omissions and conclude that, in 'most cases' involving 'delicts of action' (*Handlungsdelikte*), the 'mere objective violation of a norm of international law' suffices for responsibility to attach; in some cases, they say, proof of intent or negligence could however be required. See: Alfred Verdross and Bruno Simma, *Universelles Völkerrecht* (Duncker & Humblot, Berlin 1984) 852 (also discussing other doctrinal approaches to the subject at 850-5). Other authors, after giving careful consideration to the arguments against Strupp's approach, have observed that, '[while critics are] surely correct in rejecting any distinction between acts and omissions of States on the basis of the principle of fault, [...] the decisional trends outside the European courts have that precise effect'. See: Gordon Christenson, 'The Doctrine of Attribution in State Responsibility' in Richard Lillich (ed), *International Law of State Responsibility for Injuries to Aliens* (University Press of Virginia, Charlottesville VA 1983) 321, 362. On this approach cf. also Karl Doehring, *Völkerrecht. Ein Lehrbuch* (C. F. Müller Verlag, Heidelberg 2004) 371-2.

[104]Franck Latty, 'Actions and Omissions' in James Crawford, Alain Pellet and Simon Olleson (eds), *The Law of International Responsibility* (Oxford University Press, New York 2010) 355, 361 (following a rather 'objectivist' line of argument according to which 'there is no general requirement of any specific intention in order for there to be a breach of an international obligation'). For a detailed critical analysis of Strupp's argument see: Adolf Jess, *Politische Handlungen Privater gegen das Ausland und das Völkerrecht* (Verlag von M. & H. Marcus, Breslau 1923) 129-33. For another critical voice see: Ian Brownlie, *System of the Law of Nations. State Responsibility* (Clarendon Press, Oxford 1983) 42-3.

[105]Georg Dahm, *Völkerrecht* (Volume 3: W. Kohlhammer Verlag, Stuttgart 1961) 224-32. Decades after Dahm's death, Jost Delbrück and Rüdiger Wolfrum published a revised edition of his treatise (2002). This new edition does not include fault as an element of the internationally wrongful act and contains a rather descriptive introduction to the subject. See: Jost Delbrück and Rüdiger Wolfrum, *Völkerrecht. Begründet von Georg Dahm* (Volume 3: De Gruyter, Berlin 2002) 944-8.

connection, he went on to observe that fault is a human attribute, so that 'only a legal fiction makes it possible to speak of fault by the state'.[106]

A different version of the theory appeared in the works of Gaetano Morelli, a well-known Italian international lawyer who would serve as ICJ judge from 1961 to 1970. According to Morelli, fault (*colpa*) designates a 'psychological relationship between agent and event'.[107] As a consequence of its inherent subjective character, fault is unavoidably human.[108] Strictly speaking it is hence not the state that incurs in fault, but a human being who happens to wear the guise of a state organ.[109] Therefore, Morelli explained, it is inaccurate to say that fault is imputed to the state.[110] Rather, the presence of *culpa* could be described as a *prerequisite* for the (subsequent) imputation of a specific course of conduct to the state.[111] Morelli believed that this condition already enjoyed acceptance within the international community.[112] In this vein, he resorted to the customary obligation to prevent and punish private injuries to aliens as an example.[113]

A young Roberto Ago expressed, too, support for a general requisite of fault ('*colpa*' or '*faute*') in an article published in 1939 and his Hague Lecture of that year.[114] To-date, Ago's work is generally regarded as one of the most significant modern

---

[106] Author's translation. The original German text is: "Nur eine rechtliche Fiktion macht es möglich, von einem Verschulden des Staates zu sprechen." Georg Dahm, *Völkerrecht* (Volume 3: W. Kohlhammer Verlag, Stuttgart 1961) 224 (also making reference to Lauterpacht at n. 2).

[107] Author's translation. The original Italian text is: "[con questo termine si indica] una relazione psicologica che intercorre fra l'agente e l'evento." Gaetano Morelli, *Nozioni di diritto internazionale* (CEDAM – Casa Editrice Dott. A. Milani, Padua 1958) 339. Morelli's definition is thoroughly similar to the one advanced by Roberto Ago in 1939. See: Roberto Ago, *La colpa nell'illecito internazionale* (CEDAM – Casa Editrice Dott. A. Milani, Pavia 1939) 3, 16; Roberto Ago, 'Le délit international' (1939) 68 RCADI 415, 486.

[108] Gaetano Morelli, *Nozioni di diritto internazionale* (CEDAM – Casa Editrice Dott. A. Milani, Padua 1958) 339.

[109] Gaetano Morelli, *Nozioni di diritto internazionale* (CEDAM – Casa Editrice Dott. A. Milani, Padua 1958) 339.

[110] Gaetano Morelli, *Nozioni di diritto internazionale* (CEDAM – Casa Editrice Dott. A. Milani, Padua 1958) 339-40.

[111] Gaetano Morelli, *Nozioni di diritto internazionale* (CEDAM – Casa Editrice Dott. A. Milani, Padua 1958) 340. Morelli's clarification could give the impression of being a mere legal subtlety. Nonetheless, the distinction between the *imputation of fault* and the *imputation of guilty conduct* was actually a response to Anzilotti's objective approach to state responsibility (cf. Sect. 12.3.3).

[112] Gaetano Morelli, *Nozioni di diritto internazionale* (CEDAM – Casa Editrice Dott. A. Milani, Padua 1958) 341.

[113] Gaetano Morelli, *Nozioni di diritto internazionale* (CEDAM – Casa Editrice Dott. A. Milani, Padua 1958) 341-2.

[114] Roberto Ago, *La colpa nell'illecito internazionale* (CEDAM – Casa Editrice Dott. A. Milani, Pavia 1939) 3-32 (particularly at p. 32); Roberto Ago, 'Le délit international' (1939) 68 RCADI 415, 459 *et seq.* For a critical analysis of Ago's early conception of fault see: Pavlos Alextrandou Zannas, *La responsabilité internationale des Etats pour les actes de négligence* (Ganguin & Laubscher, Geneva 1952) 38-40.

contributions to the subject.[115] It remains however unclear whether his views changed with the passage of time. Ago's *Second* and *Third Reports on State Responsibility* (1970–1971) give the impression that, at least to some extent, they actually did.[116]

Beyond these scholars, many other authors considered fault as a general requisite of state responsibility without elaborating much on the subjective or psychological character of the concept. Indicative examples appear in academic publications of Franz von Liszt,[117] Julius Hatschek,[118] Ignaz Seidl-Hohenveldern[119] and Philip Jessup.[120] Others, like Alf Ross, recognized the element of fault, but believed it to be of limited practical relevance.[121] The theory of fault did not only enjoy acceptance among academic publicists. The *Institut de Droit International* adopted in 1927 a draft submitted by Leo Strisower, which conditioned international responsibility for injuries to aliens upon faulty conduct by the host state.[122] In the *Corfu*

---

[115]Riccardo Pisillo Mazzeschi, *"Due diligence" e responsabilità internazionale degli stati* (Giuffrè Editore, Milan 1989) 61 *et seq.*; Riccardo Pisillo-Mazzeschi, 'The Due Diligence Rule and the Nature of the International Responsibility of States' in René Provost (ed), *State Responsibility in International Law* (Ashgate Publishing Co., Burlington VT 2002) 97, 99-101.

[116]In his Third Report on State Responsibility, Ago did not include fault as a separate element of the internationally wrongful act and moreover avoided the use of the notion. In addition, the Report contains at this point some approving references to the works of Dionisio Anzilotti. Anzilotti, as will be explained in Sect. 12.3.3, was the fiercest critic of the fault-based theories of state responsibility. See: Roberto Ago, 'Second Report on State Responsibility – The Origin of International Responsibility (A/CN.4/233)' (10 April 1970) 2 *Yearbook of the International Law Commission – 1970* 177, 187-95 [31-55]; Roberto Ago, 'Third Report on State Responsibility – The Origin of International Responsibility (A/CN.4/246 and Add. 1-3)' (1971) 2(1) *Yearbook of the International Law Commission – 1971* 199, 214-23 [49-75]. For an analysis of the influence of Ago's early conception of fault on the ILC Articles on State Responsibility see: Andrea Gattini, 'Smoking/No Smoking: Some Remarks on the Current Place of Fault in the ILC Draft Articles on State Responsibility' (1999) 10(2) EJIL 397, 398 (arguing that Ago 'let ashes [of fault] fall on many places, some of them discreetly concealed in various folds of the Draft Articles, others apparently inadvertently spread over the surface').

[117]Franz von Liszt, *Das Völkerrecht systematisch dargestellt* (Verlag von O. Häring, Berlin 1906) 193.

[118]Julius Hatschek, *Völkerrecht im Grundriss* (A. Deichertsche Verlagsbuchhandlung Dr. Werner Scholl, Leipzig 1926) 188.

[119]Ignaz Seidl-Hohenveldern, *Völkerrecht* (Carl Heymanns Verlag, Berlin 1997) 315 (fault as a requisite for state responsibility) and 322 (protection obligation). See also the later edition of Seidl-Hohenveldern's manual, coauthored with Torsten Stein: Ignaz Seidl-Hohenveldern and Torsten Stein, *Völkerrecht* (Carl Heymanns Verlag, Berlin 2000) 317 and 324.

[120]Philip Jessup, *A Modern Law of Nations* (The Macmillan Company, New York 1949) 103-4 (particularly referring to the law of aliens and, more specifically, to the customary protection obligation).

[121]Alf Ross, *A Textbook of International Law. General Part* (Longmans, Green and Co., London 1947) 256 (concluding that 'International Law [...] as a main rule makes the culpa rule the basis for responsibility, though it does not acquire the same importance as in civil law).

[122]Institut de Droit International, 'Résolutions votées par l'Institut au cours de sa XXXI Vᵉ Session – Responsabilité internationale des États à raison des dommages causés sur leur territoire à la personne ou aux biens des étrangers (XIIIᵉ Commission)' (1927) 33(II) Annuaire de l'Institut de Droit International 330, 331 ("Cette responsabilité de l'Etat n'existe pas si l'inobservation de

Channel Case (1949),[123] the *culpa* principle found express support in the dissenting opinions of ICJ Judges Bohuslav Ečer (*ad hoc*),[124] José P. de Barros e Azevedo[125] and Sergei B. Krylov.[126]

12.3.2.2 Objectivist Approaches

A second group of academic approaches to the question of fault was signalized by the common purpose of 'objectivizing' the assessment of conduct without renouncing to the concept of *culpa*. This goal could be achieved through different dogmatic devices. At least two approaches were developed in this connection.

A first line of argument consisted in introducing a *presumption of fault*. A representative example appears in Samuel Pufendorf's *De iure naturae et gentium*

---

l'obligation n'est pas la conséquence d'une faute de ses organes, à moins que, dans le cas dont il s'agit, une règle conventionnelle ou coutumière, spéciale à la matière, n'admette la responsabilité sans faute"). See also the Special Rapporteaur's analysis of the subject: Leo Strisower, 'Responsabilité internationale des États à raison des dommages causés sur leur territoire à la personne ou aux biens des étrangers' (1927) 33 Annuaire de l'Institut de Droit International 455, 465-71.

[123] There has been some debate as to whether the ICJ impliedly accepted the principle of fault in this case. See generally: Antoine Favre, 'Fault as an Element of the Illicit Act' (1963-4) 52 Geo. L. J. 555, 563-4 (providing an overview of the debate and concluding that the court made an analysis of 'objective fault', in terms of due diligence); Francisco García Amador, 'International Responsibility: Fifth Report by F. V. García Amador, Special Rapporteur (A/CN.4/125)' (9 February 1960) 2 *Yearbook of the International Law Commission – 1960* 41, 62-3 [85-7] (considering that the question is a 'matter interpretation' and making specific reference to the dissenting opinions); Ian Brownlie, *System of the Law of Nations. State Responsibility* (Clarendon Press, Oxford 1983) 47-8 (suggesting that the ICJ did neither accept nor reject the element of fault); Maglosia Fitzmaurice, 'The Corfu Channel Case and the Development of International Law' in Nisuke Ando, Edward McWhinney and Rüdiger Wolfrum (eds), *Liber Amicorum Judge Shigeru Oda* (Volume 1: Kluwer Law International, The Hague 2002) 119, 138-9 (suggesting that, despite not expressly recognizing the element of fault, the ICJ 'rejected the concept of absolute liability and based Albania's responsibility upon its failure to act as it should have done – clearly a matter of fault'); Ingo von Münch, *Das völkerrechtliche Delikt in der modernen Entwicklung der Völkerrechtsgemeinschaft* (P. Keppler Verlag, Frankfurt 1963) 154 *et seq.* (noting that the judgment did not take a clear stance on the question of fault and also discussing the dissenting opinions); Malcolm Shaw, *International Law* (Cambridge University Press, New York 2003) 699-700 (rejecting this interpretation of the ICJ judgment); Rosalyn Higgins, *Problems & Process. International Law and How We Use It* (Clarendon Press, Oxford 1994) 160 (suggesting that 'the judgment is neutral on *culpa*' and discussing the dissenting opinions at n. 43).

[124] *Corfu Channel Case (UK v Albania)* [1949] ICJ Rep 4, Dissenting Opinion by Dr. Ečer 115, 127-8.

[125] *Corfu Channel Case (UK v Albania)* [1949] ICJ Rep 4, Dissenting Opinion by Judge Azevedo 78, 85-6.

[126] *Corfu Channel Case (UK v Albania)* [1949] ICJ Rep 4, Dissenting Opinion by Judge Krylov 68, 71-2.

(1672).[127] Pufendorf accepted the fundamental premise of the severability of the sovereign from its individual subjects, and further recognized that responsibility could attach on account of *patientia* or *receptus*.[128] Referring to the concept of *patientia*, Pufendorf was moreover explicit in making accountability contingent upon the sovereign having both knowledge of the subject's offences and the power to prevent their misendeavors: *scientia & facultas prohibendi*.[129] So far, Pufendorf's theory fully resembles Grotius' approach. Pufendorf however added an important caveat. According to him, the state's awareness of the injurious action and its power to prevent it shall be *presumed*:[130]

> [T]he Governors of Commonwealths are presumed to know what their Subjects openly and frequently commit, and their Power to hinder it is always supposed, unless the Want of it be manifestly proved.[131]

This caveat is of great importance. The presumption of both knowledge and power to prevent has the practical effect of creating a *presumption of responsibility*. Simply put, Pufendorf turned Grotius' general rule of *non-responsibility* into a general *responsibility* rule.[132]

---

[127] On the reception of Grotius in the writings of Samuel Pufendorf see: Riccardo Pisillo Mazzeschi, *"Due diligence" e responsabilità internazionale degli stati* (Giuffrè Editore, Milan 1989) 30.

[128] See: Samuel Pufendorf, *Of the Law of Nature and of Nations in Eight Books* (1672) (Mr. Carew tr., I. Walthoe et al. London 1729) 842. For the original Latin text see: Samuel Pufendorf, *De jure naturae et gentium. Libri octo* (Sumtibus Adami Junghans, Lund 1672) 1169 [Book VIII, Chap. VI § 12]. This work uses at this instance an early translation of Pufendorf's work, which appeared in London in 1729. This translation is different to the one used in Ch. 3, which corresponds to the English edition prepared by Michael Seidler in 1994. While Seidler's translation is generally more accurate, it only covers some selected sections of Pufendorf's work. The passages included in the 1994 translation do not include the one referring to the concepts of *patientia* and *receptus*.

[129] See: Samuel Pufendorf, *Of the Law of Nature and of Nations in Eight Books* (1672) (Mr. Carew tr., I. Walthoe et al. London 1729) 842. For the original Latin text see: Samuel Pufendorf, *De jure naturae et gentium. Libri octo* (Sumtibus Adami Junghans, Lund 1672) 1170 [Book VIII, Chap. VI § 12].

[130] On this fundamental difference between the approaches of Grotius and Pufendorf see: Riccardo Pisillo Mazzeschi, *"Due diligence" e responsabilità internazionale degli stati* (Giuffrè Editore, Milan 1989) 30. See also: Ago, *La colpa nell'illecito internazionale* (CEDAM – Casa Editrice Dott. A. Milani, Pavia 1939) 5; Margarete Kuhn, *Verschuldens- oder Verursachungshaftung der Staaten im allgemeinen Völkerrecht* (Imprimerie Photo-Landa, Frankfurt 1961) 78-9.

[131] Samuel Pufendorf, *Of the Law of Nature and of Nations in Eight Books* (1672) (Mr. Carew tr., I. Walthoe et al. London 1729) 842. The original Latin text is unmistakably clear in respect of this presumption. The relevant passage reads as follows: "Sciri autem à rectoribus civitatum praesumuntur, quae à subditis aperte & frequenter patrantur. Facultas prohibendi Semper praesumitur, nisi ejus defectus manifeste probetur." Samuel Pufendorf, *De jure naturae et gentium. Libri octo* (Sumtibus Adami Junghans, Lund 1672) 1169 [Book VIII, Chap. VI § 12].

[132] In this connection, some authors have argued that Pufendorf did not create a presumption of fault, but rather a *presumption of a wrongful conduct* (*Vermutung eines rechtswidrigen Verhalten*). See: Margarete Kuhn, *Verschuldens- oder Verursachungshaftung der Staaten im allgemeinen Völkerrecht* (Imprimerie Photo-Landa, Frankfurt 1961) 79.

The second 'objectivist' approach corresponds to the theory of *normative fault*. This model retained *culpa* as a *conditio sine qua non* for a finding of responsibility but, at the same time, wiped out the subjective or psychological element through an *objective definition of fault*.[133] At the heart of the normative theory was the assimilation of *culpa* to the *breach of duty* (or *wrongful act*). Bin Cheng, one of the best-known representatives of this school, explained that 'failure to observe one's duty constitutes the fault which is the sole basis of responsibility, and this fault is, therefore, equivalent to the notion of an unlawful act'.[134] In Cheng's view, the importance of fault lies in the fact that it embodies the 'element of freedom of action' as a fundamental ingredient of the 'unlawful act'.[135]

Cheng was not alone in his attempt to give *culpa* an 'objective' shape. In an article published in the early 1960s, Antoine Favre delivered one of the most detailed presentations of the 'normative' understanding of the concept of fault and the corresponding revisited function of the notion in the international law of state responsibility.[136] Like Cheng, Favre defined fault as 'the violation of a duty'.[137] In this line of argument, he went on to observe:

> Fault results from behavior which constitutes a transgression of the norm of conduct prescribed by the rule of law by a failure of the wrongdoer's volition; the wrongdoer could have, and should have, acted other than as he did. He is thus charged with the act – he is liable for it. The failure to observe the legal duty justifies the reprobation of the wrongdoer and brings a legal claim for redress; it takes on a moral tint.[138]

Favre's definition of fault was clearly objectivist.[139] The significance of this characterization of the concept becomes conspicuous in Favre's statement that '[a] State's responsibility resulting from a violation of an international obligation

---

[133]For a detailed presentation of the concept of normative fault and its evolution in international legal thought see: Riccardo Pisillo Mazzeschi, *"Due diligence" e responsabilità internazionale degli stati* (Giuffrè Editore, Milan 1989) 70-2 (also providing a brief overview of the approaches suggested by Bin Cheng and Hildebrando Accioly). See also: Riccardo Pisillo-Mazzeschi, 'The Due Diligence Rule and the Nature of the International Responsibility of States' in René Provost (ed), *State Responsibility in International Law* (Ashgate Publishing Co., Burlington VT 2002) 97, 101 (providing an English summary of the argument). Cf. also: Francisco García Amador, 'International Responsibility: Fifth Report by F. V. García Amador, Special Rapporteur (A/CN.4/125)' (9 February 1960) 2 *Yearbook of the International Law Commission – 1960* 41, 61 [81] (making specific reference to Bin Cheng's views on the subject).

[134]Bin Cheng, *General Principles of Law as Applied by International Courts and Tribunals* (Cambridge University Press, New York 2006) 219 [first edition: 1953].

[135]Bin Cheng, *General Principles of Law as Applied by International Courts and Tribunals* (Cambridge University Press, New York 2006) 219 [first edition: 1953].

[136]Antoine Favre, 'Fault as an Element of the Illicit Act' (1963-4) 52 Geo. L. J. 555, 557 *et seq.*

[137]Antoine Favre, 'Fault as an Element of the Illicit Act' (1963-4) 52 Geo. L. J. 555, 560.

[138]Antoine Favre, 'Fault as an Element of the Illicit Act' (1963-4) 52 Geo. L. J. 555, 560.

[139]Despite being a strong adherent of 'objective fault', Favre believed that subjective fault (in the sense of 'negligence' or 'an intentional act') could constitute an aggravating factor. In addition, he considered that the fault principle admits some exceptions. See: Antoine Favre, 'Fault as an Element of the Illicit Act' (1963-4) 52 Geo. L. J. 555, 564-5 and 567-9.

can be found even though the personal fault of the agent or agency is not established – on the basis of objective fault'.[140] Favre's understanding of 'objective fault' evinces a gradual terminological shift from 'fault' to 'due diligence'. In fact, he considered diligence to be the key for properly identifying faulty conduct:

> Fault [. . .] consists in a violation of diligency. Thus, one can speak of fault in an objective sense or of objective fault, a responsibility which is not merely causal, evoked by the injury, but one which proceeds from an act which is reproachable because it was committed in violation of an obligation of diligency. The notion of objective fault is as valid in international law as it is in other fields of law [. . .] The act is illicit because it is faulty and it is faulty to the extent that it discloses a lack of diligency such as to justify reproach.[141]

This approach might sound familiar to lawyers with a civil law background. The 'normative' approach roots in municipal law and, particularly, French civil law.[142] Hence, private law inspired the normative theory of fault. This understanding of *culpa* certainly takes distance from the Grotian analogy. What is more, some versions of the theory openly broke with the Grotian tradition. The writings of the Brazilian diplomat Hildebrando Accioly provide a clear example of this detachment.

In a lecture delivered at The Hague Academy of International Law in 1959, Accioly argued that the concept of fault does not refer to a subjective, wrongful intention (*intention fautive*) but to a 'wrongful act committed by a state organ and consisting in a violation of a legal rule'.[143] This statement earned Accioly the reputation of being a strong adherent to the theory of normative fault.[144] A look into his *Manual de Direito Internacional Publico*, which fourth edition appeared in São Paulo just one year before his Hague Lecture, indicates, however, that Accioly was not entirely convinced that fault should play any role whatsoever in the law of state responsibility. In his assessment of state responsibility for acts of individuals, Accioly took into consideration the Grotian theory of fault.[145] His analysis

---

[140]Antoine Favre, 'Fault as an Element of the Illicit Act' (1963-4) 52 Geo. L. J. 555, 564-5 and 569.

[141]Antoine Favre, 'Fault as an Element of the Illicit Act' (1963-4) 52 Geo. L. J. 555, 561-2.

[142]The private law origins of the notion become conspicuous in Bin Cheng's recourse to French legal literature in this connection. See: Antoine Favre, 'Fault as an Element of the Illicit Act' (1963-4) 52 Geo. L. J. 555, 557 (quoting Jean-Paulin Niboyet, Henri and Léon Mazeud, and André Tunc to justify the need for the concept of fault in the law of state responsibility) and 561 (quoting Henri Capitant and Ambroise Colin); Bin Cheng, *General Principles of Law as Applied by International Courts and Tribunals* (Cambridge University Press, New York 2006) 219 n. 2 [first edition: 1953] (quoting in this connection the works of Henri Capitant, and Marcel Planiol and Georges Ripert).

[143]In this vein, Accioly stated: "il semble que la principale difficulté dans l'acceptation générale de la faute, comme base de la responsabilité internationale, résulte de certaines différences sur le sens précis du mot. Vraiment, on pourra dire qu'il ne s'agit pas d'une intention fautive, mais [. . .] d'un acte illicite, commis par un organe de l'Etat et consistant dans la violation d'une règle de droit." Hildebrando Accioly, 'Principes généraux de la responsabilité internationale d'après la doctrine et la jurisprudence' (1959) 96 RCADI 349, 369.

[144]Riccardo Pisillo Mazzeschi, *"Due diligence" e responsabilità internazionale degli stati* (Giuffrè Editore, Milan 1989) 71 (quoting Accioly as a representative of the theory of normative fault).

[145]Hildebrando Accioly, *Manual de Direito Internacional Publico* (São Paulo, Edição Saraiva 1958) 79 and 88-9.

concluded that 'contemporary international law supports an entirely different point of view'.[146] Accioly's own approach to the subject can be best depicted as eclectic or, perhaps more accurately, skeptic:

> As regards to this subject, which has sown so much debate, particularly because international scholars themselves disagree as to the meaning of the term *culpa*, a reasonable solution could be achieved through the idea of the *wrongful act*. It would not be sufficient to say that it [the wrongful act] is that which violates duties or obligations. We could resort, for example, to a concept provided by our Civil Code, according to which '[the person] who, as a result of its willful action or omission, negligence or imprudence, violates the right or causes damages to others is obliged to repair the damage'. Here we have the subjective and objective elements, with a simple subjection of the duty to make reparation to a causal link between the agent's action or omission, and the harm or wrongful act that has been committed. Whether fault is considered as an essential condition of responsibility, or [responsibility] is established upon a purely objective criterion, the opposition between the two notions [...] is of merely academic interest: equivalent results could be achieved with any of the two systems.[147]

Hence, Accioly went much further than Cheng or Favre. He did not only 'objectivize' the notion of fault, but additionally questioned its practical relevance. Accioly's views can therefore be taken as an epilogue to the theories of fault. At the same time, his words might serve as an introduction to those approaches which definitively renounced to the Grotian analogy, replacing the disputed notion of *culpa* with the much less contentious concept of *due diligence*. The following sections address these *objective theories of diligence* in detail.

12.3.3 Responsibility Without Fault. The 'Objective Turn' in the International Law of State Responsibility

In the late nineteenth and early twentieth centuries, international law scholars became increasingly skeptical about the role of fault in the international law of

---

[146] Author's translation. The original Portuguese text reads: "o direito internacional contemporâneo sustenta ponto de vista completamente diverso." Hildebrando Accioly, *Manual de Direito Internacional Publico* (São Paulo, Edição Saraiva 1958) 88.

[147] Author's translation. The original Portuguese text reads: "Nessa matéria, que tem sido tão debatida, especialmente porque os próprios internacionalistas muita vez divergem sôbre o sentido da palavra *culpa*, talvez se pudesse chegar a uma solução razoável partindo-se da idéia de *ato ilícito*. Não bastaria dizer-se que êste é o que viola deveres ou obrigações. Poderíamos recorrer, por exempli, a um conceito contido em nosso Código Civil, segundo o qual "aquêle que, por ação ou omissão voluntária, negligência ou imprudência, violar direito ou causar prejuízo a outem fica obrigado a reparar o dano". Assim, temos aí reunidos os elementos subjetivo e objetivo, com a simples subordinação do dever de reparação a um nexo causal entre a ação ou omissão do agente e o dano ou ato ilícito praticado. Como quer seja, ou se considere a culpa como condição essencial da responsabilidade, ou se funde esta cum critério puramente objetivo, a oposição entre as duas noções [...] só apresenta um interêsse teórico: resultados equivalentes poderão ser alcançados com qualquer dos dois sistemas." Hildebrando Accioly, *Manual de Direito Internacional Publico* (São Paulo, Edição Saraiva 1958) 79.

state responsibility.[148] The genesis of this 'objective turn' is not easy to establish, though, at least not with precision and accuracy. Perhaps it was the German constitutional law scholar Georg von Jellinek who sowed the seed of skepticism. Jellinek observed in 1892 that every state has an obligation to prevent those who are subject to its jurisdiction from causing harm to other states.[149] In this vein, he noted that states are responsible even in the absence of fault, and went on to draw a parallel between international responsibility and the private law notion of the quasi-delict.[150] At the *Institut de Droit International*, Emilio Brusa (1898)[151] and Paul Fauchille (1900)[152] brought the idea of 'responsibility without fault' into the debate on state responsibility for injuries inflicted to aliens in the course of insurrections and civil disorders.

In spite of these important precedents, credit for the objective theory of state responsibility should go to Dionisio Anzilotti.[153] In a monograph written in 1902 and subsequent publications, Anzilotti presented a meticulous argument against the elevation of fault to a general requirement of state responsibility.[154] Anzilotti began

---

[148]On the 'objective turn' see generally: Awalou Ouedraogo, 'L'évolution du concept de faute dans la théorie de la responsabilité internationale des États' (2008) 21(2) Revue québécoise de droit international 129, 149 *et seq.*; Giuseppe Palmisano, 'Fault' in Rüdiger Wolfrum (ed), *The Max Planck Encyclopedia of Public International Law* (Volume 3: Oxford University Press, New York 2012) 1128, 1129 *et seq.*; Ingo von Münch, *Das völkerrechtliche Delikt in der modernen Entwicklung der Völkerrechtsgemeinschaft* (P. Keppler Verlag, Frankfurt 1963) 152 *et seq.*; Margarete Kuhn, *Verschuldens- oder Verursachungshaftung der Staaten im allgemeinen Völkerrecht* (Imprimiere Photo-Landa, Frankfurt 1961) 81 *et seq.*; Riccardo Pisillo Mazzeschi, *"Due diligence" e responsabilità internazionale degli stati* (Giuffrè Editore, Milan 1989) 33 *et seq.* and 55 *et seq.* For an overview of the historic evolution of the law of state responsibility, cf. James Crawford, *State Responsibility. The General Part* (Cambridge University Press, Cambridge 2013) 3 *et seq.* (see particularly pp. 20 *et seq.*); Robert Kolb, *The International Law of State Responsibility. An Introduction* (Edward Elgar Publishing, Northampton MA 2017) 1 *et seq.*

[149]Georg Jellinek, *System der subjektiven öffentlichen Rechte* (Akademische Verlagsbuchhandlung von J.C.B. Mohr 1892) 313.

[150]Georg Jellinek, *System der subjektiven öffentlichen Rechte* (Akademische Verlagsbuchhandlung von J.C.B. Mohr 1892) 313. For a critical discussion of the use of the private law concept of quasi-delicts (*Quasi-Delikte*) in the context of international law see: Ingo von Münch, *Das völkerrechtliche Delikt in der modernen Entwicklung der Völkerrechtsgemeinschaft* (P. Keppler Verlag, Frankfurt 1963) 17-8.

[151]Emilio Brusa, 'Responsabilité des États à raison des dommages soufferts par des étrangers en cas d'émeute ou de guerre civile' (1898) 17 Annuaire de l'Institut de Droit International 96, 99 *et seq.* and 135.

[152]Institut de Droit International, 'Neuvième Commission d'étude – Responsabilité des États à raison des dommages soufferts par des étrangers en cas d'émeute ou de guerre civile' (1900) 18 Annuaire de l'Institut de Droit International 233, 234-5 and 243.

[153]For an overview of Anzilotti's contribution to the international law of state responsibility see: Pierre Marie Dupuy, 'Dionisio Anzilotti and the Law of International Responsibility of States' (1992) 3 EJIL 139, 139-48.

[154]Dionisio Anzilotti, *Teoria generale della responsabilità dello stato nel diritto internazionale* (F. Lumachi Libraio-Editore, Florence 1902) 153 *et seq* (quoting Jellinek at p. 156 n. 1); Dionisio Anzilotti, 'La responsabilité internationale des états a raison des dommages soufferts par des étrangers' (1906) 13 RGDIP 285, 285-309. A summarized version of the argument appears in

by observing that, despite widespread generalizations, fault had only played a major role in the specific area of state responsibility for private injuries to aliens.[155] A look into the reality behind this private law terminology revealed, however, that even in that specific context the term 'fault' was misguided.[156] In the cases in question, Anzilotti observed, responsibility was not established on the basis of the agent's volition, but on the ground that the state *objectively* failed to fulfill its duties of protection.[157] Thus, the threshold issue was not whether the state is at fault, but whether its acts correspond to the course of conduct required by the applicable norm of international law.[158] In this vein, he emphasized that 'not fault, but the act contrary to international law, obliges [the state]'.[159]

To be sure, Anzilotti recognized that specific norms of international law could require a state to exercise *due diligence* (*dovuta diligenza/diligence nécessaire*).[160] Still, in his view, this *diligence* does not resemble the notion of *fault*, in the private law sense of the term: *due diligence* appears here as the content of a specific international obligation, not as an additional condition of responsibility.[161] This

---

Anzilotti's handbook of international law. See: Dionisio Anzilotti, *Lehrbuch des Völkerrechts* (Volume 1: Walter de Gruyter, Berlin/Leipzig 1929) 386-94.

[155] Dionisio Anzilotti, *Teoria generale della responsabilità dello stato nel diritto internazionale* (F. Lumachi Libraio-Editore, Florence 1902) 155-9 and 170.

[156] Dionisio Anzilotti, *Teoria generale della responsabilità dello stato nel diritto internazionale* (F. Lumachi Libraio-Editore, Florence 1902) 172-3.

[157] Dionisio Anzilotti, *Teoria generale della responsabilità dello stato nel diritto internazionale* (F. Lumachi Libraio-Editore, Florence 1902) 172-3.

[158] Dionisio Anzilotti, *Teoria generale della responsabilità dello stato nel diritto internazionale* (F. Lumachi Libraio-Editore, Florence 1902) 178; Dionisio Anzilotti, 'La responsabilité internationale des états a raison des dommages soufferts par des étrangers' (1906) 13 RGDIP 285, 291 *et seq.*

[159] Author's translation. The original Italian text reads: "Non la colpa, ma il fatto contrario al diritto internazionale lo obbliga." Dionisio Anzilotti, *Teoria generale della responsabilità dello stato nel diritto internazionale* (F. Lumachi Libraio-Editore, Florence 1902) 172.

[160] Dionisio Anzilotti, *Teoria generale della responsabilità dello stato nel diritto internazionale* (F. Lumachi Libraio-Editore, Florence 1902) 174-5 n. 1; Dionisio Anzilotti, 'La responsabilité internationale des états a raison des dommages soufferts par des étrangers' (1906) 13 RGDIP 285, 291.

[161] Dionisio Anzilotti, 'La responsabilité internationale des états a raison des dommages soufferts par des étrangers' (1906) 13 RGDIP 285, 290-1 ("L'idée que la responsabilité internationale de l'État a sa base dans une faute, bin que s'expliquant à origine par l'influence du droit romain, ainsi que nous l'avons remarqué, a rencontré dans la suit un soutien apparent dans l'analogie qu'on peut trouver entre le contenu de certains devoirs internationaux et ce qu'on a traditionnellement regardé comme le trait caractéristique de la faute en droit civil, c'est-à-dire le défaut de diligence dans la prévoyance des conséquences pouvant dériver d'une conduite déterminée. Il est des devoirs internationaux qui consistent à exercer sus individus soumis à la autorité de l'État une vigilance correspondante aux fonctions et aux pouvoirs dont l'État est investi. Celui-ci n'est pas internationalement obligé d'empêcher d'une façon absolue que certains faits se réalisent ; mais il est tenu d'exercer, pour les empêcher, la vigilance qui rentre dans ses fonctions ordinaires. Il ne sera donc pas responsable si un fait a lieu, il sera au contraire responsable s'il n'a pas employé la diligence nécessaire pour que ce fait ne se produise pas. Le défaut de diligence est une inobservation

conclusion is a direct consequence of Anzilotti's objective approach to state responsibility:

> International law does not consider the intention of the agent in the violation of the rights of others as an essential element of responsibility. On the contrary, it attaches the greatest importance to the *fact* of the unjust violation of rights of others. In some cases, every subjective consideration of the agent's volition is excluded by the very nature of the legal directive. In other [cases], in which a concurrence of intentions appears to be required, such [subjective element] coincides with the content of the state's international obligation.[162]

Anzilotti's objective theory captured the attention of the most brilliant international legal scholars of his time and won several adherents among them. A prominent supporter of the idea was Hans Kelsen.[163] In an academic article published in 1932, Kelsen delivered a lengthy analysis of the role of fault in international law and concluded:

> [Responsibility] is not dependent on some psychological relationship between the physical person acting as a state organ and the violation of international law. Even in the absence [of fault], responsibility attaches to the state.[164]

In this connection, Kelsen further stated that the *negligence* (*Fahrlässigkeit*) or *diligence* (*diligentia*) attached to the definition of numerous delicts of omission is not a form of *fault* (*Schuld*).[165] According to him, *negligence* is determined *objectively* through the comparison of a subject's course of conduct against some objective

---

du devoir imposé par le droit international, sans qu'il y ait alors à parler de faute au sens propre du mot. L'État qui a usé de la diligence qu'il devait n'est point responsable ; mais sont défaut de responsabilité ne tient pas à une absence de faute, il vient de ce qu'il n'y aucun acte contraire au droit des gens"). A similar argument appears in Anzilotti's monograph of 1902. Making particular reference to the due diligence obligations of neutral states, as formulated in the Treaty of Washington of 1871, Anzilotti observed that due diligence does not appear as a 'subjective element of responsibility' (*elemento subiettivo della responsabilità*), but as the 'content' (*contenuto*) of an international obligation. Dionisio Anzilotti, *Teoria generale della responsabilità dello stato nel diritto internazionale* (F. Lumachi Libraio-Editore, Florence 1902) 174-5 n. 1.

[162] Author's translation. The original Italian text reads: " il diritto internazionale non considera come un elemento essenziale della responsabilità 1' *animo* dell'agente nella violazione del diritto altrui, e dà invece la maggiore importanza al *fatto* della ingiusta violazione del diritto altrui, tanto che in alcuni casi ogni considerazione subiettiva dell'animo dell'agente rimane esclusa dall' indole stessa del precetto giuridico, ed in altri, nei quali sembra richiesto un determinato concorso di volontà, questo si confonde col contenuto del dovere internazionale dello stato." Dionisio Anzilotti, *Teoria generale della responsabilità dello stato nel diritto internazionale* (F. Lumachi Libraio-Editore, Florence 1902) 178.

[163] For some additional examples of authors following Anzilotti and a general description of Kelsen's views on state responsibility see: Andrea Gattini, *Zufall und force majeure im System der Staatenverantwortlichkeit anhand der ILC-Kodifikationsarbeit* (Duncker & Humblot, Berlin 1989) 22-5 (particularly focusing on Kelsen's concept of attribution). Gattini also provides an overview of Anzilotti's objective theory at pp. 20-2.

[164] Author's translation. The original German text reads: "[a]uf irgend eine spezifische seelische Beziehung des als Organ fungierenden Menschen zu dem Unrechtstatbestand kommt es in Wahrheit gar nicht an. Auch wenn sie fehlt, haftet der Staat". Hans Kelsen, 'Unrecht und Unrechtsfolge im Völkerrecht' (1932) 12 ZöR 481, 544.

[165] Hans Kelsen, 'Unrecht und Unrechtsfolge im Völkerrecht' (1932) 12 ZöR 481, 544-5 n. 2.

parameter, such as the *diligentia diligentis patris familia*.[166] For that very same reason, he believed that, in the final analysis, '[responsibility for] negligence remains strict liability'.[167] Decades later, in his *General Theory of Law and State* (1945), Kelsen would summarize this idea in the following terms:

> Failure to exercise the care prescribed by the law is called negligence; and negligence is usually considered to be another kind of "fault" (*culpa*) [. . .] [Negligence, however] is not the specific qualification of a delict, it is a delict itself, the omission of certain measures of precaution, and that means the non-exercise of the degree of care that ought to be exercised according to the law. Negligence is a delict of omission, and responsibility for negligence is rather a kind of absolute responsibility than a type of culpability.[168]

In later publications,[169] Kelsen would further observe that an internationally wrongful act could certainly consist in the faulty conduct of state agents.[170] And yet, he said, responsibility *of the state* remains *absolute* in character.[171] Kelsen conceived the state as a collective body of physical persons who are subject to a particular *legal order*, that is to say, as a *corporation*.[172] As a result, the individuals who conform the state (and assume responsibility) do not entirely coincide with those who commit an internationally wrongful act (i.e. the physical persons wearing the guise of a state organ).[173] For that reason, according to Kelsen, 'the international responsibility of the state has, with respect to the individuals collectively responsible, the character of absolute responsibility, but with respect of the individuals whose conduct constitutes the international delict, in principle, the character of culpability'.[174]

---

[166]Hans Kelsen, 'Unrecht und Unrechtsfolge im Völkerrecht' (1932) 12 ZöR 481, 544-5 n. 2.

[167]Author's translation. The original German text reads: "[aber] Erfolgshaftung bleibt die Fahrlässigkeit [trotzdem]." Hans Kelsen, 'Unrecht und Unrechtsfolge im Völkerrecht' (1932) 12 ZöR 481, 545 n. 2.

[168]Hans Kelsen, *General Theory of Law and State* (Anders Wedberg tr., Lawbook Exchange, Clark NJ 2009) 66 [first edition: 1945].

[169]Many of these ideas were already present in Kelsen's article of 1932. Nonetheless, this section relies at this point on the condensed version of the theory Kelsen presented in his handbook on international law (1952).

[170]Hans Kelsen, *Principles of International Law* (The Lawbook Exchange, Clark NJ 2007) 122-4 [first edition: 1952].

[171]Hans Kelsen, *Principles of International Law* (The Lawbook Exchange, Clark NJ 2007) 122-4 [first edition: 1952]. See also Kelsen's observations on 'absolute responsibility' and 'culpability' at pp. 11-3.

[172]Hans Kelsen, *Principles of International Law* (The Lawbook Exchange, Clark NJ 2007) 100-1 [first edition: 1952]. See also pp. 96 *et seq.* (on the notion of the 'corporation').

[173]Hans Kelsen, *Principles of International Law* (The Lawbook Exchange, Clark NJ 2007) 11-3 and 122-3 [first edition: 1952].

[174]Hans Kelsen, *Principles of International Law* (The Lawbook Exchange, Clark NJ 2007) 123 [first edition: 1952].

The objective theory soon gained considerable influence not only among continental international lawyers, but also in the English-speaking world.[175] For present purposes, it is fundamental to underscore that the 'objective turn', initiated by Anzilotti and strengthened by Kelsen's theory, went hand-in-hand with a conceptual and terminological shift. The 'objective' notion of *due diligence* gradually substituted the concept of *fault*, which had dominated legal analysis on state responsibility for acts of individuals since Grotian times. As a matter of fact, since Anzilotti, international legal scholars often draw a sharp conceptual line between the notions of fault and due diligence.[176] This approach found clear expression in the *First Report* of the ILA Study Group on Due Diligence in International Law (2014), according to which the 'standard of behaviour' required by due diligence should be looked for in applicable 'primary rules of conduct' and not in the notion of fault.[177]

12.4   The Indirect or Direct Character of State Responsibility for Private Injuries to Aliens

Academic discussions about the concept of fault, however important, were not the only shaping factor of the present-day understanding of due diligence in international law. A second dogmatic struggle played its part in the development of the notion, namely, the debate on the *direct* or *indirect* nature of state responsibility for acts of individuals. The threshold issue was whether international law holds the state accountable, *directly* or *indirectly*, for the *injuries inflicted by private individuals* as such, or for its *own conduct* in respect of private harmful acts.[178] The writings of leading publicists in this area could be classified in three main tendencies. The first

---

[175]See, for example: Joseph Gabriel Starke, 'Imputability in International Delinquencies' (1938) 19 BYIL 104, 112 *et seq*. For Starke's views on state responsibility for injuries caused by individuals, cf. also Joseph Gabriel Starke, *Introduction to International Law* (Butterworths, London 1984) 296-7 [First Edition: 1947].

[176]See, for example: Joachim Wolf, 'Die gegenwärtige Entwicklung der Lehre über die völkerrechtliche Verantwortlichkeit der Staaten. Untersuchung am Beispiel des Urteils des Internationalen Gerichtshofs in der Teheraner Geiselaffaire' (1983) 31 ZaöRV 481, 520-1 (arguing that due diligence liability is different from liability based on fault and underscoring that the measure of due diligence has an objective character); Paul Guggenheim, 'Les principes de droit international public' (1952) 80 RCADI 2, 149-9 (observing that the law of aliens requires states to exercise a *diligentia quam in suis* in the protection of aliens and underscoring that, even in such cases, the 'fault of omission' does not refer to the 'subjective negligence of the [state] organ' but to an 'objective rule', so that the 'subjective notion of culpability' serves no practical purpose).

[177]ILA Study Group on Due Diligence in International Law, 'First Report by Mr. Tim Stephens (Rapporteur) and Mr. Duncan French (Chair)' (7 March 2014) 3-4.

[178]For the sake of accuracy, scholarly approaches to this second question were often embedded within the parallel debate on the role of fault in the law of state responsibility. For that very same reason, as will be shown throughout this section, both issues cannot be entirely divorced from each other.

intellectual trend corresponds to theories holding the state *indirectly responsible* for the acts of private individuals, provided certain conditions are given.

A second approach developed in specific connection with injuries caused in the course of revolutions and civil wars. The core of the argument was that foreigners scourged by such situations sacrifice their private interests for the public good. Some authors went on to argue that revolutions crystalize risks that belong to the state. On these grounds, they concluded that the host state bears a direct compensation obligation.

A third group of scholars considered that international responsibility arises out of the *acts of the state* only. In cases involving private injuries to foreign nationals, responsibility is thus not predicated upon the conduct of the private wrongdoer as such, but upon the host state's *own acts*. These acts, if internationally wrongful, constitute an *autonomous delict* that is legally, though not factually, detached from the private harmful act. This approach could therefore be portrayed as the *separate delict theory*.

12.4.1 The Theories of 'Indirect' Responsibility

For a long time, influential publicists in the law of nations considered that the question of state responsibility for acts of individuals involved the attribution of the acts of private persons to the state. Responsibility was hence *not* predicated on an omission of the host state, considered as a *separate* wrong, but on the very private harmful conduct at issue. Multiple dogmatic approaches shared this common ground. The perhaps most influential of them was the so-called *theory of complicity*, which was proposed by Emer de Vattel in 1758:

> [T]he sovereign who refuses to cause reparation to be made for the damage done by his subject, or to punish the offender, or, finally, to deliver him up, renders himself in some measure an *accomplice* in the injury, and becomes responsible for it.[179]

Vattel's use of the word 'accomplice' (*complice* in the original French edition)[180] was of great theoretical importance. Scholars have observed that complicity 'concerns an actor's participation on wrongdoing committed by another actor'.[181] The

---

[179]Emphasis added. Emer de Vattel, *The Law of Nations or Principles of the Law of Nature Applied to the Conduct and Affairs of Nations and Sovereigns* (1758) (G.G. and J. Robinson, London 1797) 163.

[180]For the original French text see: Emer de Vattel, *Le droit des gens ou principes de la loi naturelle appliqués à la conduit et aux affaires des Nations et des Souverains* (1758) (Carnegie Institution, Washington 1916) 312 ('Le Souverain qui refuse de faire réparer le dommage cause par son Sujet, ou de punir le coupable, ou enfin de le livrer, se rend en quelque façon complice de l'injure, & il en devient responsable.').

[181]Miles Jackson, *Complicity in International Law* (Oxford University Press, Oxford 2015) 10. See also: Vladyslav Lanovoy, *Complicity and its Limits in the Law of International Responsibility* (Hart Publishing, Portland OR 2016) 3-4.

obvious implication is that there is only *one* wrongdoing (that of the private actor), in which the host state *participates*. As far as this participation consummates in a *failure of redress*, resort to the local judiciary unavoidably becomes a substantive condition of state responsibility. Vattel's theory of complicity found some support in scholarly writings throughout the years. A prominent follower of the 'complicity approach' was Carlos Calvo who, in reference to Vattel, stated that 'it is impossible to deny the justice of these conclusions'.[182]

Other authors, while avoiding the complex notion of complicity, shared the fundamental idea that the wrong for which the state takes responsibility is neither materially nor conceptually different from the private injury that was inflicted on an alien. A few scholars resorted in this connection to the phrase *indirect liability*. A clear example of this jargon appears in the works of Franz von Liszt:

> The state is *indirect subject of liability* in respect of faulty, wrongful actions committed within its territory against a foreign state or against foreign nationals, provided it has failed to prevent or repress [such actions] in an internationally wrongful manner [. . .] [The state] is *indirectly responsible* if the actions are undertaken by individual private persons. In virtue of its territorial sovereignty it is responsible, too, for the actions of foreigners within its territory; in contrast and for that very same reason, it is not responsible for those actions whose perpetrator [is] extraterritorial, that is to say, not subject to its sovereign authority.[183]

Liszt's concept of indirect responsibility (*mittelbare Haftung*) implies that, as a general rule, the host state is responsible for any injury inflicted upon an alien within its dominions. Liszt's source of responsibility was not the failure to prevent or redress the injury, but the host state's territorial authority. The notions of *patientia* and *receptus* did thus not take the character of separate international delinquencies. Rather, they came into play as manifestations of the requirement of *fault*.

---

[182]Author's translation. The original Spanish text reads: "[e]s imposible negar la justicia de estas conclusiones." Carlos Calvo, *Derecho internacional teórico y práctico de Europa y América* (Volume 1: D'Amyot Librairie Diplomatique & Durand et Pedone, Paris 1868) 397. See also: Carlos Calvo, *Le droit international théorique et pratique précédé d'un exposé historique des progrès de la science du droit des gens* (Volume 3: Rousseau, Paris 1896) 134-5. Some authors considered that there was no material difference between Vattel and Grotius in this regard. According to them, there is a 'Grotian-Vattelian theory of state responsibility'. For an indicative example see: Han Tao Wu, *Responsibility of States for Injuries Sustained by Aliens on Account of Acts of Insurgents* (University of Illinois, Urbana IL 1930) 5.

[183]Emphasis added. Author's translation. The original German text reads: "Der Staat ist *mittelbares Deliktsubjekt* bei allen übrigen auf seinem Gebiete gegen einen fremden Staat oder gegen fremde Staatsangehörige begangenen schuldhaften, rechtswidrigen Handlungen, vorausgesetzt, daß er deren Hinderung oder Bestrafung völkerrechtswidrig unterläßt [. . .] Er *haftet mittelbar*, wenn die Handlungen von einzelnen Privatpersonen [. . .] vorgenommen werden. Er haftet kraft seiner Territorialgewalt auch für die von Staatsfremden auf seinem Gebiete vorgenommenen Handlungen; er haftet aber eben darum nicht für diejenigen Handlungen, deren Täter extraterritorial, also seiner Staatsgewalt gar nicht unterworfen ist" Franz von Liszt, *Das Völkerrecht systematisch dargestellt* (Verlag von O. Häring, Berlin 1906) 192.

12.4.2 The Theories of 'Direct' Responsibility

In the last decades of the nineteenth and first years of the twentieth century, a few scholars submitted groundbreaking proposals for the assessment of private injuries to aliens, making particular reference to acts of revolutionaries. Their theories of responsibility could be characterized as 'direct' in the sense that they created an immediate compensation obligation on the part of the host state. Interestingly, such 'direct' obligation was not based on a direct attribution of the acts of private individuals to the state. Rather than focusing on the traditional question of attribution, these publicists sought an alternative basis for compensation, which was largely inspired by institutions of municipal administrative law.

A first example appears in a report on state responsibility for acts of insurgents, which the Italian scholar Emilio Brusa submitted to the *Institut de droit international* in 1898. Brusa considered that the basis for state responsibility for revolutionary damages had to be looked for in public law, and not in analogies to the private law notion of fault.[184] He further underscored that responsibility could attach even to a state whose conduct is 'irreproachable'.[185] The reason was that compensation is not due as a result of faulty conduct or direct violations of international law.[186] Brusa believed that foreigners who suffer the rigors of a revolution or a civil war are, in the final analysis, bearing the burden of the public interest.[187] Their losses contribute to the fulfillment of the state's sovereign duties and the consolidation of its authority.[188] For that very same reason, he argued that the state reaping the benefits of their sacrifice is also pledged to grant them adequate compensation.[189] The core of Brusa's theory therefore lies in the assimilation of these cases to the logic of an expropriation in which the taking of private property serves, at least in theory, a public purpose:

> Le droit de l'endommagé peut bien, en un certain sens, se comparer au droit du propriétaire exproprié, au droit de la victime d'une erreur judiciaire, ou de tout autre particulier innocent

---

[184]Emilio Brusa, 'Responsabilité des États à raison des dommages soufferts par des étrangers en cas d'émeute ou de guerre civile' (1898) 17 Annuaire de l'Institut de Droit International 96, 97. See also p. 99-100, 102, 109-11, 113 and 120. See also Brusa's Draft Resolution at p. 135 art. 1(b).

[185]Emilio Brusa, 'Responsabilité des États à raison des dommages soufferts par des étrangers en cas d'émeute ou de guerre civile' (1898) 17 Annuaire de l'Institut de Droit International 96, 97.

[186]Emilio Brusa, 'Responsabilité des États à raison des dommages soufferts par des étrangers en cas d'émeute ou de guerre civile' (1898) 17 Annuaire de l'Institut de Droit International 96, 103. See also Brusa's Draft Resolution at p. 135 art. 1(b).

[187]Emilio Brusa, 'Responsabilité des États à raison des dommages soufferts par des étrangers en cas d'émeute ou de guerre civile' (1898) 17 Annuaire de l'Institut de Droit International 96, 103.

[188]Emilio Brusa, 'Responsabilité des États à raison des dommages soufferts par des étrangers en cas d'émeute ou de guerre civile' (1898) 17 Annuaire de l'Institut de Droit International 96, 108. See also Brusa's remarks at pp. 114 and 116. See also Brusa's Draft Resolution at p. 135 art. 2.

[189]Emilio Brusa, 'Responsabilité des États à raison des dommages soufferts par des étrangers en cas d'émeute ou de guerre civile' (1898) 17 Annuaire de l'Institut de Droit International 96, 103. See also Brusa's Draft Resolution at p. 135 art. 2.

dont les biens, la personne ont été sacrifiés pour le bien général de l'État. Toujours est-il que ces limitations du droit des particuliers sont imposées dans l'intérêt de la collectivité, to toujours celle-ci est tenue à indemnité pour la même raison de l'avantage et du profit qu'elle en retire.[190]

According to Brusa, while *force majeure* could justify the state's conduct, even in such extraordinary events the state would be required to compensate those who have sacrificed their own welfare for the realization of the public good.[191] Brusa qualified his conclusion by emphasizing that the amount of compensation must always be assessed on the basis of 'a just consideration of all circumstances' (*une juste appreciation de toutes les circonstances*).[192] In addition, he excluded any obligation to compensate moral and indirect damages.[193] The obligation, he said, is 'correlative' to the actual 'benefit' obtained.[194] In addition, he underscored that diplomatic intervention generally requires the previous exhaustion of local remedies.[195] Nonetheless, if harm was caused by faulty conduct on the part of the host state, Brusa said, 'the indemnity is more rigorously due' and 'official diplomatic intervention is direct.'[196]

A second example appears in the minutes of the Neuchâtel Session of the *Institut de Droit International* (1900), in which Brusa's proposal was discussed.[197] On that

---

[190]Emilio Brusa, 'Responsabilité des États à raison des dommages soufferts par des étrangers en cas d'émeute ou de guerre civile' (1898) 17 Annuaire de l'Institut de Droit International 96, 106. See also pp. 108-9 and 113.

[191]Emilio Brusa, 'Responsabilité des États à raison des dommages soufferts par des étrangers en cas d'émeute ou de guerre civile' (1898) 17 Annuaire de l'Institut de Droit International 96, 108.

[192]Emilio Brusa, 'Responsabilité des États à raison des dommages soufferts par des étrangers en cas d'émeute ou de guerre civile' (1898) 17 Annuaire de l'Institut de Droit International 96, 111.

[193]Emilio Brusa, 'Responsabilité des États à raison des dommages soufferts par des étrangers en cas d'émeute ou de guerre civile' (1898) 17 Annuaire de l'Institut de Droit International 96, 137 art. 13.

[194]Emilio Brusa, 'Responsabilité des États à raison des dommages soufferts par des étrangers en cas d'émeute ou de guerre civile' (1898) 17 Annuaire de l'Institut de Droit International 96, 111 and 116. See also Brusa's remarks on the calculation of the proper amount of compensation at pp. 111 *et seq.* See also p. 135 art. 4.

[195]Emilio Brusa, 'Responsabilité des États à raison des dommages soufferts par des étrangers en cas d'émeute ou de guerre civile' (1898) 17 Annuaire de l'Institut de Droit International 96, 127 *et seq.* See also Brusa's additional remarks on the conditions for diplomatic interposition at pp. 103-4, 112, 116-8, 119 and 123 *et seq.* See also Brusa's Draft Resolution at pp. 136-7 art. 9. It should be noted that Brusa considered that the obligation to compensate revolutionary damages is always subsidiary (*subsidiaire*) to denial of justice or other violations of international law (see particularly p. 135 art. 3).

[196]See, particularly: Emilio Brusa, 'Responsabilité des États à raison des dommages soufferts par des étrangers en cas d'émeute ou de guerre civile' (1898) 17 Annuaire de l'Institut de Droit International 96, 135 art. 3 ("L'indemnité est plus rigoureusement due dans le cas d'une vraie responsabilité coupable de la part de l'État ou de ses autorités; cette responsabilité se fait alors valoir en première ligne envers l'État auquel les étrangers lésés appartiennent. Aussi, dans ce cas, l'intervention diplomatique officielle est directe").

[197]Institut de Droit International, 'Neuvième Commission d'étude – Responsabilité des États à raison des dommages soufferts par des étrangers en cas d'émeute ou de guerre civile' (1900) 18 Annuaire de l'Institut de Droit International 233, 234-5. For an overview of the different

occasion, Paul Fauchille proposed the notion of *risque étatif* as a possible basis for establishing international responsibility for private injuries to aliens.[198] Fauchille's idea of *risque étatif* was an adaptation of the French administrative law concept of *risque administratiff*.[199] This approach departed from the assumption that states always obtain an advantage from the presence of foreign nationals within their territory.[200] Their industries, he observed, could be considered as an additional 'source of revenues' (*source de profits*) for the public purse.[201] Fauchille underlined that, if this premise is correct, then it is logical for the state to assume an obligation to compensate damages caused in the course of revolutions or civil disorders.[202] Invoking the maxim *ubi emolumentum ibi onus esse debet*, he explained that compensation is due because, if it is the state who reaps the benefits of foreign investments, it should also be the state who bears the costs.[203] He however conditioned this responsibility upon the foreign victims *not* being at fault.[204] Fauchille summarized his argument with the following statement:

> L'État, tirant profit des étrangers que sont sur son territoire, est tenu de réparer los dommages causés à ces étrangers par les émeutes ou les guerres civiles souvenues sur ce territoire, à

---

approaches to state responsibility for injuries to aliens that were proposed at the Neuchâtel Session of the Institut see: Pavlos Alextrandou Zannas, La responsabilité internationale des Etats pour les actes de négligence (Ganguin & Laubscher, Geneva 1952) 59-60.

[198]Institut de Droit International, 'Neuvième Commission d'étude – Responsabilité des États à raison des dommages soufferts par des étrangers en cas d'émeute ou de guerre civile' (1900) 18 Annuaire de l'Institut de Droit International 233, 234. For a detailed critical analysis of the theory of *risque étatif* see: Jacques Dumas, 'La responsabilité des États a raison des crimes et délits commis sur leur territoire au préjudice d'Étrangers' (1931) 36 RCADI 183, 211 *et seq.* (also discussing the subsequent debate of the notion at the *Institut*).

[199]Institut de Droit International, 'Neuvième Commission d'étude – Responsabilité des États à raison des dommages soufferts par des étrangers en cas d'émeute ou de guerre civile' (1900) 18 Annuaire de l'Institut de Droit International 233, 234. For the French law notion of *risque administratif* see: Léon Duguit, *Les transformations du droit public* (Librairie Armand Colin, Paris 1913) 255 *et seq.*

[200]Institut de Droit International, 'Neuvième Commission d'étude – Responsabilité des États à raison des dommages soufferts par des étrangers en cas d'émeute ou de guerre civile' (1900) 18 Annuaire de l'Institut de Droit International 233, 234-5.

[201]Institut de Droit International, 'Neuvième Commission d'étude – Responsabilité des États à raison des dommages soufferts par des étrangers en cas d'émeute ou de guerre civile' (1900) 18 Annuaire de l'Institut de Droit International 233, 234-5.

[202]Institut de Droit International, 'Neuvième Commission d'étude – Responsabilité des États à raison des dommages soufferts par des étrangers en cas d'émeute ou de guerre civile' (1900) 18 Annuaire de l'Institut de Droit International 233, 235.

[203]Institut de Droit International, 'Neuvième Commission d'étude – Responsabilité des États à raison des dommages soufferts par des étrangers en cas d'émeute ou de guerre civile' (1900) 18 Annuaire de l'Institut de Droit International 233, 234-5.

[204]Institut de Droit International, 'Neuvième Commission d'étude – Responsabilité des États à raison des dommages soufferts par des étrangers en cas d'émeute ou de guerre civile' (1900) 18 Annuaire de l'Institut de Droit International 233, 234-5.

moins qu'il n'établisse que les lesdits dommages ont été occasionnés par une faute, une imprudence ou une négligence des étrangers que en sont victimes.[205]

This view was not without criticism. At the *Institut*, the French international law scholar and later Nobel Peace Prize laureate Louis Renault expressed serious doubts as to both the accuracy and the usefulness of Fauchille's analogy.[206] Renault emphasized that, strictly speaking, not even French municipal law imposed a legal obligation upon the state to pay compensation for damages arising out of the acts of insurgents.[207]

12.4.3   The 'Separate Delict' Theory

In spite of their innovative elements and undeniable potential for transformation, Brusa's and Fauchille's approaches to revolutionary damages had a very modest influence in the subsequent development of the law of aliens. Theories of indirect responsibility fared no better. By the turn of the twentieth century, Vattel's notion of complicity was at the heart of an intense academic debate.

The perhaps most direct opponent to the complicity theory was the German international law scholar Heinrich Triepel. The reasons for this disagreement were deeply rooted in Triepel's own view of international law. Triepel conceived the law of nations as a legal order that governs different relationships (*Lebensverhältnisse*) and has different legal sources (*Rechtsquellen*) than municipal law.[208] According to him, individuals are subjects of *domestic law* and not of *international law*.[209] The implication is striking. If the state and the individual do not simultaneously belong to the same legal order,[210] it turns conceptually impossible for them to be *accomplices* in the violation of the same legal norm:

---

[205]Institut de Droit International, 'Neuvième Commission d'étude – Responsabilité des États à raison des dommages soufferts par des étrangers en cas d'émeute ou de guerre civile' (1900) 18 Annuaire de l'Institut de Droit International 233, 235.

[206]Institut de Droit International, 'Neuvième Commission d'étude – Responsabilité des États à raison des dommages soufferts par des étrangers en cas d'émeute ou de guerre civile' (1900) 18 Annuaire de l'Institut de Droit International 233, 235-5.

[207]Institut de Droit International, 'Neuvième Commission d'étude – Responsabilité des États à raison des dommages soufferts par des étrangers en cas d'émeute ou de guerre civile' (1900) 18 Annuaire de l'Institut de Droit International 233, 236.

[208]Heinrich Triepel, *Völkerrecht und Landesrecht* (Verlag von C. L. Hirschfeld, Leipzig 1899) 7-10.

[209]Heinrich Triepel, *Völkerrecht und Landesrecht* (Verlag von C. L. Hirschfeld, Leipzig 1899) 20.

[210]Heinrich Triepel, *Völkerrecht und Landesrecht* (Verlag von C. L. Hirschfeld, Leipzig 1899) 328-9.

If it is true that the individual can be only object, and never subject, of obligations under international law, then it is unthinkable that individuals could ever infringe a 'norm' of international law.[211]

In addition to this formal argument, Triepel expressed serious doubts as to whether a *failure of redress* could be properly styled as *participation* in the unredressed injury.[212] In Triepel's words:

[This theory] imputes to the state a participatory conduct which an unbiased eye would be unable to recognize. Even assuming that a failure to react against the wrongdoer actually constitutes an approval of his conduct, such an approval does not amount to participation. Where on earth is the one who fails to discipline the offender called an "associate" in his crime?! By this means [this theory] fabricates a [form of] complicity where there can be nothing but an autonomous, separate fault.[213]

These words fell on fertile ground. Dionisio Anzilotti expressed clear support for the argument in 1902.[214] The rejection of complicity prepared the ground for definitively wiping the concept of fault out of the law of state responsibility. After describing the 'traditional' theory of complicity,[215] which he considered to be 'unacceptable',[216] Anzilotti observed:

The act of the individual does not constitute a violation of international law by itself. Responsibility derives only from the duty placed upon the state in respect of the acts in question; however, these [private acts], as such, are legally irrelevant from an international standpoint [...] the state is not responsible on the ground that its own volition directly or indirectly coincides with the act of the individual. [It is not responsible] for a reproachable, willful or negligent intention, but for failing to adopt the course of conduct required by international law: for having failed to fulfill its duty towards other states, [a duty] which consists in not tolerating the [private] act and punishing [the offenders] if it occurs.[217]

---

[211] Author's translation. The original German text reads: "wenn es richtig ist, [...] dass das Individuum nur Objekt, nicht Subjekt völkerrechtlicher Pflichten sein könne, so ist es undenkbar, dass eine "Norm" des Völkerrechts von Einzelnen übertreten werde." Heinrich Triepel, *Völkerrecht und Landesrecht* (Verlag von C. L. Hirschfeld, Leipzig 1899) 329.

[212] Heinrich Triepel, *Völkerrecht und Landesrecht* (Verlag von C. L. Hirschfeld, Leipzig 1899) 328.

[213] Author's translation. The original German text reads: "[Diese Theorie] dichtet dem Staate eine Theilnahme an, die für ein unbefangenes Auge nicht zu erkennen ist. Denn selbst einmal zugegeben, es sei die Unterlassung der Reaktion gegen den Delinquenten wirklich eine Billigung seines Verhaltens, so ist doch eine Billigung keine Theilnahme. Wo in aller Welt nennt man den, der einen Missethäter nicht züchtig, den Genossen seiner That! So fingirt man eine Mitschuld, wo doch nur eine selbstständige eigene Schuld vorliegen kann." Heinrich Triepel, *Völkerrecht und Landesrecht* (Verlag von C. L. Hirschfeld, Leipzig 1899) 328-9.

[214] Dionisio Anzilotti, *Teoria generale della responsabilità dello stato nel diritto internazionale* (F. Lumachi Libraio-Editore, Florence 1902) 171-2.

[215] Dionisio Anzilotti, *Teoria generale della responsabilità dello stato nel diritto internazionale* (F. Lumachi Libraio-Editore, Florence 1902) 171-2.

[216] Dionisio Anzilotti, *Teoria generale della responsabilità dello stato nel diritto internazionale* (F. Lumachi Libraio-Editore, Florence 1902) 172.

[217] Author's translation. The original Italian text reads: "il fatto dell'individuo non è mai di per sé una violazione del diritto internazionale; la responsabilità deriva soltanto dal dovere internazionale che incombe allo stato riguardo ai fatti di cui se parla, mentre questi, in sé considerati, sono, dal

Following a similar line of argument, Hans Buxbaum forcefully rejected the theory of complicity in 1915.[218] Buxbaum observed that the notion of *complicity* necessarily implies *volition* (*Willen*).[219] In order for the host state to be properly qualified as an accomplice, Buxbaum stated, a failure of redress would need to constitute *intentional conduct* (*vorsätzliches Handeln*).[220] In the case of private violence against foreigners, however, such element is missing: "How can there be intention, if there is no willful resolution directed at aiding and abetting?"[221] In this line of argument, Buxbaum concluded:

> The inaccuracy of this theory comes to light in view of the fact that, on the one hand, participation must take place either before or at the same time as the main conduct and, on the other hand, that participation always presupposes the will to take part in the main conduct and jointly commit a delict.[222]

If these observations are correct, an obvious question arises: on what account, if not complicity, may the host state be held accountable for the injuries inflicted by private individuals upon foreign nationals? Triepel and his followers had a simple answer: on no account at all. Their argument was precisely that the state is *not* responsible for the private injury *as such* (e.g. destruction of foreign property by a mob), but for *its own* omissions with regard to such injury (e.g. omissions in the prevention or redress of the mob injury). In their view, the harmful conduct of private individuals is legally and conceptually different from the host state's omissions. In light of the foregoing, this theory has been described as the *separate delict theory*.[223]

---

punto di vista internazionale, giuridicamente irrilevanti [. . .] lo stato è responsabile non per il concorso diretto o indiretto della sua volontà al fatto dell' individuo, non per un'intenzione doloso o colposa che gli possa rimproverare, ma per non avere tenuto il contegno che gli era imposto dal diritto internazionale, per aver violato il dovere suo versi gli atri stati, consistente nel non tollerare il fatto o nel punirlo se accaduto." Dionisio Anzilotti, *Teoria generale della responsabilità dello stato nel diritto internazionale* (F. Lumachi Libraio-Editore, Florence 1902) 172. See also: Karl Strupp, *Grundzüge des positiven Völkerrechts* (Ludwig Röhrscheid, Bonn 1922) 128-9.

[218] Hans Buxbaum, *Das völkerrechtliche Delikt* (E Th. Jacob, Erlangen 1915) 16 *et seq.*

[219] Hans Buxbaum, *Das völkerrechtliche Delikt* (E Th. Jacob, Erlangen 1915) 16-7.

[220] Hans Buxbaum, *Das völkerrechtliche Delikt* (E Th. Jacob, Erlangen 1915) 17.

[221] Author's translation. The original German text reads: "Wie kann man aber von Vorsatz sprechen, wenn überhaupt keine auf Begünstigung gerichtete Willensentschliessung vorliegt?" Hans Buxbaum, *Das völkerrechtliche Delikt* (E Th. Jacob, Erlangen 1915) 17.

[222] Author's translation. The original German text reads: "Die Unrichtigkeit dieser Auffassung erhellt schon daraus, dass einerseits die Teilnahmehandlung entweder vor oder gleichzeitig mit der Haupthandlung erfolgen muss, andererseits aber die Teilnahme immer noch den Willen voraussetzt, die Teilnahmehandlung mit der Haupthandlung zu gemeinsamen Verbrechensbegehung zu verbinden." Hans Buxbaum, *Das völkerrechtliche Delikt* (E Th. Jacob, Erlangen 1915) 16-7.

[223] For the sake of accuracy, the notion of a 'separate delict' does not necessarily imply that two international wrongful acts are at stake. As a rule, the private act originating the injury (usually an action) does not constitute an international delinquency. It is the omission of the state and not the acts of the individuals what contravenes international law. For a contemporary author using this

Nonetheless, terminology is not entirely consistent in this regard. In the mid-1970s some scholars coined the expression 'responsibility for secondary state conduct' (*Haftung für sekundäres Organverhalten*) to designate state responsibility arising in connection with the acts of non-state actors.[224] This new category served the purpose of drawing a line between the aforesaid scenario and 'indirect responsibility' (*mittelbare Haftung*) properly so-called, which was predicated upon the acts of other subjects of international law (e.g. complicity of the state in the acts of another state).[225] This approach, while interesting, was somewhat misleading. Once it is agreed that the violation of a primary due diligence obligation is a separate delict, there is no reason to depict such breach as 'secondary'. In substance, however, this theory also acknowledged that the host state's reaction towards private acts of violence is severable from those acts.[226]

The *separate delict theory* had a remarkable influence in the subsequent evolution of this area of international law. Francisco García Amador's *Second Report of State Responsibility* (1957) bears witness to its importance:

> In the circumstances envisaged in this chapter of the draft [acts of individuals and internal disturbances], the author of the act which directly causes the injury to the alien is not an organ, or official, of the State but a person, or group of persons, acting in a private capacity. *As it is one of the fundamental principles of international law on the subject of responsibility that the State cannot be held responsible except for "its own acts or omissions", its responsibility and the duty to make reparation can only arise in these cases if there is a second act or omission imputable to an organ of the State, or to one of its officials.*[227]

These words' resemblance to Triepel's conclusion is striking. Still, contemporary international law does not fully reflect Triepel's original version of the theory. Triepel's formal argument rested on the premise that *individuals* are not subjects of international obligations and, as a corollary, cannot commit a violation of international law.[228] Despite the fact that authoritative voices continue to rely on this dualistic reasoning,[229] the argument is no longer entirely straightforward.

---

terminology see: Tal Becker, *Terrorism and the State: Rethinking the Rules of State Responsibility* (Hart Publishing, Portland OR 2006) 24 *et seq.* Terminology is however not uniform. Cf., for example: Vincent-Joël Proulx, *Institutionalizing State Responsibility: Global Security and UN Organs* (Oxford University Press, Oxford 2016) 293 *et seq.* (still using the term 'indirect responsibility').

[224]Hans-Jürgen Schlochauer, 'Die Entwicklung des völkerrechtlichen Deliktsrechts' (1975) 16 AVR 239, 259-62.

[225]Hans-Jürgen Schlochauer, 'Die Entwicklung des völkerrechtlichen Deliktsrechts' (1975) 16 AVR 239, 259-62.

[226]Hans-Jürgen Schlochauer, 'Die Entwicklung des völkerrechtlichen Deliktsrechts' (1975) 16 AVR 239, 259.

[227]Emphasis added. Francisco García Amador, 'International Responsibility: Second Report by F. V. García Amador, Special Rapporteur (A/CN.4/106)' (15 February 1957) 2 *Yearbook of the International Law Commission – 1957* 104, 121 [1].

[228]Heinrich Triepel, *Völkerrecht und Landesrecht* (Verlag von C. L. Hirschfeld, Leipzig 1899) 329.

[229]In its Report to the General Assembly of 1975, the ILC used Triepel's formal argument in this connection. See: ILC, 'Report of the International Law Commission on the Work of its Twenty-

Non-state actors have come to be recognized—to a greater or lesser extent—as *subjects of* or, at least, *participants in* international law.[230] This opens the door for complicity between a state and a non-state actor.[231] Another issue pertains to the question of intention, that is to say, whether a failure of redress could be reasonably said to express the host state's actual *will* to participate in the original private wrong (i.e. Triepel's second objection to the theory of complicity). This problem is associated to the debate on the subjective element of the notion of complicity and the distinction, if any, between state responsibility on account of complicity and a breach of due diligence obligations.

Roberto Ago's *Fourth Report on State Responsibility* (1972) provides a useful introduction to the contemporary guise of the debate. On that occasion, Ago expressed some doubts as to whether complicity between a state and a private person could be excluded on the sole ground that individuals have not been traditionally considered to be subjects of obligations under international law.[232] In this vein, he explained:

> [W]hen the State endorses the act of the individual it is the State itself which acts, both through the individual and through the organs which are "accomplices"; the idea of such complicity would thus be quite conceivable [...] the conclusion envisaged should always include the idea that the State endorses the act of the individual as such, where certain State organs have in some way connived at that act. The action of the individual would be the basis of the internationally wrongful conduct of the State, and the State would violate international law through the action of an individual in which certain organs were merely accomplices.[233]

Ago's idea of 'endorsement' would finally crystalize in Article 11 of the ILC's *Articles on State Responsibility* (2001).[234] The provision in question entails a rule of

---

Seventh Session – State Responsibility' (1975) 2 *Yearbook of the International Law Commission – 1975* 51, 73 [11] (expressly dismissing the characterization of state responsibility for private injuries to aliens as 'indirect' or 'vicarious' on the same grounds outlined by Triepel).

[230]For an overview see: Cedric Ryngaert, 'Imposing International Duties on Non-State Actors and the Legitimacy of International Law' in Math Noortmann and Cedric Ryngaert (eds), Non-State Actor Dynamics in International Law. From Law-Takers to Law-Makers (Routledge, London 2016) 69, 70 et seq. On the notion of 'participants' of international law see: Rosalyn Higgins, Problems & Process. International Law and How We Use It (Clarendon Press, Oxford 1994) 50.

[231]On this issue see generally: Miles Jackson, *Complicity in International Law* (Oxford University Press, Oxford 2015) 127-31. For a different approach see: Bernhard Graefrath, 'Complicity in the Law of International Responsibility' (1996) 1996/2 Revue belge de droit international 371, 371 n. 1 (stating that '[t]he participation of a State in illegal acts of individuals against other states may raise questions of attribution *but cannot be qualified as complicity in the law of international responsibility*' – emphasis added).

[232]Roberto Ago, 'Fourth Report on State Responsibility – The Internationally Wrongful Act of the State, Source of International Responsibility (Continued) (A/CN.4/264)' (20 June 1972 and 9 April 1973) 2 Yearbook of the International Law Commission – 1972 71, 96 [63-6].

[233]Roberto Ago, 'Fourth Report on State Responsibility – The Internationally Wrongful Act of the State, Source of International Responsibility (Continued) (A/CN.4/264)' (20 June 1972 and 9 April 1973) 2 Yearbook of the International Law Commission – 1972 71, 96 [64].

[234]ILC, 'Responsibility of States for Internationally Wrongful Acts. General Commentary' (2001) 2 Yearbook of the International Law Commission – 2001 31, 52 art. 11 ("Conduct which is not

'retroactive' attribution, the foundation of which lies in a 'clear and unequivocal' adoption by the state of some private conduct as its own.[235] For present purposes, the threshold issue would be whether a failure of redress (Vattel's 'act of complicity') could fulfill these conditions and be accordingly styled as an 'endorsement' of the harmful act. This question must be answered in the negative. In his *Seventh Report on State Responsibility* (1978), Ago himself clarified that a mere lack of diligence in the prevention or redress of an injury does not constitute complicity, and should rather be seen as a 'separate' delinquency.[236] In any case, Ago's use of the term 'complicity' in this connection is unpersuasive, if not to say misleading. Strictly speaking, in these cases the state does not *participate* in the conduct of private individuals. Rather, the individuals in question are 'retroactively' declared as state agents.[237]

Notwithstanding these inaccuracies, it is striking that Ago accepted that the notions due diligence and complicity (including complicity between a state and an individual) do not only coexist, but could moreover overlap. During the past few decades, the possible juxtaposition of due diligence and complicity has taken center stage in academic debates on the subject.[238] Different criteria have been proposed in this regard.[239] A first possible approach appeared in the ICJ Judgment on the *Bosnian Genocide Case*:

---

attributable to a State under the preceding articles shall nevertheless be considered an act of that State under international law if and to the extent that the State acknowledges and adopts the conduct in question as its own").

[235] ILC, 'Responsibility of States for Internationally Wrongful Acts. General Commentary' (2001) 2 Yearbook of the International Law Commission – 2001 31, 53 art. 11 (Commentary) [6-7].

[236] In his analysis of wrongful acts committed by one state in the territory of another state, Ago confirmed the fundamental proposition that the 'mere failure [of the territorial state] to prevent and punish' constitutes 'a separate breach', which 'can certainly not be defined as a form of complicity'. Roberto Ago, 'Seventh Report on State Responsibility – The Internationally Wrongful Act of the State, Source of International Responsibility (A/CN.4/307 and Add.1 and 2)' (1978) 2(1) *Yearbook of the International Law Commission – 1978* 31, 53-4 [57] (it should be emphasized, however, that this comment pertained particularly to the question of complicity by one state in the acts of another state, and referred to a different provision of the *Articles of State Responsibility*).

[237] See generally: James Crawford, *State Responsibility. The General Part* (Cambridge University Press, Cambridge 2013) 181-8 (using the phrase '*ex post facto* adoption of conduct').

[238] See: Miles Jackson, *Complicity in International Law* (Oxford University Press, Oxford 2015) 127-32; Vladyslav Lanovoy, 'Complicity in an Internationally Wrongful Act' in André Nollkaemper and Ilias Plakokefalos (eds), *Principles of Shared Responsibility in International Law. An Appraisal of the State of the Art* (Cambridge University Press, Cambridge 2014) 134, 146-7; Vladyslav Lanovoy, *Complicity and its Limits in the Law of International Responsibility* (Hart Publishing, Portland OR 2016) 210-7.

[239] For a detailed presentation of the contemporary debate on the subject see: Vladyslav Lanovoy, *Complicity and its Limits in the Law of International Responsibility* (Hart Publishing, Portland OR 2016) 210-8. Cf. also: Vladyslav Lanovoy, 'Complicity in an Internationally Wrongful Act' in André Nollkaemper and Ilias Plakokefalos (eds), *Principles of Shared Responsibility in International Law. An Appraisal of the State of the Art* (Cambridge University Press, Cambridge 2014) 134, 146-7.

[C]omplicity always requires that some positive action has been taken to furnish aid or assistance to the perpetrators of the genocide, while a violation of the obligation to prevent results from the mere failure to adopt and implement suitable measures to prevent genocide from being committed.[240]

This criterion allows drawing a reasonably clear line between complicity and omissions in the exercise of due diligence. In the analysis of state responsibility, it would hence suffice to identify the actions and the omissions that come into play. Based on such identification, adjudicators could easily determine whether state responsibility is based on complicity or due diligence.

The issue cannot yet be considered as settled, however. The 'positive conduct' criterion has met with sharp criticism. As a matter of fact, scholars generally admit the possibility of *complicity by omission*.[241] And then the issue turns into a complex question, namely, the delicate distinction between a *want of diligence*, on the one hand, and *complicity by omission* on the other.[242] It has been suggested that international law does not exclude a concurrence of causes of action in the face of 'particularly culpable omissions that contribute significantly to the commission of harm'.[243] In such events, scholars say, '[omissions do] not only constitute a breach of that due diligence obligation but also give rise to responsibility for complicity'.[244]

For present purposes it is unnecessary to dig deeper into these intricacies. The ILC has expressly recognized that 'the responsibility of the State on the occasion of acts committed by private individuals can in no case be described as an indirect or

---

[240]*Case Concerning the Application of the Convention on the Prevention and Punishment of the Crime of Genocide (Bosnia and Herzegovina v Serbia and Montenegro)* [2007] ICJ Rep 43, 222-3 [432].

[241]See, for example: James Crawford, *State Responsibility. The General Part* (Cambridge University Press, Cambridge 2013) 219; Miles Jackson, *Complicity in International Law* (Oxford University Press, Oxford 2015) 98 *et seq.* and 155-7; Vladyslav Lanovoy, *Complicity and its Limits in the Law of International Responsibility* (Hart Publishing, Portland OR 2016) 96-7 and 332-3.

[242]See generally: Miles Jackson, *Complicity in International Law* (Oxford University Press, Oxford 2015) 157; Vladyslav Lanovoy, *Complicity and its Limits in the Law of International Responsibility* (Hart Publishing, Portland OR 2016) 210-7.

[243]Miles Jackson, *Complicity in International Law* (Oxford University Press, Oxford 2015) 157.

[244]Miles Jackson, *Complicity in International Law* (Oxford University Press, Oxford 2015) 157. For an overview on the role of fault in the concept of complicity see: Helmut Philip Aust, *Complicity and the Law of State Responsibility* (Cambridge University Press, Cambridge 2011) 232 et seq. (particularly focusing on the discussion at the ILC of the requirement of intent as an element of the notion of complicity). See also: Vladyslav Lanovoy, Complicity and its Limits in the Law of International Responsibility (Hart Publishing, Portland OR 2016) 218-40 and 333. See also the position adopted by the ICJ in connection with the crime of genocide: *Case Concerning the Application of the Convention on the Prevention and Punishment of the Crime of Genocide (Bosnia and Herzegovina v Serbia and Montenegro)* [2007] ICJ Rep 43, 218 [421] ("[T]here is no doubt that the conduct of an organ or a person furnishing aid or assistance to a perpetrator of the crime of genocide cannot be treated as complicity in genocide unless at least that organ or person acted knowingly, that is to say, in particular, was aware of the specific intent (dolus specialis) of the principal perpetrator. If that condition is not fulfilled, that is sufficient to exclude categorization as complicity.").

vicarious responsibility'.[245] Publicists addressing questions of complicity generally agree that a breach of a positive due diligence obligation is a *separate delict* for which the host state can be held accountable, regardless of whether the same facts give rise to an *additional* charge of complicity.[246]

These views provide a sharp contrast to the Vattelian notion of complicity, which purpose was precisely to build a bridge between the sovereign and the private individual who causes harm to an alien.[247] From this perspective, it was an *alternative* to *due diligence*.

A concurrence of causes of action is furthermore unlikely to arise in cases pertaining to the protection of aliens. Complicity always implies that an actor *participates* in the *international wrong* of another actor.[248] Triepel was right in stating that, as a rule, private injuries to aliens do not fit into this structure.[249] This conclusion is not necessarily dependent on the wrongdoer enjoying international legal personality. Even assuming that the private wrongdoer is a subject of international law, his or her conduct cannot be lightly qualified as *international wrong*.[250] A private individual who causes harm to an alien will, by so doing, possibly contravene his or her duties under the *municipal law* of the host state.[251] But, in most cases, such individual does not thereby commit a breach of an obligation placed upon *him or her* by *international law*. There could certainly be cases in which a 'non-state actor' is liable as a 'principal', and the host state can be properly styled as an 'accomplice'.[252]

---

[245] ILC, 'Report of the International Law Commission on the Work of its Twenty-Seventh Session – State Responsibility' (1975) 2 *Yearbook of the International Law Commission – 1975* 51, 73 [11].

[246] See: Miles Jackson, *Complicity in International Law* (Oxford University Press, Oxford 2015) 127-32; Vladyslav Lanovoy, *Complicity and its Limits in the Law of International Responsibility* (Hart Publishing, Portland OR 2016) 210-7.

[247] See Sect. 12.4.1.

[248] Miles Jackson, *Complicity in International Law* (Oxford University Press, Oxford 2015) 201-2 (further considering the conceptual difficulties arising out of injuries committed by non-state actors). For some general conceptual remarks on this subject see: Vladyslav Lanovoy, *Complicity and its Limits in the Law of International Responsibility* (Hart Publishing, Portland OR 2016) 10-1 (arguing that 'while complicity is indeed derivative at the level of the origins of responsibility – i.e. triggering or *fait générateur*', its 'legal consequences' cannot be properly styled as 'derivative').

[249] Heinrich Triepel, *Völkerrecht und Landesrecht* (Verlag von C. L. Hirschfeld, Leipzig 1899) 328-9.

[250] For a similar observation see: Miles Jackson, *Complicity in International Law* (Oxford University Press, Oxford 2015) 201-2.

[251] Heinrich Triepel, *Völkerrecht und Landesrecht* (Verlag von C. L. Hirschfeld, Leipzig 1899) 328-9.

[252] For some examples see: Miles Jackson, *Complicity in International Law* (Oxford University Press, Oxford 2015) 201 *et seq.* (particularly focusing on state complicity in genocide and making no particular reference to the law of aliens).

But this is not the general rule. This does not however mean that an overlap between complicity and a breach of FPS can never occur as a matter of principle. A case for complicity is likely to appear in some exceptional situations, such as incidents involving acts of a foreign state in the host territory.[253]

---

[253]See Sect. 8.3.2.2.

Chapter 13
Due Diligence in the Context of 'Full Protection and Security' Claims

13.1 Introductory Remarks

Investment arbitral tribunals have consistently recognized that 'full protection and security' entails a 'due diligence' obligation.[1] In spite of this consensus, the application of the due diligence standard has proven to be a true challenge for practitioners and adjudicators alike. This should not come as a surprise in view of the dogmatic intricacies surrounding the notion of diligence in international law.[2] In investment arbitral proceedings, practical difficulties have been threefold.

A first issue pertains to the burden of proof. Investors advancing FPS claims could face sheer difficulties in substantiating an allegation that the host state failed to exercise due diligence. This holds particularly true for cases involving the prevention obligation. The respondent state is usually in a better position to submit evidence of both the foreseeability of risk and its organs' ability to avert it. Arbitral tribunals will therefore struggle with the conditions upon which a claimant may be deemed to have satisfied its burden of proof and, in some cases, the extent of the respondent state's duty to cooperate in the production of evidence.

The second issue refers to the characterization of due diligence either as a *subjective* standard requiring the host state to protect foreigners with the same diligence as it protects its own interests, or as a standard requiring the host state's diligence to be measured against an *objective* yardstick. In case an objective standard is adopted, the question arises as to the formulation of the objective parameters applicable to the evaluation of the host state's conduct. The choice between different versions of the objective standard has dominated recent academic debates on the subject.

---

[1]See Sect. 11.1.
[2]See Chap. 12.

© Springer Nature Switzerland AG 2019

S. Mantilla Blanco, *Full Protection and Security in International Investment Law*,
European Yearbook of International Economic Law 8,
https://doi.org/10.1007/978-3-030-24838-3_13

The third difficulty is the absence of consensus as to the precise parameters the standard of 'due diligence' provides for the assessment of conduct. Adjudicators considering FPS claims too-often fail to make explicit the criteria they relied upon in the evaluation of the host state's diligence. Scholars might therefore feel tempted to suggest a 'due diligence test' as a means to foster certainty. This chapter argues that a 'test' is never an adequate response to the practical challenges posed by the notion of due diligence. Instead of suggesting a test, this chapter provides a non-exhaustive list of *factual circumstances* to be considered in the evaluation of the host state's conduct.

13.2   The Distribution of the Burden of Proof

A breach of FPS can never be declared in the abstract.[3] Evidence is what ultimately allows investment tribunals to properly fulfill their fact-finding function and to reach a decision on any specific claim.[4] Due diligence will often take center stage in the evidentiary phase of arbitral proceedings concerning FPS claims. A fundamental issue is therefore whether the claimant bears the burden of proving lack of diligence on the part of the host state or, alternatively, whether it is the host state that must provide evidence of its own diligence.

As a rule, each party bears the burden of bolstering its allegations with sufficient evidence; *onus probandi incumbit actori*.[5] In *AAPL v Sri Lanka*, the very first BIT-based investor-state arbitration (which involved an alleged violation of FPS), the tribunal recognized that the burden of proof rests with the claimant.[6] Along these lines, the arbitrators clarified:

---

[3]Cf. Mondev International *v* United States, Award, ICSID Case No. ARB(AF)/99/2 (11 October 2002) [118] ("When a tribunal is faced with the claim by a foreign investor that the investor has been unfairly or inequitably treated or not accorded full protection and security, it is bound to pass upon that claim on the facts and by application of any governing treaty provision").

[4]On the fact-finding function of international adjudicators see generally: Mojtaba Kazazi, *Burden of Proof and Related Issues* (Kluwer Law International, The Hague 1996) 165-6 (arguing at p. 166 that '[t]he fact-finding power of international tribunals appears to be inherent').

[5]On the recognition of this principle in the context of international adjudication see: Chittharanjan Felix Amerasinghe, *Evidence in International Litigation* (Martinus Nijhoff, Leiden 2005) 37; Joost Pauwelyn, 'Evidence, Proof and Persuasion in WTO Dispute Settlement' (1998) 1 J. Int'l Econ. L. 227, 230-3; Markus Benzing, 'Evidentiary Issues' in Andreas Zimmermann, Christian Tomuschat, Karin Oellers-Frahm and Christian Tams (eds), *The Statute of the International Court of Justice. A Commentary* (Oxford University Press, Oxford 2012) 1234, 1245; Mojtaba Kazazi, *Burden of Proof and Related Issues* (Kluwer Law International, The Hague 1996) 24-30 and 378.

[6]Asian Agricultural Products *v* Sri Lanka, Final Award, ICSID Case No ARB/87/3 (27 June 1990) [56].

The term *actor* in the principle *onus probandi actori incumbit* is not to be taken to mean the plaintiff from the procedural standpoint, but the real claimant in view of the issues involved [. . .] the burden of proof rests upon the party alleging the fact.[7]

Thus, the claimant bears the burden of presenting evidence of the facts its claims refer to.[8] In turn, the respondent must provide evidence of the facts supporting affirmative defenses.[9] In cases concerning FPS claims, the distribution of the burden of proof heavily depends on the definition of the FPS standard's normative structure.

A first possible approach would be to consider that the host state is *generally responsible* for injurious acts committed against foreigners within its territory (general responsibility rule).[10] Following this premise, the exercise of due diligence would merely *excuse* a want of protection.[11] The implication for the burden of proof is clear. An investor advancing an FPS claim would only need to provide evidence of the infliction of an injury within the host state's territory and, if the redress obligation comes into play, of the absence of adequate means of redress. The host state could then escape responsibility by showing that public authorities acted diligently in the prevention or redress of the injury. For all practical purposes, due diligence would appear as an *affirmative defense*. The burden of proof would consistently rest on the respondent state. *AMT v Zaire* (1997) provides a clear example of this approach. In that case, the arbitrators stated:

Zaire must show that it has taken all measure of precaution to protect the investments of AMT in its territory. It has not done so, by mere recognition of the existing reality of the damage caused while designating SINZA as the victim and alleging that its own national legislation has exonerated Zaire from all obligations to make reparation for the injuries sustained on its territory in the circumstances such as the ones giving rise to the present dispute.[12]

Chapter 12 has presented an argument against the aforesaid general responsibility rule.[13] The proposition advanced is that, in customary law, non-responsibility is always the general rule.[14] The state is not responsible for injuries caused by third

---

[7]Asian Agricultural Products *v* Sri Lanka, Final Award, ICSID Case No ARB/87/3 (27 June 1990) [56] (directly quoting Bin Cheng's *General Principles of Law as Applied by International Courts and Tribunals*, as well as Durward Sandifer's *Evidence before International Tribunals*).

[8]Joost Pauwelyn, 'Evidence, Proof and Persuasion in WTO Dispute Settlement' (1998) 1 J. Int'l Econ. L. 227, 230 and 232.

[9]Joost Pauwelyn, 'Evidence, Proof and Persuasion in WTO Dispute Settlement' (1998) 1 J. Int'l Econ. L. 227, 230 and 232.

[10]Cf. Sects. 12.3.2.2 and 12.4.2.

[11]Cf. Sects. 12.3.2.2 and 12.4.2.

[12]American Manufacturing & Trading Inc. *v* Zaire, Award, ICSID Case No. ARB 93/1 (21 February 1997) [6.05]. Cf. also Nicole O'Donnell, 'Reconciling Full Protection and Security Guarantees in Bilateral Investment Treaties with Incidence of Terrorism' (2018) 29(3) ARIA 293, 311-2 (suggesting that proof that the host state has taken 'all necessary measures of precaution' could provide an 'affirmative defense' in the context of FPS claims).

[13]See Chap. 12, particularly at Sect. 12.4.3.

[14]Cf. Chap. 12.

parties or natural phenomena *unless* it is established that it has *failed to exercise due diligence* in the prevention or redress of the injury.[15]

This premise necessarily implies that the *claimant* must show a lack of diligence on the part of the host state. This implication is consistent with arbitral practice. Investment tribunals have generally acknowledged that it is the investor who bears the burden of proving a breach of the FPS standard, and have consistently dismissed claims that were not supported with sufficient evidence.[16] Arbitrators have also

---

[15]Cf. Chaps. 11 and 12.

[16]Adel A Hamadi Al Tamini *v* Oman, Award, ICSID Case No. ARB/11/33 (3 November 2015) [451] (noting that the claimant had failed to submit 'credible evidence' in support of its FPS claim); AES Corporation and Tau Power B.V. *v* Kazakhstan, Award, ICSID Case No. ARB/10/16 (1 November 2013) [339] (observing that 'Claimants have failed to substantiate their claim under the FPS standard'); Ampal-American Israel Corp., Egi-Fund (08-10) Investors LLC, Egi-Series Investments LLC and BSS-EMG Investors LLC *v* Egypt, Decision on Liability and Heads of Loss, ICSID Case No. ARB/12/11 (21 February 2017) [194-6 and 216] (finding at para 196 that the investors 'have not discharged their burden of proof' in respect of the facts relevant for one of their multiple FPS claims); Crystallex International Corp. *v* Venezuela, Award, ICSID Case No. ARB (AF)/11/2 (4 April 2016) [633] (finding that the investor 'has not alleged, let alone shown, that it was subjected to a violation of physical security attributable to Venezuela); Enron Corp. and Ponderosa Assets L.P. *v* Argentina, Award, ICSID Case No. ARB/01/3 (22 May 2007) [287] (dismissing an FPS claim because the investor did not allege '[a] failure to give full protection and security to officials, employees or installations' and underscoring that '[t]he argument made in general about a possible lack of protection and security in the broader ambit of the legal and political system is not in any way proven or even adequately developed'); Gold Reserve Inc. *v* Venezuela, Award, ICSID Case No. ARB(AF)/09/1 (22 September 2014) [623] (restricting the scope of application of FPS to 'physical' protection and dismissing the claim on the ground that there was no allegation involving 'physical harm'); Jan de Nul N.V. and Dredging International N.V. *v* Egypt, Award, ICSID Case No. ARB/04/13 (6 November 2008) [270-1] ("[the Claimants] have not established that there was an actual breach to be remedied [...] irrespective of the precise scope of the standard, the Tribunal finds no breach of the Treaty"); Jan Oostergetel and Theodora Laurentius *v* Slovakia (UNCITRAL), Final Award (23 April 2012) [308] (noting that '[t]he allegation of breach of the FPS standard lacks a factual basis'); LESI S.p.A. and ASTALDI S.p.A. *v* Algeria, Sentence, ICSID Case No. ARB/05/3 (12 November 2008) [154] (noting that the Claimants did neither clearly allege nor prove that the protection granted by local authorities had been insufficient or discriminatory); Marion Unglaube and Reinhard Unglaube *v* Costa Rica, Award, ICSID Cases No. ARB/01/1 and ARB/09/20 (16 May 2012) [281 and 283] (stating at para 281 that 'the Tribunal is not persuaded that this standard has been violated by Costa Rica based on the evidence presented in this case' and explaining at para 283 what claimants are required to 'demonstrate' in order for their FPS claim to be successful; see also para 285); Mohammad Ammar Al-Bahloul *v* Tajikistan, Partial Award on Jurisdiction and Liability, SCC Case No. V 064/2008 (9 September 2009) [173 and 243-5] (rejecting two FPS claims for lack of evidence); Pantechniki S.A. Contractors & Engineers *v* Albania, Award, ICSID Case No. ARB/07/21 (30 July 2009) [83] (observing that 'specific conduct' and 'its purported effect' need to 'be alleged and proved'); Parkerings-Compagniet AS *v* Lithuania, Award, ICSID Case No. ARB/05/8 (11 September 2007) [356-9] (noting that the investor failed to 'show' or 'demonstrate' the alleged breaches of the FPS standard); Plama Consortium Ltd. *v* Bulgaria, Award, ICSID Case No. ARB/03/24 (27 August 2008) [194, 222 and 226] (noting, in respect of one of the FPS claims raised in the proceedings, that the investor 'failed to identify' a failure to exercise due diligence and did not prove any harm, thus concluding that 'the very basis of Claimant's claim [...] is not factually established'), [248-9] (observing, in respect of another FPS claim, that '[t]he factual evidence [...] is in virtually all

recognized that a want of due diligence is one of the elements a claimant must prove in order to successfully advance an FPS claim.[17]

Notwithstanding the foregoing, it must be admitted that the host state is usually in the better position to provide evidence of its own diligence. Moreover, it is often in the respondent's own interest to submit evidence of any measures adopted for the prevention or redress of the injury. Even if this was not case, the parties have a duty

---

respects contradictory' and underscoring that it was the claimant who bore the burden of proving the facts) and [279] (dismissing another FPS claim for lack of evidence); Peter A. Allard *v* Barbados (UNCITRAL), Award (27 June 2016) [252] ("[T]he Claimant has failed to establish that Barbados violated its obligations of the FPS standard"); Ronald Lauder *v* Czech Republic (UNCITRAL), Final Award (3 September 2001) [309 and 314] (finding at para 309 that 'none of the facts alleged by the Claimant constituted a violation by the Respondent of the obligation to provide full protection and security' and observing at para 314 that '[t]here is no evidence – not even an allegation – that the Respondent has violated this [redress] obligation'); Rumeli Telekom A.S. and Telsim Mobil Telekomunikasyon Hizmetleri A.S. *v* Kazakhstan, Award, ICSID Case No. ARB/05/16 (29 July 2008) [669-70] (dismissing an FPS claim on grounds that the facts alleged by the investor did not indicate a breach of the standard and that 'the record does not support' some of the claimant's contentions); Rusoro Mining Ltd. *v* Venezuela, Award, ICSID Case No. ARB(AF)/12/5 (22 August 2016) [550] (noting at 550, in respect of one of the investor's FPS claims, that '[t]he problem with this allegation is that it is unsupported in evidence') and [553] (concluding that '[t]he evidence marshalled by Rusoro is manifestly insufficient to prove its allegation'); SAUR International S.A. *v* Argentina, Décision sur la compétence et sur la responsabilité, ICSID Case No. ARB/04/4 (6 June 2012) [511] (observing that the claimant had failed to prove the facts on which a FPS claim was based); Sempra Energy International *v* Argentina, Award, ICSID Case No. ARB/02/16 (28 September 2007) [324] (stressing that the claimant's argument on legal security 'has in no way been proven'); Tecnicas Medioambientales TECMED S.A. *v* Mexico, Award, ICSID Case No. ARB(AF)/00/2 (29 May 2003) [176-7] (noting that 'Claimant has not furnished evidence' of some of its allegations and concluding 'there is no sufficient evidence supporting [the claim]'); Tokios Tokelés *v* Ukraine, Award, ICSID Case No. ARB/02/18 (26 July 2007) [123-37] (dismissing an FPS claim for lack of evidence); Toto Costruzioni Generali S.p.A. *v* Lebanon, Award, ICSID Case No. ARB/07/12 (7 June 2012) [229] (concluding that the investor 'did not demonstrate' circumstances of fact which could have provided the basis for a successful FPS claim); Vannessa Ventures Ltd. *v* Venezuela, Award, ICSID Case No. ARB(AF)04/6 (16 January 2013) [228 and 231] (noting that the Claimant had failed to submit sufficient evidence in support of its FPS claim). Please note that an ICSID Ad Hoc Committee annulled the Sempra award for reasons unrelated to this particular issue. See: Sempra Energy International *v* Argentina, Decision on the Argentine Republic's Application for Annulment of the Award, ICSID Case No. ARB/02/16 (29 June 2010) [229]. Cf. also: CME Czech Republic B.V. *v* Czech Republic (UNCITRAL), Partial Award (13 September 2001) [357] (respondent argued that the investor must 'identify [. . .] factual circumstances that could support its allegation').

[17] Asian Agricultural Products *v* Sri Lanka, Final Award, ICSID Case No. ARB/87/3 (17 June 1990) [53] (rejecting the Claimant's argument that a breach of the FPS standard could be established 'without any need to prove that the damages suffered were attributable to the State or its agents, and to establish the State's responsibility for not acting with due diligence'). Cf. also the respondent's argument in the *CME* case: CME Czech Republic B.V. *v* Czech Republic (UNCITRAL), Partial Award (13 September 2001) [357] (stating that 'CME fails to identify any factual circumstances that could support its allegation that the Czech Republic failed to provide full protection and security for its investment, or that the Czech Republic breached the obligations of full protection and security).

to collaborate with the arbitral tribunal in the clarification of relevant facts.[18] Arbitrators could draw adverse inferences from a state's reluctance to present evidence pertaining to the circumstances under which the harmful event occurred.[19]

This does not however relieve the claimant from its burden of proof. From an evidentiary standpoint, FPS claims bear some resemblance to the situation considered by the ICJ in the *Corfu Channel* case (1949). In that case, the explosion of multiple mines in Albanian territorial waters caused major damages to two British warships.[20] The ICJ found no evidence indicating that Albania had directly laid the minefield.[21] The Court acknowledged that, in this kind of cases, 'the victim of a breach of international law is often unable to furnish direct proof of facts giving rise to responsibility'.[22] It further noted that this reality 'has a bearing upon the methods of proof'.[23] Particularly, the respondent 'should be allowed a more liberal recourse to inferences of fact and circumstantial evidence'.[24] At the same time, however, the ICJ emphasized that this 'neither involves *prima facie* responsibility nor shifts the burden of proof'.[25]

There is no reason to depart from these sound principles when it comes to the proof of due diligence. The burden rests on the claimant, but arbitrators might give particular weight to the respondent's duty to cooperate and will often rely on circumstantial evidence.[26] This could have the practical effect of lowering the threshold a claimant must meet in order to successfully advance an FPS claim.

This apparent advantage is however offset by the fact that the analysis of diligence only comes into play *if* the claimant has provided sufficient evidence of: (1) the occurrence of an injurious event falling within the scope of FPS; and (2) an omission, attributable to the host state, which bears some (causal) relation to the injury. Only after these two elements have been established is it possible for the arbitrators to determine whether the host state's omission can be characterized as a failure to exercise the diligence required under the FPS standard. For that very same

---

[18]See generally: Mojtaba Kazazi, *Burden of Proof and Related Issues* (Kluwer Law International, The Hague 1996) 119-21.

[19]On the use of adverse inferences in international adjudication see generally: Mojtaba Kazazi, *Burden of Proof and Related Issues* (Kluwer Law International, The Hague 1996) 313-22. For an analysis of the use of negative inferences in the context of investment arbitration see: Michael Polkinghorne and Charles Rosenberg, 'The Adverse Inference in ICSID Practice' (2015) 30 (3) ICSID Rev. 741, 741-51.

[20]*Corfu Channel Case (UK v Albania)* [1949] ICJ Rep 4, 12-3.

[21]*Corfu Channel Case (UK v Albania)* [1949] ICJ Rep 4, 16-7.

[22]*Corfu Channel Case (UK v Albania)* [1949] ICJ Rep 4, 18.

[23]*Corfu Channel Case (UK v Albania)* [1949] ICJ Rep 4, 18.

[24]*Corfu Channel Case (UK v Albania)* [1949] ICJ Rep 4, 18.

[25]*Corfu Channel Case (UK v Albania)* [1949] ICJ Rep 4, 18.

[26]For an author considering the relevance of 'circumstantial evidence' and 'proof by inference' in the context of FPS claims see: Lucas Bastin, *State Responsibility for Omissions: Establishing a Breach of the Full Protection and Security Obligation by Omissions* (Oxford University, Oxford 2016) [D.Phil. Thesis] 247 *et seq.*

reason, adjudicators could dismiss FPS claims without specifically addressing the question of diligence.

The first step is, then, to prove that an injury has actually been inflicted.[27] Investors will be generally able to provide evidence of the occurrence of a harmful event falling within the scope of FPS. In most cases, the issue will not be whether an injury was actually inflicted, but whether the FPS standard is applicable in respect of that injury.[28] This issue is intrinsically linked to a question of law, namely, the determination of the FPS standard's scope of application. This determination is usually intertwined with the identification of the customary standard and the interpretation of specific FPS clauses.[29] As a rule, questions of law are not object of proof.[30] Adjudicators have the authority to assess the applicable law on their own initiative (*iura novit curia*).[31] Even if they find the law to be obscure, they cannot

---

[27]On the occurrence of a harmful event as a *conditio sine qua non* for a violation of FPS see Sect. 11.2.2.2.

[28]On the scope of the FPS standard see Chaps. 6–10.

[29]Chapter 14 provides a detailed assessment of the interpretation of different types of FPS clauses.

[30]Doubts may however arise as to whether the claimant bears a burden of proof with regard to the existence and scope of the customary standard. For a detailed assessment of the relevance of the maxim *iura novit curia* for the identification of international custom see: Luigi Fumagalli, 'Evidence Before the International Court of Justice: Issues of Fact and Questions of Law in the Determination of International Custom' in Nerina Boschiero, Tullio Scovazzi, Cesare Pitea and Chiara Ragni (eds), *International Courts and the Development of International Law* (Springer, The Hague 2013) 137, 143-6 (arguing that the parties are not generally required to prove universal custom, and providing references to multiple ICJ decisions and separate opinions of ICJ judges; however, Fumagalli draws a distinction between universal and regional custom). For an author considering that the claimant bears the burden of proving international custom see: Patrick Dumberry, *The Formation and Identification of Customary International Law in International Investment Law* (Cambridge University Press, Cambridge 2016) 39-42. For an overview of the debate see: Markus Benzing, *Das Beweisrecht vor internationalen Gerichten und Schiedsgerichten in zwischenstaatlichen Streitigkeiten* (Springer, Heidelberg 2010) 362-6. For an arbitral tribunal specifically requiring the claimant to prove the existence of the customary FPS standard see: ADF *v United States*, Award, ICSID Case No. ARB(AF)/00/1 (9 January 2003) [183] ("[W]e are not convinced that the Investor has shown the existence, in current customary law, of a general and autonomous requirement [. . .] to accord fair and equitable treatment and full protection and security to foreign investments"). See also the argument advanced by the United States in *Windstream Energy v Canada*: Windstream Energy LLC *v* Canada (UNCITRAL), Award (27 September 2016) [331-2].

[31]On the application of the *iura novit curia* maxim in international adjudication see: Joost Pauwelyn, 'Evidence, Proof and Persuasion in WTO Dispute Settlement' (1998) 1 J. Int'l Econ. L. 227, 230-3 and 242 (providing a general account of the issue but particularly focusing on the practice of WTO Panels and the WTO Appellate Body); Robert Kolb, 'General Principles of Procedural Law' in Andreas Zimmermann, Christian Tomuschat, Karin Oellers-Frahm and Christian Tams (eds), *The Statute of the International Court of Justice. A Commentary* (Oxford University Press, Oxford 2012) 871, 897 (presenting the maxim as an exception to the principle *ne ultra petita* and particularly referring to ICJ adjudication). For a detailed assessment of the principle of *iura novit curia* in general international law and international investment law see: Nils Börnsen, *Nationales Recht in Investitionsschiedsverfahren* (Mohr Siebeck, Tübingen 2016) 159-67

abstain from rendering judgment (*non liquet*).[32] Notwithstanding the foregoing, once a conclusion about the scope of the standard is reached, such outcome will have a decisive effect on the conclusiveness of the evidence submitted by the parties.

If it is said, for example, that the standard refers to the risk of *physical violence*, the claimant must show that *physical harm* was actually inflicted. In *Spyridon Roussalis v Romania* (2011), the arbitrators considered that a court order temporarily preventing the investor from leaving the host state's territory did not constitute a breach of the FPS standard because 'there has been no allegation that the temporary interdiction order compromised the *physical integrity* of claimant's investment against interference by use of force'.[33] In *Crystallex v Venezuela* (2016) the tribunal rejected the FPS claim on the ground that 'the Claimant has not alleged, let alone shown, that it was subjected to a violation of *its physical security*'.[34]

The tribunal could also consider that the FPS standard only grants protection against risks resulting from an event that does not originate in the host state's conduct, except for the case of collateral damages caused by state action against external threats.[35] This would coincide with the conclusion reached in Chap. 8 with regard to the customary standard. Tribunals following this approach have required the claimant to properly identify a source of risk meeting these criteria. For instance, in *Gemplus v Mexico* (2010), one of the reasons for the dismissal of an FPS claim was that 'the harm alleged by the Claimants is attributed to the Respondent itself and not to any third party'.[36] In *El Paso v Argentina* (2011), the arbitrators dismissed the investor's claim under the FPS standard on the following ground:

> El Paso did not specify or determine the duty to act against a third party that has allegedly been breached by Argentina under the BIT: all the impugned acts that allegedly violate the FPS standard are directly attributable to the GOA [Government of Argentina] and not to any third party.[37]

(arguing that arbitral tribunals have the *power* to conduct an autonomous assessment of the applicable law, but leaving the question open as to whether they also have a *duty* to do so).

[32]On the prohibition of *non liquet* in international adjudication see generally: Hersch Lauterpacht, *The Function of International Law in the International Community* (Clarendon Press, Oxford 1933) 71-7 and 135-43; Mojtaba Kazazi, *Burden of Proof and Related Issues* (Kluwer Law International, The Hague 1996) 28-9.

[33]Emphasis added. Spyridon Roussalis v Romania, Award, ICSID Case No. ARB/06/1 (7 December 2011) [609].

[34]Emphasis added. Crystallex International Corp. v Venezuela, Award, ICSID Case No. ARB(AF)/11/2 (4 April 2016) [635].

[35]See Sect. 8.3.

[36]Gemplus S.A., SLP S.A. and Gemplus Industrial S.A. de C.V. v Mexico, Award, ICSID Cases No. ARB(AF)/04/3 & ARB(AF)/04/4 (16 June 2010) [9.12]. It should be noted, however, that the tribunal did not exclude the possibility that the FPS standard could cover the risk of public injuries. As a matter of fact, the tribunal stated that, while other standards 'involve the investor and the state', 'protection provisions *also* involve the host state protecting the investment from a third party' (at para 9.11).

[37]El Paso Energy International Co. v Argentina, Award, ICSID Case No. ARB/03/15 (31 October 2011) [524]. See also: Eastern Sugar B.V. v Czech Republic, Partial Award, SCC Case

In *Oxus Gold v Uzbekistan* (2015), the absence of a clear and well-substantiated claim concerning third party conduct was the main reason for the dismissal of the FPS claims.[38] In connection with one of the investor's multiple claims under the FPS clause of the UK-Uzbekistan BIT, the arbitrators specifically observed that 'the way in which the claimant has put its claim for breach of the FPS standard is not in line with the principle that such standard may only apply with regard to actions of third parties'.[39]

The occurrence of an injurious event falling within the scope of application of the FPS standard, however important, does not suffice for the claimant to satisfy its burden of proof. As expressed by the arbitrators in *Frontier Petroleum v Czech Republic* (2010), '[t]he mere fact [. . .] that the investor lost its investment is insufficient to demonstrate a breach of full protection and security'.[40] In addition to damages, the claimant is also required to present evidence that there is a reasonable causal link between the injurious event and an act attributable to the host state. In *Marion Unglaube and Reinhard Unglaube v Costa Rica* (2012), the arbitrators stated:

> In order to prevail on this issue [an FPS claim], Claimants must demonstrate a causal connection between an improper action or failure to act of a State entity, or its agent, in violation of a legal obligation owed to Claimants, and to the detriment of Claimants or their investments.[41]

No. 088/2004 (27 March 2007) [204] (dismissing the claim on grounds that the investor was not complaining about 'acts of third parties'); Koch Minerals SÁRL and Koch Nitrogen International SÁRL *v* Venezuela, Award, ICSID Case No. ARB/11/19 (30 October 2017) [8.46] (dismissing the FPS claim because the case did 'manifestly' not refer to the prevention of physical harm by third parties); Mercer International Inc. *v* Canada, Award, ICSID Case No. ARB(AF)/12/3 (6 March 2018) [7.80] (stating that, in the absence of harm originating in a third party, an FPS claim would fail); Mobil Exploration and Development Argentina Inc. Suc. Argentina and Mobil Argentina S.A. *v* Argentina, Decision on Jurisdiction and Liability, ICSID Case No. ARB/04/16 (10 April 2013) [1004] (dismissing the FPS claims on the ground that 'Claimants did not specify or determine the duty to act against a third party that would have been breached by Argentina under the BIT'); Sergei Paushok, CJSC Golden East Co., CJSC Vostoknefte *v* Mongolia (UNCITRAL), Award on Jurisdiction and Liability (28 April 2011) [327] (requiring that the FPS claim refers to a failure to prevent 'negative action by third parties'; nonetheless, the tribunal also considered the possibility of the FPS standard being breached 'through actions of the State or its agents'); Suez Sociedad General de Aguas de Barcelona S.A. and Vivendi Universal S.A. *v* Argentina, Decision on Liability, ICSID Case No. ARB/03/19 (30 July 2010) [165] (observing at para 165 that FPS claims have 'traditionally' involved acts of third parties and physical violence, and that the claim at issue involved 'a different type of situation'; see also para 179).

[38]Oxus Gold *v* Uzbekistan (UNCITRAL), Final Award (17 December 2015) [356 *et seq.* and 834 *et seq.*].

[39]Oxus Gold *v* Uzbekistan (UNCITRAL), Final Award (17 December 2015) [839].

[40]Frontier Petroleum Ltd. *v* Czech Republic (UNCITRAL), Final Award (12 November 2010) [261] (making this general statement on the FPS standard, but subsequently focusing on the redress obligation).

[41]Marion Unglaube and Reinhard Unglaube *v* Costa Rica, Award, ICSID Cases No. ARB/01/1 and ARB/09/20 (16 May 2012) [283].

The arbitral tribunal in *Ronald Lauder v Czech Republic* (2001) similarly underscored that there was no clear link between the damages suffered by the investor, on the one hand, and the acts through which the Czech Republic allegedly breached the FPS standard on the other.[42] The assessment of causality often poses a true challenge for arbitral tribunals dealing with FPS claims. The reason is that, in cases related to responsibility for negative conduct, causality is unavoidably complex.[43] This work has advanced the proposition that the FPS standard refers to public authorities' *omissions* in respect of some *external* source of risk (a natural event or a private act), or public collateral damages.[44] The implication for causal analysis is that, as a rule, the host state's omission not the *principal*, let alone the *only*, material cause of the injury.

Approaches to causality are signalized by diversity. The possible use of 'tests' of causation inspired in domestic civil and criminal law has attracted the attention of international law scholars in the past.[45] Tribunals considering FPS claims rarely consider the question of causality in detail. A scholar observes that arbitral tribunals' approach to causation is usually 'case-specific, brief or even non-existent, and typically without reference to broader principles of causation'.[46] The problem of causation is not particular to the FPS standard, and a thorough analysis of this most intricate issue would exceed the scope of the present work.

For present purposes it shall suffice to emphasize two points. In the first place, in the context of FPS claims, the analysis of causality usually takes the form of

---

[42]Ronald Lauder *v* Czech Republic (UNCITRAL), Final Award (3 September 2001) [311 and 313]. It should be noted that the tribunal was considering an FPS claim, which was largely based on an extensive interpretation of the applicable FPS clause and pertained particularly to an alleged failure to grant 'legal security'. The tribunal observed that the damages sustained by the investor did not result from the positive or negative conduct of the host state, but from the termination of a business contract (see paras 311-4).

[43]See generally: Ilias Plakokefalos, 'Causation in the Law of State Responsibility and the Problem of Overdetermination: In Search of Clarity' (2015) 26 EJIL 471, 476-8 (underscoring the difficulties attached to causal analysis in cases involving omissions and providing an overlook of possible theoretical approaches to the subject, which are mostly inspired in American tort law).

[44]See Sect. 8.3. Cf. also Sect. 11.3.

[45]See, for example: Ilias Plakokefalos, 'Causation in the Law of State Responsibility and the Problem of Overdetermination: In Search of Clarity' (2015) 26 EJIL 471, 472-8 (particularly considering possible use in international law of causality tests developed in the context of American tort law); Sandra Stahl, *Schutzpflichten im Völkerrecht. Ansatz einer Dogmatik* (Springer, Heidelberg 2012) 169-82 (proposing the use of causality criteria developed in German criminal law); Tal Becker, *Terrorism and the State: Rethinking the Rules of State Responsibility* (Hart Publishing, Portland OR 2006) 285-360 (proposing a 'causal model of state responsibility for terrorism').

[46]Lucas Bastin, *Violation of the Full Protection and Security Obligation by Regulatory Omissions* [M.Phil. Thesis] (Oxford University, Oxford 2011) 81. In later works, Bastin has provided a detailed assessment of the question of causation in the context of FPS claims: Lucas Bastin, *State Responsibility for Omissions: Establishing a Breach of the Full Protection and Security Obligation by Omissions* (Oxford University, Oxford 2016) [D.Phil. Thesis] 150, 162 and 241 *et seq.*

counterfactual analysis.[47] In other words, the claimant is usually expected to identify a positive measure of protection which could have arguably prevented or mitigated the injury.[48] In *Parkerings v Lithuania* (2007) the arbitrators stated:

> The Claimant alleges damages to its materials due to vandalism. However, the Claimant does not show that such vandalism would have been prevented if the authorities had acted differently. The Claimant only contends that the police did not find the authors of this offence.[49]

The second point is that the claimant must establish causality to a fairly specific degree.[50] The specificity requirement found clear expression in *Pantechniki v Albania* (2009). In that case, a Greek investment had suffered significant damages as a result of mob violence.[51] The cause of the riots was the fall of fraudulent 'ponzi schemes' in which a significant portion of the local population had made substantive investments.[52] Government officials were apparently involved in the pyramid.[53] The Greek investor alleged that Albania had failed to provide the protection required under the FPS clause enshrined in the Albania-Greece BIT of 1991.[54] The claimant based the causal connection between the host state's conduct and the private acts which originated the damages on the participation of state officials in the fraudulent operations.[55] Sole Arbitrator Jan Paulsson was little impressed by the argument:

> The Claimant pushes its argument to say that Albania should be liable because powerful public officials were complicit in the pyramid schemes that had so enraged the populace. The premise of this contention is problematic in principle. *May an alleged chain of causation have so many links? This question need not be answered because the claim is simply unsubstantiated.* The Claimant has seized on a general perception that Albania's struggling public institutions were disserved by influential and unscrupulous officeholders. But a claim

---

[47]See generally: Lucas Bastin, *State Responsibility for Omissions: Establishing a Breach of the Full Protection and Security Obligation by Omissions* (Oxford University, Oxford 2016) [D.Phil. Thesis] 74 *et seq.* and 252 *et seq.*

[48]For an analysis of the 'but for' counterfactual in the context of FPS claims see: Lucas Bastin, *State Responsibility for Omissions: Establishing a Breach of the Full Protection and Security Obligation by Omissions* (Oxford University, Oxford 2016) [D.Phil. Thesis] 74 *et seq.* and 252 *et seq.*

[49]Parkerings-Compagniet AS *v* Lithuania, Award, ICSID Case No. ARB/05/8 (11 September 2007) [356].

[50]For the problem of 'remoteness' in the analysis of causation see: Lucas Bastin, *State Responsibility for Omissions: Establishing a Breach of the Full Protection and Security Obligation by Omissions* (Oxford University, Oxford 2016) [D.Phil. Thesis] 262 *et seq.*

[51]Pantechniki S.A. Contractors & Engineers *v* Albania, Award, ICSID Case No. ARB/07/21 (30 July 2009) [1].

[52]Pantechniki S.A. Contractors & Engineers *v* Albania, Award, ICSID Case No. ARB/07/21 (30 July 2009) [1].

[53]Pantechniki S.A. Contractors & Engineers *v* Albania, Award, ICSID Case No. ARB/07/21 (30 July 2009) [1 and 83].

[54]Pantechniki S.A. Contractors & Engineers *v* Albania, Award, ICSID Case No. ARB/07/21 (30 July 2009) [4 and 71-3].

[55]Pantechniki S.A. Contractors & Engineers *v* Albania, Award, ICSID Case No. ARB/07/21 (30 July 2009) [83].

before an international tribunal simply cannot be made good by casual references to general perceptions. *Specific conduct must be alleged and proved. So must its purported effect.* It is difficult to resist the impression that this contention was raised more to enlist intuitive sympathy than with a serious belief that it could prevail in this forum.[56]

Provided the Claimant has submitted evidence of an injurious event covered by the FPS standard and has furthermore established a causal link between the injury and an omission by public authorities, the threshold issue in the assessment of the FPS claim will be the characterization of the host state's omission as a failure to exercise the degree of diligence required under the FPS standard. The following sections will consider this requirement in detail.

13.3 The Subjective or Objective Character of Due Diligence

The development of 'due diligence' in international law has been signalized by an intense academic debate on the subjective or objective character of the notion.[57] In historical perspective, the bone of contention was whether the degree of diligence required by the customary protection shall be determined by reference to the diligence the host state displays in its own affairs (*subjective standard*) or, in the alternative, whether due diligence requires comparing the host state's conduct with the diligence a diligent state would exercise in a similar situation (*objective standard*).[58] This dichotomy was often explained by reference to the private law distinction between *diligentia quam in suis rebus* and the standard of a *diligens paterfamilias*.[59]

This section rejects the subjective understanding of due diligence. While historically relevant, this approach is contrary to extant principles of investment law and,

---

[56]Emphasis added. Pantechniki S.A. Contractors & Engineers *v* Albania, Award, ICSID Case No. ARB/07/21 (30 July 2009) [83]. This statement could be considered as an expression of the idea that a claim must always have some minimum degree of specificity. On this requirement see, for example: Noble Ventures *v* Romania, Award, ICSID Case No. ARB/01/11 (12 October 2005) [166] (observing that 'it is difficult to identify any *specific failure* by the Respondent to exercise due diligence in protecting the Claimant' – emphasis added); Peter A. Allard *v* Barbados (UNCITRAL), Award (27 June 2016) [251] (dismissing one of the FPS claims submitted by the investor on the ground that '[o]n no view is the claim sufficiently particularized').

[57]For an overview see: Eric De Brabandere, 'Host States' Due Diligence Obligations in International Investment Law' (2014-5) 42 Syracuse J. Int'l L. & Com. 319, 354 *et seq.*; ILA Study Group on Due Diligence in International Law, 'First Report by Mr. Tim Stephens (Rapporteur) and Mr. Duncan French (Chair)' (7 March 2014) 10.

[58]For an investment arbitral tribunal expressly recognizing the existence of these opposite approaches see: Asian Agricultural Products *v* Sri Lanka, Final Award, ICSID Case No ARB/87/3 (27 June 1990) [77].

[59]For a critical view on the use of these private law analogies see: Dionisio Anzilotti, *Lehrbuch des Völkerrechts* (Volume 1: Walter de Gruyter, Berlin/Leipzig 1929) 393.

thus, does not convey a normative character in contemporary international law. For its part, the objective standard lacks a univocal meaning. The widespread acceptance of the objective standard of diligence has given way to a wide array of modern 'objective' approaches. Debate has thus shifted from the 'objective' or 'subjective' character of due diligence to the choice between different versions of the objective standard.

13.3.1   The 'Subjective' Standard of Due Diligence

The history of international adjudication has known many attempts to define 'due diligence' through the private law notion of *diligentia quam in suis rebus*. Great Britain's arguments in the *Alabama Claims* arbitration bear witness to the long-standing tradition of this approach. In connection with the alleged breach of the duty to exercise diligence to prevent the 'fitting out, arming or equipping' of vessels for the Confederate Army within British territories,[60] the British Government stated:

> Due diligence on the part of a Government signifies that measure of care which the Government is under an obligation to use for a given purpose [...] Where the substance of the obligation consists in the prevention of certain acts within the territory of a neutral power, from the consequences of which loss might arise to foreign states or their citizens, it would not be reasonable to exact, as of right; from the Government, *a measure of care exceeding that which Governments are accustomed to exert in matters affecting their own security or that of their own citizens* [...] Where individuals are in question, the only general standards of due care which it has been possible to frame, are framed with reference either to the care which the particular individual, against whom negligence is alleged, is accustomed to exert in his own concerns, or to the care which men in general, or particular classes of men, are accustomed to exert in their own concerns. To standards of this kind, with various modifications and under different forms of expression, jurists and judicial tribunals in all countries have commonly had recourse, to assist them to a decision in cases of alleged negligence. *Where the acts or omissions of a Government are in question, it is certainly not unreasonable that the general standard of care, so far as any general standard is possible, should be drawn from the ordinary conduct of Governments in matters affecting those interests which they are primarily bound to protect.*[61]

---

[60]More specifically, the argument referred to the obligation '[t]o use due diligence to prevent the fitting out, arming or equipping, within its jurisdiction, of any vessel which it has reasonable ground to believe is intended to cruise or carry on war against a Power with which it is at peace', codified in article VI of the Treaty of Washington of 1871. Treaty of Washington between Her Britannic Majesty and the United States of America (adopted 8 May 1871, entered into force 17 June 1871) Charles Bevans (ed), *Treaties and Other International Agreements of the United States of America 1776—1949* (Volume 12: U.S. Department of State Publication, Washington 1971) 170, 173 article VI.

[61]Emphasis added. 'Argument or summary, showing the points and referring to the evidence relied upon by the Government of Her Britannic Majesty in answer to the claims of the United States presented to the Tribunal of Arbitration constituted under Article 1 of the treaty concluded at Washington on the 8th May, 1871, between Her Britannic Majesty and the United States of America' (undated) *The Argument at Geneva. A Complete Collection of the Forensic Discussions*

In the specific context of claims pertaining to the protection and security of aliens, the subjective standard found its perhaps most clear expression in the *Spanish Zone of Morocco Claims* (1924–1925).[62] The dispute concerned injuries inflicted upon British subjects and British-protected persons in the Spanish Zone of Morocco from 1913 to 1921.[63] Most of the claims involved criminal offences attributable to private individuals, such as the destruction of property and the theft of cattle and crops.[64] The governments of Great Britain and Spain agreed to submit the claims to PCIJ Judge Max Huber 'for examination and report'.[65] In his analysis of Spain's responsibility for want of diligence, Huber observed:

> Le problème [de la responsabilité de l'État] devient plus difficile quand il s'agit d'*actes de brigandage*. Le brigandage est le pillage ou le vol à main armée, habituellement exécuté par des bandes plus ou moins organisées [...] Ici, la question du degré de la vigilance exercée devient particulièrement importante. L'État territorial est-il exonérée, s'il a fait a fait ce qu'on peut raisonnablement lui demander, en tenant compte de sa situation effective? Ou est-il tenu de garantir un certain degré de sécurité, étant responsable de l'incapacité éventuelle de l'assurer? [...] La vigilance qu'au point de vue du droit international l'État est tenu de garantir, peut être caractérisée, en appliquent par analogie un terme du droit romain, comme une *diligentia quam in suis*. Cette règle, conforme au principe primordial de l'indépendance des États dans leurs affaires intérieures offre en fait aux États, pour leurs ressortissants, le degré de sécurité auquel ils peuvent raisonnablement s'attendre.[66]

Huber's shrewd analogy to the private law notion of *diligentia quam in suis rebus* provides a clear parameter for the assessment of the host state's conduct. Following this approach, an omission in the protection of aliens does not constitute an international wrong unless the diligence displayed by the host state falls below the degree of diligence which that state normally exercises in its own affairs. This premise, however appealing, is not entirely consistent with well-established principles of present-day international investment law.

The application of the *diligentia quam in suis rebus* standard implies identifying the course of conduct local authorities usually adopt in situations of risk which: (1) are comparable to those threatening foreign nationals; and (2) affect the host state's own interests. In practice, this 'usual' course of conduct is reflected in the measures public authorities commonly adopt in the protection of their *own nationals*

---

on the Part of the United States and of Great Britain before the Tribunal of Arbitration under the Treaty of Washington (Government Printing Office, Washington 1873) 257, 268 [28-30]. For a more detailed analysis of the British argument on due diligence see: Hersch Lauterpacht, *Private Law Sources and Analogies of International Law (With Special Reference to International Arbitration)* (Longmans, Green and Co. Ltd., London 1927) 217-9.

[62]*Affaire des biens britanniques au Maroc espagnol* (1 May 1925) II RIAA 615, 620-5.

[63]*Affaire des biens britanniques au Maroc espagnol* (1 May 1925) II RIAA 615, 620-5. The claims were submitted pursuant to a settlement agreement between Spain and Great Britain dated 29 May 1923 (at pp. 620-1). A schedule annexed to the agreement contains a brief description of each of the fifty-three claims filed thereunder (at pp. 621-5).

[64]*Affaire des biens britanniques au Maroc espagnol* (1 May 1925) II RIAA 615, 621-5.

[65]*Affaire des biens britanniques au Maroc espagnol* (1 May 1925) II RIAA 615, 617-21.

[66]*Affaire des biens britanniques au Maroc espagnol* (1 May 1925) II RIAA 615, 644 [4].

against a specific source of risk. Therefore, this approach ultimately defines the degree of diligence required by the customary security obligation in terms of national treatment. Early legal authorities upholding the subjective standard of diligence seemed to be conscious of this effect. For example, in its Lausanne Session (1927), the *Institut de Droit International* stated:

> L'Etat n'est responsable des dommages causés en cas d'attroupement, d'émeute, d'insurrection ou de guerre civile que s'il n'a pas cherché à prévenir les actes dommageables avec la diligence qu'il convient d'apporter normalement dans les mêmes circonstances, ou s'il n'a pas réagi avec la même diligence contre ces actes, ou s'il n'applique pas aux étrangers les mêmes mesures de protection qu'aux nationaux.[67]

Similarly, Lord McNair's *International Law Opinions* (1956) address the issue of state responsibility for insurrections in the following terms:

> A State on whose territory an insurrection occurs is not responsible for loss or damage sustained by a foreigner unless it can be shown that the Government of that State was negligent in the use of, or in the failure to use, the forces at its disposal for the prevention or suppression of the insurrection [. . .] such a State can usually defeat a claim in respect of loss or damage sustained by resident foreigners by showing that they have received the same treatment in the matter of protection or compensation, if any, as its own nationals (the plea of *diligentia quam in suis*).[68]

As far as diligence is described as and reduced to national treatment, the subjective standard of due diligence is inconsistent with the notion of the customary international minimum standard of treatment.[69] In the *Roberts* claim (1926), the US-Mexican General Claims Commission made clear that the minimum standard means that 'equality [between nationals and foreigners] is not the ultimate test of the propriety of the acts of authorities in the light of international law'.[70] Hence, the characterization of the FPS standard as an element of the international minimum

---

[67]Institut de Droit International, 'Résolutions votées par l'Institut au cours de sa XXXI Ve Session – Responsabilité internationale des États à raison des dommages causés sur leur territoire à la personne ou aux biens des étrangers (XIIIe Commission)' (1927) 33(II) Annuaire de l'Institut de Droit International 330, 332 art. 7.

[68]Arnold Duncan McNair (First Baron McNair), *International Law Opinions* (Volume 2: Cambridge University Press, Cambridge 1956) 245. In *Pantechniki v Albania* (2009) the host state relied on this opinion in response to an FPS claim concerning riot violence. The Sole Arbitrator did not consider the *diligentia quam in suis rebus* maxim in detail. See: Pantechniki S.A. Contractors & Engineers *v* Albania, Award, ICSID Case No. ARB/07/21 (30 July 2009) [74 *et seq.*]. For an author expressing support for the *diligentia quam in suis* standard see: Eric De Brabandere, 'Fair and Equitable Treatment and (Full) Protection and Security in African Investment Treaties: Between Generality and Contextual Specificity' (2017) Grotius Centre Working Paper Series 1, 22-5 (focusing, however, on the need to take into account the particular circumstances of the host state; this element is associated here to the 'modified standard' of due diligence).

[69]For a similar remark see: Elisabeth Zeitler, 'The Guarantee of Full Protection and Security in Investment Treaties Regarding Harm Caused by Private Actors' (2005) 3 SIAR 1, 21 (observing that that 'the purely subjective interpretation [of due diligence] would also go against the idea of an international minimum standard').

[70]*Harry Roberts v Mexico* (2 November 1926) IV RIAA 77, 80 [8].

standard necessarily excludes the definition of the protection obligation in terms of national treatment.[71] There can therefore be no place for the *diligentia quam in suis rebus* standard in contemporary international investment law.

13.3.2   The 'Objective' Standard of Due Diligence

In contrast to the *diligentia quam in suis rebus* standard, efforts have been made to define due diligence objectively. Municipal law analogies have not been alien to objective approaches, which have often relied on the private law notions of a *diligens paterfamilias* or an 'average prudent man'.[72] These approaches have a long tradition in the law of state responsibility for private injuries to aliens. A clear, early formulation of the 'objective standard' appears in a communication signed by US Secretary of State Thomas F. Bayard on 6th May, 1888. The note concerned the possible submission of a diplomatic claim on behalf of D. G. Negrete, an American citizen who had suffered injuries during an insurrection against the Spanish Government in Cuba.[73] In particular reference to state responsibility for acts of revolutionaries, Secretary Bayard stated:

> The measure of diligence to be exercised by a government in the repression of disorder is not that of an insurer, but such as prudent governments are, under the circumstances of the case, accustomed to exercise. To adopt the rule stated in the Code of Justinian, and as imported from the code into all modern jurisprudence, and accepted, therefore, by Spain, as well as by the United States, the law requires '*diligentiam qualem diligens paterfamilias suis rebus adhibere solet*'; remembering that '*paterfamilias*' in the sense in which it is here used, represents one whose relations to his family under the old law served to illustrate the relations of the government to the state. The decisive word in this rule is '*solet*'. It appeals to *custom*. The maxim is, that the diligence good governments are *accustomed* to exercise under the circumstances must be exercised in each case; and every government is liable to foreign powers for injuries to them or their subjects from lack of such customary diligence in the preservation of order.[74]

---

[71]For the characterization of FPS as an element of the international minimum standard see Chap. 5. On the relationship between the FPS standard and the minimum standard see Chaps. 4 and 5.

[72]On the analogy of the objective standard of due diligence to the notion of the *diligens paterfamilias* see: Eric De Brabandere, 'Host States' Due Diligence Obligations in International Investment Law' (2014-5) 42 Syracuse J. Int'l L. & Com. 319, 354 *et seq.* On the use of the notion of the 'average prudent man' for the assessment of due diligence in international law see: Hersch Lauterpacht, *Private Law Sources and Analogies of International Law (With Special Reference to International Arbitration)* (Longmans, Green and Co. Ltd., London 1927) 218-9 (commenting on the *Alabama* case).

[73]For a more detailed account of the facts of the case see: 'Mr. Bayard, Sec. of State, to Mr. Stuphen' (6 January 1888) in John Bassett Moore, *A Digest of International Law* (Volume 6: Government Printing Office, Washington 1906) 961, 961-4.

[74]Emphasis in the original. 'Mr. Bayard, Sec. of State, to Mr. Stuphen' (6 January 1888) in John Bassett Moore, *A Digest of International Law* (Volume 6: Government Printing Office, Washington 1906) 961, 962.

Almost a century later, in 1983, Ian Brownlie quoted Bayard's words in length and observed that '[t]here is good reason to believe that this exposition represents the law as it remains today'.[75] To the same effect, other authors have observed:

> As a general rule, due diligence can be measured by the average general standard of behavior of the "civilized" or "well-organized" State, just as, in some municipal legal systems, diligence is evaluated in relation to the behavior of a *bonus paterfamilias*.[76]

Following this approach, the yardstick for the evaluation of the host state's conduct must be detached from the diligence the respondent state usually exercises in the protection of its own nationals and interests, and instead be defined by reference to the course of conduct 'good governments' usually take in similar situations.

In investment arbitration practice, the 'objective' approach typically hides behind references to 'the reasonable measures of prevention which a well-administered government could be expected to exercise under similar circumstances'.[77] This formula can be traced back to a lecture delivered by Alwyn Freeman at The Hague in 1955.[78] Freeman's work was 'rediscovered' by the arbitrators in *AAPL v Sri Lanka* (1990).[79] Based on this doctrine, the *AAPL* tribunal expressed support for 'an objective standard of vigilance in assessing the required degree of protection and security with regard to what should be legitimately expected to be secured for foreign investors by a reasonably well organized modern state'.[80] Ever since *AAPL*, Freeman's formula has been continuously used in investment decisions.[81]

---

[75]Ian Brownlie, System of the Law of Nations. State Responsibility (Clarendon Press, Oxford 1983) 170. For another authority quoting Mr. Bayard's note in length see: ILC, 'Force Majeure and Fortuitous Event as Circumstances Precluding Wrongfulness: Survey of State Practice, International Judicial Decisions and Doctrine' (27 June 1977) 2(1) Yearbook of the International Law Commission – 1978 61, 115-6.

[76]Riccardo Pisillo-Mazzeschi, 'The Due Diligence Rule and the Nature of the International Responsibility of States' in René Provost (ed), *State Responsibility in International Law* (Ashgate Publishing Co., Burlington VT 2002) 97, 133. See also: Riccardo Pisillo Mazzeschi, *"Due diligence" e responsabilità internazionale degli stati* (Giuffrè Editore, Milan 1989) 398-9.

[77]Asian Agricultural Products v Sri Lanka, Final Award, ICSID Case No ARB/87/3 (27 June 1990) [77].

[78]Alwyn Freeman, 'Responsibility of States for Unlawful Acts of their Armed Forces' (1955) 88 (3) RCADI 263, 277-8.

[79]Asian Agricultural Products *v* Sri Lanka, Final Award, ICSID Case No ARB/87/3 (27 June 1990) [77].

[80]Asian Agricultural Products *v* Sri Lanka, Final Award, ICSID Case No ARB/87/3 (27 June 1990) [77].

[81]AES Summit Generation Ltd. and AES-Tisza Erömü Kft. *v* Hungary, Award, ICSID Case No. ARB/07/22 (23 September 2010) [13.3.3] (quoting a similar statement by Ian Brownlie); El Paso Energy International Co. *v* Argentina, Award, ICSID Case No. ARB/03/15 (31 October 2011) [522] (quoting Freeman and the *AAPL* award at para 522, but recognizing at para 523 that the assessment of diligence necessarily varies depending on the circumstances of the case); Hesham Talaat M. Al-Warraq *v* Indonesia (UNCITRAL), Final Award (15 December 2014) [625 and 628] (using a similar formula); Mobil Exploration and Development Argentina Inc. Suc. Argentina and

Besides the notion of a 'well-administered government', other versions of the 'objective standard of diligence' are also present in investment arbitration practice. In *Tecmed v Mexico* (2003), the tribunal resorted to the alternative criterion of a 'democratic state'.[82] In that case, the population of the Mexican vicinity of Hermosillo had engaged in protests against a landfill for industrial waste controlled by a foreign company.[83] The investor claimed that public authorities failed to 'act as quickly, efficiently and thoroughly as they should have to avoid, prevent or put an end to the adverse social demonstrations'.[84] In their analysis of the FPS claim, the arbitrators considered whether the reaction of Mexican authorities had been 'in accordance with the parameters inherent in a democratic state'.[85] This formulation, while interesting, departs from the questionable premise that the due diligence standard is intertwined with a specific form of government. Moreover, the tribunal failed to provide any indication as to which parameters of diligence are 'inherent' to democratic states, as opposed to non-democratic states.

Whichever formula is chosen to define the 'objective standard', the underlying idea seems to be that adjudicators should compare the diligence displayed by local authorities with the conduct an average diligent state would exercise in the same situation. This approach has the obvious advantage of 'objectivizing', at least to some degree, the assessment of diligence. This seems consistent with the characterization of FPS as an element of the international minimum standard. As stated by the

---

Mobil Argentina S.A. *v* Argentina, Decision on Jurisdiction and Liability, ICSID Case No. ARB/04/16 (10 April 2013) [999-1000] (quoting Freeman and the *AAPL v Sri Lanka* award); Sergei Paushok, CJSC Golden East Co., CJSC Vostoknefte *v* Mongolia (UNCITRAL), Award on Jurisdiction and Liability (28 April 2011) [323] (quoting the *AAPL* award and making reference to Alwyn Freeman in this connection); Suez Sociedad General de Aguas de Barcelona S.A. and Vivendi Universal S.A. *v* Argentina, Decision on Liability, ICSID Case No. ARB/03/19 (30 July 2010) [163] (quoting both Alwyn Freeman and Ian Brownlie in this connection). This formulation has often been used by claimants in investment arbitral proceedings. See, for example: Rumeli Telekom A.S. and Telsim Mobil Telekomunikasyon Hizmetleri A.S. *v* Kazakhstan, Award, ICSID Case No. ARB/05/16 (29 July 2008) [658] (referring to 'the degree of protection and security that should be legitimately expected from a reasonably well-organized modern State'); Saint-Gobain Performance Plastics Europe *v* Venezuela, Decision on Liability and the Principles of Quantum, ICSID Case No. ARB/12/13 (30 December 2016) [544] (using Freeman's formula in connection with an FPS claim); Teinver S.A., Transportes de Cercanías S.A. and Autobuses Urbanos del Sur S.A. v Argentina, Award, ICSID Case No. ARB/09/1 (21 July 2017) [900] (addressing the concept of due diligence and indicating that FPS '[requires] the reasonable measures of prevention which a well-administered government could be expected to exercise in the circumstances').

[82]On these different formulations of the objective standard see also: ILA Study Group on Due Diligence in International Law, 'Second Report by Mr. Tim Stephens (Rapporteur) and Mr. Duncan French (Chair)' (20 July 2016) 10 (making particular reference to the *AAPL* and *Tecmed* awards, as well as to Alwyn Freeman's formula).

[83]For a detailed account of the factual background of the case see: Tecnicas Medioambientales TECMED S.A. *v* Mexico, Award, ICSID Case No. ARB(AF)/00/2 (29 May 2003) [35-51].

[84]Tecnicas Medioambientales TECMED S.A. *v* Mexico, Award, ICSID Case No. ARB(AF)/00/2 (29 May 2003) [175].

[85]Tecnicas Medioambientales TECMED S.A. *v* Mexico, Award, ICSID Case No. ARB(AF)/00/2 (29 May 2003) [177].

arbitrators in *Glamis Gold v United States* (2009), '[a]lthough the circumstances of the case are of course relevant, the [minimum] standard is not meant to vary from state to state or investor to investor'.[86]

At the same time, however, the very idea of a 'diligent state' inspired by the private law notion of a *diligens paterfamilias* could end up turning the standard of diligence into an excessively demanding yardstick. Notions such as 'good government', 'well-administered government', 'democratic state' and their like express the idea of an *ideal* state, and not of an *average* state. In its 2005 survey of international standards of investment protection, UNCTAD concluded that arbitral decisions following an 'objective' approach to due diligence show that 'the standard of care required has been set at a fairly high level'.[87] The paradox is that this effect is inconsistent with the rationale of an international *minimum* standard. Recalling again the *Glamis* award:

> The customary international law minimum standard of treatment is just that, a minimum standard. It is meant to serve as a floor, an absolute bottom, below which conduct is not accepted by the international community.[88]

Parties in investment arbitral proceedings have emphasized that the application of the 'duty of diligence' enshrined in the FPS standard should '[reflect] the relationship between the FPS standard and the international minimum standard of treatment'.[89] Tribunals assessing FPS claims, albeit using the 'well-administered government' formula, seem to be aware of the fact that the diligence required under the FPS standard cannot be too stringent. In *Adel A Hamadi Al Tamini v Oman* (2015) the arbitrators observed:

> [I]t is broadly accepted that the minimum standard of treatment under customary international law imposes a relatively high bar for breach [. . .] [it] sets only a minimum standard [. . .] the minimum standard of treatment must be understood in this context only as the conduct expected of all States as a bare, invariable minimum.[90]

---

[86]*Glamis Gold v United States*. See: Glamis Gold *v* United States of America (UNCITRAL), Award (8 June 2009) [615].

[87]UNCTAD, *Investor-State Disputes Arising from Investment Treaties: A Review* (United Nations, New York/Geneva 2005) 40. See also the claimant's argument in *Teinver v Argentina* (2017): Teinver S.A., Transportes de Cercanías S.A. and Autobuses Urbanos del Sur S.A. v Argentina, Award, ICSID Case No. ARB/09/1 (21 July 2017) [900] (relying on the formula of 'a well-administered government' and arguing that 'the threshold for finding a violation of this standard [FPS] is low, since a mere lack of diligence will suffice and there is no need to establish malice or negligence').

[88]Glamis Gold *v* United States of America (UNCITRAL), Award (8 June 2009) [615].

[89]Saint-Gobain Performance Plastics Europe *v* Venezuela, Decision on Liability and the Principles of Quantum, ICSID Case No. ARB/12/13 (30 December 2016) [548] (argument of Venezuela; in this connection, the respondent state further described the minimum standard in terms of 'negligence, defective administration or bad faith').

[90]Adel A Hamadi Al Tamini *v* Oman, Award, ICSID Case No. ARB/11/33 (3 November 2015) [382-3] (referring to article 10.5.2 of the Oman-US FTA, which defined both the FET and the FPS standard by reference to the customary minimum standard of treatment). See also: Joseph Houben

In *AMT v Zaire* (1997), the arbitrators described FPS as 'an objective obligation which must not be inferior to the minimum standard of vigilance and care required by international law'.[91] Regrettably, the *AMT* tribunal did not elaborate further on this idea. It simply noted that there was no clarity as to 'the practical criterion to determine the level of the precautionary measure to be taken by the receiving State consistent with the minimum standard recognized by international law'.[92]

In spite of this paucity of explanation, the *AMT* award delivered a powerful idea. While presenting FPS as an 'objective' parameter for the assessment of conduct, the arbitrators managed to set the threshold of diligence at a low level. Following this view, the standard does not correspond with the conduct of an ideal and largely hypothetical 'democratic state' or 'well-administered government', but with the conduct that could be expected *as a minimum* from *any state* facing the same situation of fact as the host state.

To be sure, this is not only relevant for the obligation to exercise due diligence in the prevention injuries to aliens. It is also fundamental to the obligation of redress. In *Vannessa Ventures v Venezuela* (2013) the arbitral tribunal considered an allegation that several delays in the administration of justice constituted a breach of the FPS and FET standards.[93] The arbitrators were clear as to the high threshold international law sets in this regard:

> The question is not whether the host State legal system is performing as efficiently as it ideally could: it is whether it is performing so badly as to violate treaty obligations to accord fair and equitable treatment and full protection and security. The tribunal does not consider that the delays in this case are of an order that constitute conduct that falls below the minimum standard demanded by the Treaty.[94]

13.3.3   The Contemporary Guises of the Objective Standard of Due Diligence

The characterization of the customary FPS standard as an element of the international minimum standard of treatment has two fundamental implications for the notion of due diligence: (1) the diligence required under the customary protection obligation cannot be defined by analogy to the *diligentia quam in suis rebus*

---

v Burundi, Sentence, ICSID Case No. ARB/13/7 (12 January 2016) [175] (using the phrase 'mesures minimales nécessaires' to describe the conduct required by the FPS standard).

[91] American Manufacturing & Trading Inc. v Zaire, Award, ICSID Case No. ARB 93/1 (21 February 1997) [6.06].

[92] American Manufacturing & Trading Inc. v Zaire, Award, ICSID Case No. ARB 93/1 (21 February 1997) [6.07].

[93] Vannessa Ventures Ltd. v Venezuela, Award, ICSID Case No. ARB(AF)04/6 (16 January 2013) [217-8].

[94] Emphasis added. Vannessa Ventures Ltd. v Venezuela, Award, ICSID Case No. ARB(AF)04/6 (16 January 2013) [227].

criterion, which would entail reducing the obligation to national treatment; and (2) the assessment of FPS claims does not require comparing the diligence displayed by the host state with the conduct that could be expected from an *ideal diligent state*, but against the *minimum* degree of diligence that can be expected from an *average state*.

These two premises, albeit essential to the contemporary notion of due diligence, do not entirely clarify the concept. The question remains open as to what due diligence actually means. Different formulas have been suggested in this connection. For present purposes, three approaches merit consideration: (1) due diligence as 'reasonableness'; (2) due diligence and the notions of prudent, appropriate or necessary measures; and (3) the 'modified' objective standard of due diligence.

13.3.3.1   Due Diligence as 'Reasonableness'

International organizations, states and arbitral tribunals have often described the diligence required under the FPS standard in terms of *reasonableness*. In 1998, an UNCTAD report stated that 'the clause of full protection and security [. . .] requires that the host country should exercise *reasonable care* to protect investment'.[95] In *Ronald Lauder v Czech Republic* (2001) the arbitral tribunal concluded that 'the Treaty obliges the Parties to exercise such due diligence in the protection of foreign investment as *reasonable* under the circumstances'.[96] In *CME v Czech Republic* (2001) the respondent state argued that, under the FPS standard, '[a] government is only obliged to provide protection which is *reasonable* in the circumstances'.[97] Similarly, in *Vivendi v Argentina* (2007) reference was made to '*reasonable* protection and security'.[98] In *Frontier v Czech Republic* (2010) the tribunal specifically

---

[95]UNCTAD, *Bilateral Investment Treaties in the Mid-1990s* (United Nations, New York/Geneva 1998) 55. See also: Caline Mouawad and Sarah Vasani, 'Energy Disputes in Times of Civil Unrest: Transitional Governments and Foreign Investment Protections' in Arthur Rovine (ed), *Contemporary Issues in International Arbitration and Mediation* (Brill, Leiden/Boston 2015) 234, 242 (stating that '[FPS] requires a State to act with a *reasonable degree of diligence* and to take measures to protect foreign investors and investments that are *reasonable* under the circumstances' – emphasis added); Elisabeth Zeitler, 'The Guarantee of Full Protection and Security in Investment Treaties Regarding Harm Caused by Private Actors' (2005) 3 SIAR 1, 15-8, 22 and 25 (defining at p. 25 the standard as a duty 'to take all *reasonable and necessary measures*, taking into account its [the host state's] available resources and the conditions prevailing in the region at the particular moment' – emphasis added); Geneviève Bastid Burdeau, 'La clause de protection et sécurité pleine et entière' (2015) 119(1) RGDIP 87, 98 (referring to the duty to adopt 'mesures de prévention *raisonnables*' – emphasis added).

[96]Emphasis added. Ronald Lauder *v* Czech Republic (UNCITRAL), Final Award (3 September 2001) [308]. See also the Czech Republic's argument at para 307.

[97]Emphasis added. CME Czech Republic B.V. *v* Czech Republic (UNCITRAL), Partial Award (13 September 2001) [353].

[98]Emphasis added. Compañía de Aguas del Aconquija S.A. and Vivendi Universal S.A. *v* Argentina, Award, ICSID Case No. ARB/97/3 (20 August 2007) [7.4.15]. The discussion at this point focused, however, on the question whether FPS refers to physical security only. The

defined the content of the redress obligation in terms of reasonableness.[99] In more precise words, in *El Paso v Argentina* (2011) the arbitral tribunal stated:

> [T]he obligation to show "due diligence" does not mean that the State has to prevent each and every injury. Rather, the obligation is generally understood as requiring that the State take *reasonable actions* within its power to avoid an injury [...] the precise degree of care, of what is "*reasonable*" or "due", depends in part on the circumstances.[100]

In *Sergei Paushok v Mongolia* (2011) the arbitrators also underscored that the evaluation of reasonableness depends on the circumstances of the case.[101] In *Toto Construzioni v Lebanon* (2012) an ICSID tribunal took into consideration that the measures adopted by the host state 'were not unreasonable'.[102] In *Convial Callao v Peru* (2013) the arbitral tribunal held that the FPS standard requires a reasonable reaction to circumstances that could affect the investment.[103] In *Hesham Talaat M. Al-Warraq v Indonesia* (2014) the arbitrators found that 'the host State has an obligation to provide no more than a *reasonable* measure of prevention'.[104] In *Oxus Gold v Uzbekistan* (2015) the arbitral tribunal explained that, under FPS, 'the investor has the right to expect that the State takes *reasonable measures* within its power to prevent wrongful injuries by third parties'.[105] Similarly, the tribunal in *Joseph Houben v Burundi* (2016) stated that both the prevention obligation and the redress obligation could be understood as obligations to exercise 'reasonable diligence' (*diligence raisonnable*).[106] The arbitrators further emphasized that the

---

case concerned the guarantee of 'protection et [...] sécurité pleines et entières' in article 5 (1) France-Argentina BIT. Cf. Accord entre le Gouvernement de la République française et le Gouvernement de la République Argentine sur l'encouragement et la protection réciproques des investissements (adopted 3 July 1991, entered into force 3 March 1993) art. 5(1).

[99]Frontier Petroleum Ltd. *v* Czech Republic (UNCITRAL), Final Award (12 November 2010) [273].

[100]Emphasis added. El Paso Energy International Co. *v* Argentina, Award, ICSID Case No. ARB/03/15 (31 October 2011) [523]. See also: Electrabel S.A. *v* Hungary, Decision on Jurisdiction, Applicable Law and Liability, ICSID Case No. ARB/07/19 (30 November 2012) [7.83] (relying on this passage of the *El Paso* award); Mobil Exploration and Development Argentina Inc. Suc. Argentina and Mobil Argentina S.A. *v* Argentina, Decision on Jurisdiction and Liability, ICSID Case No. ARB/04/16 (10 April 2013) [1001] (quoting the award rendered in *El Paso*).

[101]Sergei Paushok, CJSC Golden East Co., CJSC Vostoknefte *v* Mongolia (UNCITRAL), Award on Jurisdiction and Liability (28 April 2011) [325].

[102]Toto Construzioni Generali S.p.A. *v* Lebanon, Award, ICSID Case No. ARB/07/12 (7 June 2012) [200].

[103]Convial Callao S.A. and CCI – Compañía de Concesiones de Infraestructura S.A. *v* Peru, Laudo Final, ICSID Case No. ARB/10/2 (21 May 2013) [651].

[104]Emphasis added. Hesham Talaat M. Al-Warraq *v* Indonesia (UNCITRAL), Final Award (15 December 2014) [625].

[105]Emphasis added. Oxus Gold *v* Uzbekistan (UNCITRAL), Final Award (17 December 2015) [353].

[106]Joseph Houben *v* Burundi, Sentence, ICSID Case No. ARB/13/7 (12 January 2016) [160].

determination of whether state conduct was *reasonable* (*raisonnable*) depends on both the factual background of the case and the capacities of public authorities.[107] In *Peter Allard v Barbados* (2016) the arbitrators held that the duty of protection 'is limited to *reasonable action*'.[108] To the same effect, in *Koch v Venezuela* (2017) the tribunal concluded that FPS refers to 'factual circumstances where the host State has failed to exercise *reasonable diligence*'.[109]

In addition to these statements, adjudicators have often understood due diligence as an obligation to take 'reasonable steps' to ensure the protection of the investment.[110] A few IIAs use a wording which resembles this idea. For instance, the ASEAN-China Investment Agreement of 2009 expressly provides that '[FPS] requires each Party to take such *measures as may be reasonably necessary* to ensure the protection and security of the investment'.[111] This terminology is reminiscent of the language used by some human rights bodies, which have indicated that 'lack of diligence' implies a failure to take 'reasonable steps/measures'.[112]

---

[107]Joseph Houben *v* Burundi, Sentence, ICSID Case No. ARB/13/7 (12 January 2016) [163].

[108]Peter A. Allard *v* Barbados (UNCITRAL), Award (27 June 2016) [244].

[109]Emphasis added. Koch Minerals SÁRL and Koch Nitrogen International SÁRL *v* Venezuela, Award, ICSID Case No. ARB/11/19 (30 October 2017) [8.46].

[110]Cf. AES Summit Generation Ltd. and AES-Tisza Erömü Kft. *v* Hungary, Award, ICSID Case No. ARB/07/22 (23 September 2010) [13.2.2]; Isolux Netherlands B.V. *v* Spain, Laudo, SCC Case No. V 2013/153 (17 July 2016) [817]; Peter A. Allard *v* Barbados (UNCITRAL), Award (27 June 2016) [242]. Cf. also Bernhard Friedrich Arnd Rüdiger von Pezold et al. *v* Zimbabwe, Award, ICSID Case No. ARB/10/15 (28 July 2015) [596] (expressing sympathy for the parties' submission that FPS requires 'due diligence', understood in terms of 'all reasonable measures'). See also the claimant's argument in *Saint-Gobain v Venezuela*: Saint-Gobain Performance Plastics Europe *v* Venezuela, Decision on Liability and the Principles of Quantum, ICSID Case No. ARB/12/13 (30 December 2016) [544] (using the expression 'reasonable measures of prevention'). For some indicative examples of a similar argument being advanced by a respondent state see: MNSS B.V. and Recupero Credito Acciaio N.V. *v* Montenegro, Award, ICSID Case No. ARB(AF)/12/8 (4 May 2016) [267] (arguing that competent police authorities had 'exercised due diligence and taken reasonable measures'); Teinver S.A., Transportes de Cercanías S.A. and Autobuses Urbanos del Sur S.A. *v* Argentina, Award, ICSID Case No. ARB/09/1 (21 July 2017) [901] (stating that FPS 'entails the adoption of reasonable measures'); Ulysseas Inc. *v* Ecuador (UNCITRAL), Final Award (12 June 2012) [268] (arguing that 'the [FPS] standard only requires due care and reasonable behavior').

[111]Emphasis added. Agreement on Investment of the Framework Agreement on Comprehensive Economic Cooperation between the People's Republic of China and the Association of Southeast Asian Nations (adopted 15 August 2009, entered into force 1 January 2010) art. 7(2)(b).

[112]Cf. Opuz *v* Turkey, App No 33401/02 (ECtHR: 9 June 2009) [131, 136-49 and 162] (using both the terms 'due diligence' and 'reasonable measures'); Velásquez Rodríguez *v* Honduras, Judgment on the Merits (ICtHR: 29 July 1988) [172 and 174] (referring at para 172 to responsibility for 'lack of diligence' and indicating at para 174 that '[t]he State has a duty to take reasonable steps to prevent human rights violations').

The *reasonableness* approach has not been particular to FPS claims. It has appeared frequently in the context of FET and expropriation claims.[113] In *RREEF v Spain* (2018) the tribunal held that reasonableness is 'closely linked' to proportionality.[114] Characterizing proportionality as the 'main test for reasonableness', the arbitrators described it as 'a weighing mechanism that seeks a fair balance between competing interests and/or principles'.[115] A recent study of arbitral practice concluded that 'the concept of reasonableness may be understood as a search for equilibrium and appears to require a balancing of divergent interests'.[116] Notwithstanding these general features, reasonableness does not convey an entirely clear meaning in adjudicatory practice. In this vein, the same study warns against the widespread use of the concept in investment treaty arbitration:

> Most investment tribunal decisions in this area briefly refer to reasonableness and conclude whether the measure was reasonable without further explanation, which does not shed light on the reasoning process undertaken by arbitrators [. . .] Using the concept of reasonableness as a method of review is problematic, not least because the concept is indeterminate. This method of review has attracted criticism [. . .] on the basis that it lacks a clear analytical structure and that it can conceal the subjective preferences of adjudicators and that judges have decided cases according to their own policy preferences without relying on any particular criteria.[117]

This criticism shows that 'reasonableness' could be as contentious a concept as 'due diligence'. The difficulties associated to the assessment of diligence can thus not be solved by merely rephrasing the question of diligence as a question of reasonableness. This does not however mean that all references to reasonableness are necessarily wrong or futile. The phrase 'reasonableness' could be resorted to as a gateway for introducing important *elements of analysis* to the evaluation of the host state's conduct. Arbitrators could indeed consider whether measures of protection

---

[113]See generally: Caroline Henckels, *Proportionality and Deference in Investor-State Arbitration. Balancing Investment Protection and Regulatory Autonomy* (Cambridge University Press, Cambridge 2015) 117.

[114]RREEF Infrastructure (G.P.) Ltd. and RREEF Pan-European Infrastructure Two Lux S.à.r.l. v Spain, Award, ICSID Case No. ARB/13/30 (30 November 2018) [463].

[115]RREEF Infrastructure (G.P.) Ltd. and RREEF Pan-European Infrastructure Two Lux S.à.r.l. v Spain, Award, ICSID Case No. ARB/13/30 (30 November 2018) [465].

[116]Caroline Henckels, *Proportionality and Deference in Investor-State Arbitration. Balancing Investment Protection and Regulatory Autonomy* (Cambridge University Press, Cambridge 2015) 117.

[117]Caroline Henckels, *Proportionality and Deference in Investor-State Arbitration. Balancing Investment Protection and Regulatory Autonomy* (Cambridge University Press, Cambridge 2015) 118-9. It should be noted that Henckels defines 'methods of review' as 'trade-off devices that operate as aids to problem solving and to express the reasoning processes of adjudicators' (at p. 26). Cf. also Nnaemeka Nwokedi Anozie, *The Full Security and Protection Due Diligence Obligation* (University of Ottawa, Ottawa 2016) [LL.M. Thesis] 20-1 (emphasizing that adjudicators enjoy a broad margin of discretion, and noting the difficulties of defining either reasonableness or due diligence in general terms).

were proportionate to the perceived seriousness of the situation of risk.[118] Moreover, the adoption of measures of protection often involves a policy choice between the protection of different groups of persons or interests.[119] All these issues may be arguably presented in terms of reasonableness and could certainly play a role in the assessment of due diligence. Their actual impact on a specific FPS claim depends, however, on the specific circumstances of the case.

13.3.3.2   Due Diligence and the Notions of Prudent, Appropriate or Necessary Measures

It has not been uncommon for arbitral tribunals to reduce the analysis of due diligence to the question, whether the host state adopted measures that appeared to be prudent, appropriate or necessary in the circumstances of the case. For example, in *AMT v Zaire* (1997) the arbitrators observed that the FPS standard requires local authorities to '*take all measures necessary to ensure* the full enjoyment of protection and security'.[120] In *SAUR International S.A. v Argentina* (2012) the arbitrators stated:

> L'État sera responsable s'il n'a pas adopté les mesures de protection que la prudence exige afin de protéger la propriété étrangère objet du traité.[121]

Similarly, in *OI European Group B.V. v Venezuela* (2015) the arbitral tribunal summarized the standard of liability applicable to FPS claims as follows:

> The responsibility of the State will arise if it fails to adopt the *protection measures that would be required out of prudence* to protect the foreign property covered under the treaty.[122]

The language used in these decisions bears striking resemblance to protection obligations from other areas of international law. For instance, articles 22 and 29 of

---

[118]For a detailed discussion of this element of analysis see Sect. 13.4.4.

[119]See, for example: Peter A. Allard *v* Barbados (UNCITRAL), Award (27 June 2016) [244 *et seq.*]. Section 13.4.8 discusses this element of analysis in more detail.

[120]Emphasis added. American Manufacturing & Trading Inc. *v* Zaire, Award, ICSID Case No. ARB 93/1 (21 February 1997) [6.05]. For other arbitral tribunals following a similar approach see: Plama Consortium Ltd. *v* Bulgaria, Award, ICSID Case No. ARB/03/24 (27 August 2008) [179]; Saluka Investments *v* Czech Republic (UNCITRAL), Partial Award (17 March 2006) [484]; Wena Hotels Ltd. *v* Egypt, Award, ICSID Case No. ARB/98/4 (8 December 2000) [85]. An alternative, less-usual formulation appeared in *Joseph Houben v Burundi* (2016), where the arbitrators used the French expressions 'mesures minimales nécessaires' and 'diligences nécessaires' in its assessment of the FPS standard. See: Joseph Houben *v* Burundi, Sentence, ICSID Case No. ARB/13/7 (12 January 2016) [175 and 179]. Investors in investment arbitral proceedings have also invoked the 'necessary steps' criterion. For an indicative example see: Ronald Lauder *v* Czech Republic (UNCITRAL), Final Award (3 September 2001) [306].

[121]SAUR International S.A. *v* Argentina, Décision sur la compétence et sur la responsabilité, ICSID Case No. ARB/04/4 (6 June 2012) [500].

[122]Emphasis added. OI European Group B.V. *v* Venezuela, Award, ICSID Case No. ARB/11/25 (10 March 2015) [577].

the Vienna Convention on Diplomatic Relations set forth the receiving state's obligation to 'take all appropriate steps' to protect diplomatic agents and foreign missions' premises.[123] Human rights courts have repeatedly characterized states' obligation to protect human rights within their jurisdiction as an obligation to take 'appropriate' or 'necessary' steps, and have often used these terms interchangeably with the phrase 'due diligence'.[124]

The 'appropriate steps' and similar criteria, however widespread, are unlikely to provide a suitable basis for the practical application of the concept of due diligence. It is arguable that this terminology might facilitate recourse to human rights' and

---

[123]Vienna Convention on Diplomatic Relations (adopted 18 April 1961, entered into force 24 April 1964) 500 UNTS 95, arts. 22(2) and 29. For a detailed assessment of these conventional protection obligations see: Eileen Denza, *Diplomatic Law. Commentary on the Vienna Convention on Diplomatic Relations* (Oxford University Press, Oxford 2016) 133-45, 214-6 and 219-20. For another example see: Vienna Convention on Consular Relations (adopted 24 April 1963, entered into force 19 March 1967) 596 UNTS 261, art. 31(2) and 40. In the *Teheran Hostages case* (1980) the ICJ analyzed whether Iran had taken the steps that were 'appropriate' and 'necessary' to protect the U.S. Embassy and consulates from demonstrators and militants. See: *Case Concerning United States Diplomatic and Consular Staff in Tehran (United States of America v Iran)* [1980] ICJ Rep. 3, 31-3 [62-8].

[124]The assumption of equivalence between 'due diligence' and 'necessary measures' has been particularly apparent in the jurisprudence of the ICtHR. See, for example: Familia Barrios *v* Venezuela, Judgment on Merits, Reparations and Costs (ICtHR: 24 November 2011) [124] (indicating that the state's 'duty of diligence' [deber de diligencia] requires the adoption of 'opportune and necessary measures' [medidas oportunas y necesarias]); Pueblo Bello Massacre *v* Colombia, Judgment on Merits, Reparations and Costs (ICtHR: 31 January 2006) [139] (stating that 'the State did not adopt, with due diligence, all the necessary measures'). The ECtHR often uses the phrase 'appropriate steps' in connection with the protection of human rights without express reference to the notion of 'due diligence'. Cf. L.C.B. *v* United Kingdom, App No 14/1997/798/1001 (ECtHR: 9 June 1998) [36] (referring to the state's duty 'to take appropriate steps to safeguard the life of those within its jurisdiction'); Hiller *v* Austria, App No 1967/14 (ECtHR: 22 November 2016) [47] (considering the right to life and relying on the *L.C.B.* decision); Malik Babayev *v* Azerbaijan, App No 30500/11 (ECtHR: 1 June 2017) [65] (addressing the right to life and quoting the *L.C.B.* decision in this regard); Paul and Audrey Edwards *v* United Kingdom, App No 46477/99 (ECtHR: 14 March 2002) [54] (referring to the protection of the right to life and quoting the *L.C.B.* decision in this regard); Öneryildiz *v* Turkey, App No 48939/99 (ECtHR: 30 November 2004) [71] (also referring to the right to life and quoting previous decisions on the subject). For a review of the ICtHR jurisprudence in this area see: Eduardo Ferrer Mac-Gregor and Carlos María Pelayo Möller, 'Artículo 1. Obligación de respetar los derechos' in Christian Steiner and Patricia Uribe (eds), *Convención Americana sobre Derechos Humanos. Comentario* (Konrad-Adenauer Stiftung/Editorial Temis, Bogotá 2014) 42, 49-53 (commenting on these and other decisions of the ICtHR). For a detailed analysis of protection obligations under the ECHR see: Cordula Dröge, *Positive Verpflichtungen der Staaten in der Europäischen Menschenrechtskonvention* (Springer, Heidelberg 2003) 13-84. (from a general perspective); Lucas Bastin, *State Responsibility for Omissions: Establishing a Breach of the Full Protection and Security Obligation by Omissions* (Oxford University, Oxford 2016) [D.Phil. Thesis] 55 *et seq.* (considering the practice of the ECtHR); Lucas Bastin, *Violation of the Full Protection and Security Obligation by Regulatory Omissions* [M.Phil. Thesis] (Oxford University, Oxford 2011) 28 *et seq.* (particularly referring to the 'appropriate steps' criterion, as developed by the ECtHR).

other adjudicatory bodies' jurisprudence on the subject.[125] This apparent advantage should be considered with caution. While analogies could be useful in some particular contexts, arguments advanced by human rights courts and other organs acting under specific treaty regimes cannot be automatically applied in the context of international investment law; the permissibility of analogies depends on the specific circumstances of each particular case.[126] Most importantly, it cannot be assumed that the diligence required under the customary protection obligation is the same as under other international obligations.[127]

In addition, doubts may arise as to the equivalence of the standards of 'appropriate', 'prudent', 'reasonable' or 'necessary' measures, on the one hand, and the concept of due diligence on the other. A few authorities seem to assume that the notion of 'appropriate measures' could be distinguishable from 'due diligence' but do not elaborate further on the issue.[128] Some scholars have attempted to draw a conceptual distinction between the two notions.[129] According to them, while the 'appropriate steps' criterion seems more appropriate for the assessment of obligations to attain a situation of fact which does not yet exist (e.g. eradicate hunger), 'due diligence' more suitably fits into obligations which are aimed at avoiding the alteration of an extant situation of fact (e.g. preventing interferences with a subject's bodily integrity).[130] This distinction, albeit interesting, has found little support in

---

[125]For a critical analysis of the (similar) terminology used by investment tribunals and human rights bodies in this regard see: Lucas Bastin, *State Responsibility for Omissions: Establishing a Breach of the Full Protection and Security Obligation by Omissions* (Oxford University, Oxford 2016) [D. Phil. Thesis] 56 *et seq.* (discussing possible overlaps and extant differences between 'due diligence' in the context of FPS claims and 'appropriate steps', as understood by the ECtHR). Cf. also: Lucas Bastin, *Violation of the Full Protection and Security Obligation by Regulatory Omissions* [M.Phil. Thesis] (Oxford University, Oxford 2011) 30-1.

[126]See generally: Martins Paparinskis, *The International Minimum Standard and Fair and Equitable Treatment* (Oxford University Press, Oxford 2013) 74-83 and 171-80; Martins Paparinskis, 'Analogies and Other Regimes of International Law' in Zachary Douglas, Joost Pauwelyn and Jorge Viñuales (eds), *The Foundations of International Investment Law. Bringing Theory into Practice* (Oxford University Press, Oxford 2014) 73, 79-81. Section 5.3 discusses this issue in more detail.

[127]Section 13.4.10 discusses the specific role other obligations of diligence could have in the assessment of FPS claims.

[128]See, for example: UN Human Rights Committee, *General Comment No. 31 [80]. The Nature of the General Legal Obligation Imposed on State Parties to the ICCPR*, CCPR/C/21/Rev.1/Add. 13 (26 May 2004) [8] (referring to the violation of the ICCPR by 'failing to take appropriate measures *or* to exercise due diligence to prevent, punish, investigate or redress harm by [...] acts by private persons or entities' – emphasis added).

[129]Lucas Bastin, *State Responsibility for Omissions: Establishing a Breach of the Full Protection and Security Obligation by Omissions* (Oxford University, Oxford 2016) [D.Phil. Thesis] 55 *et seq.* (particularly at pp. 59-60; also quoting the *AMT* and *Teheran Hostages* cases at p. 58). See also: Lucas Bastin, *Violation of the Full Protection and Security Obligation by Regulatory Omissions* [M.Phil. Thesis] (Oxford University, Oxford 2011) 32-3.

[130]Lucas Bastin, *State Responsibility for Omissions: Establishing a Breach of the Full Protection and Security Obligation by Omissions* (Oxford University, Oxford 2016) [D.Phil. Thesis] 59-60;

actual adjudicatory practice. Analysis of 'appropriate steps' commonly refers to obligations to prevent interferences with preexistent rights and interests, so that the measures at issue are directed at avoiding the alteration of an *extant* factual situation.[131] Furthermore, even those drawing a line between the two concepts accept the possibility of a partial overlap, in the sense that states can be expected to be 'diligent' in the adoption of appropriate measures.[132]

As far as the phrase 'all necessary measures' is concerned, the problem arises as to whether this formula is actually consistent with the characterization of FPS as a non-absolute obligation. This can be best portrayed with the example of the prevention obligation. From a causality perspective, each measure *necessary* to prevent an injury is a *necessary condition* to avoid the occurrence of the harmful event. If harm is inflicted, there are only two possible hypotheses. A first hypothesis is that the state failed to adopt the measures that were *necessary* to prevent the harmful event, which would inevitably imply that it breached the protection obligation (if such obligation is defined as a duty to take '*all* necessary measures'). The breach thus becomes apparent by the very occurrence of the event. The second hypothesis is that all possible necessary measures were actually adopted, but were still *insufficient* for the prevention of harm. This is but another way of saying the event was unavoidable by state action. The second scenario is therefore one of *impossibility* and, as a rule, the host state will thus be exempted from responsibility on grounds of *force majeure*.[133]

Hence, if the FPS standard is said to require the adoption of *all measures necessary* to prevent an injury, the state will always be responsible for the harmful event *unless* performance is actually *impossible*. Responsibility would consequently become absolute or strict, and the general non-responsibility rule for acts of third parties would be substituted by a general responsibility rule.[134]

Against this backdrop, it can only be concluded that the relationship between these standards and due diligence is unsure. Reformulating questions of diligence in terms of 'prudent', 'appropriate' or 'necessary' measures will hardly provide actual guidance for the assessment of FPS claims and could moreover lead to results inconsistent with the nature of the FPS standard. In the final analysis, these terms bring more uncertainty than certainty to the concept of due diligence.

Lucas Bastin, Violation of the Full Protection and Security Obligation by Regulatory Omissions [M.Phil. Thesis] (Oxford University, Oxford 2011) 32-3.

[131] See the examples mentioned in n. 123 and 124 above.

[132] Lucas Bastin, *State Responsibility for Omissions: Establishing a Breach of the Full Protection and Security Obligation by Omissions* (Oxford University, Oxford 2016) [D.Phil. Thesis] 59; Lucas Bastin, *Violation of the Full Protection and Security Obligation by Regulatory Omissions* [M.Phil. Thesis] (Oxford University, Oxford 2011) 31.

[133] ILC, 'Responsibility of States for Internationally Wrongful Acts. General Commentary' (2001) 2 *Yearbook of the International Law Commission – 2001* 31, 76-8 art. 23.

[134] On the general non-responsibility rule see Chap. 12.

13.3.3.3 The 'Modified' Objective Standard of Due Diligence

Recent arbitral decisions and academic publications describe the level of diligence required under FPS as a 'modified objective standard'. Credit for this terminology should go to Andrew Newcombe and Lluis Paradell. In their study of the FPS standard (2009), they stated:

> The extent of due diligence an investor may expect will vary [...] according to local conditions. This means that due diligence is limited by a state's capacity to act – a state will not be responsible when action would have been impossible. Although the host state is required to exercise an objective minimum standard of due diligence, the standard of due diligence is that of a host state in the circumstances and with the resources of the state in question. *This suggests that due diligence is modified objective standard – the host state must exercise the level of due diligence of a host state in its particular circumstances.* In practice, tribunals will likely consider the state's level of development and stability as relevant circumstances in determining whether there has been due diligence. An investor investing in an area with endemic civil strife and poor governance cannot have the same expectation of physical security as one investing in London, New York or Tokyo.[135]

This approach has permeated arbitration practice. In *Pantechniki v Albania* (2009), Sole Arbitrator Jan Paulsson presented the issue in the following terms:

> Should a state's international responsibility bear some proportion to its resources? Should a poor country be held accountable to a minimum standard which it could attain only at great sacrifice while a rich country would have little difficulty in doing so?[136]

In his analysis of these fundamental questions, Paulsson quoted Newcombe and Paradell in length, and expressed support for their view.[137] The 'modified objective standard' had a direct and material impact on the assessment of the FPS claim in *Pantechniki*. Based on the testimony of the investor's Project Manager, the Sole Arbitrator stated:

---

[135]Emphasis added. Andrew Newcombe and Lluís Paradell, Law and Practice of Investment Treaties. Standards of Treatment (Kluwer Law International, Alphen aan den Rijn 2009) 310. For another author favoring a standard of due diligence which takes into account the circumstances of the host state see: Elisabeth Zeitler, 'The Guarantee of Full Protection and Security in Investment Treaties Regarding Harm Caused by Private Actors' (2005) 3 SIAR 1, 22-3 and 33. For an author rejecting the 'modified standard of due diligence' see: Lucas Bastin, *State Responsibility for Omissions: Establishing a Breach of the Full Protection and Security Obligation by Omissions* (Oxford University, Oxford 2016) [D.Phil. Thesis] 124-6, 151, 233-8 and 278 (also pleading of an 'objective' standard at p. 265).

[136]Pantechniki S.A. Contractors & Engineers v Albania, Award, ICSID Case No. ARB/07/21 (30 July 2009) [76].

[137]Pantechniki S.A. Contractors & Engineers v Albania, Award, ICSID Case No. ARB/07/21 (30 July 2009) [81] ("My review of the cases and literature leads me [...] to adopt the more recent conclusion of Newcombe and Paradell").

[The Project Manager] testified that the police said that they were *unable* to intervene. That is crucially different from a *refusal* to intervene given the scale of the looting. I conclude that the Albanian authorities were powerless in the face of social unrest of this magnitude.[138]

The *Pantechniki* award has influenced subsequent arbitral practice. In *Joseph Houben v Burundi* (2016) the tribunal applied the 'modified standard' in its assessment of the diligence exercised by Burundian authorities in the protection of the investor's property against illegal settlers, and relied on *Pantechniki* in this regard.[139] In *Ampal v Egypt* (2017) the arbitrators also based their analysis of due diligence on the *Pantechniki* decision.[140] In this connection, the tribunal agreed that 'the adequacy of the State's response should be assessed in the light of the scale of the disorder and the extent of its resources'.[141] In regard to Egypt's reaction against terrorist threats to a major pipeline, the arbitrators stated:

> The Tribunal must now determine whether the Respondent acted diligently in preventing the attacks on the Trans-Sinai pipeline and repairing the damage caused to the pipeline. At the outset, the Tribunal acknowledges that the circumstances in the North Sinai Egypt were difficult in the wake of the Arab Spring Revolution. Armed militant groups took advantage of the political instability, security deterioration and general lawlessness that ensued in the North Sinai to perpetrate the attacks to the Trans-Sinai Pipeline.[142]

Doubts may arise as to the characterization of the 'modified' standard as an 'objective' standard. In some measure, the standard appears to be fairly subjective. Newcombe and Paradell, for example, described it as an 'objective standard' but, at the same time, relied on Huber's analogy to the private law notion of *diligentia quam in suis rebus*.[143] This characterization is misleading.

The modified objective standard, as applied by contemporary arbitral tribunals, has little to do with the notion of *diligentia quam in suis rebus*. The modified standard does not define the diligence due under FPS as that which the host state normally exercises in its own affairs. It merely suggests that the capacities and level of development of the host state are relevant for the evaluation of diligence. Adjudicators are thus required to consider how an average state, *having similar*

---

[138]Emphasis in the original. Pantechniki S.A. Contractors & Engineers *v* Albania, Award, ICSID Case No. ARB/07/21 (30 July 2009) [82].

[139]Joseph Houben *v* Burundi, Sentence, ICSID Case No. ARB/13/7 (12 January 2016) [163] (quoting *Pantechniki v Albania* in this connection) [163-4].

[140]Ampal-American Israel Corp., Egi-Fund (08-10) Investors LLC, Egi-Series Investments LLC and BSS-EMG Investors LLC *v* Egypt, Decision on Liability and Heads of Loss, ICSID Case No. ARB/12/11 (21 February 2017) [244].

[141]Ampal-American Israel Corp., Egi-Fund (08-10) Investors LLC, Egi-Series Investments LLC and BSS-EMG Investors LLC *v* Egypt, Decision on Liability and Heads of Loss, ICSID Case No. ARB/12/11 (21 February 2017) [244].

[142]Ampal-American Israel Corp., Egi-Fund (08-10) Investors LLC, Egi-Series Investments LLC and BSS-EMG Investors LLC *v* Egypt, Decision on Liability and Heads of Loss, ICSID Case No. ARB/12/11 (21 February 2017) [283-4].

[143]Andrew Newcombe and Lluís Paradell, *Law and Practice of Investment Treaties. Standards of Treatment* (Kluwer Law International, Alphen aan den Rijn 2009) 310.

resources as those available to the host state, would have reacted in a *similar situation of risk*. Nothing more.

Thus, the proposition that hides behind the somewhat flowery label 'modified objective standard' is in reality quite simple and unexceptional. Neither is it novel. It is a well-established principle that the host state's reaction against an external threat cannot be evaluated in the abstract, under the assumption that the state disposes of a perfect police machinery and unlimited resources. This idea was already present in U.S. Secretary of State Thomas F. Bayard's note on the *Negrete Affaire* (1888). In that note, Bayard delivered a textbook example of the objective notion of due diligence, which he defined as the diligence 'prudent governments' *customarily* exercise, and drew an analogy to the Roman law standard of a *diligens paterfamilias*.[144] Along these lines, Bayard also provided a quite precise formulation of the now-called 'modified' objective standard:

> What is then the custom which becomes the guide? [. . .] custom depends on conditions; so that the degree of diligence customary and reasonable in a newly and sparsely settled region of country where the police force is weak and scattered, where armed forces cannot be maintained and where custom throws on the individual, in a large degree, not only the preservation of order but the vindication of supposed rights, is very different from the degree of diligence customary in a center of population under a well-organized police, and in which armed forces could be promptly summoned in support of the law.[145]

This idea did not remain dormant in the shelves of diplomatic history. In his *Revised Draft on State Responsibility* (1961), Francisco García Amador formulated the customary rules applicable to 'negligence in the performance of the duty of protection' in the following terms:

> 1. The State is responsible for the injuries caused to an alien by illegal acts of individuals, whether isolated or committed in the course of internal disturbances (riots, mob violence or civil war), *if the authorities were manifestly negligent in taking the measures which, in view of the circumstances, are normally taken to prevent the commission of such acts.*
>
> 2. The circumstances mentioned in the foregoing paragraph shall include, in particular, the extent to which the injurious act could have been foreseen and *the physical possibility of preventing its commission with resources available to the State.*[146]

Moreover, even before the term 'modified objective standard' was used for the first time, it was common for investment tribunals to take into consideration the capacities of the host state as a fundamental ingredient of due diligence assessments. For example, in *LESI & ASTALDI v Algeria* (2008), the tribunal stated:

---

[144]'Mr. Bayard, Sec. of State, to Mr. Stuphen' (6 January 1888) in John Bassett Moore, *A Digest of International Law* (Volume 6: Government Printing Office, Washington 1906) 961, 962.

[145]'Mr. Bayard, Sec. of State, to Mr. Stuphen' (6 January 1888) in John Bassett Moore, *A Digest of International Law* (Volume 6: Government Printing Office, Washington 1906) 961, 962.

[146]Emphasis added. Francisco García Amador, 'International Responsibility: Sixth Report by F. V. García Amador, Special Rapporteur (A/CN.4/134 and Add. 1)' (26 January 1961) 2 *Yearbook of the International Law Commission – 1961* 1, 47 art. 7.

L'obligation de sécurité implique dès lors que l'Etat d'accueil fasse tout ce qui est dans son pouvoir pour éviter qu'un dommage ne soit infligé aux investissements [...] le Tribunal arbitral ne constate pas de violation de l'Accord, ni du principe tiré du droit international. La sécurité offerte au Groupement a été en proportion de ce qui était dans le pouvoir algérien de faire.[147]

It could therefore be said that the so-called 'modified objective standard of due diligence' is not a 'modified standard' at all. It is merely the new guise of an old idea, which has enjoyed widespread acceptance for a considerable period of time. The reason for the renaissance of this idea in contemporary arbitral practice and the use of the adjective 'modified' probably lies in a survey published by UNCTAD in 2005, which described the content of the FPS standard as follows:

> *Arguments of incapacity or higher priorities in responding to the circumstances of the strife have also been rejected as a basis for a defence to a claim.* In essence, while not an obligation of result, an obligation of good faith efforts to protect the foreign-owned property has been established by these recent cases, *without special regard for the resources available to do so.* This has been referred to as a standard of "due diligence" on the part of the host country. As a result, this standard should be understood as being very much a "living" one. It places a clear premium on political stability, and the obligation of host countries to ensure that any instability does not have negative effects on foreign investors, *even above the ability to protect foreign investors.*[148]

This passage of the report was quoted a few years later by the tribunal in *Biwater v Tanzania* (2008), thus having an actual impact on investment arbitration practice.[149] In spite of its moderate influence, UNCTAD's description of the standard was baseless, unsubstantiated and inaccurate. None of the three cases UNCTAD invoked in this connection contain any indication whatsoever that the FPS standard goes beyond the host state's actual ability to provide security.[150]

The standard proposed by UNCTAD was by no means novel. It bears striking resemblance to the Umpire's decision in the *Montijo* case of 1875.[151] This resemblance is significant because *Montijo* was never a case about due diligence. Quite the contrary, it was one of the few instances in which an international adjudicator interpreted the protection obligation as an absolute duty. The Umpire considered that, even in the absence of naval or military forces, public authorities had to 'find the means to make it [the state's pledge of protection] effective' and went on to hold that

---

[147]LESI S.p.A. and ASTALDI S.p.A. *v* Algeria, Sentence, ICSID Case No. ARB/05/3 (12 November 2008) [153-4].

[148]Emphasis added. UNCTAD, *Investor-State Disputes Arising from Investment Treaties: A Review* (United Nations, New York/Geneva 2005) 40-1.

[149]Biwater Gauff Ltd. *v* Tanzania, Award, ICSID Case No. ARB/05/22 (24 July 2008) 726.

[150]The 'recent cases' UNCTAD referred to were *AAPL v Sri Lanka, AMT v Zaire* and *Wena Hotels v Egypt*. See: UNCTAD, *Investor-State Disputes Arising from Investment Treaties: A Review* (United Nations, New York/Geneva 2005) 40-1 and 51-2 n. 38-9.

[151]*Case of the Steamer Montijo* (25 July 1875) in Henri La Fontaine (ed), *Pasicrisie Internationale. Histoire documentaire des arbitrages internationaux* (Stämpfli & Cie., Bern 1902) 209, 209-20.

the host state is responsible for a failure to do so *'even if by no fault of its own'*.[152] This remarkable statement did not find much support in legal theory or practice; the element of fault, which is nowadays expressed through the phrase *due diligence*, has long been acknowledged as a solid element of the protection obligation.[153] The award rendered in *Montijo* shows that there is a short distance between the assessment of diligence without regard to the actual circumstances and limitations of the host state, as suggested by UNCTAD in 2005, and the principle of absolute or strict responsibility.

The 'modified standard of due diligence' is moreover fair. The decision to make an investment is always a business decision. As such, it is usually based on a trade-off between risk and return: the higher the risk, the higher the return. Those who make a free decision to invest in a country ravaged by insecurity or, even worse, civil wars and revolutions, cannot expect local authorities to grant them the same level of protection they would enjoy in a stable and peaceful country. If local authorities have offered the security they could honestly offer, it is the investor and not the state that should bear the cost of insecurity. In the end, it is the investor who would enjoy the higher returns resulting from a risky investment. As observed by Emilio Brusa in a report submitted to the *Institut de Droit International* in 1898:

> Un émigrant qui choisit pour spéculations commerciales ou industrielles, ou même pour son activité comme pionnier ou ouvrier, un État dont le gouvernement est encore mal établi ou faible, court un plus grand risque qu'un autre, plus avisé, dont le choix est fait parmi les pays de constitution et d'administration bien solides. Il n'est, alors, que strictement juste qu'il ne s'attende pas à voir ses biens et sa personne protégés en toute circonstance et d'une manière parfaite.[154]

Consideration of the actual capacities of the host state in the assessment of diligence is therefore not only accepted under international law, but seems moreover to be justified from the standpoint of fairness and justice.

A final issue should not remain unattended. The 'modified objective standard' has been mostly applied in cases pertaining to the prevention obligation. The question might therefore arise as to whether the obligation of redress is subject to the same standard. Investment tribunals have already been confronted with this fundamental question. In *Frontier Petroleum v Czech Republic* (2010) the tribunal recognized the problem in the following terms:

> In *Pantechniki*, the tribunal applied a modified objective standard of due diligence in a situation of public violence. It found that liability in a situation involving civil strife depended on the host state's resources. However, there are no authorities which indicate

---

[152]Emphasis added. *Case of the Steamer Montijo* (25 July 1875) in Henri La Fontaine (ed), *Pasicrisie Internationale. Histoire documentaire des arbitrages internationaux* (Stämpfli & Cie., Bern 1902) 209, 219.

[153]Cf. Sect. 12.3.

[154]Emilio Brusa, 'Responsabilité des États à raison des dommages soufferts par des étrangers en cas d'émeute ou de guerre civile' (1898) 17 Annuaire de l'Institut de Droit International 96, 105 (stating at pp. 105-6 that this circumstance is relevant, in particular, for the determination of the *quantum* of compensation).

that other situations, not involving violence, would warrant the application of a relative standard.[155]

The *Frontier* tribunal's concern is understandable. In *Pantechniki*, Sole Arbitrator Jan Paulsson drew an interesting parallel between the FPS standard and denial of justice claims, suggesting that resort to an 'element of proportionality' is better justified in the context of FPS.[156] Focusing on the degree of 'consciousness' of state organs, Paulsson observed that a denial of justice typically involves normative frameworks which crystalize 'deliberate choices' by the host state.[157] In contrast, FPS comes into play in situations which, being 'unpredictable' and 'overwhelming', could pose greater challenges for weak states than for stronger states.[158] As regards to the grounds for this difference between denial of justice and FPS, the Sole Arbitrator explained:

> Two reasons appear salient. The first is that international responsibility does not relate to physical infrastructure; states are not liable for denial of justice because they cannot afford to put at the public's disposal spacious buildings or computerised information banks. What matters is rather the human factor of obedience to the rule of law. Foreigners who enter a poor country are not entitled to assume that they will be given things like verbatim transcripts of all judicial proceedings – but they are entitled to decision-making which is neither xenophobic nor arbitrary. The second is that a relativistic standard would be none at all. International courts or tribunals would have to make ad hoc assessments based on their evaluation of the capacity of each state at a given moment of its development. International law would thus provide no incentive for a state to improve. It would in fact operate to the opposite effect: a state which devoted more resources to its judiciary would run the risk of graduating into a more exacting category.[159]

This statement might suggest that the 'modified standard' is not applicable with regard to the redress obligation, which comes close to the notion of denial of justice. Such conclusion would be incorrect. There are obvious overlaps between responsibility for failures of redress and denial of justice.[160] But the fact remains that, as far as FPS is concerned, responsibility is never absolute and is always defined in terms of due diligence.[161]

The analysis of due diligence in the context of redress has certainly a different taint than in the context of the prevention obligation. The difference between the obligation to prevent and the obligation of redress, however, is not about the

---

[155]Frontier Petroleum Ltd. *v* Czech Republic (UNCITRAL), Final Award (12 November 2010) [271].

[156]Pantechniki S.A. Contractors & Engineers *v* Albania, Award, ICSID Case No. ARB/07/21 (30 July 2009) [77].

[157]Pantechniki S.A. Contractors & Engineers *v* Albania, Award, ICSID Case No. ARB/07/21 (30 July 2009) [77].

[158]Pantechniki S.A. Contractors & Engineers *v* Albania, Award, ICSID Case No. ARB/07/21 (30 July 2009) [77].

[159]Pantechniki S.A. Contractors & Engineers *v* Albania, Award, ICSID Case No. ARB/07/21 (30 July 2009) [76].

[160]See Sect. 10.3. Cf. also Sect. 2.2.3.

[161]Cf. Chap. 11.

applicable standard of liability. States have limited resources and those limitations necessarily affect the redress of injuries to aliens. While these circumstances do not necessarily relieve the host state from liability, they can never be ignored. In the *Christina Patton* case (1931), the British-Mexican Claims Commission stated:

> Even when a country passes through a period of anarchy, even when an established and recognized government is not in existence, the permanent machinery of the public service continues its activity [. . .] They [the Commissioners] might add that the Police continued to function, that it continued to regulate traffic in the capital, *to investigate crimes and to arrest criminals, as also that the Courts continued to administer justice* [. . .] *it is not denied that the performance of those duties will often have been very difficult in those disturbed times of civil war.*[162]

Due diligence does not convey a different meaning depending on whether the protection obligation is applied in its preventive or in its repressive dimension. Still, the 'modified standard' is not always the decisive factor for the assessment of alleged failures to provide adequate means of redress. While applicable as a matter of principle, the 'modified standard' will certainly play no major role where the failure of redress was caused by arbitrariness or unwillingness to offer a fair opportunity of redress. The reason is that those scenarios, which are precisely the examples mentioned by Sole Arbitrator Paulsson in the *Pantechniki* award, presuppose that the host state was, in fact, *capable* of providing redress. The 'modified standard' could however gain importance in other factual settings.

An example would be the case of delays in the administration of justice.[163] A developing country cannot be expected to offer as efficient and expeditious a justice system as a developed country. While the limited capacities of the state concerned do not excuse any delay,[164] such limitations are relevant for a fair assessment of the host state's omissions. If one were to use Paulsson's terminology in this context, it could be said that delays do not always result from a *conscious* policy choice by the host state.[165] A similar situation arises in claims pertaining to deficiencies in the investigation and punishment of crimes against foreigners. International law generally recognizes that in those events the degree of diligence required under the customary

---

[162]Emphasis added. *Christina Patton v Mexico* (8 July 1931) V RIAA 224, 226-7 [7].

[163]For an example of a delay in the administration of justice as the object of an FPS claim see: EDF International S.A., Saur International S.A. and Leon Participaciones Argentinas S.A. *v* Argentina, Award, ICSID Case No. ARB/03/23 (11 June 2012) [409]. The tribunal did not address this claim in detail, explaining that '[n]othing [. . .] suggests that the amount of damages would be different if based on a theory of denial of justice or absence of full protection and security' (at para 1112). For an additional example see: Marion Unglaube and Reinhard Unglaube *v* Costa Rica, Award, ICSID Cases No. ARB/01/1 and ARB/09/20 (16 May 2012) [286 and 288] (delays allegedly caused by two *amparo* petitions lodged with local courts; the FPS claim was however unsuccessful).

[164]Cf. *El Oro Mining and Railway Co. v Mexico* (18 June 1931) V RIAA 191, 198 [9-10].

[165]Cf. Pantechniki S.A. Contractors & Engineers *v* Albania, Award, ICSID Case No. ARB/07/21 (30 July 2009) [77].

protection obligation depends, too, on the actual circumstances of fact faced by competent authorities and the means which state agents had at their disposal.[166]

Adjudicators cannot and should not turn a blind eye to the fact that public authorities do not dispose of unlimited resources. To do otherwise would imply losing touch with reality and engaging in a rather speculative exercise. Diligence would be evaluated in an artificial and rather hypothetical factual context, different from the actual set of facts that surrounded the host state's conduct.

13.4   Factual Circumstances Relevant for the Assessment of Diligence

Chapter 12 has shown that due diligence is a functional equivalent to the notion of fault.[167] In view of the complexity of the notion, any attempt to define due diligence as a precise rule is doomed to failure. Back in 1929, Edwin Borchard observed that '[d]ue diligence is a standard, and not a definition'.[168] Borchard's opposition of the terms 'standard' and 'definition' delivers the idea of due diligence as a flexible and adaptable concept. His words remind scholars and practitioners not to look for a rule when they are looking at a standard.[169] Similarly, specifically referring to the customary duty to prevent injuries to aliens, Clyde Eagleton explained in 1928:

> Whether the state has fulfilled its obligations in this regard is measured by the rule of due diligence; and it is impossible to state this rule with precision. No clear and definitive formula has ever been promulgated: it is necessary to study the cases, and to judge according to the circumstances in any particular situation.[170]

Decades later, in his *Second Report on State Responsibility* (1957), Special Rapporteau Francisco García Amador observed:

---

[166]Cf. Amelia de Brissot et al. v. United States of Venezuela (26 August 1890) United States and Venezuelan Claims Commission. Opinions Delivered by the Commissioners in the Principal Cases (Gibson Bros., Washington 1890) 457, 486 (opinion of Commissioner Findlay, requiring an 'honest endeavor' to punish the offenders) and 482-3 (opinion of Commissioner Little, noting that a state is not responsable for a failure to punish the offenders if '[it] did all that could reasonably be required in that behalf').

[167]See Sect. 12.3.

[168]Edwin Borchard, 'The Law of Responsibility of States for Damage Done in Their Territory to the Person or Property of Foreigners. Comments to the Draft Convention' (April 1929) 23 AJIL 131, 188 art. 10. Cf. also: Lucas Bastin, *State Responsibility for Omissions: Establishing a Breach of the Full Protection and Security Obligation by Omissions* (Oxford University, Oxford 2016) [D. Phil. Thesis] 54 (underscoring the need for the standard of due diligence to be flexible).

[169]Section 6.2 explores the notion of 'standard' and considers the difference between the normative structure of 'standards' and 'rules'.

[170]Clyde Eagleton, *The Responsibility of States in International Law* (Klaus Reprint, New York 1970) 88 [first edition: 1928].

> The learned authorities are in almost unanimous agreement that the rule of "due diligence" cannot be reduced to a clear and accurate definition which might serve as an objective and automatic standard for deciding, regardless of the circumstances, whether a State was "diligent" in discharging its duty of vigilance and protection.[171]

In spite of the absence of a general definition of the diligence due under the FPS standard, it is certain that, as stated by an ICSID tribunal in *Joseph Charles Lemire v Ukraine* (2010), 'not every lack of diligence by supervisory authority opens the door to a claim under the BIT'.[172] The mere fact that an omission is attributable to the host state and has some degree of causal connection with an injury inflicted upon an alien does not suffice to establish an internationally wrongful lack of due diligence. There has to be something more. In *Noble Ventures v Romania* (2005), the arbitrators noted that, in order to be characterized as an international delinquency, a lack of diligence must be 'sufficiently grave'.[173] The extent to which an omission in the protection of foreign investors is 'grave' enough to be properly styled as a breach of FPS is a question of degree.

As a corollary, adjudicators enjoy broad discretion in the evaluation of the host state's conduct and the characterization of an omission as a failure to exercise the diligence required under FPS. In light of the foregoing, this study will not attempt formulate a general, abstract definition of due diligence. Neither will it develop a 'due diligence test'. Acknowledging that due diligence is not a fixed notion, the following subsections will focus on the circumstances of fact that could *indicate* that the host state's reaction toward some specific situation of risk fell below the diligence required by the FPS standard. Examples of the practical use of these criteria will be taken from investment arbitration decisions addressing FPS claims.

13.4.1 Material Opportunity for Positive Action

Due diligence can only be exercised where there is a real possibility of adopting positive measures of protection.[174] The investor must provide evidence indicating

---

[171]Francisco García Amador, 'International Responsibility: Second Report by F. V. García Amador, Special Rapporteur (A/CN.4/106)' (15 February 1957) 2 Yearbook of the International Law Commission – 1957 104, 122 [7].

[172]Joseph Charles Lemire *v* Ukraine, Decision on Jurisdiction and Liability, ICSID Case No. ARB/06/18 (14 January 2010) [496].

[173]Noble Ventures *v* Romania, Award, ICSID Case No. ARB/01/11 (12 October 2005) [166]. See also: SAUR International S.A. *v* Argentina, Décision sur la compétence et sur la responsabilité, ICSID Case No. ARB/04/4 (6 June 2012) [483] ("la protection de l'APRI n'entre en vigueur que lorsque la conduite de l'État, de par sa gravité et sa transcendance, et de par le caractère souverain des actes, est incompatible avec la norme internationale"). This statement of the SAUR tribunal refers to both the FET and the FPS standard.

[174]For a detailed analysis of the relevance of the state's 'capacity to act' in the context of FPS claims see: Lucas Bastin, *State Responsibility for Omissions: Establishing a Breach of the Full Protection*

that the host state had an opportunity to act.[175] In *Toto Costruzioni v Lebanon* (2012), the arbitral tribunal dismissed an FPS claim on grounds that the investor 'did not demonstrate that Lebanon *could have taken* preventive or remedial action that it failed to take, and acted negligently in relation to the owners' obstructions'.[176] Similarly, in *Noble Ventures v Romania* (2005), the arbitrators stated:

> The Claimant has failed to prove that its alleged injuries and losses *could have been prevented* had the Respondent exercised due diligence in this regard, nor has it established any specific value of the losses.[177]

The existence of a realistic possibility for positive action is necessarily dependent on the particular circumstances of the case. These circumstances include the means available to competent authorities. In the end, as expressed by Commissioner Palacio in the *Salvador Pratts* case, '[p]ossibility is, indeed, the last limit of all human obligations: the most stringent and inviolable ones cannot be extended to more'.[178] Following Palacio, this implies that 'the extent of the duties is to be commensurate with the extent of the means for performing the same, [. . .] he who has employed all the means within his reach has perfectly performed his duty, irrespective of the material result of his efforts'.[179]

Thus, for example, the presence of police units in the area where the harmful event occurred could indicate that the host state had the means and opportunity to act. In *Wena Hotels v Egypt* (2000), the arbitrators underscored that, at the moment in which the Egyptian Hotel Company forcefully seized the investor's hotels, units of the Ministry of Tourism's Police and the Kasar El-Nile Police were 'located only a few minutes away' from the investor's property.[180] In spite of the foregoing, neither unit undertook actual protective action.[181]

In determining whether the host state had an actual opportunity to act, adjudicators have also considered whether municipal law granted specific organs the powers or tools to take positive action. The *Wena* decision is again helpful to visualize this element of analysis. In that case, the tribunal observed that the Minister of Tourism enjoyed broad powers over the state-owned company that had illegally seized the investor's properties:

---

and Security Obligation by Omissions (Oxford University, Oxford 2016) [D.Phil. Thesis] 228 *et seq.*

[175]Cf. Sects. 13.2 and 13.3.3.3.

[176]Emphasis added. Toto Costruzioni Generali S.p.A. *v* Lebanon, Award, ICSID Case No. ARB/07/12 (7 June 2012) [229].

[177]Emphasis added. Noble Ventures *v* Romania, Award, ICSID Case No. ARB/01/11 (12 October 2005) [166].

[178]*Salvador Prats v United States* (undated) 3 Moore's Arb. 2886, 2894 (considering the issue in particular connection with the obligation to exercise due diligence in the protection of aliens).

[179]*Salvador Prats v United States* (undated) 3 Moore's Arb. 2886, 2894.

[180]Wena Hotels Ltd. *v* Egypt, Award, ICSID Case No. ARB/98/4 (8 December 2000) [89].

[181]Wena Hotels Ltd. *v* Egypt, Award, ICSID Case No. ARB/98/4 (8 December 2000) [88-9].

Under Law Number 97 of 1983 governing Public Sector Companies and Organizations, Minister Sultan was empowered to dismiss the Chairman and the members of the Board of EHC [. . .] Also, given its power as sole shareholder in EHC [. . .] Egypt could have directed EHC to return the hotels to Wena's control and make reparations. Instead, neither hotel was restored to Wena until nearly a year later, after decisions by the Chief Prosecutor of Egypt, which Wena asserts were only obtained as a result of diplomatic pressure on Egypt.[182]

Municipal law is one of the many factors relevant for the assessment of the options public authorities had in the face of a situation of risk. Still, municipal law will never excuse for and by itself a want of protection; the state cannot avoid responsibility by invoking its own domestic law and, possibly, its own failure to enact adequate legislation to properly avert the kind of risks the FPS standard refers to.[183]

13.4.2   Awareness About the Risk

Public authorities can only undertake positive action against a threat if they are aware of its existence.[184] No one can react against the unknown. International law generally recognizes this real-world premise. This does not however mean that ignorance about a threat necessarily excludes responsibility for lack of protection. States could be considered responsible if, in spite of being ignorant about the risk, they *ought to have been aware* of it. The question of *knowledge* often turns into a question of *foreseeability*. In such cases, the threshold issue is whether the host state could have been reasonably expected to be aware of the risk threatening a foreign national.

Knowledge and foreseeability are two fundamental ingredients for the assessment of due diligence.[185] These elements may be traced back to the Grotian notion of *patientia*,[186] and have not escaped the attention of foreign offices and international

---

[182]Wena Hotels Ltd. *v* Egypt, Award, ICSID Case No. ARB/98/4 (8 December 2000) [90-1].

[183]See Sect. 11.2.3. Cf. also Sect. 13.4.9.

[184]ILA Study Group on Due Diligence in International Law, 'Second Report by Mr. Tim Stephens (Rapporteur) and Mr. Duncan French (Chair)' (20 July 2016) 12.

[185]For some examples of academic publications addressing these two elements in connection with the FPS standard see: Finnur Magnússon, *Full Protection and Security in International Law* (University of Vienna, Vienna 2012) 166-70; Helge Elisabeth Zeitler, 'The Guarantee of Full Protection and Security in Investment Treaties regarding Harm Caused by Private Parties' (2005) 3 SIAR 1, 13-15; Lucas Bastin, *State Responsibility for Omissions: Establishing a Breach of the Full Protection and Security Obligation by Omissions* (Oxford University, Oxford 2016) [D.Phil. Thesis] 209 *et seq.* (particularly at pp. 227-8).

[186]Hugo Grotius, *The Rights of War and Peace in Three Books* (1625) (The Lawbook Exchange, Clark NJ 2004) 455 [Book 2 Chap. XXI, § II(4)]. Section 12.3.1 discusses this element of the Grotian theory of fault in more detail. The element of 'awareness' was also at the heart of Samuel Pufendorf's theory of state responsibility for acts of individuals, which entailed a presumption of both knowledge about the risk and authorities' ability to prevent harm (see Sect. 12.3.2.2).

adjudicators. In *Pantechniki v Albania* (2009), Sole Arbitrator Jan Paulsson referred in this connection to the *Cutler affair*.[187] In that case, a mob caused damages to the office of an American citizen, Marshal Cutler, in the city of Florence.[188] In its instructions to the American Embassy to the Kingdom of Italy, the Department of State explained:

> This Government cannot ask the Italian Government, or the local authorities to indemnify [. . .] unless the authorities *had knowledge, or should have had knowledge* of the impending attack and failed to take proper precautions to thwart it.[189]

Another example appears in a decision issued by the British-Mexican Claims Commission in the *Mexico City Bombardment Claims* (1930). The case involved the occupation and looting of a hotel in Mexico City, including the rooms of three British subjects, by troops of the Revolutionary General Félix Díaz (so-called '*Felicistas*').[190] The Commissioners analyzed whether Mexico could be held responsible for a breach of a treaty-based security obligation, requiring 'reasonable measures' for the prevention and redress of revolutionary damages[191]:

> In a great many cases it will be extremely difficult to establish beyond any doubt the omission or the absence of suppressive or punitive measures. The Commission realizes that the evidence of negative facts can hardly ever be given in an absolutely convincing manner. But a strong *prima facie* evidence can be assumed to exist in these cases in which *first* the British Agent will be able to make it acceptable that the facts were known to the competent authorities, either because they were of public notoriety or because they were brought to their knowledge in due time [. . .] The occupying and the looting of the building must have been known to the authorities obliged to watch over and to protect life and property; and, furthermore, the British Agent showed notes of sufficient authenticity, written in the British Legation in margin of the affidavits of the claimants, which notes satisfy the majority of the Commission that the events have been duly and without delay intimated to the public authorities.[192]

Just like mixed-claims commissions, investment arbitral tribunals addressing FPS claims usually require the claimant to provide evidence that local authorities were or should have been aware of the threat or risk. As stated in *Sergei Paushok v Mongolia* (2011):

---

[187] Pantechniki S.A. Contractors & Engineers *v* Albania, Award, ICSID Case No. ARB/07/21 (30 July 2009) [78].

[188] Green Haywood Hackworth (ed), *Digest of International Law* (Volume 5: Government Printing Office, Washington 1943) 658. For some comments on the *Cutler* affair see: Daniel Patrick O'Connell, *International Law* (Volume 2: Stevens & Sons, London 1970) 968; Richard Lillich and John Paxman, 'State Responsibility for Injuries to Aliens Occasioned by Terrorist Activities' (1977) 26(2) Am. U. L. Rev. 217, 226-7.

[189] Emphasis added. 'Instruction to the U.S. Embassy to the Kingdom of Italy [concerning the *Cutler* affair]' (5 July 1927) in Green Hackworth (ed), *Digest of International Law* (Volume 5: Government Printing Office, Washington 1943) 660-1.

[190] *Mexico City Bombardment Claims* (15 February 1930) V RIAA 76, 79-80 [6].

[191] *Mexico City Bombardment Claims* (15 February 1930) V RIAA 76, 79-80 [6].

[192] *Mexico City Bombardment Claims* (15 February 1930) V RIAA 76, 80 [6].

[T]he obligation to show "due diligence" does not mean that the State has to prevent any injury whatsoever. Rather, the obligation is generally understood as requiring that the State take reasonable actions within its power to avoid injury *when it is, or should be, aware that there is a risk of injury.*[193]

The mere fact that the state exercises actual territorial control does not imply that knowledge about potential risks threating foreign nationals can be presumed. This premise is firmly etched into the law of state responsibility. As stated by the ICJ in the *Corfu Channel* case (1949):

It is true, as international practice shows, that a State on whose territory or in whose waters an act contrary to international law has occurred, may be called upon to give an explanation. It is also true that that State cannot evade such a request by limiting itself to reply that it is ignorant of the circumstances of the act and of its authors. But it cannot be concluded from the mere fact of the control exercised by a State over its territory and waters that that state necessarily knew, or should have known, the authors.[194]

Investment arbitral tribunals may face two possible scenarios in this connection, depending on whether available evidence indicates *actual knowledge* of the situation of risk. In a first group of cases, tribunals have found evidence indicating that the host state was *actually aware* of the risk. An early example appears in *Wena Hotels v Egypt* (2000). In that case, the Egyptian Hotel Company [EHC], a local public entity, had illegally seized the investor's property.[195] In their analysis of the FPS claim, the arbitrators drew particular attention to the fact that Egypt knew about the risk of seizure:

The Tribunal agrees with Wena that Egypt violated its obligation under Article 2(2) of the IPPA [Egypt-UK Investment Promotion and Protection Agreement] to accord Wena's investment fair and equitable treatment and full protection and security. Although it is not clear that Egyptian officials other than officials of EHC directly participated in the April 1, 1991 seizures, there is substantial evidence that Egypt was aware of EHC's intentions to seize the hotels and took no actions to prevent EHC from doing so.[196]

The arbitrators provided a detailed account of the warnings received by Egyptian cabinet members,[197] and observed that '[d]espite all these warnings, Egypt took no action to protect Wena's investment'.[198] Another example appears in the award rendered in *Joseph Houben v Burundi* (2016). In that case, an ICSID tribunal stated:

---

[193]Emphasis added. Sergei Paushok, CJSC Golden East Co., CJSC Vostoknefte *v* Mongolia (UNCITRAL), Award on Jurisdiction and Liability (28 April 2011) [325]. For an almost identical statement see: El Paso Energy International Co. *v* Argentina, Award, ICSID Case No. ARB/03/15 (31 October 2011) [523]. See also: Electrabel S.A. *v* Hungary, Decision on Jurisdiction, Applicable Law and Liability, ICSID Case No. ARB/07/19 (30 November 2012) [7.83] (quoting *El Paso* in this connection).

[194]*Corfu Channel Case (UK v Albania)* [1949] ICJ Rep 4, 18.

[195]For a detailed account of the facts see: Wena Hotels Ltd. *v* Egypt, Award, ICSID Case No. ARB/98/4 (8 December 2000) [17 *et seq.*].

[196]Wena Hotels Ltd. *v* Egypt, Award, ICSID Case No. ARB/98/4 (8 December 2000) [84].

[197]Wena Hotels Ltd. *v* Egypt, Award, ICSID Case No. ARB/98/4 (8 December 2000) [85-7].

[198]Wena Hotels Ltd. *v* Egypt, Award, ICSID Case No. ARB/98/4 (8 December 2000) [88].

[L]'obligation est généralement comprise comme exigeant que l'Etat prenne des mesures raisonnables en son pouvoir lorsqu'il est, ou devrait être, au courant d'un risque de dommage.[199]

In the *Joseph Houben* case, the investor had informed competent authorities that his property had been invaded by illegal settlers, and had repeatedly requested police intervention.[200] In spite of these requests, public officials merely sent a few communications to a local administrator without taking further measures of protection.[201] The tribunal therefore concluded that Burundi had knowledge of the situation and the capacity to act.[202] The arbitrators found that local authorities' omissions in the protection of Mr. Houben's property constituted a breach of FPS:

Le Tribunal estime que le Burundi, en tant qu'Etat possédant des ressources pour faire intervenir la force publique – ce qu'il n'a pas contesté – en dehors de toute période de guerre ou de troubles publics, dès lors qu'il était au courant du risque de dommage imminent sur la propriété de M. Houben – dont il reconnaît lui-même qu'il pouvait être « irréversible » – était tout à fait à même de recourir à des mesures plus efficaces que le simple envoi de courriers à l'administrateur communal.[203]

In *Peter Allard v Barbados* (2016), the arbitrators considered an FPS claim concerning an alleged failure by the state to prevent environmental damage to a bird sanctuary operated by a Canadian investor.[204] The first step in the tribunal's analysis of due diligence was Barbados' awareness about the risk of environmental harm. In this vein, the tribunal observed that 'the record supports the Claimant's contention that Barbados was aware [of the risk]'.[205] In spite of this circumstance, the arbitrators held that 'being aware of the environmental sensitivities of the Sanctuary, Barbados took reasonable steps to protect it'.[206]

In cases where the state was actually aware of the risk, adjudicators should consider whether and to which extent public authorities had an opportunity to take action against the threat. In this connection, the *moment* in which competent authorities are informed of the situation of risk will usually be of pivotal importance. Timing should not, however, play a significant role where evidence indicates that the state was *unwilling* to act.

In *MNSS v Montenegro* (2016) members of a labor union had occupied on two occasions the headquarters of Zeljezara Niksic [ZN], a local manufacturing company in which the claimants held substantial investments.[207] The investors argued that

---

[199]Joseph Houben v Burundi, Sentence, ICSID Case No. ARB/13/7 (12 January 2016) [161].

[200]Joseph Houben v Burundi, Sentence, ICSID Case No. ARB/13/7 (12 January 2016) [164-8].

[201]Joseph Houben v Burundi, Sentence, ICSID Case No. ARB/13/7 (12 January 2016) [166].

[202]Joseph Houben v Burundi, Sentence, ICSID Case No. ARB/13/7 (12 January 2016) [171].

[203]Joseph Houben v Burundi, Sentence, ICSID Case No. ARB/13/7 (12 January 2016) [171].

[204]Peter A. Allard v Barbados (UNCITRAL), Award (27 June 2016) [232-4 and 239].

[205]Peter A. Allard v Barbados (UNCITRAL), Award (27 June 2016) [241].

[206]Peter A. Allard v Barbados (UNCITRAL), Award (27 June 2016) [242].

[207]MNSS B.V. and Recupero Credito Acciaio N.V. v Montenegro, Award, ICSID Case No. ARB (AF)/12/8 (4 May 2016) [5, 46 *et seq.* and 235].

local authorities had failed to protect their investments against the acts of the union members, and characterized this omission as a breach of the FPS clause enshrined in article 3(1) of the Netherlands-Yugoslavia BIT.[208]

The parties disagreed as to the moment in which police authorities had been informed of the threats.[209] The tribunal considered that the issue was inconsequential for the decision on the case.[210] The record indicated that authorities were unwilling to protect the investment. To begin with, the tribunal observed, 'the police took no action to dislodge the occupiers during the seven days that the occupation lasted'.[211] Moreover, the arbitrators noted that the police had taken no steps to protect the investor when the labor union announced its intention to pursue a second occupation of the premises a few months after the first occupation.[212] The testimony of ZN's CEO reinforced the impression that the host state was reluctant to take action:

> Whether the police was advised in advance or not does not seem to have made any difference in terms of preparation of the police to protect the premises. According to ZN's CEO, the police informed him that they would not attend ZN in the event of labor unrest because ZN was a private business on private property. The Respondent has not disputed this information. It is surprising that the police would not ensure the physical integrity of buildings and persons irrespective of their location or ownership. It is also surprising that Minister Vujovic [Minister of Economy] saw no reason to take steps in response to ZN's police protection request [...] The standard of "most constant protection and security" requires the Government to have a more pro-active attitude to ensure the protection of persons and property in the circumstances of ZN, particularly when it had been forewarned.[213]

In a second group of cases, the record does not provide conclusive evidence that the state had actual knowledge of the situation of risk. In those cases, a finding of responsibility is contingent upon the tribunal finding proof that the harmful event was *foreseeable*. As a rule, injuries resulting from entirely unforeseeable situations do not constitute a breach of the FPS standard. To say otherwise would imply turning FPS into an absolute guarantee and the host state into an insurer against a wide array of dangers.[214] As stated by Sole Arbitrator Paulsson in the *Pantechniki* case, 'it

---

[208]MNSS B.V. and Recupero Credito Acciaio N.V. *v* Montenegro, Award, ICSID Case No. ARB (AF)/12/8 (4 May 2016) [235].

[209]MNSS B.V. and Recupero Credito Acciaio N.V. *v* Montenegro, Award, ICSID Case No. ARB (AF)/12/8 (4 May 2016) [352]. See also the Respondent's argument at para 267.

[210]MNSS B.V. and Recupero Credito Acciaio N.V. *v* Montenegro, Award, ICSID Case No. ARB (AF)/12/8 (4 May 2016) [352].

[211]MNSS B.V. and Recupero Credito Acciaio N.V. *v* Montenegro, Award, ICSID Case No. ARB (AF)/12/8 (4 May 2016) [352].

[212]MNSS B.V. and Recupero Credito Acciaio N.V. *v* Montenegro, Award, ICSID Case No. ARB (AF)/12/8 (4 May 2016) [353].

[213]MNSS B.V. and Recupero Credito Acciaio N.V. *v* Montenegro, Award, ICSID Case No. ARB (AF)/12/8 (4 May 2016) [354-6].

[214]For a similar formulation of the non-absolute character of the so-called 'obligations of event' see: ILC, 'Draft Articles on State Responsibility with Commentaries thereto adopted by the International Law Commission on First Reading (Doc. No. 97-02583)' (January 1997) [http://legal.un.org/ilc/texts/instruments/english/commentaries/9_6_1996.pdf] 173 [6] (without making particular

seems difficult to maintain that a government incurs international responsibility for failure to plan for unprecedented trouble of unprecedented magnitude in unprecedented places'.[215]

Foreseeability can never be assessed in the abstract. It always depends on the circumstances of the case and, particularly, the information available to public officials at the time when effective preventive measures could have been taken. In some cases, a situation of risk is 'publicly notorious' and adjudicators can hence assume that ignorance about the threat could only have resulted from utter negligence by public authorities.[216] Adjudicators could also find that the host state had a duty to monitor some specific source of risk, in which case ignorance about the specific threat would necessarily result from a breach of duty and, consequently, cannot justify lack of adequate measures of protection.[217]

Another scenario arises in cases involving a series of incidents affecting the integrity of a foreign investment. Confronted with such a factual setting, arbitral tribunals could consider that the very occurrence of an unexpected and unprecedented event should turn competent authorities' attention to the source of risk and the possibility of repetition. It follows that, while the original harmful event could be fairly said to be unpredictable, subsequent incidents of a similar nature do not convey an unforeseeable character. The award issued in *Ampal et al. v Egypt* (2017) may help visualize this situation. The case was concerned with thirteen

---

reference to the FPS standard). Section 11.2.2.2 discusses the non-absolute character of the FPS standard in more detail.

[215]Pantechniki S.A. Contractors & Engineers *v* Albania, Award, ICSID Case No. ARB/07/21 (30 July 2009) [82]. See also: Ampal-American Israel Corp., Egi-Fund (08-10) Investors LLC, Egi-Series Investments LLC and BSS-EMG Investors LLC *v* Egypt, Decision on Liability and Heads of Loss, ICSID Case No. ARB/12/11 (21 February 2017) [244 and 285] (quoting Pantechniki in this connection).

[216]The British-Mexican Claims Commission often used the expression 'publicly notorious' on several occasions. For some examples see: *Christina Patton v Mexico* (8 July 1931) V RIAA 224, 226 [3] and 228 [8] (see also the British Commissioner's dissenting opinion at p. 229 [4], using the expression 'common notoriety'); *Mexico City Bombardment Claims* (15 February 1930) V RIAA 76, 80 [6]; *Santa Gertudis Jute Mill Co. Ltd. v Mexico* (15 February 1930) V RIAA 108, 112 [9]; *William E. Bowerman and Messrs. Burberry's Ltd. v Mexico* (15 February 1930) V RIAA 104, 106 [7]. In some cases, the Commission went as far as to exclude responsibility on grounds that the thread was not of 'public notoriety'. See, for example: *Buena Tierra Mining Co. Ltd. v Mexico* (3 August 1931) V RIAA 247, 251-2 [8] ("it has not been proved that there was any negligence on the part of the authorities, nor that the occurrence was of notoriety, nor that it was brought to the notice of the authorities or that they were informed thereof in due time, so as to fix responsibility on them for non-punishment"); *George Creswell Delamain v Mexico* (10 July 1931) V RIAA 229, 231 [9] ("In the present case they [the Commissioners] have not found any indication that Mr. G. C. Delamain, or his brother, advized (sic) the public authorities of the extortion, of which he had been a victim, nor can it be assumed that this crime, committed on an isolated ranch, was of such public notoriety as to come spontaneously to the knowledge of the authorities.").

[217]See generally: ILA Study Group on Due Diligence in International Law, 'Second Report by Mr. Tim Stephens (Rapporteur) and Mr. Duncan French (Chair)' (20 July 2016) 12.

terrorist attacks on the Trans-Sinai Pipeline in the context of the Arab Spring.[218] The arbitrators began by analyzing the circumstances surrounding the first attack, and concluded that it was unforeseeable and 'could not have been prevented by the Respondent and cannot amount to a breach of the full protection and security standard in itself'.[219] This did not necessarily hold true for subsequent incidents:

> [T]he Tribunal considers the thirteen attacks that were perpetrated on the Trans-Sinai Pipeline as a whole in determining whether the Respondent has breached the standard of full protection and security under the Treaty. It is apparent to the Tribunal that, when considering the totality of these attacks, a certain pattern emerges: an attack is perpetrated, to which GASCO [operator of the pipeline] reacts months later and then adopts some measures to heighten the security of the pipeline, those measures are seldom implemented (or there is no evidence on the record that they were), another attack happens, and so on [...] [The] first four first attacks should have been seen as a warning to the Egyptian State that further attacks might be carried out if security measures were not taken and implemented. It is thus clear to the Tribunal that the failure by the Egyptian authorities to take any concrete steps to protect the Claimant's investment from damage in reaction to third party attacks on the upstream pipeline system, as of the date of attack no. 5 [...] constitutes a breach of the obligation of due diligence that Egypt was required to exercise in ensuring the full protection and security of the Claimant's investment.[220]

Foreseeability and the actual existence of an opportunity to take positive action are, perhaps, the most important ingredients of any analysis of due diligence. Some scholars have gone as far as to practically reduce their assessment of due diligence to these two fundamental variables.[221] This seems also consistent with the approach adjudicatory bodies have followed in other areas of international law. For example, in the *Teheran Hostages* case (1980) the ICJ's analysis of the obligation to protect diplomatic agents and foreign mission's premises focused on the receiving state's *awareness* about the risk and the existence of *means* to take adequate measures of protection.[222] There are, however, many other circumstances of fact to be considered in this regard. The following sections provide an overview of other elements of analysis, and discuss their use in the context of FPS claims.

---

[218] Ampal-American Israel Corp., Egi-Fund (08-10) Investors LLC, Egi-Series Investments LLC and BSS-EMG Investors LLC v Egypt, Decision on Liability and Heads of Loss, ICSID Case No. ARB/12/11 (21 February 2017) [235-8 and 283 *et seq.*].

[219] Ampal-American Israel Corp., Egi-Fund (08-10) Investors LLC, Egi-Series Investments LLC and BSS-EMG Investors LLC v Egypt, Decision on Liability and Heads of Loss, ICSID Case No. ARB/12/11 (21 February 2017) [285].

[220] Ampal-American Israel Corp., Egi-Fund (08-10) Investors LLC, Egi-Series Investments LLC and BSS-EMG Investors LLC v Egypt, Decision on Liability and Heads of Loss, ICSID Case No. ARB/12/11 (21 February 2017) [286-7, 289-90].

[221] Richard Lillich and John Paxman, 'State Responsibility for Injuries to Aliens Occasioned by Terrorist Activities' (1977) 26(2) Am. U. L. Rev. 217, 241 (particularly referring to the 'duty to prevent injuries to aliens' caused by 'terrorist activities'; the authors, however, also consider likelihood of the injury as an element of the assessment of due diligence).

[222] *Case Concerning United States Diplomatic and Consular Staff in Tehran (United States of America v Iran)* [1980] ICJ Rep. 3, 32-3 [68].

13.4.3   Certainty as to the Legitimacy of the Investor's Rights and Interests

The host state cannot be expected to take positive measures of protection if, at moment protection is sought, there is no reasonable certainty as to the legitimacy of the investor's interests. This is usually the case where the claim refers to contentious or otherwise uncertain rights. In the absence of a genuine property title or a clear right, authorities could be justified in their decision not to prevent third parties from interfering with the enjoyment of property or not to undertake specific measures of protection. An indicative example appears in the award rendered in *Marion Unglaube v Costa Rica* (2012). In that case, the investors alleged that the host state had failed to protect its interests in an urbanization project in Playa Grande.[223] The arbitral tribunal observed that there was uncertainty as to the existence of 'specific development rights' on behalf of the claimants and consistently dismissed the FPS claim.[224] In this vein, the arbitrators explained:

> [T]he Tribunal finds that Claimants' general indictment regarding the alleged failure to provide full protection and security [. . .] is grounded principally on Claimants' insistence that their interpretation of the 1992 Agreement and, *inter alia* the 1995 National Park Law is the correct one. If Claimants had succeeded in establishing by appropriate evidence that they possessed certain specific development rights [. . .] then failure of Respondent to accord protection to those rights might have constituted a valid claim based on failure to provide full protection and security under Article 4(1) of the Treaty [FPS]. But [. . .] this Tribunal finds that the alleged rights and obligations regarding Claimants' remaining properties have not been proven in this proceeding.[225]

A similar situation arises in cases involving non-performance of commercial contracts. International law does not require public authorities to step into the arena of a commercial relationship and protect the economic interests of foreign citizens against other contractors. In these cases, authorities could and, in most cases, should wait until extant disputes are settled. The host state's obligation is only to provide adequate means of redress, and to properly execute any decision duly rendered in favor of the foreign investor. These principles found clear expression in *Ronald Lauder v Czech Republic* (2001) where, in its assessment of an FPS claim, the tribunal stated:

> The investment treaty created no duty of due diligence on the part of the Czech Republic to intervene in the dispute between the two companies over the nature of their legal relationships. *The Respondent's only duty under the Treaty was to keep its judicial system available*

---

[223] For a detailed account of the facts see: Marion Unglaube and Reinhard Unglaube *v* Costa Rica, Award, ICSID Cases No. ARB/01/1 and ARB/09/20 (16 May 2012) [37] *et seq.*

[224] Marion Unglaube and Reinhard Unglaube *v* Costa Rica, Award, ICSID Cases No. ARB/01/1 and ARB/09/20 (16 May 2012) [287].

[225] Marion Unglaube and Reinhard Unglaube *v* Costa Rica, Award, ICSID Cases No. ARB/01/1 and ARB/09/20 (16 May 2012) [287].

for the Claimant and any entities he controls to bring their claims, and for such claims to be properly examined and decided in accordance with domestic and international law.[226]

Another example would be the award rendered some years later in *Parkerings v Lithuania* (2007). The investor alleged that Lithuania's failure to intervene in a contractual relationship with the City of Vilnius amounted to a breach of FPS.[227] In this connection, the arbitrators stated:

> The Arbitral Tribunal considers that *the investment Treaty created no duty of due diligence on the part of the Respondent to intervene in the dispute between the Claimant and the City of Vilnius over the nature of their legal relationships.* The Respondent's duty under the Treaty was, first, to keep its judicial system available for the Claimant to bring its contractual claims and, second, that the claims would be properly examined in accordance with domestic and international law by an impartial and fair court.[228]

In *Saint-Gobain Performance Europe v Venezuela* (2016), the dispute was related to a contract for the supply of bauxite concluded with CVC Bauxilum, a state-owned Venezuelan company.[229] In 2008, CVG Bauxilum increased the price of bauxite, causing significant negative economic impact on the investor's interests.[230] The investor unsuccessfully requested the Venezuelan Ministry of Basic Industries and Mining to intervene before the company.[231] In the arbitral proceedings, the investor alleged that, by failing to protect its interests before CVG Bauxilum, the Ministry had incurred in a breach of the FPS standard.[232] The host state argued that this situation 'does not even come close to triggering a State's duty of due diligence'.[233] The respondent further observed that 'Claimant's position would render the dispute resolution clause in the Bauxite Contract pointless'.[234] The Tribunal decided in favor of Venezuela and dismissed the FPS claim:

---

[226]Emphasis added. Ronald Lauder *v* Czech Republic (UNCITRAL), Final Award (3 September 2001) [314].

[227]Parkerings-Compagniet AS *v* Lithuania, Award, ICSID Case No. ARB/05/8 (11 September 2007) [359].

[228]Emphasis added. Parkerings-Compagniet AS *v* Lithuania, Award, ICSID Case No. ARB/05/8 (11 September 2007) [359-60].

[229]Saint-Gobain Performance Plastics Europe *v* Venezuela, Decision on Liability and the Principles of Quantum, ICSID Case No. ARB/12/13 (30 December 2016) [152].

[230]Saint-Gobain Performance Plastics Europe *v* Venezuela, Decision on Liability and the Principles of Quantum, ICSID Case No. ARB/12/13 (30 December 2016) [173 *et seq.*].

[231]Saint-Gobain Performance Plastics Europe *v* Venezuela, Decision on Liability and the Principles of Quantum, ICSID Case No. ARB/12/13 (30 December 2016) [554].

[232]Saint-Gobain Performance Plastics Europe *v* Venezuela, Decision on Liability and the Principles of Quantum, ICSID Case No. ARB/12/13 (30 December 2016) [554-6].

[233]Saint-Gobain Performance Plastics Europe *v* Venezuela, Decision on Liability and the Principles of Quantum, ICSID Case No. ARB/12/13 (30 December 2016) [557] (quoting respondent's counter-memorial).

[234]Saint-Gobain Performance Plastics Europe *v* Venezuela, Decision on Liability and the Principles of Quantum, ICSID Case No. ARB/12/13 (30 December 2016) [558].

Respondent did not have an obligation to intervene in relation to the bauxite price increase and thus has not breached its obligation to accord Claimant's investment full protection and security in the manner invoked by Claimant.[235]

These statements might appear to be inconsistent with the award rendered in *Nykomb Synergetics Technology Holding AB v Latvia* (2003). In that case, the arbitrators considered a claim involving non-performance of a contract concluded between SIA Windau, a local subsidiary of a Swedish corporate investor (*Nykomb*), and Latvenergo, a Latvian state-owned company.[236] The *Nykomb* tribunal held:

> The central government of Latvia was also fully aware of Latvenergo's refusal to pay [...] There is no evidence of the government taking any further steps to protect Windau's rights under the contract [...] It must therefore be concluded that the breach of Windau's contractual rights was allowed to continue, and in that sense was caused, by the government's failure to act in order to correct the situation.[237]

In the *Saint-Gobain* case, the investor invoked the *Nykomb* decision in support of the argument that FPS entails an obligation to prevent contractual non-performance.[238] This use of the decision is misguided. A close look into the *Nykomb* award reveals that these assertions did not refer to the FPS standard.[239] Moreover, while it is true that *Nykomb* raised an FPS claim,[240] the tribunal did not declare a breach of the FPS standard.[241] The arbitrators merely established that the investor 'has been subject to a discriminatory measure in violation of [ECT] Article 10(1)'.[242] Having reached this conclusion, the *Nykomb* tribunal saw no need to decide on other claims, including the FPS claim.[243]

Generally speaking, the prevention obligation, albeit theoretically applicable, will be of little practical significance in cases involving contentious rights.[244] It cannot be

---

[235] Saint-Gobain Performance Plastics Europe *v* Venezuela, Decision on Liability and the Principles of Quantum, ICSID Case No. ARB/12/13 (30 December 2016) [560].

[236] Nykomb Synergetics Technology Holding AB *v* Latvia (SCC), Arbitral Award (16 December 2003) 1.

[237] Nykomb Synergetics Technology Holding AB *v* Latvia (SCC), Arbitral Award (16 December 2003) 30.

[238] Saint-Gobain Performance Plastics Europe *v* Venezuela, Decision on Liability and the Principles of Quantum, ICSID Case No. ARB/12/13 (30 December 2016) [555].

[239] Nykomb Synergetics Technology Holding AB *v* Latvia (SCC), Arbitral Award (16 December 2003) 29-31.

[240] Nykomb Synergetics Technology Holding AB *v* Latvia (SCC), Arbitral Award (16 December 2003) 32.

[241] Nykomb Synergetics Technology Holding AB *v* Latvia (SCC), Arbitral Award (16 December 2003) 34.

[242] Nykomb Synergetics Technology Holding AB *v* Latvia (SCC), Arbitral Award (16 December 2003) 34.

[243] Nykomb Synergetics Technology Holding AB *v* Latvia (SCC), Arbitral Award (16 December 2003) 34.

[244] Cf. also Tulip Real Estate Investment and Development Netherlands B.V. *v* Turkey, Award, ICSID Case No. ARB/11/28 (10 March 2014) [432] (rejecting an FPS claim concerning the invasion of physical premises, and noting that the alleged invader 'came into the site in the belief

reasonably expected that local authorities take preventive measures of protection until competent adjudicators have determined the existence and scope of the rights for which protection is requested (typically property or contractual rights). To be sure, local law could provide for the protection of contentious rights before a dispute has been definitively settled (e.g. through precautionary measures). It must be acknowledged, however, that domestic authorities enjoy broad discretion in the appreciation of the facts supporting a request for interim protection. Except in cases of discrimination, arbitrariness or similar situations, the availability and extent of interim protection should remain a matter of municipal law, and not of international law.

13.4.4   Seriousness of the Situation of Risk

Local authorities cannot be expected to react against every situation of risk affecting the interests of foreign nationals. Neither can they be expected to react in the same manner against every threat. The threat of a terrorist attack is not comparable to the risk of ordinary burglary. In the end, everything is a question of degree. In his 1955 Hague Lecture, Alwyn Freeman recalled in this connection Judge Benjamin Cardozo's idea that, in cases of negligence, 'the risk reasonably to be perceived defines the duty to be obeyed'.[245] According to Freeman, a similar reasoning should apply to the customary protection obligation:

> [I]n international responsibility, the degree of danger measures the nature and amount of the diligence a Government must take to prevent injurious acts to another Government or its citizens.[246]

There is merit to this idea. The diligence required from local authorities should be proportionate to the seriousness of the situation of risk or, using Freeman's terminology, the 'degree of danger' they perceived at the time positive measures of protection could have been adopted. The seriousness of the situation of risk depends on both the likelihood of a harmful event and the significance of its potential effects. As to the first point, there can be no doubt that the higher probability of the harmful

---

that [. . .] it could exercise its contractual rights to repossess the site in circumstances where it was the owner of the land').

[245] *Helen Palsgraf v The Long Island Railroad Co.* (1928) 248 NY 339. See also: Alwyn Freeman, 'Responsibility of States for Unlawful Acts of their Armed Forces' (1955) 88(3) RCADI 263, 278. For another author relying on Cardozo's formulation in the context of international due diligence obligations see: Dinah Shelton, 'Private Violence, Public Wrongs, and the Responsibility of States' (1989) 13(1) Fordham Int'l L.J. 1, 23; Dinah Shelton, *Regional Protection of Human Rights* (Volume 1: Oxford University Press 2010) 358. See also: Lidsey Cameron and Vincent Chetail, *Privatizing War. Private Military and Security Companies under Public International Law* (Cambridge University Press, Cambridge 2013) 227 (quoting Freeman).

[246] Alwyn Freeman, 'Responsibility of States for Unlawful Acts of their Armed Forces' (1955) 88 (3) RCADI 263, 278.

event, the higher the degree of diligence that can be expected from the state. As expressed by Riccardo Pissillo-Mazzeschi, the assessment of due diligence should consider 'the degree of predictability of the harm'.[247] This premise has found fertile ground not only in the context of FPS,[248] but also in connection with other international due diligence obligations.[249]

The second point is equally important for the assessment of FPS claims. The evaluation of the host state's conduct must take into account the degree of potential harm, that is to say, the impact that the potential injury would have on the protected interests. Arbitral tribunals have rejected FPS claims in which the alleged injury did not have a 'sufficiently severe' character. For example, in *SAUR v Argentina* (2012), competent authorities had ordered the 'administrative intervention' of Obras Sanitarias de Mendoza S.A. [OMS], a local corporation providing water supply services in the Province of Mendoza.[250] A French investor indirectly held substantive participation in the company.[251] The investor claimed that, in the 'brutal' application of the measure, police officers had prohibited internal communications between its employees and had furthermore 'confiscated' some of their personal belongings.[252] The arbitral tribunal noted that the claimant failed to prove these allegations.[253] Most importantly, it observed that, even if evidence had been submitted, the effects of acts in question were not 'sufficiently serious' as to constitute a breach of the FPS standard:

> Ces allégations n'ont pas été prouvées mais, même si elles l'avaient été, elles ne revêtiraient en aucun cas la gravité suffisante pour constituer une violation des garanties ayant la nature de droit international énoncées dans l'APRI.[254]

---

[247]Riccardo Pisillo-Mazzeschi, 'The Due Diligence Rule and the Nature of the International Responsibility of States' in René Provost (ed), *State Responsibility in International Law* (Ashgate Publishing Co., Burlington VT 2002) 97, 132.

[248]See, for example: Finnur Magnússon, *Full Protection and Security in International Law* (University of Vienna, Vienna 2012) 170.

[249]See, for example: Joanna Kulesza, *Due Diligence in International Law* (Brill, Leiden 2016) 259 (particularly referring to the obligation to prevent transboundary harm).

[250]SAUR International S.A. *v* Argentina, Décision sur la compétence et sur la responsabilité, ICSID Case No. ARB/04/4 (6 June 2012) [26 and 174 *et seq.*].

[251]SAUR International S.A. *v* Argentina, Décision sur la compétence et sur la responsabilité, ICSID Case No. ARB/04/4 (6 June 2012) [25-7].

[252]SAUR International S.A. *v* Argentina, Décision sur la compétence et sur la responsabilité, ICSID Case No. ARB/04/4 (6 June 2012) [467, 508 and 511].

[253]SAUR International S.A. *v* Argentina, Décision sur la compétence et sur la responsabilité, ICSID Case No. ARB/04/4 (6 June 2012) [511].

[254]SAUR International S.A. *v* Argentina, Décision sur la compétence et sur la responsabilité, ICSID Case No. ARB/04/4 (6 June 2012) [511] (particularly referring to the prohibition of internal communications and the confiscation of personal belongings).

The tribunal did not take any specific position as to the scope of the FPS standard and, particularly, its application to public violence.[255] Nonetheless, the statement quoted above indicates that, in order for a failure to prevent an injury to constitute a violation of FPS, the impairment of the investor's interests must have a fairly severe character.[256]

13.4.5   Conduct of the Investor

The investor's conduct is perhaps one of the less obvious, albeit most significant, factual circumstances to be considered in the assessment of the host state's due diligence. Particular weight should be given to evidence indicating that the investor assumed a risk or was reckless about a threat. The record could show that, at the time the investment was made, the investor had knowledge of the existence of some specific risk and was additionally aware of the host state's limited ability to undertake proper preventive or punitive action. Under such circumstances, if the risk materializes, it should be the investor who bears the consequences of the harmful event. Investors could be keen to make risky decisions in pursuit of higher returns.[257] But, as a rule, they cannot expect states to assume the costs of their own gambles.

This idea has some tradition in international affairs. A good historical example may be found in a speech delivered by Ludwig von Bar at the *Reichtag* session of March 16th, 1893. In reference to the FPS clause of the FCN Agreement negotiated between the German Empire and Colombia, Von Bar highlighted that 'those who settle in a country in which there is reason to fear unrests could be said to take such risk, which is also borne by the citizens of that state'.[258] To be certain, Von Bar was well acquainted with international law. He was not only a German politician, but also a law Professor and a Member of the *Institut de Droit International*.[259]

Contemporary arbitral decisions have echoed this risk-assumption idea. An example would be the award rendered in *LESI & ASTALDI v Algeria*. In its analysis of an alleged violation of the FPS standard, the tribunal took into account the fact that the investors were well aware of the 'general state of insecurity' (*état*

---

[255]SAUR International S.A. *v* Argentina, Décision sur la compétence et sur la responsabilité, ICSID Case No. ARB/04/4 (6 June 2012) [501].

[256]SAUR International S.A. *v* Argentina, Décision sur la compétence et sur la responsabilité, ICSID Case No. ARB/04/4 (6 June 2012) [511].

[257]See generally: Sergey Ripinsky and Kevin Williams, *Damages in International Investment Law* (British Institute of International and Comparative Law, London 2008) 326 and 350.

[258]Author's translation. The original German text reads: "Wer in einem Lande sich niederläßt, in dem Unruhen zu befürchten sind, nimmt eben das Risiko auf sich, das auch die Angehörigen des Landes selbst tragen." Reichstag, 'Protokoll – 68. Sitzung' (16 March 1893) *Stenographische Berichte über die Verhandlungen des Reichtags, VIII. Legislaturperiode, II. Session 1892/3* (Volume 3: Verlag der Norddeutschen Buchdruckerei, Berlin 1893) 1671, 1672.

[259]'In Memoriam: Ludwig von Bar' (1914) 8(2) AJIL 346, 346-7.

d'insécurité générale) that existed in Algeria at the time when the investment was made.[260] Similarly, in *Pantechniki v Albania*, Sole Arbitrator Jan Paulsson gave weight to the testimony of a Project Manager who 'depicted in striking terms an environment of desolation and lawlessness which she and her team encountered upon arrival'.[261] This circumstance was fatal to the investor's FPS claim. In words of the Sole Arbitrator, '[t]he Claimant cannot say today that it felt entitled to rely on a high standard of police protection'.[262]

Another example would be the ICC Award rendered in the case *East Mediterranean Gas Co. S.A.E. v Egyptian General Petroleum Corp., Egyptian Natural Gas Holding Co. and Israel Electric Corp.* (2015).[263] The case concerned a contractual dispute pertaining to the construction of a pipeline in Egypt.[264] In its Final Award, the ICC tribunal observed:

> At the beginning of the XXI century, when the construction of the Pipeline was undertaken, EGAS and GASCO (the Pipeline operator) must have been aware that a pipe crossing a historically conflictive zone, which was (at least partially) intended for the supply of gas to Israel, was open to attack. The awareness of some risk is evidenced by the fact that EGAS decided to adopt at least certain protective measures.[265]

---

[260]LESI S.p.A. and ASTALDI S.p.A. *v* Algeria, Sentence, ICSID Case No. ARB/05/3 (12 November 2008) [154].

[261]Pantechniki S.A. Contractors & Engineers *v* Albania, Award, ICSID Case No. ARB/07/21 (30 July 2009) [82].

[262]Pantechniki S.A. Contractors & Engineers *v* Albania, Award, ICSID Case No. ARB/07/21 (30 July 2009) [82]. For another Albanian case in which the tribunal took into consideration that, at the time of making its investment, the investor was aware of the situation of the host country see: Mamidoil Jetoil Greek Petroleum Products Societe S.A. *v* Albania, Award, ICSID Case No. ARB/11/24 (30 March 2015) [822] (emphasizing that 'Claimant decided to make its investment under these conditions of insecurity').

[263]See: East Mediterranean Gas Co. S.A.E. *v* Egyptian General Petroleum Corp., Egyptian Natural Gas Holding Co. and Israel Electric Corp., Final Award, ICC Case No. 18215/GZ/MHM (4 December 2015). The award was issued in one of several parallel commercial and investment arbitrations referring to the same factual background, including the ICSID case *Ampal v Egypt* (2017). The ICC award is not public. The present work relies on lengthy excerpts from the ICC award reproduced in the *Decision on Liability and Heads of Loss* issued in *Ampal v Egypt* (2017). For an overview of the commercial arbitrations see: Ampal-American Israel Corp., Egi-Fund (08-10) Investors LLC, Egi-Series Investments LLC and BSS-EMG Investors LLC *v* Egypt, Decision on Jurisdiction, ICSID Case No. ARB/12/11 (1 February 2016) [10 *et seq.*]; Ampal-American Israel Corp., Egi-Fund (08-10) Investors LLC, Egi-Series Investments LLC and BSS-EMG Investors LLC *v* Egypt, Decision on Liability and Heads of Loss, ICSID Case No. ARB/12/11 (21 February 2017) [8-10 and 15].

[264]See n. 263 above.

[265]*East Mediterranean Gas Co. S.A.E. v Egyptian General Petroleum Corp., Egyptian Natural Gas Holding Co. and Israel Electric Corp.*, Final Award, ICC Case No. 18215/GZ/MHM (4 December 2015) [760] (reproduced at p. 62 of the *Ampal* decision; see n. 263 above).

In *Isolux v Spain* (2016) the investor alleged that Spain's regulatory changes in the solar energy sector contravened the FPS clause of the ECT.[266] The arbitral tribunal disagreed with the investor's broad understanding of the FPS standard.[267] In addition, the arbitrators noted that *Isolux Corsán S.A.*, a parent company of the investor, had pursued a lawsuit in Spain *before* the investment was made.[268] In a declaration submitted to the Spanish Supreme Court of Justice, *Isolux Corsán S.A.* had sharply criticized Spain's constant legislative reforms.[269] In the declaration, the company went on to state that '[those legislative changes] have turned Spain into a country without legal security for investors, which provokes our international discredit'.[270] The arbitral tribunal considered this declaration to be of fundamental importance for the assessment of the FPS claim:

> A party who decides to invest in a country which, according to [that party], does not provide legal security, cannot then complain that it has not been given such [legal] security.[271]

There are also cases in which it is impossible to establish that the investor had actual knowledge about a risk at the time of making the investment. In such situations, the question arises as to whether the investor should have been aware of it. Due diligence is not a one-way street. Arbitral tribunals have recognized that 'prudent investment practice requires that any investor exercise due diligence before committing funds to any particular investment proposal'.[272] This rationale has particular weight when it comes to an FPS claim. For instance, in *Plama v Bulgaria* (2008), the investor alleged that a reform to Bulgarian environmental law entailed a breach of both the 'fair and equitable' standard and the 'most constant

---

[266]For a detailed account of the facts see: Isolux Netherlands B.V. *v* Spain, Laudo, SCC Case No. V 2013/153 (17 July 2016) [84 *et seq.*].

[267]Isolux Netherlands B.V. *v* Spain, Laudo, SCC Case No. V 2013/153 (17 July 2016) [817].

[268]Isolux Netherlands B.V. *v* Spain, Laudo, SCC Case No. V 2013/153 (17 July 2016) [818].

[269]Isolux Netherlands B.V. *v* Spain, Laudo, SCC Case No. V 2013/153 (17 July 2016) [818].

[270]Author's translation. The original Spanish text reads: "[los cambios legislativos] convierten a España en un país carente de seguridad jurídica para los inversores lo que provoca nuestro descredito internacional." Isolux Netherlands B.V. *v* Spain, Laudo, SCC Case No. V 2013/153 (17 July 2016) [818] (quoting the lawsuit filed by Isolux Corsán S.A. before the Spanish Supreme Court of Justice).

[271]Author's translation. The original Spanish text reads: "Una parte que decide invertir en un país que, según ella, carece de seguridad jurídica, no puede después quejarse que tal seguridad no le fue asegurada." Isolux Netherlands B.V. *v* Spain, Laudo, SCC Case No. V 2013/153 (17 July 2016) [818].

[272]Alasdair Ross Anderson et al. *v* Costa Rica, Award, ICSID Case No. ARB(AF)/07/3 (19 May 2010) [58] (considering the issue in connection with the requirement that foreign investors to diligently ensure that their activities fulfill local legislation; for the sake of accuracy, the tribunal was not addressing an FPS claim at this point).

protection and security' clause enshrined in the ECT.[273] In connection with this claim, the arbitrators stated:

> [The investor] was aware that Bulgarian law at the time [the investment was made] did *not* protect Nova Plama against liability for past pollution but failed to negotiate the contractual guarantees he believed necessary to avoid such risk. While Claimant criticizes Bulgaria for the inadequacy of its environmental law in this regard, Claimant was, of course, aware of, or should have been aware of, the state of Bulgarian law when it invested in Nova Plama [. . .] It is [. . .] unclear how Respondent's conduct in this context could amount to a violation of the obligation to provide constant protection and security. Even accepting the approach that this standard includes an obligation to provide legal security, the Tribunal has established that Claimant failed fully to appreciate the scope and specificities of Bulgarian legislation.[274]

In addition to a possible assumption of risk at the time the investment was made, adjudicators should consider whether the investor's subsequent conduct shows recklessness about risks potentially affecting its rights or interests. As argued by the respondent in *Garanti Koza v Turkmenistan* (2016), '[FPS] certainly does not indemnify investors for their own negligence, poor performance, misconduct or bad luck'.[275] Arbitral tribunals have been receptive to this idea.

In *Adel A Hamadi Al Tamini v Oman* (2015), an American investor alleged that the Sultanate of Oman had failed to protect his property from vandalism and, by so doing, had committed a breach of the FPS clause of the US-Oman FTA.[276] Al Tamini was able to produce evidence that 'expensive equipment' had been taken from a quarry site.[277] The circumstances of the taking were however unclear because the events occurred *after* the investor's personnel abandoned the place.[278] The only evidence of vandalism was a photograph showing that certain elements were no longer in the site, and the statement of a witness who had 'heard' that a looting took place.[279]

The tribunal considered that there was 'no credible evidence' showing 'that the Respondent was responsible for any loss or damage to any property at the Claimants

---

[273]Plama Consortium Ltd. *v* Bulgaria, Award, ICSID Case No. ARB/03/24 (27 August 2008) [194]. It should be noted that, in the *Plama* arbitration, the investor raised various FPS claims, each of which was related to a different factual aspect of the case.

[274]Plama Consortium Ltd. *v* Bulgaria, Award, ICSID Case No. ARB/03/24 (27 August 2008) [220, 222]. The arbitral tribunal followed a similar line of argument in respect of another FPS claim (at paras 270-1).

[275]Garanti Koza LLP *v* Turkmenistan, Award, ICSID Case No. ARB/11/20 (19 December 2016) [324]. In this case, the tribunal refrained from addressing these arguments, noting that the FPS claim was 'duplicative' of the 'other claimed breaches of the BIT' (at para 392).

[276]Adel A Hamadi Al Tamini *v* Oman, Award, ICSID Case No. ARB/11/33 (3 November 2015) [448].

[277]Adel A Hamadi Al Tamini *v* Oman, Award, ICSID Case No. ARB/11/33 (3 November 2015) [449].

[278]Adel A Hamadi Al Tamini *v* Oman, Award, ICSID Case No. ARB/11/33 (3 November 2015) [449].

[279]Adel A Hamadi Al Tamini *v* Oman, Award, ICSID Case No. ARB/11/33 (3 November 2015) [449].

quarry site, or otherwise failed to act reasonably to protect the Claimant's property'.[280] The arbitrators went on to observe that nothing indicated that the respondent state 'encouraged or fostered any looting or vandalism'.[281] Perhaps most importantly, the arbitrators gave great weight to the investor's lack of diligence in the protection of his own property:

> The scope of a State's full protection and security obligations under the minimum standard simply cannot extend to providing physical protection in perpetuity to an investment that has been expressly "abandoned" by its owner [...] To the extent that the Claimant was willing to abandon his property, he cannot equally assert that the Respondent failed to take steps to preserve it. The Tribunal also recalls the evidence that [...] OMCO [Oman Mining Company/state-owned] had repeatedly informed the Claimant that he was to remove all equipment and installations from the site within weeks, given that [...] the Claimant and his property remained at the site illegally.[282]

In *Gea Group Aktiengesellschaft v Ukraine* (2011), the investor claimed that a substantial amount of finished products had been stolen from its premises.[283] The claimant argued that, even if the theft were attributable to private wrongdoers, the authorities' omissions in the prevention of the event and the punishment of the culprits would entail a breach of the FPS standard.[284] Ukraine underscored that competent authorities were not aware of the situation.[285] Most importantly, no complaint had been filed with the local police.[286] This lack of diligence on the part of the investor was fatal to its FPS claim:

> In the Tribunal's view, no matter what legal standard the question is examined, the Claimant's contentions under this heading must fail. The Claimant's case on this issue entails a fundamental double standard. Over the course of its contractual relationship [...] GEA never considered it necessary to file a criminal complaint for the taking of its Products. Yet within the context of this arbitration, GEA now insists that Ukraine has breached its violations under the BIT for doing the very same.[287]

In *Tenaris v Venezuela* (2016), the investor alleged that local authorities had failed to protect its premises and personnel from several attacks by members of a

---

[280]Adel A Hamadi Al Tamini v Oman, Award, ICSID Case No. ARB/11/33 (3 November 2015) [451].

[281]Adel A Hamadi Al Tamini v Oman, Award, ICSID Case No. ARB/11/33 (3 November 2015) [451].

[282]Adel A Hamadi Al Tamini v Oman, Award, ICSID Case No. ARB/11/33 (3 November 2015) [450-1].

[283]Gea Group Aktiengesellschaft v Ukraine, Award, ICSID Case No. ARB/08/16 (31 March 2011) [47].

[284]Gea Group Aktiengesellschaft v Ukraine, Award, ICSID Case No. ARB/08/16 (31 March 2011) [243].

[285]Gea Group Aktiengesellschaft v Ukraine, Award, ICSID Case No. ARB/08/16 (31 March 2011) [244].

[286]Gea Group Aktiengesellschaft v Ukraine, Award, ICSID Case No. ARB/08/16 (31 March 2011) [244].

[287]Gea Group Aktiengesellschaft v Ukraine, Award, ICSID Case No. ARB/08/16 (31 March 2011) [246-7].

labor union.[288] Among other elements of analysis, the arbitrators took into account that, in the case at hand, 'none of alleged attacks on personnel in 2009 was reported to the National Guard'.[289] In *Peter Allard v Barbados* (2016), the investor considered that the host state's failure to properly enforce local environmental legislation constituted a breach of the FPS standard.[290] In their assessment of this FPS claim, the arbitrators gave weight to the fact that 'the Claimant appears not to have informed Barbados of the need for enforcement of the *Act* at any time before this arbitration'.[291]

In other cases, the record shows diligence on the part of the investor. Such diligence will usually help the investor's case. For example, in *Siag v Egypt* (2009), the tribunal underlined the fact that the investors had expressly and timely requested the protection of local authorities:

> Claimants have provided detailed submissions and evidence that, upon learning that Resolution No. 83 was about to be implemented and Claimants' investment seized, both Mr Siag and Dr Abou Zeid Fahmy made explicit requests of the Nuweibaa Police that Claimants' investment be protected [. . .] Egypt has not denied that the asserted requests for protection were made.[292]

Claimants in investment arbitral proceedings will seek to convince the arbitral tribunal of their own diligence in the protection of the investment. *Plama v Bulgaria* (2008) provides, once again, a good example. In that case, one of the multiple FPS claims submitted by the investor referred to the alleged failure by local police forces to 'adequately to protect' an oil refinery from 'worker riots'.[293] The investor underscored that '*[d]espite reporting these events to the Bulgarian Government*, Nova Plama received no police assistance to restore order'.[294] The arbitral tribunal took cognizance of these allegations, but found no evidence that could support a finding of liability.[295]

The conduct of the investor might also be relevant in connection with the obligation of redress. In *Marion Unglaube and Reinhard Unglaube v Costa Rica* (2012), the claimants alleged that several local judicial proceedings had caused

---

[288]Tenaris S.A. and Talta-Trading E Marketing Sociedade Unipessoal Lda. *v* Venezuela, Award, ICSID Case No. ARB/11/26 (29 January 2016) [426].

[289]Tenaris S.A. and Talta-Trading E Marketing Sociedade Unipessoal Lda. *v* Venezuela, Award, ICSID Case No. ARB/11/26 (29 January 2016) [446].

[290]Peter A. Allard *v* Barbados (UNCITRAL), Award (27 June 2016) [239 and 251]. It should be noted that this was one of multiple FPS claims that were raised in the case.

[291]Peter A. Allard *v* Barbados (UNCITRAL), Award (27 June 2016) [251].

[292]Waguih George Siag and Clorinda Vecchi *v* Egypt, Award, ICSID Case No. ARB/05/15 (1 June 2009) [446].

[293]Plama Consortium Ltd. *v* Bulgaria, Award, ICSID Case No. ARB/03/24 (27 August 2008) [236].

[294]Emphasis added. Plama Consortium Ltd. *v* Bulgaria, Award, ICSID Case No. ARB/03/24 (27 August 2008) [236].

[295]Plama Consortium Ltd. *v* Bulgaria, Award, ICSID Case No. ARB/03/24 (27 August 2008) [248-55].

significant delay to their investment project.[296] The respondent argued that the investors had themselves played a substantial part in the delay.[297] While the arbitrators considered the host state's contention to be unfounded,[298] Costa Rica's argument shows the impact that an investor's conduct in the context of local court proceedings could eventually have on a subsequent FPS claim.

13.4.6 Differences in the Protection Afforded to Different Groups of Persons

The FPS standard is nowadays generally considered as an element of the customary minimum standard of treatment.[299] As explained in Chap. 4, from a legal-historical perspective, the minimum standard is the opposite to the doctrine of equality.[300] This does not however mean that the level of protection enjoyed by the local population is immaterial for the assessment of diligence. The only implication of the minimum standard is that the host state cannot escape liability for lack of protection by merely providing evidence that foreigners were granted the same level of security as its own citizens.[301]

Arbitrators deciding on FPS claims should not ignore the existence of different degrees of protection for different groups of persons. On the one side of the spectrum, differential treatment could indicate that public authorities were both aware of a threat and capable to properly react against it. This will be the case where the state failed to protect a foreign investor, but managed to protect its own nationals or other groups of persons facing a similar situation. On the other side of the spectrum, the absence of differential treatment could reinforce the impression that the host state could not have reasonably reacted to the threat in a different manner.[302]

---

[296]Marion Unglaube and Reinhard Unglaube v Costa Rica, Award, ICSID Cases No. ARB/01/1 and ARB/09/20 (16 May 2012) [285].

[297]Marion Unglaube and Reinhard Unglaube v Costa Rica, Award, ICSID Cases No. ARB/01/1 and ARB/09/20 (16 May 2012) [288].

[298]Marion Unglaube and Reinhard Unglaube v Costa Rica, Award, ICSID Cases No. ARB/01/1 and ARB/09/20 (16 May 2012) [288] ("To be sure, the Tribunal wishes to make clear that it does not accept Respondent's argument that the delay and frustration, of which Claimants complain, was caused in its entirety by Claimants' own strenuous and repeated recourse to administrative and judicial challenges. But neither does it find persuasive evidence that Respondent has failed to provide Claimants or their investments with full protection and security").

[299]See Chap. 5.

[300]See Sects. 4.2 and 4.3.

[301]See Sect. 5.4.

[302]For a respondent state underscoring the absence of differential treatment in the context of an FPS claim see: Pantechniki S.A. Contractors & Engineers v Albania, Award, ICSID Case No. ARB/07/21 (30 July 2009) [74-5].

Surprisingly, arbitral tribunals have only rarely given weight to differential treatment in the context of FPS claims. A noteworthy exception would be the award rendered in *LESI & ASTALDI v Algeria* (2008). In that case, the Tribunal analyzed whether the protection granted to the foreign investor's working site was discriminatory in respect of the level of protection given to other construction sites in Algeria.[303] The fact that no evidence of discriminatory treatment had been submitted was one of the reasons leading to the dismissal of the FPS claim.[304] In this connection, the arbitrators pointed out that the security measures adopted by local authorities could not be depicted as arbitrary.[305] This reference to arbitrariness shows that the mere existence of different levels of protection does not necessarily imply discriminatory treatment. The threshold issue is always whether, in the specific circumstances of the case, differential treatment was justified.

13.4.7 Public Support to Private Wrongdoers

A few arbitral tribunals, while admitting that the FPS standard only imposes a diligence obligation, have required evidence of some form of participation of the host state's authorities in the acts which directly originated the injury. A remarkable passage of the award rendered in *Tecmed v Mexico* (2003) provides an example of this approach.[306] The case pertained to the social demonstrations against the operation of a landfill for industrial waste in Hermosillo.[307] In their assessment of the FPS claim, the arbitrators held:

> The Arbitral Tribunal considers that the Claimant has not furnished evidence to prove that the Mexican authorities, regardless of their level, have encouraged, fostered, or contributed their support to the people or groups that conducted the community and political movements against the Landfill, or that such authorities have participated in such movement. Also, there

---

[303]LESI S.p.A. and ASTALDI S.p.A. *v* Algeria, Sentence, ICSID Case No. ARB/05/3 (12 November 2008) [154].

[304]LESI S.p.A. and ASTALDI S.p.A. *v* Algeria, Sentence, ICSID Case No. ARB/05/3 (12 November 2008) [154].

[305]LESI S.p.A. and ASTALDI S.p.A. *v* Algeria, Sentence, ICSID Case No. ARB/05/3 (12 November 2008) [154] ("il n'a pas été prouvé par les Demanderesses que leur chantier bénéficiait d'un traitement discriminatoire par rapport aux autres chantiers en Algérie. Enfin, les décisions prises par l'Etat algérien en matière de sécurité ne sont pas arbitraires.").

[306]For an analysis of this award from the standpoint of complicity see: Helge Elisabeth Zeitler, 'The Guarantee of Full Protection and Security in Investment Treaties regarding Harm Caused by Private Parties' (2005) 3 SIAR 1, 8.

[307]Tecnicas Medioambientales TECMED S.A. *v* Mexico, Award, ICSID Case No. ARB(AF)/00/2 (29 May 2003) [35]. Section 13.3.2 also discusses the analysis of diligence conducted by the *Tecmed* tribunal.

is not sufficient evidence to attribute the activity or behavior of such people or groups to the Respondent pursuant to international law.[308]

The *Tecmed* tribunal focused on whether the acts of private individuals could be imputed to the host state on account of participation or encouragement. In contrast, the possible existence of an internationally wrongful omission which is *related to* but *autonomous from* those private acts does not seem to have played any significant role in the assessment of the FPS claim. This statement bears striking resemblance with the Vattelian theory of complicity (as opposed to the separate delict theory).[309] The main issue in *Tecmed* was not the host state's *direct responsibility* for its own omissions in the protection of aliens, but a possible *indirect responsibility* for the private acts which originally affected the enjoyment of the claimant's investment.[310]

In *Rumeli Telekom v Kazakhstan* (2008) the arbitral tribunal considered that the FPS standard could be applicable in respect of the denial of access to information and premises of a locally incorporated company in which the investor held substantial participation.[311] The arbitrators dismissed the claim on the ground that the individuals blamable for the acts in question 'were not acting upon instructions of the State authorities'.[312]

Chapter 12 has presented a detailed argument against the Vattelian theory of complicity.[313] In this vein, it argued that participation is not a condition necessary for a finding of liability under the customary protection obligation.[314] This conclusion finds support in arbitral practice. In contrast to *Tecmed*, other arbitral tribunals have recognized that a breach of FPS does not require proof of complicity. In *Wena Hotels v Egypt* (2000) the arbitrators found that Egypt had violated the FPS standard on the following basis:

> *Even if Egypt did not instigate or participate in the seizure of the two hotels,* as Wena claims, there is sufficient evidence to find tat (sic) Egypt was aware of EHC's [i.e., the state-owned Egyptian Hotel Company's] intentions and took no actions to prevent the seizures or to immediately restore Wena's control over the hotels[315]

---

[308]Tecnicas Medioambientales TECMED S.A. *v* Mexico, Award, ICSID Case No. ARB(AF)/00/2 (29 May 2003) [176]. For a similar approach see: Eureko B.V. *v* Poland (*Ad Hoc* Arbitration), Partial Award (19 August 2005) [237]. Cf. also: Gea Group Aktiengesellschaft *v* Ukraine, Award, ICSID Case No. ARB/08/16 (31 March 2011) [258 and 262].

[309]Cf. Sects. 12.4.1 and 12.4.3.

[310]Cf. also Sect. 12.4.1 (on the notion of 'indirect responsibility').

[311]Rumeli Telekom A.S. and Telsim Mobil Telekomunikasyon Hizmetleri A.S. *v* Kazakhstan, Award, ICSID Case No. ARB/05/16 (29 July 2008) [1-12].

[312]Rumeli Telekom A.S. and Telsim Mobil Telekomunikasyon Hizmetleri A.S. *v* Kazakhstan, Award, ICSID Case No. ARB/05/16 (29 July 2008) [669-70].

[313]See Sect. 12.4.1 *et seq.*

[314]See Sect. 12.4.3.

[315]Emphasis added. Wena Hotels Ltd. *v* Egypt, Award, ICSID Case No. ARB/98/4 (8 December 2000) [85] (see also para 84 in this connection).

While participation is certainly not a requirement for a finding of liability under the FPS standard, evidence indicating that public authorities gave direct or indirect support to a private wrongdoer bears significant weight in the assessment of the host state's diligence.[316] Investors advancing FPS claims might therefore be prone to submit arguments about participation of state agents. For example, in *Convial Callao v Peru* (2013) the investors alleged that the state had 'instigated and facilitated' violent opposition to a toll.[317] This claim was however rejected for lack of evidence.[318]

In 1928, Clyde Eagleton observed that '[t]he participation of authorities of the state is conclusive proof of the failure of the state to use the means at its disposal for preventing the injury'.[319] Some contemporary investment arbitral decisions are reminiscent of Eagleton's line of argument. In *OAO Tatneft v Ukraine* (2014), the investor alleged that it had been the victim of a 'corporate raid' orchestrated by a Ukrainian businessman who had 'systematically' taken over its rights over the locally-incorporated company which operated the Kremenchug refinery in central Ukraine.[320] The investor's loss of managerial control had indeed been the result of a series of events, including multiple judicial decisions, the forceful occupation of the refinery and the placing of security forces ascribed to the Ministry of Interior, which—according to the investor—effectively secured the position of the 'corporate raiders'.[321] The investor described this 'raider action' as 'the combination of a criminal seizure of property by an organized group and the involvement of the State through the issuance of unlawful court decisions, the assistance of enforcement officers of the State and the support of the State actors in the illegal acts'.[322]

The presence of armed officers of the Ministry of Interior at the refinery was a key issue in the assessment of the FPS claim.[323] The investor argued that the host state

---

[316]Section 8.3.2.4 discusses the distinction between responsibility for the actions of host state agents supporting private wrongdoers, and omissions in the prevention and redress of private injuries.

[317]Convial Callao S.A. and CCI – Compañía de Concesiones de Infraestructura S.A. v Peru, Laudo Final, ICSID Case No. ARB/10/2 (21 May 2013) [648].

[318]Convial Callao S.A. and CCI – Compañía de Concesiones de Infraestructura S.A. v Peru, Laudo Final, ICSID Case No. ARB/10/2 (21 May 2013) [649-50].

[319]Clyde Eagleton, *The Responsibility of States in International Law* (Klaus Reprint, New York 1970) 92 [first edition: 1928]. Cf. also: Lucas Bastin, *State Responsibility for Omissions: Establishing a Breach of the Full Protection and Security Obligation by Omissions* (Oxford University, Oxford 2016) [D.Phil. Thesis] 137 (commenting on the *Eureko v Poland* case and noting that '[i]f a State authors or instigates conduct which causes damage, then that will constitute persuasive evidence that it has failed to act with due diligence').

[320]For a detailed account of the facts of the case see: OAO Tatneft v Ukraine (UNCITRAL), Award (29 July 2014) [55 *et seq.*]. On the 'corporate raid' see particularly [69].

[321]OAO Tatneft v Ukraine (UNCITRAL), Award (29 July 2014) [63 *et seq.*]. The presence of the Ministry of Interior's troops is described in detail at [123-5].

[322]OAO Tatneft v Ukraine (UNCITRAL), Award (29 July 2014) [69]. See also [99].

[323]OAO Tatneft v Ukraine (UNCITRAL), Award (29 July 2014) [416-7, 421-2 and 428].

was an accomplice of the 'corporate raiders'.[324] In response, the state argued that 'military forces and other military forces – such as the Ministry of Interior troops – are authorized to carry out commercial activities in Ukraine, which include the provision of security services'.[325] The arbitral tribunal did not engage in a deep analysis of the charge of complicity as such.[326] Nonetheless, it found that the participation of state agents evidenced an internationally wrongful want of protection:

> The Tribunal has discussed in connection with the facts of this case the events surrounding the seizure of the Kremenchug refinery and the change in the company's management that followed, which is the basis for the Claimant's assertions about the breach by the Respondent of full protection and security. The participation of Ukrainian authorities in those events [...] [has] also been discussed [...] The anomalies that the Tribunal has noted in this respect, in spite of the evidence being in some respects incomplete, are sufficient to conclude that indeed the Respondent failed to provide the appropriate police protection to the officials at the refinery at the time. Particularly telling are the subsequent participation of the Ministry of the Interior's troops in such events and the scant credibility of the argument that they intervened in the capacity of private security at the service of the company. The forceful entry into the premises of the refinery and the retention of certain officials in their offices, just like the carrying of weapons, are all pointing in the direction of a breach of full protection and security in the realm of police protection and physical security.[327]

An additional example appears in the award rendered in *Joseph Houben v Burundi* (2016). In that case, the arbitrators gave weight to the fact that local authorities had 'encouraged' illegal settlers to invade the foreign investor's property and, to some extent, 'participated' in their acts.[328] In this vein, they stated:

> Il est par conséquent établi que les autorités burundaises, qui étaient au courant des atteintes à l'investissement de M. Houben, ont non seulement omis de prendre les mesures minimales nécessaires pour protéger cet investissement, mais y ont également directement contribué [...] Pour les raisons qui précèdent, le Tribunal considère qu'en ne mettant pas en œuvre les diligences nécessaires pour protéger l'investissement de M. Houben contre les atteintes physiques commises par les usurpateurs, et en y participant, le Burundi a violé le standard de sécurité et protection constantes prévu à l'article 3 du TBI.[329]

This statement shows that the arbitrators gave considerable importance to the participation of public authorities in the harmful events. Still, responsibility was established on account of a lack of diligence *directly* attributable to the host state, and not on account of an *indirect* responsibility for the acts of private individuals. This seems consistent with the fact that the award expressly recognized that the core

---

[324]OAO Tatneft *v* Ukraine (UNCITRAL), Award (29 July 2014) [124].

[325]OAO Tatneft *v* Ukraine (UNCITRAL), Award (29 July 2014) [125].

[326]OAO Tatneft *v* Ukraine (UNCITRAL), Award (29 July 2014) [428].

[327]OAO Tatneft *v* Ukraine (UNCITRAL), Award (29 July 2014) [428].

[328]Joseph Houben *v* Burundi, Sentence, ICSID Case No. ARB/13/7 (12 January 2016) [173 and 179].

[329]Joseph Houben *v* Burundi, Sentence, ICSID Case No. ARB/13/7 (12 January 2016) [175 and 179].

of FPS refers to protection against private harm.[330] Participation was thus taken as *evidence* of a want of diligence. The reasoning of the tribunal comes therefore strikingly close to the approach Eagleton suggested in the early twentieth century.

13.4.8   Balance Between Private Interests and the Public Interest

At the time measures of protection are adopted, decision-makers will usually have no certainty as to their efficacy and potential collateral effects. In some cases, the decision to protect a foreign investor could create new dangers for the local population or otherwise affect the public interest. Moreover, states have limited resources.[331] Thus, taking security measures against some particular risk often comes at the cost of leaving other potential threats or public needs unattended.

Host states cannot be expected to give priority to foreign citizens' private interests over the public good, or to endanger their own population or environment for the sole purpose of ensuring their safety. Competent authorities must balance the benefits that would be obtained from a specific course of conduct against the risks and costs the intended measures would entail. As a rule, the state will not have failed in its duty to exercise diligence in the protection of aliens if authorities have made a reasonable policy choice.[332]

The award rendered in *AES v Hungary* (2010) provides a representative example of this line of argument. In that case the investors alleged that an amendment to Hungary's Electricity Act and a series of Pricing Decrees had 'substantially devalued their investment'.[333] The claimants considered that these measures entailed a violation of the host state's duty under the ECT to grant investors 'the most constant protection and security'.[334] The arbitrators noted that the standard does not impose

---

[330]Joseph Houben *v* Burundi, Sentence, ICSID Case No. ARB/13/7 (12 January 2016) [157].

[331]State entities may certainly enter into contractual obligations to provide special protection to an investment, but the degree of protection required under such obligations does not necessarily coincide with that required under the FPS standard. Cf. Convial Callao S.A. and CCI – Compañía de Concesiones de Infraestructura S.A. *v* Peru, Laudo Final, ICSID Case No. ARB/10/2 (21 May 2013) [659] (distinguishing between the degree of protection required under a concession agreement and the protection required under the FPS standard).

[332]On the possible conflict between different rights or interests; cf. also: Elisabeth Zeitler, 'The Guarantee of Full Protection and Security in Investment Treaties Regarding Harm Caused by Private Actors' (2005) 3 SIAR 1, 24-5.

[333]AES Summit Generation Ltd. and AES-Tisza Erömü Kft. *v* Hungary, Award, ICSID Case No. ARB/07/22 (23 September 2010) [13.1.2].

[334]AES Summit Generation Ltd. and AES-Tisza Erömü Kft. *v* Hungary, Award, ICSID Case No. ARB/07/22 (23 September 2010) [13.3.2].

'strict liability'.[335] In this vein, they explained that FPS 'does not protect against a state's right (as was the case here) to legislate or regulate in a manner which may negatively affect a claimant's investment, provided that the state acts *reasonably* in the circumstances and with a view to achieving objectively *reasonable* public policy goals'.[336]

In *Peter Allard v Barbados* (2016) the investor alleged that Barbados failed to regularly and adequately operate a sluice gate, which regulated the entry of salt water from the ocean into his (private) nature reserve.[337] He also argued that the state had failed to adopt specific measures that would have decreased the 'run-off of contaminants into the Sanctuary'.[338] The tribunal gave consideration to the complexity of the situation faced by Barbados and concluded that, in the circumstances of the case, local authorities had exercised the diligence required under the FPS standard:

> The [FPS] obligation is limited to reasonable action, and a host State is not required to take any specific steps that an investor asks of it [. . .] Here, it is established that Barbadian officials implemented procedures to prevent environmental damage to the Sanctuary both on their own initiative and in response to the Claimant's complaints [. . .] the issues concerning repair and operation of the Sluice Gate and the passing of water between the Sanctuary and the sea are not the simple matters the Claimant suggests they are. There is a wider group of stakeholders [. . .] The Sluice Gate's operation would affect the Sanctuary, the surrounding lands, including government lands, as well as the public beach [. . .] It was therefore no easy issue to establish the hydrology of the whole area and to administer it in the interests of all the stakeholders. Under these circumstances, Barbados' approach in addressing the Sluice Gate and general pollution issues at the Sanctuary as part of its governance of the entire area does not fall short of what is appropriate and sufficient for purposes of the duty of due diligence required by Article II(2)(b) of the BIT [full protection and security].[339]

An additional example would be the Partial Award rendered in *Saluka v Czech Republic* (2006). The Czech Securities Commission [CSC] had issued an injunction suspending trading of a major bank's shares.[340] This decision was followed by an amendment to the Czech Securities Act, which closed the possibility of pursuing a challenge against the injunction.[341] The investor claimed that these measures were in breach of the FPS clause of the Czech Republic-Netherlands BIT.[342] The tribunal

---

[335]AES Summit Generation Ltd. and AES-Tisza Erömü Kft. *v* Hungary, Award, ICSID Case No. ARB/07/22 (23 September 2010) [13.3.2].

[336]Emphasis added. AES Summit Generation Ltd. and AES-Tisza Erömü Kft. v Hungary, Award, ICSID Case No. ARB/07/22 (23 September 2010) [13.3.2]. See also: Isolux Netherlands B.V. *v* Spain, Laudo, SCC Case No. V 2013/153 (17 July 2016) [817] (quoting this passage of the AES award).

[337]Peter A. Allard *v* Barbados (UNCITRAL), Award (27 June 2016) [34 and 233-4].

[338]Peter A. Allard *v* Barbados (UNCITRAL), Award (27 June 2016) [239].

[339]Peter A. Allard *v* Barbados (UNCITRAL), Award (27 June 2016) [244-5 and 247-9].

[340]Saluka Investments *v* Czech Republic (UNCITRAL), Partial Award (17 March 2006) [135 and 486].

[341]Saluka Investments *v* Czech Republic (UNCITRAL), Partial Award (17 March 2006) [488].

[342]Saluka Investments *v* Czech Republic (UNCITRAL), Partial Award (17 March 2006) [485-8].

did not enter into the intricate question of the applicability of the FPS standard to this factual setting.[343] Rather, it held:

> Even assuming that the suspension of trading of shares may be State conduct within the scope of the "full security and protection" clause, the Tribunal, without deciding that question, finds that this claim of the Claimant is without merit [. . .] *The reasoning behind the CSC's suspension decisions cannot be said to have been totally devoid of legitimate concerns relating to the securities market.* The suspensions of trading in IPB [i.e. the bank] shares were at least justifiable on regulatory grounds. Also, the elimination of shareholders' right of appeal does not per se transcend the limits of a legislator's discretion. Shareholder's rights vary greatly in different jurisdictions. *The amendment of the Czech Securities Act cannot be said to be totally unreasonable and unjustifiable by some rational legal policy.*[344]

In other cases involving FPS claims, adjudicators recognized the host state's margin of discretion without making particular reference to the notion of due diligence. The case *Spyridon Roussalis v Romania* (2011) may serve as an example in this regard. Mr. Spyridon Roussalis, a Greek investor, alleged that the issuance of interdiction orders temporarily preventing him from returning to Greece or otherwise traveling abroad entailed a breach of the FET and FPS standards.[345] The arbitrators dismissed the claims.[346] In reaching this decision, they stated:

> Regarding the underlying policy permitting the issuance of the interdiction orders, the Tribunal notes that such policies are commonplace in many countries and promote the rational public policy of preventing the accused of fleeing the country in avoidance of criminal prosecution.[347]

The public interest could justify the absence or insufficiency of positive measures of protection. Still, inconsistencies in the adoption of measures aimed at the protection of such public interests could be fatal to the respondent's case, revealing a disguised violation of the FPS standard. A good example of this situation would be the case *Wena v Egypt* (2000). In *Wena*, the host state did not only fail to prevent an illegal seizure of two hotels which belonged to a foreign investor.[348] It additionally failed to timely adopt measures in order to return the investments to their rightful owner.[349] When the properties were finally restituted to the investor, the Ministry of Tourism revoked the operation license of one of the hotels.[350] Egypt argued that this

---

[343] Saluka Investments *v* Czech Republic (UNCITRAL), Partial Award (17 March 2006) [490].

[344] Emphasis added. Saluka Investments *v* Czech Republic (UNCITRAL), Partial Award (17 March 2006) [490]. See also the Tribunal's conclusion at para 505.

[345] Spyridon Roussalis *v* Romania, Award, ICSID Case No. ARB/06/1 (7 December 2011) [535 *et seq.*, 551 *et seq.* and 596].

[346] Spyridon Roussalis *v* Romania, Award, ICSID Case No. ARB/06/1 (7 December 2011) [610].

[347] Spyridon Roussalis *v* Romania, Award, ICSID Case No. ARB/06/1 (7 December 2011) [606].

[348] Wena Hotels Ltd. *v* Egypt, Award, ICSID Case No. ARB/98/4 (8 December 2000) [84-8].

[349] Wena Hotels Ltd. *v* Egypt, Award, ICSID Case No. ARB/98/4 (8 December 2000) [84 and 88-90].

[350] Wena Hotels Ltd. *v* Egypt, Award, ICSID Case No. ARB/98/4 (8 December 2000) [92].

measure was intended to ensure compliance with applicable fire safety regulations.[351] The arbitrators were not impressed by this argument:

> [J]ust two days before the Nile Hotel was returned to Wena, the Ministry of Tourism
> withdrew that hotel's operating license because of alleged fire safety violations. Although
> [. . .] these safety violations had pre-dated EHC's seizure of the hotel in April 1991, it is
> noteworthy that the Ministry of Tourism allowed EHC to operate the Nile Hotel from April
> 1991 through February 1992, despite these violations, and revoked the license only on
> February 23, 1992, just prior to restoring the hotel to Wena's control.[352]

Thus, the utterly inconsistent application of fire safety protocols rendered Egypt's
defense unsuccessful. In the *Wena* case, this inconsistency was aggravated by the
fact that the investment had been made inoperable by the host state's decision to
revoke the operation license.[353] In addition, the properties returned to the investor
had been vandalized and those responsible for the illegal seizure were never
punished.[354] In light of these circumstances, the arbitrators declared that Egypt
had violated not only the obligation to prevent injuries to aliens, but also the
obligation of redress.[355]

13.4.9 Compliance with Relevant Municipal Law

There can be no doubt that, as in the case of any other international obligation, a
breach of the FPS standard shall be determined on the basis of international law, and
not of municipal law.[356] Notwithstanding the foregoing, domestic legal provisions
are certainly part of the factual setting in which a harmful event occurs. As such, they
could be of paramount importance for the evaluation of the diligence displayed by
the host state. On the one hand, local laws often express what investors may
reasonably expect from public authorities in some specific situations of risk. On
the other hand, failures to comply with domestic regulations could reveal taints of
discrimination, arbitrariness or utter recklessness in the respondent state's conduct.
    Investment arbitral tribunals dealing with FPS claims have often taken into
consideration whether the host state acted in compliance with its own domestic
legislation.[357] A good example would be the award rendered in *SAUR v Argentina*

---

[351]Wena Hotels Ltd. *v* Egypt, Award, ICSID Case No. ARB/98/4 (8 December 2000) [92].

[352]Wena Hotels Ltd. *v* Egypt, Award, ICSID Case No. ARB/98/4 (8 December 2000) [92].

[353]Wena Hotels Ltd. *v* Egypt, Award, ICSID Case No. ARB/98/4 (8 December 2000) [92].

[354]Wena Hotels Ltd. *v* Egypt, Award, ICSID Case No. ARB/98/4 (8 December 2000) [92-4].

[355]Wena Hotels Ltd. *v* Egypt, Award, ICSID Case No. ARB/98/4 (8 December 2000) [84 and 95].

[356]ILC, 'Responsibility of States for Internationally Wrongful Acts. General Commentary' (2001)
2 *Yearbook of the International Law Commission – 2001* 31, 36 art. 3 (Commentary) [1]. See also:
Zachary Douglas, 'The Hybrid Foundations of Investment Treaty Arbitration' (2003) 74 BYIL
151, 199. Cf. also Sect. 13.4.9.

[357]For some examples see: American Manufacturing & Trading Inc. *v* Zaire, Award, ICSID Case
No. ARB 93/1 (21 February 1997) [6.06] (underscoring the importance of municipal law without

(2012). In that case, the investor argued that the presence of the police at the investor's premises in the course of an 'administrative intervention' contravened the FPS clause enshrined in the Argentina-France BIT.[358] For its part, the respondent state emphasized that the intervention had been conducted under strict observance of applicable regulations.[359] In its analysis of the case, the tribunal gave weight to the fact that Argentinean law authorized the deployment of police force in that context:

> Le Tribunal arbitral coïncide avec la position maintenue par la Défenderesse et, sur ce point, rejette la demande de Sauri [...] la République a démontré, de manière convaincante, que le décret d'intervention lui-même autorisait l'office notarial à « demander l'aide de la force publique, jusqu'à ce que l'administrateur judiciaire désigné prenne possession du poste », ce qui justifie la présence de la force publique conformément à la règlementation en vigueur [...] Le Tribunal estime que la simple présence policière lors de l'intervention auprès d'une entreprise fait partie des mesures conservatoires qu'un gestionnaire public peut légitimement adopter pour garantir le bon déroulement de la prise de contrôle.[360]

Compliance with domestic law has also played a significant role in connection with alleged breaches of the redress obligation. For instance, in *Marion Unglaube and Reinhard Unglaube v Costa Rica* (2012), constitutional actions (*amparo* actions) filed by environmental activists before Costa Rican courts had significantly delayed a major construction project.[361] The investors considered that the 3-year delay was a consequence of local courts' failure to provide 'full protection and security' to their investment.[362] The arbitrators dismissed the FPS claim on the following grounds:

> Claimants, understandably, have experienced frustration at the three-year delay occasioned by the 2005 *amparo* petition as well as the subsequent nine-month delay resulting from the 2008 *amparo* petition. However this Tribunal finds that both court proceedings were

---

digging deeper into the issue); Sergei Paushok, CJSC Golden East Co., CJSC Vostoknefte *v* Mongolia (UNCITRAL), Award on Jurisdiction and Liability (28 April 2011) [323] (referring to the FPS clause of the Moldova-Russian Federation BIT, which makes express reference to municipal law, and quoting the *AMT* award in this connection); Iurii Bogdanov et al. *v* Moldova (SCC), Arbitral Award (22 September 2005) 15 (referring to the FPS clause of the Moldova-Russian Federation BIT, which makes express reference to municipal law); Marion Unglaube and Reinhard Unglaube *v* Costa Rica, Award, ICSID Cases No. ARB/01/1 and ARB/09/20 (16 May 2012) [286] (discussed later in this section); SAUR International S.A. *v* Argentina, Décision sur la compétence et sur la responsabilité, ICSID Case No. ARB/04/4 (6 June 2012) [508-10] (discussed later in this section). Section 14.3 discusses the interpretation of FPS clauses making express reference to municipal law in more detail.

[358]SAUR International S.A. *v* Argentina, Décision sur la compétence et sur la responsabilité, ICSID Case No. ARB/04/4 (6 June 2012) [508 and 510].

[359]SAUR International S.A. *v* Argentina, Décision sur la compétence et sur la responsabilité, ICSID Case No. ARB/04/4 (6 June 2012) [508 and 510].

[360]SAUR International S.A. *v* Argentina, Décision sur la compétence et sur la responsabilité, ICSID Case No. ARB/04/4 (6 June 2012) [509-10].

[361]Marion Unglaube and Reinhard Unglaube *v* Costa Rica, Award, ICSID Cases No. ARB/01/1 and ARB/09/20 (16 May 2012) [285].

[362]Marion Unglaube and Reinhard Unglaube *v* Costa Rica, Award, ICSID Cases No. ARB/01/1 and ARB/09/20 (16 May 2012) [285-6].

conducted in accordance with Costa Rican law. The Tribunal finds no evidence that either these court proceedings [...] involved impropriety, corruption or discrimination against the Claimants. Thus, the Tribunal concludes that Claimants have not demonstrated an improper failure of the Respondent to provide full protection and security to the Claimants.[363]

These cases show that, while the breach of the obligation to provide protection and security to aliens is a matter of international law, municipal law is one of the many elements to be considered in the assessment of the diligence displayed by local authorities. This holds true in respect of both the obligation to prevent injuries to aliens and the obligation to provide adequate means for the redress of such injuries.

13.4.10 Compliance with Other Due Diligence Obligations Under International Law

The notion of due diligence has developed in the most diverse areas of international law, including international environmental law, the law of armed conflict, the law of diplomatic relations and human rights law.[364] FPS claims often arise out of factual settings which involve other obligations of diligence. For example, a want of diligence in the protection of foreign property against paramilitary groups does not only pertain to international investment law, but also to human rights law. Against this backdrop, the question arises as to the relevance of those other international obligations of due diligence for the assessment of FPS claims.

Investment arbitral tribunals have generally avoided drawing a parallel between the diligence required under the FPS standard and that required by other international obligations. The case *Peter Allard v Barbados* (2016) provides a representative example of this restrain. In that case, the claimant alleged that the Government of Barbados had breached the FPS standard by failing to 'take reasonable care to protect' a bird and nature sanctuary from environmental damage.[365] The investor invoked in this connection the *Convention on Biological Diversity* and the *Ramsar*

---

[363]Marion Unglaube and Reinhard Unglaube *v* Costa Rica, Award, ICSID Cases No. ARB/01/1 and ARB/09/20 (16 May 2012) [286].

[364]See generally Sect. 12.1. For an author addressing the possible synergies and contradictions between the law of armed conflict and the FPS standard see: Ofilio Mayorga, *Arbitrating War: Military Necessity as a Defense to the Breach of Investment Treaty Obligations* (Harvard Program on Humanitarian Policy and Conflict Research, Cambridge MA 2013) 1-10 (arguing that, in situations such as counterinsurgency operations, arbitrators applying the FPS standard should seek guidance in the law of armed conflict; Mayorga additionally submits that states should be allowed to invoke, for example, 'military necessity'). Cf. also Petr Stejskal, 'War: Foreign Investments in Danger – Can International Humanitarian Law or Full Protection and Security Always Save It?' (2017) 8 CYIL 529, 529 *et seq.* On the interplay between human rights obligations and the FPS standard cf. Maria Fanou and Vassilis Tzevelekos, 'The Shared Territory of the ECHR and International Investment Law' in Yannick Radi (ed), *Research Handbook on Human Rights and Investment* (Edward Elgar Publishers, Northampton MA 2018) 93, 127-8.

[365]Peter A. Allard *v* Barbados (UNCITRAL), Award (27 June 2016) [232].

Convention.[366] According to the investor, those environmental instruments 'heighten the level of diligence required' from Barbados.[367] The arbitral tribunal was strikingly cautious in its analysis of the claimant's argument:

> The obligation [FPS] is limited to reasonable action, and a host State is not required to take any specific steps that an investor asks of it. The fact that Barbados is a party to the *Convention on Biological Diversity* and the *Ramsar Convention* does not change the standard under the BIT, although consideration of a host State's international obligations may well be relevant in the application of the standard to particular circumstances.[368]

Other examples appear in the context of FPS claims pertaining to failures of redress. In these cases, the question of due diligence is often interlocked with allegations of procedural unfairness and denial of justice. The legal issues at stake are therefore thoroughly similar to questions discussed in other areas of international law. For instance, the ICtHR has developed detailed criteria for the evaluation of diligence in the context of criminal and civil judicial proceedings.[369] The ECtHR has also considered the notion of due diligence in connection with the right to due process and the avoidance of excessively lengthy detentions without trial.[370] In investment claims involving judicial proceedings, administrative investigations and their like, it might therefore be tempting to analyze due diligence through the prism of the rich jurisprudence of human rights bodies.

---

[366]Peter A. Allard *v* Barbados (UNCITRAL), Award (27 June 2016) [230].

[367]Peter A. Allard *v* Barbados (UNCITRAL), Award (27 June 2016) [230].

[368]Peter A. Allard *v* Barbados (UNCITRAL), Award (27 June 2016) [244].

[369]See, for example: Gonzalez Llui et al. *v* Ecuador, Judgment on Preliminary Objections, Merits, Reparations and Costs (ICtHR: 1 September 2015) [293-327 and 339-40] (referring to due diligence in the context of both criminal and civil judicial proceedings); Masacre de las Dos Erres *v* Guatemala, Judgment on Preliminary Objection, Merits, Reparations and Costs (ICtHR: 24 November 2009) [136-49 and 233(c)] (in reference to failures to investigate a massacre); Rosendo Cantú et al. *v* Mexico, Judgment on Preliminary Objections, Merits, Reparations and Costs (ICtHR: 31 August 2010) [168 *et seq.* and 177-82] (referring to due diligence in the investigation and punishment of sexual violence against women, in connection with article 8 of the AHRC and article 7.b of the Belem do Pará Convention for the Prevention, Punishment and Eradication of Violence against Women); Suárez Peralta *v* Ecuador, Judgment on Preliminary Objections, Merits, Reparations and Costs (ICtHR: 21 May 2013) [94-106] (particularly referring to due diligence in criminal proceedings).

[370]Humen *v* Poland, App No 26614/95 (ECtHR: 15 October 1999) [67-9] (considering the issue of due diligence in the conduct of judicial proceedings); Rumpf *v* Germany, App No 46344/06 (ECtHR: 2 September 2010) [41-46] (referring to delay in the administration of justice as a possible violation of the due process clause enshrined in article 6(1) of the ECHR, and making particular reference to due diligence at para 44). See also the ECtHR's case law on article 5 of the ECHR (right to liberty and security): A et al. *v* United Kingdom, App No 3455/05 (ECtHR: 19 February 2009) [164] (referring to due diligence in the commencement of extradition or deportation proceedings); Khalifa et al. *v* Italy, App No 16483/12 (ECtHR: 15 December 2016) [90] (considering the issue of due diligence in the prosecution of extradition or deportation, and the avoidance of unreasonably lengthy detention before trial); Kudła *v* Poland, App No 30219/96 (ECtHR: 26 October 2000) [106-17] (referring to reasonable duration of detention before trial under article 5(3) of the ECHR, and analyzing local authorities' due diligence in this connection).

Arbitral tribunals have been generally skeptical about human rights analogies. In *Mondev v United States* (2002) the investor alleged that 'for a NAFTA party to confer on one of its public authorities immunity from suit in respect of wrongful conduct affecting the investment was in itself a failure to provide full protection and security to the investment'.[371] In connection with this claim, the parties invoked the jurisprudence of the ECtHR on governmental immunities.[372] The arbitral tribunal had difficulty in accepting the analogy:

> These decisions concern the 'right to a court', an aspect of the human rights conferred on all persons by the major human rights conventions and interpreted by the European Court in an evolutionary way. They emanate from a different region and are not concerned, as Article 1105(1) of NAFTA is concerned, specifically with investment protection. At most, they provide guidance by analogy as to the possible scope of NAFTA's guarantee of 'treatment in accordance with international law, including fair and equitable treatment and full protection and security'.[373]

The award rendered in *Spyridon Roussalis v Romania* (2011) provides another example of this widespread skepticism. In that case, the Romanian General Prosecutor filed a challenge against a lower court's decision which favored the investor's interests.[374] The Supreme Court of Justice annulled the lower court's judgment.[375] The investor alleged that the acts of the Prosecutor and the Supreme Court's decision were contrary to the FPS standard and Article 6(1) of the ECHR (due process).[376] In this vein, the investor specifically invoked the case *Brumărescu v. Romania* (1999).[377] In that case, the ECtHR analyzed the rule which allowed the Procurator-General of Romania to apply, at any time, for the annulment of final judgments.[378] In *Brumărescu* the ECtHR held that, by admitting one such request, 'the Supreme Court of Justice infringed the principle of legal certainty'.[379]

In response to the investor's human rights argument, the state contended that '[w]hether Romania's Supreme Court applied Romanian civil procedure law in a manner consistent with the European Convention is not an issue that Romania agreed to

---

[371]Mondev International *v* United States, Award, ICSID Case No. ARB(AF)/99/2 (11 October 2002) [140].

[372]Mondev International *v* United States, Award, ICSID Case No. ARB(AF)/99/2 (11 October 2002) [141-3].

[373]Mondev International *v* United States, Award, ICSID Case No. ARB(AF)/99/2 (11 October 2002) [144]. Cf. also: Sebastián Mantilla Blanco, *Justizielles Unrecht im internationalen Investitionsschutzrecht* (Nomos, Baden-Baden 2016) 82-3.

[374]Spyridon Roussalis *v* Romania, Award, ICSID Case No. ARB/06/1 (7 December 2011) [149].

[375]Spyridon Roussalis *v* Romania, Award, ICSID Case No. ARB/06/1 (7 December 2011) [150].

[376]Spyridon Roussalis *v* Romania, Award, ICSID Case No. ARB/06/1 (7 December 2011) [149-57].

[377]Brumărescu *v* Romania, App No 28342/95 (ECtHR: 28 October 1999).

[378]Brumărescu *v* Romania, App No 28342/95 (ECtHR: 28 October 1999) [56 *et seq.*].

[379]Brumărescu *v* Romania, App No 28342/95 (ECtHR: 28 October 1999) [62]. In *Spyridon Roussalis v Romania* investor invoked this particular passage of the *Brumărescu* decision. See: Spyridon Roussalis *v* Romania, Award, ICSID Case No. ARB/06/1 (7 December 2011) [156-7].

arbitrate under the Treaty [i.e. the Greece-Romania BIT]'.[380] The host state further argued that, in any case, the decision of the Supreme Court would not contravene the principle of legal certainty.[381] The applicable provisions were in force at the moment in which the court proceedings had been initiated and,[382] in any case, 'the principle of legal certainty does not absolutely prohibit reopening final judgments'.[383]

The arbitrators took notice of the parties' arguments on the right to due process, as set forth in the ECHR.[384] Nonetheless, they considered that the provisions of the BIT provided investors a 'higher and more specific level of protection' than the ECHR.[385] In their analysis of the claims, the arbitrators concluded that the General Prosecutor's actions and the Supreme Court's decision did not entail a violation of the BIT.[386] The tribunal found that 'Respondent's conduct did not infringe the principles of legal certainty and proportionality in violation of the full protection and safety clause contained in article 2(2) of the BIT'.[387] The arbitrators further underscored that, in *Brumărescu*, the proceedings before the Supreme Court were initiated after the lower court's judgment enforcement.[388] The situation was hence not comparable with the facts of the case.[389]

These arbitral decisions show that, in spite of some similarities and possible convergences, FPS does not necessarily overlap with other international obligations. Neither does the diligence required under the FPS standard coincide with that which is required under other due diligence obligations in international law. The ILA has explained that '[d]ue diligence is imbued with differing content according to the specific area of international law in which it is invoked'.[390]

This does not however mean that other due diligence obligations are entirely irrelevant in the context of FPS claims. If it is established that public authorities

---

[380]Spyridon Roussalis v Romania, Award, ICSID Case No. ARB/06/1 (7 December 2011) [275]. The host state also addressed the specifics of the *Brumărescu* decision at paras 270-1, pointing out the differences between that case and the one submitted to the arbitral tribunal.

[381]Spyridon Roussalis v Romania, Award, ICSID Case No. ARB/06/1 (7 December 2011) [259-65].

[382]Spyridon Roussalis v Romania, Award, ICSID Case No. ARB/06/1 (7 December 2011) [261].

[383]Spyridon Roussalis v Romania, Award, ICSID Case No. ARB/06/1 (7 December 2011) [263].

[384]Spyridon Roussalis v Romania, Award, ICSID Case No. ARB/06/1 (7 December 2011) [331].

[385]Spyridon Roussalis v Romania, Award, ICSID Case No. ARB/06/1 (7 December 2011) [312] (particularly referring to the possibility of applying human rights instruments through the non-derogation clause set forth in article 10 of the BIT).

[386]Spyridon Roussalis v Romania, Award, ICSID Case No. ARB/06/1 (7 December 2011) [348-59].

[387]Spyridon Roussalis v Romania, Award, ICSID Case No. ARB/06/1 (7 December 2011) [358].

[388]Spyridon Roussalis v Romania, Award, ICSID Case No. ARB/06/1 (7 December 2011) [359].

[389]Spyridon Roussalis v Romania, Award, ICSID Case No. ARB/06/1 (7 December 2011) [359].

[390]ILA Study Group on Due Diligence in International Law, 'Second Report by Mr. Tim Stephens (Rapporteur) and Mr. Duncan French (Chair)' (20 July 2016) 4. It should be noted, however, that the ILA considers that due diligence is, at the same time, a 'general principle [. . .] underlying more specific rules of due diligence' which, in any case, does not contradict 'more specific expressions of due diligence in sub-branches of international law' (at p. 6).

exercised the diligence imposed by other international obligations, it is unlikely that their acts will fall short of the conduct expected under the customary FPS standard. As a rule, the customary security obligation requires a lower degree of diligence than other international obligations. The reason is that FPS is an element of the minimum standard of treatment.[391] Consequently, the level of diligence it requires is a *minimum*, that is to say, a bottom-line.[392] FPS clauses could certainly impose a 'higher' degree of diligence.[393] But in such case treaty language must make clear the parties' intention to deviate from customary law.

---

[391] See Chap. 5.

[392] See Sects. 13.3.2 and 13.3.3.

[393] Cf. Spyridon Roussalis v Romania, Award, ICSID Case No. ARB/06/1 (7 December 2011) [312] (stating, in general reference to the Greece-Romania BIT, that the 'level of protection' granted under the BIT was higher than that afforded under the ECHR). See also para 364.

Part IV
'Full Protection and Security' Clauses in International Investment Agreements

Chapter 14
'Protection and Security' Clauses in Investment Treaties: A Typology

14.1 Preliminary Remarks

FPS clauses are generally similar, but rarely identical. The formulation of the FPS standard in investment treaties is fairly diverse. Academic assessments of the FPS standard have too-often neglected this diversity. Some scholars have stressed that 'arbitration practice does not seem to attach a significant importance to the wording of the applicable treaty in the obligation of granting full protection and security'.[1] Along these lines, they conclude that '[t]he wording of the treaty is often the starting

---

[1]Giuditta Cordero Moss, 'Full Protection and Security' in August Reinisch (ed), *Standards of Investment Protection* (Oxford University Press, New York 2008) 131, 134.

© Springer Nature Switzerland AG 2019
S. Mantilla Blanco, *Full Protection and Security in International Investment Law*,
European Yearbook of International Economic Law 8,
https://doi.org/10.1007/978-3-030-24838-3_14

point for the tribunal's reasoning, but it does not seem to play a decisive role in the result'.[2] A few tribunals have agreed with this opinion.[3]

This view, however widespread, should be considered with caution.[4] To begin with, it departs from a false premise. While *some* arbitral decisions have indeed stated, implied or assumed that the varied wordings of FPS clauses do not convey different meanings, many awards have actually given weight to the specific words used by the applicable FPS clause. For instance, in some cases the adjectives *full* and *legal* have been held to justify the interpretation of the FPS standard as a wide-ranging obligation, which encompasses a guarantee of a stable and predictable legal system.[5]

In the final analysis, protection and security clauses pose a complex hermeneutic challenge. On the one hand, it is counterintuitive to say that inconsistent language has not, or should not have, any effect on the interpretation of investment treaties. The proposition that phrases such as *full protection and security* or *most constant protection and security* entail no difference of substance requires justification beyond mere arguments of authority. On the other hand, it is insufficient to merely state that these terms have different meanings. If there is a difference, it must be identified and explained in precise terms.

The real challenge is to develop a *typology* of FPS clauses and, carefully considering their similarities and differences, determine their content and scope. This challenge represents an old and recurrent problem of legal science. For instance, domestic legal institutions generally bear some resemblance or similarity, but they

---

[2]Giuditta Cordero Moss, 'Full Protection and Security' in August Reinisch (ed), *Standards of Investment Protection* (Oxford University Press, New York 2008) 131, 134. See also: J. Anthony VanDuzer, 'Full Protection and Security' in Thomas Cottier and Krista Nadakavukaren Schefer (eds), *Elgar Encyclopedia of International Economic Law* (Edward Elgar Publishing, Northampton MA 2018) 212, 213; Heather Bray, 'SOI – Save Our Investments! International Investment Law and International Humanitarian Law' (2013) 14 J. World Investment & Trade 578, 582; Noah Rubins and N. Stephan Kinsella, *International Investment, Political Risk and Dispute Resolution. A Practitioner's Guide* (Oceana Publications, New York 2005) 219. For a similar, but slightly more cautious approach, see: Kenneth Vandevelde, *Bilateral Investment Treaties: History, Policy, and Interpretation* (Oxford University Press, New York 2010) § 6(3)(1) (observing that the different formulations used in investment treaty practice 'have not been treated as creating a substantive difference in the standard of care required of the host country'). Cf. also Nartnirun Junngam, 'The Full Protection and Security Standard in International Investment Law: What and Who is Investment Fully[?] Protected and Secured From?' (2018) 7(1) AUBLR 1, 87-8 (observing that the different formulations of the standard 'do not necessarily produce different results', but also recognizing that the adjectives used in FPS clauses could enhance the level of protection required under the standard). Interestingly, Ms. Cordero Moss acted as sole arbitrator in a case where the specific wording of the applicable FPS clause actually had a material and direct effect on the decision on the claim. See: Iurii Bogdanov et al. *v* Moldova (SCC), Arbitral Award (22 September 2005) 15. Section 14.3 discusses this case in more detail.

[3]See, for example: Parkerings-Compagniet AS *v* Lithuania, Award, ICSID Case No. ARB/05/8 (11 September 2007) [354]. See also: Frontier Petroleum Ltd. *v* Czech Republic (UNCITRAL), Final Award (12 November 2010) [260] (quoting the *Parkerings* award in this connection).

[4]Cf. also: Lucas Bastin, *State Responsibility for Omissions: Establishing a Breach of the Full Protection and Security Obligation by Omissions* (Oxford University, Oxford 2016) [D.Phil. Thesis] 105 (stating that these views 'oversimplify reality').

[5]See Sects. 14.4.1 and 14.4.3.

are never entirely identical from one municipal legal system to another. The threshold issue is to find an adequate technique to properly compare them.

In his *Allgemeine Staatslehre* (1900), Georg Jellinek masterly addressed this methodological question.[6] Despite the fact that Jellinek focused on the concept of *state*, his method might be useful for analyzing other social and legal phenomena.[7] Jellinek's method consisted in creating *empirical typologies*.[8] An *empirical type* is, in the essence, a summary of the features (*Merkmale*) different social or normative phenomena have in common.[9] The task of scholars consists in identifying such typical features, detach them from the single individuals, and subsequently present and analyze them *in abstracto*.[10] Therefore, empirical types can only be ascertained through inductive reasoning.[11] Once identified, these typical features provide a helpful organizing device for the study of a legal institution's diverse manifestations.[12]

Jellinek's notion of empirical types provides a useful technique for the analysis of the manifold manifestations of the FPS standard in investment treaties. No FPS clause is entirely identical to another. Even if two clauses employ the same language, their context and purpose could vary from one treaty to another. Despite their differences, however, they can be grouped in general categories and examined through their common features.

This chapter seeks to classify FPS clauses in *empirical types*, which are defined by features that are common to some group of FPS clauses, distinguishing them from other FPS provisions. Relevant arbitral decisions have also been classified on the basis of the treaty provisions they addressed. The typical categories identified in this chapter correspond to well-known formulations of the FPS standard. They do not intend to be exhaustive. While an effort has been made to discuss the treaty language that has been most relevant for investment arbitration practice, there might be clauses that do not perfectly fit into any of these categories. Conversely, some clauses could fall into more than one typical category.

---

[6]Georg Jellinek, *Allgemeine Staatslehre* (Verlag von O. Häring, Berlin 1914) 34-42 [first edition: 1900].

[7]Georg Jellinek, *Allgemeine Staatslehre* (Verlag von O. Häring, Berlin 1914) 36 (underscoring the significance of typologies in human thinking processes and in the formation of paradigms).

[8]Georg Jellinek, *Allgemeine Staatslehre* (Verlag von O. Häring, Berlin 1914) 34-5 [first edition: 1900]. It must be observed that Jellinek drew a careful distinction between an *ideal type* (*idealer Typus*) and an empirical type (*empirischer Typus*). *Ideal types* refer to a genre's perfect being (*vollkommene Wesen einer Gattung*), understood in terms of a platonic otherworldly idea, which may only be seen through imperfect manifestations (at p. 34). The *ideal type* has, broadly speaking, a rather teleological meaning; it is the abstract τέλος of an institution; it is hence not real (*Seiendes*) but ideal (*Seinsollendes*) (at pp. 34-5). In the particular case of the general theory of the state, Jellinek observed, *ideal types* could be identified with the constant attempts to define or describe an ideal or perfect state (at p. 35). According to Jellinek, these ideal types do not usually result from scientific research (*wissenschaftliche Forschung*) but from speculation (*Spekulation*) (at p. 35). In the end, the subject of science is the *Seiendes* and not the *Seinsollendes*, i.e., the *real* and not the *ideal* (at p. 35).

[9]Georg Jellinek, *Allgemeine Staatslehre* (Verlag von O. Häring, Berlin 1914) 36.

[10]Georg Jellinek, *Allgemeine Staatslehre* (Verlag von O. Häring, Berlin 1914) 36.

[11]Georg Jellinek, *Allgemeine Staatslehre* (Verlag von O. Häring, Berlin 1914) 37.

[12]Georg Jellinek, *Allgemeine Staatslehre* (Verlag von O. Häring, Berlin 1914) 39-42.

The purpose of this classification is to determine whether and to which extent particular elements of protection and security clauses could indicate the contracting parties' intention to merely incorporate the customary standard into the treaty or, alternatively, to derogate from customary law. Taking into consideration this guiding question, a first section considers the difference between clauses making express reference to customary law, and clauses containing no such express reference. In this vein, it analyzes the possible roles customary law could play in the application of FPS clauses, depending on the specific wording employed by the treaty. A second section addresses the qualification of the protection obligation through references to national law, and its possible effect in the definition of the content and scope of the protection obligation. Finally, a third section examines the use of adjectives such as *full*, *constant* or *legal* in protection and security clauses, as well as the possible significance of the absence of a qualifying adjective.

14.2   References to Customary Law and General International Law in Protection and Security Clauses

Protection and security clauses often include express references to customary law or general international law. This section examines the effect such references could have for the interpretation and application of the FPS standard. The argument consists of two parts. Section 14.2.1 addresses the interpretation of FPS clauses which explicitly refer to the customary standard. In this vein, it acknowledges that not every reference to customary law serves the same purpose. States may certainly codify custom in an international treaty, and often do so. Nonetheless, the mere fact that customary law is mentioned in a treaty clause does not necessarily rule out the autonomy of the treaty provision. States could refer to customary law, for example, as a means to define specific aspects of an autonomous treaty-based obligation. It is, therefore, crucial to analyze the precise wording of FPS clauses referring to customary law, in order to ascertain the function they ascribe to the customary protection obligation.

Section 14.2.2 considers the no less important question, whether the *absence* of any reference to customary law could or should be read as an expression of the parties' intention to create an independent treaty-based standard. If such treaty provisions are deemed to be autonomous from the customary protection obligation, the question arises as to the role customary law could play, if any, in the interpretation and application of an autonomous FPS clause.

14.2.1   Protection and Security Clauses Making Express Reference to Customary Law or General International Law

A look into FPS clauses from BITs and FTAs shows that references to customary or general international law have taken diverse forms, which could convey different meanings. It is, in fact, not the same to grant protection 'in accordance with' customary law than to grant protection 'no less' than required under customary law. In order to properly address this diversity of wording, the argument will be presented in two separate subsections. The first unit discusses FPS clauses in which the treaty-based standard coincides with the customary standard. In this connection, it draws particular attention to decisions rendered by NAFTA tribunals. A second subsection considers other functions express references to customary law could have in specific treaty frameworks.

14.2.1.1   Treaties Defining the Protection and Security Obligation by Reference to Customary Law

An increasing number of investment treaties indicate that the treaty-based FPS standard coincides with the customary protection obligation. Representative examples can be found in the many IIAs negotiated on the basis of the United States' Model BITs of 2004 and 2012:

Article 5. Minimum Standard of Treatment.

1. Each Party shall accord to covered investments treatment in accordance with customary international law, including fair and equitable treatment and full protection and security.

2. For greater certainty, paragraph 1 prescribes the customary minimum standard of treatment of aliens as the minimum standard of treatment to be afforded to covered investments. The concepts "fair and equitable treatment" and "full protection and security" do not require treatment in addition to or beyond that which is required by that standard, and do not create additional substantive rights. The obligation in paragraph 1 to provide [. . .] b) "full protection and security" requires each Party to provide the level of police protection required under customary international law.[13]

---

[13]U.S. Model BIT (2004) art. 5(1) and (2)(b); U.S. Model BIT (2012) art. 5(1) and (2)(b). The 2004 and 2012 Model BITs additionally include an annex, which reads as follows: "The Parties confirm their shared understanding that "customary international law" generally and as specifically referenced in Article 5 [Minimum Standard of Treatment] [. . .] results from a general and consistent practice of States that they follow from a sense of legal obligation. With regard to Article 5 [Minimum Standard of Treatment], the customary international law minimum standard of treatment of aliens refers to all customary international law principles that protect the economic rights and interests of aliens." U.S. Model BIT (2004) Annex A; U.S. Model BIT (2012) Annex A. Cf. also the wording of the USMCA of November 2018: Agreement between the United States of America, the United Mexican States, and Canada (adopted 30 November 2018) art. 14.6 (2) (b) (stating that FPS 'requires each Party to provide the level of police protection required under

This approach is not particular to U.S. investment agreements. Treaties using this wording have become increasingly common. This language is spreading fast not only in the treaty practice of developed western states, but also in treaties between countries from other latitudes.[14]

These treaty provisions leave little room for interpretation. They clearly indicate that the treaty-based FPS standard is the same as the customary standard. In *Adel A Hamadi Al Tamini v Oman* (2015), the tribunal was constituted under Chapter 10 of the U.S.-Oman FTA of 2006, which contains an FPS clause identical to article 5 of the U.S. Model BIT of 2004.[15] The parties accepted that a clause using this language 'refers to the customary international minimum standard and not an autonomous treaty standard'.[16] The arbitrators agreed with this interpretation, and explained:

> [This] conclusion is compelled by article 10.5.2, which expressly provides that the Treaty's standards of fair and equitable treatment and full protection and security *"do not require treatment in addition to or beyond that which is required by [the minimum standard of treatment]"* [. . .].[17]

In *Koch v Venezuela* (2017), the arbitrators considered the reference to international law in article 4(1) of the Switzerland-Venezuela BIT of 1993, which qualifies FPS with the phrase '[i]n accordance with the rules and principles of international law'.[18] The tribunal found that 'these words import the customary international minimum standards [FPS and FET], rather than any autonomous higher standards'.[19] The arbitrators went on to explain:

---

customary international law'). Cf. also Annex 14-A of the USMCA (definition of 'customary international law').

[14]For some indicative examples see: Free Trade Agreement between the Government of the People's Republic of China and the Government of the Republic of Korea (adopted 1 June 2015, entered into force 20 December 2015) art. 12.5(1) and (2)(b); Free Trade Agreement between the Republic of China (Taiwan) and the Republic of Nicaragua (adopted 23 June 2006, entered into force 1 January 2008) art. 10.05(1) and (2)(b); Free Trade Agreement between the Republic of Korea and the Republic of Peru (adopted 14 November 2010, entered into force 1 August 2011) art. 9.5(1) and (2)(b); Reciprocal Investment Promotion and Protection Agreement between the Government of the Kingdom of Morocco and the Government of the Federal Republic of Nigeria (adopted 3 December 2016) art. 7(1) and (2)(b).

[15]Free Trade Agreement between the United States of America and the Sultanate of Oman (adopted 19 January 2006, entered into force 1 January 2009) art. 10.5(1) and (2)(b).

[16]Adel A Hamadi Al Tamini *v* Oman, Award, ICSID Case No. ARB/11/33 (3 November 2015) [380].

[17]Emphasis in the original. Adel A Hamadi Al Tamini *v* Oman, Award, ICSID Case No. ARB/11/33 (3 November 2015) [380].

[18]Agreement between the Swiss Confederation and the Republic of Venezuela on the Reciprocal Promotion and Protection of Investments (adopted 18 November 1993, entered into force 30 November 1994) art. 4(1). Cf. Koch Minerals SÁRL and Koch Nitrogen International SÁRL *v* Venezuela, Award, ICSID Case No. ARB/11/19 (30 October 2017) [8.42 *et seq.*].

[19]Koch Minerals SÁRL and Koch Nitrogen International SÁRL *v* Venezuela, Award, ICSID Case No. ARB/11/19 (30 October 2017) [8.42].

In the Tribunal's view, this additional express wording is conclusive in confirming the meaning of the FET and FPS standards as duties imposed by customary international law and in precluding any independent or autonomous meaning.[20]

NAFTA arbitral tribunals have dealt with a similar wording. NAFTA article 1105 guarantees 'treatment *in accordance with* international law, *including* fair and equitable treatment and *full protection and security*'.[21] On July 31st, 2001, the NAFTA Free Trade Commission issued a Note of Interpretation clarifying the meaning of NAFTA article 1105 in the following terms:

> The concepts of "fair and equitable treatment" and "full protection and security" do not require treatment in addition to or beyond that which is required by the customary international law minimum standard of treatment to aliens.[22]

NAFTA article 1131(2) provides that an interpretation by the FTC has a binding character.[23] Scholars have suggested that, under the interpretative note, customary law can be depicted as the 'ceiling' of the protection granted under the treaty.[24] This observation seems to be right at the outset. But then the question arises as to whether the treaty-based standard truly grants a *lesser* degree of protection than the customary standard and, if so, to which extent this treaty clause actually differs from the customary protection obligation.

NAFTA arbitral decisions generally coincide in stating that the Note of Interpretation, combined with the phrase 'in accordance with international law, including [. . .] full protection and security' in article 1105(1), incorporates the customary standard into the treaty. Plainly stated, in the context of NAFTA, customary law is not the *ceiling* of the protection obligation, but represents and exhausts the content of the treaty standard.[25] In *Mondev v United States* (2002) the arbitral tribunal concluded that this wording expressed the NAFTA parties' will to 'incorporate principles of customary international law'.[26] Similarly, in *Loewen v United States* (2003) the tribunal stated that, as a result of the FTC Note, the FET and the FPS standards 'are not free-standing obligations'.[27] The *Loewen* tribunal added that '[FPS and

---

[20]Koch Minerals SÁRL and Koch Nitrogen International SÁRL *v* Venezuela, Award, ICSID Case No. ARB/11/19 (30 October 2017) [8.44].

[21]Emphasis added. North American Free Trade Agreement (adopted 17 December 1992, entered into force 1 January 1994) art. 1105.

[22]NAFTA Free Trade Commission, *Notes of Interpretation of Certain Chapter 11 Provisions* (31 July 2001) [http://www.sice.oas.org/tpd/nafta/Commission/CH11understanding_e.asp].

[23]North American Free Trade Agreement (adopted 17 December 1992, entered into force 1 January 1994) art. 1131 (2). See also: Andrea Bjorklund, 'NAFTA Chapter 11' in Chester Brown (ed), *Commentaries on Selected Model Investment Treaties* (Oxford University Press, Oxford 2013) 465, 484 and 520-1.

[24]Giuditta Cordero Moss, 'Full Protection and Security' in August Reinisch (ed), *Standards of Investment Protection* (Oxford University Press, New York 2008) 131, 136.

[25]See also Sect. 14.2.2.

[26]Mondev International *v* United States, Award, ICSID Case No. ARB(AF)/99/2 (11 October 2002) [111] (quoting multiple statements by the NAFTA contracting states at paras 111 and 112).

[27]Loewen Group Inc. and Raymond L. Loewen *v* United States, Award, ICSID Case No. ARB(AF)/98/3 (26 June 2003) [128].

FET] constitute obligations only to the extent that they are recognized by customary international law'.[28]

In *Grand River Enterprises v United States* (2011), the arbitrators held that the language of NAFTA 'makes clear that the controlling element in applying Article 1105 is international law'.[29] As a corollary, the arbitrators explained, '[FPS and FET] do not exist as independent, free-standing concepts drawing content from sources such as equity or the policy preferences of individual arbitrators'.[30] On the contrary, 'their content is determined by international law'.[31] According to the *Grand River* tribunal, the FTC note clarified that only *customary law* is relevant for the assessment of the content of the protection obligation.[32] Hence, in the NAFTA framework, FPS and FET 'refer to existing elements of customary international law regarding the treatment of aliens and do not add to that standard'.[33]

In *William Ralph Clayton et al. v Canada* (2015) the arbitrators also recognized that, under NAFTA, FPS 'cannot be regarded as autonomous' and is accordingly limited to customary law.[34] In *Mesa Power Group v Canada* (2016) the arbitral tribunal underscored that 'the FTC Note is clear that the Tribunal must apply the customary international law standard of the international minimum standard of treatment, and nothing else'.[35] The *Mesa Power* tribunal additionally observed that '[t]here is thus no scope for autonomous standards to impose additional requirements on the NAFTA Parties'.[36] Finally, in *Eli Lilly v Canada* (2017) the arbitrators acknowledged that NAFTA tribunals must 'determine the content, under customary law, of the minimum standard of treatment requirement for purposes, inter alia, of interpreting and applying [. . .] [the standard of] full protection and security'.[37]

An express reference to customary law must be read harmoniously with other terms used in the relevant clause. In *Windstream Energy v Canada* (2016), a NAFTA

---

[28]Loewen Group Inc. and Raymond L. Loewen *v* United States, Award, ICSID Case No. ARB(AF)/98/3 (26 June 2003) [128].

[29]Grand River Enterprises Six Nations Ltd. et al. *v* United States of America (UNCITRAL), Award (12 January 2011) [174].

[30]Grand River Enterprises Six Nations Ltd. et al. *v* United States of America (UNCITRAL), Award (12 January 2011) [174].

[31]Grand River Enterprises Six Nations Ltd. et al. *v* United States of America (UNCITRAL), Award (12 January 2011) [174].

[32]Grand River Enterprises Six Nations Ltd. et al. *v* United States of America (UNCITRAL), Award (12 January 2011) [175-6].

[33]Grand River Enterprises Six Nations Ltd. et al. *v* United States of America (UNCITRAL), Award (12 January 2011) [176].

[34]William Ralph Clayton, William Richard Clayton, Douglas Clayton, Daniel Clayton and Bilcon of Delaware Inc. *v* Canada (UNCITRAL), Award on Jurisdiction and Liability, PCA Case No. 2009-05 (17 March 2015) [432].

[35]Mesa Power Group LLC *v* Canada (UNCITRAL), Award, PCA Case No. 2012-17 (24 March 2016) [503].

[36]Mesa Power Group LLC *v* Canada (UNCITRAL), Award, PCA Case No. 2012-17 (24 March 2016) [503].

[37]Eli Lilly and Co. *v* Canada (UNCITRAL), Award, Case No. UNCT/14/2 (16 March 2017) [106].

case, the Canadian Government argued that 'to prove a breach of Article 1105 requires proving a breach of a customary international law standard, such as denial of justice or a breach of an investor's full protection and security'.[38] In this line of argument, Canada implied that a treatment that is not fair and equitable does not amount to a breach of NAFTA unless it constitutes, too, a breach of a customary standard:

> [T]he practice of states does not support the proposition that standalone FET clauses have become part of the customary international law minimum standard of treatment.[39]

The arbitral tribunal, while acknowledging that NAFTA article 1105 refers to the customary minimum standard, emphasized that the specific wording of the clause must also be taken into consideration.[40] Thus, the FTC Note '[cannot] be taken to mean that a NAFTA tribunal must entirely disregard the terms "fair and equitable" and "full protection and security" in Article 1105(1)'.[41] Rather, it must be understood that the parties considered that FPS and FET are elements of the customary standard and must be interpreted and applied in a manner that 'is in accordance, or consistent, with the [customary] standard'.[42]

In some cases, doubts have arisen as to whether clauses assuring protection and security 'in accordance with' international law, without further specification, can truly be regarded as a mere codification of the customary protection obligation. In recent years, the issue has arisen in at least two cases filed under the Canada-Venezuela BIT. Article 2(2) of the treaty reads as follows:

> Each Contracting Party shall, *in accordance with the principles of international law*, accord investments or returns of investors of the other Contracting Party fair and equitable treatment and *full protection and security*.[43]

In *Crystallex v Venezuela* (2016) the arbitral tribunal concluded that, notwithstanding the treaty's reference to 'principles of international law', 'full protection and security is a distinct treaty standard whose content is not to be equated to the minimum standard of treatment'.[44]

---

[38]Windstream Energy LLC *v* Canada (UNCITRAL), Award (27 September 2016) [311].

[39]Windstream Energy LLC *v* Canada (UNCITRAL), Award (27 September 2016) [311].

[40]Windstream Energy LLC *v* Canada (UNCITRAL), Award (27 September 2016) [355-7].

[41]Windstream Energy LLC *v* Canada (UNCITRAL), Award (27 September 2016) [357].

[42]Windstream Energy LLC *v* Canada (UNCITRAL), Award (27 September 2016) [356].

[43]Emphasis added. Agreement between Canada and the Republic of Venezuela for the Promotion and Protection of Investments (adopted 1 July 1996, entered into force 28 January 1998) art. II(2).

[44]Crystallex International Corp. *v* Venezuela, Award, ICSID Case No. ARB(AF)/11/2 (4 April 2016) [632].

A more careful approach was followed in *Gold Reserve v Venezuela* (2014). In that case, the respondent state argued that article 2(2) of the Canada-Venezuela BIT does not grant protection beyond customary law.[45] Venezuela's argument, as summarized by the arbitral tribunal, was as follows:

> [A]s made evident by the reference of the BIT provision to the "principles of international law", the full protection and security standard in the BITs codifies the general duty to provide for protection and security of aliens under the customary international law minimum standard of treatment [. . .] the standard of protection and security under customary international law requires a host State to exercise due diligence to protect foreigners and their property from "physical" harm, not to provide legal or economic security.[46]

The arbitral tribunal considered that the respondent's interpretation of the FPS clause was the 'more traditional, and commonly accepted view'.[47] At the same time, however, the arbitrators made no explicit statement about the BIT's reference to the 'principles of international law'.[48] In any case, while avoiding any express declaration that the FPS clause was a codification of customary law, the *Gold Reserve* tribunal did actually adopt a restrictive interpretation of FPS, thus ensuring that the degree of security required under the BIT would not exceed that which is customarily required.[49]

The holding of the *Gold Reserve* tribunal bears some resemblance to the award rendered some years earlier in *PSEG v Turkey* (2008). In that case, the FPS claim had been raised under article II(3) of the US-Turkey BIT, which guarantees 'full protection and security, in a manner consistent with international law'.[50] While the *PSEG* tribunal did not enter into a detailed assessment of the customary protection obligation, it expressed the view that 'this particular standard has developed in the context of physical safety of persons and installations'.[51] Noting that the case did not pertain to physical security, the arbitrators dismissed the FPS claim.[52]

---

[45] Gold Reserve Inc. *v* Venezuela, Award, ICSID Case No. ARB(AF)/09/1 (22 September 2014) [618-9].

[46] Gold Reserve Inc. *v* Venezuela, Award, ICSID Case No. ARB(AF)/09/1 (22 September 2014) [618-9].

[47] Gold Reserve Inc. *v* Venezuela, Award, ICSID Case No. ARB(AF)/09/1 (22 September 2014) [622].

[48] Gold Reserve Inc. *v* Venezuela, Award, ICSID Case No. ARB(AF)/09/1 (22 September 2014) [622].

[49] Gold Reserve Inc. *v* Venezuela, Award, ICSID Case No. ARB(AF)/09/1 (22 September 2014) [622].

[50] Agreement between the United States of America and the Republic of Turkey concerning the Reciprocal Encouragement and Protection of Investments (adopted 3 December 1985, entered into force 18 May 1990) art. II(3).

[51] PSEG Global Inc. and Konya Ilgin Elektrik Üretim ve Ticaret Limited Şirketi *v* Turkey, Award, ICSID Case No. ARB/02/5 (19 January 2007) [258].

[52] PSEG Global Inc. and Konya Ilgin Elektrik Üretim ve Ticaret Limited Şirketi *v* Turkey, Award, ICSID Case No. ARB/02/5 (19 January 2007) [259].

The abovementioned decisions indicate that adjudicators have given full effect to FPS clauses defining the extent of the treaty-based FPS standard by reference to customary international law or general international law. This holds also true where the contracting parties issue a joint declaration to this effect. The interpretation of phrases such as '[FPS] *in accordance with* international law' is not univocal, though. According to some tribunals, this wording does not *per se* exclude the autonomy of the treaty-based standard from customary law.

14.2.1.2   Other References to Customary International Law

Not every reference to customary law in an investment treaty is aimed at incorporating the customary FPS standard into the treaty, so that the treaty-based standard is defined by reference to the customary protection obligation. Scholars have argued that the relationship between customary law and FPS is much more complex than it seems:

> There are three theoretical approaches to the question: that the standard of customary international law represents the ceiling for the obligations contained in the treaty, that it represents the floor, or that it is equivalent.[53]

The previous section has considered the third 'theoretical approach' in detail. This section will briefly discuss the remaining two approaches. The notion of customary law as a 'ceiling' seems to be clearer in theory than in practice. U.S. BITs and the NAFTA Note of Interpretation are often presented as examples of this approach.[54] As explained beforehand, these treaties clarify that FPS '[does] not require treatment in addition to or beyond that which is required by that [customary minimum] standard'.[55] Nonetheless, this explanation is often preceded by the phrase '[f]or greater certainty'.[56] Many FPS clauses refer to protection and

---

[53]Giuditta Cordero Moss, 'Full Protection and Security' in August Reinisch (ed), *Standards of Investment Protection* (Oxford University Press, New York 2008) 131, 136.

[54]Cf. Giuditta Cordero Moss, 'Full Protection and Security' in August Reinisch (ed), *Standards of Investment Protection* (Oxford University Press, New York 2008) 131, 136 (mentioning NAFTA article 1105(1) as an example).

[55]Free Trade Agreement between the United States of America and the Republic of Colombia (adopted 22 November 2006, entered into force 15 May 2012) art. 10.5(2). See also: NAFTA Free Trade Commission, *Notes of Interpretation of Certain Chapter 11 Provisions* (31 July 2001) [http://www.sice.oas.org/tpd/nafta/Commission/CH11understanding_e.asp].

[56]Free Trade Agreement between the United States of America and the Republic of Colombia (adopted 22 November 2006, entered into force 15 May 2012) art. 10.5(2). See also: NAFTA Free Trade Commission, *Notes of Interpretation of Certain Chapter 11 Provisions* (31 July 2001) [http://www.sice.oas.org/tpd/nafta/Commission/CH11understanding_e.asp] (stating that the Note shall serve as a means 'to clarify and reaffirm the meaning' of some NAFTA clauses).

security 'in accordance with customary international law'.[57] In some agreements, it is further provided that '[FPS] requires each party to provide the level of police protection required under customary international law'.[58]

Read in context, these references to international law do not indicate that customary law is a 'ceiling'. Rather, custom is both floor and ceiling. In other words, customary law defines the content and scope of the treaty-based standard. Consequently, these IIAs do not provide for a lesser degree of protection than that which is customary. Quite the contrary, they equalize the protection granted under the treaty to the customary standard. This view is consistent with the leading interpretation of NAFTA article 1105(1).[59]

It is, of course, possible that a treaty clause grants a lesser degree of protection than that which is provided under customary law. But then it must be clear from the treaty provision which aspects of the customary obligation are being contracted out. This could be the case, for example, of treaties expressly referring to customary law and further defining FPS as a duty 'to take such measures as may be reasonably necessary to ensure the *physical* protection and security of covered investments'.[60] If it is agreed that the customary protection obligation grants protection against *physical* and *nonphysical* harm, this clause could indeed be read as reducing the scope of the security obligation.[61] While these treaty clauses are still rare, it is arguable that the continuous use of this wording could influence the future evolution of the customary standard.[62]

Moving on to the second 'theoretical approach' to the relationship between customary law and FPS clauses, it must be observed that numerous protection and security clauses define the scope and content of the security obligation as 'no less' than the protection required under customary international law. Article II(2)(a) of the

---

[57]Free Trade Agreement between the United States of America and the Republic of Colombia (adopted 22 November 2006, entered into force 15 May 2012) art. 10.5(1). See also: North American Free Trade Agreement (adopted 17 December 1992, entered into force 1 January 1994) art. 1105(1) (using the phrase 'in accordance with international law').

[58]For an indicative example see: Free Trade Agreement between the United States of America and the Republic of Colombia (adopted 22 November 2006, entered into force 15 May 2012) art. 10.5 (2)(b).

[59]See Sect. 14.2.1.1.

[60]Emphasis added. Free Trade Agreement between Malaysia and Australia (adopted 22 May 2012, entered into force 1 January 2013) art. 12.7. Sect. 9.2 provides further examples of this type of clauses. Cf. also Sect. 14.4.1.2.

[61]Chapter 9 considers the physical-nonphysical divide in more detail.

[62]The extent to which BITs have influenced or could influence the evolution of customary law has been the subject of intense academic debate. See: Stephen Schwebel, 'Investor-State Disputes and the Development of International Law. The Influence of Bilateral Investment Treaties on Customary International Law' (2004) 98 ASIL Proceedings 27, 27-30 (arguing that BITs have 'reshaped' customary law); Patrick Dumberry, *The Formation and Identification of Customary International Law in International Investment Law* (Cambridge University Press, Cambridge 2016) 188 *et seq.* (presenting a summary of the ongoing debate on the subject and expressing skepticism towards Schwebel's argument).

Argentina-United States BIT provides a representative example of these treaty provisions:

> Investment shall at all times be accorded fair and equitable treatment, shall enjoy full protection and security *and shall in no case be accorded treatment less than that required by international law.*[63]

In investment arbitration practice, this type of clauses has given rise to at least two hermeneutic approaches. In some cases, it has been considered that customary law has the function of determining the *minimum* degree of protection required under an autonomous treaty-based standard. This interpretation implies that, while a violation of the customary protection obligation necessarily entails a breach of the treaty, compliance with customary law does not necessarily mean that the treaty obligation has been fulfilled. The award rendered in *Azurix v Argentina* (2006) provides a good example of this line of argument. In reference to the Argentina-US BIT, the tribunal stated:

> [This wording] ensures that, whichever content is attributed to the other two standards [FET and FPS], the treatment accorded to investment will be no less than required by international law. The clause, as drafted, permits to interpret fair and equitable treatment and full protection and security as higher standards than required by international law. The purpose of the third sentence is to set a floor, not a ceiling, in order to avoid a possible interpretation of these standards below what is required by international law.[64]

Other tribunals have held that the content of treaty clauses using this wording does not differ from customary law. In *El Paso v Argentina* (2011), another case filed under the Argentina-US BIT, the arbitrators held that the treaty standard coincided with 'the traditional obligation to protect aliens under international customary law' and consistently found that the obligation requires the exercise of due diligence in the protection of aliens against third party violence, and no more.[65]

Another example of this approach appears in *Noble Ventures v Romania* (2005). In that case, the arbitral tribunal considered article II(2)(a) of the Romania-US BIT, which uses the same language as article II(2)(a) of the Argentina-US BIT.[66] As regards to the interpretation of the FPS clause, the arbitrators observed:

---

[63]Emphasis added. Treaty between the United States of America and the Argentine Republic concerning the Reciprocal Encouragement and Protection of Investment (adopted 14 November 1991, entered into force 20 October 1994) art. II(2)(a).

[64]Azurix Corp. *v* Argentina, Award, ICSID Case No. ARB/01/12 (14 July 2006) [361]. See also: Impregilo S.p.A. *v* Argentina, Award, ICSID Case No. ARB/07/17 (21 June 2011) [288] (quoting this passage of the *Azurix* award, in particular connection with the FET standard); Cargill Inc. *v* Poland, Final Award, ICSID Case No. ARB(AF)/04/2 (29 February 2008) [453] (interpreting article II:6 of the US-Poland Business and Economic Relations Treaty, and quoting the *Azurix* award; the *Cargill* tribunal was particularly concerned with the FET standard).

[65]El Paso Energy International Co. *v* Argentina, Award, ICSID Case No. ARB/03/15 (31 October 2011) [522].

[66]Treaty between the United States of America and the Government of Romania concerning the Reciprocal Encouragement and Protection of Investment (adopted 28 May 1992, entered into force 15 January 1994) art. II(2)(a).

[I]t seems doubtful whether that provision can be understood as being wider in scope than the general duty to provide for protection and security of foreign nationals found in the customary international law of aliens.[67]

At first sight, the interpretation advanced in *El Paso* and *Noble Ventures* seems to leave the phrase '[no] less' without effect. A closer look might challenge this initial impression. In the treaties analyzed in *El Paso* and *Noble Ventures*, the reference to customary law appeared in a separate sentence. After referring to the FET and FPS standards, both treaties provided that '[investment] shall in no case be accorded treatment less than that required by international law'.[68] It is, thus, plausible to think of this phrase, not as a qualification of the FPS and FET standards, but as an *additional obligation* to grant treatment consistent with *other* customary obligations. The last sentence would hence fulfill a gap-filling function for cases where the measures at stake do not fit within the scope of application of neither the FET standard nor the FPS standard.

Against this backdrop, it seems that the approaches followed in *Azurix*, on the one hand, and *El Paso* and *Noble Ventures*, on the other, are both plausible. It is not possible to express support for one or the other approach in the abstract. The answer will always depend on the language and context of the applicable treaty.

14.2.2   Protection and Security Clauses Making No Express Reference to Customary Law or General International Law

FPS clauses do not always make reference to customary or general international law. This type of treaty provisions poses the question, whether the absence of any such reference indicates the contracting states' intention to derogate from customary law. Investors pursuing far-reaching interpretations of the FPS standard have argued that this circumstance should be regarded as evidence of the FPS clause's autonomous character. A representative example would be the Memorial submitted by the investor in *ADF v United States*, which addressed the interpretation of NAFTA article 1105(1). The Memorial was filed on 1 August 2001, one day after the NAFTA Free Trade Commission issued a binding declaration stating that article 1105(1),

---

[67]Noble Ventures *v* Romania, Award, ICSID Case No. ARB/01/11 (12 October 2005) [164]. Cf. also: Geneviève Bastid Burdeau, 'La clause de protection et sécurité pleine et entière' (2015) 119(1) RGDIP 87, 99 (quoting this passage of the *Noble Ventures* award).

[68]Treaty between the United States of America and the Argentine Republic concerning the Reciprocal Encouragement and Protection of Investment (adopted 14 November 1991, entered into force 20 October 1994) art. 2(2)(a); Treaty between the United States of America and the Government of Romania concerning the Reciprocal Encouragement and Protection of Investment (adopted 28 May 1992, entered into force 15 January 1994) art. 2(2)(a).

including the FPS clause, constitute a codification of customary law.[69] In its analysis
of NAFTA, the investor explained:

> To read "full protection and security" and "fair and equitable treatment" as mere examples of
> the meager protection provided under "customary international law" would be to change the
> meaning of those terms to "protection and security from the most egregious of government
> action" and "full protection and security from actions that would shock the international
> community". That is not what the language of Article 1105 says and that is not what NAFTA
> requires in order to attain its objectives.[70]

In its response, the United States emphasized that, under NAFTA, FPS and FET
'depend upon the rule of the customary law minimum standard of treatment'.[71]
Particularly, the Respondent considered that '[t]he treaty term "full protection and
security" refers to the minimum level of police protection against criminal conduct
that is required under customary international law'.[72] The respondent additionally
underscored the binding character of the FTC's interpretation of NAFTA article
1105.[73] The arbitrators observed that the FPS and FET standards set forth in NAFTA
must be interpreted in accordance with the FTC Declaratory Note:

> [W]e have the Parties [of NAFTA] themselves – all the Parties speaking to the Tribunal. No
> more authentic and authoritative source of instruction on what the Parties intended to convey
> in a particular provision of NAFTA, is possible [. . .] any general requirement to accord "fair
> and equitable treatment" and "full protection and security" must be disciplined by being
> based upon State practice and judicial or arbitral case law or other sources of customary or
> general international law.[74]

While accepting that the content of NAFTA article 1105(1) is determined by
customary international law, the *ADF* tribunal was of the view that 'the issue relating
to the structure and content of the customary international minimum standard of
treatment has not been adequately litigated'.[75] The arbitrators added that 'neither the

---

[69]Free Trade Commission, *Notes of Interpretation of Certain Chapter 11 Provisions* (31 July 2001)
[http://www.sice.oas.org/tpd/nafta/Commission/CH11understanding_e.asp].   Section   14.2.1
addresses the impact of the Note of Interpretation on NAFTA cases in detail.

[70]ADF *v* United States, Memorial of the Investor, ICSID Case No. ARB(AF)/00/1 (1 August 2001)
[238]. See also: ADF *v* United States, Award, ICSID Case No. ARB(AF)/00/1 (9 January 2003)
[70-1] (summarizing the Claimant's argument).

[71]ADF *v* United States, Post-Hearing Submission of Respondent United States of America on
Article 1105(1) and *Pope & Talbot*, ICSID Case No. ARB(AF)/00/1 (27 June 2002) 2. See also:
ADF *v* United States, Award, ICSID Case No. ARB(AF)/00/1 (9 January 2003) [110].

[72]ADF *v* United States, Post-Hearing Submission of Respondent United States of America on
Article 1105(1) and *Pope & Talbot*, ICSID Case No. ARB(AF)/00/1 (27 June 2002) 3. See also:
ADF *v* United States, Award, ICSID Case No. ARB(AF)/00/1 (9 January 2003) [110].

[73]ADF *v* United States, Post-Hearing Submission of Respondent United States of America on
Article 1105(1) and *Pope & Talbot*, ICSID Case No. ARB(AF)/00/1 (27 June 2002) 8 *et seq.* See
also: ADF *v* United States, Award, ICSID Case No. ARB(AF)/00/1 (9 January 2003) [111].

[74]ADF *v* United States, Award, ICSID Case No. ARB(AF)/00/1 (9 January 2003) [177 and 184].
Cf. Waste Management *v* Mexico, Award, ICSID Case No. ARB(AF)/00/3 (30 April 2004)
[96] (quoting the *ADF* award in this connection).

[75]ADF *v* United States, Award, ICSID Case No. ARB(AF)/00/1 (9 January 2003) [183].

Investor nor the Respondent has been able to persuasively demonstrate the correctness of their respective contentions'.[76] In the *ADF* case, the FTC Note of Interpretation resolved any doubt as to the relationship between FPS, FET and the minimum standard of treatment. The issuance of such statement in the course of the arbitral proceedings is, however, a rather extraordinary, if not to say unique, circumstance.

In other cases, arbitral tribunals have actually given weight *absence* of an express reference to the customary minimum standard. In *Cervin v Costa Rica* (2017) the arbitrators considered the interpretation of article 4(1) of the Costa Rica-Switzerland BIT, which contains both the FPS and FET clauses. Making specific reference to the FET standard, the tribunal stated:

> [T]he arbitral tribunal notes that the text of the BIT contains no reference whatsoever to neither customary international law nor to a "minimum level of treatment". This has significant importance because the Parties to the BIT could have expressly referred to any of such [notions] within the [FET] standard included in the BIT. The absence of these phrases gives a particular meaning to the fair and equitable treatment obligation under the BIT. In light of the foregoing, the Tribunal sees no reason to equalize this obligation with the minimum standard of treatment under customary international law. It agrees with the Parties' [contention] that the fair and equitable treatment standard of Article 4.1 refers to an autonomous standard.[77]

Whether this approach is correct depends on the wording of the specific treaty clause under consideration. For example, there are treaties that refer to customary law in respect of the FET standard but not in respect of the FPS standard. In those cases, it is arguable that the parties could have intended to accord customary law a different role in respect of each standard. An example would be article III(1) of the BIT between Canada and the Czech and Slovak Federal Republic of 1990:

> Investments or returns of investors of either Contracting Party shall at all times be accorded fair and equitable treatment in accordance with principles of international law and shall enjoy full protection and security in the territory of the other Contracting Party.[78]

In *Frontier Petroleum v Czech Republic* (2010), the arbitral tribunal gave careful consideration to the wording of this FPS clause, and observed:

---

[76] ADF *v* United States, Award, ICSID Case No. ARB(AF)/00/1 (9 January 2003) [183].

[77] Author's translation. The original Spanish text reads: "[E]l Tribunal Arbitral nota que el texto del APPRI no hace referencia alguna al derecho internacional consuetudinario, ni a un "nivel mínimo de trato". Esto tiene particular importancia dado que las Partes Contratantes del APPRI pudieron haber referido el estándar incluido en el APPRI expresamente a cualquiera de ellos. La ausencia de estas expresiones confiere un significado particular a la obligación de trato justo y equitativo bajo el APPRI. En vista de lo anterior, el Tribunal no ve razones para equiparar esta obligación con el estándar de nivel mínimo de trato bajo el derecho internacional consuetudinario. Coincide así con las Partes en que el estándar de trato justo y equitativo del Artículo 4.1 se refiere a un estándar autónomo." Cervin Investissements S.A. and Rhone Investissements S.A. *v* Costa Rica, Laudo, ICSID Case No. ARB/13/2 (7 March 2017) [452-3].

[78] Agreement between Canada and the Government of the Czech and Slovak Federal Republic for the Promotion and Protection of Investments (adopted 15 November 1990, entered into force 9 March 1992, terminated 22 January 2012) art. III(1).

On the basis of the wording of Article III(1) of the BIT, "full protection and security" and general international law appear as two discrete standards. By contrast, the fair and equitable treatment clause of Article III(1) is supplemented by the words "in accordance with principles of international law". Whatever the exact meaning of this reference, the fact that it does not qualify the full protection and security standard is an argument against the latter standard being regarded as equivalent to customary international law.[79]

Whatever the merits of this interpretation of the BIT, it should be noted that Canada and the Czech Republic concluded a new BIT in 2009, which expressly recognizes that FPS is an element of the 'customary international minimum standard of treatment of aliens' and '[does] not require treatment in addition to or beyond' the minimum standard.[80]

Other treaties provide a clear indication that it was the parties' intention to establish a treaty-based standard, which does not necessarily correspond to the customary standard. Thus, in recently negotiated treaties, the European Union has defined FPS in terms of 'physical security' and avoided any reference to customary law. This pattern appears in CETA,[81] the EU-Singapore Investment Agreement,[82] and the EU-Vietnam Investment Agreement.[83] Commenting on these treaties, scholars have explained this practice as a 'reaction' against broad interpretations of the standard and, particularly, against arbitral decisions stating that FPS encompasses a guarantee of legal security.[84]

Even if it is concluded that a specific FPS clause is autonomous from customary law, the customary protection obligation could still be relevant for the interpretation of the treaty. Article 31(3)(c) of the Vienna Convention on the Law of Treaties provides that the interpretation of an international treaty shall take into consideration '[a]ny relevant rules of international law applicable in the relations between the parties'.[85] Scholars have suggested that, when the contracting parties use phrases

---

[79]Frontier Petroleum Ltd. v Czech Republic (UNCITRAL), Final Award (12 November 2010) [268].

[80]Agreement between Canada and the Czech Republic for the Promotion and Protection of Investments (adopted 6 May 2009, entered into force 22 January 2012) art. III(1).

[81]Comprehensive Economic and Trade Agreement between Canada and the European Union (signed 30 October 2016, provisionally entered into force 21 September 2017) art. 8.10(5).

[82]European Union – Singapore Investment Protection Agreement (adopted 15 October 2018) arts. 2.4(1) and (5).

[83]European Union – Vietnam Investment Protection Agreement (negotiated draft; version of September 2018) arts. 2.5(1) and (5).

[84]Peter-Tobias Stoll, Till Patrik Holterhus and Henner Gött, *Investitionsschutz und Verfassung* (Mohr Siebeck, Tübingen 2017) 23-4.

[85]Vienna Convention on Diplomatic Relations (adopted 18 April 1961, entered into force 24 April 1964) 500 UNTS 95, art. 31(3)(c). For a detailed, general academic study of this provision see: Panos Merkouris, *Article 31(3)(c) VCLT and the Principle of Systemic Integration* (Brill, Leiden 2015) 15 *et seq.* For an analysis of this provision in particular connection with international investment law see: Daniel Rosentreter, *Article 31(3)(c) of the Vienna Convention on the Law of Treaties and the Principle of Systemic Integration in International Investment Law and Arbitration* (Nomos, Baden-Baden 2015) 247 *et seq.*; Tarcisio Gazzini, *Interpretation of International Investment Treaties* (Hart Publishing, Portland OR 2016) 210 *et seq.*

which 'have a well-recognised meaning in customary international law', as would be the case of *full protection and security*, there is a strong indication that the parties intended to incorporate such customary norm into the treaty framework.[86] The threshold issue is, then, to which extent specific formulations of the FPS standard entail a reference to customary law or derogate from the customary standard. The following sections address this fundamental question in connection with the most common articulations of the FPS standard.

14.3 References to Domestic Law in Protection and Security Clauses

A few protection and security clauses contain explicit references to municipal law. These treaty provisions can be classified in two groups. In a first group of clauses, reference is made to both domestic law and general international law. A textbook example would be article II(4) of the BIT between the United States and the Republic of Zaire (now Democratic Republic of Congo):

> Investments of nationals and companies of either Party shall at all times be accorded fair and equitable treatment and shall enjoy *protection and security* in the territory of the other Party. The treatment, *protection and security of investment shall be in accordance with applicable national laws, and may not be less than that recognized by international law.*[87]

In *AMT v Zaire* (1997), the arbitral tribunal held that this treaty clause did not allow the host state to rely on domestic law to escape responsibility for wants of diligence in the protection of covered investments.[88] In this vein, the arbitrators explained:

> These treatments of protection and security of investment required by the provisions of the BIT of which AMT is beneficiary must be in conformity with its applicable national laws and must not be any less than those recognized by international law. For the tribunal, this last requirement is fundamental for the determination of the responsibility of Zaire. It is thus an objective obligation which must not be inferior to the minimum standard of vigilance and of care required by international law.[89]

---

[86]Campbell McLachlan, 'The Principle of Systemic Integration and Article 31(3)(c) of the Vienna Convention' (2005) 54(2) ICLQ 279, 312 (making particular reference to the phrase 'full protection and security' in this connection).

[87]Emphasis added. Treaty between the United States of America and the Republic of Zaire concerning the Reciprocal Encouragement and Protection of Investment (adopted 3 August 1984, entered into force 28 July 1989) art. II(4).

[88]American Manufacturing & Trading Inc. *v* Zaire, Award, ICSID Case No. ARB 93/1 (21 February 1997) [6.04].

[89]American Manufacturing & Trading Inc. *v* Zaire, Award, ICSID Case No. ARB 93/1 (21 February 1997) [6.05].

Other tribunals have followed a similar approach. In *Ampal v Egypt* (2017), an ICSID arbitral tribunal applied the FPS clause of the Egypt-US BIT, which uses a similar language as the US-Zaire BIT.[90] In their analysis of the claims, the arbitrators characterized FPS as 'one important element of the international law standard'.[91] This approach is correct. There can be no doubt that this conclusion is warranted whenever the applicable clause, despite referring to national law, expressly requires compliance with the minimum dictated by international law.

The second group of clauses poses greater difficulties. In the treaty practice of some states, the protection obligation is frequently qualified with an express reference to municipal law, without any reference to customary or general international law. Examples may be found in multiple Russian BITs, which provide that '[e]ach Contracting Party shall guarantee, *in accordance with its legislation*, full and unconditional legal protection'.[92] These clauses pose a fascinating hermeneutic problem. They indeed raise the question of whether *legal protection* is defined on the sole basis of domestic law, the potential implication being that the extent of the protection obligation depends on the vicissitudes of domestic affairs and, ultimately, on the will of the host state. Investment arbitral tribunals have followed different approaches in this regard.

In some cases, arbitrators have considered that the language of these treaty provisions grants no protection from local legislation. They have accordingly reduced the security obligation to compliance with domestic law. Thus, in *Iurii Bogdanov v Moldova* (2005), the arbitral tribunal interpreted article 2(2) of the Modova-Russian Federation BIT as follows:

> The wording of article 2(2) of the BIT makes clear that the full protection principle is not to be considered as corrective of the host country's legislation, but has to be applied in accordance with the host country's law. As long as the restrictions [...] are in accordance with Moldovan law, therefore, the full protection standard of the BIT may not be deemed violated [...] the Arbitral Tribunal finds that the conduct of the Respondent does not violate Moldovan law; therefore, the Respondent's conduct is not in violation of the full protection standard contained in article 2 of the BIT.[93]

---

[90]Cf. Treaty between the United States of America and the Arab Republic of Egypt concerning the Reciprocal Encouragement and Protection of Investments (adopted 11 March 1986, entered into force 27 June 1992) art. II(4).

[91]Ampal-American Israel Corp., Egi-Fund (08-10) Investors LLC, Egi-Series Investments LLC and BSS-EMG Investors LLC *v* Egypt, Decision on Liability and Heads of Loss, ICSID Case No. ARB/12/11 (21 February 2017) [240]. It should be observed, however, that the arbitrators did not provide any elaboration on the effect of the BIT's explicit reference to 'national legislation'.

[92]Emphasis added. Agreement between the Government of the Russian Federation and the Government of the Republic of Cyprus Regarding the Promotion and Mutual Protection of Investments (adopted 11 April 2007) art. 2(2); Agreement between the Government of the Russian Federation and the Government of the Republic of Moldova Regarding the Promotion and Mutual Protection of Investments (adopted 17 March 1998, entered into force 18 July 2001) art. 2(2). For an author commenting on this treaty language see: Geneviève Bastid Burdeau, 'La clause de protection et sécurité pleine et entière' (2015) 119(1) RGDIP 87, 90 (also citing the example of Russian BITs).

[93]Iurii Bogdanov et al. *v* Moldova (SCC), Arbitral Award (22 September 2005) 15 (referring to the FPS clause of the Moldova-Russian Federation BIT).

The opposite approach was followed in *Sergei Paushok v Mongolia* (2011). The case referred to the Mongolia-Russian Federation BIT, the same treaty considered in the *Iurii Bogdanov* case.[94] The *Sergei Paushok* tribunal rejected the restriction of the clause's scope of protection to 'physical protection', but did not specify whether this treaty wording could be said to guarantee a stable legal environment.[95] The tribunal quoted in length the *AMT* tribunal's conclusion that, under the FPS standard, protection must be 'in conformity' with the host state's municipal law but, at the same time, cannot fall below the level of protection required under international law.[96] The tribunal failed to see, however, that the treaty applied in the *AMT* case expressly established that international law defined the minimum level of protection required from local authorities.[97] No such indication appears in the Moldova-Russian Federation BIT. The *Paushok* tribunal's reliance on the *AMT* award is therefore questionable.

In other cases filed under Russian BITs, arbitral tribunals have drawn a distinction between protection from local legislation as such, and protection against the unlawful or deficient application of such legislation. An example would be the award rendered in *OAO Tatneft v Ukraine* (2014). The case concerned an FPS claim submitted under the Russia-Ukraine BIT, which guarantees legal protection 'in conformity with the legislation'.[98] In their assessment of the claim, the arbitrators stated:

> [T]he text of Article 2 2. of the Ukraine-Russia BIT provides greater clarity on this discussion as it guarantees unconditional legal protection of Claimant's investments "in accordance with its legislation". There is here a specific link to the legal protection of the investment which is not often found in BITs. While the legislation in itself might not amount to a breach of this guarantee, this is something that might happen in the context of how the legislation is implemented or applied.[99]

---

[94] Sergei Paushok, CJSC Golden East Co., CJSC Vostoknefte *v* Mongolia (UNCITRAL), Award on Jurisdiction and Liability (28 April 2011) [322-7].

[95] Sergei Paushok, CJSC Golden East Co., CJSC Vostoknefte *v* Mongolia (UNCITRAL), Award on Jurisdiction and Liability (28 April 2011) [326-7]. This finding was, however, more related to the use of the adjective 'legal' than to the reference to domestic law. Section 14.4.3 explores this aspect of the *Sergei Paushok* award in more detail.

[96] Sergei Paushok, CJSC Golden East Co., CJSC Vostoknefte *v* Mongolia (UNCITRAL), Award on Jurisdiction and Liability (28 April 2011) [323] (directly quoting the award rendered in *AMT v Zaire*, discussed above).

[97] Treaty between the United States of America and the Republic of Zaire concerning the Reciprocal Encouragement and Protection of Investment (adopted 3 August 1984, entered into force 28 July 1989) art. II(4).

[98] Agreement between the Government of the Russian Federation and the Cabinet of Ministers of the Ukraine on the Encouragement and Mutual Protection of Investments (adopted 27 November 1998, entered into force 27 January 2000) art. 2(2) ("Each Contracting Party shall guarantee, *in conformity with the legislation*, the complete and unconditional legal protection of investments of investors of the other Contracting Party").

[99] OAO Tatneft *v* Ukraine (UNCITRAL), Award (29 July 2014) [425].

It is plausible that these clauses grant security *as provided by* domestic law, rather than *from* domestic law. They certainly do not require the host state to adopt new legislation, to modify extant regulations or to abstain from doing so. But they do require the host state to enforce its own laws, so that the protection granted by the law to foreign investors is not rendered illusory. If public authorities fail to do so, international responsibility attaches.

These provisions can be better understood as entailing a *renvoi* to municipal law, in a twofold sense.[100] On the one hand, they only protect rights and interests recognized by municipal law. On other hand, once local law has recognized a right or interest, the protection promised by domestic legislation is not only a matter of municipal law, but also of international law. Thus, for example, in most domestic legal systems property owners are entitled to police protection against third parties who interfere with the enjoyment of property. Investors holding a property title acquired *in conformity with local law* are entitled to such police protection as a matter of domestic law. If competent authorities deny investors the protection provided for by municipal law, international responsibility under an FPS clause of this type could attach.

The question remains open, however, as to whether the minimum standard of treatment is still a parameter for the assessment of the host state's conduct, as suggested by the *Sergei Paushok* tribunal. If the minimum standard is applicable, an omission in the protection of aliens, even if consistent with domestic law, could still constitute a breach of this type of clauses. This question can hardly be assessed in the abstract, and heavily depends on the particular context of the treaty under consideration.

In practice, however, the issue seems to be much less important as might seem at first sight. As indicated by the *OAO Tatneft* tribunal, clauses requiring the host state to provide protection 'in accordance with its legislation' do not impose responsibility for legislation as such, but for its enforcement. *On the paper*, the protection afforded by the domestic legal system only rarely falls below the minimum standard of treatment. Quite the contrary, many jurisdictions *formally* afford foreigners a level of protection *beyond* the minimum standard. Not surprisingly, breaches of the customary FPS standard do not usually arise from legislation as such. The host state does not normally fail at its legislation, but at the implementation of its legislation.

From this perspective, even if interpreted as a derogation from the minimum standard, these treaty clauses are a double-edged sword. Treaty drafters might expect references to domestic law to reduce the risk of the host state being held accountable for a breach of FPS. However, these treaty provisions unquestionably impose upon the host state an obligation to ensure the effectiveness of the protection granted by its

---

[100]For an overview of the notion of *renvoi* (to municipal law) in international investment law see: Monique Sasson, *Substantive Law in Investment Treaty Arbitration* (Kluwer Law International, Alphen aan den Rijn 2010) xxviii-xxxi and 202-8; Nils Börnsen, *Nationales Recht in Investitionsschiedsverfahren* (Mohr Siebeck, Tübingen 2016) 81 *et seq.*

own legislation. As a rule, this protection, as defined by municipal law, reaches far beyond the minimum required by the customary law of aliens.

14.4   Qualifying Adjectives in Protection and Security Clauses

One of the most striking features of FPS clauses is the wide variety of adjectives that qualify the standard. Among these many adjectives, three are particularly relevant for the analysis of investment arbitral decisions: *full*, *constant* and *legal*. Other adjectives are, in fact, far less common in investment treaty practice.[101] This section provides an overview of the interpretation of these three terms. In addition, it considers the interpretation of protection and security clauses that do not employ any qualifying adjective.

14.4.1   The Adjective Full

The term 'full' is the adjective that most commonly qualifies the nouns 'protection' and 'security' in investment treaties. FPS claims frequently refer to clauses using the phrase '*full* protection and security' or its equivalent in another language (e.g. '*protection et [...] sécurité pleines et entières*'[102] in French or '*plena protección y seguridad*'[103] in Spanish). Examples may be found in cases decided

---

[101]For an example of a security clause using another adjective see: Agreement on Promotion, Protection and Guarantee of Investments among Member States of the Organisation of the Islamic Conference (adopted 5 June 1981, entered into force 23 September 1986) art. 2 ("The invested capital shall enjoy *adequate* protection and security [...]"- emphasis added). On the interpretation of the adjective 'adequate' in the OIC Agreement cf. Hesham Talaat M. Al-Warraq *v* Indonesia (UNCITRAL), Final Award (15 December 2014) [630] (stating that the guarantee of 'adequate protection and security' does not provide a lesser degree of protection than a clause using the adjective 'full'). Cf. also the parties' arguments at paras 423-4 (claimant) and 431 (respondent).

[102]See, for example: Accord entre le Gouvernement de la République française et le Gouvernement de la République Argentine sur l'encouragement et la protection réciproques des investissements (adopted 3 July 1991, entered into force 3 March 1993) art. 5(1).

[103]See, for example: Tratado entre el Gobierno de la República de Costa Rica y el Gobierno de la República Federal de Alemania sobre el fomento y recíproca protección de inversiones (adopted 13 September 1994, entered into force 24 March 1998) art. 4(1).

under multilateral agreements,[104] as well as under bilateral treaties concluded by major capital-exporting countries, such as Canada,[105] France,[106] Germany,[107] the

---

[104]NAFTA cases provide indicative examples in this regard. See: ADF *v* United States, Award, ICSID Case No. ARB(AF)/00/1 (9 January 2003) [175 *et seq.*, 191 and 193]; Loewen Group Inc. and Raymond L. Loewen *v* United States, Award, ICSID Case No. ARB(AF)/98/3 (26 June 2003) [128]; Mercer International Inc. *v* Canada, Award, ICSID Case No. ARB(AF)/12/3 (6 March 2018) [7.80]; Waste Management *v* Mexico, Award, ICSID Case No. ARB(AF)/00/3 (30 April 2004) [91 and 96]. The USMCA of 2018 also uses the adjective 'full'. See: Agreement between the United States of America, the United Mexican States, and Canada (adopted 30 November 2018) arts. 14.6 (1) and (2)(b).

[105]Some recent awards have referred to the 'full protection and security' clause in art. II(2) of the Canada-Venezuela BIT. See, for example: Crystallex International Corp. *v* Venezuela, Award, ICSID Case No. ARB(AF)/11/2 (4 April 2016) [632-5]; Gold Reserve Inc. *v* Venezuela, Award, ICSID Case No. ARB(AF)/09/1 (22 September 2014) [622-3]; Rusoro Mining Ltd. *v* Venezuela, Award, ICSID Case No. ARB(AF)/12/5 (22 August 2016) [542-54] (the case also involved an allegation under the guarantee of 'full protection and legal security' ['seguridad y protección jurídica plenas'] set forth in art. 4 of the Uruguay-Venezuela BIT, which was invoked on the basis of the MFN clause of the Canada-Venezuela BIT); Vannessa Ventures Ltd. *v* Venezuela, Award, ICSID Case No. ARB(AF)04/6 (16 January 2013) [216-32]. For cases concerning other Canadian FPS clauses see: Frontier Petroleum Ltd. *v* Czech Republic (UNCITRAL), Final Award (12 November 2010) [260-73] (referring to the guarantee of 'full protection and security' in art. III (1) of the Canada-Czech Republic BIT); Peter A. Allard *v* Barbados (UNCITRAL), Award (27 June 2016) [239-52] (referring to the guarantee of 'full protection and security' in art. II(2)(b) of the Canada-Barbados BIT).

[106]Multiple cases have referred to the guarantee of 'protection et [. . .] sécurité pleines et entières' in art. 5(1) of the France-Argentina BIT. See: Compañía de Aguas del Aconquija S.A. and Vivendi Universal S.A. *v* Argentina, Award, ICSID Case No. ARB/97/3 (20 August 2007) [7.4.13-7.4.17]; EDF International S.A., Saur International S.A. and Leon Participaciones Argentinas S.A. *v* Argentina, Award, ICSID Case No. ARB/03/23 (11 June 2012) [403-20 and 1108-12]; SAUR International S.A. *v* Argentina, Décision sur la compétence et sur la responsabilité, ICSID Case No. ARB/04/4 (6 June 2012) [499-501 and 508-11]; Suez Sociedad General de Aguas de Barcelona S.A. and Vivendi Universal S.A. *v* Argentina, Decision on Liability, ICSID Case No. ARB/03/19 (30 July 2010) [158 *et seq.*] (the case additionally involved the interpretation of FPS clauses using a different wording); Total S.A. *v* Argentina, Decision on Liability, ICSID Case No. ARB/04/1 (27 December 2010) [343]. For cases concerning other French BITs see: Gemplus S. A., SLP S.A. and Gemplus Industrial S.A. de C.V. *v* Mexico, Award, ICSID Cases No. ARB(AF)/ 04/3 & ARB(AF)/04/4 (16 June 2010) [9.9-9.14] (referring to the guarantee of 'full and complete protection and safety' in art. 4(3) of the France-Mexico BIT, as well as to the guarantee of 'full legal protection' ['plena protección legal'] in art. 3(2) of the Argentina-Mexico BIT); Saint-Gobain Performance Plastics Europe *v* Venezuela, Decision on Liability and the Principles of Quantum, ICSID Case No. ARB/12/13 (30 December 2016) [543-65] (referring to the guarantee of 'protection et [. . .] sécurité pleines et entières' in art. 3(2) of the France-Venezuela BIT; the case also involved an allegation under the guarantee of 'full legal protection' ['seguridad y protección jurídica plenas'] set forth in art. 4 of the Uruguay-Venezuela BIT, which was invoked on the basis of the MFN clause of the France-Venezuela BIT).

[107]Bernhard Friedrich Arnd Rüdiger von Pezold et al. *v* Zimbabwe, Award, ICSID Case No. ARB/10/15 (28 July 2015) [593-9] (referring to the guarantee of 'full protection and security' in art. 4(1) of the Germany-Zimbabwe BIT as well as art. 4(1) of the Switzerland-Zimbabwe BIT); Deutsche Bank AG *v* Sri Lanka, Award, ICSID Case No. ARB/09/02 (31 October 2012) [535] (referring to the guarantee of 'full protection and security' in art. 4(1) of the Germany-Sri Lanka

Netherlands,[108] the United Kingdom,[109] and the United States.[110] These provisions

BIT); Gea Group Aktiengesellschaft *v* Ukraine, Award, ICSID Case No. ARB/08/16 (31 March 2011) [242-67] (referring to the guarantee of 'full protection and full security' ['vollen Schutz und volle Sicherheit'] in art. 4(1) of the Germany-Ukraine BIT); Marion Unglaube and Reinhard Unglaube *v* Costa Rica, Award, ICSID Cases No. ARB/01/1 and ARB/09/20 (16 May 2012) [280-8] (referring to the guarantee of 'full protection and security' ['plena protección y seguridad'] in art. 4(1) of the Costa Rica-Germany BIT); Siemens AG *v* Argentina, Award, ICSID Case No. ARB/02/8 (6 February 2007) [301-3] (referring to the guarantee of 'full protection' ['*plena protección*'] and 'legal security' ['seguridad jurídica'] in the Spanish text of art. 4(1) of the Argentina-Germany BIT).

[108]Numerous cases have addressed the guarantee of 'full security and protection' in art. 3(2) of the Netherlands-Czech and Slovak Federal Republic BIT. See, for example: Achmea B.V. *v* Slovakia (UNCITRAL), Award on Jurisdiction, Arbitrability and Suspension, PCA Case No. 2008-13 (26 October 2010) [259-63 and 284]; CME Czech Republic B.V. *v* Czech Republic (UNCITRAL), Partial Award (13 September 2001) [351-8 and 613]; Eastern Sugar B.V. *v* Czech Republic, Partial Award, SCC Case No. 088/2004 (27 March 2007) [201-7]; Jan Oostergetel and Theodora Laurentius *v* Slovakia (UNCITRAL), Final Award (23 April 2012) [305-8]; Saluka Investments *v* Czech Republic (UNCITRAL), Partial Award (17 March 2006) [483-96 and 505]. For cases referring to other Dutch treaties see: Eureko B.V. *v* Poland (*Ad Hoc* Arbitration), Partial Award (19 August 2005) [236-7] (referring to the guarantee of 'full security and protection' in art. 3(2) of the Netherlands-Poland BIT); OI European Group B.V. *v* Venezuela, Award, ICSID Case No. ARB/11/25 (10 March 2015) [571-81] (referring to the guarantee of 'full physical security and protection' in art. 3(2) of the Netherlands-Venezuela BIT).

[109]Anglia Auto Accessories Ltd. *v* Czech Republic, Final Award, SCC Case No. V 2014/181 (10 March 2017) [190] (referring to the guarantee of 'full protection and security' in art. 2(2) of the Czech Republic-UK BIT); Anglo American PLC *v* Venezuela, Award, ICSID Case No. ARB(AF)/14/1 (18 January 2019) [473-85] (referring to the guarantee of 'full protection and security' in art. 2 (2) of the Venezuela-UK BIT); Asian Agricultural Products *v* Sri Lanka, Final Award, ICSID Case No. ARB/87/3 (17 June 1990) [45 *et seq.*] (referring to the guarantee of 'full protection and security' in art. 2(2) of the Sri Lanka-UK BIT); Biwater Gauff Ltd. *v* Tanzania, Award, ICSID Case No. ARB/05/22 (24 July 2008) [729-30] (referring to the guarantee of 'full protection and security' in art. 2(2) of the Tanzania-UK BIT); I.P. Busta and J.P. Busta *v* Czech Republic, Final Award, SCC Case No. V 2015/014 (10 March 2017) [165 and 422] (referring to the guarantee of 'full protection and security' in art. 2(2) of the Czech Republic-UK BIT); Oxus Gold *v* Uzbekistan (UNCITRAL), Final Award (17 December 2015) [348 *et seq.* and 829 *et seq.*] (referring to the guarantee of 'full protection and security' in art. 2(2) of the Uzbekistan-UK BIT); Rumeli Telekom A.S. and Telsim Mobil Telekomunikasyon Hizmetleri A.S. *v* Kazakhstan, Award, ICSID Case No. ARB/05/16 (29 July 2008) [669-70] (referring to the guarantee of 'full protection and security' in art. 2(2) of the Kazakhstan-UK BIT, which was invoked on the basis of the MFN clause of the Turkey-Kazakhstan BIT); Wena Hotels Ltd. *v* Egypt, Award, ICSID Case No. ARB/98/4 (8 December 2000) [83-95 and 134] (referring to the guarantee of 'full protection and security' in art. 2(2) of the Egypt-UK BIT).

[110]Several cases have referred to the guarantee of 'full protection and security' enshrined in art. II(2) (a) of the Argentina-US BIT. See, for example: Azurix Corp. *v* Argentina, Award, ICSID Case No. ARB/01/12 (14 July 2006) [408]; Azurix Corp. *v* Argentina, Decision on the Application for Annulment of the Argentina Republic, ICSID Case No. ARB/01/12 (1 September 2009) [182-4]; El Paso Energy International Co. *v* Argentina, Award, ICSID Case No. ARB/03/15 (31 October 2011) [522-5]; Enron Corp. and Ponderosa Assets L.P. *v* Argentina, Award, ICSID Case No. ARB/01/3 (22 May 2007) [284-7]; Impregilo S.p.A. *v* Argentina, Award, ICSID Case No. ARB/07/17 (21 June 2011) [334] (in this case the FPS clause of the Argentina-US BIT was invoked on the basis of the MFN clause of the Argentina-Italy BIT); Mobil Exploration and Development

have also been considered in disputes under Spanish[111] and Italian BITs,[112] as well as under treaties between countries traditionally classified as capital importing economies.[113]

Argentina Inc. Suc. Argentina and Mobil Argentina S.A. *v* Argentina, Decision on Jurisdiction and Liability, ICSID Case No. ARB/04/16 (10 April 2013) [988-1005]; Sempra Energy International *v* Argentina, Award, ICSID Case No. ARB/02/16 (28 September 2007) [321-4]. Other cases have referred to the guarantee of 'full protection and security' in art. II(3)(a) of the Ecuador-US BIT. See, for example: M.C.I. Power Group L.C. and New Turbine Inc. *v* Ecuador, Award, ICSID Case No. ARB/03/6 (31 July 2007) [245-6 and 252]; Occidental Exploration and Production Co. *v* Ecuador, Final Award, LCIA Case No. UN 3467 (1 July 2004) [187]; Ulysseas Inc. *v* Ecuador (UNCITRAL), Final Award (12 June 2012) [271-4]. For cases involving FPS clauses of other American IIAs see for example: Adel A Hamadi Al Tamini *v* Oman, Award, ICSID Case No. Arb/11/33 (3 November 2015) [380, 382 and 448-52] (referring to the 'full protection and security' clause in art. 10.5 of the Oman-US FTA); Joseph Charles Lemire *v* Ukraine, Decision on Jurisdiction and Liability, ICSID Case No. ARB/06/18 (14 January 2010) [246] (referring to the guarantee of 'full protection and security' in art. II(3) of the US-Ukraine BIT); Noble Ventures *v* Romania, Award, ICSID Case No. ARB/01/11 (12 October 2005) [164-7] (referring to the guarantee of 'full protection and security' in art. II(2)(a) of the Romania-US BIT); PSEG Global Inc. and Konya Ilgin Elektrik Üretim ve Ticaret Limited Şirketi *v* Turkey, Award, ICSID Case No. ARB/02/5 (19 January 2007) [257-9] (referring to the guarantee of 'full protection and security' in art. II(3) of the US-Turkey BIT); Ronald Lauder *v* Czech Republic (UNCITRAL), Final Award (3 September 2001) [305-14] (referring to the guarantee of 'full protection and security' in art. II(2) (a) of the US-Czech Republic BIT). See also the NAFTA cases quoted in n. 104 above.

[111]Tecnicas Medioambientales TECMED S.A. *v* Mexico, Award, ICSID Case No. ARB(AF)/00/2 (29 May 2003) [175-81] (referring to the guarantee of 'full protection and security' ['*protección y seguridad plenas*'] in art. IV(1) of the Mexico-Spain BIT, but focusing on other provisions of the BIT).

[112]See, for example: LESI S.p.A. and ASTALDI S.p.A. *v* Algeria, Sentence, ICSID Case No. ARB/05/3 (12 November 2008) [152-4] (referring to the guarantee of 'constant, full and complete protection and security' ['protezione e sicurezza costanti, piene ed intere'] in art. 4 (1) of the Algeria-Italy BIT); Toto Costruzioni Generali S.p.A. v Lebanon, Award, ICSID Case No. ARB/07/12 (7 June 2012) [226-30] (referring to the guarantee of 'full protection and security' in art. 4(1) of the Italy-Lebanon BIT); Waguih George Siag and Clorinda Vecchi *v* Egypt, Award, ICSID Case No. ARB/05/15 (1 June 2009) [445-8] (referring to the guarantee of 'full protection' in art. 4(1) of the Italy-Egypt BIT).

[113]Československá Obchodní Banka A.S. *v* Slovakia, Award, ICSID Case No. ARB/97/4 (29 December 2004) [63, 71, 161, 170 and 183] (referring to the guarantee of 'full protection and security' in art. 2(2) of the Czech Republic-Slovakia BIT); Gemplus S.A., SLP S.A. and Gemplus Industrial S.A. de C.V. *v* Mexico, Award, ICSID Cases No. ARB(AF)/04/3 & ARB(AF)/04/4 (16 June 2010) [9.9-9.14] (referring to the guarantee of 'full legal protection' ['plena protección legal'] in art. 3(2) of the Argentina-Mexico BIT; the case also involved the guarantee of 'full and complete protection and safety' in art. 4(3) of the France-Mexico BIT); Pantechniki S.A. Contractors & Engineers *v* Albania, Award, ICSID Case No. ARB/07/21 (30 July 2009) [71-84] (referring to the guarantee of 'full protection and security' in art. 4(1) of the Albania-Greece BIT); Spyridon Roussalis *v* Romania, Award, ICSID Case No. ARB/06/1 (7 December 2011) [319-22] (referring to the guarantee of 'full protection and security' in art. 2(2) of the Greece-Romania BIT); Tokios Tokelés *v* Ukraine, Award, ICSID Case No. ARB/02/18 (26 July 2007) [85-6 and 123 *et seq.*] (referring to the guarantee of 'full protection and security' in art. 2(2) of the Lithuania-Ukraine BIT). See also the allegations under the guarantee of 'full legal protection' ['*seguridad y protección jurídica plenas*'] set forth in art. 4 of the Uruguay-Venezuela BIT, which

Despite its widespread use and the many arbitral decisions that have addressed this treaty language, the actual meaning and implications of the adjective *full* remain somewhat unclear. In some cases, investment tribunals have held that *full* has the effect of incorporating a guarantee of legal stability into the FPS standard. They have thus understood *full security* as *legal security*. Other tribunals have adopted the view that the term *full* does not entail a departure from the traditional core of the FPS standard, and have gone on to define such core in terms of *physical* protection. The result is that *full security* is taken to mean *physical security*. Arbitrators have also held that the phrase *full security* manifests the spirit of the treaty and, as such, is relevant for the analysis of other treaty provisions. In this vein, at least one arbitral tribunal gave weight to the wording of a BIT's FPS clause in the interpretation of the treaty's dispute settlement provisions.

This section begins by presenting these three lines of argument (Sects. 14.4.1.1–14.4.1.3). After careful consideration of these approaches, it argues that, as a rule, formulas such as *full protection and security* and *full protection* are merely terms of art designating the customary protection obligation (Sect. 14.4.1.4).

14.4.1.1 *Full* Security as *Legal* Security

There is an ongoing debate as to whether FPS ensures the stability of the invest-ment's regulatory framework.[114] Several tribunals advancing the broad understand-ing of the standard have referred to clauses using the adjective *full*. For example, in *CME v Czech Republic* (2001) the arbitral tribunal interpreted an FPS clause using this language as a guarantee against regulatory changes or administrative actions having a negative economic impact on the investment.[115]

In some cases, the adjective *full* has been the key to such extensive interpreta-tions. In *Azurix v Argentina* (2006) the arbitral tribunal considered that the term *full*, as used in article II(2)(a) of the Argentina-US BIT, justified a broad interpretation of the FPS standard:

> The Tribunal is aware that in recent free trade agreements signed by the United States, for instance, with Uruguay, full protection and security is understood to be limited to the level of

---

was invoked *via* the MFN standard in the *Rusoro* and *Saint-Gobain* cases: Rusoro Mining Ltd. *v* Venezuela, Award, ICSID Case No. ARB(AF)/12/5 (22 August 2016) [542-54]; Saint-Gobain Performance Plastics Europe *v* Venezuela, Decision on Liability and the Principles of Quantum, ICSID Case No. ARB/12/13 (30 December 2016) [543-65].

[114]See Sects. 9.2 and 9.3.

[115]CME Czech Republic B.V. *v* Czech Republic (UNCITRAL), Partial Award (13 September 2001) [613]. For a recent example of a broad interpretation of a clause using the phrase '*full* protection and security' cf. Anglo American PLC *v* Venezuela, Award, ICSID Case No. ARB(AF)/14/1 (18 January 2019) [482].

police protection required under customary international law. However, *when the terms "protection and security" are qualified by "full" and no other adjective or explanation, they extend, in their ordinary meaning, the content of this standard beyond physical security.*[116]

The holding of the *Azurix* tribunal influenced the award rendered a few years later in *Biwater v Tanzania* (2008):

> The Arbitral Tribunal adheres to the Azurix holding that *when the terms "protection" and "security" are qualified by "full", the content of the standard may extend to matters other than physical security. It implies a State's guarantee of stability in a secure environment, both physical, commercial and legal.* It would in the Arbitral Tribunal's view be unduly artificial to confine the notion of "full security" only to one aspect of security, particularly in light of the use of this term in a BIT, directed at the protection of commercial and financial investments.[117]

The *Biwater* tribunal additionally rejected the view that the 'full security standard' imposes a prevention obligation with regard to 'actions by third parties' only.[118] Rather, according to the arbitrators, the term 'full' indicates that FPS 'extends to actions by organs and representatives of the State itself'.[119]

The tribunal in *Total v Argentina* (2010) followed a similar line of argument. The case concerned the interpretation of the phrase '*protection et [. . .] sécurité pleines et entières, en application du principe de traitement juste et équitable*' in article 5(1) of the Argentina-France BIT.[120] In this regard, the arbitral tribunal held:

> A plain reading of the terms used in Article 5(1) of the BIT [. . .] shows that the protection provided for by Article 5(1) to covered investors and their assets *is not limited to physical protection but includes legal security.* The explicit linkage of this standard to the fair and equitable treatment standard supports this interpretation.[121]

Other tribunals have been much more cautious in this regard. In *Marion Unglaube v Costa Rica* (2012), the arbitral tribunal took cognizance of the broad interpretations advanced in the *Azurix* and *Biwater* awards.[122] In reference to the '*full* protection and security' clause in article 4(1) of the Costa Rica-Germany BIT, the arbitrators stated:

---

[116]Emphasis added. Azurix Corp. *v* Argentina, Award, ICSID Case No. ARB/01/12 (14 July 2006) [408].

[117]Emphasis added. Biwater Gauff Ltd. *v* Tanzania, Award, ICSID Case No. ARB/05/22 (24 July 2008) [729].

[118]Biwater Gauff Ltd. *v* Tanzania, Award, ICSID Case No. ARB/05/22 (24 July 2008) [730].

[119]Biwater Gauff Ltd. *v* Tanzania, Award, ICSID Case No. ARB/05/22 (24 July 2008) [730].

[120]Accord entre le Gouvernement de la République française et le Gouvernement de la République Argentine sur l'encouragement et la protection réciproques des investissements (adopted 3 July 1991, entered into force 3 March 1993) art. 5(1). See also: Total S.A. *v* Argentina, Decision on Liability, ICSID Case No. ARB/04/1 (27 December 2010) [343].

[121]Emphasis added. Total S.A. *v* Argentina, Decision on Liability, ICSID Case No. ARB/04/1 (27 December 2010) [343].

[122]Marion Unglaube and Reinhard Unglaube *v* Costa Rica, Award, ICSID Cases No. ARB/01/1 and ARB/09/20 (16 May 2012) [280].

As with any complex legal standard stated in a brief phrase, the words "full protection and security" allow for a broad range of possible meanings. *This Tribunal accepts, as urged by Claimants, that "full protection" may, in appropriate circumstances, extend beyond the traditional standard* [. . .] However, the Tribunal is not persuaded that this standard has been violated by Costa Rica.[123]

Besides these cases, arbitral tribunals have been generally reluctant to accept the proposition that the guarantee of 'full protection' entails a promise of legal stability, as often argued by investors.[124] In *EDF v Argentina* (2012), another case filed under the Argentina-France BIT, the investor alleged that '[h]ad Argentina and France wished to devise the meaning of "security" narrowly so as to preclude obligations to legal security, they would expressly indicated so in the treaty'.[125] The investor further observed that 'the countries agreed to "full" security which [. . .] should be broadly defined so as to include legal protection'.[126] In the proceedings, the claimant additionally submitted a legal opinion by Professor Rudolf Dolzer supporting the view that '[the term] "full security", when given its ordinary meaning, runs afoul with a narrow interpretation limiting the scope of application to strictly physical aspects'.[127] The arbitrators dismissed the FPS claim.[128] As regards to the investor's interpretation of the FPS clause, they observed:

Nothing in the Argentina-France BIT incorporates a duty to maintain a stable legal and commercial environment, apart from the impact that such an environment may have in connection with fulfillment of other treaty obligations.[129]

The interpretation of *full security* as *legal security* lacks a firm legal foundation. The extension of the FPS standard to legal security is one of the most controversial issues pertaining to the interpretation of FPS clauses.[130] It therefore seems that, if states were willing to introduce the notion of legal protection into the FPS standard, they would expressly do so. This interpretation further entails a significant deviation from the customary standard.[131] When states designate a treaty obligation in terms

---

[123]Emphasis added. Marion Unglaube and Reinhard Unglaube *v* Costa Rica, Award, ICSID Cases No. ARB/01/1 and ARB/09/20 (16 May 2012) [281].

[124]Evidence of this reluctance is provided by the many cases in which *full security* has been confined to *physical security*. For a detailed presentation of these cases see Sect. 14.4.1.2.

[125]EDF International S.A., Saur International S.A. and Leon Participaciones Argentinas S.A. *v* Argentina, Award, ICSID Case No. ARB/03/23 (11 June 2012) [404].

[126]EDF International S.A., Saur International S.A. and Leon Participaciones Argentinas S.A. *v* Argentina, Award, ICSID Case No. ARB/03/23 (11 June 2012) [404].

[127]EDF International S.A., Saur International S.A. and Leon Participaciones Argentinas S.A. *v* Argentina, Award, ICSID Case No. ARB/03/23 (11 June 2012) [404]. Professor Dolzer's legal opinion was cited in the award, but is not among the publicly-available documents of the case.

[128]EDF International S.A., Saur International S.A. and Leon Participaciones Argentinas S.A. *v* Argentina, Award, ICSID Case No. ARB/03/23 (11 June 2012) [1108-12].

[129]EDF International S.A., Saur International S.A. and Leon Participaciones Argentinas S.A. *v* Argentina, Award, ICSID Case No. ARB/03/23 (11 June 2012) [1109].

[130]Cf. Sects. 9.2 and 9.3.

[131]See Sect. 9.3.2.

that recall a well-established customary obligation, any intended deviation from customary law should be made explicit.[132] Against this backdrop, this all-encompassing reading of the phrase 'full protection and security' seems to go far beyond the obligation states actually consented to. The adjective *full* should, in sum, not be used as a means to extend the FPS standard to every conceivable risk, from all thinkable sources and of any nature, including legal and even purely commercial risks.

14.4.1.2   *Full* Security as *Physical* Security

A significant number of investment tribunals have considered that the adjective 'full' merely refers to protection against physical violence, the implication being that it does not entail a guarantee of legal stability. In some cases, this approach results from an express treaty provision. As a matter of fact, a few BITs combine the adjectives *full* and *physical*. A representative example would be article 8.10(5) of CETA, which contains the following clarification:

> For greater certainty, "full protection and security" refers to the Party's obligations relating to the *physical security* of investors and covered investments.[133]

Further examples appear in Dutch BITs. For instance, article 3(2) of the Netherlands-Venezuela BIT accords covered investments '*full physical* security and protection'.[134] In *OI European Group B.V. v Venezuela* (2015), an ICSID tribunal considered an FPS claim under this treaty provision. In their assessment of the claim, the arbitrators began by presenting the ongoing debate on the scope of FPS:

> It has been widely argued whether the primary scope of protection of the FPP standard, which only covers physical security, can also be extended to legal certainty. If such extension were accepted, any arbitrary modifications to the legal and regulatory framework could also give rise to violations of the FPP standard. In the case before us, the matter is resolved by the language of Article 3(2) itself.[135]

---

[132]See Sect. 14.2.2.

[133]Emphasis added. Comprehensive Economic and Trade Agreement between Canada and the European Union (signed 30 October 2016, provisionally entered into force 21 September 2017) art. 8.10(5).

[134]Emphasis added. Agreement on Encouragement and Reciprocal Protection of Investments between the Kingdom of the Netherlands and the Republic of Venezuela (adopted 22 October 1991, entered into force 1 November 1993, terminated 1 November 2008) art. 3(2). For an additional example see: Agreement between the Kingdom of the Netherlands and the Republic of Mozambique concerning the Encouragement and the Reciprocal Protection of Investments (adopted 18 December 2001, entered into force 1 September 2004) art. 3(1).

[135]OI European Group B.V. *v* Venezuela, Award, ICSID Case No. ARB/11/25 (10 March 2015) [575-6].

The arbitral tribunal considered that, despite being an element of the more-general FET standard, the FPS standard has a limited scope of application, which specifically pertains to 'physical' security.[136] In this vein, the arbitrators emphasized that this understanding of the standard was consistent with the wording of the Netherlands-Venezuela BIT:

> The language itself in Article 3(2) of the BIT confirms this interpretation: it expressly uses the adjective "physical" to describe the security it guarantees. A literal interpretation, favored by Article 31(1) of the CVDT [VCLT], unavoidably leads to the conclusion that Article 3(2) of the Treaty is limited to guaranteeing full physical security and protection.[137]

There can be no doubt that, where the parties to the applicable treaty have explicitly agreed to limit the scope of FPS to '*physical* security', such agreement must be given full effect. This stipulation is however rather uncommon in investment treaties.

Even in the absence of an allusion to physical security, many arbitral tribunals have understood *full security* clauses as referring to *physical security*. An example would be the award issued in *Spyridon Roussalis v Romania* (2011). The *Spyridon Roussalis* tribunal took notice of the fact that the phrase '*full* protection and security' has been interpreted as a guarantee that 'reaches beyond safeguard from physical violence and requires legal protection for the investor'.[138] The arbitrators however followed the 'physical protection' approach and dismissed the FPS claim on the ground that it did not pertain to the investment's 'physical integrity'.[139]

Similarly, in *Toto Costruzioni v Lebanon* (2012) the arbitral tribunal construed the 'full protection and security' clause of the Italy-Lebanon BIT as exclusively referring to the investment's 'physical integrity'.[140] In *Crystallex v Venezuela* (2016) the arbitrators held that the 'full protection and security' clause in article 2(2) of the Canada-Venezuela BIT 'only extends to the duty of the host state to grant physical protection and security',[141] and added that '[s]uch interpretation best accords with the ordinary meaning of the terms "protection" and "security"'.[142] The tribunal

---

[136]OI European Group B.V. *v* Venezuela, Award, ICSID Case No. ARB/11/25 (10 March 2015) [576]. See also Sect. 15.2.2.

[137]OI European Group B.V. *v* Venezuela, Award, ICSID Case No. ARB/11/25 (10 March 2015) [576].

[138]Spyridon Roussalis *v* Romania, Award, ICSID Case No. ARB/06/1 (7 December 2011) [321] (quoting the Biwater award as an example).

[139]Spyridon Roussalis *v* Romania, Award, ICSID Case No. ARB/06/1 (7 December 2011) [609].

[140]Toto Costruzioni Generali S.p.A. *v* Lebanon, Award, ICSID Case No. ARB/07/12 (7 June 2012) [228-9].

[141]Crystallex International Corp. *v* Venezuela, Award, ICSID Case No. ARB(AF)/11/2 (4 April 2016) [632].

[142]Crystallex International Corp. *v* Venezuela, Award, ICSID Case No. ARB(AF)/11/2 (4 April 2016) [632]. See also the reference to the 'ordinary meaning' of the phrase 'full protection and security' at para 634.

additionally referred to 'a line of cases involving the same or a similar phrase', which followed the physical security approach.[143]

It must be noted that the interpretation of *full security* clauses in terms of *physical security* is by no means based on the idea that the adjective *full* is equivalent to the adjective *physical*. As the decisions quoted above show, the argument is rather that the term *full* does not add anything to the traditional protection obligation, which is in turn construed in terms of *physical security*.

14.4.1.3 *Full* Security as the Object and Purpose of Other Treaty Provisions

The phrase 'full security' has occasionally been said to enshrine a manifestation of the applicable BIT's object and purpose, the implication being that FPS clauses are relevant for the interpretation of other treaty provisions. In *Millicom v Senegal* (2010) the arbitral tribunal considered that the phrase 'full security' (*sécurité intégrale*), as used in the FPS clause of the Netherlands-Senegal BIT, expressed the 'spirit' of the BIT and, particularly, of its dispute settlement clause.[144] According to the arbitrators, the FPS clause reinforced the tribunal's conclusion that Senegal had consented to ICSID arbitration:

> *The spirit of the rule* [the ISDS provision] confirms this interpretation. The purpose of a treaty such as that in question [i.e. the Netherlands-Senegal BIT] is indeed to guarantee efficient and full protection. This purpose is made clear, in particular, by Articles 3 and 4 of the *Accord*, whose objective is "*sécurité intégrale*" ("full security") (Article 4, paragraph 1). Such objective, however, cannot be truly attained unless investors, the primary beneficiaries of the protection, dispose of legal means enabling them to obtain compliance therewith. To admit the contrary would amount to making the *Accord* a "*lex imperfecta*" whose application in the end would be left to the discretion of the State benefiting from the investment, since it could give or refuse its consent as it pleases. This could not have been the intention of the Contracting Parties. Moreover, there is nothing extraordinary about the rule to the extent that it implies nothing else for the State involved except to agree to submit itself to an arbitration proceeding under the aegis of ICSID by independent arbitrators, in a proceeding during which it shall have every opportunity to defend its positions.[145]

This statement of the *Millicom* tribunal is misleading and unsound. The obligation to provide full security to an investment is an autonomous *substantive* guarantee, which refers to protection *by the host state* against specific risks.[146] Its function has never been to ensure protection against other treaty breaches through the dispute

---

[143]Crystallex International Corp. *v* Venezuela, Award, ICSID Case No. ARB(AF)/11/2 (4 April 2016) [633] (quoting, among others, *Saluka Investments v Czech Republic* and *Rumeli Telekom v Kazakhstan*; see also the cases referred to in n. 863-5).

[144]Millicom International Operations B.V. and Sentel GMS SA *v* Senegal, Decision on Jurisdiction of the Arbitral Tribunal, ICSID Case No. ARB/08/20 (16 July 2010) [65].

[145]Emphasis in the original. Millicom International Operations B.V. and Sentel GMS SA *v* Senegal, Decision on Jurisdiction of the Arbitral Tribunal, ICSID Case No. ARB/08/20 (16 July 2010) [65].

[146]Cf. Chaps. 7 and 8.

settlement mechanisms envisaged by the applicable treaty. The FPS standard has nothing to do with consent to arbitration. As rightly observed by a scholar commenting on the *Millicom* decision:

> The fact that the treaty in general and Articles 3 and 4 in particular aim to provide efficient and full protection to the investors of the parties does not necessarily imply that the parties have expressed their consent beforehand with regard to any dispute relating to the relevant obligations [...] One question is to define the substantive obligations the parties have undertaken in the treaty. A completely different one is to establish the jurisdiction of the Tribunal with regard to the related disputes.[147]

It thus seems that the *Millicom* tribunal went too far in its reliance on the FPS clause for jurisdictional purposes. This does not however mean that FPS clauses are always irrelevant for the interpretation of other treaty provisions or for ascertaining a treaty's object and purpose. For instance, the interpretation of other standards of investment protection should not lead to a result that leaves the FPS clause ineffective (*effet utile*); this could be of particular importance in cases where FPS claims are interlocked with FET claims.[148]

14.4.1.4 *Full* Security as a Reference to the Customary Protection Obligation

The phrase '*full* protection and security' could be considered as a mere reference to the law of aliens' customary protection obligation. This approach is particularly justified where the applicable treaty combines the adjective *full* with an explicit and unambiguous reference to customary law or to general international law.[149] Arbitrators applying this kind of clauses will unlikely extend the FPS standard beyond its customary core.[150]

In the absence of a direct reference to customary law, however, doubts may arise as to whether the characterization of an FPS clause as a mere codification of customary law is consistent with the wording of the treaty and, particularly, with

---

[147]Tarcisio Gazzini, *Interpretation of International Investment Treaties* (Hart Publishing, Portland OR 2016) 166-7.

[148]See Sect. 15.2.1.

[149]Cf. Sect. 14.2.1.1.

[150]See, for example: Adel A Hamadi Al Tamini *v* Oman, Award, ICSID Case No. ARB/11/33 (3 November 2015) [380 *et seq.* and 450] (addressing the notion of the minimum standard at paras 380 *et seq.* and associating the customary standard to the notion of physical security at para 450); ADF *v* United States, Award, ICSID Case No. ARB(AF)/00/1 (9 January 200) [177-9 and 184] (construing NAFTA art. 1105(1) in accordance with the FTC's Interpretative Note of 2001); Koch Minerals SÁRL and Koch Nitrogen International SÁRL *v* Venezuela, Award, ICSID Case No. ARB/11/19 (30 October 2017) [8.42 and 8.44] (stating that the treaty's reference to international law is a 'conclusive' indication that the customary standard was incorporated by reference into the BIT); Noble Ventures *v* Romania, Award, ICSID Case No. ARB/01/11 (12 October 2005) [164] (noting that the extension of the FPS clause beyond the customary protection obligation 'seems doubtful').

the use of the adjective *full*. In *AAPL v Sri Lanka* (1990) the investor alleged that 'the ordinary meaning of the words full protection and security points to an acceptance by the host State of strict or absolute liability'.[151] In their assessment of this argument, the arbitrators considered the possible effect of the term *full* in article 2 (2) of the Sri Lanka-UK BIT and reached the following conclusion:

> In the opinion of the present Arbitral Tribunal, the addition of words like "constant" or "full" to strengthen the required standards of "protection and security" could justifiably indicate the Parties' intention to require within their relationship a standard of "due diligence" higher than the "minimum standard" of general international law. But, the nature of both the obligation and ensuing responsibility remain unchanged, since the added words "constant" or "full" are by themselves not sufficient to establish that the Parties intended to transform their mutual obligation into a "strict liability".[152]

This statement is twofold. In the first place, the *AAPL* tribunal held that that the word *full* is insufficient to 'transform' the FPS standard into an absolute obligation. This conclusion seems right. The adjective *full* has a long tradition in international treaty practice. States do not seem to have ever understood the word 'full' as imposing strict liability. Quite the contrary, some nineteenth century FCN agreements were quite explicit in this regard. A representative historical example would be the FCN agreement between the Sultan of Borneo and Great Britain of 1847:

> His Highness [the Sultan] engages that such British subjects shall, *as far as lies in his power* within his dominions, enjoy *full and complete protection and security* for themselves and for any property which they may so acquire in the future, or which they may have acquired already, before the date of the present Convention.[153]

The phrase 'as far as lies in his power' makes clear that the adjectives *full* and *complete*, as used in this clause, did not create an absolute obligation on the part of the Sultan. This wording was not peculiar to British treaties. For example, the United States-Borneo FCN Agreement of 1850 contained a provision that was virtually identical to the FPS clause of the British treaty of 1847.[154] These historical examples show that the adjective 'full' cannot be hastily assumed to entirely change the substance of the FPS standard.

---

[151]Asian Agricultural Products *v* Sri Lanka, Final Award, ICSID Case No. ARB/87/3 (17 June 1990) [26] (quoting the claimant).

[152]Asian Agricultural Products *v* Sri Lanka, Final Award, ICSID Case No. ARB/87/3 (17 June 1990) [50].

[153]Emphasis added. Treaty of Friendship and Commerce, and for the Suppression of the Slave Trade, between Great Britain and Borneo (adopted 27 May 1847) 34 St. Pap. 14, 15 art. III.

[154]Treaty of Peace, Friendship, Commerce and Navigation, between the United States of America and Borneo (adopted 23 June 1850, entered into force 11 July 1853) Charles Bevans (ed), *Treaties and Other International Agreements of the United States of America 1776–1949* (Volume 5: U.S. Department of State Publication, Washington 1971) 1080, 1081 art. III. In *Suez v Argentina* (2010) the arbitral tribunal discussed the wording of the US-Borneo FCN Agreement in its analysis of the historical origins of the FPS standard. See: Suez Sociedad General de Aguas de Barcelona S.A. and Vivendi Universal S.A. v Argentina, Decision on Liability, ICSID Case No. ARB/03/19 (30 July 2010) [161].

Doubts may arise, however, with regard to the second element. The *AAPL* tribunal was wrong in holding that the adjective *full* could 'justifiably' enhance the degree of protection beyond the international minimum standard of treatment.[155] Many IIAs use the adjective *full* and, at the same time, limit the scope of the obligation to the protection required under the minimum standard. If it were true that the adjective *full* conveys the meaning of protection *beyond* the minimum standard, many investment treaties, including NAFTA and CAFTA-DR,[156] would contain a blatant contradiction. Every treaty using the term *full* and simultaneously declaring that the clause containing it is a codification of customary law, expresses the contracting states' understanding that the adjective *full* does not *per se* entail a deviation from the customary standard. In *Windstream Energy v Canada* (2016), the arbitral tribunal noted that the contracting states of NAFTA defined the FET and FPS standards by reference to the customary minimum standard of treatment.[157] In this vein, the arbitrators explained:

> The State parties to NAFTA must have considered, when using the terms "fair and equitable treatment" and "full protection and security" that it is these terms, and not any others, that best reflect the content of the minimum treatment set out in the provision.[158]

Numerous investment arbitral tribunals share the view that the adjective *full* constitutes no derogation from customary law. Examples may be found in the many awards stating that *full* security means only *physical* security.[159] As explained beforehand, the adoption of the 'physical security' approach in those cases was not the consequence of the adjective *full* as such. The arbitrators simply considered that the applicable FPS clause incorporated the 'traditional' core of the FPS standard, and defined this 'core' as physical security. Chapter 9 has shown that the FPS standard has traditionally and customarily referred, too, to nonphysical harm originating in third party acts. This approach has not been alien to the interpretation of the phrase '*full* protection and security'. Several arbitral tribunals have concluded that this

---

[155]Asian Agricultural Products *v* Sri Lanka, Final Award, ICSID Case No. ARB/87/3 (17 June 1990) [50].

[156]Free Trade Agreement between CACM, the Dominican Republic and the United States of America (adopted 5 August 2004, entered into force 1 January 2009) art. 10.05(1) and (2); North American Free Trade Agreement (adopted 17 December 1992, entered into force 1 January 1994) Art. 1105(1); NAFTA Free Trade Commission, *Notes of Interpretation of Certain Chapter 11 Provisions* (31 July 2001) [http://www.sice.oas.org/tpd/nafta/Commission/CH11understanding_e.asp] (on the interpretation of NAFTA art. 1105). For some additional examples see: Free Trade Agreement between the United States of America and the Republic of Colombia (adopted 22 November 2006, entered into force 15 May 2012) art. 11.5(1) and (2); Free Trade Agreement between the United States of America and the Republic of Korea (adopted 30 June 2007, entered into force 15 March 2012) art. 11.5(1) and (2); Free Trade Agreement between the United States of America and the Sultanate of Oman (adopted 19 January 2006, entered into force 1 January 2009) art. 11.5(1) and (2).

[157]Windstream Energy LLC *v* Canada (UNCITRAL), Award (27 September 2016) [347 *et seq.*].

[158]Windstream Energy LLC *v* Canada (UNCITRAL), Award (27 September 2016) [357].

[159]See Sect. 14.4.1.2.

treaty language refers to protection against third parties.[160] For present purposes, these authorities reinforce the impression that the term *full* adds nothing to the customary standard.

The question remains, however, as to whether the word *full* serves or served any purpose whatsoever in international treaty practice. Why to qualify the guarantee of protection and security with an adjective, if that adjective has no effect on the substance of the legal obligation? The reason may be found in the shelves of legal history.

The phrase '*full* protection and security' grew with the standard throughout the centuries. The adjective *full* could have played a much more significant role in the past as it does today. A look into historical sources indicates that it most likely served a twofold purpose.

In the first place, the adjective *full* emphasized that foreigners enjoyed the protection of the law, as subjects of rights and obligations, and could assert their rights before the local judiciary against the natives and other aliens. Plainly stated, this terminology was to some extent related to the obligation of redress. Nineteenth century FCN agreements provide some evidence of this underlying purpose. For instance, the FCN Agreement between Colombia and the German Empire of 1892 contained the following clause:

> Germans in Colombia, and Colombians in Germany, shall be given full and constant protection in their persons and property; they shall enjoy free access to all courts for the assertion and defense of their rights.[161]

It is striking that there was a close linkage between the protection obligation and the right of access to the local judiciary. German scholarly writings from that period confirm this link. In a treatise published in 1896, Paul Heilborn argued that FPS clauses entailed an obligation to recognize foreigners as subjects of law, which necessarily implied that they could acquire rights and enforce them in court. In Heilborn's words:

> The international obligation to recognize, as a matter of public law, foreigners as subjects of rights and obligations, *is expressed in many international agreements through [clauses]*

---

[160]See, for example: Eastern Sugar B.V. *v* Czech Republic, Partial Award, SCC Case No. 088/2004 (27 March 2007) [203] (referring to both third party violence and the notion of 'physical security'); El Paso Energy International Co. *v* Argentina, Award, ICSID Case No. ARB/03/15 (31 October 2011) [522-5] (taking the third-party approach); Koch Minerals SÁRL and Koch Nitrogen International SÁRL *v* Venezuela, Award, ICSID Case No. ARB/11/19 (30 October 2017) [8.46] (combining the 'physical protection' criterion and the 'third party' approach, and emphasizing the express reference to international law in the FPS clause).

[161]Author's translation. The original German text reads: "Den Deutschen soll in Columbien und den Columbianern soll in Deutschland vollständiger und immerwährender Schutz ihrer Personen und ihres Eigenthums zu Theil werden; sie sollen freien Zutritt zu allen Gerichten behufs Verfolgung und Vertheidigung ihrer Rechte haben." Freundschafts-, Handels- und Schifffahrtsvertrag zwischen dem Deutschen Reich und dem Freistaat Columbien (adopted 23 July 1892, entered into force 12 April 1894) Felik Stoerk (ed), *Martens Nouveau Recueil Général des Traités, 2me Série* (Volume 19: Librairie Dietrich, Göttingen 1895) 831, 833-4 art. 4.

> *assuring the citizens of each contracting party full protection in their person and property in the territory of the other party.*[162]

In treaties concluded by the German Empire, the use of the adjective 'full' (*vollständig, vollkommen* or *voll*)[163] seems consistent with Heilborn's observation. By the time these treaties were negotiated, German public law scholars drew a careful distinction between 'fully protected rights' (*vollkommen geschützte Rechte*) and 'not-fully protected rights' (*unvollkommen geschützte Rechte*). The distinction was based on an analogy to private law. In the very same year in which the German-Colombian FCN agreement was concluded, Georg Jellinek explained the difference in the following terms:

> A right enjoys, in any case, the most perfect protection where enforcement through the state is available for its fulfillment. But a more-moderate protection may also be taken as a guarantee. As a result, there are more- or less-protected rights [...] What occurs in private law, namely, the difference between fully protected rights and not-fully protected rights (*leges imprefectae*, natural obligations), may be perceived in a much higher degree in the public law arena.[164]

From this standpoint, the adjective 'full' does not seem to be a mere ornament. There are good reasons to believe that it served the purpose of avoiding any misconception that the rights of aliens constituted non-justiciable moral obligations.

---

[162]Emphasis added. Author's translation. The original German text reads: "Der völkerrechtlichen Pflicht zur staatsrechtlichen Anerkennung der Ausländer als Rechtssubjekte wird in Staatsverträgen vielfach dadurch Ausdruck verliehen, daß den beiderseitigen Unterthanen in dem Gebiet des anderen Teils vollständiger Schutz für Person und Eigentum zugesichert wird." Paul Heilborn, *Das System des Völkerrechts entwickelt aus den völkerrechtlichen Begriffen* (Verlag von Julius Springer, Berlin 1896) 74.

[163]These adjectives were usual in FCN treaties concluded by the German Empire. See, for example: Freundschafts-, Handels- und Schifffahrtsvertrag zwischen dem Deutschen Reich und dem Königreich der Hawaiischen Inseln (adopted 19 September 1879) Friedrich Heinrich Geffcken (ed) *Martens Recueil Manuel et Pratique de Traités et Conventions, 2me Série* (Volume 3: F. A. Brockhaus, Leipzig 1888) 6, 6 art. 2 (using the adjectives '*voll*' [full] and '*vollkommen*' [full/complete]); Freundschafts-, Handels- und Schifffahrtsvertrag zwischen dem Deutschen Reich und Samoa (adopted 24 January 1879) Friedrich Heinrich Geffcken (ed) *Martens Recueil Manuel et Pratique de Traités et Conventions, 2me Série* (Volume 3: F. A. Brockhaus, Leipzig 1888) 1, 1 art. 2 (using the adjectives '*vollständig*' [complete/full] and '*immerwährend*' [constant]). It should be noted that contemporary German treaties normally use the adjective *voll*. For an indicative example see: Vertrag zwischen der Bundesrepublik Deutschland und der Ukraine über die Förderung und den gegenseitigen Schutz von Kapitalanlagen (adopted 15 February 1993, entered into force 29 June 1996) art. 4(1) (using the expression 'volle[r] Schutz und volle Sicherheit'). For an arbitral award addressing this treaty clause see: Gea Group Aktiengesellschaft *v* Ukraine, Award, ICSID Case No. ARB/08/16 (31 March 2011) [242-67].

[164]Author's translation. The original German text reads: "Wo staatliche Exekution zur Verwirklichung bereit steht, ist allerdings das Recht am Besten geschützt, aber auch minderer Schutz ist bereits als Garantie aufzufassen. Es giebt demnach mehr oder minder geschützte Rechte [...] Was bereits innerhalb des Privatrechtes stattfindet, der Unterschied von vollkommen und unvollkommen geschützten Rechten (leges imperfectae, Naturalobligationen), das lässt sich in noch viel höherem Masse im öffentlichen Rechte wahrnehmen." Georg Jellinek, *System der subjektiven öffentlichen Rechte* (J.C.B. Mohr, Freiburg 1892) 334.

Besides ensuring protection of rights through local courts, strong expressions such as *full security* or *full protection* also underscore the binding character of the protection obligation as such. This wording may be plausibly said to reflect the idea that the protection of aliens is not a mere act of mercy or grace, but a legal duty upon the host state, the breach of which gives rise to a legally-binding reparation obligation. This was of particular historical significance.

During the nineteenth and early twentieth centuries, state responsibility for acts of insurgents and civil disturbances was one of the most contentious areas of international law.[165] Pressured by western powers to pay compensation for such damages, some states still sought to avoid accepting responsibility for acts of insurgents and outlaws, and characterized the compensation awarded as a mere act of grace (*ex gratia*). The perhaps most clear example of this practice appears in the claims conventions signed by the Mexican Government with several European powers in the aftermath of the Mexican Revolution (1910–1920). The Claims Convention concluded with Great Britain provided:

> [I]t is sufficient [...] that it be established that the alleged damage actually took place, and was due to any of the causes enumerated in article 3 of this Convention [negligence in respect of injuries occurred in the course of the Mexican Revolution], for Mexico to feel moved *ex gratia* to afford such compensation.[166]

In many treaties the adjective *full* could have been intended to reinforce the idea that aliens enjoy a legal right to security, the violation of which gives rise to legal and not merely moral reparation obligations. Be as it may, present-day international law leaves no doubt as to the binding character of the protection obligation. The adjective 'full' might therefore have lost much of its practical significance. Nonetheless, it continues to be a firmly-etched element of the perhaps most widespread formulation of the FPS standard, which is best interpreted as a term of art designating the customary protection obligation delivered by the tradition of the law of aliens.

---

[165]See Sects. 8.3.1 and 8.3.2.1. Cf. also Chap. 4.

[166]Claims Convention between Great Britain and Mexico (adopted 19 November 1926, entered into force 8 March 1928) V RIAA 7, 8 art. 2. The Convention was amended in 1930 in order to express 'with greater clarity' some of its provisions. This provision introduced a slight modification to article 2. The amended version reads as follows: "it is sufficient [...] that it be established that the alleged damage actually took place, and was due to any of the causes enumerated in article 3 of this Convention, that it was not the consequence of a lawful act and that its amount be proved for Mexico to feel moved *ex gratia* to afford such compensation". See: Claims Convention between Great Britain and Mexico (adopted 5 December 1930, entered into force 9 March 1931) V RIAA 10, 11 art. 2. For some additional examples, see: Claims Convention between France and Mexico (adopted 25 September 1924, entered into force 29 December 1924) V RIAA 313, 314 art. 2; Claims Convention between France and Mexico (adopted 2 August 1930, entered into force 6 February 1931) V RIAA 318, 318 Preamble. Compensations *in gratia* continue to be an issue in other areas of international law, such as the obligation to take steps to protect the premises of a diplomatic mission under article 22 of the Vienna Convention on Diplomatic Relations. See generally: Eileen Denza, *Diplomatic Law. Commentary on the Vienna Convention on Diplomatic Relations* (Oxford University Press, Oxford 2016) 138.

14.4.2   The Guarantee of Constant Protection and Security

An impressive number of investment agreements qualify the protection granted to covered investments and investors with the adjectives *constant*[167] or *continuous*.[168] A few agreements combine the adjectives *full* and *constant*.[169] Clauses using the phrase *most constant protection and security* have some tradition in international law. In U.S. treaty practice, this formula can be traced back to the earliest American commercial treaties. A historically significant example would be the Jay Treaty of 1794.[170] FCN agreements concluded from the eighteenth to the twentieth centuries bear witness to the continued use of this language throughout the

---

[167]For some indicative examples of investment treaties using the phrases 'most constant protection and security' or 'constant protection and security' see: Agreement between Japan and the Republic of Turkey concerning the reciprocal promotion and protection of investment (adopted 12 February 1992, entered into force 12 March 1993) art. 5(1); Agreement between the Government of the Czech and Slovak Federal Republic and the Government of the Kingdom of Thailand for the Promotion and Protection of Investments (adopted 12 February 1994, entered into force 4 May 1995) art. 3(2); Agreement between the Government of the People's Republic of China and the Portuguese Republic on the Encouragement and Reciprocal Protection of Investments (adopted 9 December 2005, entered into force 26 July 2008) art. 2(2); Agreement on Encouragement and Reciprocal Protection of Investments between the Kingdom of the Netherlands and the Federal Republic of Yugoslavia (adopted 29 January 2002, entered into force 1 March 2004) art. 3(1). Further examples are provided throughout this section.

[168]For a treaty using the phrase '*continuous* protection and security' see: Agreement between the Arab Republic of Egypt and the Belgo-Luxembourg Economic Union on the Encouragement and Reciprocal Protection of Investments (adopted 28 February 1977, entered into force 20 September 1978, terminated 24 May 2002) art. I(2). It must be noted that this BIT was replaced by a new one, which uses the French phrase '*protection constante*'. In *Jan de Nul v Egypt* (2008) the arbitral tribunal translated the French adjective '*constante*' as '*continuous*'. See: Jan de Nul N.V. and Dredging International N.V. v Egypt, Award, ICSID Case No. ARB/04/13 (6 November 2008) [268]. For the new treaty see: Accord entre l'Union économique belgo-luxembourgeoise et la République arabe d'Egypte concernant l'encouragement et la protection réciproques des investissements (adopted 28 February 1999, entered into force 24 May 2002) art. 3(2).

[169]The typical formulation is '*full* and *constant* protection and security'. For some indicative examples see: Agreement between the Government of the Republic of Finland and the Government of Mongolia on the Promotion and Protection of Investments (adopted 15 May 2007, entered into force 19 June 2008) art. 2(2); Agreement between the Government of the Slovak Republic and the Government of the Republic of Kenya for the Promotion and Reciprocal Protection of Investments (adopted 14 December 2011) art. 2(2); Agreement between the Swiss Confederation and Serbia and Montenegro on the Promotion and Reciprocal Protection of Investments (adopted 7 December 2005, entered into force 20 July 2007) art. 4; Agreement for the Promotion and Protection of Investment between the Republic of Austria and the Federal Republic of Nigeria (adopted 8 April 2013) art. 3(1).

[170]Treaty of Amity, Commerce, and Navigation between the United States and Great Britain (adopted 19 November 1794, entered into force 28 October 1795) Hunter Miller (ed), *Treaties and Other International Acts of the United States of America* (Volume 2: Government Printing Office, Washington 1931) 245, 257 art. 14 (using the phrase 'most constant protection and security').

years.[171] This was moreover the formula employed in the Abs-Shawcross Convention of 1959[172] as well as in the OECD Draft Conventions on the Protection of Foreign Property of 1963 and 1967.[173] This wording, however widespread, was often perceived as ambiguous and uncertain. Commenting on U.S. treaties, Anthony Benton observed in 1965:

> The phrase "the most constant protection and security" seems fair enough on its face, but in the absence of further definition or elaboration, the concept is so vague that it is difficult to imagine this provision as the basis of a claim that one of the parties had violated the treaty.[174]

Benton could not have foreseen in 1965 that the clause he was describing would come to be tested by a wide array of international adjudicatory bodies, ranging from the ICJ to multiple arbitral tribunals, constituted under multilateral and bilateral investment treaties. In the *Elettronica Sicula* case (1989), the ICJ considered a claim concerning the 'most constant protection and security' clause enshrined in article V of the U.S.-Italy FCN Agreement.[175] In the subsequent decades, this treaty language was at the heart of countless investment disputes. The reason lies to some extent in the fact this is the phrase used by article 10(1) of the ECT,[176] which has been one of the most-litigated protection and security clauses in the past decades.[177]

---

[171]See generally: Kenneth Vandevelde, *The First Bilateral Investment Treaties: U.S. Postwar Friendship, Commerce and Navigation Treaties* (Oxford University Press, New York 2017) 413-4 (particularly focusing on FCN agreements concluded after World War II); Robert Renbert Wilson, *United States Commercial Treaties and International Law* (The Houser Press, New Orleans LA 1960) 119-21.

[172]'Abs-Shawcross Draft Convention on Investment Abroad' (April 1959) in Martins Paparinskis, *Basic Documents on International Investment Protection* (Hart Publishing, Portland OR 2012) 37, 37 art. 1.

[173]OECD Draft Convention on the Protection of Foreign Property (1963) in Martins Paparinskis, *Basic Documents on International Investment Protection* (Hart Publishing, Portland OR 2012) 63, 63 art. 1(a); OECD Draft Convention on the Protection of Foreign Property (1967) in Martins Paparinskis, *Basic Documents on International Investment Protection* (Hart Publishing, Portland OR 2012) 67, 68 art. 1(a).

[174]Anthony Benton, 'The Protection of Property Rights in Commercial Treaties of the United States' (1965) 25 ZaöRV 50, 64.

[175]*Case Concerning Elettronica Sicula S.p.A. (ELSI) (United States of America v Italy)* [1989] ICJ Rep 15, 63-5 [102-8].

[176]Energy Charter Treaty (adopted 17 December 1994, entered into force 16 April 1998) art. 10(1).

[177]For ECT cases involving FPS claims see: AES Summit Generation Ltd. and AES-Tisza Erömü Kft. *v* Hungary, Award, ICSID Case No. ARB/07/22 (23 September 2010) [13.3]; AES Corporation and Tau Power B.V. *v* Kazakhstan, Award, ICSID Case No. ARB/10/16 (1 November 2013) [337-9] (case under the ECT and the Kazakhstan-US BIT; it should be noted that the BIT uses the phrase 'full protection and security'); Electrabel S.A. *v* Hungary, Decision on Jurisdiction, Applicable Law and Liability, ICSID Case No. ARB/07/19 (30 November 2012) [7.145-7 and 7.80 *et seq.*]; Isolux Netherlands B.V. *v* Spain, Laudo, SCC Case No. V 2013/153 (17 July 2016) [816-9]; Liman Caspian Oil BV and NCL Dutch Investment BV *v* Kazakhstan, Award, ICSID Case No. ARB/07/14 (22 June 2010) [289]; Mamidoil Jetoil Greek Petroleum Products Societe S.A. *v* Albania, Award, ICSID Case No. ARB/11/24 (30 March 2015) [799-829]; Mohammad Ammar Al-Bahloul *v* Tajikistan, Partial Award on Jurisdiction and Liability, SCC Case No. V

At least two issues have arisen in connection with the interpretation of these treaty clauses. The first issue pertains to the choice between a broad interpretation of the standard, which typically leads to the inclusion of the guarantee of legal security as an element of the constant security clause, and a narrow interpretation thereof. This first issue is often interlocked with the question, whether constant security clauses deviate from customary law, or are rather a mere codification of the customary protection obligation. The second issue is whether and to which extent clauses using the adjective *constant* convey a different meaning than clauses employing alternative formulas, such as *full protection*. The following sections examine these two issues in detail.

14.4.2.1 The Choice Between a Broad and a Narrow Interpretation of *Constant Security* Clauses

In investment arbitration, the interpretation of constant security clauses has not been characterized by consistency and predictability. Quite the contrary, arbitral decisions leave the impression this treaty language conveys a rather elusive and slippery meaning. From the outset, submitting a claim under a constant security clause might therefore appear as a venture of unpredictable outcome.

In some cases, tribunals have interpreted this wording broadly. On occasions, adjudicators have gone as far as to state that this treaty language encompasses a guarantee of legal security. This approach has been followed in some ECT cases. In *Plama v Bulgaria* (2008), the arbitral tribunal held that '[t]he [most constant protection and security] standard includes [. . .] an obligation to create a framework that grants security'.[178] A more careful approach appeared in *AES v Hungary* (2010). In that case, the arbitral tribunal considered that the standard 'can, in appropriate circumstances, extend beyond physical security'.[179] However, it underscored that the obligation of constant security does not prevent the adoption of *reasonable* regulatory measures, even if they have an impact on the investor's interests.[180]

In *Mohammad Ammar Al-Bahloul v Tajikistan* (2009), another ECT case, the arbitrators expressed support for an interpretation of article 10(1) which incorporates

---

(064/2008) (9 September 2009) [243-7]; Plama Consortium Ltd. *v* Bulgaria, Award, ICSID Case No. ARB/03/24 (27 August 2008) [179-81].

[178]Plama Consortium Ltd. *v* Bulgaria, Award, ICSID Case No. ARB/03/24 (27 August 2008) [180]. It must be noted that the *Plama* tribunal acknowledged that 'the standard has been developed in the context of physical security' (at para 180). It however underscored that 'some tribunals have also included protection concerning legal security' (at para 180).

[179]AES Summit Generation Ltd. and AES-Tisza Erömü Kft. *v* Hungary, Award, ICSID Case No. ARB/07/22 (23 September 2010) [13.3.2].

[180]AES Summit Generation Ltd. and AES-Tisza Erömü Kft. *v* Hungary, Award, ICSID Case No. ARB/07/22 (23 September 2010) [13.3.2]. See also: Isolux Netherlands B.V. *v* Spain, Laudo, SCC Case No. V 2013/153 (17 July 2016) [817] (relying on the *AES v Hungary* award).

the notion of 'legal security' into the constant protection obligation.[181] Nonetheless, the *Al-Bahloul* tribunal was not particularly concerned with the question of legal stability, but with the application of the standard to an alleged 'miscarriage of justice' (i.e. the obligation of redress):

> While the concept of protection and security in investment treaties has developed principally in the context of physical security, some tribunals have applied it more broadly to encompass legal security as well. Therefore, it could arguably cover a situation in which there has been a demonstrated miscarriage of justice.[182]

In the ECT context, a few academic studies have expressed support for the broad interpretation of the protection obligation. A prominent exponent of this approach was the late Professor Thomas Wälde:

> The ECT refers to a reinforced standard – "most constant protection and security" – and links this in one sentence to the concepts of "impairment of property enjoyment, discrimination and unreasonable". There is therefore an argument to view the standard as encompassing more than a low-level standard of police protection in a merely physical sense of security and rather to link it to the "economic police" (in traditional sense), now more commonly termed "economic regulatory", powers of the State.[183]

Broad interpretations of this treaty language have also been advanced outside the framework of the ECT. In *National Grid v Argentina* (2008) the arbitral tribunal held that the 'protection and constant security' clause in article 2(2) of the Argentina-UK BIT could extend beyond physical protection.[184] The arbitrators highlighted that the BIT provided a comprehensive definition of investment, which covered both physical and nonphysical assets.[185] They also noted that the FET and FPS standards were enshrined in the same treaty provision.[186] As regards to the wording of the BIT, the tribunal observed:

[181]Mohammad Ammar Al-Bahloul *v* Tajikistan, Partial Award on Jurisdiction and Liability, SCC Case No. V 064/2008 (9 September 2009) [246].

[182]Mohammad Ammar Al-Bahloul *v* Tajikistan, Partial Award on Jurisdiction and Liability, SCC Case No. V 064/2008 (9 September 2009) [246].

[183]Thomas Wälde, 'Energy Charter Treaty-based Investment Arbitration. Controversial Issues' (2004) 5 J. World Investment & Trade 373, 391. For other authors endorsing this broad interpretation of art. 10(1) of the ECT see: Alexandra Diehl, The Core Standard of International Investment Protection: Fair and Equitable Treatment (Kluwer Law International, Alpen aan den Rijn 2012) 110-1; Kaj Hobér, 'Investment Treaty Arbitration and the Energy Charter Treaty' (2010) 1 (2) J. Int'l Disp. Settlement 153, 158-9. Cf. also: Thomas Roe and Matthew Happold, *Settlement of Investment Disputes under the Energy Charter Treaty* (Cambridge University Press, Cambridge 2011) 115-6. Section 9.4 has also discussed Wälde's views on the subject.

[184]National Grid P.L.C. *v* Argentina (UNCITRAL), Award (3 November 2008) [187-9].

[185]National Grid P.L.C. *v* Argentina (UNCITRAL), Award (3 November 2008) [187].

[186]National Grid P.L.C. *v* Argentina (UNCITRAL), Award (3 November 2008) [187 and 189].

> The Tribunal concludes that the phrase "protection and constant security" as related to the subject matter of the Treaty does *not* carry with it the implication that this protection is inherently limited to protection and security of physical assets.[187]

On the other side of the spectrum, several tribunals have interpreted constant security clauses narrowly. An example would be the Final Award rendered in *BG v Argentina* (2007). The claim was filed under the Argentina-UK BIT, which uses the phrase 'protection and *constant* security'.[188] The tribunal found that this treaty clause referred to 'physical security' only.[189] It consistently rejected the view that this wording could encompass the guarantee of a 'secure legal environment'.[190] In *Liman v Kazahstan* (2010), an ECT case, the arbitral tribunal followed a similar approach:

> With regard to the standard of most constant protection and security, the Tribunal holds that this provision [...] provides a standard which does not extend to any contractual rights but whose purpose is rather to *protect the integrity of an investment against interference by the use of force and particularly physical damage.*[191]

In other cases, tribunals have followed a narrow approach by holding that constant security clauses grant protection against risks that do not originate in the conduct of the host state. Thus, for example, in *Electrabel v Hungary* (2012) the arbitral tribunal stated that the 'most constant protection and security' guarantee in article 10(1) of the ECT only requires the host state to exercise due diligence in the protection of the investment against acts of third parties.[192]

Other tribunals have considered that the customary protection obligation refers to protection against acts of third parties, but have left the question open as to whether the terms *most constant* grant protection beyond this customary core. An example would be the award rendered in *Joseph Houben v Burundi* (2016). The *Houben* tribunal was constituted under the BIT between the Belgium-Luxembourg Economic Union and Burundi. Article 3(2) of the BIT provided:

---

[187]Emphasis added. National Grid P.L.C. *v* Argentina (UNCITRAL), Award (3 November 2008) [189].

[188]Emphasis added. Agreement between the Government of the United Kingdom and the Government of the Republic of Argentina for the Promotion and Protection of Investments (adopted 11 December 1990, entered into force 19 February 1993) art. 2(2).

[189]BG Group *v* Argentina (UNCITRAL), Final Award (24 December 2007) [324-7].

[190]BG Group *v* Argentina (UNCITRAL), Final Award (24 December 2007) [326].

[191]Emphasis added. Liman Caspian Oil BV and NCL Dutch Investment BV *v* Kazakhstan, Award, ICSID Case No. ARB/07/14 (22 June 2010) [289].

[192]Electrabel S.A. *v* Hungary, Decision on Jurisdiction, Applicable Law and Liability, ICSID Case No. ARB/07/19 (30 November 2012) [7.83]. For a commentary on this decision see: Max Baumgart and Sebastián Mantilla Blanco, 'Electrabel v. Ungarn: Aktuelle Entwicklungen beim Schutz von Auslandsinvestitionen nach dem Vertrag über die Energiecharta' (2016) 7(3) KSzW 179, 183.

> Ces investissements et activités jouissent d'une *sécurité et d'une protection constantes*, excluant toute mesure injustifiée ou discriminatoire qui pourrait entraver, en droit ou en fait, leur gestion, leur entretien, leur utilisation, leur jouissance ou leur liquidation.[193]

The arbitrators held that the broad language used in the final part of the clause could indicate that the protection obligation extends beyond physical harm, and could even encompass the notion of legal security.[194] They however avoided digging any deeper into this question.[195] In this vein, they recognized that the essence of the standard refers to protection against physical violence by third parties,[196] and noted that this was precisely the kind of violence the case was about:

> [L]e Tribunal observe cependant que l'article 3.2 du TBI est rédigé de façon plus large que les clauses relatives au standard de sécurité et protection constantes généralement insérées dans d'autres traités. L'article 3.2 du TBI prévoit en effet que l'obligation d'accorder à l'investisseur la sécurité et protection constantes exclut toute mesure injustifiée ou discriminatoire qui pourrait entraver « en droit ou en fait, [la] gestion, [l']entretien, [l'] utilisation, [la] jouissance ou [la] liquidation » de l'investissement. Une telle formulation indique que la protection offerte par le TBI au titre du standard de sécurité et protection constantes ne se limite pas à une protection contre les atteintes physiques à l'investissement, puisqu'elle fait référence à de possibles atteintes « en droit » à la jouissance de l'investissement. Toutefois, dans la mesure où la seule question invoquée par les parties dans cette affaire, sous la rubrique du standard de sécurité et protection constantes, est celle des atteintes physiques à la propriété de M. Houben, par l'installation d'usurpateurs sur sa propriété, le Tribunal n'estime pas nécessaire d'examiner la question de savoir si la protection due sous ce standard en vertu du TBI s'étend au-delà d'une protection contre l'usage de la force et les atteintes physiques à la propriété des étrangers par des tiers.[197]

The linkage of constant security clauses with third party violence has not been without controversy.[198] In *AES v Hungary* (2010), the tribunal held that the standard protects investors against 'harassment by third parties and/or state actors'.[199] In *Isolux v Spain* (2016) the arbitral tribunal considered that the 'most constant protection and security' clause of the ECT serves the purpose of ensuring protection against 'harmful acts' ('*actos dañinos*') of both the host state's authorities and third parties.[200]

---

[193]Emphasis added. Convention entre l'Union Economique Belgo-Luxembourgeoise et la République du Burundi concernant l'encouragement et la protection réciproques des investissements (adopted 13 April 1989, entered into force 12 September 1993) art. 3(2).

[194]Joseph Houben v Burundi, Sentence, ICSID Case No. ARB/13/7 (12 January 2016) [160].

[195]Joseph Houben v Burundi, Sentence, ICSID Case No. ARB/13/7 (12 January 2016) [160].

[196]Joseph Houben v Burundi, Sentence, ICSID Case No. ARB/13/7 (12 January 2016) [157 and 159].

[197]Joseph Houben v Burundi, Sentence, ICSID Case No. ARB/13/7 (12 January 2016) [160].

[198]For a historical source considering that the phrase 'most constant protection and security' also refers to protection against state action see: OECD, *Draft Convention on the Protection of Foreign Property. Notes and Comments* (OECD, Paris 1962) 9 [5] (but also stating that the obligation is always one of 'due diligence').

[199]AES Summit Generation Ltd. and AES-Tisza Erömü Kft. v Hungary, Award, ICSID Case No. ARB/07/22 (23 September 2010) [13.3.2].

[200]Isolux Netherlands B.V. v Spain, Laudo, SCC Case No. V 2013/153 (17 July 2016) [817].

Chapters 8 and 9 above have argued that the customary protection obligation is inextricably attached to the notion of third party violence. If this proposition is correct, then the interpretation of constant security clauses advanced in the *Electrabel* case seems consistent with the view that this treaty language reflects the customary standard.

There are good reasons to believe that, as a rule, these clauses entail a *renvoi* to customary law. The continuous use of the phrase *most constant protection and security* in FCN agreements from the late eighteenth century onwards suggests that this formula grew with the customary standard, and was never intended to be deviation from it. Furthermore, FCN agreements often combined the adjective *constant* with express references to international law.

In some treaties, customary law was the *minimum* degree of protection granted under the treaty. This was the effect of the often-employed phrase 'most constant protection and security, *in no case less than that required by international law*'.[201] In other treaties, the content of the constant security obligation was defined by reference to general international law. This approach was particularly common during the interwar period. The FCN Agreement between the United States and the German Empire of 1923 contains a typical security clause from those years:

> The nationals of each High Contracting Party shall receive within the territories of the other, upon submitting to the conditions imposed upon its nationals, the *most constant protection and security* for their persons and property, *and shall enjoy in this respect that degree of protection that is required by international law*.[202]

---

[201] For some indicative examples see: Treaty of Friendship, Commerce and Navigation between the United States of America and Israel (adopted 23 August 1951, entered into force 3 April 1954) 219 UNTS 237, art. III(1); Treaty of Friendship, Commerce and Navigation between the United States of America and Japan (adopted 2 April 1953, entered into force 30 October 1953) 206 UNTS 191, art. II(1); Treaty of Friendship, Commerce and Navigation between the United States of America and the Republic of Korea (adopted 28 November 1956, entered into force 7 November 1957) 302 UNTS 281, art. III(1). For a treaty using a similar language see: Treaty of Friendship, Commerce and Navigation between the United States of America and Ireland (adopted 21 January 1950, entered into force 14 September 1950) 206 UNTS 269, art. VIII(2). These and other treaties have also been discussed in Sect. 7.2.2.

[202] Emphasis added. Treaty of Friendship, Commerce and Consular Rights between the United States of America and the German Empire (adopted 8 December 1923, entered into force 14 October 1925) Charles Bevans (ed), *Treaties and Other International Agreements of the United States of America 1776–1949* (Volume 8: U.S. Department of State Publication, Washington 1971) 153, 154 art. 1. For some additional examples see: Treaty of Friendship, Commerce and Consular Rights between the United States of America and the Kingdom of Norway (adopted 5 June 1928, entered into force 13 September 1932) Charles Bevans (ed), *Treaties and Other International Agreements of the United States of America 1776–1949* (Volume 10: U.S. Department of State Publication, Washington 1972) 481-97, 482, art. I; Treaty of Peace, Amity, Navigation, and Commerce between the United States of America and the Republic of Liberia (adopted 8 August 1938, entered into force 21 November 1939) Charles Bevans (ed), *Treaties and Other International Agreements of the United States of America 1776–1949* (Volume 9: U.S. Department of State Publication, Washington 1972) 595-606, 596 art. I.

By the 1950s the U.S. State Department described the phrase *most constant protection and security* as a 'time-honored' formula and confidently regarded it as a codification of customary law.[203]

As in the case of the phrase *full protection*, the question may arise as to the reasons why states intending no obligation beyond the customary standard would employ the term *constant* in the first place. The use of the adjective *constant* seems to emphasize the applicability of the protection obligation in the context of civil disorders, revolutions and similar factual settings. As such, it underscores that the duty to exercise diligence in the protection of aliens does not cease with the emergence of groups that disregard, question or threat the sitting government's authority.[204] This entails no departure from customary law. Quite the contrary, these factual scenarios were precisely the breeding ground of the customary standard in the law of aliens.[205]

This understanding of the adjective *constant* has already been advanced in the context of investment arbitral proceedings. In *MNSS v Montenegro* (2016), the claimant contended that the phrase 'most constant protection and security' in article 3(1) of the Netherlands-Yugoslavia BIT imposed 'a particularly high standard of treatment'.[206] The respondent disagreed with this interpretation and argued that this treaty clause '[merely] stress[es] that protection and security shall be accorded to foreign investors permanently throughout the existence of the BIT'.[207] The tribunal agreed with the respondent's emphasis on this 'temporal element' and was explicit in stating that this wording does not create a guarantee of security beyond general international law[208]:

> As regards the meaning of "most constant", the plain meaning of "constant" is "unchanging", "that remains the same." Thus, the level of protection and security should not change for the duration of the investment. *But the expression "most constant" does not increase the level of protection and security as understood under international law.*[209]

---

[203]Kenneth Vandevelde, *The First Bilateral Investment Treaties: U.S. Postwar Friendship, Commerce and Navigation Treaties* (Oxford University Press, New York 2017) 414 (referring to communications exchanged in connection with the negotiation of American FCN agreements in the 1950s).

[204]The application of the standard in these situations is however conditional upon the state exercising actual territorial control. See Sect. 7.3.

[205]See Sect. 8.3.

[206]MNSS B.V. and Recupero Credito Acciaio N.V. *v* Montenegro, Award, ICSID Case No. ARB (AF)/12/8 (4 May 2016) [235].

[207]MNSS B.V. and Recupero Credito Acciaio N.V. *v* Montenegro, Award, ICSID Case No. ARB (AF)/12/8 (4 May 2016) [277].

[208]MNSS B.V. and Recupero Credito Acciaio N.V. *v* Montenegro, Award, ICSID Case No. ARB (AF)/12/8 (4 May 2016) [348 and 351].

[209]Emphasis added. MNSS B.V. and Recupero Credito Acciaio N.V. *v* Montenegro, Award, ICSID Case No. ARB(AF)/12/8 (4 May 2016) [351].

14.4.2.2 *Constant Security* Clauses and Other Formulations of the Protection Obligation

There seems to be no certainty as to whether the use of the adjective *constant* in protection and security clauses has any particular and distinguishable effect on the substance of the protection obligation, as opposed to alternative formulations of the standard. In *AAPL v Sri Lanka* (1990) the arbitral tribunal noted that the words *most constant* were 'similar' but at the same time 'stronger' than the adjective *full*.[210] Nonetheless, the tribunal did not explain to which extent the choice of one or other of these terms affects the substance of the security obligation. Moreover, the arbitrators denied that either expression could, by itself, turn the FPS standard into a standard of 'strict liability'.[211]

In most cases, parties and arbitrators have said or implied that the adjectives *full* and *constant* denote the same substantive obligation. In *CME v Czech Republic* (2001) the state referred to '[t]he requirement to provide *constant or full* security and protection' and assessed the scope and content of the standard without distinguishing between both adjectives.[212] In *BG v Argentina* (2007), the arbitrators used the terms *full protection and security* and *protection and constant security* interchangeably, without drawing any material distinction between the two phrases.[213]

In *Tenaris v Venezuela* (2016) the FPS claims were raised under two different BITs. The language of the applicable FPS clauses was slightly different. The BIT between Venezuela and the Belgium-Luxembourg Economic Union used the phrase 'constant protection' (*protection constante*).[214] For its part, the Portugal-Venezuela BIT required each party to 'protect' (*protegerá*) covered investments, without further qualification.[215] The arbitrators did not address the possible differences in the protection granted under each of the applicable treaties and, particularly, the

---

[210]Asian Agricultural Products *v* Sri Lanka, Final Award, ICSID Case No. ARB/87/3 (17 June 1990) [47].

[211]Asian Agricultural Products *v* Sri Lanka, Final Award, ICSID Case No. ARB/87/3 (17 June 1990) [50]. See also: Jan de Nul N.V. and Dredging International N.V. *v* Egypt, Award, ICSID Case No. ARB/04/13 (6 November 2008) [269] (also stating that this treaty language imposes a due diligence obligation only).

[212]Emphasis added. CME Czech Republic B.V. *v* Czech Republic (UNCITRAL), Partial Award (13 September 2001) [353].

[213]BG Group *v* Argentina (UNCITRAL), Final Award (24 December 2007) [324] (referring to 'protection and constant security' and 'full protection and security' without drawing any distinction between these two types of FPS clauses).

[214]Accord entre l'Union économique belgo-luxembourgeoise et le gouvernement de la République du Venezuela concernant la promotion et la protection réciproques des investissements (adopted 17 March 1998, entered into force 29 April 2004) art. 3(2). For the English translation of this clause see: Tenaris S.A. and Talta-Trading E Marketing Sociedade Unipessoal Lda. *v* Venezuela, Award, ICSID Case No. ARB/11/26 (29 January 2016) [436].

[215]Acordo entre o Governo da República Portuguesa e o Governo da República da Venezuela sobre a promoção e proteção mútua de investimentos (adopted 17 June 1994, entered into force 7 October 1995) art. 2(2). For the English translation of this FPS clause see: Tenaris S.A. and Talta-Trading E

potential effect that the adjective *constant* could have on the standard's scope of protection.[216] In its assessment of the FPS standard, the tribunal further relied on arbitral decisions pertaining to the interpretation of '*full* protection and security' clauses.[217] This suggests that the *Tenaris* tribunal assumed that there was no material difference between the expressions *protection, constant protection* and *full protection*.

Many other arbitral decisions appear to share this assumption. Arbitral tribunals have often interpreted *full protection and security* clauses on the basis of decisions addressing *most constant protection and security* clauses,[218] and vice-versa.[219] This practice indicates that these tribunals did not ascribe a different substantive meaning to each of these phrases.

This approach is consistent with the conclusion reached above: the phrases *full protection* and *constant protection* do not, by themselves, entail any derogation from customary law.[220] As far as both expressions point to the customary security obligation, they do not seem to convey different meanings.

Marketing Sociedade Unipessoal Lda. *v* Venezuela, Award, ICSID Case No. ARB/11/26 (29 January 2016) [437].

[216]Tenaris S.A. and Talta-Trading E Marketing Sociedade Unipessoal Lda. *v* Venezuela, Award, ICSID Case No. ARB/11/26 (29 January 2016) [438-49].

[217]Tenaris S.A. and Talta-Trading E Marketing Sociedade Unipessoal Lda. *v* Venezuela, Award, ICSID Case No. ARB/11/26 (29 January 2016) [438-9] n. 348-50 (quoting *AAPL v Sri Lanka, Biwater v Tanzania*, and *Frontier Petroleum v Czech Republic*).

[218]Asian Agricultural Products *v* Sri Lanka, Final Award, ICSID Case No. ARB/87/3 (17 June 1990) [49] (quoting the *ELSI* decision in support of the tribunal's interpretation of art. 2(2) of the Sri Lanka-UK BIT, which uses the formula '*full* protection and security'); Noble Ventures *v* Romania, Award, ICSID Case No. ARB/01/11 (12 October 2005) [165] (relying on the *ELSI* decision in connection with art. II(2)(a) of the Romania-US BIT, which uses the adjective 'full').

[219]Indicative examples appear in several ECT cases. See: Electrabel S.A. *v* Hungary, Decision on Jurisdiction, Applicable Law and Liability, ICSID Case No. ARB/07/19 (30 November 2012) [7.83] (heavily relying on *El Paso v Argentina*, which referred to a '*full* protection and security' clause); Mohammad Ammar Al-Bahloul *v* Tajikistan, Partial Award on Jurisdiction and Liability, SCC Case No. V(064/2008) (9 September 2009) [248] (relying on the *Tecmed v Mexico* award, which referred to the phrase 'protección y seguridad *plenas*'); Plama Consortium Ltd. *v* Bulgaria, Award, ICSID Case No. ARB/03/24 (27 August 2008) [179 and 181] (relying *inter alia* on the cases *Tecmed v Mexico, Saluka v Czech Republic*, and *Wena Hotels v Egypt*, all of which referred to FPS clauses using the adjective *full*). For other examples see: BG Group *v* Argentina (UNCITRAL), Final Award (24 December 2007) [324] (relying *inter alia* on the cases *AAPL v Sri Lanka* and *Wena Hotels v Egypt*, which referred to FPS clauses using the adjective *full*); Joseph Houben *v* Burundi, Sentence, ICSID Case No. ARB/13/7 (12 January 2016) [158-63] (relying *inter alia* on the cases *AAPL v Sri Lanka, El Paso v Argentina, Pantechniki v Albania, Saluka v Czech Republic*, and *Tecmed v Mexico*, all of which referred to FPS clauses using the adjective *full*).

[220]See Sects. 14.4.1.4 and 14.4.2.1.

14.4.3   The Guarantee of Legal Protection and Security

A few investment agreements qualify the guarantee of protection and security with the adjective *legal*. This terminology is fairly new. The term *legal* began to be employed in FCN agreements and other international treaties in the second half of the twentieth century. Early examples of this treaty language appear in the FCN agreements negotiated by the United States with France (1959),[221] Belgium (1961)[222] and Luxembourg (1962).[223] Article I of the France-US FCN Agreement was as follows:

> Each High Contracting Party shall accord equitable treatment to nationals and companies of the other High Contracting Party, both as to their persons and as to their property, enterprises and other interests, *and shall assure them within its territories full legal and judicial protection.*[224]

The Belgian treaty of 1961 and the Luxembourg treaty of 1962 contained three different FPS clauses.[225] The first clause referred only to 'effective protection'.[226] The second clause used the expression 'full legal and judicial protection' but focused the right of access to the local judiciary and other aspects of redress:

> 1. Nationals of either Contracting Party within the territories of the other Party shall be accorded *full legal and judicial protection for their persons, rights and interests.* Such nationals shall be free from molestation and *shall receive constant protection in no case less than that required by international law. 2. To this end they shall in particular have right of access,* on the same basis and on the same conditions as nationals of such other Party, *to the courts of justice and administrative tribunals and agencies in all degrees* of jurisdiction and shall have right to the services of competent persons of their choice.[227]

---

[221]Convention of Establishment between the United States of America and France (adopted 25 November 1959, entered into force 21 December 1960) 401 UNTS 75, 76 art. I. Interestingly, this treaty was concluded the very same day as the first BIT (between Germany and Pakistan).

[222]Treaty of Friendship, Establishment and Navigation between the United States of America and Belgium (adopted 21 February 1961, entered into force 3 October 1963) 480 UNTS 150, 153 art. 3 and 157 art. 4.

[223]Treaty of Friendship, Establishment and Navigation between the United States of America and Luxembourg (adopted 23 February 1962, entered into force 28 March 1963) 474 UNTS 3, 6 art. III and 10 art. IV.

[224]Emphasis added. Convention of Establishment between the United States of America and France (adopted 25 November 1959, entered into force 21 December 1960) 401 UNTS 75, 76 art. I.

[225]For an author discussing the three FPS clauses of the Belgium-US FCN Agreement of 1961 see: George Foster, 'Recovering "Protection and Security": The Treaty Standard's Obscure Origins, Forgotten Meaning, and Key Current Significance' (2012) 45(4) Vand. J. Transnat'l L. 1095, 1134-5.

[226]Treaty of Friendship, Establishment and Navigation between the United States of America and Belgium (adopted 21 February 1961, entered into force 3 October 1963) 480 UNTS 150, 151 art. 1.

[227]Emphasis added. Treaty of Friendship, Establishment and Navigation between the United States of America and Belgium (adopted 21 February 1961, entered into force 3 October 1963) 480 UNTS 150, 153 art. 3 (1) and (2); Treaty of Friendship, Establishment and Navigation between the United

Finally, the third clause provided that '[p]roperty that nationals and companies of either Party own within the territories of the other Party shall enjoy *constant security therein through full legal and judicial protection*'.[228]

These clauses represented a change in the traditional wording of American commercial treaties, which until then had normally employed the phrase *most constant protection and security* or, in some cases, *full protection and security*.[229] The change did not go unnoticed. Writing in 1965, Anthony Benton welcomed this new phrasing as a means of giving the protection obligation 'at least a minimum amount of legal substance'.[230] As to the meaning of the clauses, he said:

> Although opinions may vary widely on what constitutes full legal and judicial protection, the provision can reasonably be read to require the existence of a judicial remedy for unreasonable or arbitrary governmental interference with the security of the property of treaty aliens. And implicit in the existence of such a remedy is the idea that the property is a right requiring some minimum amount of recognition and respect on the part of the state, a right not easily impaired by the invocation of social considerations.[231]

More recent publications have sought to link this change in American treaty practice to the contemporary debate on whether the FPS standard grants protection against physical harm only, or encompasses the notions of nonphysical and legal security.[232] Commenting on the Belgian treaty, George Foster depicted this wording as 'the most extreme recognition within the corpus of US FCN treaties that the duty of protection and security contemplated more than police protection'.[233]

A recent historical study on the 1959 French treaty's negotiation record suggests that the motives behind the change were somewhat different. The parties originally intended to use the traditional phrase *most constant protection and security*, but the clause was modified at the request of the French negotiators, who sought to avoid any risk that such vague language could be interpreted as imposing strict responsibility.[234] The French understood the redrafted clause as '[putting] each Party under

---

States of America and Luxembourg (adopted 23 February 1962, entered into force 28 March 1963) 474 UNTS 3, 6 art. III (1) and (2).

[228]Emphasis added. Treaty of Friendship, Establishment and Navigation between the United States of America and Belgium (adopted 21 February 1961, entered into force 3 October 1963) 480 UNTS 150, 147 art. 4(1); Treaty of Friendship, Establishment and Navigation between the United States of America and Luxembourg (adopted 23 February 1962, entered into force 28 March 1963) 474 UNTS 3, 10 art. IV.

[229]See Sects. 14.4.1 and 14.4.2.

[230]Anthony Benton, 'The Protection of Property Rights in Commercial Treaties of the United States' (1965) 25 ZaöRV 50, 64.

[231]Anthony Benton, 'The Protection of Property Rights in Commercial Treaties of the United States' (1965) 25 ZaöRV 50, 64.

[232]George Foster, 'Recovering "Protection and Security": The Treaty Standard's Obscure Origins, Forgotten Meaning, and Key Current Significance' (2012) 45(4) Vand. J. Transnat'l L. 1095, 1134-5.

[233]George Foster, 'Recovering "Protection and Security": The Treaty Standard's Obscure Origins, Forgotten Meaning, and Key Current Significance' (2012) 45(4) Vand. J. Transnat'l L. 1095, 1135.

[234]Kenneth Vandevelde, *The First Bilateral Investment Treaties: U.S. Postwar Friendship, Commerce and Navigation Treaties* (Oxford University Press, New York 2017) 351.

the responsibility of having laws and a system of protection that will assure the safety and security of the treaty-alien and his belongings'.[235] Therefore, there is merit to the idea that these treaty clauses were specifically intended to ensure protection under the law and through the local justice system, rather than to create a guarantee of legal stability.

While the United States readily abandoned this treaty language, and returned to former formulations of the standard, France continued to use the phrase '*pleine protection légale et judiciaire*' in conventions of establishment concluded with several countries.[236] At the multilateral level, the same wording appears in article 7 of the European Convention on Establishment of 1955,[237] and article 26(1) of the European Convention on the Status of Migrant Workers of 1977.[238]

On the other side of the Atlantic, the Spanish expression '*plena protección legal*' was employed in some BITs between Latin American states,[239] as well as in a few treaties concluded with states outside the region.[240] Most importantly, this wording was used in the Colonia Protocol to the Treaty of Asunción, which was envisaged as

---

[235]Kenneth Vandevelde, *The First Bilateral Investment Treaties: U.S. Postwar Friendship, Commerce and Navigation Treaties* (Oxford University Press, New York 2017) 351 (directly quoting an airgram from the U.S. Embassy in Paris to the Department of State, dated 14 May 1959).

[236]For some indicative examples see: Convention d'établissement entre le Gouvernement de la République Française et le Gouvernement de la République Centrafricaine (adopted 26 September 1994, entered into force 1 May 1996) 1980 UNTS 221, 223 art. 4; Convention d'établissement entre le Gouvernement de la République Française et le Gouvernement de la République du Mali (adopted 26 September 1994, entered into force 1 April 1996) 1980 UNTS 189, 191 art. 4. For an additional example of this wording being used in a French treaty see: Accord entre le Gouvernement de la République Française et le Gouvernement de la République Populaire du Congo sur les droits fondamentaux des nationaux (adopted 1 January 1974, entered into force 1 November 1981) 1309 UNTS 79, 80 art. 4.

[237]European Convention on Establishment (adopted 13 December 1955, entered into force 23 February 1965) 529 UNTS 141, 148 art. 7 (assuring treaty aliens 'full legal and judicial protection of their persons and property and of their rights and interests').

[238]European Convention on the Legal Status of Migrant Workers (adopted 24 November 1977, entered into force 1 May 1983) 1496 UNTS 3, 12 art. 26(1) (assuring migrant workers 'full legal and judicial protection of their persons and property and of their rights and interests').

[239]For some indicative examples see: Acuerdo entre el Gobierno de la República de Venezuela y el Gobierno de la República Argentina para la promoción y protección recíprocas de inversiones (adopted 16 November 1993, entered into force 1 July 1995) art. 4(2); Acuerdo entre el Gobierno de los Estados Unidos Mexicanos y el Gobierno de la República Argentina para la promoción y protección recíproca de las inversiones (adopted 13 November 1996, entered into force 22 June 1996) art. 3(2); Convenio entre la República de Bolivia y la República del Ecuador para la promoción y protección recíproca de inversiones (adopted 25 May 1995, entered into force 15 August 1997) art. 3(2); Convenio entre la República de Costa Rica y la República del Ecuador para la promoción y protección recíproca de inversiones (adopted 6 December 2001) art. II(6).

[240]See, for example: Agreement between the Government of the Kingdom of Denmark and the Government of the Republic of Argentina concerning the Promotion and Reciprocal Protection of Investments (adopted 6 November 1992, entered into force 2 February 1995) art. 3(2); Tratado entre la República Federal de Alemania y la República Argentina sobre promoción y protección recíproca de inversiones (adopted 9 April 1991, entered into force 8 November 1993) art. 4(1).

the legal instrument applicable to the protection of investments within Mercosur, but would never enter into force.[241] In April 2017, the members of Mercosur signed a new Protocol in Buenos Aires; this new instrument expressly excludes the FPS and FET standards from its scope of application.[242]

Only a few investment arbitral tribunals have considered claims referring to *legal protection* or *legal security* clauses. To-date, the perhaps most significant arbitral decision on the subject is the award rendered in *Siemens v Argentina* (2007). In that case, the investor argued that an FPS clause using the adjective 'legal' should be interpreted broadly.[243] For its part, the respondent state maintained that the standard 'refers only to physical security'.[244] The arbitral tribunal observed that, in its submissions, the host state 'did not address the fact that security was qualified by "legal" in this instance'.[245] In the eyes of the tribunal this word was the clue to the interpretation of the treaty:

> In the instant case, "security" is qualified by "legal". In its ordinary meaning, "legal security" has been defined as the "quality of the legal system which implies certainty in its norms and, consequently, their foreseeable application." It is clear that in the context of this meaning the Treaty refers to security that it is not physical.[246]

While this interpretation seems plausible, the *Siemens* tribunal failed to adequately justify its approach. The arbitrators based their understanding of *legal security* on a definition taken from the Spanish Dictionary of the Royal Spanish Academy.[247] Dictionaries could be helpful in the interpretation of treaties. Still, relying on a dictionary as the only source for the interpretation of the treaty clause seems insufficient, if to say the least. In the context of the WTO, the Appellate Body has rightly noted that 'dictionaries are important guides to, but not dispositive of, the meaning of words appearing in treaties'.[248]

---

[241]Protocolo de Colonia para la Promoción y Protección Recíproca de Inversiones en el Mercosur (Intrazona) (adopted 17 January 1994) in Martins Paparinskis, *Basic Documents on International Investment Protection* (Hart Publishing, Portland OR 2012) 350, 352 art. 3(3) (using the phrase 'plena protección legal'). A few months later, the member states of Mercosur concluded another Protocol on the protection of investments from third countries, which contains an FPS clause using the phrase 'plena protección' (without the adjective *legal*). Protocolo de Buenos Aires sobre Promoción y Protección de Inversiones Provenientes de Estados no Partes del Mercosur (adopted 5 August 1994) in Martins Paparinskis, *Basic Documents on International Investment Protection* (Hart Publishing, Portland OR 2012) 356, 358 art. 2(C)(2).

[242]Protocolo de Buenos Aires de Cooperación y Facilitación de Inversiones Intra-Mercosur (adopted 7 April 2017) [online] http://apc.mef.gub.uy/innovaportal/file/21186/2/protocolo-de-cooperacion-y-facilitacion-de-inversiones.pdf, art. 4(3).

[243]Siemens AG v Argentina, Award, ICSID Case No. ARB/02/8 (6 February 2007) [301].

[244]Siemens AG v Argentina, Award, ICSID Case No. ARB/02/8 (6 February 2007) [301].

[245]Siemens AG v Argentina, Award, ICSID Case No. ARB/02/8 (6 February 2007) [302].

[246]Siemens AG v Argentina, Award, ICSID Case No. ARB/02/8 (6 February 2007) [303].

[247]Siemens AG v Argentina, Award, ICSID Case No. ARB/02/8 (6 February 2007) [303] n. 114.

[248]China – Measures Affecting Trading Services and Distribution Services for Certain Publications and Audiovisual Entertainment Products, Appellate Body Report, WT/DS363/AB/2 (21 December 2009) [348]. For an overview of the use of dictionaries in the WTO see: David Pavot, 'The Use of

The *Siemens* tribunal went a step further and noted that the adjective *legal* could raise doubts as to whether the FPS clause grants physical protection. In the tribunal's words:

> [O]ne may question given the qualification of the term "security", whether the Treaty covers physical security at all. Arguably it could be considered to be included under "full protection", but that is not an issue in these proceedings.[249]

The implication is that, in the Argentina-Germany BIT, *legal security* refers to the guarantee of a 'certain' and 'foreseeable' legal system, whereas *full protection* could 'arguably' cover physical harm. The *Siemens* tribunal seems to have focused on the Spanish (authentic) version of article 4(1) of the Argentina-Germany BIT. A word-to-word translation of the treaty clause would be as follows:

> Investments of nationals or corporations of one of the Contracting Parties shall enjoy *full protection* and *legal security* within the territory of the other Contracting Party.[250]

In proposing this interpretation, the arbitrators ignored the slightly different wording used by the other authentic version of the treaty, in German language. In the German text of the treaty, the adjectives *full* (*voll*) and *legal* (*rechtlich*) qualify *protection* (*Schutz*) as well as *security* (*Sicherheit*). A literal translation of the German text would be as follows:

> Investments of nationals or corporations from a Contracting Party shall enjoy within the territory of the other Contracting Party *full legal protection* and *full legal security*.[251]

This wording is fairly common in German BITs concluded from the 1960s through the 1990s. A look into German legal literature from that period indicates that the adjective *rechtlich* was not understood as excluding the customary core of the protection obligation. Making reference to the Germany-Liberia BIT of 1961, which also used the phrase *rechtliche Sicherheit*, a scholar observed in 1974 that FPS

Dictionary by the WTO Appellate Body: Beyond the Search of Ordinary Meaning' (2013) 4 (1) J. Int'l Disp. Settlement 29, 29-46.

[249] Siemens AG v Argentina, Award, ICSID Case No. ARB/02/8 (6 February 2007) [303].

[250] Author's translation. The original Spanish text reads as follows: "Las inversiones de nacionales o sociedades de una de las Partes Contratantes gozarán de plena protección y seguridad jurídica en el territorio de la otra Parte Contratante." Tratado entre la República Federal de Alemania y la República Argentina sobre promoción y protección recíproca de inversiones (adopted 9 April 1991, entered into force 8 November 1993) art. 4(1).

[251] Author's translation. The original German text reads as follows: "Kapitalanlagen von Staatsangehörigen oder Gesellschaften einer Vertragspartei genießen im Hoheitsgebiet der anderen Vertragspartei vollen rechtlichen Schutz und volle rechtliche Sicherheit." Vertrag zwischen der Bundesrepublik Deutschland und der Argentinischen Republik über die Förderung und den gegenseitigen Schutz von Kapitalanlagen (adopted 9 April 1991, entered into force 8 November 1993) art. 4(1).

clauses pertain to the protection of investments from a 'static-legal standpoint' (*statisch-juristischer Standpunkt*).[252] In this connection, he explained:

> Legal protection and legal security means, first, in a formal sense, the free access and the secured legal position of the investor before local courts for the defense of his investment. This seems natural since, in contrast to FCN agreements, the German treaty system does not contain any specific provision addressing the means for the investor's legal protection [...] In a substantive sense, the meaning of the conceptual pair *protection and security* shall be linked to the preservation of the external components of the investment against destruction or damage. In this connection, it should be thought of the criminal and police protection of the offices, warehouses and industrial premises of the investor against attacks of state agents and private individuals, as in the case of demonstrations or strike violence.[253]

This passage shows that the use of the adjective 'legal' does not necessarily imply that the customary protection obligation was substituted with a different treaty-based standard. While it is arguable that 'legal security' could entail some additional guarantee of legal stability, such extension of the FPS standard should not come at the expense of the standard's customary core. Furthermore, it is plausible that the main concern behind the expression 'legal' (*rechtlich*) was to ensure protection by the law and, particularly, access to the local judiciary. This seems consistent with the use of the adjective *legal* in FCN agreements concluded by the United States in the 1950s, discussed above.

In addition to the *Siemens* tribunal, other arbitral tribunals have also addressed the interpretation of security clauses using the adjective *legal*. In *Convial Callao v Peru* (2013) the arbitrators interpreted article 4(1) of the Peru-Argentina BIT, which uses the phrase 'full legal protection and security' ('*plena protección y seguridad jurídica*').[254] The tribunal recognized that the adjective 'legal' had an effect on the scope of the FPS clause, noting that '[t]he text of the article clearly shows that the

---

[252]Helmut Frick, *Bilateraler Investitionsschutz in Entwicklungsländern. Ein Vergleich der Vertragssysteme der Vereinigten Staaten von Amerika und der Bundesrepublik Deutschland* (Duncker & Humblot, Berlin 1975) 207.

[253]Author's translation. The original German text reads: Rechtsschutz und Rechtssicherheit wird zunächst in formeller Hinsicht ungehinderten Zugang zu und gesicherte Rechtsstellung vor innerstaatlichen Gerichten für den Investor in Verteidigung seiner Kapitalanlage bedeuten. Das liegt deswegen nahe, weil das deutsche Vertragssystem im Gegensatz zu den FHS-Verträgen keine spezifische Bestimmung über die Rechtsschutzmöglichkeiten des Investors enthält [...] In materieller Hinsicht ist die Bedeutung des Begriffspaares Schutz und Sicherheit auf die Wahrung und Verteidigung des äußeren Bestandes der Kapitalanlage, auf Schutz gegen Zerstörung oder Beschädigung zu beziehen. Hierbei ist vor allem an die straf- und polizei-rechtliche Absicherung der Geschäftsräume, der Lager- und Fabrik-gebäude des Investors gegen Übergriffe sowohl staatlicher Organe als auch von Privatpersonen etwa bei Demonstrationen oder Streikexzessen zu denken." Helmut Frick, *Bilateraler Investitionsschutz in Entwicklungsländern. Ein Vergleich der Vertragssysteme der Vereinigten Staaten von Amerika und der Bundesrepublik Deutschland* (Duncker & Humblot, Berlin 1975) 207.

[254]Convenio entre el Gobierno de la República del Perú y el Gobierno de la República Argentina sobre Promoción y Protección Recíproca de Inversiones (adopted 10 November 1994, entered into force 24 October 1996) art. 4(1). Cf. also Convial Callao S.A. and CCI – Compañía de Concesiones de Infraestructura S.A. *v* Peru, Laudo Final, ICSID Case No. ARB/10/2 (21 May 2013) [641].

protection guaranteed includes both the physical protection of the investment and its legal protection'.[255] In *Sergei Paushok v Mongolia* (2011) the arbitrators considered the guarantee of 'full legal protection' in article 2 of the Mongolia-Russian Federation BIT. As regards to the use of the adjective 'legal', the tribunal observed:

> The "legal protection" clause has been raised in a number of BIT cases and has sometime been interpreted, as a stand-alone clause; as aimed at the physical protection of persons or assets against illegal actions by third parties. Further, some BITs provide simply for "full physical protection and security" of investments. However, in the present instance, the Treaty provides clearly for "full legal protection to investments of investors of the other Contracting Party." There is therefore no reason to limit the protection guaranteed to mere physical protection.[256]

It must be noted that the *Sergei Paushok* tribunal refrained from drawing a specific definition of the treaty clause, albeit rejecting the 'physical security' approach.[257] Rather, it noted that the claim would fail regardless of the interpretation adopted.[258]

While the *Siemens*, *Convial* and *Paushok* decisions advanced a broad interpretation of clauses employing the adjective *legal*, other arbitral tribunals have concluded that the phrase 'full legal protection' does not convey a different meaning than other formulations of the FPS standard. An example is the award rendered in *Gemplus v Mexico* (2010). In that case, the tribunal considered the meaning of the phrase 'full legal protection' in article 3(2) of the Argentina-Mexico BIT.[259] The arbitrators considered that this clause was 'materially similar' to the FPS clause of the France-Mexico BIT,[260] which does not use the adjective *legal*.[261] The *Gemplus* tribunal further stated that these provisions provide protection against third parties and do

---

[255] Author's translation. The original Spanish text reads: "el texto del artículo deja ver claramente que la protección garantizada incluye tanto la protección física de la inversión como su protección jurídica". Convial Callao S.A. and CCI – Compañía de Concesiones de Infraestructura S.A. *v* Peru, Laudo Final, ICSID Case No. ARB/10/2 (21 May 2013) [642].

[256] Sergei Paushok, CJSC Golden East Co., CJSC Vostoknefte *v* Mongolia (UNCITRAL), Award on Jurisdiction and Liability (28 April 2011) [326].

[257] Sergei Paushok, CJSC Golden East Co., CJSC Vostoknefte *v* Mongolia (UNCITRAL), Award on Jurisdiction and Liability (28 April 2011) [326-7].

[258] Sergei Paushok, CJSC Golden East Co., CJSC Vostoknefte *v* Mongolia (UNCITRAL), Award on Jurisdiction and Liability (28 April 2011) [327].

[259] Author's translation. The original Spanish text reads 'plena protección legal'. Acuerdo entre el Gobierno de los Estados Unidos Mexicanos y el Gobierno de la República Argentina para la promoción y protección recíproca de las inversiones (adopted 13 November 1996, entered into force 22 June 1996) art. 3(2).

[260] Gemplus S.A., SLP S.A. and Gemplus Industrial S.A. de C.V. *v* Mexico, Award, ICSID Cases No. ARB(AF)/04/3 & ARB(AF)/04/4 (16 June 2010) [9.9].

[261] Cf. Agreement between the Government of the Republic of France and the Government of the United Mexican States on the Reciprocal Promotion and Protection of Investments (adopted 12 November 1998, entered into force 12 October 2000) art. 4(3) (using the phrase 'full and complete protection and safety').

under no circumstances create a strict liability.[262] In *CC/Devas v India* (2016) the arbitral tribunal applied the guarantee of 'full legal protection and security' of the India-Serbia BIT *via* the MFN clause of the India-Mauritius BIT.[263] Despite the use of the adjective 'legal', the arbitrators considered that the clause pertained only to the protection of investments against acts of third parties.[264]

These remarks should suffice as an overview of the possible interpretations of FPS clauses using the adjective *legal*. This section has shown that the interpretation of these treaty provisions is not always as straightforward as it might seem at first sight. Particularly, the mere use of the term *legal* does not *necessarily* mean that the protection obligation includes the guarantee of a stable and foreseeable legal environment. Historical sources suggest that, in the treaty practice of some states, this wording was primarily intended to ensure protection under the local legal system and the availability of adequate mechanisms of redress. It was neither aimed at imposing strict liability on the host state, nor at excluding the traditional areas of application of the FPS standard (e.g. mob violence, revolutionary damages, etc.).

To be sure, states are free to derogate from customary law, and could surely extend the protection obligation beyond its customary core. They may certainly agree on a protection obligation which includes a broadly-defined guarantee of legal stability. The question before competent adjudicators will always be whether the parties to the applicable treaty have actually consented to such comprehensive obligations. In the context of a specific treaty, adjudicators could find good reasons to conclude that the adjective *legal* is a manifestation of such an intention. Still, the meaning of the treaty provision must be considered on a case-by-case basis, in order to ascertain the actual will of the parties.

14.4.4 Protection and Security Clauses Using No Qualifying Adjectives

Not every investment treaty formulates the protection obligation using a qualifying adjective. It is not uncommon for treaties to merely assure *protection*,[265] or

---

[262]Gemplus S.A., SLP S.A. and Gemplus Industrial S.A. de C.V. *v* Mexico, Award, ICSID Cases No. ARB(AF)/04/3 & ARB(AF)/04/4 (16 June 2010) [9.10-9.12].

[263]CC/Devas (Mauritius) Ltd., Devas Employees Mauritius Private Ltd. and Telcom Devas Mauritius Ltd. *v* India (UNCITRAL), Award on Jurisdiction and Merits, PCA Case No. 2013-09 (25 July 2016) [496].

[264]CC/Devas (Mauritius) Ltd., Devas Employees Mauritius Private Ltd. and Telcom Devas Mauritius Ltd. *v* India (UNCITRAL), Award on Jurisdiction and Merits, PCA Case No. 2013-09 (25 July 2016) [497-9].

[265]See, for example: Acuerdo para la promoción y la protección recíproca de inversiones entre el Reino de España y la República Argentina (adopted 3 October 1991, entered into force 28 September 1992) art. 3(1).

protection and security.[266] The question arises as to whether the *absence* of qualifying adjectives has any implication on the scope and content of the security obligation. To-date, only a few arbitral tribunals have elaborated on this issue. Case law on the subject is divided.

In a first group of cases, investment tribunals have actually given weight to the absence of a specific qualifying adjective. The perhaps most clear example of this approach is the *Decision on Liability* rendered in *Suez v Argentina* (2010). In the *Suez* case, multiple investors raised different FPS claims, respectively invoking the Argentina-France BIT, the Argentina-Spain BIT and the Argentina-UK BIT.[267] The investors argued that the FPS standard entailed a guarantee of legal stability, and relied in this connection on the *Azurix v Argentina* and *CME v Czech Republic* cases.[268] The arbitral tribunal underscored the differences between the wording of the FPS clauses applied in those cases and the applicable BITs:

> The CME tribunal was interpreting Article 3(2) of the Netherlands-Czech Republic BIT, stipulating that "each Contracting Party shall provide to such investments full security and protection" [. . .] That treaty formulation is somewhat different from the BIT provisions applicable to the present case. *The Argentina-Spain and Argentina-U.K. BITs refer only to "protection" and to "protect" without the qualifying word "full" or "fully," while the Argentina-France BITs states that investors shall be "fully protected." Does the difference in formulation affect the scope of protection afforded by the BITs?* The tribunal in *Azurix* implied that it did, for it justified on that basis that the Argentina-United States BIT providing for "full protection and security" applied only to measures taken by a government and was not limited to physical actions [. . .] Thus, *Azurix* seemed to suggest that *the omission of "full" or "fully," as in the case with two of the applicable BITs in the present cases, restricted the scope of protection only to physical security and protection. The tribunal in Biwater adhered to the same line of argument.*[269]

Commenting on the *Siemens* case, the arbitrators stated:

---

[266]See, for example: Treaty between the United States of America and the Republic of Zaire concerning the Reciprocal Encouragement and Protection of Investment (adopted 3 August 1984, entered into force 28 July 1989) art. II; Treaty between the United States of America and the Arab Republic of Egypt concerning the Reciprocal Encouragement and Protection of Investments (adopted 11 March 1986, entered into force 27 June 1992) art. II(4).

[267]Suez Sociedad General de Aguas de Barcelona S.A. and Vivendi Universal S.A. *v* Argentina, Decision on Liability, ICSID Case No. ARB/03/19 (30 July 2010) [59]. For the sake of accuracy, it must be observed that, while art. III(1) of the Argentina-Spain BIT did not employ any qualifying adjective, art. 5(1) of the Argentina-France BIT and art. 2(2) of the Argentina-UK BIT did actually use qualifying adjectives. In any case, as explained in the main text, the tribunal gave considerable weight to the *absence* of some particular adjectives.

[268]Suez Sociedad General de Aguas de Barcelona S.A. and Vivendi Universal S.A. *v* Argentina, Decision on Liability, ICSID Case No. ARB/03/19 (30 July 2010) [165-6].

[269]Emphasis added. Suez Sociedad General de Aguas de Barcelona S.A. and Vivendi Universal S.A. *v* Argentina, Decision on Liability, ICSID Case No. ARB/03/19 (30 July 2010) [168]. As regards to the wording of the Argentina-France BIT (which actually uses the adjective 'full'), the tribunal focused on the relationship between the FPS and the FET standards (at paras 170-1). Section 15.2.2 addresses this aspect of the *Suez* award in greater detail.

None of the three BITs concerned [i.e., the BITs applicable in the *Suez* case] refers to "legal security". Therefore, this Tribunal is of the opinion that the various formulations of protection and security employed in the present BITs cannot extend to an obligation to maintain a stable and secure legal and commercial environment.[270]

After this detailed analysis of previous arbitral decisions, the *Suez* tribunal noted that '[o]ther tribunals have given less weight to the precise language used in the treaty when determining the scope of full protection and security'.[271] Notwithstanding the foregoing, the arbitrators considered that, as a rule, the extension of the standard beyond physical security is not justified where the applicable clause does not expressly provide so; this should hold particularly true for treaties in which the nouns 'protection' and 'security' are not even qualified with the term 'full'.[272] In this vein, the arbitrators explained:

> As far as this Tribunal is concerned, it is inclined to think that the absence of the word "full" or "fully" in the full protection and security provisions in the Argentina-Spain and the Argentina-UK BITs supports the view of an obligation limited to physical protection and legal remedies for the Spanish and U.K. Claimants and their assets.[273]

In a second group of cases, arbitral tribunals have concluded that, as such, the absence of a qualifying adjective has no significant effect on the content and scope of the protection obligation. Thus, in *Parkerings v Lithuania* (2007) the arbitrators stated:

> Article III of the Treaty [Lithuania-Norway BIT] only mentions the term *protection*. In a number of decisions, Tribunals make reference to the standard of "*full protection and security*." It is generally accepted that the variation of language does not make a significant difference in the level of protection a host State is to provide. Moreover, *in casu*, the Parties make systematically reference to the standard of "*full protection and security*." Therefore, the Arbitral Tribunal intends to apply the standard of "*full protection and security*".[274]

In *Teinver v Argentina* (2017) the arbitral tribunal considered the differences between the 'protection' obligation under article III(1) of the Argentina-Spain BIT and guarantee of 'full protection and security' in article II(2)(a) of the Argentina-US

---

[270]*Suez Sociedad General de Aguas de Barcelona S.A. and Vivendi Universal S.A. v Argentina*, Decision on Liability, ICSID Case No. ARB/03/19 (30 July 2010) [176]. See also para 179.

[271]*Suez Sociedad General de Aguas de Barcelona S.A. and Vivendi Universal S.A. v Argentina*, Decision on Liability, ICSID Case No. ARB/03/19 (30 July 2010) [169].

[272]*Suez Sociedad General de Aguas de Barcelona S.A. and Vivendi Universal S.A. v Argentina*, Decision on Liability, ICSID Case No. ARB/03/19 (30 July 2010) [175-6 and 179]. Cf. also Sect. 14.2.

[273]*Suez Sociedad General de Aguas de Barcelona S.A. and Vivendi Universal S.A. v Argentina*, Decision on Liability, ICSID Case No. ARB/03/19 (30 July 2010) [175]. See also the tribunal's emphasis on the absence of the adjective 'legal' (at paras 176 and 179). On this issue see Sect. 15.2.2.

[274]*Parkerings-Compagniet AS v Lithuania*, Award, ICSID Case No. ARB/05/8 (11 September 2007) [354].

BIT.[275] Their conclusion was that there was 'no significant difference' from one treaty to the other.[276] At the same time, however, they did not exclude the possibility that the phrase 'full protection and security' could require a degree of protection which is 'more favorable' to foreign investors.[277]

Other tribunals, while following a similar line of argument, have been less explicit in this regard. An example would be the award rendered in *Ampal v Egypt* (2017). The *Ampal* tribunal considered a treaty provision assuring 'protection and security' without using any qualifying adjective.[278] The absence of an adjective did not play any significant role in the interpretation and application of the standard. Quite the contrary, the arbitrators heavily relied on arbitral decisions pertaining to FPS clauses using the adjectives *full* and *constant*.[279] This indicates, albeit implicitly, that it was the tribunal's understanding that, as a rule, the different formulations of FPS have no effect on the standard's scope and content.

These arbitral decisions show that the absence of a qualifying adjective has not been interpreted as justifying the extension of the FPS standard beyond customary law. The prevailing view seems to be that this feature of FPS clauses has little or no significance for the definition of the standard. While in some cases arbitrators have highlighted the absence of some specific adjectives, these tribunals have not interpreted such treaty language as a derogation from customary international law. Taking the *Suez* case as an example, one observes that the emphasis on the absence of the terms *full* and *legal* served the purpose of reinforcing the tribunal's restrictive interpretation of the standard.

---

[275]Teinver S.A., Transportes de Cercanías S.A. and Autobuses Urbanos del Sur S.A. *v* Argentina, Award, ICSID Case No. ARB/09/1 (21 July 2017) [897].

[276]Teinver S.A., Transportes de Cercanías S.A. and Autobuses Urbanos del Sur S.A. *v* Argentina, Award, ICSID Case No. ARB/09/1 (21 July 2017) [897].

[277]Teinver S.A., Transportes de Cercanías S.A. and Autobuses Urbanos del Sur S.A. *v* Argentina, Award, ICSID Case No. ARB/09/1 (21 July 2017) [897]. For another tribunal referring to the 'protection' obligation of the Argentina-Spain BIT see: Emilio Agustín Maffezini *v* Spain, Award, ICSID Case No. ARB/97/7 (13 November 2000) [83].

[278]Cf. Treaty between the United States of America and the Arab Republic of Egypt concerning the Reciprocal Encouragement and Protection of Investments (adopted 11 March 1986, entered into force 27 June 1992) art. II(4).

[279]Ampal-American Israel Corp., Egi-Fund (08-10) Investors LLC, Egi-Series Investments LLC and BSS-EMG Investors LLC *v* Egypt, Decision on Liability and Heads of Loss, ICSID Case No. ARB/12/11 (21 February 2017) [242] (quoting the *ELSI* case, which referred to the guarantee of '*most constant* protection and security' in art. V of the Italy-US FCN Agreement), [243] (quoting *AAPL v Sri Lanka*, which referred to the guarantee of '*full* protection and security' in art. 2(2) of the Sri Lanka-UK BIT) and [244 and 285] (quoting *Pantechniki v Albania*, which referred to the guarantee of '*full* protection and security' in art. 4(1) of the Albania-Greece BIT). For another case giving no substantive importance to the absence of a qualifying adjective in the applicable FPS clause see: American Manufacturing & Trading Inc. *v* Zaire, Award, ICSID Case No. ARB 93/1 (21 February 1997) [6.06 *et seq.*].

Chapter 15
'Full Protection and Security' Clauses and Other Treaty Provisions

15.1 Preliminary Remarks

In investment treaties, 'full protection and security' clauses are normally embedded within a complex web of broadly worded substantive standards of investment protection. Notwithstanding the rapid growth in the number of investment disputes the world has witnessed during the past few decades, the interplay between the substantive provisions of investment treaties remains somewhat unclear. Arbitral tribunals face sheer difficulties in assessing the possible overlap of different standards, and do not always succeed in drawing a meaningful distinction between them. In some cases, while the difference between standards was not essential to the decision on the case, doubts arose as to the possible relevance of one standard for the interpretation and application of another.

This chapter considers the relationship between the FPS standard, on the one hand, and other substantive obligations commonly found in investment treaties on the other. In this vein, it provides an outlook of the specific problems at stake, as they have appeared in arbitral practice, and discusses current theories about the interplay between FPS and other treaty provisions. The clauses examined in this chapter include: (1) fair and equitable treatment; (2) expropriation; (3) protection against arbitrary measures; (4) national treatment; (5) most-favored-nation treatment; and (6) war clauses.

© Springer Nature Switzerland AG 2019
S. Mantilla Blanco, *Full Protection and Security in International Investment Law*,
European Yearbook of International Economic Law 8,
https://doi.org/10.1007/978-3-030-24838-3_15

15.2 'Full Protection and Security' and 'Fair and Equitable Treatment'

Investment treaties often manage to compress different obligations in a few sentences of a short treaty provision. As observed by the arbitral tribunal in *Lemire v Ukraine* (2010):

> It is a rule of Delphic economy of language, which manages in just three sentences to formulate a series of wide ranging principles: FET standard, protection and security standard, international minimum standard and prohibition of arbitrary or discriminatory measures.[1]

This holds particularly true for the FPS and the FET standards, which are usually enshrined in the same treaty clause. This circumstance raises the question, whether there is a special connection between the two standards.[2] This question turns particularly relevant in view of the fact that no substantive obligation in international investment law has been more often litigated or more intensively theorized than the FET standard.[3] The vaguely worded guarantee of 'fair and equitable treatment' has been applied in the most diverse contexts, from arbitrariness in the administration of justice to the protection of legitimate expectations.[4] A look into arbitral decisions and scholarly writings leaves the impression that the FET standard is ever-present in contemporary international investment law. Scholars have gone as far as to state that '[t]he FET standard may be characterized as the pivotal, the core investment protection standard'.[5]

The relationship between FPS and FET has drawn the attention of adjudicators and scholars alike.[6] At least three approaches have been suggested in this

---

[1]Joseph Charles Lemire *v* Ukraine, Decision on Jurisdiction and Liability, ICSID Case No. ARB/06/18 (14 January 2010) [246] (in reference to the article II(3) of the Ukraine-USA BIT and the U.S. Model BITs of 1992 and 1994).

[2]For an arbitral tribunal giving weight to this circumstance see: National Grid P.L.C. *v* Argentina (UNCITRAL), Award (3 November 2008) [189].

[3]Cf. Katia Yannaca-Small, 'Fair and Equitable Treatment Standard: Recent Developments' in August Reinisch (ed), *Standards of Investment Protection* (Oxford University Press, New York 2008) 111, 111-3.

[4]For an overview see: Marc Jacob and Stephan Schill, 'Fair and equitable treatment: Content, Practice, Method' in Marc Bungenberg, Jörn Griebel, Stephan Hobe and August Reinisch (eds), International Investment Law (Nomos, Baden-Baden 2015) 700, 700-63; Matthias Herdegen, *Principles of International Economic Law* (Oxford University Press, New York 2016) 455-66; Ronald Kläger, *'Fair and Equitable Treatment' in International Investment Law* (Cambridge University Press, New York 2011) 154 *et seq.*; Rudolf Dolzer and Christoph Schreuer, *Principles of International Investment Law* (Oxford University Press, New York 2012) 145-60.

[5]Alexandra Diehl, *The Core Standard of International Investment Protection: Fair and Equitable Treatment* (Kluwer Law International, Alpen aan den Rijn 2012) 9.

[6]Sections 15.2.1–15.2.3 provide examples of arbitral decisions addressing this question. For academic publications on the subject see: Carsten Kern, *Schiedsgericht und Generalklausel: Zur Konkretisierung des Gebots des fair and equitable treatment in der internationalen Schiedsgerichtsbarkeit* (Mohr Siebeck, Tübingen 2017) 158-62; Christoph Schreuer, 'Fair and

regard.[7] The first approach considers that FPS and FET are not separate obligations, but constitute a single substantive standard (equating approach). A second approach departs from a broad understanding of the FET standard as an all-encompassing obligation, and characterizes FPS as a particular element of such general standard (general-particular approach). For its part, the third approach emphasizes that FPS has its own meaning, which is distinct and autonomous from the FET obligation.

This section provides a critical overview of these approaches. In this vein, it argues that FPS and FET should be viewed as independent, albeit correlated, international obligations. Based on the conclusion reached with regard to the FPS standard's scope and content, this section submits an alternative explanation of the relationship between FPS and FET in international investment law.

15.2.1 The Equating Approach

There has been a tendency to place the FPS and the FET standards on equal footing, as a single substantive obligation. This trend is by no means a recent phenomenon.

Equitable Treatment (FET): Interactions with Other Standards' in Graham Coop and Clarisse Ribeiro (eds), *Investment Protection and the Energy Charter Treaty* (Juris Publishing, Huntington NY 2008) 63, 66-9; Christoph Schreuer, 'Full Protection and Security' (2010) 1(2) J. Int'l Disp. Settlement 353, 365-6; Finnur Magnússon, *Full Protection and Security in International Law* (University of Vienna, Vienna 2012) 203-7; Giuditta Cordero Moss, 'Full Protection and Security' in August Reinisch (ed), *Standards of Investment Protection* (Oxford University Press, New York 2008) 131, 146-9; J. Anthony VanDuzer, 'Full Protection and Security' in Thomas Cottier and Krista Nadakavukaren Schefer (eds), *Elgar Encyclopedia of International Economic Law* (Edward Elgar Publishing, Northampton MA 2018) 212, 214; Katia Yannaca-Small, 'Fair and Equitable Treatment Standard: Recent Developments' in August Reinisch (ed), *Standards of Investment Protection* (Oxford University Press, New York 2008) 111, 118-9; Lucas Bastin, *State Responsibility for Omissions: Establishing a Breach of the Full Protection and Security Obligation by Omissions* (Oxford University, Oxford 2016) [D.Phil. Thesis] 111 *et seq.*; Marc Jacob and Stephan Schill, 'Fair and equitable treatment: Content, Practice, Method' in Marc Bungenberg, Jörn Griebel, Stephan Hobe and August Reinisch (eds), International Investment Law (Nomos, Baden-Baden 2015) 700, 758-60; Nartnirun Junngam, 'The Full Protection and Security Standard in International Investment Law: What and Who is Investment Fully[?] Protected and Secured From?' (2018) 7 (1) AUBLR 1, 75-81 and 96-9; Nicole O'Donnell, 'Reconciling Full Protection and Security Guarantees in Bilateral Investment Treaties with Incidence of Terrorism' (2018) 29(3) ARIA 293, 303-4; Onyema Awa Oyeani, *The Obligation of Host States to Accord the Standard of "Full Protection and Security" to Foreign Investments under International Investment Law* (Brunel University, London 2018) [D.Phil. Thesis] 200 *et seq.*; Ralph Alexander Lorz, 'Protection and Security (Including the NAFTA Approach)' in Marc Bungenberg, Jörn Griebel, Stephan Hobe and August Reinisch (eds), International Investment Law (Nomos, Baden-Baden 2015) 764, 786-8; Ronald Kläger, *'Fair and Equitable Treatment' in International Investment Law* (Cambridge University Press, New York 2011) 291-5.

[7]For a short description of some of these approaches see: Katia Yannaca-Small, 'Fair and Equitable Treatment Standard: Recent Developments' in August Reinisch (ed), *Standards of Investment Protection* (Oxford University Press, New York 2008) 111, 118-9.

As early as 1961, in his *Critical Commentary* to the Abs-Shawcross Convention of 1959, Georg Schwarzenberger explained the content of the protection and security obligation in terms of fair and equitable treatment:

> The emphasis in Article I of the Draft Convention on protection and security of foreign property being "most constant" and being granted "at all times" does not appear to add any undue rigidity to the obligations expected to be undertaken by capital-importing States. *What is promised at all times is merely the grant of equitable treatment.*[8]

The so-called 'equating approach' has found its way into investment arbitral decisions. The award rendered in *Occidental v Ecuador* (2004) provides the perhaps clearest example of this line of argument. In their analysis of the FPS standard, the arbitrators stated:

> The Tribunal [. . .] holds that the Respondent has breached its obligation to accord fair and equitable treatment under Article II(3)(a) of the Treaty. In the context of this finding the question of whether in addition there has been a breach of full protection and security under this Article becomes moot as *treatment that is not fair and equitable automatically entails an absence of full protection and security of the investment.*[9]

In *National Grid v Argentina* (2008) the claimant argued that, as enshrined in the Argentina-UK BIT, 'the general duty to protect investments is linked to fair and equitable treatment'.[10] Based on this contention and noting that the BIT contained a broad definition of investment, which included both tangible and intangible assets, the investor concluded that the FPS clause could not be limited to the guarantee of physical protection.[11]

The tribunal was convinced by the claimant's submissions, and rejected the idea that FPS is limited to physical protection.[12] In this connection, the arbitrators noted that '[t]his conclusion is reinforced by the inclusion of this commitment in the same article of the Treaty as the language on fair and equitable treatment'.[13] The tribunal went on to declare a violation of the FPS standard on grounds that Argentina had modified the investment's regulatory framework, thus causing 'uncertainty'.[14] According to the tribunal, such measures 'are contrary to the protection and constant security which the respondent agreed to provide for investments under the Treaty'.[15] For that very same reason, the arbitrators declared that 'the Respondent breached its

---

[8]Emphasis added. Georg Schwarzenberger, 'The Abs-Shawcross Draft Convention on Investments Abroad: A Critical Commentary' (1961) 14(1) Current Legal Problems 213, 221.

[9]Emphasis added. Occidental Exploration and Production Co. *v* Ecuador, Final Award, LCIA Case No. UN 3467 (1 July 2004) [187].

[10]National Grid P.L.C. *v* Argentina (UNCITRAL), Award (3 November 2008) [181].

[11]National Grid P.L.C. *v* Argentina (UNCITRAL), Award (3 November 2008) [181-2].

[12]National Grid P.L.C. *v* Argentina (UNCITRAL), Award (3 November 2008) [189].

[13]National Grid P.L.C. *v* Argentina (UNCITRAL), Award (3 November 2008) [189].

[14]National Grid P.L.C. *v* Argentina (UNCITRAL), Award (3 November 2008) [189].

[15]National Grid P.L.C. *v* Argentina (UNCITRAL), Award (3 November 2008) [189].

obligation to provide protection and constant security on the same date as it breached its undertaking to treat investments fairly and equitably'.[16]

A few tribunals have followed a more careful approach by observing that an overlap between both standards only occurs when FPS is interpreted broadly, so as to encompass the notion of legal stability. In *Plama v Bulgaria* (2008) the arbitrators noted that, when FPS is said to comprise the guarantee of a stable legal environment, 'the standard becomes closely connected with the notion of fair and equitable treatment'.[17] A similar statement was made in *Achmea v Slovakia* (2010):

> Where, as here, the complaint is essentially that the investment was not protected against government policies, the question whether there has been a breach of the Treaty is inseparable from the question whether the policies in question were fair and equitable.[18]

In *Spyridon v Romania* (2011) the tribunal expressed the view that, where this broad interpretation is adopted, 'the [FPS] standard is also covered by Fair and Equitable Treatment'.[19] Other tribunals, albeit advancing a broad interpretation of the FPS standard, have avoided taking a stance on the equating approach. For instance, in *Siemens v Argentina* (2007) the tribunal stated:

> The Tribunal first notes that, although the parties have argued the application of this standard as a single standard, the Treaty provides for the fair and equitable treatment and full protection and security under two different Articles. The parties do not seem to have found this separation to be significant and the Tribunal will not dwell further on this point.[20]

In other cases, arbitral tribunals, having reached a conclusion regarding the FET standard, found it unnecessary to give further consideration to the FPS standard. These decisions should be read with caution. They do not usually express support for the equating approach as such, but merely apply the principle of procedural economy.

A good example would be *Murphy v Ecuador* (2016/2017). In its Partial Final Award the tribunal considered that a finding of liability under the FET standard turned further consideration of the investor's FPS claim unnecessary.[21] The tribunal's reasoning was heavily based on procedural economy.[22] In a later stage of the proceedings, the claimant requested the arbitrators to 'reconsider' this

---

[16]National Grid P.L.C. *v* Argentina (UNCITRAL), Award (3 November 2008) [190].

[17]Plama Consortium Ltd. *v* Bulgaria, Award, ICSID Case No. ARB/03/24 (27 August 2008) [180].

[18]Achmea B.V. *v* Slovakia (UNCITRAL), Award on Jurisdiction, Arbitrability and Suspension, PCA Case No. 2008-13 (26 October 2010) [284] (further noting that there was 'no need' to address the FPS separately from the FET claim).

[19]Spyridon Roussalis *v* Romania, Award, ICSID Case No. ARB/06/1 (7 December 2011) [321].

[20]Siemens AG *v* Argentina, Award, ICSID Case No. ARB/02/8 (6 February 2007) [302].

[21]Murphy Exploration & Production Co. *v* Ecuador (UNCITRAL), Partial Final Award (6 May 2016) [294].

[22]Murphy Exploration & Production Co. *v* Ecuador (UNCITRAL), Partial Final Award (6 May 2016) [294].

approach.[23] The arbitrators explained that they had already established 'the extent of the Respondent's liability [. . .] under the aegis of the Treaty's FET standard'.[24] In this vein, they emphasized that '[i]t would be an unnecessary and duplicative reexamination of the merits if the Tribunal were to consider anew whether the Respondent breached the Treaty's non-FET provisions'.[25]

Another example is the award issued in *AES v Kazakhstan* (2013).[26] In that case, the arbitrators observed that the claims raised under both standards were identical.[27] Having dismissed the FET claim, the arbitrators stated that '[the tribunal] sees no additional element in or aspect of Respondent's conduct that constitutes a breach of the FPS standard'.[28] To be sure, procedural economy is not a one-way street. Just as finding of responsibility under the FET standard could turn further analysis of the FPS standard irrelevant, substantive analysis of the FET standard could turn out unnecessary as a result of a finding of liability under the FPS standard.[29] In *Anglo American PLC v Venezuela* (2019), the investor claimed that a set of measures was contrary to both the FET and the FPS standards for similar reasons.[30] Since the Tribunal had rejected the investor's argument as regards to the FET standard, it also dismissed the FPS claim.[31]

In sum, besides the *Occidental* and *National Grid* cases, there is scarce authority in support of the equating approach. Investors have usually been unsuccessful in advancing this line of argument. In *Rumeli Telekom v Kazakhstan* (2008) the

---

[23]Murphy Exploration & Production Co. *v* Ecuador (UNCITRAL), Final Award (10 February 2017) [22].

[24]Murphy Exploration & Production Co. *v* Ecuador (UNCITRAL), Final Award (10 February 2017) [32].

[25]Murphy Exploration & Production Co. *v* Ecuador (UNCITRAL), Final Award (10 February 2017) [32].

[26]AES Corporation and Tau Power B.V. *v* Kazakhstan, Award, ICSID Case No. ARB/10/16 (1 November 2013) [337-9].

[27]AES Corporation and Tau Power B.V. *v* Kazakhstan, Award, ICSID Case No. ARB/10/16 (1 November 2013) [339].

[28]AES Corporation and Tau Power B.V. *v* Kazakhstan, Award, ICSID Case No. ARB/10/16 (1 November 2013) [339].

[29]For an indicative example see: Ampal-American Israel Corp., Egi-Fund (08-10) Investors LLC, Egi-Series Investments LLC and BSS-EMG Investors LLC *v* Egypt, Decision on Liability and Heads of Loss, ICSID Case No. ARB/12/11 (21 February 2017) [291] ("[I]n view of the Tribunal's finding of a breach by the Respondent of the full protection and security standard and for the sake of procedural economy, the Tribunal need not analyse whether [. . .] [the events] are in breach of the FET standard or the umbrella clause under the Treaty or whether they constitute an unlawful expropriation of the Claimants' investment under Treaty").

[30]Anglo American PLC *v* Venezuela, Award, ICSID Case No. ARB(AF)/14/1 (18 January 2019) [483].

[31]Anglo American PLC *v* Venezuela, Award, ICSID Case No. ARB(AF)/14/1 (18 January 2019) [484-5].

claimant argued that the breach of the FET standard 'automatically entails' a failure to provide FPS.[32] The respondent state acknowledged that '[FPS] is closely related to the fair and equitable standard'.[33] Still, the respondent insisted that the investor's claims could be more adequately assessed under other standards of investment protection, so that there was no 'proper claim' under the FPS standard.[34] The arbitral tribunal underscored 'the limited scope of application of the full protection and security standard',[35] and linked FPS to the notions of 'physical damage' and 'interference[s] by use of force'.[36] Based on this interpretation, the tribunal found that most of the claims raised under the FPS standard did not actually pertain to the protection obligation.[37]

In *PSEG v Turkey* (2007) the investor invoked the *Occidental* award and advanced the argument that 'the breach of fair and equitable treatment automatically entails the absence of full protection and security'.[38] The arbitrators took a cautious approach in this regard. They began by noting that where the FPS standard is said to grant legal security, 'the connection with fair and equitable treatment becomes a very close one'.[39] At the same time, however, they held that such extension was 'exceptional' and expressed support for a more restrictive understanding of the FPS standard, implying that FPS must be a separate source of responsibility.[40] The tribunal finally dismissed the FPS claim on the following grounds:

> The Tribunal does not find that in the present case there has been any question of physical safety and security, not has any been alleged. Neither does the Tribunal find that there is an exceptional situation that could qualify under this standard as a separate heading of liability. The anomalies that have been found are all included under the standard of fair and equitable treatment [. . .] This heading of liability is accordingly dismissed.[41]

---

[32]Rumeli Telekom A.S. and Telsim Mobil Telekomunikasyon Hizmetleri A.S. *v* Kazakhstan, Award, ICSID Case No. ARB/05/16 (29 July 2008) [658].

[33]Rumeli Telekom A.S. and Telsim Mobil Telekomunikasyon Hizmetleri A.S. *v* Kazakhstan, Award, ICSID Case No. ARB/05/16 (29 July 2008) [663].

[34]Rumeli Telekom A.S. and Telsim Mobil Telekomunikasyon Hizmetleri A.S. *v* Kazakhstan, Award, ICSID Case No. ARB/05/16 (29 July 2008) [666-7].

[35]Rumeli Telekom A.S. and Telsim Mobil Telekomunikasyon Hizmetleri A.S. *v* Kazakhstan, Award, ICSID Case No. ARB/05/16 (29 July 2008) [669].

[36]Rumeli Telekom A.S. and Telsim Mobil Telekomunikasyon Hizmetleri A.S. *v* Kazakhstan, Award, ICSID Case No. ARB/05/16 (29 July 2008) [668].

[37]Rumeli Telekom A.S. and Telsim Mobil Telekomunikasyon Hizmetleri A.S. *v* Kazakhstan, Award, ICSID Case No. ARB/05/16 (29 July 2008) [669].

[38]PSEG Global Inc. and Konya Ilgin Elektrik Üretim ve Ticaret Limited Şirketi *v* Turkey, Award, ICSID Case No. ARB/02/5 (19 January 2007) [257].

[39]PSEG Global Inc. and Konya Ilgin Elektrik Üretim ve Ticaret Limited Şirketi *v* Turkey, Award, ICSID Case No. ARB/02/5 (19 January 2007) [258].

[40]PSEG Global Inc. and Konya Ilgin Elektrik Üretim ve Ticaret Limited Şirketi *v* Turkey, Award, ICSID Case No. ARB/02/5 (19 January 2007) [259].

[41]PSEG Global Inc. and Konya Ilgin Elektrik Üretim ve Ticaret Limited Şirketi *v* Turkey, Award, ICSID Case No. ARB/02/5 (19 January 2007) [259].

The equating approach was the subject of intense debate between the parties in *EDF v Argentina* (2012). The investor underlined that the applicable FPS clause made express reference to the FET standard and concluded that, as enshrined in the BIT, 'the concept of full protection and security is closely linked to that of Fair and Equitable Treatment'.[42] For its part, Argentina argued that 'it is impossible to put the two standards in the same footing in the sense that violation of Fair and Equitable Treatment equals breach of full protection and security'.[43] According to the host state, 'if such were the case, the existence of one of the two standards would become unnecessary'.[44] The arbitral tribunal did not address the FPS standard in detail.[45]

In *Mobil v Argentina* (2013) the investors also relied on the equating approach.[46] According to the claimants' argument, 'measures which violate the fair and equitable treatment standard also violate the state's obligation to provide investors with full protection and security as well'.[47] The tribunal rejected this view and underscored the importance of avoiding a 'confusion' between both standards.[48]

In *Eurogas v Slovakia* (2017) the investor contended that 'acts and omissions identified as being in violation of the fair and equitable treatment standard also constitute a violation of the standard of full protection and security'.[49] The respondent rejected the equalization of the two standards, and argued that FPS solely refers to omissions in the protection of investors against third party violence.[50] The *Eurogas* tribunal declared that it lacked jurisdiction over the dispute and, therefore, did not assess the substance of the FPS claim.[51]

---

[42]EDF International S.A., Saur International S.A. and Leon Participaciones Argentinas S.A. *v* Argentina, Award, ICSID Case No. ARB/03/23 (11 June 2012) [405].

[43]EDF International S.A., Saur International S.A. and Leon Participaciones Argentinas S.A. *v* Argentina, Award, ICSID Case No. ARB/03/23 (11 June 2012) [413].

[44]EDF International S.A., Saur International S.A. and Leon Participaciones Argentinas S.A. *v* Argentina, Award, ICSID Case No. ARB/03/23 (11 June 2012) [413].

[45]EDF International S.A., Saur International S.A. and Leon Participaciones Argentinas S.A. *v* Argentina, Award, ICSID Case No. ARB/03/23 (11 June 2012) [1108-12].

[46]Mobil Exploration and Development Argentina Inc. Suc. Argentina and Mobil Argentina S.A. *v* Argentina, Decision on Jurisdiction and Liability, ICSID Case No. ARB/04/16 (10 April 2013) [988].

[47]Mobil Exploration and Development Argentina Inc. Suc. Argentina and Mobil Argentina S.A. *v* Argentina, Decision on Jurisdiction and Liability, ICSID Case No. ARB/04/16 (10 April 2013) [988].

[48]Mobil Exploration and Development Argentina Inc. Suc. Argentina and Mobil Argentina S.A. *v* Argentina, Decision on Jurisdiction and Liability, ICSID Case No. ARB/04/16 (10 April 2013) [1002].

[49]Eurogas Inc. and Belmont Resources Inc. *v* Slovakia, Award, ICSID Case No. ARB/14/14 (18 August 2017) [364].

[50]Eurogas Inc. and Belmont Resources Inc. *v* Slovakia, Award, ICSID Case No. ARB/14/14 (18 August 2017) [365].

[51]Eurogas Inc. and Belmont Resources Inc. *v* Slovakia, Award, ICSID Case No. ARB/14/14 (18 August 2017) [476].

While it is usually the investor who expresses support for the equating approach, respondent states have also advanced this understanding of the standard in a few cases. For example, in *Sergei Paushok v Mongolia* (2011) the host state contended that FPS 'amounts to a reiteration of fair and equitable treatment'.[52] Thus, according to the state, the FPS claim could be dismissed on the same basis as the FET claim.[53] The arbitral tribunal, while dismissing the FPS claim, was careful not to expressly take a stance on the equating approach.[54] In its analysis of the FPS claim, the tribunal did however take into consideration its finding that Mongolia had not breached the FET standard.[55]

These cases show that arbitral tribunals have been somewhat skeptical with regard to the equating approach. The generally accepted view seems to be that each standard has a different normative content. As expressed by the tribunal in *Liman v Kazakhstan* (2010), an ECT case, '[FPS] must have a meaning beyond, and distinct from, the standard of fair and equitable treatment'.[56] Similarly, in *Vannessa Ventures v Venezuela* (2013) the arbitrators underlined that '[FPS and FET] are two *distinct* standards of protection of an investor's rights'.[57] To the same effect, in *Mamidoil v Albania* (2015) the arbitral tribunal underscored that 'the obligation to provide constant protection and security must not be confounded with the obligation to provide fair and equitable treatment'.[58]

Parties advancing narrow interpretations of the FPS standard in investment arbitral proceedings have highlighted the need to avoid overlaps between the FPS and the FET standards. Just to mention a representative example, in *Saint Gobain v Venezuela* (2016) the respondent state argued that FPS 'relates primarily, and perhaps exclusively, to the physical integrity of the investment'.[59] Venezuela added that 'this limitation is required in order to maintain a meaningful distinction between the FPS standard and other protection standards set out in the treaty [i.e., the

---

[52] Sergei Paushok, CJSC Golden East Co., CJSC Vostoknefte *v* Mongolia (UNCITRAL), Award on Jurisdiction and Liability (28 April 2011) [278].

[53] Sergei Paushok, CJSC Golden East Co., CJSC Vostoknefte *v* Mongolia (UNCITRAL), Award on Jurisdiction and Liability (28 April 2011) [278].

[54] Sergei Paushok, CJSC Golden East Co., CJSC Vostoknefte *v* Mongolia (UNCITRAL), Award on Jurisdiction and Liability (28 April 2011) [322-7].

[55] Sergei Paushok, CJSC Golden East Co., CJSC Vostoknefte *v* Mongolia (UNCITRAL), Award on Jurisdiction and Liability (28 April 2011) [327].

[56] Liman Caspian Oil BV and NCL Dutch Investment BV *v* Kazakhstan, Award, ICSID Case No. ARB/07/14 (22 June 2010) [289].

[57] Emphasis added. Vannessa Ventures Ltd. *v* Venezuela, Award, ICSID Case No. ARB(AF)04/6 (16 January 2013) [216]. It must be noted, however, that the tribunal considered the FET and FPS claims in the same section of the award (at paras 216-32).

[58] Mamidoil Jetoil Greek Petroleum Products Societe S.A. *v* Albania, Award, ICSID Case No. ARB/11/24 (30 March 2015) [819].

[59] Saint-Gobain Performance Plastics Europe *v* Venezuela, Decision on Liability and the Principles of Quantum, ICSID Case No. ARB/12/13 (30 December 2016) [549].

France-Venezuela BIT], in particular the FET standard'.[60] The tribunal dismissed the FPS claim, but avoided making a general statement as to the precise scope of the protection obligation.[61]

Even where an FPS clause is interpreted broadly, so as to encompass the notion of legal stability, the 'equalization' of the FPS and FET standards should be avoided. The reason is that, if FET and FPS were said to convey the same meaning, one of the standards would be deprived from any meaningful content.[62] Hence, the equating approach runs afoul of the *effet utile* principle of interpretation. The award and the annulment decision rendered in the *Azurix v Argentina* case (2006/2009) provide an excellent introduction to the *effet utile* argument. In that case, the arbitral tribunal, giving particular weight to the use of the adjective *full* in the FPS clause of the Argentina-United States BIT, reached the following conclusion:

> The Tribunal is persuaded of the interrelationship of fair and equitable treatment and the obligation to afford the investor full protection and security [. . .] full protection and security was understood [in other cases] to go beyond protection and security ensured by the police. It is not only a matter of physical security; the stability afforded by a secure investment environment is as important from an investor's point of view *[. . .] the Tribunal, having held that the Respondent failed to provide fair and equitable treatment to the investment, finds that the Respondent also breached the standard of full protection and security under the BIT*.[63]

In the annulment proceeding, Argentina argued that '[i]f the standard of full protection and security were the same as the standard of fair and equitable treatment under the Treaty, there would be no *effet utile* for the second standard'.[64] The Annulment Committee considered that the arbitral award did not 'necessarily' imply that both standards are identical, but could also be read as indicating that FPS is a 'sub-category' of FET.[65] As to the *effect utile* argument, the Committee made the following observation:

> Argentina's argument that the Tribunal's findings in this respect leave no *effet utile* for the full protection and security standard might, if accepted, support a conclusion that the Tribunal was wrong in law. However, mere error of law, even if this could be established,

---

[60]Saint-Gobain Performance Plastics Europe *v* Venezuela, Decision on Liability and the Principles of Quantum, ICSID Case No. ARB/12/13 (30 December 2016) [547].

[61]Saint-Gobain Performance Plastics Europe *v* Venezuela, Decision on Liability and the Principles of Quantum, ICSID Case No. ARB/12/13 (30 December 2016) [553].

[62]For an author making a similar observation see: Christoph Schreuer, 'Fair and Equitable Treatment (FET): Interactions with Other Standards' in Graham Coop and Clarisse Ribeiro (eds), *Investment Protection and the Energy Charter Treaty* (Juris Publishing, Huntington NY 2008) 63, 68; Christoph Schreuer, 'Full Protection and Security' (2010) 1(2) J. Int'l Disp. Settlement 353, 365-6.

[63]Emphasis added. Azurix Corp. *v* Argentina, Award, ICSID Case No. ARB/01/12 (14 July 2006) [408]. See also the tribunal's reliance on *Occidental v Ecuador* at paras 406-7.

[64]Azurix Corp. *v* Argentina, Decision on the Application for Annulment of the Argentina Republic, ICSID Case No. ARB/01/12 (1 September 2009) [134 and 182].

[65]Azurix Corp. *v* Argentina, Decision on the Application for Annulment of the Argentina Republic, ICSID Case No. ARB/01/12 (1 September 2009) [183].

is not a ground for annulment. The Committee considers that the Tribunal's reasoning, right or wrong, is quite clear. The Committee therefore considers that there is no basis for annulling this finding under Article 52(1)(e) of the ICSID Convention ['failure to state reasons'].[66]

Arbitral tribunals have often resorted to the *effet utile* argument as the basis for the distinction between the FPS and the FET standards. Thus, in *Electrabel v Hungary* (2012) the arbitrators explained:

In the Tribunal's view, given that there are two distinct standards [FPS and FET] under ECT, they must have, by application of the legal principle of "effet utile", a different scope and role.[67]

Similarly, in *Crystallex v Venezuela* (2016) the tribunal considered that 'full protection and security' does not extend beyond physical security, and observed:

[A] more extensive reading of the "full protection and security" standard would result in an overlap with other treaty standards, notably FET, which in the Tribunal's mind would not comport with the "*effet utile*" principle of interpretation.[68]

Even where the *effet utile* principle is not expressly mentioned, avoiding overlaps between FPS and FET has been a recurrent concern of arbitrators interpreting FPS clauses. Arbitral tribunals have often warned about the risk that extensive interpretations of FPS clauses could lead to a complete overlap between the FPS and FET standards.[69]

15.2.2 The General-Particular Approach

Parties in investment arbitral proceedings might seek to strengthen their case by alleging that the duty to provide protection and security does not constitute a separate head of liability, properly so-called, but a mere element of the obligation to provide fair and equitable treatment.[70] Similarly, some academic studies have addressed the

---

[66]Azurix Corp. *v* Argentina, Decision on the Application for Annulment of the Argentina Republic, ICSID Case No. ARB/01/12 (1 September 2009) [184].

[67]Electrabel S.A. *v* Hungary, Decision on Jurisdiction, Applicable Law and Liability, ICSID Case No. ARB/07/19 (30 November 2012) [7.83].

[68]Crystallex International Corp. *v* Venezuela, Award, ICSID Case No. ARB(AF)/11/2 (4 April 2016) [634]. Cf. also Oxus Gold *v* Uzbekistan (UNCITRAL), Final Award (17 December 2015) [354].

[69]Cf. Enron Corp. and Ponderosa Assets L.P. *v* Argentina, Award, ICSID Case No. ARB/01/3 (22 May 2007) [286]; Sempra Energy International *v* Argentina, Award, ICSID Case No. ARB/02/16 (28 September 2007) [323].

[70]See, for example, the investor's argument in *Urbaser v Argentina* (2016): Urbaser S.A. and Consorcio de Aguas Bilbao Bizkaia, Bilbao Biskaia Ur Partzuergoa *v* Argentina, Award, ICSID Case No. ARB/07/26 (8 December 2016) [560] (invoking '[t]he requirement of protection *as included* in the fair and equitable treatment test' and advancing the proposition that '[t]he fair and

protection obligation as an item of the FET standard.[71] Arbitral decisions provide some authority for this line of argument. In some cases, this interpretation has resulted from the particular wording of the applicable BIT. This has been the case of awards referring to Article 5(1) of the France-Argentina BIT, which reads as follows:

> Les investissements effectués par des investisseurs de l'une ou l'autre des Parties contractantes bénéficient, sur le territoire et dans la zone maritime de l'autre Partie contractante, *d'une protection et d'une sécurité pleines et entières, en application du principe de traitement juste et équitable* mentionné à l'article 3 du présent Accord.[72]

In *Vivendi v Argentina* (2007), the tribunal held that this treaty clause grants protection beyond physical security.[73] In this vein, it drew particular attention to the embedding of the FPS standard within the BIT:

> [T]he scope of the Article 5(1) protection should be interpreted to apply to reach any act or measure which deprives an investor's investment of protection and full security, providing, in accordance with the Treaty's specific wording, the act or measure also constitutes unfair and inequitable treatment. Such actions or measures need not threaten physical possession or the legally protected terms of operation of the investment.[74]

The *Total v Argentina* case (2010) was also concerned with the interpretation of Article 5(1) of the France-Argentina BIT. In their *Decision on Liability*, the arbitrators held that the close connection between the FPS and the FET standards confirmed the interpretation of the FPS clause as encompassing the notion of 'legal security'.[75] The tribunal stated:

> [T]he obligation set forth in Article 5(1) [FPS] forms part of the fair and equitable treatment standard, so that a finding of breach of that obligation would form part of the breach of

---

equitable treatment standard and the right to full protection and certainty must be viewed *as a whole* and cannot be interpreted in isolation' – emphasis added).

[71] Katia Yannaca-Small, 'Fair and Equitable Treatment in International Investment Law' in OECD, *Working Papers on International Investment* (OECD, Paris 2004) 26-8. For a similar view cf. Carsten Kern, *Schiedsgericht und Generalklausel: Zur Konkretisierung des Gebots des fair and equitable treatment in der internationalen Schiedsgerichtsbarkeit* (Mohr Siebeck, Tübingen 2017) 162 (arguing that, while a breach of FPS typically entails a violation of FET, not every breach of the FET standard constitutes a breach of the FPS standard).

[72] Emphasis added. Accord entre le Gouvernement de la République française et le Gouvernement de la République Argentine sur l'encouragement et la protection réciproques des investissements (adopted 3 July 1991, entered into force 3 March 1993) art. 5(1).

[73] Compañía de Aguas del Aconquija S.A. and Vivendi Universal S.A. v Argentina, Award, ICSID Case No. ARB/97/3 (20 August 2007) [7.4.13-7.4.17].

[74] Compañía de Aguas del Aconquija S.A. and Vivendi Universal S.A. v Argentina, Award, ICSID Case No. ARB/97/3 (20 August 2007) [7.4.15]. For another case concerning the interpretation of article 5(1) of the Argentina-France BIT see: EDF International S.A., Saur International S.A. and Leon Participaciones Argentinas S.A. v Argentina, Award, ICSID Case No. ARB/03/23 (11 June 2012) [405, 413 and 1108-12]. Section 15.2.1 considers this aspect of the *EDF* award in more detail, in connection with the 'equating approach'.

[75] Total S.A. v Argentina, Decision on Liability, ICSID Case No. ARB/04/1 (27 December 2010) [343].

Article 3 [FET] rather than be an independent finding of breach. The Tribunal has already found such a breach in respect of the same facts so that no additional finding of breach of Article 5(1) is warranted. Moreover, no further damages would result from following a different approach.[76]

A similar approach was followed in *Suez v Argentina* (2010). Making particular reference to the wording of the France-Argentina BIT, the arbitrators explained:

The present Tribunal [...] takes the view that under Article 3 [FET], quoted above, the concept of full protection and security is included within the concept of fair and equitable treatment, but that the scope of full protection and security is narrower than the fair and equitable treatment. Thus, State action that violates the full protection and security clause would of necessity constitute a violation of fair and equitable treatment under the French BIT. On the other hand, all violations of fair and equitable treatment are not automatically also violations of full protection and security. Under the French BIT, it is possible for Argentina to violate its obligation of fair and equitable treatment toward the Claimants without violating its duty of full protection and security. In short, there are actions that violate fair and equitable treatment that do not violate full protection and security.[77]

Based on this holding, the *Suez* tribunal explained that the notion of 'legal security' could be placed within FET standard, but not within the FPS standard.[78] According to the arbitrators, the security obligation particularly pertains to 'physical' protection, notwithstanding the fact that it also encompasses a duty of redress.[79] In this vein, the tribunal emphasized the need to avoid an entire overlap between the FET and FPS standards:

[T]his Tribunal [...] believes that an overly extensive interpretation of the full protection and security standard may result in an overlap with the other standards of investment protection, which is neither necessary nor desirable.[80]

A few years later, in *SAUR International S.A. v Argentina* (2012), another ICSID tribunal considered, once again, the interpretation of article 5(1) of the France-Argentina BIT.[81] The tribunal characterized FPS as a 'species' within the FET standard, which was consistently described as a 'genus'.[82] The species-genus relationship between these two standards logically implied that the FPS standard must

---

[76]Total S.A. *v* Argentina, Decision on Liability, ICSID Case No. ARB/04/1 (27 December 2010) [343].

[77]Suez Sociedad General de Aguas de Barcelona S.A. and Vivendi Universal S.A. *v* Argentina, Decision on Liability, ICSID Case No. ARB/03/19 (30 July 2010) [171].

[78]Suez Sociedad General de Aguas de Barcelona S.A. and Vivendi Universal S.A. *v* Argentina, Decision on Liability, ICSID Case No. ARB/03/19 (30 July 2010) [173 and 176].

[79]Suez Sociedad General de Aguas de Barcelona S.A. and Vivendi Universal S.A. *v* Argentina, Decision on Liability, ICSID Case No. ARB/03/19 (30 July 2010) [173]. On this aspect of the *Suez* decision see Sect. 10.3.

[80]Suez Sociedad General de Aguas de Barcelona S.A. and Vivendi Universal S.A. *v* Argentina, Decision on Liability, ICSID Case No. ARB/03/19 (30 July 2010) [174].

[81]SAUR International S.A. *v* Argentina, Décision sur la compétence et sur la responsabilité, ICSID Case No. ARB/04/4 (6 June 2012) [499-501 and 508-11].

[82]SAUR International S.A. *v* Argentina, Décision sur la compétence et sur la responsabilité, ICSID Case No. ARB/04/4 (6 June 2012) [500].

have a narrower scope of application than the FET standard.[83] In this line of thought, the *SAUR* tribunal concluded that the FPS standard has primarily and traditionally referred to 'physical violence and civil strife'.[84] In the words of the arbitrators:

> L'art. 5.1 de l'APRI garantit les PSPE [protection et sécurité pleines et entières] « en application du principe de traitement juste et équitable mentionné à l'art. 3 ». Dans son sens ordinaire – premier principe herméneutique de la Convention de Vienne – la PSPE constituent donc une espèce au sein du genre du TJE, qui est applicable si la sécurité de l'investissement est menacée par la violence physique ou des troubles civils.[85]

The *SAUR* tribunal additionally took note of the ongoing discussion on the possible extension of FPS beyond this 'primary scope of application' (*champ de protection primaire*), so as to include the notion of 'legal security' (*sécurité juridique*).[86] Nonetheless, the arbitrators did not find it necessary to dig any deeper into the debate; the claim referred to physical violence and, thus, to the 'most traditional and strict concept of the FPS standard'.[87]

Besides the France-Argentina BIT, many other investment treaties characterize FPS as an element or particular application of the FET standard. This wording is particularly usual in Dutch IIAs. A representative example would be article 3 of the BIT between the Netherlands and the Czech and Slovak Federal Republic (1991):

> Each Contracting Party shall ensure fair and equitable treatment to the investments of investors of the other Contracting Party [. . .] *More particularly*, each Contracting Party shall accord to such investments full security and protection.[88]

In *Jan Oostergetel v Slovakia* (2012), an UNCITRAL arbitral tribunal interpreted this treaty provision. The investor raised 'identical' claims under the FPS and FET standards.[89] The arbitrators concluded that Slovakia's conduct had been consistent

---

[83]SAUR International S.A. *v* Argentina, Décision sur la compétence et sur la responsabilité, ICSID Case No. ARB/04/4 (6 June 2012) [500].

[84]SAUR International S.A. *v* Argentina, Décision sur la compétence et sur la responsabilité, ICSID Case No. ARB/04/4 (6 June 2012) [500-1].

[85]SAUR International S.A. *v* Argentina, Décision sur la compétence et sur la responsabilité, ICSID Case No. ARB/04/4 (6 June 2012) [500].

[86]SAUR International S.A. *v* Argentina, Décision sur la compétence et sur la responsabilité, ICSID Case No. ARB/04/4 (6 June 2012) [501].

[87]Author's translation. The original French text refers to 'le concept plus traditionnel et plus strict du príncipe de PSPE'. SAUR International S.A. *v* Argentina, Décision sur la compétence et sur la responsabilité, ICSID Case No. ARB/04/4 (6 June 2012) [501]. The tribunal additionally noted that the protection of legitimate expectations under the FET and FPS standards is only relevant where the legal conditions that the host state has guaranteed to the investor are 'arbitrarily modified', and considered that the discussion was irrelevant for the resolution of the dispute between the parties (at pp. 495-8).

[88]Emphasis added. Agreement between the Kingdom of the Netherlands and the Czech and Slovak Federal Republic on the Encouragement and Reciprocal Protection of Investments (adopted 24 April 1991, entered into force 1 October 1992) arts. 3(1) and 3(2).

[89]Jan Oostergetel and Theodora Laurentius *v* Slovakia (UNCITRAL), Final Award (23 April 2012) [307].

with the FET standard.[90] This finding, coupled with the wording of the BIT, led the tribunal to dismiss the FPS claim:

[T]he Tribunal found no breach of FET. Given that the facts alleged are the same, *and given that in the BIT full protection and security appears as a specific application of the general FET standard*, the Tribunal considers it unnecessary to analyze these allegations again separately [...] In the context of the present case, if no violation of Article 3.1 of the BIT [FET] was found, there was no violation of Article 3.2 [FPS] either.[91]

Another example would be the award rendered in *OI European Group B.V. v Venezuela* (2015). The case pertained to the interpretation of article 3 of the Netherlands-Venezuela BIT, which used the following wording:

Article 3. 1. Each Contracting Party shall ensure fair and equitable treatment of the investments of nationals of the other Contracting Party [...] 2. *More particularly*, each Contracting Party shall accord to such investments full physical security and protection which in any case shall not be less than that accorded either to investments of its own nationals or to investments of nationals of any third State, whichever is more favourable to the national concerned.[92]

In its analysis of this treaty provision, the arbitral tribunal concluded:

The precept [article 3(1)] is similar to a specific application of the FET standard, given that it is immediately inserted after the FET guarantee (contained in Article 3(1)) and leads with the phrase "more particularly." As such, a literal reading of the BIT indicates that *there is a general classification – FET under Article 3(1) – and a more specific type – FPP under Article 3(2)*. Whereas the general classification covers acts that violate legal certainty, the specific type Centers (sic) on physical security [...] In summary, *Article 3(2) of the BIT [FPS] deals with a specific type within the general classification of FET that applies when the security of an investment is impaired by physical violence or civil strife*.[93]

The general-particular approach has also been adopted in cases filed under treaties that do not expressly envisage a particular connection between the FPS and the FET standards. In *LESI v Algeria* (2008) the investor submitted multiple claims under the FET standard, including a claim pertaining to 'security' (*sécurité*).[94] The tribunal thus considered the possible violation of the FPS standard as an item of the more-

---

[90] Jan Oostergetel and Theodora Laurentius *v* Slovakia (UNCITRAL), Final Award (23 April 2012) [304].

[91] Emphasis added. Jan Oostergetel and Theodora Laurentius *v* Slovakia (UNCITRAL), Final Award (23 April 2012) [308].

[92] Emphasis added. Agreement on Encouragement and Reciprocal Protection of Investments between the Kingdom of the Netherlands and the Republic of Venezuela (adopted 22 October 1991, entered into force 1 November 1993, terminated 1 November 2008) art. 3(2).

[93] Emphasis added. OI European Group B.V. *v* Venezuela, Award, ICSID Case No. ARB/11/25 (10 March 2015) [576-7].

[94] LESI S.p.A. and ASTALDI S.p.A. *v* Algeria, Sentence, ICSID Case No. ARB/05/3 (12 November 2008) [152].

general FET claim.[95] In this context, the arbitrators used the expression 'traitement juste et equitable en matière de sécurité'.[96]

In *OAO Tatneft v Ukraine* (2014) the arbitral tribunal agreed on a broad interpretation of the FPS standard and observed that 'the issue of failure to guarantee the legal protection envisaged might equally bring in a close relationship with fair and equitable treatment'.[97] The arbitrators took cognizance of a 'line of jurisprudence' according to which '[FPS] is subsumed into the concept of fair and equitable treatment'.[98] The tribunal went on to observe that '[relevant] cases do not exclude the possibility that both standards might have a standing of their own while mutually reinforcing each other'.[99] Nonetheless, the arbitrators failed to identify the specific features of each standard. Their argument came close to the equating approach. In particular reference to the redress obligation, the *OAO Tatneft* tribunal observed that '[i]ssues concerning the role of the judiciary are particularly difficult to distinguish as to whether they should be treated under one standard or the other, or both'.[100] The arbitrators further noted that allegations concerning the obligation of redress 'are inseparable from the context of fair and equitable treatment [...] as they are intertwined with the contents of this other standard'.[101]

The general-particular approach also found expression, at least implicitly, in *Rusoro Mining v Venezuela* (2016). In that case, the investor alleged that regulatory measures adopted by Venezuela constituted a breach of both the FET and the FPS clauses of the Canada-Venezuela BIT.[102] In their assessment of one of the FPS claims, the arbitrators stated:

> [T]he Tribunal has already concluded that [...] [the measures] did not amount to a breach of the FET standard; *consequently, such measures can never imply a breach of the FPS standard, however widely interpreted.*[103]

In *Teinver v Argentina* (2017) the investor underscored the 'close relationship between the full protection and security standard and the fair and equitable treatment standard'.[104] For its part, the respondent emphasized that the FET and FPS standards

---

[95]LESI S.p.A. and ASTALDI S.p.A. *v* Algeria, Sentence, ICSID Case No. ARB/05/3 (12 November 2008) [154].

[96]LESI S.p.A. and ASTALDI S.p.A. *v* Algeria, Sentence, ICSID Case No. ARB/05/3 (12 November 2008) [154].

[97]OAO Tatneft *v* Ukraine (UNCITRAL), Award (29 July 2014) [426].

[98]OAO Tatneft *v* Ukraine (UNCITRAL), Award (29 July 2014) [427].

[99]OAO Tatneft *v* Ukraine (UNCITRAL), Award (29 July 2014) [427].

[100]OAO Tatneft *v* Ukraine (UNCITRAL), Award (29 July 2014) [427].

[101]OAO Tatneft *v* Ukraine (UNCITRAL), Award (29 July 2014) [429].

[102]Rusoro Mining Ltd. *v* Venezuela, Award, ICSID Case No. ARB(AF)/12/5 (22 August 2016) [527 *et seq.* and 546].

[103]Emphasis added. Rusoro Mining Ltd. *v* Venezuela, Award, ICSID Case No. ARB(AF)/12/5 (22 August 2016) [548].

[104]Teinver S.A., Transportes de Cercanías S.A. and Autobuses Urbanos del Sur S.A. *v* Argentina, Award, ICSID Case No. ARB/09/1 (21 July 2017) [900].

appeared in different clauses of the applicable treaty, so that 'the Parties must have intended them to mean two different things'.[105] The arbitral tribunal addressed the question shortly:

> In the Treaty, the provisions regarding protection of investments and fair and equitable treatment are contained in two different articles, which leads to the conclusion that the Parties must have intended them to address different things. As a result, the Tribunal believes that these two standards should be given distinct meanings and fields of application. Nevertheless, the Tribunal accepts there is considerable overlap between the concepts of fair and equitable treatment and full protection and security, as submitted by Claimants. *In the Tribunal's view, the fair and equitable standard is broader than that of full protection and security. As a result, while a breach of the full protection and security clause would likely constitute a violation of fair and equitable treatment, the converse is not necessarily the case. Not all violations of the fair and equitable treatment standard automatically constitute violations of the full protection and security standard.*[106]

Based on this reasoning, the tribunal gave considerable weight to its previous findings on the FET claims, which had been successful in part only; the FPS claims were dismissed in their entirety.[107]

In other cases, arbitral tribunals have underscored that the FPS standard does not provide protection beyond the FET standard, without making any statement as to whether the standards stand in a particular-to-general relationship. An example would be the award rendered in *Isolux v Spain* (2016), where the arbitral tribunal rejected the investor's argument on legal security on the following grounds:

> [T]he Claimant presents the [FPS] standard in a manner that overlaps with [the] FET [standard] and the issue of foreseeability of [regulatory] measures, despite the fact that the main purpose of the [FPS] standard is to protect the investor against harmful acts from third parties and state agents. The Claimant has not alleged that it has been the victim of such acts. *The standard of protection and security cannot intervene to protect the investor against changes in the legal framework in cases where protection under the obligation to ensure FET is not justified.*[108]

Compared to the equating approach, the general-particular approach has the obvious advantage of giving the FPS standard a meaningful content in respect of the FET standard. This approach should be considered with caution, though. This

---

[105]Teinver S.A., Transportes de Cercanías S.A. and Autobuses Urbanos del Sur S.A. *v* Argentina, Award, ICSID Case No. ARB/09/1 (21 July 2017) [901].

[106]Emphasis added. Teinver S.A., Transportes de Cercanías S.A. and Autobuses Urbanos del Sur S.A. *v* Argentina, Award, ICSID Case No. ARB/09/1 (21 July 2017) [904-5].

[107]Teinver S.A., Transportes de Cercanías S.A. and Autobuses Urbanos del Sur S.A. *v* Argentina, Award, ICSID Case No. ARB/09/1 (21 July 2017) [906-10].

[108]Emphasis added. Author's translation. The original Spanish text reads: "la demandante hace del estándar [de protección y seguridad] una presentación que se confunde con el TJE [trato justo y equitativo] y el tema de la previsibilidad de las medidas, cuando la principal finalidad del estándar es garantizar al inversor contra actos dañinos de terceros y de agentes del Estado. La Demandante no ha sostenido que fue víctima de tales actos. El estándar de protección y seguridad no puede intervenir para proteger al inversor contra modificaciones del marco jurídico en casos que no justifican su protección por la obligación de asegurar el TJE." Isolux Netherlands B.V. *v* Spain, Laudo, SCC Case No. V 2013/153 (17 July 2016) [817].

view is reminiscent of older theories, which sought to elevate specific legal institutions of the law of aliens into all-encompassing obligations that could virtually cover the whole body of this area of international law. The pattern has repeated itself, over and over again, throughout history. In the first decades of the twentieth century, this tendency crystalized in all-embracing definitions of denial of justice.[109] Later on, the umbrella function was ascribed to the minimum standard of treatment.[110] And, finally, in the past few decades, enthusiastic scholars and a few arbitral tribunals are striving to transform fair and equitable treatment into a new umbrella concept.[111]

As regards to the relationship between FPS and FET, this approach comes across the fact that the two standards do not share a common origin and, moreover, have followed different lines of development. The conditions upon which a breach of FET can be established do not coincide with those applicable to the FPS standard. Particularly, while the notion of due diligence dominates the assessment of FPS claims, it plays no significant role in the analysis of FET claims.

The general-particular approach is dangerous because it typically leads to the dismissal of FPS claims on the sole ground that there was no breach of the FET standard. It seems to be a matter of sheer logic that, if there was no violation of the general obligation (FET), there can be no breach of one of its constituent elements (FPS). The argument is however misleading. The reality that hides behind this veil of apparent logic is that adjudicators dismiss FPS claims without losing a single word about the substance of the FPS standard, including the notion of due diligence.

It could be argued that, in order to avoid this undesirable effect, tribunals following the general-particular approach should begin their analysis with FPS. An assessment of other elements of the FET standard (genus) will only be needed where no breach of FPS (species) could be established. This chain of argument is certainly better as a matter of substance. However, if this approach is followed, the characterization of FPS as an element of FET will generally be of minor practical significance. Two scenarios must be distinguished in this regard.

First, if it is concluded that no violation of the FPS standard has occurred, the tribunal will need to assess the FET standard on an independent basis. Thus, regardless of whether FPS is said to be an element of the FET standard, the two standards will be analyzed in a separate manner.

The second possible scenario is that the tribunal declares a breach of FPS. In such case, if it is assumed that FPS is an element of FET, it will certainly be unnecessary to give further consideration to other elements of the FET standard. However, the efficiency achieved through this interpretation could also be reached without classifying FPS under the FET standard. In the end, the issue is one of procedural

---

[109]See Sect. 2.2.3.

[110]The FPS standard is generally considered as a part of the minimum standard of treatment. See Chap. 5.

[111]It has been argued, for example, that the FET standard coincides with the international minimum standard of treatment; for an account and critical assessment of this approach see: Ronald Kläger, 'Fair and Equitable Treatment' in International Investment Law (Cambridge University Press, New York 2011) 55 et seq.

economy: a finding of responsibility under an international obligation turns it pointless to consider further heads of liability in respect of the same set of facts.

15.2.3 'Full Protection and Security' and 'Fair and Equitable Treatment' as Independent Standards

While the equating approach and the general-particular approach have enjoyed some support in the past, the most widely accepted view is that the FPS standard is different and independent from the FET standard. This conclusion seems convincing as a matter of principle.[112] The real issue, however, lies in the determination of the precise difference between the two obligations. Some arbitral tribunals have rightly observed that, while the FET standard is not attached to any particular standard of liability, there is widespread agreement that a breach of FPS requires a failure to exercise due diligence.[113] As explained by the arbitrators in *Jan de Nul v Egypt* (2008):

> The notion of continuous protection and security is to be distinguished here from the fair and equitable standard since they are placed in two different provisions of the BIT, even if the two guarantees can overlap. As put forward by the Claimants, this concept relates to the exercise of due diligence by the State.[114]

In *Gemplus v Mexico* (2010) the arbitral tribunal also drew a careful distinction between the FPS and the FET standards. The arbitrators considered that the difference between them is twofold. In the first place, FPS '[does] not generally impose strict liability on a host state under international law'.[115] Secondly, in its core, each standard refers to a different source of risk:

> [T]hese BIT provisions [FPS] are directed at different kinds of unlawful treatment from that proscribed by other provisions of the two BITs [i.e. the Argentina-Mexico BIT and the France-Mexico BIT], particularly those regarding FET and Expropriation. *The latter involve the investor and the host state, whereas the 'protection' provisions also involve the host state protecting the investment from a third party.*[116]

Other arbitral decisions have followed a similar line of argument. In *El Paso v Argentina* (2011) the arbitrators noted that, where the acts the investor complains

---

[112]For a similar observation see: Christoph Schreuer, 'Full Protection and Security' (2010) 1 (2) J. Int'l Disp. Settlement 353, 366; Finnur Magnússon, *Full Protection and Security in International Law* (University of Vienna, Vienna 2012) 207.

[113]Chapter 11 considers this element of the protection obligation in more detail.

[114]Jan de Nul N.V. and Dredging International N.V. v Egypt, Award, ICSID Case No. ARB/04/13 (6 November 2008) [269].

[115]Gemplus S.A., SLP S.A. and Gemplus Industrial S.A. de C.V. v Mexico, Award, ICSID Cases No. ARB(AF)/04/3 & ARB(AF)/04/4 (16 June 2010) [9.10].

[116]Emphasis added. Gemplus S.A., SLP S.A. and Gemplus Industrial S.A. de C.V. v Mexico, Award, ICSID Cases No. ARB(AF)/04/3 & ARB(AF)/04/4 (16 June 2010) [9.11].

about 'emanated from the state itself', international responsibility must be determined under standards other than FPS.[117] While the tribunal did not mention any other standard in particular, it is conspicuous that its conclusion is especially relevant for the assessment of the relationship between the FPS standard and the FET standard.

In *Electrabel v Hungary* (2012) the arbitral tribunal held that the FPS standard is not the same as the FET standard.[118] In this vein, it concurred with the *El Paso* tribunal's finding that FPS protects investments against acts of third parties.[119] The implication is that, while the FET standard refers to direct injuries committed by state organs, the FPS standard imposes a positive obligation to protect foreign investors from harmful events that do not originate in the host state's conduct.

In *Ulysseas v Ecuador* (2012) the investor argued that the FPS and the FET standards should be assessed jointly because 'both treatments require the State to provide stability and predictability'.[120] The arbitrators were not convinced by the investor's approach:

> The Tribunal does not share this view. Full protection and security is a standard of treatment other than fair and equitable treatment, as made manifest by the separate reference made to the two standards by Article II(3)(a) of the BIT.[121]

The *Ulysseas* tribunal observed that, as opposed to the FET standard, FPS establishes a 'due diligence' obligation, which comprises the prevention and redress of injuries originating in the conduct of entities other than the host state.[122]

In *Mobil v Argentina* (2013) the arbitrators limited the scope of the FPS standard to protection against acts which stem from third parties rather than state agents,[123] also acknowledging the standard's preventive and repressive functions.[124] The tribunal considered this approach justified 'for the FPS standard to keep its own

---

[117]El Paso Energy International Co. *v* Argentina, Award, ICSID Case No. ARB/03/15 (31 October 2011) [524].

[118]Electrabel S.A. *v* Hungary, Decision on Jurisdiction, Applicable Law and Liability, ICSID Case No. ARB/07/19 (30 November 2012) [7.83].

[119]Electrabel S.A. *v* Hungary, Decision on Jurisdiction, Applicable Law and Liability, ICSID Case No. ARB/07/19 (30 November 2012) [7.83].

[120]Ulysseas Inc. *v* Ecuador (UNCITRAL), Final Award (12 June 2012) [271]. See also para 260.

[121]Ulysseas Inc. *v* Ecuador (UNCITRAL), Final Award (12 June 2012) [272].

[122]Ulysseas Inc. *v* Ecuador (UNCITRAL), Final Award (12 June 2012) [272].

[123]Mobil Exploration and Development Argentina Inc. Suc. Argentina and Mobil Argentina S.A. *v* Argentina, Decision on Jurisdiction and Liability, ICSID Case No. ARB/04/16 (10 April 2013) [999].

[124]Mobil Exploration and Development Argentina Inc. Suc. Argentina and Mobil Argentina S.A. *v* Argentina, Decision on Jurisdiction and Liability, ICSID Case No. ARB/04/16 (10 April 2013) [1002].

identity' and explained that '[g]oing beyond this would lead to the confusion of this standard with other standards, particularly with the FET standard'.[125]

In *Oxus Gold v Uzbekistan* (2015) the arbitral tribunal found that, as a rule, FPS serves the function of providing protection against third party conduct.[126] As regards the relationship between FPS and FET, the arbitrators explained:

> [U]nless otherwise expressly defined in a specific BIT, the general FPS standard complements the FET standard by providing protection towards acts of third parties, i.e. non-state parties, which are not covered by the FET standard. Thus, where an incriminated act is done by a State-organ, the applicable standard is the FET standard, whereas where such act is done by a non-state entity, the applicable standard becomes the FPS standard.[127]

The *Oxus Gold* tribunal consistently held that the 'nature and scope' of the FPS standard do not coincide with those of the FET standard.[128] The arbitrators observed that 'a State is not in a position to ensure the level of commitment with regard to the conduct of non-state parties [. . .] compared with the conduct of its own organs'.[129] Accordingly, they said, the FPS standard does not guarantee a 'fair and equitable treatment by non-state entities'.[130] Rather, it prescribes duties of prevention and redress with regard to third party conduct.[131]

In *CC/Devas v India* (2016) the arbitral tribunal held that FPS is applicable only in respect of acts of third parties.[132] The arbitrators added that '[i]f, on the other hand, the acts can be attributed to the Government, then the FET standard would apply'.[133] The award rendered in *Koch v Venezuela* (2017) follows a similar approach, as it links the FET standard to good faith and the absence of arbitrariness,[134] and FPS to protection against physical violence by third parties.[135]

---

[125]Mobil Exploration and Development Argentina Inc. Suc. Argentina and Mobil Argentina S.A. *v* Argentina, Decision on Jurisdiction and Liability, ICSID Case No. ARB/04/16 (10 April 2013) [1002].

[126]Oxus Gold *v* Uzbekistan (UNCITRAL), Final Award (17 December 2015) [353].

[127]Oxus Gold *v* Uzbekistan (UNCITRAL), Final Award (17 December 2015) [353].

[128]Oxus Gold *v* Uzbekistan (UNCITRAL), Final Award (17 December 2015) [353 and 834].

[129]Oxus Gold *v* Uzbekistan (UNCITRAL), Final Award (17 December 2015) [353]. Cf. also para 834.

[130]Oxus Gold *v* Uzbekistan (UNCITRAL), Final Award (17 December 2015) [353]. Cf. also para 834.

[131]Oxus Gold *v* Uzbekistan (UNCITRAL), Final Award (17 December 2015) [353]. Cf. also para 834.

[132]CC/Devas (Mauritius) Ltd., Devas Employees Mauritius Private Ltd. and Telcom Devas Mauritius Ltd. *v* India (UNCITRAL), Award on Jurisdiction and Merits, PCA Case No. 2013-09 (25 July 2016) [499].

[133]CC/Devas (Mauritius) Ltd., Devas Employees Mauritius Private Ltd. and Telcom Devas Mauritius Ltd. *v* India (UNCITRAL), Award on Jurisdiction and Merits, PCA Case No. 2013-09 (25 July 2016) [499].

[134]Koch Minerals SÁRL and Koch Nitrogen International SÁRL *v* Venezuela, Award, ICSID Case No. ARB/11/19 (30 October 2017) [8.43].

[135]Koch Minerals SÁRL and Koch Nitrogen International SÁRL *v* Venezuela, Award, ICSID Case No. ARB/11/19 (30 October 2017) [8.46].

In sum, two features define the line between FPS and FET: the applicable standard of liability and the source of risk. Bearing the foregoing in mind and taking inspiration from the awards cited above, this section argues that, in the final analysis, each standard refers to a different function of the state.

In his seminal work *Das Grundrecht auf Sicherheit* (*The Fundamental Right to Security*), the German public law scholar Josef Isensee stressed that, in western legal and political thought, arguments about the legitimacy of public power evolved through three stages.[136] The first stage corresponds to the Hobbesian legitimation argument and coincides with the idea of a security state, which serves the function Thomas Hobbes envisaged for seventeenth century absolute monarchies.[137] In words of Isensee:

> Fear from reciprocal violence and civil war reigns at the first stage, the Hobbesian stage. This fear is averted by the unity of power and peace, [which is embodied] in the modern state and its monopoly of force.[138]

The Hobbesian state is all about security, and the security it provides comes often at the price of liberty. According to Isensee, once the security state has consolidated its authority, the individual's fear from her fellow citizens twists into fear from the almighty state.[139] The state, created as a protective power (*Schutzmacht*), risks turning into an oppressive power (*Unterdrückungsmacht*).[140] It is precisely for this reason that the second stage corresponds to the constitutional state (*Rechtsstaat*).[141] The constitutional state is concerned with the protection of individuals from public power, and accordingly seeks the subjection of the sovereign to the rule of law.[142] The *Rechtsstaat* did not however provide a clear response to the threat of economic want.[143] Fear from economic risks originates Isensee's third legitimation stage: the

---

[136]Josef Isensee, *Das Grundrecht auf Sicherheit. Zu den Schutzpflichten des freiheitlichen Verfassungsstaates* (Walter de Gruyter, Berlin 1983) 17.

[137]Josef Isensee, *Das Grundrecht auf Sicherheit. Zu den Schutzpflichten des freiheitlichen Verfassungsstaates* (Walter de Gruyter, Berlin 1983) 17.

[138]Author's translation. The original German text reads: "Auf der ersten, der hobbesianischen Stufe, herrscht die Furcht vor wechselseitiger Gewalttätigkeit, die Bürgerkriegsfurcht. Sie wird gebannt in der Macht- und Friedenseinheit des gewaltmonopolistischen, modernen Staates."Josef Isensee, *Das Grundrecht auf Sicherheit. Zu den Schutzpflichten des freiheitlichen Verfassungsstaates* (Walter de Gruyter, Berlin 1983) 17.

[139]Josef Isensee, *Das Grundrecht auf Sicherheit. Zu den Schutzpflichten des freiheitlichen Verfassungsstaates* (Walter de Gruyter, Berlin 1983) 17.

[140]Josef Isensee, *Das Grundrecht auf Sicherheit. Zu den Schutzpflichten des freiheitlichen Verfassungsstaates* (Walter de Gruyter, Berlin 1983) 17.

[141]Josef Isensee, *Das Grundrecht auf Sicherheit. Zu den Schutzpflichten des freiheitlichen Verfassungsstaates* (Walter de Gruyter, Berlin 1983) 17.

[142]Josef Isensee, *Das Grundrecht auf Sicherheit. Zu den Schutzpflichten des freiheitlichen Verfassungsstaates* (Walter de Gruyter, Berlin 1983) 17.

[143]Josef Isensee, *Das Grundrecht auf Sicherheit. Zu den Schutzpflichten des freiheitlichen Verfassungsstaates* (Walter de Gruyter, Berlin 1983) 17.

social state (*Sozialstaat*).[144] These three stages are not incompatible with one another; on the contrary, each one of them builds up on the preceding stages.[145]

For present purposes, attention can be focused on the first two stages. The relationship between the FPS standard and the FET standard, as they have evolved in international investment law, bears striking resemblance to the relationship between the Hobbesian security state (*Sicherheitsstaat*) and the constitutional state (*Rechtsstaat*).

If the proposition advanced in Chap. 8 above is correct, the customary FPS standard specifically pertains to security from third parties and natural phenomena.[146] Protection from state action is only covered by the FPS standard when the host state takes action against external sources of risk (typically private acts of violence), but fails to mitigate collateral damage.[147] The FPS standard could hence be said to ensure that aliens enjoy the basic guarantee of security embodied in the Leviathan. This seems further consistent with early eighteenth-century theories explaining the host state's duty to protect foreign subjects through the notion of a tacit agreement, by means of which the foreigner obtained the benefits of the social contract in exchange for a pledge of obedience to the local sovereign.[148]

For its part, the FET standard is usually invoked and applied in respect of abuses of public power.[149] There is a strong link between the FET standard and the rule of law.[150] Based on a detailed analysis of arbitral case law on the FET standard, Stephan Schill observes:

> [I]nvestment tribunals have interpreted fair and equitable treatment as encompassing sub-elements the rule of law is associated with in various domestic legal systems, including stability and predictability of the legal framework, consistency in decision-making, the principle of legality, the protection of confidence, due process, the prohibition of denial of justice, transparency and proportionality.[151]

---

[144]Josef Isensee, *Das Grundrecht auf Sicherheit. Zu den Schutzpflichten des freiheitlichen Verfassungsstaates* (Walter de Gruyter, Berlin 1983) 17.

[145]Josef Isensee, *Das Grundrecht auf Sicherheit. Zu den Schutzpflichten des freiheitlichen Verfassungsstaates* (Walter de Gruyter, Berlin 1983) 18.

[146]See Sect. 8.3.

[147]See Sect. 8.3.3.1.

[148]See Sects. 3.3 and 3.4.

[149]Cf. Stephan Schill, *The Multilaterization of International Investment Law* (Cambridge University Press, Cambridge 2009) 80-1.

[150]See generally: Stephan Schill, 'Fair and Equitable Treatment, the Rule of Law and Comparative Public Law' in Stephan Schill (ed), *International Investment Law and Comparative Public Law* (Oxford University Press, New York 2010) 151, 151-82; Marc Jacob and Stephan Schill, 'Fair and equitable treatment: Content, Practice, Method' in Marc Bungenberg, Jörn Griebel, Stephan Hobe and August Reinisch (eds), International Investment Law (Nomos, Baden-Baden 2015) 700, 700-63.

[151]See generally: Stephan Schill, 'Fair and Equitable Treatment, the Rule of Law and Comparative Public Law' in Stephan Schill (ed), *International Investment Law and Comparative Public Law* (Oxford University Press, New York 2010) 151, 182.

Schill argues that these 'sub-elements' 'can be understood as and united under the concept of the rule of law (*Rechtsstaat, état de droit*)'.[152] Thus, according to him, the FET standard could be regarded as 'an embodiment of the rule of law'.[153]

The relationship between the FPS and the FET standards can thus be described by analogy to the relationship between the Hobbesian security state and the constitutional state. This explanatory model shows that each standard has its own meaning, addresses different risks and represents a distinguishable state function. FPS refers to the consolidation and diligent exercise of the monopoly of force. By contrast, FET pertains to the limitation and constrain of public power. The two standards, albeit interrelated, serve different purposes.

15.3 'Full Protection and Security' and Expropriation

The protection of foreign property is the quintessence of international investment law. Investment claims are often about expropriation. It has been rightly observed that '[e]xpropriation is the most severe form of interference with property'.[154] In the end, '[a]ll expectations of the investor are destroyed if the investment is taken without adequate compensation'.[155] While international law does not prohibit expropriatory measures as such, it sets out the conditions upon which an expropriation may be undertaken.[156] The contemporary notion of expropriation is broad in scope. It does not only refer to direct expropriations, in which the investor's property is forcefully taken and formally transferred to the host state, but also to measures that have an effect equivalent to formal takings of property.[157]

---

[152]See generally: Stephan Schill, 'Fair and Equitable Treatment, the Rule of Law and Comparative Public Law' in Stephan Schill (ed), *International Investment Law and Comparative Public Law* (Oxford University Press, New York 2010) 151, 154.

[153]See generally: Stephan Schill, 'Fair and Equitable Treatment, the Rule of Law and Comparative Public Law' in Stephan Schill (ed), *International Investment Law and Comparative Public Law* (Oxford University Press, New York 2010) 151, 155. See also: Marc Jacob and Stephan Schill, 'Fair and equitable treatment: Content, Practice, Method' in Marc Bungenberg, Jörn Griebel, Stephan Hobe and August Reinisch (eds), International Investment Law (Nomos, Baden-Baden 2015) 700, 760-3.

[154]Rudolf Dolzer and Christoph Schreuer, *Principles of International Investment Law* (Oxford University Press, New York 2012) 98.

[155]Rudolf Dolzer and Christoph Schreuer, *Principles of International Investment Law* (Oxford University Press, New York 2012) 98.

[156]See generally: August Reinisch, 'Legality of Expropriations' in August Reinisch (ed), *Standards of Investment Protection* (Oxford University Press, New York 2008) 171, 171-204; Rudolf Dolzer and Christoph Schreuer, *Principles of International Investment Law* (Oxford University Press, New York 2012) 98.

[157]See generally: Anne Hoffmann, 'Indirect Expropriation' in August Reinisch (ed), *Standards of Investment Protection* (Oxford University Press, New York 2008) 151, 151-70; Rudolf Dolzer and Christoph Schreuer, *Principles of International Investment Law* (Oxford University Press,

This section analyzes the relationship between expropriation clauses and full protection and security clauses.[158] A first part of the argument considers possible overlaps between the two notions, and seeks to identify plausible differentiation criteria. The second part of the argument provides a critical analysis of arbitral decisions concerning the interplay between the two standards.

15.3.1 The Substantive Difference Between Protection and Security Clauses and Expropriation Clauses

Expropriation provisions are related to protection and security clauses. A broad interpretation of an FPS clause as a guarantee of legal stability could certainly lead to a partial overlap between the FPS standard and the notion of indirect expropriation. Thus, in *Enron v Argentina* (2007) the arbitral tribunal observed that the interpretation of the FPS clause of the Argentina-US BIT as extending beyond physical protection could turn it 'difficult' to draw a distinction between FPS and 'some form of expropriation'.[159]

Moreover, both expropriation and FPS clauses serve the purpose of protecting foreign property.[160] Some treaties go as far as to place the FPS standard under the headline 'expropriation'. An example would be article 4(1) of the Albania-Greece BIT,[161] which was the basis of the FPS claim in the *Pantechniki v Albania* case

---

New York 2012) 101-26; UNCTAD, *Expropriation: A Sequel* (United Nations, New York/Geneva 2012) 6 *et seq.*; Ursula Kriebaum, *Eigentumsschutz im Völkerrecht* (Duncker & Humblot, Berlin 2008) 272 *et seq.*; Ursula Kriebaum, 'Expropriation' in Marc Bungenberg, Jörn Griebel, Stephan Hobe and August Reinisch (eds), *International Investment Law* (Nomos, Baden-Baden 2015) 959, 970 *et seq.* A few treaties contain an express provision excluding indirect expropriation from their scope of application. For a representative example see: Protocolo de Buenos Aires de Cooperación y Facilitación de Inversiones Intra-Mercosur (adopted 7 April 2017) [online] http://apc.mef.gub.uy/innovaportal/file/21186/2/protocolo-de-cooperacion-y-facilitacion-de-inversiones.pdf, art. 6(6).

[158]For another author analyzing the relationship between expropriation clauses and FPS see: Finnur Magnússon, *Full Protection and Security in International Law* (University of Vienna, Vienna 2012) 207-13. Cf. also Nartnirun Junngam, 'The Full Protection and Security Standard in International Investment Law: What and Who is Investment Fully[?] Protected and Secured From?' (2018) 7 (1) AUBLR 1, 83-4.

[159]Enron Corp. and Ponderosa Assets L.P. *v* Argentina, Award, ICSID Case No. ARB/01/3 (22 May 2007) [286]. See also: Suez Sociedad General de Aguas de Barcelona S.A. and Vivendi Universal S.A. *v* Argentina, Decision on Liability, ICSID Case No. ARB/03/19 (30 July 2010) [174] (quoting the *Enron* award in this connection).

[160]For an academic publication recognizing this shared purpose see: Herman Walker, 'The Post-War Commercial Treaty Program of the United States' (1958) 73(1) Pol. Sci. Q. 57, 69.

[161]Agreement between the Hellenic Republic and the Government of the Republic of Albania for the Encouragement and Reciprocal Protection of Investments (adopted 1 August 1991, entered into force 4 January 1995) art. 4(1).

(2009).[162] In other treaties, the FPS standard and the expropriation clause appear in separate paragraphs of the same treaty provision. This is the case of numerous German BITs.[163] Scholars commenting on these treaties have argued that FPS constitutes a 'general clause' within the expropriation article, which protects investors against a broad category of risks, including private violence. Credit for this interpretation must go to Justus Alenfend, who advanced it as early as 1971.[164] Over a decade later, in a monograph published in 1988, Michael Banz delivered a more detailed presentation of the argument:

> As a rule, injuries to investments committed by private individuals do not fall within the property protection provisions [i.e. expropriation clauses] of investment treaties. They can, however, be relevant in the context of the treaty, if the host state made possible the injury through a faulty violation of the general clause of the expropriation article, according to which the foreign investment enjoys full protection and security.[165]

---

[162]Pantechniki S.A. Contractors & Engineers *v* Albania, Award, ICSID Case No. ARB/07/21 (30 July 2009) [71-84]. It must be noted that, while the Sole Arbitrator assessed the FPS claim in detail, the headline of article 4 did not play any role in the decision.

[163]This wording has been usual in German treaties, from the late 1950s up to the present day. For some indicative examples see: Treaty for the Promotion and Protection of Investments between Pakistan and the Federal Republic of Germany (adopted 25 November 1959, entered into force 28 April 1962) art. 3(1) (FPS) and (2) (expropriation); Vertrag zwischen der Bundesrepublik Deutschland und dem Königreich Griechenland über die Förderung und den gegenseitigen Schutz von Kapitalanlagen (adopted 27 March 1961, entered into force 15 July 1963) art. 3(1) (FPS) and (2) (expropriation); Treaty between the Federal Republic of Germany and the Republic of Haiti concerning the Promotion and Reciprocal Protection of Capital Investment (adopted 14 August 1973, entered into force 1 December 1975) art. 3(1) (FPS) and (2) (expropriation); Agreement between the Federal Republic of Germany and the People's Republic of Bangladesh concerning the Promotion and Reciprocal Protection of Investments (adopted 6 May 1981, entered into force 14 September 1986) art. 3(1) (FPS) and (2) (expropriation); Tratado entre la República Federal de Alemania y la República de Chile sobre fomento y recíproca protección de inversiones (adopted 21 October 1991, entered into force 8 May 1999) art. 4(1) (FPS) and (2) (expropriation); Agreement between the Federal Republic of Germany and the Palestine Liberation Organization for the benefit of the Palestinian Authority concerning the Encouragement and Reciprocal Protection of Investments (adopted 10 July 2000, entered into force 19 September 2008) art. 4(1) (FPS) and (2) (expropriation); Agreement between the Federal Republic of Germany and the Hashemite Kingdom of Jordan concerning the Encouragement and Reciprocal Protection of Investments (adopted 13 November 2007, entered into force 28 August 2010) art. 4(1) (FPS) and (2) (expropriation). See also: German Model BIT (2008) art. 4(1) (FPS) and (2) (expropriation).

[164]Justus Alenfeld, *Die Investitionsförderungsverträge der Bundesrepublik Deutschland* (Athenäum Verlag, Frankfurt am Main 1971) 112. See also: Rudolf Dolzer and Yun-i Kim, 'Germany' in Chester Brown (ed), *Commentaries on Selected Model Investment Treaties* (Oxford University Press, Oxford 2013) 289, 310 (commenting on Alenfend's interpretation and noting that '[s]o far, the issue does not seem to have attracted attention').

[165]Author's translation. The original German text reads: "Grundsätzlich fallen Eingriffe in ausländische Kapitalanlagen, die von Privatleuten begangen werden, nicht unter die Eigentumsschutzregelung der Investitionsförderungsverträge. Sie können jedoch dann im Rahmen der Abkommen relevant werden, wenn der Kapitalanlagestaat den Eingriff dadurch ermöglicht hat, daß er schuldhaft die Generalklausel des Enteignungsartikels verletzt hat, nach der die ausländische Kapitalanlage vollen Schutz und Sicherheit genießt." Michael Banz, *Völkerrechtlicher Eigentumsschutz durch Investitionsschutzabkommen. Insbesondere die Praxis der Bundesrepublik*

The characterization of FPS as a 'general clause' should be considered with some restraint. FPS and expropriation clauses do not stand in a general-to-particular relationship. An expropriation does not necessarily entail a breach of FPS. Claimants in investment arbitrations might be prone to argue that the very occurrence of an expropriation implies that the investment was not given adequate protection. Still, the argument is unsound and normally unsuccessful. In *Teinver v Argentina* (2017), for example, the investor claimed that the 'unlawful expropriation' of an airline entailed a breach of the FPS standard.[166] While the arbitral tribunal did not rule out the possibility of an overlap, it held that the facts could be 'more appropriately considered' under the expropriation clause and the FET standard.[167]

Alenfeld and Banz were however right in noting that private injuries should be assessed under the FPS standard rather than expropriation clauses. This observation could be the clue to the distinction between both standards. While both provisions protect foreign property, they refer to different sources of risk. In *Gemplus v Mexico* (2010) the arbitrators suggested that the distinction between FPS and expropriation could be based on the same criteria as the distinction between FPS and FET.[168] According to the *Gemplus* tribunal, the decisive elements for the distinction would be the fact that FPS does not create a strict liability and, perhaps most importantly, the fact that FPS grants protection against third parties.[169] This view is consistent with the content and scope of the customary protection obligation.[170] It is moreover useful. As a matter of fact, if this approach is followed, there should be little place for an overlap between FPS and expropriation clauses.

15.3.2 The Interplay Between Protection and Security Claims and Expropriation Claims in Investment Arbitration

Despite FPS clauses are distinct and autonomous from expropriation clauses, there has been a recurrent interplay between FPS claims and expropriation claims. This interplay has not always been fortunate. Adjudicators too-often fail to recognize the

---

Deutschland seit 1959 (Duncker & Humblot, Berlin 1988) 83 (also relying on Alenfeld's monograph in this connection).

[166]Teinver S.A., Transportes de Cercanías S.A. and Autobuses Urbanos del Sur S.A. *v* Argentina, Award, ICSID Case No. ARB/09/1 (21 July 2017) [899].

[167]Teinver S.A., Transportes de Cercanías S.A. and Autobuses Urbanos del Sur S.A. *v* Argentina, Award, ICSID Case No. ARB/09/1 (21 July 2017) [906 and 910]. The *Teinver* award also addressed the relationship between the FPS and the FET standard. This aspect of the decision is discussed in Sect. 15.2.2.

[168]Gemplus S.A., SLP S.A. and Gemplus Industrial S.A. de C.V. *v* Mexico, Award, ICSID Cases No. ARB(AF)/04/3 & ARB(AF)/04/4 (16 June 2010) [9.10-9.12] (particularly at para 9.11).

[169]Gemplus S.A., SLP S.A. and Gemplus Industrial S.A. de C.V. *v* Mexico, Award, ICSID Cases No. ARB(AF)/04/3 & ARB(AF)/04/4 (16 June 2010) [9.10-9.11].

[170]See Sect. 8.3. Cf. also Chap. 11.

substantive differences between the two standards. The award rendered in *Siag v Egypt* (2009) provides a clear example of the shortcomings of arbitral decisions addressing the subject. In the *Siag* case, the arbitral tribunal held that a breach of the FPS standard could arise out of the failure to prevent an unlawful expropriation and to promptly return the expropriated properties to their rightful owner:

> In the present case Claimants investment was expropriated by force and in opposition of explicit pleas of protection. The Egyptian courts on several subsequent occasions cancelled the Resolutions or decrees that purported to give legitimacy to the expropriation, yet Claimants' investment has not been returned to them in the 12 years following expropriation [...] *The Tribunal is of the view that the conduct of Egypt fell well below the standard of protection that the Claimants could reasonably have expected, both in allowing the expropriation to occur and in subsequently failing to take steps to return the investment to Claimants following repeated rulings of Egypt's own courts that the expropriation was illegal.* This is indeed the most egregious element of the whole affair. Accordingly the Tribunal finds that Egypt has contravened Article 4(1) of the Italy-Egypt BIT.[171]

It is hard to agree with the *Siag* tribunal's findings. To begin with, it is artificial to say that Egypt breached the FPS standard by 'allowing' the occurrence of an expropriation. This statement entails a self-reference problem. The expropriation was conducted by Egypt's state organs; it was Egypt's own doing. Thus, to say that Egypt is responsible for 'allowing the expropriation to occur' is the same as saying that A is responsible for 'allowing the occurrence of an action of A'. Following the *Siag* tribunal's reasoning one could then state that a burglar is responsible for having 'allowed' his hands to commit the burglary. The *Siag* tribunal recognized that the FPS standard only imposes an obligation of 'due diligence'.[172] The idea that Egypt failed to exercise diligence in order to prevent its own organs from committing an expropriation is incongruous, if to say the least.

As to the failure to return the properties for a period of 12 years, it is doubtful whether such omission can be accurately styled as a breach of FPS. The *Siag* tribunal relied in this regard on the award issued a few years earlier in *Wena v Egypt* (2000):

> The Tribunal notes in this respect the decision in the *Wena Hotels* case, wherein the seized investments were returned to Claimants after a year, yet the Tribunal in that case ruled that the full protection clause of the relevant BIT had been breached.[173]

The *Siag* tribunal overlooked a fundamental difference between the dispute it was deciding upon and the *Wena* case. In *Wena Hotels v Egypt* the arbitral tribunal was concerned with the illegal seizure of the investor's hotels by the Egyptian Hotel Company [EHC], which was described in the award as 'a company of the Egyptian Public Sector'.[174] However, the arbitrators treated EHC as an entity *separate* from

---

[171]Emphasis added. Waguih George Siag and Clorinda Vecchi *v* Egypt, Award, ICSID Case No. ARB/05/15 (1 June 2009) [447-8].

[172]Waguih George Siag and Clorinda Vecchi *v* Egypt, Award, ICSID Case No. ARB/05/15 (1 June 2009) [447].

[173]Waguih George Siag and Clorinda Vecchi *v* Egypt, Award, ICSID Case No. ARB/05/15 (1 June 2009) [448].

[174]Wena Hotels Ltd. *v* Egypt, Award, ICSID Case No. ARB/98/4 (8 December 2000) [17 *et seq.*].

the Egyptian state.[175] This characterization of EHC played a fundamental role in the *Wena* tribunal's assessment of the FPS claim.[176] The arbitrators found that Egyptian authorities, despite having knowledge of EHC's plans to seize the investment, 'took no action to prevent the seizures or to immediately restore Wena's control over the hotels'.[177] The *Wena* tribunal also held that, by failing to punish EHC, 'Egypt condoned ECH's actions'.[178] These statements would be semantically odd if EHC had been considered as an organ of the Egyptian state.

By contrast to *Wena*, the *Siag* expropriation resulted from acts of the Minister of Tourism, the Prime Minister and the very President of Egypt, and was moreover directly executed by agents of the Egyptian state.[179] None of the events considered by the *Siag* tribunal originated in a source other than the host state's own conduct. Thus, if the argument advanced in Chap. 8 is correct, none of the risks involved in the *Siag* case was actually covered by the FPS standard.[180] The *Siag* tribunal's finding that the failure to return the properties constitutes a breach of FPS is therefore unsound.

In other cases, the parties to the dispute have described FPS as a default provision, which could be invoked to obtain relief where an expropriation claim would be unfounded. An example appears in the parties' submissions in *I.P. Busta and J.P. Busta v Czech Republic* (2017). The *I.P. Busta* case was signalized by the fact that the applicable dispute settlement clause excluded the FET and the FPS provisions from the arbitral tribunal's jurisdiction.[181] For this reason, the investors sought to present their claims as expropriation claims.[182] The problem was that the expropriation would have affected only a part of the investment.[183] The respondent state argued that no expropriation had taken place.[184] The argument of the Czech Republic was that 'expropriation requires the entirety of the investor's investment to

---

[175]For a detailed account of Egypt's relationship to EHC see: Wena Hotels Ltd. *v* Egypt, Award, ICSID Case No. ARB/98/4 (8 December 2000) [65-9]. On the question of attribution see also: Wena Hotels Ltd. *v* Egypt, Decision on Annulment, ICSID Case No. ARB/98/4 (5 February 2002) [30].

[176]Wena Hotels Ltd. *v* Egypt, Award, ICSID Case No. ARB/98/4 (8 December 2000) [82 *et seq.*] (drawing a distinction between Egypt's omissions and EHC's acts). See also the language used in respect of the expropriation claim at para 99.

[177]Wena Hotels Ltd. *v* Egypt, Award, ICSID Case No. ARB/98/4 (8 December 2000) [85].

[178]Wena Hotels Ltd. *v* Egypt, Award, ICSID Case No. ARB/98/4 (8 December 2000) [94].

[179]Waguih George Siag and Clorinda Vecchi *v* Egypt, Award, ICSID Case No. ARB/05/15 (1 June 2009) [33-42, 47-8, 65-71, 76-80, 83-4].

[180]See Sect. 8.3.

[181]I.P. Busta and J.P. Busta *v* Czech Republic, Final Award, SCC Case No. V 2015/014 (10 March 2017) [165].

[182]I.P. Busta and J.P. Busta *v* Czech Republic, Final Award, SCC Case No. V 2015/014 (10 March 2017) [356 *et seq.*].

[183]Cf. I.P. Busta and J.P. Busta *v* Czech Republic, Final Award, SCC Case No. V 2015/014 (10 March 2017) [374 and 388-90].

[184]I.P. Busta and J.P. Busta *v* Czech Republic, Final Award, SCC Case No. V 2015/014 (10 March 2017) [373 *et seq.*].

have been taken [...] expropriation of only part of the investment is not suffi-cient'.[185] While denying the occurrence of an expropriation, the host state conceded that 'investors whose assets had been partially expropriated could nevertheless find relief under the standards of fair and equitable treatment and full protection and security'.[186] The Czech Republic however underscored that, in light of the applica-ble ISDS clause, 'an investor under this BIT case would not be able to enforce claims for breaches of those standards [i.e., FPS and FET]'.[187] The tribunal declared that it only had jurisdiction on the expropriation claim, and dismissed the case on the merits for lack of evidence.[188]

The Czech Republic's argument in the *I.P. Busta* proceedings poses the question of whether FPS clauses could provide a gateway for the ongoing discussion about the possibility of a partial expropriation.[189] This line of argument is more provoc-ative than plausible. The acts that give rise to an expropriation, whether total or partial, are unlikely to provide the basis for a successful FPS claim. FPS typically refers to risks that do *not* originate in the host state's conduct.[190] In contrast, the risk of expropriation is *par excellence* a public risk.[191] Moreover, while FPS is a delict of omission, expropriations typically result from state action.[192] The notion of 'expro-priation by omission' is controversial in theory and rarely alleged in practice.[193]

---

[185]I.P. Busta and J.P. Busta v Czech Republic, Final Award, SCC Case No. V 2015/014 (10 March 2017) [374].

[186]I.P. Busta and J.P. Busta v Czech Republic, Final Award, SCC Case No. V 2015/014 (10 March 2017) [375].

[187]I.P. Busta and J.P. Busta v Czech Republic, Final Award, SCC Case No. V 2015/014 (10 March 2017) [375].

[188]I.P. Busta and J.P. Busta v Czech Republic, Final Award, SCC Case No. V 2015/014 (10 March 2017) [421-2 and 437].

[189]On this issue see generally: Ursula Kriebaum, *Eigentumsschutz im Völkerrecht* (Duncker & Humblot, Berlin 2008) 385-405; Ursula Kriebaum, 'Expropriation' in Marc Bungenberg, Jörn Griebel, Stephan Hobe and August Reinisch (eds), *International Investment Law* (Nomos, Baden-Baden 2015) 959, 993-5.

[190]See Sect. 8.3.

[191]Cf. Sect. 15.3.1.

[192]On the characterization of FPS as a delict of omission see Sect. 11.3.

[193]For international adjudicatory bodies holding that expropriation can only arise out of positive state action see: Eudoro Armando Olguín v Paraguay, Award, ICSID Case No. ARB/98/5 (26 July 2001) [84] ("Expropriation [...] requires a teleologically driven action for it to occur; omissions, however egregious they may be, are not sufficient for it to take place"); Sea-Land Service Inc. v Iran, Award, Case No. 33 (20 June 1984), 6 Iran-US Cl. Trib. Rep. 149, 166 (dismissing an expropriation claim on grounds that expropriation requires 'deliberate governmental interference' and further noting that '[a] claim founded substantially on omissions and inaction [...] can hardly justify a finding of expropriation'). Other tribunals admit the possibility of an expropriation arising out of an omission, or from a combination of actions and omissions, see: Eureko B.V. v Poland (*Ad Hoc* Arbitration), Partial Award (19 August 2005) [238 *et seq.* and 260] (holding that 'actions and inactions' of Polish authorities were 'expropriatory in effect'); Waste Management v Mexico, Award, ICSID Case No. ARB(AF)/00/3 (30 April 2004) [174] (stating that 'one could envisage conduct tantamount to expropriation which consisted of acts and omissions'); I.P. Busta and

The arguments described above failed to recognize that the FPS standard and expropriation refer to different kinds of risk. The acknowledgment of this fundamental premise is a precondition for any plausible analysis of the interaction between the two standards. A genuine interplay between FPS and expropriation clauses may occur, for example, in cases concerning the protection of the investor from labor unions or other groups of persons in the context of an expropriation or nationalization process. Investment tribunals have considered these situations in several cases filed against the Bolivarian Republic of Venezuela.

In *Saint Gobain v Venezuela* (2016) a French corporation had established a plant for the production of bauxite-made 'ceramic proppants' for the hydrocarbons industry through a fully owned, locally incorporated subsidiary.[194] The investor argued that two increases in the price of bauxite had a significant impact on the investment.[195] In addition, a dispute with a labor union had lead to unrests and to the 'temporary takeover of the plant' by former workers.[196] President Hugo Chávez addressed the situation of the plant in a public event and announced the Government's intention to transform the investor's company into a 'state-controlled' corporation.[197] He further ordered to 'transfer it [the company] to the hands of Petróleos de Venezuela [PDVSA]'.[198] The definitive takeover of the plant followed.[199] The National Guard and an official commission accompanied the workers participating in the takeover.[200] The Government subsequently issued an official expropriation decree.[201]

J.P. Busta *v* Czech Republic, Final Award, SCC Case No. V 2015/014 (10 March 2017) [398-9] (discussing the *Olguín* and *Eureko* cases). See also: Anne Hoffmann, 'Indirect Expropriation' in August Reinisch (ed), *Standards of Investment Protection* (Oxford University Press, New York 2008) 151, 160 (providing an overview of the subject); Campbell McLachlan, Laurence Shore and Mattew Weiniger, *International Investment Arbitration: Substantive Principles* (Oxford University Press, Oxford 2008) 291-2 (rejecting the notion of 'expropriation by omission' and quoting in this connection the *Olguín* and *Sea-Land Service* cases).

[194] Saint-Gobain Performance Plastics Europe *v* Venezuela, Decision on Liability and the Principles of Quantum, ICSID Case No. ARB/12/13 (30 December 2016) [135-7].

[195] Saint-Gobain Performance Plastics Europe *v* Venezuela, Decision on Liability and the Principles of Quantum, ICSID Case No. ARB/12/13 (30 December 2016) [173-86].

[196] Saint-Gobain Performance Plastics Europe *v* Venezuela, Decision on Liability and the Principles of Quantum, ICSID Case No. ARB/12/13 (30 December 2016) [198-215].

[197] Saint-Gobain Performance Plastics Europe *v* Venezuela, Decision on Liability and the Principles of Quantum, ICSID Case No. ARB/12/13 (30 December 2016) [216].

[198] Saint-Gobain Performance Plastics Europe *v* Venezuela, Decision on Liability and the Principles of Quantum, ICSID Case No. ARB/12/13 (30 December 2016) [216].

[199] Saint-Gobain Performance Plastics Europe *v* Venezuela, Decision on Liability and the Principles of Quantum, ICSID Case No. ARB/12/13 (30 December 2016) [216-28].

[200] Saint-Gobain Performance Plastics Europe *v* Venezuela, Decision on Liability and the Principles of Quantum, ICSID Case No. ARB/12/13 (30 December 2016) [219].

[201] Saint-Gobain Performance Plastics Europe *v* Venezuela, Decision on Liability and the Principles of Quantum, ICSID Case No. ARB/12/13 (30 December 2016) [245].

The investor filed a claim under the France-Venezuela BIT, alleging that Venezuela had breached the expropriation clause as well as the FET and FPS standards.[202] As regards to FPS, the investor unsuccessfully claimed that the increase of the bauxite price entailed a failure to provide legal security.[203] Most importantly, the investor argued that, regardless of whether the expropriation was internationally wrongful, the takeover of the plan by the workers and its subsequent administration by a state-owned company (PDVSA) *prior* to the expropriation decree constituted a breach of FPS.[204] In response to this claim, Venezuela stressed that the presence of PDVSA during that period '[was] both appropriate and necessary given the dangers associated with the Plant'.[205] It further underlined the dangers of leaving the plant 'in the hand of unsupervised workers'.[206]

The arbitral tribunal recalled that 'the expropriation process' had begun *before* the issuance of the expropriation decree.[207] Noting that this FPS claim was alternative to the expropriation claim, which had been successful, the arbitrators considered it unnecessary to address the FPS standard in more detail.[208] In spite of this finding, it is arguable that the host state's omissions in respect of the takeover of a plant by organized workers could fall within the scope of the FPS standard. While the risk of expropriation as such is not covered by FPS,[209] the protection of property against third parties is a classic area of application of the security obligation.[210]

Another relevant case is *Tenaris v Venezuela* (2016). The claimants were *Tenaris S.A.*, a Luxembourgian company, and *Talta Ltd.*, a Portuguese company.[211] The case involved the nationalization of two locally incorporated companies: SIDOR (2008) and Matesi (2009).[212] According to the investors, the SIDOR Nationalization Decree, issued by the Venezuelan Government in April 2008, was followed by a

---

[202] Saint-Gobain Performance Plastics Europe *v* Venezuela, Decision on Liability and the Principles of Quantum, ICSID Case No. ARB/12/13 (30 December 2016) [270 *et seq.*].

[203] Saint-Gobain Performance Plastics Europe *v* Venezuela, Decision on Liability and the Principles of Quantum, ICSID Case No. ARB/12/13 (30 December 2016) [289 and 559-60].

[204] Saint-Gobain Performance Plastics Europe *v* Venezuela, Decision on Liability and the Principles of Quantum, ICSID Case No. ARB/12/13 (30 December 2016) [288 and 561-2].

[205] Saint-Gobain Performance Plastics Europe *v* Venezuela, Decision on Liability and the Principles of Quantum, ICSID Case No. ARB/12/13 (30 December 2016) [563].

[206] Saint-Gobain Performance Plastics Europe *v* Venezuela, Decision on Liability and the Principles of Quantum, ICSID Case No. ARB/12/13 (30 December 2016) [563].

[207] Saint-Gobain Performance Plastics Europe *v* Venezuela, Decision on Liability and the Principles of Quantum, ICSID Case No. ARB/12/13 (30 December 2016) [565].

[208] Saint-Gobain Performance Plastics Europe *v* Venezuela, Decision on Liability and the Principles of Quantum, ICSID Case No. ARB/12/13 (30 December 2016) [565].

[209] See Sect. 15.3.1.

[210] See Sect. 8.3.

[211] Tenaris S.A. and Talta-Trading E Marketing Sociedade Unipessoal Lda. *v* Venezuela, Award, ICSID Case No. ARB/11/26 (29 January 2016) [1].

[212] Tenaris S.A. and Talta-Trading E Marketing Sociedade Unipessoal Lda. *v* Venezuela, Award, ICSID Case No. ARB/11/26 (29 January 2016) [55 *et seq.*] (nationalization of SIDOR) and [63 *et seq.*] (nationalization of Matesi).

'serious labor unrest', which took place in November-December 2008.[213] These events occurred *after* the nationalization of SIDOR but *before* the nationalization of Matesi.[214] As a result of the unrest, the investors' personnel were unable to access the premises.[215] Many employees were assaulted.[216] In addition, twenty administrative employees were '[held] against their will' during an incident.[217]

In the investors' view, 'an expropriation that occurs in the face of pleas for protection amounts to a breach of this standard [i.e. the FPS standard]'.[218] The claimants moreover stressed that the Government of Venezuela 'was in collusion' with a labor union and had encouraged violence.[219] According to the investors, the measures of protection taken by Venezuela had been 'deliberately ineffectual'.[220] In response, the host state argued that there was no proof of collusion and that the acts of the labor unions could not be attributed to the state.[221] The state also emphasized that 'freedom of association was a fundamental democratic right enshrined in Venezuelan and international law'.[222] In addition, Venezuela contended that local authorities had made a serious effort to protect the investment.[223]

The arbitral tribunal dismissed the FPS claims.[224] In this vein, it observed that the FPS claims had been filed as claims for declaratory relief.[225] The arbitrators further explained that the evidence submitted was in any case insufficient to make a

---

[213]Tenaris S.A. and Talta-Trading E Marketing Sociedade Unipessoal Lda. *v* Venezuela, Award, ICSID Case No. ARB/11/26 (29 January 2016) [425 *et seq.*].

[214]Tenaris S.A. and Talta-Trading E Marketing Sociedade Unipessoal Lda. *v* Venezuela, Award, ICSID Case No. ARB/11/26 (29 January 2016) [441-2].

[215]Tenaris S.A. and Talta-Trading E Marketing Sociedade Unipessoal Lda. *v* Venezuela, Award, ICSID Case No. ARB/11/26 (29 January 2016) [425].

[216]Tenaris S.A. and Talta-Trading E Marketing Sociedade Unipessoal Lda. *v* Venezuela, Award, ICSID Case No. ARB/11/26 (29 January 2016) [426].

[217]Tenaris S.A. and Talta-Trading E Marketing Sociedade Unipessoal Lda. *v* Venezuela, Award, ICSID Case No. ARB/11/26 (29 January 2016) [425].

[218]Tenaris S.A. and Talta-Trading E Marketing Sociedade Unipessoal Lda. *v* Venezuela, Award, ICSID Case No. ARB/11/26 (29 January 2016) [426].

[219]Tenaris S.A. and Talta-Trading E Marketing Sociedade Unipessoal Lda. *v* Venezuela, Award, ICSID Case No. ARB/11/26 (29 January 2016) [426].

[220]Tenaris S.A. and Talta-Trading E Marketing Sociedade Unipessoal Lda. *v* Venezuela, Award, ICSID Case No. ARB/11/26 (29 January 2016) [435].

[221]Tenaris S.A. and Talta-Trading E Marketing Sociedade Unipessoal Lda. *v* Venezuela, Award, ICSID Case No. ARB/11/26 (29 January 2016) [427].

[222]Tenaris S.A. and Talta-Trading E Marketing Sociedade Unipessoal Lda. *v* Venezuela, Award, ICSID Case No. ARB/11/26 (29 January 2016) [427].

[223]Tenaris S.A. and Talta-Trading E Marketing Sociedade Unipessoal Lda. *v* Venezuela, Award, ICSID Case No. ARB/11/26 (29 January 2016) [434].

[224]Tenaris S.A. and Talta-Trading E Marketing Sociedade Unipessoal Lda. *v* Venezuela, Award, ICSID Case No. ARB/11/26 (29 January 2016) [449].

[225]Tenaris S.A. and Talta-Trading E Marketing Sociedade Unipessoal Lda. *v* Venezuela, Award, ICSID Case No. ARB/11/26 (29 January 2016) [441-2].

declaration of liability under the FPS standard.[226] In spite of this finding, the *Tenaris* case shows that the poisoned political and social environment that often surrounds major nationalization programs could be a fertile ground for the kind of violence the FPS standard refers to.

Notwithstanding the fact that expropriation and FPS claims could be closely intertwined, a breach of FPS must always be established on a separate basis. The mere fact that a taking is surrounded by violence or turmoil does not suffice for a declaration of liability under FPS. This holds true even if the police intervenes in the taking. Arbitral tribunals are unlikely to interpret the participation of the police as evidence of a violation of FPS. Quite the contrary, the presence of the police will be often considered as an indication of the host state's diligence. The award rendered in *OI European Group B.V. v Venezuela* (2015) provides a good example in this regard. The case pertained to a direct expropriation order issued by President Hugo Chavez on live television.[227] The words of the President were clear:

> The expropriation of that glass company, what's it called? – Owens Illinois! – is already all set. Let it be expropriated! Elías [Jaua – Vice President of Venezuela], proceed. Owens-Illinois, a North American Company that has been exploiting the workers here for years, destroying the environment there in. . . there in. . . in Trujillo. Go see the mountains they've destroyed. And taking the Venezuelan people's money. Hitcher [Minister of the Environment], do an environmental study; all the environmental damage. Proceed as indicated, Vice President.[228]

An official expropriation decree followed.[229] The measure affected two glass manufacturing plants.[230] A small contingent of the Venezuelan National Guard (*Guardia Nacional Bolivariana*—GNB) was sent 'to monitor access to the Plants and safeguard the expropriated properties'.[231] The investor alleged that 'the deployment of the GNB at the Plants caused an atmosphere in which the employees of the Plants were threatened and intimidated and had no other alternative than to obey the orders of Respondent or face legal action for sabotage'.[232] In the investor's view, such a measure could be characterized as 'a breach of the duty to protect the physical

---

[226]Tenaris S.A. and Talta-Trading E Marketing Sociedade Unipessoal Lda. *v* Venezuela, Award, ICSID Case No. ARB/11/26 (29 January 2016) [443-8].

[227]OI European Group B.V. *v* Venezuela, Award, ICSID Case No. ARB/11/25 (10 March 2015) [110].

[228]OI European Group B.V. *v* Venezuela, Award, ICSID Case No. ARB/11/25 (10 March 2015) [110] (square brackets in the original).

[229]OI European Group B.V. *v* Venezuela, Award, ICSID Case No. ARB/11/25 (10 March 2015) [111-3].

[230]OI European Group B.V. *v* Venezuela, Award, ICSID Case No. ARB/11/25 (10 March 2015) [85-8].

[231]OI European Group B.V. *v* Venezuela, Award, ICSID Case No. ARB/11/25 (10 March 2015) [114].

[232]OI European Group B.V. *v* Venezuela, Award, ICSID Case No. ARB/11/25 (10 March 2015) [564].

safety of its investments'.[233] The arbitrators were not convinced by this argument. In their assessment of the FPS claim, they made the following finding:

> The mere presence of the GNB during the takeover of the Companies is a component of the precautionary measures a government authority legitimately can and should take to ensure that control is assumed in an orderly manner, precisely for the purpose of guaranteeing FPP [i.e., FPS] of the investment. It is contradictory to allege that the actions of the State's security forces, which ensure physical security, constitute a violation of the FPP standard.[234]

This conclusion bears some resemblance to the findings of the tribunal in *Saur International S.A. v Argentina* (2012). In the *SAUR* case, the tribunal found that Argentina had committed an internationally wrongful direct expropriation through a series of measures, including an 'administrative intervention'.[235] Specifically, the administrative intervention involved the physical takeover of a locally incorporated company, which was executed in the presence of the local police.[236] The investor argued that the 'brutal' manner how the intervention took place entailed a breach of the FPS standard.[237] The tribunal held that the mere presence of the police was not sufficient for a declaration of liability under the FPS standard.[238]

In sum, the risk of expropriation is not covered by the FPS standard. The reason is that FPS refers to risks that do not originate in the host state's conduct, such as private violence. It is however possible that a breach of FPS occurs in the context of an expropriation or nationalization process. While in such events the FPS claim could be entangled with an expropriation claim, a breach of FPS must always be established on a separate basis.

---

[233]OI European Group B.V. *v* Venezuela, Award, ICSID Case No. ARB/11/25 (10 March 2015) [564].

[234]OI European Group B.V. *v* Venezuela, Award, ICSID Case No. ARB/11/25 (10 March 2015) [580].

[235]SAUR International S.A. *v* Argentina, Décision sur la compétence et sur la responsabilité, ICSID Case No. ARB/04/4 (6 June 2012) [362 *et seq.*]. For an account of the expropriatory measures at stake see para 384. The Argentine Republic subsequently challenged the finding on expropriation before an ICSID Annulment Committee. The claim was unsuccessful. See: SAUR International S.A. *v* Argentina, Décision relative à la demande d'annulation de la république argentine, ICSID Case No. ARB/04/4 (19 December 2016) [57-63, 128-31, 264-90 and 341].

[236]SAUR International S.A. *v* Argentina, Décision sur la compétence et sur la responsabilité, ICSID Case No. ARB/04/4 (6 June 2012) [193].

[237]SAUR International S.A. *v* Argentina, Décision sur la compétence et sur la responsabilité, ICSID Case No. ARB/04/4 (6 June 2012) [508-11].

[238]SAUR International S.A. *v* Argentina, Décision sur la compétence et sur la responsabilité, ICSID Case No. ARB/04/4 (6 June 2012) [509].

15.4 'Full Protection and Security' and the Prohibition of Discriminatory and Arbitrary Measures

Numerous IIAs expressly proscribe discriminatory and arbitrary measures against investors and covered investments.[239] This widespread guarantee has been described as one of the 'classical standards' of international investment law.[240] A few IIAs set forth this obligation in the same treaty provision as the FPS standard. The 2008 version of the Colombian Model BIT provides a good example in this regard:

> Each Contracting Party *shall protect* within its territory investments made in accordance with its law by investors of the other Contracting Party *and shall not impair with discriminatory measures the management, maintenance, use, enjoyment, extension, sale and liquidation of said investments.*[241]

The relationship between the prohibition of discriminatory and arbitrary measures and other standards of treatment has drawn the attention of scholars and adjudicators alike. In particular, there is extensive literature and case law on the link between this prohibition and the FET standard.[242] Little has been said, however, as to its relation to the FPS standard.[243] While it has not been unusual for parties in investment arbitral proceedings to emphasize the arbitrary or non-arbitrary character of the

---

[239]Cf. Federico Ortino, 'Non-Arbitrariness' in Thomas Cottier and Krista Nadakavukaren Schefer (eds), *Elgar Encyclopedia of International Economic Law* (Edward Elgar Publishing, Northampton MA 2018) 207, 207-8; Jörn Griebel, *Internationales Investitionsrecht* (C.H. Beck, Munich 2008) 73; Rudolf Dolzer and Christoph Schreuer, *Principles of International Investment Law* (Oxford University Press, New York 2012) 191-7; Ursula Kriebaum, 'Arbitrary/Unreasonable or Discriminatory Measures' in Marc Bungenberg, Jörn Griebel, Stephan Hobe and August Reinisch (eds), *International Investment Law* (Nomos, Baden-Baden 2015) 790, 790-1; Veijo Heiskanen, 'Arbitrary and Unreasonable Measures' in August Reinisch (ed), *Standards of Investment Protection* (Oxford University Press, New York 2008) 87, 87-9.

[240]Rudolf Dolzer and Christoph Schreuer, *Principles of International Investment Law* (Oxford University Press, New York 2012) 191.

[241]Emphasis added. Colombian Model BIT (2008) art. III(2). It should be noted, however, that the Model BIT contained a more detailed regulation of the FPS standard in arts. III(3) and (4). For a more traditional enunciation of the prohibition of arbitrary and discriminatory measures see: German Model BIT (2008) art. 2(3).

[242]Cf. Christoph Schreuer, 'Fair and Equitable Treatment (FET): Interactions with Other Standards' in Graham Coop and Clarisse Ribeiro (eds), *Investment Protection and the Energy Charter Treaty* (Juris Publishing, Huntington NY 2008) 63, 69-76; Christoph Schreuer, 'Protection against Arbitrary or Discriminatory Measures' in Catherine Rogers and Roger Alford (eds), *The Future of Investment Arbitration* (Oxford University Press, New York 2009) 183, 189-92; Ronald Kläger, *'Fair and Equitable Treatment' in International Investment Law* (Cambridge University Press, New York 2011) 290-1; Ursula Kriebaum, 'Arbitrary/Unreasonable or Discriminatory Measures' in Marc Bungenberg, Jörn Griebel, Stephan Hobe and August Reinisch (eds), *International Investment Law* (Nomos, Baden-Baden 2015) 790, 794-7.

[243]For an author briefly addressing the relationship between FPS and the prohibition of discriminatory measures, as developed in investment awards cf. Nartnirun Junngam, 'The Full Protection and Security Standard in International Investment Law: What and Who is Investment Fully[?] Protected and Secured From?' (2018) 7(1) AUBLR 1, 82.

measures of protection adopted by the host state,[244] only a few arbitral decisions have specifically addressed the relationship between the two standards.

An example would be the Final Award issued in *Ronald Lauder v Czech Republic* (2001). The case concerned an American investment in the Czech broadcasting industry.[245] The investor claimed that the respondent state had breached several provisions of the US-Czech Republic BIT, including the guarantee against discriminatory and arbitrary measures, enshrined in article II(2)(b) of the treaty, and the standard of full protection and security set forth in article II(2)(a) of the BIT.[246] The arbitral tribunal concluded that some, but not all, of the measures challenged by the investor could be characterized as 'arbitrary or discriminatory'.[247] The FPS claims, however, pertained to measures that were neither discriminatory nor arbitrary.[248] This circumstance was of pivotal importance for the tribunal's decision on the FPS standard:

> The Arbitral Tribunal holds that none of the facts alleged by the Claimant constituted a violation by the Respondent of the obligation to provide full protection and security under the Treaty. Here again, in order to avoid redundancy, the Arbitral Tribunal refers to the findings made under the chapter addressing the issue of prohibition against arbitrary and discriminatory measures [. . .] for most of the arguments denying the existence of any arbitrary or discriminatory measure from the Czech Republic [. . .] also apply to the Respondent's compliance with the obligation to provide full protection and security.[249]

Based on this general observation, the *Ronald Lauder* tribunal analyzed the FPS claims raised by the investor, which referred to six different measures.[250] The arbitral tribunal recognized that FPS entails an obligation to exercise due diligence.[251] Nonetheless, it applied the standard of due diligence only in respect of one of the six measures, which was also the only one involving the conduct of

---

[244]See for example the respondent's argument in *Rumeli Telekom v Kazakhstan*: Rumeli Telekom A.S. and Telsim Mobil Telekomunikasyon Hizmetleri A.S. *v* Kazakhstan, Award, ICSID Case No. ARB/05/16 (29 July 2008) [667].

[245]For a detailed account of the facts see: Ronald Lauder *v* Czech Republic (UNCITRAL), Final Award (3 September 2001) [43 *et seq.*].

[246]Ronald Lauder *v* Czech Republic (UNCITRAL), Final Award (3 September 2001) [236].

[247]Ronald Lauder *v* Czech Republic (UNCITRAL), Final Award (3 September 2001) [214 *et seq.*].

[248]Ronald Lauder *v* Czech Republic (UNCITRAL), Final Award (3 September 2001) [310 *et seq.*].

[249]Ronald Lauder *v* Czech Republic (UNCITRAL), Final Award (3 September 2001) [310].

[250]Ronald Lauder *v* Czech Republic (UNCITRAL), Final Award (3 September 2001) [305].

[251]Ronald Lauder *v* Czech Republic (UNCITRAL), Final Award (3 September 2001) [308].

private parties.[252] By contrast, the notion of arbitrary measures took center stage in the assessment of measures that were unrelated to non-state actors.[253]

This monograph has argued that the FPS standard primarily refers to protection against non-state risks (e.g. private violence). If this premise is correct, it could be said that most of the measures discussed in the *Ronald Lauder* case did not actually pertain to the FPS standard: only one out of six measures referred to a third party.[254] The tribunal was right in assessing just this one measure through the prism of due diligence.[255]

This shows that an overlap between FPS and the prohibition of arbitrary or discriminatory measures should not occur where there is no link between the measures challenged by the investor and a source of risk other than the host state's conduct.[256] An intersection between the two standards cannot be ruled out as a matter of principle, though. A possible overlap could occur, for example, where persons facing similar risks and under similar circumstances are given different degrees of protection. In their analysis of due diligence, adjudicators could and should consider whether differential treatment was justified. A finding of arbitrariness or discrimination in the protection afforded could lead a tribunal to declare that a want of diligence was internationally wrongful.[257] Nonetheless, even in such events, the notions of arbitrariness and discrimination are mere elements in the analysis of diligence, and not substitutes for the due diligence standard of liability.

15.5 'Full Protection and Security' and National Treatment

Most investment treaties require the host state to treat covered investors and their investments at least as favorably as its own nationals and their property.[258] This obligation has a long tradition in international law. National treatment clauses have

---

[252]Ronald Lauder *v* Czech Republic (UNCITRAL), Final Award (3 September 2001) [314] (referring to the alleged failure by Czech authorities to 'intervene' in a dispute between the investor and other private parties). For the sake of accuracy, the tribunal additionally mentioned the notion of due diligence in connection with the FET standard (at para 292) and in its general description of the FPS standard (at para 308).

[253]See, particularly: Ronald Lauder *v* Czech Republic (UNCITRAL), Final Award (3 September 2001) [310-2].

[254]Ronald Lauder *v* Czech Republic (UNCITRAL), Final Award (3 September 2001) [305 and 314].

[255]Ronald Lauder *v* Czech Republic (UNCITRAL), Final Award (3 September 2001) [314].

[256]It should be noted, however, that this conclusion only holds true as far as the applicable FPS clause does not derogate from customary law. Attention should also be drawn to the notion of public collateral damages, discussed in Sect. 8.3.3.1.

[257]Cf. Sect. 13.4.6.

[258]See generally: August Reinisch, 'National Treatment' in Marc Bungenberg, Jörn Griebel, Stephan Hobe and August Reinisch (eds), *International Investment Law* (Nomos, Baden-Baden 2015) 846, 847 and 850-1; David Collins, 'National Treatment in Emerging Market Investment

been traced back to the European Middle Ages.[259] In the essence, national treatment implies comparing the situation of foreign investors with that of domestic investors placed in 'like circumstances'.[260] A breach of the standard occurs where the treatment given to foreign investors is less favorable than that afforded to local investors, and there is no justification for differential treatment.[261]

FPS clauses are frequently entangled with references to national treatment. Such references serve different purposes. In some agreements, national treatment is used as a means to define the *minimum* level of protection investors are entitled to. Article 3(2) of the Netherlands-Czech and Slovak Federal Republic BIT of 1991 provides a good example of this type of clauses:

> [E]ach Contracting Party shall accord to such [covered] investments *full security and protection which in any case shall not be less than that accorded either to investments of its own investors* or to investments of investors of any third state, whichever is more favourable to the investor concerned.[262]

This formulation grants covered investments protection beyond the customary FPS standard. The reason is that customary law requires states to afford foreigners a *minimum* level of security, regardless of whether such minimum goes beyond or falls

---

Treaties' in Anselm Kamperman Sanders (ed), *The Principle of National Treatment in International Economic Law: Trade, Investment and Intellectual Property* (Edward Elgar, Northampton MA 2014) 161, 161-8 and 181; Leïla Choukroune, 'National Treatment in International Investment Law and Arbitration: A Relative Standard for Autonomous Public Regulation and Sovereign Development' in Anselm Kamperman Sanders (ed), *The Principle of National Treatment in International Economic Law: Trade, Investment and Intellectual Property* (Edward Elgar, Northampton MA 2014) 183, 183 *et seq.*; Matthias Herdegen, *Principles of International Economic Law* (Oxford University Press, New York 2016) 450-2.

[259]Cf. Todd Weiler, *The Interpretation of International Investment Law: Equality, Discrimination, and Minimum Standards of Treatment in Historical Context* (Brill, Leiden 2013) 415 n. 1225; August Reinisch, 'National Treatment' in Marc Bungenberg, Jörn Griebel, Stephan Hobe and August Reinisch (eds), *International Investment Law* (Nomos, Baden-Baden 2015) 846, 848.

[260]Rudolf Dolzer and Christoph Schreuer, *Principles of International Investment Law* (Oxford University Press, New York 2012) 199-200. On the likeness requirement see also: Andrea Bjorklund, 'National Treatment' in August Reinisch (ed), *Standards of Investment Protection* (Oxford University Press, New York 2008) 29, 38-48; August Reinisch, 'National Treatment' in Marc Bungenberg, Jörn Griebel, Stephan Hobe and August Reinisch (eds), *International Investment Law* (Nomos, Baden-Baden 2015) 846, 856-60; David Collins, 'National Treatment in Emerging Market Investment Treaties' in Anselm Kamperman Sanders (ed), *The Principle of National Treatment in International Economic Law: Trade, Investment and Intellectual Property* (Edward Elgar, Northampton MA 2014) 161, 163 *et seq.*; Leïla Choukroune, 'National Treatment in International Investment Law and Arbitration: A Relative Standard for Autonomous Public Regulation and Sovereign Development' in Anselm Kamperman Sanders (ed), *The Principle of National Treatment in International Economic Law: Trade, Investment and Intellectual Property* (Edward Elgar, Northampton MA 2014) 183, 207-13.

[261]Rudolf Dolzer and Christoph Schreuer, *Principles of International Investment Law* (Oxford University Press, New York 2012) 199-203.

[262]Emphasis added. Agreement between the Kingdom of the Netherlands and the Czech and Slovak Federal Republic on the Encouragement and Reciprocal Protection of Investments (adopted 24 April 1991, entered into force 1 October 1992) art. 3(2).

below the security enjoyed by the host state's citizens.[263] The reference to national treatment in the Netherlands-Czech and Slovak Federal Republic BIT does not relieve the host state from its obligation to provide investors the minimum protection required under customary international law, even if the host state's nationals do not enjoy the same level of security. But where the host state's citizens are given protection *beyond* this minimum, the treaty clause creates an obligation to extend such higher degree of protection to the foreign investor.

In other treaties, resort to national treatment is made to limit the degree of protection required under the FPS standard. Any finding of responsibility under such clauses therefore depends on the existence of differential treatment between foreigners and nationals. The historical record shows that provisions of this kind have been present in commercial treaties for centuries. The Chile-US FCN Agreement of 1832 provides an early example of this treaty practice.[264] A more recent example would be article III(4)(e) of the Colombian Model BIT of 2008, which reads as follows:

> The "Full protection and security" standard does not imply, in any case, a better treatment to that accorded to nationals of the Contracting Party where the investment has been made.[265]

This clause has serious implications for the substance of the protection obligation. As far as the FPS standard is *limited* to national treatment, it cannot be a part of the customary minimum standard of treatment. The essence of the minimum standard, as formulated by the General Claim Commission in the *Roberts Claim* (1926), is that 'equality [between nationals and aliens] is not the ultimate test of the propriety of the acts of authorities in the light of international law'.[266] Article III(3) of the Colombian Model BIT seems to confirm the autonomous character of the FPS clause. In fact, it defines the FET standard, but not the FPS standard, by reference to customary international law.[267]

The drafters of the Colombian Model BIT however introduced an additional reference to the minimum standard, which is inconsistent with the abovementioned clauses. Article III(4)(a) of the Model BIT provides:

---

[263] See Sect. 5.4.

[264] Treaty of Peace, Amity, Navigation, and Commerce between the United States of America and the Republic of Chile (adopted 16 May 1832, entered into force 29 April 1834) Hunter Miller (ed), *Treaties and Other International Acts of the United States of America* (Volume 3: Government Printing Office, Washington 1971) 671, 677-8 art. 10. Section 4.3.1 discusses this treaty in greater detail.

[265] Colombian Model BIT (2008) art. III(4)(e). An identical provision appears in a new Model BIT released in 2011 (only available in Spanish): Colombian Model BIT (2011) art. VI(6).

[266] Cf. *Harry Roberts v Mexico* (2 November 1926) IV RIAA 77, 80 [8]. See also Sects. 5.3 and 5.4.

[267] Colombian Model BIT (2008) art. III(3) ("Each Party shall accord *fair and equitable treatment in accordance with customary international law, and full protection and security* in its territory to investments of investors of the other Contracting Party" – emphasis added). This provision changed in the new version of the Colombian Model BIT, which refers the minimum standard in respect of both FPS and FET. See: Colombian Model BIT (2011) art. VI(1).

> The concepts of "fair and equitable treatment" and "full protection and security" do not require additional treatment to that required under the minimum standard of treatment of aliens in accordance with the standard of customary international law.[268]

Interpreters will face the sheer difficulty of reconciling the inclusion of *both* the minimum standard and national treatment as the 'ceiling' of the FPS standard. In a commentary to this treaty provision, a former Colombian Government official stressed that, while the linkage between national treatment and FPS in the Colombian Model BIT is 'unorthodox', it actually enhances the protection enjoyed by foreign investors:

> [B]y adding the legal caveat that – apart from assuring the minimum standard of full protection and security dictated by custom – the host Party shall also extend to foreign investments any better protection and security granted to investments of its nationals, Colombia gives foreign investors a positive signal which is consistent with the non-discrimination principle.[269]

This interpretation does violence to the language of article III(4)(e) of the 2008 Colombian Model BIT, which does certainly *not* impose an obligation to extend to foreign investors the same degree of protection enjoyed by domestic investors. The Model BIT is quite explicit in providing that FPS does *not* require protection beyond national treatment. If the drafters' intention was to expand the scope of protection of the FPS standard they could and should have used a different formulation. Fortunately, this remarkably confusing language is most unusual in investment treaties.

The interplay between FPS and national treatment goes beyond treaties explicitly establishing a link between the two standards. For instance, in *Pantechniki v Albania* (2009), a case involving riot violence,[270] the respondent state argued that the treatment received by the investor was 'equivalent to that of all other victims of the events'.[271] Equal or unequal treatment could be strong arguments in the context of FPS claims.[272] From the standpoint of due diligence, the very existence of different levels of protection could indicate that the host state had the resources to provide some form of security, and denied the foreign investor the protection it was able and willing to afford to other groups of persons. Conversely, equal treatment could reinforce the impression that the state provided the security it was honestly able to offer in a given situation.

Another case worth mentioning is *ADF v United States* (2003). In the proceedings, *ADF* invoked the standard of national treatment set forth in NAFTA article

---

[268]Colombian Model BIT (2008) art. III(4)(a). Cf. also Colombian Model BIT (2011) art. VI(2).

[269]José Antonio Rivas, 'Colombia' in Chester Brown (ed), *Commentaries on Selected Model Investment Treaties* (Oxford University Press, Oxford 2013) 183, 217.

[270]Pantechniki S.A. Contractors & Engineers *v* Albania, Award, ICSID Case No. ARB/07/21 (30 July 2009) [70 *et seq.*]. For a detailed account of the facts of the case see paras 12 *et seq.*

[271]Pantechniki S.A. Contractors & Engineers *v* Albania, Award, ICSID Case No. ARB/07/21 (30 July 2009) [75]. The Sole Arbitrator did not address this argument in his assessment of the case.

[272]Section 13.4.6 discusses the relevance of differential treatment for the analysis of due diligence in more detail.

1102, arguing that it was entitled to receive a treatment as favorable as that which the United States claims for its own investors under other IIAs.[273] The claimant observed that several BITs concluded by the United States assured American investors protection and security not limited to the customary minimum standard of treatment.[274] Based on this observation, *ADF* contended that, as a Canadian investor in the United States, it was entitled to such better treatment under NAFTA article 1102.[275] The tribunal was skeptical about the argument.[276] *ADF's* statements bear resemblance to arguments typically advanced under MFN provisions. The next section discusses this aspect of the case in more detail.

15.6 'Full Protection and Security' and Most-Favored-Nation Treatment

Besides the national treatment clause, most IIAs include a most-favored-nation treatment [MFN] provision.[277] A representative example would be article 8.4 of the Korea-Colombia FTA of 2013, which reads as follows:

> Each Party shall accord to investors of the other Party treatment no less favorable than that it accords, in like circumstances, to investors of any non-Party with respect to the

---

[273] ADF *v* United States, Investor's Reply to the Counter-Memorial of the United States of America on Competence and Liability, ICSID Case No. ARB(AF)/00/1 (28 January 2002) [242-6]. See also the arbitrators' description of the investor's argument: ADF *v* United States, Award, ICSID Case No. ARB(AF)/00/1 (9 January 2003) [80].

[274] ADF *v* United States, Investor's Reply to the Counter-Memorial of the United States of America on Competence and Liability, ICSID Case No. ARB(AF)/00/1 (28 January 2002) [242-6] (specifically invoking the US-Albania BIT and the US-Estonia BIT). See also: ADF *v* United States, Award, ICSID Case No. ARB(AF)/00/1 (9 January 2003) [80 and 197-8].

[275] ADF *v* United States, Investor's Reply to the Counter-Memorial of the United States of America on Competence and Liability, ICSID Case No. ARB(AF)/00/1 (28 January 2002) [244-6]. See also: ADF *v* United States, Award, ICSID Case No. ARB(AF)/00/1 (9 January 2003) [80 and 197]. The investor's interpretation of the national treatment clause was based on a passage of the jurisdictional decision rendered in *Maffezini v Spain* (2000). See: Emilio Agustín Maffezini *v* Spain, Decision on Objections to Jurisdiction, ICSID Case No. ARB/97/7 (25 January 2000) [61] ("While this clause [national treatment] applies to national treatment of foreign investors, it may also be understood to embrace the treatment required by a Government for its investors abroad").

[276] Cf. ADF *v* United States, Award, ICSID Case No. ARB(AF)/00/1 (9 January 2003) [197-8].

[277] See generally: August Reinisch, 'Most Favoured Nation Treatment' in Marc Bungenberg, Jörn Griebel, Stephan Hobe and August Reinisch (eds), *International Investment Law* (Nomos, Baden-Baden 2015) 807, 808 *et seq.*; Matthias Herdegen, *Principles of International Economic Law* (Oxford University Press, New York 2016) 452-5; Yas Banifatemi, 'The Emerging Jurisprudence on the Most-Favoured-Nation Treatment in Investment Arbitration' in Andrea Bjorklund, Ian Laird and Sergey Ripinsky (eds), *Investment Treaty Law* (British Institute of International and Comparative Law, London 2009) 241, 246 *et seq.*

establishment, acquisition, expansion, management, conduct, operation, and sale or other disposition of investments in its territory.[278]

The *ADF v United States* arbitration (2003), discussed above in connection with the national treatment standard, provides an excellent example of the interplay between MFN clauses and the FPS standard. In the *ADF* case, the investor advanced broad interpretations of both the FPS and FET provisions of NAFTA.[279] The arbitral proceedings were still pending as the NAFTA Free Trade Commission released its Note of Interpretation on NAFTA Article 1105(1), which expressly limited the scope of the FET and FPS clauses to customary law.[280] In a memorial submitted after the issuance of the FTC Note, *ADF* observed that other IIAs concluded by the United States (particularly the US-Albania BIT and the US-Estonia BIT) did not restrict FPS and FET to the treatment due under customary international law and, accordingly, could be said to offer a 'better treatment' than NAFTA.[281] *ADF* claimed that it was entitled to such better treatment under NAFTA Article 1103 (MFN).[282]

For its part, the United States argued that *ADF's* contentions were based on a misinterpretation of the FPS clauses of the US-Albania and the US-Estonia BITs.[283] In the host state's view, the wording used in those treaties entails no derogation from customary law; on the contrary, '[that wording] sets out a minimum standard of treatment based on standards found in customary international law or based on customary international law'.[284] After careful consideration of the parties' submissions, the arbitrators rejected the claimant's argument:

> The Investor's theory assumes the validity of its own reading of the relevant clauses of the treaties with Albania and Estonia. That reading, as observed in some detail earlier, is that the

---

[278]Free Trade Agreement between the Republic of Korea and the Republic of Colombia (adopted 21 February 2013, entered into force 15 July 2016) art. 8.4(1). It must be noted that the MFN clause of the Korea-Colombia FTA is not applicable to the treaty's ISDS clause (as provided in n. 2).

[279]ADF v United States, Memorial of the Investor, ICSID Case No. ARB(AF)/00/1 (1 August 2001) [238-9]. See also: ADF v United States, Award, ICSID Case No. ARB(AF)/00/1 (9 January 2003) [70-1] (summarizing the Claimant's argument).

[280]NAFTA Free Trade Commission, *Notes of Interpretation of Certain Chapter 11 Provisions* (31 July 2001) [http://www.sice.oas.org/tpd/nafta/Commission/CH11understanding_e.asp].

[281]ADF v United States, Investor's Reply to the Counter-Memorial of the United States of America on Competence and Liability, ICSID Case No. ARB(AF)/00/1 (28 January 2002) [221-41]. See also: ADF v United States, Award, ICSID Case No. ARB(AF)/00/1 (9 January 2003) [75-80].

[282]ADF v United States, Investor's Reply to the Counter-Memorial of the United States of America on Competence and Liability, ICSID Case No. ARB(AF)/00/1 (28 January 2002) [221]. See also: ADF v United States, Award, ICSID Case No. ARB(AF)/00/1 (9 January 2003) [75-80]. A similar argument was advanced on the basis of the national treatment standard. Section 15.5 discusses this aspect of the *ADF* case.

[283]ADF v United States, Rejoinder of Respondent United States of America on Competence and Liability, ICSID Case No. ARB(AF)/00/1 (29 March 2002) 40 *et seq.* See also: ADF v United States, Award, ICSID Case No. ARB(AF)/00/1 (9 January 2003) [107].

[284]ADF v United States, Rejoinder of Respondent United States of America on Competence and Liability, ICSID Case No. ARB(AF)/00/1 (29 March 2002) 40-1. See also: ADF v United States, Award, ICSID Case No. ARB(AF)/00/1 (9 January 2003) [107].

"fair and equitable treatment" and "full protection and security" clauses of the two treaties establish broad, normative standards of treatment distinct and separate from the specific requirements of the customary international law minimum standard of treatment. We have, however, already concluded that the Investor has not been able persuasively to document the existence of such autonomous standards, and that even if the Tribunal assumes hypothetically the existence thereof, the Investor has not shown that the U.S. measures are reasonably characterized as in breach of such standards.[285]

Another example would be the award rendered in *Rumeli Telekom v Kazakhstan* (2008). The *Rumeli* tribunal was constituted under the Kazakhstan-Turkey BIT of 1992, which contains no FPS clause.[286] Due to this circumstance, the investors relied on the FPS clause of the Kazakhstan-UK BIT, which they considered to be applicable by virtue of article II(2) of the Kazakhstan-Turkey BIT (MFN).[287] In their decision on the case, the arbitrators observed:

[T]he parties agree that in view of the MFN clause contained in the BIT, Respondent's international obligations assumed in other bilateral treaties, and in particular the United Kingdom-Kazakhstan BIT, are applicable to this case, such obligations including [...] the obligation to accord full protection and security.[288]

A few years later, in *Impregilo v Argentina* (2011), the investor sought to rely on the FPS clause of the Argentina-US BIT by invoking the MFN clause of the Argentina-Italy BIT.[289] The arbitral tribunal found no need to consider this contention in detail because it had already declared a violation of the FET standard.[290]

In *EDF v Argentina* (2012) the investors contended that, even if the tribunal were to find that the FPS clause of the Argentina-France BIT did not ensure the stability of the investment's legal framework, Argentina would be under an obligation to give to their investments the more-favorable treatment granted to other investments under the Argentina-Germany BIT, which explicitly refers to 'legal security'.[291] To this effect, the investors invoked the MFN clause of the Argentina-France BIT.[292] In response, Argentina argued that 'incorporation of other treaty standards by way of

---

[285] ADF *v* United States, Award, ICSID Case No. ARB(AF)/00/1 (9 January 2003) [194].

[286] Agreement between the Republic of Turkey and the Republic of Kazakhstan concerning the Reciprocal Promotion and Protection of Investments (adopted 1 May 1992, entered into force 10 August 1995).

[287] Rumeli Telekom A.S. and Telsim Mobil Telekomunikasyon Hizmetleri A.S. *v* Kazakhstan, Award, ICSID Case No. ARB/05/16 (29 July 2008) [560].

[288] Rumeli Telekom A.S. and Telsim Mobil Telekomunikasyon Hizmetleri A.S. *v* Kazakhstan, Award, ICSID Case No. ARB/05/16 (29 July 2008) [575].

[289] Impregilo S.p.A. *v* Argentina, Award, ICSID Case No. ARB/07/17 (21 June 2011) [122(d), 157, 192(d), 332(b), 334].

[290] Impregilo S.p.A. *v* Argentina, Award, ICSID Case No. ARB/07/17 (21 June 2011) [334] and Finding D (at p. 86).

[291] EDF International S.A., Saur International S.A. and Leon Participaciones Argentinas S.A. *v* Argentina, Award, ICSID Case No. ARB/03/23 (11 June 2012) [407]. For the investors' main contention (pertaining to the interpretation of the Argentina-France BIT) see para 405.

[292] EDF International S.A., Saur International S.A. and Leon Participaciones Argentinas S.A. *v* Argentina, Award, ICSID Case No. ARB/03/23 (11 June 2012) [407].

the MFN clause [...] would run afoul of the intentions of the contracting states'.[293] The tribunal took note of the parties' arguments but found it unnecessary to consider the substance of the FPS claim, since a finding on this matter would have had no impact on the quantum of damages awarded to the investor.[294]

In *Hesham Talaat M. Al-Warraq v Indonesia* (2014) the investor alleged that the guarantee of 'full protection and security' in the Indonesia-UK BIT was applicable to the case, basing its argument on the MFN clause of the OIC Agreement.[295] The arbitrators agreed on the applicability of the FPS clause, but considered that the Indonesia-UK BIT did not provide a 'higher standard' of security than article 2 of the OIC Agreement, which refers to 'adequate protection and security'.[296]

In *CC/Devas v India* (2016) the claimants contended that the guarantee of 'full legal protection and security' in article 3(2) of the Serbia-India BIT was applicable to the dispute by virtue of the MFN clause of the India-Mauritius BIT.[297] India opposed the argument, arguing that the investors' use of the MFN clause 'entailed creating a standard that is not present in the applicable Treaty'.[298] The arbitrators dismissed the state's contention and, following the investor's line of argument, applied the FPS clause of the Serbia-India BIT.[299] Still, they did not reach a finding of liability under the FPS standard, and dismissed the claim.[300]

In *Rusoro Mining v Venezuela* (2016) the claimant alleged that several regulatory measures adopted by Venezuela were inconsistent with the FPS clause of the Canada-Venezuela BIT.[301] For its part, the respondent argued that FPS referred

---

[293]EDF International S.A., Saur International S.A. and Leon Participaciones Argentinas S.A. *v* Argentina, Award, ICSID Case No. ARB/03/23 (11 June 2012) [417].

[294]EDF International S.A., Saur International S.A. and Leon Participaciones Argentinas S.A. *v* Argentina, Award, ICSID Case No. ARB/03/23 (11 June 2012) [1110-2].

[295]Hesham Talaat M. Al-Warraq *v* Indonesia (UNCITRAL), Final Award (15 December 2014) [424]. Cf. Agreement on Promotion, Protection and Guarantee of Investments among Member States of the Organisation of the Islamic Conference (adopted 5 June 1981, entered into force 23 September 1986) art. 8 (MFN).

[296]Hesham Talaat M. Al-Warraq *v* Indonesia (UNCITRAL), Final Award (15 December 2014) [630].

[297]CC/Devas (Mauritius) Ltd., Devas Employees Mauritius Private Ltd. and Telcom Devas Mauritius Ltd. *v* India (UNCITRAL), Award on Jurisdiction and Merits, PCA Case No. 2013-09 (25 July 2016) [486 and 488-9].

[298]CC/Devas (Mauritius) Ltd., Devas Employees Mauritius Private Ltd. and Telcom Devas Mauritius Ltd. *v* India (UNCITRAL), Award on Jurisdiction and Merits, PCA Case No. 2013-09 (25 July 2016) [490]. Cf. also para 487.

[299]CC/Devas (Mauritius) Ltd., Devas Employees Mauritius Private Ltd. and Telcom Devas Mauritius Ltd. *v* India (UNCITRAL), Award on Jurisdiction and Merits, PCA Case No. 2013-09 (25 July 2016) [496].

[300]CC/Devas (Mauritius) Ltd., Devas Employees Mauritius Private Ltd. and Telcom Devas Mauritius Ltd. *v* India (UNCITRAL), Award on Jurisdiction and Merits, PCA Case No. 2013-09 (25 July 2016) [500].

[301]For a detailed account of the measures in question see: Rusoro Mining Ltd. *v* Venezuela, Award, ICSID Case No. ARB(AF)/12/5 (22 August 2016) [546].

only to 'physical security' and was therefore irrelevant for the assessment of the measures challenged by the claimant.[302] In response to this argument, the investor submitted that, even if the arbitral tribunal were to accept that the FPS clause of the Canada-Venezuela BIT was limited to 'physical security', the treaty's MFN clause would allow Canadian investors to claim the same 'full protection and *legal* security' promised to Uruguayan investors under the Uruguay-Venezuela BIT.[303] The tribunal dismissed the FPS claims without digging deeper into the MFN argument.[304] They merely noted that 'even assuming *arguendo* the widest possible construction of the FPS standard, there can be no doubt that Venezuela never incurred in a breach'.[305]

In *Saint Gobain v Venezuela* (2016) the investor advanced an extensive interpretation of the FPS clause set forth in article 3(2) of the France-Venezuela BIT.[306] As in the *Rusoro* case, Venezuela stressed that the FPS standard 'related primarily, and perhaps exclusively, to the physical security of the investment'.[307] As an alternative to its broad interpretation of the applicable FPS provision, the investor relied on the MFN standard to invoke the guarantee of 'legal security' provided in article 4 of the Uruguay-Venezuela BIT.[308] The tribunal did not address the issue in detail. The arbitrators merely observed that the legal security claim had already been considered and dismissed in connection with other allegations (in particular, the FET claim).[309]

In *Ampal v Egypt* (2017) the tribunal was constituted under the Egypt-US BIT,[310] which uses the phrase 'protection and security' without further qualifying

---

[302]Rusoro Mining Ltd. *v* Venezuela, Award, ICSID Case No. ARB(AF)/12/5 (22 August 2016) [545].

[303]Rusoro Mining Ltd. *v* Venezuela, Award, ICSID Case No. ARB(AF)/12/5 (22 August 2016) [544].

[304]Rusoro Mining Ltd. *v* Venezuela, Award, ICSID Case No. ARB(AF)/12/5 (22 August 2016) [547].

[305]Rusoro Mining Ltd. *v* Venezuela, Award, ICSID Case No. ARB(AF)/12/5 (22 August 2016) [547].

[306]Saint-Gobain Performance Plastics Europe *v* Venezuela, Decision on Liability and the Principles of Quantum, ICSID Case No. ARB/12/13 (30 December 2016) [544-5].

[307]Saint-Gobain Performance Plastics Europe *v* Venezuela, Decision on Liability and the Principles of Quantum, ICSID Case No. ARB/12/13 (30 December 2016) [549].

[308]Saint-Gobain Performance Plastics Europe *v* Venezuela, Decision on Liability and the Principles of Quantum, ICSID Case No. ARB/12/13 (30 December 2016) [546].

[309]Saint-Gobain Performance Plastics Europe *v* Venezuela, Decision on Liability and the Principles of Quantum, ICSID Case No. ARB/12/13 (30 December 2016) [559-60].

[310]The claim had been originally raised by four American companies and a German national. The German investor invoked the protection of the Egypt-Germany BIT. However, the arbitral tribunal declared that it lacked jurisdiction *ratione personae* over the German investor. See: Ampal-American Israel Corp., Egi-Fund (08-10) Investors LLC, Egi-Series Investments LLC and BSS-EMG Investors LLC *v* Egypt, Decision on Jurisdiction, ICSID Case No. ARB/12/11 (1 February 2016) [1 and 209-27].

adjectives.[311] The investors invoked the FPS clause of the Egypt-UK BIT,[312] which employs the formula '*full* protection and security'.[313] According to the investors, the clause of the British BIT could be applied *via* the MFN clause of the Egypt-US BIT.[314] The MFN argument had no actual impact on the assessment of the case. The arbitrators' analysis focused on the FPS clause enshrined in the Egypt-US BIT.[315]

In *Teinver v Argentina* (2017) the claims were submitted under the Spain-Argentina BIT of 1991, which does not contain a typical FPS clause but merely provides that '[e]ach Party shall *protect* within its territory the investments made in accordance with its legislation by investors of the other Party'.[316] For that reason, the Spanish investor relied on the FPS clause of the Argentina-US BIT, arguing that said treaty provision was applicable on the basis of the MFN clause of the Argentina-Spain BIT.[317] The MFN clause was as follows:

> Article IV. Treatment. 1. Each Party shall guarantee in its territory *fair and equitable treatment* to investments made by investors of the other Party.
>
> 2. In all matters governed by this Agreement, *such treatment shall be no less favourable than that accorded by each Party to investments made in its territory by investors of a third country*."[318]

---

[311]Treaty between the United States of America and the Arab Republic of Egypt concerning the Reciprocal Encouragement and Protection of Investments (adopted 11 March 1986, entered into force 27 June 1992) art. II(4). See also Sect. 14.4.4.

[312]Ampal-American Israel Corp., Egi-Fund (08-10) Investors LLC, Egi-Series Investments LLC and BSS-EMG Investors LLC *v* Egypt, Decision on Liability and Heads of Loss, ICSID Case No. ARB/12/11 (21 February 2017) [68(iv)]. It should also be noted that the claimants had originally invoked, too, the FPS clause enshrined in article 4(1) of the Egypt-Germany BIT. See: Ampal-American Israel Corp., Egi-Fund (08-10) Investors LLC, Egi-Series Investments LLC and BSS-EMG Investors LLC *v* Egypt, Decision on Jurisdiction, ICSID Case No. ARB/12/11 (1 February 2016) [74(d)].

[313]Agreement between the Government of the United Kingdom and the Arab Republic of Egypt for the Promotion and Protection of Investments (adopted 11 June 1975, entered into force 24 February 1976) art. 2(2).

[314]Ampal-American Israel Corp., Egi-Fund (08-10) Investors LLC, Egi-Series Investments LLC and BSS-EMG Investors LLC *v* Egypt, Decision on Liability and Heads of Loss, ICSID Case No. ARB/12/11 (21 February 2017) [68(iv)].

[315]Ampal-American Israel Corp., Egi-Fund (08-10) Investors LLC, Egi-Series Investments LLC and BSS-EMG Investors LLC *v* Egypt, Decision on Liability and Heads of Loss, ICSID Case No. ARB/12/11 (21 February 2017) [240 *et seq.*].

[316]Emphasis added. Teinver S.A., Transportes de Cercanías S.A. and Autobuses Urbanos del Sur S.A. *v* Argentina, Award, ICSID Case No. ARB/09/1 (21 July 2017) [866 *et seq.*]. For the text of the treaty see: Acuerdo para la promoción y la protección recíproca de inversiones entre el Reino de España y la República Argentina (adopted 3 October 1991, entered into force 28 September 1992) art. III(1). This English translation of article III(1) of the BIT appears at paras 879 and 911 of the award.

[317]Teinver S.A., Transportes de Cercanías S.A. and Autobuses Urbanos del Sur S.A. *v* Argentina, Award, ICSID Case No. ARB/09/1 (21 July 2017) [866 *et seq.*].

[318]Emphasis added. Acuerdo para la promoción y la protección recíproca de inversiones entre el Reino de España y la República Argentina (adopted 3 October 1991, entered into force

The respondent argued that the phrase 'such treatment' in article IV(2) of the BIT provided a clear indication that the MFN clause referred only to the FET standard, and not to the FPS standard.[319] In addition, Argentina considered that the MFN clause was inapplicable with regard to the FPS standard because the Argentina-Spain BIT contained no FPS clause, properly so-called.[320] The arbitral tribunal considered both arguments in detail.[321] As regards to the first argument, the arbitrators stated:

> Article IV(2) of the Treaty [i.e., the Argentina-Spain BIT] expressly refers to "all matters governed by this Agreement", which the Tribunal has found to be unambiguously inclusive. This broad language is inconsistent with the notion that only fair and equitable treatment was intended to be the subject of the most favorable nation treatment. If such were the case, then the MFN Clause would apply only to more favorable FET provisions contained in other BITs. In the Tribunal's view, the plain or ordinary meaning of the language does not sustain this interpretation [. . .] Accordingly, the Tribunal finds that the MFN Clause contained in Article IV(2) of the Treaty is not restricted to fair and equitable treatment provisions and can be used in respect of all matters governed by the Treaty to incorporate more favorable provisions from other BITs concluded by Argentina.[322]

With regard to the second argument, the arbitral tribunal made the following finding:

> In the Tribunal's view, in interpreting the scope of the MFN Clause contained in Article IV (2) of the Treaty, meaning must be given to the critical words "[i]n all matters governed by this Agreement". According to Claimants, this language should be interpreted as referring generally to the protection of foreign investors. This interpretation is too broad and disregards the reference to all "matters" governed by the Treaty. In the Tribunal's view, the plain and ordinary meaning of this language is to refer to the various rights or forms of protection contained in the individual provisions of the Treaty [. . .] Article III(1) of the Treaty contains an obligation that each Party shall protect within its territory investments made by investors of the Party. As a result, protection of investments is a matter governed by the Treaty and, for the reasons set out above, the MFN Clause contained in Article IV(2) of the Treaty permits Claimants to invoke the full protection and security provision contained in Article II(2)(a) of the US-Argentina BIT.[323]

---

28 September 1992) arts. IV(1) and (2). For this English translation of the MFN clause see: Teinver S.A., Transportes de Cercanías S.A. and Autobuses Urbanos del Sur S.A. *v* Argentina, Award, ICSID Case No. ARB/09/1 (21 July 2017) [868].

[319]Teinver S.A., Transportes de Cercanías S.A. and Autobuses Urbanos del Sur S.A. *v* Argentina, Award, ICSID Case No. ARB/09/1 (21 July 2017) [877].

[320]Teinver S.A., Transportes de Cercanías S.A. and Autobuses Urbanos del Sur S.A. *v* Argentina, Award, ICSID Case No. ARB/09/1 (21 July 2017) [878]. See also Argentina's comments on the protection obligation under article III(1) of the BIT at para 879.

[321]Teinver S.A., Transportes de Cercanías S.A. and Autobuses Urbanos del Sur S.A. *v* Argentina, Award, ICSID Case No. ARB/09/1 (21 July 2017) [880 *et seq.*].

[322]Teinver S.A., Transportes de Cercanías S.A. and Autobuses Urbanos del Sur S.A. *v* Argentina, Award, ICSID Case No. ARB/09/1 (21 July 2017) [880-1].

[323]Teinver S.A., Transportes de Cercanías S.A. and Autobuses Urbanos del Sur S.A. *v* Argentina, Award, ICSID Case No. ARB/09/1 (21 July 2017) [884 and 896].

The arbitral tribunal however considered that, in respect of FPS, the difference between the treaties concluded with Spain and the U.S. was not 'significant'.[324] Notwithstanding this observation, the arbitrators held:

> [T]o the extent the standard of "full protection and security" may be more favorable, the Tribunal applies that standard as set out in Article II(2)(a) of the US-Argentina BIT.[325]

The cases presented throughout this section show that investors have often invoked MFN clauses to obtain a greater degree of security than that envisaged by the IIA concluded between their home state and the host state. In most cases, the MFN argument has met with rejection or skepticism.[326] Even in the few instances where the investor managed to successfully invoke the FPS provision of another IIA *via* an MFN clause, the argument had no recognizable impact on the tribunal's decision. Newly negotiated IIAs suggest that states are reacting against this use of MFN clauses. Examples may be found in treaties recently negotiated by the European Commission. For instance, CETA article 8.7 qualifies MFN with the following caveat:

> Substantive obligations in other international investment treaties and other trade agreements do not in themselves constitute "treatment", and thus cannot give rise to a breach of this Article [MFN], absent measures adopted or maintained by a Party pursuant to those obligations.[327]

---

[324]Teinver S.A., Transportes de Cercanías S.A. and Autobuses Urbanos del Sur S.A. *v* Argentina, Award, ICSID Case No. ARB/09/1 (21 July 2017) [897].

[325]Teinver S.A., Transportes de Cercanías S.A. and Autobuses Urbanos del Sur S.A. *v* Argentina, Award, ICSID Case No. ARB/09/1 (21 July 2017) [897].

[326]Cf. also the respondent state's argument in *Italba Corp. v Uruguay* (2019): Italba Corporation *v* Uruguay, Award, ICSID Case No. ARB/16/9 (22 March 2019) [127] ("[t]he clear intention of the State Parties regarding the definition of this obligation [FPS clause referring to 'police protection'], which was a fundamental condition of their agreement to the BIT, cannot be annulled by importing a contrary definition in another treaty by mere operation of a most favored nation clause").

[327]Comprehensive Economic and Trade Agreement between Canada and the European Union (signed 30 October 2016, provisionally entered into force 21 September 2017) art. 8.7(4). Cf. also: European Union – Vietnam Investment Protection Agreement (negotiated draft; version of September 2018) art. 2.4(5).

15.7 'Full Protection and Security' and War Clauses

Investment treaties normally include clauses specifically addressing the risk of armed conflict.[328] These treaty provisions are commonly known as 'war clauses' or 'war and civil disturbance clauses'.[329] War clauses may be classified in two general categories: *simple war clauses* and *extended war clauses*.[330] Simple war clauses grant covered investors national treatment and most-favored-nation treatment as regards to compensation for losses resulting from armed conflict and similar factual circumstances.[331] A typical example of this kind of clauses would be article 9 of the ASEAN-China Investment Agreement, which reads as follows:

> Article 9. Compensation for losses. Investors of a Party whose investments in the territory of another Party suffer losses owing to war or other armed conflict, revolution, a state of emergency, revolt, insurrection or riot in the territory of the latter Party shall be accorded by the latter Party treatment, as regard restitution, indemnification, compensation or other

---

[328] See generally: Caline Mouawad and Sarah Vasani, 'Energy Disputes in Times of Civil Unrest: Transitional Governments and Foreign Investment Protections' in Arthur Rovine (ed), *Contemporary Issues in International Arbitration and Mediation* (Brill, Leiden/Boston 2015) 234, 248-9; Christoph Schreuer, 'The Protection of Investments in Armed Conflicts' in Freya Baetens (ed), *Investment Law within International Law* (Cambridge University Press, Cambridge 2013) 3, 3-20; Geneviève Bastid Burdeau, 'La clause de protection et sécurité pleine et entière' (2015) 119 (1) RGDIP 87, 93 *et seq.*; Jeswald Salacuse, *The Law of Investment Treaties* (Oxford University Press, Oxford 2015) 367-70; Petr Stejskal, 'War: Foreign Investments in Danger – Can International Humanitarian Law or Full Protection and Security Always Save It?' (2017) 8 CYIL 529, 529 *et seq.*

[329] For this terminology see: Christoph Schreuer, 'The Protection of Investments in Armed Conflicts' in Freya Baetens (ed), *Investment Law within International Law* (Cambridge University Press, Cambridge 2013) 3, 12 *et seq.* (using the phrase 'war clauses'); Sempra Energy International & Camuzzi International S.A. v Argentina, Opinion of José E. Álvarez, ICSID Cases No. ARB/02/16 and ARB/03/02 (12 September 2005) [75] (using the phrase 'war and civil disturbance clauses').

[330] For this classification of 'war clauses' see: Christoph Schreuer, 'The Protection of Investments in Armed Conflicts' in Freya Baetens (ed), *Investment Law within International Law* (Cambridge University Press, Cambridge 2013) 3, 12 *et seq.*; Petr Stejskal, 'War: Foreign Investments in Danger – Can International Humanitarian Law or Full Protection and Security Always Save It?' (2017) 8 CYIL 529, 532-3; Walid Ben Hamida, 'Investment Treaties and Democratic Transition: Does Investment Law Authorize Not to Honor Contracts Concluded with Undemocratic Regimes?' in Stephan Schill, Christian Tams and Rainer Hoffmann (eds), *International Investment Law and Development: Bridging the Gap* (Edward Elgar Publishers, Northampton MA 2015) 309, 310-1. It must be noted that most authors use the terms 'war clauses' and 'extended war clauses'. Schreuer describes the first group of clauses as war clauses 'in their simple form' (at p. 12). This chapter employs the phrase '*simple* war clauses' to avoid any confusion between the first and the second category.

[331] See generally: Christoph Schreuer, 'The Protection of Investments in Armed Conflicts' in Freya Baetens (ed), *Investment Law within International Law* (Cambridge University Press, Cambridge 2013) 3, 12-3.

settlement, no less favourable than that which the latter Party accords, in like circumstances, to investors of any third country or its own nationals, whichever is more favourable.[332]

Similar clauses appear in countless investment treaties,[333] and are a standard provision in the Model BITs of numerous states.[334] At the outset, these treaty clauses seem to have a potential for overlap with FPS. In its customary core, the FPS standard refers to the protection of aliens in circumstances that could well fall within the notion of 'armed conflict', such as severe civil disorders, revolutions, or acts of other states in the host state's territory.[335] In *L.E.S.I. and Astaldi v Algeria* (2008) an ICSID arbitral tribunal characterized the relationship between FPS clauses and war clauses as a general-to-particular relationship.[336] In this line of argument, the arbitrators stated that the war clause of the Algeria-Italy BIT constituted a *lex specialis* in respect of the treaty's FPS clause.[337] The implication was that war clauses are applicable to the exclusion of the more-general FPS standard.[338] In the tribunal's words:

Le Tribunal arbitral considère que les événements survenus sur le territoire de l'Etat de l'Algérie entrent, en raison de leur gravité et leur persistance, dans les prévisions d'1 article 4.5 de l'Accord bilatéral, visant les situations de conflit armé, d'état d'urgence national et de révolte. Il en conclut que l'Algérie n'état de faire bénéficier les Demanderesses que d'un traitement non moins favorable que celui accordé à ses propres nationaux ou personnes morales ou à ceux de la nation la plus favorisée en application des termes de l'Accord bilatéral [. . .] L'article 4.5 de l'Accord est donc applicable au cas d'espèce. Etant donné que cette disposition est une *lex specialis*, elle exclut toute application de l'article 4.1. de

---

[332] Agreement on Investment of the Framework Agreement on Comprehensive Economic Cooperation between the People's Republic of China and the Association of Southeast Asian Nations (adopted 15 August 2009, entered into force 1 January 2010) art. 9.

[333] For some representative examples see: Comprehensive Economic and Trade Agreement between Canada and the European Union (signed 30 October 2016, provisionally entered into force 21 September 2017) art. 8.11; Energy Charter Treaty (adopted 17 December 1994, entered into force 16 April 1998) art. 12(1); North American Free Trade Agreement (adopted 17 December 1992, entered into force 1 January 1994) art. 1105(2).

[334] Austrian Model BIT (2008) art. 8; Canadian Model BIT (2004) art. 12(1); French Model BIT (2006) art. 5(3); German Model BIT (2008) art. 4(3) and (4); Italian Model BIT (2003) art. IV; Korean Model BIT (2001) art. 4(1); Netherlands Model BIT (2004) art. 7; U.K. Model BIT (2008) art. 4(1); U.S. Model BIT (2012) art. 5(4). Some model agreements refer only to national treatment in this regard. For an indicative example see: Colombian Model BIT (2011) art. IX (available in Spanish only); Colombian Model BIT (2008) art. VII.

[335] Cf. Sect. 8.3. For a definition of 'armed conflict' see: ILC, 'Effects of Armed Conflicts on Treaties (A/66/10)' (2011) 2(2) *Yearbook of the International Law Commission* 173, 175 art. 2 (b) ("armed conflict means a situation in which there is resort to armed force between States or protracted resort to armed force between governmental authorities and organized armed groups").

[336] LESI S.p.A. and ASTALDI S.p.A. *v* Algeria, Sentence, ICSID Case No. ARB/05/3 (12 November 2008) [175 and 177].

[337] LESI S.p.A. and ASTALDI S.p.A. *v* Algeria, Sentence, ICSID Case No. ARB/05/3 (12 November 2008) [177].

[338] LESI S.p.A. and ASTALDI S.p.A. *v* Algeria, Sentence, ICSID Case No. ARB/05/3 (12 November 2008) [177].

l'Accord [protection et sécurité constantes]. Il s'ensuit que la protection que la Défenderesse doit assurer à l'investisseur doit être équivalente à celle garantie aux nationaux.[339]

This approach is misleading. In spite of their apparent resemblance, war clauses are quite different from FPS provisions. To begin with, the compensation obligation is not triggered by the risk of injuries to aliens as such, but by the host state's decision to compensate its own nationals or third-party nationals for such losses.[340] Borrowing the words of the arbitral tribunal in *El Paso v Argentina* (2011), '[a war clause] applies to measures adopted in response to a loss, not to measures that cause a loss'.[341]

War clauses do not impose a duty of due diligence in the prevention or redress of the injuries, but a non-discrimination obligation.[342] Some instruments are quite explicit in this regard. The Canada Model BIT of 2004, for example, requires

---

[339]LESI S.p.A. and ASTALDI S.p.A. *v* Algeria, Sentence, ICSID Case No. ARB/05/3 (12 November 2008) [177]. The tribunal's references to article 4(5) of the Algeria-Italy BIT should be read as references to article 4(6) of the BIT: Accordo tra il Governo della Repubblica Italiana ed il Governo della Repubblica Algerina Democratica e Popolare sulla promozione e protezione degli investimenti (adopted 15 May 1991, entered into force 26 November 1993) art. 4(6).

[340]Cf. Céline Lévesque and Andrew Newcombe, 'Canada' in Chester Brown (ed), *Commentaries on Selected Model Investment Treaties* (Oxford University Press, Oxford 2013) 53, 92. Cf. also: Jeswald Salacuse, *The Law of Investment Treaties* (Oxford University Press, Oxford 2015) 369.

[341]El Paso Energy International Co. v Argentina, Award, ICSID Case No. ARB/03/15 (31 October 2011) [559] (making particular reference to the war clause enshrined in article IV(3) of the Argentina-US BIT).

[342]There seems to be widespread agreement among scholars that the core obligation of war clauses is non-discrimination. See generally: Caline Mouawad and Sarah Vasani, 'Energy Disputes in Times of Civil Unrest: Transitional Governments and Foreign Investment Protections' in Arthur Rovine (ed), *Contemporary Issues in International Arbitration and Mediation* (Brill, Leiden/ Boston 2015) 234, 249; Christoph Schreuer, 'The Protection of Investments in Armed Conflicts' in Freya Baetens (ed), *Investment Law within International Law* (Cambridge University Press, Cambridge 2013) 3, 12; Jeswald Salacuse, *The Law of Investment Treaties* (Oxford University Press, Oxford 2015) 368. Numerous commentaries to specific treaties and model BITs have shared this interpretation. See: Andrea Bjorklund, 'NAFTA Chapter 11' in Chester Brown (ed), *Commentaries on Selected Model Investment Treaties* (Oxford University Press, Oxford 2013) 465, 483 (commenting on art. 1105(2) of NAFTA); August Reinisch, 'Austria' in Chester Brown (ed), *Commentaries on Selected Model Investment Treaties* (Oxford University Press, Oxford 2013) 15, 33 (commenting on article 8 of the Austrian Model BIT of 2008); José Antonio Rivas, 'Colombia' in Chester Brown (ed), *Commentaries on Selected Model Investment Treaties* (Oxford University Press, Oxford 2013) 183, 229 (commenting on art. VII of the Colombian Model BIT of 2008); Lee Caplan and Jeremy Sharpe, 'United States' in Chester Brown (ed), *Commentaries on Selected Model Investment Treaties* (Oxford University Press, Oxford 2013) 755, 786 (commenting on article 5.4 of the 2012 U.S. Model BIT); Michael Schmid, 'Switzerland' in Chester Brown (ed), *Commentaries on Selected Model Investment Treaties* (Oxford University Press, Oxford 2013) 651, 678 (commenting on art. 7 of the China-Switzerland BIT); Nico Schrijver and Vid Prislan, 'The Netherlands' in Chester Brown (ed), *Commentaries on Selected Model Investment Treaties* (Oxford University Press, Oxford 2013) 535, 578 (commenting on article 7 of the Dutch Model BIT of 2004); Thomas Roe and Matthew Happold, *Settlement of Investment Disputes under the Energy Charter Treaty* (Cambridge University Press, Cambridge 2011) 134 (commenting on article 12 of the ECT).

'non-discriminatory treatment with respect to measures [...] relating to losses [...] owing to armed conflict, civil strife or a natural disaster'.[343] In *Bernardus H. Funnekotter v Zimbabwe* (2009) the arbitrators explained that war clauses are nothing but 'a further guarantee of equal treatment with nationals of the Contracting Party or nationals of Third States'.[344]

As a corollary, war clauses do not impair the application of other treaty provisions, such as FPS, neither as *lex specialis* nor as exceptions. The non-discrimination obligation is *additional* to any other obligations under the treaty or applicable customary law. In *EDF v Argentina* (2012), for example, the arbitrators noted that that war clauses leave obligations emanating from the customary law of aliens 'untouched'.[345] In a legal opinion addressing the interpretation of article IV (3) of the Argentina-US BIT, José Álvarez provided a clear explanation of these provisions' true nature:

> This clause is what is commonly referred to as a "war and civil disturbance" clause. Article IV(3) does not authorize the parties to revoke or suspend the protection for foreign investment at any time; rather, it provides that a party must accord non-discriminatory treatment [...] [I]t merely confirms that a state continues to be obligated to afford foreign investors most-favored-nation and national treatment in respect of compensatory measures. Article IV(3) provides further assurance to foreign investors; it is not a further exception permitting derogations from the treaty. Thus, Article IV(3) will not provide a party a means for evading the obligations imposed under other sections of the BIT.[346]

This opinion reflects what seems to be the prevailing view on the subject.[347] The non-discrimination obligation imposed by war clauses is applicable regardless of

---

[343]Canadian Model BIT (2004) art. 12(1). For an additional, representative example see: North American Free Trade Agreement (adopted 17 December 1992, entered into force 1 January 1994) art. 1105(2).

[344]Bernardus Henricus Funnekotter *et al.* v Zimbabwe, Award, ICSID Case No. ARB/05/6 (22 April 2009) [104].

[345]EDF International S.A., Saur International S.A. and Leon Participaciones Argentinas S.A. v Argentina, Award, ICSID Case No. ARB/03/23 (11 June 2012) [1158-9].

[346]Sempra Energy International & Camuzzi International S.A. v Argentina, Opinion of José E. Álvarez, ICSID Cases No. ARB/02/16 and ARB/03/02 (12 September 2005) [75]. The tribunal agreed with this view. See: Sempra Energy International v Argentina, Award, ICSID Case No. ARB/02/16 (28 September 2007) [319-21] (stating at para 120 that the sole effect of the war clause 'is to provide a minimum treatment to foreign investments suffering losses in the host country by the simultaneous interplay of national and most favored nation treatment' and further noting that the clause applies to 'corrective or compensatory measures' only).

[347]For a representative example see: Impregilo S.p.A. v Argentina, Award, ICSID Case No. ARB/07/17 (21 June 2011) [339] (holding that '[a]rticle 4 [of the Argentina-Italy BIT] provides for no exception from the obligations of the State in whose territory an investment was made but merely gives the investor a right to national treatment and most-favored-nation treatment in respect of damages'). The Argentine Republic unsuccessfully challenged this finding in the subsequent annulment proceedings. See: Impregilo S.p.A. v Argentina, Decision on the Application for Annulment, ICSID Case No. ARB/07/17 (24 January 2014) [68-9] (argument of Argentina) and [150] (determination of the ad hoc Committee). Similar statements appear in the arbitral decisions rendered in several Argentinean cases: BG Group v Argentina (UNCITRAL), Final Award

whether an international wrongful act was committed in connection with the original injury. As observed by the arbitral tribunal in *Total v Argentina* (2010):

> [The war clause] is aimed at granting to the investments [...] an additional guarantee in respect of situations in which the host State, *even if not internationally obliged to do so*, has provided for compensation for the losses suffered due to certain events to its own nationals or investors of third States.[348]

Some authors have gone as far as to state that the 'main purpose' of war clauses is precisely to assure non-discriminatory treatment where the host state bears no responsibility for the harmful event.[349] This suggests that war clauses are particularly relevant where foreign investors have suffered losses due to armed conflict, but

---

(24 December 2007) [382-3] (characterizing this type of clauses as 'a specific expression of the national treatment and most favored nation standard'; the *BG* tribunal referred in this connection to art. 4 of the Argentina-UK BIT); CMS Gas Transmission Co. *v* Argentina, Award, ICSID Case No. ARB/01/8 (12 May 2005) [375] (stating, without particular reference to the FPS standard, that the 'compensation for losses' rule enshrined in article IV(3) of the Argentina-US BIT 'does not derogate from the Treaty rights but rather ensures that any measures directed at offsetting or minimizing losses will be applied in a non-discriminatory manner'); EDF International S.A., Saur International S.A. and Leon Participaciones Argentinas S.A. *v* Argentina, Award, ICSID Case No. ARB/03/23 (11 June 2012) [1157] (stating that article 5(3) of the Argentina-France BIT 'serves as a non-discrimination provision, not as a shield against host state liability for treaty violation'); El Paso Energy International Co. *v* Argentina, Award, ICSID Case No. ARB/03/15 (31 October 2011) [559] (concluding, in reference to art. IV(3) of the Argentina-US BIT, that '[t]he plain meaning of the provision is that the standards of treatment of the BIT – national treatment and most favored nation treatment – have to be applied when a State tries to mitigate the consequences of war or another emergency'). See also the parties' arguments in *Continental Casualty v Argentina* (2008): Continental Casualty Co. *v* Argentina, Award, ICSID Case No. ARB/03/9 (5 September 2008) [58] (argument of Argentina) [75] (argument of the investor). On the assessment of war clauses in investment disputes related to the Argentinian economic crisis of 2001 see: Jeswald Salacuse, *The Law of Investment Treaties* (Oxford University Press, Oxford 2015) 369 (citing these and numerous other Argentinian cases in this connection); Caline Mouawad and Sarah Vasani, 'Energy Disputes in Times of Civil Unrest: Transitional Governments and Foreign Investment Protections' in Arthur Rovine (ed), *Contemporary Issues in International Arbitration and Mediation* (Brill, Leiden/Boston 2015) 234, 249 (referring to the *CMS* and *BG* awards). For an example unrelated to the Argentinian crisis see: Bernardus Henricus Funnekotter et al. *v* Zimbabwe, Award, ICSID Case No. ARB/05/6 (22 April 2009) [104] (stating that the war clause enshrined in article 7 of the Netherlands-Zimbabwe BIT 'does not exonerate Contracting Parties from their obligation under Article 6 [expropriation] in case of national emergency or riot').

[348]Emphasis added. Total S.A. *v* Argentina, Decision on Liability, ICSID Case No. ARB/04/1 (27 December 2010) [230] (particularly referring to art. 5(3) of the Argentina-France BIT).

[349]See: Michael Schmid, 'Switzerland' in Chester Brown (ed), *Commentaries on Selected Model Investment Treaties* (Oxford University Press, Oxford 2013) 651, 678 (commenting on art. 7 of the China-Switzerland BIT). For a similar view see: Walid Ben Hamida, 'Investment Treaties and Democratic Transition: Does Investment Law Authorize Not to Honor Contracts Concluded with Undemocratic Regimes?' in Stephan Schill, Christian Tams and Rainer Hoffmann (eds), *International Investment Law and Development: Bridging the Gap* (Edward Elgar Publishers, Northampton MA 2015) 309, 310-1. On this function of war clauses see also: Rudolf Dolzer and Yun-i Kim, 'Germany' in Chester Brown (ed), *Commentaries on Selected Model Investment Treaties* (Oxford University Press, Oxford 2013) 289, 311.

the host state has not engaged in an internationally wrongful want of diligence in respect of the prevention or redress of the injuries.[350]

As opposed to *simple* war clauses, *extended* war clauses go beyond a mere non-discrimination obligation and provide precise rules about requisition and destruction of property.[351] A typical example of this second group of clauses would be article 4(2) of the UK Model BIT of 2008, which reads as follows:

> Without prejudice to paragraph (1) of this Article [non-discrimination as regards to compensation for losses in the event of armed conflict], nationals or companies of one Contracting Party who in any of the situations referred to in that paragraph suffer losses in the territory of the other Contracting Party resulting from: (a) requisitioning of their property by its forces or authorities; or (b) destruction of their property by its forces or authorities, which was not caused in combat action or was not required by the necessity of the situation, shall be accorded restitution or adequate compensation. Resulting payments shall be freely transferable.[352]

To-date, only a few arbitral decisions have considered the interplay between extended war clauses and the FPS standard.[353] A representative example would be the award rendered in *AMT v Zaire* (1997). In that case, the arbitral tribunal described the extended war clause enshrined in article IV(2)(b) of the US-Zaire BIT as a 'reinforcement' of the treaty's FPS provision:[354]

> [The extended war clause serves] to reinforce further the engagement of the responsibility of the State of Zaire for ensuring the protection and security of the investment made by AMT on the Zairian territory in accordance with Article II paragraph 4 of the BIT [FPS], as well as

---

[350]Cf. Nico Schrijver and Vid Prislan, 'The Netherlands' in Chester Brown (ed), *Commentaries on Selected Model Investment Treaties* (Oxford University Press, Oxford 2013) 535, 578 (noting that the war clause set forth in article 7 of the Dutch Model BIT of 2004 takes into consideration that, in the absence of a lack of diligence in breach of FPS, losses caused by armed conflict do not normally give rise to state responsibility).

[351]For the notion of 'extended war clauses' see: Caline Mouawad and Sarah Vasani, 'Energy Disputes in Times of Civil Unrest: Transitional Governments and Foreign Investment Protections' in Arthur Rovine (ed), *Contemporary Issues in International Arbitration and Mediation* (Brill, Leiden/Boston 2015) 234, 249 n. 51; Christoph Schreuer, 'The Protection of Investments in Armed Conflicts' in Freya Baetens (ed), *Investment Law within International Law* (Cambridge University Press, Cambridge 2013) 3, 13 *et seq*.

[352]U.K. Model BIT (2008) art. 4(2).

[353]For an overview of investment cases addressing extended war clauses see: Christoph Schreuer, 'The Protection of Investments in Armed Conflicts' in Freya Baetens (ed), *Investment Law within International Law* (Cambridge University Press, Cambridge 2013) 3, 13 *et seq*. (particularly referring to the *AAPL v Sri Lanka* and *AMT v Zaire* awards).

[354]American Manufacturing & Trading Inc. *v* Zaire, Award, ICSID Case No. ARB 93/1 (21 February 1997) [6.12 *et seq*.]. Article IV(2) of the US-Zaire BIT reads as follows: "In the event that such damages [i.e. damages caused by armed conflict or war] result from: (a) a requisitioning of property by the other Party's forces or authorities, or (b) destruction of property by the other Party's forces or authorities which was not caused in combat action, the national or company shall be accorded restitution or compensation in accordance with Article III [Expropriation]." Treaty between the United States of America and the Republic of Zaire concerning the Reciprocal Encouragement and Protection of Investment (adopted 3 August 1984, entered into force 28 July 1989) art. IV(2).

the obligation to prevent the occurrence of any act of violence on its territory. It is the duty or obligation to prevent the occurrence of a given event that is at issue.[355]

The arbitrators specifically held that the extended war clause confirmed that the host state's responsibility could attach in cases involving injuries inflicted by third parties within Zairian jurisdiction.[356] The *AMT* tribunal was additionally confronted with the question of whether the extended war clause could provide an additional cause of action, different from the FPS standard and other treaty obligations.[357] The arbitrators found, however, that this latter question had no 'usefulness' for the resolution of the dispute.[358]

The *AMT* award leaves the impression that extended war clauses are inescapably entangled with the FPS standard. This proposition is inaccurate. Extended war clauses are neither an element nor a 'reinforcement' of the FPS standard. A close look into the wording of an extended war clause suffices to confirm that these treaty provisions are more closely related to expropriation clauses than to FPS. A scholar has observed that these clauses treat the requisition or unjustified destruction of foreign property 'in analogy to expropriation'.[359] Thus, by contrast to FPS, 'extended war clauses' normally refer to risks that originate in the actions of the host state and which could hence be said to be of a public nature.[360]

The *AAPL v Sri Lanka* award of 1990 confirms this conclusion. The *AAPL* tribunal analyzed the wording of article 4(2) of the UK-Sri Lanka BIT, which is similar to the extended war clause of the 2008 UK Model BIT (quoted above).[361] In this connection, the arbitrators explained that investors relying on a clause of this kind must prove, among others, 'that the *governmental forces and not the rebels* caused the destruction'.[362] In other words, even when the case pertains to the

---

[355]American Manufacturing & Trading Inc. *v* Zaire, Award, ICSID Case No. ARB 93/1 (21 February 1997) [6.14].

[356]American Manufacturing & Trading Inc. *v* Zaire, Award, ICSID Case No. ARB 93/1 (21 February 1997) [6.12-6.14].

[357]American Manufacturing & Trading Inc. *v* Zaire, Award, ICSID Case No. ARB 93/1 (21 February 1997) [6.15-6.19].

[358]American Manufacturing & Trading Inc. *v* Zaire, Award, ICSID Case No. ARB 93/1 (21 February 1997) [6.19].

[359]Christoph Schreuer, 'The Protection of Investments in Armed Conflicts' in Freya Baetens (ed), *Investment Law within International Law* (Cambridge University Press, Cambridge 2013) 3, 13. Cf. also: August Reinisch, 'Austria' in Chester Brown (ed), *Commentaries on Selected Model Investment Treaties* (Oxford University Press, Oxford 2013) 15, 33 (particularly referring to art. 8 of the Austrian Model BIT of 2008).

[360]For the characterization of the risk of expropriation as a public risk see Sect. 15.3.

[361]Asian Agricultural Products *v* Sri Lanka, Final Award, ICSID Case No. ARB/87/3 (17 June 1990) [54-5 and 57-8]. On the evolution of British war clauses see: Chester Brown and Audley Sheppard, 'United Kingdom' in Chester Brown (ed), *Commentaries on Selected Model Investment Treaties* (Oxford University Press, Oxford 2013) 697, 731-3.

[362]Emphasis added. Asian Agricultural Products *v* Sri Lanka, Final Award, ICSID Case No. ARB/87/3 (17 June 1990) [58].

destruction of property, extended war clauses refer to the *actions of state agents* and not to failures to prevent *third party violence*.[363]

Nonetheless, a partial overlap between extended war clauses and the FPS standard cannot be ruled out as a matter of principle. The reason is that FPS requires the host state to exercise due diligence in the mitigation of collateral damages caused by state action against external sources of risk (e.g. insurgents).[364] The existence and extent of an overlap cannot be determined in the abstract. The issue depends on the scope of the war clause applicable in the each particular case. Attention should be drawn, for example, to war clauses that exclude 'combat action' from their scope of application (such as article 4(2) of the UK Model BIT).[365]

In spite of this potential for partial overlap, extended war clauses should have no effect on scope and content of the FPS standard. The *AAPL* case provides, once again, a good example in this regard. In the arbitral proceedings, the investor argued that a treaty containing a war clause granted less favorable treatment than a treaty containing no such clause.[366] Particularly, *AAPL* contended that, in the absence of a war clause, the FPS standard would impose strict liability.[367] The investor underscored that the Sri Lanka-Switzerland BIT also provided for FPS, but did not include a war clause.[368] For that reason, *AAPL* stressed that this more-favorable standard was applicable via the MFN clause of the Sri Lanka-UK BIT.[369] The arbitrators found the investor's argument unsound:

> By invoking the absence in the Sri Lanka/Switzerland Treaty of a text similar to Article 4 providing for a "war clause" or "civil disturbance" exception form (sic) the full protection and security standard, the Claimant based its argument on two implicit assumptions:
>
> (i) – that the Sri Lanka/Switzerland BIT provides equally for a "strict liability" standard of protection in case of losses suffered due to property destruction; and

---

[363] See: Christoph Schreuer, 'The Protection of Investments in Armed Conflicts' in Freya Baetens (ed), *Investment Law within International Law* (Cambridge University Press, Cambridge 2013) 3, 16 (relying in this connection on the *AAPL* and *AMT* cases).

[364] See Sect. 8.3.3.1.

[365] U.K. Model BIT (2008) art. 4(2). Cf. also the application of art. IV(2)(b) of the US-Zaire BIT in *AMT v Zaire* (1997): American Manufacturing & Trading Inc. *v* Zaire, Award, ICSID Case No. ARB 93/1 (21 February 1997) [6.15 *et seq.*] (referring to art. IV of the US-Zaire BIT, but noting at para 6.16 that 'the damages and injuries sustained by AMT were not caused in combat actions').

[366] Asian Agricultural Products *v* Sri Lanka, Final Award, ICSID Case No. ARB/87/3 (17 June 1990) [26(D) and 54].

[367] Asian Agricultural Products *v* Sri Lanka, Final Award, ICSID Case No. ARB/87/3 (17 June 1990) [26(D) and 54].

[368] Asian Agricultural Products *v* Sri Lanka, Final Award, ICSID Case No. ARB/87/3 (17 June 1990) [26(D) and 54]; Agreement between the Government of the Swiss Confederation and the Government of the Democratic Socialist Republic of Sri Lanka for the Reciprocal Promotion and Protection of Investments (adopted 23 September 1981, entered into force 12 February 1982) art. 3 (2).

[369] Asian Agricultural Products *v* Sri Lanka, Final Award, ICSID Case No. ARB/87/3 (17 June 1990) [26(D) and 54].

(ii) – that the rules of general international law are totally excluded and replaced exclusively by the Treaty's "strict liability" standard.

Both assumptions are unfounded, as the Tribunal has no reasons to believe that the Sri Lanka/Switzerland Treaty adopted a "strict liability" standard, and the Tribunal is convinced that, in the absence of a specific rule provided for in the Treaty itself as *lex specialis*, the general international law rules have to assume their role as *lex generalis*.[370]

In light of the foregoing, the *AAPL* tribunal concluded that 'it is not proven that the Sri Lanka/Switzerland Treaty contains rules more favourable than those provided for under the Sri Lanka/UK treaty'.[371] This finding is correct. There is no reason why the existence or absence of a war clause should turn the protection obligation into a strict liability. While both war clauses and FPS clauses are concerned with armed conflict and civil strife, they have a different and autonomous normative content.

---

[370] Asian Agricultural Products *v* Sri Lanka, Final Award, ICSID Case No. ARB/87/3 (17 June 1990) [54].

[371] Asian Agricultural Products *v* Sri Lanka, Final Award, ICSID Case No. ARB/87/3 (17 June 1990) [54].

Chapter 16
Conclusion: The Night Watchman State

The introduction to this monograph recalled a long forgotten unrest that took place in a marketplace of Panama City on April 15th, 1856. By refusing to pay a street peddler for a watermelon slice, an American citizen brought upon himself and his countrymen the fury of the local population, which by the end of the day had left an upsetting trail of blood and destruction throughout the city.[1] The killing of American nationals and the burning down of their properties during this day resulted in a tense diplomatic controversy between the Republic of New Granada and the United States.[2] The legal guise of the watermelon crisis was a lively dispute about New Granada's obligation to ensure the safety of U.S. citizens within its territory.[3] This security obligation is nowadays commonly designated with a firmly etched term of art: *full protection and security—FPS*.

The watermelon riot was but one of many instances in which this security obligation took center stage in the arena of international politics. The significance of the obligation has not diminished with the passage of time. Quite the contrary, in the specific area of international investment law, the FPS standard has been one of frequent application. Notwithstanding its practical importance, FPS has been a rather neglected topic in contemporary investment law scholarship. Perhaps as a corollary of this neglect, the application of the standard in investment cases is signalized by inconsistency and ambiguity. For that very same reason, the FPS standard has the fascinating feature of being simultaneously classic and unexplored, fundamental and contested. This monograph represents an effort to explore the FPS standard both in customary international law and in investment treaty provisions.

---

[1]Chapter 1 provides a more detailed account of the facts as well as complete references to the relevant sources.

[2]For a compilation of the relevant documents see: Luis Santamaría (ed), *Final Diplomatic Controversy relating to the Occurrences that Took Place at Panama on the 15th of April, 1856* (Mail Office, Liverpool 1857). See also Introduction, pp. 1–4.

[3]Cf. Introduction, pp. 1–4.

© Springer Nature Switzerland AG 2019
S. Mantilla Blanco, *Full Protection and Security in International Investment Law*,
European Yearbook of International Economic Law 8,
https://doi.org/10.1007/978-3-030-24838-3_16

The core of the argument is that, as the watermelon incident already suggests, the customary FPS standard is concerned with the effective exercise of the monopoly of force against those who subvert, or threaten to subvert, peace and tranquility.[4] The FPS standard requires the host state to fulfill, to the benefit of foreign nationals, the most basic function of the modern state: the maintenance of public order and security. This function resembles the Hobbesian idea of a security state.[5] The FPS standard is not concerned with protection *from* the state, but with protection *through* the state.[6] FPS requires the host state to be vigilant of the observance of the *neminem laedere* principle (i.e. 'harm no one') in respect of foreign nationals, and to duly consider the interests of aliens when taking action against external threats.[7] The closest one can get to a vivid figure of the standard is hence to think of the host state as the 'night watchman state', which Ferdinand Lasalle satirically portrayed in his *Working Man's Programme (Arbeiterprogramm)* of 1863, in the following terms:

> The Bourgeoisie understands the moral purpose of the state as follows: [it] consists solely and only in giving protection to the personal freedom and property of the individual. This is the idea of a night watchman, gentlemen. [And it is] the idea of a night watchman because, under this conception, the state can only be visualized as a night watchman, whose entire function consists in the prevention of theft and burglary. If the Bourgeoisie were consistent, it would have to concede that, under its own understanding [of the state], the state would be unnecessary in the absence of thieves and bandits.[8]

It might seem naïve to think that Lasalle's political satire can actually provide an image of a complex institution of the law of aliens, such as FPS. But most fundamentals of the customary notion of FPS are actually present in Lasalle's words. Pursuant to the customary protection obligation, the host state must wear the cloak of a night watchman and be prepared to wipe a truncheon against those who disturb peace, as well as to do justice whenever tranquility is broken.[9]

---

[4]For an arbitral tribunal linking the FPS standard to the idea of the 'monopoly' of force see: Eastern Sugar B.V. *v* Czech Republic, Partial Award, SCC Case No. 088/2004 (27 March 2007) [203–4].

[5]For an analysis of the Hobbesian security state as a stage in the development of the modern state see: Josef Isensee, *Das Grundrecht auf Sicherheit. Zu den Schutzpflichten des freiheitlichen Verfassungsstaates* (Walter de Gruyter, Berlin 1983) 17.

[6]See Sect. 8.3. Cf. also Sect. 15.3.

[7]See particularly Sect. 8.3.

[8]Author's translation. The original German text reads as follows: "[Entsprechend diesem Unterschiede], faßt die Bourgeoisie den sittlichen Staatszweck so auf: er bestehe ausschließend und allein darin, die persönliche Freiheit des einzelnen und sein Eigentum zu schützen. Dies ist eine Nachtwächteridee, meine Herren, eine Nachtwächteridee deshalb, weil sie sich den Staat selbst nur unter dem Bilde eines Nachtwächters denken kann, dessen ganzen Funktion darin besteht, Raub und Einbruch zu verhüten [...] Wollte die Bourgeoisie konsequent ihr letztes Wort aussprechen, so müßte sie gestehen, daß nach diesen ihren Gedanken, wenn es keine Räuber und Diebe gebe, der Staat ganz überflüssig sei". Ferdinand Lasalle, *Arbeiterprogramm. Ueber den besonderen Zusammenhang der gegenwärtigen Geschichtsperiode mit der Idee des Arbeiterstandes* (Meyer & Zeller, Zürich 1863) 39.

[9]On the preventive and repressive functional dimensions of the FPS standard see Chap. 10.

More precisely, FPS requires states to diligently undertake positive action in the prevention and redress of physical and nonphysical injuries to the acquired values of foreign citizens, provided such impairments arise out of an external threat or are incidental to the host state's reaction against an external threat (e.g. collateral damages).[10] The host state's responsibility is engaged, not upon the mere occurrence of harm, but on account of a failure to exercise due diligence which produces an injury.[11] The law further recognizes that our night watchman has limited resources.[12] He is neither ubiquitous nor almighty. The diligence he is customarily pledged to display is a minimum and not a maximum.[13]

Security is only one of many functions of modern states.[14] And so, too, FPS is only one of many obligations of states in international investment law. The understanding of the FPS standard as a reference to the 'security state' does not justify wrongdoings that cannot be properly styled as wants of protection, leaving foreign investors to their fate even in the most extreme scenarios of despotism and arbitrariness.[15] In these cases, *other* standards of investment protection come into play, such as the standard of 'fair and equitable treatment'—FET, which is often characterized as an expression of the 'rule of law'.[16] As far as the FPS clauses are interpreted in the light of the customary core of the standard,[17] there will be little space for overlaps with other standards.[18] FPS and other standards complement each other,[19] just as the different functions of the state are coexistent and coherent.[20]

---

[10]See Chaps. 8 and 9.

[11]See Chap. 11.

[12]See Sect. 13.3.3.3.

[13]See Sects. 13.3.2 and 13.3.3.

[14]Cf. Josef Isensee, *Das Grundrecht auf Sicherheit. Zu den Schutzpflichten des freiheitlichen Verfassungsstaates* (Walter de Gruyter, Berlin 1983) 17.

[15]Cf. Sect. 8.3.1.

[16]For this characterization of the FET standard see: Stephan Schill, 'Fair and Equitable Treatment, the Rule of Law and Comparative Public Law' in Stephan Schill (ed), *International Investment Law and Comparative Public Law* (Oxford University Press, New York 2010) 151, 155. See also: Marc Jacob and Stephan Schill, 'Fair and equitable treatment: Content, Practice, Method' in Marc Bungenberg, Jörn Griebel, Stephan Hobe and August Reinisch (eds), International Investment Law (Nomos, Baden-Baden 2015) 700, 760–3. These views are discussed in Sect. 15.2.3.

[17]On the interpretation of FPS clauses see Chap. 14.

[18]Cf. Chap. 15.

[19]See Chap. 15.

[20]Cf. Josef Isensee, *Das Grundrecht auf Sicherheit. Zu den Schutzpflichten des freiheitlichen Verfassungsstaates* (Walter de Gruyter, Berlin 1983) 17.

Table of Legal Instruments

Treaties

Friendship, Commerce and Navigation Treaties

- Additional and Explanatory Convention to the Treaty of Peace, Amity, Commerce and Navigation concluded in the City of Santiago on the 16th Day of May of 1832 between the United States of America and the Republic of Chile (adopted 1 September 1833, entered into force 29 April 1834) Hunter Miller (ed), *Treaties and Other International Acts of the United States of America* (Volume 3: Government Printing Office, Washington 1971) 695-99.
- Convention between the United States and the Republic of Panama for the Construction of a Ship Canal to Connect the Waters of the Atlantic and Pacific Oceans (adopted 18 November 1903, entered into force 26 February 1904) *Papers relating to the Foreign Relations of the United States with the Annual Message of the President* (Government Printing Office, Washington 1905) 543-52.
- Convention between the United States of America and the Republic of New Granada (adopted 10 September 1857, entered into force 5 November 1860) Charles Bevans (ed), *Treaties and Other International Agreements of the United States of America 1776—1949* (Volume 6: U.S. Department of State Publication, Washington 1971) 888-92.
- Convention of Establishment between the United States of America and France (adopted 25 November 1959, entered into force 21 December 1960) 401 UNTS 75.
- Freundschafts-, Handels- und Schifffahrtsvertrag zwischen dem Deutschen Reich und dem Freistaat Columbien (adopted 23 July 1892, entered into force 12 April 1894) Felik Stoerk (ed), *Martens Nouveau Recueil Général des Traités, 2me Série* (Volume 19: Librairie Dietrich, Göttingen 1895) 831-48.

© Springer Nature Switzerland AG 2019
S. Mantilla Blanco, *Full Protection and Security in International Investment Law*,
European Yearbook of International Economic Law 8,
https://doi.org/10.1007/978-3-030-24838-3

- Freundschafts-, Handels- und Schifffahrtsvertrag zwischen dem Deutschen Reich und dem Königreich der Hawaiischen Inseln (adopted 19 September 1879) Friedrich Heinrich Geffcken (ed) *Martens Recueil Manuel et Pratique de Traités et Conventions, 2me Série* (Volume 3: F. A. Brockhaus, Leipzig 1888) 6-19.
- Freundschafts-, Handels- und Schifffahrtsvertrag zwischen dem Deutschen Reich und Samoa (adopted 24 January 1879) Friedrich Heinrich Geffcken (ed) *Martens Recueil Manuel et Pratique de Traités et Conventions, 2me Série* (Volume 3: F. A. Brockhaus, Leipzig 1888) 1-6.
- Treaty of Amity and Commerce between the United States of America and the Kingdom of France (adopted 6 February 1778, entered into force 17 July 1778) Hunter Miller (ed), *Treaties and Other International Acts of the United States of America* (Volume 2: Government Printing Office, Washington 1931) 3-47.
- Treaty of Amity and Commerce between the United States of America and the Kingdom of Prussia (adopted 10 September 1785, entered into force 17 May 1786) Hunter Miller (ed), *Treaties and Other International Acts of the United States of America* (Volume 2: Government Printing Office, Washington 1931) 162-84.
- Treaty of Amity and Commerce between the United States of America and the Netherlands (adopted 8 October 1782, entered into force 23 June 1783) Hunter Miller (ed), *Treaties and Other International Acts of the United States of America* (Volume 2: Government Printing Office, Washington 1931) 59-95.
- Treaty of Amity, Commerce, and Navigation between the United States and Great Britain (adopted 19 November 1794, entered into force 28 October 1795) Hunter Miller (ed), *Treaties and Other International Acts of the United States of America* (Volume 2: Government Printing Office, Washington 1931) 245-74.
- Treaty of Friendship and Commerce between the United States of America and Pakistan (adopted 12 November 1959, entered into force 12 February 1961) 404 UNTS 259.
- Treaty of Friendship and Commerce, and for the Suppression of the Slave Trade, between Great Britain and Borneo (adopted 27 May 1847) 34 St. Pap. 14-7.
- Treaty of Friendship, Commerce and Consular Rights between the United States of America and the German Empire (adopted 8 December 1923, entered into force 14 October 1925) Charles Bevans (ed), *Treaties and Other International Agreements of the United States of America 1776—1949* (Volume 8: U.S. Department of State Publication, Washington 1971) 153-70.
- Treaty of Friendship, Commerce and Consular Rights between the United States of America and the Kingdom of Norway (adopted 5 June 1928, entered into force 13 September 1932) Charles Bevans (ed), *Treaties and Other International Agreements of the United States of America 1776—1949* (Volume 10: U.S. Department of State Publication, Washington 1972) 481-97.
- Treaty of Friendship, Commerce and Navigation between the Kingdom of the Netherlands and the United States of America (adopted 27 March 1956, entered into force 5 December 1957) 285 UNTS 231.

- Treaty of Friendship, Commerce and Navigation between the United States of America and Ireland (adopted 21 January 1950, entered into force 14 September 1950) 206 UNTS 269.
- Treaty of Friendship, Commerce and Navigation between the United States of America and the Italian Republic (adopted 2 February 1948, entered into force 26 July 1949) Charles Bevans (ed), *Treaties and Other International Agreements of the United States of America 1776—1949* (Volume 9: U.S. Department of State Publication, Washington 1971) 261-88.
- Treaty of Friendship, Commerce and Navigation between the United States of America and the Republic of Liberia (adopted 8 August 1938, entered into force 21 November 1939) Charles Bevans (ed), *Treaties and Other International Agreements of the United States of America 1776—1949* (Volume 9: U.S. Department of State Publication, Washington 1972) 595-606.
- Treaty of Friendship, Commerce and Navigation between the United States of America and Israel (adopted 23 August 1951, entered into force 3 April 1954) 219 UNTS 237.
- Treaty of Friendship, Commerce and Navigation between the United States of America and the Kingdom of Denmark (adopted 1 October 1951, entered into force 30 July 1961) 421 UNTS 105.
- Treaty of Friendship, Commerce and Navigation between the United States of America and Japan (adopted 2 April 1953, entered into force 30 October 1953) 206 UNTS 191.
- Treaty of Friendship, Commerce and Navigation between the United States of America and the Republic of Korea (adopted 28 November 1956, entered into force 7 November 1957) 302 UNTS 281.
- Treaty of Friendship, Commerce and Navigation between the United States of America and the Federal Republic of Germany (adopted 29 October 1954, entered into force 14 July 1956) 273 UNTS 3.
- Treaty of Friendship, Establishment and Navigation between the United States of America and Belgium (adopted 21 February 1961, entered into force 3 October 1963) 480 UNTS 150.
- Treaty of Friendship, Establishment and Navigation between the United States of America and Luxembourg (adopted 23 February 1962, entered into force 28 March 1963) 474 UNTS 3.
- Treaty of Peace, Amity, Navigation, and Commerce between the United States of America and the Republic of Chile (adopted 16 May 1832, entered into force 29 April 1834) Hunter Miller (ed), *Treaties and Other International Acts of the United States of America* (Volume 3: Government Printing Office, Washington 1971) 671-95.
- Treaty of Peace, Amity, Navigation, and Commerce between the United States of America and the Republic of New Granada (adopted 12 December 1846, entered into force 18 February 1848) Charles Bevans (ed), *Treaties and Other International Agreements of the United States of America 1776—1949* (Volume 6: U.S. Department of State Publication, Washington 1971) 868-81.

• Treaty of Peace, Friendship, Commerce and Navigation, between the United States of America and Borneo (adopted 23 June 1850, entered into force 11 July 1853) Charles Bevans (ed), *Treaties and Other International Agreements of the United States of America 1776—1949* (Volume 5: U.S. Department of State Publication, Washington 1971) 1080-2.

Claims Conventions

• Agreement for Settlement of Certain Claims of Citizens of the United States on Account of Wrongs and Injuries Committed by Authorities of Spain in the Island of Cuba (concluded 11-12 February 1871) John Haswell (ed), *Treaties and Conventions Concluded Between the United States of America and Other Powers since July 4, 1776* (U.S. Department of State, Washington 1889) 1025-7.
• Claims Convention between France and Mexico (adopted 2 August 1930, entered into force 6 February 1931) V RIAA 318-21.
• Claims Convention between France and Mexico (adopted 25 September 1924, entered into force 29 December 1924) V RIAA 313-6.
• Claims Convention between Great Britain and Mexico (adopted 19 November 1926, entered into force 8 March 1928) V RIAA 7-10.
• Claims Convention concerning the Venezuela Steam Transportation Company (adopted 19 January 1892, entered into force 28 July 1894) Charles Bevans (ed), *Treaties and Other International Agreements of the United States of America 1776—1949* (Volume 12: U.S. Department of State Publication, Washington 1971) 1098-100.
• Convention for the Adjustment of Claims of Citizens of the United States against Mexico (adopted 11 April 1839, entered into force 7 April 1840) John Haswell (ed), *Treaties and Conventions Concluded Between the United States of America and Other Powers since July 4, 1776* (U.S. Department of State, Washington 1889) 676-9.
• Convention for the Settlement of Claims against Venezuela (adopted 25 April 1866, entered into force 17 April 1867) John Haswell (ed), *Treaties and Conventions Concluded Between the United States of America and Other Powers since July 4, 1776* (U.S. Department of State, Washington 1889) 1140-3.
• Convention for the Settlement of Claims between Great Britain and the United States (concluded 8 February 1853, entered into force 26 July 1853) John Haswell (ed), *Treaties and Conventions Concluded Between the United States of America and Other Powers since July 4, 1776* (U.S. Department of State, Washington 1889) 445-8.
• Convention for the Settlement of Claims between Mexico and the United States (concluded 4 July 1868, entered into force 1 February 1869) Charles Bevans (ed), *Treaties and Other International Agreements of the United States of America 1776—1949* (Volume 9: U.S. Department of State Publication, Washington 1971) 826-30.

- Convention for the Settlement of Claims between the United States and Peru (adopted 4 December 1868, entered into force 4 June 1869) John Haswell (ed), *Treaties and Conventions Concluded Between the United States of America and Other Powers since July 4, 1776* (U.S. Department of State, Washington 1889) 872-5.
- Convention for the Settlement of Claims between the United States and Peru (adopted 12 January 1863, entered into force 12 April 1863) John Haswell (ed), *Treaties and Conventions Concluded Between the United States of America and Other Powers since July 4, 1776* (U.S. Department of State, Washington 1889) 870-2.
- Convention Reviving and Modifying the U.S.-Venezuela Convention of April 25, 1866 (adopted 5 December 1885, entered into force 3 June 1889) Charles Bevans (ed), *Treaties and Other International Agreements of the United States of America 1776—1949* (Volume 12: U.S. Department of State Publication, Washington 1971) 1085-92.
- General Claims Convention between the United States of America and the United Mexican States (adopted 8 September 1923, entered into force 1 March 1924) Charles Bevans (ed), *Treaties and Other International Agreements of the United States of America 1776—1949* (Volume 9: U.S. Department of State Publication, Washington 1971) 935-40.
- Protocol establishing a Mixed Claims Commission between Venezuela and Great Britain (adopted 13 February 1903) IX RIAA 351-3.
- Protocol establishing a Mixed Claims Commission between Venezuela and Italy (adopted 13 February 1903) X RIAA 479-81.
- Protocol of an Agreement for Submission to Arbitration of All Unsettled Claims of Spanish Subjects against the Republic of Venezuela (adopted 2 April 1903) X RIAA 737-8.
- Protocol on the Constitution of a Mixed Claims Commission between Venezuela and the German Empire (adopted 13 February 1903) X RIAA 359-60.
- Protocol on the Constitution of a Mixed Claims Commission between Venezuela and the German Empire (adopted 7 May 1903) X RIAA 361-2.
- Protocol on the Constitution of a Mixed Claims Commission between Venezuela and the Netherlands (adopted 28 February 1903) X RIAA 709-10.
- Special Agreement for the Submission to Arbitration of Pecuniary Claims Outstanding between the United States and Great Britain (adopted 18 August 1910, entered into force 26 April 1912) VI RIAA 9-11.
- Special Claims Convention between Mexico and the United States (adopted 10 September 1923, entered into force 19 February 1924) Charles Bevans (ed), *Treaties and Other International Agreements of the United States of America 1776—1949* (Volume 9: U.S. Department of State Publication, Washington 1971) 941-5.
- Washington Protocol Constituting the French-Venezuelan Claims Commission (adopted 27 February 1903) X RIAA 3-4.

International Investment Agreements[1]

- Accord entre l'Union économique belgo-luxembourgeoise et la République arabe d'Egypte concernant l'encouragement et la protection réciproques des investissements (adopted 28 February 1999, entered into force 24 May 2002).
- Accord entre l'Union économique belgo-luxembourgeoise et le gouvernement de la République du Venezuela concernant la promotion et la protection réciproques des investissements (adopted 17 March 1998, entered into force 29 April 2004).
- Accord entre le Gouvernement de la République française et le Gouvernement de la République Argentine sur l'encouragement et la protection réciproques des investissements (adopted 3 July 1991, entered into force 3 March 1993).
- Acordo entre o Governo da República Portuguesa e o Governo da República da Venezuela sobre a promoção e proteção mútua de investimentos (adopted 17 June 1994, entered into force 7 October 1995).
- Accordo tra il Governo della Repubblica Italiana ed il Governo della Repubblica Algerina Democratica e Popolare sulla promozione e protezione degli investimenti (adopted 15 May 1991, entered into force 26 November 1993).
- Acuerdo entre el Gobierno de la República de Venezuela y el Gobierno de la República Argentina para la promoción y protección recíprocas de inversiones (adopted 16 November 1993, entered into force 1 July 1995).
- Acuerdo entre el Gobierno de los Estados Unidos Mexicanos y el Gobierno de la República Argentina para la promoción y protección recíproca de las inversiones (adopted 13 November 1996, entered into force 22 June 1996).
- Acuerdo para la promoción y la protección recíproca de inversiones entre el Reino de España y la República Argentina (adopted 3 October 1991, entered into force 28 September 1992).
- Agreement between Canada and Mali for the Promotion and Protection of Investments (adopted 28 November 2014).
- Agreement between Canada and the Czech Republic for the Promotion and Protection of Investments (adopted 6 May 2009, entered into force 22 January 2012).
- Agreement between Canada and the Federal Republic of Senegal for the Promotion and Protection of Investments (adopted 27 November 2014).
- Agreement between Canada and the Government of the Czech and Slovak Federal Republic for the Promotion and Protection of Investments (adopted 15 November 1990, entered into force 9 March 1992, terminated 22 January 2012).
- Agreement between Canada and the Republic of Costa Rica for the Promotion and Protection of Investments (adopted 18 March 1998, entered into force 29 September 1999).

---

[1]*Unless otherwise indicated, the following materials are available at the IIAs Database of the United Nations Commission on Trade and Development [http://investmentpolicyhub. unctad.org/IIA].*

- Agreement between Canada and the Republic of Croatia for the Promotion and Protection of Investments (adopted 3 February 1997, entered into force 30 January 2001).
- Agreement between Canada and the Republic of Venezuela for the Promotion and Protection of Investments (adopted 1 July 1996, entered into force 28 January 1998).
- Agreement between Japan and the Oriental Republic of Uruguay for the Liberalization, Promotion and Protection of Investment (adopted 26 January 2015).
- Agreement between Japan and the Republic of Colombia for the Liberalization, Promotion and Protection of Investment (adopted 12 September 2011).
- Agreement between Japan and the Republic of Peru for the Promotion, Protection and Liberalization of Investment (adopted 22 November 2008, entered into force 10 December 2009).
- Agreement between Japan and the Republic of Turkey concerning the reciprocal promotion and protection of investment (adopted 12 February 1992, entered into force 12 March 1993).
- Agreement between New Zealand and the Separate Customs Territory of Taiwan, Penghu, Kinmen, and Matsu on Economic Cooperation (adopted 10 July 2013).
- Agreement between the Arab Republic of Egypt and the Belgo-Luxembourg Economic Union on the Encouragement and Reciprocal Protection of Investments (adopted 28 February 1977, entered into force 20 September 1978, terminated 24 May 2002).
- Agreement between the Belgium-Luxembourg Economic Union and the Republic of Colombia on the Reciprocal Promotion and Protection of Investments (adopted 4 February 2009).
- Agreement between the Federal Republic of Germany and the Hashemite Kingdom of Jordan concerning the Encouragement and Reciprocal Protection of Investments (adopted 13 November 2007, entered into force 28 August 2010).
- Agreement between the Federal Republic of Germany and the Palestine Liberation Organization for the benefit of the Palestinian Authority concerning the Encouragement and Reciprocal Protection of Investments (adopted 10 July 2000, entered into force 19 September 2008).
- Agreement between the Federal Republic of Germany and the People's Republic of Bangladesh concerning the Promotion and Reciprocal Protection of Investments (adopted 6 May 1981, entered into force 14 September 1986).
- Agreement between the Government of the Czech and Slovak Federal Republic and the Government of the Kingdom of Thailand for the Promotion and Protection of Investments (adopted 12 February 1994, entered into force 4 May 1995).
- Agreement between the Government of the Kingdom of Cambodia and the Government of the Republic of Cuba concerning the Promotion and Protection of Investments (adopted 26 September 2001).
- Agreement between the Government of the Kingdom of Cambodia and the Government of the Socialist Republic of Vietnam concerning the Promotion and Protection of Investments (adopted 1 September 2001).

- Agreement between the Government of the Kingdom of Cambodia and the Government of the Republic of the Philippines concerning the Promotion and Protection of Investments (adopted 16 August 2000).
- Agreement between the Government of the Kingdom of Denmark and the Government of the Republic of Argentina concerning the Promotion and Reciprocal Protection of Investments (adopted 6 November 1992, entered into force 2 February 1995).
- Agreement between the Government of the People's Republic of China and the Portuguese Republic on the Encouragement and Reciprocal Protection of Investments (adopted 9 December 2005, entered into force 26 July 2008).
- Agreement between the Government of the Republic of Azerbaijan and the Government of the Syrian Arab Republic on the Promotion and Reciprocal Protection of Investments (adopted 8 July 2009, entered into force 4 January 2010).
- Agreement between the Government of the Republic of Croatia and the Government of the Republic of Azerbaijan on the Promotion and Reciprocal Protection of Investments (adopted 2 November 2007, entered into force 30 May 2008).
- Agreement between the Government of the Republic of Finland and the Government of Mongolia on the Promotion and Protection of Investments (adopted 15 May 2007, entered into force 19 June 2008).
- Agreement between the Government of the Republic of Mauritius and the Government of the Arab Republic of Egypt in the Reciprocal Promotion and Protection of Investments (adopted 25 June 2014).
- Agreement between the Government of the Republic of Singapore and the Government of the Republic of Indonesia on the Promotion and Protection of Investments (adopted 16 February 2005, entered into force 21 June 2006).
- Agreement between the Government of the Republic of Turkey and the Government of the Islamic Republic of Pakistan concerning the Reciprocal Promotion and Protection of Investments (adopted 22 May 2012).
- Agreement between the Government of the Russian Federation and the Cabinet of Ministers of the Ukraine on the Encouragement and Mutual Protection of Investments (adopted 27 November 1998, entered into force 27 January 2000).
- Agreement between the Government of the Russian Federation and the Government of the Republic of Cyprus Regarding the Promotion and Mutual Protection of Investments (adopted 11 April 2007).
- Agreement between the Government of the Russian Federation and the Government of the Republic of Moldova Regarding the Promotion and Mutual Protection of Investments (adopted 17 March 1998, entered into force 18 July 2001).
- Agreement between the Government of the Slovak Republic and the Government of the Republic of Kenya for the Promotion and Reciprocal Protection of Investments (adopted 14 December 2011).
- Agreement between the Government of the Swiss Confederation and the Government of the Democratic Socialist Republic of Sri Lanka for the Reciprocal Promotion and Protection of Investments (adopted 23 September 1981, entered into force 12 February 1982).

- Agreement between the Government of the United Kingdom and the Arab Republic of Egypt for the Promotion and Protection of Investments (adopted 11 June 1975, entered into force 24 February 1976).
- Agreement between the Government of the United Kingdom and the Government of the Democratic Socialist Republic of Sri Lanka for the Promotion and Protection of Investments (adopted 13 February 1980, entered into force 18 December 1980).
- Agreement between the Government of the United Kingdom and the Government of the Republic of Argentina for the Promotion and Protection of Investments (adopted 11 December 1990, entered into force 19 February 1993).
- Agreement between the Government of the United Kingdom and the Government of the United Mexican States for the Promotion and Reciprocal Protection of Investments (adopted 12 May 2006, entered into force 25 July 2007).
- Agreement between the Government of the United Mexican States and the Government of the Republic of Belarus on the Promotion and Reciprocal Protection of Investments (adopted 4 September 2008, entered into force 27 August 2009).
- Agreement between the Government of the United Mexican States and the Government of the Republic of India on the Promotion and Protection of Investments (adopted 21 May 2007, entered into force 23 February 2008).
- Agreement between the Hellenic Republic and the Government of the Republic of Albania for the Encouragement and Reciprocal Protection of Investments (adopted 1 August 1991, entered into force 4 January 1995).
- Agreement between the Italian Republic and the Lebanese Republic on the Promotion and Reciprocal Protection of Investments (adopted 7 November 1997, entered into force 9 February 2000).
- Agreement between the Kingdom of the Netherlands and the Czech and Slovak Federal Republic on the Encouragement and Reciprocal Protection of Investments (adopted 24 April 1991, entered into force 1 October 1992).
- Agreement between the Kingdom of the Netherlands and the Macao Special Administrative Region of the People's Republic of China on Encouragement and Reciprocal Protection of Investments (adopted 22 May 2008, entered into force 1 May 2009).
- Agreement between the Kingdom of the Netherlands and the Republic of Mozambique concerning the Encouragement and the Reciprocal Protection of Investments (adopted 18 December 2001, entered into force 1 September 2004).
- Agreement between the Republic of Guatemala and the Republic of Trinidad and Tobago on the Reciprocal Promotion and Protection of Investments (adopted 13 August 2013).
- Agreement between the Republic of Turkey and the Government of the Gabonese Republic concerning the Reciprocal Promotion and Protection of Investments (adopted 18 July 2012).
- Agreement between the Republic of Turkey and the Republic of Kazakhstan concerning the Reciprocal Promotion and Protection of Investments (adopted 1 May 1992, entered into force 10 August 1995).

- Agreement between the Swiss Confederation and Serbia and Montenegro on the Promotion and Reciprocal Protection of Investments (adopted 7 December 2005, entered into force 20 July 2007).
- Agreement between the Swiss Confederation and the Republic of Venezuela on the Reciprocal Promotion and Protection of Investments (adopted 18 November 1993, entered into force 30 November 1994).
- Agreement between the United Mexican States and the Slovak Republic on the Promotion and Reciprocal Protection of Investments (adopted 26 October 2007, entered into force 8 April 2009).
- Agreement between the United States of America and the Republic of Turkey concerning the Reciprocal Encouragement and Protection of Investments (adopted 3 December 1985, entered into force 18 May 1990).
- Agreement between the United States of America, the United Mexican States, and Canada (adopted 30 November 2018).
- Agreement for the Promotion and Protection of Investment between the Republic of Austria and the Federal Republic of Nigeria (adopted 8 April 2013).
- Agreement for the Promotion and Protection of Investments between the Republic of Colombia and the Republic of India (adopted 10 November 2009, entered into force 3 July 2013).
- Agreement on Encouragement and Reciprocal Protection of Investments between the Kingdom of the Netherlands and the Dominican Republic (adopted 3 March 2006, entered into force 1 October 2007).
- Agreement on Encouragement and Reciprocal Protection of Investments between the Kingdom of the Netherlands and the Federal Republic of Yugoslavia (adopted 29 January 2002, entered into force 1 March 2004).
- Agreement on Encouragement and Reciprocal Protection of Investments between the Government of the Republic of Tajikistan and the Government of the Kingdom of the Netherlands (adopted 24 July 2002, entered into force 1 April 2004).
- Agreement on Encouragement and Reciprocal Protection of Investments between the Republic of Armenia and the Kingdom of the Netherlands (adopted 10 June 2005, entered into force 1 August 2006).
- Agreement on Encouragement and Reciprocal Protection of Investments between the Kingdom of the Netherlands and the Republic of Suriname (adopted 31 March 2005, entered into force 1 September 2006).
- Agreement on Encouragement and Reciprocal Protection of Investments between the Kingdom of the Netherlands and the Republic of Venezuela (adopted 22 October 1991, entered into force 1 November 1993, terminated 1 November 2008).
- Agreement on Encouragement and Reciprocal Protection of Investments between the Lao People's Democratic Republic and the Kingdom of the Netherlands (adopted 16 May 2003, entered into force 1 May 2005).
- Agreement on Investment of the Framework Agreement on Comprehensive Economic Cooperation between the People's Republic of China and the Association of Southeast Asian Nations (adopted 15 August 2009, entered into force 1 January 2010).

- Agreement on Promotion, Protection and Guarantee of Investments among Member States of the Organisation of the Islamic Conference (adopted 5 June 1981, entered into force 23 September 1986).
- Bilateral Investment Treaty between the Government of Canada and the Republic of Côte d'Ivoire (adopted 30 November 2014).
- Comprehensive and Progressive Agreement for Trans-Pacific Partnership (adopted 8 March 2018, partially entered into force 30 December 2018).
- Comprehensive Economic and Trade Agreement between Canada and the European Union (signed 30 October 2016, provisionally entered into force 21 September 2017).
- Comprehensive Economic Cooperation Agreement between the Government of Malaysia and the Government of the Republic of India (adopted 18 February 2011, entered into force 1 July 2011).
- Convenio entre el Gobierno de la República del Perú y el Gobierno de la República Argentina sobre Promoción y Protección Recíproca de Inversiones (adopted 10 November 1994, entered into force 24 October 1996).
- Convenio entre la República de Bolivia y la República del Ecuador para la promoción y protección recíproca de inversiones (adopted 25 May 1995, entered into force 15 August 1997).
- Convenio entre la República de Costa Rica y la República del Ecuador para la promoción y protección recíproca de inversiones (adopted 6 December 2001).
- Convention entre l'Union Economique Belgo-Luxembourgeoise et la République du Burundi concernant l'encouragement et la protection réciproques des investissements (adopted 13 April 1989, entered into force 12 September 1993).
- Energy Charter Treaty (adopted 17 December 1994, entered into force 16 April 1998).
- European Union – Singapore Investment Protection Agreement (adopted 15 October 2018).
- European Union – Vietnam Investment Protection Agreement (negotiated draft; version of September 2018).
- Free Trade Agreement between Australia and the Republic of Korea (adopted 8 April 2014).
- Free Trade Agreement between CACM, the Dominican Republic and the United States of America (adopted 5 August 2004, entered into force 1 January 2009).
- Free Trade Agreement between Malaysia and Australia (adopted 22 May 2012, entered into force 1 January 2013).
- Free Trade Agreement between the Government of the People's Republic of China and the Government of the Republic of Korea (adopted 1 June 2015, entered into force 20 December 2015).
- Free Trade Agreement between the Government of the People's Republic of China and the Government of the Republic of Peru (adopted 28 April 2009, entered into force 1 March 2010).
- Free Trade Agreement between the Government of the United States of America and the Government of Chile (adopted 6 June 2003, entered into force 1 January 2004).

- Free Trade Agreement between the Kingdom of Morocco and the United States of America (adopted 15 June 2004, entered into force 1 January 2006).
- Free Trade Agreement between the Republic of China (Taiwan) and the Republic of Nicaragua (adopted 23 June 2006, entered into force 1 January 2008).
- Free Trade Agreement between the Republic of Korea and the Republic of Peru (adopted 14 November 2010, entered into force 1 August 2011).
- Free Trade Agreement between the Republic of Korea and the Republic of Colombia (adopted 21 February 2013, entered into force 15 July 2016).
- Free Trade Agreement between the United States of America and the Republic of Colombia (adopted 22 November 2006, entered into force 15 May 2012).
- Free Trade Agreement between the United States of America and the Republic of Korea (adopted 30 June 2007, entered into force 15 March 2012).
- Free Trade Agreement between the United States of America and the Sultanate of Oman (adopted 19 January 2006, entered into force 1 January 2009).
- Free Trade Agreement between the United States of America and the Republic of Peru (adopted 12 April 2006, entered into force 1 February 2009).
- Investment Agreement for the COMESA Common Investment Area (adopted 23 May 2007).
- North American Free Trade Agreement (adopted 17 December 1992, entered into force 1 January 1994).
- Protocol on Investment to the New Zealand-Australia Closer Economic Relations Trade Agreement (adopted 16 February 2011, entered into force 1 March 2013).
- Protocol to the Agreement between the Government of Australia and the Government of the United Mexican States on the Promotion and Reciprocal Protection of Investments (adopted 23 August 2005, entered into force 21 July 2007).
- Protocolo de Buenos Aires de Cooperación y Facilitación de Inversiones Intra-Mercosur (adopted 7 April 2017) [online] http://apc.mef.gub.uy/innovaportal/file/21186/2/protocolo-de-cooperacion-y-facilitacion-de-inversiones.pdf
- Protocolo de Buenos Aires sobre Promoción y Protección de Inversiones Provenientes de Estados no Partes del Mercosur (adopted 5 August 1994) in Martins Paparinskis, *Basic Documents on International Investment Protection* (Hart Publishing, Portland OR 2012) 356-61.
- Protocolo de Colonia para la Promoción y Protección Recíproca de Inversiones en el Mercosur (Intrazona) (adopted 17 January 1994) in Martins Paparinskis, *Basic Documents on International Investment Protection* (Hart Publishing, Portland OR 2012) 350-6.
- Reciprocal Investment Promotion and Protection Agreement between the Government of the Kingdom of Morocco and the Government of the Federal Republic of Nigeria (adopted 3 December 2016).
- Trans-Pacific Partnership Agreement (adopted 4 February 2016).
- Tratado entre el Gobierno de la República de Costa Rica y el Gobierno de la República Federal de Alemania sobre el fomento y recíproca protección de inversiones (adopted 13 September 1994, entered into force 24 March 1998).
- Tratado entre la República Federal de Alemania y la República Argentina sobre promoción y protección recíproca de inversiones (adopted 9 April 1991, entered into force 8 November 1993).

- Tratado entre la República Federal de Alemania y la República de Chile sobre fomento y recíproca protección de inversiones (adopted 21 October 1991, entered into force 8 May 1999).
- Treaty between Australia and Japan for an Economic Partnership (adopted 8 July 2014).
- Treaty between the Federal Republic of Germany and the Republic of Haiti concerning the Promotion and Reciprocal Protection of Capital Investment (adopted 14 August 1973, entered into force 1 December 1975).
- Treaty between the United States of America and the Arab Republic of Egypt concerning the Reciprocal Encouragement and Protection of Investments (adopted 11 March 1986, entered into force 27 June 1992).
- Treaty between the United States of America and the Argentine Republic concerning the Reciprocal Encouragement and Protection of Investment (adopted 14 November 1991, entered into force 20 October 1994).
- Treaty between the United States of America and the Government of Romania concerning the Reciprocal Encouragement and Protection of Investment (adopted 28 May 1992, entered into force 15 January 1994).
- Treaty between the United States of America and the Republic of Ecuador concerning the Encouragement and Reciprocal Protection of Investment (adopted 17 August 1993, entered into force 11 May 1997).
- Treaty between the United States of America and the Republic of Zaire concerning the Reciprocal Encouragement and Protection of Investment (adopted 3 August 1984, entered into force 28 July 1989).
- Treaty for the Promotion and Protection of Investments between Pakistan and the Federal Republic of Germany (adopted 25 November 1959, entered into force 28 April 1962).
- Vertrag zwischen der Bundesrepublik Deutschland und dem Königreich Griechenland über die Förderung und den gegenseitigen Schutz von Kapitalanlagen (adopted 27 March 1961, entered into force 15 July 1963).
- Vertrag zwischen der Bundesrepublik Deutschland und der Argentinischen Republik über die Förderung und den gegenseitigen Schutz von Kapitalanlagen (adopted 9 April 1991, entered into force 8 November 1993).
- Vertrag zwischen der Bundesrepublik Deutschland und der Ukraine über die Förderung und den gegenseitigen Schutz von Kapitalanlagen (adopted 15 February 1993, entered into force 29 June 1996).

Other International Treaties

- Accord entre le Gouvernement de la République Française et le Gouvernement de la République Populaire du Congo sur les droits fondamentaux des nationaux (adopted 1 January 1974, entered into force 1 November 1981) 1309 UNTS 79.
- Convention d'établissement entre le Gouvernement de la République Française et le Gouvernement de la République Centrafricaine (adopted 26 September 1994, entered into force 1 May 1996) 1980 UNTS 221.

- Convention d'établissement entre le Gouvernement de la République Française et le Gouvernement de la République du Mali (adopted 26 September 1994, entered into force 1 April 1996) 1980 UNTS 189.
- Convention on the Limitation of Employment of Force for Recovery of Contract Debts (adopted 18 October 1907, entered into force 26 January 1910) in Charles Bevans (ed), *Treaties and Other International Agreements of the United States of America 1776-1949* (Volume 1: Government Printing Office, Washington 1968) 607-18.
- Convention on the Reduction of Statelessness (adopted 30 August 1961, entered into force 13 December 1975) 989 UNTS 175.
- Convention on the Rights and Duties of States (adopted 26 December 1933, entered into force 26 December 1934) 165 LNTS 19.
- Convention on the Settlement of Investment Disputes between States and Nationals of Other States (submitted 18 March 1965, entered into force 14 October 1966) 575 UNTS 159.
- Convention relating to the Status of Stateless Persons (adopted 28 September 1954, entered into force 6 June 1960) 360 UNTS 117.
- Convention Relative to the Rights of Aliens (adopted 1902) *Report of the Delegates of the United States to the Second International Conference of American States, Held at the City of Mexico from October 22, 1901, to January 22, 1902* (Government Printing Office, Washington 1902) 226-30 (Appendix GG).
- European Convention on Establishment (adopted 13 December 1955, entered into force 23 February 1965) 529 UNTS 141.
- European Convention on the Legal Status of Migrant Workers (adopted 24 November 1977, entered into force 1 May 1983) 1496 UNTS 3.
- Protocol Additional to the Geneva Conventions of 12 August 1949, and relating to the Protection of Victims of International Armed Conflicts (adopted 8 June 1977, entered into force 7 December 1978) XVI ILM 1391-441.
- Statute of the International Court of Justice (adopted 26 June 1945, entered into force 24 October 1945).
- Treaty of Washington between Her Britannic Majesty and the United States of America (adopted 8 May 1871, entered into force 17 June 1871) Charles Bevans (ed), *Treaties and Other International Agreements of the United States of America 1776—1949* (Volume 12: U.S. Department of State Publication, Washington 1971) 170-87.
- Vienna Convention on Consular Relations (adopted 24 April 1963, entered into force 19 March 1967) 596 UNTS 261.
- Vienna Convention on Diplomatic Relations (adopted 18 April 1961, entered into force 24 April 1964) 500 UNTS 95.
- Vienna Convention on the Law of Treaties (adopted 23 May 1969, entered into force 27 January 1980) 1155 UNTS 331.

Reservations

- 'Reservation of the United States of America to the Convention on the Rights and Duties of States' (26 December 1933) 165 L.N.T.S. 28.

Model International Investment Agreements

- Austrian Model BIT (2008).
- Canadian Model BIT (2004).
- Colombian Model BIT (2008).
- Colombian Model BIT (2011).
- French Model BIT (2006).
- German Model BIT (2008).
- Indian Model BIT (2015).
- Italian Model BIT (2003).
- Korean Model BIT (2001).
- Netherlands Model BIT (2004).
- U.K. Model BIT (2008).
- U.S. Model BIT (2004).
- U.S. Model BIT (2012).

Other Materials

- 'Acta de la Quinta Sesión' in *Actas y antecedentes de la primera, segunda y octava comisiones de la Séptima Conferencia Internacional Americana* (Montevideo 1933) 111.
- 'Actas de la Quinta Sesión Plenaria' (24 December 1933) in *Actas y antecedentes de las sesiones plenarias de la Séptima Conferencia Internacional Americana* (Montevideo 1933) 107.

Table of Cases

Permanent Court of International Justice

- *Mavrommatis Palestine Concessions (Greece v UK)* (Jurisdiction) [1924] PCIJ Rep Series A No 2.

International Court of Justice

- *Ahmadou Sadio Diallo (Guinea v Congo)* [2007] ICJ Rep 582.
- *Ahmadou Sadio Diallo (Guinea v Congo)* [2010] ICJ Rep 639, Separate Opinion of Judge Cançado Trindade 729.
- *Barcelona Traction Light and Power Company Ltd. (Belgium v Spain)* [1970] ICJ Rep 3.
- *Barcelona Traction Light and Power Company Ltd. (Belgium v Spain)* [1970] ICJ Rep 3, Separate Opinion of Judge Jessup 161.
- *Case Concerning Elettronica Sicula S.p.A. (ELSI) (United States of America v Italy)* [1989] ICJ Rep 15.
- *Case Concerning Pulp Mills on the River Uruguay (Argentina v Uruguay)* [2010] ICJ Rep 14.
- *Case Concerning the Application of the Convention on the Prevention and Punishment of the Crime of Genocide (Bosnia and Herzegovina v Serbia and Montenegro)* [2007] ICJ Rep 43.
- *Case Concerning United States Diplomatic and Consular Staff in Tehran (United States of America v Iran)* [1980] ICJ Rep. 3.
- *Corfu Channel Case (UK v Albania)* [1949] ICJ Rep 4, Dissenting Opinion by Dr. Ečer 115.

© Springer Nature Switzerland AG 2019

631

S. Mantilla Blanco, *Full Protection and Security in International Investment Law*, European Yearbook of International Economic Law 8, https://doi.org/10.1007/978-3-030-24838-3

- *Corfu Channel Case (UK v Albania)* [1949] ICJ Rep 4, Dissenting Opinion by Judge Azevedo 78.
- *Corfu Channel Case (UK v Albania)* [1949] ICJ Rep 4, Dissenting Opinion by Judge Krylov 68.
- *Corfu Channel Case (UK v Albania)* [1949] ICJ Rep 4.
- *Delimitation of the Maritime Boundary in the Gulf of Maine Area (Canada v United States of America)* [1984] ICJ Rep 246.
- *North Sea Continental Shelf (Germany v Denmark / Germany v Netherlands)* [1969] ICJ Rep. 3.
- *Obligation to Negotiate Access to the Pacific Ocean (Bolivia v Chile)* [2018] ICJ General List No. 153.
- *Western Sahara (Advisory Opinion)* [1975] ICJ Rep 12.

World Trade Organization

- China – Measures Affecting Trading Services and Distribution Services for Certain Publications and Audiovisual Entertainment Products, Appellate Body Report, WT/DS363/AB/2 (21 December 2009).

European Court of Justice

- Slovak Republic *v* Achmea B.V., Case C-284/16, Opinion of Advocate General Wathelet (19 September 2017).

European Court of Human Rights

- A et al. *v* United Kingdom, App No 3455/05 (ECtHR: 19 February 2009).
- Brumărescu *v* Romania, App No 28342/95 (ECtHR: 28 October 1999).
- Hiller *v* Austria, App No 1967/14 (ECtHR: 22 November 2016).
- Humen *v* Poland, App No 26614/95 (ECtHR: 15 October 1999).
- Khalifa et al. *v* Italy, App No 16483/12 (ECtHR: 15 December 2016).
- Kudła *v* Poland, App No 30219/96 (ECtHR: 26 October 2000).
- L.C.B. *v* United Kingdom, App No 14/1997/798/1001 (ECtHR: 9 June 1998).
- Malik Babayev *v* Azerbaijan, App No 30500/11 (ECtHR: 1 June 2017).
- Öneryildiz *v* Turkey, App No 48939/99 (ECtHR: 30 November 2004).
- Opuz *v* Turkey, App No 33401/02 (ECtHR: 9 June 2009).
- Paul and Audrey Edwards *v* United Kingdom, App No 46477/99 (ECtHR: 14 March 2002).
- Rumpf *v* Germany, App No 46344/06 (ECtHR: 2 September 2010).

Inter-American Court of Human Rights

- Familia Barrios *v* Venezuela, Judgment on Merits, Reparations and Costs (ICtHR: 24 November 2011).
- Gonzalez Llui et al. *v* Ecuador, Judgment on Preliminary Objections, Merits, Reparations and Costs (ICtHR: 1 September 2015).
- Masacre de las Dos Erres *v* Guatemala, Judgment on Preliminary Objection, Merits, Reparations and Costs (ICtHR: 24 November 2009).
- Rosendo Cantú et al. *v* Mexico, Judgment on Preliminary Objections, Merits, Reparations and Costs (ICtHR: 31 August 2010).
- Suárez Peralta *v* Ecuador, Judgment on Preliminary Objections, Merits, Reparations and Costs (ICtHR: 21 May 2013).
- Velásquez Rodríguez *v* Honduras, Judgment on the Merits (ICtHR: 29 July 1988).

Iran – US Claims Tribunal

- Alfred L. Short *v* Iran, Award, Case No. 11135 (14 July 1987) 16 Iran – US Cl. Trib. Rep. 76-86.
- Alfred L. Short *v* Iran, Dissenting Opinion of Justice Brower, Case No. 11135 (14 July 1987) 16 Iran – US Cl. Trib. Rep. 86-102.
- Anaconda Iran Inc. *v* Iran, Award, Case No. 167 (10 December 1986) 13 Iran – US Cl. Trib. Rep. 199-239.
- Gould Marketing Inc. *v* Ministry of National Defense, Award, Case No. 49 (17 July 1983) 3 Iran – US Cl. Trib. Rep. 147-55.
- International Technical Products Corp. *v* Iran, Award, Case No. 302 (19 August 1985) 9 Iran – US Cl. Trib. Rep. 10-45.
- Kenneth P. Yeager *v* Iran, Award, Case No. 10199 (2 November 1987) 17 Iran – US Cl. Trib. Rep. 92-113.
- Sea-Land Service Inc. *v* Iran, Award, Case No. 33 (20 June 1984), 6 Iran-US Cl. Trib. Rep. 149-218.
- Sylvania Technical Systems Inc. *v* Iran, Award, Case No. 64 (28 June 1985) 8 Iran – US Cl. Trib. Rep. 298-328.

International Tribunal for the Law of the Sea

- *Responsibilities and Obligations of States Sponsoring Persons and Entities with Respect to Activities in the Area (Advisory Opinion)* [2011] 50 ILM 458.

Claims Commissions

Italy – Venezuela Mixed Claims Commission *(Protocols of February 13th, 1903 and May 7th, 1903)*

- *De Caro Case* (1903) X RIAA 635, 635-44.
- *Guastini Case* (1903) X RIAA 561-82.
- *Guerrieri Case* (1903) X RIAA 583.
- *Poggioli Case* (1903) X RIAA 669-92.
- *Tagliaferro Case* (1903) X RIAA 592-4.
- *Sambiaggio Case* (1903) X RIAA 499-535.

France – Venezuela Commission *(Protocol of February 19th, 1902)*

- *Antoine Fabiani Case* (31 July 1905) X RIAA 83-139.
- *French Company of Venezuelan Railroads Case* (31 July 1905) X RIAA 285-355.

France – Mexico Claims Commission *(Conventions of September 25th, 1925, March 12th, 1927 and August 2nd, 1930)*

- *Georges Pinson v Mexico* (19 October 1928) V RIAA 327-466.

Great Britain – Colombia Ad Hoc Tribunal *(Convention of December 14th, 1872)*

- *Cotesworth & Powell Case* (August 1875) 4 Moore's Arb. 2050-85.

Great Britain – Mexico Claims Commission *(Conventions of November 19th, 1926 and December 5th, 1930)*

- *Buena Tierra Mining Co. Ltd. v Mexico* (3 August 1931) V RIAA 247-52.
- *Christina Patton v Mexico* (8 July 1931) V RIAA 224-9.

- *Mexico City Bombardment Claims* (15 February 1930) V RIAA 76-90.
- *El Oro Mining and Railway Co. v Mexico* (18 June 1931) V RIAA 191-9.
- *George Creswell Delamain v Mexico* (10 July 1931) V RIAA 229-31.
- *Santa Gertrudis Jute Mill Co. Ltd. v Mexico* (15 February 1930) V RIAA 108-15.
- *Sarah Bryant, Countess D'Etchegoyen v. Mexico* (6 August 1932) V RIAA 305-6.
- *The Interoceanic Railway of Mexico Ltd. et al. v Mexico* (18 June 1931) V RIAA 178-90.
- *William E. Bowerman and Messrs. Burberry's Ltd. v Mexico* (15 February 1930) V RIAA 104-8.

Great Britain – United States Arbitral Tribunal *(Special Agreement of August 18th, 1910)*

- *D. Earnshaw et al. v United States of America* (30 November 1925) VI RIAA 160-5.
- *Home Frontier and Foreign Missionary Society of the United Brethren in Christ v Great Britain* (18 December 1929) VI RIAA 42-4.
- *Luzon Sugar Refining Co. Ltd. v United States of America* (30 November 1925) VI RIAA 165.

Great Britain – Venezuela Commission *(Protocols of February 13th, 1903, and May 7th, 1903)*

- *Aroa Mines Ltd. v Venezuela* (1903) IX RIAA 402-45.
- *Bolívar Railway Company Case* (1903) IX RIAA 445-55.
- *Charles de Lemos and Guillermina Dalton de Lemos v Venezuela* (1903) IX RIAA 360-80.
- *James Crossman v Venezuela* (1903) IX RIAA 356-60 [interlocutory opinion].
- *Puerto Cabello and Valencia Railway Company Case* (1903) IX RIAA 510-33.

Great Britain – Spain Commission *(Special Convention of May 29th, 1923)*

- *Affaire des biens britanniques au Maroc espagnol* (1 May 1925) II RIAA 615-742.

Netherlands – Venezuela Commission *(Protocol of 28th February, 1903)*

- *N. H. Henriquez Case* (1903) X RIAA 713-7.
- *Salas Case* (1903) X RIAA 720-1.

United States – Colombia Special Claims Commission *(Agreement of Arbitration of August 17th, 1874)*

- *Case of the Steamer Montijo* (25 July 1875) in Henri La Fontaine (ed), *Pasicrisie Internationale. Histoire documentaire des arbitrages internationaux* (Stämpfli & Cie., Bern 1902) 209-20.

United States – Chile Claims Commission *(Convention of August 7th, 1892)*

- *Frederick H. Lovett et al. v. Chile* (10 April 1894) XXIX RIAA 319-21.

United States – Costa Rica Commission *(Claims Convention of July 2nd, 1860)*

- *George H. Bowley & Co. v Costa Rica* (21 December 1862) 3 Moore's Arb. 3032-3.

United States – France Claims Commission *(Claims Convention of January 15th, 1880)*

- *Jean Jeannaud v United States of America* (undated) 3 Moore's Arb. 3000-1.
- *Louis Castelain and Marie Castelain v United States of America* (undated) 3 Moore's Arb. 2999-3000.
- *Vidal v United States of America* (undated) 3 Moore's Arb. 2999.

United States – Panama General Claims Commission (*Convention of July 28th, 1926 and Subsequent Amendments*)

- *Cecelia Dexter Baldwin et al. v Panama* (26 June 1933) VI RIAA 328-33.
- *Charlie R. Richeson et al. v Panama* (26 June 1933) VI RIAA 325-8.
- *Hampden Osborne Banks et al. v Panama* (29 June 1933) VI RIAA 349-52.
- *Walter A. Noyes v Panama* (22 May 1933) VI RIAA 308-12.

United States – Peru Claims Commission (*Convention of January 12th, 1863*)

- *Montano v United States of America* (2 November 1863) 2 Moore's Arb. 1630-8.

United States – Venezuela Mixed Claims Commission (*Claims Convention of December 5th, 1885*)

- *Amelia de Brissot et al. v. United States of Venezuela* (26 August 1890) *United States and Venezuelan Claims Commission. Opinions Delivered by the Commissioners in the Principal Cases* (Gibson Bros., Washington 1890) 457-89.
- *Frederick Wipperman v United States of Venezuela* (10 July 1890) *United States and Venezuelan Claims Commission. Opinions Delivered by the Commissioners in the Principal Cases* (Gibson Bros., Washington 1890) 132-7.

United States – Mexico Claims Commission (*Claims Convention of February 2nd, 1842; Board Constituted by Act of the U.S. Congress of March 3rd, 1849*)

- *Case of the "Topas"* (undated) 3 Moore's Arb. 2992-3.

United States – Mexico Claims Commission (*Claims Convention of July 4th, 1868*)

- *Dunbar & Belknap v Mexico* (17 April 1875) 3 Moore's Arb. 2998.
- *Mildred Standish v Mexico* (12 March 1875) 3 Moore's Arb. 3004-6.
- *Salvador Prats v United States* (undated) 3 Moore's Arb. 2886-900.

- *Theodore Webster v Mexico* (undated) 3 Moore's Arb. 3004.
- *William W. Mills v Mexico* (6 July 1870) 3 Moore's Arb. 3033-5.

United States – Mexico General Claims Commission (*Convention of September 8th, 1923 and Extension Agreements*)

- *Agnes Connelly et al. v Mexico* (23 November 1926) IV RIAA 117-8.
- *B. E. Chattin v Mexico* (23 July 1927) IV RIAA 282-312.
- *Bond Coleman v Mexico* (3 October 1928) IV RIAA 364-8.
- *Dickson Car Wheel Co. v Mexico* (July 1931) IV RIAA 669-91.
- *Elvira Almaguer v Mexico* (13 May 1929) IV RIAA 523-9.
- *Francisco Mallén v United States* (27 April 1927) IV RIAA 173-90.
- *George Adams Kennedy v Mexico* (6 May 1927) IV RIAA 194-203.
- *Gertrude Parker Massey v Mexico* (15-16 April 1927) IV RIAA 155-64.
- *G. L. Solis v Mexico* (3 October 1928) IV RIAA 358-64.
- *Harry Roberts v Mexico* (2 November 1926) IV RIAA 77-81.
- *H. G. Venable v Mexico* (8 July 1927) IV RIAA 219-61.
- *Illinois Central Railroad Company v Mexico* (31 March 1926) IV RIAA 21-5.
- *Irma Eitelman Miller et al. v Mexico* (26 September 1928) IV RIAA 336-7.
- *J. J. Boyd v Mexico* (12 October 1928) IV RIAA 380-1.
- *John Chase v Mexico* (26 September 1928) IV RIAA 337-9.
- *Laura M.B. Janes et al. v Mexico* (16 November 1925) IV RIAA 82-98.
- *LFH Neer and Pauline Neer v Mexico* (15 October 1926) IV RIAA 60-6.
- *Lina Balderas de Díaz v United States of America* (16 November 1926) IV RIAA 106-8.
- *Louis B. Gordon v. Mexico* (8 October 1930) IV RIAA 586-93.
- *Louise O. Canahl v Mexico* (15 October 1928) IV RIAA 389-91.
- *Margaret Roper v Mexico* (4 April 1927) IV RIAA 145-8.
- *Sarah Ann Gorham v Mexico* (24 October 1930) IV RIAA 639-45.
- *Sophie B. Sturtevant v Mexico* (5 November 1930) IV RIAA 665-9.
- *Teodoro García and M. A. Garza v United States of America* (3 December 1926) IV RIAA 119-34.
- *The Home Insurance Company v Mexico* (31 March 1926) IV RIAA 48-53.
- *Thomas H. Youmans v Mexico* (23 November 1926) IV RIAA 110-7.
- *Vernon Monroe Greenlaw v Mexico* (24 October 1930) IV RIAA 626-32.

United States – Mexico Special Claims Commission (*Agreement of September 10th, 1923*)

- *Naomi Russell v Mexico* (24 April 1931) IV RIAA 805-914.

United States – Spain Claims Commission *(Convention of February 12th, 1871)*

- *Case of Thomas K. Foster* (9 May 1874) 3 Moore's Arb. 2999.

United States – Venezuela Mixed Claims Commission *(Claims Convention of February 17th, 1903)*

- *Boulton, Bliss & Dallett Case* (1904) IX RIAA 136-9.
- *Dix Case* (1903-5) IX RIAA 119-21.
- *Heny Case* (1903-5) IX RIAA 125-36.
- *Jennie L. Underhill Case* (1903-5) IX RIAA 158-61.

Other Arbitration Claims

- *Affaire des biens britanniques au Maroc espagnol* (1 May 1925) II RIAA 615-72.
- *Rosa Gelbtrunk v El Salvador* (26 April 1902) *Papers relating to the Foreign Relations of the United States with the Annual Message of the President* (Government Printing Office, Washington 1902) 876-80.

International Centre for the Settlement of Investment Disputes[2]

- Adel A Hamadi Al Tamini *v* Oman, Award, ICSID Case No. ARB/11/33 (3 November 2015).
- ADF *v* United States, Award, ICSID Case No. ARB(AF)/00/1 (9 January 2003).[3]
- ADF *v* United States, Investor's Reply to the Counter-Memorial of the United States of America on Competence and Liability, ICSID Case No. ARB(AF)/00/1 (28 January 2002).
- ADF *v* United States, Memorial of the Investor, ICSID Case No. ARB(AF)/00/1 (1 August 2001).

---

[2]*Unless otherwise indicated, the following materials are available at the Investment Treaty Arbitration Database of the University of Victoria [http://www.italaw.com].*

[3]*The memoranda submitted by the parties to the ADF tribunal are available on the official website of the U.S. State Department [https://2009-2017.state.gov/s/l/c3754.htm].*

- ADF *v* United States, Post-Hearing Submission of Respondent United States of America on Article 1105(1) and *Pope & Talbot*, ICSID Case No. ARB(AF)/00/1 (27 June 2002).
- ADF *v* United States, Rejoinder of Respondent United States of America on Competence and Liability, ICSID Case No. ARB(AF)/00/1 (29 March 2002).
- AES Corporation and Tau Power B.V. *v* Kazakhstan, Award, ICSID Case No. ARB/10/16 (1 November 2013).
- AES Summit Generation Ltd. and AES-Tisza Erömü Kft. *v* Hungary, Award, ICSID Case No. ARB/07/22 (23 September 2010).
- Alasdair Ross Anderson et al. *v* Costa Rica, Award, ICSID Case No. ARB(AF)/07/3 (19 May 2010).
- American Manufacturing & Trading Inc. *v* Zaire, Award, ICSID Case No. ARB 93/1 (21 February 1997).
- Ampal-American Israel Corp., Egi-Fund (08-10) Investors LLC, Egi-Series Investments LLC and BSS-EMG Investors LLC *v* Egypt, Decision on Jurisdiction, ICSID Case No. ARB/12/11 (1 February 2016).
- Ampal-American Israel Corp., Egi-Fund (08-10) Investors LLC, Egi-Series Investments LLC and BSS-EMG Investors LLC *v* Egypt, Decision on Liability and Heads of Loss, ICSID Case No. ARB/12/11 (21 February 2017).
- Anglo American PLC *v* Venezuela, Award, ICSID Case No. ARB(AF)/14/1 (18 January 2019).
- Asian Agricultural Products *v* Sri Lanka , Final Award, ICSID Case No ARB/87/3 (27 June 1990).
- Asian Agricultural Products *v* Sri Lanka, Dissenting Opinion of Samuel K.B. Asante, ICSID Case No. ARB/87/3 (27 June 1990), 6(2) ICSID Review 574-97.
- Autopista Concesionada de Venezuela C.A. *v* Venezuela, Award, ICSID Case No. ARB/00/5 (23 September 2003).
- Azurix Corp. *v* Argentina, Award, ICSID Case No. ARB/01/12 (14 July 2006).
- Azurix Corp. *v* Argentina, Decision on the Application for Annulment of the Argentina Republic, ICSID Case No. ARB/01/12 (1 September 2009).
- Bear Creek Mining Corp. *v* Peru, Award, ICSID Case No. ARB/14/21 (30 November 2017).
- Bernardus Henricus Funnekotter et al. *v* Zimbabwe, Award, ICSID Case No. ARB/05/6 (22 April 2009).
- Bernhard Friedrich Arnd Rüdiger von Pezold et al. *v* Zimbabwe, Award, ICSID Case No. ARB/10/15 (28 July 2015).
- Biwater Gauff Ltd. *v* Tanzania, Award, ICSID Case No. ARB/05/22 (24 July 2008).
- Burlington Resources Inc. *v* Ecuador, Decision on Jurisdiction, ICSID Case No. ARB/08/5 (2 June 2010).
- Cargill Inc. *v* Poland, Final Award, ICSID Case No. ARB(AF)/04/2 (29 February 2008).
- Cervin Investissements S.A. and Rhone Investissements S.A. *v* Costa Rica, Laudo, ICSID Case No. ARB/13/2 (7 March 2017).

- Československá Obchodní Banka A.S. *v* Slovakia, Award, ICSID Case No. ARB/97/4 (29 December 2004).
- CMS Gas Transmission Co. *v* Argentina, Award, ICSID Case No. ARB/01/8 (12 May 2005).
- Compañía de Aguas del Aconquija S.A. and Vivendi Universal S.A. *v* Argentina, Award, ICSID Case No. ARB/97/3 (20 August 2007).
- Continental Casualty Co. *v* Argentina, Award, ICSID Case No. ARB/03/9 (5 September 2008).
- Convial Callao S.A. and CCI – Compañía de Concesiones de Infraestructura S.A. *v* Peru, Laudo Final, ICSID Case No. ARB/10/2 (21 May 2013).
- Crystallex International Corp. *v* Venezuela, Award, ICSID Case No. ARB(AF)/11/2 (4 April 2016).
- Deutsche Bank AG *v* Sri Lanka, Award, ICSID Case No. ARB/09/02 (31 October 2012).
- EDF International S.A., Saur International S.A. and Leon Participaciones Argentinas S.A. *v* Argentina, Award, ICSID Case No. ARB/03/23 (11 June 2012).
- Electrabel S.A. *v* Hungary, Decision on Jurisdiction, Applicable Law and Liability, ICSID Case No. ARB/07/19 (30 November 2012).
- El Paso Energy International Co. *v* Argentina, Award, ICSID Case No. ARB/03/15 (31 October 2011).
- Emilio Agustín Maffezini *v* Spain, Award, ICSID Case No. ARB/97/7 (13 November 2000).
- Emilio Agustín Maffezini *v* Spain, Decision on Objections to Jurisdiction, ICSID Case No. ARB/97/7 (25 January 2000).
- Enron Corp. and Ponderosa Assets L.P. *v* Argentina, Award, ICSID Case No. ARB/01/3 (22 May 2007).
- Eudoro Armando Olguín *v* Paraguay, Award, ICSID Case No. ARB/98/5 (26 July 2001).
- Eurogas Inc. and Belmont Resources Inc. *v* Slovakia, Award, ICSID Case No. ARB/14/14 (18 August 2017).
- Flughafen Zürich A.G. and Gestión de Ingeniería IDC S.A. *v* Venezuela, Laudo, ICSID Case No. ARB/10/19 (18 November 2014).
- Fraport AG Frankfurt Airport Services Worldwide *v* Philippines, Award, ICSID Case No. ARB/11/12 (10 December 2014).
- Garanti Koza LLP *v* Turkmenistan, Award, ICSID Case No. ARB/11/20 (19 December 2016).
- Gea Group Aktiengesellschaft *v* Ukraine, Award, ICSID Case No. ARB/08/16 (31 March 2011).
- Gemplus S.A., SLP S.A. and Gemplus Industrial S.A. de C.V. *v* Mexico, Award, ICSID Cases No. ARB(AF)/04/3 & ARB(AF)/04/4 (16 June 2010).
- Gold Reserve Inc. *v* Venezuela, Award, ICSID Case No. ARB(AF)/09/1 (22 September 2014).
- Impregilo S.p.A. *v* Argentina, Award, ICSID Case No. ARB/07/17 (21 June 2011).

- Impregilo S.p.A. *v* Argentina, Decision on the Application for Annulment, ICSID Case No. ARB/07/17 (24 January 2014).
- Italba Corporation *v* Uruguay, Award, ICSID Case No. ARB/16/9 (22 March 2019).
- Jan de Nul N.V. and Dredging International N.V. *v* Egypt, Award, ICSID Case No. ARB/04/13 (6 November 2008).
- Joseph Charles Lemire *v* Ukraine, Decision on Jurisdiction and Liability, ICSID Case No. ARB/06/18 (14 January 2010).
- Joseph Houben *v* Burundi, Sentence, ICSID Case No. ARB/13/7 (12 January 2016).
- Karkey Karadeniz Elektrik Uretim A.S. *v* Pakistan, Award, ICSID Case No. ARB/13/1 (22 August 2017).
- Koch Minerals SÁRL and Koch Nitrogen International SÁRL *v* Venezuela, Award, ICSID Case No. ARB/11/19 (30 October 2017).
- LESI S.p.A. and ASTALDI S.p.A. *v* Algeria, Sentence, ICSID Case No. ARB/05/3 (12 November 2008).
- Liman Caspian Oil BV and NCL Dutch Investment BV *v* Kazakhstan, Award, ICSID Case No. ARB/07/14 (22 June 2010).
- Loewen Group Inc. and Raymond L. Loewen *v* United States, Award, ICSID Case No. ARB(AF)/98/3 (26 June 2003).
- Mamidoil Jetoil Greek Petroleum Products Societe S.A. *v* Albania, Award, ICSID Case No. ARB/11/24 (30 March 2015).
- Marion Unglaube and Reinhard Unglaube *v* Costa Rica, Award, ICSID Cases No. ARB/01/1 and ARB/09/20 (16 May 2012).
- M.C.I. Power Group L.C. and New Turbine Inc. *v* Ecuador, Award, ICSID Case No. ARB/03/6 (31 July 2007).
- Mercer International Inc. *v* Canada, Award, ICSID Case No. ARB(AF)/12/3 (6 March 2018).
- Millicom International Operations B.V. and Sentel GMS SA *v* Senegal, Decision on Jurisdiction of the Arbitral Tribunal, ICSID Case No. ARB/08/20 (16 July 2010).
- MNSS B.V. and Recupero Credito Acciaio N.V. *v* Montenegro, Award, ICSID Case No. ARB(AF)/12/8 (4 May 2016).
- Mobil Exploration and Development Argentina Inc. Suc. Argentina and Mobil Argentina S.A. *v* Argentina, Decision on Jurisdiction and Liability, ICSID Case No. ARB/04/16 (10 April 2013).
- Mondev International *v* United States, Award, ICSID Case No. ARB(AF)/99/2 (11 October 2002).
- Noble Ventures *v* Romania, Award, ICSID Case No. ARB/01/11 (12 October 2005).
- OI European Group B.V. *v* Venezuela, Award, ICSID Case No. ARB/11/25 (10 March 2015).
- Pantechniki S.A. Contractors & Engineers *v* Albania, Award, ICSID Case No. ARB/07/21 (30 July 2009).

- Parkerings-Compagniet AS *v* Lithuania, Award, ICSID Case No. ARB/05/8 (11 September 2007).
- Philip Morris Brands Sàrl, Philip Morris Products S.A. and Abal Hermanos S.A. *v* Uruguay, Award, ICSID Case No. ARB/10/7 (8 July 2016).
- Plama Consortium Ltd. *v* Bulgaria, Award, ICSID Case No. ARB/03/24 (27 August 2008).
- PSEG Global Inc. and Konya Ilgin Elektrik Üretim ve Ticaret Limited Şirketi *v* Turkey, Award, ICSID Case No. ARB/02/5 (19 January 2007).
- Railroad Development Corp. *v* Guatemala, Award, ICSID Case No. ARB/07/23 (29 June 2012).
- RREEF Infrastructure (G.P.) Ltd. and RREEF Pan-European Infrastructure Two Lux S.à.r.l. *v* Spain, Award, ICSID Case No. ARB/13/30 (30 November 2018).
- Rumeli Telekom A.S. and Telsim Mobil Telekomunikasyon Hizmetleri A.S. *v* Kazakhstan, Award, ICSID Case No. ARB/05/16 (29 July 2008).
- Rusoro Mining Ltd. *v* Venezuela, Award, ICSID Case No. ARB(AF)/12/5 (22 August 2016).
- Saint-Gobain Performance Plastics Europe *v* Venezuela, Decision on Liability and the Principles of Quantum, ICSID Case No. ARB/12/13 (30 December 2016).
- SAUR International S.A. *v* Argentina, Décision relative à la demande d'annulation de la république argentine, ICSID Case No. ARB/04/4 (19 December 2016).
- SAUR International S.A. *v* Argentina, Décision sur la compétence et sur la responsabilité, ICSID Case No. ARB/04/4 (6 June 2012).
- Sempra Energy International *v* Argentina, Award, ICSID Case No. ARB/02/16 (28 September 2007).
- Sempra Energy International *v* Argentina, Decision on the Argentine Republic's Application for Annulment of the Award, ICSID Case No. ARB/02/16 (29 June 2010).
- Sempra Energy International & Camuzzi International S.A. *v* Argentina, Opinion of José E. Álvarez, ICSID Cases No. ARB/02/16 and ARB/03/02 (12 September 2005).
- Siemens AG *v* Argentina, Award, ICSID Case No. ARB/02/8 (6 February 2007).
- Suez Sociedad General de Aguas de Barcelona S.A. and Vivendi Universal S.A. *v* Argentina, Decision on Liability, ICSID Case No. ARB/03/19 (30 July 2010).
- Sucz Sociedad General de Aguas de Barcelona S.A. and Vivendi Universal S.A. *v* Argentina, Separate Opinion of Arbitrator Pedro Nikken, ICSID Case No. ARB/03/19 (30 July 2010).
- Supervisión y Control S.A. *v* Costa Rica, Award, ICSID Case No. ARB/12/4 (18 January 2017).
- Spyridon Roussalis *v* Romania, Award, ICSID Case No. ARB/06/1 (7 December 2011).
- Tecnicas Medioambientales TECMED S.A. *v* Mexico, Award, ICSID Case No. ARB(AF)/00/2 (29 May 2003).

- Teinver S.A., Transportes de Cercanías S.A. and Autobuses Urbanos del Sur S.A. *v* Argentina, Award, ICSID Case No. ARB/09/1 (21 July 2017).
- Tenaris S.A. and Talta-Trading E Marketing Sociedade Unipessoal Lda. *v* Venezuela, Award, ICSID Case No. ARB/11/26 (29 January 2016).
- Tokios Tokelés *v* Ukraine, Award, ICSID Case No. ARB/02/18 (26 July 2007).
- Total S.A. *v* Argentina, Decision on Liability, ICSID Case No. ARB/04/1 (27 December 2010).
- Toto Costruzioni Generali S.p.A. *v* Lebanon, Award, ICSID Case No. ARB/07/12 (7 June 2012).
- Toto Costruzioni Generali S.p.A. *v* Lebanon, Decision on Jurisdiction, ICSID Case No. ARB/07/12 (11 September 2009).
- Tulip Real Estate Investment and Development Netherlands B.V. *v* Turkey, Award, ICSID Case No. ARB/11/28 (10 March 2014).
- Urbaser S.A. and Consorcio de Aguas Bilbao Bizkaia, Bilbao Biskaia Ur Partzuergoa *v* Argentina, Award, ICSID Case No. ARB/07/26 (8 December 2016).
- Vannessa Ventures Ltd. *v* Venezuela, Award, ICSID Case No. ARB(AF)04/6 (16 January 2013).
- Vincent J. Ryan, Schooner Capital LLC and Atlantic Investment Partners LLC *v* Poland, Award, ICSID Case No. ARB(AF)/11/3 (24 November 2015).
- Waguih George Siag and Clorinda Vecchi *v* Egypt, Award, ICSID Case No. ARB/05/15 (1 June 2009).
- Waste Management *v* Mexico, Award, ICSID Case No. ARB(AF)/00/3 (30 April 2004).
- Wena Hotels Ltd. *v* Egypt, Award, ICSID Case No. ARB/98/4 (8 December 2000).
- Wena Hotels Ltd. *v* Egypt, Decision on Annulment, ICSID Case No. ARB/98/4 (5 February 2002).

Other Arbitrations[4]

- Achmea B.V. *v* Slovakia (UNCITRAL), Award on Jurisdiction, Arbitrability and Suspension, PCA Case No. 2008-13 (26 October 2010).
- Anglia Auto Accessories Ltd. *v* Czech Republic, Final Award, SCC Case No. V 2014/181 (10 March 2017).
- BG Group *v* Argentina (UNCITRAL), Final Award (24 December 2007).
- CC/Devas (Mauritius) Ltd., Devas Employees Mauritius Private Ltd. and Telcom Devas Mauritius Ltd. *v* India (UNCITRAL), Award on Jurisdiction and Merits, PCA Case No. 2013-09 (25 July 2016).

---

[4]*Unless otherwise indicated, the following materials are available at the Investment Treaty Arbitration Database of the University of Victoria [http://www.italaw.com].*

- CME Czech Republic B.V. *v* Czech Republic (UNCITRAL), Dissenting Opinion of Arbitrator Jaroslav Hándl against the Partial Award (11 September 2001).
- CME Czech Republic B.V. *v* Czech Republic (UNCITRAL), Partial Award (13 September 2001).
- Deutsche Telekom AG *v* India (UNCITRAL), Interim Award, PCA Case No. 2014-10 (13 December 2017).
- Eastern Sugar B.V. *v* Czech Republic, Partial Award, SCC Case No. 088/2004 (27 March 2007).
- East Mediterranean Gas Co. S.A.E. *v* Egyptian General Petroleum Corp., Egyptian Natural Gas Holding Co. and Israel Electric Corp., Final Award, ICC Case No. 18215/GZ/MHM (4 December 2015). Partly reproduced in: Ampal-American Israel Corp., Egi-Fund (08-10) Investors LLC, Egi-Series Investments LLC and BSS-EMG Investors LLC *v* Egypt, Decision on Liability and Heads of Loss, ICSID Case No. ARB/12/11 (21 February 2017).
- Eli Lilly and Co. *v* Canada (UNCITRAL), Award, Case No. UNCT/14/2 (16 March 2017).
- Eli Lilly and Co. *v* Canada (UNCITRAL), NAFTA Article 1128 Submission of the United States of America, Case No. UNCT/14/2 (18 March 2016).
- Eureko B.V. *v* Poland (*Ad Hoc* Arbitration), Partial Award (19 August 2005).
- Frontier Petroleum Ltd. *v* Czech Republic (UNCITRAL), Final Award (12 November 2010).
- Gami Investments *v* Mexico (UNCITRAL), Final Award (15 November 2004).
- Glamis Gold *v* United States of America (UNCITRAL), Award (8 June 2009).
- Grand River Enterprises Six Nations Ltd. et al. *v* United States of America (UNCITRAL), Award (12 January 2011).
- Greentech Energy Systems A/S, NovEnergia II Energy & Environment (SCA) SICAR and NovEnergia II Italian Portfolio SA *v* Italy, Dissenting Opinion of Arbitrator Giorgio Sacerdoti, SCC Case No. V 2015/095 (5 December 2018).
- Gujarat State Petroleum Corp. Ltd., Alkor Petroo Ltd. and Western Drilling Contractors Private Ltd. *v* Republic of Yemen and The Yemen Ministry of Oil and Minerals, ICC Case No. 19299/MCP, Final Award (10 July 2015).
- Hesham Talaat M. Al-Warraq *v* Indonesia (UNCITRAL), Final Award (15 December 2014).
- I.P. Busta and J.P. Busta *v* Czech Republic, Final Award, SCC Case No. V 2015/014 (10 March 2017).
- Isolux Netherlands B.V. *v* Spain, Laudo, SCC Case No. V 2013/153 (17 July 2016).
- Iurii Bogdanov et al. *v* Moldova (SCC), Arbitral Award (22 September 2005).
- Jan Oostergetel and Theodora Laurentius *v* Slovakia (UNCITRAL), Final Award (23 April 2012).
- Merril & Ring Forestry L.P. *v* Canada (UNCITRAL /ICSID Administered Case), Award (31 March 2010).
- Mesa Power Group LLC *v* Canada (UNCITRAL), Award, PCA Case No. 2012-17 (24 March 2016).

- Mohammad Ammar Al-Bahloul *v* Tajikistan, Partial Award on Jurisdiction and Liability, SCC Case No. V 064/2008 (9 September 2009).
- Murphy Exploration & Production Co. *v* Ecuador (UNCITRAL), Partial Final Award (6 May 2016).
- Murphy Exploration & Production Co. *v* Ecuador (UNCITRAL), Final Award (10 February 2017).
- National Grid P.L.C. *v* Argentina (UNCITRAL), Award (3 November 2008).
- Nykomb Synergetics Technology Holding AB *v* Latvia (SCC), Arbitral Award (16 December 2003).
- OAO Tatneft *v* Ukraine (UNCITRAL), Award (29 July 2014).
- Occidental Exploration and Production Co. *v* Ecuador, Final Award, LCIA Case No. UN 3467 (1 July 2004).
- Oxus Gold *v* Uzbekistan (UNCITRAL), Final Award (17 December 2015).
- Peter A. Allard *v* Barbados (UNCITRAL), Award (27 June 2016).
- Pope & Talbot Inc. *v* Canada (UNCITRAL), Award in respect of Damages (31 May 2002).
- Ronald Lauder *v* Czech Republic (UNCITRAL), Final Award (3 September 2001).
- Saluka Investments *v* Czech Republic (UNCITRAL), Partial Award (17 March 2006).
- Sergei Paushok, CJSC Golden East Co., CJSC Vostoknefte *v* Mongolia (UNCITRAL), Award on Jurisdiction and Liability (28 April 2011).
- Spence International Investments LLC., Berkowitz et al. *v* Costa Rica (UNCITRAL), CAFTA-DR Article 10.20.2 Submission of the United States of America, Case No. UNCT/13/2 (17 April 2015).
- Ulysseas Inc. *v* Ecuador (UNCITRAL), Final Award (12 June 2012).
- William Ralph Clayton, William Richard Clayton, Douglas Clayton, Daniel Clayton and Bilicon of Delaware Inc. *v* Canada (UNCITRAL), Award on Jurisdiction and Liability, PCA Case No. 2009-05 (17 March 2015).
- Windstream Energy LLC *v* Canada (UNCITRAL), Award (27 September 2016).
- Windstream Energy LLC *v* Canada (UNCITRAL), NAFTA Article 1128 Submission of the United States of America (12 January 2016).

National Courts

United Kingdom

- *Al Rawi et al. v Foreign Secretary* [2006] EWCA Civ 1219-74.

United States

- *Baltimore & Ohio RR Co v Goodman* (1927) 275 US 66.
- *Helen Palsgraf v The Long Island Railroad Co.* (1928) 248 NY 339.
- Hum Fay et al. *v* Frank Balwin et al. (1900) *Papers relating to the Foreign Relations of the United States with the Annual Message of the President* (Government Printing Office, Washington 1901) 117-24.
- *Pokora v Wabash Rail Co* (1934) 292 US 98.

Table of State Practice

Argentina

- 'Letter of Mr. Drago, Minister of Foreign Relations of the Argentine Republic, to Mr. Mérou, Argentine Minister to the United States' (29 December 1902) in Alejandro Álvarez, *The Monroe Doctrine. Its Importance in the International Life of the States of the New World* (Oxford University Press, New York 1924) 187-93 (Annex XXIX).

Austria

- 'Note du Cabinet de Vienne' (14 April 1850) in Carlos Calvo, 'De la non-responsabilité des états a raison des pertes et dommages éprouvés par des étrangers en temps de troubles intérieurs ou de guerres civiles' (1869) 1 Revue de droit international et de législation comparée 417, 419.

Chile

- 'Antonio Varas al señor Cazotte, Encargado de Negocios de la República Francesa' (29 December 1852) in Rafael Caldera (ed), *Obras completas de Andrés Bello / Derecho internacional IV. Documentos de la Cancillería Chilena* (Volume XIII: Fundación La Casa de Bello, Caracas 1981) 490-505.
- 'Antonio Varas al señor Peyton, Enviado Extraordinario y Ministro Plenipotenciario de los Estados Unidos de América' (20 December 1852) in Rafael Caldera (ed), *Obras completas de Andrés Bello / Derecho internacional*

© Springer Nature Switzerland AG 2019
S. Mantilla Blanco, *Full Protection and Security in International Investment Law*,
European Yearbook of International Economic Law 8,
https://doi.org/10.1007/978-3-030-24838-3

IV. Documentos de la Cancillería Chilena (Vol. XIII: Fundación La Casa de Bello, Caracas 1981) 481-6.

China

- 'Chen Lan Pin to Mr. Evarts' (12 November 1880) *Papers relating to the Foreign Relations of the United States with the Annual Message of the President* (Government Printing Office, Washington 1882) 318.
- 'Chen Lan Pin to Mr. Evarts' (21 January 1881) *Papers relating to the Foreign Relations of the United States with the Annual Message of the President* (Government Printing Office, Washington 1882) 321-3.
- 'Mr. Wu to Mr. Hill' (6 July 1901) *Papers relating to the Foreign Relations of the United States with the Annual Message of the President* (Government Printing Office, Washington 1901) 100-3.
- 'Report of B. A. Bee, Chinese Consul' (8 December 1880) *Papers relating to the Foreign Relations of the United States with the Annual Message of the President* (Government Printing Office, Washington 1882) 323-4.

Colombia

- 'Extract from the Presidential Message to the Congress of New Granada' (1 February 1857) in Luis Santamaría (ed), *Final Diplomatic Controversy relating to the Occurrences that Took Place at Panama on the 15th of April, 1856* (Mail Office, Liverpool 1857) 47-50.

France

- 'Count Sartriges, French min., to Mr. Marcy, Sec. of State' (13 January 1857) in John Bassett Moore, *A Digest of International Law* (Volume 6: Government Printing Office, Washington 1906) 926-7.

Germany

- 'Der Botschafter in London Graf von Metternich an das Auswärtige Amt' (15 December 1902) in Johanes Lepsius, Albrecht Mendelssohn and Friedrich Thimme (eds), *Die Große Politik der Europäischen Kabinette 1871-1914. Sammlung der Diplomatischen Akten des Auswärtigen Amtes* (Volume 17: Deutsche Verlagsgesellschaft für Politik und Geschichte, Berlin 1924) 262-4.

- 'Der Geschäftsträger in Washington Graf von Quadt an das Auswärtige Amt' (25 November 1902) in Johanes Lepsius, Albrecht Mendelssohn and Friedrich Thimme (eds), *Die Große Politik der Europäischen Kabinette 1871-1914. Sammlung der Diplomatischen Akten des Auswärtigen Amtes* (Volume 17: Deutsche Verlagsgesellschaft für Politik und Geschichte, Berlin 1924) 256.
- 'Der Reichkanzler Graf von Bülow an Kaiser Wilhelm' (1 September 1902) in Johanes Lepsius, Albrecht Mendelssohn and Friedrich Thimme (eds), *Die Große Politik der Europäischen Kabinette 1871-1914. Sammlung der Diplomatischen Akten des Auswärtigen Amtes* (Volume 17: Deutsche Verlagsgesellschaft für Politik und Geschichte, Berlin 1924) 244-6.
- 'Der Reichkanzler Graf von Bülow an Kaiser Wilhelm' (12 December 1902) in Johanes Lepsius, Albrecht Mendelssohn and Friedrich Thimme (eds), *Die Große Politik der Europäischen Kabinette 1871-1914. Sammlung der Diplomatischen Akten des Auswärtigen Amtes* (Volume 17: Deutsche Verlagsgesellschaft für Politik und Geschichte, Berlin 1924) 258-60.
- 'Der Reichkanzler Graf von Bülow an Kaiser Wilhelm' (3 November 1902) in Johanes Lepsius, Albrecht Mendelssohn and Friedrich Thimme (eds), *Die Große Politik der Europäischen Kabinette 1871-1914. Sammlung der Diplomatischen Akten des Auswärtigen Amtes* (Volume 17: Deutsche Verlagsgesellschaft für Politik und Geschichte, Berlin 1924) 246-9.
- 'Der Staatssekretär des Auswärtigen Amtes Freiherr von Richthofen an den Botschafter in London Grafen von Metternich' (14 Dezember 1902) in Johanes Lepsius, Albrecht Mendelssohn and Friedrich Thimme (eds), *Die Große Politik der Europäischen Kabinette 1871-1914. Sammlung der Diplomatischen Akten des Auswärtigen Amtes* (Volume 17: Deutsche Verlagsgesellschaft für Politik und Geschichte, Berlin 1924) 260-1.
- 'Grossbritanien – Denkschrift über die Beschwerde gegen Venezuela' in Gustav Roloff (ed) *Das Staatsarchiv. Sammlung der offiziellen Aktenstücke zur Geschichte der Gegenwart* (Volume 68: Duncker & Humblot, Berlin 1904) 121-5.
- Reichstag, 'Protokoll – 241. Sitzung' (19 January 1903) *Stenographische Berichte über die Verhandlungen des Reichtags, X. Legislaturperiode, II. Session 1900/3* (Volume 8: Verlag der Norddeutschen Buchdruckerei, Berlin 1903) 7393-412.
- Reichstag, 'Protokoll – 242. Sitzung' (20 January 1903) *Stenographische Berichte über die Verhandlungen des Reichtags, X. Legislaturperiode, II. Session 1900/3* (Volume 8: Verlag der Norddeutschen Buchdruckerei, Berlin 1903) 7413-36.
- Reichstag, 'Protokoll – 243. Sitzung' (21 January 1903) *Stenographische Berichte über die Verhandlungen des Reichtags, X. Legislaturperiode, II. Session 1900/3* (Volume 8: Verlag der Norddeutschen Buchdruckerei, Berlin 1903) 7437-65.
- Reichstag, 'Protokoll – 244. Sitzung' (22 January 1903) *Stenographische Berichte über die Verhandlungen des Reichtags, X. Legislaturperiode,*

II. Session 1900/3 (Volume 8: Verlag der Norddeutschen Buchdruckerei, Berlin 1903) 7467-97.

- Reichstag, 'Protokoll – 287. Sitzung' (19 March 1903) *Stenographische Berichte über die Verhandlungen des Reichtags, X. Legislaturperiode, II. Session 1900/3* (Volume 10: Verlag der Norddeutschen Buchdruckerei, Berlin 1903) 8717-49.
- Reichstag, 'Protokoll – 68. Sitzung' (16 March 1893) *Stenographische Berichte über die Verhandlungen des Reichtags, VIII. Legislaturperiode, II. Session 1892/ 3* (Volume 3: Verlag der Norddeutschen Buchdruckerei, Berlin 1893) 1671-93.

Honduras

- 'Mr. Bonilla to Mr. Hunter' (2 July 1900) *Papers relating to the Foreign Relations of the United States with the Annual Message of the President* (Government Printing Office, Washington 1900) 692-3.
- 'Mr. Bonilla to Mr. Hunter' (25 April 1899) *Papers relating to the Foreign Relations of the United States with the Annual Message of the President* (Government Printing Office, Washington 1900) 679-81.
- 'Mr. Bonilla to Mr. Hunter' (30 June 1899) *Papers relating to the Foreign Relations of the United States with the Annual Message of the President* (Government Printing Office, Washington 1900) 684-5.
- Mr. Fiallos, Honduran minister of justice, to the minister of Honduras' (4 March 1899) *Papers relating to the Foreign Relations of the United States with the Annual Message of the President* (Government Printing Office, Washington 1900) 681-4.

Japan

- 'The [Japanese] Minister of Foreign Affairs to the American Ambassador' (6 October 1911) *Papers relating to the Foreign Relations of the United States with the Annual Message of the President* (Government Printing Office, Washington 1911) 323-4.

Mexico

- 'The [Mexican] Minister of Foreign Affairs to the American Ambassador' (16 May 1911) *Papers relating to the Foreign Relations of the United States with the Annual Message of the President* (Government Printing Office, Washington 1911) 493.

Soviet Union

- 'Note from the Soviet Foreign Ministry to the Turkish Embassy in Moscow' (30 August 1964) in Ian Brownlie, *System of the Law of Nations. State Responsibility* (Clarendon Press, Oxford 1983) 118.

United Kingdom

- 'Argument or summary, showing the points and referring to the evidence relied upon by the Government of Her Britannic Majesty in answer to the claims of the United States presented to the Tribunal of Arbitration constituted under Article 1 of the treaty concluded at Washington on the 8th May, 1871, between Her Britannic Majesty and the United States of America' (undated) *The Argument at Geneva. A Complete Collection of the Forensic Discussions on the Part of the United States and of Great Britain before the Tribunal of Arbitration under the Treaty of Washington* (Government Printing Office, Washington 1873) 257-370.
- 'Correspondence between Great Britain, Italy, Turkey and Greece, respecting the Capture and Murder by Brigands of the Secretaries of the British and Italian Legations at Athens (Mr. Herbert and Count de Boyl) and of other British Subjects' (1870-1871) 65 St. Pap. 667-723.
- 'Earl Russel to Mr. Adams' (26 November 1861) in John Bassett Moore, *A Digest of International Law* (Volume 1: Government Printing Office, Washington 1906) 209.
- 'Mr. Bonham to Commissioner Seu' (13 March 1849) 38 (1) St. Pap. 856-8.
- Henry John Temple (Third Viscount Palmerston), 'Intervention before the House of Commons on the Greytown Bombardment' (19 June 1857) Hansard's Parliamentary Debates CXLVI (Commons), Third Series 40-3.
- Henry John Temple (Third Viscount Palmerston), 'Speech on the *Don Pacifico* affair' (28 June 1850) Hansard's Parliamentary Debates CXII (Commons), Third Series 380-444.

United States

- 'Cabinet Meeting. Opinion on a Proclamation of Neutrality and on Receiving the French Minister' (19 April 1793) *United States National Archives: Founders Online Project* [http://founders.archives.gov/documents/Hamilton/01-14-02-0226].
- 'Communication of the U.S. Secretary of State to the Mexican Ambassador at Washington' (22 August 1938) 32(4) AJIL 191-201.

- 'Instruction to the U.S. Embassy to the Kingdom of Italy [concerning the *Cutler affair*]' (5 July 1927) in Green Hackworth (ed), *Digest of International Law* (Volume 5: Government Printing Office, Washington 1943) 660-1.
- 'Instructions from Secretary of State Livingston on the Additional and Explanatory Convention to the Treaty of Peace, Amity, Commerce and Navigation between the United States of America and the Republic of Chile' (19 April 1833) in Hunter Miller (ed), *Treaties and Other International Acts of the United States of America* (Volume 3: Government Printing Office, Washington 1971) 704.
- 'Lincoln, At. Gen.' (1802) in John Bassett Moore, *A Digest of International Law* (Volume 6: Government Printing Office, Washington 1906) 787.
- 'Message from Secretary of State Rusk to Chairman of the Ad Hoc Commission of the Congo Prime Minister Jomo Kenyatta' (16 November 1964) Jules Davids (ed), *Documents on American Foreign Relations – 1964* (Harper & Row Publishers, New York 1965) 345, 346.
- 'Message of the President of the United States to the Senate and House of Representatives' (6 December 1904) *Papers relating to the Foreign Relations of the United States with the Annual Message of the President* (Government Printing Office, Washington 1905) ix-xlviii.
- 'Message of the President of the United States, at the Commencement of the First Session of the Eighteenth Congress' 5 American State Papers: Foreign Relations (1858) 245-50.
- 'Mr. Adams to Earl Russell' (20 November 1862) *Papers relating to the Foreign Relations of the United States with the Annual Message of the President* (Government Printing Office, Washington 1863) 7-10.
- 'Mr. Bayard, Sec. of State, to Mr. Buck, min. to Peru' (13 August 1886) in John Bassett Moore, *A Digest of International Law* (Volume 6: Government Printing Office, Washington 1906) 992.
- 'Mr. Bayard, Sec. of State, to Mr. Buck, min. to Peru' (28 October 1885) in John Bassett Moore, *A Digest of International Law* (Volume 6: Government Printing Office, Washington 1906) 758-9.
- 'Mr. Bayard, Sec. of State, to Mr. Stuphen' (6 January 1888) in John Bassett Moore, *A Digest of International Law* (Volume 6: Government Printing Office, Washington 1906) 961-4.
- 'Mr. Blaine to Chen Lan Pin' (25 March 1881) *Papers relating to the Foreign Relations of the United States with the Annual Message of the President* (Government Printing Office, Washington 1882) 335-7.
- 'Mr. Evarts to Chen Lan Pin' (30 December 1880) *Papers relating to the Foreign Relations of the United States with the Annual Message of the President* (Government Printing Office, Washington 1882) 319-20.
- 'Mr. Fish, Sec. of State, to Baron Gerolt, Prussian min.' (15 April 1870) in John Bassett Moore, *A Digest of International Law* (Volume 6: Government Printing Office, Washington 1906) 937, 937-8.
- 'Mr. Fish, Sec. of State, to Mr. Foster' (16 December 1873) in Francis Wharton (ed), *A Digest of the International Law of the United States. Documents issued by*

Presidents and Secretaries of State (Volume 2: Government Printing Office, Washington 1887) 617-8.

- 'Mr. Hamm, *Chargé d'Affaires*, to Mr. Livingston, Sec. of State' (5 October 1832) Hunter Miller (ed), *Treaties and Other International Acts of the United States of America* (Volume 3: Government Printing Office, Washington 1971) 704.
- 'Mr. Hay to Mr. Bridgman' (14 March 1899) *Papers relating to the Foreign Relations of the United States with the Annual Message of the President* (Government Printing Office, Washington 1899) 105.
- 'Mr. Hay to Mr. Wu' (4 December 1901) *Papers relating to the Foreign Relations of the United States with the Annual Message of the President* (Government Printing Office, Washington 1901) 127-8.
- 'Mr. Hay, Sec. of State, to Mr. Hunter' (16 March 1899) *Papers relating to the Foreign Relations of the United States with the Annual Message of the President* (Government Printing Office, Washington 1900) 674-6.
- 'Mr. Hay, Sec. of State, to Mr. Hunter' (20 March 1900) *Papers relating to the Foreign Relations of the United States with the Annual Message of the President* (Government Printing Office, Washington 1900) 685-9.
- 'Mr. Marcy, Sec. of State, to Count Sartiges, French min.' (26 February 1857) in John Bassett Moore, *A Digest of International Law* (Volume 6: Government Printing Office, Washington 1906) 927-36.
- 'Mr. Root's South American Trip' (1907) 1(1) AJIL 143-4.
- 'Mr. Seward to Mr. Adams' (8 December 1862) *Papers relating to the Foreign Relations of the United States with the Annual Message of the President* (Government Printing Office, Washington 1863) 16-7.
- 'Mr. Seward, Sec. Of State, to Mr. Dayton, min. to France' (12 January 1864) in John Bassett Moore, *A Digest of International Law* (Volume 6: Government Printing Office, Washington 1906) 957.
- 'Mr. Seward, Sec. of State, to Mr. Smith' (9 July 1868) in John Bassett Moore, *A Digest of International Law* (Volume 6: Government Printing Office, Washington 1906) 956.
- 'Mr. Webster to Mr. Calderón' (13 November 1851) in Henry St. George Tucker, *Limitations on the Treaty Making Power under the Constitution of the United States* (Little, Brown, and Co., Boston 1915) 242-4.
- 'Mr. Webster to the President of the United States' (23 December 1851) *The Works of Daniel Webster* (Volume 6: Charles C. Little and James Brown, Boston 1851) 521-30.
- 'Mr. Wharton to the Department of State' (21 April 1885) *Papers relating to the Foreign Relations of the United States with the Annual Message of the President* (Government Printing Office, Washington 1885) 212.
- 'Murder of Charles W. Renton– Diplomatic Correspondence' (1895) *Papers relating to the Foreign Relations of the United States with the Annual Message of the President* (Government Printing Office, Washington 1895) 882-935.
- 'Note of Mr. Fish, Sec. of State, to Mr. Partidge' (27 February 1875) in Francis Wharton (ed.), *A Digest of the International Law of the United States. Documents*

issued by Presidents and Secretaries of State (Volume 2: Government Printing Office, Washington 1887) 602.

- 'Note of Mr. Frelinghuysen, Sec. of State, to Mr. Morgan' (15 November 1883) in Francis Wharton (ed.), *A Digest of the International Law of the United States. Documents issued by Presidents and Secretaries of State* (Volume 2: Government Printing Office, Washington 1887) 679-91.

- 'Note of the Legation of the United States to the Honourables Mssrs. Lino de Pombo and Florentino González, Commissioners on the part of New Granada' (26 February 1857) in Luis Santamaría (ed), *Final Diplomatic Controversy relating to the Occurrences that Took Place at Panama on the 15th of April, 1856* (Mail Office, Liverpool 1857) 37-9.

- 'Remarks on the Treaty of Amity Commerce and Navigation Lately Made between the United States and Great Britain' (9-11 July 1795) *United States National Archives: Founders Online Project* [http://founders.archives.gov/documents/Hamilton/01-18-02-0281].

- 'Reply of the House to Hutchinson's First Message' (26 January 1773) in Robert Taylor, *The Adams Papers. Papers of John Adams* (Volume 1: Harvard University Press, Cambridge MA 1977) 315-31.

- 'Reply of the House to Hutchinson's Second Message' (2 March 1773) in Robert Taylor, *The Adams Papers. Papers of John Adams* (Volume 1: Harvard University Press, Cambridge MA 1977) 331-46.

- 'Report for a Plan for the Further Support of Public Debt' (16 January 1795) *United States National Archives: Founders Online Project* [http://founders.archives.gov/documents/Hamilton/01-18-02-0052-0002].

- 'Report of Mr. Wharton to the Department of State' (18 May 1885) *Papers relating to the Foreign Relations of the United States with the Annual Message of the President* (Government Printing Office, Washington 1885) 212-3.

- 'Report on the Negotiations with Spain' (18 March 1792) *United States National Archives: Founders Online Project* [http://founders.archives.gov/documents/Jefferson/01-23-02-0259].

- 'Settlement of the Claims of Mrs. Charles W. Renton, of Ella Miller Renton, and of the Estate of Jacob Baiz' (1904) *Papers relating to the Foreign Relations of the United States with the Annual Message of the President* (Government Printing Office, Washington 1904) 352-69.

- 'Stanbery, At. Gen., in response to a request of Mr. Seward, Sec. of State, for an opinion on the claims of Wheelwright & Co. and Loring & Co. for loses of merchandises in the conflagration caused by the bombardment of Valparaiso by the Spanish fleet' (1866) in John Bassett Moore, *A Digest of International Law* (Volume 6: Government Printing Office, Washington 1906) 941-2.

- 'Statement of Harold F. Linder, Deputy Assistant Secretary of State for Economic Affairs, Department of State' (9 May 1952) *Hearing before a Subcommittee of the Committee on Foreign Relations, United States Senate, Eighty-Second Congress, 2nd Session on Treaties of Friendship, Commerce, and Navigation between the United States and Colombia, Israel, Ethiopia, Italy, Denmark, and Greece* (Government Printing Office, Washington 1952) 2-7.

- 'The American Ambassador to the Mexican Minister of Foreign Affairs' (13 May 1911) *Papers relating to the Foreign Relations of the United States with the Annual Message of the President* (Government Printing Office, Washington 1911) 492.
- 'The Secretary of State to the American Minister' (20 January 1911) *Papers relating to the Foreign Relations of the United States with the Annual Message of the President* (Government Printing Office, Washington 1911) 649-52.
- 'Turkey. Abduction by Brigands, Ransom, and Release of Miss Ellen M. Stone, An American Missionary' (5 September 1901 – 8 May 1902) *Papers relating to the Foreign Relations of the United States with the Annual Message of the President* (Government Printing Office, Washington 1902) 997-1023.
- United States Department of State, *Personal Instructions to the Diplomatic Agents of the United States* (Government Printing Office, Washington 1885).

Bibliography

Abdy, John Thomas (ed), *Kent's Commentary on International Law* (Steven & Sons, London 1878).

Accioly, Hildebrando, 'Principes généraux de la responsabilité internationale d'après la doctrine et la jurisprudence' (1959) 96 RCADI 349-441.

Accioly, Hildebrando, *Manual de Direito Internacional Publico* (São Paulo, Edição Saraiva 1958).

Ago, Roberto, 'Le délit international' (1939) 68 RCADI 415-554.

Ago, Roberto, *La colpa nell'illecito internazionale* (CEDAM – Casa Editrice Dott. A. Milani, Pavia 1939).

Alenfeld, Justus, *Die Investitionsförderungsverträge der Bundesrepublik Deutschland* (Athenäum Verlag, Frankfurt am Main 1971).

Alexandrov, Stanimir, 'The Evolution of the Full Protection and Security Standard' in Meg Kinnear, Geraldine Fischer, Jara Mínguez Almeida, Luisa Torres and Mairée Uran Bidegain (eds), *Building International Investment Law. The First 50 Years of ICSID* (Wolters Kluwer / ICSID, Alphen aan den Rijn 2016) 319-29.

Allott, Philip, 'State Responsibility and the Unmaking of International Law' (1988) 29(1) HILJ 1-26.

Alschner, Wolfgang, 'Americanization of the BIT Universe: The Influence of Friendship, Commerce and Navigation (FCN) Treaties on Modern Investment Treaty Law' (2013) 5 (2) GoJIL 455-86.

Álvarez, Alejandro, *Exposé de motifs et déclaration des grands principes du droit international moderne* (Editions Internationales, Paris 1938).

Álvarez, Alejandro, *Le droit international américain* (A. Pedone, Paris 1910).

Álvarez, Alejandro, *The Monroe Doctrine. Its Importance in the International Life of the States of the New World* (Oxford University Press, New York 1924).

Álvarez, José, *Expert Opinion in Sempra Energy International v Argentina (ICSID Case No. ARB/02/16 and ARB/03/02)* (12 August 2005).

Álvarez, José, *The Public International Law Regime Governing International Investment* (Hague Academy of International Law, The Hague 2011).

Amerasinghe, Chittharanjan Felix, *Diplomatic Protection* (Oxford University Press, New York 2008).

Amerasinghe, Chittharanjan Felix, *Evidence in International Litigation* (Martinus Nijhoff, Leiden 2005).

Amerasinghe, Chittharanjan Felix, *Local Remedies in International Law* (Cambridge University Press, Cambridge 2004).

Anghie, Anthony, 'Francisco de Vitoria and the Colonial Origins of International Law' (1996) 5 Soc. Leg. Stud. 321-36.

Anozie, Nnaemeka Nwokedi, *The Full Security and Protection Due Diligence Obligation* (University of Ottawa, Ottawa 2016) [LL.M. Thesis].

Anzilotti, Dionisio, 'La responsabilité internationale des états a raison des dommages soufferts par des étrangers' (1906) 13 RGDIP 5-29 and 285-309.

Anzilotti, Dionisio, *Lehrbuch des Völkerrechts* (Volume 1: Walter de Gruyter, Berlin/Leipzig 1929).

Anzilotti, Dionisio, *Teoria generale della responsabilità dello stato nel diritto internazionale* (F. Lumachi Libraio-Editore, Florence 1902).

Araújo, Orestes, *Las doctrinas internacionalistas de Fray Francisco de Vitoria* (Universidad de Montevideo, Montevideo 1948).

Arias, Harmodio, 'The Non-Liability of States for Damages Suffered by Foreigners in the Course of a Riot, an Insurrection, or a Civil War' (1913) 7(4) AJIL 724-66.

Aust, Anthony, *Handbook of International Law* (Cambridge University Press, Cambridge 2010).

Aust, Helmut Philip, *Complicity and the Law of State Responsibility* (Cambridge University Press, New York 2011).

Baldwin, David, 'The Concept of Security' (1997) 23 Rev. Int'l St. 5-26.

Bandeira, Galindo, George Rodrigo, 'Martti Koskenniemi and the Historiographical Turn in International Law' (2005) 16(3) EJIL 539-59.

Banifatemi, Yas, 'The Emerging Jurisprudence on the Most-Favoured-Nation Treatment in Investment Arbitration' in Andrea Bjorklund, Ian Laird and Sergey Ripinsky (eds), *Investment Treaty Law* (British Institute of International and Comparative Law, London 2009) 241-74.

Barnidge, Robert, 'The Due Diligence Principle under International Law' (2006) Int'l Comm. L. Rev. 81-121.

Bastid Burdeau, Geneviève, 'La clause de protection et sécurité pleine et entière' (2015) 119 (1) RGDIP 87-101.

Bastin, Lucas, *State Responsibility for Omissions: Establishing a Breach of the Full Protection and Security Obligation by Omissions* (Oxford University, Oxford 2016) [D.Phil. Thesis].

Bastin, Lucas, *Violation of the Full Protection and Security Obligation by Regulatory Omissions* [M.Phil. Thesis] (Oxford University, Oxford 2011).

Baumgart, Max, and Sebastián Mantilla Blanco, 'Electrabel v. Ungarn: Aktuelle Entwicklungen beim Schutz von Auslandsinvestitionen nach dem Vertrag über die Energiecharta' (2016) 7 (3) KSzW 179-87.

Baxter, Richard Reeve, 'Multilateral Treaties as Evidence of Customary International Law' (1965-6) 41 BYIL 275-300.

Baxter, Richard Reeve, 'Treaties and Custom' (1970) 129 RCADI 25-105.

Becker Lorca, Arnulf, 'Universal International Law: Nineteenth-Century Histories of Imposition and Appropriation' (2010) 51(2) HILJ 475-552.

Becker Lorca, Arnulf, *Mestizo International Law. A Global Intellectual History 1842-1933* (Cambridge University Press, New York 2014).

Becker, Florian, 'Gebiets- und Personalhoheit des Staates' in Josef Isensee and Paul Kirchhof (eds), *Handbuch des Staatsrechts* (Volume 9: C. F. Müller 2013) 193-248.

Becker, Tal, *Terrorism and the State: Rethinking the Rules of State Responsibility* (Hart Publishing, Portland OR 2006).

Behringer, Ronald, *The Human Security Agenda. How Middle Power Leadership Defied US Hegemony* (Continuum International Publishing Group, New York 2012).

Bello, Andrés, *Principios de derecho de jentes* (Valentín Espinal, Caracas 1837).

Ben Hamida, Walid, 'Investment Treaties and Democratic Transition: Does Investment Law Authorize Not to Honor Contracts Concluded with Undemocratic Regimes?' in Stephan Schill, Christian Tams and Rainer Hoffmann (eds), *International Investment Law and Development: Bridging the Gap* (Edward Elgar Publishers, Northampton MA 2015) 309-29.

Benedek, Wolfgang, 'Drago-Porter Convention' in Rüdiger Wolfrum (ed), *The Max Planck Encyclopedia of Public International Law* (Volume 3: Oxford University Press, New York 2012) 234-46.

Benjamin, Walter, *The Arcades Project* (Howard Eiland and Kevin McLaughlin tr, Harvard University Press, Cambridge MA 1999).

Benton, Anthony, 'The Protection of Property Rights in Commercial Treaties of the United States' (1965) 25 ZaöRV 50-75.

Benzing, Markus, 'Evidentiary Issues' in Andreas Zimmermann, Christian Tomuschat, Karin Oellers-Frahm and Christian Tams (eds), *The Statute of the International Court of Justice. A Commentary* (Oxford University Press, Oxford 2012) 1234-75.

Benzing, Markus, *Das Beweisrecht vor internationalen Gerichten und Schiedsgerichten in zwischenstaatlichen Streitigkeiten* (Springer, Heidelberg 2010).

Bjorklund, Andrea, 'NAFTA Chapter 11' in Chester Brown (ed), *Commentaries on Selected Model Investment Treaties* (Oxford University Press, Oxford 2013) 465-533.

Bjorklund, Andrea, 'National Treatment' in August Reinisch (ed), *Standards of Investment Protection* (Oxford University Press, New York 2008) 29-58.

Bleckmann, Albert, *Grundprobleme und Methoden des Völkerrechts* (Karl Alber, München/Frankfurt 1982).

Blocher, Joseph, 'Roberts' Rules: The Assertiveness of Rules-Based Jurisprudence' (2011) 46 TULSA L. Rev. 431-48.

Bluntschli, Johann Kaspar, *Das moderne Völkerrecht der civilisirten Staten als Rechtsbuch dargestellt* (C.H. Beck, Nördlingen 1868).

Bodansky, Daniel, 'Rules vs. Standards in International Environmental Law' (2004) 98 ASIL Proceedings 275-80.

Bodansky, Daniel, and John R. Crook, 'Symposium: The ILC's State Responsibility Articles. Introduction and Overview' (2002) 96(4) AJIL 773-91.

Bodansky, Daniel, *Rules and Standards in International Law* (New York University, New York 2003) [Preliminary Draft].

Boersma, Hanns, *Violence, Hospitality, and the Cross: Reappropriating the Atonement Tradition* (Baker Publishing, Grand Rapids MI 2004).

Borchard, Edwin, 'Basic Elements of Diplomatic Protection of Citizens Abroad' (1913) 7(3) AJIL 497-520.

Borchard, Edwin, 'The "Minimum Standard" of the Treatment of Aliens' (1940) 38(4) Mich. L. Rev. 445-61.

Borchard, Edwin, 'The Law of Responsibility of States for Damage Done in Their Territory to the Person or Property of Foreigners. Comments to the Draft Convention' (April 1929) 23 AJIL 140-218.

Borchard, Edwin, *The Diplomatic Protection of Citizens Abroad or the Law of International Claims* (The Banks Law Publishing Co., New York 1916).

Börnsen, Nils, *Nationales Recht in Investitionsschiedsverfahren* (Mohr Siebeck, Tübingen 2016).

Bourne, Mike, *Understanding Security* (MacMillan, New York 2014).

Braun, Tilmann Rudolf, 'Globalization-Driven Innovation: The Investor as a Partial Subject in Public International Law – An Inquiry into the Nature and Limits of Investor Rights' (2013) 04/13 JMWP 1-63.

Braun, Tilmann Rudolf, *Ausprägungen der Globalisierung: Der Investor als Partielles Subjekt im Internationalen Investitionsrecht* (Nomos, Baden-Baden 2012).

Bray, Heather, 'SOI – Save Our Investments! International Investment Law and International Humanitarian Law' (2013) 14 J. World Investment & Trade 578-94.

Brown Scott, James, *Cases on International Law* (West Publishing Co., St. Paul MN 1922).

Brown, Chester, and Audley Sheppard, 'United Kingdom' in Chester Brown (ed), *Commentaries on Selected Model Investment Treaties* (Oxford University Press, Oxford 2013) 697-754.

Brown, David, *Palmerston and the Politics of Foreign Policy 1846-55* (Manchester University Press, New York 2002).

Brownlie, Ian, *System of the Law of Nations. State Responsibility* (Clarendon Press, Oxford 1983).

Bruno, Giovanni Carlo, 'Collateral Damages of Military Operations: Is Implementation of International Humanitarian Law Possible Using International Human Rights Law Tools?' in Roberta Arnold and Noëlle Quénivet (eds), *International Humanitarian Law and Human Rights Law* (Brill, Leiden 2008) 295-307.

Bücheler, Gebhard, *Proportionality in Investor-State Arbitration* (Oxford University Press, Oxford 2015).

Burdick, William Livesey, *The Principles of Roman Law and Their Relation to Modern Law* (Lawbook Exchange, Clark NJ 2004).

Burgstaller, Markus, 'Nationality of Corporate Investors and International Claims against the Investor's Own State' (2006) 7 J. World Investment & Trade 857-81.

Burke-White, William, and Andreas von Staden, 'Investment Protection in Extraordinary Times: The Interpretation and Application of Non-Precluded Measures Provisions in Bilateral Investment Treaties' (2007-8) 48 Va. J. Int'l L. 307-410.

Bushnell, David, *The Making of Modern Colombia: A Nation in Spite of Itself* (University of California University Press, London 1993).

Butler, Geoffrey, and Simon Maccoby, *The Development of International Law* (Longmans, Green & Co., New York 1928).

Buxbaum, Hans, *Das völkerrechtliche Delikt* (E Th. Jacob, Erlangen 1915).

Buzan, Barry, 'Peace, Power, and Security: Contending Concepts in the Study of International Relations' (1984) 21(2) JPR 109-25.

Buzan, Barry, Ole Waever and Jaap de Wilde, *Security. A New Framework for Analysis* (Lynne Rienner Publishers, Boulder CO 1998).

Byron, Christine, 'Collateral Damage' in Vincent Parrillo (ed), *Encyclopedia of Social Problems* (SAGE Publications, Thousand Oaks CA 2008) 140-2.

Cable, James, *Gunboat diplomacy 1919-1979. Political Applications of Limited Naval Force* (McMillan, London 1994).

Caldera, Rafael, (ed), *Obras completas de Andrés Bello/Derecho internacional IV. Documentos de la Cancillería Chilena* (Volume XIII: Fundación La Casa de Bello, Caracas 1981).

Calvo, Carlos, 'De la non-responsabilité des états a raison des pertes et dommages éprouvés par des étrangers en temps de troubles intérieurs ou de guerres civiles' (1869) 1 Revue de droit international et de législation comparée 417-27.

Calvo, Carlos, 'Lettre-Circulaire à quelques-uns de ses collègues de l'Institut de France et de l'Institut de Droit International' (17 April 1903) in *La Doctrine de Monroe* (A. Eyméoud, Paris 1903) 14-5.

Calvo, Carlos, *Derecho internacional teórico y práctico de Europa y América* (Volume 1: D'Amyot Librairie Diplomatique & Durand et Pedone, Paris 1868).

Calvo, Carlos, *Le droit international théorique et pratique précédé d'un exposé historique des progrès de la science du droit des gens* (Volumes 1-3: Rousseau, Paris 1896).

Cameron, Lidsey, and Vincent Chetail, *Privatizing War. Private Military and Security Companies under Public International Law* (Cambridge University Press, Cambridge 2013).

Cançado Trindade, Antônio Augusto, 'Origin and Historical Development of the Rule of Exhaustion of Local Remedies in International Law' (1976) 12 RBDI 499-527.

Caplan, Lee, and Jeremy Sharpe, 'United States' in Chester Brown (ed), *Commentaries on Selected Model Investment Treaties* (Oxford University Press, Oxford 2013) 755-851.

Carpenter, Teresa, *The Miss Stone Affair. America's First Modern Hostage Crisis* (Simon & Schuster, New York 2003).

Carr, Edward Hallett, *What is History?* (Penguin Books, New York 1987).

Caspersen, Nina, 'Making Peace with De Facto States' in Martin Riegl and Bohumil Doboš (eds), *Unrecognized States and Secession in the 21st Century* (Springer, Cham 2017) 11-22.

Chen Daley, Mercedes, 'The Watermelon Riot: Cultural Encounters in Panama City, April 15, 1856' (1990) 70(1) HAHR 85-108.

Cheng, Bin, *General Principles of Law as Applied by International Courts and Tribunals* (Cambridge University Press, New York 2006) [first edition: 1953].

Chetail, Vincent, 'Vattel and the American Dream: An Inquiry into the Reception of the *Law of Nations* in the United States' in Vincent Chetail and Pierre Marie Dupuy (eds), *The Roots of International Law. Liber Amicorum Peter Haggenmacher* (Martinus Nijhoff Publishers, Leiden 2013) 251-300.

Chornyi, Vasyl, Marianna Nerushay and Jo-Ann Crawford, *A Survey of Investment Provisions in Regional Trade Agreements*, WTO Working Paper ERSD-2016-07 (World Trade Organization/ Economic Research and Statistics Division, Geneva 2016).

Choukroune, Leïla, 'National Treatment in International Investment Law and Arbitration: A Relative Standard for Autonomous Public Regulation and Sovereign Development' in Anselm Kamperman Sanders (ed), *The Principle of National Treatment in International Economic Law: Trade, Investment and Intellectual Property* (Edward Elgar, Northampton MA 2014) 183-219.

Christenson, Gordon, 'Attributing Acts of Omission to the State' (1990) 12 Mich. J. Int'l L. 312-70.

Christenson, Gordon, 'The Doctrine of Attribution in State Responsibility' in Richard Lillich (ed), *International Law of State Responsibility for Injuries to Aliens* (University Press of Virginia, Charlottesville VA 1983) 321-60.

Cicero, Marcus Tullius, *De Officiis* (Walter Miller tr, Macmillan Co., New York 1921).

Cicero, Marcus Tullius, *On the Republic. On the Laws* (Clinton Keyes tr, Harvard University Press, Cambridge MA 1928).

Clark, Grover, 'The English Practice with Regard to Reprisals by Private Persons' (1933) 27 (4) AJIL 694-723.

Clarke, Floyd, 'A Permanent Tribunal of International Arbitration: Its Necessity and Value' (1907) 1 AJIL 342-408.

Cohen, Amicahi, 'Rules and Standards in the Application of International Humanitarian Law' (2008) 41 Isr. L. Rev. 1-27.

Collins, David, 'Applying the Full Protection and Security Standard of Protection to Digital Investments' (2011) 12(2) J. World Investment & Trade 225-44.

Collins, David, 'National Treatment in Emerging Market Investment Treaties' in Anselm Kamperman Sanders (ed), *The Principle of National Treatment in International Economic Law: Trade, Investment and Intellectual Property* (Edward Elgar, Northampton MA 2014) 161-82.

Combs, Jerald, *The Jay Treaty: Political Battleground of the Founding Fathers* (University of California Press, Berkeley 1970).

Conforti, Benedetto, 'Cours general de droit international public' (1988) 212 RCADI 9-210.

Conklin, William, *Statelessness. The Enigma of an International Community* (Hart Publishing, Oxford 2014).

Cordero Moss, Giuditta, 'Full Protection and Security' in August Reinisch (ed), *Standards of Investment Protection* (Oxford University Press, New York 2008) 131-50.

Corwine, Amos, 'The Panama Massacre. Report of the United States Commissioner of July 18, 1856/Evidence Taken at Panama' The New York Times, September 23, 1856.

Coyle, John, 'The Treaty of Friendship, Commerce and Navigation in the Modern Era' (2013) 51 Columb. J. Transnat'l L. 302-59.

Crandall, Russell, *Gunboat Democracy. U.S. Interventions in the Dominican Republic, Grenada, and Panama* (Rowman & Littlefield, Lanham MD 2006).

Craven, Matt, 'International Law and its Histories' in Matt Craven, Malgosia Fitzmaurice and Maria Vogiatzi (eds), *Time, History and International Law* (Martinus Nijhoff, Leiden/Boston 2011) 1-25.

Crawford, James, 'Revisiting the Draft Articles on State Responsibility' (1999) 10(2) EJIL 435-60.

Crawford, James, 'The ILC's Articles on Responsibility of States for Internationally Wrongful Acts: A Retrospect' (2002) 96(4) AJIL 874-90.

Crawford, James, 'Treaty and Contract in Investment Arbitration' (2008) 24(3) Arb. Int'l. 351-74.

Crawford, James, *Brownlie's Principles of Public International Law* (Oxford University Press, Oxford 2012).

Crawford, James, *State Responsibility. The General Part* (Cambridge University Press, Cambridge 2013).

Crawford, Neta, *Accountability for Killing: Moral Responsibility for Collateral Damage in America's Post-9/11* (Oxford University Press, New York 2013).

D'Amato, Anthony, 'A Brief Rejoinder' (1988) 21 Vand. J. Transnat'l L. 489-90.

D'Amato, Anthony, 'Custom and Treaty: A Response to Professor Weisburd' (1988) 21 Vand. J. Transnat'l L. 459-72.

D'Amato, Anthony, *The Concept of Custom in International Law* (Cornell University Press, Ithaca/London 1971).

D'Amato, Anthony, *Treaties as a Source of General International Law* (1961-2) 3(2) Harv. Int'l. L. Club Bull. 1-43.

D'Aspremont, Jean, 'International Customary Investment Law: Story of a Paradox' in Tarcisio Gazzini and Eric De Brabandere (eds), *International Investment Law: The Sources of Rights and Obligations* (Martinus Nijhoff, Leiden 2012) 5-47.

D'Aspremont, Jean, 'Rebellion and State Responsibility: Wrongdoing by Democratically Elected Insurgents' (2009) 58 ICLQ 427-42.

Dahm, Georg, Jost Delbück and Rüdiger Wolfrum, *Völkerrecht* (Volumes 1-3: De Gruyter, Berlin 2002).

Dahm, Georg, *Völkerrecht* (Volume 1: W. Kohlhammer Verlag, Stuttgart 1958).

Dahm, Georg, *Völkerrecht* (Volume 3: W. Kohlhammer Verlag, Stuttgart 1961).

Dawson, Frank Griffith, 'The Influence of Andrés Bello on Latin-American Perceptions on Non-Intervention and State Responsibility' (1986) 57 BYIL 253-315.

De Brabandere, Eric, 'Fair and Equitable Treatment and (Full) Protection and Security in African Investment Treaties: Between Generality and Contextual Specificity' (2017) Grotius Centre Working Paper Series 1-25.

De Brabandere, Eric, 'Host States' Due Diligence Obligations in International Investment Law' (2014-5) 42 Syracuse J. Int'l L. & Com. 319-61.

De Brabandere, Eric, *Investment Treaty Arbitration as Public International Law. Procedural Aspects and Implications* (Cambridge University Press, Cambridge 2014).

De Frouville, Olivier, 'Attribution of Conduct to the State: Private Individuals' in James Crawford, Alain Pellet and Simon Olleson (eds), *The Law of International Responsibility* (Oxford University Press, New York 2010) 257-80.

De Quadros, Fausto, *A proteção da propriedade privada pelo direito internacional público* (Livraria Almedina, Coimbra 1998).

De Quincey, Thomas, *The Caesars* (Ticknor & Fields, Boston 1860).

De Visscher, Charles, 'Cours général de principes de droit international public' (1954) 86 RCADI 445-556.

De Visscher, Charles, 'La déni de justice en droit international' (1935) 52(2) RCADI 365-442.

De Visscher, Charles, *Théories et réalités en droit international public* (A. Pedone, Paris 1960).

DeConde, Alexander, *Herbert Hoover's Latin American Policy* (Stanford University Press, Stanford CA 1951).

Delbrück, Jost, and Rüdiger Wolfrum, *Völkerrecht. Begründet von Georg Dahm* (Volumes 1-3: De Gruyter, Berlin 2002).

Demogue, René, *Traité des obligations en général* (Volume 5: Rousseau: Paris 1925).

Denza, Eileen, *Diplomatic Law. Commentary on the Vienna Convention on Diplomatic Relations* (Oxford University Press, Oxford 2016).

Derrida, Jacques, *Adieu to Emmanuel Levinas* (Pascale-Anne Brault/Michael Naas tr, Stanford University Press, Stanford CA 1999).

Derrida, Jacques, *Of Hospitality* (Rachel Bowlby tr, Stanford University Press, Stanford CA 2000).

Diehl, Alexandra, *The Core Standard of International Investment Protection: Fair and Equitable Treatment* (Kluwer Law International, Alphen aan den Rijn 2012).

Diggelmann, Oliver, 'Fault in the Law of State Responsibility – Pragmatism *ad infinitum*?' (2006) 49 GYIL 293-305.

Dippel, Horst, 'A Nineteenth-Century Truman Doctrine *avant la lettre*? Constitutional Liberty Abroad and the Parliamentary Debate about British Foreign Policy from Castlereagh to Palmerston' in Kelly Grotke and Markus Prutsch (eds), *Constitutionalism, Legitimacy, and Power. Nineteenth-Century Experiences* (Oxford University Press, Oxford 2014) 23-48.

Doehring, Karl, 'Der Status des Fremden im Verfassungsrecht der Bundesrepublik Deutschland unter Gesichtspunkt der normativen Verschränkung von Völkerrecht und Verfassungsrecht' in Karl Doehring and Josef Isensee (eds), *Die staatsrechtliche Stellung der Ausländer in der Bundesrepublik Deutschland. Vertrauensschutz im Verwaltungsrecht* (De Gruyter, Berlin 1974) 7-44.

Doehring, Karl, 'Gewohnheitsrecht aus Verträgen' (1976) 36 ZaöRV 77-95.

Doehring, Karl, *Die allgemeinen Regeln des völkerrechtlichen Fremdenrechts und das deutsche Verfassungsrecht* (Carl Heymanns Verlag, Köln/Berlin 1963).

Doehring, Karl, *Völkerrecht. Ein Lehrbuch* (C. F. Müller Verlag, Heidelberg 2004).

Dolzer, Rudolf, and Christoph Schreuer, *Principles of International Investment Law* (Oxford University Press, New York 2012).

Dolzer, Rudolf, and Margrete Stevens, *Bilateral Investment Treaties* (Martinus Nijhoff, The Hague 1995).

Dolzer, Rudolf, and Yun-i Kim, 'Germany' in Chester Brown (ed), *Commentaries on Selected Model Investment Treaties* (Oxford University Press, Oxford 2013) 289-319.

Donoghue, Michael, 'Watermelon Riot, Panama (1856)' in Alan McPherson (ed), *Encyclopedia of U.S. Military Interventions in Latin America* (Volume 1: ABC-Clio, Santa Barbara CA 2013) 688-90.

Doswald-Beck, Louise, et al., *San Remo Manual on International Law Applicable to Armed Conflicts at Sea* (Cambridge University Press, Cambridge 1995).

Douglas, Zachary, 'Property, Investment, and the Scope of Investment Protection Obligations' in Zachary Douglas, Joost Pauwelyn and Jorge Viñuales (eds), *The Foundations of International Investment Law. Bringing Theory into Practice* (Oxford University Press, Oxford 2014) 363-406.

Douglas, Zachary, 'The Hybrid Foundations of Investment Treaty Arbitration' (2003) 74 BYIL 151-289.

Douglas, Zachary, *The International Law of Investment Claims* (Cambridge, Cambridge University Press 2009).

Drago, Luis María, 'State Loans in Their Relation to International Policy' (1907) 1(3) AJIL 692-726.

Dröge, Cordula, *Positive Verpflichtungen der Staaten in der Europäischen Menschenrechtskonvention* (Springer, Heidelberg 2003).

Dubois, Bernhard, *Die Frage der völkerrechtlichen Schranken landesrechtlicher Regelung der Staatsangehörigkeit* (Verlag Stämpfli & Cie., Bern 1955).

Duguit, Léon, *Les transformations du droit public* (Librairie Armand Colin, Paris 1913).

Dull, Jonathan, *Franklin the Diplomat: the French Mission* (The American Philosophical Society, Philadelphia 1982).

Dumas, Jacques, 'La responsabilité des États a raison des crimes et délits commis sur leur territoire au préjudice d'Étrangers' (1931) 36 RCADI 183-261.

Dumberry, Patrick, 'New State Responsibility for Internationally Wrongful Acts by an Insurrectional Movement' (2006) 17(3) EJIL 605-21.

Dumberry, Patrick, *The Formation and Identification of Customary International Law in International Investment Law* (Cambridge University Press, Cambridge 2016).

Dunn, Frederick Sherwood, *The Diplomatic Protection of Americans in Mexico* (Klaus Reprint, New York 1971) [first edition: 1933].

Dunn, Frederick Sherwood, *The Protection of Nationals. A Study in the Application of International Law* (The Johns Hopkins Press, Baltimore 1932).

Dupuy, Pierre Marie, 'Dionisio Anzilotti and the Law of International Responsibility of States' (1992) 3 EJIL 139-48.

Dupuy, Pierre Marie, 'La diligence due dans le droit international et la responsabilité' in OECD, *Aspects juridiques de la pollution transfrontière* (OECD, Paris 1977) 396-405.

Dupuy, Pierre Marie, 'Reviewing the Difficulties of Codification: On Ago's Classification of Obligations of Means and Obligations of Result in Relation to State Responsibility' (1999) 10 (2) EJIL 371-85.

Dupuy, Pierre Marie, and Jorge E. Viñuales, 'Human Rights and Investment Disciplines: Integration in Progress' in Marc Bungenberg, Jörn Griebel, Stephan Hobe and August Reinisch (eds), *International Investment Law* (Nomos, Baden-Baden 2015) 1739-67.

Dworkin, Ronald, *Taking Rights Seriously* (Bloomsbury Academic, New York 1977).

Eagleton, Clyde, 'Denial of Justice in International law' (1928) 22 AJIL 538-59.

Eagleton, Clyde, *The Responsibility of States in International Law* (Klaus Reprint, New York 1970).

Eberspächer, Cord, *Die deutsche Yangste-Patrouille. Deutsche Kanonenpolitik im Zeitalter des Imperialismus 1900-1914* (Winkler, Bochum 2004).

Eckes, Alfred, *Opening America's Market. U.S. Foreign Trade Policy Since 1776* (The University of North Carolina Press, Chapel Hill NC 1995).

Ehsassi, Ali, 'Cain and Abel: Congruence and Conflict in the Application of the Denial of Justice Principle' in Stephan Schill (ed), *International Investment Law and Comparative Public Law* (Oxford University Press, New York 2010) 213-42.

Endacott, George Beer, *A Biographical Sketch-Book of Early Hong Kong* (Hong Kong University Press, Hong Kong 2005).

Endara Flores, Francisco, 'La protección y seguridad plena de las inversiones. ¿El estándar olvidado de los tratados bilaterales de inversión?' (2009) 2 Revista de Derecho Público 443-60.

Erdmann, Ulrich, *Nichtanerkannte Staaten und Regierungen* (Institut für Völkerrecht der Universität Göttingen, Göttingen 1966).

Eustathiades, Constantin, 'La responsabilité internationale de l'état pour les actes judiciaires et le problème du déni de justice en droit international' (1936) in Constantin Eustathiades, *Études de droit international* 1929-1959 (Volume 1: Editions Klissiounis, Athens 1959) 1-458.

Fanou, Maria, and Vassilis Tzevelekos, 'The Shared Territory of the ECHR and International Investment Law' in Yannick Radi (ed), *Research Handbook on Human Rights and Investment* (Edward Elgar Publishers, Northampton MA 2018) 93-136.

Favre, Antoine, 'Fault as an Element of the Illicit Act' (1963-4) 52 Geo. L. J. 555-70.

Fenwick, Charles, 'The Authority of Vattel' (1913) 7(3) APSR 395-410.

Fenwick, Charles, 'The Progress of International Law During the Past Forty Years' (1951) 79 RCADI 1-71.

Fenwick, Charles, *International Law* (The Century Co., New York 1924).

Feres, João, *La historia del concepto "Latin America" en los Estados Unidos de América* (Universidad de Cantabria, Santander 2008).

Ferrer Mac-Gregor, Eduardo, and Carlos María Pelayo Möller, 'Artículo 1. Obligación de respetar los derechos' in Christian Steiner and Patricia Uribe (eds), *Convención Americana sobre Derechos Humanos. Comentario* (Konrad-Adenauer Stiftung/Editorial Temis, Bogotá 2014) 42-68.

Fillion, Réal Robert, *Multicultural Dynamics and the Ends of History. Exploring Kant, Hegel, and Marx* (University of Ottawa Press, Ottawa 2008).

Fiore, Pascuale, *Nouveau droit international public suivant les besoins de la civilisation moderne* (Volume 1: Charles Antoine tr, A. Durand et Pedone-Lauriel Éditeurs 1885).

Fiore, Pasquale, *Il Diritto Internazionale Codificato e la Sua Sanzione Giuridica* (Unione Tipografico-Editrice, Turin 1890).

Fisher, William, 'Texts and Contexts: The Application to American Legal History of the Methodologies of Intellectual History' (1997) 49 Stan. L. Rev. 1065-110.

Fitzmaurice, Gerald, 'The Meaning of the Term Denial of Justice' (1932) 13 BYIL 93-114.

Fitzmaurice, Maglosia, 'The Corfu Channel Case and the Development of International Law' in Nisuke Ando, Edward McWhinney and Rüdiger Wolfrum (eds), *Liber Amicorum Judge Shigeru Oda* (Volume 1: Kluwer Law International, The Hague 2002) 119-46.

Foden, Timothy, 'Back to Bricks and Mortar: The case of a "Traditional" Definition of Investment that Never Was' in Ian Laird, Borzu Sabahi, Frédéric Sourgens and Todd Weiler (eds), *Investment Treaty Arbitration and International Law* (Juris Net, Huntington NY 2015) 125-66.

Foighel, Isi, *Nationalization. A Study in the Protection of Alien Property in International Law* (Stevens & Sons, London 1957).

Foster, George, 'Recovering "Protection and Security": The Treaty Standard's Obscure Origins, Forgotten Meaning, and Key Current Significance' (2012) 45(4) Vand. J. Transnat'l L. 1095-156.

Freeman, Alwyn, 'Human Rights and the Rights of Aliens' (1951) 45 ASIL Proceedings 120-39.

Freeman, Alwyn, 'Responsibility of States for Unlawful Acts of their Armed Forces' (1955) 88 (3) RCADI 263-416.

Freeman, Alwyn, *The International Responsibility of States for Denial of Justice* (Klaus Reprint, New York 1970) [first edition: 1938].

Frick, Helmut, *Bilateraler Investitionsschutz in Entwicklungsländern. Ein Vergleich der Vertragssysteme der Vereinigten Staaten von Amerika und der Bundesrepublik Deutschland* (Duncker & Humblot, Berlin 1975).

Friedman, Samy, *Expropriation in International Law* (Steven & Sons, London 1953).

Frowein, Jochen Abr., *Das de facto-Regime im Völkerrecht. Eine Untersuchung zur Rechtsstellung nichtanerkannter Staaten und ähnlicher Gebilde* (Carl Heymanns Verlag, Köln/Berlin 1968).

Fumagalli, Luigi, 'Evidence Before the International Court of Justice: Issues of Fact and Questions of Law in the Determination of International Custom' in Nerina Boschiero, Tullio Scovazzi, Cesare Pitea and Chiara Ragni (eds), *International Courts and the Development of International Law* (Springer, The Hague 2013) 137-48.

Gagné, Renaud, *Ancestral Fault in Ancient Greece* (Cambridge University Press, Cambridge 2013).

Gaillard, Emmanuel, 'Investment Treaty Arbitration and Jurisdiction Over Contract Claims – The SGS Cases Considered' in Todd Weiler (ed), *International Investment Law and Arbitration. Leading Cases from the ICSID, NAFTA, Bilateral Investment Treaties and Customary International Law* (Cameron May, London 2005) 325-46.

Gaja, Giorgio, *Articles on the Responsibility of International Organizations* (United Nations Audiovisual Library, 2014) [Written version: http://legal.un.org/avl/ha/ario/ario.html].

Gallie, Walter Bryce, 'Essentially Contested Concepts' (1956) 56 Proceedings of the Aristotelian Society 167-98.

García Amador, Francisco, 'State Responsibility. Some New Problems' (1958) 94 RCADI 365-491.

García San Martín, Álvaro, 'Francisco Bilbao y el proyecto latinoamericano' in Andrés Kozel and Héctor Palma (eds), Heterodoxia y fronteras en América Latina (Teseo, Buenos Aires 2013) 129-46.

Gardani, Francesco, 'Affix Pleonasm' in Peter Müller, Ingeborg Ohnheiser, Susan Olsen and Franz Rainer (eds), *Word Formation. An International Handbook of the Languages of Europe* (Volume 1: Walter de Gruyter, Berlin/Boston 2015) 537-50.

Gasser, Hans-Peter, and Knut Dörmann, 'Protection of the Civilian Population' in Dieter Fleck (ed), *The Handbook of International Humanitarian Law* (Oxford University Press, Oxford 2013) 231-320.

Gattini, Andrea, 'Smoking/No Smoking: Some Remarks on the Current Place of Fault in the ILC Draft Articles on State Responsibility' (1999) 10(2) EJIL 397-404.

Gattini, Andrea, *Zufall und force majeure im System der Staatenverantwortlichkeit anhand der ILC-Kodifikationsarbeit* (Duncker & Humblot, Berlin 1989).

Gazzini, Tarcisio, *Interpretation of International Investment Treaties* (Hart Publishing, Portland OR 2016).

Gentili, Alberico, 'De iure belli libri tres' (1598) in James Brown Scott (ed), *Classics of International Law* (John C. Rolfe tr, Carnegie Institution, Washington 1917).

Geuffre de Lapradelle, Albert, and Nicolas Politis, *Recueil des arbitrages internationaux* (A. Pedone, Paris 1904).

Gilderhus, Mark, *History and Historians. A Historiographical Introduction* (Prentice Hall, Upper Saddle River NJ 2007).

Gindler, Michael, *Die local remedies rule im Investitionsschutzrecht* (Nomos, Baden-Baden 2013).

Goebel, Julius, 'The International Responsibility of States for Injuries Sustained by Aliens on Account of Mob Violence, Insurrections and Civil Wars' (1914) 8 AJIL 802-52.

Goldstein, Eduard, *Die Staatsangehörigkeit der juristischen Person* (Junge & Sohn, Erlangen 1912).

Golendukhin, Levon, 'Reference to Intellectual Property Treaty Norms in Full Protection and Security and Fair and Equitable Treatment Claims' in Ian Laird, Borzu Sabahi, Frédéric Sourgens and Todd Weiler (eds), *Investment Treaty Arbitration and International Law* (Juris Net, Huntington NY 2018) 89-110.

Gordley, James, and Arthur von Mehren, *An Introduction to the Comparative Study of Private Law* (Cambridge University Press, Cambridge 2006).

Graefrath, Bernhard, 'Complicity in the Law of International Responsibility' (1996) 1996/2 Revue belge de droit international 371-80.

Grewe, Wilhelm, *The Epochs of International Law* (Walter de Gruyter, Berlin 2000).

Griebel, Jörn, *Internationales Investitionsrecht* (C.H. Beck, Munich 2008).

Gross, Leo, 'The Peace of Westphalia 1648-1948' in ASIL, *International Law in the Twentieth Century* (Meredith Corp., New York 1969) 25-46.

Groti, Hugonis, *De iure belli ac pacis* (1625) (Leiden, A. W. Sijthoff 1919).

Grotius, Hugo, *On the Law of War and Peace* (Stephen Neff tr, Cambridge University Press, Cambridge 2012).

Grotius, Hugo, *The Rights of War and Peace in Three Books* (1625) (The Lawbook Exchange, Clark NJ 2004).

Guardiola, Óscar, *What if Latin America Ruled the World? How the South Will Take the North into the 22nd Century* (Bloomsbury Publishing Plc., London 2010).

Guggenheim, Paul, 'Les principes de droit international public' (1952) 80 RCADI 2-189.

Guggenheim, Paul, *Lehrbuch des Völkerrechts* (Volume 1: Verlag für Recht und Gesellschaft, Basel 1948).

Guterman, Simeon, 'The First Age of European Law: The Origin and Character of the Conflict of Laws in the Early Middle Ages' (1961) 7(2) NYLF 131-66.

Guzmán, Andrew, 'Why LDCs Sign Treaties That Hurt Them: Explaining the Popularity of Bilateral Investment Treaties' (1997) 38 Va. J. Int'l L. 639-88.

Hackworth, Green (ed), *Digest of International Law* (Volumes 1-8: Government Printing Office, Washington 1943).

Hackworth, Green, 'Responsibility of States for Damages Caused in their Territory to the Person or Property of Foreigners. The Hague Conference for the Codification of International Law' (1930) 24(3) AJIL 500-16.

Haggermacher, Peter, 'L'ancêtre de la protection diplomatique: les représailles de l'ancien droit' (2010) 143 Relations Internationales 7-12.

Hall, William Edward, *A Treatise on International Law* (Clarendon Press, Oxford 1890).

Hamilton, John, *Security: Politics, Humanity, and the Philology of Care* (Princeton University Press, Princeton NJ 2013).

Hannell, David, 'Lord Palmerston and the 'Don Pacifico Affair' of 1850. The Ionian Connection' (1989) 19 EHQ 495-508.

Harding, Robert, *The History of Panama* (Greenwood Press, Westport 2006).

Hasse, Johann Christian, *Die Culpa des Römischen Rechts. Eine Civilistische Abhandlung* (Akademische Buchhandlung, Kiel 1815).

Hatschek, Julius, *Völkerrecht im Grundriss* (A. Deichertsche Verlagsbuchhandlung Dr. Werner Scholl, Leipzig 1926).

Heffernan, James A., *Hospitality and Treachery in Western Literature* (Yale University Press, New Haven CT 2014).

Heidegger, Martin, *Sein und Zeit* (Max Niemeyer Verlag, Tübingen 1967).

Heilborn, Paul, *Das System des Völkerrechts entwickelt aus den völkerrechtlichen Begriffen* (Verlag von Julius Springer, Berlin 1896).

Heiskanen, Veijo, 'Arbitrary and Unreasonable Measures' in August Reinisch (ed), *Standards of Investment Protection* (Oxford University Press, New York 2008) 87-110.

Henckels, Caroline, *Proportionality and Deference in Investor-State Arbitration. Balancing Investment Protection and Regulatory Autonomy* (Cambridge University Press, Cambridge 2015).

Herdegen, Matthias, *Principles of International Economic Law* (Oxford University Press, New York 2016).

Herdegen, Matthias, *Völkerrecht* (C.H. Beck, Munich 2017).

Hernández, Gleider, 'The Interaction Between Investment Law and the Law of Armed Conflict in the Interpretation of Full Protection and Security Clauses' in Freya Baetens (ed), *Investment Law within International Law* (Cambridge University Press, Cambridge 2013) 21-50.

Hershey, Amos, *The Essentials of International Public Law and Organization* (The Macmillan Co., New York 1927).

Hessbruegge, Jan Arno, 'The Historical Development of the Doctrines of Attribution and Due Diligence in International Law' (2003/4) 36(4) JILP 265-306.

Higgins, Rosalyn, *Problems & Process. International Law and How We Use It* (Clarendon Press, Oxford 1994).

Hillgruber, Christian, 'Ist privates Eigentum ein Menschenrecht? Philosophische und verfassungshistorische Überlegungen' in Anton Rauscher (ed), *Das Eigentum als eine Bedingung der Freiheit* (Duncker & Humblot, Berlin 2013) 111-37.

Hilton Young, Edward, 'The Nationality of a Juristic Person' (1908) 22(1) Harv. L. Rev. 1-26.

Hirch, Mosche, *The Responsibility of International Organizations toward Third Parties* (Martinus Nijhoff Publishers, Dordrecht 1995).

Hobbes, Thomas, *Leviathan* (Cambridge University Press, Cambridge 1904) [first edition: 1651].

Hobe, Stephan, *Einführung in das Völkerrecht* (A. Francke Verlag, Tübingen 2014).

Hobér, Kaj, 'Investment Treaty Arbitration and the Energy Charter Treaty' (2010) 1(2) J. Int'l Disp. Settlement 153-90.

Hoffmann, Anne, 'Indirect Expropriation' in August Reinisch (ed), *Standards of Investment Protection* (Oxford University Press, New York 2008) 151-70.

Hohl, Friedrich Rudolf, *Bartolus a Saxoferrato: Seine Bedeutung für die Entwicklungsgeschichte des Repressaliensrechts* [unpublished doctoral dissertation] (Volumes 1-2: Universität Bonn, Bonn 1954).

Huffcut, Ernest Wilson, 'International Liability for Mob Injuries' (1891) 2 Annals of the Amer. Acad. of Pol. and Soc. Science 69-84.

Humphrey, John, 'The International Law of Human Rights in the Middle Twentieth Century' in Maarten Bos (ed), *The Present State of International Law. International Law Association 1873-1973* (Springer Science/Business Media, New York 1973) 75-105.

Hyde, Charles Cheney, *International Law. Chiefly as Interpreted and Applied by the United States* (Volume I: Little Brown & Co., Boston 1922).

Ipsen, Knut, *Völkerrecht* (C.H. Beck, Munich 2014).

Isay, Ernst, *Das deutsche Fremdenrecht. Ausländer und Polizei* (Verlag von Georg Stilke, Berlin 1923).

Isay, Ernst, *Die Staatsangehörigkeit der juristischen Personen* (Mohr, Tübingen 1907).

Isensee, Josef, 'Abwehrrecht und Schutzpflicht' in Josef Isensee and Paul Kirchhof (eds), *Handbuch des Staatsrechts* (Volume 9: C. F. Müller 2013) 413-568.

Isensee, Josef, *Das Grundrecht auf Sicherheit. Zu den Schutzpflichten des freiheitlichen Verfassungsstaates* (Walter de Gruyter, Berlin 1983).

Islam, Rumana, *The Fair and Equitable Treatment Standard (FET) in International Investment Arbitration* (Springer, Singapore 2018).

Jackson, Miles, *Complicity in International Law* (Oxford University Press, Oxford 2015).

Jackson, Robert, *Sovereignty. Evolution of an idea* (Polity Press, Malden MA 2007).

Jacob, Marc, and Stephan Schill, 'Fair and equitable treatment: Content, Practice, Method' in Marc Bungenberg, Jörn Griebel, Stephan Hobe and August Reinisch (eds), *International Investment Law* (Nomos, Baden-Baden 2015) 700-63.

Janmyr, Maja, *Protecting Civilians in Refugee Camps. Unable and Unwilling States, UNCHR and International Responsibility* (Martinus Nijhoff, Leiden 2013).

Jellinek, Georg, *System der subjektiven öffentlichen Rechte* (Akademische Verlagsbuchhandlung von J.C.B. Mohr 1892).

Jennings, Robert, 'State Contracts in International Law' (1961) 37 BYIL 156-82.

Jennings, Robert, and Arthur Watts (eds), *Oppenheim's International Law* (Volume 1: Longman Group, Essex 1993).

Jess, Adolf, *Politische Handlungen Privater gegen das Ausland und das Völkerrecht* (Verlag von M. & H. Marcus, Breslau 1923).

Jessup, Philip, *A Modern Law of Nations* (The Macmillan Company, New York 1949).

Jessup, Philip, 'Responsibility of States for Injuries to Individuals' (1946) 46 Colum. L. Rev. 903-28.

Jiménez de Aréchega, Eduardo, 'International responsibility' in Max Sørensen (ed), *Manual of Public International Law* (St. Martin's Press, New York 1968) 531-603.

Johnson, O. Thomas, and Jonathan Gimblett, 'From Gunboats to BITs: The Evolution of Modern International Investment Law' in Karl Sauvant (ed), *Yearbook on International Law & Policy* 649-92.

Jones, John Mervyn, 'Claims on Behalf of Nationals Who are Shareholders in Foreign Companies' (1949) 26 BYIL 225-58.

Jönsson, Christer, 'Gunboat Diplomacy' in Keith Dowding (ed), *Encyclopedia of Power* (SAGE Publications, Los Angeles CA 2011) 300.

Jörs, Paul, and Wolfgang Kunkel, *Römisches Privat Recht* (Springer, Berlin 1949).

Julliard, Patrick, 'Calvo Doctrine/Calvo Clause' in Rüdiger Wolfrum (ed), *The Max Planck Encyclopedia of Public International Law* (Volume 1: Oxford University Press, New York 2012) 1086-93.

Junngam, Nartnirun, 'The Full Protection and Security Standard in International Investment Law: What and Who is Investment Fully[?] Protected and Secured From?' (2018) 7(1) AUBLR 1-100.

Kaeckenbeeck, Georges, 'La protection internationale des droits acquis' (1937) 59(1) RCADI 317-419.

Kälin, Walter, and Jörg Künzli, *The Law of International Human Rights Protection* (Oxford University Press, New York 2010).

Kant, Immanuel, *Project for a Perpetual Peace: A Philosophical Essay* (Vernor & Hood, London 1796).

Kant, Immanuel, *Zum ewigen Frieden. Ein philosophischer Entwurf* (Frankfurt/Leipzig, 1796).

Kaplow, Louis, 'Rules versus Standards: An Economic Analysis' (1992) 42 Duke L. J. 557-627.

Kaufmann, Erich, 'Règles générales du droit de la paix' (1935) 54(4) RCADI 309-620.

Kazazi, Mojtaba, *Burden of Proof and Related Issues* (Kluwer Law International, The Hague 1996).

Kelly, J. Patrick, 'Customary International Law in Historical Context: The Exercise of Power Without General Acceptance' in Brian Lepard (ed), *Reexamining Customary International Law* (Cambridge University Press, Cambridge 2017) 47-85.

Kelsen, Hans, 'Collective and Individual Responsibility in International Law with Particular Regard to the Punishment of War Crimes' (1943) 31 Cal. L. Rev. 531-71.

Kelsen, Hans, 'Unrecht und Unrechtsfolge im Völkerrecht' (1932) 12 ZöR 481-608.

Kelsen, Hans, *General Theory of Law and State* (Anders Wedberg tr., Lawbook Exchange, Clark NJ 2009).

Kelsen, Hans, *Principles of International Law* (The Lawbook Exchange, Clark NJ 2007) [first edition: 1952].

Kennedy, David, 'The Disciplines of International Law and Policy' (1999) 12 LJIL 9-133.

Kennedy, Duncan, 'Form and Substance in Private Law Adjudication' (1976) 89 Harv. L. Rev. 1685-778.

Kern, Carsten, *Schiedsgericht und Generalklausel: Zur Konkretisierung des Gebots des fair and equitable treatment in der internationalen Schiedsgerichtsbarkeit* (Mohr Siebeck, Tübingen 2017).

Khairallah, Daoud L., *Insurrection under International Law with Emphasis on the Rights and Duties of Insurgents* (Lebanese University, Beirut 1973).

Kishoiyian, Bernard, 'The Utility of Bilateral Investment Treaties in the Formulation of Customary International Law' (1993-4) 14 Nw. J. Int'l L. & Bus. 327-75.

Kläger, Ronald, *'Fair and Equitable Treatment' in International Investment Law* (Cambridge University Press, New York 2011).

Klein, Friedrich, *Die mittelbare Haftung im Völkerrecht* (Vittorio Klostermann, Frankfurt am Main 1941).

Kleinlein, Thomas, 'Christian Wolff. System as an Episode?' in Stefan Kadelbach, Thomas Kleinlein and David Roth-Isigkeit (eds), *System, Order and International Law. The Early History of International Legal Thought from Machiavelli to Hegel* (Oxford University Press, Oxford 2017) 216-39.

Klopschinski, Simon, *Der Schutz geistigen Eigentums durch völkerrechtliche Investitionsverträge* (Carl Heymanns Verlag, Cologne 2011).

Klossowski, Pierre, *Les lois de l'hospitalité* (Gallimard, Paris 1970).

Kneer, Dominik, *Investitionsschutz und Menschenrechte. Eine Untersuchung zum Einfluss menschenrechtlicher Standards auf die Investitionssicherung* (Nomos, Baden-Baden 2012).

Koivurova, Timo, 'Due Diligence' in Rüdiger Wolfrum (ed), *The Max Planck Encyclopedia of Public International Law* (Volume 3: Oxford University Press, New York 2012) 236-46.

Kolb, Robert, 'General Principles of Procedural Law' in Andreas Zimmermann, Christian Tomuschat, Karin Oellers-Frahm and Christian Tams (eds), *The Statute of the International Court of Justice. A Commentary* (Oxford University Press, Oxford 2012) 871-908.

Kolb, Robert, *The International Law of State Responsibility. An Introduction* (Edward Elgar Publishing, Northampton MA 2017).

König, Valériane, *Präzedenzwirkung internationaler Schiedssprüche. Domatisch-empirische Analysen zur Handels- und Investitionsschiedsgerichtsbarkeit* (De Gruyter, Berlin 2013).

Korobkin, Rusell, 'Behavioral Analysis and Legal Form: Rules vs. Standards Revisited' (2000) 79 Or. L. Rev. 23-60.

Koskenniemi, Martti, 'International Law and *raison d'état*: Rethinking the Prehistory of International Law' in Benedict Kingsbury and Benjamin Straumann (eds), *The Roman Foundations of the Law of Nations. Alberico Gentili and the Justice of Empire* (Oxford University Press, New York 2010) 297-339.

Koskenniemi, Martti, 'International Legal Theory and Doctrine' in Rüdiger Wolfrum (ed), *The Max Planck Encyclopedia of Public International Law* (Volume 3: Oxford University Press, New York 2012) 976-86.

Koskenniemi, Martti, 'Into Positivism: Georg Friedrich von Martens (1756-1821) and modern international law' (2008) 15 *Constellations* 189-207.

Koskenniemi, Martti, 'The Politics of International Law – 20 Years Later' (2009) 20(1) EJIL 7-19.

Koskenniemi, Martti, 'The Politics of International Law' (1990) 1 EJIL 4-32.

Koskenniemi, Martti, *From Apology to Utopia. The Structure of International Legal Argument* (Cambridge University Press, New York 2005).

Koskenniemi, Martti, *The Gentle Civilizer of Nations. The Rise and Fall of International Law 1870-1960* (Cambridge University Press, New York 2008).

Krajewski, Markus, *Wirtschaftsvölkerrecht* (C. H. Müller, Heidelberg 2009).

Kraus, Manuela Sissy, *Menschenrechtliche Aspekte der Staatenlosigkeit* (Berliner Wissenschaftsverlag, Berlin 2013).

Kriebaum, Ursula, 'Arbitrary/Unreasonable or Discriminatory Measures' in Marc Bungenberg, Jörn Griebel, Stephan Hobe and August Reinisch (eds), *International Investment Law* (Nomos, Baden-Baden 2015) 790-806.

Kriebaum, Ursula, 'Expropriation' in Marc Bungenberg, Jörn Griebel, Stephan Hobe and August Reinisch (eds), *International Investment Law* (Nomos, Baden-Baden 2015) 959-1030.

Kriebaum, Ursula, *Eigentumsschutz im Völkerrecht* (Duncker & Humblot, Berlin 2008).

Krueger, Anna, *Die Bindung der Dritten Welt an das postkoloniale Völkerrecht* (Springer, Heidelberg 2017).

Kühler, Anne, 'Societas Humana bei Christian Wolff' in Tilmann Altwicker, Francis Cheneval and Oliver Diggelmann (eds), *Völkerrechtsphilosophie der Frühaufklärung* (Mohr Siebeck, Tübingen 2015) 117-30.

Kuhn, Margarete, *Verschuldens- oder Verursachungshaftung der Staaten im allgemeinen Völkerrecht* (Imprimiere Photo-Landa, Frankfurt 1961).

Kulesza, Joanna, *Due Diligence in International Law* (Brill, Leiden 2016).

Lalive, Pierre, 'The Doctrine of Acquired Rights' in International and Comparative Law Center, *Rights and Duties of Private Investors Abroad* (Matthew Bender & Co., New York 1965) 145-200.

Lanovoy, Vladyslav, 'Complicity in an Internationally Wrongful Act' in André Nollkaemper and Ilias Plakokefalos (eds), *Principles of Shared Responsibility in International Law. An Appraisal of the State of the Art* (Cambridge University Press, Cambridge 2014) 134-68.

Lanovoy, Vladyslav, *Complicity and its Limits in the Law of International Responsibility* (Hart Publishing, Portland OR 2016).

Lasalle, Ferdinand, *Arbeiterprogramm. Ueber den besonderen Zusammenhang der gegenwärtigen Geschichtsperiode mit der Idee des Arbeiterstandes* (Meyer & Zeller, Zürich 1863).

Lasson, Adolf, *Princip und Zukunft des Völkerrechts* (Verlag von Wilhelm Hertz, Berlin 1871).

Latty, Franck, 'Actions and Omissions' in James Crawford, Alain Pellet and Simon Olleson (eds), *The Law of International Responsibility* (Oxford University Press, New York 2010) 355-63.

Lauterpacht, Hersch, *An International Bill of the Rights of Man* (Columbia University Press, New York 1945).

Lauterpacht, Hersch, *Private Law Sources and Analogies of International Law (With Special Reference to International Arbitration)* (Longmans, Green and Co. Ltd., London 1927).

Lauterpacht, Hersch, *The Function of International Law in the International Community* (Clarendon Press, Oxford 1933).

Legnano, Giovanni, 'Tractatus De Bello, De Represaliis et De Duello' (1393) in James Brown Scott (ed), *Classics of International Law* (James Leslie Brierly tr, Carnegie Institution, Washington 1917).

Leonard, Thomas M., *Historical Dictionary of Panama* (Rowman & Littlefield, Lanham MD 2015).

Lepard, Brian, *Customary International Law. A New Theory with Practical Applications* (Cambridge University Press, New York 2011).

Lesaffer, Randall, 'International Law and its History: The Story of an Unrequired Love' in Matt Craven, Malgosia Fitzmaurice and Maria Vogiatzi (eds), *Time, History and International Law* (Martinus Nijhoff, Leiden/Boston 2011) 27-41.

Lévesque, Céline, and Andrew Newcombe, 'Canada' in Chester Brown (ed), *Commentaries on Selected Model Investment Treaties* (Oxford University Press, Oxford 2013) 53-130.

Levinas, Emmanuel, *Totalité et infini. Essai sur l'extériorité* (Brodard at Taupin, Paris 1990).

Lillich, Richard, and John Paxman, 'State Responsibility for Injuries to Aliens Occasioned by Terrorist Activities' (1977) 26(2) Am. U. L. Rev. 217-313.

Lillich, Richard, *International Claims: Postwar British Practice* (Syracuse University Press, New York 1967).

Lillich, Richard, *The Human Rights of Aliens in Contemporary International Law* (Manchester University Press, Manchester 1984).

Lint, Gregg, 'John Adams on the Drafting of the Treaty Plan of 1776' 2(4) Diplomatic History (1978) 313-20.

Lippman, Walter, *U.S. Foreign Policy: Shield of the Republic* (Little & Brown, Boston 1943).

Lissitzyn, Oliver, 'The Meaning of the Term Denial of Justice in International Law' (1936) 30 (4) AJIL 632-46.

Lissitzyn, Oliver, *International Law Today and Tomorrow* (Oceana Publications, New York 1965).

Locke, John, *Two Treatises of Government* (A. Millar et al., London 1764) [first edition: 1689].

Lorz, Ralph Alexander, 'Protection and Security (Including the NAFTA Approach)' in Marc Bungenberg, Jörn Griebel, Stephan Hobe and August Reinisch (eds), *International Investment Law* (Nomos, Baden-Baden 2015) 764-89.

Lowenfeld, Andreas, *International Economic Law* (Oxford University Press, New York 2008).

Luhmann, Niklas, *Soziale Systeme. Grundriß einer allgemeinen Theorie* (Suhrkamp Verlag, Frankfurt 1984).

Lysén, Göran, *State Responsibility and International Liability of States for Lawful Acts* (Iustus Förlag, Uppsala 1997).

Magnússon, Finnur, *Full Protection and Security in International Law* (University of Vienna, Vienna 2012).

Makarov, Alexander, *Allgemeine Lehren des Staatsangehörigkeitsrechts* (W. Kohlhammer Verlag, Heidelberg 1962).

Makonnen, Yilma, 'State Succession in Africa: Selected Problems' (1986) 200(5) RCADI 93-234.

Mann, Francis A., 'British Treaties for the Promotion and Protection of Investments' (1981) 52 BYIL 241-54.

Manning, Martin, 'Gunboat Diplomacy' in Alan McPherson (ed), *Encyclopedia of U.S. Military Interventions in Latin America* (ABC-Clio, Santa Barbara CA 2013) 261-3.

Mantilla Blanco, Sebastián, *Justizielles Unrecht im internationalen Investitionsschutzrecht* (Nomos, Baden-Baden 2016).

Martens, Georg Friedrich, *Einleitung in das positive Europäische Völkerrecht auf Verträge und Herkommen gegründet* (Johann Christian Dieterich, Göttingen 1796).

Martens, Georg Friedrich, *Précis du droit moderne de l'Europe* (Guillaumin et cir. Libraires, Paris 1858).

Martens, Georg Friedrich, *Versuch über die Existenz eines positiven Europäischen Völkerrechts und den Nutzen dieser Wissenschaft* (Johann Christian Dieterich, Göttingen 1787).

Matthews, John, 'Roosevelt's Latin-American Policy' (1935) 29 Am. Pol. Sci. Rev. 805-20.

Mayer, Theodor, 'Die Ausbildung der Grundlagen des modernen deutschen Staates im hohen Mittelalter' (1939) 159(3) Historische Zeitschrift 457-87.

Mayer, Theodor, 'Die Entstehung des "modernen" Staates im Mittelalter und die freien Bauern' (1937) 57(1) ZRG 210-88.

Mayorga, Ofilio, *Arbitrating War: Military Necessity as a Defense to the Breach of Investment Treaty Obligations* (Harvard Program on Humanitarian Policy and Conflict Research, Cambridge MA 2013).

McGilchrist, John, *Lord Palmerston. A Biography* (George Routledge & Sons, London 1865).

McGuinness, Aimes, *Path of Empire. Panama and the California Gold Rush* (Cornell University Press, New York 2008).

McLachlan, Campbell, 'Investment Treaties and General International Law' (April 2008) 57 ICLQ 361-401.

McLachlan, Campbell, 'The Evolution of Treaty Obligations in International Law' in Georg Nolte (ed), *Treaties and Subsequent Practice* (Oxford University Press, Oxford 2013) 69-81.

McLachlan, Campbell, 'The Principle of Systemic Integration and Article 31(3)(c) of the Vienna Convention' (2005) 54(2) ICLQ 279-319.

McLachlan, Campbell, Laurence Shore and Mattew Weiniger, *International Investment Arbitration: Substantive Principles* (Oxford University Press, Oxford 2008).

McNair, Arnold Duncan (First Baron McNair), *International Law Opinions* (Volume 2: Cambridge University Press, Cambridge 1956).

McPherson, Alan, *Yankee No! Anti Americanism in U.S.–Latin American Relations* (Harvard University Press, Cambridge MA/London 2003).

Merkouris, Panos, *Article 31(3)(c) VCLT and the Principle of Systemic Integration* (Brill, Leiden 2015).

Mignolo, Walter, *The Idea of Latin America* (Blackwell Publishing, Oxford 2005).

Miles, Kate, *The Origins of International Investment Law* (Cambridge University Press, New York 2013).

Mitchell, Francis, 'International Liability for Mob Injuries' (1900) 34 Am. L. Rev. 709-21.

Mitchell, Nancy, *The Danger of Dreams. German and American Imperialism in Latin America* (The University of North Carolina Press, Chapel Hill NC 1999).

Mitteis, Heinrich, *Der Staat des hohen Mittelalters. Grundlinien einer vergleichenden Verfassungsgeschichte des Lehnszeitalters* (Hermann Böhlaus, Weimar 1953).

Montt, Santiago, *State Liability in Investment Treaty Arbitration* (Hart Publishing, Oxford 2009).

Moore, John Bassett, 'The Responsibility of Governments for Mob Violence' (1892) 5 Columb. L. T. 211-5.

Moore, John Bassett, *A Digest of International Law* (Volumes 1-6: Government Printing Office, Washington 1906).

Moore, John Bassett, *History and Digest of the International Arbitrations to which the United States has been a Party* (Volumes 1-6: Government Printing Office, Washington 1898).

Morelli, Gaetano, *Nozioni di diritto internazionale* (CEDAM – Casa Editrice Dott. A. Milani, Padua 1958).

Moser, Johann Jakob, *Grundsätze des jetzt üblichen Europäischen Völkerrechts in Friedenszeiten* (Hanau 1750).

Mouawad, Caline, and Sarah Vasani, 'Energy Disputes in Times of Civil Unrest: Transitional Governments and Foreign Investment Protections' in Arthur Rovine (ed), *Contemporary Issues in International Arbitration and Mediation* (Brill, Leiden/Boston 2015) 234-50.

Muszack, Georg, *Ueber die Haftung einer Regierung für Schäden, welche Ausländer gelegentlich innerer Unruhen in ihren Landen erlitten haben* (Heiz u. Mündel, Strasbourg 1905).

Nadakavukaren Schefer, Krista, *International Investment Law. Text, Cases and Materials* (Edward Elgar Publishing, Northampton MA 2013).

Neff, Stephen, *Justice Among Nations. A History of International Law* (Harvard University Press, Cambridge MA 2014).

Nellen, Henk, *Hugo Grotius: A Lifelong Struggle for Peace in Church and State, 1583-1645* (J.C. Grayson tr., Brill, Leiden 2015).

Nelson, Timothy, et al., 'Full Protection and "Cyber" Security?' in Ian Laird, Borzu Sabahi, Frédéric Sourgens and Todd Weiler (eds), *Investment Treaty Arbitration and International Law* (Juris Net, Huntington NY 2018) 133-57.

Newcombe, Andrew, and Lluís Paradell, *Law and Practice of Investment Treaties. Standards of Treatment* (Kluwer Law International, Alphen aan den Rijn 2009).

Nicholson, David, 'Gunboat Diplomacy' in James Bradford (ed) *International Encyclopedia of Military History* (Routledge, New York 2006) 574-5.

Nussbaum, Arthur, *Geschichte des Völkerrechts in gedrängter Darstellung* (C.H. Beck, München/Berlin 1960).

Nys, Ernest, *Le droit de la guerre et les précurseurs de Grotius* (C. Muquardt, Brussels 1882).

O'Connell, Daniel Patrick, *International Law* (Volume 2: Stevens & Sons, London 1970).

O'Connell, Daniel Patrick, *The Law of State Succession* (Cambridge University Press, Cambridge 2015) [first edition: 1956].

O'Donnell, Nicole, 'Reconciling Full Protection and Security Guarantees in Bilateral Investment Treaties with Incidence of Terrorism' (2018) 29(3) ARIA 293-313.

Oden, Amy G. (ed), *And You Welcomed Me. A Sourcebook on Hospitality in Early Christianity* (Abingdon Press, Nashville TN 2001).

Odumosu-Ayanu, Ibironke, 'International Investment Law and Disasters: Necessity, Peoples and the Burden of Economic Emergencies' in David Caron, Michael Kelly and Anastasia Telesetsky (eds), *The International Law of Disaster Relief* (Cambridge University Press, New York 2014) 314-37.

Offutt, Milton, *The Protection of Citizens Abroad by the Armed Forces of the United States* (Kraus Reprint, New York 1972) [first edition: 1928].

Oosterveld, Willem Theo, *The Law of Nations in Early American Foreign Policy. Theory and Practice from the Revolution to the Monroe Doctrine* (Brill, Leiden 2015).

Oppenheim, Lassa Francis Laurence, 'The Science of International Law: Its Task and Method' (1908) 2(2) AJIL 313-56.

Oppenheim, Lassa Francis Laurence, *International Law. A Treatise* (Volume 1: Longmans, Green & Co., London 1905).

Orakhelashvili, Alexander, 'The Origins of Consensual Positivism – Pufendorf, Wolff and Vattel' in Alexander Orakhelashvili (ed), *Research Handbook on the Theory and History of International Law* (Edward Elgar Publishing, Northampton MA 2011) 93-110.

Ortino, Federico, 'Non-Arbitrariness' in Thomas Cottier and Krista Nadakavukaren Schefer (eds), *Elgar Encyclopedia of International Economic Law* (Edward Elgar Publishing, Northampton MA 2018) 207-8.

Ouedraogo, Awalou, 'L'évolution du concept de faute dans la théorie de la responsabilité internationale des États' (2008) 21(2) Revue québécoise de droit international 129-66.

Oyeani, Onyema Awa, *The Obligation of Host States to Accord the Standard of "Full Protection and Security" to Foreign Investments under International Investment Law* (Brunel University, London 2018) [D.Phil. Thesis].

Palmisano, Giuseppe, 'Fault' in Rüdiger Wolfrum (ed), *The Max Planck Encyclopedia of Public International Law* (Volume 3: Oxford University Press, New York 2012) 1128-36.

Palombino, Fulvio Maria, *Fair and Equitable Treatment and the Fabric of General Principles* (Springer, Berlin 2018).

Paparinskis, Martins, 'Analogies and Other Regimes of International Law' in Zachary Douglas, Joost Pauwelyn and Jorge Viñuales (eds), *The Foundations of International Investment Law. Bringing Theory into Practice* (Oxford University Press, Oxford 2014) 73-107.

Paparinskis, Martins, 'Fair and Equitable Treatment' in Thomas Cottier and Krista Nadakavukaren Schefer (eds), *Elgar Encyclopedia of International Economic Law* (Edward Elgar Publishing, Northampton MA 2018) 208-12.

Paparinskis, Martins, 'Investment treaty interpretation and customary investment law: Preliminary remarks' in Chester Brown and Kate Miles (eds), *Evolution in Investment Treaty Law and Arbitration* (Cambridge University Press, Cambridge 2011) 65-96.

Paparinskis, Martins, *Basic Documents on International Investment Protection* (Hart Publishing, Portland OR 2012).

Paparinskis, Martins, *The International Minimum Standard and Fair and Equitable Treatment* (Oxford University Press, Oxford 2013).

Park, William, 'Arbitrators and Accuracy' (2010) 1(1) J. Int'l Disp. Settlement 25-53.

Paulsson, Jan, 'International Arbitration Is Not Arbitration' (2008) 2 Stockholm International Arbitration Review 1-20.

Paulsson, Jan, and Georgios Petrochilos, '*Neer*-ly Misled?' (2007) 22(2) ICSID Review 242-57.

Paulsson, Jan, *Denial of Justice in International Law* (Cambridge University Press, New York 2005).

Pauwelyn, Joost, 'Evidence, Proof and Persuasion in WTO Dispute Settlement' (1998) 1 J. Int'l Econ. L. 227-58.

Pavot, David, 'The Use of Dictionary by the WTO Appellate Body: Beyond the Search of Ordinary Meaning' (2013) 4(1) J. Int'l Disp. Settlement 29-46.

Perkams, Markus, 'Protection of Legal Persons' in Marc Bungenberg, Jörn Griebel, Stephan Hobe and August Reinisch (eds), *International Investment Law* (Nomos, Baden-Baden 2015) 638-52.

Phillimore, George, 'Current Notes on International Law' (1902) 27 Law Mag. & Rev. Quart. Rev. Juris. 330-43.

Phillimore, Robert, *Commentaries upon International Law* (Volume 2: Butterworths, London 1871).

Pillet, Antoine, and Paul Fauchille (eds), 'Cronique des faits internaux' (1894) 1 RGDIP 154-81.

Pillet, Antoine, *Les lois actuelles de la guerre* (Rousseau, Paris 1901).

Pisillo Mazzeschi, Riccardo, 'The Due Diligence Rule and the Nature of the International Responsibility of States' in René Provost (ed), *State Responsibility in International Law* (Ashgate Publishing Co., Burlington VT 2002) 97-139.

Pisillo Mazzeschi, Riccardo, *"Due diligence" e responsabilità internazionale degli stati* (Giuffrè Editore, Milan 1989).

Pitt-Rivers, Julian, 'The Law of Hospitality' (2012) 2(1) HAU Journal of Ethnographic Theory 501-17.

Plakokefalos, Ilias, 'Causation in the Law of State Responsibility and the Problem of Overdetermination: In Search of Clarity' (2015) 26 EJIL 471-92.

Planas Suárez, Simón, *Los extranjeros en Venezuela. Su condición ante el derecho público y privado de la república* (Centro Tipográfico Colonial, Lisboa 1917).

Planitz, Hans, 'Studien zur Geschichte des deutschen Arrestprozesses. Der Fremdenarrest' (1919) 40 Zeitschrift der Savigny Stiftung für Rechtsgeschichte 87-198.

Podestá Costa, Luis A., 'La responsabilidad del Estado por daños irrogados a la persona o a los bienes de extranjeros en luchas civiles' (1938) 67/8 Revista de Derecho Internacional 5-103.

Polkinghorne, Michael, and Charles Rosenberg, 'The Adverse Inference in ICSID Practice' (2015) 30(3) ICSID Review 741-51.

Potestà, Michele, 'Legitimate Expectations in Investment Treaty Law: Understanding the Roots and Limits of a Controversial Concept' (2013) 28(1) ICSID Review 88-122.

Poulsen, Lauge Skovgaard, 'The Politics of South-South Bilateral Investment Treaties' in Tomer Broude, Marc Busch and Amelia Porges (eds), *The Politics of International Economic Law* (Cambridge University Press, New York 2011) 186-211.

Pound, Roscoe, 'Hierarchy of Sources and Forms in Different Systems of Law' (1933) 7(4) Tul. L. Rev. 475-87.

Pound, Roscoe, 'The Administrative Application of Legal Standards' (1919) 42 Annu. Rep. A.B.A. 445-65.

Powell, Rhonda, 'The Concept of Security' (2012) 1 Oxford Socio-Legal Review 1-29.

Pritchard, Sarah, *Der völkerrechtliche Minderheitenschutz. Historische und neuere Entwicklungen* (Duncker & Humblot, Berlin 2001).

Proulx, Vincent-Joël, *Institutionalizing State Responsibility: Global Security and UN Organs* (Oxford University Press, Oxford 2016).

Pufendorf, Samuel, 'Elementorum Jurisprudentiae Universalis Libri Duo' in James Brown Scott (ed), *Classics of International Law* (William Abbott tr, Clarendon Press, Oxford 1931).

Pufendorf, Samuel, 'Of the Law of Nature and of Nations in Eight Books' (1672) in Craig Carr (ed) *The Political Writings of Samuel Pufendorf* (Michael Seidler tr, Oxford University Press, New York 1994) 95-268.

Pufendorf, Samuel, *De jure naturae et gentium. Libri octo* (Sumtibus Adami Junghans, Lund 1672).

Pufendorf, Samuel, *Of the Law of Nature and of Nations in Eight Books* (1672) (Mr. Carew tr., I. Walthoe et al. London 1729).

Pütter, Karl Theodor, *Das praktische europäische Fremdenrecht* (J. C. Hinrichs'schen Buchhandlung, Leipzig 1845).

Rabban, David, 'The Historiography of Late Nineteenth-Century American Legal History' (2003) 4 (2) Theoretical Inquiries in Law 541-78.

Rachel, Samuel, 'De Jure Naturae et Gentium Dissertationes' (1676) in James Brown Scott (ed), *Classics of International Law* (John Pawley Bate tr, Carnegie Institution, Washington 1916).

Ralston, Jackson, *International Arbitral Law and Procedure. Being a Résumé of the Procedure and Practice of International Commissions and Including the Views of Arbitrators upon Questions arising under the Law of Nations* (Ginn & Co., Boston/London 1910).

Ralston, Jackson, *Venezuelan Arbitrations of 1903* (Government Printing Office, Washington 1904).

Ranjan, Prabhash, 'Investment Protection and Host State's Right to Regulate in the Indian Model Bilateral Investment Treaty: Lessons for Asian Countries' in Julien Chaisse, Tomoko Ishikawa and Sufian Jusoh (eds), *Asia's Changing International Investment Regime: Sustainability, Regionalization, and Arbitration* (Springer, Singapore 2017) 47-65.

Reed, Lucy, Jan Paulsson and Nigel Blackaby, *Guide to ICSID Arbitration* (Kluwer Law International, Alphen aan den Rijn 2011).

Reinisch, August, 'Austria' in Chester Brown (ed), *Commentaries on Selected Model Investment Treaties* (Oxford University Press, Oxford 2013) 15-51.

Reinisch, August, 'Internationales Investitionsschutzrecht' in Christian Tietje (ed), *Internationales Wirtschaftsrecht* (De Gruyter, Berlin 2015) 398-433.

Reinisch, August, 'Legality of Expropriations' in August Reinisch (ed), *Standards of Investment Protection* (Oxford University Press, New York 2008) 171, 171-204.

Reinisch, August, 'Most Favoured Nation Treatment' in Marc Bungenberg, Jörn Griebel, Stephan Hobe and August Reinisch (eds), *International Investment Law* (Nomos, Baden-Baden 2015) 807-45.

Reinisch, August, 'National Treatment' in Marc Bungenberg, Jörn Griebel, Stephan Hobe and August Reinisch (eds), *International Investment Law* (Nomos, Baden-Baden 2015) 846-69.

Reisman, Michael, 'Compensating Collateral Damage in Elective International Conflict' (2013) 8 Intercultural Hum. Rts. L. Rev. 1-18.

Reyes Landicho, Robert, 'Enforcing a State's International IP Obligations through Investment Law Standards of Protection – An Ill-Fated Romance' in Ian Laird, Borzu Sabahi, Frédéric Sourgens and Todd Weiler (eds), *Investment Treaty Arbitration and International Law* (Juris Net, Huntington NY 2018) 111-32.

Riggs, John, 'Investment Protection in Colombia: Can Investors Rely on the Full Protection and Security Clause?' (2014) 7(3) J. World Investment & Trade 264-73.

Ripinsky, Sergey, and Kevin Williams, *Damages in International Investment Law* (British Institute of International and Comparative Law, London 2008).

Rivas, José Antonio, 'Colombia' in Chester Brown (ed), *Commentaries on Selected Model Investment Treaties* (Oxford University Press, Oxford 2013) 183-243.

Roberts, Anthea, 'Clash of Paradigms: Actors and Analogies Shaping the Investment Treaty System' (2013) 107 AJIL 45-94.

Roberts, Anthea, 'Power and Persuasion in Investment Treaty Arbitration: The Dual Role of States' (2010) 104 AJIL 179-225.

Robins, Joshua, 'The Emergence of Positive Obligations in Bilateral Investment Treaties' (2005-6) U. Miami Int'l & Comp. L. Rev. 403-73.

Roe, Thomas, and Matthew Happold, *Settlement of Investment Disputes under the Energy Charter Treaty* (Cambridge University Press, Cambridge 2011).

Rojas Mix, Miguel, *Los cien nombres de América, eso que descubrió Colón* (Universidad de Costa Rica, San José 1997).

Roorda, Eric Paul, 'Good Neighbor Policy' in Alan McPherson (ed), *Encyclopedia of U.S. Military Interventions in Latin America* (ABC-Clio, Santa Barbara CA 2013) 235-9.

Roosevelt, Theodore, *Theodore Roosevelt. An Autobiography* (The Macmillan Company, New York 1913).

Root, Elihu, 'The Basis of Protection of Citizens Residing Abroad' (1910) 4(3) AJIL 517-28.

Root, Elihu, 'The Real Monroe Doctrine' (1914) 8 ASIL Proceedings 6-22.

Rosenfeld, Friedrich, 'The Trend from Standards to Rules in International Investment Law and its Impact upon the Interpretative Power of Arbitral Tribunals' (2014) 108 ASIL Proceedings 191-3.

Rosentreter, Daniel, *Article 31(3)(c) of the Vienna Convention on the Law of Treaties and the Principle of Systemic Integration in International Investment Law and Arbitration* (Nomos, Baden-Baden 2015).

Ross, Alf, *A Textbook of International Law. General Part* (Longmans, Green and Co., London 1947).

Roth, Hans, *The Minimum Standard of International Law Applied to Aliens* (IMP F.A.A. Sijhoff, The Hague 1949).

Rothschild, Emma, 'What is Security?' (1995) 124(3) Daedalus 53-98.

Rougier, Antoine, *Les guerres civiles et le droit des gens* (Larose & Forcel, Paris 1903).

Rousseau, Jean-Jacques, *Du contrat social ou principes du droit politique* (M.M. Rey, Amsterdam 1763) [first edition: 1762].

Roy, Guha, 'Is the Law of Responsibility of States for Injuries to Aliens a Part of Universal International Law?' (1963) 55(4) AJIL 863-91.

Rubins, Noah, and N. Stephan Kinsella, *International Investment, Political Risk and Dispute Resolution. A Practitioner's Guide* (Oceana Publications, New York 2005).

Ruegger, Paul, *Die Staatsangehörigkeit der juristischen Personen. Die völkerrechtlichen Grundlagen* (Schweizerische Vereinigung für Internationales Recht, Zürich 1918).

Ruiz Moreno, Isidoro, *Manual de derecho internacional público* (Editorial Juan Castagnola, Buenos Aires 1943).

Ryngaert, Cedric, 'Imposing International Duties on Non-State Actors and the Legitimacy of International Law' in Math Noortmann and Cedric Ryngaert (eds), *Non-State Actor Dynamics in International Law. From Law-Takers to Law-Makers* (Routledge, London 2016) 69-90.

Ryngaert, Cedric, and Holly Buchanan, 'Member State Responsibility for the Acts of International Organizations' (2011) 7(1) Utrecht Law Review 131-46.

Ryngaert, Cedric, *Jurisdiction in International Law* (Oxford University Press, Oxford 2015).

Sabahdi, Borzu, *Compensation and Restitution in Investor-State Arbitration* (Oxford University Press, New York 2011).

Salacuse, Jeswald, *The Law of Investment Treaties* (Oxford University Press, Oxford 2015).

Sánchez, Margarita, and Robert DeRise, 'The Full Measure of Full Protection and Security' in Ian Laird, Borzu Sabahi, Frédéric Sourgens and Todd Weiler (eds), *Investment Treaty Arbitration and International Law* (Juris Net, Huntington NY 2015) 99-123.

Santamaría, Luis, (ed), *Final Diplomatic Controversy relating to the Occurrences that Took Place at Panama on the 15th of April, 1856* (Mail Office, Liverpool 1857).

Sasson, Monique, *Substantive Law in Investment Treaty Arbitration* (Kluwer Law International, Alphen aan den Rijn 2010).

Scalia, Antonin, 'The Rule of Law as a Law of Rules' 55(4) U. Chi. L. Rev. 1175-88.

Schauer, Frederick, 'Rules and the Rule of Law' (1991) 14 Harv. J. L. & Pub. Pol'y 645-94.

Schill, Stephan, 'Fair and Equitable Treatment, the Rule of Law and Comparative Public Law' in Stephan Schill (ed), *International Investment Law and Comparative Public Law* (Oxford University Press, New York 2010) 151-82.

Schill, Stephan, 'International Investment Law and Comparative Public Law – An Introduction' in Stephan Schill (ed), *International Investment Law and Comparative Public Law* (Oxford University Press, New York 2010) 3-37.

Schill, Stephan, 'Ioana Tudor. The Fair and Equitable Treatment Standard in the International Law of Foreign Investment' (2009) 20 EJIL 229-39.

Schill, Stephan, *The Multilaterization of International Investment Law* (Cambridge University Press, Cambridge 2009).

Schlag, Pierre, 'Rules and Standards' (1985-6) 33 UCLA L. Rev. 379-430.

Schlochauer, Hans-Jürgen, 'Die Entwicklung des völkerrechtlichen Deliktsrechts' (1975) 16 AVR 239-77.

Schmid, Michael, 'Switzerland' in Chester Brown (ed), *Commentaries on Selected Model Investment Treaties* (Oxford University Press, Oxford 2013) 651-96.

Schöbener, Burkhard, Jochen Herbst and Markus Perkams, *Internationales Wirtschaftsrecht* (C.F. Müller, Heidelberg 2010).

Schoen, Paul, *Die völkerrechtliche Haftung der Staaten aus unerlaubten Handlungen* (J. U. Kern's Verlag, Breslau 1917).

Schorkopf, Frank, *Staatsrecht der internationalen Beziehungen* (C.H. Beck, Munich 2017).

Schreuer, Christoph, 'Fair and Equitable Treatment (FET): Interactions with Other Standards' in Graham Coop and Clarisse Ribeiro (eds), *Investment Protection and the Energy Charter Treaty* (Juris Publishing, Huntington NY 2008) 63-100.

Schreuer, Christoph, 'Full Protection and Security' (2010) 1(2) J. Int'l Disp. Settlement 353-69.

Schreuer, Christoph, 'Protection against Arbitrary or Discriminatory Measures' in Catherine Rogers and Roger Alford (eds), *The Future of Investment Arbitration* (Oxford University Press, New York 2009) 183-98.

Schreuer, Christoph, 'The Protection of Investments in Armed Conflicts' in Freya Baetens (ed), *Investment Law within International Law* (Cambridge University Press, Cambridge 2013) 3-20.

Schrijver, Nico, and Vid Prislan, 'The Netherlands' in Chester Brown (ed), *Commentaries on Selected Model Investment Treaties* (Oxford University Press, Oxford 2013) 535-91.

Schüle, Adolf, 'Methoden der Völkerrechtswissenschaft' (1959/60) 8 AVR 129-50.

Schultz, Thomas, 'Against Consistency in Investment Arbitration' in Zachary Douglas, Joost Pauwelyn and Jorge Viñuales (eds), *The Foundations of International Investment Law. Bringing Theory into Practice* (Oxford University Press, Oxford 2014) 297-316.

Schwarzenberger, Georg, 'The Abs-Shawcross Draft Convention on Investments Abroad: A Critical Commentary' (1961) 14(1) Current Legal Problems 213-46.

Schwarzenberger, Georg, *Foreign Investments and International Law* (Stevens & Sons, London 1969).

Schwarzenberger, Georg, *The Inductive Approach to International Law* (Stevens & Sons, London 1965).

Schwebel, Stephen, 'Investor-State Disputes and the Development of International Law. The Influence of Bilateral Investment Treaties on Customary International Law' (2004) 98 ASIL Proceedings 27-30.

Scott Smith, R., and Stephen Trzaskoma, *Apollodorus' Library and Hyginus' Fabulae* (Hackett Publishing, Indianapolis IN 2007).

Seidl-Hohenveldern, Ignaz, and Torsten Stein, *Völkerrecht* (Carl Heymanns Verlag, Berlin 2000).

Seidl-Hohenveldern, Ignaz, *Collected Essays on International Investments and on International Organizations* (Kluwer Law International, The Hague 1998).

Seidl-Hohenveldern, Ignaz, *Völkerrecht* (Carl Heymanns Verlag, Berlin 1997).

Seydel, Max, *Commentar zur Verfassungs-Urkunde für das Deutsche Reich* (A. Stuber's Buchhandlung, Würzburg 1873).

Shaw, Malcolm, *International Law* (Cambridge University Press, New York 2003).

Shelton, Dinah, 'Private Violence, Public Wrongs, and the Responsibility of States' (1989) 13 (1) Fordham Int'l L.J. 1-34.

Shelton, Dinah, *Regional Protection of Human Rights* (Volume 1: Oxford University Press 2010).

Silvanie, Haig, *Responsibility of States for the Acts of Unsuccessful Insurgent Governments* (AMS Press, New York 1968) [first edition: 1939].

Slomanson, William, *Fundamental Perspectives on International Law* (Wadsworth, Boston 2010).

Smith, Adam, *The Theory of Moral Sentiments* (1759) (Cambridge University Press, Cambridge 2002).

Sornarajah, Muthucumaraswamy, 'A Coming Crisis: Expansionary Trends in Investment Treaty Arbitration' in Karl Sauvant (ed), *Appeals Mechanism in International Investment Disputes* (Oxford University Press, New York 2008) 39-80.

Sornarajah, Muthucumaraswamy, *The International Law on Foreign Investment* (Cambridge University Press, New York 2010).

Sornarajah, Muthucumaraswamy, *The Pursuit of Nationalized Property* (Martinus Nijhoff Publishers, Dordrecht 1986).

Spiegel, Hans, 'Origin and Development of Denial of Justice' (1938) 32(1) AJIL 63-81.

Stahl, Sandra, *Schutzpflichten im Völkerrecht. Ansatz einer Dogmatik* (Springer, Heidelberg 2012).

Starke, Joseph Gabriel, 'Imputability in International Delinquencies' (1938) 19 BYIL 104-17.

Starke, Joseph Gabriel, *Introduction to International Law* (Butterworths, London 1984) 296-7 [first Edition: 1947].

Stejskal, Petr, 'War: Foreign Investments in Danger – Can International Humanitarian Law or Full Protection and Security Always Save It?' (2017) 8 CYIL 529-49.

Stephen, James Fitzjames, *A History of the Criminal Law of England* (Volume 3: Macmillan & Co., London 1883).

Stevenson, Robert Louis, *The Strange Case of Dr. Jekyll and Mr. Hyde* (Longmans, Green and Co., London 1901) [first edition: 1886].

Still, Judith, *Derrida and Hospitality. Theory and Practice* (Edinburgh University Press, Edinburgh 2013).

Stoerk, Felix, 'Staatsunterthanen und Fremde' in Franz von Holtzendorff (ed), *Handbuch des Völkerrechts auf Grundlage europäischer Staatspraxis* (Volume 2: Verlag von F. F. Richter, Hamburg 1887) 582-671.

Stoll, Peter-Tobias, Till Patrik Holterhus and Henner Gött, *Investitionsschutz und Verfassung* (Mohr Siebeck, Tübingen 2017).

Stone, Lawrence, 'The Revival of Narrative: Reflections on a New Old History' (1979) 85 Past & Present 3-24.

Storey, Moorfield, *The Recognition of Panama* (Geo. H. Ellis Co. Printers, Boston 1904).

Strupp, Karl, *Grundzüge des positiven Völkerrechts* (Ludwig Röhrscheid, Bonn 1922).

Strupp, Karl, *Handbuch des Völkerrechts. Das völkerrechtliche Delikt* (Volume 3: Verlag von W. Kohlhammer 1920).

Subedi, Surya, *International Investment Law. Reconciling Policy and Principle* (Hart Publishing, Portland OR 2012).

Sullivan, Kathleen, 'Foreword: The Justices of Rules and Standards' (1992) 106 Harv. L. Rev. 22-123.

Tadjbakhsh, Shahrbanou, 'In Defense of the Broad View of Human Security' in Mary Martin and Taylor Owen (eds), *Routledge Handbook of Human Security* (Routledge, New York 2014) 43-57.

Talmon, Stefan, 'Determining Customary International Law: The ICJ's Methodology between Induction, Deduction and Assertion' (2015) 26(2) EJIL 417-43.

Talmon, Stefan, *Recognition of Governments in International Law. With Particular Reference to Governments in Exile* (Clarendon Press, Oxford 1998).

Ten Cate, Irene, 'The Costs of Consistency: Precedent in Investment Treaty Arbitration' (2013) 51 Columb. J. Transnat'l L. 418-78.

Thomas, Caroline, 'Globalization and Human Security' in Anthony McGrew and Nana K. Poku, *Globalization, Development and Human Security* (Polity Press, Cambridge 2007) 107-31.

Tiburcio, Carmen, *The Human Rights of Aliens under International and Comparative Law* (Martinus Nijhoff Publishers, The Hague 2001).

Titi, Catharine, 'Full Protection and Security, Arbitrary or Discriminatory Treatment and the Invisible EU Model BIT' (2014) 14 J. World Investment & Trade 534-50.

Tollope, Anthony, *Lord Palmerston* (Wm. Isbister Ltd., London 1882).

Torres Caicedo, José María, 'Importante cuestión de derecho de gentes. A propósito del conflicto venezolano-hispano en 1860' in José María Torres Caicedo, *Unión Latino-Americana* (Librería de Rosa y Bouret, Paris 1865) 307-81.

Torres Caicedo, José María, *Religión, patria y amor. Colección de versos escritos* (Th. Ducessoirs, Paris 1860).

Tourme Jouannet, Emmanuelle, and Anne Peters, 'The Journal of the History of International Law: A Forum for New Research' (2014) 16 JHIL 1-8.

Triepel, Heinrich, *Völkerrecht und Landesrecht* (Verlag von C. L. Hirschfeld, Leipzig 1899).

Tudor, Ioana, *The Fair and Equitable Treatment in the International Law of Foreign Investment* (Oxford University Press, New York 2008).

Van Harten, Gus, *Investment Arbitration and Public Law* (Oxford University Press, Oxford 2008).

Vandevelde, Kenneth, 'A Brief History of International Investment Agreements' (2005) 12 U. C. Davis J. Int'l L. & Pol'y 157-94.

Vandevelde, Kenneth, *Bilateral Investment Treaties: History, Policy, and Interpretation* (Oxford University Press, New York 2010).

VanDuzer, J. Anthony, 'Full Protection and Security' in Thomas Cottier and Krista Nadakavukaren Schefer (eds), *Elgar Encyclopedia of International Economic Law* (Edward Elgar Publishing, Northampton MA 2018) 212-4.

Vasciannie, Stephen, 'Bilateral Investment Treaties and Civil Strife: The AAPL/Sri Lanka Arbitration' (1992) 39 (3) NILR 332, 345-54.

Vattel, Emer, *Le droit des gens ou principes de la loi naturelle appliqués à la conduit et aux affaires des Nations et des Souverains* (1758) (Carnegie Institution, Washington 1916).

Vattel, Emer, *The Law of Nations or Principles of the Law of Nature Applied to the Conduct and Affairs of Nations and Sovereigns* (1758) (G.G. and J. Robinson, London 1797).

Verdross, Alfred, 'Les règles internationales concernant le traitement des étrangers' (1931) 37 (3) RCADI 322-412.

Verdross, Alfred, 'Theorie der mittelbaren Staatenhaftung' (1948) 1 ÖZÖR 388-423.

Verdross, Alfred, and Bruno Simma, *Universelles Völkerrecht* (Duncker & Humblot, Berlin 1984).

Vermeer-Künzli, Annemarieke, 'Nationality and Diplomatic Protection. A reappraisal' in Alessandra Annoni and Serena Forlati (eds), *The Changing Role of Nationality in International Law* (Routledge, New York 2013) 76-95.

Vernmeer-Künzli, Annemarieke, 'As If: The Legal Fiction in Diplomatic Protection' (2007) 18 (1) EJIL 37-68.

Vitoria, Francisco, 'De Indis et de Iure Belli Reflectiones' (1532) in James Brown Scott (ed), *Classics of International Law* (John Pawley Bate tr, Carnegie Institution, Washington 1917).

Von der Heydte, Friedrich August, *Die Geburtsstunde des souveränen Staates. Ein Beitrag zur Geschichte des Völkerrechts, der allgemeinen Staatslehre und des politischen Denkens* (Druck und Verlag Josef Habbel, Regensburg 1952).

Von Fisch, Hans, *Die Staatsrechtliche Stellung der Fremden* (Carl Heymanns Verlag, Berlin 1910).

Von Gierke, Otto, *Der Humor im Deutschen Recht* (Weidmannsche Buchhandlung, Berlin 1871).

Von Jhering, Rudolf, *Scherz und Ernst in der Jurisprudenz* (Breitkopf & Härtel, Leipzig 1885) [first edition: 1884].

Von Liszt, Franz, *Das Völkerrecht systematisch dargestellt* (Verlag von O. Häring, Berlin 1906).

Von Münch, Ingo, *Das völkerrechtliche Delikt in der modernen Entwicklung der Völkerrechtsgemeinschaft* (P. Keppler Verlag, Frankfurt 1963).

Von Ranke, Leopold, *Geschichten der romanischen und germanischen Völker von 1494 bis 1514* (Leipzig, Ducker & Humblot 1885) [first edition: 1824].

Von Ullmann, Emanuel, *Völkerrecht* (J. C. B. Mohr, Tübingen 1908).

Von Waldkirch, Eduard Otto, *Das Völkerrecht in seinen Grundzügen dargestellt* (Verlag von Helbing & Lichtenhahn, Basel 1926).

Wälde, Thomas, 'Energy Charter Treaty-based Investment Arbitration. Controversial Issues' (2004) 5 J. World Investment & Trade 373-412.

Walker, Alexandra, 'Conscious and Unconscious Security Responses' in Hitoshi Nasu and Kim Rubenstein, *Legal Perspectives on Security Institutions* (Cambridge University Press, Cambridge 2015) 27-46.

Walker, Herman, 'Provisions on Companies in United States Commercial Treaties' (1956) 50 (2) AJIL 373-93.

Walker, Herman, 'The Post-War Commercial Treaty Program of the United States' (1958) 73 (1) Pol. Sci. Q. 57-81.

Walker, Herman, 'Treaties for the Encouragement and Protection of Foreign Investment: Present United States Practice' (1956) Am. J. Comp. L. 229-47.

Wallace, Don, 'Fair and Equitable Treatment and Denial of Justice in *Loewen v. US* and *Chattin v. Mexico*' in Todd Weiler (ed), *International Investment Law and Arbitration. Leading Cases from the ICSID, NAFTA, Bilateral Investment Treaties and Customary International Law* (Cameron May, London 2005) 669-700.

Washington Crichfield, George, *American Supremacy. The Rise and Progress of the Latin American Republics and their Relations to the United States under the Monroe Doctrine* (Volume 2: Bentano's, New York 1908).

Watson, Alan, *Legal Transplants: An Approach to Comparative Law* (University of Georgia Press, Athens GA 1993) [first edition: 1974].

Weiler, Todd, *The Interpretation of International Investment Law: Equality, Discrimination, and Minimum Standards of Treatment in Historical Context* (Brill, Leiden 2013).

Weisburd, Arthur, 'A Reply to Professor D'Amato' (1988) 21 Vand. J. Transnat'l L. 473-88.

Weisburd, Arthur, 'Customary International Law: The Problem of Treaties' (1988) 21 Vand. J. Transnat'l L. 1-46.

Wharton, Francis (ed), *A Digest of the International Law of the United States, taken from Documents issued by Presidents and Secretaries of State and Decisions of Federal Courts and Opinions of Attorneys-General* (Volume 2: Government Printing Office, Washington 1887).

Whittaker, Simon, 'The Law of Obligations' in John Bell, Sophie Boyron and Simon Whittaker (eds), *Principles of French Law* (Oxford University Press, New York 2008) 294-452.

Wiechmann, Gerhard, 'Die Königlich Preußische Marine in Lateinamerika 1851 bis 1867. Ein Versuch deutscher Kanonenbootpolitik in Übersee' in Sandra Carreras and Günter Maihold (eds), *Preußen und Lateinamerika. Im Spannungsfeld von Kommerz, Macht und Kultur* (LIT Verlag, Münster 2004) 105-44.

Wiesse, Carlos, *Le droit international apliqué aux guerres civiles* (B. Benda Libraire-Éditeur, Lausanne 1898).

Wiesse, Carlos, *Reglas de derecho internacional aplicables á las guerras civiles* (Imp. Torres Aguirre, Lima 1905).

Wolf, Joachim, 'Die gegenwärtige Entwicklung der Lehre über die völkerrechtliche Verantwortlichkeit der Staaten. Untersuchung am Beispiel des Urteils des Internationalen Gerichtshofs in der Teheraner Geiselaffaire' (1983) 31 ZaöRV 481-536.

Wolfers, Arnold, 'National Security as an Ambiguous Symbol' (1952) 67(4) Pol. Sci. Q. 481-502.

Wolff [Freiherr von], Christian, *Ius gentium methodo scientifica perpractatum* (Officina libraria Rengeriana, Magdeburg 1740).

Wolff, Christian, 'Jus gentium methodo scientifica pertractactum' (1749) in James Brown Scott (ed), *Classics of International Law* (Joseph Drake tr, Clarendon Press, Oxford 1934).

Wolfrum, Rüdiger, 'Obligations of Result Versus Obligations of Conduct: Some Thoughts About the Implementation of International Obligations' in Mahnoush Arsanjani, Jacob Katz Cogan, Robert Sloane and Siegfried Wiessner (eds), *Looking into the Future. Essays on International Law in Honor of W. Michael Reisman* (Martinus Nijhoff, Leiden/Boston 2011) 363-83.

Woolf, Cecil Sidney, *Bartolus of Sassoferrato. His position in the History of Medieval Political Thought* (Cambridge University Press, Cambridge 1913).

Wrobleski, Jessica, *The Limits of Hospitality* (Liturgical Press, Collegeville MN 2012).

Wu, Han Tao, *Responsibility of States for Injuries Sustained by Aliens on Account of Acts of Insurgents* (University of Illinois, Urbana IL 1930).

Yannaca-Small, Katia, 'Fair and Equitable Treatment in International Investment Law' in OECD, *Working Papers on International Investment* (OECD, Paris 2004).

Yannaca-Small, Katia, 'Fair and Equitable Treatment Standard: Recent Developments' in August Reinisch (ed), *Standards of Investment Protection* (Oxford University Press, New York 2008) 111-30.

Zannas, Pavlos Alextrandou, *La responsabilité internationale des Etats pour les actes de négligence* (Ganguin & Laubscher, Geneva 1952).

Zedner, Lucia, *Security* (Routledge, New York 2009).

Zeitler, Helge Elisabeth, 'Full Protection and Security' in Stephan Schill (ed), *International Investment Law and Comparative Public Law* (Oxford University Press, New York 2010) 183-212.

Zeitler, Helge Elisabeth, 'The Guarantee of Full Protection and Security in Investment Treaties regarding Harm Caused by Private Parties' (2005) 3 SIAR 1-34.

Zellweger, Edward, *Die völkerrechtliche Verantwortlichkeit des Staates für die Presse unter besonderer Berücksichtigung der schweizerischen Praxis* (Polygraphischer Verlag, Zurich 1949).

Zemanek, Karl, 'Schuld- und Erfolgshaftung im Entwurf der Völkerrechtskommission über Staatenverantwortlichkeit. Zugleich Bemerkungen zum Prozess der Kodifikation im Rahmen der Vereinten Nationen' in Emanuel Diez, Jean Monnier, Jörg Müller, Heinrich Reimann and Luzius Wildhaber (eds), *Festschrift für Rudolf Bindschedler zum 65. Geburtstag am 8. Juli 1980* (Verlag Stämpfli & cie., Bern 1980) 315-31.

Zemanek, Karl, Gerhard Hafner and Stephan Wittich, 'Die völkerrechtliche Verantwortlichkeit und die Sanktionen des Völkerrechts' in Hanspeter Neuhold, Waldemar Hummer and Christoph Schreuer (eds), *Österreichisches Handbuch des Völkerrechts* (Volume 1: Manz, Vienna 2004) 505-32.

Others

Documents of the International Law Association[5]

ILA, 'Mandate of the Study Group on Due Diligence in International Law' (n.d.).

ILA Study Group on Due Diligence in International Law, 'First Report by Mr. Tim Stephens (Rapporteur) and Mr. Duncan French (Chair)' (7 March 2014).

ILA Study Group on Due Diligence in International Law, 'Second Report by Mr. Tim Stephens (Rapporteur) and Mr. Duncan French (Chair)' (20 July 2016).

Documents of the *Institut de Droit International*

Resolutions

Institut de Droit International, 'Résolutions votées par l'Institut au cours de sa XXXI Ve Session – Responsabilité internationale des États à raison des dommages causés sur leur territoire à la personne ou aux biens des étrangers (XIIIe Commission)' (1927) 33(II) Annuaire de l'Institut de Droit International 330-5.

Institut de Droit International, 'Règlement sur la responsabilité des États à raison des dommages soufferts par les étrangers en cas d'émeute, d'insurrection ou de guerre civile' (1900) 18 (I) Annuaire de l'Institut de Droit International 254-6.

---

[5]*The following materials are available at the website of the International Law Association [http://www.ila-hq.org/index.php/study-groups].*

Reports

Emilio Brusa, 'Responsabilité des États à raison des dommages soufferts par des étrangers en cas d'émeute ou de guerre civile' (1898) 17 Annuaire de l'Institut de Droit International 96–137.

Emilio Brusa, 'Responsabilité des États à raison des dommages soufferts par des étrangers en cas d'émeute ou de guerre civile. Nouvelles thèses présentées par MM. Brusa, rapporteur, et L. de Bar' (1900) 18 Annuaire de l'Institut de Droit International 47–9.

Leo Strisower, 'Responsabilité internationale des États à raison des dommages causés sur leur territoire à la personne ou aux biens des étrangers' (1927) 33(I) Annuaire de l'Institut de Droit International 455–98.

Minutes

Institut de Droit International 'Neuvième Commission d'étude – Responsabilité des États à raison des dommages soufferts par des étrangers en cas d'émeute ou de guerre civile' (1900) 18 Annuaire de l'Institut de Droit International 233–54.

Documents of the International Law Commission

Diplomatic Protection

ILC, 'Documents of the Fifty-Eighth Session – Comments and Observations received from Governments on Diplomatic Protection' (2006) 2(1) *Yearbook of the International Law Commission – 2006* 34-63.

ILC, 'Report of the International Law Commission on the Work of its Fifty-Eighth Session - Diplomatic Protection' (2006) 2(2) *Yearbook of the International Law Commission – 2006* 23-55.

Effects of Armed Conflicts on Treaties

ILC, 'Effects of Armed Conflicts on Treaties (A/66/10)' (2011) 2(2) *Yearbook of the International Law Commission* 173-217.

Identification of Customary Law

Michael Wood, 'Second Report on Identification of Customary International Law (A/CN.4/672)' (22 May 2014) [http://legal.un.org/ilc/documentation/english/a_cn4_672.pdf].

International Organizations

ILC, 'Responsibility of International Organizations, with Commentaries (A/66/10)' (2011) [http://legal.un.org/ilc/texts/instruments/english/commentaries/9_11_2011.pdf].

Protection of Persons in the Event of Disasters

Eduardo Valencia-Ospina, 'Preliminary Report on the Protection of Persons in the Event of Disasters (A/CN.4/598)' (5 May 2008) 2(1) *Yearbook of the International Law Commission – 2008* 143-54.

ILC, 'Draft Articles on the Protection of Persons in the Event of Disasters (A/71/10)' (2016) [http://legal.un.org/ilc/texts/instruments/english/commentaries/6_3_2016.pdf].

ILC, 'Protection of Persons in the Event of Disasters: Memorandum by the Secretariat (A/CN.4/590)' (11 December 2007) [http://legal.un.org/docs/?symbol=A/CN.4/590].

ILC, 'Protection of Persons in the Event of Disasters: Statement of the Chairman of the Drafting Committee' (26 July 2013) [http://legal.un.org/docs/?path=../ilc/sessions/65/pdfs/protection_of_persons_dc_statement_2013.pdf&lang=E].

ILC, 'Protection of Persons in the Event of Disasters' (2006) 2(2) *Yearbook of the International Law Commission – 2006* 206-28.

ILC, 'Report of the International Law Commission on the Work of its Sixtieth Session – Protection of Persons in the Event of Disasters' (2008) 2(2) *Yearbook of the International Law Commission – 2008* 129-41.

State Responsibility – ILC Articles/Drafts and Commentaries

ILC, 'Draft Articles on State Responsibility with Commentaries thereto adopted by the International Law Commission on First Reading (Doc. No. 97-02583)' (January 1997) [http://legal.un.org/ilc/texts/instruments/english/commentaries/9_6_1996.pdf].

ILC, 'Responsibility of States for Internationally Wrongful Acts. General Commentary' (2001) 2 *Yearbook of the International Law Commission – 2001* 31-143.

ILC, 'Revised Draft on the Responsibility of States for Injuries Caused in its Territory to the Person or Property of Aliens' (1961) 2 *Yearbook of the International Law Commission – 1961* 46-54.

State Responsibility – Reports and other Documents of the ILC

ILC, 'Force Majeure and Fortuitous Event as Circumstances Precluding Wrongfulness: Survey of State Practice, International Judicial Decisions and Doctrine' (27 June 1977) 2(1) *Yearbook of the International Law Commission – 1978* 61-227.

ILC, 'Report of the International Law Commission on the Work of its Twenty-Seventh Session – State Responsibility' (1975) 2 *Yearbook of the International Law Commission – 1975* 51-106.

ILC, 'Report of the International Law Commission on the Work of its Twenty-Ninth Session – State Responsibility' (1977) 2(2) *Yearbook of the International Law Commission – 1977* 5-50.

ILC, 'Report of the International Law Commission on the Work of its Fifty-First Session – State Responsibility' (1999) 2(2) *Yearbook of the International Law Commission – 1999* 48-88.

State Responsibility – Reports of the Special Rapporteurs

Francisco García Amador, 'International Responsibility: Report by F. V. García Amador, Special Rapporteur (A/CN.4/96)' (20 January 1956) 2 *Yearbook of the International Law Commission - 1956* 173-231.

Francisco García Amador, 'International Responsibility: Second Report by F. V. García Amador, Special Rapporteur (A/CN.4/106)' (15 February 1957) 2 *Yearbook of the International Law Commission – 1957* 104-30.

Francisco García Amador, 'International Responsibility: Fourth Report by F. V. García Amador, Special Rapporteur (A/CN.4/119)' (26 February 1959) 2 *Yearbook of the International Law Commission – 1959* 1-36.

Francisco García Amador, 'International Responsibility: Fifth Report by F. V. García Amador, Special Rapporteur (A/CN.4/125)' (9 February 1960) 2 *Yearbook of the International Law Commission – 1960* 41-68.

Francisco García Amador, 'International Responsibility: Sixth Report by F. V. García Amador, Special Rapporteur (A/CN.4/134/Add. 1)' (26 January 1961) 2 *Yearbook of the International Law Commission – 1961* 1-54.

Roberto Ago, 'Second Report on State Responsibility – The Origin of International Responsibility (A/CN.4/233)' (10 April 1970) 2 *Yearbook of the International Law Commission - 1970* 177-97.

Roberto Ago, 'Third Report on State Responsibility – The Origin of International Responsibility (A/CN.4/246 and Add. 1-3)' (1971) 2(1) *Yearbook of the International Law Commission - 1971* 199-274.

Roberto Ago, 'Fourth Report on State Responsibility – The Internationally Wrongful Act of the State, Source of International Responsibility (Continued) (A/CN.4/264)' (20 June 1972 and 9 April 1973) 2 *Yearbook of the International Law Commission – 1972* 71-160.

Roberto Ago, 'Sixth Report on State Responsibility – The Internationally Wrongful Act of the State, Source of International Responsibility (A/CN.4/302 and Add.1-3)' (1977) 2(1) *Yearbook of the International Law Commission – 1977* 3-43.

Roberto Ago, 'Seventh Report on State Responsibility – The Internationally Wrongful Act of the State, Source of International Responsibility (A/CN.4/307 and Add.1 and 2)' (1978) 2(1) *Yearbook of the International Law Commission – 1978* 31-60.

James Crawford, 'First Report on State Responsibility (A/CN.4/490 and Add. 1-7)' (April-August 1998) 2(1) *Yearbook of the International Law Commission – 1998* 1-80.

James Crawford, 'Second Report on State Responsibility (A/CN.4/490 and Add. 1-7)' (1999) 2(1) *Yearbook of the International Law Commission – 1999* 3-96.

Succession of States

Mohammed Bedjaoui, 'Sixth Report on Succession of States in respect of Matters other than Treaties (A/CN.4/267)' (20 May 1973) 2 *Yearbook of the International Law Commission – 1973* 3-73.

Summary Records

ILC, 'Summary Records of the 370th Meeting' (19 June 1956) 1 *Yearbook of the International Law Commission – 1956* 226-33.
ILC, 'Summary Records of the 372nd Meeting' (21 June 1956) 1 *Yearbook of the International Law Commission – 1956* 239-45.
ILC, 'Summary Records of the 415th Meeting' (12 June 1957) 1 *Yearbook of the International Law Commission – 1957* 162-8.
ILC, 'Summary Records of the 1309th Meeting' (14 May 1975) 1 *Yearbook of the International Law Commission – 1975* 28-33.
ILC, 'Summary Records of the 1476th Meeting' (10 May 1978) 1 *Yearbook of the International Law Commission – 1978* 4-9.
ILC, 'Summary Records of the 1477th Meeting' (11 May 1978) 1 *Yearbook of the International Law Commission – 1978* 9-13.
ILC, 'Summary Records of the 1478th Meeting' (12 May 1978) 1 *Yearbook of the International Law Commission – 1978* 13-9.
ILC, 'Summary Records of the 1513th Meeting' (6 July 1978) 1 *Yearbook of the International Law Commission – 1978* 206-9.

Other United Nations Documents

United Nations Development Programme, *Human Development Report 1994* (Oxford University Press, New York 1994).

UNCTAD Documents

UNCTAD, *Bilateral Investment Treaties in the Mid-1990s* (United Nations, New York/Geneva 1998).
UNCTAD, *Expropriation: A Sequel* (United Nations, New York/Geneva 2012).
UNCTAD, *International Investment Agreements: Key issues* (Volume 1: United Nations, New York/Geneva 2004).
UNCTAD, *Investor-State Disputes Arising from Investment Treaties: A Review* (United Nations, New York/Geneva 2005).
UNCTAD, *South-South Cooperation in International Investment Arrangements* (United Nations, New York/Geneva 2005).

League of Nations Documents

League of Nations, 'Bases of Discussion drawn up in 1929 by the Preparatory Committee of the Conference for the Codification of International Law (Doc. Nr. C.75.M.69.1929.V)' in Martins Paparinskis, *Basic Documents on International Investment Protection* (Hart Publishing, Portland OR 2012) 20-6.
League of Nations, 'Questionnaire No. 4/Responsibility of States for Damage done in their Territories to the Person or Property of Foreigners (Doc. Nr. C. 46.M.23.126.V)' in Shabtai

Rosenne (ed), *League of Nations Committee of Experts for the Progressive Codification of International Law [1925-1928]* (Volume 2, Oceana Publications, New York 1972) 118-31.

League of Nations, 'Text of Articles Adopted in First Reading by the Third Committee of the Conference for the Codification of International Law (Doc. Nr. C.351(c).M.145(c).929.V)' in Martins Paparinskis, *Basic Documents on International Investment Protection* (Hart Publishing, Portland OR 2012) 26-8.

Other Draft International Instruments

'Abs-Shawcross Draft Convention on Investment Abroad' (April 1959) in Martins Paparinskis, *Basic Documents on International Investment Protection* (Hart Publishing, Portland OR 2012) 37-9.

'Responsibility of States for Damage done in their Territory to the Person and Property of Foreigners' (1929) 23 AJIL 131-9.

OECD Draft Convention on the Protection of Foreign Property (1963) in Martins Paparinskis, *Basic Documents on International Investment Protection* (Hart Publishing, Portland OR 2012) 63-7.

OECD Draft Convention on the Protection of Foreign Property (1967) in Martins Paparinskis, *Basic Documents on International Investment Protection* (Hart Publishing, Portland OR 2012) 67-72.

OECD, *Draft Convention on the Protection of Foreign Property. Notes and Comments* (OECD, Paris 1962).

Documents of the NAFTA Free Trade Commission

NAFTA Free Trade Commission, *Notes of Interpretation of Certain Chapter 11 Provisions* (31 July 2001) [http://www.sice.oas.org/tpd/nafta/Commission/CH11understanding_e.asp].

National Legislation

Constitución del Estado Plurinacional de Bolivia (adopted 7 February 2009) [https://www.oas.org/dil/esp/Constitucion_Bolivia.pdf].

Grundgesetz für die Bundesrepublik Deutschland (23 May 1949) BGBl. 1.

Regulations for the Government of the Navy of the United States (Government Printing Office, Washington 1913).

Verfassung des deutschen Reiches (11 August 1929) (Reichszentrale für Heimatdienst, Berlin 1929).

Statesmen's Personal Correspondence and Documents

'A Course of Reading for Joseph C. Cabell' (September 1800) *United States National Archives: Founders Online Project* [http://founders.archives.gov/documents/Jefferson/01-32-02-0110].

'Benjamin Franklin to Andreas Peter Graf von Bernstorff' (22 December 1779) *United States National Archives: Founders Online Project* [http://founders.archives.gov/documents/Franklin/01-31-02-0175].

'Benjamin Franklin to James Bowdoin' (24 March 1776) *United States National Archives: Founders Online Project* [http://founders.archives.gov/documents/Franklin/01-22-02-0231].

'John Adams to Benjamin Rush' (24 July 1789) *United States National Archives: Founders Online Project* [http://founders.archives.gov/documents/Adams/99-02-02-0700].

'John Adams to George Washington Adams' (13 January 1822) *United States National Archives: Founders Online Project* [http://founders.archives.gov/documents/Adams/99-03-02-3995].

'John Adams to George Washington Adams' (9 December 1821) *United States National Archives: Founders Online Project* [http://founders.archives.gov/documents/Adams/99-03-02-3989].

'John Adams to Richard Cranch Norton' (20 March 1812) *United States National Archives: Founders Online Project* [http://founders.archives.gov/documents/Adams/99-03-02-2127].

'John Adams to Richard Rush' (14 April 1811) *United States National Archives: Founders Online Project* [http://founders.archives.gov/documents/Adams/99-02-02-5631].

'John Adams to William Cranch' (30 December 1790) *United States National Archives: Founders Online Project* [http://founders.archives.gov/documents/Adams/99-02-02-1118].

'John Jay to George Washington' (28 August 1790) *United States National Archives: Founders Online Project* [http://founders.archives.gov/documents/Washington/05-06-02-0170].

'John Quincy Adams to John Adams' (3 December 1794) *United States National Archives: Founders Online Project* [http://founders.archives.gov/documents/Adams/99-02-02-1610].

'John Quincy Adams to John Adams' (9 November 1794) *United States National Archives: Founders Online Project* [http://founders.archives.gov/documents/Adams/99-02-02-1580].

'No Jacobin No. II' (5 August 1793) *United States National Archives: Founders Online Project* [http://founders.archives.gov/documents/Hamilton/01-15-02-0145].

'Original Letter from Dr. Franklin to Monsieur Dumas' (9 December 1775) 45 *The European Magazine and London Review* (1804) 347-9.

'September 15th' in Robert Taylor & Marc Fredlaender, *The Adams Papers. Diary of John Quincy Adams* (Volume 2: Harvard University Press, Cambridge MA 1981) 289.

'September 22nd' in Robert Taylor & Marc Fredlaender, *The Adams Papers. Diary of John Quincy Adams* (Volume 2: Harvard University Press, Cambridge MA 1981) 292-3.

'Thomas Jefferson to Edmond Charles Genet' (17 June 1793) *United States National Archives: Founders Online Project* [http://founders.archives.gov/documents/Jefferson/01-26-02-0276].

'Thomas Jefferson to Edmund Pendleton' (14 February 1799) *United States National Archives: Founders Online Project* [http://founders.archives.gov/documents/Jefferson/01-31-02-0024].

'Thomas Jefferson to George Hammond' (20 May 1792) [http://founders.archives.gov/documents/Jefferson/01-23-02-0506].

'Thomas Jefferson to James Madison' (28 April 1793) *United States National Archives: Founders Online Project* [http://founders.archives.gov/documents/Madison/01-15-02-0013].

'Thomas Jefferson to James Madison' (3 August 1793) *United States National Archives: Founders Online Project* [http://founders.archives.gov/documents/Madison/01-15-02-0044].

'Thomas Jefferson to John Adams' (11 June 1790) *United States National Archives: Founders Online Project* [http://founders.archives.gov/documents/Jefferson/01-16-02-0278].

'William Short to Thomas Jefferson' (31 August 1792) *United States National Archives: Founders Online Project* [http://founders.archives.gov/documents/Jefferson/01-24-02-0313].

Other Sources

'action, n' (October 2016) *Oxford English Dictionary Online* [http://www.oed.com/view/Entry/1938?rskey=k9Re6P&result=1&isAdvanced=false#eid].

'action' in *Merriam Webster Collegiate Dictionary* (Merriam-Webster, Springfield MA 2004) 12.

'In Memoriam: Ludwig von Bar' (1914) 8(2) AJIL 346-7.

'omission, n' (October 2016) *Oxford English Dictionary Online* [http://www.oed.com/view/Entry/ 131211?redirectedFrom=omission#eid].

'communitas' in *Mediae Latinitatis Lexicon Minus – Medieval Latin Dictionary* (Volume 1: Brill, Leiden 2002) 1027.

'communitas' in *Glossarium Mediae et Infimae Latinitatis* (Volume 2: Niort, L. Favre 1886) 459.

'community, n' (January 2017) *Oxford English Dictionary Online* [http://www.oed.com/view/ Entry/37337?redirectedFrom=community#eid].

'protection, n' (June 2015) *Oxford English Dictionary Online* [http://www.oed.com/view/Entry/ 153134?redirectedFrom=protection].

'security, n' (June 2015) *Oxford English Dictionary Online* [http://www.oed.com/view/Entry/ 174661?redirectedFrom=security&].

'physical, adj.' (May 2016) *Oxford English Dictionary Online* [http://www.oed.com/view/Entry/ 143120?rskey=KMtVVv&result=2&isAdvanced=false#eid].

'physical' in *Merriam Webster Collegiate Dictionary* (Merriam-Webster, Springfield MA 2004) 935.

'Rector' in *Mediae Latinitatis Lexicon Minus – Medieval Latin Dictionary* (Volume 2: Brill, Leiden 2002) 1164-5.

'Rector' in *Glossarium Mediae et Infimae Latinitatis* (Volume 7: Niort, L. Favre 1886) 61.

'The Aigues-Mortes Massacre. Story of the Assaults Upon Italian Workmen Told Anew' The New York Times, December 29, 1893.

Printed by Printforce, the Netherlands